A
PEOPLE'S
HISTORY
OF THE
AMERICAN
REVOLUTION

A
NEW
AGE
NOW
BEGINS

Page Smith

VOLUME TWO

McGRAW-HILL BOOK COMPANY

New York / St. Louis / San Francisco

Düsseldorf / Toronto / Mexico

Half-title page: Great Seal of the United States, reverse side.
Courtesy of the Library of Congress #44633/2784.

Book design by Stanley Drate.

VOLUME TWO

1 2 3 4 5 6 7 8 9 KPKP 7 9 8 7 6 5

Library of Congress Cataloging in Publication Data

Smith, Page.
    A new age now begins.

    Includes index.
    1. United States—History—Revolution, 1775–1783.
2. United States—History—Revolution, 1775–1783—
Campaigns and battles.   I. Title.
E208.S67   973.3   75-8656
ISBN 0-07-059097-4

CONTENTS

VOLUME TWO

 Part VII

1. *Howe Tries the Jerseys Again* 875

2. *Burgoyne's Invasion* 891

3. *Forts Stanwix and Oriskany* 908

4. *Bennington* 915

5. *Saratoga* 922

6. *Brandywine* 948

7. *The Paoli Massacre and Germantown* 959

8. *Foreign Volunteers* 972

9. *Forts Mifflin and Mercer* 978

10. *The Army Goes into Winter Quarters,*
    1777–78 992

11. *The Conway Cabal* 1019

12. *The British in Philadelphia* 1031

13. *The French Alliance* 1044

14. *England* 1060

v

Part VIII

1. *Monmouth*   *1079*
2. *The Battle of Rhode Island*   *1106*
3. *Winter Quarters, 1778–79*   *1123*
4. *Meanwhile Congress . . .*   *1137*
5. *Border Warfare: The Wyoming Valley*   *1150*
6. *Sullivan's Expedition*   *1163*
7. *Border Warfare: New York*   *1178*
8. *George Rogers Clark*   *1190*
9. *The Capture of Vincennes*   *1201*
10. *The Southern Frontier*   *1212*
11. *The Sandusky Expedition*   *1219*
12. *The End of the Border War*   *1228*
13. *The War on the High Seas*   *1238*
14. *Naval "Militia" and Privateers*   *1261*
15. *John Paul Jones*   *1268*
16. *The Continuing War at Sea*   *1288*

Part IX

1. *From Savannah to Brier Creek*   *1301*
2. *Prevost Threatens Charles Town*   *1317*
3. *Failure at Savannah*   *1331*
4. *Stony Point and Paulus Hook*   *1338*
5. *Fort Wilson*   *1361*

6. *Parliament Takes Stock*   *1370*

7. *The Surrender of Charles Town*   *1380*

8. *From the Waxhaw Massacre to Ramsour's Mill*   *1393*

9. *Camden*   *1407*

10. *King's Mountain*   *1419*

11. *Greene Takes Command*   *1435*

12. *Cowpens*   *1449*

13. *Greene Runs*   *1464*

14. *Guilford Court House*   *1478*

15. *Hobkirks Hill*   *1486*

16. *Greene Turns South*   *1496*

Part X

1. *Morristown: 1779–80*   *1513*

2. *Springfield and After*   *1526*

3. *Parliament*   *1541*

4. *General Arnold and the British*   *1555*

5. *Treason*   *1571*

6. *The Mutiny of the Pennsylvania Line*   *1600*

7. *Lafayette in Virginia*   *1624*

8. *Congress*   *1637*

9. *The Episode at Green Spring Farm*   *1646*

10. *To Virginia*   *1656*

11. *The Battle of the Capes*   *1672*

12. *The Seige of Yorktown*   *1693*

13. *Parliament Reacts*   *1717*

14. *Peace Negotiations*   *1725*

15. *The Aftermath of Yorktown*   *1746*

16. *Congress: A Rope of Sand*   1762
17. *The Army Disbands*   1783
18. *Blacks in the Revolution*   1798
19. *Women in the Revolution*   1808
20. *Novus Ordo Seclorum*   1815

BIBLIOGRAPHIC NOTE   1833

INDEX   1841

ACKNOWLEDGMENTS   1901

List of Maps

FACING PAGE

Burgoyne's Saratoga Campaign	*932*
Battle of Bennington	*916*
Battle of Freeman's Farm	*922*
Battle of Bemis Heights	*930*
Surrender of Burgoyne	*940*
Battle of Brandywine	*948*
Battle of Germantown	*960*
Lafayette at Barren Hill	*1080*
Battle of Monmouth	*1090*
Siege of Newport	*1108*
Siege of Savannah	*1332*
Siege of Charleston	*1380*
Battle of Springfield	*1526*
Battle of Camden	*1408*
Battle of Cowpens	*1452*
Battle of Guilford	*1478*
Battle of Hobkirk Hill	*1492*
Battle of Eutaw Springs	*1690*
Siege of Yorktown	*1694*

A
NEW
AGE
NOW
BEGINS

PART VII

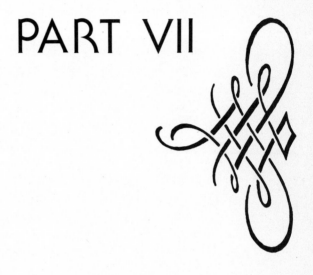

Howe Tries the Jerseys Again

W_E left Washington after the Battle of Princeton hard pressed by Howe, his men exhausted by the campaigning that marked the last months of 1776 but exhilarated by their modest victories over the British. After Princeton Howe returned his army to winter quarters, and on January 7, 1777, Washington's army reached Morristown in New Jersey and prepared its own winter quarters there. The men built huts of logs chinked with moss and clay and made themselves comparatively snug. Washington established his headquarters at the Freeman Tavern on the town square.

The greater part of New Jersey, only a few days before seemingly secure in British hands, had been recaptured. Morristown, which threatened the British post at New Brunswick, was protected by hilly and wooded terrain to the south and afforded easy routes of escape to the north if Howe should resume the offensive. Washington once again turned his attention to reconstituting his army, or rather, to preserving a remnant of it. The practical American soldier could see little point in merely being present. It seemed clear that there was to be no fighting and the men began to go home in large numbers; soon there were hardly more than two thousand, supplemented by militia, left in the army at Morristown.

Washington sent Henry Knox to New England to supervise the casting of more cannon for the army and to encourage the manufacture of powder. He also dispatched a series of expeditions to root out any stray detachments of British or Hessian soldiers and to emphasize to the inhabitants, by the freedom with which his forces scoured New Jersey, that the British had abandoned the pretense of holding any substantial portion of the state outside of New Brunswick and Perth Amboy.

Washington had instructed General William Heath to attack the Hessian position at Fort Independence north of King's Bridge, New York. On January 18, Heath drew up his division near Spuyten Duyvil Creek, a few miles from Fort Independence. General Benjamin Lincoln, who had advanced down the Hudson River Road, was on his right, and General Charles Scott, who had come by way of White Plains, was on his left with Generals David Wooster and Samuel Parsons, who had been based at New Rochelle and Eastchester. Together the American force numbered nearly six thousand. Facing them were some two thousand Hessians in strong defensive positions. The movement of the four divisions had been so well coordinated that the Americans arrived at the advance Hessian posts almost at the same moment and took the enemy completely by surprise. Heath informed the startled Hessians that they had "twenty minutes to surrender or abide the consequences."

When the Hessians failed to surrender, Heath's threat turned out to be empty. Washington had, to be sure, instructed Heath to "act with great precaution" while taking "every favorable opportunity of attacking the enemy, when you can do it to advantage." The cautionary note was hardly necessary; Heath was the converse of reckless. Pompous (in his memoirs he always refers to himself in the third person as "our General") and lacking in energy, Heath was not one of the brighter lights among Washington's officer corps. On this occasion, having demanded a surrender in twenty minutes, he loitered about for ten days, firing a few rounds of artillery at the fort and making a feint here and there, until the Hessians, emboldened by such tactics, sallied out and sent several regiments of militia flying. Finally, on January 29, signs of an impending storm completed the rout of the American forces, who withdrew to their encampments north of Spuyten Duyvil Creek to find shelter from the elements.

Heath's maneuvers around Fort Independence and King's Bridge, inept as they were, served the purpose of distracting Howe and removing from his mind any thought of attacking Washington at Morristown. Heath's decision, in which his officers all concurred, not to attack the well-defended fort with a force made up largely of inexperienced militiamen offended Washington less than the fact that Heath had managed to make himself an object of ridicule in the process. Washington thus wrote "our General" a curt reprimand. "This letter," he observed, " . . . is to hint to you . . . that your conduct is censured (and by men of sense and judgment who have been with you on the expedition to Fort Independence) as being fraught with too much caution: by which the army has been disappointed and in some degree disgraced. Your summons, as you did not attempt to fulfill your threats, was not only idle but farcical, and will not fail of turning the laugh exceedingly upon us."

Washington's letter surely had a hidden purpose. He knew Heath's limitations, knew that he was an old fuddy-duddy and that he was inadequate to the assignment that Washington had given him. Aware of the political complications of sacking him, Washington probably was trying to drive Heath to resign his command or, in the event that Heath failed to do so, was paving the way for firing him. The letter also demonstrates clearly Washington's own sensitivity to criticism or ridicule. "Your threats," he wrote, " . . . will not fail of turning the laugh exceedingly upon *us.*"

Washington instructed Generals Joseph Spencer and Benedict Arnold, in command of some four thousand Continental soldiers of the Northern Department at Providence, to augment their force with militia and attempt to recapture Newport, but the militia failed to materialize and the scheme was dropped. The Connecticut general Samuel Parsons was dispatched on a recruiting expedition in his home state in hopes of raising a sufficient force to mount an attack on Long Island, across the Sound from Connecticut. Again it proved to be impossible to round up a force adequate to the task. General Philip Schuyler was urged to try and draw from New England an army sufficient to repel the advance of Sir Guy Carleton from Canada because "troops of extreme sections could not be favorably combined."

General William Maxwell had occupied Elizabethtown after the flight of the Hessians and Highlanders, and from there he exercised a restraining influence on the numerous New Jersey Tories and kept a close eye on the British. Perhaps the most encouraging event was the arrival in Portsmouth, New Hampshire, in March of a French shipment of 12,000 muskets, 1,000 barrels of powder, blankets, and much-needed military supplies of various kinds. A few weeks later 11,000 muskets reached Philadelphia. These were among the first of a constantly growing stream of arms, ammunition, and military stores to be supplied by France through a dummy trading company presided over by Pierre Augustin Caron, who took the name Beaumarchais. The French composer, adventurer, poet, and jewelry-maker had taken a particular interest in the American cause. Of course, it was not the interest of Beaumarchais that caused the steadily mounting supply of French goods. The king, Louis XVI, and his ministers could not resist the opportunity to weaken Great Britain. The obvious way to accomplish this—short of a war for which France was not yet ready—was by clandestine shipments of desperately needed military equipment to Washington's army. It was certainly cheaper and safer for the French to equip the Americans to fight the British than for them to undertake the task themselves. If the Americans, with French aid, could cause a constant drain of British soldiers, sailors, ships, and money, there was no telling what gains might accrue to France.

The situation of Washington's army by early spring can best be gauged by the general's own account to Robert Morris, the Philadelphia financier. He estimated that Howe had no less than 10,000 soldiers available for duty in New Jersey. The total American force there did not exceed 4,000—2,000 of Washington's Continentals plus a roughly equal number of militia. "His," Washington wrote, "are well disciplined, well officered, and well supplied; ours, raw militia, badly officered and under no government." The prospective American advantage lay in the fact that while Howe's force "can not be in a short time augmented, ours must be very considerably, and by such troops as we can have some reliance upon, or the game is at an end." Washington was convinced that Howe, as soon as the weather and the roads improved, would strike for Philadelphia. "With what propriety," he asked, "can he miss so favorable an opportunity of striking a capital stroke against a city from whence we derive so many advantages, the carrying of which would give such eclat to his arms, and strike such a damp to ours?"

If the recruiting and training of a new army went, as always, with disheartening slowness, the officer corps took shape as the more able and experienced were advanced and the weak and inefficient were shifted to jobs where they could do little harm. There was one unfortunate portent: Lord Stirling, Thomas Mifflin, Adam Stephen, Arthur St. Clair, and Benjamin Lincoln were advanced to major general, but Benedict Arnold was inexplicably omitted. On his military record he deserved to be promoted. Furious, he submitted his resignation, but Washington convinced him to retract it.

A large group of colonels who had performed excellent service—among them John Glover, Anthony Wayne, Edward Hand, Joseph Reed, and Charles Scott—were promoted to brigadier general. As before, the order in which they were listed, which determined their precedence over each other within rank, was the cause of endless petty squabbles and jealousies. Timothy Pickering took Reed's place as adjutant general when Reed resigned his commission. General Alexander MacDougall, the New York radical of "Wilkes and '45" fame, took over command of the American forces at Peekskill. Heath, who had taken a brief leave, was ordered to assume command of the Eastern Department in Massachusetts from Artemas Ward.

Typical of the problems Washington had with his generals was John Sullivan's petulant complaint that he had not been given an independent command, though Heaven knows he had done little enough to deserve one. "Why these unreasonable, these unjustifiable suspicions, which can answer no other end than to poison your own happiness and add vexation to that of others?" Washington wrote, like a father admonishing a sullen child, adding, "I shall quit with an earnest expostulation that you will not suffer yourself to be teased with evils that only exist in the imagination, and with slights that have no existence at all. . . ." If any independent commands became available, Washington reminded Sullivan, there were other generals "before you in point of rank who have a right to claim preference."

Throughout the spring, there were frequent small engagements with the British and Hessians. Intermittent raids by Washington's soldiers inflicted steady losses on the battalion of Seventy-first Highlanders, stationed at Bonham Town between Perth Amboy and New Brunswick. In April, Cornwallis attacked General George Clinton, who was stationed at Bondwick, seven miles from New Brunswick, drove him out of the town, and captured some one hundred Americans. Early in May, General Stephen with two thousand men launched a surprise attack on the Forty-second Regiment at Piscataway and was driven off with heavy casualties. Stephen reported the raid as a great success, claiming to have felled at least two hundred British, but Washington caught him in the lie.

Besides his concern about Howe's movement toward Philadelphia, Washington was very much aware of the possibility that Howe would send a strong force up the Hudson to make contact with Burgoyne, who was reportedly driving down from the north. This was a strategy widely discussed and indeed anticipated by many of the officers of Howe's staff. Lord Germain had, in addition, sent what was subsequently to become a very famous and controversial letter to Howe, saying that he "expected" Howe to move up the Hudson to make connection with Burgoyne. Since Germain's words appeared more in the form of a suggestion (or at least Howe chose to interpret them in this way) than an order, Howe ignored them. The truth was that Howe was countersuggestible. If someone proposed a course of action, he was likely to reject it. But none of this, of course, was known to Washington, and he, with his usual prudence and foresight, collected a substantial force of New Englanders, both Continentals and militia, at Peekskill to oppose any move up the river by land. An enormous chain had been forged to be stretched some eighteen hundred feet across the river below Peekskill, in order to deny passage to British warships and transports. The forging and placing of the chain was a herculean task that turned out to be an example of misplaced American ingenuity. The links kept breaking and the chain kept pulling loose from its moorings.

As spring wore on, as spongy roads began to dry out and streams and rivers to fall, Washington redoubled his preparations for renewed campaigning. The soldiers, like hibernating animals, began to emerge from the makeshift huts in which they had sought refuge from the rigors of a winter encampment. The case of our old friend Joseph Martin is apropos. After White Plains, Martin had been sent to Norwalk as nurse to sick soldiers, and when his term of enlistment had ended he had returned home. As he put it: "The spring of 1777 arrived. I . . . begun to think again about the army. In the month of April as the weather warmed, the young men began to enlist." Now the prospect was of enlisting for three years, or for the duration of the war. One of Martin's best friends had enlisted for the duration with the rank of sergeant and had been assigned to recruiting service "and was every time he saw me, which was often," Martin noted, "harassing me with temptations to engage in the service again." Finally, as Martin put it, "he so far overcame my resolution as to get me into the scrape again. . . ." As soon as Martin had enlisted, he regretted his decision. He had been overpersuaded. He went to his sergeant friend "and told him I repented my bargain." The friend asked his captain to release Martin, and the captain consented.

Relieved, Martin enrolled in the town militia, only to find that each militia unit was required to "furnish a man for the army, either by hiring or by sending one of their own number." Martin had a cousin by marriage who was a lieutenant in the Continental Army, and this officer, anxious to recruit Martin, urged the men of his squad to try to enlist him, "and they accordingly attacked me front, rear and flank." At last Martin agreed, if his fellow militiamen would make up a proper purse for him. At the next militia muster Martin "kept wandering about till the afternoon, among the crowd, when I saw the lieutenant, who went with me into a house where the men of the squad were, and there I put my name to the enlisting indentures for the last time. And now I was hampered again. The men gave me what they agreed to, I forget the sum, perhaps enough to keep the blood circulating during the short space of time which I tarried at home after I had enlisted. They were now freed from any further trouble, at least for the present, and I had become the scapegoat for them."

The men of Martin's newly recruited regiment assembled from all over the western part of Connecticut at the home of their Colonel, John Chandler. There "Uncle Sam" supplied them with arms and ammunition, which he "was always careful to supply us with . . . even if he could not give us anything to eat, drink, or wear." And so it went in hundreds of towns and thousands of militia squads; slowly Washington's army filled up, often with men who, like Martin, had given a good account of themselves in earlier actions.

Before Martin could even join the main army, Benedict Arnold marched him and his militia unit, along with a number of others from adjacent towns, off to intercept a British raiding party that had burned and sacked the town of Danbury.

The British-Hessian force of almost two thousand men had landed near the mouth of the Saugatuck River, some four miles from Norwalk. From there they marched twenty-five miles inland to Danbury, where they destroyed 1,700 barrels of pork, fifty barrels of preserved beef, 700 barrels of flour, thirty barrels of fat, and a number of hogsheads of rum and wine. In addition, 1,600 bushels of grain were burned up, along with a supply of desperately needed tents and ten new wagons. Much of the town was set afire, and those people who remained in it, Tory or patriot, were harassed and abused by the British and Hessian soldiers. An eyewitness, Mrs. Thaddeus Burr, who, hoping to protect her home from pillaging, had stayed behind in the town when others fled, told of finding British soldiers in her bedroom. The redcoats, she wrote, "fell to stripping and tearing her curtains to pieces, and then with their bayonets cut and slashed her dressing glass with the bureau table. . . . They damned her and . . . robbed her of her buckles and searched her pockets and took her sleeve buttons and everything she had about her. . . ." After the British troops were gone, a detachment of Hessians "came to her house, abused her most shamefully by insulting her, told her she had a gold watch and then went to searching her again, ordered her if she had a mind to save anything to do it in so many minutes, for her house was to be fired directly. . . . they abused old Mrs. Rawland very much, dragged her about by the hair of her head, tore her clothes off and swore they would kill her. . . . They murdered old Mr. S. Sturgis and old Mr. J. Gold in a most inhuman manner. . . ."

Arriving on the heels of the departing British, Martin noted that "the town had been laid in ashes, a number of the inhabitants murdered and cast into their burning houses, because they presumed to defend their persons and property, or to be avenged on a cruel, vindictive invading enemy. I saw the inhabitants, after the fire was out, endeavoring to find the burnt bones of their relatives amongst the rubbish of their demolished houses. The streets, in many places, were thereby flooded by the fat which ran from the piles of barrels of pork burnt by the enemy."

During the raid, and as the British and Hessians began their withdrawal, Benedict Arnold had been scouring the country for militia and had gathered several hundred men and a six-pound artillery piece. This gun he rushed to a rise by the Saugatuck River, near where the British were to be picked up by transports waiting in Long Island Sound. A half-hour later the British appeared, and as soon as they were within range, Arnold ordered the six-pounder fired, producing considerable confusion and alarm in the British ranks. A party of redcoats moved up to outflank the American positions, and Arnold, in turn, tried to flank the flankers, but the task was too demanding for the untrained militia, and the British succeeded in emplacing several artillery pieces on an elevation that commanded the American positions, forcing Arnold's men to withdraw. "General Arnold," one observer wrote, "exerted every power & faculty in order to excite the Troops to a manly discharge of their duty. Indeed, he exposed himself, almost to a fault. . . ." When the British tried to resume their march, Arnold, now joined by a force under General Wooster, pursued and harassed them. For a time it looked as though there might be a reenactment of the retreat from Lexington and Concord. Some of the British and Hessians, without sleep or rest for three days and nights, dropped in their tracks from exhaustion. But when it seemed the Americans might rout the weary British, the carriage of the six-pounder collapsed, and two others, brought by Wooster, ran out of ammunition.

At the landing site, the Americans again pressed hard to trap the enemy, but the British General William Erskine led a desperate counter-attack that routed the Americans. Once more Arnold distinguished himself. Riding up "to our front line in the full force of the Enemy's fire, of Musquetry & Grape shot, [he] encouraged them from right to left." As the British advanced to drive back their tormenters, Arnold "conjured [his men] by the love of themselves, posterity and all that is sacred not to desert him," Martin wrote, "but it was all to no purpose, their nerves were unstrung at the shot of the artillery, and having no officers of spirit among them . . . they became panic struck, and there was no stopping them. . . ." Colonel John Lamb, who had rivaled Arnold in bravery and enterprise, was wounded by grapeshot, and General Wooster was so badly injured that his life was despaired of. American estimates of the British casualties were some one hundred and fifty killed or wounded, including ten officers; American losses were ten or twelve killed and as many wounded, the most serious casualties, of course, being Lamb and Wooster. As Martin expressed it, "we had some pretty severe scratches with them; killed some, wounded some, and took some prisoners." The principal credit for the American attack went, properly, to Benedict Arnold, who assumed command of the militia and, during the action, was reported to have had two horses shot out from under him.

Whatever damage the British inflicted on the Americans at Danbury by their destruction of supplies was largely negated by the indignation aroused by the wanton looting and burning carried out by the invaders. Like the burning of Falmouth and Norfolk, the punitive spirit in which the foray against Danbury was carried out served, if anything, to stiffen patriot resolve and rally more recruits to the army and the local militia forces.

After the Danbury raid, Washington, still concerned over the possibility of a move north by Howe, sent Nathanael Greene to inspect the American positions in the "highlands" around Peekskill. Greene arrived at almost the same time that Joseph Martin's regiment reached the town after its attempt to block the British withdrawal from Danbury. Perhaps Greene, too, was kept awake by the "continual roar" of the whippoorwills that began "their imposing music in the twilight and continue it till ten or eleven o'clock, and commence again before the dawn. No man, unless he were stupified," Martin wrote, "could get a wink of sleep during the serenade."

One of the measures Washington took to prepare for the summer campaigns ahead was to give all the new soldiers who had not had smallpox an inoculation against it under carefully controlled and supervised conditions. Martin and his fellows were placed in a large barn and there inoculated by having their arms scratched and and a fresh smallpox scab placed on the wound. The immunity that they received as the result of such a course of treatment was not due to the so-called inoculation, but to the fact that they actually had a case of smallpox, hopefully a mild one. Fasting and frequent purgatives were considered an essential part of the regimen. A small stream ran in front of the improvised hospital where Martin and his fellows were quartered. The weather was warm; his smallpox pustules itched and smarted. He and a friend could not resist the temptation to slip into the cool water to fish for suckers. Stealing out of the hospital, they left their clothes on the riverbank and, equipping themselves with short rods from which bare hooks were suspended, made their way up the stream, hooking plump suckers as they went. "We continued at this business three or four hours," Martin noted, "and when we came out of the water, the pustules of the smallpox were well cleansed." His expedition was not what the doctor had ordered, and during the night Martin was violently ill—he was lucky, he thought, to survive.

Immune to smallpox, he had dysentery followed by a severe attack of the boils: "Good old Job could scarcely have been worse handled by them than I was," he wrote. "I had eleven at one time upon my arm, each as big as half a hen's egg, and the rest of my carcas was in much the same condition."

By May, Washington's army, increased by the arrival of Joseph Martin and hundreds like him, numbered almost eight thousand men; they were organized into five divisions of two brigades each—a total of forty-three regiments from Pennsylvania, Virginia, Maryland, Delaware, Connecticut, and New Jersey. The division commanders were Greene, Stephen, Sullivan, Lincoln, and Stirling. At the end of May, Washington, anticipating a drive into the Jerseys by Howe, moved his headquarters from Morristown to Middlebrook, some twelve miles south of Morristown, where a long wooded ridge, running roughly east and west, provided a natural defensive position. The Raritan River also ran along the front of Washington's lines, making an attack still more difficult. Washington placed Arnold, now a major general and apparently placated, in command of Philadelphia in case Howe should move in that direction.

In New York, the Tories and the British regained the optimism that had been dampened by Washington's winter offensive in the Jerseys. A Boston Tory told Ambrose Serle that New England "was distressed beyond Measure for Clothing and dry Goods; that they were at absolute Variance among themselves, without Law, without Administration of Justice, without Constitution; that they lost full 9000 men by Battle & Sickness in their Expedition to Canada; that the People are discontented, & begin to wish matters were in the old Channel; . . . that they can scarce obtain any Recruits for their Army; and that the whole Country is running, fast into Beggary & Ruin." In May, 1777, two deserters told Serle that Washington's whole force at Bound Brook and Morristown did not exceed seven thousand men, and that a maidservant in Washington's headquarters at Morristown had reported to them "that she has frequently caught [the general] in Tears about the House, and that, when he is alone, he appears constantly dejected and unhappy. . . ."

It was June 12 before Howe marched from New Brunswick toward Princeton. He obviously felt no press of time. It was far more important to stitch up the rebels thoroughly than to do so hastily. His army consisted of nearly seventeen thousand well-trained and well-equipped soldiers. It set out at eleven o'clock at night, hoping thereby to surprise Sullivan's brigade, which was thought to be at Princeton. Cornwallis was sent on to Hillsborough to protect Howe's flank, and Von Heister turned off the Princeton road toward the Raritan and the front of Washington's position at Middlebrook. Contrary to Washington's expectations, Howe did not intend to "occupy" New Jersey once more, nor to march on Philadelphia. His "only object," he wrote Germain, "was to bring the American army to a general action." Besides being counter-suggestible, Sir William was a slow learner. He should have known by now that Washington was as anxious to avoid a "general action" as Howe was to bring one on.

The movement that Howe in fact executed was to anchor his right flank at New Brunswick and rest his left on Millstone Creek just above (or south of) the point where it flowed into the Raritan. Two redoubts were built at Somerset Court House facing Middlebrook, and Howe settled down—apparently to wait for an attack by Washington. Sullivan, observing the movement of Howe's army, simply withdrew to the northwest to Flemington. Washington, confident now that Howe had no immediate intention of advancing up the Hudson, ordered the troops under MacDougall, Parsons, and Glover at Peekskill to march, one division at a time, to his support at Middlebrook; Putnam was left with four Massachusetts regiments ready to move north to help intercept Burgoyne, who, Washington learned on June 20, was approaching St. John's in command of an army of some thirteen thousand. The fact that Howe had left his heavy baggage, provisions, and boats at New Brunswick confirmed Washington in his opinion that Howe's objective was not, in fact, the Delaware and, beyond it, Philadelphia.

On the morning of the nineteenth, Howe abandoned his positions in front of Middlebrook and retired to New Brunswick. Washington sent General William Maxwell on a forced march to take up a position between New Brunswick and Perth Amboy in the event that Howe planned a maneuver against the relatively exposed American left. Greene was dispatched with three brigades to follow the north bank of the Raritan and attack the British rear if the opportunity arose. On June 22, Howe started out from New Brunswick to Perth Amboy. His rear guard of Hessians had hardly cleared the town when it was vigorously attacked by Anthony Wayne and Daniel Morgan, whose men drove them back to the main body. Greene's plan to join with Maxwell in an attack on the column as it approached Piscataway miscarried when Maxwell failed to get Greene's message, but Washington, half-persuaded by his officers that the retreat was a genuine one rather than a feint to draw him out of his strong positions at Middlebrook, advanced his main body to Quibbletown. The American forces were therefore deployed along the left flank of Howe's column in a line roughly parallel to the Brunswick-Amboy road, and echeloned to the north.

As soon as it was clear that Washington had reacted to the feint, Howe swung his columns sharply to the left and north and headed for Scotch Plains and Westfield, hoping thereby to outflank Washington, separate his main army from the detachments that had harassed the British line of march, and take the high ground in the rear of Middlebrook, making that post untenable. The ultimate hope was to force Washington into a general engagement.

On June 26 Cornwallis was dispatched through Woodbridge in an encircling movement intended to outflank the American left and effect Howe's plan for driving Washington out of his entrenched positions at Middlebrook. Howe, meanwhile, led the British left forward to Metuchen Meeting House with the hope of pinning down the American left so that Cornwallis could carry through his encircling movement. A third detachment was sent to make a feint at the American right at Bonham Town, where Greene and Wayne were stationed. Howe did not know that Stirling had moved his division well beyond Metuchen in the direction of Woodbridge. Cornwallis had hardly passed beyond the town when he encountered Stirling's men, who, outnumbered two to one, made a stiff fight of it, only giving ground when Cornwallis's heavier and more numerous artillery drove them back. Stirling's division lost more than two hundred men killed, wounded, and captured, while the British losses were no more than seventy, but the clash won valuable time and allowed the main body of Washington's army to retire to the Middlebrook positions. Howe's elaborate stratagem had failed, and he was back where he had started from a week earlier. In the words of Charles Stedman, who served on Howe's staff, Howe "made use of every possible effort to induce [Washington] to quit his position and hazard an engagement. The American general, however, easily penetrated into the designs of the commander in chief, and eluded them all by his cool, collected, and prudent conduct."

In Henry Knox's words, the British "conduct was perplexing. It was unaccountable that people who the day before gave out in very gasconading terms that they would be in Philadelphia in six days should stop short when they had gone only nine miles."

The people of New Jersey, roused from their cautious neutrality by the plundering and insolence of the British army, were, Knox wrote, "all fire, all revenge." Howe's withdrawal was beset by the Americans, who buzzed around like angry bees, constantly sniping at officers and men, cutting off stragglers, and taking prisoners whenever the opportunity offered. Among the prisoners were two lieutenants of the grenadiers and an officer of the light horse. "This little march of General Howe's," Knox noted, "fully proves that no people can be permanently conquered when the inhabitants are unanimous in opposition."

Howe, unwilling to press the attack on Middlebrook, decided to abandon the Jerseys. He moved his army to Perth Amboy, then across to Staten Island, and began to load his soldiers on transports. Compared to this muddled and pointless foray into the Jerseys, Howe's earlier operations were quite splendid. Again in the words of Stedman: "Thus the British general retreated before an enemy greatly inferior in force; and, after obtaining great advantages, altered the plan of operation which he himself had proposed, and the British minister of war had approved [which was to move on Pennsylvania through the Jerseys]. Why (it was asked) did he make such extensive preparations for crossing the Delaware, without making use of them? Why did he pass on the south side of the Raritan, and take positions in which he could neither assail his enemy nor the enemy him, if disposed to do so? Why did he not march round either on the north or south to the rear of that enemy where [the enemy] might have been assaulted without any other hazard than such as must, in the common course of war, be unavoidably incurred? If the enemy was, in his judgment, so strongly posted as to render an attack on his camp a measure too bold and desperate, why did he not intercept his convoys, cut off his supplies of provisions, and reduce him under his power by famine; or cross the Delaware, and destroy his posts and magazines?"

If Stedman, who was an aide to Howe, could not answer these questions, it is not surprising that subsequent historians have found Howe's actions a puzzle. The answers are locked in the mystery of Sir William's own temperament. Even Howe's explanation of his movements are not consistent. He spoke at one point of hesitating to attack Washington because he (Howe) realized that he was outnumbered, but Stedman, who was in a position to know, listed the British forces in June, 1777, at thirty thousand and the "rebels" at eight thousand.

By June, 1777, Serle and his Tory friends were deeply depressed. "Much dejected in my Mind at the Appearance of Affairs," Serle wrote. "Had a long, pensive Walk with Mr. Galloway," he added the next day, ". . . in wch we discoursed upon the Dejection of our Army, the Elevation of the Rebels, & the present posture of Affairs. We were very melancholy upon the whole, and parted with wishing for better Times." Two weeks later Galloway reported to Serle a conversation with Lord Howe, "who gave up every Hope of obtaining America by Arms. We agreed," Serle added, "that if affairs go on as they have lately done, He will certainly be in the right." In another diary entry in June, he wrote despairingly: "Follies and Blunders without end!"

The most spectacular episode of the summer of 1777 was undoubtedly Major William Barton's capture of the British general Richard Prescott at his Rhode Island headquarters. The reader will recall the capture of Charles Lee at Basking Ridge the preceding fall. Captured officers were commonly exchanged, rank for rank, but the Americans had no British general to exchange for Lee, who thus languished in captivity. Meanwhile Major Barton of the Rhode Island line, who was stationed at Tiverton on the eastern shore of Narragansett Bay, learned that General Richard Prescott, who was in command of the British troops that occupied Rhode, Canonicut, and Prudence islands, had established his headquarters on the west side of Rhode Island. From a captured British soldier Barton learned the exact location of Prescott's house and its relation to the British positions. Barton conceived the notion of kidnapping Prescott and got permission from his commanding officer to recruit a picked force of raiders to help him.

He selected forty men and two officers, and on July 4, 1777, they embarked in long boats for Bristol, where they spent the day and reconnoitered. On the night of the fifth, Barton and his men landed at Warwick Neck; a severe storm delayed them for four days, but on July 9, with the weather at last clearing, they set sail for Rhode Island, slipping between the British warships anchored in the bay. Guards were left with the boats and the remainder of the party divided into five groups. The distance from the landing spot to the general's headquarters was about a mile. The house had three doors, and three groups were assigned to block these exits. One group was to guard the road as a line of retreat, and the fifth was to stand by in case of emergency. Arriving at Prescott's house, the lead group was challenged by a sentry who called out, "Who goes there?" "Friends," Barton replied. "Advance and give the countersign." "We have no countersign," Barton answered, continuing to advance on the uncertain sentry; "Have you seen any rascals tonight?" By this time, Barton was an arm's length from the sentry, and before the latter could speak or move, the major had seized his musket and hissed to him that he had better not make a sound on pain of death. The other groups moved quickly to their posts, and Barton, with threats, extracted from the sentry the information that Prescott was indeed in the house.

When Barton knocked on the front door, the owner, one Perwig, insisted that the general was away. A hasty search of the lower rooms failed to turn up Prescott, whereupon Barton declared in a loud voice that he would burn the house down if necessary. At this point a voice with a decidedly English accent called down from the upstairs hall to ask what the commotion was. Barton and his men dashed up the steps to find a drowsy Prescott, still in his bedclothes. Barton addressed him as General Prescott, and the man admitted his identity. "You are my prisoner," Barton informed him. "I acknowledge that I am," Prescott replied. He was given a minute to draw on trousers and shoes and was then hustled off, his coat and hat in his hand, down the stairs and out into the darkness.

While Barton and his men had been searching the house, one of the British guards, dressed in his nightshirt, had managed to escape and had run off to spread the alarm. He informed the sentry on duty at a nearby cavalry post, but when that soldier in turn tried to pass on the story to the officer of the guard, it was dismissed as too ridiculous to credit.

Barton and his little party, hastily assembled, set out for the boats, hurrying the general along with them. Before they embarked, Prescott was permitted to finish dressing, so that he might appear as a proper British general rather than as a half-clothed prisoner. The raiders had hardly pushed off before a discharge of cannon and three sky rockets spread the alarm. The British ships in the harbor failed to respond to the signal, and the boats got safely back to Bristol. When they landed, Prescott is reported to have said to Barton, "Sir, you have made an amazing bold push tonight." "We have been fortunate," Barton replied, with considerable truth.

The episode was one of the most daring and dramatic of the war. Barton and his men became instant heroes, and General Charles Lee eventually was exchanged for Prescott.

On July 5, thirty-six battalions of British and Hessian troops, including a regiment of light horse, were loaded on transports, "where both foot and cavalry remained pent up, in the hottest season of the year, in the holds of vessels" until July 23. There we will leave Howe and his army for the moment, quite literally stewing in their own juices.

2

Burgoyne's Invasion

WHILE Washington tried to penetrate Sir William Howe's strange maneuvers and obscure strategies, "Gentleman Johnny" Burgoyne began his fateful campaign to end the war by splitting the rebellious colonies in two. This was to be accomplished by driving down from Canada to Lake Champlain, Lake George, and the Hudson River, thus splitting New England off from the middle and southern colonies.

On March 26, 1777, a letter was dispatched from Lord Germain to Sir Guy Carleton, instructing him, after the Americans had been driven from Canada, to reserve a force sufficient to defend the province and to send all other available troops under Burgoyne "with all possible expedition to join General Howe. . . . With a view of quelling the rebellion as soon as possible, it had become highly necessary," Germain declared, "that the most speedy juncture of the two armies should be effected." Burgoyne should press on to Albany, where he might expect to join forces with elements of Howe's army moving up from New York. Lieutenant Colonel Barry St. Leger was to make a diversionary move into the Mohawk Valley, supported by Indian auxiliaries, and give heart to the numerous Tories in that area.

Germain's instructions were remarkably detailed as to the particular units designated to undertake the expedition, but understandably vague as to how it was to be done. Some 3,770 men, carefully enumerated, were to remain in Canada for its defense; 7,173 were to accompany Burgoyne, and 675 soldiers were assigned to St. Leger.

The trouble with Germain was that he fancied himself a general. His long, tedious, and impractical orders to Carleton directed him to recruit Indians. This "corps of savages, supported by detachments of light regulars," he wrote, "should be continually on foot to keep [the Americans] in alarm and within their works, to cover the reconnoitering of general officers and engineers, and to obtain the best intelligence of their strength, position and design." "These ideas," Germain wrote at the end of his long screed, "are formed upon the supposition that it be the sole purpose of the Canada army to effect a junction with General Howe."

That was fine on paper. But in Canada there were practical difficulties that not even the zeal and energy of Carleton could surmount. Instead of a thousand Canadians, one hundred and fifty were mustered up. It proved to be difficult to recruit the corvées, the workmen whose task it would be to build roads through the wilderness for Burgoyne's baggage and artillery to pass over. Even drivers for the wagons were hard to find.

Germain's proposal was, in the main, based on Burgoyne's own suggestions as revised by the king, who also considered himself a military strategist. It was the king himself who specified the exact number of troops to be used in Burgoyne's expedition and the number to be retained in Canada.

One of the problems was that Howe had already written Sir Guy Carleton to inform him that he had "but little expectation that I shall be able, from the want of sufficient strength in this army, to detach a corps in the beginning of the campaign to act up Hudson's River." Carleton should, therefore, expect "little assistance from hence to facilitate [the] approach of any force coming down from Canada." Howe was confident, however, that the "friends of Government" in upper New York "will be found so numerous and so ready to give every aid and assistance in their power that it will prove no difficult task to reduce the more rebellious parts of the province." Howe would then give what assistance he could by attempting "to open the communication for shipping" on the Hudson by seizing the forts that presently guarded the river.

How easy and how wrong, to try and direct the war from the vicinity of St. James's Palace! And Howe was not helping the situation by his casual attitude toward the rebel's jugular—the Hudson River—and by his false perception of the strength of Tory sentiment. The British view of the Tories was incorrect because their contacts were among the prosperous colonial upper classes who contained in their ranks a disproportionate number of Loyalists. The British had few dealings with the common people, who they believed in their hearts to be of no consequence. It was simply beyond their comprehension that the great mass of the American people stood, in the matter of political judgments and opinions, on their own feet. The same thing was, of course, to a large degree true of the American Tories themselves. They had much the same aristocratic view of the commonalty (indeed they had learned it from the mother country). When they reported that "all substantial men" in their town or county supported the Crown, they simply left out of account, as being of *no* account, the feelings of most of their more humble neighbors—if, indeed, they knew what those feelings were.

Howe, who was constantly collecting soldiers from every point of the compass in order to descend on Washington, was the last man to be depended upon to bail out Burgoyne by dispatching a proper army to meet him at Albany. But even though Carleton was on notice that Burgoyne could expect no assistance from Howe, he gave Gentleman Johnny godspeed and sent him on his way, perhaps comforting himself with the thought that Germain, who was precise when he should have been vague and vague when he should have been precise, would straighten things out with Howe.

Underlying the confusion and uncertainty of Burgoyne's campaign was the simple and ultimately crucial fact that the British still could not take American military capabilities seriously. It did not occur to anyone that, with Washington preoccupied with Howe in the Jerseys, General Schuyler and his tattered legions could offer any serious resistance to Burgoyne's army. Given such a frame of mind, the British undertook ventures that they had little hope of carrying through successfully, or that, if successful, were seldom worth the effort expended.

There were, indeed, plenty of critics, British and American, who considered Burgoyne's expedition doomed from the start. Richard Henry Lee wrote to Sam Adams on July 27, 1777: "The success of Burgoyne thus far, I own I did expect, if he made the attempt. . . . But I am also inclined to think that if our Cards are well plaid, it may prove his ruin. There is nothing so delusive as prosperity, and I take Burgoyne's mind to be one of those most likely to be injured by its impressions; he may therefore be hurried into some fatal mistake provided we are ready to profit from his errors." Lee's comments proved a shrewd analysis of the British general's character.

There was also, of course, the fact that Burgoyne was an ass. This is not an absolute disqualification in a military leader—there have certainly been asses who made good generals. But it was in no sense an advantage, and Burgoyne seemed determined to establish his asininity at the very start of the campaign. He began his operation by cooking up a piece of literary bombast, which he prefaced with a list of his various titles and honors. Burgoyne left it to the judgment of his readers "whether the present unnatural Rebellion has not been made the Foundation of the compleatest System of Tyranny that ever God, in his Displeasure, suffered, for a Time, to be exercised over a froward and stubborn Generation." Having listed the numerous villainies of the rebels, he added, "To consummate these shocking Proceedings the Profanation of Religion is added to the most profligate Prostitution of common Reason! The Consciences of Men are set at naught, and the Multitude are compelled not only to bear arms, but also to swear Subjection to an Usurpation they abhor." The general, benign even to rascals and traitors, invited all the repentant to rally to him, confident that they would be forgiven and protected from harm. But if, despite such a generous and humane offer, there still remained those who were caught in "the Phrenzy of Hostility . . . the Messengers of Justice and of Wrath await them in the Field, and Devastation, Famine, and every concomitant Horror . . . will bar the Way."

The American "poet laureate," Francis Hopkinson, entertained his readers with a satire on Burgoyne's proclamation:

> By John Burgoyne and Burgoyne, John, Esq.,
> And graced with titles still more higher,
> For I'm Lieutenant-general, too,
> Of George's troops both red and blue,
> On this extensive continent;
> And of Queen Charlott's regiment
> Of light dragoons the Colonel . . .
> And furthermore, when I am there,
> In House of Commons I appear
> (Hoping ere long to be a Peer).

Hopkinson then compared Burgoyne to Don Quixote and, after mocking his pompous phrases, ended:

They'll [the British] scalp your heads, and kick your shins,
And rip your ass, and flay your skins,
And of your ears be nimble croppers,
And make your thumbs tobacco-stoppers.
If after all these loving yearnings,
You remain as deaf as an adder,
Or grow with hostile rage the madder
I swear by George and by St. Paul
I will exterminate you all.

With St. Leger going from Montreal by way of the St. Lawrence to Lake Ontario and then along the shore to Fort Oswego, Burgoyne loaded his army's baggage—including 128 pieces of artillery and mortars—on transports for passage down Lake Champlain to Ticonderoga and the headwaters of Lake George. "It is almost impossible to get an idea of the excessive amount of baggage carried along with the army," wrote DuRoi, a Hessian officer. "An army which is of any use in these parts, must be almost without baggage, and with no more tents than can be taken by boats."

In the British army was the Baron Friedrich Adolph von Riedesel and his wife—"my dear angel"—who, with her three children, Friedericke, Caroline, and Gustava, had made the arduous trip to America from Brunswick to join her husband, commander of the Brunswicker mercenaries on the expedition. The baroness, an observant lady, put future historians much in her debt by keeping a journal of the march. Lieutenant Thomas Anburey likewise kept a running account, and Burgoyne, to defend himself against charges of cowardice and incompetence, also composed a narrative of the expedition, entitled *A State of the Expedition from Canada*, published in London in 1780. With these and other letters and documents we have a reasonably full account of the campaign.

Burgoyne's force, which began moving south at the end of June, 1777, numbered 3,700 British regulars, 3,000 Hessians and Brunswickers, 470 artillerymen, 400 Indians, and some 250 Canadians and American Tories. The main body of the army marched along the west shore of Lake Champlain south toward Crown Point. The force moved by brigades, some seventeen to twenty miles a day, with each brigade occupying the campsite of the brigade that had preceded it. The supplies and heavy equipment, as well as the Indian auxiliaries and a portion of the troops, moved by boat over the mirrorlike waters of beautiful Lake Champlain. The flotilla of more than one hundred

vessels made, for Lieutenant Anburey, "one of the most pleasing spectacles I ever beheld." The lake was "remarkably fine and clear, not a
breeze stirring, when the whole army appeared at one view in such
perfect regularity, as to form the most compleat and splendid regatta
you can possibly conceive. . . . In the front, the Indians went with their
birch canoes, containing 20 to 30 in each, then the advanced corps in a
regular line, with the gun-boats, then followed the *Royal George* and
Inflexible, . . . with the other brigs and sloops following; after them the
first brigade in a regular line, then the Generals Burgoyne, Phillips, and
Riedesel in their pinnaces; next to them were the second brigade,
followed by the German brigades, and the rear was brought up with the
sutlers and followers of the army [for the most part, women]." The
army, in Anburey's opinion, was "in the best condition that can be
expected or wished, the troops in the highest spirits, admirably disciplined, and remarkably healthy."

At the Bouquet River on the shores of Lake Champlain, Burgoyne
arranged for a meeting with the chiefs and principal warriors of the
Algonquins, Iroquois, Abnaki, and Ottawa, some four hundred in
number. They listened patiently to an interpreter who read to them,
with, it may be imagined, some modest alterations, General Burgoyne's
address:

"Chiefs and Warriors, the great King, our common father and
patron of all who seek and deserve his protection, has considered with
satisfaction the general conduct of the Indian tribes from the beginning
of the troubles in America. Too sagacious and too faithful to be deluded
or corrupted, they have observed the violated rights of the parental
power they love, and burned to vindicate them . . . Warriors, you are
free—go forth in might and valour of your cause—strike at the common enemies of Great Britain and America, disturbers of public order,
peace and happiness, destroyers of commerce, parricides of state."

Then, having invited them to attack the Americans, Burgoyne
added a cautionary note. It would be the responsibility of the British
and Hessian officers "from the dictates of our religion, the laws of our
warfare and the principles and interest of our policy, to regulate your
passions when they over bear, to point out where it is nobler to spare
than to revenge, to discriminate degrees of guilt, to suspend the uplifted
stroke, to chastise and not destroy. . . . Aged men, women and children
must be held sacred from the knife or hatchet." Scalps might be taken,
but only from those who were dead; on no account from "the wounded
or even dying," and the Indians must not kill the wounded or prisoners

in order to get their scalps. Nor must they tell lies and say that one of the enemy was already dead when they in fact had really killed him in order to get his scalp.

When the speech was finally finished, an old chief of the Iroquois rose to assure the general that the Indians had listened attentively, were pleased with the address, and would fight bravely by the side of the British. "After the Chief of the Iroquois had finished," a British officer noted, "they all, as before, cried out *'Etow! Etow! Etow!'*" and the meeting broke up.

After the treaty meeting, the Indians were provided with rum and staged a war dance in which, as young Lieutenant Anburey described it, "they throw themselves in various postures, every now and then making the most hideous yells; as to their appearance, nothing more horrid can you paint to your imagination, being dressed in such an *outre* manner, some with the skins of bulls with the horns upon their heads, others with a great quantity of feathers, and many in a state of total nudity. . . ."

Burgoyne was delighted with his own speech and with the council and promptly sent off copies of his address to England, where Edmund Burke, speaking in the House of Commons, made great fun of it. "Suppose," he asked the members, "there was a riot on Tower Hill. What would the keeper of his Majesty's lions do? Would he not fling open the dens of the wild beasts and then address them thus: 'My gentle lions—my humane bears—my tender-hearted hyenas, go forth! But I exhort you, as you are Christians, and members of civil society, take care not to hurt any man, woman or child.'"

Burgoyne's final pronouncement was a relatively mild bit of gasconade issued in the form of an order to his troops at Crown Point: "The army embarks to-morrow to approach the enemy. The services required of this particular expedition are critical and conspicuous. During our progress occasions may occur, in which, no difficulty, nor labour, nor life are to be regarded. This army must not retreat."

General Philip Schuyler had been in command of the Americans' Northern Department until March, 1777, when Horatio Gates, who coveted the post, intrigued with his supporters in Congress and managed to get the assignment for himself. Schuyler, however, rallied the New York Congressional delegation to his cause and, after appearing before Congress to argue his case, was restored to his command. Returning to his headquarters early in June, Schuyler offered Gates direction of the post at Ticonderoga, the most vital point in his command. But Gates, who had done little in the period he was in command, had not resigned himself to being superseded and refused the post. "If General Schuyler is solely to possess all powers, all the intelligence, and that particular favorite, the military chest, and constantly reside in Albany, I cannot, with any peace of mind, serve at Ticonderoga," he wrote.

Gates had been Charles Lee's confidant, and we have already noted his dissatisfaction with Washington after the fall of Fort Washington and his insinuations that Lee should replace the commander in chief. Now Gates wrote petulantly to James Lovell, one of the Massachusetts delegates in Congress, complaining about lack of support from Washington, adding, "Either I am exceedingly dull, or unreasonably jealous if I do not discern by the style and tenor of the letters from Morristown, how little I have to expect from thence. Generals are like parsons, they are all for christening their own children first; but let an impartial moderating power decide between us, and do not suffer southern prejudice to weigh heavier in the balance than northern."

Schuyler, back in command of the department, did all he could to augment the defenses of Fort Ticonderoga as well as of Fort Edward and the lower posts on Lake George. Arthur St. Clair was the senior officer at Ticonderoga, supported by Fermoy, Poor, and Patterson, with twenty-five hundred Continental soldiers and about nine hundred militia. Schuyler, on an inspection trip, found the situation at Ticonderoga deplorable. The men were short on military supplies and their clothing was in rags. They had only a few hundred bayonets for three thousand muskets and little to eat besides salt pork and flour. It was decided in a council of war that Ticonderoga would not resist long against a siege by a superior force. St. Clair, if attacked, as it now seemed certain he would be, was to try to hold out long enough to give reinforcements time to come to his assistance and then, when the position was no longer tenable, was to try to carry away all his supplies.

On July 1, after Schuyler had returned to Albany, he wrote to a friend, expressing his doubts about the ability of the defenders to hold the fort without being trapped in it. "The insufficiency of the garrison," he noted, " . . . the imperfect state of the fortifications, and the want of discipline in the troops, give me great cause to apprehend that we shall lose that fortress, but as a reinforcement is coming up from Peekskill, with which I shall move up, I am in hopes that the enemy will be prevented from any further progress."

Arriving at Crown Point on June 27, Burgoyne pushed on to

Ticonderoga, reaching that post three days later. Opposite Fort Ticonderoga was Mount Independence, which commanded the water passage between Lake Champlain and Lake George. It had been heavily fortified by the Americans. The strait itself was blocked by twenty-two large timbers, connected by floats of logs fifty feet long and twelve feet wide. These in turn were bound by chains and secured to timber piers. At the northern entrance to Lake George, the South River branches to the east. Between the river and the lake is a tongue of land known as Sugar Loaf Hill, a point some seven hundred feet high that overlooks both Ticonderoga and Mount Independence. The Americans had considered Sugar Loaf impossible to fortify because of the steepness of its sides, but Lieutenant Twiss of the British engineers hacked out a path to the summit; it was occupied by the British, and cannons were hauled up with great effort. The promontory was named Fort Defiance, and a battery of guns soon looked out over the headwaters of Lake George.

When he saw the British battery on Sugar Loaf Hill, St. Clair and his council of war decided that both Ticonderoga and Fort Independence were indefensible, that a "retreat ought to be undertaken as soon as possible, and that we shall be fortunate to effect it." Both forts were almost surrounded by Burgoyne's forces, with only South River (really a large lake) remaining as an avenue of escape. On the night of July 5, the soldiers were given the order to prepare to evacuate both forts. The sick, ammunition, and supplies were quietly loaded on 220 bateaux tied up in the South River and sent down the lake to Skenesboro. Artillery fire was kept up on the British positions on Sugar Loaf Hill, and every effort was made to suggest normal camp routines.

St. Clair directed a battery of guns on Mount Independence to be loaded with grape and canister and aimed at the makeshift bridge spanning the straits between the forts and the eastern shore. Four soldiers with lighted wicks were detailed to wait at the guns until the British started across in pursuit of the retiring Americans. They were then to fire the cannon and make their escape. ("Had these men obeyed their instructions," Anburey noted lated, "they would, situated as our brigade was, have done great mischief; but allured by the sweets of plunder and liquor, instead of obeying their orders, we found them dead drunk by a cask of Madeira." But while Anburey was congratulating himself on this turn of events, a curious Indian picked up a still-smoldering wick and touched it to a cannon, which went off with a roar, narrowly missing the men of the Ninth Regiment, who were at that moment crossing the bridge.)

At three in the morning, the American garrison at Ticonderoga made its way across the bridge. Joining with the defenders of Fort Independence, they took the road southeast to Castleton. Before the last elements had cleared Fort Independence, a house was set afire, and in the light from the blaze, the British could see that the Americans were slipping away.

Dr. James Thacher, accompanying the women and the sick soldiers in the bateaux, which were under the command of Colonel Long and contained a sizable detachment of troops, observed that "the night was moon light and pleasant, the sun burst forth in the morning with uncommon lustre, the day was fine, the water's surface serene and unruffled," the whole scene "enchantingly sublime." Fifes and drums were broken out to provide music for "enlivening our spirits," and among the hospital stores some ingenuous soul discovered "many dozens of choice wine"—sisters, no doubt, to the Madeira that had overcome the artillery men at Mount Independence. In Thacher's words, "we cheered our hearts with the nectareous contents." They would hardly have been so cheery if they had known that the British were in hot pursuit.

As soon as the British discovered that the Americans had evacuated the two forts, Brigadier General Simon Fraser took command of a hastily assembled column of light infantry and gave chase, followed by General von Riedesel with three battalions of Brunswickers. Major General William Philips loaded a division on boats to pursue the American vessels that had sailed for Skenesboro. The bridge was soon cut, and the British frigates *Inflexible* and *Royal George,* with the fastest of the gunboats, all under the personal command of Burgoyne, started up the South River. By reacting swiftly, and by moving by both water and land along the east side of Lake George, Burgoyne had gotten ahead of St. Clair by nightfall.

Long's force had hardly arrived at Skenesboro at three in the afternoon when Burgoyne's frigates hove into view and opened fire on the galleys and bateaux tied at the wharf. Soon British soldiers and their Indian allies could be seen landing. Colonel Long and his officers tried to rally the regiments that had been assigned to guard the sick and the supplies, but "this was found impossible, every effort proved unavailing, and in the utmost panic they were seen to fly in every direction for personal safety." Thacher took some of his medical instruments and drugs from his medicine chest and joined in the retreat through the woods to Fort Anne. Wood Creek was navigable from Skenesboro to

Fort Anne, and some of the invalids and military baggage escaped by this route, but all the cannon and provisions, and several of the invalids, fell into the hands of the British.

With the British Ninth Regiment in close pursuit, Long arrived at Fort Anne. Meanwhile Schuyler, at the head of a small relief column, spent the night at Fort Edward, thirteen miles farther south. Hearing that Long was at Fort Anne, Schuyler hurried reinforcements to him, and Long, thus strengthened, turned on his pursuers next morning.

The Americans attacked at ten behind a "heavy and well directed fire." While the British front was engaged, a detachment of Americans took positions in a thick wood on the British left and from there began to sift toward their rear. To avoid being surrounded, the British withdrew to a high knoll, where they were again hard pressed by "a very vigorous attack and they certainly would have forced us," a British officer wrote, "had it not been for some Indians that arrived and gave the Indian whoop." The arrival of the Indians, with their bloodcurdling howls, demoralized the Americans, who withdrew to Fort Anne, bringing with them as captives a surgeon, a wounded captain, and twelve or fifteen privates. The surgeon, it turned out, had in his possession medical books and supplies that had been taken from Thacher's abandoned chest the day before, and several of the captured soldiers produced some of the doctor's private letters.

As more British reinforcements came up, the Americans burned the blockhouse and sawmill of a notorious Tory named Skene, and then fell back to Fort Edward to join forces with Schuyler. Long's men had given an excellent account of themselves, attacking with skill and resolution and inflicting heavy casualties on the British advance guard.

To the east, St. Clair, pursued by Fraser, left Colonel Turbott Francis with some thirteen hundred men to hold off the British pursuit. At five in the morning the British scouts came on the Americans cooking breakfast. General James Grant, the British commander of the detachment, promptly attacked and drove in the American pickets, but when he mounted a stump to look over the ground ahead a rifle ball struck him dead. General Fraser had to move his men down a forward slope to engage the Americans. Colonel Francis, probably wisely, did not wait to receive Fraser's assault but, taking advantage of higher ground, attacked. The fire of the Americans was especially severe on two regiments of the light infantry. The grenadiers moved to cut off the Castleton Road as a line of retreat and then scrambled and climbed to the summit of a steep hill that covered the British left. This movement caused confusion in the American ranks. One regiment fled from the field, leaving Francis and Colonel Seth Warner to face the British grenadiers and light infantry with some nine hundred men, as opposed to Fraser's eight hundred and fifty.

With conventional maneuvers made almost impossible by the nature of the terrain, the Americans fought skillfully and persistently from behind fallen trees, rocks, and stumps. They were, indeed, in the process of turning Fraser's left when Von Riedesel, who had hurried forward at Fraser's urging, arrived on the scene. Taking in the situation on the battlefield, Von Riedesel ordered his band to strike up a martial tune and moved to the attack with a company of his riflemen, who caught the American right flank just as they were about to take Fraser's regiments in the rear. The unexpected attack with bayonets scattered the Americans, whose own rear was suddenly threatened. After a brief skirmish they gave way. Francis had been killed in the American attack on the British left, and Warner's men were so dispersed in their retreat that he was only able to assemble 80 men when he joined St. Clair at Rutland. The British had lost 183 men and officers killed and wounded. The Brunswick casualties were 22. The Americans had 40 men and officers killed and 350 wounded or taken prisoner.

Perhaps the most impressive aspect of these figures is the clear evidence that the Americans could sustain heavy casualties and still persist in an attack against an equal force of British, carrying it to a point where the enemy was saved from defeat only by the arrival of reinforcements. In two separate engagements in the same twenty-four-hour period the Americans had attacked strong British forces with great resolution, and in both instances the British had been rescued by reinforcements. It was not an encouraging sign for Burgoyne, and in his report of Fraser's engagement, Burgoyne plainly misstated the case. According to his account of the battle, Fraser had attacked "two thousand rebels strongly fortified" and driven them from their position. Riedesel, by this account, arrived in time to share "in the honor of the victory." Lieutenant James Hadden of the Royal Artillery understood the significance of the engagement, if Burgoyne did not. "The corps," he wrote, "certainly discovered that neither they were invincible nor the Rebels all poltroons. On the contrary many of them acknowledged the enemy behaved well, and looked upon General Riedesel's fortunate arrival as a matter absolutely necessary."

How well Burgoyne's injunctions to the Indians to refrain from all acts of wanton violence and terrorism worked is suggested by the fact that General Fraser, having to send back the prisoners captured near Hubbardtown under a very small guard, told them if they tried to escape, "no quarter would be shown them, and that those who might elude the guard, the Indians would be sent in pursuit of, and scalp them."

Burgoyne soon had cause to regret his Indian allies. They infested Ticonderoga and attempted to carry away everything movable as part of their legitimate spoils of war. "Those who have the management and conduct of them," Anburey wrote, "are, from interested motives, obliged to indulge them in all their caprices and humors, and, like spoiled children, are more unreasonable and importunate upon every new indulgence granted them: but there is no remedy; were they left to themselves, they would be guilty of enormities too horrid to think of. . . ."

The British, for their part, were incensed by the fact that the Americans did not fight like gentlemen or observe the proper rules of warfare. An example, cited by Lieutenant Anburey, was the behavior in one engagement of some sixty Americans, who marched across a field toward two companies of grenadiers with their muskets clubbed (with the butts of the muskets over their shoulders). To the British this was an indication that they wished to surrender, and the British therefore held their fire, but when the Americans were only a few yards away, they presented their pieces, fired point-blank at the grenadiers, and took to their heels.

Lieutenant Anburey, who was in Fraser's corps, found the fighting far different from the Continental wars: "In this the life of an individual is sought with as much avidity as the obtaining a victory over an army of thousands." After Riedesel's rescue of Fraser, a group of British officers was standing on a promontory reading the papers that had been taken from Colonel Francis's dead body when one of them fell to the ground crying, "I have been wounded"; he was the victim of a sniper. Such was the "immoral" behavior of the Americans.

The general reaction to the abandonment of Ticonderoga and Mount Independence is indicated in James Thacher's journal. "It had," he wrote, "occasioned the greatest surprise and alarm. No event could be more unexpected nor more severely felt throughout our army and country. This disaster has given to our cause a dark and gloomy aspect. . . . The conduct of General St. Clair on this occasion has rendered him very unpopular, and subjected him to general censure and reproach; there are some, indeed, who even accuse him of treachery;

but time and calm investigation must decide whether he can vindicate himself as a judicious and prudent commander." Some "well informed and respectable characters," Thacher noted, among whom he plainly counted himself, predicted "that this event, apparently so calamitous, will ultimately prove advantageous, by drawing the British army into the heart of our country, and thereby place them more immediately within our power."

One clear benefit was that Burgoyne's army, marching in pursuit of St. Clair's remnant, committed itself to moving down the east side of Lake George, where his path could be more readily impeded by felled trees and where it was difficult if not impossible to supply his army by water. An advance down the west side of the lake over well-worn roads would have been infinitely easier and quicker.

After the engagements at Fort Anne and Castleton, Fort Edward, where Schuyler was in command, was the next point of resistance. St. Clair, his escape assured by Francis's courageous fight, arrived with his hungry and exhausted men at Fort Edward on July 12. Long was already there with his detachment. Burgoyne established his headquarters at Skenesboro and there showed his usual ingenuity in strengthening the hand of his enemies. He accomplished this by calling on the people of certain townships to return to British allegiance by the fifteenth of the month "under pain of military execution on failure to pay obedience to such order."

The only response came from Tories who came into Burgoyne's army every day, offering to serve as soldiers. Since only a few had guns, the rest were assigned to clearing roads and building bridges. But nowhere was there any sign of the general rising of Loyalists on which Burgoyne had so confidently counted.

Schuyler responded to Burgoyne's proclamation with his own warning "to all traitors who should in any way assist, give comfort to, or hold correspondence with, or take protection from the enemy," and pressed ahead with his efforts to impede and delay the progress of Burgoyne's army from Skenesboro to Fort Edward. Schuyler sent out parties to collect all the livestock and food supplies in the country through which the British must march. Much of the land was swampy, and creeks were blocked with brush and timber so that they would overflow their banks and flood the adjacent land. Bridges were destroyed, streams were diverted to intersect the route of march, and large trees were cut down to block trails and roads. In such tasks, the Americans were at their best. The results were all Schuyler could have asked. Burgoyne was forced to build forty bridges, chop his way through innumerable trees, and construct more than two miles of cord road in order to move his army forward by a few hundred yards—or feet—at a time. "You would think it almost impossible," Anburey wrote, "but every ten or twelve yards great trees are laid across the road . . . We lie under many disadvantages in prosecuting this war, from the impediments I have stated. . . ."

Anburey pointed out that the British soldier was hardly equipped for a rapid march through enemy territory, since he "generally carries during a campaign . . . a knapsack, a blanket, a haversack that contains his provision, a canteen for water, a hatchet, and a proportion of the equipage belonging to his tent; these articles (and for such a march there cannot be less than four days provision) added to his accouterments, arms and 60 rounds of ammunition, make an enormous bulk, weighing about 60 pounds." The Germans were even more encumbered, their grenadiers wearing a cap with "a very heavy brass front, a sword of enormous size, a canteen that cannot hold less than a gallon, and their coats are very long skirted." Often the soldiers, bowed down by such a weight, trudging through rain and slipping in the mud or sweating profusely under a merciless summer sun, threw away their heavy rations, exclaiming, as Anburey put it, "Damn the provisions, we shall get more at the next encampment; the General won't let his soldiers starve."

As the invading force advanced, problems of supply became Burgoyne's major preoccupation. In Anburey's words, "For one hour that he can devote in contemplating how to fight his army, he must allot twenty to contrive how to feed it!" Another handicap that the campaign had to bear was Burgoyne's contempt for the Germans under his command. The principal liability of the Germans was that they were not English. They were competent and well-trained troops who usually gave a good account of themselves in battle. But Baron Riedesel, a brave and experienced officer who was popular with his soldiers and was by all accounts a kind and generous man, was left out of Burgoyne's councils and given, or so it seemed to him, the less demanding and thus less honorable assignments.

Baroness von Riedesel, a pious lady, was scandalized by Burgoyne's way of life, in which he persisted despite the hardships of the march. "He spent half the nights," she noted disapprovingly, "in singing and drinking, and amusing himself with the wife of a commissary, who was his mistress, and who, as well as he, loved champagne." The fact that

Burgoyne took his commissary officer's wife as his mistress in the middle of the American wilderness tells as much about the British class system as it does about Burgoyne himself.

While Burgoyne's army was making its tortuous way toward Fort Edward, an episode took place that provided a great incentive for the recruitment of militia in all the neighboring areas of New England and New York. A young woman named Jane McCrea, who was engaged to one of the Tories attached to Burgoyne's army, was seized by a band of marauding Indians led by a chief named Wyandot Panther. In a dispute over which Indian had captured her, she was tomahawked, stripped of her clothing, and scalped. The Indians took her scalp, along with that of an American officer, back to camp, and in the evening they had a victory dance. Later the girl's body was discovered, and soon word of the killing spread through the British army.

Burgoyne was caught in a trap of his own making. If he executed the guilty savage, as he was first disposed to do, he might turn his Indian allies into enemies. If, on the other hand, he took no action, he would seem to condone the murder. He chose the latter course; he pardoned the murderer and gave the Indians a stern lecture on restraint. Far from being grateful for his clemency, the Indians resented Burgoyne's efforts to interfere with their ways of waging war, and "their ill humor and mutinous disposition strongly manifested itself." A few days later a large number of them departed, "loaded with such plunder as they had collected. . . ." In the words of Du Roi: "It did not make any difference to the Indians, if they attacked a subject loyal to the king, or one friendly to the rebels; they set fire to all their homes, took away everything, killed the cattle, leaving them dead on the spot. . . . It would certainly have been better, if we had not had the Indians with us."

The Americans were horrified at the death of Jane McCrea. It was, to be sure, only one of numerous instances of murderous action by Burgoyne's Indians, but it touched a doleful and romantic chord. The story spread throughout the states, north and south, with astonishing speed. Washington, hearing it, wrote urging the Massachusetts and Connecticut militia to "repel an enemy from your borders, who, not content with hiring mercenaries to lay waste your country, have now brought savages, with the avowed and expressed intention of adding murder to desolation." Suffice it to say that for this, as well as for other reasons, the New England militia responded.

It should be pointed out that Indian atrocities were by no means confined to the British Indians. An American officer, Oliver Boardman, noted in his journal that "this Afternoon a scout of our Indians [in Gates's army] took a Tory, the Genl. gave him to them for a while they took him & Buried him up to his Neck & had their Pow wow around him, after that they had him up and Laid him a side of a great fire & turn'd his head & feet a while to the fire, hooting & hollowing round him then he was hand Cuff'd & sent to Albany Gaol."

On July 30, Burgoyne at last reached Fort Edward; it had taken him twenty-four days to travel twenty-three miles. At the approach of Burgoyne's army, Schuyler withdrew all of his forces to Saratoga. Warner meanwhile was in Manchester, New Hampshire, trying to fill up his depleted ranks, and Glover arrived from the south with less than a thousand men. Massachusetts rounded up some two thousand militiamen, but these did little more than take the place of those whose terms of enlistment had expired. Schuyler remained woefully undermanned. Washington, watching for Howe's next move, could give him little assistance.

However, all was not as black as it looked. Washington did send Arnold to help in the task of collecting an army to oppose Burgoyne, and he wrote to Schuyler, "Though our affairs have for days past worn a dark and gloomy aspect, I yet look forward to a fortunate and happy change. I trust General Burgoyne's army will meet sooner or later an important check, and as I have suggested before . . . that the success he has had will precipitate his ruin." Burgoyne's practice of "acting in detachments" would certainly, Washington noted shrewdly, "give room for enterprise on our part and expose his parties to a great hazard. Could we be so happy as to cut one of them off, though it should not exceed four, five, or six hundred men," Washington wrote, "it would inspirit the people and do away with much of this present anxiety. In such an event they would lose sight of past misfortunes; and, urged at the same time by a regard for their own security, they would fly to arms and afford every aid in their power." The letter proved to be a remarkably accurate analysis and prediction; it demonstrated once more, if any demonstration was needed, the soundness of Washington's own strategic instincts.

3

Fort Stanwix and Oriskany

O<small>N</small> August 2, while Burgoyne was ensconced at Fort Edward, issuing a stream of self-congratulatory orders and pronouncements, Colonel Barry St. Leger, having made the arduous journey from Montreal with a force of some eighteen hundred men (in one historian's words, "a composite army of regulars, Hessian chasseurs, Royal-greens [Tories], Canadians, axe-men, and non-combatants") arrived at Fort Schuyler (old Fort Stanwix) at the head of the Mohawk Valley. The fort was defended by Colonel Peter Gansevoort with seven hundred and fifty men. Gansevoort was only twenty-nine but he was courageous and intelligent and determined to hold the fort, and he was backed up by Lieutenant Colonel Marinus Willett, an experienced Continental officer.

There was, to be sure, an added incentive for the Americans. Only a foolish man would readily surrender to an army whose Indian auxiliaries were constrained with difficulty from murdering prisoners. Prowling around the fort on their arrival, St. Leger's Indians came on three young girls picking berries. They shot, killed, and scalped two while the third, wounded in the shoulder, ran to the fort. It was a grim reminder of the nature of Indian warfare.

Gansevoort, anxious to keep up morale in his beleaguered garrison, was determined to fly a flag, and one was made by cutting the white stripes out of ammunition sacks, the red out of "pieces of stuff procured from one another of the garrison," and the blue out of a camlet cloak captured from the enemy at Peekskill.

On August 4, the Indians encircled the fort and "commenced a terrible yelling, which was continued at intervals the greater part of the night." All the next day Indians prowled outside the fort, taking cover behind bushes, weeds, and even potato plants, and keeping up a constant fire on the fort; they killed one man and wounded six. The next day brought more of the same, but on the sixth three militiamen who had made their way past the Indian outposts brought a letter from General Nicholas Herkimer, a veteran militia officer. Herkimer, who was ten miles away at Oriskany, was on the march with eight hundred militia; in his letter he requested help from Fort Stanwix in penetrating St. Leger's lines. If the messengers got through, Gansevoort was to fire three cannon as a signal. He did so, with three cheers from the fort, and as soon as the men could be turned out, Gansevoort sent two hundred soldiers under the command of Willett to make contact with Herkimer.

Willett and his men had gone scarcely half a mile when they came on one of St. Leger's encampments, attacked it, killed fifteen or twenty of the enemy, dispersed the rest, and returned to camp triumphantly with four prisoners, three of them wounded, and "a number of blankets, brass kettles, powder and ball, a variety of clothes and Indian trinkets and hard cash. . . ." So unexpected had the American foray been that Sir John Johnson, Leger's second-in-command, had fled in his shirtsleeves, leaving all his personal papers behind. Included in the booty were four fresh scalps, two of them belonging to the young girls. Four colors were captured and run up defiantly under the Continental flag. An unfortunate consequence of the raid was that the British were alerted to Willett's movements, and the hope of joining forces with Herkimer was thus destroyed.

Herkimer had intended to wait for the sortie from the fort to distract the British and Indians and cover his advance, but the officers under his command were too confident of their own strength and too impatient to wait for the agreed-upon signal. They insisted on advancing, and when Herkimer refused to budge, four of his regimental commanders—Ebenezer Cox, Isaac Paris, Richard Visscher, and Peter Bellinger—reportedly overrode his objections by accusing him of timidity and suggesting that he had Tory sympathies (one of his brothers was with St. Leger's force). Reluctantly Herkimer gave in, placed himself at the head of the column, and moved forward without advance or flanking parties.

When St. Leger's scouts brought him word that Herkimer's force was on the march, he sent Joseph Brant, the Mohawk chief, and four hundred Indians, along with John Butler's Tory Rangers and John Johnson's Royal Greens, to ambush the Americans at a spot six miles from the fort, where a ravine two hundred yards wide could be crossed only by a log road or causeway. Butler's Rangers and Johnson's Royal Greens concealed themselves in the thick underbrush at the head of the ravine, and the Indians were deployed to strike the American flanks and rear as Herkimer's force crossed the causeway.

Herkimer was not, of course, totally without "eyes." He had dispatched sixty Oneida Indians as scouts, but they, inexplicably, failed to detect the ambush, and the American column, almost a mile long, moved out along the causeway, the supply wagons close behind the leading elements. At a signal, the Tories and Indians poured a devastating fire into the exposed column. Most of the American officers were cut down in the first volley. Herkimer's leg was badly shattered by a musket ball. Cox, one of those who had been so impatient for action, was killed almost instantly. Visscher's regiment, acting as a rear guard, ran at the moment of attack. The other regiments, trapped, fought back furiously. It is said that Herkimer, propped up on his saddle against a tree, with his life's blood ebbing away, lit a pipe and calmly directed the men whom his caution would have saved from ambush.

As the battle developed, there was no semblance of order on either side. Much of the fighting was hand-to-hand, and small groups of soldiers defended themselves as best they could. After several hours of desperate and inconclusive fighting, the battle was interrupted by a violent thunderstorm. Under its cover the Americans pulled their force together, and when the rain stopped they had formed a makeshift defensive position on high ground. Soon the sound of firing in the distance, which signaled Willett's attack on the British camp, gave them fresh courage. But the British had another stratagem. John Butler, once of the ubiquitous and deadly Butler family, who commanded the Royal Greens, so named because of their green coats, ordered his men to reverse their jackets so as to appear to be part of a relief force from Fort Stanwix. He led them thus disguised up to the American defensive positions and was almost inside them before the ruse was accidentally discovered. One of the patriot militiamen, believing an advancing Tory was an old friend, ran forward to greet him with his hand outstretched. His hand was seized, and he was claimed as a prisoner. His captain,

Gardenier, ran to his rescue, wounding the Tory captor with his spear. When other Tories closed in on the captain, Gardenier killed one with his spear and wounded a third; then, his spurs catching in the under-brush, he fell, and before he could extricate himself, bayonets were thrust through both legs. As another bayonet was aimed at his chest, Gardenier seized the blade, deflected it, and pulled his assailant down on top of him, using him as a shield. Meantime, Adam Miller, a soldier in Gardenier's company, came to the captain's rescue, distracting the attackers and giving Gardenier an opportunity to retrieve his spear with his lacerated hand and kill the man who had fallen on top of him.

Stephen Watts, a dashing Tory officer and brother-in-law of John Butler, was knocked down by a clubbed musket, and the British attack was once more beaten off. The Indians, thoroughly disheartened by their own heavy losses, slipped off, and the Tories had no choice but to retreat as best they could. The Americans were in no condition to pursue them. Both sides had sustained very heavy casualties. As was usually the case when Americans fought Americans, the fighting had been bitter and relentless. One of the American militia officers, a Major John Frey, was captured by Brant's men. William Stone, the nineteenth-century historian, tells us that when Frey was taken to Butler's camp, the prisoner's brother, a Tory in the British service, tried to kill him but was prevented by the intervention of other officers.

The Americans lost almost half their number killed, wounded, or taken prisoner. Herkimer died soon after the battle, and the survivors made their way back to Albany as best they could. On the British side, the heaviest losses were sustained by the Indians. The Seneca lost seventeen killed, among them some of their chief warriors, and had sixteen wounded. The losses to the other tribes were almost as severe. Somewhere in the neighborhood of sixty to eighty Indians were killed or wounded. One writer attributed the heavy losses among the Indians to the fact that in order to prevail upon them to join the ambush, the British officers had given them generous amounts of rum, and many of them were intoxicated when the battle started.

A British scout who returned to the scene of the battle several days later wrote, "I beheld the most shocking sight I had ever witnessed. The Indians and white men were mingled with one another, just as they had been left when death first completed his work. Many bodies had also been torn to pieces by wild beasts."

Considering the numbers of men engaged at Oriskany, it was one of the bloodiest and most bitterly fought battles of the Revolution.

With Herkimer's force checked, St. Leger returned to Fort Stanwix and requested a parley. Colonel Butler, who commanded the Indians with Brant, and two other officers were brought blindfolded into the fort and conducted to Gansevoort's quarters. The windows of the room were blacked out, and candles were lit. A table was spread with crackers, cheese, and wine. The American colonels and the British officers were seated at the table, and the rest of the room was soon filled with the other officers of the fort. After some perfunctory drinking of wine and the exchange of formal courtesies, one of the British officers declared: "I am directed by Colonel St. Leger . . . to inform the commandant, that the colonel has, with much difficulty, prevailed on the Indians to agree, that if the garrison, without further resistance shall be delivered up . . . the officers and soldiers shall have all their baggage and private property secured to them. . . ." If they surrendered promptly, not a "hair of the head of one of they shall be hurt." Then, turning to a fellow officer, he said, "That, I think was the expression they made use of, was it not?" "Yes," the other officer replied.

The first officer then went on to say that the defeat of Herkimer made any hope of relief illusory; Burgoyne was already in Albany. "Colonel St. Leger, from an earnest desire to prevent bloodshed, hopes these terms will not be refused; as in this case, it will be out of his power to make them again. It was with great difficulty the Indians consented to the present arrangement, as it will deprive them of plunder which they always calculate upon, on similar occasions. Should then, the present terms be rejected, it will be out of the power of the colonel to restrain the Indians, who are very numerous, and much exasperated, not only from plundering the property, but destroying the lives of, probably, the greater part of the garrison." Indeed, the Indians were so inflamed that they had threatened "to march down the country. . . . In this case, not only men, but women and children, will experience the sad effects of their vengeance."

Willett, looking full in the face of the British officer, replied for the garrison. "Do I understand you, Sir? I think you say, that you come from a British colonel . . . and by your uniform, you appear to be an officer in the British service. You have made a long speech on the occasion of your visit, which, stript of all its superfluities, amounts to this, that you come from a British colonel, to the commandant of this garrison, to tell him, that if he does not deliver up the garrison into the hands of your Colonel, he will send his Indians to murder our women and children. You will please to reflect, sir, that their blood will be on your head, not on ours. We are doing our duty; this garrison is committed to our charge, and we will take care of it. After you get out of it, you may turn around and look at its outside, but never expect to come in again, unless you come as a prisoner. I consider the message you have brought, a degrading one for a British officer to send, and by no means reputable for a British officer to carry. For my own part, I declare, before I would consent to deliver this garrison to such a murdering set as your army, by your account consists of, I would suffer my body to be filled with splinters, and set on fire, as you know has at times been practiced, by such hordes of women and children killers, as belong to your army."

At this splendid speech, the officers of the garrison applauded loudly. St. Leger's offer suggested that the besiegers were disheartened and hoped to get by threats what they feared they could not accomplish by arms. With the British suggestion that a three-day truce be called Gansevoort and Willett complied, since they were anxious to conserve their meager supply of ammunition.

During the truce, Willett and a Major Stockwell decided to try to slip through the Indian lines to summon help. With nothing but two eight-foot spears, a few crackers, several pieces of cheese apiece, and a quart canteen of rum, and with only the stars to guide them, they made their way past the Indian sentinels and traveled, without pausing or eating, until the following night, when, not daring to light a fire, "they lay down wrapped in each other's arms." The next afternoon, having stopped to refresh themselves in a patch of raspberries and blackberries, they reached Fort Dayton, a distance of fifty miles from Stanwix. There they found that General Schuyler had already sent a brigade of Massachusetts troops under General Ebenezer Learned to the relief of Fort Stanwix.

With the truce at an end, Gansevoort continued to stall for time. He asked for St. Leger's terms in writing. The letter came, and the American officer wrote a reply: "I have only to say that it is my determined resolution with the forces under my command, to defend this fort, at every hazard, to the last extremity, in behalf of the United States who have placed me here to defend it against all their enemies." The British began to bombard the fort at once. Shells fell all during the night, but only one man was killed and one wounded.

Meanwhile Schuyler had directed Benedict Arnold and the First New York Regiment to accompany Willett back to Fort Schuyler. Lieutenant Colonel Brooks, at the head of an advance party from Learned's brigade, came on a group of Tories holding a meeting at Shoemaker's

House and captured Major Walter Butler, John Butler's brother and a close friend of Brant and Colonel Guy Johnson and a powerful influence on the Indians of the Mohawk Valley. Also captured was Hon Yost Schuyler, a prominent Tory, who was seized as a spy.

Brooks proposed to Arnold that the captured Schuyler be prevailed upon, by promise of a pardon and the restoration of his lands, to return to St. Leger's camp and inform the Indians that their friend and leader, Walter Butler, had been captured and would doubtless be hung, "and make such an exaggerated report of General Arnold's force as to alarm them and put them to flight." Several friendly Indians offered to cooperate in the plan. Bullet holes were made in Schuyler's jacket to suggest a narrow escape; he then headed for the Indian camp and told his story, which was confirmed an hour or so later by one of the friendly Indians. "The Indians," James Thacher wrote, "instantly determined to quit their ground and make their escape; nor was it in the power of St. Leger . . . to prevent it." When St. Leger tried to argue with them, they replied, "When we marched down, you told us there would be no fighting for us Indians; we might go down and smoke our pipes; but now a number of our warriors have been killed, and you mean to sacrifice us." Abandoned by five or six hundred of his mercurial allies, St. Leger felt it was futile to persist. He was alarmed himself by the report of Arnold's imminent arrival and decided he had no recourse but to join the Indians, departing "in the greatest hurry and confusion, leaving his tents with most of his artillery and stores in the field."

An incident told of St. Leger's flight is revealing of the Indian sense of humor. As St. Leger and Sir John Johnson rode along, each attempting to blame the other for the failure of their mission, two of the Indian chiefs directed a young warrior to loiter in the rear until the officers approached a bog of clay and mud; he was then to run suddenly, as if alarmed, while calling out, "They are coming, they are coming." "On hearing this the two commanders, in a fright, took to their heels, rushing into the bog, frequently falling and sticking in the mud" whereupon their Indians friends seized the packs off their backs and threw them away. Indian humor could be almost as demoralizing as Indian cruelty—indeed, they were closely related.

In such fashion was Fort Stanwix and its resolute garrison saved and Burgoyne's ill-conceived plan to take the Americans on their western flank defeated. Arnold and Learned turned back to join General Schuyler at Stillwater, where he had established his headquarters.

4

Bennington

Aт Fort Edward, Burgoyne's orderly book told the true story of his accumulating difficulties: "August fifth. Victually of the army *out* this day, and from difficulties of the roads and transportation, no provisions came in this night. Sixth August. At Ten o'clock this morning, not quite enough provisions for the consumption of two days." The army was plagued with desertions, and Burgoyne, according to Du Roi, gave his Indian allies permission to kill and scalp all the British deserters they encountered.

Philip Skene, a Tory, reported to the anxious Burgoyne that a substantial depot of supplies was stored at nearby Bennington, Vermont, and Burgoyne decided to organize an expedition to seize these supplies. He gave orders to round up some 1,500 horses—1,300 to mount Riedesel's dragoons and 200 for general use. Explaining his decision to raid Bennington, Burgoyne wrote: "I knew that Bennington was the great deposit of corn, flour, and store cattle, that it was only guarded by militia, and every day's account tended to confirm the persuasion of the loyalty of one description of the inhabitants and the panic of the other. Those who knew the country best were the most sanguine in this persuasion."

A force of Germans was detached under the command of Lieuten-

ant Colonel Frederich Baum, supplemented by some of Fraser's marksmen, a detachment of Tories, and some Canadian volunteers. The
original plan of a movement against Seth Warner at Manchester, Vermont, followed by a raid on Bennington, was changed at the last
moment by Burgoyne over Riedesel's objections. To leave Warner
undisturbed on the left of the expeditionary force seemed to the Hessian general an unnecessary risk; Bennington was more than twenty-five
miles away over bad roads and rough terrain.

Baum departed on August 12 with some five hundred men and
marched from Battenkill to Cambridge, where he met and routed a
force of forty or fifty Americans who were guarding cattle and captured
eight prisoners, a modestly auspicious beginning.

The Indians who accompanied Baum were skillful in rounding up
horses, but they demanded to be paid for them, and if they were not
they slashed the horses hamstring muscles and made them useless.
Baum was also told that some fifteen hundred militia were at Bennington, "but are supposed to leave at our approach. . . . The savages cannot
be controlled. They ruin and take everything they please," he noted.

The situation of the British-German force was compromised by the
fact that, in the words of one of his junior officers, Baum had "listened
with complacency to . . . previous assurances that in Bennington a large
majority of the populace were our friends." In addition, Burgoyne had
instructed the officers to try to recruit friendly natives during their
advance. Thus Baum had issued muskets to a number of farmers who
appeared and expressed loyalty to His Majesty George III and avowed
their determination to fight for his cause.

At Bennington there were not the inexperienced militia that Baum
expected to encounter, but well-trained soldiers under the command of
an officer who had first distinguished himself at the Battle of Bunker
Hill. John Stark had resigned his commission as general in the Continental Army when junior officers were promoted over his head and had
retired to New Hampshire. When word came of Burgoyne's invasion,
Stark accepted a command in the military establishment of his native
state on the condition that he would not be required to serve in the main
army. When General Schuyler asked him to report for duty with the
army at Stillwater, Stark refused, but he went to Bennington where
Colonel Gregg was in command of the militia force guarding the supply
depot. He was there on the night of August 13 when word came that a
party of Indians was in the neighborhood of Cambridge. Gregg sent out
two hundred men to intercept the Indians and got back word during

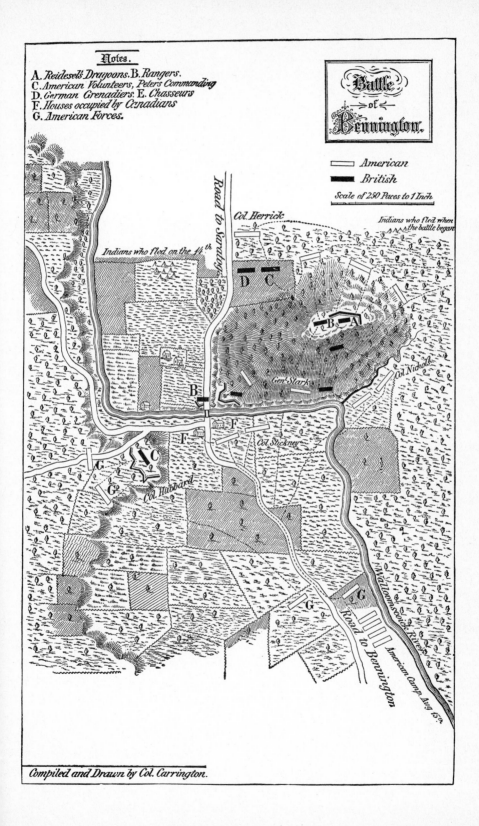

the night that a large detachment of British, of which the Indians were only an advance party, was moving in the direction of Bennington. Gregg, meanwhile, sent word to Warner at Manchester asking for help.

On August 14, Baum made camp four miles from Bennington. Seeing that the Americans were numerous—and being under instructions from Burgoyne not to attack if faced by a resolute foe—he occupied a high and thickly wooded hill situated at a bend in the Walloomscoick River and began to dig in. On the fifteenth, Burgoyne, hearing that Baum had encountered resistance on the road north of Bennington, dispatched Lieutenant Colonel Heinrich von Breyman from Cambridge.

Breyman encountered a succession of obstacles. A torrential rain turned the roads into quagmires, and his troops, consisting of a battalion of chasseurs, one of grenadiers, a rifle company, and two pieces of artillery, made no better than half a mile an hour. An artillery cart overturned, the guide lost the way, and the party was only seven miles from Cambridge by nightfall.

The rain that impeded Breyman prevented any direct engagement on the fifteenth and provided time for Warner to march down from Manchester and Colonel Symonds to move up from Bennington with a regiment of Berkshire militia. Thus Stark had, by the morning of the sixteenth, some two thousand men under his command.

Besides Baum's force of Brunswick dragoons on the hill, a company of grenadiers with some Canadian rangers held a position beyond the bridge on the Bennington Road. The Canadians, with a detachment of American Tories, or Royalists as they preferred to call themselves, were stationed in several houses south of the bridge. Another detachment of grenadiers and Royalists covered the British left on the road to Saratoga. The Indians had fled on the fourteenth, as soon as it had become apparent that a substantial American force intended to give battle. Stark assigned regiments to attack each of the British exterior positions—front, both flanks, and rear—and took charge himself of the attack on the main British line at the top of the hill.

Despite ample evidence of hostile intentions, Baum was so convinced that Bennington held a large body of Tories that when the Americans advanced against the British positions on the Bennington Road, Baum ordered his men to hold their fire in the expectation that the approaching figures were coming to offer their support. Thus the Americans were almost on the British before it was clear that their intent was hostile in the extreme. In addition, the Americans who had secured muskets and insinuated themselves among the British and Brunswickers under the guise of friends turned their weapons on the defenders and revealed the enemy within.

The American attack was led by Colonel Moses Nichols, with two hundred New Hampshire militiamen. This force constituted the right wing. Soon after Nichols reached the dragoon redoubt, a flanking force of Vermonters led by Colonel Samuel Herrick hit the enemy's rear while a third column made a double envelopment against the Tory positions.

One of the German officers described the attack on the hill in these words: "Our little band, which had hitherto remained in column, was instantly ordered to extend, and the troops lining the breastworks replied to the fire of the Americans with extreme celerity and considerable effect. So close and destructive, indeed, was our first volley that assailants recoiled before it, and would have retreated, in all probability, within the woods; but ere we could take advantage of the confusion produced, fresh attacks developed themselves, and we were warmly engaged on every side and from all quarters. Not one of our dispositions had been concealed from the enemy, who, on the contrary, seemed to be aware of the exact number of men stationed at each point, and they were one and all threatened with a force perfectly adequate to bear down opposition. . . . All, moreover, was done with the sagacity and coolness of veterans, who perfectly understood the nature of the resistance to be expected and the difficulties to be overcome, and who, having well considered and matured their plans, were resolved to carry them into execution at all hazards and at every expense of life."

The Tories and Canadians fled at the first onslaught of the Americans, but the Brunswickers, beleaguered as they were, gave a good account of themselves for almost an hour, using their artillery effectively until a stray shot from the attackers ignited a tumbrel containing all the spare ammunition, which blew up with such violence that the ground shook. The Americans, witnessing the explosion and guessing its cause, gave a great cheer and rushed the British position and broke through. "For a few seconds," the Brunswick officer wrote, "the scene which ensued defies all power of language to describe. The bayonet, the butt of the rifle, the sabre, the pike, were in full play, and men fell as they rarely fall in modern war, under the direct blows of their enemies." Outnumbered, their ranks broken and they themselves demoralized, the defenders fled or surrendered. Colonel Baum was mortally wounded.

Almost at the instant of the American triumph, word came that

Breyman was finally approaching the field of battle. Fortunately Colonel Warner, who had paused at Bennington after a forced march from Manchester, arrived at the same time and engaged Breyman. Stark, busy rounding up the remnants of the British-German force, sent what units he could spare to reinforce Warner. Breyman gave ground in what threatened to be a rout, but Warner's pursuit was interrupted by darkness, and Breyman's main body escaped after abandoning four brass cannon, several hundred muskets, drums, and swords. Counting Baum's losses, the Americans took more than 600 prisoners and killed 207 of the enemy. Stark, reporting the action, estimated that forty Americans had been killed and almost as many wounded. The men of his command, he wrote, "fought through the midst of fire and smoke, mounted two breastworks that was well-fortified and supported with cannon. I can't particularize any officer as they all behaved with the greatest spirit and bravery," perhaps partly because Stark had promised them "all the plunder taken in the enemy camp."

The victory at Bennington filled Washington's prescription exactly: it was just the tonic needed to strengthen the resolution of New Englanders. The feeling spread that Burgoyne's army was doomed, and militiamen from all over the eastern states hurried toward Saratoga to be in at the kill.

At this point, Horatio Gates once more replaced Schuyler as commander of the Northern Department. Gates was indefatigable in soliciting advancement and in manipulating Congress through his sponsors there, primarily the delegates from New England who showed none of the proverbial Yankee shrewdness in their infatuation with Gates and with his fellow Englishman, Lee.

When Gates's earlier importunings had succeeded for a time in gaining him command of the Northern Department, he had been insolent and overbearing to Schuyler; and when Congress, responding to a troubled conscience, had restored Schuyler, Gates had dashed off to Philadelphia, where he had managed to get an audience with Congress on the grounds that he was bringing valuable information—and had then used the opportunity to denigrate those he considered his rivals. His performance before Congress was a dismal one. He alternately boasted, whined, and, at one point, wept. At least one member of Congress believed that he was a man "who had manifestly lost his head." Not knowing how to handle the problem of the lachrymose general, Congress had passed it on to Washington.

At this point the news came of the abandonment of Ticonderoga, and the blame was placed on Schuyler and St. Clair. It was a perfect moment for Gates's partisans to push him forward once more. Since most of his supporters were New Englanders, and since Burgoyne's invasion was so plainly a New England problem, Gates carried the day. He arrived at Stillwater on August 19 to reap the benefits of all that had been done before his arrival. Alternately arrogant and unctuous, resolute only in promoting his own interests, he remains, despite the efforts of several biographers to rehabilitate him, one of the least appealing figures of the American Revolution.

The courtesy and cooperativeness with which Philip Schuyler received Gates showed the New Yorker at his best—a man always in possession of himself, who, if he did not have the attributes of a fighting general, had a largeness of spirit and a capacity for taking endless and, on the whole, ill-acknowledged pains for the cause, and who showed none of that spirit of petty rivalry and wounded pride that was so rife among the officers of the Continental Army.

One of Gates's first official acts was to write an insolent letter to Burgoyne accusing him of being personally responsible for the death of Jane McCrea (which in a sense, of course, he was). Miss McCrea, Gates wrote, was "dressed to receive her promised husband, but met her murderer employed by you." Burgoyne was an ass but not a knave. He indignantly rejected Gates's charge that he paid his Indian allies for scalps or had in any way encouraged them to murder Americans.

The news of Bennington brought daily augmentation of Gates's ranks. Daniel Morgan's riflemen were sent, at the direction of Congress, to join the constantly growing force at Stillwater. Burgoyne meanwhile lay at Saratoga as one paralyzed, struggling with the problem of supply for his demoralized army, hoping desperately for some assistance from Howe. The Americans grew constantly bolder. They sniped at soldiers and engineers repairing bridges, and when a group of British soldiers were rooting up potatoes, a scouting party fired on them, wounding thirty.

After Bennington, Burgoyne was well aware of the hazardousness of his situation. With St. Leger frightened off and little prospect of any help from Howe, he knew that his head was in a noose. "Wherever the king's forces point," he wrote, "militia to the amount of three or four thousand assemble in twenty-four hours, and bring their subsistence with them, and the alarm over, they return to their farms. . . . The Hampshire Grants, in particular, a country unpeopled and almost unknown in the last war, now abounds in the most active and rebellious men of the continent, and hangs like a gathering storm on my left."

On August 20, Burgoyne wrote a letter to Lord Germain in which might be plainly read, if Germain had had the wit to so read it, the fate of his army. No more than four hundred Tories had appeared in all the territory Burgoyne had traversed. "The great bulk of the country," he wrote, "is undoubtedly with the Congress, in principle and in zeal; and their measures are executed with a secrecy and dispatch that are not to be equalled."

"When I wrote more confidently," he added, "I little foresaw that I was to be left to pursue my way through such a tract of country and hosts of foes, without any co-operation from New York." The letter was not entirely candid. Even before he left Canada, Burgoyne was well aware that there was little prospect of support from Howe. He simply had underrated the difficulties and hazards of his mission; now he was preparing the ground for the failure that his letter anticipated: "Whatever may be my fate . . . when all the motives become public . . . I rest in the confidence that, whatever decision may be passed upon my conduct, my good intent will not be questioned." This anxious petition was a far cry from the windy bombast with which Burgoyne had announced his intention to punish the American rebels.

5

Saratoga

 B Y the middle of September, Burgoyne realized that his only hope was to push on to Albany and at least open a line of communication there with a British expedition from New York. He pressed through Saratoga, past General Philip Schuyler's abandoned mansion there, and on toward the American positions at Stillwater. On the nineteenth, Burgoyne divided his army into three divisions and deployed it for an attack on the force that Gates now commanded. Simon Fraser, with a corps of British light infantry and a corps of Hessian grenadiers, plus Indian and Tory auxiliaries (some twenty-two hundred in all), was to attack to the right, toward a clearing at Freeman's Farm. The British center was to move south and west to join Fraser. The left, commanded by Baron von Riedesel, was to take the river road.

It was 11 A.M. before Burgoyne's force was ready to attack. After an hour's march, the British advance scouts encountered a substantial body of Americans in an outpost at Freeman's Farm. Behind and to the left, at Bemis Heights, were the main American positions laid out by the Polish engineer, Thaddeus Kosciusko, who had joined the Continental Army as a volunteer. Kosciusko, who had absorbed the ideals of the French philosophers, had borrowed money to come to America and join the fight for freedom. The skill with which he had fortified the Dela-

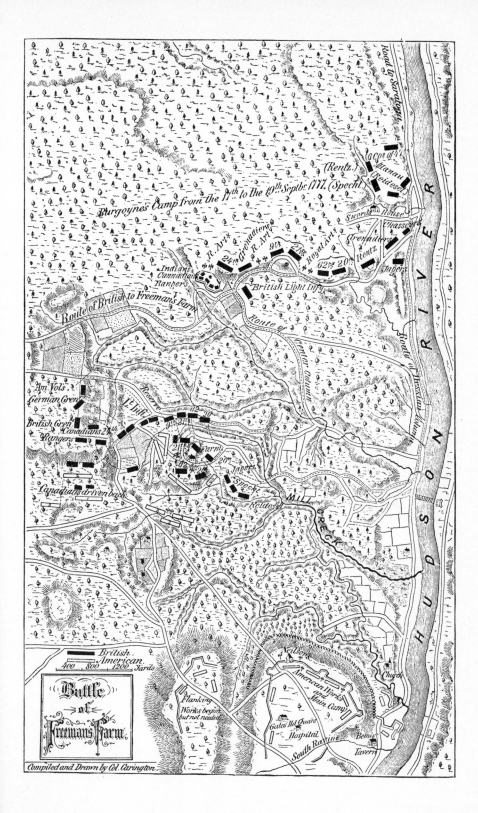

Battle of Freeman's Farm

Compiled and Drawn by Col. Carington.

ware River forts below Philadelphia in the summer of 1776 had won him a commission as colonel of engineers. Here he had chosen high ground near the river and had directed the building of breastworks in a semicircle about a half-mile in length. An old barn, built of logs, was strongly reinforced, and earthworks in the meadow below the hill had also been constructed.

General Enoch Poor's brigade, consisting primarily of New York and New Hampshire regiments and Connecticut militia, along with Daniel Morgan's riflemen and Henry Dearborn's light infantry, made up the American left; positioned nearly a mile from the river, it was under the command of Benedict Arnold. Ebenezer Learned's brigade, consisting of Massachusetts and New York regiments, had been assigned to a small plateau on the left of the main American positions. Gates, with John Nixon's, John Paterson's, and John Glover's brigades, made up the right wing, which dipped down to the river. Eight other brigades, made up largely of New England militia, were used to reinforce the American positions.

Three ravines intersected the Americans and British lines. One ran from the river directly behind the American defenses, a second in front of the main fortifications, and one directly in front of the British army at Freeman's Farm.

One of the principal purposes of Burgoyne's foray was to provide cover for parties sent out to collect wheat and hay for the horses and whatever food might have escaped the attention of Gates's army. It was this aspect of the plan, in fact, that led to the initial encounter. Colonel James Wilkinson, Gates's aide, hearing that British soldiers were on the move, rode forward and observed a foraging party, protected by a strong detachment, cutting wheat in a field on the left of the American positions. After watching them for a time and assuring himself that they had no aggressive intentions, Wilkinson reported back to Gates, who asked his aide's opinion of the ground and the advisability of an attack.

"Their front is open," Wilkinson replied, "and their flanks rest on the woods, under the cover of which they may be attacked. . . ."

"Well, then, order on Morgan to begin the game."

When Wilkinson brought the word to Morgan, the Virginian, who knew the terrain, decided to move through the woods to a high position on the right of the British, from which he could attack advantageously. He would wait until fire was commenced against the British left; he would take this as his signal to attack. The plan was followed. When the confused British and German soldiers tried to change positions to meet the attack from their flank, Dearborn "pressed forward with ardour and delivered a close fire; then leapt the fence, shouted, charged and gallantly forced them to retire in disorder."

Riding up to the scene of the skirmish just after the British had retreated, Wilkinson saw a "scene of complicated horror and exultation. In the space of twelve or fifteen yards," he wrote, "lay eighteen grenadiers in the agonies of death, and three officers propped up against stumps of trees, two of them mortally wounded, bleeding and almost speechless." Further on, by the captured British guns, Colonel Joseph Cilley was sitting astride a brass twelve-pounder shouting in triumph.

There are conflicting accounts of the opening of the engagement. Ebenezer Mattoon, a Continental officer, reported that Arnold was with Gates when word arrived that contact had been made between Morgan's riflemen and some Indians. Mattoon reports that Arnold declared: "That is nothing; you must send a strong force," to which Gates, understandably irritated, answered, "General Arnold, I have nothing for you to do; you have no business here." Benjamin Lincoln repeated Arnold's advice, and the additional reinforcements from Learned's and Nixon's brigades were sent to support Morgan and Dearborn. By another account, when Tories and Canadians, decked out in Indian regalia, began to harass the American lines from the cover of a wood filled with down-timber, Arnold, who had persuaded Gates to allow the Americans to advance to meet the British right, rode up to the man who had marched with him to Quebec and said, "Colonel Morgan, you and I have seen too many redskins to be deceived by that garb of paint and feathers; they are asses in lions' skins, Canadians and Tories, let your riflemen cure them of their borrowed plumes." The "Indians" were promptly driven off by the accuracy of the Virginia riflemen.

The first major contact seems to have been with the Canadians on the extreme British right, who were moving in advance of the grenadiers and light infantry (which moved laterally westward) to skirt the ravines that covered the American front. The Canadians were driven back but rallied as General Fraser's corps came up in support of them and, keeping the higher ground, turned directly south toward the American lines. Burgoyne led the center column through the first ravine and formed it in a line of battle on the level ground beyond. Major General Phillips and Von Riedesel moved the British left down the road that ran parallel to the river, ready to deploy as Burgoyne might direct. At one o'clock, when each division was in place, a gun was fired to signal the beginning of a coordinated attack on the American lines. Fraser moved rapidly ahead and drove a small detachment of Americans off the high ground on the British right, thus affording protection for Burgoyne's advance.

A battle seldom develops according to plan. As the action unfolds, a particular feature of the terrain, natural or manmade, often becomes the focal point for the subsequent action. Victory or defeat then rests on the ability of one side or the other to exploit the changing circumstances on the field of combat itself. Fraser's corps, turning south and east, headed for the little cluster of buildings that marked Freeman's Farm—where the battle concentrated—hoping to turn the American left by a determined attack. Some five regiments joined in the assault, supported by the light infantry on Burgoyne's right. Major Forbes, commanding the advance pickets, was "attacked with great vigor from behind rail fences and a house by a body of riflemen and light infantry." The Americans pressed both the right and left flanks of the attacking British aggressively.

Typical of the nature of the action that day was the small portion of the battlefield on which Lieutenant Anburey directed his men. Anburey was sitting on a log talking to a captured American officer when a volley of musket balls came from a little clump of woods to his front. Those not struck in the first volley took cover wherever they could find it, and an artillery piece was brought up to fire on the woods. "Shortly after this," Anburey noted, "we heard a most tremendous firing upon our left, where we were attacked in great force, and in the very first fire . . . Lieutenant Don of the 21st regiment received a ball through his heart . . . when he was wounded, he sprung from the ground, nearly as high as a man." The Americans were driven off once more by cannon fire, and the fighting swayed back and forth in this fashion through most of the afternoon.

As the British pressed the American left, principally Morgan's riflemen and Colonel Alexander Scammel's regiment, Arnold strongly reinforced the units there until the battle in that sector was stalemated. The action then shifted to the British center, and here, as one participant put it, "the conflict was dreadful; for four hours a constant blaze was kept up, and both armies seemed to be determined to death or victory." "Such an explosion of fire I never had any idea of before," a British lieutenant of the Shropshire Regiment wrote, "and the heavy artillery joining in concert like great peals of thunder, assisted by the echoes of the woods, almost deafened us with the noise. . . . The crash of cannon and musketry never ceased till darkness parted us. . . ."

When Von Riedesel arrived at Freeman's Farm with his relief force, he found that the British artillery was out of ammunition and that there were indeed few artillerymen left. The Americans had attacked six times and were preparing for a final assault that promised to carry everything before it. Riedesel led his men forward on the double, with drums beating and the men shouting.

Reinforced by several new regiments, the British charged with their dreaded bayonets, but accurate American fire and the advantage of the terrain forced the British back several times until the Americans finally gave way and took up positions on the high ground between Freeman's Farm and Chatfield House. At this point darkness brought an end to the fighting, and the British hastily dug defensive positions at and around Freeman's Farm.

The central British regiments that had been under fire throughout the long afternoon, while the maneuvering on the British right around Freeman's Farm took place, had received heavy casualties. Of the eleven hundred men in this corps, more than half were killed or wounded, including a large number of officers. In the Twentieth and Sixty-second regiments "the survivors did not probably exceed fifty, besides four or five officers," according to British estimates. Captain Jones, who commanded four artillery pieces, had thirty-six men killed or wounded out of forty-eight. For this slaughter Burgoyne must bear the blame. He placed almost a third of his force in an exposed position from which they could not effectively engage the enemy, and he kept them there in the face of withering fire.

Benedict Arnold's energy and initiative in reinforcing Morgan on the American left was an essential element in the American victory; and an American victory it certainly was, although the British claimed victory because they were in possession of the field at the end of the day. Lieutenant Anburey expressed general misgivings when he wrote, "The only apparent benefit gained, is that we keep possession of the ground where the engagement began." He added, "Not withstanding the glory of the day, I am fearful the advantage resulting from this hard-fought battle, will rest on that of the Americans, our army being so much weakened by this engagement, as not to be of sufficient strength to venture forth and improve the victory, which may, in the end, put a stop to our intended expedition. . . ."

Most depressing of all to the British was the courage and tenacity of the Americans, who, to "the astonishment of every one," returned time and again to the action. "We are now become fully convinced," Anburey wrote a friend, "that they are not that contemptible enemy we had hitherto imagined them. . . . Instead of a disheartened and flying enemy, we have to encounter a numerous, and . . . a resolute one, equally disposed as ourselves to maintain their ground, and commanded by Generals, whose activity leave no advantages unimproved." Anburey was in command of the burial detail next day and had to supervise the grim task of digging large pits and burying the dead in mass graves. "I however," he noted, "observed a little more decency than some parties had done, who left heads, legs and arms above ground. . . . Our army abounded with young officers, in the subaltern line, and in the course of this unpleasant duty three of the 20th regiment were interred together, the age of the eldest not exceeding seventeen." Even more painful to Anburey was the sight of the wounded—many of whom were in terrible pain, "perishing with cold and weltering in their blood . . . some upon the least movement . . . put in the most horrid tortures. . . . . [they] were bumped and jostled over the rough ground for a mile to the hospital tents in the rear."

It should be emphasized that it is impossible to gain more than a very general idea of the course of this battle, which was characterized by bitter engagements of squads and companies in rough and wooded terrain. In this kind of fighting the determination and tenacity of the individual soldier is a major element, as, of course, is leadership on the company level. Indeed, such combat is decided by the courage and resourcefulness displayed by officers and men in the lower echelons. The general officers, once initial deployment is made, have little control over the battlefield situation. This, of course, was especially true when communications were far more rudimentary than with a modern army. Generals could do little more than commit their reserves quickly and skillfully in response to the ebb and flow of the fighting. Thus Gates had little effect on the outcome, and Arnold was distinguished principally in that he hurried reinforcements to that part of the field where they were most needed. And this, plus the courage of the individual soldiers and the officers immediately commanding them, carried the day for the Americans, who were not content to simply await the British attack but who came forward to press the battle on their own initiative.

The Americans lost 65 killed, 218 wounded, and 38 missing, for a casualty total of 321. They were convinced that only the arrival of Riedesel with his Brunswickers and the coming of darkness enabled the

British to escape a complete rout. The Americans could be forgiven some exultation over the outcome of the battle. "I trust," Henry Dearborn wrote, "we have convinced the British butchers that the 'cowardly' Yankees can, and where there is a call for it, will fight."

The most unfortunate aftermath of the battle from the American point of view was a bitter altercation between Gates and Arnold. They were both quarrelsome and ambitious men—although Arnold was at least a real soldier. He was furious that Gates seemed determined to rob him of any credit for the day's action. Indeed, Gates was not content to let the matter rest there. He accused Arnold of disobeying orders and removed Morgan's men from his command. Three days after the battle, Arnold wrote Gates a letter reviewing his actions at Freeman's Farm and stating that he had been "received with the greatest coolness at headquarters, and often treated in such a manner as must mortify a person with less pride than I have, and in my station in the army." Arnold asked to be relieved of his command and given permission to join Washington.

The news that Arnold was affronted by his treatment at Gates's hands and determined to leave caused dismay in all ranks. Colonel Henry Livingston wrote to Schuyler that he was distressed at Arnold's intentions "to retire from the army at this important crisis. His presence was never more necessary," Livingston added. "He is the life and soul of the troops. Believe me, Sir, to him and to him alone is due the honor of our late victory. . . . He enjoys the confidence and affection of officers and soldiers. They would, to a man, follow him to conquest or death."

The advocates and detractors of Gates and Arnold respectively have, almost since the end of the battle of Freeman's Farm, contended over the merits and demerits of the two generals. Arnold was touchy, ambitious, and arrogant. But he was also a fine soldier and a courageous leader. In battle after battle and campaign after campaign he performed with distinction. The case was quite the reverse with Gates. Although he had been a more than competent junior officer, he never displayed outstanding qualities as a general. Even the ultimate treacheries of the two men are revealing of their characters. Gates's sly maneuverings to replace the man who had sponsored and befriended him seem, at least to me, as reprehensible as Arnold's outright treachery, which, it might be argued, required a good deal more boldness and initiative.

Livingston so resented Gates's treatment of Arnold that he decided to leave with him and resign his commission. A petition circulated among the officers requesting Arnold to stay and thanking him for his leadership "during the late action." Arnold's own officers thus gave him their strongest vote of confidence, and it must be assumed that they, much more than historians, were the proper judges of his conduct at Freeman's Farm.

The battle was over, but nothing was settled. The American army was demoralized by the unhappy quarrel between Gates and Arnold; the British, for their part, were daily more aware of the desperateness of their situation. As Sergeant Lamb of the Welsh Fusiliers wrote, "difficulty and danger appeared to grow out of it [the battle]. The intricacy of the ground before us increased at every step. Our scouting, reconnoitering and foraging parties encountered perils uncalculated and unseen before." Those few Indians who were left, and who were invaluable for scouting, stole away. They had no obligation to go down with a sinking ship in a war that was of little consequence to them. They had been enticed to come by promises of plunder and glory, but there was little of either.

Burgoyne kept his army busy building fortifications in anticipation of an American counterattack. Freeman's Farm was surrounded by breastworks, and the high ground to the northwest of it, assigned to Colonel Breyman and his Brunswickers, was crowned by a strong redoubt. Von Riedesel's main force was distributed along the road that ran laterally from the Hudson River westward, in front of the British positions. The British grenadiers and light infantry extended this line to Freeman's Farm. Along the line was a series of breastworks and gun emplacements. The British left on the Hudson was echeloned to the northeast, facing the river and supporting Riedesel's corps.

But even as they constructed fortifications, the British were not allowed to forget their predicament. Their lines were constantly harassed by raiding parties, and musket and rifle fire thumped and snapped night and day. American sharpshooters worked their way into range and seldom missed an opportunity to fire at a soldier who exposed himself. "We are now become so habituated to fire," Anburey wrote, "that the soldiers seem to be indifferent to it, and eat and sleep when it is very near them; the officers rest in their cloaths, and the field officers are up frequently in the night. . . . You could scarcely believe it, but the enemy had the assurance to bring down a small piece of cannon, to fire their morning gun, so near to our quarter-guard, that the wadding rebounded against the works." In addition to the noise of gunfire, the sleep of the British was disturbed by what sounded like the howling of dogs. At first it was assumed that they were the officers' dogs, and orders went out for all officers to keep their dogs in their tents. When the howling continued, a scouting party discovered the grim truth. The howls came from wolves busy digging up the bodies of soldiers that Anburey had buried.

The fact that in history events happen simultaneously, while in a narrative account the historian can only tell of one event at a time, creates a problem for which there is no solution. At this point we must leave the two armies facing each other below Bemis Heights while we take note of the British effort to afford Burgoyne relief.

In this regard it is necessary to say something, however brief, about Sir Henry Clinton's seizure of the forts guarding the Hudson. The two forts, Montgomery and Clinton (the latter named after the New York patriot leader, Governor George Clinton), were both on the west side of the Hudson, just north of Peekskill. Fort Clinton, the smaller of the two and the southernmost, was situated above a sharp bend in the river. Beyond it, and across Poplopen's Creek, was Fort Montgomery. Five miles to the south, on the opposite bank of the river, was Fort Independence, under the command of Israel Putnam. From Fort Montgomery a boom and heavy iron chain extended across the Hudson, blocking the passage of British warships. Colonel John Lamb was in command of Fort Montgomery, where a company of artillery and a few poorly equipped militia were stationed. Fort Clinton was in the charge of Brigadier General James Clinton (father of George), who commanded a handful of regulars and some militia recruited from the surrounding countryside. (The Clintons are almost as difficult to sort out as the Lees.)

When word reached Governor George Clinton that Sir Henry intended an attack on the highlands and the forts guarding the river, he rounded up a substantial number of militia and sent them on to Putnam, who had command of the defenses of the area. Since it was harvest time and no enemy was in sight, Putnam furloughed the men. Governor Clinton tried to countermand the order so that at least half would remain on duty, but before this change could take effect, Sir Henry Clinton had already started to move. In Stedman's words, "The enterprise was entirely spontaneous on the part of Sir Henry Clinton—was conducted with more energy than most of the military operations that took place in America." The purpose was not to come to the relief of Burgoyne, the precariousness of whose position was still not fully com-

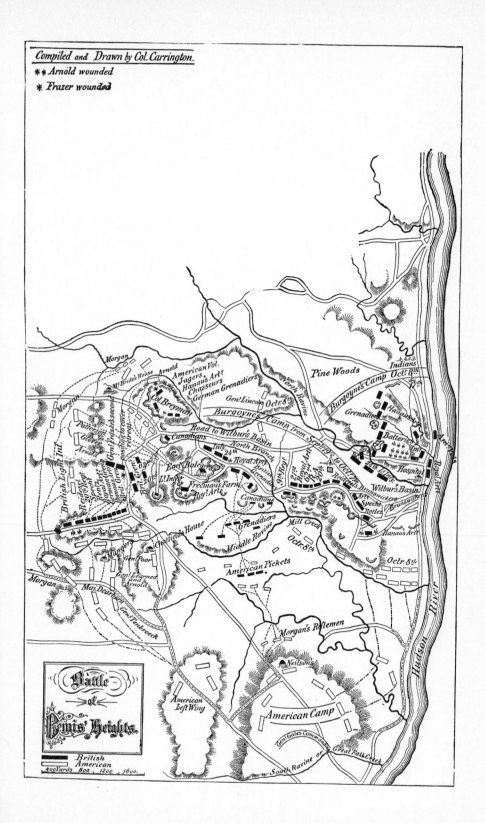

Compiled and Drawn by Col. Carrington.

✳✳ Arnold wounded

✳ Frazer wounded

Morgan

Pine Woods

Indians

Burgoyne's Camp Octr 8th

McBride's House

Arnold

American Vol.
Jagers,
Hanau Arty
Chasseurs
German Grenadiers

Col. Breyman

North Ravine

Genl Lincoln Octr 8th

Burgoyne's Camp from Sept 19 to Octr 7th

Grenadiers

Hanau Regt

Battery

Hospital

Morgan

Patterson & Glover
Arnold

British Light Inf.

Reid's Regt

Road to Wilbur's Basin

Canadians

North Branch

Inf. 24th

24th Royal Arty

British Grenadiers

47th

20th

21st

Royal Artillery

62d

Regt Nettler

Wilbur's Basin

Brunswickers
Arty
Specht
Nettler

Brunswick

62d

Lt Inf.

Freeman's Farm
Roy! Arty.

Canadians

Hanau Arty

Munger's

Chatfield's House

Grenadiers

Middle Ravine

Mill Creek

Octr 8th

Octr 8th

Genl Poor

Genl Learned
and
Arnold

American Pickets

Morgan

Maj. Dearborn

Genl Tenbroeck

Morgan's Riflemen

Neilson's

American
Left Wing

American Camp

Genl Gates Commands

South Ravine or Great Fall Creek

Hudson River

Battle
of
Bemis' Heights.

| | British |
| | American |
400 Yards 800 1200 1600.

prehended, but simply to open up a line of communication between New York and Albany in anticipation of Burgoyne's arrival in that town.

On October 3, eleven hundred British were transported to Tarrytown. A second division of approximately the same number marched from King's Bridge to Tarrytown by land. A third division left New York on the following day in transports convoyed by three warships. From Tarrytown, the troops were carried on flatboats up the river to Verplanck's Point. On October 5, Sir Henry Clinton loaded a good portion of his command on flatboats and began what looked like a move against Fort Independence, where Putnam had some twelve hundred Continental soldiers under his command.

Governor Clinton meanwhile had adjourned the New York legislature, meeting at Kingston, and had hurried to Fort Montgomery to take command there. Sir Henry Clinton, under the cover of his feint toward Fort Independence and with the assistance of a thick fog, got his force across the river to Stony Point. The British moved by interior roads, with roughly half the force sent to assault Fort Clinton and the remainder continuing on to attack Fort Montgomery.

As soon as Governor Clinton got word of the British advance, he sent out a party to try to seize a crucial pass at Dunderberg Mountain, but the British were already in possession of the ground. The governor then appealed to Putnam for reinforcements and directed a resourceful defense of the roads leading to Fort Clinton. The Americans were, however, constantly pressed back by the much larger British force; they finally took refuge in the fort itself, and when the British attacked with bayonets at dusk, most of the Americans escaped in the darkness. Again the principal British losses were among the officers; some 40 of the attackers were killed and 150 wounded. The American losses were estimated at almost 300 killed, wounded, and missing, roughly twice the British casualties. The statistics suggest two points: that the Americans fought with considerable courage and tenacity against a vastly superior force; and that, as we have often seen before, the losses of the attackers were much smaller than those of the defenders. Two hundred and sixty Americans were taken prisoner, and some 400 escaped.

By capturing Forts Clinton and Montgomery, Sir Henry was able to clear away the obstructions in the river. An alarmed Putnam abandoned both his headquarters at Peekskill and the two forts on the east side of the river, Fort Independence and Fort Constitution. Sir Henry Clinton had thus in a few days, by a skillfully coordinated attack, opened the river. William Tryon, the royal governor of New York, wished to make a dash for Albany, with the troops alternately marching and sailing to speed their progress and preserve their strength; Clinton, however, felt his force was too small to permit such an expedition. General Sir John Vaughan did sail up the river to Kingston, which he burned on October 16, and then to Livingston's Manor, at which point his pilots refused to carry him further. Finally, Howe ordered Clinton to proceed up the Hudson in an effort to effect a junction with Burgoyne.

Burgoyne must now have pinned whatever hopes he had of extricating himself from his unhappy situation on a letter from Sir Henry Clinton, written in cipher, which he received a few days after the battle of Freeman's Farm. Clinton informed Burgoyne that he intended to attack the forts guarding the Hudson in about ten days. British warships and supply vessels could then sail up the Hudson to Albany and meet Burgoyne there, or dispatch a force to march to his relief. It was a dim hope but the only one, and it provided an incentive to try to hang on for a few weeks more.

When word reached Saratoga of Clinton's advance with, it was rumored, four thousand men, there was general apprehension in the American camp. With Clinton at Albany, the American army would be caught between two fires. If Gates detached sufficient troops to meet Clinton, he would give Burgoyne the opportunity to drive through the remaining Americans and join up with Clinton. But if Gates remained at Stillwater, he might find himself surrounded. "In either event," James Thacher wrote, "the consequences must be exceedingly disastrous to our country. We tremble with apprehensions."

At Bemis Heights the Americans, in addition to constantly harassing the British army, took several steps to cut off Burgoyne's greatly extended supply line to Canada. A detachment of 500 infantry marched to a landing point on Lake George, a few miles below Ticonderoga and some forty miles behind the British lines. Two other small forces were directed to Mount Independence, Fort Anne, and Fort Edward. The Americans took the outposts around Ticonderoga—Mount Defiance and Mount Hope—capturing 200 bateaux, a sloop, several gunboats, and some 300 prisoners. Although they were unable to capture the fort itself, they demonstrated the vulnerability of Burgoyne's supply lines.

By October 7, Burgoyne's food supplies were once more so low that he felt he must make one final desperate effort to break through the American lines and struggle on to Albany. A retreat was still theoretically possible, but it would be a measure equally desperate, and it would,

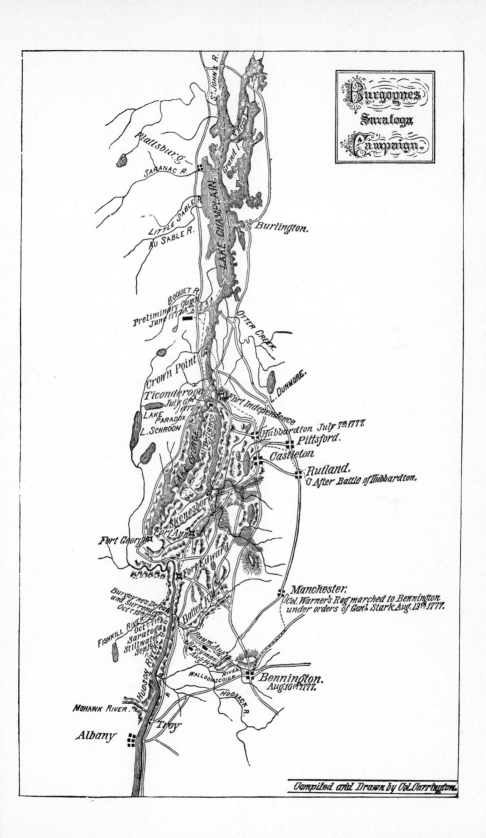

in addition, free a substantial part of the American army to give its attention to Sir Henry Clinton, now making his way up the Hudson. Moreover, a retreat, just at the moment when it seemed possible that a juncture might be effected between the two forces—Burgoyne's and Clinton's—would have sacrificed everything that had been fought for. Alternately, to do nothing was to face starvation and, finally, surrender.

The discussion among the British staff officers and general officers centered on the question of whether to make an all-out frontal attack on the American positions, and thus force a way through to the south, or to attempt what would really be a raid in force with the hope of so crippling and demoralizing the Gates army that it could not prevent the escape of the main British force. The latter plan was agreed upon as the one offering the best hope of success. Fifteen hundred of the best British and German soldiers were chosen. Burgoyne himself was to lead them, accompanied by Phillips, Fraser, and Von Riedesel. Two six-pounders, two twelve-pounders, and two howitzers were attached.

The intention was to turn the American left beyond Freeman's Farm; penetrate the rear of the main defensive positions at Neilson's Farm, where Gates's headquarters were located; and so scatter and confuse the Americans that they would, at least for a period of days, be rendered ineffective as an offensive force.

The British force moved off late in the morning of October 7, thus sacrificing the element of surprise that an early morning attack would have afforded. The intention in delaying the attack may have been to give the British a chance to withdraw under cover of darkness that evening, since the foray was not designed to seize and hold positions within the American lines but simply to put Gates on the defensive and thus allow Burgoyne's army time to escape. But the Americans seized the initiative, and before the British plan of battle could be put into operation, five American regiments—accompanied by Arnold, who had been persuaded to remain and now fought as a volunteer in the division he had earlier commanded—launched a heavy attack on the British right. Slowly the grenadiers under Major John Acland were forced back, and before the Germans in the center could be shifted to support the right, they were under attack themselves.

The American assault was so sudden and so well sustained that the entire British front began to give way, and the order came from Burgoyne to withdraw to the main redoubts. Sir Francis Clerke, the officer who brought the message, was fatally wounded as he delivered it, and General Fraser, who took a position on the right to cover the retreat, was struck by a musket ball soon afterward. It was said that Daniel Morgan, seeing Fraser rallying the British, called two of his best marksmen and said, "Do you see that gallant officer? that is General Fraser—I respect and honor him; but it is necessary he should die." The first rifle bullet cut the crupper of the grey gelding Fraser was riding. Another clipped the horse's mane, and Fraser's aide urged him to take cover. Fraser replied, "My duty forbids me to fly from danger," and a few seconds later a bullet struck him in the chest. It proved to be a mortal wound.

Major Acland, shot through the legs, begged a friend, Captain Simpson, to carry him back to the British lines so that he would not be captured by the Americans. Simpson hoisted him on his back, but Acland was a heavy man, and Simpson, seeing that the Americans were about to overtake him and his burden, put the major down and made his own escape. Acland "cried out to the men who were running by him, that he would give fifty guineas to any soldier who would convey him into camp. A stout grenadier instantly took him on his back, and was hastening into camp when they were overtaken by the enemy. . . ." Colonel James Wilkinson, an American officer, soon heard an English voice calling out, "Protect me, Sir, against this boy." Wilkinson turned his head and saw a boy, hardly more than twelve or thirteen years old by the look of him, aiming a musket at the wounded major. Wilkinson rescued Acland.

Everywhere the pressure of the Americans was constant and unrelenting. Moving singly or in small groups, firing, loading their pieces and firing again, keeping their momentum and maintaining contact in the best of all ways—by advancing toward the enemy—they dominated the battlefield. They were fighting on their own ground, where every ditch, gully, and fold offered temporary cover or a rallying point for another rush forward against an enemy accustomed to wheeling and firing as a body, to splendid maneuvers requiring precision and discipline—an enemy that loved level earth, preferably flat as a parade ground and as open.

The British, indeed, had little notion of how to cope with the terrain on which they found themselves. Classic battle maneuvers were impossible; units became separated and scattered, and individual soldiers took refuge wherever they could find a hiding place. The Brunswick artillery officer, Captain Georg Pausch, fired his cannon until they were too hot to touch—but to little effect besides smoke and noise. When, abandoned by the infantry who were supposed to protect his artillerymen, Pausch tried to retreat in the face of advancing rebels, he found the road already occupied by the Americans, who fought without any regard to convention; "the bushes were full of them, they were hidden behind the trees." Leaving his guns, he ducked into the heavy brush and found a path. "Here," he noted, "I met all the different nationalities of our division running pell-mell. . . . In this confused retreat all made for our camp and our lines."

Six guns were abandoned, and as the British re-entered their main lines, "the works were stormed with great fury by the Americans, who rushed on under a severe fire of grapeshot and small arms." Arnold again was in the thick of the action, his conduct marked by "intemperate rashness." At one point, while waving his sword and urging the soldiers forward, he struck one of his own officers on the head and inflicted a painful wound.

The Earl of Balcarres, in command on the right, held fast at Freeman's Farm, but the Americans swept past him and attacked the redoubt defended by Colonel Breyman and his Brunswickers. It was here that Arnold, leading a party around the rear of the fortifications, was struck in the leg by a musket bullet and his horse was killed under him. Frustrated and furious, he had fought like a man possessed or a man inviting death. Breyman was killed in the assault, and the Brunswickers fled for their lives, abandoning guns and equipment; a number of them were captured in the redoubt itself. Only darkness saved Burgoyne's army from being completely overrun.

Two hundred of the British were captured, among them three officers, and they lost more than 600 killed and wounded as well as nine cannon and a large supply of ammunition. The American losses were some 30 or 40 killed and 100 wounded.

General Fraser was buried with military honors. When he had been brought back to the British camp on October 7, severely wounded by a ball that had passed through his chest and out his back, he had asked the surgeon who dressed the fearful wound, "Tell me, son, to the best of your skill and judgment, if you think the wound is mortal." The surgeon replied, "I am sorry, sir, to inform you that it is, and that you cannot possibly live four and twenty hours." Fraser had borne the news with great fortitude, distributed some mementos to the officers of his staff, and ordered that he be taken to the general hospital with the other men wounded during the battle. His funeral was a bitter occasion and portent for the army. The procession was a modest one that took place in view of both armies, and Anburey noted that "the enemy, with an inhumanity peculiar to Americans, cannonaded the procession as it passed, and during the service over the grave."

On the eighth there was some skirmishing, and General Lincoln's division relieved the American regiments that had carried the brunt of the assault the previous day. Burgoyne meanwhile decided that his positions were disadvantageous for defense, and on the night of the eighth he withdrew to the north in a heavy rain, abandoning his wounded and most of his baggage. Baroness von Riedesel and her children moved with the retreating army. Like the soldiers, they were all soaked to the skin. But when they stopped for the night, after a short march, she was distressed that they had not pushed on farther. While she was sitting by a fire, warming her chilled bones and preparing the children for sleep on a bed of straw, General Phillips walked up, and the baroness asked him "why we did not continue our retreat while there was yet time. . . ."

"Poor woman," Phillips answered, "I am amazed at you! completely wet through, have you still the courage to wish to go further in this weather! Would that you were . . . our commanding general! He halts because he is tired, and intends to spend the night here and give us a supper."

Burgoyne's crossing of the Fishkill River, a tributary of the Hudson, was delayed while a bridge was constructed. Across the Hudson itself, a sizable American force kept up continual artillery fire on the bateaux that held the last of the British supplies. On the tenth, Burgoyne finally got his army over the Fishkill. He made an effort to push a party of infantry and carpenters farther up the river beyond Saratoga, but they were driven back by men of Poor's and Learned's brigades, who had moved beyond the British encampment and had occupied the high ground to the northwest. The British began one final digging in. Substantial earthworks were thrown up on three hills—one to the southwest, a few hundred yards from the river, covering what was the British left; one to the north, which constituted the right; and a third at the juncture of the Hudson and Fishkill. All roads north and south were now cut by the Americans. General Fellows and his brigade guarded the east bank of the Hudson. Morgan's rifle corps covered the British front on a line that ran north and south, parallel to the river. The Americans numbered some 13,000; the British 5,763.

The string of the bag was drawn tight; within it was a prize almost too rich to be believed: a British army, diminished though it might be, with all its paraphernalia, its ancient regiments, its blue-blooded officers, its battle standards, its splendid equipment only slightly tarnished by months of arduous campaigning. Rations were down to a three days' supply, and only thirty-four hundred men were fit for duty. The last hope was Sir Henry Clinton. Even at the moment he might be disembarking four or five thousand fresh soldiers at Albany. But no such word reached the British lines. Instead, "by day and night grape shot and rifle shot reached the lines . . . the men had become so worn out, and at the same time so accustomed to the incessant firing, that a part slept while other watched," Anburey wrote.

By the time the army had gotten back to Saratoga, Baroness von Riedesel was the only wife whose husband had not been either killed or wounded, and she was in a constant state of worry for his safety. She found refuge with her children in the cellar of a house near the riverbank and helped to convert it into a hospital. The Americans, apparently suspecting that the house was being used as a headquarters, or perhaps having nothing better on which to practice their marksmanship, bombarded it with their cannon from the east bank of the Hudson. "Eleven cannon balls went through the house," she wrote, "and we could plainly hear them rolling over our heads. One poor soldier, whose leg they were about to amputate, having been laid upon a table for this purpose, had the other leg taken off by another cannon ball, in the very middle of the operation." Water was soon so scarce that the only way it could be brought into the British camp was by a brave woman whose sex saved her from being fired at by the Americans across the river.

On the tenth, the baroness wrote that "the greatest misery and the utmost distress prevail in the army. The commissaries had forgotten to distribute provisions among the troops. There were cattle enough, but not one had been killed, more than thirty officers came to me, who could endure hunger no longer. I had coffee and tea made for them, and divided among them all the provisions with which my carriage was constantly filled; for we had a cook who, although an arrant knave, was fruitful in all expedients, and often in the night crossed small rivers in order to steal from the country people sheep, poultry and pigs."

One of the strangest sights of wartime was to see, in houses near the lines where troops were quartered, the excrement of those who, through fear of the enemy or simple indifference, were unwilling to step outside to relieve themselves. This rather minor act of desecration expressed in an especially vivid way for the baroness the horror of war.

Burgoyne had one last card to play. Perhaps if he could lure the Americans into an assault on his lines and inflict heavy casualties, he might still make his escape. On the eleventh, Gates was told by a double agent that Burgoyne had started for Fort Edward. Without reconnaissance, he ordered Morgan, Nixon, and Glover to cross the Fishkill in pursuit. The first two brigades had passed over the creek and started up the steep hill beyond when they picked up a deserter who told them that the British, far from having evacuated their camp, were waiting with artillery and loaded muskets to pour a withering fire on the Americans. Nixon and Morgan at once began to withdraw. Both commands suffered casualties from the British artillery, but Burgoyne's last stratagem had failed.

On October 12, the British general officers and staff concurred in the opinion that the only possible course was surrender, and the following day an officer went under a flag of truce to request a formal council or "convention" governing the terms of surrender. Gates replied curtly that the British must surrender unconditionally. Burgoyne refused. He would fight to the last man before he would consider such a disgraceful capitulation. Gates then reconsidered, and after brief discussions the conditions of the surrender were agreed upon.

The terms of the surrender stipulated that the British troops were to march out of camp with the honors of war and stack their arms "by word of command of their own officers." They were to be allowed "a free passage" to Great Britain on the pledge that they would never again be employed in the American war. Meanwhile, they were to march to Boston and there await transportation to England. "I call it," Burgoyne wrote, putting the best face on disaster, "saving the army, because if sent home, the State is thereby enabled to send forth troops now destined for her internal defence; if exchanged they become a force to Sir William Howe, as effectually as if any other junction had been made."

Article VII of the convention provided that "all sailors, working men, drivers, volunteer companies and other persons, being in, and belonging to the army of General Burgoyne, shall be considered as British subjects, and shall, in every way, be considered as included in this article—no matter of what country they may be." It was under this article that the notorious Tory Philip Skene, who had been lieutenant governor of Ticonderoga and a major, placed his name, adding "a poor follower of the British army," and thus secured immunity. Otherwise he would surely have been hanged.

After the negotiations had started, news reached Burgoyne that must have given him some agonizing last-minute reflections: it was the word that Clinton had captured Forts Clinton and Montgomery and advanced up the Hudson as far as Kingston. Burgoyne called his general officers together to get their advice on whether to break the capitulation. "It was finally decided," in Baroness Riedesel's words, "that this was neither practicable nor advisable. . . ." It was too late. The news really gave no hope of deliverance. The Americans would not rest on their arms while Clinton or the advance units of his army made their way up the Hudson River. Long before a British force could possibly reach the beleaguered army, the Americans would come down on Burgoyne like vengeance itself.

The final act of this particular drama was played with a touch of flamboyance and derring-do that recalled the start of the ill-fated campaign. After the fall of Fort Clinton, Sir Henry Clinton sent a message to Burgoyne, embedded in a silver bullet. "*Nous y voici,*" it read, "and nothing now between us but Gates. I sincerely hope this little success of ours may facilitate your operations." Daniel Taylor, Sir Henry's messenger, was captured by the Americans and was caught in the act of swallowing the bullet. George Clinton, the American general, ordered him given an emetic that promptly produced the bullet. When the bullet was opened, the message was revealed and poor Taylor was hanged as a spy.

General Heath with his division had been assigned to march along the banks of the Hudson and keep pace with Clinton's ships sailing to Burgoyne's rescue. Early in the morning of October 18, Joseph Martin, one of Heath's men, was among the soldiers who heard "forward of us a most tremendous shout, soon followed by another thundering shout on the west side of the river. What it all meant we could not imagine," Martin wrote, "but in a few minutes another shout still louder, and we were perfectly astonished, for the fleet was moving on very peacibly and quietly." Just then a postrider passed, "crying in a loud voice 'Burgoyne has surrendered and all his army prisoners of war,' and then the ground trembled with the roar of voices on both sides of the river."

The next morning the British fleet put about and headed back down the river, "very sad and still." A brig bringing up the rear came close to the bank where two Connecticut soldiers were standing. "We agreed," Martin wrote, "to hurl each of us a stone as the brig's deck was full of British troops. When she came near enough we hurled our stones in among the red coats." The reply was a broadside that sent the two bold soldiers scrambling into a ditch, where a cannonball covered them with dirt.

It remained to Lieutenant William Digby of the Shropshire Regiment to record the details of Burgoyne's surrender in his journal. "October 17," he wrote, *"A day famous in the annuals of America."* Burgoyne called his officers together and in a voice choked with emotion reviewed and excused his own actions. It was the failure of Clinton to move north to Albany earlier that had brought them all to this pass. The articles of convention (the surrender) were, Burgoyne told them, better than they had any right to expect, considering the desperateness of their situation.

At two o'clock the British marched out of their fortifications with drums beating; to Lieutenant Digby and his fellows, "the drums seemed to have lost their former inspiriting sounds, and though we beat the Grenadiers march, which not long before was so animating, yet then it seemed by its last feeble effort as if almost ashamed to be heard on such an occasion."

Some of the officers and soldiers wept. The Americans stood in silence as if they too were astonished at the spectacle, awed and moved at the sight of British might so humbled. Burgoyne was attired in full court dress, "as if going to assist in some gala occasion," one of the Brunswick officers noted somewhat bitterly, adding, "he wore costly regimentals bordered with gold, and a hat with streaming plumes . . . he looked like a dandy rather than a warrior." Gates, by contrast, was dressed in a plain blue overcoat without insignia of rank. The two generals advanced toward each other and halted a few steps apart. Burgoyne removed his plumed hat with a flourish, bowed, and said, "General, the caprice of war has made me your prisoner." Gates bowed in turn and replied, "You will always find me ready to testify that it was not brought about through any fault of your excellency."

These formalities completed, Burgoyne and his general officers sat down to lunch with Gates and his staff. The meal was a simple one—the drink was cider and rum mixed with water. Burgoyne was talkative and expansive, full of compliments to the Americans whom he had not long before denounced as the most wretched of traitors. He startled his own officers, as well as the Americans, by proposing a toast to General Washington, a toast that Gates doubtless drank with some reluctance; not to be outdone in this exchange of courtesies, the American general replied with a toast to George III. While Burgoyne was garrulous, Gates was quiet and preoccupied.

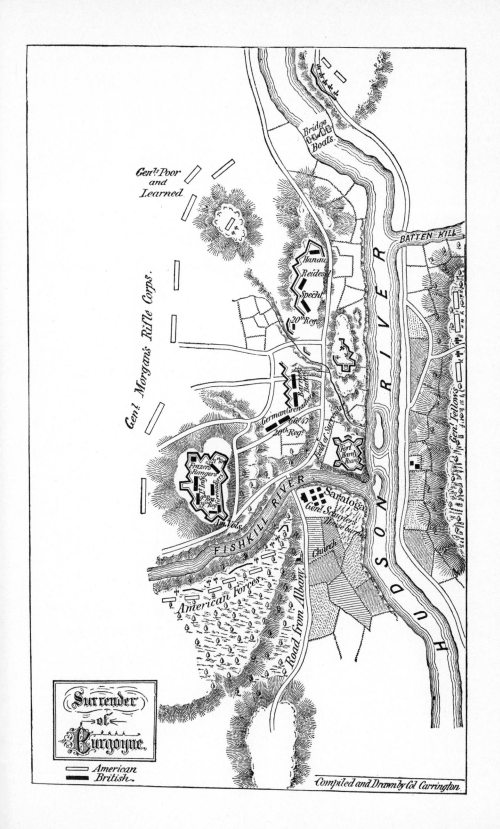

Gen.ls Poor
and
Learned

Gen.l Morgan's Rifle Corps.

Bridge
of
Boats

BATTEN KILL

Hanau
Reidesel
Specht
20th Reg.t

German Grenadiers
Col. 47
2nd Reg.t

Fort of Surrender

Fort
Hardy
Ruin

Fraser's
Rangers
9th Reg.t
Vols.

FISHKILL RIVER

Saratoga
Gen.l Schuyler's
House burnt

Church

American Forces

Road from Albany

HUDSON RIVER

Gen.l Fellows

Surrender
of
Burgoyne

American
British.

Compiled and Drawn by Col. Carrington.

It might have seemed to an uninformed observer that the English officer was the victor and the American the conquered. "Thus," Digby wrote in his journal, "ended all our hopes of victory, honour, glory, etc. Thus was Burgoyne's army sacrificed to either the absurd opinions of a blundering ministerial power, the stupid inaction of a general [Howe] who, from lethargic disposition, neglected every step he might have taken to assist their operations, or lastly, perhaps, his [Burgoyne's] own misconduct in penetrating so far as to be unable to return, and tho I must own my own partiality to him is great, yet if he or the army under his command are guilty, let them suffer to the utmost extent. . . ."

Du Roi, the Hessian officer, was convinced that the campaign was doomed from the moment when Germain, jealous of Carleton, chose Burgoyne's plan of invasion. Du Roi, indeed, gave a good résumé of the problems faced by the British and Hessians, not merely in the Saratoga campaign but in all operations against the Americans. The British "came over to fight the rebels," he wrote, "and the rebels can always select the best places from which to defend themselves. Whenever an attack proves too serious, they retreat, and to follow them is of little value. It is impossible on account of the thick woods, to get around them, cutting them off from a pass, or force them to fight. Never are they so much to be feared as when retreating. Covered by the woods, the number of enemies with which we have to deal, can never be defined. A hundred men approaching may be taken for a corps. The same are attacked, they retreat fighting. We think ourselves victors and follow them; they flee to an ambush, surround and attack us with a superior number of men and we are defeated. These are drawbacks which the royal army cannot avoid under the circumstances. . . . The scouting parties of the rebels . . . go out in small troops without baggage and little provisions. In case of need they live on roots and game. They are fit to undertake the longest incursions all around the royal army, while we have no troops who can do so." The Indians, intended for this purpose, had proved too unreliable and mercurial.

We might allow Dr. James Thacher to speak for the patriots: "We have now brought to a glorious termination a military campaign, pregnant with remarkable vicissitudes and momentous events," he wrote, "the result of which, seemed for a time to poise on a pinnacle of sanguine hopes and expectations on one side, and the most appalling apprehensions on the other. All gratitude and praise be ascribed to Him who alone limits the extent of human power, and decrees the destiny of nations!"

With the surrender of Burgoyne, the suffering of his army was near its end. The men still had a hard march ahead of them to Boston. General Schuyler took Baroness von Riedesel and her children under his protection. "You are certainly," that grateful lady said, unaware of her benefactor's identity, "a husband and a father, since you show me so much kindness."

Schuyler's hospitality extended to Burgoyne, who had, for no good military reason, ordered Schuyler's house near Saratoga burned down during his retreat from Bemis Heights. Schuyler put Burgoyne up in his handsome Albany home, where, according to the baroness, the defeated general said: "Is it to *me,* who have done you so much injury, that you show so much kindness!"

"That is the fate of war," Schuyler replied; "Let us say no more about it."

After Saratoga, Albany was filled with the sick and wounded. The attention given the wounded varied greatly. James Thacher was impressed by "the skill and dexterity" of the British surgeons. The Germans, on the other hand, with few exceptions, were "the most uncouth and clumsy operators" that Thacher had ever witnessed. To him they appeared "to be destitute of all sympathy and tenderness toward the suffering patient." Thacher, working from early morning until eleven at night to patch up the wounded Americans, wrote, "Here is a fine field for professional improvement. Amputating limbs, trepanning fractured skulls, and dressing the most formidable wounds, have familiarized my mind to scenes of woe. A military hospital is peculiarly calculated to afford examples for profitable contemplation, and to interest our sympathy and commiseration. If I turn from beholding mutilated bodies, mangled limbs and bleeding, incurable wounds, a spectacle no less revolting is present, of miserable [men] languishing under afflicting diseases of every description."

The British and German prisoners began their long, weary march, to Cambridge; then, after almost a year in Massachusetts, when Congress rejected the article in the Saratoga convention that allowed the prisoners to be carried back to England, they were sent on for six hundred more miles to Virginia. They were treated alternately with kindness or spite, depending on the dispositions of the Americans through whose towns and villages they passed and the temperament and efficiency of those in charge. But their plight was miserable at best. Food was often in short supply; their uniforms were rotting away on their emaciated bodies, their shoes wore out, they fell ill and died far from the consolations of home and family and friends. The most fortunate were those who simply became Americans, who here and there dropped out and became farmers or carpenters or blacksmiths.

When the Hessian prisoners finally reached the German country of Pennsylvania, they looked forward to being received hospitably by their former countrymen. "The inhabitants are very wealthy," Du Roi wrote. "They came as poor people from all parts of Germany. The houses are very clean inside and the way of living is exactly like that in Germany. Our hopes of being received in this town by our countrymen in a hospitable manner were cruelly deceived. . . . On the whole we were ashamed of being Germans, because we had never met so much meanness in one spot as from our countrymen." However, at Hanover "all the German maidens came to a ball given by us and danced with our officers" on Christmas Day. Du Roi was pleased that, despite the fact that the German "girls did their best to keep them for husbands," only four hundred of the Hessian prisoners deserted on the long march from Saratoga to their barracks at Charlottesville, Virginia. According to Du Roi, even the officers got proposals of marriage from German girls, and he professed to know of some "to whom girls were offered with a fortune of $3000 to $4000."

It might be argued that Burgoyne, "sunk in mind and body," was more sinned against than sinning. It was inevitable that he should be bitterly criticized. He had presided over the unthinkable: the surrender of a British army to the scorned and hated rebels. Returned to England in April, 1778, he demanded a court-martial to clear his reputation, but to no effect. He appeared in Parliament and gave a long and emotional (and quite persuasive) defense of his conduct; he even published a book that contained an account of his downfall. But he could not recall his address to the Indians or his proclamation to the inhabitants of the northern provinces, and he could not eradicate the image of himself as a pompous ass. Pompous asses can be endured as long as they are successful; unsuccessful ones, whatever the cause of their failure, can expect little mercy. Burgoyne never received another command.

Saratoga, of course, was not his fault—except as he promoted the scheme. He was the scapegoat, not simply for Germain and for the king himself, for North and his ministry, for Howe and for Clinton, but for all Englishmen who nourished illusions about the nature of the American resistance, who continued to believe in that perpetual will-o'-the-wisp, a large-scale Tory uprising; who cherished the notion that Americans were motivated solely by self-interest and ambition and were led (or misled rather) by a few fanatics who maintained a precarious hold over them by threats and blandishments. Men come by a very hard road to face those facts that they do not wish to face. Poor Gentleman Johnny, vain and foolish as he was, nevertheless was very little worse than those he served. Indeed, he had some qualities that most of his superiors lacked. He was, in fact, a gentleman, courteous to his opponents, thoughtful and considerate of his officers and men, courageous in battle, a basically decent man far out of his depth.

The consequences of Saratoga were of course considerable. It revived the spirits of Americans at the very moment when the unhappy situation of Washington's own army near Philadelphia had cast a general gloom over everyone. But it did not do what Americans hoped beyond hope that it would: it did not convince the British that they had embarked on an ultimately hopeless venture. (Writing to his wife a few days after the surrender, Gates observed, "If old England is not by this lesson taught humility, then she is an obstinate old slut, bent upon her ruin.") It did not persuade the British to seek an end to the conflict on terms acceptable to their American cousins, and it had one unhappy consequence: by making Horatio Gates a hero and the apparent savior of the American cause, it vastly increased his potential for mischief and thereby added to the numerous burdens that Washington already bore.

It has been customary to speak of Saratoga as "the turning point in the American Revolution," a victory that, by inducing the French to enter into a military alliance with the Americans, insured the eventual triumph of the cause of independence. The matter could be argued somewhat differently. While Gates's success was doubtless a factor in the decision of the French Crown to openly support the American patriots, Vergennes, the French foreign minister, was more impressed by the near-victory of Washington's army at Germantown, a battle that occurred at almost the same time as Burgoyne's surrender. Beyond that, I am inclined to argue that the French military alliance was an actual disservice to the American cause. Moreover, the Saratoga disaster, far from disheartening the British, called forth a renewed effort. In the words of the Duke of Grafton, "The majority both in and out of Parliament, continued in a blind support of the measures of Administration. Even the great disgrace and total surrender of General Burgoyne's army at Saratoga was not sufficient to awaken them from their follies." In this atmosphere, Lord Chatham's motion to repeal the most oppressive acts passed by Parliament against the colonies since 1763 was brushed aside, and war supplies amounting to almost thirteen million pounds sterling were voted with little debate.

When North tried to resign after Saratoga, the king replied, "I should have been greatly hurt at the inclination expressed by you to retire, had I not known, however you may now and then be inclined to despond, yet you have too much personal affection for me, and a sense of honour, to allow such a thought to take any hold on your mind. You must feel how very entirely I have confided in you since you have presided at the Treasury . . . how sincerely you are loved and admired by the House of Commons, and how universally esteemed by the public. . . ." In short, George III would not hear of North resigning.

Yet North, worn out and demoralized, had no heart for the job, and he tried again to step aside. If he were to do so, it was clear that the only man capable of forming a new government would be Lord Chatham, somewhat recovered from a long illness, and the king would not accept Chatham. North could have Chatham only as a member of his ministry. The king would never speak to or deal directly with him. "No advantage to this country," he wrote North, "nor personal danger to myself, can ever make me address myself to Lord Chatham, or to any other branch of opposition. Honestly, I would rather lose the Crown I now wear than bear the ignominy of possessing it under their shackles. . . . Men of less principles and honesty than I pretend to may look on public measures and opinions as a game," the king added, "I always act from conviction; but I am shocked at the base arts all these men have used, therefore cannot go toward them; if they come to your assistance I will accept them."

The curious exchange continued, with North showing unusual persistence in pressing for a new ministry and the king stubbornly refusing to "change one jot" whatever the circumstances. North protested once more, argued, implored. The king replied that "whilst any ten men in the kingdom will stand by me, I will not give myself up into bondage." (In other words, he would not act as the Whigs believed a constitutional monarch must act.) Finally, some eight days later, after a dozen letters, the king closed the correspondence by asking North, "If I will not by your advice take the step I look on as disgraceful to myself and destruction to my country and family, are you resolved, agreeable to the example of the D. of Grafton, at the hour of danger to desert me?" North had done what he could to free himself from his bondage and give the country an opportunity to extricate itself from the useless and dangerous war. He acquiesced.

"Turning point" or not, there is no question of the importance of the surrender of Burgoyne's army. If it raised false hopes of an imminent end to the war, Saratoga put new heart in the patriots. The victory became the subject of numerous patriotic songs and ballads and of a satiric ode by an English friend to the American cause that appeared in the *London Magazine*. With the British, the author suggested, good form was everything:

> What though America doth pour
> Her millions to Britannia's store,
> Quoth Grenville, that won't do—for yet,
> Taxation is the etiquette.
>
> The tea destroy'd, the offer made
> That all the loss should be repaid—
> North asks not justice, nor the debt,
> But he must have the etiquette.
> . . .
> At Bunker's Hill the cause was tried,
> The earth with British blood was dyed;
> Our army, though 'twas soundly beat,
> We hear, bore off the etiquette.

So in every situation, etiquette, not common sense had been the guide.

> Of Saratoga's dreadful plain—
> An army ruin'd; why complain?
> To pile their arms as they were let,
> Sure they came off with etiquette!
>
> God save the King! and should he choose
> His people's confidence to lose,
> What matters it? they'll not forget
> To serve him still—through etiquette.

When Sir Henry Clinton received word at Livingston Manor of Burgoyne's surrender, he decided it would be both practical and desirable to retain control of the Hudson; but at this point he received an urgent dispatch from his commander in chief, General Howe, directing him to send "without delay" a major part of the troops still under his command to New York, "even notwithstanding I might be gone up the North River . . . except I should be on the eve of accomplishing some very material and essential stroke. . . ." Clinton concluded that he had no choice but to hurry the troops Howe had requested south. This order was followed by instructions from Howe to abandon Fort Clinton and return to New York.

Sir Henry wrote, in an understandably aggrieved tone, that he "was not a little hurt and disappointed when I found my move up the North River so contrary to the Commander in Chief's views . . . because I had flattered myself with hopes that, as soon as he found I had opened the important door of the Hudson, he would have strained every nerve to keep it so and prevent the rebels from ever shutting it again—even though he had been obliged to place the back of his whole army against it. And I hope I shall be pardoned if I presume to suggest that, had this been done, it would have most probably finished the war."

6

Brandywine

DURING the summer months of 1777, while Burgoyne was making his laborious way southward, Sir William Howe in New York was busy planning his next military move. We left Howe dithering about in New York Bay, his sweltering men and animals packed in overcrowded transports whose destination Washington could only guess at. On July 20, Howe drafted a letter purporting to be to Burgoyne, and arranged to have it fall into Washington's hands as though by unhappy chance. In it Howe referred to his intended expedition to "B———" as taking the place of the drive up the Hudson. "If," Howe added, "according to my expectations, we may succeed rapidly in the possession of B———, the enemy having no force of consequence there, I shall, without loss of time, proceed to cooperate with you in the defeat of the rebel army opposed to you. Clinton is sufficiently strong to amuse Washington and Putnam. I am now making a demonstration southward, which I think will have the full effect of carrying our plan into execution."

The ironic thing about this plan, which was intended to send Washington flying to New England to save Boston, was that it would actually have been a far better course for Howe than the strategy it was supposed to mask. Washington, in any event, was not taken in. Howe headed for the Delaware, planning to sail up that river and to land

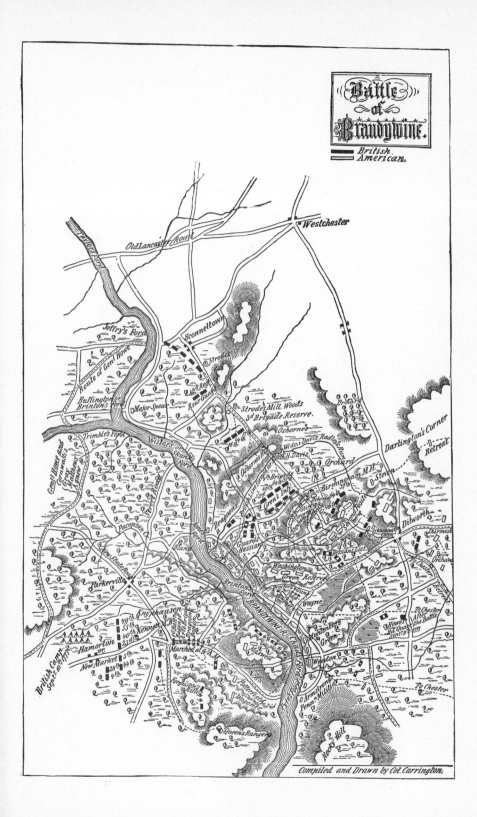

Battle of Brandywine

British.
American.

Compiled and Drawn by Col. Carrington.

seventeen miles from Philadelphia. His purpose, he later stated, was to thereby take "the surest road to peace, the defeat of the regular rebel army." If Howe wished to destroy Washington's army, a sea voyage to Philadelphia was a strange way to do it. The British general embarked his army for Philadelphia because, having withdrawn from the front of Washington's army and thus plainly avoided the battle he insisted he was seeking, he had to do something—and he could think of nothing better to do.

The plain fact is that Howe feared a showdown with Washington. He thus tried to lure him north to Boston while he headed south. Having decided to go to Philadelphia, Howe then invented a number of reasons to justify the action. He had, to be sure, received permission from Germain to make the expedition. Philadelphia, like New York, was reputed to be a stronghold of Tories as well as a nest of rebels. Seizing the city would deny the Americans their capital—the largest and most prosperous city in North America, the seat of Congress, the geographical center of the rebelling states. In New York, Howe was constantly assured by such prominent and articulate Tories as Joseph Galloway and the Allens that the Pennsylvanians would greet his army as deliverers and that he would find Philadelphia Loyalists ready to do all in their power to aid the royal cause.

After Howe set sail from New York, his fleet anchored off Sandy Hook for two weeks of perishing heat and boredom. Here he cooked up his stratagem to deceive Washington, who, to be sure, waited most uneasily for some word of his intentions. On July 5, Washington received a message from John Hancock that a portion of the British fleet had been sighted off the capes of the Delaware the preceding day. Washington immediately started his army for Philadelphia. On July 23, Howe finally sailed for the Delaware River, without adequate reconnaissance and in the face of adverse winds that kept his fleet tacking back and forth for another weary week.

On July 31, a belated survey of the hazards of the river—natural and man-made—convinced Howe that it would be impractical to attempt to sail up the Delaware and make a landing. He might have ascertained this quite easily before ever embarking his troops, and while it may have been that his original plan for sailing up the river was nullified by the obstructions placed in the river by the Americans and the defenses erected to cover them, it is hard to believe that Howe could not have landed his forces on the west side of the Delaware Bay and marched to Philadelphia in a few days.

But Howe was never the man to do things in a direct and simple way if there was a circuitous and difficult way to do them. Again in the face of prevailing winds, he directed his fleet for the headwaters of the Chesapeake, a voyage of some three hundred miles that took another three weeks and brought him on August 24 to the Elk River, only a few miles from Delaware Bay. In the middle of June, Howe had been some twenty miles from Princeton, perhaps sixty miles from Philadelphia. Now, nine weeks later, he was approximately the same distance from Philadelphia but to the south, and, of course, considerably farther from his base of operations in New York City. His army had been packed on ships for so long that the soldiers were exhausted and debilitated; many of the horses had died and been thrown overboard. After the British disembarked, they turned the remaining animals, some three hundred, into a cornfield, where the hungry horses so gorged themselves that half died of the colic.

The British made their landing without opposition, and Howe issued a proclamation offering pardon and protection to all who would place themselves under the jurisdiction of His Majesty's forces. Few responded to the invitation. Most of the Marylanders in the area preferred to abandon their farms and homes and carry off as many of their possessions and as much of their stock as they could.

Washington, given ample time by Howe's inscrutable maneuvers, marched out through Philadelphia to meet him, his soldiers decorated with evergreens in an attempt to lend a jaunty note to their threadbare attire. Alexander Hamilton wrote, "I would not only fight them, but I would attack them, for I hold it an established maxim that there is three to one in favor of the party attacking."

Washington, with about 11,000 men fit for duty (out of 14,000), sent Maxwell with an infantry corps of some 3,000, armed mostly with rifles, to remove supplies from a point on the Elk River; the British, however, were there before Maxwell, and after a skirmish the Americans withdrew to Iron Hill, where the rugged terrain favored the defense, "having," as a Continental captain put it, "a great quantity of woods, large morasses they must pass through, and many commanding hills. . . ." Raiding parties of Americans captured small groups of soldiers who had wandered from their camps searching for food or forage.

General Anthony Wayne and his corps were given the job of constructing defensive positions at Wilmington, and Wayne was reported to be "like a mad bear. . . . he heartily wishes all engineers at the devil." Maxwell's corps, whose function was primarily to delay

Howe, was forced back from Iron Hill, and on September 8, the whole British army took up its advance on Philadelphia in two columns. Washington had established himself across the British line of advance at Red Clay Creek. There the British moved against Washington's right flank and threatened to pin him against the Delaware River. A council of officers agreed unanimously that the position was a disadvantageous one, and at two o'clock on the morning of the ninth, Washington pulled his army back to positions that had been selected by General Greene on Brandywine Creek near Chadds Ford, Pennsylvania. Chadds Ford was some ten miles northwest of Wilmington and on the Delaware, and Washington chose the position in order to be able to attack the British lines if the opportunity offered. Acting on Howe's order, Knyphausen and Cornwallis joined forces at Kennett Square, some seven miles south of Chadds Ford. Knyphausen then advanced directly toward the American positions to hold Washington's attention while Howe, taking command of the divisions of generals Cornwallis, Grey, Matthews, and Agnew, began a long flanking march of some seventeen miles that carried him well beyond Washington's right.

The American center, composed of Anthony Wayne's, George Weedon's, William Maxwell's, and Peter Muhlenberg's brigades, was under the command of Greene. A redoubt and earthworks were hastily constructed and artillery emplaced. Washington had put his best general officers at this spot under Greene's direction because he hoped to be able to launch a strong attack upon the British. The Pennsylvania militia made up the American left, running along the creek to Pyle's Ford. The right wing was made up of three divisions: that of John Sullivan on the left, Adam Stephen in the center, and Lord Stirling on the right. American pickets were stationed well up the Brandywine.

Before the morning of September 11, Washington had withdrawn Weedon's and Muhlenberg's brigades to constitute a reserve, their place being taken by an extension of Wayne's brigade to the left. Maxwell crossed the Brandywine early on the eleventh, and his troops maintained a constant harassing fire on Knyphausen's advance guard until they were pushed back to the creek by the much more numerous enemy. Reinforced, Maxwell then drove the British off a low hill near Chadds Ford, and two regiments of Continentals under Porterfield and Waggoner joined him across the creek, moving to the left and attacking Ferguson's rifles and a portion of the Twenty-eighth Regiment, who were constructing artillery emplacements. Thus beset, Knyphausen was forced to bring up two brigades with artillery to hold off Maxwell.

Meanwhile a strong detachment was dispatched by the Hessian general to Brinton's Ford, a mile or so above Chadds Ford, to threaten Maxwell's right and force him to withdraw across the Brandywine. The maneuver succeeded and Maxwell withdrew. The Americans had fought effectively. They had inflicted some one hundred and thirty casualties on the British and Hessian troops at the cost of less than sixty to themselves. But Knyphausen's advance was, after all, diversionary; the American resistance had accomplished little more than to help mask the movement of Howe's main force.

Word reached Washington early on the eleventh that Cornwallis had moved out of Kennett Square to the north, as though to attempt a crossing higher up the Brandywine, but Washington, confident that Sullivan would push his scouts along the creek and keep him informed of the British movements, determined to attack Knyphausen while Cornwallis was otherwise occupied.

A fog obscured the initial movements of the British, but some time between nine and ten in the morning, Colonel Theoderick Bland crossed Jones's Ford with some light horse and spotted Cornwallis nearing Trimble's Ford on the west fork of the Brandywine. He sent word at once to Sullivan, and the message was followed by a more explicit report from Lieutenant Colonel James Ross, who wrote at eleven o'clock, that "a large body of the enemy, from every account five thousand, with sixteen or eighteen field-pieces, marched along the road just now. . . . I believe General Howe is with this party, as Joseph Galloway is here known by the inhabitants with whom he spoke, and told them that General Howe was with them." Included was a description of the roads on the west side of the Brandywine that were available to the British.

Washington ordered Sullivan to cross the Brandywine with his three divisions on the American right and to attack the British force. Meantime the main army under Greene would make a direct attack on Knyphausen. Greene was already on the move with his advance guard across the creek when Washington received a second dispatch from Sullivan. Major Spear, who also had the assignment of watching the fords for any sign of the British and who was stationed at Brinton's Ford, had been to several taverns on the west or south side of the Brandywine and had heard nothing of any movement of the enemy and was, consequently, "confident that they are not in that quarter. . . ."

When in a military engagement there is conflict in reports—one stating that the enemy have been seen in a certain area and the other stating that they have not been—the presumption, assuming that the reports are both from reliable sources, must be heavily in favor of the sighting, since one is much less likely to see something that is not in fact there than not to see something that is. Pursuing the point a step further: it was much more hazardous for Sullivan to act as though the British were not moving to turn the American flank than for him to act as though they were. In the first instance he could be charged with nothing more serious than carrying out an order based on incorrect information. In the second, he was open to the charge that by his dilatoriness he had exposed the whole army not only to defeat but to destruction. At the very least, he should have immediately undertaken to discover the true situation before sending a dispatch to Washington that could do no more than obscure and obfuscate the general's own picture of the situation. Sullivan had been instrumental in losing the Battle of Long Island; he now was to contribute substantially toward losing the Battle of Brandywine. One is reminded of an axiom: "Bad generals do not improve with age." A few moments of reflection would have made apparent to Sullivan that the route referred to in Ross's communique was nearly a mile beyond the fork of the Brandywine, so that Spear's report was no proof that the statement of Ross was not also true.

On receiving Sullivan's report, Washington recalled Greene and countermanded his order to Sullivan to cross the Brandywine and attack Howe. He could hardly attack someone who was not there. The fact that the opportunity was missed does not mean, of course, that it would have succeeded. It could be argued that Washington's plan was an unnecessarily reckless one. (Washington did not know that Cornwallis's corps was made up of fully two-thirds of the entire British force.) Indeed Cornwallis's troops exceeded in numbers Washington's whole command. While the chances for the success of Greene's divisions against Knyphausen were good, Sullivan was surely no match for Howe and Cornwallis. A victory over the British center at Chadds Ford would have certainly been balanced, if not overbalanced, by a sharp rebuff on the American right and the advance of Howe's force to the American rear. It is just conceivable that Washington was saved from disaster by the ineptness of Sullivan. Certainly he was tempted to undertake tactical moves that strained his always inadequate staff and inexperienced officers and men to the limit of their capacities or beyond.

Washington at this point ordered Colonel Bland to move farther west in an effort to search out the British, and at two o'clock in the afternoon Bland reported two brigades moving rapidly to the rear of Sullivan's right flank and added that he had observed a large cloud of dust on the horizon for more than an hour, indicating that the advance brigades were supported by a much larger force. Some three hours had thus been lost between Ross's first sighting and Bland's alarming report. Those three hours proved fatal to any hope of discomforting the British. Sullivan subsequently had any number of plausible reasons for his failure to detect Howe's movement, just as every unsuccessful commander does, but no argument he advanced could exonerate him from having reacted as he did to Major Spear's faulty intelligence. It was perhaps too much to expect Sullivan to detect the fallacy in Spear's message by a process of reasoning similar to that which I have described; but a good general would have known instinctively where the real issue lay.

Information of Howe's maneuver was received by Sullivan well enough in advance of his actual attack to allow the Americans to make adequate dispositions to meet him. At the same time, Howe must be given credit once more for doing brilliantly what he was clearly best at—maneuvering an army in the field. He had brought his force, undetected, on a forced march of seventeen miles, had crossed Jeffries Ford well above the juncture of the forks of the Brandywine, and by three o'clock was in position to attack Stirling's right, at the extreme right of the American lines. Howe formed three brigades, two in the attack and one in reserve; the grenadier guards were on the right, the First British Grenadiers to their left. The Hessian grenadiers and two battalions of light infantry, with Hessian and Anspach chasseurs along with the fourth brigade, formed the second line.

The Americans opposed them on high ground near Birmingham Meetinghouse. "Both flanks were covered by very thick woods, and the artillery was advantageously disposed." The British attack was so heavy and well-sustained, depending once more on the bayonet, that the Americans quickly gave way, taking refuge in the woods on either side of their main line, and the "Guards, First British Grenadiers and Hessian grenadiers . . . having in pursuit got entangled in very thick woods, were no further engaged during the day." But the second line swept to the town of Dilworth, almost directly in the American rear.

Knyphausen, who had "kept the enemy amused with cannon," as a British officer put it, moved to the attack when Howe hit the American rear, and the defenders of Chadds Ford were soon routed. Washington, at the beginning of Howe's assault, ordered Sullivan to oppose him with the entire American right. Wayne was left to direct the brief defense of the creek line, and Greene was placed in charge of the reserve. Sullivan, confused and uncertain, fought his division badly. His men scattered, and he and his officers failed to rally them. From his own account of his actions it is plain enough that he had a very inadequate notion of what was going on and no resources to cope with the situation when he did. Stirling's and Stephen's divisions, on the other hand, fought well and inflicted heavy casualties on the British before they fell back in good order, taking their baggage and artillery with them. General Prud-homme de Borre's brigade on the right of the American line offered only token resistance, but Hazen's, Ogden's and Dayton's regiments on the American left made a determined and effective fight.

The demoralization of Sullivan's division became a matter of special attention after the battle, because it gave the British an opportunity to cut in between Wayne's force at Chadds Ford and the main American army now deployed to face Howe's attack. As the battle turned more and more decisively against Washington, it appeared that Howe was at last on the verge of what he had so laboriously sought, an engagement in the field, where his disciplined troops, well-trained staff, and experienced officers could destroy the main American army and thus, they hoped, bring the war to an end. Washington himself must have felt something close to despair. When he received word that the British were concentrating their attack at the Birmingham Meetinghouse, he was anxious to ride to that point to see for himself how the action was going, but no one on his staff knew the way. Finally an old man named Joseph Brown turned up. Washington asked Brown to guide him to the meetinghouse. When the old man refused, "one of Washington's suite dismounted from a fine charger, and told Brown if he did not instantly get on his horse and conduct the General by the nearest and best route to the place of action, he would run him through on the spot." Brown, thus encouraged, set off at a gallop, across hills and fields, taking the fences in stride, with Washington close behind and his staff following in the rear, "the General continually repeating to him, 'Push along, old man—Push along, old man.'"

Quickly taking in the situation at Birmingham Meetinghouse, Washington called for Greene's division to support the American right, but it arrived too late; it could do no more than help to cover the retreat of Stephen's and Stirling's divisions. Washington, in a skillfully executed maneuver, placed the reserve at Dilworth and there kept open a line of withdrawal for both Wayne and the units on the right that were being driven back by sheer weight of numbers. The militia brigade under General John Armstrong, which had been posted at Pyle's Ford (below Chadds Ford), pulled out to the east with Maxwell and Wayne and joined in the general retreat toward the town of Chester.

Among the little contingent of French volunteers who fought at Brandywine, the most famous was the young Marquis de Lafayette, scion of one of the great families of France, who had been appointed major general by Congress "by way of a compliment," though he was little more than a boy. Lafayette, serving as Washington's aide-de-camp, was wounded in the leg by a musket ball while trying to rally troops on the right near the brigade of his countryman, Prudhomme de Borre. Captain Louis Teissedre de Fleury, another French officer, distinguished himself by his gallantry, and the Baron St. Ovary was taken prisoner as he tried to check the flight of a group of Americans.

By eleven o'clock at night the weary Americans had reached Chester and had been sorted out, organized, and fed. Washington sat down to write an account of the day's action to John Hancock, who was presiding over Congress. The Americans had been defeated once more by a superior force led in a classic envelopment by an officer whose genius was for battlefield tactics, not grand strategy. They had, for the most part, fought courageously. Maxwell's men early in the day had done all that might be expected of trained professional soldiers. Numerous other units, squads, companies, and regiments had performed well, had held their positions until forced back by superior numbers, and had retreated in good order. Sullivan had, once more, proved to be the weakest of the general officers, but, as we have seen, his ineptitude may in fact have saved the Americans from a far worse defeat. Most important, the army was still virtually intact. The British casualties numbered some six hundred killed, wounded or missing; American losses were several hundred greater, with four hundred taken prisoner. Brandywine deserves special notice because the Continental Army and its militia auxiliaries fought a conventional battle of maneuver and emerged very much alive—though badly singed, to be sure. It was an encouraging prelude to the battles of Freeman's Farm and Bemis Heights, soon to be fought in the Northern Department.

Of course it did not seem encouraging to Congress or to most patriots, who saw the action at Brandywine simply as another disheartening setback. A whole series of investigations and inquisitions tried to establish blame for a defeat that could hardly, in any circumstances, have been a victory. Thomas Burke, a member of Congress from North

Carolina who was present at the battle, wrote to Sullivan, who had certainly fought with courage if not with skill, "I heard officers on the field lamenting in the bitterest terms that they were cursed with such a commander and I overheard numbers during the retreat complain of you as an officer whose evil conduct was forever productive of misfortunes to the army." Burke planned to urge Congress to remove a person so "unqualified" and so "void of judgment and foresight. . . . My objection to you is want of sufficient talents, and I consider it as your misfortune, not fault."

War has many dimensions, and any history that tells of war is obliged to try to convey a sense of how war affects the lives of ordinary people. It was after the Battle of Brandywine that Sally Wister, a Quaker girl living in a village nearby, heard "a great noise" and rushing to the door saw "a large number of waggons, with about three hundred of the Philadelphia militia. They begged for drink," she wrote her friend, Deborah Norris, "and several pushed into the house. One of those that entered was a little tipsy, and had a mind to be saucy." Sally, who was fifteen, fled, "all in a shake with fear; but after a little, seeing the officers appeared gentlemanly and the soldiers civil," her fears were "in some measure dispelled, tho' my teeth rattled, and my hands shook like an aspen leaf. They did not offer to take their quarters with us; so with many blessings, and as many adieus, they marched off." A few days later, the Wister house in Gwynedd became the headquarters of General William Smallwood and his staff of Maryland officers. Sally was atingle with excitement. The general's arrival was announced by "the greatest drumming, fifing, and rattling of waggons that she had heard." Soon there was "a large guard of soldiers, a number of horses and baggage-waggons, the yard and house in confusion, and glittered with military equipments." The general and his staff entered the house and introduced themselves to the Wisters while Sally watched wide-eyed. "They retired about ten, in good order," she wrote Deborah, adding, "How new is our situation! I feel in good spirits, though surrounded by an army, the house full of officers, the yard alive with soldiers—very peaceable sort of people tho'. They eat like other folks, talk like them, and behave themselves with elegance; so I will not be afraid of them, that I won't. Adieu. I am going to my chamber to dream, I suppose, of bayonets and swords, sashes, guns and epaulets."

Colonel Line, an unmarried officer, became Sally's favorite. "He is monstrous tall and brown," she wrote Debbie, "but has a certain something in his face and conversation very agreeable; he entertains the highest notions of honour, is sensible and humane, and a brave officer; he is only seven and twenty years old, but, by a long indisposition and constant fatigue, looks vastly older, and almost worn to a skeleton, but very lively and talkative." Captain Furnival, a young artillery officer in the Maryland line, had, Sally noted, "excepting one or two, the handsomest face I ever saw, a very fine person; fine light hair, and a great deal of it, adds to the beauty of his face." Three of the officers dined with the Wisters, and Sally "was dress'd in my chintz, and looked smarter than the night before," when she had been surprised by the arrival of the officers. Major Stoddert, who was nineteen years old and was reputed to have a private fortune, was incurably bashful. Although Sally set herself to drive away that bashfulness, she found it a difficult campaign: "Fifth day, Sixth day, and Seventh day pass'd," she wrote Debbie. "The General still here; the Major still bashful."

Finally, besieged for almost a month, the major surrendered. He asked Sally to sing. Sally denied she could, "for my voice is not much better than the voice of a raven," but the ice was broken at last, and Sally noted that they "talk'd and laugh'd for an hour. He is clever, amiable, and polite. He has the softest voice, never pronounces the *r* at all." The next night after dinner the major drew his chair close to Sally's at the fire "and entertain'd me most agreeably. Oh, Debby" she added, "I have a thousand things to tell thee. I shall give thee so droll an account of my adventures that thee will smile. 'No occasion of that, Sally,' methinks I hear thee say, 'for thee tells me every trifle.' But, child, thee is mistaken, for I have not told thee half the civil things that are said of us *sweet* creatures at 'General Smallwood's Quarters.'"

Six weeks after their arrival, the general and his officers—the amiable Major Stoddert among them—departed to join Washington's army. "With daddy and mammy they shook hands very friendly," Sally reported; "to us they bow'd politely. Our hearts were full. I thought the Major was affected. 'Good-bye, Miss Sally,' spoken very low. We stood at the door to take a last look, all of us very sober." The major was the last to leave. "We look'd at him till the turn in the road hid him from our sight. 'Amiable major,' 'Clever fellow,' 'Good young man,' was echoed from one to the other. I wonder if we shall ever see him again." And a few days later she wrote: "It seems strange not to see our house as it used to be. We are very still. No rattling of waggons, glittering of musquets. The beating of the distant drum is all we hear." It was thus that Sally Wister experienced the war.

7

The Paoli Massacre and Germantown

From Chester, Washington marched promptly to Philadelphia to reorganize and re-equip his army. Then he moved to Germantown, just a few miles north of the city, and made camp. He sent orders to the French engineer, Monsieur Tronson de Coudray, to finish the fortifications along the Delaware as soon as possible; to General Armstrong to erect defensive positions with his Pennsylvania militia along the line of the Schuylkill, south of the city; and to General Putnam at Peekskill to send him fifteen hundred Continental soldiers, among them, as it turned out, our friend, Joseph Martin.

Howe, meanwhile, made various feints—west toward Reading, north toward Philadelphia, and finally to Chester and Wilmington on the Delaware. He had on his hands almost one thousand wounded men; he needed quarters for them and surgeons to attend their wounds. Washington, for his part, was determined to keep his army on the move and to take advantage of any opportunity that Howe might offer for battle—on terms favorable to the Continental Army, of course. September 15, Washington recrossed the Schuylkill to the west (or south) side and moved out on the Lancaster Road in a position on Howe's left. Howe moved to Westchester a few miles away and made preparations for battle. Again avoiding the direct attack that Washington invited,

Howe moved on the American right, trying to pin the Americans against the Schuylkill. The moment seemed opportune to Washington for an attack, but before the Americans could take the offensive, a heavy rain soaked both armies to the skin and destroyed more than four hundred thousand cartridges, "a most terrible stroke" forcing Washington to retire. The cartridges were ruined, Knox wrote his wife, "owing entirely to the badness of the cartouch-boxes which had been provided for the army."

Washington left Wayne in a remote and well-hidden spot near Paoli, with fifteen hundred men and instructions to be ready to attack Howe's rear while Washington shadowed Howe's army, trying to divine the British general's inscrutable intentions. Anticipating a move to Reading by Howe, Washington marched to Yellow Springs and from there to Warwick; then, satisfied that the British general's plan was to occupy Philadelphia, he crossed the Schuylkill and made camp on the Perkiomen. In the words of Enoch Anderson, an officer in the Delaware line, "We marched all this day, keeping near the British army. When they marched, we marched; when they stopped, we stopped. Our guide was the beating of drums. Night came on, there was no house we dare go into; we had no tents. I had no blanket even and must make no fire. . . . The night was very cold. I kept myself tolerably comfortable by walking about but was very sleepy and could not sleep for the cold. . . . This day [September 26] . . . brought us safe to headquarters, being nine days out, during which time we never had our clothes off, lodged in no house, in a manner on half allowance of provisions and had to beg on the road."

Alexander Hamilton was sent to Philadelphia to collect shoes by whatever means necessary, short of taking them off the feet of the inhabitants.

Meanwhile, a Tory informer told the British the location of Wayne's camp, and on the evening of September 20 three British regiments, moving with the utmost stealth and secrecy, took his sleeping men by surprise and, attacking with bayonets, killed a number of them before they could defend themselves. Those who rallied were in many instances shot down as they were silhouetted against the campfires. The shadows seemed haunted by redcoats with their merciless bayonets. It was a minor miracle that Wayne managed to collect a major portion of his men and artillery and escape into the welcome darkness. In the morning, the Paoli villagers counted 53 mangled bodies. The British had carried off 71 prisoners, 40 of whom were so badly injured that they

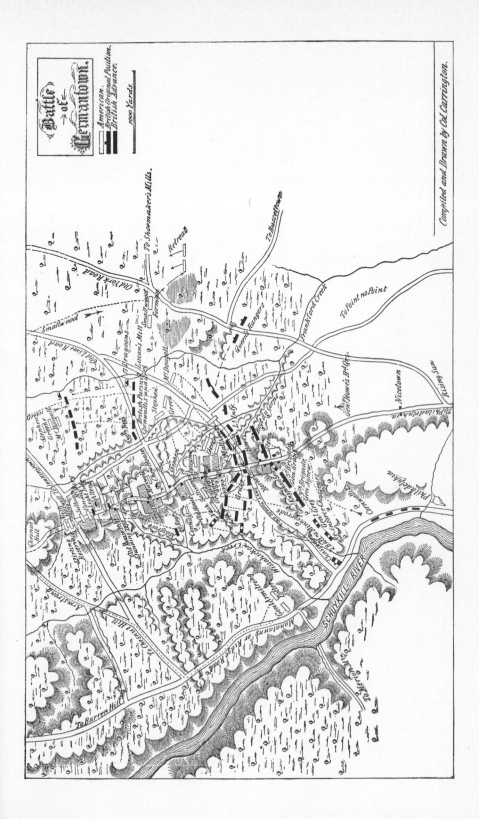

Battle
of
Germantown.

American. →
British Original Position.
British Advance.

1000 Yards.

Compiled and Drawn by Col. Carrington.

had to be left by the way. In total the Americans suffered more than 300 casualties in what came to be known as the Paoli Massacre.

The disaster to Wayne disheartened an already weary and apprehensive Washington. People with short memories who had hailed him as the savior of the cause after Trenton began to grumble that the commander in chief was less of a general than his reputation made him out to be; that he was vacillating and dilatory. The criticisms of Gates, Conway, and other disenchanted officers began to circulate more widely. Washington had numerous critics in Congress, especially among the New Englanders. John Adams, for one, was indignant at his decision to put the Schuylkill between himself and Howe. "It is a very injudicious movement" he wrote. "If he had sent one brigade of his regular troops to have headed the militia he might cut to pieces Howe's army in attempting to cross any of the fords. Howe will not attempt it. . . . He will wait for his fleet in Delaware River. O! Heaven! grant us one great soul! One leading mind would extricate the best cause from that ruin which seems to await it!"

Even Nathanael Greene felt that Washington was displaying some of the hesitation and uncertainty that had characterized him at the time of Fort Washington. When Greene stopped at a watering place one night with the new adjutant general, Timothy Pickering, Pickering remarked, "Before I came to the army, I entertained an exalted opinion of General Washington's military talents, but I have since seen nothing to enhance it." Greene's answer was not reassuring: "Why the general does want decision; for my part I decide in a moment." Baron Johann de Kalb, a Bavarian who had served with distinction in the French army and had come to America on the same ship with Lafayette as a volunteer, was even more critical. "Washington," he wrote "is the most amiable, kindhearted and upright of men; but as a General he is too slow, too indolent and far too weak; besides he has a tinge of vanity in his composition, and overestimates himself. In my opinion, whatever success he may have will be owing to good luck and the blunders of his adversaries, rather than to his abilities. I may even say that he does not know how to improve upon the grossest blunders of the enemy."

Washington was not unaware of the criticisms, but he must have wondered what the critics expected him to do. He had fewer than seven thousand men, almost a thousand of whom had no shoes; he was faced by an army almost twice the size of his own. For the moment he could only do as he had done so often before, labor ceaselessly to augment his ragged army with more men who could march and dig and fire a musket. He had, certainly, every reason to despond. He did not, because he had acquired confidence in his own powers and faith in the ability of his soldiers, properly led, to fight the British on equal terms. Brandy-wine was plainly a defeat. But the battle could be read in more ways than one. Whatever others might think, Washington chose to find reassurance in the way many units had performed. And if he was cautious at times, he could also be reckless. If he was subject to fits of depression, he was far more hopeful for the most part than the circumstances of his army would seem to have warranted.

Washington meanwhile anticipated the arrival of Alexander Mac-Dougall's brigade from New York, a thousand militia from Virginia, and an equal number from New Jersey, as well as Heath's Massachusetts line and the return of Morgan's riflemen when Gates no longer needed them.

As Howe's army approached Philadelphia, Thomas Paine was active in trying to persuade the capital's inhabitants to erect defenses across the roads leading to the city. He observed very shrewdly that "notwithstanding the knowledge military gentlemen are supposed to have . . . they move exceedingly cautiously on new ground, and are exceedingly suspicious of villages and towns, and more perplexed at seemingly little things which they cannot clearly understand than at great ones which they are fully acquainted with. . . ." But Paine was unable to rouse the citizens of the city to any resolute measures of self-defense. A strange lethargy, indeed a kind of paralysis, seized Philadelphia and the adjacent towns. Colonel John Bayard, trying to collect militia, wrote to the Philadelphia Council of Safety: "We are greatly distressed to find no more of the militia of our State joining General Washington at this time; for God's Sake what shall we do; is the cause deserted by our State, and shall a few Brave men offer their Lives as a Sacrifice . . . without assistance. . . . I am far from thinking our cause desperate, if our people would but turn out. . . ."

Paine went to General Thomas Mifflin to urge that efforts be made to round up two or three thousand men. Mifflin promised help, but when Paine came back several hours later, the general had left the city. Paine had no choice but to depart himself. Had he been able to rally support, he might well have become additionally famous as the first modern practitioner of street fighting in defense of a city. If Howe had been met by determined Pennsylvania militia blocking the access roads at the edge of the city, with Washington's army in his rear, he might very well have abandoned his plan to occupy Philadelphia. Paine's perception that "military gentlemen," however skillful in dealing with conventional situations, were unnerved at unorthodox ones was a very penetrating one. In addition, Howe's native caution might well have made him particularly reluctant to undertake such a novel venture as trying to invest a large city whose inhabitants seemed determined to fight.

Congress, expecting Howe to occupy Philadelphia, departed on September 19 for Lancaster and then moved on to York. In anticipation of the occupation of the city, they ordered the most essential military supplies moved fifty miles northwest to Reading. It was therefore to Reading that Washington made his way to get food and supplies for his weary army. From there he crossed the Schuylkill and marched down the left bank of the river to a spot three miles north of Valley Forge. On the eighteenth, Cornwallis and Knyphausen captured a quantity of supplies in a depot at Valley Forge, and three days later Howe marched north toward the Schuylkill. Washington, assuming that Howe's goal was Philadelphia, had expected the British to cross the river near the city. Now he decided that Howe's objective was Reading and the American supplies. Washington assigned Sullivan to guard the fords and moved the rest of his army to block Howe's advance. Under the cover of darkness, Howe turned back along the right bank, secured the fords at Flatland and Gordon, scattered the defenders, and crossed the river on the night of September 22. Four days later Cornwallis's division, with drums beating, fifes tooting, and flags flying, entered Philadelphia, where they received a warm greeting from the Tories of that city. When Franklin was told that Howe had captured Philadelphia, he replied, "No, Philadelphia has captured Howe!"

Howe, with the balance of his army, established his headquarters at Germantown, a village some six miles from Philadelphia that consisted of a hundred or so dwellings extending along the Skippach Road for nearly two miles.

Washington and his weary army had been badly outmaneuvered. Moreover, in the fortnight between Brandywine and Cornwallis's entry into Philadelphia, his footsore, cold, and hungry army had marched one hundred and forty miles in wretched weather; in the process it had dwindled through desertion, illness, and the expiration of enlistments to scarcely six thousand men, approximately half the number that had opposed Howe on the Brandywine.

The situation was, in many ways, similar to that which had faced Washington and his army prior to the attack on Trenton. Despite the miserable condition of his army, Washington was determined to make an attack on Howe. Considerably strengthened by the arrival of MacDougall's division and encouraged by word that Howe had dispatched a sizable detachment to help reduce the forts along the Delaware, Washington called his general officers together to propose the attack on Germantown. The tactic was to be a double envelopment—a strong movement on the British center with flanking forces advancing on the left and right of the Skippach Road; the intention was to scoop up the whole British command. The council of war voted unanimously to make the attack. Stephen, Greene, and MacDougall were to make up the American left; Sullivan and Wayne would comprise the center, supported by Maxwell and Nash under Stirling as a reserve; Armstrong would be on the right. Smallwood's and Forman's brigades, with the Maryland and Virginia militia, were to follow the Old York Road in an effort to move on the extreme British right.

The American army was at Pennypack's Mill, some twenty miles from Philadelphia. Washington's intention was to advance by the main roads to the vicinity of Germantown under the cover of darkness, move his divisions into their jumping-off positions, allow them some time to rest, and make his attack at daybreak.

At dawn on October 4, Conway's brigade led the advance on the north end of the town and promptly encountered the British pickets, who were soon reinforced by light infantry. Sullivan brought up his own division, driving the British advance units back one hundred yards or more; his men cried out, "Have at the bloodhounds! Revenge Wayne's affair." The Fortieth British Regiment, one of the regiments that had participated in the Paoli Massacre, was brought up by its commanding officer, Colonel Thomas Musgrave. As he moved forward, he encountered the British advance guard and the light infantry falling back under a well-sustained attack.

The opening phase of the battle is well described by a British officer, Lieutenant Sir Martin Hunter, who noted that the British returned the initial American charge with shouts and cheers of their own. "On our charging, they gave way on all sides, but again and again renewed the attack with fresh troops and greater force. We charged them twice, until the battalion was so reduced by killed and wounded that the bugle was sounded to retreat; indeed had we not retreated at the very time we did, we should all have been taken or killed, as two columns of the enemy had nearly got round our flank." This was the most significant moment of the battle; the British had never before retreated in open battle before the attack of American troops. "It was with great difficulty," Hunter wrote, "we could get our men to obey our orders."

Howe came up as the light infantry were retiring and "seeing the battalion retreating all broken, he got into a passion and exclaimed: 'For shame, Light Infantry! I never saw you retreat before. Form! form! it's only a scouting party.'" A little cluster of officers gathered about Howe under a large chestnut tree to try to persuade him that they had been forced back by a large force of Americans. Just then the column of enemy soldiers appeared with a cannon that was quickly wheeled into action and fired at the most conspicuous target—Howe and the party around him. "I think I never saw people enjoy a charge of grape before," Lieutenant Hunter wrote, "but we really all felt pleased to see the enemy make such an appearance, and to hear the grape rattle about the commander-in-chief's ears, after he had accused the battalion of running away from a scouting party."

Joseph Martin was a soldier in Sullivan's division that morning, and as the British pickets were engaged, his brigade deployed to the right of the Skippach Road and advanced toward a line of redcoats drawn up behind a rail fence. "Our orders," he wrote, "were not to fire till we could see the buttons upon their clothes, but they were so coy that they would not give us an opportunity to be so curious, for they hid their clothes in fire and smoke before we had either time or leisure to examine their buttons. . . . The enemy were driven quite through their camp. They left their kettles, in which they were cooking their break-fasts, on the fires, and some of their garments were lying on the ground, which the owners had not time to put on."

At this point things were going well for the Americans, but there was no sign yet of Greene's or Armstrong's maneuvers on the left and right. As Colonel Musgrave retreated with the Fortieth, he came to the house of Benjamin Chew, one of the leading men in Pennsylvania, a person of generally Tory inclinations. The house was a handsome, sturdily built stone mansion with thick walls. Making a quick decision, Musgrave decided to occupy the house, which, situated as it was on a slight rise, might serve as a kind of improvised fort. He ordered six companies of his regiment into the house. It was one of those sponta-neous, individual decisions, impossible to anticipate, that so often change the whole course of a battle. Sullivan's men, finding themselves under heavy fire from an enemy it seemed impossible to dislodge, recoiled on the Skippach Road. Confusion was compounded by a heavy fog that obscured much of the town. Conway was directed to deploy his men to the right on the west of the town, and Wayne, in the absence of Greene, was moved to the left to protect the east side of the town. The crucial decision was whether to stop, bring up artillery, and try to destroy the little garrison in the Chew house, or to by-pass it and move on in the main attack, allowing rear units to deal with the house. If the American attack was successful, the Chew house must inevitably surrender. Even if the Americans were forced back, they could easily detour around that spot.

At a house near the Chew mansion, Captain Timothy Pickering found Washington and a group of officers discussing the strategy of moving forward and leaving the Chew house uncaptured. It was Knox who, at least on this occasion, knew too much military theory and who insisted that it was contrary to all sound practice to leave a castle in one's rear. An effort should be made to persuade the garrison in the mansion to surrender. Lieutenant Colonel Smith, a Virginian and a deputy adjutant general, volunteered to advance under a white flag to demand the capitulation. Other officers objected to the plan as a useless and dangerous enterprise, but Knox persisted and Washington acquiesced. Smith started forward with the flag, but as he reached the lawn of the Chew mansion he was hit by a musket ball and fell. Maxwell's brigade, reinforced with four six-pounders, was then given the mission of reducing the house. The artillery was ineffective against the thick stone walls; under the cover of artillery and musket fire, platoons of infantry tried repeatedly to work their way close to the house. Time and again they were driven back by fire from the windows. The two New Jersey regiments involved in the assault lost forty-six officers and men. Chevalier Maduit de Plessis, a French engineer who had come to America with Lafayette, and John Laurens made several daring efforts to set fire to the house, and one of the members of Sullivan's staff, Major White, was fatally injured in the same enterprise. But all efforts failed; the mansion remained a thorn in the side of the attacking Americans. It is clear in retrospect that Maxwell's brigade could have been used to much better advantage elsewhere.

For a crucial hour or more, Musgrave had delayed the advance of those Continental units that might have exploited the success of the initial attack. Timothy Pickering wrote that Chew's house "annoyed us prodigiously and absolutely stopped our pursuit—not necessarily but we mistook our true interest." In attack, momentum is everything.

There was still no word of Greene. Stephen's division, without orders from Greene, had peeled off from Greene's left toward the noise of muskets and artillery near the Chew house. Here Stephen's men struck the rear of Wayne's brigade and, mistaking the Americans in the fog for British, began a startling and demoralizing fire on Wayne's rear. The effect was to neutralize both Wayne's and Stephen's forces. Greene, moving along the Lime Kiln Road, had to echelon his division to his right to avoid the strong British force that was advancing on the right to try to envelop the American center. He passed the left of the British advance and Sullivan's division, still struggling to extricate itself from the battle that swirled around the Chew house. As Sullivan's advance elements moved in the direction of the markethouse at the center of Germantown, Greene was also converging toward that point. Here Washington had to take stock of the situation. Wayne and Stephen were immobilized. Armstrong had failed to make an effective movement on the British left. The American right had only MacDougall's division to cover it, and contact had been lost with him. The fog, which persisted all morning, made communication between the various American units difficult if not impossible. "Officers and men got much separated from each other, neither (in numerous instances) knowing where to find their own," Pickering wrote.

The reserve was useless, having been deflected (or distracted) by the problem of the Chew house. Demoralizing rumors circulated. One, which of course was more than a rumor, concerned the disastrous clash of Stephen's division and Wayne's brigade. All hope of a coordinated attack had been lost by the fog, the delay occasioned by the defense of the Chew house, Greene's failure to come up on time, and the weak behavior of General Armstrong; the latter, after "cannonading" from the heights on each side of the Wissahickon, had been forced to march three miles before making contact "with a superior body of the enemy, with whom we engaged about three-quarters of an hour," he reported, "but their grape shot and ball soon intimidated and obliged us to retreat, or rather file off." (The fact that Armstrong's division lost "not quite twenty" men with thirty-nine wounded must raise the suspicion that it fought rather faintheartedly.) At this point, many soldiers were retreating, and Washington felt he had no choice but to order a general withdrawal, which, with the aid of the fog, was accomplished with a fair degree of dispatch. Martin thought the American retreat came about because some soldiers called out that their ammunition was gone and the British, overhearing them, stopped their own retreat and, urged on by their officers, moved to the attack, forcing the Continentals back and spreading confusion in the American ranks.

The British losses, dead and wounded, were 535, including General James Agnew. The American losses were listed at 673. Four hundred Americans were captured during the retreat. These were high losses out of a mere 7,000 men.

Two things seem clear enough. The delay at the Chew house was unfortunate, if not disastrous. Equally disabling was Stephen's unauthorized movement, which entangled him with Wayne's brigade. Stephen was apparently drunk, though whether intoxication was the reason for his error is not clear. In any event, he was made the scapegoat, court-martialed, and dismissed from the army.

The effect of the Battle of Germantown is difficult to assess. Washington's plan of attack, while it followed classic military precepts, was a demanding one for inexperienced troops and officers to carry out. Timothy Pickering, the new adjutant general, made perhaps the best critique of the plan itself. "This disposition," he wrote, "appears to have been well made; but to execute such a plan requires great exactness in the officers conducting the columns, as well as punctuality in commencing the march, to bring the whole to the point of action at once; and for this end it is absolutely necessary that the length and quality of the roads be perfectly ascertained, the time it will take to march them accurately calculated, and guides chosen who are perfectly acquainted with the roads." There was, apparently, no opportunity for the kind of careful reconnaissance that should precede any major attack. One of the principal problems of an inexperienced army is maintaining contact or communication. Without proper communication, an army is like a man groping about in the dark. The astonishing thing is that despite all this Washington almost succeeded in driving the British from the field and inflicting a major defeat on Howe. This fact confirms the maxim of Hamilton (and of course many others) that "there is three to one in favor of the party attacking."

T. Will Heth, another Continental officer, was more enthusiastic than Pickering. "It was a grand enterprize," he wrote a friend, "an inimitable plan, which nothing but its God-like author could equal." If Heth was perhaps a little too fervent in regard to the practicality of Washington's plan of battle, he was close to the truth when he wrote, "Tho we gave away a complete victory, we have learned this valuable truth: [that we are able] to beat them by vigorous exertion, and that we are far superior [in] point of swiftness. We are in high spirits. Every action [gives] our troops fresh vigor and a greater opinion of their own strength."

The same confusion that hampered the American attack was, if anything, even more demoralizing to the British. In an engagement of this kind the courage and resourcefulness of the individual American soldier was fully revealed, while the dependence of the British and Hessians upon order, discipline, and unquestioning obedience rendered them less effective. If Washington's attack could come so near success, one is tempted to say that the outcome of battles is determined not by the elaborate strategies of generals but by the courage and shrewdness of individual officers and men; to say, in short, that any resolute attack smiled on by the gods of war has an excellent chance of success.

A British officer wrote a letter after the battle, declaring that "this may well be called an unfortunate war for us all. Hardly an officer but is now lamenting the loss of one of his brave friends, and no man can look at the instruments of their misfortune without pitying them still more for having died by the hands of fellows who have hardly the form of men, and whose hearts are still more deformed than their figures." On the other hand, it was reported that a British soldier on a burial detail for American dead said, "Don't bury them thus, and cast dirt in their faces, for they also are mothers' sons."

After his unsuccessful efforts to rouse the citizens of Philadelpha to a defense of the city, Thomas Paine rode about for almost a week looking for Washington's army. Finally, in the early stages of the Battle of Germantown, he came up with it and discovered that the British were being driven back in disorder. As he rode forward he began to encounter demoralized patriots in full retreat, "a promiscuous crowd of wounded and otherwise." He was warned that if he advanced farther he would be seized by the British. "I never could, and cannot now, learn," he wrote Franklin six months later, "and I believe no man can inform truly the cause of that day's miscarriage. The retreat was as extraordinary. Nobody hurried themselves. Every one marched at his own pace. . . . The army had marched the preceding night fourteen miles, and having full twenty to march back were exceedingly fatigued. They appeared to me," Paine added, "to be only sensible of a disappointment, not a defeat; and to be more displeased at their retreating from Germantown, than anxious to get to their rendezvous."

Paine had breakfast with Washington the next morning and found the general's mood much like that of the army. He was equally at a loss to explain the reason for "the accidents of the day." Washington told Paine that, confident that the attack had succeeded, he was about to give orders to the army to push on toward Philadelphia when "he saw most unexpectedly a part (I think) of the artillery hastily retreating. This partial retreat," Paine wrote, "was I believe misunderstood, and soon followed by others. The fog was frequently very thick, the troops young, and unused to breaking and rallying, and our men rendered suspicious to each other, many of them being in red. A new army once disordered, is difficult to manage, and the attempt dangerous." Paine also shared the feeling of many others that there was "prudence in not putting matters to too hazardous a trial." Men must learn fighting "by practice and by degrees." Though the attack had ultimately failed, "it had this good effect that [the soldiers] seemed to feel themselves more important after, than before, as it was the first general attack they had ever made." Paine's analysis was an excellent one.

When all is said and done, the remarkable fact is that despite the impediment of the Chew mansion and the confusion created at a critical junction by Stephen's attack on Wayne's brigade, the Americans came close to winning. The battle, it seems, ultimately turned on some minor point of confusion and misunderstanding at the company level. In conventional terms it is hard to believe that the attack could be justified. Yet many Americans were dazzled by the fact that it almost succeeded, and Count de Vergennes, the French foreign minister, who had advised Louis XVI not to make a military alliance with the Americans on the grounds that they could not hold out much longer against the full force of British military power, was as much impressed by the American attack at Germantown as by Gates's more spectacular victory at Saratoga. "Nothing," he wrote, "has struck me so much as Gen. Washington's attacking and giving battle to Gen. Howe's army. To bring troops, raised within the year, to do this, promises everything." In General Armstrong's words, "The triumphing Tories again shook at the center, the drooping spirits of the Whigs, a little relieved—thus God supports our otherwise sinking spirits. . . ."

After the retreat at Germantown, Washington pulled his weary men back to Pennypack's Mill. "I had now to travel the rest of the day," Joseph Martin wrote, "after marching all the day and night before and fighting all the morning. I had eaten nothing since the noon of the preceding day, nor did I eat a morsel till the forenoon of the next day, and I needed rest as much as victuals. . . . I was tormented with thirst all the morning, fighting being warm work. . . ." Martin's account of Washington's movements after Germantown has the virtue of simplicity! "After the army had collected again and recovered from their panic, we were kept marching and counter-marching, starving and freezing, nothing else happening, although that was enough, until we encamped at a place called the White Marsh."

Major Stoddert was back sooner than Sally Wister could have dared to hope. Exhausted and feverish after the Battle of Germantown, he had been sent back to the hospitable Wisters to recuperate. There Sally tried her charms on him again, but she found him often silent and preoccupied, and once he clasped her hand and exclaimed, "Oh, my God, I wish this war was at an end."

Foreign Volunteers

SOMETHING might be said here about the foreigners who came as volunteers to fight with the Americans. The largest number of such volunteers came from France, many of them scions of that country's most aristocratic families. It is easy to be cynical about these young men; to say that they were simply the idle rich who liked to fight, who were bored with the court life of a corrupt monarchy and yearned for excitement and military glory; that fighting in America became a fad for energetic young French aristocrats. Undoubtedly such sentiments entered into the decisions of those adventurous spirits who offered their services to the Continental Congress. Few human motives are entirely pure. But a stronger consideration with them, and with the Poles and Germans who joined them, was a genuine idealism, a devotion to what to their romantic minds seemed to be the principles of freedom and justice.

The clearest evidence of the brotherhood of man is that tyranny and injustice arouse the resentment not simply of those who suffer it, but of every man and woman of conscience, regardless of their race or nation. It was another of those historical paradoxes, with which we are now so familiar, that members of a notorious aristocracy should wish to cast their lot with revolutionaries who made no attempt to hide their hostility toward hereditary class distinctions and many of whom fought in the name of democracy.

Well before France signed its treaty of amity and concord with the envoys of the Continental Congress, young Frenchmen were slipping out of the country to join Washington's ragged little army. The most famous was Lafayette, but he was only one of a rapidly growing company. We have mentioned Plessis and Fleury, Armand and Laumoy. The Chevalier de Chastellux helped the Baron de Montesquieu get to America. He was, after all, the grandson of that Montesquieu whose great work on the spirit of the laws was one of the texts that all Americans with scholarly or intellectual pretensions knew well, one of the sources of the revolution. "The Americans who hold M. de Montesquieu in veneration," Chastellux wrote to the French war minister, "will hasten to meet his grandson and rejoice in that acquaintance." Indeed, it was like history coming to life.

Armand Tufin, Marquis de la Rouërie, was a comparatively mature twenty-five when he arrived in America in the first group of French volunteers. He had been a member of the elite Garde du Corps but was forced to resign after wounding the king's cousin in a duel. When his family made him break off an affair with a beautiful actress, he retired to a Trappist monastery. From there he set sail for America on a ship that escaped British pursuers in Chesapeake Bay by the narrowest of margins. In America he adopted the name Charles Armand because he thought his aristocratic titles were inappropriate to someone fighting in a republican cause. Washington, impressed by his ardor and military experience, gave Armand permission to try to raise a corps of volunteers. Ordinary Americans have always regarded Frenchmen, it is to be feared, as effete "frog eaters" and/or enterprising seducers of innocent virgins. Many of the Frenchmen who came in a spirit of enthusiastic republicanism encountered such prejudices among the common ranks, however warmly they may have been received by a flattered Congress. Armand, apparently in part for this reason and more importantly because American soldiers wished to be commanded by officers they knew, was unsuccessful in raising a corps of volunteers. But he was determined to fight in the American cause, and, having vast wealth, he simply bought a group of French soldiers that had been recruited by a Swiss major. He led them with conspicuous skill and courage. At Red Bank he was second-in-command to Lafayette and distinguished himself in the action against Cornwallis's rear guard.

The story of Lafayette himself is a familiar but perpetually fascinating one. Lafayette's father, a colonel of the grenadiers, had been killed at the battle of Minden while Lafayette himself was still an infant. His mother had died when he was thirteen, leaving him heir to the family's considerable fortunes. He had entered the royal army when he was fourteen and two years later had married the daughter of one of the most powerful and important families in France. At a dinner with the Duke of Gloucester soon after word had reached Europe of the Battle of Bunker Hill, Lafayette was struck by the Englishman's sympathy for the Americans. The Duke of Gloucester lit a spark within the Frenchman that soon flamed into a passionate and romantic attachment to the American cause.

Lafayette was a rather odd-looking young man: inclined to stoutness, rather awkward, with a strangely "bent" face and sharp nose. As one American officer put it, his nose "does not appear to correspond perfectly with his person." The queen of France had laughed cruelly at his clumsy efforts to dance at Versailles. He was a moody romantic, this poorly assembled boy; restless and ill at ease at the court, conscious that he was an object of ridicule to many in that polished and glittering company. "The moment I heard of America," he wrote, "I loved her; the moment I knew she was fighting for freedom, I burned with a desire of bleeding for her."

Lafayette applied to Silas Deane, the agent of Congress in France, for help in getting to America and for assurance that he would be commissioned at a proper rank. In view of his wealth and position (and four years of nominal military service), he felt he should be given the rank of major general. Deane, greatly impressed with the social eminence of his young importuner, equipped Lafayette with a letter promising him, in the name of Congress, a commission as major general. Lafayette departed under the protection of Johann de Kalb, a grizzled old veteran of fifty-five who, starting life as the son of a Bavarian peasant, had risen to the rank of major during the Seven Years' War, married a wealthy heiress, and become a self-proclaimed baron and a gentleman scholar.

De Kalb was an excellent mentor for young Lafayette. He had traveled in America in 1768 as a secret agent for the Duc de Choiseul, the French foreign minister, reporting to his superior on the feelings of the colonists toward Great Britain. Since he reported what he observed rather than what Choiseul wanted to hear, he was, in the manner of many such candid observers, recalled. He returned to the army with the rank of brigadier general and then, like Lafayette, secured a commission from Silas Deane. He and the young Frenchman had sailed together for America in April, 1777.

When Lafayette and de Kalb reached America, they found Congress more than a little embarrassed by Deane's generosity. After some backing and filling, the delegates made the nineteen-year-old Lafayette a major general without command and sent him off to join Washington. De Kalb, having only considerable military experience to commend him, found Congress not disposed to honor the commission that Silas Deane had so recklessly promised him. He was understandably indignant and threatened to sue Congress for breach of contract. Finally, after several months of indecision, that body voted to commission him as major general, and he, too joined Washington in November at his headquarters near Philadelphia.

Washington found the stream of foreign volunteers, a number of whom were soldiers of fortune who went wherever there was promise of some military glory, a heavy burden. They appeared at almost weekly intervals to request or to insist on commands appropriate, in their view, to their experience or, as in the case of Lafayette, to their social standing. Some spoke English imperfectly, and all suffered the substantial handicap of simply not being Americans and thus being, in most cases, too exotic for the American temperament. After they had been tested and proved themselves in battle, they were, by and large, accepted with the regard that brave men have for each other, a regard that transcends differences of race and nationality. But there were still very considerable difficulties of a practical kind, and, with some notable exceptions, the most successful and useful of this colorful and romantic band were those who, like Plessis, had specialized experience as military engineers.

Perhaps the principal embarrassment inflicted on Congress and Washington by the assiduous Silas Deane was Philippe Charles Tronson de Coudray, who arrived in Boston with eighteen other officers and ten sergeants and a contract from Deane promising him the rank of major general of artillery and ordnance. Coudray's brother was Marie Antoinette's lawyer, and he himself had tutored the Comte d'Artoise (the future Charles X of France) in the art of war. Washington, more than satisfied with General Knox, warned Congress that if they honored Coudray's contract, Knox would resign and the whole officer corps would be turned upside down. Knox had "deservedly acquired the character of one of the most valuable officers in the service, and . . . combatting the almost innumerable difficulties in the department he fills, has placed the artillery upon a footing that does him the greatest honor." Coudray's demands were an acute embarrassment to the delegates in Congress. Fortunately the French officer, who had already alienated many Americans by his imperious ways, rode his horse full tilt onto the Schuylkill ferry, slipped over the side, and drowned—"a dispensation," as John Adams put it dryly, "that will save us much altercation."

When Lafayette presented himself to Washington, the latter suppressed whatever irritation he may have felt and promptly fell under the spell of the Frenchman. The Virginian, an aristocrat himself, had never met anyone like this vivid and charming boy, so enthusiastic, so open and expressive. He was irresistible to the older man, and Washington, who already regarded the very different but almost equally charming Hamilton as a "son," adopted Lafayette as another. (After the battle at Brandywine, where Lafayette was wounded, Washington told his surgeon, "Treat him as if he were my son, for I love him as if he were.") And Lafayette, the orphan who had never known a father, responded with a kind of puppy-dog affection, embarrassing and pleasing the reserved Washington with his Gallic effusiveness. (Another French volunteer, Comte de More, Chevalier de Pontgibaud, wrote of Lafayette, "He possessed . . . those external advantages which a man born to command should have; tall stature, a noble face, gentleness in his glance, amenity in his language, simplicity in his gestures and expressions. A calm, firm bearing harmonized perfectly with these attributes.")

What the other "son," Hamilton, thought of the rapid advancement of his new rival is not recorded. He was exactly the same age as Lafayette—twenty. After having served with courage and skill as an artillery officer at Long Island, Harlem, and White Plains, and having been through the arduous Jersey campaign at Trenton and Princeton, Hamilton had become Washington's aide-de-camp in March and had been promoted to lieutenant colonel a few months later. Washington became more and more dependent upon the young man's brilliance, his inexhaustible energy, his skill as a writer, and his gifts of intrigue and political maneuver. Sullivan gave a vivid description of Hamilton in this period of his life: "He was under middle size, thin in person, but remarkably erect and dignified in his deportment. His hair was turned back from his forehead, powdered, and collected in a club behind. His complexion was exceedingly fair, and varying from this only by the almost feminine rosiness of his cheeks, he might be considered, as to figure and colour, an uncommonly handsome face. When at rest, it had a rather severe and thoughtful expression; but when engaged in conversation, it easily assumed an attractive smile." Hamilton would have been more than human had he not experienced some pangs of envy at the readiness with which Washington took Lafayette into his inner circle.

When Lafayette rejoined Washington after convalescing from the wound he received at Brandywine, Washington wrote to Congress that "the Marquis de LaFayette is extremely solicitious of having a command equal to his rank. I do not know in what light Congress will view the matter, but it appears to me, from consideration of his illustrious and important connections, the attachment which he has manifested for our cause, and the consequences which his return in disgust might produce, that it will be advisable to gratify his wishes, and the more so as several gentlemen from France who came over here under some assurances have gone back disappointed in their expectations. . . . Besides he is sensible, discreet in his manners, has made great proficiency in our language, and from the dispositions he discovered at the battle of Brandywine possesses a large share of bravery and military ardor." Washington might have added that since generals are born and not made, Lafayette's lack of experience was not the obstacle that it might have been.

We will encounter other foreign volunteers as the war progresses, but none whose contribution to the American cause was as notable as that of the Marquis de Lafayette.

9

Forts Mifflin and Mercer

Washington's relative success at Germantown roused the hopes of patriots that he would attack Howe in Philadelphia and deliver the city from the British. The possibility of forcing the British to abandon Philadelphia rested primarily on holding the forts that controlled the Delaware River, thereby denying supplies and reinforcements to Howe. This effort by the Americans to maintain their defensive positions around Philadelphia produced some of the most dramatic episodes of the war.

On October 20, the British watched a jubilant celebration in the rebel encampment. "They say," Serle wrote, "that Gen. Burgoyne was taken Prisoner, as he was reconnoitring between Saratoga and Stillwater. Their Leaders often make Triumphs on imaginary Victories, to keep up the Spirits of the deluded People." However, the report continued to circulate that Burgoyne was defeated, and Serle wrote in his journal: "My Mind is torn with anxiety upon that Subject, as the Event seems too probable from his unsupported State in a wild, rugged, difficult Country." And when the word was confirmed, he wrote: "This is the most fatal Blow we have yet felt, and will I fear occasion every sort of Chagrin & Uneasiness at Home. GOD save & bless my King & Country from the wicked Conspiracies of all their Enemies!"

Howe fully realized the importance of the forts below the city that blocked access to Philadelphia by the Delaware, and he was determined to capture them. At Billingsport, on the New Jersey shore, an American redoubt covered a *chevaux-de-frise*. (A British officer described the American *chevaux-de-frise* in these words: "This kind of chevaux de frise consists of large timbers, like the main mast of a ship, at the top of which are three branches armed and pointed with iron, spreading out fanwise. . . . fifteen feet asunder. The main beam is fixt at an elevation to the frame of a float or stage, composed of vast logs, bound together as fast as possible; then covered with plank to the top and calked. When the machine is towed to its place, it is loaded with about thirty tuns of stones, secured in cases which, by taking the plugs out of the deck to admit the water into the float, sinks it down and keeps it firm and steady. . . . the points of the branches are about six or seven feet under the surface of the water; and they spread in front thirty feet. A row of these chevaux de frise are sunk sixty feet asunder from each other and another row behind in their intervals, to form a range.")

These formidable barricades extended from the village of Billingsport to Billing's Island, which was really two small adjacent islands. Slightly to the west were three more islands. The largest was Hog Island. Beyond it lay Mud Island, close to the mouth of the Schuylkill and heavily fortified; the guns of Fort Mifflin on the island were directed primarily to covering the downstream approaches of the Delaware.

Fort Mercer, at Red Bank in New Jersey, along with an American redoubt on a small offshore island, provided further defense of the river and of the *cheveaux-de-frise* that extended out from Hog and Mud Islands into the channel of the river. Two other redoubts were interspersed along the Jersey shore between Billingsport and Red Bank. Galleys and floating batteries with mounted cannon, under Commander John Hazelwood, were anchored in such a manner as to assist in blocking the river.

Beyond the *chevaux-de-frise* was the *Delaware,* a frigate of twenty-eight guns, twelve- and nine-pounders; the *Province* with eighteen nine-pounders; large brigs of ten and eight guns; some ten small-armed vessels; thirteen galleys, each with one eighteen-pounder on board; two floating batteries of ten and nine eighteen-pounders respectively; seventeen fire ships, primed with powder and dry brush; and a large number of fire rafts loaded with combustible material. The *Washington* and the *Effingham* (the latter named after the British lord who resigned his commission rather than serve against the Americans) were still uncompleted. They had no guns or crews.

These ships were cockleshells and peashooters compared with the British vessels under Admiral Richard Howe, waiting at New Castle for the river to be cleared of obstructions, but they were a large part of the total naval force available to the Americans, and the cannon alone were a very precious resource. The Americans, lacking foundries, had excruciating difficulty replacing any armament, especially heavy naval ordnance and artillery.

It was this network of fortifications, on which the Americans had expended great energy with pick and shovel under the direction of the French engineer Plessis, that Howe intended to sweep away, and in whose impregnability the Americans had great faith. Colonel Christopher Greene of Rhode Island, a cousin of Nathanael's, who had distinguished himself at Bunker Hill and on the march to Quebec, undertook to defend Fort Mercer. Greene was described by a fellow officer as "stout and strong," cheerful, good-natured, and respected by his men. Lieutenant Colonel Samuel Smith of Baltimore was given the assignment of defending Fort Mifflin on Mud Island with a contingent of some four hundred Maryland troops.

Howe, in preparation for an attack on the forts, emplaced guns on the few spots of dry ground near the mouth of the Schuylkill. These pieces commanded the rear—the least adequately defended portion—of Fort Mifflin. The Hessians were to attack Fort Mercer with five regiments of the line and a detachment of infantry chasseurs.

The first British foray was disconcertingly easy. On October 9, Colonel Sterling, with the Forty-second Regiment and part of the Seventy-first crossed the river, attacked from the rear, and seized Billingsport. The defenders of the unfinished fort there spiked the guns, set fire to everything that would burn, and took to their heels. Meanwhile the British frigate *Roebuck* smashed the laboriously constructed *chevaux-de-frise,* clearing the channel for the passage of British warships.

The Hessian Colonel, Von Donop, had requested of Howe the honor of attacking Fort Mercer. He set out with battalions of grenadiers, a regiment of infantry, and four companies of chasseurs, twelve mounted chasseurs, eight fieldpieces, and two English howitzers. Reportedly, Von Donop requested more artillery and was told that if he could not take the fort with his Hessians the British would do the job, to which he replied to the officer who brought Howe's message: "Tell your general that the Germans are not afraid to face death." Turning to his staff, he declared, "Either the fort will soon be called Fort Donop, or I shall have fallen."

The fort was five-sided, surrounded by a ditch protected by abatis. Woods came within four hundred yards of the fort and afforded cover for the attackers. The fort was defended by between three and four hundred of Greene's Rhode Islanders with fourteen cannon.

Under a flag of truce, Von Donop demanded the surrender of the garrison. His aide-de-camp was preceded by a drummer "as insolent as his officer." "The King of England," his message to Greene read, "commands his rebellious subjects to lay down their arms and they are warned that if they wait until the battle, no quarter will be granted." Greene replied that he refused to surrender, and would ask or give no quarter. He had disposed his men so that few were visible, and the aide-de-camp who carried Von Donop's demand for surrender reported that the garrison was apparently a very small one.

The Hessian commander anchored the right flank of his attacking force on the river, with the three-pounders and the howitzers protected by a battalion of grenadiers and by chasseurs. Sappers and one hundred men with fascines, commanded by an officer, preceded the infantry to bridge the ditches and protect the advancing troops against artillery fire from the fort. At four o'clock in the afternoon, with only a hour or so left till dark, the Hessians were finally in position to launch the attack. Donop exhorted the officers to fight with the bravery for which they were famous. They dismounted, drew their swords, and took their places at the head of their troops. Observing the Americans withdrawing from the outer works of the fort and assuming that they were already in retreat, the Hessians came on at the double. Pausing as they passed the outer works, they shouted "Vittoria" and threw their hard, round black hats into the air, convinced that the fort was theirs.

As they began to pull up or to try to cut away the branches of the abatis that faced them in front of the main fort, "they were overwhelmed with a shower of musket shot. . . . The officers were seen continually rallying their men, marching them back to the abatis, and falling amidst the branches they were endeavoring to cut."

The south column passed through the abatis and crossed the ditch on their fascines, but they were stopped by the pointed stakes that Plessis had erected there. While the German hesitated, they saw the northern column repulsed and fleeing from the field, and they followed suit.

Another attack was mounted, and this time the galleys and floating batteries in the river delivered a warm fire from the flanks that once more drove the Hessians back in disorder. The momentum of the attack carried some of the Germans over the ramparts, but they were quickly beaten back with clubbed muskets and bayonets. Von Donop was wounded by a musket ball that struck him in the groin, and Lieutenant Colonel Minnigrode fell beside him. Twenty-two officers were killed or wounded, including all the battalion commanders, and the demoralized soldiers turned and ran, leaving almost a third of their number dead, injured, or captured. The cannon were dumped in the river so that their carriages could be used to bring off some of the wounded. The American casualties were reported as fourteen killed and twenty-three wounded. In addition to the Hessians who fell in the assault, two British warships that attempted to assist ran aground. The *Augusta* was set on fire by red-hot shot from the American galleys and blew up. The British abandoned the *Merlin* and set it on fire to prevent its capture by the Americans.

After nightfall an American working party came out to repair the fortifications and tend the wounded. They found twenty frightened Germans "glued against the face of the parapet" and brought them into the fort. As Plessis was directing the working party, the wounded Von Donop called out to him from the dark in his gutteral accents, "Whoever you may be, take me from here." He was carried into the fort, and as he passed the soldiers one of them called out, "Well, is it settled that no quarter is to be given?"

"I am in your hands," Von Donop replied. "You can avenge your-selves." The soldiers and others who had chimed in to bait the Hessian officer were rebuked by Plessis. "Sir," said Von Donop, "you appear to be a stranger; who are you?" "A French officer," Plessis replied. Von Donop, with that fine eighteenth-century instinct for last words, answered in French: "I am content, I die in the arms of honor itself."

The line, if orotund, was premature. Von Donop lived three days and talked frequently with Plessis. He asked the French officer to warn him when he was near death, and when Plessis told him that the time had come, Von Donop had another dying speech ready: "This is finishing a noble career early," he declared, "but I die the victim of my ambition and of the avarice of my sovereign."

It was certainly a strange war in which a German officer, fighting for Great Britain, found comfort in the friendly concern of a French officer fighting for the Americans.

The victory at Fort Mercer was a striking one for the Americans. Christopher Greene and his Rhode Islanders, defending the fortifica-tions whose reconstruction Plessis had skillfully supervised, gave an excellent account of themselves, destroying a substantial portion of the Hessian soldiers and, more important, of the officers under Howe's command. If the story of Von Donop's request for more artillery is correct, Howe must, again, bear a major part of the blame for the Hessian disaster. Not only were the cannon refused, but they were refused in such an insulting manner that Von Donop felt impelled to press an attack under conditions that he knew were far from ideal. If we place beside his expressed determination to vindicate his bravery and that of his men his statement to Plessis that he was a victim of his own ambition (as well as the avarice of his sovereign), it is plain enough that he knew he had acted in part out of vanity and thus most unwisely. In the words of Joseph Martin: "Here was fought as brilliant an action as was fought during the Revolutionary War, considering the numbers engaged, Bunker Hill 'to the contrary notwithstanding.' . . . Why it has not been more noticed by historians of the times I cannot tell."

In contrast to the circumstances of Von Donop's attack, the preparations that Howe made to take Fort Mifflin, a fortification of approximately the same size and defended by roughly the same number of Continental soldiers, seem grandiose. Perhaps Howe might be said to have learned from the fate of the Hessian force that he had so cavalierly dispatched to Red Bank. He left nothing undone in his well-planned and skillfully coordinated attack on Fort Mifflin. On November 10 he began a bombardment of Mud Island with four 32-pounders from the *Somerset,* six 24-pounders from the *Eagle,* and one 13-inch mortar, plus the artillery pieces already emplaced at Province Island and the mouth of the Schuylkill. In addition to this crushing armory, six British frigates as well as a number of smaller vessels took part in the act. The *Vigilant* of sixteen guns and a vessel converted into a floating battery with three eighteen-pounders took up a position in the river from which sharpshooters in the rigging picked off American gunners in the fort. (Von Donop, we recall, had only eight three-pounders for the attack on Fort Mercer.)

A Major Thayer had succeeded Lieutenant Colonel Samuel Smith in command of Fort Mifflin, but, as at Fort Mercer, the construction and repair of the fortifications were in the hands of a French engineer, François Louis Teissèdre de Fleury. Fleury was a member of one of the noblest families of France, and one of the first Frenchmen to volunteer his services to the American cause. He was hardly more than a boy, but he soon became known as a brave and resourceful officer, popular with the American officer corps and respected by the Continental troops he commanded. Young Fleury tried to requisition fascines and palisades to help shore up the defenses of the fort, and he asked that a chain be stretched across the river to the Pennsylvania shore to prevent the easy passage of British men-of-war past the fort. Both requests proved fruitless. The soldiers, Fleury wrote, "are overwhelmed with fatigue."

The rising moon silhouetted the American defenses and brought a barrage of cannon fire from the shore batteries on Province Island. Fleury noted on the third day of the bombardment that he had employed his exhausted soldiers "in covering the two western block-houses with joists within and without and filling the interstices with rammed earth. I have closed the breaches made in our palisades with planks, centry-boxes, rafters, and strengthened the whole with earth. . . . It is impossible with watery mud alone to make works capable of resisting the enemy's 32-pounders."

A day later, with many of the men of the little garrison wounded and ill, Fleury still insisted that if he had proper equipment for strengthening the fortifications, the island could not be taken. "The fire of the enemy will never take the fort," he wrote; "it may kill us men but this is the fortune of war. And all their bullets will never render them masters of the island if we have courage enough to remain on it."

Joseph Martin was one of the defenders of Fort Mifflin. "Here," he wrote, "I endured hardships sufficient to kill half a dozen horses." In the "cold month of November" he and his fellows found themselves without food, and Martin and a number of others were "without . . . a scrap of either shoes or stockings to my feet or legs. . . ."

On the eastern side of the fort was a zigzag stone wall built long before the Revolution. At the southeast end were several 18-pounders, and at the southwestern angle, four or five 12- or 18-pounders and a 32-pounder. At the northwest corner there were three 12-pounders. In addition, there were three blockhouses within the crude fortification. On the western side, facing Province Island, was a row of barracks running half the length of the fort. Another row of barracks ran across the northern end of the island from east to west. "In front of the barracks and other necessary places were parades and walks; the rest of the ground was soft mud." Those enemy shells that struck the mud often sank in so far that their explosion could not be heard, only the shaking of the earth. When they burst nearer the surface, they would throw mud fifty feet in the air and leave any nearby defenders coated with muck.

The American guns were protected by works made of old spars and timber, laid up in parallel lines and filled with mud and dirt. "The British batteries in the course of the day," Martin wrote, "would nearly level our works, and we were, like the beaver, obliged to repair our dams in the night. As the American defenders made repairs, a soldier would stand guard and when he saw the muzzle flash of a British artillery piece, he would call out 'a shot'—upon which everyone endeavored to take care of himself, yet they would ever and anon, in spite of all of our precautions, cut up some of us," Martin noted.

Martin described Fleury as "a very austere man" who "kept us constantly employed day and night; there was no chance of escaping from his vigilance." In one protected little dugout, the defenders gathered the splinters broken off the palisades by the British cannonballs and shrapnel and kept a small fire going. When they could escape from Fleury, they would "run into this place for a moment or two's respite from fatigue and cold." Finally, Fleury, noticing the gradual attrition of his work force, would come to the entrance and call the weary soldiers out. "He had always his cane in his hand, and woe betide him he could get a stroke at," Martin noted.

The barracks were too dangerous to sleep in, and the mud made an impossible bed. Martin swore he did not sleep a wink in bed in the two weeks that he was under bombardment in the fort. He and his companions had to make do with cat naps while sitting on the ground or leaning against a wall.

The defenders of Fort Mifflin had a 32-pounder, but there was no ammunition for it. The American artillery officers offered a gill of rum to any soldier who could retrieve a British cannonball to use in the American cannon. As Martin put it, "I have seen from 20 to 50 men standing on the parade waiting with impatience the coming of the shot, which would often be seized before its motion had fully ceased and conveyed off to our gun to be sent back again to its former owners. When the lucky fellow who had caught it had swallowed his rum, he would return to wait for another, exulting that he had been more lucky or more dexterous than his fellows."

What little food the defenders had—corned beef and hard bread for the most part—was cooked by the recuperating wounded at Red Bank and brought to the island at night in old flour barrels.

On November 14, four days after the bombardment had begun, the British maneuvered ten warships into the western channel within pistol shot of the fort; six of them were 64-gun frigates. These vessels and the shore batteries all bombarded the fort. A signal flag was hoisted to request aid from Hazelwood's galleys, anchored up the river, but no help came, and the defenders of the fort were left to shift for themselves. In Martin's words: "The enemy's shot cut us up. I saw five artilleryists belonging to one gun cut down by a single shot, and I saw men who were stooping to be protected by the works, but not stooping low enough, split like fish to be broiled."

By nightfall "the whole area of the fort was completely ploughed as a field. The buildings of every kind [were] hanging in broken fragments, and the guns all mismounted. . . . If ever destruction was complete, it was here."

When orders came to remove the heavy cannon to the Jersey shore and abandon the fort, Fleury insisted that the Jersey side of the river had disadvantages over Mud Island that were not compensated for by its relative safety. The stubborn young Frenchman may well have been right. Although the Americans had taken heavy losses, the dead and wounded could be evacuated at night and replacements sent in with tools and timbers to shore up the defenses. The fury of the British attack was the best indication of the importance they attached to the island's defenses. "We must have men to defend the ruins of the fort. Our ruins will serve us as breast-works," Fleury wrote. "We will defend the ground inch by inch, and the enemy shall pay dearly for every step—but we want a commanding officer; ours is absent and forms projects for our defence at a distance. . . . We are so much neglected that we have been 7 days without food, and at present have only cartridges of eighteen-pounders for a piece of 32 which does considerable mischief to the enemy."

But without sufficient men to man the defenses, without shelter, or protection from the incessant fire of the British batteries, and with precious little sleep, the weary Americans were finally forced to evacuate the island. Fleury, who was badly wounded shortly before the withdrawal, was critical of the decision to withdraw the remnants of the garrison rather than reinforce it. The American gunners had given an excellent account of themselves against heavy odds. Properly supplied and augmented, they could, he felt, have held the island indefinitely. But Washington, remote from the scene of the action, had to depend on the reports of his staff officers, and they, unnerved by the growing casualty lists and the visible destruction of the fort, advised evacuation. Congress subsequently presented Fleury with a medal, which can be seen today in the Bibliothèque Nationale in Paris.

Martin, staying behind with a party of seventy or eighty men to destroy and burn all that remained of the supplies of the fort, saw a British vessel pass so close to the fort that he could hear sailors on board talking—"We will give it to the damned rebels in the morning"—and thought to himself, "The damned rebels will show you a trick which the devil never will; they will go off and leave you." Martin found some hogsheads of rum, and before he destroyed them, he prudently decided to fill his canteen. He had left it that morning with his best friend and messmate, and when he went looking for it he found his friend's body piled among those waiting to be carried to the Jersey shore and buried.

When the fort was set afire, the light revealed the boats carrying off the last of the defenders, and the British batteries let loose a hail of fire that fell all around the fleeing boats.

It must be said that the defense of Fort Mifflin was seriously compromised by Robert White, an engineer charged with placing the *chevaux-de-frise*—the line of sunken obstructions—across the river. White, a Tory at heart, left a channel open on the Pennsylvania side, so that British warships could pass and open fire on the fort. When the stubborn resistance of the defenders had disheartened the British and convinced them that the island was too strongly held to take, it was apparently White, coming over to the British lines, who told them that the fort could not hold out much longer and persuaded them to renew the assault.

As late as November, Howe's position in Philadelphia had seemed a highly precarious one. The attack on Fort Mercer had failed, Von Donop had been killed, and the Hessians had suffered heavy losses. Fort Mifflin on Mud Island had seemed impregnable, and with Mifflin in rebel hands, the problems of supplying Howe's forces in the city were greatly complicated. James Allen reported that John Adams, who had passed through Bethlehem on his way to York, spoke of the evacuation of Philadelphia "as a certain event, & said the struggle was past & that Independence was now unalterably settled; the Crisis was over. . . . Even the Tories believed Genl Howe, thus circumstanced must quit the City. . . ."

The single event, in Allen's opinion, that enabled Howe to maintain himself in Philadelphia was the destruction of Fort Mifflin by the battery on Province Island. It is apparently to a traitor, Robert White, that the principal credit for the reduction of Fort Mifflin must go.

The loss to the British was thirteen killed and twenty-four wounded in the siege of Mud Island or Fort Mifflin, which was occupied on November 16 by the Royal Guards.

Washington in his report to Congress wrote: "The defense will always reflect the highest honor upon the officers and men of the garrison. The works were entirely beat down; every piece of cannon was dismounted, and one of the enemy's ships came so near that she threw grenades into the fort and killed men upon the platform, from her tops, before they quitted the island."

It was Martin's opinion, recorded some thirty years afterward, that so little attention had been paid to the battles at Fort Mercer and Fort Mifflin because "there was no Washington, Putnam, or Wayne there. Had there been, the affair [Fort Mifflin's defense] would have been extolled to the skies. No, it was only a few officers and soldiers who accomplished it in a remote quarter of the army. . . . Great men get great praise; little men, nothing." The Connecticut private's observations on this, as on so many other points, are more than slightly convincing.

On November 18, two days after the British occupied Fort Mifflin, Howe dispatched Cornwallis and some two thousand men to the Jersey shore by way of Billingsport with orders to take Fort Mercer from the land side. Washington sent Nathanael Greene to command the American troops in New Jersey and to try to block Cornwallis's movement against the fort.

Joseph Martin was in one of Greene's regiments, quartered near Haddonfield, New Jersey. There he and his comrades spent their time trying to find some food. A dozen of them had been assigned to a single room that was barren of furniture except for an old quill wheel and a chair frame. They scavenged some firewood, got a thick board, and placed it over the wheel and the chair frame to make a rough bench, "and all sat down to regale ourselves with the warmth, when the cat happening to come under the bench to partake of the bounty, the board bending by the weight upon it, both ends slipped off at once and brought us all slap to the floor. Upon taking up the board to replace it again we found the poor cat, pressed as flat as a pancake, with her eyes started out two inches from her head. We did not eat her although my appetite was sharp enough to have eaten almost anything that could be eaten." Their exteriors warmed, the soldiers turned their attention to getting some food. "After several plans had been devised, many 'resolves proposed and all refused a passage,'" two or three soldiers were dispatched "to procure something by foraging." They were back shortly with a hissian, the soldiers' code word for a goose. There was nothing in the room to hold the feathers. The solution was to pluck the bird over the fire and burn up the incriminating evidence. In Martin's words, "we dressed her and divided her amongst us. If I remember rightly, I got *one wing*. Each one broiled his share and ate it, as usual without bread or salt." The next morning the evidence of their thievery was broadcast. Instead of burning, the feathers had been carried up the chimney and now littered the street outside.

Two days after Cornwallis began his movement against Fort Mercer, the fort was abandoned without a shot being fired, and all its buildings and supplies were burned. Why the fort was evacuated without a fight remains one of the minor mysteries of the Revolutionary War. An attack by twelve hundred seasoned Hessian troops had been beaten off decisively. The garrison had since been reinforced. General Greene was on hand to assist in protecting it from Cornwallis. While it was true that Mud Island and the ruins of Fort Mifflin were now in British hands and British warships could sail up the river as far as Red Bank, the principal damage done to Fort Mifflin had been by the shore batteries on Province Island. The Americans still had the galleys and gunboats that had destroyed the *Augusta* and the *Merlin*. Contemporary accounts and later historians have treated the abandonment of Fort Mercer in the most casual way, with no more than passing mention. In Henry Carrington's words: "On the eighteenth Cornwallis landed at Billingsport in force; . . . the demonstration was so formidable that the garrison abandoned the works on his approach." What "demonstration"? Were the Americans, having fought with notable resolution, suddenly to be routed by "demonstrations"?

All that can be said is that Fort Mercer had received the wounded and demoralized men from Fort Mifflin and that the defenders had watched across the water while Mifflin was pounded into ruin. The decision to abandon Fort Mercer must have been related in some way to the morale of its defenders. Americans were always alarmed by heavy cannon and artillery fire. General Nathanael Greene, in consultation with Colonel Christopher Greene, may have felt that the spirit of the soldiers gave little prospect of a successful defense. To defend the fort with the British in control of the Delaware would be to risk having the entire force trapped between Cornwallis's soldiers and the river.

Perhaps the most notable thing about the operations around Fort Mercer was that the young Marquis de Lafayette, recovered from the wound received at Brandywine, was given a modest command by General Greene—150 riflemen, ten light horse, and a handful of militia.

The newly arrived French colonels, Charles Armand and the Chevalier de Laumoy, were with Lafayette, as was the Chevalier de Plessis.

Scouting the terrain around Red Bank, Lafayette encountered a detachment of some three hundred Hessians operating in the rear of Cornwallis's force, attacked them, and drove them back to the main body. Pursued in turn by a much larger body, Lafayette narrowly escaped and joined Greene near Haddonfield. His first independent command was thus hardly brilliant, but he had kept his head and extricated his men from a dangerous position.

Washington next planned a raid by Wayne and Morgan on the British batteries on Province Island, but it was called off at the last moment as impractical. While Cornwallis operated in Jersey, occupying the abandoned Fort Mercer, Washington repeatedly polled his general officers for their opinion about the desirability of attacking Howe's remaining force in Philadelphia. Only four out of eleven officers supported the notion. A sharp defeat might mean the virtual end of Washington's army. The odds in such an engagement were simply too great to run the risk. So Washington remained in camp at Whitemarsh, some twelve miles from Philadelphia. As Washington put the matter to Greene: "Our situation . . . is distressing from a variety of irremediable causes, but more especially from the impracticability of answering the expectations of the world without running hazards which no military principles can justify, and which, in case of failure, might prove the ruin of our cause; patience and a ready perseverance in such measures as appear warranted by sound reason and policy must support us under the censure of the one, and dictate a proper line of conduct for the attainment of the other; that is the great object in view."

Washington had much on his mind in November, 1777. One of the most pressing issues was court-martial action against those officers who had failed to perform their duty properly at Brandywine and Germantown. In addition there were the perpetual problems of expiring enlistments and desertions. As winter came on, the lack of blankets, shoes, warm clothing, and adequate food became increasingly onerous to the tired and ragged soldiers in Washington's army. "There are now in this Army," he wrote Congress, "by a later return 4000 men wanting blankets, near 2000 of which have never had one, although some of them have been twelve months in service." One of Washington's officers had complained in August: "The deficiency—from desertion and other causes is almost incredible. . . . in the instance of the two independent Companies, they are returned sixty and when they first joined they were about 140 strong." The militia who had joined with the Continental Army for the Pennsylvania campaign now began to drift away. The discharge day of nine Virginia regiments was approaching, and Washington's hopes of recruiting Pennsylvanians to replace them seemed doomed to disappointment. "This State," he wrote his brother, "acts most infamously, the people of it I mean as we derive little or no assistance from them." His efforts to get help from Gates were frustrated by that officer's stubborn determination to operate as an independent command. Hamilton, dispatched to persuade Gates to send reinforcements to Washington, found, in Douglas Freeman's words, that he was treated like "an agent sent to a foreign court to solicit an alliance. . . ." Nathanael Greene wrote a friend in Rhode Island: "I think I never saw the Army so near dissolving since I have belonged to it."

The officers who faced court-martial included the Frenchman Prudhomme de Borre, who had been inefficient and cowardly at Brandywine; John Sullivan, for his poor performance at Staten Island and at Brandywine; Anthony Wayne, for the so-called Paoli Massacre; Adam Stephen, for misconduct and drunkenness at the Battle of Brandywine, and William Maxwell for similar offenses at Germantown. Prudhomme de Borre resigned before his case was tried. Sullivan was acquitted unanimously; his shortcomings were hardly chargeable under the articles of war. Wayne was vindicated with the "highest honor." Maxwell was not convicted either, but Stephen was found guilty of "unofficerlike behavior" and drunkenness. He pleaded for reinstatement, and when that plea was refused, he wrote to Congress that his only crime was that he had become "the object of hatred of a person of high rank for no other reason that I know, but for delivering my sentiments on the measures pursued in this campaign with [the] candor . . . [of] an old officer of experience who has the interests of America at heart." Congress was unmoved.

Lafayette replaced Stephen in command of his division. But a number of officers nourished grievances over lack of promotion or because foreigners were promoted above them by Congress. "My feelings," Washington wrote Congress, "are every day wounded by the discontent, complaints and jarring of officers, not to add resignations."

10

The Army Goes into Winter Quarters, 1777-78

Howe was under enormous pressure to use his well-equipped and well-supplied troops against the dwindling Continental Army at White-marsh. On December 4, with Cornwallis back from New Jersey, Howe marched out with fourteen thousand men to Chestnut Hill, some three miles from the American right wing. The next day he sent Sir Robert Abercrombie out with the Second Battalion and a detachment of the First Light Infantry for a reconnaissance in force. The American outposts were driven in, General William Irvine was captured, and some casualties were suffered on both sides.

Whatever advantage there might have been rested with the British, but Howe failed to follow up Abercrombie's foray. Two days later the British army changed directions, marching around to Edge Hill on the *left* of the American positions. Here General Daniel Morgan and his rifle corps, detached with difficulty from Gates and just arrived, joined with Colonel Mordecai Gist and the Maryland militia to engage the First Battalion of light infantry and the Thirty-third Regiment, commanded by Cornwallis. The Hessian chasseurs, the Queen's Rangers, and one brigade of British regulars advanced on the American left, inflicting casualties and causing some momentary confusion in the Continental lines. The advance seemed a prelude to a general engagement, and both armies made the requisite deployments. Lieutenant General Charles Grey, the villain of Paoli in American eyes, moved his light infantry so rapidly that an American outpost was almost surrounded and, in making their escape, came under heavy fire from Grey's center.

Washington's position was a strong one, and he invited the British to attack. Howe, on the other hand, professed to believe that Washington had been reinforced by four thousand men and might thus be tempted to come forth and give battle in the open field. But Washington had no such notion. As he wrote, "reason, prudence and every principle of policy, forbade us quitting our post to *attack them.*" So on December 8 Howe withdrew to Philadelphia. Of the eleven thousand men nominally under Washington's command, De Kalb estimated that not more than seven thousand were present for duty; the rest were sick or incapacitated by lack of proper clothing and equipment. The Americans and British each suffered between forty and fifty killed and wounded. Of the inconclusive engagement at Chestnut Hill, Private Martin wrote: "We . . . wished nothing more than to have them engage us, for we were sure of giving them a drubbing, being in excellent fighting trim, as we were starved and cross and ill-natured as curs."

Howe's demonstration in front of Washington's lines marked the end of the Pennsylvania campaign of 1777. He withdrew to the warmth, the pleasures, and the gaiety of Philadelphia. Washington's dilemma was whether to yield to the pressure of Pennsylvania patriots, indignant at the loss of Philadelphia, and make at least a gesture toward ousting Howe from the city, or to acknowledge the impracticality of such a maneuver and put his hungry and exhausted army in winter quarters.

Colonel John Laurens wrote to his father early in December weighing the pros and cons of going into winter quarters. Winter campaigns, Laurens pointed out, were "ominous to the best appointed and best disciplined armies. The miseries incident to them occasions desertion and sickness which waste their numbers." The Continental Army, on the other hand, required "exemption from fatigue in order to compensate for their want of clothing; relaxation from the duties of a campaign, in order to allow them an opportunity of being disciplined and instructed. . . ."

On Howe's withdrawal from Whitemarsh, Washington finally decided to march his chilblained army to Valley Forge. On the way the soldiers camped at Gulph, a town near Matson's Ford. They were there when Congress ordered a day of Thanksgiving. "We must now have what Congress said," Martin wrote, "a sumptuous Thanksgiving to close the year of high living we had now seen brought nearly to a close. . . . Our country, ever mindful of its suffering army, opened her sympathizing heart so wide, upon this occasion, as to give us something to make the world stare. And what you think it was, reader? Guess. You cannot guess. . . . I well tell you; it gave each and every man *half a gill* of rice and a *tablespoonful* of vinegar!!"

After this repast the soldiers were summoned to hear a sermon on the text, "And the soldiers said unto him, And what shall we do? And he said unto them, Do violence to no man, nor accuse anyone falsely." The soldiers knew the text—an odd choice at best—as well as the preacher did. He omitted the balance of the verse from Luke 3: 14, which read, "And be content with your wages," and when he had finished, "it was shouted from a hundred tongues" with certain rude amendments, after which the soldiers returned to their areas "to make our . . . supper as usual, upon a leg of nothing and no turnips."

Ambrose Serle, viewing the matter from a very different perspective than Joseph Martin, found the Congressional proclamation of a day of Thanksgiving "one of the most extraordinary Performances I ever read. It is full of Falsehood, Bravado, and Despair. To say, that it contradicts itself is only saying half the Truth: It contradicts the knowledge & Experience of every man of Sense throughout the Colonies. I cannot help calling it one of the dying Groans of Rebellion."

Washington's first winter in command of the Continental Army at Cambridge had been spent in the nerve-racking task of trying to "new-model" the army. His second winter had been retrieved from disaster by the most daring military maneuvers of the war—the brilliant attacks on Trenton and Princeton. Now the third was to be devoted to preserving the remnant of his ragged force and trying to turn it into the tough core of a professional army. And this had to be done in face of mounting criticism of his leadership, in Congress and out; in the face of an especially bitter winter; and with the distracting and unpleasant business that came to be called the Conway Cabal to contend with.

When the Pennsylvania assembly chided him for going into winter quarters without making an effort to drive Howe out of Philadelphia, Washington replied with some warmth. "Gentlemen," he wrote, "reprobate the going into winter quarters as much as if they thought the soldiers were made of sticks, or stones. I can assure these gentlemen that it is a much easier and less distressing thing to draw remonstrances in a comfortable room, than to occupy a cold bleak hill, and sleep under frost and snow, without clothes or blankets. However, although they seem to have little feeling for the naked and distressed soldiers, I feel superabundantly for them, and from my soul I pity their miseries which it is neither in my power to relieve or prevent." This was as sharp a retort to importuning civilians as Washington ever allowed himself, but it was sharp enough.

Albigence Waldo, a surgeon of the Connecticut line, spoke for most of the men when he noted derisively in his diary that people were complaining that Washington had not rushed into the lightly held city of Philadelphia while Howe was scavenging the countryside. "Why don't His Excellency rush in and retake the city, . . . ? Because he knows better than to leave his post and be caught like a damned fool cooped up in the city. He has always acted wisely hitherto. His conduct when closely scrutinized is uncensurable. Were his inferior Generals as skillful as himself, we should have the grandest choir of officers ever God made."

Most of the criticisms of Washington's inactivity were made by people who believed the report that Washington had twice as many men as Howe. Such inaccuracies, Waldo declared, brought "blame on His Excellency, who is deserving of the greatest encomium" and "disgrace on the Continental troops, who have never evidenced the least backwardness in doing their duty, but on the contrary have cheerfully endured a long and very fatiguing campaign." Washington, "by opposing little more than an equal number of young troops to old veterans, has kept the ground in general, cooped them [the British] up in the city, prevented their making any considerable inroads upon him, killed and wounded a very considerable number of them in different skirmishes, and made many proselytes to the shrine of Liberty by these little successes, and by the prudence, calmness, sedateness, and wisdom with which he facilitates all his operations. This being the case, and his not having wantonly thrown away the lives of his soldiers, but reserved them for another campaign (if another should open in the spring) which is of the utmost consequence, ours cannot be called an inglorious campaign. If he had risked a general battle and should have proved unsuccessful, what in the name of Heaven would have been our case this day? . . . If this army is cut off where should we get another as good?"

Waldo is an appealing figure. Fond of music, painting, and drawing, generous and compassionate, he watched with distress while illness and disease decimated the men under his care. He himself fell ill early in December. "I am prodigious sick," he wrote in his diary, "and cannot get anything comfortable. What in the name of Providence am I to do with a fit of sickness in this place where nothing appears pleasing to the sickened eye and nausiating stomach? But I doubt not Providence will find a way for my relief. But I cannot eat beef if I starve, for my stomach positively refuses to entertain such company, and how can I help that?"

On December 12 at Whitemarsh, Waldo noted despairingly, "Sun set—we were ordered to march over the river—It snows—I'm sick—eat nothing—no whiskey—no forage—Lord—Lord—Lord." Two days later he observed, "Prisoners and deserters are continually coming in. The army which has been surprisingly healthy hitherto, now begins to grow sickly from the continued fatigues they have suffered this campaign. Yet they still show a spirit of alacrity and contentment not to be expected from so young troops. I am sick—discontented—out of humour. Poor food—hard lodging—cold weather—fatigue—nasty cloathes—nasty cookery—vomit half the time—smoaked out of my senses—the Devil's in't—I can't endure it—why are we sent here to starve and freeze? What sweet felicities have I left at home: A charming wife—pretty children—good beds—good food—good cookery—all agreeable—all harmonious! Here all confusion—smoke and cold—hunger and filthyness—pox on my bad luck! Here comes a bowl of beef soup, full of burnt leaves and dirt, sickness enough to make a Hector spue—away with it boys!—I'll live like the chameleon upon air."

"Poh! Poh! crys Patience within me, you talk like a fool," Waldo continued, "Your being sick covers your mind with a melancholic gloom, which makes everything about you appear gloomy. See the poor soldier when in health—with what cheerfulness he meets his foes and encounters every hardship. If barefoot, he labours thro' the mud and cold with a song in his mouth extolling War and Washington. If his food be bad, he eats it notwithstanding with seeming content—blesses God for a good stomach and whistles it into digestion."

For soldiers who were sick there were none of the familiar remedies. They got "mutton and grog and a capital medicine once in a while, to start the disease from its foundations at once," but "no piddling pills, powders, Bolus's Linctus's cordials and all such insignificant matters whose powders are only rendered important by causing the patient to vomit up his money instead of his disease," Waldo noted. And strangely enough, "few of the sick men die."

On December 21 Varnum's brigade had had no meat for forty-eight hours and no bread for a longer period. Sullivan's men, whose brigade area was near the river, dredged up some clams. When an officer came upon soldiers boiling a stone and inquired the reason he was told: "They say there's strength in a stone, if you can get it out."

Hungry but full of humor, the men laughed at the expression on the officer's face.

Under such conditions, it is hardly surprising that soldiers were continually on the verge of mutiny. One militia regiment assigned to outpost duty entertained itself by giving false alarms of enemy activity. When Colonel Aaron Burr was dispatched to straighten out the troublesome regiment, he was greeted with such insolent threats against his life that he slashed off the ringleader's arm with his sword—an act that had a sobering effect on the rest of the troublemakers.

Joseph Martin wrote in much the same vein as Waldo. "I had experienced what I thought sufficient of the hardships of a military life the year before," he noted, "although nothing in comparison to what I had suffered in the present campaign. We had engaged in the defense of our injured country and were willing, nay, we were determined to persevere as long as such hardships were not altogether intolerable. . . . But we were now absolutely in danger of perishing, and that too, in the midst of a plentiful country."

On the night of December 19 the army arrived at Valley Forge, and Martin was so thirsty that he bought a drink of water from two soldiers for three pence, Pennsylvania currency—his last pennies. In two nights and one day, he had eaten only half of a small, half-cooked pumpkin.

At Valley Forge, some twenty-one miles west of Philadelphia, Washington was in a position to counter any British expeditions into the area, and there he finally went into winter quarters with "two thousand eight hundred and ninety-eight men . . . unfit for duty, because barefoot and otherwise naked." The size of his army, he noted, had "decreased two thousand, from hardships and exposure in three weeks. . . . Only eight thousand two hundred men were present fit for duty," Washington wrote Congress, adding, "we have not more than three months in which to prepare a great deal of business. If we let them slip, or waste, we shall be laboring under the same difficulties all next campaign as we have been in this, to rectify mistakes and bring things to order. Military arrangements and movements, in consequence, like the mechanism of a clock, will be imperfect and disordered by the want of a part."

Washington ordered a detachment of American cavalry under General Pulaski to take their posts at Trenton. Casimir Pulaski was a Polish nobleman who had fought the Russians and had fled from Poland when his homeland was partitioned in 1772. He went to Turkey and then Paris, where there was a small colony of refugee Poles. In Paris he was directed to Benjamin Franklin, who sent the count to America as another in that growing company of international volunteers. Pulaski was an experienced cavalry officer, and Washington, impressed by his knowledge and obvious competence, decided in the fall of 1777 to give him command of four regiments of mounted dragoons recently authorized by Congress. The thirty-nine-year-old officer was given the title of commander of the horse and the rank of brigadier general. He spoke no English, but nonetheless managed to be constantly embroiled with his officers—most acrimoniously with one of his regimental commanders, Stephen Moylan, whom he court-martialed for "disobedience to the orders of General Pulaski, a cowardly and ungentlemanly action in striking Mr. Zielinski, a gentleman and officer in the Polish service [and another of those military acolytes that every foreign officer felt himself entitled to bring with him when he left for America] when disarmed . . . and giving irritating language to General Pulaski." For all his arrogance and touchiness, Pulaski was a stern disciplinarian and kept his detachment at Trenton under strict control.

Valley Forge lay at the junction of the Schuylkill River and Valley Creek. It was not, in fact, a valley at all but high ground—a thickly wooded slope some two miles long above the river. At the western end of the ridge was a modest promontory named Mount Joy. The forward slope of the ridge was well fortified with a line of entrenchments extending from the Schuylkill on the left to Mount Joy and Valley Creek on the right. Knox's artillery was emplaced on the high ground above the creek. By late winter the camp at Valley Forge was virtually impregnable. Duportail had laid the fortifications out so skillfully that General Grey, after a thorough reconaissance, declared with British understatement that an attack would be "unjustifiable."

Upon arrival at Valley Forge, the soldiers were divided into parties of twelve to build their huts. Washington offered a prize of twelve dollars for the best and most rapidly constructed hut in each regiment. Tom Paine, who wrote his fifth *Crisis* essay at Valley Forge, observed the soldiers building their huts "like a family of beavers, every one busy; some carrying logs, others mud, and the rest plastering them together. The whole was raised in a few days," he wrote Franklin, "and it is a curious collection of buildings, in the true rustic order." Paine, like so many others, was convinced that the "fighting was nearly over, for Britain, mad, wicked and foolish, has done her utmost. The only part for her now to act is frugality, and the only way to get out of debt is to lessen her Government expenses." With the war in its presumably final stages, Paine looked forward to "advising" with Franklin, "respecting the history of the American Revolution, as soon as a turn of affairs make it safe for me to take a passage to Europe." Paine's "design" was "a history in three quarto volumes, and to publish one each year from the time of the beginning, and to make an abridgement afterwards in an easy, agreeable language for a school-book."

The huts built by the soldiers measured sixteen feet long by fourteen feet wide, with walls six-and-a-half feet in height. Three bunks were built into each corner for a total of twelve. Straw, moss, and mud were used to fill the chinks between the logs; as often as the holes were chinked up, rain washed much of the crude mortar out and let the cold wind whistle in. Again Washington offered a prize—this time one hundred dollars for the best roofing material the soldiers could devise. Even the ingenuity of the American soldier had its limits. There was nothing better to be found than brush, straw, and turf, supplemented here and there by an old piece of tent. It did well enough for snow, but very badly for rain. The doors were made of split oak boards. Oiled paper let some dim light into the windows, and a few of the more ambitious structures had stone chimneys. Most cabins had chimneys and fireplaces built of wood and lined with eighteen inches of clay. The cabins of the officers were behind those of the men. They were similar in construction. Each general had a hut to himself; the field-grade officers of each regiment—majors, colonels, and lieutenant colonels—shared one, and the company-grade officers were quartered together, two officers to a hut. The slopes and the adjacent woods were soon denuded of trees to construct more than one thousand huts, which provided crude quarters for the fourteen brigades that made up the army.

As long as any of his men lacked huts to live in, Washington himself lived near the top of Mount Joy in his headquarters tent with its blue flag bearing thirteen stars. After his men were housed, he moved to the Isaac Potts house in the little hamlet of Valley Forge. His Negro slave, Billy, served him in these cramped quarters.

Colonel Timothy Pickering was one of the more fortunate officers. He found quarters "in a little cabin in a corner of a warm chamber," where he slept on a straw pallet with a bag of straw for a pillow and for a blanket his greatcoat and all his other clothes piled on top of him.

Charles Willson Peale, the young patriot and painter, who was a refugee from Philadelphia, painted Washington's portrait on bedticking, since no canvas was available.

Martha Washington arrived at Valley Forge around the middle of February and brought with her the comfortable ministrations of a devoted wife. She put the Potts house in proper order, had a dining room (or more properly, cabin) built onto the house for Washington's staff, and gave a party for the general's forty-sixth birthday, with music by a military band to which she scrupulously paid fifteen shillings. Other officers' wives began to join the camp, and Martha promptly organized them into a corps of seamstresses who assembled every morning in her drawing room to patch and mend and darn. Every afternoon she went faithfully with an attendant and "a basket of comforts" to minister to the soldiers who lay in the crude hospital huts.

There were also social evenings in the Potts house, presided over by the general's wife. Those ladies and those officers who could sing or play a musical instrument were prevailed on to do so. General Knox's "darling" made the long, arduous trip from Boston to be with him, and although some critics found her "meddlesome," she cheered everyone with her wit and plump prettiness. Handsome "Lady" Stirling and her pretty daughter, "Lady Kitty," seconded the efforts of Mrs. Nathanael Greene. Mrs. Greene's recently learned French made her a special favorite with homesick French officers, who bickered with each other constantly but found solace in her good-humored struggles with their language. James Monroe was one of the young officers who enjoyed Martha Washington's hospitality, as was John Marshall. Gouverneur Morris, Joseph Reed (Washington's former adjutant general), and Charles Carroll of Carrollton were also part of the modest but lively social life created by the commanding officer's lady. The officers' morale was vastly improved by these touches of civilization. Most important of all, Washington himself took a more cheerful view of life. As Pierre Etienne Duponceau, a recent French arrival, wrote of one such occasion: "I could not keep my eyes from that imposing countenance; grave, yet not severe; affable, without familiarity. Its predominant expression was calm dignity, through which you could trace the strong feelings of the patriot, and discern the father, as well as the commander of his soldiers. I have never seen a picture that represents him to me as I saw him at Valley Forge, and during the campaigns in which I had the honor to follow him."

A bridge was built across the Schuylkill River to expedite the collection of provisions for the army. It was quickly put to use by bands of marauding soldiers who stole everything that was not nailed down and evoked a storm of indignant protests from nearby farmers whose premises had been raided. Washington's response was to prescribe punishment for anyone absent from camp without leave and to chastise those who engaged in looting. Desertion was a problem also, and the penalty for those caught was commonly one hundred lashes. Two chronic deserters were hanged on the parade ground in front of detachments from every brigade.

Washington also had to deal with the problem of officers fraternizing with their men. It was the New England officers, many of whom had friends and relatives among the enlisted men, who were the particular offenders. Some clearly preferred drinking and brawling with their men to the company of their fellow officers.

Officers themselves were not infrequently charged with infractions of the rules that Washington had established for the proper order of the camp, such as the prohibition against playing at cards and dice for stakes. A commissary officer, convicted of stealing from the meager larder, was tied backward on a horse with his hands bound and drummed out of camp. An officer convicted of "infamously stealing" and "association with a private" had his sword broken over his head at a formation. A captain who had stolen a hat was dismissed from the service with a dishonorable discharge, and his crime was advertised in his hometown newspaper.

When cloth was obtained, those soldiers who had some experience as tailors were excused from duty to make crude uniforms for their comrades, and in the town of Lancaster patriotic ladies made 1,200 shirts for the soldiers at Valley Forge. Officers, like men, had come to the end of their wardrobes, and some were forced to take guard duty in their dressing gowns or wrapped in blankets. One shipment of clothes arrived without buttons, and the morning reports for February showed 3,989 men not fit for duty because of no shoes or inadequate clothing; out of a nominal strength of 10,000, the effective strength was a mere 5,012. When a soldier had to go on guard duty, his hut mates often lent him their clothes to bundle up in against the cold; an officer inspecting the guard came on a soldier standing in his hat to keep his cloth-wrapped and chilblained feet off the icy ground. Joseph Martin made himself a pair of moccasins out of a piece of cowhide, which, while the rough edges galled his ankles, at least kept his feet off the ground.

Most distressing of all was the lack of blankets to cover the sick.

They lay on bare slats in crude and drafty cabins where they must freeze or choke on smoky fires that barely kept off the chill. Soldiers who had never had smallpox were ordered, like Martin at Peekskill earlier, to receive inoculation so that they might be immune, but in their weakened condition many died of the remedy. Lice and, for those lucky enough to have crude beds, bedbugs were a constant misery. The itch was endemic, and Martin and his companions made up a mixture of sulphur and tallow as a salve, "not forgetting to mix in a plenty of hot whiskey toddy." Stirring up a hot fire and lying down beside it on an oxhide, they piled "each other's outsides with brimstone and tallow and the inside with hot whiskey sling." Two sick soldiers, numb with alcohol, lay naked all night beside the dead fire and almost froze to death. Some soldiers went insane. Some fingers and toes were so badly frostbitten that they had to be amputated: the only anesthetic was a bottle of whiskey. The general hospital for the most serious cases was at Bethlehem, fifty miles away. Many soldiers who were sent off on that jolting journey failed to survive. Those who did were faithfully attended by the Moravian inhabitants of the town, who seemed "to vie with each other in humility and brotherly kindness." They had already taken devoted care of the wounded from Brandywine and Germantown, and in the middle of winter the little village was filled with often desperately ill soldiers. The Hostel for Single Brethren, the town's bachelor quarters—built to accommodate 250 men—was jammed with 750 patients lying a few feet apart on straw pallets. Out of forty soldiers from one disease-prone regiment, only three survived the winter.

Ironically, being sent to a military hospital was, in itself, a sentence of death. The hospitals were sinks of contagion, where the "putrid fever" spread like wildfire and nine out of ten who caught it died. Benjamin Rush, who was the physician general of the army's medical department, resigned in protest over the hopeless conditions in the hospitals and wrote a bitter letter to Washington condemning them as charnel houses. Soldiers knew their reputations and did their best to avoid being sent to them.

In the cold and rain, the wry humor of soldiers helped to sustain them: "Good morning, Brother Soldier. How are you?"

"All wet I thank'e, hope you are so," came the reply.

The typical evening ration was a watery gruel, and the doleful cry rang out and echoed among the trees, "No meat! No meat!" to the imitation of crows cawing and the hooting of owls.

"What have you for your dinner, boys," was a cheerful inquiry from an officer.

"Nothing but fire cake and water, Sir."

And again at night: "What is your supper, lads?"

"Fire cake and water, Sir."

"The Lord send that our Commissary of Purchases may live [on] fire cake and water till their glutted guts are turned to pasteboard," Waldo wrote in his diary.

Among all the miseries, hunger was certainly the most demoralizing and persistent. Nathanael Greene proposed, as a substitute for meat, that the men cook up a "firmity" of wheat and sugar. Fresh vegetables were almost impossible to get, and Washington tried with little success to persuade the soldiers to eat salads. One order read: "As there is plenty of French and Common Sallid, Lamb's Quarter and Water Cresses growing about camp, and as these vegetables are very conducive to health and to prevent scurvy and all Putrid disorders, the General recommends to the soldiers the constant use of them as they make an agreeable Sallid and have the most Salutary effect."

Colonel John Brooks of Massachusetts wrote to a friend describing vividly the hardships of Valley Forge, of "our poor brave fellows living in tents [the huts had not yet been finished] bare-footed, bare-legged, bare-breeched . . . in snow, in rain, on marches, in camp, and on duty." It was his opinion that "nothing but virtue has kept our army together through this campaign. There has been that great principle, the love of our country, which first called us into the field, and that only ought to influence us. But this will not last always. Some other motives must cooperate with us in order to keep an army together any length of time. I know of no reason why one part of the community should sacrifice their all for the good of it, while the rest are filling their coffers. We have this consolation, however, that it cannot be said we are bought or bribed into the service."

What the soldiers had difficulty understanding was how they could be starving in the midst of comparative plenty. In the bitter words of Colonel Brooks, "The States of Pennsylvania and Maryland do not seem to have any more idea of liberty than a savage has of civilization. What," Brooks asked with the sectional feeling that was so often the bane of the patriot cause, "would have been the situation of New England at this moment had they shown the same disposition towards Genl. Burgoyne which the cringing, non-resisting, ass-like fools of this State [Pennsylvania] have done towards Howe?"

De Kalb wrote on Christmas day to his friend and patron Count Charles-Francis de Broglie expressing a pessimism that was general among the officers and men of Washington's army. De Kalb's initial opinion of the commander in chief was not a flattering one. The decision to go into winter camp at Valley Forge, was, in the view of the German-born officer, a bad one "discussed in all its length and breadth —a bad practice to which they are addicted here—and good advice [i.e. De Kalb's] was not taken." It seemed to De Kalb that the determination to "lie in shanties" could only have been put into Washington's head "by an interested spectator or a disaffected man" who wished harm to the patriot cause. "It is unfortunate that Washington is so easily led," De Kalb added. "He is the bravest and truest of men, has the best intentions and a sound judgment. . . . It is a pity he is so weak and has the worst of advisers in the men who enjoy his confidence. If they are not traitors, they are certainly gross ignoramuses."

De Kalb, like the other foreign officers, was amused and disconcerted by the democracy of the American army. In Europe officers were, virtually without exception, members of the aristocracy (the exception were some aggressive climbers like De Kalb himself), and it was strange to them to see officers who, in social terms, were indistinguishable from the men they commanded. "My blacksmith is a captain!" De Kalb informed De Broglie. "The very numerous assistant-quartermasters are for the most part men of no military education whatever, in many cases ordinary hucksters, but always colonels. . . . It is safe to accost every man as a colonel who talks to me with familiarity; the officers of a lower rank are invariably more modest. In a word the army teems with colonels."

Duportail believed that the Americans had been spoiled by their luxurious life in peacetime, when they "enjoyed in abundance every requisite to make life comfortable and happy"; they thus passed the "great part of their time either in smoking, drinking tea or spirituous liquors." It was not surprising, therefore, that so many of them "should prefer the yoke of the English to a liberty purchased at the expense of the comforts of life." The Americans would never, Duportail wrote to the French minister of war, be firm in the cause of liberty until France furnished them with all the luxuries that they so missed. "True," he wrote, "it will cost some millions," but it would be money well spent if, by encouraging the resistance of the Americans, it annihilated "the power of England, which, when bereft of her colonies, without a navy and without commerce, will lose her consequence in the world, and leave France without a rival." There was, he assured his correspondent, "a hundred times more enthusiasm for this revolution in any one coffee-house at Paris, than in all the Thirteen Provinces united."

By the end of December, officers began to resign by the dozen—fifty in Nathanael Greene's division alone. It seemed the last straw. Waldo, who requested a furlough himself, best tells us why they went: "When an officer has been fatigued through wet and cold and returns to his tent he finds a letter directed to him from his wife, filled with the most heart-aching tender complaints a woman is capable of writing; acquainting him with the incredible difficulty with which she procures a little bread for herself and children—and finally concluding with expressions bordering on despair, of procuring a sufficiency of food to keep body and soul together through the winter . . . she begs of him to consider that charity begins at home, and not suffer his family to perish with want in the midst of plenty. When such, I say, are the tidings they constantly hear from their families, what man is there, who has the least regard for his family, whose soul would not shrink within him? Who would not be disheartened from persevering in the best of causes—the cause of his country—when such discouragements as these lie in his way, which his country might remedy if she would?"

As the resignations continued, it almost seemed as though Washington would be left alone with his soldiers to survive, as best he could, the rigors of the winter. Waldo's request for a furlough met with a plea to him to stay on a while longer, at least until the regimental hospitals were finished. He decided to stay. Suddenly things looked a bit brighter. The huts were at last completed. "We got some spirits," he noted in his diary, "and finished the year with a good drink and thankful hearts in our new hut. . . . In the evening I joyfully received a letter from my good and loving wife," and on New Year's Day he could write: "I am alive. I am well. Huts go on briskly, and our camp begins to appear like a spacious city." Waldo applied for a furlough once more and was once more refused and so "came home sulky and cross-stormed at the boys and swore round like a piper and a fool till 'most night, when I bought me a bearskin, dressed with the hair on; this will answer me to lie on."

Two of the most persistent problems were keeping the soldiers busy in camp and keeping the camp clean. A simple armory was built, and soldiers were assigned to making cartridges; another hastily constructed building was equipped as a blacksmith's shop, and here a detail of men were put to work making spitoons—interminable spitting was a particularly unattractive characteristic of American soldiers, most of whom either chewed tobacco or dipped snuff. Field latrines or vaults had to be constantly dug in the frozen soil, burned out, filled in, and dug again, and a constant campaign had to be waged against "committing nuisances" everywhere about the camp. The farm boys who made up 90 per cent of the private soldiers at Valley Forge were inclined to relieve themselves wherever they could find a log, a tree stump, or some convenient spot. On a cold night, soldiers were very apt to relieve themselves outside their huts rather than go stumbling off through the dark to the vaults. Such behavior, unchecked, would soon have made the camp an infectious pesthole. After exhortations and threats had failed, the soldiers on guard duty in one brigade were ordered to fire on any man "easing himself anywhere else than at ye vaults."

The soldiers' huts and the hospital buildings had to be constantly inspected and repaired, and the orderly books were filled with the mention of dead horses left unburied and of offal that rotted when the weather turned warm, of "much filth and nastiness."

Efforts were made to observe Benjamin Rush's principles for "preserving the Health of Soldiers." Rush, visiting behind the English lines to arrange the exchange of wounded prisoners, had been greatly impressed by the efficiency and good order of the British medical service. "It would take a volume," he wrote John Adams, "to tell you of the many things I saw and heard which tend to show the extreme regard that our enemies pay to discipline, order, economy and cleanliness among their soldiers." The American service was a dismal contrast. Arriving at the headquarters of General Washington at night, Rush was not even challenged by a sentry, and this lack of discipline was exemplified by the hospital. "The sick suffer," he wrote, "but no redress can be had for them. Upwards of 100 of them were drunk last night. We have no guards to prevent this evil. In Howe's army a captain's guard mounts over every 200 sick. Besides keeping their men from contracting and prolonging distempers by rambling, drinking, and whoring, guards keep up at all times in the minds of the sick a sense of military subordination. . . . One month in our hospitals would undo all the discipline of a year, provided our soldiers brought it with them from the army."

Inspired by the example of the British, Rush produced a pamphlet on "preserving the Health of Soldiers" by means of attention to "I. Dress. II. Diet. III. Cleanliness. and IV. Encampments." In this eminently sensible document, Rush laid out a regimen that, had it been followed, would certainly have saved the lives of thousands of soldiers who died in camp of one of a multitude of diseases. "Too much cannot be said in favor of *Cleanliness*," Rush wrote. "If it were possible to convert every blade of grass on the continent into an American soldier, the want of cleanliness would reduce them in two or three campaigns to a handful of men. It should extend 1. To the *body* of a soldier. He should be obliged to wash his hands and face at least once every day, and his whole body twice or three times a week, especially in summer. The cold bath was part of the military discipline of the Roman soldiers and contributed much to preserve their health." Clothes should likewise be kept clean, and the same concern for cleanliness should extend to the soldier's food: "Great care should be taken that the vessels in which he cooks his victuals should be carefully washed after each time of their being used. . . . The environs of each tent and of the camp in general should be kept perfectly clean of the offals of animals and of filth of all kinds. They should be buried or carefully removed every day beyond the neighborhood of the camp." All these are the most rudimentary principles of sanitation in a modern army. That Rush had to argue them makes it clear that far too little attention was paid to them at Valley Forge and elsewhere.

In February, the army was so desperately hungry that Washington was forced to authorize extreme measures to collect food if his soldiers were not to starve. General Greene led a foraging party along the Brandywine, taking everything he found from farmers already reduced to bare subsistence. Those suspected of Tory sympathies received the special attention of the foraging soldiers. The woods were scoured for horses and livestock hidden there. "Harden your hearts," Greene instructed his men, "we are in the midst of a damn nest of Tories." General Wayne used the same tactics in New Jersey, and he collected such a haul of livestock that when his little force appeared driving herds of sheep and cattle he promptly acquired the nickname "Wayne the Drover."

Joseph Martin was sent on a foraging expedition with a lieutenant, a sergeant, a corporal, and eighteen other privates. Their mission: procuring "provisions from the inhabitants for the men in the army . . . at the point of a bayonet." The first night out the little party stopped at a farmhouse, where a soldier was forced to trade his shirt for some gravy to go on their tough beef. After the family had retired to bed, the soldiers tapped the cider keg in the cellar and repossessed the shirt. The next morning they were off before daylight, much pleased with themselves.

The foraging duty was Martin's best fortune in the army. "We fared much better," he wrote, "than I had ever done in the army before, or ever did afterwards. We had very good provisions all winter and generally enough of them. Some of us were constantly in the country with the wagons; we went out by turns and had no one to control us . . . We had no guards to keep; our only duty was to help load the wagons with hay, corn meal, or whatever they were to take off, and when they were thus loaded, to keep them company until they arrived at the commissary's. . . ."

Amid all the hardship and suffering at Valley Forge, one piece of good fortune was in the offing. This was the arrival of Freidrich Wilhelm Augustus von Steuben (the "von," a mark of nobility, was somewhat dubious), the son of an army engineer. He had been educated by the Jesuits at Breslau and had become, at seventeen, an officer in the Prussian army. He had served in the Seven Years' War and had subsequently been a member of the staff of Frederick the Great. Frederick might be said to have virtually invented the modern army staff, and "Von" Steuben had thus attended the best military school in the world. Discharged from the army as a captain in 1763, he became chamberlain at the court of Hohenzollern-Hechingen and somehow acquired the title of "baron." The court, and Von Steuben with it, became so involved in debt that the baron had to find other employment. He was referred to Benjamin Franklin, who had been sent to Paris by Congress to impose some restraints on Silas Deane. With the endorsement of the French minister of war and a loan from Beaumarchais' dummy company, Hortalez & Company, Steuben sailed for America.

From Portsmouth, New Hampshire, where he landed, he wrote a letter to the Continental Congress, declaring, "The honor of serving a respectable Nation, engaged in the noble enterprise of defending its rights and liberty, is the only motive that brought me over to this Continent. I ask neither riches nor titles. I am come here from the remotest end of Germany at my own expense, and have given up an honorable and lucrative rank. . . . My only ambition is to serve you as a Volunteer, to deserve the confidence of your General in Chief . . . and if I am Possessor of some talents in the Art of War, they should be much dearer to me, if I could employ them in the service of a Republick. . . . I should willingly purchase at my Blood's Expence, the honor of seeing one Day my Name after those of the Defenders of your Liberty." With that he set out for Pennsylvania.

Congress, flattered and impressed by the baron's letter, "cheerfully" accepted his offer to serve in the cause of liberty. At York, where he stopped to meet the congressmen, he made a fine figure in his ornate uniform. He had a large nose and ruddy cheeks, lively grey eyes, and an expressive mouth. He was courtly with a kind of gruff Germanic charm and had a quick, if rather elemental, sense of humor. Congress gave him a handsome dinner, applauded "the generosity of his propositions in thus risking his fortune on that of the United States," and sent him off to Valley Forge—which was, in turn, to make him as famous as he could have wished and doubtless far more so than he had expected.

Before he left New York, Steuben took some pains to reach an understanding on what his remuneration as a "volunteer" was to be. The terms were by no means ungenerous to Steuben (nor apparently very clearly understood by Washington). With Steuben, as part of his "staff," came three French officers who had also to be provided for by Congress—DePontiere, Du Ponceau and L'Enfant. Pierre Étienne Du Ponceau acted as Steuben's interpreter and remained in America to become a leading citizen of Philadelphia after the war. And Pierre L'Enfant, a gifted engineer-artist, was destined to become the principal designer of the new national capitol, the city of Washington.

The baron's somewhat inflated reputation had preceded him. Washington himself rode out to greet the distinguished volunteer, and a guard of honor met him at his quarters. His name was designated as the watchword of the day. The next day he reviewed the ragged and poorly equipped little army, a tatterdemalion force, ill-shod, if shod at all, ill-clothed, bearded and dirty, and displaying only the barest rudiments of military order.

John Laurens, immediately impressed, wrote to his father that the baron "appears to be a man profound in the science of war, and well disposed to render his best services to the United States. . . . Steuben seems to understand what our soldiers are capable of, and is not so staunch a systematist as to be averse from adapting established forms to stubborn circumstances." This, indeed, was a sensitive point on which Washington wished to satisfy himself before placing the training of his army in the hands of the Prussian officer. He would, Laurens noted, "not give us the perfect instructions absolutely speaking, but the best which we are in a condition to receive. . . ."

Nathanael Greene, the ardent student of military history, was dazzled at the prospect of learning more of his craft from an officer who had served under the great Frederick, the leading military genius of Europe. The baron made a fine figure as he rode about the camp in his handsome uniform on a spirited horse. Private Ashbel Greene wrote in later life, "Never before, or since, have I had such an impression of the ancient fabled God of War as when I looked on the baron; he seemed to me a perfect personification of Mars. The trappings of his horse, the enormous holsters of his pistols, his large size [he looked in all his regalia considerably larger than life, which in fact was a moderate five feet nine inches or so] and his striking martial aspect, all seemed to favor the idea."

The baron made a careful inspection of the ragged men and their rusty weapons. Half-starved and half-frozen, filthy and wretchedly equipped as the soldiers were, the baron was struck by the grim jocularity with which they bore their miseries. It was the first time the baron in all his extensive military experience had seen citizen soldiers fighting for a cause in which they believed. He was a good enough soldier himself to be deeply impressed. No professional army in Europe, he told Washington, could have been held together under such conditions.

Young Laurens, inspired by the baron's martial air, confided to his father that "[my] desire of gaining fame, leads me to wish for the command of men," rather than for the position of staff officer that he occupied. He longed to be at the head of "those dear ragged Continentals, whose patience will be the admiration of future ages, and glory in bleeding with them. . . ." But since that was not to be, for the time being at any rate, he had the pleasure of working with Baron von Steuben, who "has had the fortune to please uncommonly, for a stranger, at first sight. . . ." Von Steuben, Laurens added, wished to have no actual command until he knew the "language and the genius and manners of the people."

It was a month before Von Steuben, with the assistance of Hamilton and Greene, had drawn up a uniform code of drill. Time was short; winter was near an end, and soon Howe must bestir himself in Philadelphia. As Von Steuben and his assistants finished each drill lesson, it was passed on to the troops. Von Steuben wrote the drills in French. Du Ponceau translated them into English and Laurens and Hamilton turned them into American, so to speak. Once the drills had been written out, the problem of distributing them to the soldiers had to be faced. Washington had no printing press with the army and only the most modest secretarial staff. Hundreds of fair copies would have to be made. The solution was to appoint "brigade inspectors" from each of the fourteen infantry brigades. Each of them made a copy of the first chapter of the drill regulations, and this in turn was copied in the brigade orderly book and then in its regimental counterpart, and on down to the company level, where every officer and drillmaster could make his own copy. As Steuben expressed it: "I dictated my dispositions in the night; in the day I had them performed." Steuben could not read his own drill instructions. Yet it was essential for him to give the commands in English and supervise the drills personally if they were to have the best effect. He thus learned them by rote, reciting them aloud like a schoolboy in his broken English with a variety of French and German oaths.

Having mastered the English version of his own drill instructions, Steuben then collected a model company made up of men who would act as drill sergeants for their own units. On March 17, Washington included the following paragraph in his order of the day: "One hundred chosen men are to be annexed to the Guard of the Commander in Chief for the purpose of forming a corps to be instructed in the Maneuvers to be introduced into the Army and serve as a model for the execution of them. . . ."

The first item was the "position of the soldier," and here Steuben showed the men what was wanted and then walked the line and corrected their posture—head up, chin in, chest out, stomach (or what there was of it) in, shoulders back—the classic posture that every American soldier since has assumed on the drill field. Then he taught them how to dress right, with the left arm extended and fingers touching the next man's shoulders. And then, "foorrwarrrd march!" And the cadence, "Von, Two, Tree, Four," until the men could pick up the count and at the command "in cadence, count!" sing out, as they swung along, "hup, two, three, fuh," a powerful chant that locked them together in a fundamental rhythm that would ring forever in their memories—"hup, two, three, fuh," the incantation of their brotherhood.

They faced right and left, snapping their scarred and calloused heels together smartly, and faced about, placing the toe to the right foot behind the heel of the left and swinging around quite neatly, a simple maneuver to be sure, but a satisfying one to master. They were all simple movements, but Steuben—sly, fraudulent old "Von" Steuben— was a skilled impresario. Soldiers and officers gathered by the hundreds to watch the engaging spectacle, to laugh at Von Steuben's accent, and to applaud the efforts of their fellows. Squad by squad, the men drilled and drilled, training their reflexes until they could obey the commands without thinking. At the end of the drill the whole model company was re-formed, marched to the front, ordered "about face," and marched back again. They faced right and left. And in the afternoon, they learned the more exacting "wheel to the right" and "wheel to the left."

The next day it was more of the same. And the next. Joseph Martin got back from his foraging detail just in time for the new drill. "After I had joined my regiment," he noted, "I was kept constantly when off other duty, engaged in learning the Baron de Steuben's new Prussian exercise. It was a continual drill."

From the drill manual, the baron proceeded to the manual of arms. He eliminated some parade-ground flourishes, but it still consisted of these commands: "Secure your cartridges; handle your muskets; prime your firing pans [the top was torn off by the soldier's teeth, and he sprinkled a small portion of the powder into the firing pan of the musket]; close your firing pans; charge your musket [the cartridge was placed in the muzzle of the musket]; remove ramrods [they were withdrawn from the groove beneath the barrel]; ram down cartridge; replace ramrod; present firelock; aim firelock; fire." What might seem to the modern mind a very tedious and impractical way of preparing to fire a musket served a definite purpose. Eighteenth-century military tactics called for massed infantry aligned in successive ranks to fire volleys on command, drop back, load, and then advance and fire again. In actual combat such formations usually broke down rapidly, but it was essential to master them, especially those steps involved in loading the musket. Unless the routines were imprinted on his reflexes, a frightened and nervous soldier might well (and often did) omit, in his frenzied haste to reload before a British bayonet pricked him, some essential step (such as priming the firing pan). His weapon was cranky enough in any case, and there were, under the best of conditions, numerous misfires (when the powder in the firing pan itself failed to ignite from the sparks struck by the contact of the flint with the face of the firing pan). Often a soldier, in his haste, failed to remove his ramrod from the barrel of his musket after having rammed down his cartridge. The ramrod would thus be fired with the bullet. It made a lethal projectile, but it left the soldier without a ramrod to use in reloading his piece. The more automatic the actions of the soldier, the better.

From wheeling and moving to the flank and by half-right and half-left in mass, the battalions and brigades went on to marching in column and deploying from column into line. The army had most commonly moved in a column of files—single men marching in succession. This meant long strung-out lines, hard for officers to control. To march in a column of fours was much more efficient, especially over short distances; it prevented straggling and, on contact with the enemy, made it possible to deploy much more rapidly. A major handicap for the Continentals at Brandywine and Germantown had been the length of time it took them to come into battle line at crucial points.

After four weeks, Von Steuben wrote, "My Enterprize Succeeded better than I had dared to expect, and I had the Satisfaction . . . to see not only a regular Step introduced in the Army, but I also made maneuvers with ten and twelve Battalions with as much precision as the Evolution of a Single Company." The Baron discovered, however, that the American soldier could not be treated like his European counterpart. "The genius of this nation," he wrote an old military friend, "is not the least to be compared with that of the Prussians, Austrians, or French. You say to your [European] soldier, 'Do this, and he doeth it'; but I am obliged to say, 'This is the reason why you ought to do that: and then he does it.'" Steuben was astonished, moreover, that the Continental soldier learned so fast.

Washington announced the inauguration of the new program in a general order: "The Importance of establishing an uniform system of useful maneuvers, and regularity of discipline, must be obvious; the deficiencies of our army in those respects must be equally so; but the time we probably shall have to introduce the necessary reformation is short. With the most active exertion, therefore, of officers of every class, it may be possible to effect all the improvement that may be essential to the success of the ensuing campaign. Arguments surely need not be multiplied to kindle the zeal of officers in a matter of such great moment to their own homes, the advancement of the service, and the prosperity of our arms."

The basic drills having been mastered, the troops were directed to spend some time each day "in charging the enemy by platoons," firing, advancing, and, most important of all, rushing the enemy with fixed bayonets, something the Americans had shown little aptitude for— partly, of course, because they seldom had bayonets. But of all military drills, the one concerned with the use of the bayonet is perhaps the most arduous and the most important, requiring, as it does, great discipline and precision. As important as the bayonet drill was training the Continental soldiers to face a bayonet attack with at least a degree of equanimity. Their principal use for bayonets had been as tent pegs or for barbecuing tough meat over a smoky fire. Now they were drilled to fight with them.

As important as the drill itself was the fact that the baron, with his good humor and ebullience, made the whole thing fun. The soldiers grumbled, as soldiers do, at having to engage in all this parade-ground nonsense, but they took pleasure in their growing mastery and were soon caught up in the compelling experience of even that moderate degree of unified and rhythmic action demanded by the baron's drill. The effect on morale was remarkable. The gaunt and tattered Continentals began to feel like an army, and even, if one could ignore their lack of proper uniforms, to look a bit like one. Most were, by this time, decently shod and somewhat better fed. And Von Steuben was irresistible. His grin was infectious, and he mixed profanity and laughter in equal proportions. When his charges fouled up a maneuver, he would swear in French and in German and then call on one of his aides to curse a bit in English: *"Viens*, Walker, *mon ami, mon bon ami! sacre!* Goddam *de gaucheries of dese badauts. Je ne suis plus.* I can curse them no more."

On at least one occasion he gave an order in English and followed it with one in German that no one could understand. The confused soldiers began to march in different directions as Von Steuben shouted in a bewildering combination of German and French and the whole formation broke up.

The baron not only raised the spirits of the soldiers, he cheered up the officers as well. His French aides, with his permission, invited a number of young officers to dine at the baron's quarters "on the condition," as Du Ponceau tells it, "that none should be admitted that had on a whole pair of breeches. This was of course understood as *pars pro toto;* but torn clothes were an indispensible requisite for admission, and in this the guests were very sure not to fail." Each guest contributed his own ration to the feast, and, again in Du Ponceau's words, "we dined sumptuously on tough beefsteak and potatoes, with hickory nuts for our desert. Instead of wine, we had some kind of spirits, with which we made 'Salamanders,' that is to say, after filling up our glasses, we set the liquor on fire and drank it up, flame and all. Such a set of ragged and, at the same time, merry fellows, were never brought together." Von Steuben called the young officers his "sansculottes," or "men without kneebreeches," since many of the officers, like the men, wore ragged trousers.

John Laurens wrote his father: "The Baron discovers the greatest zeal, and an activity which is hardly to be expected of his years [he was forty-eight]. The officers in general seem to entertain a high opinion of him, and he sets them an excellent example in descending to the functions of a drill-sergeant."

The Prussian officer had turned out to be more "democratic" than the officers of Washington's "republican army." Indeed, what can you say of a man who years later wrote so disarmingly to Alexander Hamilton: "If, however, I should be charged with having made use of illicit stratagems to gain admission into the service of the United States, I am sure I have obtained my pardon of the Army and I flatter myself, of the citizens of this Republic in general."

The problem of a proper title and rank for Von Steuben was solved at the end of April, when Thomas Conway resigned as inspector general. Von Steuben was ideally suited for the post, and Washington immediately recommended him to Congress.

Washington himself was an attentive observer of Von Steuben's reforms. It was always his practice to be much with his troops, and his presence was constantly felt by the ordinary soldier during the long and bitter winter at Valley Forge. Simply seeing his splendid figure about was an enormous comfort to officers and men alike. To hear a word of comfort or exhortation from him was antidote for cold and hunger and general misery. Coming on Private John Brantley and some of his companions drinking precious and doubtless stolen wine and already a little tipsy, Washington was invited to "drink some wine with a soldier."

"My boy, you have no time for drinking wine," Washington replied.

"Damn your proud soul," Brantley answered. "You are above drinking with soldiers."

Washington, who had started to ride away, turned his chestnut sorrel about and said, "Come I will drink with you." He put the jug to his mouth, took a swig, and handed it back to the startled Brantley.

"Give it to your servants," Brantley said, indicating Washington's aides. The jug was passed around and returned to Brantley.

"Now," said that bold young man, "I'll be damned if I don't spend the last drop of my heart's blood for you."

The story went about, of course, as all such stories will in camp, and strengthened the affection of the soldiers for their commander.

Despite such pleasant incidents, the situation at Valley Forge in the spring of 1778 was anything but bright. All units were below strength. One company was reduced to a single healthy enlisted man, and one regiment counted only thirty privates fit to bear arms. The officer corps was still far below strength. New enlistments were slow coming in.

Howe's army, rested and well fed, might be expected to take the field any week.

The general depletion of the army created problems for the baron's new drill. How did a one-man company function in relation to a company nearer normal size? Steuben had, for the purposes of his drill, to divide men up into companies and brigades without regard to their actual units. One unanticipated dividend from this procedure was that it mixed men from different units and different lines—Connecticut men with Virginia men, Rhode Island men with Pennsylvanians—thus bringing about a measure of the reform that Washington had labored to achieve at Cambridge two winters before when he undertook to "new-model" the army in the face of stubborn opposition from the individual states.

The tough and seasoned corps that Steuben and his aides hammered and coaxed into some form of military order could be counted on to do as well as soldiers could do. The real question was whether they would have to do it alone. "It would enchant you to see the enlivened scene on our Campus Martius," John Laurens wrote to his father. "If Mr. Howe opens his campaign with his usual deliberation, and our recruits or drafts come in tolerably well, we shall be infinitely better prepared to meet them than ever we have been."

Recruits did, at last, begin to come in and were quickly integrated into the veteran units—although there is no record of what happened to the company that had only one soldier left in it. An officer wrote a letter, printed in the *New Jersey Gazette,* that gave an encouraging picture of conditions in Washington's camp: "The Army grows stronger every day. It increases in numbers . . . there is a spirit of discipline among the troops that is better than numbers. Each brigade is on parade almost every day for several hours. You would be charmed to see the regularity and exactness with which they march and perform their maneuvers."

"The troops were so harassed with marches [campaigns] last year that there was little discipline among them," the writer continued, and "it was almost impossible to advance or retire in the presence of an enemy without disordering the line and falling into confusion. That misfortune, I believe, will seldom happen again . . . for the troops are instructed in a new and so happy a method of marching that they will soon be able to advance with the utmost regularity, even without musick and on the roughest grounds."

Surgeon Waldo, back from his furlough, proclaimed the improved conditions in the campus with a verse:

> Camp, hills and dales with mirth resound;
> All with clean clothes and powdered hair
> For sport and duty now appear,
> Here squads in martial exercise,
> There whole brigades in order rise.
> . . . .
> Where all the varying glitters show
> Of guns and bayonets polished bright.
> . . . .
> One choix at Fives are earnest here
> Another furious at Cricket there.

Washington himself so far threw off the cares of his office as to join with his officers in a game of cricket, and a pageant, or Grand Parade, complete with Maypoles for every regiment, was put on to celebrate May Day with "mirth and jollity." The soldiers put dogwood blossoms in their hats and paraded through the camp streets, escorting a sergeant attired as an Indian chief accompanied by thirteen other sergeants dressed as Indian braves. The band proceeded to Washington's headquarters, where they were informed that the general was sick in bed, so back they marched "with the greatest decency and regularity."

In the unifying rhythm of close-order drill even more than in combat, where they had, after all, fought for the most part in units made up of men from their own colony or town, Washington's soldiers achieved the sense of belonging, finally, to a Continental Army. What Washington had started three years earlier at Cambridge—the new-modeling of the army—came to fruition at Valley Forge. It is a commonplace, of course, to say that the American army was "forged" at Valley Forge. The fact was that the most notable military actions involving colonial soldiers had occurred prior to the winter of 1777–78: Lexington and Concord, Bunker Hill, Harlem Heights, White Plains, Trenton, Brandywine, Germantown, Princeton, the defense of Forts Mercer and Mifflin, Freeman's Farm, and Saratoga.

In what sense then can we say that the Continental Army was "forged" at Valley Forge? The army had been kept together by a series of desperate expedients. Time and again it had been questionable whether the army as an army would survive (as distinguished from the question of whether armed resistance against Great Britain would continue). In December of 1777, when Howe, after his demonstrations at Chestnut Hill and Edge Hill, retired to Philadelphia and went into winter quarters with his army, the Continental Army, which had so often experienced crisis before, touched rock bottom. It was clear that there would be no more serious fighting until spring. Prudence and common sense suggested that the wretchedly clothed and miserably fed soldiers return to comfortable homes and friends and wives and children rather than shiver at Valley Forge. But Washington had managed to get Congressional approval for enlistments for the duration of the war, and beyond that, he prevailed upon many soldiers and a substantial number of officers, by the force of his own implacable will, to remain with him at Valley Forge. Washington and those men who remained with him that winter formed a bond of unity that could never be broken. There they first endured and then triumphed, and the name Valley Forge became a magic and talismanic word, an essential part of that primal memory that nourished a nation. There was a scriptural phrase that embodied it: "men and nations are forged in the fires of adversity."

What Valley Forge settled once for all was whether there was to be an army, and that, in turn, settled whether there was to be a Continental Congress and, in fact, a nation.

11

The Conway Cabal

THROUGHOUT the fall and early winter of 1777, Washington was preoccupied by the so-called Conway Cabal. We have already observed the
seeds of the cabal in the machinations of Gates, Conway, Charles Lee,
and some of the delegates in the Continental Congress. Gates's triumph
at Saratoga had given fresh impetus to the movement. Gates himself
became little short of insubordinate, sending his reports and dispatches
directly to Congress rather than passing them "through channels" to
Washington. Washington had, indeed, received no official account of
the surrender at Saratoga from Gates, and when Colonel James Wilkinson finally arrived with dispatches, they were addressed to Congress
rather than to Washington.

Thomas Conway, Gates's coadjutor, was another of the officers who
had been signed up by Deane in Paris. (Born in Ireland, Conway had
served in the French army for thirty years.) Like Gates, Conway viewed
Washington as an inexperienced and incompetent amateur who should
be replaced by a professional soldier—Gates. In addition to his detractors in the army, Washington had a number of critics in Congress.
Samuel Adams, Richard Henry Lee, Thomas Mifflin, and Benjamin
Rush were among those who had developed sincere misgivings about
Washington's ability as a military leader. They helped to circulate an

anonymous paper, entitled "Thoughts of a Freeman," that criticized Washington's performance as a general and attacked the growth of a cult that seemed determined to deify him. "The people of America," it read, "have been guilty of making a man their God."

James Lovell, in a letter to Samuel Adams, expressed pleasure over the "smartness in a Resolve which was meant to rap a Demi G___ over the Knuckles," and complained about his fellow delegates as "privy Councillors to one great Man whom no Citizen *shall* dare even to talk about, say the Gentleman of the Blade"—a reference to the readiness of Washington's officers to challenge his detractors to a duel.

Much of the evidence of the "cabal" comes from Henry Laurens' letters to his son, who was one of Washington's staff officers. Under the circumstances, they were mischief-making letters. Although Laurens, the South Carolinian who became president of Congress in November, 1777, was careful to mention no names, his letters were full of allusions to enemies of Washington in Congress, which was made up of "prompters and Actors, accommodators, Candle snuffers, Shifters of scene and Mutes." There was a member whose "fawning mild address and obsequiousness procured him toleration from great Men on both sides." This individual's "idleness, duplicity and criminal partialities in a certain Circle laid the foundations," Laurens wrote his son, "of our present deplorable State." There was, according to Laurens, one particular delegate who was the pivot of "the late mischiefs." Laurens was inclined to believe that "there were Agents from our Enemies if not within Doors, yet too closely connected with some who sat there." This man was one of whom Washington held "the most favorable sentiments."

Laurens must have known that his son would carry such stories to Washington, and that the general, in turn, would suspect some innocent men. The wonder is that Washington, under such circumstances, preserved his remarkable equanimity.

Conway, who had performed well at Brandywine (Sullivan wrote of him: "His regulations in his Brigade are much better than any in the Army, and his knowledge of military matters far exceeds any officer we have"), was constantly pestering Congress to promote him from brigadier to major general. Several weeks after Brandywine, he had written a long, boastful, and querulous letter to Congress, listing his qualifications to become a major general, ending: "Your very speedy and categorial answer will very much oblige. . . ." And Alexander Graydon heard him say, "No man was more a gentleman than General Washington, or appeared to more advantage at his table, or in the usual intercourse of life; but as to his talents for the command of an Army, they were miserable indeed."

When Washington heard that there was a plan afoot in Congress to promote Conway, he wrote to Richard Henry Lee protesting the appointment. "General Conway's merit . . . as an officer, and his importance in this army exists more in his imagination than in reality: For it is a maxim with him, to leave no service of his untold, nor to want any thing which is to be obtained by importunity." It could hardly have been said better. Then Washington added, "I have been a Slave to the service; I have undergone more than most Men are aware of, to harmonize so many discordant parts; but it will be impossible for me to be of any further service, if such insuperable difficulties are thrown in my way."

The hint that the promotion of Conway would bring his resignation was plain enough for anyone to read. That Washington should have put the matter in this way clearly reveals the bitterness of his own feelings. He had put a weapon in the hands of those who might wish to replace him. Although the threat to resign was not categorical, it was certainly implied.

Lee's answer was evasive. Conway would not be promoted to major general "whilst it is likely to produce the evil consequences you suggest." Congress was discussing the reorganization of the Board of War. Joseph Reed and Timothy Pickering were favored for the board, along with Robert Harrison, Washington's secretary. The thought was that Conway might then take Pickering's place as Washington's adjutant general. It is hard to believe that there was not some malice in the suggestion. Were the members of Congress so obtuse as to think that Washington would accept as his adjutant general a man who was his constant detractor? Perhaps the delegates who supported the idea had such lack of confidence in Washington's generalship that they were willing to risk his resignation to force him to accept on his staff an officer whose experience and abilities they apparently regarded more highly than Washington's. Washington replied with restraint to Lee's letter, reviewing in detail Conway's qualifications for the laborious administrative duties of the adjutant general.

Into this brew was stirred another ingredient. The sinuous Wilkinson, Gates's aide, stopped by at the headquarters of Lord Stirling for the night and, perhaps attempting to sound out Stirling's staff, passed on word of Conway's dissatisfaction with Washington. It was a disastrous blunder on Wilkinson's part. A few days later Stirling, writing to Washington, enclosed a statement made by Wilkinson to an officer named

McWilliams that showed "such wicked duplicity of conduct" that he felt bound to report it. The comment read: "In a letter from Genl. Conway to Genl. Gates he says—'Heaven has been determined to save your country; or a weak General and bad Councellors would have ruined it.'"

Washington, anxious to get some sense of how widespread the resistance to his leadership might be, wrote a brief note to Conway beginning, "Sir: A Letter which I received last Night, contained the following paragraph," and enclosing Stirling's report of Conway's communication to Gates. Conway wrote back at once defending himself. He had, he admitted, criticized the operations of the Continental Army, but he denied that he had used the phrase "a weak General" and declared, "I defy the most keen and penetrating detractor to make it appear that I leveled at your bravery, honesty, patriotism or judgment, of which I have the highest sense." He was willing to have Washington read his original letter to Gates to prove his case. "My opinion of you, sir," he wrote, "without flattery or envy is as follows: You are a brave man, an honest man, a patriot and a man of good sense. Your modesty is such that although your advice is commonly sound and proper you have often been influenced by men who were not equal to you in point of experience, knowledge or judgment."

The letter had an insultingly condescending tone that certainly did not escape Washington. Moreover, to put down a general's staff as incompetent, as Conway's letter seemed to do, was almost as insulting as direct personal criticism. Conway's specious compliments might well be read as a confirmation of the phrase "weak General." Young John Laurens described the letter accurately enough when he wrote, "The perplexity of his [Conway's] style, the evident insincerity of his compliments, betray his real sentiments and expose his guilt."

Conway then wrote to Congress and submitted his resignation. He cited among his reasons his failure to be promoted, the letter quoted by Washington, and the promotion over him of De Kalb, who had been junior to him in the French army. If he accepted De Kalb's superior rank, "it might be concluded in France that I misbehaved and, indeed, Congress, instead of looking on me as an officer who enjoyed some esteem and reputation in the French infantry, must take me for a vagabond who fled here to get bread." Congress took no action but passed Conway's letter on to the Board of War, which was headed by Mifflin (Gates was soon to be its president). When no action was taken by the board, Congress in December established the position of inspector general and appointed Conway to fill the office.

Ironically, the notion of an inspector general had originated with Washington himself, based on a suggestion by a foreign volunteer, Baron D'Arendt. The notion was that a particular officer given that title could devote the full time of himself and his staff to preparing a training manual, a plan of maneuvers, and an appropriate list of military regulations, as well as to supervising their implementation. The change that Congress, at Conway's suggestion, worked in Washington's proposal was a crucial one. By Congress's plan the inspector general would be independent of the commander in chief and would report directly to the Board of War. With Gates as president of the Board of War and Conway as the inspector general, Washington would be neatly boxed in.

It is hard to see how the delegates could have expected that Washington's reaction could have been anything but indignation. Congress had advanced over the heads of twenty-three brigadier generals senior to him in rank an officer who was strongly suspected of having been critical of Washington, if not openly disloyal, and moreover had placed him in a position where, as the instrument of Congress, he could be of particular embarrassment to Washington. There was either malice or stupidity in the act, perhaps a bit of both.

When Conway appeared at Valley Forge in his new role as inspector general, Washington received him with a cold correctness that masked deep anger. Conway was alarmed and disconcerted to feel the full force of Washington's wrath underneath the carefully observed formalities. When Washington wrote to ask him how he intended to perform his new duties, Conway replied that "if my appointment is productive of any inconvenience or anyways disagreeable to your excellency . . . I am very ready to return to France where I have pressing business. . . ." Washington then notified Conway that the brigadiers were determined to protest Conway's promotion by Congress, adding, "By consulting your own feelings upon the appointment of the baron de Kalb you may judge what must be the Sensations of those Brigadiers who by your Promotion are Superceded." Washington himself, however, would accept and respect the decision of Congress.

At this point Conway gave free reign to his own resentment of Washington. "The general and universal merit which you wish every promoted officer might be endowed with is a rare gift," Conway wrote. "We know but the great Frederick in Europe and the great Washington in this continent. I certainly never was so rash as to pretend to such a prodigious height. However, sir, by the complexion of your letter and by the reception you have honored me with since my arrival, I perceive that I have not the happiness of being agreeable to your Excellency and that I can expect no support in fulfilling the laborious duty of an Inspector General."

One of the morals of this exchange is that if you give an unstable and vindictive man enough opportunity, he will hang himself. The letter, with its tone of calculated insolence, could hardly have served Conway's cause. If Conway had confined himself to the charge that Washington had received him coolly and failed to cooperate with him, he would have been on firmer ground. The spitefulness cast doubts on the specific complaints. Washington resented especially the accusation that he could not be counted on to support Conway in the performance of his duties. This struck directly at Washington's code of respect for the authority of Congress and of obedience to its directions, so far as that was possible. On January 2 Washington sent the correspondence to Congress with a covering letter. "If General Conway means, by cool receptions . . . that I did not receive him in the language of a warm and cordial friend, I readily confess the charge . . . my feelings will not permit me to make professions of friendship to a man I deem my enemy. . . . At the same time, Truth authorizes me to say that he was received and treated with proper respect to his official character, and that he has had no cause to justify the assertion that he could not expect any support for fulfilling the duties of his appointment."

Conway, meanwhile, had traced the original tattling to Colonel Wilkinson, the highest-ranking messenger boy in the Continental Army, who denied that he had ever spoken the words relayed to Washington. Conway reported the conversation to Mifflin, who was dismayed by the casualness of Gates's care for his private papers and warned Gates to be more cautious. Gates, trying to find a convenient red herring to drag across the trail, made the mistake of implicating Hamilton. Hamilton, he declared, had been left alone in Gates's room during a visit to his headquarters and had undoubtedly copied the incriminating material from Gates's unguarded correspondence. Gates wrote in this vein to Washington. Conway's letters to him had been "stealingly copied." The culprit must be a member of Washington's staff. The general could do "a very important service, by detecting the wretch who may betray me, and capitally injure the very operations" that Washington was directing. He was sending a copy of this letter to Congress, Gates wrote.

It was a foolish and reckless act, a wicked imputation of Hamilton's honor that under different circumstances would doubtless have led to a duel. But Hamilton had a more lethal weapon available—his pen, which as Washington's aide he used with devastating effect. Washington at once informed Congress that the report of the letter had come from Gates's own staff. Wilkinson at first succeeded in shifting suspicion to another of Gates's aides, Lieutenant Colonel Robert Troup, who had carried Conway's letter to Gates. When Gates was finally convinced that Wilkinson was the culprit, he abused him so bitterly that Wilkinson challenged his commanding officer to a duel.

Throughout the unpleasant controversy, Lafayette served Washington well by his prestige among the French officers and his good standing with Congress. But Hamilton was undoubtedly Washington's principal strategist. Of course, Washington himself had a sure instinct for navigating in stormy political waters. Nine brigadiers signed a "memorial" to Congress protesting Conway's promotion, and the colonels who had been passed over when Congress had promoted Wilkinson at Gates's request likewise protested. In the light of the behavior of all three men, Congress found itself in a most awkward position. They had preferred fools to worthy men; they were now thoroughly discomfited, and the officers whose cause they had been inclined to champion were discredited.

There was a final act to be played. Conway and Gates had decided to try to bluff their way through. On January 19, Gates arrived at York, Pennsylvania, with the original of the letter that had caused so much trouble. Conway declared himself anxious to have the letter published to prove his innocence. But he and Gates refused to let Washington or Henry Laurens read the letter, and Laurens, after seeing a copy from some other source, wrote a friend that although the quotation from Conway's letter was not verbatim, it was "ten times worse in every way."

The underlying question remains whether there was in fact a cabal or conspiracy to replace Washington as commander in chief. If there was, the evidence to prove it is lacking. What evidence there is indicates that the ambitions of Gates and the unsavory Conway came into conjunction with a latent dissatisfaction in some members of Congress over Washington's performance. Richard Henry Lee, a fellow Virginian, was among those who questioned Washington's competence. Samuel Adams was another; Thomas Mifflin of Pennsylvania was a third. John Adams clearly had doubts of his own, but these were directed, as were his cousin's, more at his fears that the deification of Washington would prepare the way for a military dictatorship than at Washington's competence. Such anxieties were by no means improper ones. A general of less rectitude than Washington would certainly have represented a real threat to Congress. And who in 1777 knew the limits of Washington's own self-restraint? Blind adulation of a military figure is bound to make civilian authority uneasy. History is full of examples of the ease with which generals have assumed supreme authority in times of national crisis. If indeed Washington had shortcomings as a military leader, it was the responsibility of Congress to consider whether a more skillful tactitian might be found to replace him. To have such reflections was surely no conspiracy. And if Washington was to be replaced, who was a more likely candidate than Gates, an experienced general who had just won the most spectacular victory of the war at Saratoga—a victory so dazzling that it was counted on to win the eagerly sought French aid? The members of Congress could hardly be blamed for not knowing what historians are still disputing—that Gates deserved much less credit for Burgoyne's surrender than he was given by most people in their delight at the desperately needed victory.

Throughout the winter at Valley Forge, the tensions between Washington and Congress occasioned by the Conway affair were aggravated by other misunderstandings, or more plainly, conflicts. Washington's constant requests for supplies for his army, with their implied rebukes to Congress for its failure to be an adequate provider, exacerbated Congressional nerves, and two other issues rose to further trouble the relations between Washington and Congress. To the committee appointed to confer with Washington on the reform of the army, Washington brought his proposal for half-pay for life for those officers who served until the end of the war, this benefit to be extended to the widows of officers who died in the service of their country. Washington's main argument in support of half-pay was that "at present the Officers have no permanent interest in their Commissions, it is not possible to reduce them to discipline because whenever the necessary strictness and severity is observed they threaten to resign a Commission which affords them no prospects but of pain, danger, fatigue, and ruin to their private fortunes."

The committee was also drawn into discussions about the terms of a proposed exchange of prisoners. According to Elias Boudinot, a New Jersey delegate, the members of the Congressional committee took the line that it was a bad time to exchange prisoners and urged Washington to undertake the negotiation simply "for the purpose of satisfying the Army and throwing the blame on the British," but with no intention of actually making an exchange. Washington, who had heard dismal reports of the suffering of American prisoners in British hands, was outraged. He and the officers he had appointed "would not be made Instruments in so dishonorable a measure." Washington told the chagrined politicians that he personally resented the suggestion. "His Troops looked up to him as their protector, and . . . he would not suffer an opportunity to be lost of liberating every Soldier who was then in Captivity let the Consequence be what it might."

To the committee, such talk smacked of insubordination. The issue of the prisoner exchange was further complicated by the fact that the British insisted that Loyalists captured by the Americans be treated as prisoners of war rather than as traitors, and Washington was willing to concur in order to make the exchange possible. These two inflammatory issues were presented by the committee, more than a little annoyed by the dressing-down they had received from Washington, in a manner designed to cause irritation and hostility toward the general. Buried resentments and old animosities were brought to the surface at once, and produced what was probably the most severe crisis between the Congress and the general of the entire war.

Thomas Burke of North Carolina, who supported the half-pay measure, declared that it was "unjust to sacrifice the time and property of the men whose lives are every day exposed for us without any prospect of compensation, while so many who are protected by their valor and exertions are amassing princely fortunes. . . ." Indeed, it was the opinion of Washington and those who supported the proposal "that unless something of this kind is done we cannot long expect to have an Army, because the Officers being unable even to subsist on their pay have already expended much of their private property and would be entirely ruined were they to continue; in a word . . . that without it we can have no discipline, and almost no army."

From the first, the idea of half-pay for life aroused bitter opposition among many members of Congress. Henry Laurens, who usually supported Washington staunchly, wrote, "Had I heard of the Loss of half my Estate, the amount would not have involved my mind in such fixed concern as I feel from the introducing of this untoward project." To Laurens, whose own son would of course be a beneficiary of half-pay, the measure seemed "unjust, unconstitutional, unseasonable, a compliance under menace, dangerous, the reasoning from loss of virtue and insufficiency of the present pay not convincing." Laurens was not alone in resenting the fact that heavy pressure had been brought to bear on the delegates on the grounds that to refuse half-pay would be to lose the army. It seemed to him "unjust in the extreme, to compel thousands of poor industrious Inhabitants by contributions to pamper the Luxury of their fellow citizens many of whom will step out of the Army in the repossession of large acquired or inherited Estates. . . ." Laurens wrote extensively to William Livingston of New Jersey on the subject, ending with the comment that "a whole quire of paper would be too narrow to range in, upon the topic." It was fortunate for Livingston "that Genl. Gates an English Newspaper and two or three members of Congress steped in and knocked out of my head more than would have filled another sheet."

William Ellery of Rhode Island believed that the issue was so important that it ought to be "referred to the consideration of the states." The opponents of the measure argued that officers should serve from motives of patriotism, not of gain; that they "ought to distain motives of private interest. . . ." Granting half-pay might well be the first step in creating an armed force subservient to the wishes of Congress. Furthermore the role of the states in appointing regimental officers would be "reduced to nothing" (which was doubtless most desirable from Washington's point of view), and finally, "its effect will be to keep a great number of People idle Pensioners on the public who ought to be restored to useful industry. . . ."

There were many militia officers who had served as loyally and bravely as officers of the Continental Army, and they were bound to be affronted by such discrimination. Burke himself was willing to support half-pay if it were limited to those officers who "shall have regular Troops to command." "The arguments drawn from Patriotism and public spirit may be fine and specious," he wrote to the governor of North Carolina, "but I choose to trust to some principles of more certain, lasting and powerful influence for the defence of our country."

The debate on the half-pay issue grew so heated that a paper was circulated asking each member of Congress to pledge himself "to support order and preserve decency and politeness" in all discussions. The president of Congress nevertheless had to admonish "the House against disorder and intemperate reflections." In the words of the Connecticut delegates, "most disagreeable and serious debate resulted in a majority of eight states in favor of half-pay." The four states who were in the negative insisted on "the dangerous tendency of such a measure as being totally inconsistent with free States, repugnant to the principals [sic] in which this great controversy was begun and by which it must and ought to be defended." The opposition was intractable, and a compromise was finally reached: half-pay was approved for a period of seven years after the end of the war. Almost two months had been occupied with the question. Now, Laurens wrote, it had at last been "by the Grace of God . . . rid to Death, and from the Ashes, the inclosed Act of Congress of the 15th May, produced." (The vote for half-pay for seven years did not really settle the matter, however. Washington raised the issue again in August, 1780, and two months later he pressed Congress still another time. Finally, in October, 1780, Congress adopted half-pay for life.)

Washington's willingness to regard captured Tories as prisoners of war rather than as traitors also met "with very great and almost general opposition and indignation in Congress," one delegate wrote. It was attacked as "betraying our independence and in effect giving a license to the enemy to recruit in our country." The consequence was a letter, drafted by a Congressional committee, that seemed to Thomas Burke unnecessarily sharp and unpleasant in its tone. He and those members most loyal to Washington found it "exceptionable in many parts . . . and also in several charges against the General of suffering the Dignity and Honor of the United States to be injured. The whole indeed appeared . . . to indicate in the framers a disposition not friendly to the General, nor such as so good, so Important, so public spirited and Disinterested a Character deserves," Burke wrote. Although Burke was "not of the opinion that any individual is absolutely Essential to the success of our Cause," he admired Washington and was convinced that if he were to find himself unable to work with Congress and to submit his resignation, "his loss would be very severely felt, and would not be easily supplied." Burke therefore strongly objected to the wording of the letter and, finding his arguments to no avail, resorted to the expedient of absenting himself from Congress, thereby depriving it of a quorum and making it impossible for the delegates to approve the letter. This strategy infuriated James Lovell, the Massachusetts delegate, who wrote to Joseph Trumbull, "The Sickness or *Will* of one man out of those now here destroys [Congress's] existence."

Meanwhile Thomas Conway, who had been sent on useless errands to keep him occupied, wrote a querulous letter to Gates offering to resign "if you have no occasion for my services." Conway had become a distinct liability to Gates, who passed his letter on to Congress. His support there had almost dwindled away. This was the moment his opponents had been waiting for. Gouverneur Morris wrote to Washington that, afraid that "his [Conway's] Merits and our Misfortune in loosing him would become the Topick of Declamation," he had taken "the earliest Opportunity to express in the very strongest Terms my Satisfaction my Joy at the Receipt of the Letter from him and of Consequence to assign the Reasons why this event gave me so much pleasure." At this "Panegyrick dwindled to Apology and no Opposition was made to the main point of accepting his Resignation."

After Congress accepted Conway's resignation, that officer hung about blackguarding Washington until General Cadwalader challenged him to a duel and "stopped his lying mouth" with a bullet that wounded him in the face and neck. Believing that his wound was fatal, Conway wrote a letter of apology to Washington for the trouble he had caused him. When he recovered, Conway returned to France, served as governor of the French colonies in India, fought against the armies of the French Revolution, and died in exile in 1800.

The resignation of Conway and the temporary resolution of the question of half-pay for officers marked the end of the crisis between Congress and the commander in chief of the Continental Army. Those delegates who still had doubts about Washington banished or suppressed them, and Washington regained his famous equanimity.

The British in Philadelphia

THERE was, of course, general rejoicing among the thousand or more Tories in Philadelphia at the investment of that city by Howe and his army in September of 1777. They did not doubt the outcome of the rebellion in any event. Few of them could imagine that Washington's wretched legions could long continue to evade the crushing defeat that Howe's splendidly trained and equipped army must at last inflict on them. But they had had to endure the insolence and the persistent harassment of patriots or to lie very low, which had not been good for their morale. Now, with the British among them—the brilliant and aristocratic officers, the sturdy-looking soldiers in the splendid uniforms, the ample cannon, the invincible warships anchored in the river—the end of the insurrection seemed nearer at hand than ever. Joseph Galloway, back from New York, assumed the leadership of the Tory faction in the city. He and Ambrose Serle reinforced each other's confidence that those Americans who had betrayed their sovereign by their treacherous behavior would soon be brought to account.

Galloway and Serle discussed at length a scheme for seizing the members of Congress. Galloway had contact with a number of spies who assured him that, given sufficient financial support, they could recruit a force of Tories who would corral the delegates and carry them off to the

British lines. Indeed, he was assured that one hundred men had taken an oath to do the deed. "I never met a man with whom I could more perfectly agree in politics than Mr. Galloway," Serle noted, "nor one who more coolly investigates the Causes and Order of public Affairs." They were both convinced that without the authority of Great Britain, "America, unsettled and disputing with itself, would become first a Field of Blood, and then the Domain of some arbitrary Despot at the Head of an Army."

The British army, with all its multitudinous parts, made itself as comfortable in the city as it could. The degree of comfort depended, as it does in most armies, on the rank of the individuals involved. The officers, for the most part, fared well; the soldiers, on the whole, poorly. The Hessians were particularly uncomplimentary about the city itself. A Lieutenant Wiederhold described Philadelphia as "a meetingplace of all religions and nations, and consequently a mishmash of all sects and beliefs, and not less a *confluens canaillorum*" that "does not yield to Sodom and Gomorrah in respect to all the vices." Another Hessian officer was equally critical. The plants and animals were all undersized and the people sickly and prone to madness, "a craziness of the senses coming rather from poor than from overheated blood. . . . Not one person in a hundred has a healthy color." The Americans manufactured little, in this officer's opinion, and that of poor quality, but "the American, and particularly the Philadelphian, is so conceited as to think that no country on earth is more beautiful, happier, richer, or more flourishing than his hardly budding state. . . . If the honorable Count Penn would give me the whole country in exchange for my commission, with the condition that I should live here all my life, I would hardly take it."

Although the Hessian officers were far from complimentary about Philadelphia, the British were generally delighted to have fallen heir to such comfortable winter quarters. Besides the unspecified vices that were available to the enterprising, there were dances, concerts, ice-skating parties on the Schuylkill, and, after heavy snows, sleighing expeditions. The officers, much lionized by Tory ladies and their pretty daughters, found themselves involved in a constant round of parties. To keep up their end of things, the officers organized weekly balls at Smith's City Tavern. There were horse races on the common, at which the dashing Banastre Tarleton, who had performed such a valuable service for the American cause by capturing General Lee at Basking Ridge, distinguished himself and doubtless broke the hearts of a number of Philadelphia belles. Captain John André and Captain Oliver

Delancey of the Seventeenth Dragoons became the leading impresarios of the city, taking over the theater on South Street and producing *No One's Enemy But His Own* and *The Deuce Is In Him,* entertaining light comedies, for which Delancy painted the scenery. They were followed by *Henry IV, Part I,* and another comedy, *The Wonder,* or *A Woman Who Kept A Secret.* The proceeds from the sale of tickets were contributed to the relief of widows and orphans of British soldiers killed in the American service. The plays were so popular that servants had to be sent at four in the afternoon to hold seats for the performances at seven.

The theater company had its greenroom at the City Tavern, in whose handsome chambers the members of the cast and their guests dined after the theater. Gambling was endemic. Several young officers lost so heavily that they had to sell their commissions and return to England penniless. Then there were wild dinners at the Indian Queen and at the Cockpit in Moore's Alley, and it was rumored among the soberer citizens that the parties at the Bunch of Grapes Tavern were rough and bawdy. Some officers kept mistresses quite openly, and besides the local tarts the soldiers enjoyed the attentions of a shipload of amiable females imported from England for their pleasure. Two officers advertised for a young woman "who can occasionally put her hand to anything." The wages were high, and "no character" references were required. The implication was plain enough. Some Philadelphia serving girls had the intoxicating experience of being set up in quite handsome style by aristocratic young Englishmen. Major Williams of the artillery apparently picked out of the shipment of females a strikingly handsome girl "whom he displayed at retreat formation attired in regimental colors and riding in a carriage drawn by handsome horses and attended by a coachman and footman."

While the officers caroused and entertained themselves, discipline and good order among the troops understandably suffered. The best of armies with time on its hands is vulnerable to the pleasures of an occupied city and ingenuous in searching out dangerous diversions. Some soldiers were court-martialed and hanged for stealing (a sentence much more likely when the victim turned out to be a prominent Tory). Others were flogged to death.

The Hessians were a special problem. Their officers had a more casual attitude toward looting and wanton destruction than their British counterparts, who usually did their best to prevent it, if only because such acts might turn Tories into rebels. The Hessian soldiers, isolated by their inability to speak English and often bitterly resentful at having been shipped off to a foreign country to play second fiddle to the British—who continually condescended to them when they did not openly misuse them, as at Fort Mercer—became notorious for their acts of destructiveness. They quartered horses in commandeered homes and chopped holes in the floors to shovel the manure into the cellar. It was estimated that the damage to property by British and Hessian soldiers in Philadelphia during the occupation of that city amounted to one hundred and eighty thousand pounds, a huge sum for that day. In the words of Charles Stedman, who had grown up in Philadelphia and had returned as an officer on Howe's staff, "A want of discipline and proper subordination pervaded the whole army; and if disease and sickness thinned the American army encamped at Valley Forge, indolence and luxury perhaps did no less injury to the British troops at Philadelphia. . . . Dissipation . . . spread through, and indolence, and want of subordination, its natural concomitants."

Archibald Robertson, a young Scotsman of good family but without influential friends or relatives, was a skilled engineer, a gifted amateur artist, and a conscientious journal keeper. Robertson's brother, who was barrack master for the British army in Philadelphia, was simply relieved of his office without "any Accusation or granting a hearing in any respect and replaced by an officer with influence," Robertson wrote in his journal. "This . . . plainly shews the wide Difference of a Desspotical and Monarchial Government. Lord have mercy on the Poor People that are always subject to the peevish spleenitical whims of an unreasonably headstrong Despot."

Robert Morton, a sixteen-year-old Quaker, kept a diary during the period of Howe's occupation of Philadelphia. A Tory in his sympathies, he had watched helplessly as those among his friends who were considered pro-British had been shipped off to Winchester, Virginia, by the rebels. "O Philada, my native City," he wrote, "thou that hast heretofore been so remarkable for the preservation of thy Rights, now sufferest those who were the Guardians, Protectors, and Defenders of thy Youth, and who contributed their share in raising thee to thy present state of Grandeur and magnificence with a rapidity not to be paralleled in the World, to be dragged by a licentious mob from their near and dear connections, and by the hand of lawless power. . . ."

But the British soldiers proceeded to systematically pillage the vegetable gardens of the inhabitants of the city, and young Robert Morton's diary took on an increasingly critical and finally hostile note toward the redcoats and their officers. When he went to complain about the theft of his mother's cabbages and potatoes, he was treated rudely by the officer to whom he complained, and scarcely a month after the occupation of the city he wrote: "The ravages and wanton destruction of the soldiery will, I think, soon become irksome to the inhabitants, as many who depended upon their vegetables, etc. for the maintenance of their families, are now entirely and effectually ruined by the soldiers being permitted, under the command of their officers, to ravage and destroy their property. I presume the fatal effects of such conduct will shortly be very apparent by the discontent of the inhabitants, who are now almost satiated with British clemency, and numbers of whom, I believe, will shortly put themselves out of the British protection. . . ." It was plain that the arrogance of the British galled young Morton, and he could not resist taking pleasure in news of the success of Gates at Saratoga. His countrymen had "always appeared contemptible in the eyes of men who have uniformly dispised the Americans as a cowardly insignificant set of People."

When James Allen, in exile at Bethlehem, finally got a pass from Washington to enter Philadelphia (where his wife had preceded him), he wrote, "Here I feel an ease, security & freedom of speech, that has been long denied me . . . in many places in Bucks county & Jersey, the Tories have risin & brought their oppressors prisoners here. . . . This City is filled with fugitives from the country. The military have lived a very gay life the whole winter, & many very expensive entertainments given, at most of which I have been." With the country devastated and prices exorbitant in the city, Howe was preoccupied with social life, and "little regard is paid," Allen noted, "to the discontents of the people, & no satisfaction for the injury of their property. . . . It is evident the conduct of this war on the part of Gr Britain has been a series of mistakes both in the cabinet & the field."

Much of the blame for all this must of course be placed at Howe's door. Charles Lee, with his gift for the sharp phrase—a gift considerably greater than his military skills—wrote: "Howe shut his eyes, fought his battles, drank his bottle, had his little whore, advis'd his Counsellors, receiv'd his orders from North and Germane, one more absurd than the other, shut his eyes and fought again."

Francis Hopkinson wrote of Howe:

> Sir William he, snug as a flea,
> Lay all the time a snoring,
> Nor dreamed of harm as he lay warm
> In bed with Mrs. *L—ng*.

Mrs. Loring, "a flashing blonde" known in the army as the "Sultana," was the wife of Howe's commissary of prisoners, a man who neglected and abused his charges and was paid at Howe's direction the equivalent of some thirty thousand dollars for acquiescing in this extramarital arrangement. Indeed, we can speculate on whether both Burgoyne and Howe might not have done considerably better than they did if they could have managed to do without their mistresses, who at the very least were major distractions for both these susceptible officers. Living in General Cadwalader's handsome house on Second Street, Howe grew fatter and more indolent by the month. Rumor had it that he was to be relieved of his command and thereby, in a measure, disgraced. In wartime the most common way that politicians have of covering up their own blunders is by firing the generals whom they have assigned to carry them out. But in Howe's own mind, he was satisfied that he had done his best in a war with which he had little sympathy; a war run by idiots and bunglers in England who, knowing nothing of conditions in the colonies, expected him, much as Congress had expected Washington, to do impossible things with inadequate means. It was easier for Howe to issue proclamations calling on Americans "to repair to the British standard, promising them remission of their political sins," than to bestir himself in his comfortable quarters.

The administration of the whole army reflected its commander's self-indulgence and inattention. Graft, peculation, and corruption were rampant. It was rumored that Howe himself profited from an agreement with a military supplier named Coffin. Large fortunes were made by those with contracts to provide the army with food and supplies, and the soldiers were, at the same time, poorly fed. "A pack of self-interested puppies" waxed fat, while the graft that went on was, in the opinion of one observer, "enormous . . . indecent . . . both the troops and the treasury robbed." The hospitals were in the most dismal state of neglect, and in the military prison at Sixth and Walnut streets those prisoners of war who did not starve would have frozen to death if it had not been for gifts of clothing and food from the Quakers. The American prisoners were in the charge of Provost Marshal William Cunningham, a coarse and brutal man. More than two thousand American prisoners under his care died from disease and malnutrition. He was reported to have hanged some two hundred and fifty more for petty offenses without a trial of any kind. The prisoners were crowded into unventilated rooms without the most rudimentary sanitation; they were allowed a daily ration of four to six ounces of pork and a half-pound biscuit. Despite all

Washington's efforts to arrange for the exchange of prisoners, Howe was obdurate, and the Americans in Philadelphia continued to die of disease and starvation all through the winter of 1777–78.

Both British and Tories were much encouraged by American deserters who came into the British lines. In Captain John Montresor's journal, hardly a day passed without mention of deserters: "Deserted to us this morning a Sloop with 2 guns and 30 armed men. Also several deserters and a Trumpeter of Rebel Light Horse. Deserted to us 30 armed men with a Galley which they run ashore below Gloucester Point, while their Captain was gone for Orders." And again the next day: "Several deserters from the rebels came in by 4s and 6s." The following day: "About 50 deserters chiefly from General Wayne's brigade." Two days later, 60 "rebels" deserted. And so the record ran until one wondered that there could be any soldiers or sailors left in the Continental Army and Navy.

Ambrose Serle found additional comfort in a set of calculations about rebel manpower. Serle estimated that "not less than 50,000 rebels have perished . . . by Sickness & the Sword, the People here not having the requisite *Stamina* to endure the Rigors of Campaigns." Serle's arithmetic proved to his satisfaction that there were 150,000 male Americans of military age left. Of these, "one third at least may be estimated *Blacks*," which left 100,000. And if these were divided into "Friends, Enemies, and moderate Neuters," it must be assumed that half fell into the latter category, leaving some 50,000 white males able to bear arms, of whom at least 20,000 must be presumed to be loyal to the Crown. It followed from this that Washington must fill up his army from the scant 30,000 left. These figures proved to Serle "*why* Mr. Washington's Army is so low an Ebb. . . . It also proves, that the present British Force, duly exerted, has but little to fear; and that this unnatural Outrage, deprived of foreign Assistance & destitute of internal Succors, could not possibly last long, and of course that Peace might soon be restored to this distracted Land."

Yet even Serle grew sour at the perpetual assurances of the Tories. When William Allen, father of James and former chief justice of Pennsylvania, told him he was "positive that three fourths of the People are against Independency" and were ready to kick over the Congressional traces, Serle noted, "But, alas, they all prate & profess much; but, when You call upon them, they will *do* nothing. . . . To govern America, it must be conquered; and it must be no lax Government to retain the Conquest."

Needless to say, there was widespread criticism of Howe's inactivity in England. One wag proposed that he be elevated to the peerage with the title of Lord Delay-ware. Howe's days were, in any event, numbered. Lord North's new policy was to harass New England and the middle colonies by coastal raids, while concentrating the main military effort in the South, where, he was informed, thousands of loyal subjects waited only for some encouragement from the mother country to rise in arms and overthrow their oppressors. It was this notion—that large numbers, perhaps a substantial majority, of Americans were loyal to the Crown— that had been an important if not guiding assumption in turning the major British military effort first to New York and then to the Jerseys, both reputed to be teeming with Tories, and then finally to Pennsylvania. Since the hopes had been, for the most part, defeated in these areas, there was only the South left in which to pursue this *ignis fatuus*. This clutching at straws is, of course, characteristic of politicians fighting to save their political lives. Under such circumstances the limits of self-delusion seem virtually boundless. Each defeat is explained away as being somehow a triumph if only it were properly understood, and when the speciousness of these arguments becomes too transparent even for those who so solemnly affirm them, they quite readily find a scapegoat on whom to place the blame.

Howe had asked to be relieved in November. The word that his request had been granted reached him in April, and soon thereafter Clinton arrived from New York to assume command. Howe, despite his inactivity, retained his popularity with his men and officers.

It remained for a member of Howe's own staff, Charles Stedman, to make one of the most accurate analyses of the general's failure: "With one of the best appointed, in every respect, and finest armies (consisting of at least fourteen thousand effective men) ever assembled in any country, a number of officers of approved service, wishing only to be led to action, this dilatory commander . . . dragged out the winter, without doing any one thing to obtain the end for which he was commissioned."

Lieutenant Colonel Allan MacLean, a member of Howe's staff, gave a slightly more charitable character analysis. He described Howe as "a very honest man . . . and I believed a disinterested one" as well as a brave one who would make "a very good executive officer under another's command, but," he added, "he is not by any means equal to a C. in C." "I do not know of any employment," MacLean continued, "that requires so many great qualifications either natural or acquired as the Commander in Chief of an Army." Moreover, Howe had "none but silly fellows around about him—a great parcel of old women—most of them improper for American service." MacLean was careful to exempt Hugh Percy, Earl Cornwallis, Alexander Leslie, and Sir William Erskine.

Thus Sir William Howe, who did his best in the field and his worst in winter quarters, was recalled, and Sir Henry Clinton arrived in Philadelphia to replace him. The British had to exhaust their generals as well as the strategic possibilities before they would be ready to admit defeat. Howe prepared to leave for England, and Captain John André, displaying an arrogance that was eventually to prove fatal, arranged a grand party, a "Meschianza" or mock tournament, in his honor. The beautiful seventeen-year-old Peggy Shippen, soon to be the bride of General Benedict Arnold, had rehearsed a part in the pageant, but at the last moment her father had put his foot down and, in a tearful scene, forbade her participation; most of the other belles of Philadelphia, Whig and Tory alike, were present. (They paid the price by being omitted from the guest list when a ball was given some weeks later to celebrate the American occupation of the city.)

Two handsome pavilions were erected on either side of the square where the jousting was to take place. In one were seven young ladies "wearing dazzling Turkish costumes"; attached to their turbans were favors that they would award to the successful knights. The knights, dressed in red and white silk garments and mounted on splendidly caparisoned grey horses, took their positions in front of the ladies. Then their heralds, announced by trumpets, advanced to the center of the square and proclaimed the challenge:

"Knights of the Blended Rose, by me their Herald, proclaim and assert that the Ladies of the Blended Rose excel in wit, beauty and every accomplishment those of the *whole world;* and should any Knight or Knights be so hardy as to dispute or deny it, they are ready to enter the lists with them . . . according to the laws of ancient chivalry."

At this another herald with four trumpeters, dressed in black and orange and representing the Knights of the Burning Mountain, advanced to accept the challenge. The gauntlet was thrown down and picked up, the knights received lances from their pages, and "making a general salute to each other by a graceful movement of their lances, dashed at each other with their spears, then on a second charge fired their pistols and finally engaged each other with their swords." With honor satisfied, the ladies expressed the wish that the battle not be pressed to the death, and a procession was formed, accompanied by bands of music, to march through two triumphal arches. The first emphasized a naval theme in honor of Admiral Lord Howe—Neptune above, images of sailors with drawn cutlasses on either side. The second celebrated the glorious victories of his brother, the general. At the summit stood the figure of Fame "and various military trophies."

At the end of the second arch, the knights and Turkish ladies proceeded into a spacious hall made of panels painted (doubtless by Captain Delancey) in imitation of Siena marble. There the company seated itself to partake of "tea, lemonade and other cooling liquor." From here they proceeded to a ballroom, "decorated in a light, elegant style of painting. . . . These decorations were heightened by 85 mirrors, decked with rose-pink silk ribbands and artificial flowers; and in the intermediate space were 34 branches with wax-lights."

The dancing continued until ten o'clock, when the windows of the ballroom were thrown open "and a magnificent bouquet of rockets began the fire-works," some twenty different exhibitions arranged by the chief engineer. At the end came the most spectacular display of all. The triumphal arch "was illuminated amidst an uninterrupted flight of rockets and bursting of balloons. The military trophies on each side assumed a variety of transparent colours. The shell and flaming heart on the wings sent forth Chinese fountains, succeeded by fire-pots. Fame appeared at top, spangled with stars, and from her trumpet blowing the following device in letters of light, *Tes Lauriers sont immortels* (Your laurels are immortal)."

André had written a poem to be declaimed in praise of Howe:

> Chained to our arms, while Howe the battle led,
> Still round those files her wings shall Conquest spread.
> Loved though he goes, the spirit still remains
> That with him bore us o'er these trembling plains.

Clinton had his more modest lines:

> Nor fear but equal honors shall repay
> Each hardy deed where Clinton leads the way.

The fireworks and declamation were followed by a magnificent supper at midnight. Sumptuous food was served at richly laid tables lighted by several thousand candles, again reflected in 56 large mirrors; 430 places were set, and there were 1,200 dishes, "24 black slaves in oriental dresses, with silver collars and bracelets . . . bending to the ground as the General and Admiral approached the saloon . . . a *coup d'oeil* beyond description magnificent." It was also beyond description in bad taste. There was, for one thing, a serious doubt that Howe's laurels were immortal. He himself must have been a singularly insensitive man if he did not feel very keenly the irony of the whole lavish performance. The frivolity, extravagance, and ostentation of the Meschianza were entirely inappropriate in a city where many people had experienced the distresses of war, and where American prisoners were starving in their fetid cells.

The Meschianza, performed two weeks after the Grand Parade at Valley Forge, said a good deal, little of it complimentary, about the quality of British life. The more austere Tories, and especially the Quakers among them, were appalled at the vulgarity of spirit. Even Galloway called it "a farce of Knight errantry," and a Philadelphia Whig reported hearing a British officer, asked by a little boy the difference between the two companies of knights, reply: "Why, child, the Knights of the Burning Mountain are Tom Fools, and the Knights of the Blended Rose are damned fools. I know of no other difference between 'em."

"What will Washington think of all this?" Galloway asked a Tory friend. No one, certainly, could have been more severe than the Tory historian of New York, Thomas Jones. Jones, who blamed the Howes for not having brought the Revolution to a quick end by resolute campaigning, called it a "ridiculous farce." "The exhibition of this 'triumphal Meschianza' will be handed down to posterity," he added, "as one of the most ridiculous, undeserved, and unmerited triumphs ever performed. Had the General been properly rewarded for his conduct while Commander-in-Chief in America, an execution, and not a Meschianza, would have been the consequence."

It is unfortunate for Howe that our last view of him is as the administrator of an occupied city. Howe was plainly no garrison soldier. His laziness and self-indulgence revealed him, in that situation, at his worst. He deserves to be remembered at his best—as the skillful and sometimes brilliant tactician who bested Washington in half-a-dozen engagements, who fought his army well, and who was beloved by his officers and men. He had an abundance of human failings, but it can hardly be counted among them that he was a staunch Whig who was favorably disposed to the colonists that he had been charged with subduing. He wished, therefore, to subdue them as gently and considerately as possible. He continued to hope that after each setback they (and the North ministry as well) would come to their senses and agree to an "imperial system" that would substantially guarantee their essential liberties within the British empire.

He was certainly far from a vindictive or ruthless conqueror. He was an English gentleman conscious of being sent on a distasteful mission to put down some unruly members of the family. He was also a professional soldier, so he did that job, by and large, as well as he knew how. Since the cowardly colonials were expected to flee for their lives, he got little credit for his victories. Where one victory against a European army would probably have been enough to insure his fame as a great general, all his victories in America served to do little more than raise the question of why the Continental Army continued to exist. Its survival was blamed on Howe's lack of vigor and repeated failure to pursue a defeated enemy.

The facts were rather different and more complex. The American soldiers had, from the beginning, fought on occasion with what seemed to the British a surprising ferocity. And Washington, if he was not Howe's match as a tactician, was a tenacious and stubborn opponent, always dangerous and especially resourceful in selecting strong defensive positions. It is important to keep in mind that Howe was most often criticized for failing to attack Washington. But in an attack against fortified positions every advantage that the British had, except for their superiority in artillery, was nullified or at least greatly diminished. The superior British staffwork, which was an important and in some cases critical factor in open battles of maneuver, was rendered nugatory, as were the better order and discipline of the British soldiers, the skill of a trained and experienced officer corps, and, finally, the vastly greater experience of the British army at all levels of command. The Americans had demonstrated in the most conclusive fashion at Bunker Hill, and had reaffirmed at Fort Mercer, that, properly entrenched in stout fortifications and well officered, they could take a deadly toll of anyone who attacked them. (There were certainly notable exceptions, such as Fort Washington.) If in the face of such evidence, Howe had made reckless attacks that resulted in disastrous casualties, he would have properly received far more scathing criticism and experienced an even prompter eclipse of his military reputation. The principal charge of dilatoriness that his critics leveled against him had to do with his failure to attack Washington's wretched army at Valley Forge. But, while Washington overestimated the number of Howe's troops, Howe in turn overestimated Washington's force. Howe had the positions at Valley Forge carefully reconnoitered by experienced officers, and they were strongly of the opinion that if the position was not impregnable, an attack on it would be very costly. Moreover, the weather conditions were far from favorable for a campaign—snow, rain, and mud were constant impediments; and the British soldiers and officers were not trained for winter operations or accustomed to the rigors of the severe American weather. Nor could they as professional soldiers be expected to accept the hardships endured by the Americans in the cause of liberty.

Beyond all this, Howe's intelligence source encouraged him to believe what the Americans themselves greatly feared—that Washington's army would simply disintegrate under the terrible rigors of a winter at Valley Forge. There were no laurels to be won in an arduous attack against starving, ill, half-naked soldiers that could compensate for the fact that these men, fighting like cornered rats, might destroy a large part of Britain's finest army.

13

The French Alliance

THE most significant event of the spring of 1778 was the alliance between Congress and the French court. It had been the major goal of American diplomacy since the beginning of the war. As early as December of 1775, Franklin had written to a friend at The Hague to ask him on behalf of Congress to make discreet inquiries in diplomatic circles about the disposition "of the several courts with respect to . . . assistance or alliance." "We have hitherto applied to no foreign power," Franklin wrote. "We are using the utmost industry in endeavoring to make saltpeter, and with daily increasing success. Our artificers are also every where busy in fabricating small arms, casting cannon, etc. Yet both arms and ammunition are much wanted. . . ."

There were two views in Congress and throughout the states about the desirability of foreign alliances. Richard Henry Lee, one of the more radical of the patriot leaders, was convinced that a military alliance with the French was, ultimately, the only hope of securing American independence. On the other hand Thomas Paine in *Common Sense* had warned against European wars and intrigues, and there was certainly a degree of provincialism in all the states that was generally opposed to foreign entanglements. France was, after all, the traditional and bitter enemy of the American colonists. They had fought a series of costly wars with the French and their Indian allies in Canada. Many Americans had lost their lives in these constantly renewed and generally inconclusive contests—brought on, usually, by events across the ocean that had little to do with the colonists themselves. Above all, France was the center of Catholic power in Europe and in the New World as well, and Catholicism was, to devout Protestants, the antichrist, the creature of the devil, determined to root up and destroy the true Protestant faith.

Thus reasons of state, pure and simple, rather than any tenderness of sentiment toward the French induced Congress to try initially to secure supplies, especially guns and powder, from the French, and then to seek a military and naval alliance. And it was no sentimental attachment to republican principles that induced the French to give aid to the Americans. In the French view, every British soldier who fell on American soil, killed or wounded by a French musket and French powder and ball in the hands of an American rebel, strengthened France as surely as if the bullet had been fired by a French grenadier—and at much less cost to France than if the damage had been directly inflicted by a French soldier. Cannon and muskets and powder, even in large quantities, were much less expensive than soldiers. As John Adams wrote in an autobiographical fragment, "Some gentlemen [in Congress] doubted of the sentiments of France; thought she would frown upon us as rebels, and be afraid to countenance the example." To this argument, Adams pointed out that "it was the unquestionable interest of France that the British Continental Colonies should be independent." Not only were French pride and jealousy engaged, but also France's "rank, her consideration in Europe and even her safety and independence were at stake." In Adams' words, "The interest of France was so obvious, and her motives so cogent, that nothing but a judicial infatuation of her councils could restrain her from embracing us. . . ."

Certain individuals involved in politics cannot follow a policy or line of action without committing themselves to it heart and soul. If expediency dictates a particular course, these idealists must persuade themselves that it is a noble and unimpeachable course. They must believe that the expedient ally is, like them, prompted by the most exalted motives, and that the people who inhabit the country with whose government the alliance has been or is to be made are exemplary people—just, friendly, generous to a fault. On the other side there are those cynical souls, more experienced in the ways of the world, who cling stubbornly to the notion that marriages of convenience are just that. They are not, by definition, love affairs; they are mutually beneficial arrangements entered into for the achievement of particular ends. To encumber them with a great baggage train of superficial and irrelevant sentiments is to complicate them and place those who insist on dragging such baggage around with them at a substantial disadvantage.

These diverse views were to be found in the Continental Congress, of course, and they had a conspicuous influence on the conduct of American foreign policy. While the military struggle continued on land and sea, the ideological war went on in Congress between those delegates who, having committed themselves to the French alliance, wished to repose perfect trust and confidence in that nation, and those who, accepting the necessity of the alliance, had no illusions about the French motives in making it. In France much the same kind of division existed with this important exception: in that nation it was the liberal intellectuals, the radicals, the reformers, and the prospective revolutionaries who loved the honest American farmers and virtuous republicans; but they had little to do with the formation of French policy, which was in the hands of tough, shrewd, unsentimental politicians like Vergennes—who did not give a fig for American independence unless it clearly served the interests of France. And one certainly could not fault him for that; that was his job; that was why he was the king's minister. The result, however, was that those Americans charged with the practical, on-the-scene diplomacy were like men with one hand tied behind their backs. They were, for the most part, as tough and shrewd as their French counterparts, but they were inhibited by those sentimental politicians in Congress who were so moved by the generosity, majesty, benignity, and power of France that they were willing to abandon their foreign policy to the direction of this Exalted Majesty's ministers rather than support the laborious efforts of their own emissaries, who, as John Adams noted bitterly, were often in the position of swimmers negotiating for their lives in the midst of a school of sharks.

But on the initial steps there was little dispute. Americans needed military supplies desperately, especially powder, and to a slightly lesser degree, flints and lead and muskets. There was no inclination to quibble about the source.

The French position was a simple one. She wished to do all within her power to encourage American independence as the surest means of weakening her rival, Great Britain. On the other hand, it would be disastrous for France to involve itself if it turned out that England could quickly and easily subdue the colonies, for the British would then have the opportunity and the excuse to complete the destruction of French power and influence already carried so far by her successes in the Seven Years' War. It thus followed quite naturally that French policy was to give as much aid as possible to the Americans unofficially, being careful to provide the British with no excuse to treat France as a belligerent until that day when it became evident that Great Britain had little chance of subduing the colonists and was indeed so deeply involved in America as to be fair game for France. Then the French could safely enter the fray.

Meantime, the Comte de Vergennes encouraged that astonishing adventurer Pierre Augustin Caron de Beaumarchais to provide assistance to the Americans. Beaumarchais, the author of the play *The Marriage of Figaro,* later set to music by Mozart, proclaimed the coming of a new day of equality when every Frenchman would be proud to be called simply "citizen," and hereditary titles and privileges would be discarded. His imagination had been fired by the determined resistance of American patriots to the vast power of Great Britain, and he had written the king in September, 1775: "I say, Sire, that such a nation must be invincible." A few months later he again wrote to Louis XVI, "The famous quarrel between America and England, imposes upon each power the necessity of examining well in what manner the event of this separation can influence it, and either serve it or injure it. . . ." Beaumarchais went on to argue that *"the Americans must be assisted."* Britain could triumph over America if at all only "by an enormous expenditure of men and money." In order to compensate for such losses, the British would surely seize the remaining French islands in the Caribbean. On the other hand, if Britain forced the colonies to submit, the Americans would blame the French for not coming to their aid and unite their arms with those of Britain against the French possessions in America. The true policy of France was to prevent England and America "from completely triumphing over the other." This could only be done by giving such aid to the Americans as would "put their forces on an equality with those of England, but nothing beyond." By this means France, in controlling the outcome of the conflict, would be able to impose terms that would greatly strengthen it in relation to both England and America.

Beaumarchais had conferred with Arthur Lee, an American diplomat, in London, and in June of 1776, with the encouragement of Vergennes and the covert financial backing of the government, he had set up a private trading company under the name of Roderique Hortalez et Compagnie to "send help to your friend in the shape of powder and ammunition in exchange for tobacco." Beaumarchais wrote to Congress in the summer of 1776, "The respectful esteem that I bear towards that brave people who so well defend their liberty . . . has induced me to form a plan concurring in this great work, by establishing an extensive commercial house, solely for the purpose of serving you in Europe . . . to supply you with necessaries of every sort, to furnish you expeditiously and certainly with all articles—clothes, linens, powder, ammunition, muskets, cannon, or even gold for the payment of your troops. . . . Your deputies . . . will find in me a sure friend, an asylum in my house, money in my coffers, and every means of facilitating their operations, whether of a public or a secret nature." Beaumarchais—as good as his word—had secured for Congress 200 brass four-pound cannon; 200,000 pounds of powder; 20,000 muskets; and innumerable bombs, cannonballs, bayonets, clothes, and lead for musket balls.

Congress, Beaumarchais advised, should channel everything through him. It should have no other French representatives or agents "in order that there may be no idle chattering or time lost," and ships carrying American goods should be assigned to his commercial house. His agents would arrange for prohibited cargoes from America to be landed in French ports, and he would smooth away every difficulty and problem. "Notwithstanding," he wrote, "the open opposition which the King of France, his ministers and the agents of administration show, and ought to show, to everything that carries the appearance of violating foreign treaties and the internal ordinances of the kingdom, I dare promise to you, gentlemen, that my indefatigible zeal shall never be wanting to clear up difficulties, soften prohibitions, and, in short, facilitate all operations of a commerce which my advantage, much less than yours, has made me undertake with you." In return, Beaumarchais wrote, "I request of you, gentlemen, to send me next spring, if it is possible for you, ten or twelve thousand hogsheads, or more if you can, of tobacco from Virginia of the best quality. . . ."

It is small wonder that Congress was dazzled by such a missive, hinting, as it did, of almost limitless influence in high places and presenting as evidence of that influence a marvelous assortment of acutely needed supplies. Gratitude is one of the noblest (if, as it sometimes seems, one of the least frequent) human sentiments, and it is to the credit of Congress that it should have felt vast relief and an accompanying gratitude at this largess showered upon them. At the same time, it was a startling letter to delegates unschooled in the intricacies of European diplomatic intrigue.

The whole arrangement seemed thoroughly unbusinesslike. Was the tobacco in payment for the supplies that Beaumarchais was furnishing? If so, it was entirely inadequate. Did this hint at payment not mentioned in the letter? Or was it simply expected that Congress would do its best and Beaumarchais and the French court would do their best? It was hard to believe that the French king (if, indeed, he was the source of the supplies) was interested in ten or twelve thousand hogsheads of tobacco. Arthur Lee believed, on the basis of his discussions with Beaumarchais, that the supplies were in effect gifts of the French government. Silas Deane believed otherwise. And Beaumarchais, who could, presumably, have easily cleared the matter up, left things in a state of uncertainty that in the end reflected on his motives and, by analogy, on those of Deane. Some members of Congress were convinced that Hortalez and Company was a scheme by which both Deane and Beaumarchais lined their own pockets.

What is clear is that Beaumarchais received a large secret subsidy from both France and Spain in his role as a supplier of military equipment for the American colonies. The supplies were desperately needed. Beaumarchais had first persuaded the king to give support to the Americans; he then became the channel through which those supplies flowed. In this manner he performed an essential service for the American cause.

One important consequence of the concern of many members of Congress with the maneuvers of Beaumarchais and Deane was that Benjamin Franklin and Arthur Lee were sent to check up on them. Franklin came, almost at once, to embody for French intellectuals the spirit of republican America. He was already one of the most famous literary and scientific figures of the day, and he had just those qualities that Frenchmen found endearing. That shrewd and not infrequently immoral moralist seemed to represent all the virtues of the simple farmer. They saw in him Crèvecoeur's American farmer, a new type of human being, uncowed by hereditary authority, secular or ecclesiastic, his mind unclouded by false teachings and priestly superstitions. Crèvecoeur of course had not dreamed up this idealized and idolized figure by himself. The French intellectuals, who drew their inspiration from Rousseau's natural man, had fashioned him—a figure of natural virtue, uncorrupted by the sophistries and elegant vulgarities of a decadent European society. Crèvecoeur had merely discovered him in the American wilderness.

Franklin, a man as subtle and devious as a French diplomat, as sophisticated in his tastes as the most decadent aristocrat, was nonetheless cast by the French in the role of a simple American agriculturist. And Franklin—editor, author, courtier, scientist, inventor, sensualist, and roué—played the role with zest. He even wore a beaver cap, which was more enchanting to his admirers than the most bejeweled crown could have been. Everywhere in Paris he was feted, admired, and acclaimed. His picture was reproduced on snuffboxes, plates, vases, and commodes and sold by the thousands. Enterprising businessmen sold seats at places where the people of Paris could watch him ride by in his coach. Elegant ladies vied for his favors. He lay in bed much of the morning receiving visits from countesses and baronesses, and, of course, he was escorted to the Academy of Sciences, the Valhalla of French intellectual life. At the Academy was the grand master of French philosophy, Voltaire. The members raised "a general cry" that the two great philosophers be introduced to each other. "This was done," John Admas reported, "and they bowed and spoke to each other. This was no satisfaction; there must be something more. Neither of our Philosophers seemed to divine what was wished or expected; they, however, took each other by the hand. But this was not enough; the clamor continued, until the explanation came out. *'Il faut s'embrasser, a la Française,'* The two aged actors," Adams noted, "upon this great theatre of philosophy and frivolity then embraced each other, by hugging one another in their arms, kissing each other's cheeks, and then the tumult subsided. And the cry immediately spread through the whole kingdom, and, I suppose, over all Europe, *'Qu'il etait charmant de voir embrasser Solon et Sophocle!'* . . ." The reference to Solon was a tribute to Franklin's role in the framing of the much-admired Pennsylvania constitution of 1776.

The tableau, some suggested, marked the emergence of a new era that would be distinguished by a reign of Reason. John Adams, who did not believe that Reason could ever rule in affairs of man and certainly did not believe that it was present in the Pennsylvania constitution, was a somewhat cynical observer of the scene.

It was Adams' view then and later that Franklin was a consummate artist in the nascent field of personal publicity. His fame, according to Adams, was the result of "more artificial modes of diffusing, celebrating and exaggerating his reputation than were ever before or since practiced in favor of any individual. . . . Franklin's fame was universal. His name was familiar to government and people, to kings, courtiers, nobility, clergy and philosophers, as well as plebians, to such a degree that there was scarcely a peasant or a citizen, a *valet de chambre*, coachman or footman, a lady's chambermaid, or a scullion in a kitchen who was not familiar with it, and who did not consider him as a friend to human kind. . . . He was considered as a citizen of the world, a friend to all men and an enemy to none."

He was in fact the first universal hero, the first great democratic figure of modern times. The popular imagination, as much as it distorted the actual Franklin, that master of satire and irony, was right in its perception that he was the archetypal man of the new epoch, who, with his precepts of thrift and hard work, was to place his mark on the American psyche as surely as Washington himself.

The fact that the French loved him so passionately did not change the outcome of the American struggle for independence, but it did help to keep open the purse strings, loosened originally by nothing more exalted than calculating self-interest. While it was certainly the case that the French government supported the American rebels out of self-interest rather than sentiment, Franklin's enormous popularity may have helped to augment the flow of goods to the Continental Congress.

When Franklin and Lee joined Deane, the ill-assorted trio tried to agree on a course of action. Important as it was to maintain the flow of supplies, the commissioners had been charged with attempting to secure a military alliance. Deane was in favor of simply going to Vergennes and saying, in effect, "If you don't come to our aid with soldiers and ships as well us supplies and money, we will be forced to capitulate to Great Britain." Franklin was opposed to such an extreme position. It might well alarm the French and convince them that the American cause was doomed in any event. "He was clearly of the opinion that we could maintain the contest, and successfully too, without any European assistance."

Lee was also opposed, on the grounds that, thus confronted, the French might stop the assistance they were already giving through Beaumarchais. The important thing was to maintain this flow and, if possible, to increase it. Developments were, as it turned out, to outrun their expectations.

On December 6, 1777, the three Congressional commissioners met Vergennes' secretary at Passy. The news of the Battle of Germantown had encouraged the French to believe that the Americans were capable of encountering the British in conventional warfare and of giving an excellent account of themselves. The word of Burgoyne's surrender at Saratoga made it clear that the British had a long war ahead of them. The moment that Vergennes had been waiting for had arrived.

Through his secretary he sent his congratulations and the crucial word: "He said as there now appeared no doubt of the ability and resolution of the states to maintain their independency, he could assure them it was wished they would reassume their former position of an alliance . . . and that it could not be done too soon. . . ." If France's ally, Spain, was willing, a treaty might be concluded promptly, and French troops might well be in the field in a few months.

Six days later the Americans met at Versailles with Vergennes. The French minister was agreeable, even charming. The terms of the treaty proposed by the Americans were, in the main, acceptable. France was too generous, Vergennes implied, to take advantage of the desperate needs of Congress to drive a hard bargain and impose conditions that the Americans "might afterwards repent and endeavor to retract." However, there was a joker. Spain's interests must be considered, and Spain was sensitive to the fact that Virginia claimed land running to the Pacific Ocean and thus conflicting with Spain's claim to California. The commissioners answered that they thought it better to omit all discussions of the area west of the Mississippi. Vergennes acquiesced and left his secretary, Conrad Gerard, to work out the details of the treaty.

The next day Vergennes sat down to write to the French ambassador at Madrid. The time was ripe and Spain, like France, must seize the moment lest it pass. The Spanish indeed stood to gain more than the French, since, according to Vergennes, the mainland possessions of the Spanish in the Caribbean were far more tempting to British greed than the French islands. Spain might also recover Florida, since it was natural to assume that the Americans could not "care much about a thing which they do not yet possess, and which does not even seem of major importance to them." Finally, separating the American colonies from their British masters in the long run was so important a consideration that even a war waged under certain disadvantages would be a modest price to pay. It was, therefore, "*aut nunc aut nunquam* [now or never]." "Events," Vergennes wrote, "have surprised us; they have marched much more rapidly than we could have expected. . . ."

On January 9, Conrad Gerard reported to Vergennes on the results of his conference with the commissioners. He had begun by pledging them to secrecy. He then informed them that His Majesty Louis XVI had decided to support the American struggle and that "he only desired to bring about irrevocably and completely the independence of the United States; that he would find therein his essential interest in the weakening of his natural enemy, and that this important and permanent interest would render the American cause in future common to France. . . ." However, His Majesty could not yet announce an action that would have the effect of a declaration of war with Great Britain. Meanwhile, the United States must by no means enter into any sort of agreement with Great Britain that would compromise their independence in the slightest degree, especially any commercial treaty by means of which Britain might reserve American trade for itself.

Franklin had alarmed Gerard by his assumption that the treaty "inferred an immediate war." That was absolutely out of the question, Gerard replied. It seemed to Franklin that the French wanted too much. They wished to bind the hands of the Americans against entering into any treaty negotiations with Great Britain that did not include "the recognition of full and absolute independence both in politics and trade," but at the same time, the French government was unwilling to make any public declaration of war. The Americans asked for time to consider—a day perhaps. Gerard proposed an hour. The Americans conferred, and when Gerard returned Franklin was busy framing a statement, the general effect of which was that "the immediate conclusion of a treaty of commerce and alliance would induce the Deputies [the Commissioners] to close their ears to any proposal which should not have as its basis entire liberty and independence, both political and commercial. . . ."

This was the concession that Gerard had been instructed to exact. Now that he had secured it, he could announce, he told the surprised commissioners, that he had been instructed by His Majesty to tell them that they might have a treaty whenever they thought it would be necessary. This was precisely what the commissioners had been striving for. But there was another catch. It was the king's wish that there should be two treaties; the first, the public one, would provide for "peace, friendship and commerce, and the second . . . eventual alliance." The first would have the effect of recognizing American independence. The second might then be worked out more carefully, taking into account the particular needs of the Americans. "The Deputies [the American commissioners]," Gerard reported to Vergennes, "applauded this recital with a sort of transport. . . ."

By the terms of the treaty of amity and commerce, France recognized the independence of the states and undertook to provide Congress with supplies. Although this was tantamount to a declaration of war on England, no such declaration was made. The treaty of alliance was kept secret. It provided for naval and military assistance, but it would only become effective in the event of actual fighting between England and France. Thus Vergennes left it to England to provoke hostilities, knowing that the British ministry could not ignore the French challenge. The treaty of alliance gave Congress a free hand to try to seize Canada and Bermuda and accepted the French interest in the British West Indies. Neither country was to conclude a treaty without the other's consent. And Congress was to agree to no peace that did not recognize American independence.

When news of the French alliance reached the Americans in April, there was general rejoicing. Tench Tilghman, one of Washington's aides, expressed a common conviction when he wrote, "It seems agreed on all hands that the American War cannot be supported [by England] in conjunction with a French one." Most patriots were confident that the entry of France into the war "must unhorse the present Ministry and all their Connections" and thereby bring a speedy end to the war.

The committee for foreign affairs wrote to the Congressional commissioners at Paris: "Our Affairs have now a universally good appearance. Everything at home and abroad seems verging towards a happy and permanent Period. We are preparing for either War or Peace, for altho' we are fully persuaded that our Enemies are wearied, beaten and in despair, yet we shall not presume too much on that belief, and the rather it is our fixt determination to admit no terms of Peace but such as are fully in Character with the dignity of Independent States and consistent with the Spirit and intention of our alliances on the Continent of Europe."

Patrick Henry belonged to the Richard Henry Lee camp of idealistic patriots for whom France could do no wrong. "I look at the past condition of America," he wrote Lee, "as a dreadful precipice from which we have escaped by means of the generous French, to whom I will be everlastingly bound by the most heartfelt gratitude. . . . Salvation to America depends upon our holding fast our attachment to them."

Not all Americans were so sanguine, however. Some of the delegates who had serious misgivings about a treaty between a republic and a Catholic monarchy far more authoritarian then England herself, suppressed such feelings because they wished to see England driven out of Canada and thought a French alliance the best way to insure such an outcome. William Ellery of Rhode Island was typical of this group. He was convinced that the treaty would result in war between France and England "unless Britain can bring down her proud stomache to relish sound policy, to acknowledge our independence, and make peace with us. Whether the haughty insolent Thane can stoop to this or not you are a good judge. I should with you, perhaps, have been willing that France should have continued in her usual way to have supported us, had I not in contemplation the divesting of Britain of every foot of land upon this Continent. I think it absolutely necessary to a future, lasting peace that we should be possessed of Canada, Nova Scotia and the Floridas, which we cannot so well effect without the open assistance of France. . . ."

Samuel Mather of Massachusetts wrote to Sam Adams in April, 1778, "The Benevolence, generous Benevolence, tendered from France, must needs be as acceptable, as it was seasonable. . . . But you know, my honored Friend that, as Kings govern Kingdoms, Interest governs Kings. Therefore the Grand Monarque and his Ministry, no Doubt, will from the Motive of Interest, endeavor to engross the Whole Trade of these American States." The question was, should America consent "to be monopolized by any Power, however inclined and able to supply and help us?"

Andrew Adams, a delegate to Congress from Connecticut, was even more skeptical. "I must freely own," he wrote, "I don't feel myself so compleatly flush'd upon this Occasion as many do: I cant say but it be attended with the happy Consiquences expected; but when I view the Matter upon a larger Scale sundry Questions suggest themselves for our Condideration; I was fully of Oppinion that the War was drawing to a speedy issue . . . upon this View of the Case I would quere wither the arrival of this Fleet will not be a Means of lengthining out the War, and also ley us under an Obligation of affording France an arm'd force in Case they Need it . . . besides would it not be much to our Advantage had we settled the present Controversy in our favour without a foreign Aid. Under such Idears I have never been fond of the Assistance of any foreign Power: However I am no Adept in Politicks . . . and leave the Decision to abler Politicians or future time."

If some members of Congress had doubts about the wisdom of the French alliance, these were not shared by Washington. A staff officer noted that the news of the treaty broke Washington's iron reserve; he seemed near tears of relief and joy, and he decided to celebrate the great event with a military review and appropriate ceremonies by the revitalized army. There should be a splendid *feu de joye*. Orders for the Grand Parade were issued on the same day. "It having pleased the Almighty Ruler of the Universe," the orders began, "propitiously to defend the Cause of the United American States & finally, by raising us up a powerful Friend among the Princes of the Earth, to establish our

Liberty & Independence upon lasting Foundations, it becomes us to set apart a day for gratefully acknowledging the divine Goodness & celebrating the important Event which we owe to his benign interposition."

At nine o'clock in the morning there was to be a religious service of Thanksgiving. After this the brigades were to be formed into battalions of equal strength, and after a signal by cannon shot, they were to march to their places in the line of battle, the right of the first line to be commanded by Major General Lord Stirling, the left wing by the Marquis de Lafayette, and the Baron de Kalb commanding the second line. Moreover, "Each man is to have a gill of rum."

According to the report of John Laurens, "the line was formed with admirable rapidity and precision. Three salutes of artillery thirteen [guns] each, and three discharges of a running fire by the musquetry where each company fired in uninterrupted succession around the hollow formation of lines facing each [other] were given in honour of the King of France, the friendly European powers, and the United American States."

Laurens rhapsodized over "the order with which the whole was conducted, the beautiful effect of the running fire which was executed to perfection, the martial appearance of the troops [which] gave sensible pleasure to everyone present" and demonstrated most dramatically the effect of Von Steuben's reforms.

After the *feu de joye*, the officers gathered under a canopy with those wives who were in camp for a "cold collation," and "triumph beamed on every countenance. The greatness of mind and policy of Louis XVI were extold, and his long life toasted with as much sincerity as that of the British king used to be in former times." Washington, having against all odds survived the cruel winter, "received such proofs of the love and attachment of his officers as must have given him the most exquisite feelings." Those who had doubted him were ashamed of themselves and loved him more fervently than ever. As young John Laurens wrote his father: "If ever there was a man in the world whose moderation and patriotism fitted him for the command of a Republican army he is. . . ."

It was certainly a moment of exultation for Washington. Now, with the iron clutch of winter relaxed, with spring flowers and budding trees, with the dogwood whitening those patches of brush and saplings too insignificant to attract the soldiers' axes, the army, like the stirring earth, had come back to life. It was indeed a kind of resurrection—the army dead and now reborn out of Washington's patient endurance. And the nation was somehow created in that rebirth, so that memory, which knew better than historians the nature of essences, would not let it go. Like grass out of the bleak earth, love had grown out of suffering and despair. That was all Washington's doing. So as the soldiers, somewhat refurbished but still ragged enough, now fired their muskets so precisely, Washington must have felt that however long the outcome of the struggle might be delayed, it was now assured.

Amid all the celebration there was one sour note. The strained relations between Washington and Congress over the issue of half-pay and prisoner exchange were reflected in the fact that Congress did not see fit to inform Washington of the secret articles of the French treaty, which he knew only through rumor. John Laurens, who regularly acted as a kind of private hot line between Washington and his father, the president of Congress, had hinted to the senior Laurens that it was "a galling circumstance, for him to collect the most important intelligence piece-meal, and as they choose to give it, from gentlemen who come from York . . . he merits unrestrained confidence."

Henry Laurens wrote back that he had "suffered not a little Chagrin" over the reluctance of Congress to convey the secret clauses to Washington. He certainly had as much right to hear them as "the Member who lay snoring fuddled [drunk] on one of the Benches while those papers were reading." Laurens was convinced "the omission was not the effect of design in a majority who love and Esteem that valuable Man. . . ." Laurens thought that the committee on foreign affairs had, indeed, not always been as frank and open as they might have been. "This is unpleasant ground to walk on," Laurens concluded, "I must retire from it. Much former history should be recited, the State of parties introduced and other circumstances extremely disagreeable to me, in order to give you a tolerable understanding of matters alluded to."

For the British and Tories in Philadelphia, the hope that the Americans would be "deprived of foreign Assistance" was shattered by word of the French treaty of amity and commerce, and "in consequence a War with that Power, & therefore with Spain, was inevitable." It was to God alone that the British must now trust. "Surely, the righteous One," Ambrose Serle the tireless diarist wrote, would not "prosper the Iniquity of our Enemies, nor suffer a Cause, founded in Falsehood, Baseness, & Rebellion, to succeed."

Word of the French alliance was followed by even more disheartening news. The rumor spread through the city that Germain, afraid that the French fleet might sail up the Delaware and trap the British army there, had ordered the troops to be withdrawn from Philadelphia. Howe, it was reported, had told a dismayed Joseph Galloway that he had best try to make his peace with the rebels, "who, he supposed, would not treat [him] harshly; for that it was probable that, on account of the French War, the troops would be withdrawn." "The information," Ambrose Serle wrote, "chilled me with horror, and with some indignation when I reflected upon the miserable circumstances of the Rebels, etc."

Confirmation of the British withdrawal reached Philadelphia on May 22, the day before the Meschianza, and Serle took his unhappiness to his diary, where he wrote gloomily of the situation of his friend Galloway, forced to give up an estate worth seventy thousand pounds— he was a millionaire by the standards of the day—and "left to wander like Cain upon the earth without home and without property." Serle was convinced that the decision to evacuate Philadelphia was in practical fact the end of the effort to subdue the rebellious colonies. "I now look upon the contest as at an end," he wrote. "No man can be expected to declare for us when he cannot be assured of a fortnight's protection. Every man, on the contrary, whatever might have been his primary inclinations, will find it to his interest to oppose and drive us out of the country." For Galloway, it was clear, nothing remained "but to attempt reconciliation with (what I may now venture to call) the *United States of America*. . . . O Thou righteous GOD, where will all this villainy end!" Serle and Galloway took one of their gloomier strolls, and their conversation "turned on the misery of the Times & on the Loss of that Happiness (perhaps the greatest ever enjoyed by human Society in this depraved State of things), which had been wantonly thrown away in Gratification of the dishonest & ambitious Views of smuggling merchants and turbulent Demagogues."

Sir William Erskine declared to Serle that the abandonment of Philadelphia, "so void of all Honor, Spirit & Policy, made him miserable in himself & ashamed of the name of a Briton; That he never was accused of Rashness, but wd, answer with his Life, either to crush the Rebels, if they stayed in their Works, in 48 hours, or disperse & drive them entirely out of this Province over the Susquehannah in 10 Days. . . . That the Rebels were nothing compared with our Army in any respect; and that . . . we might even now (as we could have done long since) 'put our Foot upon them' & soon settle the Controversy." But hope still flickered. "Many People come in," Serle wrote, "who assert that nine tenths of the People are weary of the Rebellion and the tyrannical oppression of their new Governors, and wd. take up arms in our Behalf, if they had them."

14

England

T HE British were well aware that a treaty between France and America was in the making, and Lord North was determined to take measures to thwart such an alliance if possible. The condition that North had exacted as the price of remaining in office after the news of Saratoga was that new offers of conciliation be made to the Americans. Now, if ever, was the time. The London stock market had fallen to new lows in the autumn of 1777. Germany would not provide any more mercenaries, and the British manpower barrel had long been empty, or near it. North's majority in Parliament had diminished, and Edward Gibbon noted that even before news of Saratoga sentiment for peace had begun to make headway. The Earl of Chatham (the elder William Pitt) had taken the occasion of Saratoga to make one of his most brilliant attacks on the conduct of the war. Again and again he returned to the theme that the British and the Americans were cousins who belonged together. A reconciliation might still be effected. "America," he declared, "is in an ill-humor with France on some points that have not entirely answered her expectations; let us wisely take advantage of every possible moment of reconciliation. Her natural disposition still leans towards England, and to the old habits of connection and mutual interest that united both countries. . . . The security and permanent prosperity of both countries" could only be secured by union. "America and France cannot be congenial; there is something decisive and confirmed in the honest American that will not assimilate to the futility and levity of Frenchmen." Parliament should remain in session and take such action as might end the conflict. But the members of Parliament were too impatient to be home for the pleasures and festivities of the Christmas holiday. Fresh efforts at conciliation must wait.

During the holidays, rumors of the impending alliance stimulated British maneuvers to bring an end to hostilities before such a consummation could take place. A series of informal diplomatic efforts were launched. In January, Benjamin Franklin was approached in Paris by an English friend named James Hutton with hints that he was empowered to explore the possibilities of peace. Hutton, who described himself as "a loving volunteer," was one of those amateur diplomats who appear in the course of all great conflicts and whose efforts are seldom, if ever, crowned with success. Hutton protested to Franklin that as "a friend of peace; a hater of discord" he wished only to see the Americans "secure in your liberties, and guarded forever against all apprehensions." He was convinced, he told Franklin, that "anything short of absolute independency would almost be practicable, and could take place."

To Hutton, his "Dear Old Friend," Franklin gave some advice. "I think it is Ariosto," he wrote, "who says that all things lost on earth are to be found in the moon; on which somebody remarked that there must be a great deal of good advice in the moon." Franklin, confident that his letter would be read by the king's ministers and doubtless by Lord North himself, then told his friend a few home truths. "You have lost by this mad war," he declared, "and the barbarity with which it has been carried on, not only the Government and commerce of America, and the public revenues and private wealth arising from that commerce, but what is more, you have lost the esteem, respect, friendship and affection of all that great and growing people, who consider you at present, and whose posterity will consider you, as the worst and wickedest nation upon earth. A peace you may undoubtedly obtain by dropping all your pretensions to govern us; and to your superior skill in huckstering negociations, you may possibly make such an apparently advantageous bargain as shall be applauded in your Parliament. . . ." But unless Great Britain could bring itself to make a fair and generous peace that would offer some recompense for all its bullying and barbarity, it could never win back the affection of the American people or restore true harmony. The handsome thing, Franklin advised, would be to offer America

Canada, Nova Scotia, and East and West Florida as part of a peace agreement. These vast areas would serve as a form of indemnity for all the damage the British had caused in America. He was under no illusions, Franklin wrote, that the British government would see the utility of such measures, but Hutton had asked for his views and he had complied. The ministers to whom Franklin's opinions were communicated were doubtless startled indeed.

Shortly afterward another Englishman, William Pultney, contacted the Pennsylvanian with pacific overtures. Franklin replied more curtly: "I see by the propositions you have communicated to me that the ministers cannot yet divest themselves of the idea that the power of Parliament over us is constitutionally absolute and unlimited." Only recognition of American independence could terminate the war.

Upon the reconvening of Parliament, the House of Commons once more took up the matter of America. As Horace Walpole put it: "Disappointed, defeated, disgraced, alarmed, but still depending on a majority in both Houses, and on the blindness and indifference of the nation," North appeared in the House to announce a dramatic reversal of government policy. The military situation had reached a point where, in Walpole's words, England "must stoop to beg peace of America *at any rate.*"

This, at least, is how the terms of North's conciliatory proposals appeared to many members of the House of Commons who were in no sense friends of the war. The North ministry seemed ready to abandon any pretension to govern America if only it could preserve the *name* of dependency. Even some of the ministers were disgusted at the concessions proposed by North, and in the discussions within the cabinet North was reported to have stated "he would treat with the Congress, with anybody—*would even allow the independence of the Colonies—not verbally, yet virtually.*"

The Whigs were, for the most part, glad to accept the terms of the commission, and some of the Rockinghamites went so far as to urge that complete independence be recognized.

As soon as North had formally presented his plan, Charles James Fox rose, "and after pluming himself on having sat there till he had brought the noble Lord to concur in sentiments with him and his friends," startled North by asking him if it was not true that a commercial treaty between France and America had been signed in Paris within the past ten days. If this indeed was the case, Fox continued, there was little else that the House could do except "concur with the propositions, though probably now they would have no effect." An angry murmur ran through the House, and North sat stunned and motionless, at a loss for words.

George Grenville, doubtless recalling his own misfortunes in attempting to deal with the American colonists, had a good deal to say about the "ignominious posture of his country in such humiliating concessions . . . *He felt the humiliating blush that must spread the cheek of his Sovereign when he should be called to give his assent to these bills."*

Edmund Burke, reminding Lord North that his proposals were virtually the same ones that he, Burke, had offered two years earlier, called on that unhappy minister to tell the House what he knew of the French treaty. "Still the Minister was silent," Walpole wrote, "till George Savile rose and told him it would be criminal to withold a reply, and a matter of impeachment, and ended with crying, 'An answer! an answer! an answer!'"

Finally North answered with a series of equivocations. He had no official word. It might all be rumor. France had denied the existence of such a treaty some time ago. "Such evasive answers rather convinced everybody of truth," Walpole noted wryly, adding, "Such an avowal, in effect, of criminality, ignorance, and incapacity in the Ministers had never been equalled—nor, since King John surrendered his Crown at the Nuncio's feet, could a more ignominious instance of the debasement of a great monarch be quoted." The stricture was perhaps excessive, but it is nonetheless eloquent testimony to the feelings aroused within Parliament and without by what many saw as a gesture of abasement—a gesture that was not only degrading but, what was infinitely worse, futile; an effort at conciliation prompted by fear of the French much more than by an acceptance of the right of Americans to be independent; an effort to nullify the effect of the French-American alliance by abandoning the principles for which the war had ostensibly been fought.

As Walpole put it, "The Ministers had stigmatized the whole body of colonists as cowards, and boasted they could traverse the whole continent of America with 5000 men; and in four years stooped to offer terms infinitely beyond what would have glutted the most sanguine or presumptious wishes of the insurgents but two years ago! . . . how could England but fall into disgrace and contempt, when Ministers, by turns so audacious, so criminal, and so mean, remained yet undisturbed in their posts?"

Walpole was not alone in believing that the conciliation bills were not sincere efforts at peace but were designed primarily to confuse and demoralize the Americans; to appeal to those who were neutral, those who had remained at least covertly loyal to the Crown, and those who were simply weary of the war. This assumption would certainly have been strengthened if the members of Parliament had been privy to the various intrigues that the North government was busy promoting, such as Hutton's approach to Franklin.

North's plan was denounced by Barré as a "shameful imposture," a "scandalous deceit . . . a cheat . . . of the most gross kind . . . meant as a trick on the public, to divide, distract, and sow divisions. . . ." The debates grew so heated that the dying Lord Chatham appeared once more in Parliament. On crutches, swathed in flannel, supported by his son-in-law and by his son—who would soon rival his father as a Parliamentary leader—he was like a ghost haunting the scene of his great days. He was, he told the members, especially offended by the air of expediency that enveloped North's proposals. America had always been the kingpin of his policy. He had been the agent of the French defeat and humiliation in the Seven Years' War. Now, in his dying hour, he saw the major work of his life crumbling into ruin: The American colonies, whose patron he had been for so long, who had, in turn, adored him, were now allied to England's immemorial enemy! How had that happened? He knew very well the long chain of bunglings and ineptitudes that had brought about this tragic day. Weak as he was, Chatham's old eloquence lighted up the house once more. "My Lords . . . I rejoice that the grave has not yet closed upon me; that I am still alive to lift up my voice against the dismemberment of this ancient and most noble monarchy!" Opponent of George III, Chatham was champion of the constitution and of the principle of kingship as a part of that constitution. "While I have sense and memory," he declared, "I will never consent to deprive the royal offspring of the House of Brunswick . . . of their fairest inheritance. Where is the man who will dare to advise such a measure? My Lords, his Majesty succeeded to an empire as great in extent as its reputation was unsullied. Shall we tarnish the lustre of this nation by an ignominious surrender of its rights and fairest possessions? Shall this great kingdom, that has survived whole and entire the Danish depredations, the Scottish inroads, and the Norman conquest, that has stood threatened invasion of the Spanish Armada, now fall prostrate before the House of Bourbon? . . . Shall a people that seventeen years ago was the terror of the world, now stoop so low as to tell its ancient inveterate enemy, Take all we have only give us peace? It is impossible!"

A continuing war was far better than a peace without honor. "But, my Lords," Chatham concluded, "any state is better than despair. Let us at least make one effort; and if we must fall, let us fall like men!" The same words in the mouth of another man would perhaps have sounded like windy bombast. In Chatham's mouth they had a power given them by the speaker's great services to his country, by his long-time dominance of Parliamentary debate, and by his illness. What is perhaps most interesting about those words is Pitt's bitterness toward what he saw as capitulation not to American independence but to the threat of French intervention. It was the apparent willingness of the ministers to give up America for fear of the French that in Pitt's mind measured the real decline in British greatness.

After the reply of the Duke of Richmond, Chatham tried to rise once more but fainted. Carried from the House, he lingered on a month longer and died on May 11, asking his son just before his death to read him the passage from Homer telling of the funeral of Hector and the "despair of Troy."

The drama of Pitt's last appearance in the House of Lords made a profound impression on his colleagues and on Englishmen everywhere. He was ineradicably identified with the most glorious moments in modern British history—England's triumph in the Seven Years' War—and his patriotism, eloquence, and political skill had made him the dominant figure of his age. He received a public funeral. Parliament annexed an annuity of four thousand pounds a year to his title in perpetuity and voted a monument in Westminster Abbey, which the king took as "rather an offensive measure to me personally."

North's conciliatory bills, which passed the House of Commons on March 16, were denominated the "Royal Instructions to the Peace Commission of 1778." The peace commission was to be made up of the Earl of Carlisle, the Howe brothers, William Eden (now a commissioner for Trade and Plantations), and George Johnstone, a captain in the navy and former governor of West Florida, who had once fought a duel with Germain. It took its name from the Earl of Carlisle, whom Walpole described as "a young man of pleasure and fashion, fond of dress and gaming, by which he had greatly hurt his fortune . . . totally unacquainted with business, and though not void of ambition had but moderate parts, and less application." It was this frivolous young man who became the principal figure in a new effort at negotiation.

The most able member of the Carlisle peace commission was its secretary, a Scottish historian and philosopher named Adam Ferguson, author of *The History of Rome*. The purpose of the commission was to quiet "the disorders now subsisting in certain of our colonies, plantations, and provinces in North America." The commissioners were authorized to negotiate with any appropriate individual or governmental body in the colonies and to address them by "any style or title" that would be most acceptable to them. They were to meet anywhere that the colonists might designate and, during the subsequent negotiations, to "admit of any claim or title to independency . . . during the time of the treat." The commissioners might assure those with whom they negotiated that Great Britain wished to promote "a full and permanent reconciliation between Great Britain and the said colonies" and as proof of its sincerity had already repealed the tea duty and the Massachusetts Government Act. Furthermore, the commissioners had the power to promise the colonists that all acts passed since 1763 would be suspended pending the outcome of negotiations.

Beyond this they might promise that the former mother country, to establish maternal ties once more, would make "every proper concession"—among them pledges that no standing army would be kept in the colonies "in time of Peace without their consent" and that "none of the antient governments or constitutions" would ever be altered unless at the express request or with the consent of the colony itself.

While the commissioners had broad powers to negotiate a general treaty, their instructions made it plain that if Congress (or Washington) should prove recalcitrant, the commissioners were to do their best to detach any former colonies from the American confederation.

After the concessions there followed a list of restrictions regarding the conditions of a possible cease-fire agreement. These covered such points as a continuing embargo on goods shipped to America, no augmentation of the forces of either army during the treaty discussions, and so on. The colonies, if they were willing to return to their allegiance to Great Britain, might even preserve a substantial degree of continental self-government by preserving the mode prescribed in the Articles of Confederation, the new constitution recently sent to the states for ratification. The Declaration of Independence need not be repealed, since it would automatically become a dead letter if the colonies assumed once more their proper allegiance to the Crown.

And then, finally, despite any conditions or qualifications stated in their instructions, if the commissioners had "a reasonable prospect of bringing the treaty to a happy conclusion" they were "not to lose so desirable an end, by breaking off the negociation on the [colonists'] absolutely insisting on some point which you are hereby directed, or which, from your own judgment and discretion, you should be disposed, not to give up or yield to, provided the same be short of open and avowed independence (except such independence as relates only to the purpose of the treaty)."

Put simply, the commissioners were authorized to concede outright or to negotiate every point at dispute between Great Britain and her colonies since 1763. If Britain could go so far in 1778, it could have gone so far in 1775 or 1776. Had it gone so far, or even, indeed, part way, the vast majority of colonists would have gratefully accepted, and would have seen the concessions as that return to reason on the part of the mother country so fervently desired and so long prophecied.

Sir John Dalrymple, commenting on the instructions to the British commissioners, observed, sensibly enough, that England should renounce all restraints on American manufacturers since these restraints could not, in any event, be enforced. Moreover, restrictions concerning paper money should be ended. It was certainly not worth waging a war to "prevent Americans from cheating each other, or even a few of ourselves, in their modes of payment." After these practical suggestions, Dalrymple presented a foolish one. Since Washington was "a man of principle" who had "no son, daughter, brother or sister, so that his ambition must be limited to himself," would it not be a good policy for the king to write "a private letter" to Washington suggesting that if Washington proposed "fair and just" peace terms, he would be rewarded with a dukedom?

Lord George Germain, who had an almost infinite capacity for self-delusion—a quality apparently essential to public officials of limited intelligence—was convinced that the great majority of Americans would be dazzled by the generosity of the terms. Writing to Sir Henry Clinton to inform him that he had been appointed General Howe's successor, Germain foresaw a speedy end to the war. There was, he asserted, "no room to doubt that the generous terms now held out . . . will be gladly embraced"; and negotiations would undoubtedly proceed so rapidly "as to supersede the necessity of another campaign."

The commissioners departed from Portsmouth, England, on April 16. William Eden brought his wife, four months' pregnant, who found "the servants and baggage past all belief." Another member of the party (though not a commissioner) was Anthony Morris Storer, "known as the best dancer and skater in London." Cornwallis, who had been on leave in England, was also on board, returning to become Sir Henry Clinton's second-in-command.

Rumors of the conciliatory proposals reached America well before the commissioners themselves. As early as April, Henry Laurens had anticipated some effort at reconciliation on the part of Great Britain; "and who," he wrote, "can dry eyed contemplate submission?" Laurens originally believed the proposals to be spurious and urged that they be returned "decently tarred and feathered." Indeed, the anxiety they aroused among members of Congress is revealing, for it indicates that the delegates had rather less faith in the resolution of their constituents than they often professed to have. For them, the bills were a "political stroke," an "insidious scheme" designed to "mislead the ignorant and alienate the minds of the wavering." The manifest intention, Samuel Chase wrote, "is to amuse us with a Prospect of Peace and relax our Preparations." He had been impatient to return to Maryland, but, he noted, "I believe I shall stay and see it out. The Hour to try the Firmness and prudence of Man is near at Hand. . . ." John Henry, Chase's colleague from Maryland, dreaded "the impression it will make upon the minds of many of our people. If it should . . . make its appearance in the form of a Law [as opposed to a rumor] it will prove more dangerous to our cause than ten thousand of their best Troops."

Even before it was clear that the conciliatory bills were authentic, Gouverneur Morris was commissioned to prepare some "observations" for public distribution. He declared "that these United States cannot, with propriety, hold any conference or treaty with any commissioners on the part of Great Britain, unless they shall, as a preliminary thereto, either withdraw their fleets and armies, or else, in positive and express terms, acknowledge the independence of the said states." Some patriots in and out of Congress were afraid such bold words might discourage serious peace negotiations, but Henry Laurens was "averse." "We have made an excellent move on the Table," he wrote a friend. "Rest until we see or learn the motives on the other side." To make some conciliatory gesture "would be a dangerous Act, encourage our Enemies and alarm our friends."

Patrick Henry, alarmed at the appointment of the Carlisle commission with its obvious intention of undoing the French alliance, wrote to Richard Henry Lee in Congress urging him to stand fast. Great Britain was "baffled, defeated, disgraced," he noted, "or at least in her extreme humiliation, which . . . cannot happen until she is deluged with blood, or thoroughly purged by a revolution, which shall wipe from existence the present king with his connexions, and the present system with those who aid and abet it. . . . We are undone if the French alliance is not religiously observed."

Washington likewise was dismayed, seeing the commission's instructions as intended "to poison the minds of the people, and detach the wavering at least from our cause."

Gouverneur Morris was convinced that "Great Britain seriously means to treat," and that if skilled negotiators from England and France were on hand, "I am a blind politician if the thirteen States (with their extended territory) would not be in peaceable possession of their independence three months from this day. As it is," he added, "expect a long war." Morris did not expect it would "require such astonishing efforts after this campaign to keep the enemy at bay." Doubtless the French-American treaty had been signed; "if not, a spark hath fallen upon the train which is to fire the world. Ye gods! what havoc doth ambition make among your works. . . ."

The commissioners themselves were disconcerted to find that Germain had ordered Philadelphia evacuated on the eve of their arrival, creating, as Johnstone wrote Germain, "a tendency the most prejudicial to the conduct of our negotiation." Johnstone's letter points up the mistake of the secretary at war in directing Howe to abandon Philadelphia. It was clearly a panic reaction. As events were to prove, it would in all probability have been several years before the French could have joined Washington's army in a major campaign to recapture the city. With Philadelphia and New York in British hands, American resistance must have been both complicated and weakened. The evacuation of the city was not called for by any compelling military need or imminent danger. Its principal effect was to raise the spirits of the patriots everywhere, and in conjunction with the Carlisle commission, it convinced them that the British were at the end of their rope and must soon sue for peace. "The withdrawing of His Majesty's troops from this province . . . is the more to be lamented," Johnstone added, "as the army under the command of General Washington is reported to be sickly and ill provided, whilst His Majesty's Forces are in the best condition both in respect to health, numbers and preparation for the field."

The actual dispatches of the commissioners did not reach Congress until June 11. The delegates were still considering them when a packet arrived from Carlisle. "This," Laurens said, "might prove an attempt to amend the whole." The address came under "triple Seals," with the

representation in the sealing wax of "a fond Mother embracing returning Children." Laurens read two paragraphs of the address before he
came to a demeaning reference to their friend and ally, the king of
France. At this point Gouverneur Morris "opposed going on with it, and
laboured hard to send it back with contempt." The commissioners
should be instructed to delete all "insolent" references to the great and
good king of France, "thereby striking conviction to the souls even of
Tories, that G B is reduced to implore a peace from America." Thomas
McKean wrote exultantly, "I have lived to see the day when, instead of
'Americans licking the dust from the feet of a British Minister,' the
tables are turned."

The reply of Congress to the Carlisle commissioners was notably
brief and to the point. Congress had shown a good deal of tolerance in
even consenting to read proposals "so derogatory to the honor of an
independent nation." They were clearly based "on the idea of dependence, which is utterly inadmissible." Congress would be pleased, of
course, to enter into negotiations when Great Britain "shall demonstrate
a sincere disposition for that purpose." And the only "solid proof of this
disposition will be an explicit acknowledgment of the independence of
these states, or the withdrawing of his fleets and armies."

The frustrated commissioners, unable to make any headway with
Congress, threatened to take their case to the people, a threat that
moved Gouverneur Morris, under the pen name of "An American," to
write: "There is but one way to sink still lower, and thank God you have
found it out. You are about to publish! Oh my Lord! you are indeed in a
mighty pitiful condition. You have tried fleets and armies, and proclamations, and now you threaten us with newspapers."

The fact was that the commissioners were both inexperienced and
stupid. Having failed to open formal discussions with Congress, they
tried a little discreet bribery. George Johnstone, who, in Stedman's
words, had "not only been a uniform but a strenuous advocate in the
British Parliament for the rights originally claimed by Americans,"
wrote to a number of individual members of Congress hinting that their
good offices to promote peace and reconciliation on the terms offered
by the commissioners would bring ample rewards from a grateful
monarch. He wrote to, among others, Francis Dana, Joseph Reed, and
Robert Morris. He realized that it would not be easy to bring their fellow
delegates around to the idea of a reunion with Great Britain. "In all such
transaction," he wrote, "there is risk, and I think that whoever ventures
should be secured, at the same time that honour and emolument should

naturally follow the fortune of those who have steered the vessel in the storm, and brought her safely to port. I think that Washington and the president [of Congress] have a right to every favour that grateful nations can bestow, if they could once more unite our interests, and spare the miseries and devastations of war."

Joseph Reed received a letter from a Mrs. Ferguson, wife of a Tory in whose house Johnstone had lodged, asking him to visit her. Reed did so, and the lady revealed that Johnstone had authorized her to promise Reed a gift of ten thousand pounds sterling to facilitate negotiations on the basis of the Carlisle commission proposals. It was a very large sum, but Reed did not hesitate in his answer: "That I was not worth purchasing, but such as I was, the King of Great-Britain was not rich enough to do it." When some of Johnstone's letters, with their mention of "honour and emolument" for those who united "our interest," were published, he hastily resigned from the commission, accusing Congress of using his letters to discredit the commission. The charge was certainly true, but it was Johnstone who had so injudiciously placed the weapons in their hands.

Lord Carlisle may have been a giddy and foppish young man, but he had enough sense to see that his mission was an abortive one based on a totally inadequate understanding of the true situation in America. "The arrival of this fleet," he wrote Lady Carlisle on July 21, 1778, of the Comte d'Estaing's appearance in American waters with a French fleet, "makes every hope of success in our business ridiculous." A pompous and silly "Proclamation to the People" had been issued, calling on Americans to return to their allegiance to the British Crown, but Carlisle was under no illusions that it would have any effect. "The common people hate us in their hearts," he wrote, "notwithstanding all that is said of their secret attachment to the mother country."

With the French treaty approved, the Carlisle commission, Laurens wrote, "will perceive a necessity for taking a new departure from the Tower of Independence." But the Congressional delegates remained uneasy about the popular reaction. It would be well, the members concluded, to publish an address to the people explaining the rebuff of the Carlisle commission and exhorting all good patriots to stand firm. "The God of battles in whom was our trust," the document read, "hath conducted us through the paths of danger and distress to the thresholds of security . . . if we have courage to persevere, we shall establish our liberties and independence. The haughty prince, who spurned us from his feet with contumely and distain, and the parliament which proscribed us, now descend to offer terms of accomodation. . . . What, then, is their intention? Is it not to lull you with fallacious hopes of peace, until they can assemble new armies to prosecute their nefarious designs? . . . Be not, therefore, deceived. You have still to expect one severe conflict. . . . Arise then! To your tents, and gird for the battle! It is time to turn the headlong current of vengeance upon the head of the destroyer. . . . If you exert the means of defence which God and nature have given you, the time will soon arrive when every man shall sit under his own vine and under his own fig-tree, and there shall be none to make him afraid. . . . Thus shall the power and happiness of these sovereign, free and independent states, founded on the virtue of their citizens, increase, extend and endure, until the Almighty shall blot out all the empires of the earth."

That was certainly a mouthful. Aside from noting its rather feverish rhetoric and the now familiar biblical reference to "every man sitting under his own vine," perhaps only two points need be made. First, there was no indication of substantial popular sentiment in patriot quarters for returning, under any circumstances, to the fold of Great Britain. Thus the exhortation, if it was not unheeded, was in fact unneeded. Secondly, the promise of independence "soon" was a highly optimistic prediction that would return to haunt the members in the long years of war that remained.

The conciliatory bills proved far less divisive and troublesome than Washington had feared. Congress ordered them printed and circulated, and it was soon apparent that most Americans, in their own minds, had crossed the Rubicon of independence and, having experienced the intoxicating elixir of being "free and independent," had no disposition to retrace their steps. At Providence, Rhode Island, the conciliatory bills were burned at the public gallows, and in many other towns there were similar expressions of contempt for what most Americans saw as a woefully belated gesture, prompted far more by dismay at the French alliance than by genuine benevolence.

The commissioners had arrived at Philadelphia just as it was being evacuated by Clinton's army. It was a most inauspicious moment. "As long," Carlisle wrote, "as we had the army to back us, we had hopes of success; but this turning our backs upon Mr. Washington will certainly make them reject offers that perhaps the fear of what that army could have done would have made them listen to."

Once again poor timing and inept planning negated British policy. If the proposals of the Carlisle commission had come even two or three months earlier, before the conclusion of the French alliance gave the Americans more confidence than was actually warranted, and if they had been accompanied by aggressive action against Washington's army or even obvious preparations for an aggressive campaign, they might possibly have met with success. Even that is highly conjectural. It is hard to imagine that Congress, having declared independence almost two years earlier, could have brought itself to return the country to the British fold under any circumstances. At the same time it is interesting to note how fearful many Americans, including Washington himself, were that the terms proposed by the Carlisle commissioners would prove irresistible to their war-weary countrymen. I have stated a number of times that I believe that all genuine revolutions are, in an important sense, irreversible. They may, in time, go bad. They all, inevitably, make peace at last with the old order; but they make that peace on their own terms or at least on terms very different from those that characterized the order against which they originally revolted. Henry Laurens spoke for the great majority of ordinary patriots when he wrote Horatio Gates, "If all the fine things now offered had been tendered some time ago, admitting their solidity, there can be no doubt that the people of America would joyfully have embraced the proposition, but now what answer can be given but that which was returned to the foolish Virgins?–'the door is shut.'" Not only did the proposals come too late, they were subject to final ratification by Parliament. "Here," Laurens added, "a boy's card house [is] tumbled down by a breath. . . . They seem to mistake our understanding as once they did our resolution."

If the Carlisle commission was unable to persuade Congress to consider negotiations short of independence, it may have worked some mischief by reporting to North that it was the commissioners' "belief that the acknowledgement of Independency in case the nation [Britain] should be so far reduced or sunk as to think of it, would not . . . contribute to procure peace." They had "repeated informations" to confirm this opinion. America was now bound to France and was determined to use that connection to "add . . . the remaining British possessions on this Continent" to the thirteen revolting provinces. The commissioners had strong reason to believe that if independence were granted, the Americans would next demand "a similar separation and Independence to the remaining Colonies on this Continent"—Florida, Nova Scotia, and Canada most conspicuously. If the British government were to grant this demand, Congress would then insist on indemnity "for the losses and expenses of the war." Perhaps the most serious error made by the commissioners was to be attentive to the Tories, especially those of Philadelphia, who assured them that the rebel cause was fast wasting away and that a little firmness on the part of Great Britain would soon carry the day.

The commissioners departed in November, after firing off a threatening proclamation that declared that the Americans had, by the French alliance, altered the character of the war. "The question is," the proclamation read, "how far Great Britain may by every means in her power destroy or render useless a connection contrived for her ruin and for the aggrandizement of France. Under such circumstances the laws of self-preservation must direct the conduct of Great Britain; and if the British colonies are to become an accession to France, will direct her to render that accession of as little avail as possible to her enemy." This silly and bad-tempered statement, seeming to promise a systematic devastation of America as part of British policy, simply strengthened the hands of the patriots and further weakened the Loyalists.

The Carlisle commission demonstrated once more how far the British ministry, and for that matter most of the Whig opposition, were from understanding the temper of the Americans in rebellion. Lexington and Concord might have instructed the British, if they had been willing to learn, that the Americans were determined to fight for what they understood to be their liberties. Bunker Hill confirmed that fact. Trenton and Princeton demonstrated not only Washington's brilliance as a military leader but the resilience of the patriots, whose most striking success came at the apparent nadir of their fortunes. The fate of Burgoyne made clear that the interior of the northern states could not be "conquered." The Battle of Germantown gave evidence that the Americans could fight a conventional battle of maneuver and come close to defeating the finest army in the world.

Now the abortive efforts of the royal commissioners made plainer than ever what had, indeed, been abundantly plain before: that the "rebels" could not be diverted from their determination to be independent, and that on this issue at least there was remarkable solidarity among all degrees and conditions of those men and women who called themselves patriots.

The king, triumphant over his enemies, turned his attention once more to the conduct of the war with that cheerful confidence that was one of his most marked and unfortunate characteristics. The failure of the North conciliatory proposals came as no surprise to him. "Farther concession is a joke," he wrote North. For the time being "we must content ourselves with distressing the rebels, and not think of any other conduct until the end of the French, which, if successful, will oblige the rebels to submit to more reasonable [terms] than can at this hour be obtained." And several months later, the king, pushing plans for a decisive naval showdown with the French, wrote to John Robinson giving him suggestions as to how North and, in turn, his party might be stirred out of their apparent lethargy. He took an admonitory tone with North himself for not having prepared a plan to insure a respectable turnout in Parliament. North must "cast off his indecision, and bear up," the king wrote Robinson, "or no plan can succeed." To North, the king praised the "beauty, excellence and perfection of the British constitution as by law established." He was determined to contribute toward its preservation by defending the powers of the executive branch. North could always count on his confidence and support, "but the times require vigour, or the state will be ruined," he concluded.

It sometimes seemed to George III as if the whole weight of the war rested on his shoulders alone. He was poorly served by his ministers, constantly if indirectly attacked by the wretched and treacherous opposition, and even on occasion criticized in the press. There were endless things to attend to—supplies for the army and navy, rumors of corruption in the letting of contracts, faint-hearted officers of the Crown to be encouraged, and, of course, North himself, often a cross in spite of his loyalty, but doubtless, sluggish "old fat fellow" though he was, the best instrument that he could find among a company of faithless and inept servants. So, conscious of his own rectitude, his own devotion to the constitution, his own courage and perserverence in the face of adversities that discouraged lesser men, the king plodded on, determined to save the honor of his country, to overcome sloth, indifference, and timidity at home and his enemies abroad.

While the Carlisle commission blundered about in America, alienating even Tories by their clumsy efforts to bribe patriot leaders, the British campaign of intrigue was pushed in France. An agent of the North ministry with the improbable *nom de plume* of Charles de Weissenstein wrote a letter to Franklin at the end of June with peace proposals and the suggestion that peerages and large pensions would be given to prominent Americans who helped to bring about peace short of complete independence. Franklin rejected "the crooked, dark paths" that his correspondent proposed. If Weissenstein was as sincere in his wishes for peace as he professed to be, Franklin declared, he should have addressed his letter "to your sovereign and his venal Parliament. He and they, who wickedly began, and madly continue, a war for the desolation of America. . . . Your Parliament never had a right to govern us, and your King has forfeited it by his bloody tyranny."

Weissenstein had proposed to meet Franklin at Notre Dame—he would be recognized by a rose in his hat—and there receive his reply. Franklin's response was scathing: "I may be indiscreet enough in many things," he wrote, but even if he were disposed to enter into such an improper negotiation, "I should never think of delivering them to the Lord knows who, to be carried to the Lord knows where, to serve no one knows that purposes. Being at this time one of the most remarkable figures in Paris, even my appearance in the church of Notre Dame, where I cannot have any conceivable business, and especially being seen to leave or drop any letter to any person there . . . might . . . have very mischievous consequences to our credit here. . . ." For the promises of pensions and peerages, Franklin reserved his special scorn. No American could accept a pension paid by the British Crown "without deserving, and perhaps obtaining a SUS-*pension.*" As for peerages: "Alas! Sir, our long observation of the vast servile majority of your peers, voting constantly for every measure proposed by a minister, however weak or wicked, leaves us small respect for that title. We consider it as a sort of *tar-and-feather* honour, or a mixture of foulness and folly, which every man among us who would accept it from your King would be obliged to renounce, or exchange for that conferred by the mobs of their own country, or wear it with everlasting infamy."

The British, in short, proved themselves more inept in promoting peace than in waging war, whatever their shortcomings might have been in the latter area. The curious events of the winter and spring of 1778 that culminated in the departure of the Carlisle commission served to demonstrate to the world the moral and political disarray of the British government. These events thus encouraged Britain's enemies (since it had no friends, it could not discourage them). Beyond that, they revealed how far the North ministry had to travel before it might finally comprehend the true situation in America—or, perhaps more accurately, since it never would really understand the true situation in America, how much blood and gold it must expend before it would come to accept what it could not, from its very nature, understand.

PART VIII

PART VII

1

Monmouth

WASHINGTON had promised Lafayette that he would give him command of an expedition against Canada. The young Frenchman therefore set off for the Northern Department in February, 1778, but when he arrived at Albany he found that instead of the expected twenty-five hundred soldiers ready to march, there were barely a thousand—and these, in Thomas Conway's words, "most naked, destitute of every necessary article for the march and extremely dissatisfied; being five months & some of them eight months without pay." The New Hampshire and Vermont militia, who had been counted on to augment the Continental troops under Lafayette, declared that they would not join the expedition without "*double* pay and rations, and the benefit of *plunder!*" In addition, Philip Schuyler and Benjamin Lincoln persuaded Lafayette that early spring thaws had made it impossible to move an army north. Thoroughly disappointed, the French general returned to Valley Forge after a wild-goose chase of some six weeks.

Washington, perhaps to raise his spirits and give a portion of the army an opportunity to take the field, sent the marquis with three thousand men to take a position at Barren Hill on the Schuylkill, seven miles from Valley Forge. Washington may have hoped that Howe would attack in force and in so doing make himself vulnerable. If so, the move was perhaps too successful. Lafayette was hardly established at Barren Hill on May 20 when five thousand British soldiers under General Grant set out from Philadelphia on a forced night march that brought them at daybreak to a point between Valley Forge and Lafayette's positions. Another detachment of British troops under Colonel Grey marched along the west bank of the Schuylkill and took up a position guarding a ford two or three miles in front of Lafayette's right flank. At dawn Lafayette was virtually surrounded by a superior force, with Matson's Ford, some distance to his right rear, the only avenue of escape.

Lafayette was talking, in his broken English, with a young woman on her way to Philadelphia to spy on the British when he received word that redcoats had been seen in the woods to his rear and on the road from Whitemarsh to Swede's Ford. Either Lafayette's security was lax or the British had been lucky. There was little time in which to regroup his forces, but Lafayette reacted with the instinct of a born soldier. The men were quickly redeployed to face the threat from the Whitemarsh–Swede's Ford Road, and Lafayette made a feint as though he intended to attack Grant. The British officer, meanwhile, halted to wait for the arrival of his whole division. The column under Grey, which was advancing up the Ridge Road toward what had been Layfayette's front, also halted to determine whether Grant had reached the position for a coordinated attack. At this point, the road to Matson's Ford was hidden from British view by trees and a slight defilade. It was by this route that Lafayette made a hasty retreat through the woods to the ford. General Grant, who was in an ideal position to cut off the retreating Americans, chose instead to advance on the Barren Hill positions. He found them abandoned, but by this time it was too late to overtake Lafayette, who got his troops across the river minus some of their artillery and disposed them in battle formation to cover the ford.

Washington, watching the advance of the British through a spyglass, had some agonizing moments before he saw Lafayette's division arrive at the ford just ahead of its pursuers. In Stedman's words: "The British generals advancing to the Ford, perceived that La Fayette was so advantageously posted on the other side of the river, with his artillery on the high and broken grounds which arose from the water's edge, that nothing further could be attempted against him." Even the presence of mind of Lafayette would hardly have extricated his battalions if Grant had not been so stubborn in his determination to advance on Barren Hill. Charles Lee, still the prisoner of the British, declared, according to Serle, that "Grant deserved to be hanged for his Conduct in the attempt

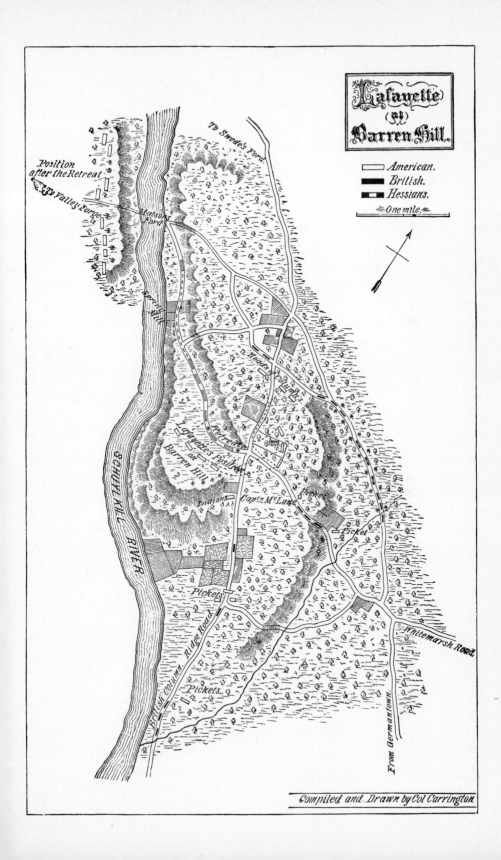

Lafayette at Barren Hill.

☐ American.
▬ British.
▭ Hessians.
≈ One mile. ≈

To Swede's Ford

Position after the Retreat

To Valley Forge

Matson's Ford

Barren Hill

Schuylkill River

Heart's Church

Retreat

Lafayette's Position on Barren Hill

Indians

Capt. McLane

Picket

Picket

Pickets

British Colum. Ridge Road

Pickets.

Whitemarsh Road.

From Germantown.

Compiled and Drawn by Col Carrington

upon Fayette's Corps, who were actually surrounded or cut off in their Retreat by our Troops, when he suffered them to escape . . . & that not one of them cd. have got away if there had been but ordinary management, an Event wch wd. have entirely ruined them, as they were the best of their army."

The dispatch of Lafayette to Barren Hill was one of those quixotic acts, inexplicable in terms of any known military doctrine, of which Washington was sometimes capable. By it he came hair-raisingly close to squandering most of what he had labored so long and hard to create. If the British could have evacuated Philadelphia with the Marquis de Lafayette as a prisoner, along with several thousand soldiers of Washington's painstakingly reconstituted little army, much of the bitterness of their withdrawal would have been assuaged, and the Continental Army would have suffered a severe, if not disastrous, blow.

Despite Lafayette's setback at Barren Hill, a cautious optimism was evident in the spring of 1778. Word circulated that Governor Richard Caswell of North Carolina was on his way to join Washington with five thousand volunteers, and five thousand more were reported to have been recruited in Virginia. In the words of one delegate to Congress (Francis Lewis of New York), "If the public reports we have from abroad be true, we have nothing more to do than to exert ourselves this campaign, and our Independence will have a permanent establishment."

Following the escape of Lafayette's division, Washington had two unwelcome additions to his army. General Thomas Mifflin, who had been involved in the scheming against Washington and had simply abandoned his duties as quartermaster general, presented himself and requested a command. Washington, as he put it in a letter to Gouverneur Morris, was surprised "to find a certain gentleman, who some time ago, when a heavy cloud of darkness hung over us and our affairs looked gloomy, was desirous of resigning, now stepping forward in the line of the army. . . . I must think that gentleman's stepping in and out, as the sun happens to beam forth or become obscure, is not *quite* the thing, nor *quite* just, with respect to those officers who take the bitter with the sweet."

Close on Mifflin's heels came General Charles Lee, finally exchanged for Colonel Prescott. Lee had spent several weeks in Philadelphia fraternizing with the enemy, so to speak, and talking in a manner very close to treasonable. He was a warm advocate of peace, he told anyone who would listen, and he would do all in his power to promote it. He had earlier drawn a plan for the Howes that he believed would result in a speedy British victory. Lee had gone so far as to write to the Carlisle commissioners, declaring: "It appears to me that by the continuance of the war, America has no chance of obtaining its ends." It thus remained only to terminate the war as quickly and painlessly as possible, he wrote, so that a just peace could be concluded. "I think myself not only justifiable, but bound in conscience in furnishing all the light I can, to enable 'em to bring matters to a conclusion in the most commodious manner." If Maryland was reduced "and the people of Virginia are prevented or intimidated from marching aid to the Pennsylvania army, the whole machine is divided," Lee wrote, "and a period put to the war." He was so confident of the success of his plan that he would "stake my life on the issue."

Lee had written off Washington as "not fit to commmand a sergeant's guard," and Washington, if he had not heard this particular phrase, was well aware that Lee had a low opinion of his generalship. He nevertheless welcomed Lee like a returning hero, riding out four miles from camp to greet him "as if he had been his brother," in Elias Boudinot's words. The general officers waited two miles from camp, and soldiers were drawn up on both sides of the road leading to Valley Forge. That night there was an elegant dinner with music, and a room was assigned to Lee "back of Mrs. Washington's sitting room, and all his baggage was stored in it." The next morning he lolled in bed while Washington waited breakfast for him. When Lee emerged very late from his room, Boudinot noted that "he looked as dirty as if he had been in the street all night." And Boudinot discovered that "he had brought a miserable dirty hussy with him from Philadelphia (a British sergeant's wife) and had actually taken her into his room by a back door and she had slept with him that night." It was not an auspicious beginning.

Lee had hardly unpacked his bags before he was in communication with Howe and Clinton. To Clinton he wished "all possible happiness and health and begs, whatever may be the event of the present unfortunate contest, that he will believe General Lee to be his most respectful and obliged humble servant." He then proceeded to scold Congress for promoting other generals while he was a prisoner, and he wrote with almost intolerable arrogance to Washington proposing that, since the Americans could not hope to defeat the British army in battle, he build a huge fort at Pittsburgh to hold the Continental funds and the old men, women, and children, and that he send Congress down the Mississippi to a safe refuge in Spanish territory. This proposal falling on deaf ears, Lee urged Washington to move south, giving it as his opinion that Clinton intended to "go to Maryland or Delaware or some other independent field" where he could control "water communication, and act in harmony with frontier Indian aggression." Those historians who believe in Lee's outright treason have emphasized that his recommendation to Washington would have prevented the commander in chief from pursuing Clinton's army into New Jersey and is thus prima facie evidence of Lee's treasonable intention. The validity of this argument rests, of course, on whether Lee knew that Clinton planned to march north from Philadelphia. There is no evidence that he did, and since there is no indication that the British trusted Lee or paid any attention to his unsolicited advice, it is highly unlikely. Lee's case seems to be quite simply that he had lost whatever faith he may have had in an American victory and wished to establish himself with the British as a sincere friend of reconciliation. Lee, one suspects, lacked the courage and consistency to be a genuine traitor in the mold of Benedict Arnold. He was too mercurial and unbalanced, too vain and foolish, to be steady in any cause except his own.

Washington, replying to Lee's proposal of a campaign into Maryland, thanked him for candidly submitting his views, adding, in a plain rebuke, "I only beg that they may come directly to myself. The custom which many officers have of speaking freely of things, and reprobating measures which upon investigation may be found to be unavoidable, is never productive of good, but often of very mischievous consequences."

The question that might appropriately catch our attention at this juncture is why Washington, who is often described as an unerring judge of character, tolerated such behavior and such a man. In the case of Lee, Washington showed an almost embarrassing deference to an individual whose whole manner proclaimed him a charlatan or, perhaps more accurately, mentally unbalanced.

Washington had held a council of war a few days before Lee arrived in camp. It was only the most recent of a series of discussions about the best plan for the Continental Army to follow in the coming months. In an early council Wayne, Patterson, and Maxwell gave their support to an effort to capture Philadelphia. Knox, Poor, Varnum, and Muhlenberg believed New York to be the better theater of operations. Greene urged an attack on New York City by the regulars and the New England militia under Washington's command, with the main army remaining at Valley Forge. Lord Stirling supported a plan to attack both Philadelphia and

New York, while the foreign generals, Lafayette, Von Steuben, and Duportail, advised Washington to make no offensive moves until his army had been substantially strengthened or the British had disclosed their own intentions. Washington himself had felt this last proposal to be much the wisest course. Now clear evidence that the British planned to evacuate Philadelphia substantially changed the situation. By Washington's calculations the effective British force at Philadelphia numbered some 10,000. In addition there were 4,000 in New York and 2,000 at Newport. His own army, including the sick and those who could be called on in an emergency, came to 11,800. Washington in fact seriously underestimated the size of Clinton's army, which was much closer to 20,000 than to 10,000, a very substantial difference. (There were 10,456 British soldiers in New York.) Although it was clear that the British intended to evacuate Philadelphia, it was by no means certain whether Clinton would move his army north to New York or south to launch the rumored Southern campaign.

The crucial question for Clinton was: How should the British evacuate Philadelphia? If they were to go down the Delaware to New Castle and up along the coast to New York, they would run the risk of being attacked at sea by a French fleet from Toulon reported to be on the way to American waters, a formidable fleet under the command of Comte d'Estaing, carrying four thousand French soldiers and officers. In addition, a movement by sea that was attended by any delay because of adverse winds or an encounter with the French would leave New York open to an attack by Washington. Clinton therefore decided to move his army by land across New Jersey to New Brunswick, sending his baggage and a sizable contingent of Tories by sea.

The scene that took place when the British evacuated Boston was repeated in Philadelphia. The streets of the city were full of carts, chaises, wagons, and wheelbarrows carrying the most prized possessions of prosperous Tories to the wharves to be loaded on British transports; the sidewalks were filled with household goods waiting to be conveyed to the docks along the Delaware. In Serle's words, "The town in great distress was occupied in preparing for our departure." The Tory refugees of Philadelphia, men, women, and children, came to more than three thousand. With those of their belongings that they could carry with them, they filled a substantial number of vessels, and the loading went on day after day through the end of May and early June. A wealthy Tory who applied to a British officer for help was told, rather shortly, to seek passage on board one of the British vessels in the river.

To which the Tory replied, "But what the Devil shall I do with my estate?" He got a brutal answer: "Damn you, why did you not stay at home and fight to defend it with your country?" In the words of James Allen, the British "have been unrelenting where they should have been relaxed, & vice versa. The consequence is all their late concessions are attributed justly to their weakness." With the evacuation of Philadelphia, the Allen family was, in the words of James, "totally unhinged." He himself took the oath of loyalty "to the mob-government of Pennsylvania & the united states" to prevent the confiscation of his property, but he was nonetheless indicted for high treason when the Americans reoccupied the city.

Perhaps the principal beneficiaries of the British occupation of Philadelphia were the Tory belles. One of them wrote on the eve of Clinton's departure:

> O halcyon days, forever dear,
> When all were happy, all were gay,
> When winter did like spring appear,
> And January fair as May!
> . . . .
> Still danced the frolic hours away,
> While heart and feet alike were light,
> Still hope announced each smiling day,
> And Mirth and Music crown'd each night.

Clinton, always thorough and methodical, had made careful plans for moving his army out of the city. He knew very well that unless precautions were taken, such an evacuation could leave his troops very vulnerable, both in their exodus and in their marching order. He ordered redoubts built on the New Jersey shore and posted strong detachments to cover the crossing of the Delaware. On June 18, at three o'clock in the morning, the evacuation of the city began, and by ten o'clock the entire army was on the Jersey side of the river and moving out on the road to New Brunswick, the baggage train alone extending over twelve miles. The crossing of the river, based on meticulous staffwork, was carried out with impressive skill and dispatch.

Washington, who was well informed of Clinton's movements, dispatched Arnold, still largely incapacitated from the wounds that he had suffered at Saratoga, to enter the city on the heels of the British. General Maxwell, with a contingent of militia, engaged Clinton's advance guard outside Haddonfield.

Maxwell's harassment, plus the blistering heat of June, made British progress slow and tiring; but Clinton, always expeditious, pressed hard on Maxwell's brigade, and his light-infantry skirmishers drove the Americans back with little delay to Mt. Holly. There Joseph Martin's company waited for the rest of their battalion to join them. Martin, who had gone without food for almost two days, found a barrel with some salt in it and filled his pockets—"salt was as valuable as gold with the soldiers"—then went looking for something to put it on. "In the yard and about it," he wrote, "was a plenty of geese, turkeys, ducks, and barn-door fowls." Martin found some corn, and sitting himself on some boards, he soon had a "fine battalion" of fowls around him. He caught one, wrung its neck, dressed and washed it in a nearby stream, and "stalked into the first house that fell in my way, invited myself into the kitchen, took down the gridiron and put my fowl to cooking upon the coals. The women of the house were all the time going and coming to and from the room. They looked at me but said nothing. 'They asked me no questions and I told them no lies.' When my game was sufficiently broiled, I took it by the *hind* leg and made my exit from the house with as little ceremony as I had made my entrance. When I got into the street I devoured it after a *very* short grace and felt as refreshed as the old Indian did when he had eaten his crow roasted in the ashes with the feather and entrails."

Washington meanwhile moved north and crossed the Delaware some forty miles above Philadelphia. Believing that Clinton wished to draw him into a full-scale battle, Washington moved very cautiously with his main body, sending out detachments of picked men to hang on the flanks of Clinton's army and sound out his intentions. For his part Clinton, very well aware of the hazard of his situation, had no thought in mind except getting his cumbersome and vastly extended column of troops safely to New York. When there was no indication that the British general intended to make a stand, Washington reinforced his detachments until amost a third of his command had advanced to a point where they were in a position to make rapid contact with the British column. First he sent Morgan with six hundred men to reinforce Maxwell's brigade, and then Brigadier General Charles Scott with fifteen hundred more. In a council of war the day before Clinton's army began to move out of the city, Lee had strongly opposed Washington's suggestion of a full-scale attack on Clinton. Such a plan, Lee insisted, would be little short of "criminal." Hamilton, who wrote the minutes of the meeting, was disgusted when Lee prevailed. The discussion, he wrote scathingly, "would have done honor to the most honorable society of midwives, and to them only." Nathanael Greene wrote to Washington after the council had adjourned: "People expect something from us and our strength demands it."

Washington, who had allowed himself to be persuaded against his better judgment to adopt a policy of caution, decided to place the detached troops under the command of a general officer eager to do battle with Clinton. Lafayette was his choice for the assignment, but Lee, who outranked the Frenchman, stood in the way. Washington offered the command to Lee, making clear his preference for the marquis, and Lee deferred to Lafayette, then decided he wished the command, then stepped aside and placed the reins in Lafayette's hands once more, stating that he "was well pleased to be freed from all responsibility for a plan he was sure would fail."

The British army went into camp near Freehold, New Jersey, with Knyphausen to the east at Imlay's Town and Cornwallis's division at Allentown to the north. There Clinton, receiving word that a large Continental force was advancing in battle order, deployed troops to cover his march and pushed on toward Monmouth. Washington marched with the main body to Princeton, from there to Hopewell, five miles away, and then to Kingston, where he received word that Clinton was headed for Monmouth. At this news, Washington sent a third detachment there—a thousand men under General Wayne. Lafayette went along to take command of the combined force, including Maxwell's brigade and Morgan's contingent, with orders to "take the first fair opportunity to attack the rear of the enemy."

Upon assuming command, Lafayette sent a series of messages to Washington informing him of his position and the movement of Clinton's army. From Robin's Tavern on June 26, he wrote that he had "consulted the general officers of the detachment; and the general opinion seems to be that I should march in the night near them, so as to attack the rear guard on the march." Lafayette reminded Washington that he was only three miles farther from Monmouth than "we are in this place." Some British stragglers had been captured, "and deserters," he wrote, "come in amazing fast . . . I believe a happy blow would have the happiest effect."

At five o'clock in the afternoon he wrote again, ending his letter: "I have no doubt but if we overtake them we possess a very happy chance." At seven in the evening Lafayette encountered Hamilton, who had been carrying on a kind of personal reconnaissance. Hearing that Clinton's rear elements were only eight miles away, Lafayette ordered Maxwell and Wayne to advance and move obliquely with Scott's and Jackson's regiments towards the British left.

Meanwhile Lee, realizing that Lafayette would be in a position to attack Clinton, wrote him a whining kind of letter, begging him in effect to allow him to assume command. "It is my fortune and my honor that I place in your hands," the Englishman wrote; "you are too generous to cause the loss of either." Lafayette's response was indeed a generous one: if Washington wished to send General Lee with several thousand more soldiers to take command of the entire detachment, Lafayette would be willing to serve under him. Armed with Lafayette's letter, Lee went to Washington and insisted that as a general senior to the Frenchman he had the right to assume command of the advance units. Washington, inexplicably, consented. The next day Lee, with two brigades, joined Lafayette at the village of Cranbury, where the American detachment had camped for the night, and took command of a force that now numbered some five thousand men, or roughly half of Washington's command.

Washington's orders to Lee when he left the main army to join the divisions under Lafayette's command were to attack the British at the first opportunity. Washington further directed Lee to call his general officers together "to concert some mode of attack." Lee set the time of the meeting for half past five on the afternoon of the twenty-seventh. But he failed to appear. General Scott, encountering Lee that evening, reminded him of the missed appointment and asked if he had any orders. "He said that he had none," Scott recalled.

With Lee had gone a letter from Washington to Lafayette. He had, he told the Frenchman, obtained from Lee "a promise . . . that when he gives you notice of his approach and command, he will request you to prosecute any plan you may have already concerted for the purpose of attacking or otherwise annoying the enemy. . . ." This was the only way, Washington declared, that he could think of to reconcile Lee's determination to hold the command with Lafayette's desire to launch a bold assault on the British. It was certainly not a very good way; to send one officer, whom Washington knew to be opposed to an attack, with instructions to make use of any plan that might have been formulated by the officer he was superseding was very bad procedure at best. The letter was, indeed, even more ambiguous. Washington's precise words to Lafayette were, "he[Lee] will request *you* to prosecute any plan you may have already concerted. . . ." Did this mean that if Lafayette had a well-conceived plan for an attack, Lee was to empower him to carry it out? Or did it mean that Lee was to carry it out, or simply that Lafayette was to "complete any plan" and submit it to Lee? The latter interpretation is the weakest one, but the one that would have certainly been the most acceptable to Lee himself. Beyond all this we do not know exactly what Washington told Lee, or how Lee heard and interpreted what Washington told him. To criticize Washington has often been judged akin to criticizing the Almighty Himself, but the fact is that Washington was human and that he made mistakes, some of them serious. This was one such occasion. A basic military principle is that one should never send a general to do a job that he believes cannot be done; essential to success in military combat is the conviction that you will triumph over your adversary. Regardless of Lee's claim on the command or Lafayette's generosity in conceding it to him, Washington's first error was to give the command to Lee. It was a strong man's weak decision, stemming from Washington's unwarrantably high opinion of Lee, which in turn stemmed from some attitude or emotion in Washington too deep and obscure for us to penetrate. Having allowed Lee to claim the command, Washington then compounded the original error by sending him off with confusing and ambiguous, or, if he made himself entirely clear to Lee, improper orders. He could not in good conscience expect Lafayette to direct Lee's army for him, or Lee to stand by while he did so.

Washington thus appears, as we approach the Battle of Monmouth, to have acted indecisively in his troop dispositions, doing things piecemeal and with an unnecessary degree of improvisation; to have failed to insure adequate reconnaissance; and to have placed a crucial command in the hands of a man not fit or not disposed to exercise it, and one who, moreover, had made abundantly clear his conviction that the operation was doomed from the outset. It is hard to see how the American action could have begun under less favorable circumstances. If Washington felt that military protocol demanded that he accede to Lee's importunings (which, in fact, it did not), he could have solved the dilemma very simply by assuming command of the detachment himself and leaving Lee in charge of the main body.

Lafayette, increasingly concerned at Lee's inaction, came to his headquarters on the evening of the twenty-seventh to ask if any troop dispositions had been made for the following morning. "Lee thought it would be better to act according to the circumstances," Lafayette later reported, "and had no plans." Between one and two o'clock, Washington sent an order that six or eight hundred men from Scott's and

Varnum's commands should be sent forward at once "to lie very near the enemy as a party of observation, in case of their moving off, to give the earliest intelligence of it; to skirmish with them, so as to produce delay and give time for the rest of the troops to come up"; he also directed Lee "to write to Morgan to make a similar attack." No such message ever reached Morgan, although Lee's aide-de-camp stated at Lee's court-martial that he sent one. Here again, in a matter of such importance, good military practice would have required that Morgan verify that he had received the message; and in the absence of such verification, further efforts should have been made until contact was established. Properly speaking, a staff officer should have carried the message.

On the evening of the twenty-seventh, the main body of Clinton's army had camped with its right extending a mile and a half beyond the Monmouth Court House and its left along the Allentown-Monmouth Road. Right and left were protected by marshy ground and woods. The British lines ran in a southeasterly direction, while the Americans advanced from the northwest. Early on the morning of the twenty-eighth, Clinton, in anticipation of an attack by Washington, gave Knyphausen orders to move at daylight and make all possible speed to Middletown and the sea. He himself took command of a division of selected troops to protect Knyphausen's march.

At four o'clock in the morning, Lafayette, sensing that things were not as they should be, went again to Lee's headquarters to get the latest word. One brigade was already marching, he was told. Where should he, Lafayette, go, he asked? With the selected troops, Lee replied, and Lafayette, suppressing his misgivings, went off in the growing light of dawn to find his unit.

At five o'clock Philemon Dickinson, who commanded a contingent of New Jersey militia sent word to Washington and to Lee from his position on the British right that the enemy had commenced their march. Washington sent orders to Lee at once to "move forward and attack the enemy, unless very powerful reasons prevented." The main body "had thrown aside their packs and was advancing to his support."

The soldiers themselves were eager to engage the British. The captain commanding Joseph Martin's platoon told his men when they were formed up: "Now, you have been wishing for some days past to come up with the British you have been wanting to fight,—now you shall have fight enough before the night." Even the sick and the lame, according to Martin, were determined to get into the fray, and when the

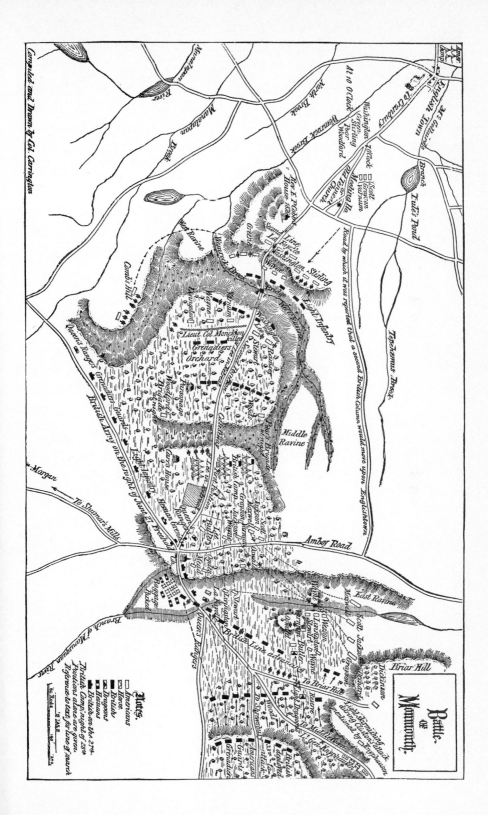

captain detailed them to stay behind as guards and instructed them to give their arms to "those who were going into the field, they would not part with them. 'If their arms went,' they said, *they* would go with them at all events.'"

Lee's response to Washington's order was simply to start his troops forward. He did not himself oversee their movement. If such an attack was to succeed, speed and force were the most essential elements. But the army moved forward in a confused and halting manner. Orders were vague and seemed on more than one occasion to have miscarried or to have been directly contradictory. General Scott's account of the movement of his brigade may be taken as typical: "Had orders about five o'clock to follow Maxwell's brigade;—passed Englishtown; was ordered to halt; received an order from one of General Lee's aides to march in the rear of General Wayne's detachment. About this time there was a halt of an hour; marched to the Meeting-house, where there was a second halt; advanced a mile and then halted, when several pieces of cannon were fired, and some small arms, in front of the column."

Clinton, pressed by Dickinson's force, dispatched skirmishers to give the illusion of an attack and hide the withdrawal of the main army. A series of skirmishes quickly developed. The first two were inclusive, although the British were observed after the second retreating "in very great disorder." The third skirmish, according to Wayne, who was in the thick of it, was the most promising. An attack by British cavalry was beaten off and the horsemen driven back on an infantry detachment that likewise broke and ran. British artillery fire delayed Wayne, and his own artillery was beginning to reply when word came that Lee had ordered the Americans to retire. Wayne, dismayed at the order, went off to find Lee, and, failing, sent an aide "to request that the troops might again be returned to the place they had left." The British, observing the confusion in the American lines and various units in retreat, began a counterattack. The battle was clearly out of Lee's control. He did not wait to supervise the withdrawal "but fell back with the retreating troops, then a mile in the rear."

John Laurens, also dismayed at the order to retreat, tried repeatedly to convince Lee that the situation warranted not a retreat but a determined advance. He also sent word off to Washington describing the situation as far as his presence on the field enabled him to ascertain it. But Lee gave orders and counterorders that soon approached a burlesque. In Lauren's words: "One order succeeded another with a rapidity and indecision calculated to ruin us. . . . All this disgraceful retreating, passed without the firing of a musket, over ground which might have been disputed inch by inch." The initial stages of the battle were most confused. Intelligence of the enemy was lacking, and the American movements were tentative and uncertain. Interestingly enough, the course of the battle is so obscure primarily because we have so much information about it, more perhaps than any other engagement of the Revolution. This is because of Lee's subsequent court-martial, in which most of the general officers and many others down to the rank of captain recollected the events of the day. When relatively little is known about a battle, the historian is free to arrange his little rectangles representing opposing units with an air of assurance. The more we know about most battles the clearer becomes the confusion and disorder that pervade all battlefields.

What emerges most plainly about the early phases of the Battle of Monmouth is that Lee, as might have been expected, did little to advance the action in any bold and decisive way, and at the first indication of real British resistance ordered a general retreat. What remains rather obscure is the nature of an intended envelopment of the British rear-guard position with a force led by Lee himself. It is clear that Lee undertook such a maneuver, leaving Wayne to engage the enemy front. Apparently, when the British rear guard advanced toward Monmouth Court House, Lee halted his envelopment on the grounds that the redcoats, by advancing on the Americans, had left Lee in their rear. However, he failed to take advantage of the opportunity offered to him to attack the rear or flank of the British, and instead began a general retreat that seriously exposed some units who were not promptly informed of the withdrawal. Lee later declared that "the retreat in the first instance was contrary to my intentions, contrary to my orders, contrary to my wishes." Clinton reacted sharply to the American movement because he thought it was directed at Knyphausen's vulnerable baggage train.

It was not until a general retreat had begun that a messenger arrived from Morgan asking for orders. There were no orders to be had other than that the Americans were in retreat. By eleven o'clock, the British division, which had been retreating under American pressure down the Middletown Road, had, as we have seen, formed between that road and Briar Hill Road and then begun to advance. Lee's withdrawal was made without notifying Washington, who received only scattered and sketchy reports of the retreat, which was not surprising in view of the general confusion that enshrouded the American and British movements for several hours.

As in numerous other engagements, the weather was an important factor. When Joseph Martin's unit moved from the road on which they had been marching into a cornfield surrounded by "thick tall trees," it was as though they had entered "the mouth of a heated oven . . . it was almost impossible to breathe." Only in the shade of the woods did it seem possible to draw a breath. They had been there a few minutes when they received orders to retreat, and, Martin added, "grating as this order was to our feelings, we were obliged to comply."

During the morning's fighting Washington had moved his main body forward, with Greene in command of the right wing and Lord Stirling of the left. Near a bridge at the west ravine, Washington and his staff began to encounter the first indications of a general retreat—first a farmer on horseback and then a frightened young fifer, sure that the British devils were breathing down his neck. "After a few paces, two or three more persons said that the continentals were retreating." Washington at once sent two of his aides forward to try to discover what was happening. They met a major who said, simply, "They are flying from a shadow." More and more men and officers passed over the bridge; most of them, like Martin's unit, had not even engaged the enemy or seen a shot fired in anger, and none knew why they were retreating, other than the rumor that "the whole British army was just behind."

Retreating through a muddy defile, Martin and his fellows stopped to let the artillery pass and promptly sat down to rest along the roadside. Flushed and sweating and disheartened, the soldiers saw Washington and his staff ride up and ask an officer "'By whose order the troops were retreating,' and being answered 'by General Lee's,' he said something but as he was moving forward all the time this was passing, he was too far off for me to hear it distinctly," Martin wrote, but companions who were nearby said that the words were an uncharacteristic "damn him." It was hard for Martin to believe that the general had so lost his self-possession as to swear out loud, but it was certainly true that "he seemed at the instant to be in a great passion; and his looks if not his words seemed to indicate as much."

As he had done before at the Battle of Kip's Bay, Washington rode recklessly forward on his old English charger in an open field where British artillery fell all around him and where he could see the British advancing under the cover of a sharp cannonading. After surveying the terrain for a few anxious moments, Washington turned back, overtook the two Connecticut brigades along with some Rhode Islanders, and ordered them to hold a fence line in order to give the American artillery and retreating troops time to make their way through the defile. Thus covered, the American artillery was formed up on high ground and returned the enemy fire.

Whatever errors Washington may have made in the days leading up to the battle, he redeemed them at the moment of his arrival on the field. The very sight of him, looming up so splendidly, so erect and commanding, put heart into the weary and dispirited soldiers, and the decisiveness and skill with which he assigned the retreating soldiers to defensive positions across the line of the British advance gave the officers new resolution. The doubt and uncertainty that hung over the army like a cloud evaporated in minutes. Washington was always at his best in the midst of battle, where personal courage, physical energy, and self-possession counted for so much. Colonel Willett, who had first fought with Washington on Braddock's ill-fated campaign, wrote: "I have seen him in a variety of situations, and none in which he did not appear great; but never did I see him when he exhibited such greatness as on this day." Under the circumstances it would perhaps be captious to ask why he had not been in the thick of things from the first moment of contact with Clinton's troops, and to speculate on the outcome of the battle if he had been. He might then have won a dazzling victory; as it was, it was too late to do more than prevent a humiliating defeat.

Soon after Washington had brought the retreating soldiers on line to a defensive position, Lee appeared and demanded to know why his orders for a general retreat were not being obeyed. When he was told that Washington had made the dispositions himself, it was characteristic of Lee that his first reaction should have been one of offended dignity. He searched out Washington to ask for orders, but the sight of Lee was enough to stoke Washington's rage. Riding up with a manner of surprised reproach, Lee encountered a Washington he had never known before. The coldness of Washington's tone, his flushed face and barely suppressed fury, overwhelmed him. When Washington demanded an explanation of the retreat, Lee could only stammer, "Sir—sir," and then, as Washington asked the question again, Lee pulled himself together enough to say, haltingly, that "the contradictory reports as to the enemy's movements brought about a confusion he could not control." Washington's expression betrayed his reaction to the lame answer, and Lee, seeking desperately to excuse himself and to mitigate the rage that pressed upon him like a smothering weight, reminded Washington that the whole operation "was contrary to his opinion, that he was averse to an attack, or general engagement, and was against it in council,—that while the enemy were so superior in cavalry we could not oppose them." Why, then, Washington asked, had he undertaken the command? "Whatever his opinion might have been, he expected his orders would have been obeyed."

Washington's fury may have stemmed, in part, from his sense that he was the architect of his own undoing. He must have already doubted more than once the wisdom of putting Lee in charge of the advance detachment, of assigning such a crucially important mission to an officer who had no faith in it, and he must have considered and rejected the notion that he himself should be in command of that most vital element of the entire operation.

Washington terminated this strange dialogue by asking Lee if he would take command of the American defensive positions while Washington himself undertook to form the rest of the army in the rear. Under the circumstances, it was an odd request. Lee replied that he would take the command and, if overwhelmed by the British, would be the last to leave the field. At this Hamilton flourished his sword and called out, "in a flustrated manner and phrenzy of valor," as Lee put it, "That's right, my dear General, and I will stay and we will all die here, on the spot."

"I am responsible to the General and to the continent, for the troops I have been entrusted with," Lee replied. "When I have taken proper measures to get the main body in a good position, I will die with you, on the spot, if you please."

Greene's and Stirling's divisions came quickly and in good order onto line out of their marching formation, Greene still on the right and Stirling on the left. High ground in Stirling's area permitted the advantageous emplacement of artillery. A second line was formed with Lafayette in command. Greene detached five artillery pieces to Combs' Hill, the highest ground in his sector, where they could bring enfilade fire on the British advancing against Wayne's lines. At this point Clinton, persuaded that a "general engagement" in which the Americans might be soundly beaten was possible, sent to Knyphausen for two brigades of British and Hessian light dragoons to cover his right flank while he mounted a sharp attack by the grenadiers on the American lines. Ramsay's and Stewart's regiments of Stirling's division were driven back by the force of the British assault. Greene's division also fell back, though in good order, to the second line commanded by Lafayette and supported by a well-positioned battery of artillery.

Meanwhile the Connecticut soldiers at the fence, Joseph Martin among them, held their ground until they were about to be overwhelmed by the vastly larger British attacking force; even then, when their officers ordered them to fall back by platoons, "they had to force them to retreat," Martin recalled, "so eager were they to be revenged on the invaders of their country and rights." When the British had seized the fence line, they brought up an artillery battery and began "a violent attack" upon the American artillery positions and Martin's Connecticut companions, but the well-aimed fire of the Americans prevailed, and the British "reluctantly crawled back from the height which they had occupied and hid themselves from our sight."

This small episode may well have marked a turning point in the battle. As we have noted of other engagements, the key to most battles usually lies in some incident, typically involving a handful of soldiers who, quite outside the view of their commanding general, attack or defend in what subsequently turns out to have been the crucial action of the whole engagement. We cannot, of course, say this with certainty of the clash in which Martin was involved (though he is such an appealing figure and we are so beholden to him for his vivid accounts of this and other battles that it would be most satisfying if we could), but it is plainly the case that it was one of the actions that bought precious time for the rest of Washington's army, helped to prevent a disgraceful rout, and permitted the American forces to be rested and re-formed.

The heat of the day continued to be more devastating than enemy fire. Soldiers on both sides fainted from heat exhaustion, with the British soldiers suffering most because of their thick uniforms and cumbersome battle attire, as well as their generally poor physical condition; the clothes of the Americans were much better ventilated.

While Martin's regiment protected the artillery, elements on the British right had avanced across a low meadow and a brook and occupied an orchard that extended to the left of the Americans and threatened their flank. There the redcoats scattered under the trees to get some protection from "weather . . . almost too hot to live in." With the British artillery silenced, the British in the orchard were vulnerable to attack, and Colonel Joseph Cilley of New Hampshire passed along and gathered up the Connecticut and Rhode Island men. "'Ah!,' said he, 'you are the boys I want to assist in driving those rascals from yon orchard.'"

Rounding up some five hundred men, Cilley led his force through intervening woods and then, when there was no more cover, marched them into the open field and formed them for an attack. The British, without waiting to exchange fire, promptly withdrew, and Cilley ordered three or four platoons to pursue them and keep them preoccupied until additional forces could be brought up to press the attack. Passing through the orchard in a hasty and disorganized pursuit of the enemy, Martin saw numerous dead soldiers killed by American artillery fire. The New Englanders were soon on the heels of the retreating British, and Martin could see every detail of their uniforms and equipage clearly. He picked out a redcoat and took aim directly between his shoulders. "He was a good mark," Martin wrote, "being a broad-shouldered fellow. . . . One thing I know, that is, I took as deliberate aim at him as ever I did at any game in my life." He fired but the smoke from his musket obscured the target. "After all," Martin wrote later, "I hope I did not kill him, although I intended to at the time."

Reinforcements came up with the pursuing platoons as the redcoats rallied and formed on higher ground, supported by a small artillery piece called a grasshopper, which at its first shot "cut off the thigh bone of a captain, just above the knee and the heel of a private in the rear of him." Under a well-directed American fire the British again fell back toward their main body, and Colonel Cilley, seeing them in retreat, shouted, "'Come, my boys, reload your pieces, and we will give them a set-off. . . .' We then laid ourselves down under the fences and bushes to take breath, for we had need of it," Martin wrote, "I presume everyone has heard of the heat of that day, but none can realize it that did not feel it."

In the lull, Martin, going to a nearby well to get water, encountered the captain who had had his leg severed. His sergeant was busy looting the bodies of the dead British soldiers, and Martin heard the captain pleading with him to help him get to a doctor before he bled to death. "He said he would directly." "Directly!" Martin said, "why he will die directly," offering to help carry the officer to a meetinghouse nearby that had been converted into a field hospital. At the hospital Martin lingered long enough to see "two or three limbs amputated" by rough surgery, while the wounded men, if they were lucky, got a stiff shot of whiskey and a piece of wood to bite on.

Among the incidents of the long, stifling day of combat, one in particular caught Martin's eye. The wife of a Pennsylvania artillery private, Mary Ludwig Hays, "who smoked, chewed tobacco and swore like a trooper," helped her husband at his task as he loaded his piece. As Martin tells it, "While in the act of reaching a cartridge and having one of her feet as far before the other as she could step, a cannon shot from the enemy passed directly between her legs without doing any damage than carrying away the lower part of her petticoat. Looking at it with apparent unconcern, she observed that it was lucky it did not pass a little higher, for in that case it might have carried away something else, and continued her occupation." History knows her as Molly Pitcher.

While Martin's unit operated on the American left, the center and right of the American line moved to the attack. At the line of the hedgerow on the left of the road to Monmouth, Livingston's and Varnum's brigade gave such a good account of themselves that the Second Battalion of British grenadiers suffered heavy losses, among them their commanding officer, Lieutenant Colonel Monckton. The grenadiers made three attacks without breaking the American line or retrieving Monckton's body and then withdrew, while Wayne, to straighten the American line, pulled his division back behind the ravine, where it took up positions under the cover of Lafayette's guns. Clinton tried to turn the American flanks, but Greene and Stirling turned him back, and Wayne's division in the center exacted a heavy toll of British casualties.

With Clinton's retreat, this time beyond the middle ravine, word was sent to General Von Steuben, who had been busy reforming those troops that had been in the vanguard of the original retreat, to bring as many as were in good order forward. General Maxwell's brigade and part of General Scott's were gathered at Englishtown, along with three brigades under General Paterson and Smallwood's second brigade. It was here that Von Steuben received word from Washington that the British were retiring, if not retreating, and asking for reinforcement. Leaving Maxwell in command of the troops remaining at Englishtown, Von Steuben started off with three brigades to join Washington. As Von Steuben was leaving Englishtown he encountered General Lee, who asked him where he was going. Von Steuben repeated Washington's orders. The British were retreating in confusion. "Upon that word *confusion,*" Von Steuben recalled, "he [Lee] took me up, and said that they were only resting themselves. . . . I am sure there is some misunderstanding in your being [directed] to advance with these troops." It took some time to convince Lee that the cessation of firing was the consequence of the British withdrawal rather than of the defeat and flight of Washington's army.

At nightfall Washington moved Woodford's comparatively fresh brigade forward on the right and Poor's on the left as a preliminary to a renewed attack on the British the next morning. But during the night Clinton, with nothing to gain and much to lose from resuming the battle, quietly decamped.

The casualties in the two armies were roughly equal, some three hundred officers and men killed and wounded. In the British army three sergeants and fifty-six privates died of heat prostration, while on the American side a hundred and twenty-six soldiers were reported missing, most of whom had been overcome by the heat and later rejoined their units. A burial detail sent out by Washington to bury the British dead reported four British officers, including Monckton, and two hundred and forty-two privates, a number much in excess of Clinton's figures. Since body counts are notoriously inaccurate, the figure is probably somewhere between Clinton's figures and those published by the Americans. In addition, some estimates of British desertions ran as high as two thousand. While Clinton believed Washington to have twenty thousand men under his command, and Washington in turn underestimated Clinton's force by several thousand, approximately twelve thousand troops were engaged on each side.

Two obvious points about the battle might be emphasized. Every maneuver was inhibited by the terrible heat, which undoubtedly had a major effect on the outcome of the battle. Since the British apparently suffered more from its effects than the Americans, it seems reasonable to assume that Clinton's failure to press his attack on Washington's lines beyond the west ravine was due to the exhaustion of his soldiers as much as to the obstinacy of the American defense. Such factors seldom receive their proper weight in formal accounts of military action, but they are often decisive. The other point is that the toll of British deserters was remarkably high. If the tally of two thousand is even approximately correct, one must assume a very severe loss of morale among the British troops engaged, or a degree of heat prostration severe enough to make many soldiers prefer to desert rather than struggle to keep up with their units. Such disproportionate losses reinforce an earlier observation on Valley Forge and other campaigns that the Americans were willing to bear far greater physical hardship than the professional British soldier. There was something very substantial in the fact that the Americans were fighting for their liberties and for their country, while the British soldiers were fighting, by and large, for their wretchedly low pay. The British fought, as might be expected, much more professionally, but this advantage was largely negated by the fact the Americans on the whole fought much harder, or one might say made up in stamina and simple endurance what they lacked in soldierly qualities.

The practical military gains of the Battle of Monmouth were minimal. Clinton was forced to pay a moderately severe price for the difficult maneuver of extricating his army from Philadelphia. But the American army missed an opportunity for a notable victory, a feat at least theoretically within Washington's power. If Clinton's army had been badly beaten, the effects on British morale and perhaps on the duration of the war might have been considerable. Monmouth was certainly not Washington's most impressive effort—far from it. It was mismanaged from the beginning, so that what promised at least the possibility of a substantial success became instead a rescue operation. But again it could be said that, leadership aside, the American soldiers fought well under the most trying conditions; that they preserved, for the most part, their coherence as functioning units in the face of a bewildering series of marches and countermarches, advances and retreats that might have demoralized far more experienced troops. Perhaps, when all is said and done, Monmouth was important for one reason: The army that had been so painstakingly built at Valley Forge was used. To have let Clinton slip away without an engagement, however inconclusive, would have caused widespread disapproval and grumbling, not least in the army itself.

Charles Stedman's criticisms of the American tactics were sound ones. Washington, he wrote, "ought to have attacked so encumbered an army with all his light troops, and, in spite of partial defeats, contended, in such favorable circumstances, for ultimate victory. The check that the advanced guard of the American army sustained did not, it was said, appear to be so great as to justify a declination of all further attempts against the British army, even at that very time. . . . The American [general] suffered the important occasion to pass by, when he might have terminated the war with one great and decisive effort."

In other words, Stedman, who was with Clinton's army, felt that even after the mismanagement of the battle by General Lee, it was a serious mistake for Washington not to have pressed Clinton harder. It seems clear to me, however, that Washington's initial errors rendered the destruction of Clinton's army impossible. His extreme caution and tentativeness in his pursuit of Clinton, his acquiesing in Lee's determination to command the advance detachment (which was, in large part, a consequence of his not taking command of that body himself), and the confusing orders he gave to Lee were the major factors in the American failure at Monmouth. After Clinton's counterattack had been halted, the American army was too exhausted to carry on an effective pursuit. But the basic point remains: Washington lost a splendid opportunity to destroy Clinton's army after the evacuation of Philadelphia, and the failure to do so was by no means attributable solely to Charles Lee's less-than-inspired performance.

What is difficult for a modern student of the battle to understand is why Washington did not organize his army in such a way as to establish a mobile reserve and take charge himself of the pursuit of Clinton. To try to direct things through Lafayette and then through Lee was an awkward arrangement at best. Washington moved his own force to within three miles of Lee's detachment and five miles of the British rear. Morgan's riflemen had meanwhile moved around to the British right some three miles south of Monmouth, at Richmond's Mills. There Morgan rested his little corps and awaited orders, which apparently never came. In addition to dividing his force, apparently without reference to any systematic tactical plan, Washington failed to press his reconnaissance as aggressively as he might have, so the leaders of the various units that had been detached on special assignments had as inadequate a notion of the terrain as did Washington himself. The American army thus groped its way forward, only dimly aware of the position and relationship of the various units moving toward an engagement. Again the fault was primarily poor staffwork, or, more plainly, no staffwork at all. As we have seen, Hamilton had been riding desperately about the countryside trying to collect information about the enemy's movements, but his place was with Washington, not spying out the lay of the land. All he accomplished was to wear himself out and leave Washington without his services when he needed them most.

Whatever Washington's errors may have been, they were compounded by Lee. It was Lee who was, after all, in direct contact with the enemy, and it was he who should have moved with resolution and expedition. It was incumbent upon him to keep his divisions in hand, to push forward his scouts and advance units, to give spirit and energy to the force under his command. Lafayette, who accompanied Lee as a volunteer, recalled that even after Lee had received Washington's orders to attack, he procrastinated. Lafayette rode up to urge him to outflank the British rear, and Lee replied, "Sir, you do not know British soldiers; we cannot stand against them; we shall certainly be driven back at first, and we must be cautious." Lafayette replied warmly that British soldiers had been beaten before and could be beaten again. Lafayette subsequently had some shrewd observations about Lee, describing him as never an American at heart but simply "a violent Whig," far more interested in embarrassing the North ministry than in "fighting for the independence of the colonies. . . . He always expressed contempt of the American soldiers, and usually spoke of them with a sneer." Giving support to Lafayette's analysis of Lee is a letter Lee wrote in June, 1781, to Robert Morris, who had upbraided him for associating with Tories. He had, Lee declared, been strongly opposed to the accumulation of power in the hands of the British monarch. He had therefore supported the colonists in their resistance to, as he saw it, the unjust and improper influence of the Crown through Parliament. He had been alarmed by the Declaration of Independence and keenly disappointed at the reception of the Carlisle commission, which, in his view, had granted the colonies all they had demanded. In addition to rejecting the generous terms offered through the commission, the Americans had made a treaty of alliance with France and were, from that point on, "fighting the Battles of the House of Bourbon, not her own." "The true spirit of Whiggism," Lee continued, "is now absolutely a stranger to the breast and systems of those who at present take the lead in every state of the continent, and those who are branded with the name of Tories are now the only true Whigs. . . ." "Is the disenfranchisement of the great part of the Pennsylvania Citizens, a Whiggish law?" he asked Morris. If the individuals responsible were Whigs and such laws Whiggish, "I and my associates are undoubted Tories and we glory in the name of it. . . ." Lee and those who were of a like mind lived in Virginia, he wrote, not under "Monarchy, Aristocracy nor Democracy" but where "a Macocracy, that is a banditti of Scotch, Irish Servants or their immediate descendants (whose names generally begin with Mac) are our Lords and Rulers." Lee insisted that he only associated with "true Whigs," those who detested the "tyrannical and felonious measures of our present misrulers [Congress] as much as the meditated tyrannical schemes of the British Ministry."

The aftermath of Monmouth was unsavory. General Lee, when he had recovered his wits, began to try to retrieve his reputation, which proved to be considerably more difficult. With his fatal instinct for the wrong move, he undertook to do this by writing two challenging and insolent letters to Washington a few days after the battle. Haunted by the memory of his humiliation, he could not be quiet but had to make a difficult position impossible. Washington would doubtless have preferred to forget the whole thing; he certainly should have felt some complicity in Lee's downfall. But Lee made the mistake of demanding that Washington, who had doubtless been influenced "by some of those dirty earwigs who will forever insinuate themselves near persons in high office," give an explanation of his treatment of him. Washington replied that Lee should have an opportunity to clear his name of any suggestion of failure to obey orders if he wished. Lee answered rudely with a reference to Washington's "tinsel dignity," and demanded a court-martial, which convened almost instantly (the second of July, five days after the battle) and which found Lee guilty of disobeying orders, of "making an unnecessary, disorderly and shameful retreat," and of disrespect toward Washington. He was sentenced to be suspended from his command for a year.

The verdict of the court-martial had to be reviewed by Congress, and the now desperate Lee began a backstairs campaign among his supporters in that body to win a reversal of its decision. For a time it seemed as though he might be successful in reviving what Colonel John Laurens called "the *old faction*," which included his fellow Virginian Richard Henry Lee and Sam Adams, and Gouverneur Morris wrote gloomily to Washington that "General Lee's Affair hangs by the Eye Lids. . . . Granting him guilty of all the Charges is too light a Punishment. And if he is not guilty . . . there would be an Injustice in [delegates] not declaring their Opinion." The arguments were not unreasonable ones; although a residue of animus toward Washington undoubtedly influenced some delegates, the first two charges were difficult to sustain on the basis of the evidence. The fact that the sentence of suspension was too light if the charges were true indicates most clearly the uneasiness of the court-martial board itself. But it is hard to feel much sympathy for Lee. It was he, after all, who had forced the issue and done it in such a way that the challenge to Washington's leadership had to be considered calculated and deliberate.

Benjamin Rush, one delegate who was no friend to Washington, complained that the waverers were being swayed by "talk of *state necessity* and of making justice yield in some case to policy." Nevertheless, after much agonizing the verdict was confirmed by a vote of fifteen to seven.

Alexander Graydon wrote that "if he [Lee] committed a fault it was because he was too respectful of the enemy; and that he was too scientific, too much of a reasoner. . . ." That was only part of his trouble; I suspect that the most charitable and the most accurate thing that can be said about Lee was that he was more than a little mad. Boudinot, who knew Lee as well as any man, wrote, "Genl Lee had considerable Military knowledge & did very well on a small scale, but I have no doubt that whenever any thing on a very large scale struck him, that a partial Lunacy took place." Indeed, an officer reported to Boudinot after Monmouth that Lee had asked him during the engagement: "Colonel have you seen anything improper in my Conduct this morning? . . . Such an Extraordinary question," Boudinot added, "from a Commander in Chief of a division, under such Extraordinary Circumstances, is full proof that he must have felt something unusual in himself." What is perhaps most remarkable about Lee is the influence that he exerted on many eminently sane and practical patriots, Washington by no means the least among them. And that may indeed be the clue to the riddle of Charles Lee. Individuals who are mad, as long as their madness does not reveal itself in some unmistakable manner, often exercise a strong influence on the normal people with whom they come daily into contact. In their very instability, in their mad self-confidence and their occasional piercing insights, there is just enough admixture of genius to awe and impress their more mundane contemporaries. Lee did, to be sure, place a genuine charge upon the consciences of Americans by his trenchant, passionate advocacy of the American cause in the early years of the revolutionary crisis; but then, like a reckless card player, he squandered that capital. Finally, with little or nothing left in his hand, he insisted on raising the ante until his career and reputation were the last stake he had to throw into the pot. At the heart of most madness, and beneath its restless assertiveness, lies some terrible kernel of self-doubt, a suicidial impulse, if you will, that makes such individuals, whatever their gifts, totally unfit to command. The fact is that the command of others requires relatively modest talents if the commander has great stability of character; what is valued by those who are to be commanded more than any other quality is steadiness and predictability in their leaders.

If the Battle of Monmouth accomplished nothing else, it rid Washington and the cause of the burden of Charles Lee. The Americans claimed the battle as a victory. It was clear in any event that Washington's courage and resolution had saved the day. So far as the battle had a hero, it was clearly he. Henry Laurens wrote congratulating him "on the success of the American Arms under Your Excellency's immediate Command," adding, "It is not my design to attempt encomiums upon Your Excellency. I am as unequal to the task as the Act is unnecessary. Love and respect for Your Excellency is impressed on the heart of every grateful American, and your Name will be revered by posterity."

Lee retired to his Virginia farm, where he lived in that strange squalor that seemed most congenial to him: in a filthy house without glass in the windows, and with hypothetical rooms marked out in chalk on the floor of the drafty, barnlike structure. (The filthiness and the disorder in which Lee preferred to live and which were so often commented on by his contemporaries were clear indications that he was a psychotic.) He wrote a bitter, hectoring letter to Congress and was dismissed from the army. He denounced Alexander Hamilton as the "son of a bitch" who had ruined him by committing perjury at his trial, and he publicly continued to attack Washington until John Laurens wounded him in a duel (Wayne had also challenged him). Later, he distracted himself with plans for a Utopian military colony in the West. When he died in 1782, a widespread rumor alleged that he had committed suicide.

2

The Battle of Rhode Island

AFTER the Battle of Monmouth, Washington moved his army by "easy marches"—breaking camp at three in the morning to avoid the full heat of day, marching some ten miles, and making camp again in the late morning or early afternoon. He proceeded in this manner to New Brunswick and then north along the Hudson to Kings Ferry, where the army was carried across in boats to the east bank. Washington once more established his headquarters at White Plains. Joseph Martin, who was assigned to one of the boats as a ferryman, had the good fortune to have a sturgeon seven or eight feet in length leap from the water into his boat. He delivered it to his messmates with instructions to boil it and save him his proper share.

Almost two years before, Martin and some of his companions had fought at White Plains, and now they went together to walk over the field and rehash the battle. Crude graves dotted the rolling land, and some soldiers had been buried in such shallow and hastily dug pits that dogs or hogs had rooted them up, and "the skulls and other bones and hair were scattered about the place." "Here," wrote Martin, "were Hessian skulls as thick as a bombshell. Poor fellows! They were left unburied in a foreign land. They had, perhaps, as near and dear friends to lament their sad destiny as the Americans who lay buried near them.

But they should have kept at home; we should then never have gone after them to kill them in their own country. But, the reader will say, they were forced to come and be killed here, forced by their rulers who have absolute power of life and death over their subjects. Well then, reader," Martin added, "bless a kind Providence that has made such a distinction between *your* condition and *theirs*. And be careful, too, that you do not allow yourself ever to be brought to such an abject, servile and debased condition."

While Washington established himself in strong defensive positions at White Plains, Clinton held New York City, Staten Island, and Newport, Rhode Island. "It is not a little pleasing," Washington wrote, "nor less wonderful to contemplate that, after two years Manoeuvring . . . both Armies are brought back to the very point they set out from." That this was so was the measure of Washington's achievement. Over a period of three long years he had fought the British army to a standstill.

The British ministry, as we have seen, had decided that the key to a final victory lay in joining forces with the supposedly numerous Southern Loyalists to bring the South under firm control. With that task speedily accomplished, the Eastern states might finally be dealt with as they deserved. Such hopes were, of course, dimmed by the entry of the French into the conflict. The alliance meant a much-increased flow of arms and ammunition and military supplies of all kinds from France to America. In addition, a formidable French fleet of twelve ships and four frigates under the Comte D'Estaing arrived in American waters on the eighth of July after a discouragingly lengthy crossing of eighty-seven days.

D'Estaing's fleet, led by the *Languedoc* of ninety guns, arrived in American waters too late to intercept Clinton's transports. The slowness of the crossing lost the French the opportunity to intercept Admiral Lord Howe's less heavily armed squadron and the vast baggage of Clinton's army. Had D'Estaing arrived in time to engage Howe and— what is somewhat less probable, given D'Estaing's subsequent performance as a naval commander—had he inflicted a decisive defeat on the much inferior British fleet, it is hard to see how Clinton could have maintained his hold on New York. The war might then have ended, for all practical purposes, in 1778 instead of five years later. But D'Estaing was just a few days too late.

D'Estaing's major ships outgunned the British by a substantial margin. Besides the *Tonnant* with 80 guns, there was the *Caesar*, the *Guerriere*, and the *Protecteur*, each with 74, two ships with 64, and one with

54. The British had six with 64, three with 50, and two with 40. Unfortunately the heaviest of the French warships drew too much water to enter New York Harbor. For a time the French gathered in a rich harvest of British supply ships that arrived off New York unaware that a French fleet blocked the harbor. A squadron had been dispatched from England to reinforce Howe at New York, but on the basis of a rumor that D'Estaing's original destination was the West Indies, the fleet had been recalled.

D'Estaing's arrival off New York had been announced by an effusive letter to Washington. The count had been given by His Majesty "the glorious task of giving his allies, the United States of America, the most striking proofs of his affection." D'Estaing assured Washington that he was flattered to have the opportunity "of concerting my operations with a general such as Your Excellency. The talents and great actions of General Washington," he wrote, "have insured him in the eyes of all Europe, the title, truly sublime, of Deliverer of America." He looked forward to being known as a friend of the great Washington: "it is prescribed to me by my orders, and my heart inspires it. . . ."

In addition to his fleet, D'Estaing carried four thousand French soldiers, somewhat the worse for wear, it may be assumed, after such a protracted crossing. Washington's aides, John Laurens and Alexander Hamilton, located pilots who conferred with D'Estaing on the problems of getting his deep-draft vessels into New York Harbor and, as the French officer put it, "destroyed all illusion." "These experienced persons," D'Estaing wrote, "unanimously declared, that it was impossible to carry us in. I offered, in vain, a reward of fifty thousand crowns to any one who would promise success. All refused, and the particular soundings which I caused to be taken, myself, too well demonstrated that they were right."

In New York Clinton, dismayed at the condition of the garrison, which was badly in need of supplies, and unnerved by the proximity of the French fleet, contemplated abandoning the city. He wrote to Lord Germain at the end of July that he "might be compelled to evacuate the city and return to Halifax." Captain Mackenzie of the Royal Welsh Fusiliers was indignant at Clinton's apparent lack of decision. "So extraordinary an event as the present certainly never before occurred in the history of Britain! An army of 50,000 men [the British forces in America came to more than 35,000 at this time] and a fleet of nearly 1000 ships and armed vessels are prevented from acting offensively by the appearance on the American coast of a French squadron of 12 sail of

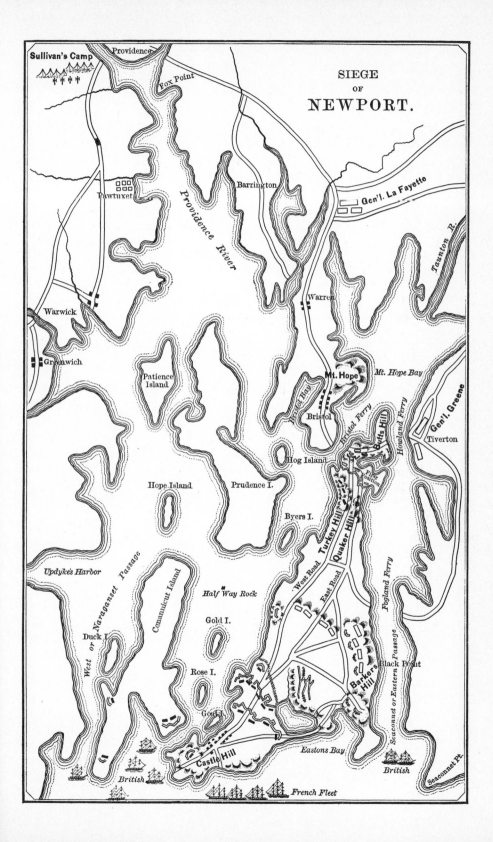

Sullivan's Camp   Providence

SIEGE
OF
NEWPORT.

Fox Point

Pawtuxet

Barrington

Gen'l. La Fayette

Providence River

Taunton R.

Warwick

Warren

Greenwich

Patience
Island

Mt. Hope Bay

Mt. Hope

Bristol Bay

Bristol

Bristol Ferry

Butts Hill

Howland Ferry

Gen'l. Greene

Tiverton

Hog Island

Hope Island

Prudence I.

Fort

Byers I.

Quaker Hill

Turkey Hill

West Road

East Road

Fogland Ferry

Updyke's Harbor

West or Naraganset Passage

Cannunicut Island

Half Way Rock

Gold I.

Duck I.

Barkers
Hill

Seaconnet or Eastern Passage

Black Point

Rose I.

Gold I.

Castle Hill

Eastons Bay

British

Seaconnet Pt.

British

French Fleet

the line and 4 frigates, without troops [the French had, as we have noted, 4,000 troops]. Some unpardonable faults have been committed somewhere"; Mackenzie added, "and those whose duty it is to watch the motions of the enemy in every quarter should answer with their heads for risquing the fate of so large a portion of the national force by their supineness and total want of intelligence."

What Mackenzie did not know, of course, was that in March Lord Germain had sent the following secret instructions to General Clinton: "If you shall find it impracticable to bring Mr. Washington to a general & decisive Action early in the Campaign, you will relinquish the Idea of carrying on offensive Operations within Land & as soon as the Season will permit embark such a Body of Troops as can be spared from the Defence of the Post you may think necessary to maintain, on Board of Transports under the Conduct of a proper Number of the King's Ships, with Orders to attack the ports on the Coast from New York to Nova Scotia . . . so as to incapacitate the Rebels from raising a Marine or continuing their Depredations upon the Trade of this Kingdom."

Meanwhile the most practical use of the French force seemed to Washington to be to move in a combined land and sea operation of French and American soldiers and sailors against Newport, Rhode Island, where the British, it will be recalled, had a garrison of somewhat less than four thousand men. The command of the American forces was given to General Sullivan, with Greene and Lafayette serving under him. Sullivan's force, to be made up largely of militia, was to rendevous with the French north of Newport for an attack on the city while D'Estaing opened a heavy bombardment from the harbor. Such closely coordinated actions are always difficult to bring off. They require cooperation, excellent discipline, and, perhaps above all, good luck. The Newport campaign was lacking all three.

The call for militia brought an enthusiastic response. Jonathan Trumball wrote from Connecticut to General Sullivan: "the men enlist freely and with alacrity, notwithstanding the peculiar difficulties of the Season, which calls them to the labours of the Field." But the militia further to the north were much slower to appear, many of them doubtless lingering to bring in the harvest before they departed.

When the militia straggled into Tiverton—a Rhode Island town north of Newport—Sullivan described them as a "motley and dissaranged Chaos. . . ." He proposed, however, to arrange "with more precision, the dismembered Parts of this unwieldly Body—if any Power less than the Almightly fiat, could reduce them to order. . . ."

When D'Estaing reached Newport Harbor, Sullivan came aboard his flagship to make plans for the joint attack on the town. D'Estaing, who outranked Sullivan, agreed graciously to place the French forces at his disposal, and he put up good-naturedly with Sullivan's New England abruptness. After their conference on August 2, D'Estaing wrote Sullivan: "I fear that you left on my table a plan, which I have had the presumption to keep, because anything made by yourself is too precious a keepsake to be allowed to slip through one's fingers . . . I beg you, Sir, to be kind enough to accept some pineapples and two barrels of fresh lemons. . . ." The plan that D'Estaing and Sullivan agreed upon was for the French to force the Middle Passage between Canonicut Island and Newport, running the British defenses on the eighth of August. On the night of the ninth and the early morning of the tenth, Sullivan was to move his troops from Tiverton to the northeast tip of Rhode Island, on which Newport is situated, and the next morning the French were to land on the west side of the island and join in the assault.

The brigades of Varnum and Glover were assigned to Sullivan as the nucleus of his force; the militia would increase the American strength to some ten thousand men. The British garrison, which had been augmented after Clinton's evacuation of Philadelphia, was believed to consist of slightly less than six thousand men under Major General Robert Pigot. When D'Estaing's fleet arrived in the outer harbor, three British frigates of thirty-two guns were burned along with the *King-Fisher* of sixteen guns, and the *Flora* (thirty-two guns) and the *Falcon* (eighteen guns) were sunk to keep them from being captured. The French troops, which had been on transports for nearly five months, should have been invited ashore at once and provisions made for quartering them, but Sullivan was too preoccupied with his own plans and problems to pay those courtesies and attentions to D'Estaing and his French officers. They had arrived in a friendly and fraternal spirit to help free the Americans from the yoke of their oppressors, and they found themselves treated with what seemed rather like disdain or indifference.

On the night of the eighth, D'Estaing, according to plan, brought his fleet through the Middle Passage into Narragansett Bay. The night of August 9–10 was the time set by Sullivan for the attack. The Americans were to cross on that night from Tiverton at Howland's Ferry, and the French were to land simultaneously on the west side across from Byer's Island. Learning that the British had evacuated the positions opposite Tiverton, Sullivan, without notifying D'Estaing, brought his troops over on the morning of the ninth. The movement of troops was quickly and skillfully executed, but of course it made impossible the combined operation that had been planned for the following day and enabled the British to concentrate their attention on the French landing. D'Estaing, obviously disconcerted by Sullivan's premature action, came ashore to confer with the American general. "Knowing that there are moments which must be eagerly seized in war," he later wrote to the president of Congress, "I was cautious of blaming any overthrow of plans, which nevertheless astonished me ... although accumulated circumstances might have rendered the consequences very unfortunate." In the unsympathetic words of Henry Laurens: "This measure gave much umbrage to the French officers. They conceived their troops injured by our landing first, and talked like women disputing precedence in a country dance, instead of men engaged in pursuing the common interest of two great nations." It was certainly not a promising beginning for a joint operation.

D'Estaing had hardly concluded his talk with Sullivan before the morning mist burned away to reveal a British fleet off the harbor, some thirty-six ships in all. Clinton, learning of the joint French-American plan to attack Newport, had dispatched Admiral Richard Howe to the rescue with a substantial fleet, including eight line-of-battle 64's, five 50's, and two 44's.

With the arrival of the British fleet, D'Estaing insisted on taking the French soldiers who had been detailed to cooperate in the attack on Newport back on board ship. Sullivan protested vigorously but to no effect.

A strong south wind prevented D'Estaing, his troops aboard, from leaving the harbor; but during the night the wind shifted to the northeast and D'Estaing sailed out of the channel, taking up a position to the windward, where Howe, outnumbered three to two, refused to attack with the wind against him. The next twenty-four hours passed with that elaborate maneuvering for the advantage of the wind that was an almost inevitable prelude to any naval warfare before the age of steam. Then came a violent three-day storm that made any formal naval engagement impossible. The wind was hardly short of a hurricane. The ninety-gun *Lanquedoc* lost all her masts and her rudder, and the *Tonnant* of eighty guns had only one mast standing. Several of the ships actively engaged during the intervals of the storm—the *Marseilles* of eighty guns and the *Preston* of fifty fought for several hours—and the less heavily gunned and better handled British ships came off somewhat better than their opponents, although terribly battered by the storm. Whatever modest laurels there were to be distributed went to the British.

Sullivan maintained that he had been about to attack the British in Newport, "finding my own Troops numbers have Increased Sufficiently to warrant my advancing to the Town without waiting for the Return of the Fleet . . . but Fortune Still Determined to Sport Longer with us, brought down a Storm so violent That it Last Night Blew Down & Tore & almost Ruined all the Tents I had. . . . My men," Sullivan wrote to Washington, "are mostly Lying under the Fences half Covered with water without Ammunition & with Arms rendered useless. . . . Should the Enemy come out to attack us our Dependance must be upon the Supcriority of our numbers & the Point of the Bayonet—how our militia may behave on Such an Occasion I am unable to Determine [but plainly his hopes were not high]; to Retreat is impossible; therefore we must Conquer or perish. . . . Several men have perished with the Severity of the weather & I Expect more will as I See no possibility of thc Storm Ceasing." Then Sullivan added a revealing and disarming sentence: "To Combat all these misfortunes & to Surmount all those Difficulties Requires a degree of Temper and persevering fortitude which I could never boast of & which few possess in so ample a manner [as] Your Excellency."

Many of Sullivan's letters had a complaining, querulous quality, full of self-doubt and lamentations about his bad fortune. Washington had not hesitated, on receiving such a letter from Sullivan on the eve of the Battle of Long Island, to replace him with a more resolute general—in that case Greene. Sullivan meanwhile had done nothing to bolster Washington's confidence in him. His service had been undistinguished at Brandywine, to say the least, and it will be recalled that there had been a hearing, which had cleared him of anything worse than poor judgment and indecision. Under the circumstances it was most surprising that Washington gave him a detached command of such heavy responsibility. Several possibilities suggest themselves. Sullivan was still very popular in New England; he was a political general who knew and enjoyed the confidence of those officials to whom he would have to appeal for militia levies. Without substantial augmentation of Greene's and Lafayette's divisions by militia, the operation against Newport would not be practical. Washington had, if anything, less confidence in the other New England generals—Heath and Putnam—who had sufficient rank. By sending two of his best division commanders—Greene and Lafayette—to support him, Washington doubtless hoped to compensate for Sullivan's basic timidity and lack of confidence. Thus, if Sullivan was a poor choice, he may have been, everything considered, the best one available to Washington. We certainly cannot say, as we could of Washington's appointment of Lee to command the advance detachment at Monmouth, that Washington simply made the wrong decision. The choice of Sullivan was a dramatic demonstration of what might be called the extramilitary problems that Washington had to contend with. Every political general—that is to say, every important revolutionary politician who became a general—had to be treated with considerable care. They were prominent and (in the case of Sullivan) often beloved figures in their home states. They had friends and supporters in Congress from other states as well as their own (many New Englanders beyond the boundaries of New Hampshire admired Sullivan, for example), and they had often (again like Sullivan) been members of Congress themselves and might very well be delegates again. It was also assumed that they would, in the future, play a vital role in the laborious task of creating a nation. In any properly run professional army, an incompetent general could be retired (with an extra medal or two to sweeten his retirement), cashiered if he had been hopelessly derelict, or switched to some assignment, like graves registration or PX management, where his bumbling could do no harm; but in Washington's army, political considerations often outweighed military ones. Indeed, as we have seen in the case of Sullivan, the political implications of his assignment had an essential military dimension—that is, his political influence was essential to the mustering of any substantial number of militia.

When the storm, which lasted almost three days, was over and the army and its arms had had a chance to dry out, Sullivan urged D'Estaing to resume the original plan of attack. But D'Estaing wrote, "I should be culpable in my duty to America herself if I could for a moment think of not preserving a squadron destined for her defense." D'Estaing hinted that Sullivan was in large part responsible for his present uncomfortable position by virtue of the fact that he had carried his troops over to the island a day ahead of the agreed-on joint operation. Even so, D'Estaing wrote, "I should be greatly affected to know that you are in danger. . . . To decide upon your motives is a wrong which I have not committed; and the twelve thousand men now under your command will probably prove the correctness of the step, by a success which I desire as a citizen, and as an admirer of your bravery and talents."

Certainly D'Estaing's primary responsibility was to get his disabled ships to Boston for refitting, but it is hard to believe that he could not have placed a sizable portion of his soldiers under the command of Lafayette and left a few of his more seaworthy frigates to assist in the assault on the British works. When Sullivan received D'Estaing's refusal, which he had in a measure already anticipated, he dispatched a letter signed by his general officers urging D'Estaing in the strongest terms to reconsider his decision to sail for Boston and speaking of the "ruinous consequences" that must result. Nine reasons were listed why D'Estaing should remain at Newport, the first being, "Because the expedition against Rhode Island was undertaken by agreement with the Count D'Estaing. An army has been collected, and immense stores brought together, for the reduction of the garrison; all of which will be liable to be lost should he depart with his fleet. . . ."

The ninth point made in Sullivan's letter was perhaps the most telling: it noted "the Count D'Estaing's taking with him the land forces which he has on board, and which might be of great advantage in the expedition, and of no possible use to him at Boston."

Sullivan was told by Lafayette, who went on board D'Estaing's flagship with Greene to try to prevail on the French admiral to alter his plans, that D'Estaing wished to support the attack on Newport but was overruled by his officers, who "are So Incensed at the Count . . . being put over them he being but a Land officer that they are Determined to prevent his Doing any thing that may redound to his Credit or our advantage." Greene and Lafayette had asked only that D'Estaing agree to remain at Newport forty-eight hours, long enough for the combined forces to launch an immediate attack, but the French were adamant.

The departure of D'Estaing left Sullivan in an awkward position. The British, free to re-establish their control over the harbor and to reinforce the Newport garrison, were also in a position to block the escape of Sullivan's army from Newport Island and thus deal a severe blow to the Americans. Sullivan, already obsessed by anxieties and misgivings, issued a general order to his troops declaring, "The General yet hopes the event will prove America able to procure that by her own arms, to which her allies refuse to assist in obtaining."

Sullivan's letters to Henry Laurens and to Washington were filled with bitter complaints about D'Estaing's behavior. The departure of the storm-battered French fleet for Boston had, he told Laurens, "raised every voice against the French nation, revived all those ancient prejudices against the faith and sincerity of that people, and inclines them [the Americans] most heartily to curse the new alliance." The fact was that the great majority of the American people had, prior to the French alliance, viewed Frenchmen as sly and devious and, most unforgivable of all, the enemies of the Protestant religion. No wonder it took a bit of time to accept them as allies and, much more, as agents of the Almighty, sent to preserve their liberties. Sullivan, in his letter to Laurens, added, "I do most cordially resent the conduct of the Count. . . . He well knows that the original plan was for him to land his own troops with a large detachment of mine . . . under the fire of some of his ships, while with the rest I made an attack in front, but his departure has reduced me to the necessity of attacking their works in front or of doing nothing. . . . Your brave and worthy son" he added, "is a fellow-sufferer with me in this fatal island."

Sullivan's gloomy review of his situation on the sixteenth was, to be sure, not far from the truth. With a force of somewhat more than eight thousand men, three-fourths of them highly unreliable militia, he had to attack a defending force of almost six thousand, led by experienced officers and an able general. "My feelings as an officer cause me to hesitate." So he hesitated, which was in fact the worst policy, while his army, impatient at the delay, began to trickle away despite his exhortations. Most of them had enlisted for fifteen days and could not, Sullivan wrote bitterly, be "prevailed upon to remain One hour after the expiration of that time, tho' the establishing of American Independence had been their Reward."

When Sullivan solicited the views of his general officers as to the best course of action, General William Whipple expressed an opinion common to a number of his fellows: "A retreat without attempting anything further would be followed by such consequences as would make it very difficult to raise an army on any future emergency. . . . On the whole, sir . . . I must give my Opinion in favor of an attack. . . ." Nathanael Greene's response, contained in a letter to Sullivan, was the clearest and most cogently argued. It demonstrated that, political considerations aside, Greene should have commanded the attack on Newport. The thoroughness and force of the letter indicate moreover that had Greene indeed commanded the American forces, the outcome might have been a far different one. His suggestions cut through to the heart of the matter. Rulling out a slow-siege operation on obvious grounds, he pointed out to Sullivan that a decision either to storm the British lines or to retreat involved identical preparations—the collecting and removal of baggage, and measures to protect the lines of supply in the event of a successful storming or of withdrawal in the event of a repulse or of a decision not to attack at all. In other words, whether the island was to be evacuated without an attack or by an attack, the initial steps were the same. Therefore these should be taken with the greatest expedition. The reasons for retreat were certainly "strong & many," Greene wrote, "you have the flower of all New England in your Army, your regular force is small, and your whole strength not very great; should you meet with a misfortune the blow will be terrible to these States—You have a prodigious quantity of valuable stores here, the loss of which by a precipitate retreat would greatly distress us." The whole operation had been planned "upon the single condition that the French fleet & forces should cooperate with ours. . . ." It would be folly to attack "6,000 regular troops in Redoubts." To hope for success in such an operation "would require 15,000 Troops of equal or superior quality. . . ."

Only by some stratagem could the British be dislodged. Greene's suggestion was that a sudden bayonet assault on the redoubt at Easton's Beach be launched by three hundred chosen men, with the rest of the army prepared to exploit the opening in the British lines if the redoubt were carried. This attack on the key point in the British lines would be accompanied by "sham attacks along their Lines." Of course, only an officer of Greene's skill would have had any chance of carrying off so complex and demanding an assault.

The consensus of the general officers was clearly opposed to a general assault on the British defenses. Two of the officers proposed that a retreat be conducted in such a manner as to "draw the Enemy out if possible," with the hope of a general engagement on terms more favorable to the Americans. General Varnum took the occasion to write, after comments on the "inexplicable" maneuvers of Comte D'Estaing: "A Sentiment of Dean Swift is constantly with me That every Tub should stand upon its own Bottom; From this consideration, we are to advise the Measures best calculated to promote the rising Glory of America, abstrackted from those complex Views which make up national Connections," i.e., the French alliance.

Greene had evidently discussed the idea of a bayonet attack on the Easton redoubt with Varnum and Glover, because these officers also proposed it, each mentioning an attacking force of three hundred men. Sullivan, vacillating as usual, began to prepare defensive positions. He established his own headquarters at Gibbs Farm, some five miles from Newport, with General Greene's division at Middletown and Lafayette adjacent to him. John Hancock commanded the second line and Colonel West the reserve. The exterior line ran a quarter of a mile in front of the main positions facing eastward; the interior, or main line, extended from the sea to the north end of the island. A strong redoubt had been built between Easton's Bay and Easton's Pond. A second redoubt, a hundred and fifty feet to the north, covered the high ground near the pond. Abatis crossed the island in front of the British defenses.

From the fifteenth to the twenty-third, both armies prepared for battle, the Americans by emplacing batteries to command the British lines and the British by strengthening their defenses. Sullivan was industrious in seeking additional supplies of men and fresh contingents of militia to take the place of those who had departed for home.

On the twenty-eighth Washington wrote from White Plains with the news that Admiral Howe was again on the move, apparently with the intention of reinforcing Newport. Under the circumstances a speedy retreat seemed the only recourse. Washington added a word of caution. Should the expedition fail through the abandonment of the French fleet, the Americans would undoubtedly be loud in their complaints and accusations. "But prudence dictates that we should put the best face on the matter, and to the world attribute the removal to Boston to necessity. The reasons," Washington added, "are too obvious to need explaining. The principal one is that our British and internal enemies would be glad to improve the least matter of complaint and disgust against and between us and our new allies into a serious purpose."

Acting on the advice of his council of war, Sullivan had completed the removal of the heavy baggage and supplies of food and had actually begun to fall back and fortify the north end of the island, while Lafayette was sent to Boston to make a final effort to persuade Count D'Estaing to return to Newport.

By dawn on the morning of August 29, Quaker Hill and Turkey Hill were held by the advance guard under Livingston, and the main American lines had been established across the end of the island, hinged on a strong position on Butt's Hill. At this point the British in Newport under Pigot's command began an attack on the retreating Americans, almost as though they were acting out the script written by Sullivan's staff. Livingston and Lawrence engaged the leading British elements moving along the east and west roads. The fighting was surprisingly sharp and bitter. As the engagement began, General Glover, in command of the American forces on Quaker Hill, was sitting at a table in his headquarters on the reverse side of the hill finishing a hasty breakfast. When the firing broke out, he sent his young aide-de-camp, Rufus King, to find out what was up. As King left the table another officer named

Sherburne took his place. He was hardly seated before a cannonball flew through the window, narrowly missing Glover but smashing Sherburne's leg. The leg had to be amputated later, and Sherburne wrote wryly, "The loss of a leg might be borne but to be condemned all future life to say I lost my leg under a breakfast table, is too bad."

The firing from Quaker Hill was by Colonel Edward Wigglesworth's regiment, which was under heavy artillery bombardment. Moreover the Hessians, moving rapidly up the west road, had outflanked Wigglesworth's position and were turning east to cut off his retreat. Sullivan sent his own aide-de-camp, John Trumbull, son of the Connecticut governor and later one of the most famous painters of the new republic, to warn Wigglesworth of his danger. "Colonel Wigglesworth," Trumbull said, "do you see those troops crossing obliquely from the west road towards your rear?"

"Yes," replied Wigglesworth, "they are Americans coming to our support." "No, sir," Trumbull shouted above the thump of cannon and musket fire, "those are Germans; mark, their dress is blue and *yellow,* not buff; they are moving to fall into your rear, and to intercept your retreat. Retire instantly—don't lose a moment, or you will be cut off." Wigglesworth gave the command, and the Americans abandoned their positions on the hill as fast as they could. Immediately to the rear of Wigglesworth, in the main American line, was General Glover's brigade, with Tyler's on the right and Christopher Greene's on the left. Greene's brigade included a regiment of Negro troops enlisted in Rhode Island. Glover opened up with his own artillery on the advancing British and Hessians to cover Wigglesworth's retreat. His brigade stood firm, and the British regiments fell back to Quaker Hill, where they kept up a heavy fire on the American positions.

Meanwhile several British frigates had moved up the river and taken positions where they could bring their fire to bear on the right flank of the American lines. This fire was accompanied by an attack of Hessian chasseurs on the right of the American lines, an attack directed particularly at a redoubt somewhat in advance of the main American positions. Here Christopher Greene advanced with two or three regiments and drove the Hessians, now reinforced, back. The British reformed and attacked again, and again they were repulsed. In Sullivan's words: "officers & our soldiers behaving with uncommon Fortitude & not giving up an Inch of Ground through the whole Day."

By four o'clock in the afternoon the British had begun to withdraw.

It was to Nathanael Greene in command of the right wing that the principal credit for repulsing the British attack should go. Greene's troops led the counterattack that routed the British and Hessians—"I had the pleasure to see them run in worse disorder," he wrote Washington, "than they did at the battle of Monmouth." General Sullivan's euphoric account of the battle, ending with the words, "The victory on our side was Compleat. . . ," rather overstated the case, but it was certainly true that the Americans had performed most creditably. (To Washington, Sullivan wrote, "The Enemy were oblig'd to retire in great disorder, leaving us in full possession of the Field of Action.") The British, by attacking, had permitted Sullivan and his generals to retrieve a slim measure of triumph from what had been a series of bitter disappointments and frustrations. In his pompous letter to Congress, Sullivan described the course of the battle in terms that made it sound more like a formal pageant than the bitter and at times confused engagement that it was, but in this he was little different from other commanding officers. "I hope," he added toward the end of his letter, "my Conduct through the expedition may merit the approbation of Congress." Sullivan indeed seemed much more assiduous in conveying information to that body than to his own commanding general, Washington. He had let almost a week pass without sending Washington a line, a week of crucial importance during which Washington waited with growing uneasiness for some word from Rhode Island. The account of the battle that Sullivan sent to Washington, although written the same day, was considerably briefer than that to the president of Congress and contained the following sentence (after describing the reasoning behind his decision to retreat): "I therefore (after making use of some little Maneuvres, which effectually deceiv'd the Enemy) gave orders about six oClock last evening. . . ." Nathanael Greene wrote to Washington the same day, and his brief and lucid account of the engagement is in striking contrast to Sullivan's report.

Word reached Sullivan the day after the battle that Clinton was apparently on his way with five thousand more soldiers, making it imperative that Sullivan evacuate the island. Tents were erected in sight of the British, and parties of Americans could be seen strengthening the defenses. But as soon as darkness fell, the ferrying of the army across to the mainland at Bristol and Howland began under the management of the Salem amphibians. Lafayette, who had covered the sixty miles to Boston in seven hours and returned in less, was placed in command of the rear guard, and by early morning the entire American force with its baggage and equipment had been carried over. Sullivan had escaped from his "fatal island."

The initial attempt at cooperation between the Americans and their French allies was certainly not an encouraging one. A Tory satirist published a poem in Rivington's *Royal Gazette* at New York City making fun of the Franco-American campaign to capture Newport. The arrival of the French fleet, the author declared, had enabled the American Jonathan to overcome his fear of the British:

> So Yankee Doodle did forget
> The sound of British drum, sir,
> How oft it made him quake and sweat,
> In spite of Yankee rum, sir.
>
> He took his wallet on his back,
> His rifle on his shoulder.
> And vowed Rhode Island to attack
> Before he was much older.
>
> In dread array their tattered crew
> Advanced with colors spread, sir,
> Their fifes played Yankee doodle, doo,
> King Hancock at their head, sir . . .
>
> As Jonathan so much desired
> To shine in martial story,
> D'Estaing with politesse retired,
> To leave him all the glory.
>
> He left him what was better yet,
> At least it was more use, sir,
> He left him for a quick retreat,
> A very good excuse, sir . . .
>
> Another cause with these combined,
> To throw him in the dumps, sir,
> For Clinton's name alarmed his mind
> And made him stir his stumps, sir.

There was soon another unhappy episode to further strain relations between the new allies. On the night of September 17, in Boston, where D'Estaing was refitting his fleet, a bitter fight broke out between French and American sailors and longshoremen in which a number of the French were beaten and wounded; and the Chevalier de Saint Sauveur was killed trying to break up a fight. The next day the Massachusetts general assembly, anxious to do something to placate its furious guests, directed that a monument be erected to his memory. A reward of three hundred dollars was offered for any information about who had provoked the riot, and the Boston papers did their not-particularly-successful best to put the blame on captured British seamen and deserters from Burgoyne's army who had enlisted as American privateers.

A few weeks later, French and American seamen in Charles Town, South Carolina, clashed in a bloody brawl that left a number on both sides killed and wounded. The Frenchmen, driven from the docks to their ships, opened fire with cannon and small arms, while the Americans replied from the shore.

In the meantime, the British fleet was waging what George Mason rightly described as "a predatory, vindictive War" on the coastal towns of the northeast. On the morning of August 30, a hundred British ships appeared with reinforcements for the Newport garrison. Vice Admiral James Gambier, Admiral Howe's successor, then turned to New London with the intention of bombarding that town in compliance with Germain's orders to Clinton to carry out punitive raids on the New England coast, but unfavorable winds made it impossible for the British ships to enter the harbor. A raiding party under General Grey sailed to the Acushnet River, landed, and destroyed some seventy American boats along the river. On September 4 a raid that involved forty-five British warships and four thousand troops descended on American shipping at Buzzards Bay and Martha's Vineyard off Cape Cod. At New Bedford and Fair Haven, dozens of American ships were destroyed along with twenty-six storehouses, twenty ships and twenty-two houses. Germain's undersecretary, William Knox, was delighted by the news of the New Bedford expedition. "It was always clear in speculation," he wrote, "that the Militia would never stay with Washington or quit their homes, if the coast was kept in alarm, but the experiment having now been made, the effect is reduced to certainty. Surely somebody will ask Lord Howe why he has never attempted anything of the kind." If Admiral Byron could destroy D'Estaing's fleet at Boston and burn that city, he added, "then everything will succeed with us."

The British fleet accordingly appeared off Boston hoping to lure General D'Estaing into a naval engagement, but the count remained in the harbor, where he was immune to attack. His intention was to sail for the West Indies, where he would at least be free of the complications and embarrassments of combined operations with the Americans. Several days before he was to sail, the British fleet appeared once more, this time commanded by Admiral Byron. Before the two fleets could engage, another violent storm blew up and inflicted so much damage on the British ships that Byron was forced to sail to Newport to repair and refit his vessels. Twice in a period of less than two months the weather had played the major role in military and naval operations. Byron had had his fleet scattered and buffeted on the Atlantic crossing; that portion that had accompanied Howe to Newport had also been badly mauled by the storm that started on the eleventh of August and battered both French and British ships mercilessly. Now, attempting once more to bring D'Estaing to an engagement, Byron's fleet was so severely damaged that even after a stay at Newport it was poorly equipped for further campaigning. While D'Estaing set sail for the West Indies, Byron returned to New York.

It was to be more than a year before the French and Americans tried once more to combine forces in a military engagement against the British.

3

Winter Quarters, 1778–79

AFTER the successful retreat from Newport, Sullivan established his headquarters at Providence, and General Greene, in his capacity as quartermaster general, went to Boston to try to facilitate the purchase of supplies for the French fleet. Washington, at White Plains, enjoyed his first breathing spell in many months. "The hand of Providence," he wrote, "has been so conspicuous, that he must be worse than an infidel that lacks faith; and more than wicked, that has not gratitude enough to acknowledge his obligation."

Making early preparations for going into winter quarters, Washington was determined that his army should at last be comfortable and well supplied, and that their positions should deny free movement to the British at New York. Nine brigades were stationed on the west side of the Hudson, the key to whose defense was the fort at West Point. The New Jersey brigade on the Continental Line took its position at Elizabethtown (on the east side of the river) to secure the central part of New Jersey. Seven brigades were encamped near Middle Brook, on the Raritan west of Elizabethtown, and six brigades remained on the east side of the Hudson River in the area bounded by the Highlands, Fishkill, and West Point. The remaining three brigades were posted in the vicinity of Danbury, Connecticut, to protect that portion of the state against British raids and to come to the support of the troops in the Highlands if Clinton should make any serious move in that direction. General Putnam was given command of the forces at Danbury and Alexander MacDougall was placed in charge of the units in the Highlands, while Washington eventually established his own headquarters near Middle Brook.

Clinton's own army was stripped by order of the British ministry, which directed him to send five thousand soldiers to the West Indies to defend the British Caribbean islands against the French; three thousand additional soldiers were dispatched to Florida. In Clinton's words: "With an army so much diminished at New York, nothing important can be done; especially as it is also weakened by sending seven hundred men to Halifax, and three hundred to Bermuda." The British did, however, mount raids. General Grey, who had "massacred" Wayne's detachment at Paoli, caught Colonel George Baylor's light horse by surprise at Tappan and inflicted heavy casualties. Lieutenant Colonel John Simcoe led British cavalry in forays north of New York City, and Cornwallis, with five thousand men, penetrated into New Jersey between the Hudson and the Hackensack, while Knyphausen and his Hessians (or those who had not deserted after Monmouth) made Westchester County the center of raiding operations, collecting what supplies they could for the British garrison in New York. Colonel Ferguson of the Seventieth British Regiment, with three thousand redcoats and the Third New Jersey Volunteers, hit Little Neck in New Jersey at night and caught Count Pulaski's brigade by surprise, inflicting a "loss of fifty killed, nine wounded." Ferguson wrote: "It being a night attack, little quarter could of course be given; so that there are only five prisoners."

In the annals of the Revolution, these were minor engagements that seem to merit no more than a passing mention in military histories. This is true partly because, as Joseph Martin suggested in regard to the defense of Fort Mercer against Von Donop's Hessians, there were no famous American generals involved. It is also true that these encounters were almost uniformly disastrous for the Americans, thus reducing the incentive to recount them in any detail. It seems safe to assume that if Pulaski, alerted by spies or scouts, had ambushed Ferguson's force and killed fifty of them, historians would have provided us with an ample account of the victory. There are two points that might be made here. The first is that few military objectives are more difficult than keeping a garrison sufficiently alert over an extended period to avoid a skillfully executed surprise attack. We have seen such attacks succeed time after time. The second point is to remind the reader that as obscure as these engagements may have been and as unimportant in the total course of the war, they were nonetheless bitterly fought, and those who died were quite as dead as their comrades who fell in famous battles, and were as surely martyrs to the cause of liberty. The American infantryman bayoneted in bed at Paoli or Little Neck died a particularly unpleasant death. But those two clashes involved considerable forces on both sides; three thousand or five thousand men were, in the Revolution, the equivalent of fifty or a hundred thousand in terms of modern warfare. There were hundreds, indeed thousands of smaller clashes—many of them, of course, between Loyalist groups and patriots—that involved from half a dozen to half a hundred men, and the records of those encounters, if they are preserved at all, are hidden in some local archive, in half-legendary stories passed on from one generation to the next, or in a brief notice in a seldom-read newspaper. These, however, were the grim facts of war and revolution as the great majority of Americans experienced them. Comparatively few were involved in the famous battles that took place on center stage; most labored in the wings and experienced in very acute form the hunger, the fear, the continual and corrosive anxiety, the bitter divisions between friends and neighbors, the scattered incidents of violence, the demoralizing effect of rumor that were part of the daily lives of Americans, patriot or Tory, during the years of the war.

Joseph Martin again gives us a vivid picture of just such an encounter. His regiment of light infantry was dispatched from White Plains on a scouting expedition. The men marched all night and then at dawn took up positions on either side of a road, concealing themselves in the bushes. Word had been brought that an enemy foraging party was nearby. Soon a group of Hessian horsemen appeared down the road. When they were abreast of the American ambush, an officer stood up "and very civilly" ordered them to halt. Seeing only one man, the Hessians hesitated, and then their leader gave the signal to the patrol to wheel about. At this the American officer called to the Hessian officer "in a voice like thunder, *'Come here, you rascal!'*" But the Hessian, according to Martin, "paid very little attention to the colonel's summons and began to endeavor to free himself from what, I suppose, he thought a bad neighborhood. Upon which our colonel ordered the whole regiment to rise from their ambush and fire upon them." A detachment of American cavalry helped seal off the Hessian line of retreat. Thirty were captured and a number killed, with no losses to the Americans.

After the brief skirmish was over, one of the light infantrymen, an Irishman, seeing a wounded Hessian lying in the road, "took pity on him, as he was in danger of being trodden upon by the horses, and having shouldered him was staggering off with his load, in order to get him to a place of more safety." Crossing a small bridge over a muddy stream, the Irishman jostled his burden, who cried out in pain, "Good rebel, don't hurt poor Hushman." "Who do you call a rebel, you scoundrel?" the Irishman replied, "and tossed him off his shoulders as unceremoniously as though he had been a log of wood." The unfortunate Hessian fell head down in the mud, and as Martin passed him he saw him struggling for life, "but," Martin wrote, "I had other business on my hands than to stop to assist him. I did sincerely pity the poor mortal, but pity was all I could then do."

Soon after, Martin was again detached, this time with some eighty men, to try to capture a gang of "cowboys" (the name given to Loyalist irregulars) who had destroyed a cache of American supplies at the town of Bedford near King's Bridge. Again they marched at night, and as they marched they could hear the sound of Tories firing on the American sentries. Two free blacks were suspected of being part of the gang, and Martin and some of his fellows, guided by several militia officers, went to the house where the two men lived. The occupants professed to know of no such persons, "but some of the men inquiring of a small boy belonging to the house, he very innocently told us that there were such men there and that they lay in a loft over the hogsty." The birds had flown, but the soldiers routed them out from some bushes in the yard and carried them off. At another house a mile or two away, also reputed to be a Tory hide-out, they found no Tories but "plenty of good bread, milk and butter," and "hungry as Indians," Martin and his companions gorged themselves on the spot. That night they resumed their search for the Tory cowboys, "over brooks and fences, through swamps, mire and woods, endeavoring to keep as clear of the inhabitants as possible. . . . I shall never forget how tired and beat out I was," Martin wrote later. By this means they came to the village of Westchester, split up into groups of five or six, "and immediately entered all the suspected houses at once. . . . There were several men in the house into which I was led, but one only appeared to be obnoxious. . . . This man was a Tory Refugee, in green uniform; we immediately secured him. An old man as blind as a bat came out of a bedroom, who appeared to be in great distress for fear there would be murder committed, as he termed it. I told him," Martin recalled "that it was impossible to commit murder with Refugees."

With twelve or fourteen prisoners, the Americans, knowing that they were in enemy territory, so to speak (surrounded by Tory sympathizers), hurried back to Bedford. As they passed a house, an elderly woman standing in a doorway and "seeing among the prisoners some that she knew . . . began to open her batteries of blackguardism upon us for disturbing what she termed the king's peaceable subjects. Upon a little closer inspection, who should her ladyship spy amongst the herd but one of her own sons. Her resentment was then raised to the highest pitch and she had a drenching shower of imprecations let down upon our heads. 'Hell for war!' said she, 'why, you have got my son Josey, too.' Poor old simpleton! She might as well have saved her breath to cool her porridge."

On another mission to intercept a British raiding party, Joseph Martin's regiment made a forced march at night and, finding no enemy, turned around to march back to White Plains. At nightfall, in Martin's words, "We were conducted into our bedroom, a large wood, by our landlords, the officers, and left to our repose, while the officers stowed themselves away snugly in the houses of the village, about half a mile distant." About midnight a soaking rain began that put out the campfires and wakened the cold and hungry soldiers, who, after enduring several hours of the downpour, began to express their displeasure at being abandoned by their officers by firing their muskets "louder and louder," until the officers "came running from their warm dry beds . . . exclaiming, 'Poor fellows! Are you not almost dead?'" "We might have been," Martin added, "for aught they knew or cared."

Marching into winter quarters with the detachment at Danbury, Connecticut, Joseph Martin watched while, as he put it, "some of our *gentleman officers* [doubtless a reference to their being Southerners] . . . took such a seasoning" at a tavern "that two or three of them became 'quite frisky'. . . . They kept running and chasing each other backward and forward by the troops, as they walked along the road, acting ridiculously," and finally ending up in a bitter fight "to the no small diversion of the soldiers, for nothing could please them better than to see the officers quarrel amongst themselves."

The soldier's entertainment was sometimes brutal. Irishmen, denominated "Old Countrymen," were notorious for getting drunk and "boxing with each other in good fellow ship," as Joseph Martin put it.

Martin witnessed such a fray on "a cold, frosty day in the month of December." The two drinking companions "stripped to the buff, and a broad ring was directly formed for the combatants . . . when they prepared for battle. The first pass they made at each other, their arms drawing their bodies forward, they passed without even touching each." They were too drunk to do much damage, and the only blood that was drawn was by the frozen ground when one or the other fell upon it. Finally, one of the combatants cried out, "I am too drunk to fight," and headed for the sutler's hut and more whiskey. "The other followed, both as bloody as butchers, to drink friends again, where no friendship had been lost. And there I left them and went back to my tent, thankful that Yankees, with all their follies, lacked such a *refined* folly as this."

Of their camp near Danbury, Martin wrote: "We . . . went on in our old Continental line of starving and freezing. We now and then got a little bad bread and salt beef [chiefly horsemeat]. . . . Our condition, at length, became insupportable. We concluded that we *could* not or *would* not bear it any longer. We were now in our own state and were determined that if our officers would not see some of our grievances redressed, the state should." After roll call, the soldiers turned out without their arms and paraded in front of their huts as a form of dramatic protest. "We had hardly got paraded," Martin wrote, "before all our officers, with the colonel at their head, came in front of the regiment, expressing a great deal of sorrow for the hardships we were compelled to undergo, but much more for what they were pleased to call our mutinous conduct."

The expression proved an unfortunate one, and an angry murmur began to rise from the ranks. At this the officers "changed their tone and endeavored to soothe the Yankee temper they had excited. . . ." The soldiers were persuaded with some difficulty to return to their tents, but they had ingenious notions of how to make their discontent felt. Firing muskets in camp was forbidden, under the threat of severe punishment. Knowing that the sound of gunfire would keep their officers in a turmoil, the soldiers took an old gun barrel, loaded it with a charge, placed it in an unfinished hut, put a slow match to it, and stole away quietly to their own huts. The gun fired, the officers came "running and scolding but none knew who made the noise or where it came from. This farce was carried on the greater part of the night; but at length the officers tired of running so often to catch Mr. Nobody . . . that they . . . gave up the chase. . . . We fared a little better for a few days after this memento to the officers. . . ." But things soon became unbearable again, according to Martin. This time the soldiers decided to turn out with their arms, appoint one of their number as commander, and simply march off to Hartford to demand redress of their grievances from the assembly; if their requests were denied, they intended to "disperse to our homes, in presence of as many of our fellow citizens as chose to be spectators." As the men were forming up the adjutant came by and, realizing that something serious was afoot, summoned the officers of the brigade, "all of whom were soon upon the parade."

The sergeant whom the soldiers had appointed to act as their commander ordered his mutinous little force to shoulder arms, present arms, and order arms. At this point the major addressed the newly elected commander: "Well, Sergeant, you have got a larger regiment than we had this evening at roll call, but I should think it would be more agreeable for the men to be asleep in their huts this cold night, than to be standing on the parade. . . ."

"Yes, sir," the sergeant replied, "Solomon says that 'the abundance of the rich will not suffer *him* to sleep,' and we find that the abundance of poverty will not suffer us to sleep." By this time the colonel had joined the major, "and the old mode of flattery and promising was resorted to and produced the usual effect. We all once more returned to our huts and fires, and there spent the remainder of the night, muttering over our forlorn condition." One result of the soldiers' agitation was that many of them were furloughed, Martin among them. He set out to cover the thirty miles to his home in a day; "the hopes of soon seeing my friends and the expectation of there filling my belly . . . buoyed up my spirits."

At the last ferry crossing, the boat was frozen to the bank and covered with snow. There Martin found the ferryman's daughter, who was the wife of the drum major of his regiment. "She made a bitter complaint to me," Martin wrote, "against her husband, said he came home from the army and spent all her earnings, gave the whole family the itch, and then went off to camp, leaving her and her children to shift for themselves as well as they could." "I could have told her a little more of his *amiable* conduct than she knew," Martin observed dryily, "but I thought she might as well get her information from some other quarter."

Home at last, Martin had "an opportunity of seeing the place of my boyhood, visit old acquaintance, and ramble over my old haunts; but my time was short, and I had, of course, to employ every minute to the best advantage."

Back in camp after the blessed respite, it was freeze and starve once more—"we had nothing to eat except now and then a little miserable beef or a little fresh fish and a very little bread . . . which had some villainous drug incorporated with it that took all the skin off our mouths" and "some clams, which kept us from absolutely dying."

In the early weeks of winter, Washington could hardly be said to have had a headquarters of his own. Rather, he made constant circuits of his dispersed units. A hospital had been established at the abandoned home of a prominent Tory, Beverley Robinson, near West Point, and on October 8 Washington made a visit to the hospital, which was in the charge of our old friend, Dr. Thacher. Thacher described Washington in almost clinical detail: "The appearance of our Commander in Chief, is that of the perfect gentleman and the accomplished warrior. He is remarkably tall, full six feet, erect and well proportioned. The strength and proportion of his joints and muscles appear to be commensurate with the preeminent powers of his mind. The serenity of his countenance, and majestic gracefulness of his deportment, impart a strong impression of that dignity and grandeur, which are his peculiar characteristics, and no one can stand in his presence without feeling the ascendancy of his mind, and associating with his countenance the idea of wisdom, philanthropy, magnanimity, and patriotism. There is a fine symmetry in the features of his face indicative of a benign and dignified spirit. . . . He wears his hair in a becoming cue, and from his forehead it is turned back and powdered in a manner which adds to the military air of his appearance. He displays a native gravity, but devoid of all appearance of ostentation. His uniform dress is a blue coat, with two brilliant epaulettes, buff colored under clothes, and a three-corned hat with a black cockade. He is constantly equipped with an elegant small sword, boots and spurs, in readiness to mount his noble charger."

Thacher's description is worth presenting in full because it gives a vivid if familiar picture of Washington and serves to remind us how much his mere appearance among his scattered brigades meant in preserving morale and how much he embodied, quite literally, the Continental Army.

With Clinton's forces too widely dispersed to be a serious threat, Washington's thoughts turned once more to an invasion of Canada. "The question of the Canadian expedition, in the form in which it now stands," he wrote the president of Congress, "appears to me one of the most interesting that has hitherto agitated our national deliberations." The notion was that French and American forces should combine in such a campaign. The example of the attempt at Newport was not an encouraging one, however, and John Jay, among others, urged against such an effort. In December, leaving MacDougall in command of the troops in the Highlands, Washington established his headquarters in Middle Brook or Bound Brook near the main body of his army. From Bound Brook he rode on to Philadelphia to confer with Congress on plans for campaigns that might be undertaken in the spring, and while in the city he joined in a celebration by the "Most ancient and worshipful Society of Free and accepted Masons." Washington, himself a Mason, was given the principal place in the procession, accompanied by the grand master. In the service at handsome Christ Church, the preacher spoke of him as the Cincinnatus of America, a reference to the famous Roman general who left his plow as a simple farmer to lead the armies of Rome to victory over their enemies.

Behind his inscrutable façade, Washington suffered one of his not infrequent spells of depression. The signs of comfortable and even lavish living in Philadelphia while his own soldiers were suffering from the lack of adequate food and clothing distressed him. He wrote to Benjamin Harrison in December: "If I were called upon to draw a picture of the times and of men from what I have seen, heard, and in part know, I should in one word say that idleness, dissipation, extravagance seems to have laid fast hold of most of them—That speculation—peculation—and an insatiable thirst for riches seems to have got the better of every other consideration and almost of every order of Men—That party disputes and personal quarrels are the great business of the day whilst the momentous concerns of an empire—a great and accumulating debt—ruined finances—depreciated money—and want of credit (which in their consequences is the want of everything) are but secondary considerations and postponed from day to day—from week to week as if our affairs wore the most promising aspect. . . . Our money is now sinking 50 per cent. a day in this city . . . and yet an assembly—a concert—a dinner or supper will not only take men off from acting in this business, but even from thinking of it—while a great part of the officers of our army are quitting the service, and the more virtuous few, rather than do this, are sinking by sure degrees into beggary and want . . .—after drawing this picture, which from my Soul I believe to be a true one, I need not repeat to you that I am alarmed and wish to see my countrymen roused."

Not only was Congress unable, in the face of the refusal of the states to make any substantial contributions to the Continental treasury, to supply Washington's army adequately with the barest necessities; it was unable to control a ruinous inflation that it in fact had created by the desperate expedient of printing more and more paper money. In October Washington had complained that the boniest horse cost at least two hundred pounds, a saddle thirty, and boots twenty. Abigail Adams complained to her husband a few months later that meat cost from a dollar to eight shillings a pound and corn twenty-five dollars a bushel, and common labor six to eight dollars a day. Washington wrote, "Our affairs are in a more distressed, ruinous, and deplorable condition than they have been since the commencement of the war. . . . The common interests of America are mouldering and sinking into irretrievable ruin if a remedy is not soon applied."

Having been summoned to Philadelphia to confer with Congress, Washington was detained as an unwilling guest of that body for over a month while the delegates argued over strategy and continued their fruitless debates over how to supply the Continental Army. Washington employed some of the time sitting for a portrait by Charles Willson Peale, the Philadelphia artist; the finished picture was to be hung in the chamber of the supreme executive council of Pennsylvania. The itinerant French artist, Pierre Eugène du Simitière, also made "a drawing in black lead . . . in profile of his Excellency" to be used in striking a medal. At the end of January Washington complained to Congress of his "long and unexpected stay in this City" and asked for permission to return to his headquarters at Middle Brook. He was back in time for "a splendid entertainment" given by the Knoxes in celebration of the French alliance. The occasion was marked by a handsome parade and "a very beautiful set of fire works," followed by a ball, which was opened by Washington "having for his partner the lady of General Knox." "We danced all night," Knox wrote his brother "—an elegant room, the illuminating fire works, etc., were more than pretty."

There was an ironic undertone to the celebration given by the Knoxes. The French alliance, on which Washington and many others had placed such great hopes, was a bitter disappointment. The fleets of France and Spain together had failed to inflict a decisive defeat on the British in the year since the treaty had been concluded. "We ought not to deceive ourselves," he wrote. "The maritime resources of Great Britain are more substantial and real than those of France and Spain united. . . ." It seemed that all the advantages were on the side of the British. "In modern wars," he noted, "the longest purse must chiefly determine the event. I fear that of the enemy will be found so." Britain's great commercial and industrial resources must prevail in the long run, "and then what would become of America?" Washington asked, and then answered his own question: "I see one head gradually changing into thirteen. I see one army branching into thirteen, which, instead of looking up to Congress as the supreme controlling power of the United States, are considering themselves as dependent on their respective states. In a word, I see the power of Congress declining too fast for consideration and respect." Washington would gladly be rid of all Frenchmen except Lafayette, he declared.

The disillusionment with the alliance was mutual. Vergennes, basing his views in large part on the very negative reactions of some of the French officers attached to Washington's army, spoke scathingly of American cowardice and inefficiency. He expressed himself as astonished that the British had not crushed the rebellion long ago and feared that even French intervention might not prevent the dissolution of the patriot cause. He doubted "their talents, their views and their love of country. . . . Their republic if they fail to correct its vices will always be a body capable of very little activity. . . . I swear to you I have only faint confidence in the energy of the United States," he wrote.

A few days after the Knoxes' celebration, Dr. Thacher, who had last encountered Washington at the hospital, was a guest at the general's headquarters, and once more he noted in his diary Washington's "cheerful open countenance, simple and modest deportment," which commanded such "veneration and respect." "He is feared," Thacher wrote, "even when silent, and beloved even while we are unconscious of the motive . . . a placid smile is frequently observed on his lips, but a loud laugh, it is said, seldom if ever escapes him. . . . Mrs. Washington combines in an uncommon degree, great dignity of manner with the most pleasing affability, but possesses no striking marks of beauty."

Back at Middle Brook Washington gave his principal attention to recruiting. One of the major difficulties in recruiting Continental soldiers in New England was that they were unwilling to serve under regular officers, many of whom were Southerners. David Cobb, a sometime aide to Washington, wrote a friend in 1780 that "the curse of slander" prevailed "that the Continental officers are so cruel and severe that the men can never be got to serve under 'em. . . . You can't meet a man of any Influence from the Country, but he'll tell you that they never shall be able to raise their men unless they appoint their officers, for the men, they say, will never serve under Continental officers, because they have been so badly treated by 'em. . . . This is a prejudice that must be combated with all the force of art and Intrigue, for I conceive that this will have the most fatal tendency to the opposition of this Country, of anything that has happened during the contest." But Cobb himself was most unhappy at the rumor that the army was to be new-modeled, and that he would, in consequence, find himself "serving in a different corps than what I have heretofore serv'd in. . . . I shall be chas'd into some other Regt. that will make me very unhappy & consequently defeat all my pleasure, as it is from the agreeableness of connection that I continu'd in the service. . . ."

The dislike of New England soldiers for Continental officers was related to the bitter sectional feelings. Alexander Graydon, the Philadelphian, noted in his memoirs that the New Englanders were viewed with contempt by the Southerners. "Even the celebrated General Putnam," he wrote, "riding with a hanger belted across his brawny shoulders, over a waistcoat without sleeves (his summer costume), was deemed much fitter to head a band of sickle-men or ditchers, than musketeers." One officer noted that the animosity between the soldiers from different sections had risen "to such a height, that the Pennsylvania and New-England troops would as soon fight each other as the enemy. Officers of all ranks are indiscriminately treated in a most contemptible manner, and whole colonies traduced and villified as cheats, knaves, cowards, poltroons, hypocrites, and every term of reproach, for no other reason, but because they are situated east of New-York. Every honor is paid to the merit of good men from the south; the merit, if such be possible, from the north is not acknowledged; but if too apparent to be blasted with falsehood, is carefully buried in oblivion."

After Monmouth, when Washington's army encamped at White Plains, Joseph Martin had been assigned to a light-infantry corps made up of picked soldiers from the whole army. The idea, which was Washington's, was that these men should have special training and be used for particularly dangerous and difficult assignments. Martin's description of the corps gives a vivid picture of sectional conflict on the level of the private soldier. "It was a motley group," Martin wrote, "— Yankees, Irishmen, Buckskins, [Virginians] and what not. The regiment that I belonged to was made up of about one half New Englanders and the remainder were chiefly Pennsylvanians—two sets of people as opposite in manners and customs as light and darkness. Consequently there was not much cordiality subsisting between us, for, to tell the sober truth, I had in those days as lief have been incorporated with a tribe of western Indians as with any of the southern troops, especially of those which consisted mostly, as the Pennsylvanians did, of foreigners. But I *was* among them and in the same regiment too . . . and had to do duty with them. To make a bad matter worse, I was often, when on duty, the only Yankee that happened to be on the same tour for several days together. 'The bloody Yankee,' 'the damned Yankee,' was the mildest epithets that they would bestow upon me at such times. It often made me think of home, or at *least* of my regiment of fellow Yankees." Martin found that "southern women" had a "queer idea of Yankees. . . . They seemed to think that they were a people quite different from themselves, as indeed they were in many respects." When Martin, on a foraging expedition for Washington's army, stopped with a wagoner at the home of a Pennsylvania woman, the wagoner complemented her on the gentleness and beauty of her four-year-old daughter. The mother replied that the child had been "quite cross and crying all day. 'I have been threatening' said she, 'to give it to the Yankees.' 'Take care,' said the wagoner, 'how you speak of the Yankees, I have one of them here with me.' 'Law!' said the woman. 'Is he a Yankee? I thought he was a Pennsylvanian. I don't see any difference between him and other people.'"

Although Washington deplored sectional feeling, he was not, as we have seen, entirely free of it himself. He wrote to John Custis, his brother-in-law, "It is painful to me to hear of such illiberal reflections upon the Eastern States as you say prevails in Virginia. I always have and always shall say that I do not believe any of the States produce better men, or persons capable of making better soldiers, but it is to be acknowledged that they [the New Englanders] are (generally speaking) most wretchedly officered. To this, and this only, is to be attributed their demerits. The policy of those States has been to level men as much as possible to one standard . . . whenever a Regiment is well officered, their men have behaved well—when otherwise, ill-conduct or cowardly behavior always originating with the officers who have set the example. Equal injustice is done them, in depriving them of merit in other respects; for no people fly to arms readier than they do, or come better equipped, or with more regularity into the field than they do."

It was small wonder that, under such circumstances, the recruiting went badly. Supporters of the Crown in England and America took heart from the reports of the miserable state of Washington's army. An American Tory in England wrote a friend in America that he had heard that in New York many gentlemen of "Influence & property, who had been laying on their oars, to see which way the game would finally go . . .

have lately come in," that is to say, affirmed their loyalty to the Crown. The writer continued that as a result of the "unexampled Tyranny of Congress, and their sub-Devils [the state legislatures] the almost universal poverty & distress of the people, and the general aversion to french connections, the quondam union of the 13 States is upon the point of Dissolution, and that nothing is wanting but a single effort to Crush the Rebellion, root & branch."

4

Meanwhile Congress . . .

Aꜰᴛᴇʀ Clinton's evacuation of Philadelphia, Congress returned to that city and immediately spent considerable time trying to decide how to receive the French plenipotentiary, (or "Plenipo," as the delegates promptly nicknamed him), Monsieur Conrad Alexandre Gérard. It was important to receive him with sufficient simplicity as to appear properly "republican," but yet with such show and dignity as befitted the representative of the great nation who had come so graciously to America's rescue. It was, at least in the minds of the delegates themselves, a delicate matter. Finally it was resolved to virtually everyone's satisfaction. As Elias Boudinot described the scene to his wife: "Our President was seated in a Mahogany armed chair on a platform raised about two feet, with a large table covered with a green cloth and the secretary along side of him. The Members were all seated round within the Bar and a large armed chair in the middle opposite the President for the Plenipo." At twelve sharp the stagecoach of Congress, drawn by six handsome horses, "waited on the Minister at his quarters. He was preceded by his own Chariot . . . with his Secretaries. The Minister was attended by two Members who introduced him thro' the crowd and seated him in the chair; He then sent to the President (by his Secretary) the Letters from the King of France to Congress, which was opened and read aloud first in French and then in English. It was then announced to the house by the waiting Members, that the stranger introduced was the Minister Plenipotentiary from His most Christian Majesty, upon which the Minister arose and bowed to the President and then to the House and the House rising returned the Compliment. The Minister then addressed the Congress and was answered by the President, on which, the bowing again took place and the whole concluded. A public Dinner succeeded at which was a band of musick and the firing of Cannon. The whole was plain, grand and decent. The Minister was much pleased as well as the Audience."

Henry Marchant, a delegate to Congress from Rhode Island, wrote fervently, "The Scene brightens, grows more and more interesting, and calls for new and fresh exertions of Senatorial Wisdom. We advance into the Circle and Standing of mighty Nations—Adepts in all the Policy of Peace and War. May Heaven protect our Youth and prove the Friend, Protector and Counsellor of America!" Another enthusiastic congressman wrote, "I never was Witness to a more elevating and unspeakably joyous Interview than that between the Plenipotentiary of His most Christian Majesty, and the President of Congress in the Name and Behalf of the thirteen United States of America. It was reciprocally graceful Endearing and Noble. May it presage a happy Issue to the American Struggle and a growing and undecaying Glory that shall diffuse its grateful Influences thro' the World."

In some ways the most vexing, or at least the most depressing, issue faced by Congress was the bitter wrangle between Arthur Lee and Silas Deane, an issue that troubled Congress for more than a year. Indeed, that body might be said to have never entirely recovered from the rancors and animosities stirred up by that unhappy quarrel. Deane, whatever else might be said for or against him, was an impulsive man of poor judgment; he had plagued Congress by sending to America, in addition to some notable officers, a seemingly endless flood of impecunious and arrogant soldiers of fortune, the castoffs or, more typically, the unemployed veterans of a half-dozen European armies. They descended on America with expensive retinues and outmoded notions, exotic reminders of the Old World culture that Americans had rejected. They importuned Congress weekly with exaggerated accounts of their military accomplishments and with demands for high rank and for important commands. Deane was apparently impressed by all of them, indiscriminately, and he sent them off to America with promises that could not have been honored without triggering wholesale resignations in the American officer corps, and with letters of introduction that usually took them at their own inflated valuation.

All this was, in large measure, compensated for by the fact that through Beaumarchais and his Hortalez and Company, Deane also produced a steady flow of desperately needed supplies. And he did this without any money from Congress. Ironically, the French alliance deprived Deane of his most useful function, for it transferred the whole matter of providing supplies and equipment for the Continental Army from the clandestine trading company to the French ministry of war. Coincident with this, Arthur Lee's long campaign of innuendo against Deane blossomed into direct charges of improper conduct in his office. Lee found a ready ally in the South Carolinian Ralph Izard, who, writing from Paris, did his best to undermine the confidence of Congress in both Deane and Franklin. Of Deane he wrote, "Search the World thro' and a more unfit Person could not be found . . . he is totally unqualified for the post he has filled, and not to be trusted in the future . . . and as to Franklin, he is a crafty old Knave . . . in my conscience I believe he has neither honor nor honesty. . . ."

Franklin, well aware of the intrigues of his enemies, wrote to Lee in April, 1780: "It is true that I have omitted answering some of your letters, particularly your angry ones in which you, with very magisterial airs, schooled and documented me, as if I had been one of your domestics. I saw in the strongest light the importance of our living in decent civility towards each other, while our great affairs were depending here. I saw your jealous, suspicious, malignant and quarrelsome temper, which was daily manifesting itself against Mr. Deane and almost every other person you had any concern with. I, therefore, passed your affronts in silence, did not answer them, but burnt your angry letters, and received you, when I next saw you, with the same civility as if you had never written them."

John Adams, arriving in France in April, 1778, was dismayed to find that the American agents of Congress were at swords' points. There were "animosities between Mr. Deane and Mr. Lee; between Dr. Franklin and Mr. Lee; between Mr. Izard and Dr. Franklin; between Dr. Bancroft and Mr. Lee; between Mr. Carmichael and all. It is a rope of sand. . . . Parties and divisions among the Americans must have disagreeable, if not pernicious, effects." Lee had clearly given offense "by an unhappy disposition, and by indiscreet speeches before servants and others concerning the French nation and government—despising and cursing them. . . . The public business has never been methodically conducted. There never was, before I came, a minute book, a letter book or an account book; and it is not possible to obtain a clear idea of our affairs. Mr. Deane lived expensively, and seems not to have had much order in his business, public or private; but he was active, diligent, subtle and successful, having accomplished the great purpose of his mission to advantage."

By the summer of 1778, the anti-Deane faction in Congress had gained sufficient strength to have Deane recalled. He got back to Philadelphia not long after the evacuation of that city by the British in the late spring of 1778, and he began, almost at once, to appear before Congress to explain and justify his action as their commissioner, "reporting from Notes and Memory his own transactions separately as well as conjunctly with his Colleagues. . . ." Deane was determined to present his case in person, although, in an effort to stem the apparently endless recital, some members tried to have his report submitted in written form. The most complicated and controversial aspect of Deane's recital was his insistence that the constant flow of supplies (which Congress had been so happy to receive under the illusion that they were, in effect, gifts of the benign monarch at Versailles who did not yet wish to declare himself publicly as a friend of the Revolution) were, in fact, charges against Congress by a private contractor, namely Beaumarchais. This was very bad news, since Congress had no money to pay the bills that Deane presented to it; it also inevitably raised the suspicion that Beaumarchais, with the interested cooperation of Deane, was trying to shake down Congress by deliberately misrepresenting the nature of Hortalez and Company.

The most remarkable aspect of the affair of Silas Deane was that with the exception of the question of half-pay for officers, it split Congress more deeply and bitterly than any other issue that came before it during the course of the Revolution. As Henry Laurens wrote to the governor of South Carolina, he soon discovered "that my fellow labourers had as absolutely taken sides as it can be supposed Gentleman are capable of in a *pure unbiased* Assembly." What Deane's enemies could not effect—an interruption of his recital—was forced by the press of more urgent matters. Week after week Deane cooled his heels while the delegates struggled with military and monetary problems. He made constant pleas that Congress resume its inquiry into the conduct of his office and release him. When Congress failed month after month to respond, Deane made up his mind to carry his "case" to the general public through the pages of the *Pennsylvania Packet*. He did this in the form of an address "to the free and virtuous citizens of America." On the principle that the best defense is a strong offense, he leveled a series of charges against Arthur Lee and his brother William, a commercial agent of Congress in Paris, who, he charged, had joined in the conspiracy against him.

To his enemies, Deane's action, taken while his case was still pending before Congress, was rude and improper. Whatever else its effect, it certainly increased the resentments against Deane in that body. "This Appeal," Laurens wrote, "this rash unnecessary appeal I trust will this day be attended to in Congress ... the honor and interests of these United States call upon every Delegate in Congress for support. If therefore other Men shall be silent, I will deliver my sentiments on this very extraordinary circumstance and I have in prospect the production of much good out of this evil." Laurens' disgust with the response of Congress, and perhaps with the whole affair, seems to have led directly to his resignation as president of Congress in December, 1778.

At last, in an odd kind of compromise, Deane was directed to make his report in writing, as he should, of course, have done initially, but he was allowed to read it to Congress and to reply to questions raised by his account. He began reading the document on the twenty-second of December and finished it by the end of the month. Meanwhile, outside the halls of Congress, the case was hotly argued in the public press. Tom Paine, secretary of the committee for foreign affairs, attacked Deane over the pen name of "Common Sense." Richard Henry Lee also joined in under an assumed name. Deane, in turn, found defenders as vigorous as his defamers.

Francis Lightfoot Lee, writing to Arthur, told him that his enemies were part of a "very dangerous party who think it necessary to their designs, to remove all the old friends of Liberty and Independence, for which purpose every Lie their invention can furnish, is circulated with the Air of certainty, and the blackest colorings given to Actions in themselves indifferent or accidental." In Lee's view, this faction was "composed of the Tories, all those who have rob'd the public, are now doing it, and those who wish to do it, with many others, whose design, I fear, is of a much more alarming nature, and a few who wish to succeed to Offices abroad. All these together form a very powerful body. Having prepared the minds of the people, by a number of understrappers, who have circulated their insinuations and falsehoods thro' the Country with great industry. . . ."

Many delegates to Congress made determined efforts to be fair to both men and labored to collect and assimilate the evidence, pro and con. If, on reading the vast accumulation of material on this basically uninteresting and unimportant controversy, one does not emerge with any clear notion of who was right and who wrong, one does get a vivid picture of the patience and pertinacity with which the delegates pursued the question, as well as a renewed sense of their humanness, struggling as they did, albeit not particularly successfully, to make their heads rule their hearts, trying, as Elbridge Gerry said rather plaintively, "to act with becoming Freedom and Independence." So one alternates between irritation and admiration. Lee and Deane, as many of the delegates came rather soon to feel, were not really worthy of the time and energy expended on them by Congress, but clearly the principle of trying "to do justly" *was,* at least for those delegates not blinded by their prejudices.

Early in 1779 Congress appointed a committee made up of a member from each state to review the whole field of foreign affairs. A month later the committee brought in its report, with the hardly surprising statement that "in the course of this committee's examination and enquiry they find many complaints against the Commissioners," and that "suspicions and animosities highly prejudicial to the honor and interests of these United States" had arisen among them. The committee's recommendation was "that the appointments of the said Commissioners be vacated and that new appoints be made."

Initially, the committee's report simply added fuel to an already hot fire. Ralph Izard, Arthur Lee, and William Lee were now on the griddle. The partisans of both factions tried to maneuver Gérard, the French plenipotentiary, into stating that Arthur Lee had (or did not have, as the case might be) the complete confidence of the French court. After Sam Adams hinted that Gérard had said that Lee was the object of just such confidence, Drayton of South Carolina and Paca of Maryland reported that they had gotten a different impression from the French minister. In Laurens' words: "Mr. Lee . . . was put into the Court Alembrick, what came forth? a jealous troublesome, but honest Man."

To the modern reader it will seem strange that our Revolutionary ancestors, men whose wisdom and vision we have been taught to venerate, should have become hopelessly bogged down in such a sordid squabble and done so in the midst of the country's desperate struggle for survival against an implacable enemy. At this distance in time it seems more difficult than ever to measure out blame between the rivals themselves—Arthur Lee and Silas Deane—and between the factions that gathered around them. And fortunately it is not necessary. William Houston of New Jersey reported to Governor Livingston of his home state on his examination into Lee's character. "The result," he wrote, "is this: I take Mr. Arthur Lee to be a man of jealous, suspecting, difficult disposition; trusty, capable and industrious. Indefatigable above others in procuring and transmitting intelligence; accurate and frugal in expenses and money matters; simple, severe, and republican in manners, so much so, as to be thought by many sour and inimical." Deane, perhaps equally devoted to the public good as he understood it, was a more florid, pompous man, as touchy and vain as Lee and clearly as contentious. He was, in addition, something of a fool, strident where Lee was acidulous, naive where Lee was suspicious. And Deane, in fact, was more sinned against than sinning as far as Arthur and William Lee were concerned. It was not until the last stages of the controversy that Deane and his supporters turned their guns full on the Lee faction. Moreover, poor Deane was surely unfortunate in his adversaries. The Lees made up the largest and most ubiquitious clan of patriots in America. The family, Richard Henry in particular, had numerous uncashed checks drawn on the loyalties and affections of patriot leaders in every state; on Samuel Adams, for instance, in Massachusetts, and Thomas Burke in North Carolina, to mention only two among many.

The delegates to Congress thus found themselves embroiled in a conflict that penetrated far behind the conflict between the Deane and Lee factions. It was nourished by a dozen old battles, rousing echoes of personal and sectional feuds whose history extended back to the early days of revolutionary agitation. It involved, in time, the whole notion of the nature of American independence, and it stimulated uneasiness on the part of many Congressmen, since it brought to the foreground the question of the intentions of France toward America and the whole issue of the degree to which Congress should accept the direction of the French ministers in those matters of common concern. The crisis created by Deane's campaign to clear his name soon dissipated, but the question of French influence continued to trouble the delegates to Congress.

On June 20, 1778, Congress had taken up once more the Articles of Confederation. And Richard Henry Lee wrote to John Adams, "The friends to the future happiness and glory of America are now urging the Confederation to a close, and I hope it will be signed in a few days." The small states that were delaying would "undoubtedly fall in." The delegates of one such state, Rhode Island, expressed similar sentiments, "For this," they wrote, "is the Grand Corner Stone." By the end of the session on June 25, the delegates from all the states seemed ready to suspend their various objections to particular articles and vote for ratification, leaving amendment to another day. However, just as the delegates were about to sign the document some inaccuracies were discovered, and the signing was postponed until such time as Congress should convene in Philadelphia. It was July 7 before a quorum was present in the recently evacuated city. But this time more serious misgivings had taken root in some of the members. The unanimity of the twenty-fifth had disappeared. John Mathews of South Carolina wrote despondently to John Rutledge: "This I am clear in, from what I have seen, and know, since I have been in Congress, that if we are to have no Confederation until the Legislatures of the Thirteen States agree to one, that we shall never have one, and if we have not one, we are to have no Confederation until the Legislatures of the Thirteen that will follow at the end of this war." July 9 the delegates of eight states placed their signatures on the Articles of Confederation. North Carolina and Georgia followed suit, but Maryland, New Jersey, and Delaware all remained obdurate. One of the New Jersey members, embarrassed by the unwillingness of the legislature of his state to permit its delegates to ratify the articles, wrote to the speaker of the New Jersey assembly, "These States have actually entered into a Treaty with the Court of Versailles as a Confederated People, and Monsieur Girard, their Ambassador Plenipoteniary to Congress is now on our Coast with a powerful Fleet of Ships, which have taken a Pilot on Board for Delaware. He probably may be landed by this Time, and will at all Events be in Philadelphia in a few Days. How must he be astonished and confounded, and what may be the fatal Consequences to America when he discovers (which he will immediately do) that we are *ipso facto* unconfederated, and consequently, what our Enemies have called us, 'A Rope of Sand'?" In November New Jersey ratified, and in the early months of 1779 Delaware followed. But Maryland, uneasy about Virginia's extensive land claims and determined to oppose them by every possible means, continued to refuse.

The problem of what to do about "the people Stiling themselves the Inhabitants of Vermont" was a constant headache for Congress. New York claimed the area, and New York land speculators were much interested in holding fast to it. On the other hand there were a number of independent and contentious settlers in the area, most typically the

Green Mountain Boys; when their natural leader, Ethan Allan, returned from a British prison, he wanted nothing to do with New York and insisted that they constituted a separate state. Every petition to be recognized as such by Congress was, however, turned back by the assiduous efforts of the New York delegates. In July, 1778, Congress reaffirmed its opposition to statehood for those settlers living in what they chose to call "Vermont." (The area, which had originally been called New Connecticut, was named Vermont in 1777 by Dr. Thomas Young, who apparently intended to suggest, in abbreviated form, Vertes Monts, or Green Mountains.) "Resolved," the resolution of congress read, "that no number or body of people within any part of these United States can be Justified in Attempting to form and Establish any new Independent States within any part of the United States without the Consent of the State or States in which they are and were Included at the time the Congress were at first Elected." The settlers in the region, notoriously militant, were further admonished "in the Strongest terms . . . to refrain from all Acts of violence and coercive measures as they regard the peace and welfare of these United States."

Beyond or beneath all such troubling issues lay the most persistent and unremitting problem of all—money. Not only was Congress issuing money that had no hard currency behind it and indeed nothing but Congress's promise to pay when it could; the states were trying to solve their financial dilemmas the same way. By the fall of 1778, the monetary situation was too serious to be swept under the Congressional rug any longer. The delegates resolved to turn to the matter of finances "precisely at one o'clock, until the same be finished, and this rule not to be broken unless by unanimous consent." For the next six weeks Congress struggled with the problem. The principal features of the policy it finally hammered out were that fifteen million dollars were to be raised by taxes during 1779 and six million a year thereafter for eighteen years. Certain issues of money, amounting to some forty-one million, were to be called in and exchanged for loan-office certificates of new bills. This latter measure was directed primarily at the emissions of the states and was immediately resisted by some delegates as an infringement on the sovereignty of the states.

Henry Laurens had been elected president of Congress in November, 1777. Through all the quarrels, the dissensions, and the frequent crises and alarms that marked the deliberations of the Continental Congress, Laurens, whom we first encountered, the reader will recall, defending his house and his sick wife against the Sons of Liberty, steered a wise and judicious course. He seems to have made a conscientious effort to avoid intrigue and to remain above factional squabbles, although his private comments on the delegates were often caustic. He was a large man with an impressive "presence"; his plump, amiable face seldom betrayed his emotions. As president he could not engage in debate, but he made his very substantial weight felt in numerous small ways. The official correspondence of Congress passed through his discreet and tactful hands, and in hundreds of private letters he smoothed ruffled feathers and dropped hints of important matters to people who he felt should have such hints; perhaps most important of all, through his son, Colonel John Laurens, Washington's devoted young staff officer, he kept open a crucially important line of indirect communication with the commander in chief. It is a commonplace that some of the most significant vectors of history lie outside the historian's view, or, if visible, are blurred and diffuse. Reading of the tortuous and often acrimonious debates of Congress on such matters as the "Conway Cabal," the prisoner-of-war exchange, half-pay, and the Deane-Lee controversy, it is hard to avoid the feeling that Laurens' role, especially in the winter and spring of 1778, was a crucial one. A less firm and temperate man, or one who enjoyed less respect and indeed affection, might have lost control of the situation entirely. Moreover, the importance of the happy accident of Laurens' son's relationship to Washington can hardly be overestimated. The relations between Washington and Congress were never before or later so severely strained as they were from the summer of 1777 to the summer of 1778. The fact that Washington trusted Laurens was of course not unrelated to the fact that he was like another father to Laurens' son. Through his son, Laurens was kept aware of Washington's own moods and of those things that particularly chafed him—as he could never have been through official correspondence—and, as we have seen, Laurens was able to apply a soothing lotion when it was most needed.

There was another unpleasant, if minor, episode toward the end of 1778 that revealed the touchiness of Congress. General William Thompson, indignant at the delay in arranging his exchange as a British prisoner, was accused of having declared loudly and emphatically in public at the Coffee House that Congress was "a Rascally set and a Set of Rascals ... particularly applying the approbrious term to the Chief Justice of the State [Thomas McKean]." Thompson, called to account by an angry Congress, denied he had called its members rascals but reaffirmed his applying the term to McKean. In the words of one delegate,

Thompson "wantonly adds Villain, and twice repeats that he had said that Gentleman was a Rascal and a Villain. . . ." That simply made the matter worse. Congress voted him guilty of a breach of privilege.

In summarizing the developments of 1778 in Congress, the most thorough student of that body has written: "The year had been witness to great abuses in the conduct of public business, and, not the least of evils, of exasperating deficiencies within the halls of Congress. Something had been accomplished toward the cure of these several ills, but much more remained to be done." The grossest illusion that Congress and, it is to be feared, much of the country labored under (largely as a consequence of the French entry into the war) was that "one good campaign more and the thing is done."

The year 1779 opened in Congress with a continuing effort to bring some kind of order and control to financial affairs. The only possible solution seemed to be to once more make a desperate appeal to the states. Additional taxes must be laid and collected (Congress even went so far as to consider attempting to tax citizens directly) if the patriot cause was to survive. John Dickinson penned a lengthy document describing in detail the critical need for money, the consequences of not getting it, and the suggested means for collecting it on the state level. At the end came a classic Dickinsonian exhortation: "Rouse yourselves, therefore, that this campaign may finish the great work you have so nobly carried on for several years past. What nation has ever engaged in such a contest under such complication of disadvantages, so soon surmounted many of them, and in so short a period of time had so certain a prospect of a speedy and happy conclusion. . . . Fill up your battalions . . . place your several quotas in the continental treasury; lend money for public uses; sink the [paper money] emissions of your respective states; provide effectually for expediting the conveyance of supplies for your armies and fleets, and for your allies . . . and may you be approved before Almighty God worthy of those blessings we devoutly wish you to enjoy."

The address was too long and, in the opinion of Charles Carroll of Carrollton, "too late by six months," but it was all that Congress could bring itself to do. It was increasingly clear that the endless printing of paper money, far from being a remedy, only brought the patient nearer death. "A Stoppage of the press once effected," William Ellery wrote, "our liberties are established and an end put to the war. The enemy's whole dependence now rests upon our being crushed with the weight of Rheams of depretiated paper money. Once remove that ground of

Hope and they will offer us, as proud and haughty as they may be, honorable terms of peace." This suggested a whole new strategy: Britain need not be defeated in the field, it could be defeated simply by sound currency.

The rapid depreciation of money encouraged, of course, the most reckless speculation. It was such, in the words of Benjamin Rush, as would "corrupt a community of Angels." Prices in three weeks rose over 100 per cent. "This," as Daniel of St. Thomas Jenifer, a Maryland delegate, wrote, "has made those Vermin the Speculators become the object of resentment, and a Mob has assembled to regulate prices. What will be the issue God knows." Nathaniel Scudder, a new delegate from New Jersey, wrote to Richard Henry Lee: "What shall I say as to the great Business of our Finances? I cannot yet determine that I have learned any Thing concerning them, much indeed I have unlearned; for although an amazing Deal of Time has been spent on this important Subject; tho one Hypothesis has been piled upon another like Pelion on Ossa; tho Scheme has been tacked to Scheme, and System succeeded System, while the speculative Genius and playful Fancies of some of our Brethren have again and again in amendments and a variety of Substitutes exhausted themselves, and finally, when all their pretty wiredrawn Plans were crumbled away in the handling, have often in common Consent assisted to sweep away the rubbish, and begin *de novo;* I say I have ranged in this Way the boundless Field of Finance and with great Labor and Diligence too, I have for my own Part obtained no more than to determine what will *not do* for the Support of our public Credit and the prevention of a general Depreciation. When I shall be happy enough to determine what *will do* Heaven only knows—my Enthusiasm only remains."

A journalist who called himself Leonidas exhorted Congress to "Rouse . . . to a sense of danger of these infant States that are committed to your care. Let us read something more than 'Yeas' and 'Nays', and questions for re-committing and postponing business in your journals. Your money—our money—demands every thought and every hour. . . . I conjure you therefore immediately to bind yourselves to each other by an oath, not to eat, drink or sleep till you have arrested your money in its progress towards destruction, and fixed it upon a permanent foundation." The article, which appeared in the July 3, 1779, issue of the *Pennsylvania Packet,* caused such indignation in Congress that a number of members agreed with Elbridge Gerry that the editor should be unmasked and taken to law for slander and disrespect of Congress. "Gentlemen talk," John Penn said, "of imprisoning the Printer or Author. I will undertake to say, if you have the power, which I doubt, and were to imprison them for six months, they would come out far greater [better known] Men than they went in."

Henry Laurens resigned as president and was succeeded by John Jay. James Lovell, typically for him, made a suggestive comparison between the two: "The Manners of the Men differ. One was flush of Pen and Ink [Laurens] the other quite the Reverse; one was with his Candle burning in the Morning almost thro the year, the other [Jay] has lovely Wife to amuse him in these Hours."

Border Warfare: The Wyoming Valley

I N history, as we remarked earlier, events crowd in upon each other, many important events taking place simultaneously. It is necessary, therefore, to leave Congress to its deliberations and Washington at his winter headquarters in Middle Brook to take a look at the border or frontier warfare that raged from Canada to Georgia and involved the lives and hopes of thousands of patriots.

Although the British had made sporadic use of Indian allies, particularly in Burgoyne's campaign and St. Leger's move to Oriskany, the ministers in England, like the British commanders in the field, were deeply divided in their feelings about employing Indians against the American rebels. Most of them viewed the Indians as the colonists did: as savages who, once turned loose, could not easily be kept within the bounds of civilized warfare. The Indian propensity for massacre and pillage was well known. Especially in the early stages of the war, when British hopes of reconciliation were stronger, there was a disinclination to employ methods of warfare that might alienate the Americans. In addition, there was the simple fact that the Indians, like most partisan or guerrilla fighters, were unreliable in prolonged and arduous campaigns. It was, first of all, not the Indians' fight; secondly, their concept of warfare was that of stealthy raids, with a brief explosion of fierce fighting and a rich harvest of loot. They had no stomach for long-drawn-out engagements, and their undisciplined methods of fighting were not easily coordinated with the white man's rather formal and cumbersome tactics. On the other hand, the Indians were superb scouts and raiders, and the psychological effects of their use were often more devastating than the practical effects. Americans, particularly those who inhabited isolated frontier settlements, lived in constant fear of Indian attacks. Their dreams were haunted by images of painted savages sweeping out of the forest to murder, burn, scalp, and rape. In such sudden assaults, the fortunate were those who were tomahawked where they lay; the unfortunate survived to be tortured to death. White feelings are perhaps best indicated by the fact that New Hampshire in 1776 offered seventy pounds for each scalp of a hostile male Indian, and thirty-seven pounds, ten shillings for each scalp of a woman or of a child over twelve years old.

In New York and "the Old Northwest," the region north of the Ohio River, there was a close alliance between the Tories and the Indians, most notably various tribes of the Iroquois Confederacy. The Tories' bitter hatred drove them to stir up the Indians against the patriots whenever possible and to try to persuade the British to make full use of the capacity of the Indians for spreading terror and demoralization in the white settlements.

Massachusetts had enrolled the Stockbridge Indians in the Minutemen, but that was rather a special case, and the Indians, during the siege of Boston, had become restless and unhappy with the routines of camp life and army training.

Congress had the subject of the Indians constantly in mind. Various measures were proposed to keep the Indians neutral. In July, 1775, not long after the Battle of Bunker Hill, Congress had divided the colonies into three departments—northern, middle, and southern—and had appointed eleven commissioners to supervise Indian affairs in the three areas. The commissioners were to have "power to treat with the Indians in their respective departments, in the name, and on behalf of the united colonies, in order to preserve peace and friendship with the said Indians, and to prevent their taking any part in the present commotions."

James Duane, a New York delegate, saw the hostility of the Onondagas as justifying the seizure of their lands after the Revolution ended. The Indian tribes, he advised the commissioners of the Northern Department, should be notified that if they engaged in hostilities against the Americans, the result would be the confiscation of their lands. "The Indians," Duane added, "are sufficiently sensible of the value of their lands. No other consideration will keep them within the bounds of humanity or good faith. . . . I flatter myself that the venal and disgraceful system hitherto practiced, of courting and bribing them to lay down their arms after the most wanton barbarities will never be revived. Let justice be done to them as reasonable beings: but let them know that they shall not injure us with impunity. This alone can secure our future tranquility; especially if Britain should retain Canada on a pacification."

The issue of the Indians was a particularly sensitive one. Every colony had had a different experience with the Indians; each one had its own interest in exploiting the savages, and often these interests were in sharp conflict. South Carolina, which profited from a rich trade in deerskins with the Indians, was fearful that Congress might try to regulate or impede her commerce with the Indians. Georgia, exposed to the raids of the Southern tribes, was anxious to have all possible help from Congress. James Wilson, a Pennsylvania delegate and a large land speculator, insisted on the autonomy of Congress in dealing with the Indians. There could be no peace with the savages unless that peace was made by one body. "No such language as this ought to be held out to the Indians. 'We are stronger, we are better, we treat you better than another colony.' No power ought to treat with the Indians, but the United States." The Indians knew at first hand the "striking benefits of confederation"; they had an extraordinary example in the union of the Six Nations. "None should trade with the Indians," Wilson concluded, "without a license from Congress. A perpetual war would be unavoidable, if everyone was allowed to trade with them."

In October, 1775, the commissioners for the Middle Department met at Fort Pitt with a number of Indian chiefs—Silver Heels; Blue Jacket, a famous warrior; Cornstalk, chief of the Shawnees and one of the most noted Indians in America; Kilbuck, a Delaware chief; and Kyashota of the Senecas. The Indians loved such parleys. There were always fine speeches and presents and a good deal of drinking. The chiefs, when the treaty meeting began, wore their most elegant trappings, a strange mixture of soiled English and native finery—deerskin mantles rubbed soft and white, beaver top hats, coats of red broadcloth trimmed with gold lace, and flowered white vests.

The Indians agreed to remain neutral, and White Eyes, a principal Delaware chief, returned to Philadelphia to meet the members of Congress and assure them of the friendship of his tribe. Congress, for its part, undertook to support several young Indians at the College of New Jersey at Princeton, but the experiment was somewhat less than a success. When one of the Indians made a white girl pregnant, her indignant father applied to Congress for compensation.

Treaty discussions also were carried on between Congressional commissioners, among them William Duer, and Indians in the Northern Department. When the commissioners arrived at the site of the council they found the "Chiefs all in one House to receive us," as the secretary, Tench Tilghman wrote, "and the men all seated in a Circle in an adjoining Orchard the Women & Children standing at a little distance. Seats were set for us in the area of the Circle. When we entered there was a mutual solemn salutation of How do you do or something of that kind and then a profound silence." Interpreters informed the assembled chiefs of the business on which the commissioners had come, but nothing could be done since the Mohawk chiefs had not arrived. On word that they would be provided with drink and tobacco, the chiefs brightened up "and assured us in general," Tilghman wrote, "that their Brothers the Americans should find them fast friends." Tilghman continued, "The Behaviour of the poor Savages at a public meeting ought to put us civilized people to the Blush. The most profound silence is observed, no interruption of a speaker. When any one speaks the rest are attentive." The Indians smoked the tobacco that the commissioners gave them with a quiet, deliberate air. "When drink was served round it was in the same manner, no Man seemed anxious for the Cup. One of them made a speech and set forth the bad effects of drinking at a time of Business and desired that the White people might not have liberty to sell rum to their Young Men."

"An Indian Treaty, by the by," Tilghman wrote, "is but dull entertainment owing to the delay and difficulty of getting what you say, delivered properly to the Indians. The Speech is first delivered in short sentences by one of the Commissioners, then an Interpreter tells an Indian what the Commissioner has been saying. After this has been repeated to the Indian he speaks it to the six nations, so that a speech that would not take up twenty minutes in the delivery will from the necessary delays employ us two or three hours." An additional difficulty was that the formal language of Congress had to be altered and amended "and put . . . into such mode & Figure as would make intelligible to the Indians for in its original form, you might almost as well have read them a Chapter out of Locke or any of your most learned reasoners."

In the evening the commissioners turned a bull loose for the "young Indians to hunt and kill after their manner, with arrows, knives and hatchettes. The Beast," Tilghman added, "was not of the furious spanish breed for he suffered himself to be despatched in a very few minutes without ever turning upon his assailants." Then there was a foot race run for "two laced Hats." The Indians entertained the commissioners by singing, but Tilghman found the voices of the women too shrill. The Stockbridge Indian girls, Christianized and trained in hymn singing by the missionaries, Tilghman found "pretty and extremely cleanly they speak tolerable English too. . . ."

After several days of parleying, the negotiations were transferred to Albany for the convenience of the Indians, but Tilghman found that town uncomfortably and dangerously crowded with soldiers and Indians. "It is hard to say which is the most irregular and Savage," he noted. "The former are mutinous for want of liquor the latter for want of pay, without which they refused to march. The troops raised in and about New York are a sad pack. They are mostly old disbanded Regulars and low lived foreigners."

After an interval of several days, the Indians replied to the proclamations of Congress that had been delivered by the commissioners. "It is amazing," Tilghman wrote, "with what exactness these people recollect all that has been said to them. The speech which delivered took up nine or ten pages of folio Paper, when they came to answer they did not omit a single head and on most of them repeated our own words. . . . They are thorough bred politicians. They know the proper time of making demands."

"It was soon evident that the most influential Indian in the council was Molly, the squaw or mistress of the famous and beloved Sir William Johnson, now deceased, British Commissioner for the Northern Indians." A woman of noble bearing, "she saluted us," Tilghman wrote, "with an air of ease and politeness, she was dressed after the Indian Manner, but her linen and other Cloathes the finest of their kind." She reproached Kirkland, an Oneida missionary present at the meeting, for not having visited her since her husband's death—"the poor and unfortunate were always neglected." Tilghman guessed that she would be the principal impediment to a treaty with the assembled tribes. She had thrown her considerable weight, it was rumored, with Guy Johnson and the British. "It is plain," Tilghman wrote at the end of the treaty meeting, "that the Indians understand their game, which is to play into both hands."

In the Southern Department a similar meeting with the chiefs of local tribes took place, at which presents were distributed and promises of neutrality exacted in return.

As the war dragged on month after month and as the British sense of frustration increased, their policy of employing Indians cautiously and for primarily military ends was gradually replaced by one of using them to punish and frighten the Americans. In the fall of 1776, Lord George Germain wrote to the British Indian agent in the South, John Stuart, urging him to press on in his negotiations with the Creeks and Choctaws and to try to get them to join with the Cherokees in raiding the Carolina and Virginia frontier. At the outbreak of hostilities, it was rumored that the South Carolina assembly had offered bounties for Indian scalps and had stated that Indian children "of a certain age which may be taken prisoners [shall be] the slaves of their captors. . . ." Such policy, Germain assured Stuart, would help to recruit the Indian tribes to fight against the American rebels.

Six months later Governor Tryon, from his refuge in New York, was urging the British ministry to "loose the savages against the miserable Rebels in order to impose a reign of terror on the frontiers. . . ." Indeed, his proposal soon became government policy. When North tried to defend it in Parliament on the grounds that the British were obliged to use such means as "God and nature put into our hands," Chatham was stirred to one of his most eloquent flights of rhetoric. He was, he declared, "astonished to hear such principles confessed! . . . Principles equally unconstitutional, inhuman, and unchristian! . . . What! to attribute the sacred sanction of God and nature to the massacres of the Indian scalping knife? to the cannibal savage, torturing, murdering, roasting and eating; literally, my lords, *eating* the mangled victims of his barbarous battles! Such horrible notions shock every precept of religion, divine or natural, and every generous feeling of humanity . . . they shock me as a lover of honorable war, and a detester of murderous barbarity. . . . We turn loose these savage hell-hounds against our brethren and countrymen in America, of the same language, laws, liberty and religion, endeared to us by every tie that should sanctify humanity."

Washington, who had his own problems, wrote to the commissioners of Indian affairs, in the name of Congress, asking them to enlist a "body of four hundred Indians, if they can be procured upon proper terms. Divesting them of the Savage customs exercised in their Wars against each other, I think they may be made of excellent use, as scouts and light troops, mixed with our own Parties."

While such matters of policy were debated, small-scale but bitter fighting between patriots and those Indians who were willing to throw in their lot with the British broke out along the American frontier. It was a time of settlers murdered in their beds, of frontier cabins and lean-tos put to the torch, of children abducted, and of reprisals as savage as the raids that provoked them.

The most devastating of these raids was directed at the Wyoming Valley, which lay along the Susquehanna near Wilkes-Barre (named of course after John Wilkes and Colonel Issac Barré of Sons of Liberty fame). The area, which made up roughly the northern quarter of Pennsylvania, was claimed by Connecticut also, and every effort by Pennsylvania to oust the Connecticut settlers had resulted in open warfare. The valley settlers were strong patriots, and most of the able-bodied men had enlisted in the Connecticut Line.

Major John Butler's Tory Rangers and their Indian allies chose the Wyoming Valley as the object of an attack designed to wreak vengeance and provide a rich haul of plunder. Led by Butler, a combined force of over twelve hundred Indians and Tories set out from Niagara. The march to western Pennsylvania was marked by looting and murder. In the words of Hector St. John Crèvecoeur, who lived near the plundered towns, "it was easy to surprise defenceless isolated families who fell an easy prey to their enemies. . . . Many families were locked up in their houses and consumed with their furniture. Dreadful scenes were transacted which I know not how to retrace."

The raiders took the settlements of the Wyoming Valley by surprise. The only defense was provided by Colonel Zebulon Butler, who with some three hundred boys and old men occupied Forty Fort. On the morning of June 28, 1778, the Tories and Indians, principally Senecas and White Eyes' Delawares, came, in the words of a Tory carpenter, Richard McGinnis, "to a mill belonging to the Rebels. The Savages burnt the mill and took 3 prisoners, two white men and a Negro whom they afterwards murdered in their own camp." The hungry raiders were supplied by local Tories, the Wintermots, who brought fourteen head of fat cattle into their camp. The Wintermots told Sir John Butler they came from a fort that bore their name, which was ready to surrender if given assurance that the women and children would be safe from the Indians. Butler then sent a flag of truce to Forty Fort and Jenkins' Fort calling for their capitulation on the same terms. Jenkins' Fort followed the example of Wintermot, but the defenders of Forty Fort, under Zeb Butler, sent word that they never "would give it over to Tories and savages but stand it out to the last and defend it to the last extremity."

The Tories and Indians surrounded the fort and waited. Finally, on July 3 at five o'clock in the afternoon, Sir John Butler ordered his men to set fire to Wintermot's Fort, intending to give the impression that he and his raiders were retreating. Zeb Butler took the bait; the patriots issued from Forty Fort in hot pursuit, calling to the enemy, concealed in the woods, "Come out, ye villainous Tories! Come out, if ye dare, and show your heads, if ye durst, to the brave Continental Sons of Liberty!" With the patriots dispersed in pursuit, the waiting Tories and Indians sprang their trap. At first the patriots held their ground, but after they had fired their muskets, the Indians rushed on them with spears and tomahawks, and the inexperienced men turned and fled for their lives. Many of them jumped into the Susquehanna, where the Indians, naked and better swimmers, overtook them and killed them in the water, "and for a long time afterwards the carcasses became offensive, floated and infested the banks of the Susquehanna as low as Shamokin," Crèvecoeur wrote. "The other party, who had taken their flight towards their forts, were all either taken or killed. It is said that those who were then made prisoners were tied to small trees and burnt the evening of the same day." Crèvecoeur, who, of course, was no sympathizer with the Revolution, added, "Thus the ill-judged policy of these ignorant people and the general calamities of the times overtook them and extirpated them even out of that wilderness which they had come twelve years before to possess and embellish. Thus the grand contest entered into by these colonies with the mother-country has spread everywhere, even from the sea-shores to the last cottages of the frontiers." The losses to the raiders were given as one Indian killed and two white men wounded. "Thus," a Tory wrote, "did loyalty and good order that day triumph over confusion and treason, the goodness of our cause aided and assisted by the blessing of Divine Providence. . . ." The defenders of Forty Fort paid for their temerity with their property as well as, in many instances, their lives. There was, again in Richard McGinnis's words, "a total confiscation of property, such as oxen, cows, horses, hogs, sheep and every thing of that kind. Thus did Rebellion get a severe shock."

The Wyoming Valley Massacre, as it was immediately called, aroused a storm of fury against the Indians and the Tories. The ruthless destruction carried out by the attackers was grist for the patriot press. There were enough atrocity stories, many of them true, many not, to keep printer's devils busy for weeks setting type. The fort had been set on fire, it was said, and the captured prisoners thrown into the flames, or pinned down with pitchforks and slaughtered by the tomahawk of an Indian queen of notorious cruelty. At dark, it was said, fires had been kindled, and those prisoners who had survived were chased, naked, through the flames until they dropped from exhaustion. Thus the Wyoming Valley Massacre became a byword for Tory and Indian brutality. They made, indeed, an ugly combination. As we have seen, the Tories were apt to be particularly vindictive. Their sense of outrage at the actions of the patriots in resisting the authority of the mother country were, for the most part, not tempered by any respect for the rules of warfare. The Tories usually neither gave nor expected any quarter, and when this vengeful spirit was augmented by the Indian propensity for total war, the results were almost invariably grim.

The Mohawk Valley and western New York north to Michilmac was soon largely emptied of its inhabitants, becoming a wasteland of charred houses whose desolate chimneys marked spots where villages and farmhouses had once stood. Settlers of English, Irish, and French Huguenot descent had occupied the area in the decades prior to the outbreak of the war. Goshen, Minisink, and Warwarsing had become thriving communities, even though they were situated in the middle of Indian country; savages and settlers had lived in a kind of armed and wary peace. The Revolution turned the area into a battleground, a center of British power. Tory and Indian irregulars from Canada swept through the Mohawk Valley in endless raids. Strongly built houses were used as forts, and the residents of the area kept their muskets nearby day and night. The premier Indian chief of the region was Joseph Brant, or Thayendanegea, a Mohawk who had been educated at Eleazar Wheelock's Indian Charity School and had then become secretary to Guy Johnson, the Indian superintendent. Brant, who had been in England in the spring of 1776, became a friend of James Boswell, had his portrait painted by Romney, and returned to fight against the Americans in the home territory he knew so well.

Brant chose as his objective a cluster of villages in the Cherry Valley, an area of western New York. The valley had first been settled by the family of a New Yorker, John Lindsay, in 1740. From the spring of 1778 on, rumors circulated that Brant and his Mohawks intended to raid the valley, which was protected primarily by a fortified house belonging to Colonel Samuel Campbell. In July Colonel Ichabod Alden and his Seventh Massachusetts Regiment, consisting of some two hundred and fifty soldiers, arrived to provide for the defense of the valley and speed the building of an adequate fort. Alden was an inefficient martinet who paid little attention to the advice or the needs of the inhabitants of the region. He was warned by friendly Indians in November that a "great meeting of Indians and Tories" had taken place on the Tioga River and that a decision had been made to attack Cherry Valley. With a new fort finished, the settlers, who had also heard reports of the projected raid, requested permission from Alden to move into it with their families or at least to store their most important possessions there. Alden refused on the strange grounds that his soldiers would be tempted to steal the settlers' goods.

Meanwhile Brant, hearing that the officers of the Seventh Massachusetts were quartered outside the fort, made plans for a surprise attack on the morning of November 11. He was aided by a heavy fog that shrouded the fort and concealed the approach of his force. Just as he was ready to launch an assault, a farmer came jogging by on his way to the fort. He saw Brant's silent warriors just as they spied him. The Indians fired and wounded him, but he galloped off in time to give a few minutes' warning to the sleepy garrison. Close on his heels came a party of Senecas, who were auxiliaries to Brant's Mohawks. Their mission was to seize the Wells house, some four hundred yards from the fort. Alden, asleep in the Wells house, awoke and ran for the fort, but he was killed as he ran. His second-in-command was captured, and other officers and men of Alden's staff who tried to put up some resistance were quickly struck down.

After four or five hours spent in skirmishing, it became clear to Brant that there was little chance of reducing the fort, and he withdrew his men. Baffled in their primary object, the Indians in Brant's force then turned on the defenseless inhabitants, burning and pillaging the nearby settlements. There were some forty farmhouses in the area, and in six of these the occupants, mostly women and children, were killed without mercy. Captain Walter Butler, whose name was anathema because of his father's role in the Wyoming Valley Massacre, was held accountable for the atrocities, and Joseph Brant's biographers have been at pains to depict him as rushing about to check the Senecas' slaughter of the innocent. Timothy Dwight, when he visited the valley years later, was told the story of Butler's men entering a house where a women had just given birth to a child and ordering both mother and child to be killed. "At that moment Brant, coming up, cried out, 'What, kill a woman and child! No, that child is not an enemy to the King, nor a friend to Congress. Long before he is big enough to do any mischief, the dispute will be settled.'" A guard was set at the door and the child and mother saved.

At the height of the destruction, Captain McDonnell led some of his men out of the fort and rescued a number of terror-stricken settlers who had taken refuge in the woods. Besides the thirty-some settlers killed, seventy-one prisoners were taken by Brant and Butler. They spent the night in fear of their lives, but most were released the next day. Butler kept two women and seven children as hostages to exchange for his own mother and wife, who were prisoners in Albany, and also took with him some twenty Negro slaves, who doubtless went willingly.

The wanton killing of unarmed residents and the methodical pillaging of the Cherry Valley settlements added to the bitter indignation over the Wyoming Valley Massacre and increased the pressure for a campaign that would crush the Indians and Tories once for all. Thus began the tedious work of collecting and equipping an expeditionary force to sweep the Indian country. While it was being assembled, Brant struck again, this time at the little town of Minisink in the Mohawk Valley, which had been left defenseless when Count Pulaski was ordered south to reinforce General Lincoln at Charles Town. Brant, with a force of sixty Indians and twenty-seven Tories disguised as Indians, attacked the little settlement on the twenty-second of July, 1779, setting fire to several buildings while most of the settlers were still sound asleep. The first warning of the attack came from the howls of the Indians and Tories and the explosions of dry and burning wood. The inhabitants, mostly women and children and males too young or old to be recruited into the army, fled for the woods. The small fort, the mill, and twelve houses were fired, a few people were killed or taken prisoner, the orchards were chopped down, the farms were laid waste, and the livestock were driven off.

When word of the raid reached Goshen twelve miles away, Colonel Tustin, head of the local militia, sent word to the officers of his regiment scattered through the adjacent communities to collect as many volunteers as they could and meet him the following day at Minisink. The next morning Tustin counted a hundred and forty-nine boys and men, "many of these . . . principal gentlemen of the vicinity." A council of war decided, over the objections of Tustin, to pursue Brant, and while the colonel was still expostulating, his second-in-command, a Major Meeker, mounted his house, flourished his sword, and called out the kind of challenge no group of raw and inexperienced soldiers could resist: "Let the *brave* men follow me; the *cowards* may stay behind!" The first day, the little force made seventeen miles and gained on the enemy, encumbered by their loot. The next morning, the pursuers came on the still-smoldering ashes of the Indian campfires. There were indications that the force was a large one, and Tustin again urged the men to turn back, but he was once more overruled. By nine the advance scouts came to the ridge overlooking the Delaware River near the Lackawaxen. Below they could see the Indians, genuine and bogus, moving toward a ford on the river. Colonel Hathorn, a militia officer senior to Tustin who had arrived with a detachment of militia and taken command of the combined forces, decided to ambush the Indians and cut off their line of retreat. He disposed his men beside the trail, but Brant had observed the maneuver and, slipping through a ravine, he brought his force behind the Americans, thus in effect ambushing the ambush. When the Indians failed to appear at the point where the militia expected them, they went to search them out, and a battle ensued. Hathorn's party was completely outmaneuvered and surrounded. The Indians had the advantage of high ground and kept up a constant, harassing fire during the whole day, while the ammunition of the militia dwindled away and their casualities mounted. At dusk the Indians attacked and broke the crude square that the defenders had formed. The militia fled for their lives with the Indians in close pursuit. Tustin, who was a doctor as well as a militia officer, had set up a primitive field hospital to care for the wounded. There he and seventeen of his patients were cut down and scalped. Some of the militia tried to escape by swimming the Delaware, and the Indians shot them in the water like ducks.

Of the group of something more than a hundred and seventy men, only thirty returned to the settlements from which they had set out so boldly. The nineteenth-century historian Benson Lossing says that they were heavily outnumbered, but the only figures we have for Brant's force are sixty Indians and twenty-seven Tories for a total of eighty-seven, while the militia had almost twice as many. The Indian and Tory force, moreover, suffered only a handful of casualties.

During the battle Major Wood, a militia officer from Goshen, inadvertently made, according to Lossing, the sign of the Masonic order. Brant, who was a Mason, took special care after the American lines were broken to see that Wood's life was spared and that he was well treated as a prisoner. When the Indian leader questioned Wood and discovered that he was not a Mason, he thought that Wood had given the sign as a ruse to save his life and was furious at this betrayal of the order. He spared the terrified officer's life, however, and as soon as Wood was exchanged the major lost no time in becoming a Mason.

The fact was that the loss of life in the initial attack on Minisink was relatively small; it was the foolish persistence of the militia in pursuing a party of Indians led by a chief famous for his skill as a warrior that led to the disastrous toll of deaths. But the defenseless village of Minisink was hardly a proper military target. To exterminate a community of sleeping farmers was no bold and warlike thrust. The effect was purely punitive and all the more bitterly resented in consequence.

6

Sullivan's Expedition

THE Wyoming Valley and Cherry Valley massacres and Brant's attack on Minisink, less than fifty miles from West Point and Morristown, speeded the launching of an expedition under General Sullivan against the Indians of the region. The plan of the campaign called for a three-pronged invasion of the Indian stronghold. Sullivan, in command of twenty-five hundred men, would move up the Susquehanna to the southern border of New York. General James Clinton, with fifteen hundred soldiers, would drive into the Mohawk Valley to Lake Otsego, at the head of the Susquehanna, and then proceed down that river, while six hundred men under the command of Colonel Daniel Brodhead would move from Fort Pitt up the Allegheny River. Sullivan and Clinton were to join forces at Tioga (now Athens, Pennsylvania) and then move north to Niagara, joining Brodhead at Genesee, near Cuylerville.

Sullivan's mission, assigned by Washington, was "the total destruction and devastation" of the Iroquois settlements and "the capture of as many prisoners of every age and sex as possible. It will be essential to ruin their crops now in the ground and prevent their planting more." Querulous, cranky Sullivan was far from the ideal man for the job, but the officer to whom, for reasons of seniority, the expedition had first been offered, Horatio Gates, would have been even worse. Washington did his best to offset Sullivan's deficiencies by a constant stream of exhortation and advice. Recalling his own experience in Indian warfare, Washington urged Sullivan to "make rather than receive attacks." The attacks should be "attended with as much impetuosity, shouting and noise as possible, and to make the troops act in as loose and dispersed a way as is consistent with a proper degree of government concert and mutual support—It should be previously impressed upon the minds of the men wherever they have an opportunity, to rush on with the war whoop and fixed bayonet—Nothing will disconcert and terrify the Indians more than this—" Again and again Washington, knowing the inclinations of his cautious general, emphasized to Sullivan the importance of speed: "Your operations should be as rapid ... as will be consistent with efficacy—"

Sullivan was certainly industrious and did his best to hasten preparations for the campaign, but it was the eighteenth of June, 1779, before his column was ready to move, and once on the move it dawdled along in the Wyoming Valley for almost a month. In the first nine days of July the army moved fifty-five miles, scarcely six miles a day, and small wonder. Sullivan had loaded himself down with a hundred and twenty boats, twelve hundred packhorses, and seven hundred cattle.

While Sullivan made his snail-like progress through Pennsylvania, Clinton did little better. As heavily burdened as Sullivan, Clinton carried more than two hundred bateaux in his baggage train. "He goes incumbered with useless supplies," Washington wrote, and then discovered that Clinton was simply acting on Sullivan's orders. There was little that Washington could do except to keep up a steady stream of exhortatory missives. Sullivan's own letters to Washington were loaded with the familiar apprehensions and complaints: not enough men, not enough supplies, not enough time—and, though he did not say so, not enough talent. Most of the letters contained touching little signs of the general's insecurity, affirmations of his admiration for Washington, and assurances that he valued most highly his commander's advice and suggestions. One of the principal reasons for Sullivan's endless reiteration of his problems was, as he himself put it, that he wished "to avoid censure in case of misfortune," a strange frame of mind for a general preparing to lead his men on a critical campaign, but one quite typical of this officer.

On the twenty-ninth of July, Washington wrote urging on his laggard general: "I cannot but repeat my intreaties, that you will hasten your operations with all possible dispatch; and that you will disencumber yourself of every article of baggage and stores which is not necessary to the expedition. . . . 'Tis a kind of service in which both officers and men must expect to dispense with conveniences and endure hardships. . . ."

Brodhead wrote to Sullivan on the sixth of August that he had been instructed by Washington to proceed against the Seneca towns and to cooperate with Sullivan as far as possible. He was accompanied by twelve Seneca warriors, and a number of Cherokee chiefs had pledged their support. "The Indians," he wrote, "sometimes take a scalp from us, but my light parties which I dress & paint like Indians have retaliated in several instances."

Meanwhile Clinton demonstrated that freed from Sullivan's restraints, he could move his force with expedition. From his base at Canajoharie on the Mohawk River he had begun his operations in April, making a six-day raid that covered a hundred and eighty miles. One of his officers, Colonel Goose Van Schaick, led five hundred soldiers and a few Indians from Fort Stanwix into the country of the Onondagas, destroying in the process one of the principal settlements of that tribe, capturing thirty-seven prisoners, killing more than twenty warriors, and seizing a hundred British muskets.

On the seventeenth of June, Clinton began dragging his bateaux over the twenty-mile portage to Lake Otsego. The movement took some thirteen days, and on the thirtieth he wrote to Sullivan that he was ready to start for Tioga.

The British were well informed of the expedition that was being mounted against their Indian allies. John Butler was alarmed by word of Van Schaick's raid and the rumor that one of Brant's children had been captured. "This stroke of theirs," he wrote, "has every appearance as if they mean to take hold of Oswego for by having this Indian in their hands, they conjecture the Indians will not presume to molest them in such an enterprise." A few days later he received word that a column of Americans was moving up the Allegheny (Brodhead's force), and then that "a body of rebels were on their way from Albany to make another attempt against the Indians." The principal error on the part of the British was their refusal to believe that the Americans could muster an army as large as the combined forces of Sullivan, Clinton, and Brodhead for a campaign into the Indian country. Sir Frederick Haldimand, who had succeeded Sir Guy Carleton as governor of Canada and commander in chief in that province, wrote on the twenty-third of July to the commander of the British garrison at Niagara, Lieutenant Colonel Bolton: "It is impossible the Rebels can be in such force as has been represented by the deserters to Major Butler upon the Susquehanna. He would do well to send out intelligent white men to be satisfied of the truth of those reports. If anything is really intended against the Upper Country I am convinced Detroit is the object, and that they show themselves and spread reports of expeditions in your neighborhood merely to divert the Rangers and Indians from their main purpose— Major Butler should be aware of this." As I have so often observed before, military intelligence is usually rendered useless by the fact that commanding officers almost invariably twist it to conform to what they believe to be the enemy's intentions. The above is a perfect example.

Butler did send out two reliable agents, Lieutenant Henry Hare, who was caught and executed as a spy, and Sergeant William Newberry, a notorious Tory who was hung in retribution for atrocities he had committed in the Cherry Valley Massacre. But by the eleventh of August there was intelligence enough. Sullivan finally arrived at Tioga, on the border between Pennsylvania and New York, only a few miles from the important Indian town of Chemung, and the next day John Butler ordered his son, Walter, to march immediately for Tioga with every man he could round up. Sullivan, meanwhile, had sent a force ahead under General Edward Hand to try to close off the avenue of escape from the town. The prey eluded Hand, however, and he found an empty village. "Finding it impossible to bring them to an engagement," Sullivan wrote, "I directed their Town to be burnt, which consumed between 30 and 40 Houses some of them large and neatly finish'd; particularly a Chapel and Council House. I also caus'd their Fields of Corn which were of a considerable extent, and all their Gardens which were repleted with Herbiage to be destroy'd . . ." along with "great quantities of potatoes, pumpkins, squashes. . . ." In the desultory fighting that followed the evacuation of the Indians and Tories from Chemung, seven Americans were killed and thirteen wounded.

At Tioga, Clinton's and Sullivan's combined forces built Fort Sullivan to defend the head of the Wyoming Valley and the western approaches to West Point. Then, on the twenty-sixth of August, leaving some two hundred and fifty men to defend the new fort, Sullivan, Clinton, and some twenty-five hundred men set out from Chemung. The interval between the destruction of the town and the movement of Sullivan's army had given Butler time to muster a substantial force and build a breastwork near Newtown to block Sullivan's advance. Sullivan's force consisted of the brigades of Edward Hand, William Maxwell, and Enoch Poor. Maxwell's brigade (the First) was made up of Oliver Spencer's New Jersey Regiment and the First and Second New Jersey Regiments. The Second Brigade (Poor's) included the First, Second, and Third New Hampshire and the Seventh Massachusetts, which had been under the command of Ichabod Alden at Cherry Valley. Hand's Third Brigade was made up of the Fourth and Eleventh Pennsylvania Regiments, Colonel Thomas Proctor's Fourth Artillery Regiment (four three-pounders, two six-pounders, and two howitzers), a detachment of Morgan's riflemen under Major James Parr, Captain Anthony Selin's Independent Rifle Company, and a group of Wyoming Valley militia. Clinton's division numbered about fifteen hundred men, made up largely of the Second, Third, Fourth, and Fifth New York Regiments and a company of the Second Artillery Regiment.

Major Parr, sent on ahead with his riflemen as a scouting party, reported the ambush that Butler had prepared and had "endeavored to mask in a very artful manner. . . ." The enemy position was on a bend of the Susquehanna, forming, with the river, a semicircle. A deep brook ran in front of the works, parallel to the high ground on which the enemy were entrenched. A large detachment waited, on still higher ground a mile in the rear, to fall on the American right when it became engaged with the main defensive positions. General Hand formed the light corps in the woods some four hundred yards from the enemy works, while the riflemen engaged in constant skirmishing with the Indians and Tories, who time and again dashed out, fought briefly, and retired, apparently intending to draw the Americans into hasty pursuit. Poor, constituting the right wing of the army, deployed his men in the rear of Hand's division. Maxwell's brigade took its place abreast of Poor but in column, ready to move wherever it might be needed. As the action developed, Poor was dispatched to secure a line of hills on the American right and rear, where, Sullivan guessed, the enemy might also be waiting to attack once his troops were engaged in a frontal assault on the British positions. Clinton was ordered to "turn off and follow the rear of General Poor to sustain him in case of necessity. . . ."

The opening of artillery fire against the main enemy positions was to signal a general attack. Poor, delayed by a swamp, arrived in front of the line of hills assigned as his objective at the moment the artillery began to fire. He encountered sharp resistance, and his men fired and then charged with bayonets, which proved heavy going, since the Indians and Tories fell back, shooting from behind trees, "keeping up an incessant fire, until [Poor's] troops had gained the summit of the hill." Clinton reinforced Poor and followed with the remainder of his brigade.

At the main position, the failure of the ambush plus the fire of the artillery demoralized the defenders and, in Sullivan's words, "occasioned them instantly to abandon their works in the greatest confusion. They fled in the greatest disorder, leaving eleven of their Indian warriors and one female dead on the ground, with a great number of packs, blankets, arms, camp equipage and a variety of their jewels, some of which are of considerable value."

Sullivan's men took two prisoners, one a Tory, the other an enlisted Negro in one of the Tory companies. According to them there were five companies of white men and a large number of Indian warriors of the Six Nations, members of the Iroquois Confederacy. They had been waiting eight days for the Americans to fall into their carefully constructed trap. Both the Butlers (Colonel John Butler of Wyoming Valley infamy and his son, Walter, leader with Brant of the Cherry Valley raid) had been involved in the action. Brant was also one of those commanding. Most of the wounded had been carried off on horseback, and Sullivan was convinced that many of the dead must also have been carried off, "as we found many bloody packs, coats, shirts, and blankets. . . ."

The American losses were three killed and thirty-nine wounded, most of these in Poor's brigade. "I cannot help saying," Sullivan wrote in his report to Washington, "that the disposition of the enemy's troops and the construction of their works would have done honor to much greater officers than the unprincipled wretches who commanded them."

The Indian settlement at Newtown was so large that the whole army spent the better part of a day destroying the "extensive fields of the best corn and beans." It appeared to Sullivan that Newtown was the principal supply center of the Indians. Twenty houses were burned there, and two miles east another thirty were discovered and destroyed, bringing the number of Indian villages that had been burned down by Clinton and Sullivan since the beginning of the campaign to some fourteen, "some of them considerable, others inconsiderable."

After Sullivan's success at Newtown, he made an effort to form an alliance with the Oneidas. His message hinted at some doubts as to their loyalty to the Americans. These doubts could only be removed if the warriors of the Oneidas were to join his expedition, especially such as "have a perfect knowledge of the country through which I am to pass." If he received such proof of their "attachment to the American cause . . . the army which I have the honor to command will be able totally to extirpate our common enemy [the Iroquois], and leave you in a perfect state of tranquility, enable you to enjoy your possessions and carry on with the Americans a commerce which will tend to the mutual advantage of both." The Oneidas, thus threatened, offered cautious assistance.

Everywhere, as Sullivan advanced, he found abandoned villages and no sign of Indians. At Catherinetown, the Americans found two old women of the Cayuga tribe, one of whom had been shot by an advance party of Americans. Sullivan ordered that a keg of pork and some biscuits be left "for the old creature to subsist on, although," as an officer noted resentfully, "it [the pork] was so scarce an article that no officer under the rank of a field officer had tasted any since leaving Tioga. . . ." The squaw was glad to tell whatever she knew. The morning after the fight at Newtown the warriors had arrived there. She heard them "tell their women they were conquered & must fly, that they had a great many killed & vast numbers wounded. . . . They kept runners on every mountain to observe the march of our army. . . ." At word of the approach of the American force, "all those who had not been before sent off, fled with precipitation leaving her without any possible means of escape." Brant had taken the wounded up the Tioga in canoes. Estimates of the number of the Indians and Tories varied from eight hundred to fifteen hundred, the latter being Sullivan's own estimate and undoubtedly somewhat too generous.

At another abandoned Indian town, Kendaia, Sullivan found one of the survivors of the Wyoming Valley Massacre, who had escaped from his captors and who gave a graphic account of the demoralization of the Indians. Here, again, the army spent almost a day destroying cornfields and ancient fruit trees, "of which there was a great abundance." Pushing on to Canadasaga on Seneca Lake, they found a white child about three years old and carried it along with the army. Canadasaga consisted of fifty houses and a great number of fruit trees that were, once again, destroyed with the town. Another town, Canandaigua, was unusual among the Indian villages in that it contained twenty-three "very elegant houses, mostly framed" after the white man's style. The fields of corn and groves of fruit trees were so extensive that two days were required to complete the work of destruc-

Genesee, "the grand capital" of the Indian country, was the final objective. Because it was the most remote of the villages, it had been chosen as the central Indian granary. The Indians of all nations had spent the spring there planting the crops that would nourish them through the winter and enable them to carry out raids against the white border settlements. Even the Tory rangers and some British troops, the story went, had been active in helping to plant corn and squash.

Sullivan's force reached the vicinity of Genesee on the fourteenth of September. It had been a strange march; everywhere the Indians hovered about, but they were unwilling to attempt another organized stand against Sullivan's force, which was certainly larger than any collection of warriors and Tories that could be rallied to oppose it. They thus had to watch as their villages and fields were obliterated and the food that they depended on to carry them through a long, bitter winter was systematically destroyed. The Indians received, of course, no substantial help from their British friends.

But the Indians and Tories had one dramatic success. Lieutenant Thomas Boyd, with a scouting party of twenty-six men, including several Indians, surprised some enemy Indians near Genesee and killed two. But while Boyd's men argued over who should have the right to scalp the Indians they had just killed, Walter Butler and several hundred Indians and Tories rose out of an ambush. They killed or captured twenty-two of the party. Boyd, who had been wounded in the fighting, was questioned by Butler and then turned over to the Indians, who tortured him to death. Along with Boyd was an Oneida Indian, Han Yerry, a famous marksman, who was "literally hewn to pieces" by his captors.

When Sullivan's men found Boyd's body, it was apparent that he had been mercilessly whipped, and that his fingernails had been pulled out, his nose and tongue cut off, one of his eyes put out, and his body pierced with spears in various places. His genitals had been cut off, and there had been other tortures, Sullivan wrote, "which decency will not permit me to mention." As the *coup de grâce,* he had been skinned alive and his head had been cut off.

Genesee was an impressive town of a hundred and twenty-eight houses, "most very large and elegant." The village, in Sullivan's words, "was beautifully situated almost encircled with a clear flat, which extends for a number of miles, where the most extensive fields of corn were and every kind of vegetable that can be conceived." Once again the work of destruction went on: "apples, peaches, cucumbers, watermelons, fowls, etc." A white woman appeared who had been hiding outside the village.

She also had been captured at Wyoming, and she had interesting information for Sullivan. There was, understandably, much bitterness between the Indians and their Tory leaders. Some Indians, she reported, had attempted to shoot Colonel Guy Johnson "for the false-hoods by which he had deceived and ruined them." She had overheard Butler telling Johnson that it was impossible to keep the Indians together after the Newtown battle; their crops were being destroyed and they could not count on Canada to supply them with food. For his own part, Butler declared that he would not even try to get the warriors together to assist in the defense of Niagara, which, in his opinion, would be the final objective of Sullivan's march.

But Sullivan had less ambitious notions. Complaining regularly of a shortage of food (though never explaining why his soldiers were not dining like lords on the pillage of the Indian villages), Sullivan declared that his supplies were too meager to press on to Niagara. Instead he turned northeast along the southern shore of Lake Ontario to work havoc in the Cayuga country. The Oneidas, apparently at the behest of the Cayugas, who had often been their enemies, tried to persuade Sullivan to spare the Cayuga villages, but Sullivan insisted it was too late. There were too many black marks against the Cayugas. Sullivan detached Lieutenant Colonel Peter Gansevoort, who had so distinguished himself earlier at the seige of Fort Stanwix, Lieutenant Colonel William Butler, and Colonel Henry Dearborn to systematically destroy the Cayuga towns. Dearborn burned six and took an Indian boy and three women prisoners, "one of the women being very ancient & the Lad a cripple"—hardly a very impressive haul. The officer in command ordered that one house be left to provide shelter for them, but after the troops had begun to move out, "some of the soldiers taking an opportunity when not observed set the house on fire, after securing and making the door fast . . . and . . . the house was consumed together with the savages. . . ."

Colonel Philip Van Cortlandt on a similar mission "destroyed several fields of corn, & burnt several houses." Lieutenant Colonel William Butler destroyed five principal towns "and a number of scattering houses, the whole making about one hundred in number, exceedingly large & well built," along with "two hundred acres of excellent corn, with a number of orchards, one of which, had in it 1500 fruit trees." Sullivan estimated that forty towns had been destroyed and a hundred and sixty thousand bushels of corn, "with a vast quantity of vegetables of every kind." "I am well persuaded," Sullivan wrote to Congress after his return to Tioga, "that except for one Town ... there is not a single Town left in the Country of the five nations."

This had all been accomplished, Sullivan pointed out, with the loss of only forty men. He had moved his army without adequate maps or experienced guides over a country "abounding in woods, creeks, rivers, mountains, morasses & defiles," hacking out roads as they went. Yet they had managed to average ten to fifteen miles a day, "when not detained by rains, or employed in destroying settlements."

Sullivan had not been able to engage the enemy in a major encounter, if we except the action at Newtown. That was hardly his fault; the savages were too elusive. He had captured only a handful of women and, so far as the record discloses, one crippled "lad." Yet he had carried out to the letter his instructions from Washington to devastate the Indian country and destroy all food supplies.

Sullivan's greatest error lay in his failure to attack and destroy Niagara. That was the hornet's nest, the point from which the British supplied and encouraged the Indians in New York and in the Ohio country to the west. A little more enterprise, a little more expedition, a little more resolution, and Niagara might very well have fallen into American hands like a ripe plum, but it was useless, as Washington certainly knew by now, to expect such qualities from Sullivan. There was no protest from Washington. Perhaps he was relieved and a bit surprised that his general had accomplished as much as he had, and conscious of the justice of Nathanael Greene's observation that much of Sullivan's delay was due to poor prior planning by Washington's own staff. Moreover, while the capture of Niagara was part of the original plan, Washington had not specifically ordered Sullivan to attack Niagara, perhaps because he lacked confidence in him.

Sullivan's campaign was the most ruthless application of a scorched-earth policy in American history. It bears comparison with Sherman's march to the sea or the search-and-destroy missions of American soldiers in the Vietnam war. The Iroquois Confederacy was the most advanced Indian federation in the New World. It had made a territory that embraced the central quarter of New York State into an area of flourishing farms with well-cultivated fields and orchards and sturdy houses. Indeed, I believe it could be argued that the Iroquois had carried cooperative agriculture far beyond anything the white settlers had achieved. In a little more than a month all of this had been wiped out, the work of several generations of loving attention to the soil, which promised a new kind of Indian society, one not dependent on nomadic wandering or exclusively on hunting, but one that, while preserving the rich Indian culture virtually intact, also created a stable and orderly society able to hold its own against white encroachments. The Iroquois never recovered from that blow.

It must be pointed out, however, that ruthless as the action of the Americans was, it had been provoked by numerous incidents of Indian savagery, most dramatically, of course, the episodes in the Wyoming Valley and Cherry Valley. The Americans conceived themselves to be fighting for their lives as well as their liberties. They had taken, out of self-interest to be sure, substantial steps to try to keep the border Indians neutral, and they had, for the most part also out of self-interest, avoided trying to make allies of those tribes who were the traditional enemies of the nations that made up the Iroquois Confederacy. Despite the skill and enterprise with which the Iroquois embraced agricultural life, they retained their warlike tradition. Indeed, without it their whole culture would have collapsed. So they were more than a constant threat to the Americans; they resisted the efforts of the more responsible British officials like Sir Guy Carleton to keep them neutral and listened instead to the blandishments of Tory leaders like the Butlers, who were both ruthless and shortsighted.

The fallaciousness of the British policy was well expressed by Edward Abbott, lieutenant governor of Canada and in command at Detroit, who wrote to Sir Guy Carleton in June, 1778: "Your Excellency will plainly perceive the employing Indians on the Rebel frontiers has been of great hurt to the cause, for many hundreds would have put themselves under His Majesty's protection was there a possibility; that not being the case, these poor unhappy people are forced to take up arms against their Sovereign or be pillaged & left to starve; cruel alternative. This is too shocking a subject to dwell upon; Your Excellency's known humanity will certainly put a stop if possible to such proceedings as it is not people in arms that Indians will ever daringly attack, but the poor inoffensive families who fly to the deserts to be out of trouble, & who are inhumanly butchered sparing neither women or children."

When the major raids at Wyoming and Cherry valleys, which were largely punitive and had no real military purpose and which, without Tory initiative, would hardly have been attempted, provoked retaliation, neither the Tories nor the British regular army could, or took the trouble to, do anything to protect the Indian country from the devastation that Sullivan's army visited upon it. As we have noted, Haldimand, commander in chief in Canada, had ample warning of the projected campaign and chose to ignore that warning, in part at least because it came from Indians (and was thus presumptively unreliable); beyond that, one cannot help feeling that he did not really care about the fate of the Indians. They were a convenience and were to be used when it was clearly expedient to do so, but they were not, after all, Englishmen. So, having been ruthlessly exploited, they were abandoned to their fate. British strategic plans did not include defending the country of their Indian allies.

As for the Sullivan campaign itself, one is astonished at the facility of it; a territory almost as large as the state of New Hampshire and occupied by people famous for their warlike qualities was ravaged in a few weeks by a motley army, operating in unfamiliar terrain and led by a general not notable for skill or resolution. The truth is that Sullivan's expedition revealed most dramatically the basic weakness in the Indians' tribal organization, at least as it related to sustained warfare. The Indians, warlike as they were, were not prepared for protracted campaigning. Their "wars" were wars of stealthy raids and individual acts of heroism that expressed their warrior skills and validated them as brave men. They did not intend to inflict heavy casualties; or at least they were unwilling to sustain heavy casualties themselves. As warfare was an almost constant state with them, fighting that resulted in many warriors being killed or disabled would destroy a tribe in which virtually every male member was a warrior. The Indians certainly displayed great personal bravery—that was at the heart of their "ethic"; but they did not have the will to persist in the face of unfavorable odds or to sustain heavy casualties. As we have seen in St. Leger's expedition, they fought for glory and spoils, not for "victory" in the white man's terms. At the same time, they were volatile and naive and were, in consequence, constantly manipulated by white men who played skillfully upon their baser emotions of greed, hate, and fear. Beyond this, Indians, with few exceptions, were capable of just one form of military action—attack. In an attack, especially at night or at daybreak, their terrifying appearance, their speed and agility, their paralyzing howls, their strength and the ferocity with which they fought in close combat, their skill with tomahawk and knife made them highly effective auxiliaries. But as we have seen on numerous occasions, the difficulty of restraining or controlling them when they were once aroused made them difficult allies in any conventional military operation.

In defensive situations they were virtually useless. There were few if any engagements where substantial bodies of Indians stood fast in the face of sustained attacks by superior forces. The only instances were when they were surrounded and were faced with death or surrender. Then, almost invariably, they chose death. Again, it was not a matter of courage but of the fact that their temperament, their mode of warfare, and even their "consciousness" made them incapable of the particular kind of discipline, or effort of will, required to defend a position against enemy attack. Part of the problem was that the Indians, not having or being used to artillery, could not withstand its fire. Thus one cannon would be enough to put a large force of Indians to flight. It is only by taking into account these aspects of Indian culture that we can understand why it was that the Iroquois nations stood by and saw their "country" destroyed without being able to muster any effective opposition to the invader. Any resolutely led force of whites, fighting in its own territory, could almost certainly have delayed Sullivan's cumbersome army for months until it was finally immobilized by winter. While it is true that the Indians were heavily outnumbered, they could certainly have put up more of a defense than they did. Their casualties at Newtown, despite Sullivan's optimistic calculations, were apparently not very heavy. Had any substantial number of them decided to die in defense of their "homeland," the outcome of Sullivan's campaign might have been very different.

Describing the expedition, Major Jeremiah Fogg wrote: "Not a single gun was fired for eighty miles on our march out or an Indian seen on our return. Then we expected the greatest harassment—a hundred might have saved half their country by retarding us until our provisions were spent; and a like number hanging on our rear in the return would have occasioned the loss of much baggage and taught us an Indian dance." Weather had also favored the expedition to a remarkable degree, Fogg noted. He ended his account of the expedition on what proved a prophetic note: "The question will naturally arise, What have you to show for your exploits? Where are your prisoners? To which I reply that the rags and emaciated bodies of our soldiers must speak for our fatigue, and when the querist will point out a mode to tame a partridge, or the expediency of hunting wild turkeys with light horses, I will show them our prisoners. The nests are destroyed, but the birds are still on the wing."

Sullivan concluded his report to Congress on the expedition with the following observation: "It would have been very pleasing to this army to have drawn the enemy to a second engagement, but such panic seized them after the first action that it was impossible, as they never ventured themselves in reach of the Army, nor have they fired a single gun at it, on its march or in quarters, tho, in a Country exceeding well calculated for ambuscades."

On the third of October, Washington wrote to Sullivan ordering him to march "with all possible dispatch" to join him for, hopefully, a joint operation against New York with the fleet of the Count D'Estaing. The campaign against the Indian country was over. The Iroquois, their homes and fields laid waste, must depend on the British at Niagara for sufficient food to keep them from starving. They huddled miserably through the winter in makeshift camps, thirsting for revenge.

In retrospect, Washington must bear a part of the blame for the inept Indian policy. Sullivan's, Clinton's and Brodhead's campaigns kept almost five thousand men, a number as large as the entire army of the Southern Department and more than half the size of the Continental Army under Washington, tied up from April to early October, 1779, a period of almost six months. The only tangible result of the scorched-earth policy that Washington ordered Sullivan to undertake was the destruction of the Iroquois society, but without doing serious damage to the warlike potential of those embittered savages. The expedition also ensured, of course, a winter on the frontier free from Indian attacks.

Two other lines of action certainly would have produced better results. A mobile force of some five hundred experienced Indian fighters (one-tenth of the force mobilized for Sullivan's campaign), led by an officer who knew his business and headquartered at Tioga, could have made periodic raids into the edges of the Indian country—on such towns as Chemung and Newtown—and done a great deal to neutralize the Indians and Tories of the area.

Once the decision had been made to raise a force the size of Sullivan's, a far better strategy than the one employed would have been to penetrate deep into Indian territory to Genesee, destroy it, move on to invest Niagara, and then, having impressed the Indians with American strength and the impotence of their British allies, try to bring the Iroquois to a peace meeting. Sullivan's campaign was simply a vengeful, punishing reaction to the raids on the Wyoming and Cherry valleys; and as we have argued elsewhere, punitive actions are always self-defeating. The Iroquois were left with a sense of grievance that could not be assuaged, with wounds that would, quite literally, never heal. The poisonous combination (poisonous to frontier and to the Indians alike) of Tory and Indian remained intact; indeed, by forcing the Indians to depend on the British for their survival, the Indian-Tories-British alliance was sealed beyond undoing. All that Sullivan's expedition accomplished was to let loose a storm of Indian vengeance on the frontier come spring. Acting under Washington's instructions, Sullivan had sown the wind and left the settlers to reap the whirlwind.

7

Border Warfare: New York

THE headquarters of the Western Department were at Pittsburgh, and the command there was in the hands of a Scottish-born officer, General Lachlan McIntosh, from Charles Town, South Carolina. McIntosh, who was contentious and quarrelsome and not notably efficient, had a dreary tale to tell Washington of Indian raids against the frontier settlements of western Pennsylvania that his fort was supposed to protect. Simon Girty, an American soldier turned renegade, had led a small party of Mingoes or Senecas in an ambush of a Captain Clark and fifteen men of the Eighth Pennsylvania Regiment who were returning from Fort Laurens. Clark was driven back to the fort in the fighting that ensured, and two of his men were killed and one captured. A few weeks later a scalping party killed or carried off eighteen men, women, and children from Turtle Creek, a little settlement only twenty miles from Pittsburgh. Word came also from Fort Laurens that a wagoner who had been sent out of the fort to haul wood with an escort of eighteen men was attacked by Indians who killed and scalped the entire party within sight of the fort and then laid siege to the post.

Much the same disheartening story was repeated throughout the spring and summer, while Colonel Daniel Brodhead, who relieved McIntosh, struggled to recruit and equip a force large enough to carry the war to the enemy. Brodhead, who had joined Sullivan in his raids against the Iroquois settlements, was an experienced officer of the Pennsylvania Line and a veteran of the Battle of Long Island. He was a martinet, imperious and overbearing, but he had the drive and energy that were lacking in McIntosh, and he launched his little force of five or six hundred men in an expedition into Indian country.

Marching in single file along the banks of the Allegheny, Lieutenant Harding, commanding an advance party of fifteen whites dressed and painted to look like Indians. and eight Delawares, came on twice as many hostile Indians landing from their canoes in a clearing ahead of them. Harding quickly formed his men into a crude semicircle, and with tomahawks in their hands they dashed to the attack "with such irresistible fury . . . that the savages could not long sustain the charge, but fled with the utmost horror and precipitation, some plunging themselves into the river, and others, favored by the thickness of the bushes, made their escape on the main, leaving five dead. . . ." Three of the attackers were slightly wounded; the dead Indians were promptly scalped.

That was the only engagement of the campaign, although in the course of thirty-three days, Brodhead's force marched almost four hundred miles. In the words of one soldier, the men advanced "through a country almost impassable by reason of stupendous heights and frightful declivities with a continued range of craggy hills, overspread with fallen timbers, thorns and underwood. . . ." Brodhead's little army "burnt ten of the Mingo, Munsey and Seneca towns . . . containing one hundred and sixty-five houses, and destroyed fields of corn, computed to be five hundred acres."

Back at Pittsburgh, the Wyandot chief, Doonyontat, came to treat with Brodhead. *"Brother,"* the Indian declared, "it grieves me to see you with tears in your eyes. I know it is the fault of the British. *Brother,* I wipe away all those tears, and smooth down your hair, which the English and the folly of my young men has ruffled. . . . *Brother,* I see your heart twisted, and neck and throat turned to one side, with the grief and vexation which my young men have caused, all which disagreeable sensations I now remove, and restore you to your former tranquility, so that now you may breathe with ease, and enjoy the benefit of your food and nourishment. . . . *Brother,* I gather up the bones of all our young men on both sides, in this dispute, without any distinction of party. . . . *Brother,* I now look up to where our Maker is, and think there is still some darkness over our heads, so that God can hardly see us, on account of the evil doings of the King over the great waters. All these thick clouds, which have been raised on account of that bad King, I now entirely remove, that God may look and see in our treaty of friendship, and be a witness to the truth and sincerity of our intentions."

The speech, a long ritual interspersed with the solemn presentation of wampum, was answered by Brodhead the next day. "*Brother,* the Chiefs of the Wyandot have lived too long with the English to see things as they ought to do. They must have expected when they were councilling that the Chief they sent to this council fire would find the Americans asleep. But the sun which the Great Spirit has set to light this island discovers to me that they are much mistaken." The Americans were not to be taken in by easy promises and smooth words. What Brodhead wished as pledges of good faith were hostages from the Hurons. He continued, "As I said before, unless they have killed and taken as many from the English and their allies as they have killed and taken from the Americans, and return whatever they have stolen from their brothers, together with their flesh and blood, and on every occasion join us against their enemies—upon these terms . . . they and their posterity may live in peace and enjoy their property without disturbance from their brethren of this island, so long as the sun shines or the waters run. *Brothers,* I have spoken from my heart. I am a warrior as well as a councillor; my words are few, but what I say I will perform. And I must tell you that if the Nations will not do justice, they will not be able, after the English are driven from this island, to enjoy peace or prosperity." They were hard words, but they were spoken in desperate times.

The Americans, who, in the words of Governor Clinton of New York, waited for "the overtures of peace which we had some reason to expect from them [the Indians]," heard instead disturbing rumors that the savages were planning new attacks on the border settlements. The Oneidas, whose cooperation Sullivan had enlisted, felt the full force of the initial onslaught. Supported by British regulars and Tories, the Mohawks, Senecas, and Cayugas destroyed the Oneida settlements and drove them down the Mohawk Valley. Most of them gathered near Schenectady, where they were no longer able to function as a kind of early warning line for raids on the frontier.

In March the militiamen garrisoning the fort at Skenesboro, near Lake George, were captured. Harpersfield, a little town twenty miles south of Cherry Valley, was hit by Brant a few weeks later. Most of the inhabitants had decamped, but several of those who remained were killed, and Captain Alexander Harper, after whom the village had been named, was captured along with eighteen men and women. Hearing Brant speaking about his intention of attacking Lower Fort, Harper gave him the false information that three hundred Continental soldiers were there. That stratagem must have been cold comfort to the battered survivors at Minisink, for Brant and his men returned to that village and plundered whatever was left after their earlier raid the previous spring.

It was soon evident that hostile Indians were ranging the whole length of the country from Canajoharie to the northern end of the Wyoming Valley. A blockhouse at Sacandaga was attacked by seven Indian warriors, who were all killed by the defenders of the fort. At the end of April a party of seventy-nine Indians attacked Cherry Valley again and killed and scalped several whites, but this time the settlers and the soldiers in the fort gave a good account of themselves and fought off the marauders.

In this first phase, aside from Brant's raid on Harpersfield, the attacks were largely carried out by "small unorganized parties of starving men." Much worse was to come. By May, Sir John Johnson was ready to strike at the network of small forts and blockhouses that offered at least some protection to the settlers in the Mohawk Valley. Coming down the Lake Champlain route to Crown Point with a force of four hundred Tories and two hundred Indians, Johnson reached the Johnstown settlements at the north end of the valley on May 21. From there he marched to the Sacandaga River and sent Brant to burn Caughnawaga. Two days later he burned Johnstown and rounded up forty prisoners, as well as collecting a number of the families of his Tory officers and soldiers who had been held more or less as hostages by the patriots. On the first and second of August, Brant with five hundred Tories and Indians pillaged Canajoharie, burned most of its buildings, killed a number of the inhabitants, and captured others.

Then Brant started down the Ohio, where he captured part of an advance party bringing word to George Rogers Clark that Colonel Archibald Lochry was on his way down the Ohio with a picked company of a hundred Pennsylvania volunteers to join Clark in an attack on Kaskaskia. Brant got his force across Lochry's path, and when the Pennsylvanian landed with his men below the Great Miami River, Brant sprang his ambush and virtually annihilated Lochry's detachment. Five officers and thirty-six privates were killed and forty-eight privates and twelve officers captured. Lochry, who was captured, was tortured to death along with several other prisoners, but more than half of those captured eventually made their way back to Pennsylvania. The battle, if it could be called that, was a brilliantly executed maneuver by Brant and the worst defeat suffered by Americans in the border warfare.

From the forks of the Ohio, Brant and his party, loaded with scalps, booty, and prisoners, turned back north and by forced marches joined Johnson for another expedition into Tryon County, New York, the area of the Mohawk Valley that had already seen so much bitter fighting. Haldimand explained the purpose of the campaign to Germain in a letter written on the seventeenth of September, 1780. He wished, he wrote, "to divide the strength that may be brought against Sir H. Clinton, or to favor any operations his present situation may induce him to carry on and to give His Majesty's loyal subjects an opportunity of retiring from the Province. . . ." For this purpose he had fitted out "two parties of about 600 men each, besides Indians, to penetrate into the enemy's territory by the Mohawk River and Lake George." One of the minor objectives of the campaign was Johnson Hall, the home of the famous superintendent of the Indians, Sir William Johnson, father of Sir John. At Johnson Hall, north of the conjunction of the Mohawk and Schoharie rivers, Sir John Johnson found the family silver and papers where they had been hidden when he had earlier escaped his patriot pursuers.

In September, 1780, Johnson left Oswego and advanced to Unadilla, where he met Brant, back from his brilliant victory over Lochry, and Cornplanter, son of a white trader and a Seneca woman and now one of the most famous fighting chieftains. With Brant's and Cornplanter's men, Johnson commanded a force of over a thousand Tories and Indians. He also had with him a brass three-pounder, called a "grasshopper." He slipped undetected into the Schoharie Valley, devastated that area on the fifteenth of October, then destroyed all the rebel property near Fort Hunter and marched up the Mohawk, leaving a trail of burning buildings and ruined fields on both sides of the river as far north as Canajoharie. A lieutenant colonel of militia reported to General Robert Van Rensselaer that "the enemy have burnt the whole of Schohary . . . they have fired two swivel shoots thro' the roof of the church."

By the time Van Rensselaer started in pursuit with a much smaller force, Johnson had already crossed the Mohawk River. "Harassed and fatigued as my force is by a long march," Van Rensselaer wrote, "I am apprehensive I shall not be able to pursue them with that dispatch which is necessary to overtake them. No exertion, however, shall be wanting on my part to effect it. . . ."

Behind the simple recital of villages and farms burnt lies a story of terror, suffering, and death impossible to recount. "The panic that has seized the people is incredible," General Schuyler wrote to Governor Clinton, "with all my efforts I cannot prevent numbers from deserting their habitations, and I am very apprehensive that the whole will move, unless the militia will remain above until a permanent relief can be procured."

Meanwhile Schuyler did his best to help Van Rensselaer collect a force to do battle with Johnson's invading army. Some four or five hundred militia were assembled on the lower end of the Mohawk Valley, while Clinton left his headquarters in Albany with a small, hastily gathered force to join in pursuit of Johnson. From Fort Paris, near Stone Arabia, Colonel John Brown, assured by Van Rensselaer that the latter would arrive in time to support him, came out to attack Johnson's vastly superior force with a hundred and thirty men. It was a sentence of death for many of Brown's militia. He overtook Johnson at the abandoned Fort Keyser, and in savage fighting that lasted the better part of the day, his little force was badly mauled; forty of his men were killed and the rest scattered far and wide. Johnson then looted and burned the village of Stone Arabia.

A battle like that of Fort Keyser has a very modest place in the history of the Revolution, but such casualties were devastating in a sparsely settled region where every soldier was the father or son of a family living in the area. The militiamen in Brown's company, who fought so bravely against heavy odds, fought quite literally for their lives, families, and property, and the forty dead men made up perhaps a fourth or fifth of the able-bodied men of the immediate vicinity. Like the partisan contests in the South, such fighting showed the grimmest face of war.

Van Rensselaer arrived too late to save Brown's men, but, reinforced by four hundred militia and sixty Oneidas under Colonel Lewis DuBois, he pressed so hard on Johnson's heels that the Tory leader was forced at sunset on the nineteenth to turn and fight at Fox Mills. Van Rensselaer's men needed no exhortation to attack. The fighting was intense before Johnson's force gave way and fled under cover of darkness, "leaving behind them," as Clinton reported to Washington, "their baggage, provisions and a brass three-pounder with its ammunition."

The Americans, who had marched thirty miles the day before without halting, were too exhausted to continue the pursuit, and Clinton's men, who arrived the following morning, were, in his words, "so beat out with fatigue, having marched at least 50 miles in less than 24 hours, as to be unable to proceed any further." The statistics that Clinton cited to Washington had an ironic echo: Johnson's raiders had "destroyed, on a moderate computation, 200 dwellings and 150,000 bushels of wheat, with a proportion of other grain and forage." Sullivan, in his month-long raid through Indian country the year before, had claimed 160,000 bushels of corn and forty villages destroyed. Johnson had accomplished almost as much damage in a raid that lasted five days. His raid was the whirlwind that Sullivan had sown. There were two conspicuous differences. Johnson had been opposed at Fort Keyser and caught at Fox Mills. He could not have continued his raid another week without having been overwhelmed by patriot militia, collected from a hundred miles around. While he spread fear among the inhabitants of the region and inflicted heavy damage, as soon as he was gone families, recovering their nerve, began to filter back to their ruined farms and villages. By the following spring, a traveler in the area reported that "there is a prospect of as plentiful crops as has been in the memory of man."

In addition to Johnson's raid, a detachment of the British Fifty-third Regiment hit the upper Connecticut Valley and burned some houses at Royalton, while another small force marched down the line of the Hudson and attacked Ball's Town, twelve miles north of Schenectady.

In the early months of the new year, 1781, Brant, who had been wounded at Klock's Field and put out of action for four or five months, traversed the upper Mohawk Valley with impunity. So many families had fled from the valley that there was no militia to oppose him. Cherry Valley was attacked in April, and two detachments of the Second New York Continentals were captured trying to get supplies to the hungry garrison at Fort Stanwix, which lived in a state of virtual siege.

In May Fort Stanwix, badly damaged by fire and flood waters and almost impossible to supply, was abandoned. The decision seemed a symbol of the low estate of the American cause. Since 1776, Fort Stanwix had guarded the principal line of access from Oswego on Lake Ontario to the upper Hudson, Tryon County, the heart of New England, and the headwaters of the Mohawk River. The friendly Oneidas in whose territory the fort was located had, as we have seen, been driven into the vicinity of Schenectady.

But American fortunes, as it turned out, soon took a turn for the better. Colonel Marinus Willett was sent to take command of the defense of the region. Willett was a forty-year-old graduate of King's College in New York, a successful merchant who had served as a lieutenant in the French and Indian War; he had been, the reader may recall, with Washington on Braddock's campaign. One of the leaders of the Sons of Liberty, he had taken part in the raid on the British arsenal at New York in 1775 and had been made a captain in Alexander MacDougall's First New York Regiment. He had been with Montgomery in Canada and had played a vital role at Fort Stanwix in checking St. Leger's invasion in 1777. He had also distinguished himself at the Battle of Monmouth. Three times married and the father of at least one illegitimate child, Willett was a military leader in the classic mold. When he took charge of the defense of western New York and the Mohawk Valley he assumed responsibility for some five thousand square miles of territory inhabited by roughly two thousand hardy settlers who had resisted all efforts to drive them from their land. He established his principal posts at Ball's Town, Catskill, and Fort Herkimer in German Flats; some hundred and twenty or thirty Continentals were scattered about these three posts. The main force was made up of a hundred and twenty men at Canajoharie, where Willett made his own headquarters. Because Willett had been with Sullivan in the campaign through the Indian country two years before, he knew the land and the nature of his adversaries well. Willett estimated that the country had suffered so heavily from repeated raids by Indians and Tories that its original muster of militia had shrunk from twenty-five hundred at the beginning of the Revolution to a total of less than half as many "classible inhabitants" (males above sixteen years of age). Of these, not more than two-thirds (or some eight hundred) were eligible for the militia rolls. Thus, by Willett's calculations, the number of militia had diminished, during the course of the war, by two-thirds. Of the number lost, it was Willett's estimate that "one third of them have been killed, or carried captive by the enemy; one third have removed to the interior parts of the country; and one third deserted to the enemy."

Those inhabitants who remained relied mainly on crude forts, each giving shelter of a kind to between ten and fifty families. There were twenty-four such forts in the country that Willett was charged with defending. From them the farmers sallied forth every day to till their fields, with their muskets loaded and close at hand, and to them they returned in the evening. Hardly a week passed that marauding Indians did not surprise a farmer in his fields and kill and scalp him.

Willett's first move was to rotate his soldiers among the four main posts. This would enable him to get to know them all, it would keep them fit and alert, and the appearance of activity would improve morale among the settlers themselves. Willett was well aware of the fact that nothing deteriorates so fast as a soldier in garrison. "Having troops constantly marching backwards and forwards through the country," he wrote Washington on July 6, "and frequently changing their route, will answer several purposes such as will easily be perceived by you, sir, without my mentioning them." In addition, Willett intended to personally visit every part of the region to make himself familiar with the state of the garrisons and to "observe the condition of the militia, upon whose aid I shall be under the necessity of placing considerable reliance." Willett's strategy was not to try to defend every post, but "in case the enemy should again appear this way with anything of force, to collect all the strength we can get to a point, and endeavour to beat them in the field." This meant an effective warning system and a high degree of readiness and mobility in the soldiers, regular and militia, under his command.

Shortly after his arrival at Canajoharie, Willett received a report that smoke was visible to the southeast in the direction of Corey's Town. Thirty-five Continentals had already set off on a patrol. Willett sent after them to turn them toward Corey's Town. Sixteen regulars with as many militia as they could round up were sent to the town, eleven miles away, and made such good time that they were able to extinguish some of the fires. Willett meantime rounded up a hundred more militia, who, with the regulars, brought his little force to a hundred and seventy. A scout had brought him word of where the enemy encampment was located, and Willett, assuming that they would return there, headed for the spot under cover of darkness, covering eighteen miles over rough and unmapped country and arriving at six o'clock in the morning. In the daylight the element of surprise was lost, but Willett pushed ahead. The leader of the raiders, perhaps aware that his men were far more effective in offensive actions than in defensive ones, ordered an attack on Willett's force, and the Indians and Tories advanced, yelling and shouting and firing their muskets. "This," Willett wrote, "was the fury of the Indians and nothing more; for upon the huzzas and advance of the front line, they soon gave way." At the same time the Americans were attacked on their right, but they counterattacked so vigorously that the Indians broke and fled.

The battle had lasted for an hour and a half. Willett's force had lost five killed and nine wounded. Out of a force of some two hundred, by

Willett's calculations, the enemy had lost not less than forty, among them the notorious Tory raider, Donald McDonald. It was a severe setback for the Indians and Tories. They were not able to sustain such heavy losses, and for most of the summer the country round about was free of further incursions. Equally important, the one-sided victory gave a tremendous boost to patriot morale. Willett was voted the freedom of Albany by the grateful council of that city, and every settler slept a little better for it. It was a striking demonstration of what inspired leadership can accomplish.

The fall brought a resurgence of enemy activity, however. Late in October, Willett got word that a considerable force of the enemy had appeared at Warrens Bush, some twenty miles from Canajoharie. Willett moved at once, taking all the men he dared from Fort Rensselaer and sending orders to all the regulars and militia "in the contiguous posts and settlements, to follow." He marched all night, arriving in the morning at Fort Hunter, where he learned that the enemy had crossed the river and moved on Johnstown. An exhausted British soldier, who had fallen by the roadside, told Willett that the raiding expedition consisted of some eight hundred seasoned Tories and British regulars with a hundred and twenty Indians under the command of Walter Butler. At Fort Hunter, the other contingents that Willett had ordered to that rendezvous came in, giving him a force of slightly more than four hundred men, the majority of them militia, with which to oppose a force more than twice as large. Willett got his men across the river in bateaux by afternoon and began the march to Johnstown. Two miles outside the town Willett got word that the enemy were busy slaughtering cattle. He decided to attack at once and split his force into two divisions, one to attack in front on the line of march; the other to slip around and take the enemy in the rear. Willett, in command of the right wing of the attacking echelon, moved into a field adjacent to the one where Butler's force was camped and pressed the enemy so hard that they fell back into the cover provided by nearby woods. He then ordered his men to form at skirmish line, advance, and fire, but one of those unreasoning moments of panic that we are by now so familiar with seized the soldiers, and they turned and fled despite all their furious commander could do to rally them. At this juncture, with defeat apparently certain, Major Rowley, a Massachusetts officer in command of the encircling movement, attacked with his division, composed almost entirely of militia except for some sixty regulars. This force pressed the action so resolutely that the British were finally broken and driven from the field, leaving most of their packs and baggage behind them. It was dark by this time, and the Americans by the light of torches collected the wounded of both sides and the abandoned packs. They rounded up a bag of some fifty prisoners, who, in addition to those killed, brought the enemy toll to nearly a hundred. Willett lost some forty men killed or badly wounded.

Unable to determine the enemy intentions, Willett withdrew his troops to German Flats, thereby placing them between Butler's force and their boats that they had left at Oneida Creek. Here sixty Oneida warriors joined him, together with some more militia, bringing his small army to almost five hundred men. Two days later, when it was clear that Butler had given up hope of regaining his boats and had probably started overland for Oswego, Willett, with a picked body of four hundred men equipped with five days' rations, started after Butler. After two days of forced marches, the second through a heavy snowstorm, they discovered that they were on the heels of the enemy. Willett overtook a foraging detachment of forty soldiers and a few Indians. Some were killed or wounded, some captured, and the rest scattered in every direction. Again Willett pressed on and came up with the main body, which was by this time thoroughly demoralized by exhaustion and lack of food. There were plain signs of disorganization and confusion, and after a brief, halfhearted resistance the enemy left the field, trotting in single file. It was a strange flight and pursuit. Butler must have realized that he could not flee forever. His men were at the limit of their endurance. The weather was bitter, and the snow, turning to icy slush, impeded their march. The pursuers, spurred on by the hope of vengeance on their tormentors, were almost as weary as those they pursued. Late in the afternoon, after fording Canada Creek, Butler stopped and made preparations for a battle. In the first skirmish he was severely wounded, and twenty of his men were killed. The rest fled once more, and when Willett's force made camp to get some desperately needed sleep, the British staggered on without food or blankets, determined to put as much distance as they could between themselves and the Americans. Their situation seemed hopeless. They had a seven days' march to Oswego ahead of them, without provisions or blankets to protect them from the increasingly bitter nights. Reluctantly, Willett broke off the pursuit and left the British to the mercies of the wilderness. His men had only five days' rations and would soon have been as depleted as the enemy.

The invaders' most impressive accomplishment was their flight. On a ration of half a pound of horse meat a day, after four days of grueling campaigning, the British, Tories, and Indians had moved, often at a trot, thirty miles before they stopped. Willett wrote Clinton that the wounded Butler was found by "one of our Indians, who finished his business for him and got considerable booty." The raiders were left (Willett's words) "in a fair way of receiving a punishment better suited to their merit than a musket ball, a tomahawk or captivity. . . ."—starvation in the forest.

The most important gain for the Americans was the death of Walter Butler, who with his father and Joseph Brant had been the scourge of the frontier for years. He was bitterly hated for his depredations and for his ruthlessness and cruelty. Historians have attempted to exonerate him from the worst charges against him. Trained in Albany as a lawyer, he was a handsome, graceful man. There had never been any doubt that he would cast his lot with His Majesty's forces. His father, as an Indian agent, had been a friend of the great Sir William Johnson and a faithful servant of the Crown; the son, joining forces with Sir William's son, Sir John, was true to that tradition. Four years before, Butler had been caught trying to recruit settlers to the Tory cause in Tryon County and had been sentenced to be hanged as a spy by a military court of which, ironically, Willett had been judge advocate. He had escaped. It was the opinion of Colonel Willett's son that Butler "had exhibited more instances of enterprise, had done more injury, and committed more murder, than any other man on the frontiers." To the patriot inhabitants of the Mohawk Valley his death was of greater moment and hailed with greater delight than Washington's defeat of Cornwallis.

Although small bands of Indians continued to roam the frontier and made occasional raids on isolated settlements and farmhouses, Willett's victory at Johnstown marked the end of large-scale attacks on the northern frontier. What Sullivan with five thousand men could not accomplish (indeed it could be argued he stimulated the border raids), Willett achieved with a tenth the number of troops.

8

George Rogers Clark

W HILE Sullivan, Brodhead, and finally Willett contended with the Indians and Tories who used Niagara as their base and raided out of that garrison town against the Mohawk Valley and the western boundaries of Pennsylvania, one of the most remarkable dramas of the war was taking place in the territory east of the Mississippi and north of the Ohio.

George Rogers Clark had been twenty-three years old at the time of Lexington and Concord, and his imagination had immediately been fired by dreams of personal glory as well as by ardor for the Revolutionary cause. He had grown up on a farm near Charlottesville, Virginia, son of just such a yeoman farmer as Clark's future patron, Thomas Jefferson, was to extol as the finest flower of American democracy. Clark had bright red hair, but the most arresting features of his handsome, open face were his dark, intense eyes. Strong and agile, he had had little formal schooling, but he had omnivorous and catholic intellectual interests and had read widely, especially in history and geography. At nineteen, he had begun the career of a surveyor, a classic occupation for young men drawn by the romance of the wilderness—young men who delighted in the danger and excitement of pitting their skill and resourcefulness against an intractable forest and its savage inhabitants.

When he was scarcely twenty Clark went exploring down the Ohio to its juncture with the Kanawha with a boatful of friends, and the next spring he ran down the Ohio to the mouth of Fish Creek, a hundred and thirty miles below Pittsburgh. From there he and a friend went another hundred and thirty miles down the Ohio, returned, and spent the winter on Fish Creek. He dreamed of towns in the wilderness, with himself as leader of a band of settlers. In Dunmore's War, which pitted Virginians against the Shawnees in 1774, he secured a commission as a militia captain, and after that brief episode he became a surveyor of land on the Kentucky River for the Ohio Company of Virginia, a company in which Washington and his brother were investors, along with George Mason and other prominent Virginia patriots.

But all this was unexceptional. Hundreds of young men much like George Rogers Clark ranged the frontier looking for their fortunes and for adventure. Clark was like John Laurens, Henry Lee, Alexander Hamilton, and Allan McLane, all in their early twenties at the outbreak of the Revolution, all thirsting for military glory and renown, all natural leaders of other men. Clark was distinguished from the others by the fact that his ambition burned, if anything, more intensely (with the exception, of course, of Alexander Hamilton), and because with his innate gifts as a military leader he combined a strategic imagination of great sweep and vigor and a precocious knowledge of the wild country that stretched westward farther than the imagination could reach. Of his brilliant coevals—those young warriors of the republic whom he so much resembled—Henry Lee, with his remarkable gifts as leader and his brilliant tactical instincts, was his nearest counterpart. Like Lee, George Rogers Clark never adapted to peacetime society, and like Lee he died a pathetic death, forlorn and ill, a kind of exile from the country he had done so much to create.

Clark was obsessed by the Old Northwest, the immense country that extended south of the Great Lakes, an area that was to contain the future states of Ohio, Illinois, Michigan, and Indiana. It was a region of vast forests, open plains, mighty rivers, and of course, over it all, the seemingly endless expanse of the Great Lakes. It was a region interlaced with rivers that ran out from the spine of the Ohio like the ribs of a skeleton. (From east to west, on the north of the Ohio are the Allegheny, the Muskingum, the Scioto, the Little and Great Miami, the Wabash [with the White River angling off from it to the east] and the Little Wabash, and then, of course, the Mississippi. On the south side of the Ohio are the Monongahela, forming a juncture with the Allegheny, the Kanawha [pointing at western Virginia], the Big Sandy, the Licking, the Kentucky, the Green, the Cumberland, and the Tennessee.) That great country had been the preserve of the western Indians: the Ottawas and Hurons in Michigan; the Potawatomis in western Ohio and Indiana; the Mascoutens, Kickapoos, and Illinois in what was to become Illinois; in later-day Wisconsin the Winnebagos; to the northwest, near the headwaters of the Mississippi River, the Ojibwas or Chippewas; and south and west of them the Sioux (or Dakotas), whom the Ojibwas had driven out of their homeland with the help of the French. South of the Sioux were the Sauks and the Foxes. This enormous area had first been explored by La Salle and other great seventeenth-century French adventurers and had then become the terrain of the *courier de bois,* the tough and enterprising French fur traders who roamed far into Indian country in search of beaver pelts. The Treaty of Paris, in 1763, had given control of the region, along with Canada proper, to the British, but at the outbreak of the Revolution, French settlers still lived at the old French posts of Vincennes on the Wabash and Kaskaskia and Cahokia on the Mississippi. There were other scattered posts—Fort St. Joseph at the southeastern end of Lake Michigan, Fort Miami on the Maumee, and most important of all, Fort Detroit, near the northwest tip of Lake Erie.

That splendid country, filled with sparkling lakes, broad rivers, and verdant forests, was seen by most Americans as a dark and perpetual menace. In a series of "intercolonial wars" stretching back into the preceding century, the French and their Indian allies had time and again emerged from the Northwest to ravage the border settlements.

The Indians of the Northwest, now allied with the British, posed a threat to all the western settlements as far east as Pittsburgh. George Rogers Clark's dream was to take possession of the Northwest Territory, an area almost the size of the entire continent of Europe. The first priority was, to be sure, the defense of the Kentucky country against Indian raids, especially against the attacks of the Shawnees and the Cherokees. Clark visited Williamsburg in 1776 to get help from Virginia and took an active part himself in organizing militia for the defense of the area. Almost from the beginning of hostilities, there had been schemes for an attack on Detroit. Daniel Morgan, Edward Hand, and Lachlan McIntosh had all tried to mount expeditions. Clark became convinced that the middle and upper Southern frontier could never be defended as long as the Indian sanctuary in the Northwest was inviolate. From Detroit, Lieutenant Colonel Henry Hamilton, the "Hair Buyer," incited the Indians by blandishments and bribery to undertake forays against the Americans, and from that post came a constant stream of supplies and gifts for the Indians.

If Detroit was the ultimate objective, it was also the remotest and best defended. Attacks on Kaskaskia and Vincennes would do much to neutralize that post and check Indian raids. While Clark pressed his campaign to win official approval and support for such an expedition, he sent two of the most experienced and hardy woodsmen of the frontier on a risky mission to assay the condition of Vincennes and Kaskaskia. Clark had originally picked four, but it was decided that two men could accomplish the task better. Simon Kenton, Si Harland, Ben Lyon, and Sam Moore drew lots. Moore and Lyon won and set out for the juncture of the Ohio and the Mississippi. Meanwhile, Clark rallied support for his plan. There was general approval in the Virginia assembly, but the state's resources were too meager to provide support for such an ambitious undertaking. There was also uneasiness at the idea of Virginia initiating a venture that was much more properly the business of Congress. Yet the primary reason for going to the Virginia authorities for backing was that Virginia claimed virtually the whole of the present-day United States west of the Alleghenies, including the Northwest. Thus leading Virginians, especially those involved in land speculation (and those who hoped to be), were by no means disinterested parties. As Jefferson saw it, having a Virginian capture the territory under the auspices, formal or informal, of his home state "would have an important bearing ultimately in establishing our western boundary," that is to say, the western boundary of the United States and the western boundary of Virginia. By late summer Lyon and Moore were back with encouraging news. The British garrison at Kaskaskia had been withdrawn to Detroit. Kaskaskia and the little, dependent, largely French towns near it—Misère, Ste. Geneviève, Fort de Chartres, Prairie du Rocher, and even Cahokia, further up the Mississippi—were virtually defenseless. Moreover their inhabitants had no great love for the British.

Clark wrote promptly to Governor Patrick Henry, describing the situation of the country and his plans for seizing control of it. There were, he told Henry, about one hundred French and English families at Kaskaskia, most of them engaged in trade with the Indians. In addition there were a number of Negroes who constituted a kind of militia force and worked in the fields that surrounded the town. The fort, which was a short distance below the town, was built of logs and stood some ten feet high with blockhouses at each corner, defended by several cannon. The commander at Kaskaskia, Rocheblave, had encouraged the Wabash Indians to "invade the frontiers of Kentucky; was daily treating with other nations, giving large presents and offering them great rewards for scalps." After describing the advantages that accrued to the British by possessing Kaskaskia, Clark added, "If it was in our possession it would distress the garrison at Detroit for provisions, it would fling the command of the two great rivers into our hands, which would enable us to get supplies of goods from the Spaniards [who controlled the lower Mississippi] and to carry on a trade with the Indians. . . ."

Clark followed his letter with another trip to Williamsburg. His conviction was irresistible. With the support of Jefferson, Mason, Richard Henry Lee, and Governor Henry, the Virginia assembly was persuaded to give the project its blessing on the basis of the vaguest account of Clark's actual intentions. If word got out of the grandiose nature of the enterprise, there would almost certainly be embarrassing questions in Congress. The simple fact is that it was, at best, a rather shady deal. Its only justification was that if the matter came into the purview of Congress, that body would wear out the project discussing it and doubtless veto it in the end. In any event, Clark was commissioned as colonel and authorized to raise seven companies of men. How he was to clothe and feed them was not entirely clear. He was given some money and authority to draw supplies from Fort Pitt. His ostensible orders were to defend the Kentucky country. It was not felt necessary to let many people know that this was to be done by capturing Kaskaskia, a hundred and fifty miles northwest of the Kentucky River, and, if possible, Detroit, several hundred miles farther on.

Clark sent a trusted lieutenant, Captain W. P. Smith, to the Holston River settlement to raise four companies of fifty men each. He himself recruited men in western Virginia and western Pennsylvania (which, it will be recalled, was also claimed by Virginia). Smith was to meet Clark at the Falls of the Ohio, the site of present-day Louisville, Kentucky; Clark, with the men that he had rounded up and several boats full of supplies, would come down from Fort Pitt. Clark left Redstone, Pennsylvania, on the Monongahela on May 12, 1778. The recruiting went badly from the beginning. Men were desperately needed to defend their own families and communities, and few were inclined to sign up with the enthusiastic twenty-six-year-old redhead who displayed a colonel's commission from the state of Virginia and was rather imprecise about the exact nature of his mission. When he got to the falls, he had only a hundred and fifty men with him. There was no sign of Smith. "You may easily guess at my mortification," Clark wrote to George Mason, "on being informed that he had not arrived; that all his men had been stopt by the incessant labours of the populace. . . ." In other words, many prospective recruits had simply been forced to remain at home on the not unreasonable grounds that they were more needed there than somewhere else. One thin company had arrived, some of the men having been "threatened to be put in prison if they did not return."

Clark was desperate. It seemed as though several years of planning and politicking in behalf of his grand design were to be frustrated by his inability to find men to accompany him. One problem was that given his ostensible charge—to protect the Kentucky settlers—the hardheaded frontiersmen could not see the point of draining off their best fighting men. On the other hand, how much better would Clark do if he were to reveal to his prospective recruits his real assignment—to capture the Northwest? Would they volunteer, in Clark's words, "to be taken near a thousand [miles] from the body of their country to attack a people five times their number, and merciless tribes of Indians, . . . determined enemies to us?"

Clark, in the classic manner of the obsessive, refused to despair. ("I knew that my case was desperate, but the more I reflect on my weakness the more I was pleased with the enterprise.") A few more Kentuckians drifted in. Clark gathered his little group on an island in the middle of the falls and placed a guard over the boats "to stop the desertion I knew would ensue upon the troops knowing their destination." Then he told them; despite his precautions, one contingent—a Lieutenant Hutchings and his party—escaped "after being refused leave to return." It is not hard to imagine the state of mind of the several hundred men marooned on an island in the middle of the Ohio River with their fanatical young leader. These were tough and independent characters, seasoned woodsmen and Indian fighters. They had been induced to enlist by a young zealot who had overcome their better judgment and, more important, had misrepresented the purpose of the expedition. What followed was a fierce contest of wills between the furious recruits and their stubborn leader. "On this island," Clark wrote, in a sentence heavy with unspoken implications, "I first began to discipline my little army, knowing that to be the most essential point towards success. Most of them determined to follow me. The rest seeing no probability of making their escape, I soon got that subordination as I could wish for." The self-reliant and strong-willed men who constituted that company were able to cope remarkably well with most of the problems and hazards of daily life, but they could not cope with this half-mad youth who was determined to make heroes of them or die in the attempt.

On the twenty-sixth of June, Clark loaded his men, something under two hundred in number, in flatboats, shot the rapids during a total eclipse of the sun that he tried to persuade his frightened men was a favorable omen, and, rowing double night and day, made the mouth of the Tennessee River in four days. Here they met a boatful of hunters eight days out of Kaskaskia. Clark interrogated them ("Their intiligence was not favourable," he noted) and then set out cross-country from Fort Massac through primeval forests where the men had to hack their way for fifty miles before they came out onto the level plains of lower Illinois. Clark realized that with his handful of men, the success of his expedition depended largely on secrecy. Visible sometimes for miles to hostile observation, they proceeded on a course north and west. Clark's guide felt the full weight of his leader's rage when he lost the way. Deep in enemy country on a wild venture fraught with peril, the men of the expedition watched uneasily while Clark struggled with a "passion that," in his own words, "I did not master for some time." He threatened to put the terrified guide to death "if he did not find his way that evening." Thus encouraged, the guide got Clark's party back on the right trail. By the evening of the fourth of July, Clark and his men were within three miles of Kaskaskia.

Now the Kaskaskia River was the last remaining barrier. Had the town gotten word of their march? Would the commandant, Rocheblave, have adopted a posture of defense that would make their attack far more hazardous? They marched to a farm by the river, took the inhabitants prisoners, collected boats, and in two hours were ferried across "with the greatest silence." Rocheblave, it turned out, had received a warning and had sent out scouts, but the scouts had returned to report no signs of an enemy, and the commandant had relaxed his vigilance.

Clark divided his little band in two, surrounded the town, caught Rocheblave in the fort, and in fifteen minutes "had every street secured." Runners were sent through the town "ordering the people on pane of death to keep close to their houses," and soldiers followed them collecting arms. The psychological effect on the inhabitants was all that Clark could have wished. The wild American rebels, reported to be little better than the Indians themselves, had appeared as silently as ghosts. The settlers had been taught "to expect nothing but savage treatment from the Americans," Clark noted. "Giving all for lost, their lives were all they could dare to beg for, which they did with the greatest fervancy; they were willing to be slaves to save their families."

Clark, with the instincts of a master showman, turned aside their entreaties. He had not decided yet what to do with them or to them. Rebuffed, the settlers "repaired to their houses, trembling as if they were led to execution. . . ." The next day, Clark was all friendliness and lordly affability, "for I was too weak," he wrote, "to treat them any other way. . . ."

The tactics worked like a charm. The leading men of the town explained, with Gallic effusiveness, that they had never really been properly informed about the struggle between England and her colonies. Naturally, hearing only the British side, they had accepted it. Now that they saw the Americans as they really were, splendid, magnanimous fellows, fighting for the rights of man, "they were . . . convinced that it was a cause they ought to espouse; that they would be happy of an opertunity," as Clark put it, "to convince me of their zeal, and think themselves the happyest people in the world if they were united with the Americans. . . ." This was going somewhat farther than Clark had expected. He consolidated his gains by assuring the Catholic priest, who asked if he could perform his duties, "that I had nothing to do with the churches more than to defend them from insult . . . This seemed to complete their happiness." Soon the streets were adorned with flowers and bright-colored banners, and there was singing and dancing as though in gratitude for a deliverance.

Clark issued a proclamation on December 24, 1778. Too great liberty had been enjoyed by "red and black slaves," he declared. He ordered "all persons of whatsoever quality . . . from selling to, causing to be given to, or trading with red and black slaves any intoxicating liquors under any pretext whatsoever and in any quantity. . . ." Moreover all inhabitants were forbidden to "lend or rent gratuitously to any red or black slaves their house, buildings and courts, after sunset or for the night, for the purpose of dancing, feasting, or holding nocturnal assemblies therein. . . ." And none could be out of their houses or compounds after tattoo was beaten in the evening unless provided with a pass.

Clark wished to secure Cahokia, sixty miles up the river, and he sent a detachment on horseback to accomplish this. The Americans rode off accompanied by a "considerable number" of their new friends. This happy troop marched right into the middle of the town before anyone sounded the alarm, and then the residents of Kaskaskia were called to in their native tongue "to submit to their happier fate, which they did with very little hestitation. . . ."

Rocheblave watched glumly as his charges exuberantly changed their alliance. Morose and uncooperative, he was shipped off under guard to Virginia. Father Gibault, the priest, was especially helpful. The word that France was now an ally of America was, of course, another important encouragement to friendly feelings. Gibault, with a French doctor and several other Kaskaskians, made the journey to Vincennes and returned in August with word that the town had transferred its allegiance to the state of Virginia. Clark immediately dispatched Captain Helm, one of his most trusted officers, with a small body of men to officially occupy the town and take command of the militia.

So far so good. Clark had brought off a brilliant coup by his energy and daring. But he was, after all, in the middle of an area filled with Indians traditionally hostile to the Americans. He was short of supplies and had no ready means of procuring food and ammunition for his force. Furthermore, he had to assume that the British, as soon as they were fully informed of the nature of this fleabite, would mount a strong counteroffensive from Detroit. Clark, who knew how long it took for a regular military expedition to be mustered and equipped, realized that the Indians were the first problem. If they were not dealt with, they might be down about his ears in a matter of days. With his customary directness he summoned them to a council, and there he matched his fervent oratory with their ritual eloquence and bluffed his way out of danger. On his side was the fact that Indians generally were unduly impressed by success. What counted for Clark even more than his masterful poker-playing was the fact that he had, after all, established himself in the heart of enemy territory and seemed to be in full command of the situation. Beyond that there was the disconcerting news that the French, to whom many of the tribes had given allegiance long before the British appeared on the scene, were reported to be allies of the Americans. With the Indians there was always a pull between the immediate advantages of going on the warpath and the long-term problem of who was going to emerge from the Revolution victorious. Since they quite naturally had no real interest in the white man's squabbles, except insofar as they might profit from them, they were constantly making delicate calculations of profit and loss in determining where to give their support. And since they were subject to the same vicissitudes of history as the white men, they often guessed wrong. Now, after considerable palavering, they decided it was one of those moments when they would do best to pay strict attention to their own business. If the British appeared in large force with appealing presents, it would be time enough to reconsider. So Clark was over his first and most serious hurdle.

The matter of supplies was solved by one of the shrewdest and most enterprising patriots in the states, Oliver Pollock, agent for Virginia in New Orleans, who shipped provisions up the Mississippi to Clark's "army."

There remained the threat of a British counteroffensive. Hamilton, in charge at Detroit, was a determined if inexperienced soldier. He persevered in his efforts to gather a force sufficient to regain British control of the Kaskaskia-Vincennes region, but it was October before he was ready to set out on the six-hundred-mile journey to Vincennes. His route ran southwest up the Maumee, across a long portage to the Wabash, and then down to Vincennes. His force was no more impressive than Clark's—a hundred and seventy-five soldiers, mostly French, and sixty Indians—but he could count on picking up Indian auxiliaries along the way, as indeed he did, arriving above Vincennes with some five hundred men. The trip, in the late fall and winter, was an exhausting one that took seventy-one days. The water in the Oubache, or Wabash, was frozen, and "flating ice cut the men as they worked in the water to haul the boats over shoals and rocks." The bateaux were damaged and had to be periodically unloaded and caulked. Hamilton also stopped frequently at Indian villages to hold tedious councils, to distribute presents, and to try to enlist warriors.

Above Vincennes, one of Hamilton's scouting parties captured a French lieutenant and three men who had been on a similar mission at Clark's behest. Hamilton now proved as adept at psychological warfare as Clark. He sent one of his officers to Vincennes to warn the inhabitants "that unless they quitted the Rebels and laid down their arms, there was no mercy for them." Some Indian chiefs accompanied the officer, "to show the French what they might expect if they pretended to resist." The militia that Captain Helm had so assiduously trained got the point and despite his protests laid down their arms. Hamilton's emissary immediately "secured the arms, ammunition and spirituous liquors," and Helm had no alternative but to surrender "this wretched fort," as Hamilton put it. It looked as though Clark's days were numbered. Hamilton, with a force of more than five hundred British regulars, French recruits, and Indians, was in possession of Vincennes, some one hundred and fifty miles from Clark's headquarters at Kaskaskia. Clark had had no word that the reinforcements he had requested from Virginia were on the way, and he had every reason to believe that they were not. His small force, which had been recruited to protect the Kentucky frontier and then bullied into advancing hundreds of miles into enemy territory, had been away from the familiar scenes of home for six months. The chill of winter penetrated their tattered garments. Hamilton meanwhile was, in Clark's words, "influancing all the Indians he possibly can to join him," and he had presumably sealed off Clark's line of supply and retreat by guarding the Ohio River near its junction with the Wabash. Clark, measuring Hamilton by his own impetuosity, daily "expected an attact from him."

But early in February a Spaniard named Vigo, who had been in Vincennes, reached Kaskaskia with the welcome news that Hamilton, deterred by the bitterness of the winter and the weariness of his own troops after their six-hundred-mile journey, did not plan to attack the garrison at Kaskaskia until spring. Presents and speeches had been sent to all the Indian tribes south of the Ohio to meet at a great council at the mouth of the Tennessee River "to lay the best plans for cuting of the Rebels at Illinois and Kentucky. . . ." The fort at Vincennes was being strengthened and fortified by a brass six-pounder, two four-pounders, and two swivels, along with "plenty of ammunition and provisions and all kinds of warlike stores."

The Indian allies of the British were called on to assemble at l'Arbe Croche, in Michigan country, to join forces with Hamilton at Vincennes. When the Indians held back, fearful of Clark's reputation and reluctant to undertake an arduous campaign in Illinois, Hamilton sent Charles de Langlade, a French officer serving with the British army, to try to persuade them to go on the warpath. When Langlade's arguments were unavailing, he drew on his intimate knowledge of the customs and superstitions of the Indians. He built a lodge with a door at each end in the middle of the Indian village. He had several dogs killed for the dog feast that was very popular with the savages. He then placed the still-warm hearts of the dogs on sticks at each door to the lodge and invited the warriors to the banquet. At the end he sang a war song and went around the lodge from one door to the other, tasting, at each entrance, a piece of the dog's heart. The challenge was inescapable. If the Indians present were not to appear as cowards they must follow his example, taste the dogs' hearts, and follow him to war. They dared not dishonor an ancient custom of the tribe. They joined in the war chant and took up their arms to follow Langlade into the Illinois country.

9

The Capture of Vincennes

CLARK realized that the Indian question was crucial, and that without reinforcements he could not expect to withstand a determined attack in the spring. Cut off from any retreat, he would be forced to surrender his miniature army or have them slaughtered by the British and Indians. It seemed to him that the only course open besides abandoning his post without a fight was to attack Hamilton "and risque the whole on a single battle."

First Clark sent off part of his force in a galley, with instructions to row down the Mississippi, then up the Ohio to the Wabash, and from there up that river to a point some ten leagues below Vincennes. Then he set out with the rest of his men on their perilous journey. He was, he wrote George Mason, much concerned "for those brave officers and soldiers that are determined to share my fate" on "this forlorn hope." He concluded his letter to Mason with prophetic words: "Who knows what fortune will do for us? Great things have been affected by a few men well conducted. Perhaps we may be fortunate. We have this consolation: that our cause is just, and that our cuntrey will be greatful. . . ."

The essential quality of charismatic leadership is that it can prevail on men to hazard their lives in the face of overwhelming odds. It is also near madness. It is plain enough that Clark was loaded with charisma. It must have taken all he had to put his little band in motion. Perhaps they found the very audacity of the idea irresistible. Scarcely two hundred men were setting out in the dead of winter to make a march of one hundred and fifty miles in the face of innumerable obstacles, through territory filled with potentially hostile Indians, to attack a well-fortified position manned by two or three times their number. Nothing like it had happened since Arnold's march to Quebec. On the fifth of February the army started off, conducted out of the town by the inhabitants, who had fallen under the sway of the young red-haired American. Father Gibault, the Catholic priest, preached "a very suitable" sermon to the force, which included a number of the more venturesome young Frenchmen of the town, and then gave the whole party, Protestant and Catholic alike, absolution, undoubtedly the Protestants' first experience of that office.

From the first, Clark's principal concern was to "divert the men as much as possible in order to keep up their spirits." And their spirits certainly needed sustaining. The line of march lay across country that was alternately deep in snow and drowned in black water. In such circumstances a heroic effort is required simply to exist. Attention becomes fixed on the most minute details: keeping one's toes and fingers from freezing, or the tip of one's nose; finding a dry place to make a miserable bed; and then, deciding whether to take off one's wet shoes and risk their freezing, or keep them on and freeze one's feet (the solution is usually to take off the shoes and stay under the blankets); eating with numb fingers and trying to soak up a little warmth over a meager campfire without being blinded by the smoke from damp wood. In eighteen days Clark and his men covered almost one hundred and fifty miles under the most difficult and exhausting conditions imaginable. How Clark diverted his soldiers was, in itself, a stroke of genius. He encouraged them to shoot game at every opportunity, which was not only a welcome distraction on such an arduous march but a practical measure to feed the men and conserve rations. Each evening a different company gave a feast for the whole party, using the game that had been shot during the march and engaging in Indian war dances. Clark and the senior officers exhorted "the woodsmen shouting now and then and Runing as much through the Mud and Water as any of them." Thus there came to be a kind of desperate gaiety about the venture, something of the air of an extended picnic or excursion. After wading all day through water sometimes as high as their waists or chests, the men reached dry ground, "in high spirits Each Laughing at the other in consequence of something that had happened in the course of this ferrying business as they called it and the whole at the great Exploit as they thought that they had accomplished." A "little Antick Drummer" delighted the soldiers by floating on his drum. "All this," Clark wrote, "was greatly Incouraged and they really began to think themselves superiour to other men and that neither the Rivers or seasons could stop their progress."

The most essential element was always Clark himself. He was unfailingly cheerful and optimistic, thereby causing his men "to believe that I had no doubt of suckcess which keep their Spirits."

On the thirteenth of February the party came to the most formidable obstacle that they had yet encountered. The branches of the Little Wabash had flooded, covering all the land in between to a distance of three to five miles with from three to four feet of frigid water. "This," Clark wrote, with classic understatement, "would have been enough to have stopped any set of men not in the same temper that we was. . . ." They had come too far to turn back. A "large canoe" was built to carry the men and supplies across the two riverbeds, and the rest of the way the men waded, always in water up to their waists, frequently sinking up to their shoulders, stumbling over underwater obstructions that they could not see, floundering and cursing and chilled to the very marrow of their bones. Scaffolds were built on each riverbank to hold the expedition's baggage until the horses could be gotten over to carry them across the flooded land between the rivers. They were now so close to Vincennes that it was dangerous to light fires to dry out clothes and equipment, not to mention the men themselves. Another day's march brought them to the Embarras River, which was also flooded. On one occasion, when Clark came back from scouting the way ahead, he so far forgot himself as to look serious and somewhat distracted. The effect on the men was immediate; morale collapsed as suddenly as if it had been a pricked balloon. There was a murmur of despair through the ranks of men who had come so far and suffered so much. Clark's response was characteristically ingenuous. He whispered to the officers nearest him to do what he did. He scooped up some water, mixed it with powder from his powder horn and smeared the black paste on his face, and then, giving a war whoop, he turned and marched into the water without a word. Silently, "like a flock of sheep," the weary men fell in behind him. Clark ordered the men beside him to begin a favorite song; "it soon passed through the Line and the whole went on chearfully." Just when

Clark feared that they could go no farther because of deepening water, a soldier found a path higher than the ground on either side of it, and the party was able to push forward to Sugar Island.

The weather, which had been unseasonably warm for days, now turned bitterly cold, with a half to three-quarters of an inch of ice formed on the water. "A little after sun-Rise," Clark recalled, "I Lectured the whole. . . ." A few more hours would put them within striking distance of Vincennes. Then all that they had labored and suffered for would be achieved. When Clark "amediately stept into the water without waiting for any Reply a Huza took place." Clark turned and called to one of his officers to fall in the rear and put to death any person who refused to march, "the whole gave a cry of apperbation that it was Right and on we went."

Clark judged the difficulty of the march by his own failing strength. He ordered the two or three canoes to move back and forth carrying the weakest of the men, and he sent ten or twelve of the strongest men on ahead with instructions to pass the word back that the water was growing shallower and to call out, "land," to encourage the rest of the men to continue. The stronger half dragged the weak, but the water, instead of getting shallower, got deeper. Finally the exhausted company reached the woods, and there the weakest clung to logs and trees until they were taken off by the canoes. Meanwhile "the strong and Tall" got ashore and built fires. Some who reached the shore were too exhausted to pull their bodies out of the water. Even the fires failed to revive some of the men, and the only way to restore circulation to their numb bodies was for two of the stronger men to take them by the arms and walk them about until their strength returned. "As if designed by Providence" a canoe of Indian squaws and children came by; it was captured and stripped of its provisions, which included nearly a half-quarter of buffalo, some corn, and several kettles. A broth was immediately made and distributed, first to those most in need of it. Many of the men refused to take any, giving their portion to their weaker fellows, "jocosely saying something cheary to their comrades this little refreshment and fine weather by the afternoon gave new life to the whole."

The nine miles from the Embarras to the Wabash, on whose east bank Vincennes stood, were also flooded. Clark sent a canoe down the Wabash to make contact with the party that had gone by water and to hurry them up. But he dared not wait for the boat. The army had now been almost two weeks on the march, much of it in rain. Between them and their objective lay another ten miles of flooded terrain that had somehow to be negotiated. There was no way to rest, no means to cook food or even to get supplies to the men who struggled for their lives hour after hour in cold water. All that flesh and blood could do, lashed on by the determination of a fanatic, it did. "Our suffering for four days in crossing those waters, and the manner it was done . . . is too incredible for any person to believe, except those that are well acquainted with me as you are, or had experienced something similar to it," Clark wrote. It was as hideous and interminable as a nightmare, but it came at last to an end. On the twenty-third, to the "inexpressible joy" of the men, they reached dry ground within a mile of the fort and under the cover of a grove of trees. Fortunately the sun came out and the day turned unseasonably warm, drying the clothes on the men's backs a bit. Several small, carefully concealed fires were built. Some persons coming from the town were intercepted and held prisoner; one gave them "all the intiligence we wished for."

From the prisoners Clark learned that Hamilton's original force of some six hundred men, with which he had seized Vincennes in December, had shrunk to a few hundred. The greater part of his force had been made up of Indians who had long since departed for home with Hamilton's blessings. They were of little use certainly in Fort Sackville, the British post at Vincennes. Hamilton planned to muster them up for a spring offensive against Kaskaskia, but in the town they simply got drunk whenever they could get their hands on liquor and made trouble. Clark was careful not to let the prisoners get a notion of the size of his force. As he waited at the edge of the woods "a thousand ideas" flashed through his head. Hamilton could clearly defend the fort for a considerable time, though if Clark and his men were to seize the town itself, Hamilton could hardly venture out. On the other hand, in a prolonged siege the British must undoubtedly learn of the paltry number of besiegers and send a rescue party. Not surprisingly, Clark "resolved to appear as darring as possible, that the enemy might conceive by our behaviour that we were very numerous. . . ."

He decided to write to the inhabitants of Vincennes, telling them where he was and of his plans to occupy the town. All who were friends to the States were to keep in their houses; those who favored the king of England were to report to the fort "and fight for their King; otherways there should be no mercy shown them. . . ." In order to give the impression of a much larger force than the one at his command, Clark sent the compliments of several officers "that was known to be expected to reinforce me" and whose names were familiar to residents of the town. When it was nearly sundown, he sent one of the prisoners to the town with the message and then followed not far behind. He moved his men off in the fading light with numerous faked company colors flying, and with the troops deployed in such a way as to appear from the town to be many times larger in number than they actually were. An officer was assigned to attack the fort on a signal from Clark while he, with the main body of his men, took possession of the town. Surprise was so complete that the defenders of the fort assumed the initial firing came from some drunken inhabitants until one of the members of the garrison was wounded through a firing slot in the fort. The fires of the Americans had in fact been observed, and Hamilton had sent out a scouting party, but before they could return, Clark had launched his attack.

The fort's surgeon was in the town when the attack began. The woman in whose house he was visiting was among those who had been warned by Clark's messenger, and she cried, when the first shots were heard: "There is Colonel Clarke. [He] is arrived from Illinois with 500 men."

The first reaction was the flight of a considerable number of British-allied Indians from the town itself. A steady fire was kept up on the fort, and the Kickapoo and Piankashaw Indians, who remained in the town, took up their arms and offered to march out and help Clark's force in the attack on the fort. Clark explained to the chiefs that he feared there might be confusion in the dark and asked them to wait until dawn to join in the attack. Meantime, he worked his men closer and closer to the fort itself, until "the garrison was intirely surrounded within eighty and a hundred yards beyond houses, palings and ditches, etc., etc. . . ." Clark himself, weary as he was, experienced a kind of euphoria that was shared by his men. They had triumphed over the protracted anguish of the march itself, and there was no denying them now. "All my past suffering vanished," Clark wrote. "Never was a man more happy. It wanted no encouragement from any officer to inflame our troops with a martial spirit." Hamilton was universally hated on the frontier as the "Hair Buyer," and many of the men attacking the fort had lost friends and relatives to Indian raids that they believed him to have instigated. Now they had him in a trap, and they did not mean to let him go. Clark, knowing that he could not afford to lose many members of his small army, "took the greatest care of them that I possibly could; at the same time encouraged them to be daring, but prudent."

Gradually the riflemen drove the defenders from the embrasures; whenever a port was raised to fire one of the fort's artillery pieces, so many rifles would draw on it that the artillerymen would be driven from their piece. Clark now directed the building of an entrenchment in front of the main gate. When his artillery came up by boat, he would emplace it there. The American soldiers, with their French auxiliaries from Kaskaskia, were reinforced by a number of the townspeople who took up firing positions around the fort. At eight in the morning, Clark ordered the firing to cease. It was time for more psychological warfare. He sent an officer with a flag of truce and a "hard bill" to parley with Hamilton. It was "recommended" to Hamilton that he surrender the garrison. To this Hamilton replied, rather encouragingly, that he was "not disposed to be awed into any thing unbecoming British soldiers." The implication was that he might be awed into something that was "becoming"—that is to say, not humiliating. Clark ordered the attack to be resumed, and after two hours of heavy firing, a flag appeared from the fort with a suggestion from Hamilton that a three-day cease-fire be agreed upon, with an immediate conference between the two commanding officers. "After some deliberation" Clark sent word that he would agree "to no other terms than his surrendering himself and garrison prisoners at discretion. . . ." However, if Hamilton wished a conference, he would meet him at a church outside the fort.

At the church Hamilton offered to surrender, but the two men could not agree to terms. Clark treated the Englishman with a rough contempt and hostility "as a man of his known barbarity deserved." Hamilton had best depend on the "spirit and bravery" of his men in defending the fort. That was the only thing that might persuade Clark "to treat him and his garrison with lenity" when he stormed it. Hamilton was plainly disconcerted by Clark's boldness; it gave credence to his claim to command a large force. Hamilton, although a brave and resourceful man, was also deeply disturbed by Clark's threats and his obvious hostility toward him and his officers. He did not wish to have his officers and men, nor himself for that matter, butchered by these wild Americans, whose mere presence suggested that they were more than human—or considerably less. What more could he offer? Hamilton asked a litle plaintively. Speaking bluntly, Clark told the now thoroughly demoralized Hamilton that he would like nothing better than an excuse "to put all the Indians and partisans [Tories]to death, as the greatest part of those villains was then with him." Hamilton tried one concession after another, and Clark, doubtless relishing his role, refused them all.

Would nothing do but fighting? Hamilton asked. "I know of nothing else," Clark replied.

Hamilton then asked Clark to wait until he had had a chance to return to the fort to consult with his officers. Clark, glad to have an interlude to give his troops a chance to eat and get a brief rest, allowed Hamilton an hour. (The meal that Clark's men ate during the truce was their first regular meal in six days.) During that time some Kickapoo Indians brought word that a raiding party of British Indians was returning to the town with two prisoners they had captured. Clark dispatched a body of soldiers to meet them. At the town common, the Americans saw the warriors approaching in their full regalia of warfare, painted and befeathered. The Indians thought that the Americans, with their muskets and rifles loaded and primed, were part of a welcoming committee sent out by Hamilton to honor the success of their foray. So they came on leaping, whooping, hallooing, and striking each others' breasts; "each seemed to try to out do the other in the greatest signs of joy," Clark noted. It was only when Clark's men opened fire at point-blank range that the startled savages realized that something was amiss. Six were captured, two scalped, "and the rest so wounded . . . but one lived."

Clark now had a chance to demonstrate to the Indians in the fort that British protection was a slender reed to lean upon in the Northwest Territory. The captured Indians, including an eighteen-year-old son of the great chief Pontiac, were taken to a spot in full view of the fort to be tomahawked.

One of the Indian raiders turned out to be a white man daubed with war paint. When he was asked if the white man should be toma-hawked along with his Indian companions, Clark ordered that he should receive no mercy; he was a worse miscreant than the Indians. An old French militia officer from Cahokia named St. Croix was a member of Clark's force; he stationed himself beside the white man with his sword drawn to run him through if he tried to escape. As the soldier who was assigned to execute him approached, the white man cried out, "O, save me!" and St. Croix recognized the "white Indian" as his own son. Clark, observing the scene between the father and son and antici-pating that he would be importuned to spare him, tried to slip away, but the combined supplications of the father and the French officers per-suaded Clark to spare the son's life.

As the first Indian was tomahawked, the others, anticipating their fate, began to sing their death song. One of the last to be killed was a young chief of the Ottawas, Macutte Mong. When the tomahawk was buried in his skull, he took it out and handed it back to his executioner, who struck him twice more before killing him. The execution was a brutal measure, but it had the desired effect. The Indians in the fort "upbraided the English parties in not trying to save their friends, and gave them to understand that they believed them to be liars and no warriors."

Hamilton now faced a serious problem. He knew that his Indian allies were ill-suited by temperament to withstand a prolonged siege. He believed himself surrounded by a force much larger than his own. He had witnessed the execution of the Indian warriors and observed its effects on the Indians in the fort. He thus met again with Clark to discuss terms of surrender. The second meeting was on the parade ground outside the fort. Clark appeared, in Hamilton's account, "all bloody and sweating—seated himself on the side of one of the bateaux that had some rainwater in it, and while he washed his hands and face still reeking from the human sacrifice in which he had acted as chief priest, he told me with great exultation how he had been employed."

Clark declared that he knew the number and the temper of the defenders of the fort to a man. He disconcerted Hamilton by describing very accurately the defection of the French recruits and went so far as to declare that there were only thirty-five or thirty-six men in the fort that the British officer could depend on. An unconditional surrender would be the best course under the circumstances. Hamilton replied, "Then, Sir, I shall abide the consequences, for I never will take a step so disgraceful and unprecented while I have ammunition and provision."

"You will be answerable for the lives lost by your obstinacy." Clark declared.

Nonetheless, Hamilton was determined not to surrender unconditionally. There was further parleying, and Clark consented to read such terms as Hamilton considered acceptable. The American read and rejected the articles of surrender proposed by the British commander, and that evening he sent his own, which concluded with the threat, "If any of the stores be destroyed or any letters or papers burned, you may expect no mercy, for by Heavens you shall be treated as a murtherer."

When Hamilton read his soldiers the conditions of surrender demanded by Clark and his own reply, "the English to a man declared they would stand to the last for the honour of their country, and as they expressed it, would stick to me as the shirt on my back," Hamilton recalled.

"Then they cried 'God save King George!' and gave three huzzas."

This was a sentiment that Hamilton could hardly have expected his reluctant French recruits to share. Small wonder they "hung their heads, and their serjeants first turned round and muttered with their men. Some said it was hard they should fight against their own friends and relations who they could see had joined the Americans and fired against the fort."

Part of Hamilton's problem was that he had been openly contemptuous of the French inhabitants of the town. To him, Vincennes was a mixture "of vice levity Sloth & ignorance," and it is not surprising that he found the residents less than ardent in defense of the British cause. Finally, with a "fifth of our trusty Englishmen wounded," Hamilton gave way and surrendered the fort, placing the blame on the French "traitors." The Northwest was once more securely in American hands, or, one might say, securely in the hands of George Rogers Clark, after one of the classic military expeditions in the annals of warfare.

It was a bitter moment for Hamilton. Of course, he did not know immediately that he had been hoodwinked and bluffed. But he did know that he, the lieutenant governor of Canada, an English gentleman, had been forced to surrender to an uncouth frontiersman, a man little better than a savage. "The mortification, disappointment and indignation I felt," he wrote in his journal, "may possibly be conceived. . . . Our views of prosecuting any design against the enemy totally overturned— the being captives to an unprincipled motley banditti and being betrayed and sacrificed by those very people who owed the preservation of their lives and properties to us [the French inhabitants of Vincennes]."

The next day, acting on word that a number of boats carrying provisions were on their way down the Wabash from Detroit, Clark sent out a party that intercepted them and captured forty men and seven boats loaded with provisions and gifts for the Indians. It was a substantial haul.

Hamilton was sent under heavy guard to Virginia with the British regulars. Those French who had been enlisted for the expedition in Canada were sent back to Detroit with word that Clark would soon follow them for an attack on that important post. The terrible rigors of the march from Kaskaskia continued to take a toll of Clark's soldiers for months after they were ensconced, comparatively comfortably, at Vincennes. When the effort of will that had sustained them was no longer needed, Clark wrote, "they more sensibly felt the Pains and other complaints that they had contracted during the severity of the late uncommon march to which many of those Valuable men fell . . . a sacrifice and few others perfectly recovered. . . ."

10

The Southern Frontier

Aʟᴛʜᴏᴜɢʜ the major theater of operations on the frontier—the so-called Western Department—was in the area north of the Ohio and south and east of Lakes Erie and Ontario, the Southern frontier was the scene of intermittent warfare during the years from 1775 to 1783. What distinguished this region was the fact that the fighting was, in large part, a continuation of border conflicts that went back to the colonial wars.

As early as the mid-1760's, settlers and land speculators, taking advantage of the defeat of the Cherokees, had pushed westward along the Watauga and Kentucky rivers. In 1771 James Robertson came into the Watauga Valley with his family and a small band of settlers. A year later he was joined by John "Nolichucky Jack" Sevier. Strikingly handsome, tall and fair with bright blue eyes, Sevier was a member of a prosperous Huguenot family, a literate and intelligent man, charming and gracious in his manners. When enough settlers had filtered into the area so that the need was felt for some form of government, the inhabitants met and formed the Watauga Association and elected five commissioners to govern the settlements. In August, 1776, they had addressed the North Carolina assembly thusly: "Finding ourselves on the frontiers, and being apprehensive that for want of proper legislature we might become a shelter for such as endeavored to defraud their creditors; considering the necessity of recording deeds, wills, and doing other public business; we, by consent of the people, formed a court for the purposes above mentioned, taking, by desire of our constituents, the Virginia laws as our guide, so near as the situation of affairs would permit. This was intended for ourselves, and was done by consent of every individual. . . . We pray your mature and deliberate consideration on our behalf, and that you may annex us to your Province . . . in such manner as may enable us to share in the glorious cause of liberty; enforce our laws under authority and in every respect become the best members of society. . . ."

In 1775, near the Kentucky River, James Harrod established the first permanent settlement in what was to be Kentucky, and the same year Daniel Boone started the little community of Boonesborough not many miles away. Logan's Station and Boiling Spring were also founded in 1775, and Richard Henderson, a North Carolina land speculator, tried to organize the settlements into the state of Transylvania. Such pressure was bound to bring a reaction from the Indians of the region. As early as 1769 a Shawnee chief, Captain Will, had warned Daniel Boone, "Now, brothers . . . go home and stay there. Don't come here any more, for this is the Indians' hunting ground, and all the animals, skins and furs are ours; and if you are so foolish as to venture here again you may be sure the wasps and yellow-jackets will sting you severely."

At the outbreak of the Revolution the Cherokees, the most powerful tribe in the South, were still smarting from their crushing defeat during the French and Indian War. In that campaign, Amherst had sent twelve hundred regulars along with provincial auxiliaries to break Cherokee resistance and destroy fifteen of their settlements. Thus when the war began the Cherokees, urged on by the Shawnees, with whom they had close ties, seized the opportunity to attack the frontier settlements of Georgia and South Carolina. The British agents in this instance advised against such forays and advised wisely. After the Cherokees had raided the settlements on the Watauga and the Holston and been beaten off, a counteroffensive was mounted from Georgia, the Carolinas, and Virginia. In August, 1776, General Andrew Williamson at the head of eighteen hundred troops, guided by Catawba scouts, struck at the Indian villages and cornfields. In September he was joined by General Griffith Rutherford from North Carolina with twenty-five hundred militia. The combined force pushed on, driving the Indians toward Florida, wiping out the Middle Cherokee villages and driving them westward to the Overhills. A third column of two thousand

Virginia and North Carolina militia under Colonel William Christian came down the Holston River and advanced deep into the territory of the Overhill Cherokees. The Cherokees' hope for aid from the Creeks and the British proved groundless, and from May to July, 1777, the Cherokees signed treaties ceding all their lands east of the Blue Ridge and north of the Nolichucky River.

That campaign, the largest and most ambitious mounted against the Indians during the Revolution, marked the effective end of Cherokee participation on the side of the British. James Robertson was appointed Indian agent for North Carolina. He established himself at the leading Cherokee town of Echota, and much credit goes to him for keeping the Cherokees off the warpath. A small group of irreconcilables moved to the Chickamauga Creek area, where, aided by the Creeks, they conducted raids against the frontier throughout the war. When Robertson left Echota in 1779, the Cherokees there joined the Chickamaugas and the Creeks in extensive forays. But after frontier militia defeated a Tory force at Kings Mountain, South Carolina, on October 7, 1780, John Sevier and Andrew Pickens once more laid waste to the Indian settlements.

In the summer of 1779, Spain threw in its lot with France and America against Great Britain. Spain had, if it was possible, even less interest in American independence than France, but she could not resist the notion of scooping up some loot from the beleaguered British lion, who seemed plainly on the run. The hope of recapturing Gibraltar, in which France encouraged her, was perhaps the principal incentive. In America, Spain had a strong interest in the British posts on the lower Mississippi, and Spanish troops advanced from New Orleans to seize Baton Rouge, Natchez, Mobile, and Pensacola. Patrick Sinclair, the British governor of Fort Michilimackinac (now Mackinaw City, Michigan), was determined to try to retrieve the posts and push the Spanish back to New Orleans by means of an expedition down the Mississippi. Governor Sinclair's chief reliance was on a British trader named Emmanuel Hesse. Hesse persuaded Sinclair, who was anxious to win military laurels, that a large number of Indians could be recruited for an expedition that would depart from the confluence of the Mississippi and the Wisconsin, float down the Mississippi, and seize St. Louis, thereby controlling the rich fur trade up the Missouri and establishing a base for a further thrust to Natchez and, eventually, to New Orleans itself. Sinclair's strategic imagination far outran his resources. Hesse was dispatched on his ambitious project with three hundred regular troops and nine hundred Indians, the latter consisting of Menominis, Sauks, Foxes, Winnebagos, Ottawas, and Sioux.

The Spanish commander at St. Louis was Captain Don Fernando de Leyba. Hearing that Hesse was on the move, De Leyba strengthened the fortifications of St. Louis with a wooden tower holding five cannon. He had in his command twenty-nine Spanish regulars and two hundred and eighty-one residents of the town. Hesse's attack, with an overwhelmingly superior force, came on May 26, 1780, at one o'clock in the afternoon. It was met by a heavy fire from the fort, whose defenders were stimulated by "the lamentable cries of the women and children. . . ." By nightfall it was clear that the attackers had failed of their objective; and as so often happened in similar circumstances when the Indians were frustrated in their initial attack on a fortified position and disappointed in their hopes for booty, they vented their rage on the neighboring countryside, burning farms and killing or taking captive and often torturing the farmers and their families.

Hesse's attack on St. Louis was to have been accompanied by an attack from Detroit into the Kentucky country and an expedition against New Orleans from Florida. As Hesse was approaching St. Louis, Captain Henry Bird, a brilliant British partisan leader, was on his way down the Maumee and Miami rivers with six hundred Indians and Tory irregulars, picking up another six hundred as he went. Bird's most notable accomplishment was to carry with him six artillery pieces. When he struck at the forts at Ruddle's and Martin's Station, which defended the Kentucky region between the Kentucky and Licking rivers, those forts quickly surrendered in the face of cannon fire. Captain Ruddle surrendered with Bird's assurance that the settlers crowded into his stockaded fort would not become prisoners of the Indians. It turned out that Bird was unable to keep his promise; the Indians refused to be deprived of their human booty, but Bird extracted an agreement that all future prisoners should be in the charge of the white men in the expedition. After the capitulation of Martin's Station, the Indians, delighted with their loot, were anxious to press on against Lexington, but Bird, only too well aware that a reversal of the fortunes of war might scatter his army far and wide, prevailed on them to withdraw, taking three hundred and fifty prisoners and much plunder.

George Rogers Clark, who still hoped to be able to attack Detroit, was forced to drop such plans for the moment and try to intercept Bird. Indeed, most of the credit for the collapse of the British plan must go to Clark. Bird avoided him, and Hesse, after a short skirmish with Clark's forces at Cahokia, turned back. Part of the speed with which Bird withdrew after taking Ruddle's and Martin's Station was undoubtedly due to his uneasiness about rumors of Clark's activities. His caution was well founded. As soon as Clark had learned of Bird's general plan of campaign, he had started for Fort Jefferson, and from there with two other men, for Harrodsburg. There he recruited men to counter Bird's maneuvers. In a few weeks he had collected a thousand volunteers at the mouth of the Licking. The men came not only armed but with their own rations. As we have seen, Bird evaded him, and Clark, disappointed, decided to use his newly recruited force to attack the Shawnees in their home country.

Burdened with artillery, Clark's men made only seventy miles in four days. Indian scouts kept a constant check on their movements, and when they reached the first large Shawnee settlement at Old Chillicothe, they found it abandoned. It was clear to Clark that the Indians were drawing them deeper and deeper into their own territory, waiting simply for an appropriate moment to attack. Clark's men destroyed the buildings and crops at Chillicothe and pressed on to the Pickaway settlements, which were guarded by a fort. There the Indians attacked, and a fierce battle ensued. Gradually the superior tactical skill and discipline of the Americans began to tell. The Indians—Shawnees, Mingoes, Wyandots, and Delawares—were repeatedly outflanked and forced to fall back until they were finally penned in a small wood and in an adjacent fort. Now Clark's artillery could be used with effect, and by dark the Indians were completely routed. The Americans had lost fourteen killed and thirteen wounded (a very high ratio of killed to wounded, incidentally), and the Indians, by Clark's estimate, three times as many.

In thirty-one days Clark and his men had marched 480 miles and destroyed eight hundred acres of corn in addition to large quantities of vegetables. The heat and lack of provisions made it impossible to carry the campaign further. For the remainder of the year the Kentucky settlements were undisturbed, and Clark once more revived his scheme to capture Detroit, the source of all the infection. He found ready support (but again little money) from George Mason, Patrick Henry, and Jefferson. Even Washington concurred. The capture of Detroit "would," he wrote, "be the only certain means of giving peace and security to the whole western frontier. . . ."

This time Congress assumed responsibility for the undertaking. Clark was commissioned as brigadier general of the forces "to be embodied on an expedition westward of the Ohio." It was a dubious honor. Six weeks were spent collecting supplies for the campaign. An effort to draft troops in Virginia was a failure, and Governor Jefferson had to call for volunteers. With one thing and another it was August before Clark was able to start down the Ohio with a mixed force of four hundred regulars and volunteers instead of the two thousand that had been hoped for. When Clark arrived at Louisville, it was obvious that the long-projected attack on Detroit would have to be postponed once more. Fort Nelson at the falls had been completed, but Fort Jefferson on the Mississippi below the mouth of the Ohio had been abandoned, and there were only sixty men to defend Vincennes against a rumored British attack. Clark garrisoned and strengthened Fort Nelson and reoccupied Fort Jefferson. His mere presence caused anxiety to the British, who spent much of the winter trying to prevail on the Northwest tribes to stand fast. Rumor had it that twenty-seven of the tribes were prepared to treat with Clark, but the British spared no efforts and no money to enlist the Shawnees, Wyandots, and Delawares "to prevent the inroads of the Virginians." The Indians must be "delicately managed, to prevent their favouring those rebels," an English officer wrote.

The Indians were informed that the British planned a major offensive in the spring that would capture Fort Nelson and devastate the whole frontier. Meanwhile raids were renewed against the Kentucky and Virginia settlements.

Clark, using some of his own funds when Virginia could give him no help, built four armed galleys to guard the line of the Ohio. Scouts and spies patrolled the trails leading to the settlements, but Clark labored under almost insurmountable handicaps. Militia, ordered to Fort Nelson for the relief of soldiers who had served their stint in that remote outpost, refused to go. Thirty-eight men serving on one of the galleys that Clark had built with so much trouble and expense deserted in a body. The Kentucky settlements had been hit by a succession of Indian raids, and the settlers there were in no mood to support an expedition against Detroit. Clark was bitterly disappointed.

By December, 1781, with Benjamin Harrison having succeeded Jefferson as governor, it was clear that Virginia had no resources to support a campaign against Detroit. Harrison wrote to Nathanael Greene, "The Credit of the State is lost and we have not a Shilling in the Treasury. The powers formerly given to embody and march the Militia out of the State are no longer continued to us, nor can we impress what may be necessary for you, or even for ourselves, and the last Invasion has nearly drained us of our Stock of Provisions and Refreshments of all Kinds necessary for an Army. As this is not an exaggerated but a true State of our Situation I leave you to judge whether any great Dependance can for the present be placed on this State."

The soldiers stationed in the border forts deserted in substantial numbers. They had been living in the most uncomfortable quarters, inadequately clothed and poorly fed. One of Clark's captains trenchantly described the "wretched situation of the few troops remaining Westward Many of them have been in service for two years past and never received a Shoe, Stocking, or hat & none of them any pay. . . ."

When General William Irvine succeeded Colonel Brodhead as commander of the Western Department, he reported to Washington, "I never saw troops cut so truly a deplorable, and at the same time despicable, a figure. Indeed, when I arrived no man would believe from their appearance that they were soldiers; nay, it would be difficult to determine whether they were *white men.*" It was small wonder under such circumstances that discipline was virtually nonexistent. Irvine observed, "Though nothing like general mutiny has taken place, yet several individuals have behaved in the most daring and atrocious manner, two of whom are now under sentence and shall be executed tomorrow, which I hope will check these proceedings." In the opinion of one observer, some of the Western leaders deliberately encouraged rebelliousness among the soldiers. Such was the state of the Western Department in the period immediately following Cornwallis's surrender at Yorktown.

The Sandusky Expedition

IN the early spring of 1782 an episode took place which disgraced American arms and brought savage retribution from the Indians.

David Zeisberger and John Heckewelder, two Moravian missionaries to the Delaware Indians, had Christianized a substantial number of that tribe and had prevailed on them to adopt a settled agricultural life in western Pennsylvania. Several years before the outbreak of the Revolution, the two missionaries had, in response to pleas by the Delawares, migrated to a site on the upper Tuscarawas River some one hundred miles from Fort Pitt. There they founded three prosperous little settlements: Schönbrunn, Gnadenhütten, and Salem. At the beginning of the Revolution, the missionaries and their Indian followers declared themselves neutral. In consequence they were suspected of treachery by both the British and the Americans. Because the Moravian Indians' kinship with the Delawares, who were among the tribes most loyal to the British, they were under constant pressure to favor the British side, and some of their bolder young braves joined war parties of British Indians. Finally, a party of fifty British and Indians forced them in the fall of 1781 to move from their villages to the upper Sandusky River. When they satisfied the British authorities in Detroit that they were innocent of charges of having aided the Americans, a hundred of them were allowed to return to their settlements on the Tuscarawas to harvest the corn standing in the fields.

In the meantime, a series of particularly vicious Indian atrocities on the Pennsylvania frontier aroused bitter resentment among the white settlers there. When a rumor circulated that hostile Indians had occupied the deserted villages of the Moravian Indians, a force of three hundred militia was dispatched to attack them. Conscious of their own innocence and doubtless anxious to protect their towns from being destroyed, the Christian Indians who had returned home stood their ground and took no measures for defense. The militia arrived first at Gnadenhütten. A mile from the town they met a young Indian, Schebosh, whom they killed and scalped. Two other peaceful and unarmed Indians met a similar fate. The rest were rounded up with assurances that "no harm should befall them" and were taken to the center of town, where they were all bound, "the men being put into one house, the women into another."

By now the Indians realized that they were to become sacrifices to the Americans' thirst for vengeance. The men began to pray and sing hymns "and spoke words of encouragement and consolation to one another until they were all slain." It was the turn of the women next. Christina, a Mohegan woman who knew German and English, begged for her life and those of her sisters, but to no avail.

There was an added bitter irony. On the arrival of the militia at Gnadenhütten, one of the missionaries went on to Salem to inform the Indians there. Not knowing of the fate of their fellows, they too resolved not to flee, which would have suggested that they were guilty. The next day, a party of militia arrived in Salem, disarmed the Indians, and led them back to Gnadenhütten. There they bound them and took their knives. In Zeisberger's words, "They made our Indians bring all their hidden goods out of the bush, and then took them away; they had to tell them where in the bush the bees were, help get the honey out; other [things] they also had to do for them before they were killed . . . They prayed and sang until the tomahawks struck into their heads. . . . They burned the dead bodies, together with the houses. . . ."

The militia knew very well that the Indians were "good Indians," that is to say, Indians who had not taken hostile action against the American settlements and who were not allied with the enemy. They knew, moreover, that they were Christians, and it is hard to believe that some of them were not moved by their victims' martyrlike courage in the face of certain death. What unappeasable hatreds lay in their hearts we cannot fathom. Like the soldiers of My Lai, the militia at Gnadenhütten destroyed unarmed men, women, and children and did so out of some strange reflex of fear and resentment toward people they felt were not quite human. The massacre aroused a storm of protest. The leading figures in the frontier settlements were virtually unanimous in denouncing it as an act of unparalleled barbarity. Punishment of the perpetrators was demanded. The Pennsylvania assembly investigated the episode and condemned it. And there the matter rested.

A month or so later, on May 25, an expedition under Colonel William Crawford set out from Fort Pitt for the Wyandot and Shawnee towns on the upper Sandusky, charged with destroying them "with fire and sword if practicable . . . by which we hope to give ease and safety to the inhabitants of this country. . . ," as the Pennsylvania General William Irvine wrote Washington. Among the four hundred and sixty-five Pennsylvania and Virginia frontiersmen who had signed on with Crawford were some of the men who had participated in the massacre at Gnadenhütten.

The group also included a distinguished-looking young man with a thick foreign accent who called himself John Rose. Rose was one of the foreigners who had appeared at Valley Forge to solicit the support of Washington. He would say nothing of his background or even of his native land, although the more knowledgeable identified his accent as Russian. After a brief tour of duty as a surgeon's mate, Rose was taken under the wing of Irvine, who made him a member of his staff. After experiencing many vicissitudes, including capture by the British and exchange, Rose volunteered to accompany Colonel Crawford on his ill-fated expedition into the Indian country and was given command of a company of militia.

Rose, it turned out, was really a Russian nobleman, Baron Rosenthal, who had killed a man in a duel and been forced to flee his country. Having, as he put it, danced "merrily . . . through the various scenes of this Tragic comedie," he now found himself on the most perilous venture of all. Rose was not impressed by the motley band who appeared in response to Crawford's call. He referred to them as "this undaunted party of Clodhoppers seated on their Meal Baggs and Balancing themselves in rope Stirrups" and guiding their nags "by a hair halter with but one rein. . . ." Crawford's orders to his band reinforced Rose's picture of an undisciplined gang. The colonel constantly upbraided his men for their "criminal conduct" in indiscriminately firing their guns despite the most explicit instructions to the contrary and in their failure to properly carry out their guard duties.

Rose, whose own compary was made up of twenty men (the others were not much larger), gave a shrewd analysis of his commanding officer, Crawford. He was over sixty years of age, "inured to fatigue from his childhood, and by repeated campaigns against the Indians acquainted with their manner of engaging. In his private Life, kind and exceedingly affectionate; in his military character personally Brave, and patient of hardships—As a partisan, too cautious, & frightened at appearances; always calculating the chances against. Consequently, By no means, calculated for . . . hazardous enterprises—As a Commanding Officer, cool in danger, but not systematical. Like others in the same stations, he wanted to be all in all: by trusting everything to the performance of his own abilities only, everything was but half done, and Everybody was disgusted. . . . He is somewhat capricious . . . Jealous of his military Knowledge, & Superiority, but a mere quack in the profession of a Soldier. No military Genius; & no man of Letters—." Williamson, a much younger man and second-in-command, was, in Rose's view, "brave as Caesar and active . . . Fond of thrusting himself into danger, he leaves everything else to chance—He has some obscure notions of military matters, suggested to him by mere Genius; but is quite ignorant of how to dispose of men, or how to fight them to advantage." He knew himself to be a great man in his small circle, but he was willing to listen to advice. "His Oratory," Rose added, "is suited to the taste of the people his countrymen, and their Bigotted notions stand him in lieu of arguments. It is a pity but he had no military opportunities of instruction, as his natural talents are not dispicable. . . ."

Rose wrote other striking portraits of his companions-in-arms. "Upon these Volunteer Expeditions," he noted, "every Man allmost appears on Horseback; but he takes care to mount the very worst horse he has upon his farm. This horse he loads with at least as much provisions as he is well able to carry. No man calculates the distance he is going, or how long he can possible be absent [in terms of his food]. As he has provisions enough to maintain at least three Men on the Campaign, he does not stint himself to a certain allowance. Lolling all day unemployed upon his horse, his only amusement is chewing, particularly as all noise in talking, singing & whistling is prohibited.—"

The horses, poor beasts at best, "inadequate to the load of Bread bacon & Whiskey imposed on them," had, in addition, to carry "a heavy

rider up & down hill, . . . & break a path through Weeds and thickets."
The horses, Rose observed, "render the party a heavy, unwieldy Body.
This will at first view seem a paradoxical thesis. But if we consider the
reduced state they are in, the heavy Loads they stagger under, the hills
& swamps they have to go over—nobody can deny, but what they are an
obstruction to the expedition of every military operation. Add to this
that every Man hangs upon his horse to the very moment of attack.
Then instead of being disencumbered & ready to defend himself, his first
care is his horse. Him, he must tye and look after during an engagement, because all his dependence is in his horse & his horses burthen."

The horses were then a constant problem. There was not only the
reluctance of their riders to dismount from them to fight; every
encampment was complicated by the need to find grass for them. If
there was no grass nearby they must be turned loose to graze, and then
precious time must be spent in the morning rounding them up again.
"If the horses are not done justice by," Rose added, "they are knocked
up, & your march is retarded."

In addition there was little notion of order on the march. "Regularity . . . and precaution, considering [we were] as a body, penetrating into
an ennemy's country, did seem to be looked upon as matters of mere
Moonshine," Rose noted. It was almost impossible to get the militia to
man their sentry posts, to stay awake, or, in turn, to relieve those already
on duty. When men deserted their posts to sit by the fire, there was no
way to properly discipline them, and Crawford had to be content with a
harangue. Whenever the leading companies got to a narrow pass on the
trail, they crowded into it without regard to any proper military order or
security against surprise attack.

Indeed it seemed as though every possible ineptitude or misconduct was displayed by this disorderly and undisciplined gang—it could
hardly be called a military force—and it was only saved from a greater
debacle by the exertions of a Russian nobleman who displayed all those
military and frontier characteristics, notably bravery, hardihood, caution, and a keen tactical sense, that were so conspiciously missing among
the men who slogged along behind him on their overburdened nags.

The little force made its way through thickets and open woods,
across huckleberry bushes and swamps, always alert for any sign of
Indians. Rose, reconnoitering forward of the main body, discovered the
remains of an Indian village burned the year before; "the ruins of the
lowest house in town are mixed with the calcined bones of the burnt
bodies of the Indians," he noted. Approaching the settlements of the

Moravian Indians on the trail to the Sandusky, scouts observed the tracks of some sixty Indians and saw in the distance three mounted warriors shadowing the American force. At various spots the Indians had set fire to the woods to detain the soldiers. The ground became increasingly rugged, with deep ravines and muddy creeks across their line of march. Losing a number of their horses to exhaustion and accidents along the trail, the party pushed on, making as much as twenty miles a day despite the terrain.

By the first of June Crawford's band was clearly in trouble. The Indians had discovered their movements, and it was logical to assume that they were gathering their scattered forces. Supplies were running low, and there was murmuring among the men, who were disheartened by the difficulties of the march and the sense that Indians were all around them, though few could be seen. Crawford held a council of war the same day. If they reached the Sandusky, how would they find their way back through a territory filled with hostile Indians? How would they carry out the sick or wounded, and where would they get fresh food when they had exhausted their dwindling supply? But the decision was to press on; to turn back would almost be as dangerous as to continue. Nearing the Indian town on the Sandusky that was their objective, the Americans found numerous tracks, and Rose, riding ahead to reconnoiter with a party of forty mounted horsemen, almost immediately found himself beset by a large party of savages trying to cut off his line of retreat. He immediately sent two of his men on the swiftest horses to warn Crawford of the proximity of the enemy. Meanwhile he collected his men and began to return the fire of the Indians, trying at the same time to prevent them from blocking his line of retreat. The main force under Crawford arrived as Rose was deploying his men. The two groups joined and, fighting from the cover of a small woods, kept the Indians at bay until sunset. A hasty inventory the next morning showed that two men had been killed instantly. Three more had died during the night, their groans and cries doing little to improve the morale of their companions. Nineteen more had been wounded, and of these, three had wounds that were plainly mortal. One of the Americans had been scalped, and two Indian scalps had been taken.

The next day, the fifth of June, the Indians circled the beleaguered little force, apparently trying to draw their fire and keep them pinned down until further reinforcements might arrive. At evening a body of some hundred and fifty Shawnees appeared, advancing openly in three columns and carrying a red flag. Delawares were also identified among the Indians who encircled Crawford's force. The Indians began to erect primitive defenses across the American line of retreat. Crawford and most of his officers decided to try to fight their way out under the cover of darkness. The horses were quietly saddled and the men prepared to march in two columns. But one unit, unwilling to fall in with the general plan, took another route, and so the detachment was badly split at the beginning. In the darkness confusion was compounded, one group trying to fight its way back along the trail it had advanced over two days before, the other taking a path that brought it near the Indian town. The goal was the spring where the men had camped before encountering the Indians. Crawford disappeared in the confusion, and another officer assumed command of the men. "We proceeded," Rose wrote, "with as much speed as possible through the plains, wanting to gain the Woods, fearfull of the ennemy's horses. Our front was stragling, as every Body expected a general overthrow if the ennemy did overtake us in the plains and thought the Woods could afford us a chance, against their numbers."

In spite of the effort of the Indians to intercept them, most of the party reached the temporary haven of the woods. But it was slow, hot work. After twenty hours without food or rest, the horses were worn out and their riders little better. Many of the men deserted by two and threes, believing they had a better chance to get away on their own. Resting briefly and then pushing on in their desperate flight, they heard the bloodcurdling "Scalp Halloo" from time to time, which told them that the Indians had caught a straggler or deserter and taken his scalp. Gradually, as the party got farther from the Shawnee towns, it picked up some of those who had made their way singly or in groups. "June 9th," Major Rose wrote, "A party of about 20 men joined us this morning . . . besides single Men, who came up with us constantly; and we observed in different places signs of encampments of our people of about 40 or 50 along the road—." Finally there were some three hundred and eighty of the original four hundred and sixty-five. For so many of the party to have found their way back was a remarkable testimony to their skill as woodsmen and, equally, to the inability of the Indians to maintain a sustained pursuit. A day's march from Mingo Bottom, the weary men were met by a relief party; they were carried over the Ohio in canoes and then dismissed to their homes in the nearby frontier settlements. The final tally, Rose estimated, was between forty and fifty officers and men killed and missing and twenty-eight wounded. The escape of the Americans was undoubtedly facilitated by the capture of Crawford and the doctor of the expedition, along with a number of other Americans. Many of the Indians withdrew to one of their towns to entertain themselves with their prisoners.

First Crawford and Dr. Knight were stripped of their clothes and daubed black; then they were made to run the gauntlet between two long lines of men, women, and children who beat them with clubs, sticks, and fists. The next day they were again blackened. Their hands were tied behind them, and Colonel Crawford was led to a stake surrounded by red hot coals; he was forced to walk in the hot coals while his torturers fired powder at his body at close range and prodded his body with burning sticks. This continued for two hours; when Crawford pled with Simon Girty, the American turncoat, who stood watching the spectacle, to shoot him, Girty replied, "Don't you see I have no gun?"

Finally Crawford was scalped, and with the blood pouring from the wound in his head, he fell down on the live coals while the Indian women heaped shovelfuls of coals on his body. Knight was forced to watch his friend's death, and when Crawford was scalped, the Indians "slapped the scalp over the Doctor's face, saying, 'This is your great captain's scalp; tomorrow we will serve you so.'"

Knight was to be tortured to death in another village. A single Indian was put in charge of him, and on the way to the other spot the savage, wishing a fire, untied Knight and ordered him to collect wood. With a good-sized chunk, Knight struck the Indian on the head, knocked him down, and seized his gun. When the Indian ran, Knight escaped through the woods and traveled for twenty days before he got back to Fort Pitt with his gruesome tale. The only prisoners who had been tortured were those captured by the Delawares, "who," a member of the expedition wrote a friend, "say they will shew no mercy to any white man, as they would shew none to their friends and relations, the religious Moravians."

It was Rose's opinion that Crawford never intended to attack the Shawnee towns, believing his force inadequate, but planned to make a feint in that direction and then turn back in a wide circle to distract the Indians and thereby afford relief for the frontier settlements. This notion was given support by Crawford's random progress and his lack of aggressiveness in hurrying on his party's laggard soldiers. When the frontiersmen were finally engaged by the Indians, their casualties were relatively light, and Rose was convinced they could have pressed on successfully to the Indian villages. "Five Men were only killed," he wrote sarcastically," ". . .—a vast obstruction to every military operation!" The intention of the enemy, Rose observed, was "to frighten us home and take the advantage of our confusion on the retreat. The first he did—but the latter he did not effectually do. . . ." The Indians, in Rose's view, were inferior in numbers and had simply bluffed the little frontier army out of completing its mission. "Whilst the ennemy was thus manoeuvering us out of our Wits," he wrote, "we lay motionless and in despair; wishing for the approach of the second night to run off—stuffing our Sadle Baggs with bread & bacon. . . . A singular Way, indeed, to invade an ennemy's country." To Rose it was plain that the frontiersmen had in fact "Run off Skeared at the discharge of half a dozen of Guns—& did not dare to make as much as a feint to know the Strength and situation of the place, and whether the ennemy would have dared to oppose us—."

Rose's detailed criticism of the whole expedition and especially of the weak and confused councils that followed the first attack by the Indians make fascinating and entirely convincing reading. It is a classic if minor military critique that shows very clearly that no amount of frontier hardihood could counterbalance poor leadership, lack of discipline, and failure to observe the most basic principles of sound tactics. The wonder is not that a handful of Indians routed a larger number of fabled frontier fighters, but that the American force was not entirely destroyed.

The End of the Border War

T HE defeat of Crawford brought in its wake an outburst of Indian raids along the upper Ohio. The volatile savages, cast down by defeat, were correspondingly excited by victory. Hannastown, some thirty miles beyond Pittsburgh, was surprised and burned, and twenty settlers who could not reach the fort were murdered or carried off as prisoners. All along the frontier the cry was raised for retribution for Crawford's defeat and torture and for the raids against Hannastown and other isolated settlements. If General Irvine would lead them, the settlers declared, they would raise and equip six or seven hundred men for an expedition against the Sandusky villages. Once more the machinery was set in motion to raise a force of a thousand men, stiffened by a hundred regulars, to clear out the Sandusky region and then join forces with Clark in an attack against the Shawnees.

Joseph Brant had been planning an attack against Wheeling, West Virginia, and the frontier settlements to the south. He had been joined by Simon Girty and a Captain William Caldwell, a bold and enterprising Tory officer. Brant's combined force consisted of over eleven hundred Indians, perhaps the largest Indian force assembled during the Revolution. While they were on the march word came of Clark's expedition against the Shawnee villages, and Brant was asked to turn back to help defend them. Most of the warriors wished to return, but their leaders were determined not to abandon the campaign without a foray into Kentucky country. Three hundred Wyandots and some Tory rangers thus crossed the Ohio on August 15, 1782, and surrounded Bryan's Station, five miles north of Lexington. Bryan's Station was a compound two hundred yards long and forty yards wide, containing forty cabins occupied by ninety men, women, and children. Each corner had a blockhouse two stories high; the palisades that surrounded the fort were twelve feet high. The residents of the fort soon got word that a large party of Indians was waiting to attack. The only water for the fort came from a spring at the foot of the hill below the fort, close to the point where the Indians lay in hiding. The fort's defenders decided to send the women down the hill with buckets to fetch water for cooking and washing, as though they had no suspicion that there were hostile savages about. It was an extraordinary drama. Laughing and talking, the little band of women and young girls trooped down to the spring and filled their pails. The Wyandots, taking the expedition as clear evidence that no one in the fort suspected their presence, let the women carry out their task unmolested.

Soon after the women returned, the Indians sent a small party to try to decoy the settlers out of the fort. The defenders pretended to take the bait. A small group rushed out in pursuit of the Indians, but they were careful to stay close enough to the fort to be able to quickly return to it. Girty and his warriors, confident that their ruse had worked, rushed out of the woods in an attack on the other side of the fort, only to be met by a heavy fire that drove them back in disorder. Girty then began intermittent fire on the fort and called for its surrender, promising to protect its occupants from the Indians. Young Aaron Reynolds shouted back to Girty that he was a known scoundrel and dog who was despised by every honest man. If he and his mongrel followers got inside the fort, they would be driven out with switches rather than guns. And if he remained another day, Reynolds added, a relief party would nail his dirty hide to a tree. The Indians howled with fury at Reynold's taunts. Bullets spattered against the palisades, and frequent efforts were made to set fire to it. But next day, convinced that the siege was hopeless, Girty withdrew after destroying the crops in the fields, killing the cattle, sheep, and hogs, and carrying off the horses.

Girty fell back slowly to Blue Licks on the Licking River, inviting pursuit. Soon after Girty's retreat from Bryan's Station, volunteers had arrived from Lexington, Harrodsburg, and Boonesborough, with a hundred and thirty-five militia from Lincoln County and a contingent from Fayette County, led by Daniel Boone. It was decided to pursue Girty's party at once, and a picked group of a hundred and eighty mounted riflemen started off after the Indians. At lower Blue Licks, they saw a few Indians moving along a rocky ridge less than a mile away. Some of the riflemen, Boone among them, suspected a trap and urged the party to wait until it was properly reinforced. Others were anxious to attack at once; Major Hugh McGary, a hotheaded Kentuckian, settled the debate by putting spurs to his horse and calling out, "Delay is dastardly! Let all who are not cowards follow me, and I will show them the Indians." The party, following McGary's lead, crossed a small stream and formed a line of attack with Boone in command of the left, McGary of the center. They rode to within sixty yards of the Wyandots and Tories who lay waiting for them, dismounted, and opened fire. Boone drove the Indians back on the left, but the American right gave way under the threat of being outflanked, and McGary found himself attacked on the right and from the rear. His men retreated against Boone's right, and the whole American line broke and ran for the ford. "He that could remount a horse was well off," one of the officers wrote, "and he that could not saw no time for delay." At the river they were partially intercepted by a detachment of Indians, and many were toma- hawked as they tried to swim across the stream. One of the officers saved a number of lives by rallying the men who had gotten across to cover those of their fellows who were struggling to get over. Once across, what was left of the original force continued to retreat until they met rein- forcements. At that point the Indians withdrew, and the action was broken off.

The battle of Blue Licks was the worst defeat suffered by the Kentuckians at the hands of the British Indians. Seventy were killed— more than a third of the force engaged—and twenty more captured or badly wounded. When the reinforcements reached the ford at Blue Licks, they found a number of Americans tied to trees and "butchered with knives and spears." Andrew Steele, one of the members of the relief party, wrote to Governor Benjamin Harrison of Virginia: "Through the continued series of seven years vicessitudes, nothing has happened so alarming, fatal and injurious to the interest of the Kane- tuckians. . . . To express the feelings of the inhabitants of both the counties at this rueful scene of hitherto unparalleled barbarities barre all words and cuts description short. . . . Forty seven of our brave Kane- tuckians were found in the field, the matchless massacred victims of their [the Indians'] unprecedented cruelty. . . . The ballance stand upon an equilibrium and one stroke more will cause it to preponderate to our irretrievable wo. . . ."

Steele wrote to Harrison again a few weeks later, describing the condition of the frontier. "The frequent Incursions & Hostile Depredations of a Savage Enemy upon our Exterior Posts, our Despersed Legions, our veteran army defeated, our Widows Tears & orphans cries grate strongly on the Ear. . . . I beg leave to inform you that annualy since the seventeen Hund'd & seventy eight an army of not less than three Hund'd Saveges Infested our Territories & since seventy six, Eight hundred & sixty Effective men fell, the matchless massacred victims of unprecendented Cruelty [Steele plainly liked the phrase]." If Harrison would show some concern for the frontier settlers, "the Indigent Offspring of an oppulent father," they would celebrate him as "the Illustrious Patron & Protector of our Lives, Laws & Religious Liberties," and the "annals of History will rank your name among the Bravest Patriots & Wisest Politicians & Gratitude like Torrent will flow from the Heart of every Kanetuckian. . . ."

For a time it seemed as if the whole Kentucky frontier would have to be abandoned. Clark, criticized for not protecting the Kentucky region, replied that the tragedy at Blue Licks was due to the "Extreamly Reprihensible" behavior of the officers in command, who acted recklessly in attacking before reinforcements had arrived.

The effect of Blue Licks, like the effect of similar setbacks, stirred the frontier to still another effort. By a herculean effort twelve hundred militia and regulars were collected to march under Irvine against the Indian stronghold on the Sandusky. "I am now preparing for an excursion into the Indian country," Irvine wrote to Harrison. "My troops are chiefly to be volunteer militia, who propose not only to equip & feed themselves, but also such Continental troops as I can take with me. If we succeed in burning the Shawnee, Delaware & Wyandot towns, it will put an end to the Indian war in this quarter."

Clark, with a similar force drawn from Kentucky, was to attack the Shawnee villages centered at Chillicothe, and nearly a thousand men were to be dispatched against the Indian towns in the Genesee area that Sullivan had destroyed three years before.

Early in November, 1782, weeks before Irvine's troops were ready to march, a force of a thousand and fifty mounted men under Clark's leadership set out from the mouth of the Licking to strike into Shawnee territory. Clark, characteristically, maintained strict discipline during the six days' march, but the Indians were on the alert and escaped with only ten killed and ten captured. Chillicothe and five other towns were put to the torch and ten thousand bushels of corn destroyed. Unable to bring on a general engagement with the Indians, Clark returned reluctantly to the mouth of the Licking, confident that he had at least thrown the Indians off balance and made the frontier settlements safe from raids for some months to come. The winter supplies of the Indians were wiped out, but more important, the effect of the victory at Blue Licks was negated, and the savages once more were reminded of the American capacity for retaliation. In the words of Daniel Boone, "The spirits of the Indians were damped, their connections dissolved, their armies scattered & a future invasion entirely out of their power."

A British officer wrote to Abraham De Peyster, a Loyalist officer, to the same effect: "I am endeavoring to assemble the Indians, but I find I shall not be able to collect a number sufficient to oppose them, the chiefs are now met here upon that business who desire me to inform you of their Situation requesting you will communicate it by the inclosed strings to their Brethren the Lake Indians, without speedy assistance they must be drove off from their country, the Enemy being too powerful for them."

Before Irvine could mount his more cumbersome attack on the Sandusky towns, word came from Washington that the British had assured him that all hostilities were suspended in anticipation of a treaty of peace and that the Indians had been ordered to carry out no further raids. But in the Northwest, where fear gave wings to rumor, the declared intention of Clark to attack the other enemy Indians as he had done the Shawnees kept the British-allied tribes in continual ferment. The efforts of the British to restrain their raids made them restless and uneasy, as did the sharp decline in the presents usually provided for them by the British authorities at Detroit and Niagara. Clark urged a general offensive into the Indian stronghold at the head of the Wabash and the strengthening of Fort Nelson and Vincennes to convince the Indians "that they were inferior to us, that the British assertions of our weakness was false, and that we could at all times penetrate into their Country at Pleasure. . . ." By the middle of April, 1783, word reached the frontier of the signing of preliminary peace articles at Paris. By the terms of the definitive treaty, the Old Northwest was ceded to the United States. Governor Benjamin Harrison wrote to Clark in July informing him that his services would no longer be needed. "Before I take leave of you," he added, "I feel called on in the most forciable

Manner to return to you my Thanks and those of my Council for the very great and singular services you have rendered your Country, in wresting so great and valuable a Territory out of the Hands of the British Enemy, repelling the attacks of their Savage Allies and carrying on successful war in the Heart of their Country. . . ."

It is certainly possible that the Northwest would have been conceded to the United States by the Treaty of Paris even if Clark had not dominated the region. But the possibility that it would not have been given up so readily is strengthened by the fact that the reluctance of the British to abandon their Western posts after peace was concluded was a constant source of friction between the two countries and one of the contributing factors to the War of 1812. What is incontrovertible is that Clark's achievement was the most brilliant single military accomplishment of the Revolution. The fact that it took place in the wings, so to speak, rather than on center stage does not dim the accomplishment itself. His campaigns against Kaskaskia and Vincennes will always remain among the epic military achievements, a remarkable story of the triumph of fortitude and will over apparently insurmountable obstacles. Even if, as one devoutly wishes, war comes to exist only in the memory of the race, the tale of Clark's victories will remain as a monument to and metaphor of the triumph of will and imagination over the intractable material of existence.

George Rogers Clark was the archetype of the Western hero. In him was foreshadowed every western novel or movie, every tale of hardihood, endurance, and courage in a perpetual and relentless battle with a cruel geography and a savage enemy. Behind the forest romance, only partially concealed, was the violence and cruelty of the westward movement. Clark, bullying, cajoling, and killing, his name a legend and a terror to the Indians, was a symbol of the superior powers of the white man, of his determination to subdue the Indian and dispel his frightfulness so that the white man might inhabit the Indian's land. Clark's own life outdid the most lurid romances that fiction could devise—a series of brilliant episodes, hairbreadth escapes, victories against overwhelming odds, endurance in the face of incredible hardships. He attempted after the war to found a colony in Louisiana but was rebuffed by the Spanish; he then formed an expedition to occupy disputed lands between the Yazoo River and Natchez, and when Washington blocked that venture, he accepted a commission in the French army to attack Spanish territory west of the Mississippi. The Federal government demanded that he resign his commission, and Clark found a temporary refuge in St. Louis, then in French hands. While his younger brother, William, journeyed with Meriwether Lewis on one of the great odysseys in history, George Rogers Clark was running a grist mill and acting as a land commissioner in the Illinois country. A stroke paralyzed his right leg, which then had to be amputated, and Clark, almost incapacitated, moved to his sister's home in Louisville, where he died in 1818. His final consolation was the bottle; the conqueror of the vast Northwest Territory became an eccentric recluse, a defeated visionary whose dreams and genius were too extravagant for a mundane, peacetime world.

The war in the West, or the border war as it is sometimes called, often seems a kind of footnote or addendum to the Revolution, and for good reason. It was, in a real sense, another war, a war between Indians and Americans, with the Indians aided, abetted, and egged on by the British. It had begun well before the Revolution in the numerous "Indian wars" of the colonial era, and it continued well after the end of the fighting in the east (that is, essentially, after Yorktown) and, indeed, after the Treaty of Paris in 1783, which marked the formal end of the Revolution. In many ways the most disastrous legacy of the Revolution could be found in the permanently embittered relations between the Western settlers and the Indians who confronted them. That confrontation was a difficult and dangerous one at best. The British, as we have seen, at first sporadically and then systematically promoted Indian raids on the frontier from upper New York State to Georgia. Most of these raids had only tenuous military objectives; increasingly they were punitive, a means of punishing those Americans who were most remote from any military support or reinforcement, for their presumption in revolting against the mother country. It was primarily an Indian war; without Indian allies the activity of the British in the West would have been confined to a few minor expeditions by British regulars and Tories, the latter mostly from the Mohawk Valley of New York. With the involvement of the Indians, the frontier was devastated by a ruthless and barbarous total war. Indeed the frontier settlers suffered, in the course of the raids and counterraids of the border war, more casualties than Washington's Continental Army suffered in all its major engagements. The settler who had laboriously cleared a small patch of land in the wilderness, erected a simple cabin and some crude sheds, fenced a vegetable plot, and collected, at considerable effort and expense, a horse and a few domestic animals, and who then saw the buildings put to the torch and the animals slaughtered, nursed an understandable hatred of the British and their Indian auxiliaries. If, in addition, he saw the livid crimson skull of a friend or relative who had been scalped by Indians, the lust of vengeance burned in him as long as he lived. Not only had the Indians turned on the Americans when, in a sense, they were down and fighting for their lives; they were, in practical fact, British mercenaries, to be distinguished from the Hessians only by their savage waging of total war. The British paid the Indians, with an endless stream of gifts and presents, to murder Americans. Or at least that was the American view of the matter.

Of all the policies pursued by the British in the Revolutionary era, their employment of Indians to kill Americans is the least excusable. As we have pointed out in the case of the devastation of the lands of the Iroquois Confederacy by General Sullivan, the British policy was as cruel and exploitive to the Indians as it was bloody and ruthless to the Americans. When the British departed, they left behind them a legacy of bitterness that could never be alleviated. From the Revolution on, those Americans who lived in the frontier settlements, which moved constantly westward, viewed the Indian as *the* enemy, cruel, deceitful, merciless; and they judged it a simple rule of self-preservation to match him in cunning and savagery, terror for terror, life for life, scalp for scalp, settler and savage caught in a terrible ritual of violence. At first there were distinctions made between "good" Indians and "bad" Indians, between "hostile" and "friendly" Indians. But the distinctions were crude ones and frequently not observed, and one corollary of these distinctions was that the traditional animosities between certain tribes were exacerbated, so that tribes warred with each other with a ferocity that had been rare in earlier days. They had learned the warfare of extermination from the white man.

The irony of the British policy, as Clark himself pointed out, was that most frontiersmen felt little identification with the Revolutionary "cause." They had moved to the frontier because they wished to be "free and independent" of governments, whether British or American. The prosperous lawyer of Boston or the wealthy patriot merchant or landlord of New York were to the frontier settlers as uncongenial figures as Lord North and his haughty emissaries. From the first the frontiersmen showed strong "separatist" tendencies; they wished, as in Vermont and Kentucky, Watauga, or the infant state of Franklin, to form separate states, and they were willing, in most instances, to ally themselves with any power that would grant them the independence they wished for. A group of Western settlers, for example, called for a meeting at Wheeling early in 1782, to make plans for acquiring lands on the Muskingum

River and establishing a new state to come eventually under British authority. Had the British thus restrained the Indians and cultivated the separatist tendencies so evident on the frontier, they would in all probability have created far more trouble for the "United States" than they could ever have caused by promoting border raids. As it was, their strategy seemed designed to drive the frontier settlers into the not especially hospitable arms of Congress or of the particular states. To the harassed delegates in Congress, the bloody events that kept the frontier in an uproar seemed almost as remote as if they had happened on the moon. In general, Congress had little knowledge of the frontier or little sympathy with it. When they thought of the settlers at all, they thought of them as congeries of lower-class individuals, resistant to authority, not much better in their habits and manners than the savages themselves— men and women who, by their inability to get along with their Indian neighbors and their constant pressure on Indian hunting grounds, created endless problems for Congress, which already had problems enough.

Howard Swiggett, a close student of the warfare of the Northern Indians and their Tory allies, wrote thusly of the British use of the Indians: "The irony of it all is that the Indians as fighters were worthless and the British high command were early sick of them. Time and again . . . their fighting qualities proved lower than the most worthless militia. . . . The problem of feeding them was terrific. They poured into the northwestern posts from Oswego to beyond Detroit, cold and hungry, and the £17,000 spent on them by Sir William Johnson in thirteen months was to be quintupled in a few months, and all for naught. They brought disgrace on the British arms and confusion to the management of the war." Swiggett certainly overstates the case. While the British employment of the Indians was one of the most serious of many strategic mistakes they made, the Indians, under the proper conditions, were formidable fighters. The point is that they could not be controlled or disciplined, and they fought erratically when used with regular troops. If the Revolution could have been won by a war of attrition (as the British clearly thought it could be), then the use of the Indians was an astute, if immoral, policy (immoral, as we have said, as much because of the reckless exploitation of the Indian as because of the terrible devastation and suffering that the Indians caused in the frontier settlements). "The employing of the Indians," the Marquis de Chastellux wrote in 1783, " . . . it is now pretty generally admitted, produced consequences directly opposite to the interest of Great-Britain; uniting the inhabitants of all the countries liable to their incursions as one man against them and their allies, and producing such bloody scenes of inveterate animosity and vengeance as make human nature shudder."

While exploitation of the Indian and hostility between Indians and settlers were as old as the beginnings of the colonies, there had always been men like Roger Williams, William Penn, and John Eliot—leading settlers who labored sincerely to protect the rights of the Indians and to preserve peace with them. And while there were numerous Indian wars, massacres, and countermassacres, the Indians, in large part, had managed to preserve their tribal integrity. Where they were forced out of heavily settled areas, they gave a good account of themselves in battle, fought a determined rearguard action, and withdrew to areas where they were safe, at least for the moment, from the intrusion of the whites. Some, like the Stockbridge Indians, became "civilized" and settled down in peaceful proximity to the whites. Thus in 1775 it was possible to believe that there might be a "solution" to the Indian problem; that colonists and Indians, despite the cultural gulf that separated them, might learn to live together in this vast country. But the Revolution changed all that. The wounds made in that unrelenting contest never healed. From the time of the Revolution to the end of the nineteenth century there was, for the inhabitant of the frontier, only one good Indian, and that was a dead Indian.

We are only too well aware that we live today with the consequences of this tragic legacy from the Revolution. And yet it must be remembered that the claims now submitted by blacks and Indians to us, as heirs of the Revolution, are submitted in the name of those principles for which the Revolution was fought. And it is the consciousness of this, more than anything else, that lays upon us the obligation of honoring them.

13

The War on the High Seas

Since the Americans were an ocean-oriented people, clustered pre-dominately in towns and villages along the seacoast, they were far more conscious of and concerned about the naval engagements of the Revolution than about the remote border warfare. Moreover, the hopes of many Americans for making a profit off the war centered on the activities of privateers.

The naval warfare of the Revolution is one of those topics that, like the border warfare of the West, is not readily woven into a general narrative. It involved, however, tens of thousands of American sailors, from captains to able-bodied seamen; thousands of sailing vessels of every kind; and millions of pounds sterling in ships' cargoes. There were innumerable engagements, many of them stirring battles. As in the better-known land battles, thousands were killed and wounded, and thousands more died of disease or drowned when their ships went down. Storms were as fatal and conclusive as the bitterest battles. And the naval warfare produced one famous, if slightly tainted, hero—John Paul Jones.

The reader will recall that the nucleus of an American navy appeared first in 1775, when Washington commissioned vessels to carry out raids on British shipping as a kind of adjunct to his military operations. That October, the Rhode Island delegates to Congress proposed that an American navy be established. At the same time Congress got word that two unconvoyed British vessels had sailed for Quebec loaded with military supplies. A committee of three was appointed to propose steps for intercepting the ships. Many members of Congress were alarmed at the suggestion. It was one thing to fight to defend the country from British intrusions; it was quite another thing to seize ships of His Majesty's merchant marine on the high seas. That smacked of piracy and would strike the mother country at its most sensitive point—its domination of the ocean—and thus make reconciliation more difficult than ever.

The proposal from the general assembly of Rhode Island stated that since the ministry, "lost to every sentiment of justice, liberty and humanity, continue to send troops and ships of war into America, which destroy our trade, plunder and burn our towns, and murder the good people of these colonies," every proper measure should be taken for defense. "And amongst other measures . . . this Assembly is persuaded that the building and equipping an American fleet, as soon as possible, would greatly and essentially conduce to the preservation of the lives, liberty and property of the good people of this colonies. . . ."

The Rhode Island proposal brought on a hot debate in Congress. John Adams, who at once became the leading advocate of a navy, recalled that, traveling the circuit of the Massachusetts courts in the seacoast towns of his native colony, he had gotten a very favorable opinion of "the activity, enterprise, patience, perseverance and daring intrepidity of our seamen. I had formed," he wrote, "a confident opinion that, if they were once let loose upon the ocean, they would contribute greatly to the relief of our wants, as well as to the distress of the enemy."

Those delegates who opposed the notion considered it "the most wild, visionary, mad project that ever had been imagined. It was an infant, taking a mad bull by his horns, and what was more profound it . . . would ruin the character, and corrupt the morals of all our seamen. It would make them selfish, piratical, mercenary, bent wholly on plunder. . . ." A week later the committee of three brought in the recommendation that "a swift sailing vessel, to carry ten guns and a proportional number of swivels, with eighty men, be fitted with all possible dispatch for a cruise of three months, and that the commander be instructed to cruise eastward, for intercepting such transports as may be laden with warlike stores and other supplies for our enemies. . . ."

Pleased by their boldness, the delegates resolved to outfit three more such vessels with the same mission, the largest to carry between twenty and thirty-six guns. A committee made up of seven members of Congress was thereupon appointed to carry into execution "with all possible expedition" the resolutions of Congress in regard to establishing a "navy." A little more than a month later, the committee brought in a draft of rules for the government of an American navy, and Congress officially created a naval arm to complement its military arm. Adams later recalled his services on the naval committee as the pleasantest of his four-year-long labors in Congress. "Mr. Lee, Mr. Gadsden [members of the committee] were sensible men, and very cheerful, but Governor Hopkins of Rhode Island, about seventy years of age, kept us all alive. Upon business, his experience and judgment were very useful. But when the business of the evening was over, he kept us in conversation till eleven, and sometimes twelve o'clock. His custom was to drink nothing all day, nor till eight o'clock in the evening, and then his beverage was Jamaica spirit and water. It gave him wit, humor, anecdotes, science and learning. He had read Greek, Roman and British history and was familar with English poetry, particularly Pope, Thomson and Milton, and the flow of his soul made all his reading our own and seemed to bring recollection in all of us of all we had ever read. . . . Hopkins never drank to excess, but all he drank was immediately not only converted into wit, sense, knowledge and good humor, but inspired us with similar qualities."

On the British side, the number of naval vessels of all classes at the outset of the Revolution was 270, including 131 ships of the line—ships carrying sixty or more guns on two or more decks (the American navy still had no ships of the line at the time of Yorktown). By the end of the war, the British navy consisted of 468 warships, with 164 ships of the line. The number of British sailors increased in the same period from 18,000 to 110,000. By the third year of the war, when the French alliance was concluded, the British had ninety-two warships on station in the coastal waters of North America, thirteen at Newfoundland, and forty-one in the West Indies.

Against this vast superiority in numbers of naval vessels must be placed the fact that Britain by 1778 was involved in a global war, that it had to supply a large army in America and patrol several thousand miles of coastline in addition to keeping a substantial force in the Indies. As we have already noted, the British navy was riddled with corruption. The Earl of Sandwich was a wretched administrator, and many of the admirals were superannuated. England, moreover, was deprived of the colonies as a source of sailors and was forced to impress many of her own seamen to secure crews for her ships.

On the matter of impressment and the harshness with which the law bore on the poor, one story will perhaps suffice for purposes of illustration. In 1777 a British seaman had been pressed—seized and carried off to serve in the British navy—leaving his wife, who was eighteen years old, and two infants, With the husband removed from the scene, his household goods were taken for an old debt, and his wife and children were turned out of their lodgings for nonpayment of rent. After begging for a living for months, the woman stole a piece of coarse linen from a draper's shop. She was caught and brought to trial. In her defense she stated that "she had lived in credit and wanted for nothing till a press-gang came and stole her husband from her, but since then she had no bed to lie on, nothing to give her children to eat, and they were almost naked. She might have done some wrong, for she hardly knew what she did." The lawyers stated that since shoplifting was a capital offense she must be hanged, and she was carried off to Tyburn with an infant nursing at her breast and there hanged.

So great was the need for sailors in the British navy after the beginning of hostilities in America that over eight hundred men were pressed in London alone in one month, and several lives were lost in the fierce struggles that took place between press gangs and their victims.

Under Sandwich's administration, "embezzlement, larceny, swindling" were the order of the day. "Vessels reported as well found and ready for sea lay in the naval harbours rotting." Between 1775 and 1782, seventy-six naval vessels, among them fourteen of sixty-four guns or more, "capsized, foundered or were wrecked." Of 175,990 men raised by the navy between 1774 and 1780, 42,000 men deserted and 18,541 died of disease, while only 1,243 were killed in action. Charles Middleton, comptroller of the navy, wrote to Sandwich in 1779, "The desertions from ships and hospitals are beyond imagination. The discipline of the service is entirely lost, and a great measure owing to admiralty indulgences, but still more to admiralty negligence. . . . For want of plan, for want of men of professional knowledge used to business . . . for want of method and execution, one error has produced another, and the whole has become such a mass of confusion, that I see no prospect of reducing it to order." The Admiralty office, Middleton wrote, "is . . . so wretchedly bad, that if I waited for official orders and kept within the mere line of duty without pressing or proposing what ought to come unasked for, we must inevitably stand still. . . . The whole system of the admiralty is rotten. . . . The dockyards . . . are in a wretched disabled state, without spirit, without discipline." To this and subsequent complaints from Middleton, Sandwich replied, "I have neither leisure nor inclination to enter into a discussion upon the subject. . . ."

Sandwich's cavalier attitude toward his responsibilities was lamented by David Hume, who complained to a friend that the first lord of the Admiralty found his amusement "in trouting during three weeks near sixty miles from the scene of business, and during the most critical season of the year." "There needs," Hume added, "but this single fact to decide the fate of the nation."

In naval warfare there had been little development in tactical doctrine for several generations. The manuals of fighting instructions for the British fleet "were hide-bound and forbade anything like originality." Commanders dared not deviate from them because if they did and suffered defeat they might expect court-martial. One British admiral—Richard Kempenfelt—wrote to the comptroller of the navy in 1780, "I believe you will with me think it is something surprising that we who have been so long a famous maritime Power should not yet have established any regular rules for the orderly and expeditious performance of the several evolutions necessary to be made in a fleet. The French have long set us an example. They have formed a system of tactics which are studied in their academies and practiced in their squadrons. . . ."

Engagements at sea almost invariably followed an established pattern. The American ship, whether a privateer or a ship of the Continental Navy or a particular state's navy, would approach another vessel warily, not flying its colors, trying to determine if possible its nationality and, more important, its size and whether it was a merchant vessel, a British naval vessel, or a privateer. This was usually the most crucial phase of the encounter. If the ship, on closer inspection, proved to be an unarmed enemy transport or a merchant vessel, the American ship would close on it, run up its colors, and order it to strike. Once the prize had surrendered, a crew would usually be sent aboard to sail the ship into its captor's home port.

If the sighted vessel proved to be armed, the fateful question was whether it carried a heavier armament than its American pursuer. Usually, the size and armament of a ship became apparent while there was still time—if it was a more heavily gunned naval vessel—to break off and avoid an engagement. But then the pursuer might become the pursued, with uncertain results. Once two ships had come within range of each other, the opening phase of the engagement might consist of the pursuer firing her bow guns, usually swivels and several cannon, and receiving return fire from stern guns. Such fire was directed at the rigging, with the hope of cutting stays and sails and thus reducing maneuverability, and at the decks to drive off sailors and marines who might be manning swivels or firing muskets as the range shortened. The pursuing vessel wished, of course, to come up on the weather gauge (to the windward) of the ship it was pursuing. In this way it could steal the wind from its victim and bear down upon it with the advantage of much greater maneuverability. The enemy vessel might, on the other hand, depending on the force and the direction of the wind and its sailing capability, come about and flee off on another tack (though to do so it must pass its pursuer and usually take a broadside in passing), or turn down and run before the wind. Indeed there were a dozen variations in which the ingenuity of the respective captains and the skill of their crew might be severely tested.

If the vessels were of approximately the same armament (it was often easy to make a mistake), their captains generally considered that honor required them to risk an engagement. In that case, instead of flight and pursuit, the ships maneuvered to gain the advantage of wind and position so that their broadsides could fire most effectively. Here the emphasis switched to four tasks: sweeping the decks clear of fighting men by canister and grape; riddling the sails and cutting the stays and shrouds with chain and shrapnel; shattering masts; and, finally and most fatefully, piercing the hull with heavy cannonballs "betwixt wind and water." Since ships running on a parallel tack into the wind, would, depending on the velocity of the wind, be heeled over to a greater or lesser degree, the cannon must be lowered or elevated to compensate for the angle at which the ship was sailing; the guns of the vessel to the leeward would thus be inclined to fire high (above the decks and into the rigging) and those of the windward vessel to fire low (into the water or at the water line). Coming about would, of course, reverse the situation, and if the leeward ship had received shot at or below the water line, a new tack would bring that lower portion of its hull under water, with dangerous consequences.

Sometimes, if evenly engaged, with a light wind, the opposing ships might come into the wind where they could trust the outcome to the skill of their gunners and the weight of iron that they could hurl against each other, and so exchange broadsides until one ship or the other was incapable of making way or was so badly hulled that it was in danger of sinking and was thus forced by a combination of casualties among its officers and crew and damage to its hull and rigging to strike its colors. It was at this latter stage of the battle that skill and tenacity counted most. Marines, or, in their absence, sailors detailed to that duty, were placed along the gunwales and even in the rigging with the mission of firing on the enemy vessel for the purpose of clearing the decks of sailors and thus diminishing the maneuverability of the ship. The larger the ship, the more extensive and complex its sails. In battle the coordination between sails and guns was, of course, crucial. The way in which the sails were handled had the most direct bearing on whether the guns were elevated or depressed, and it was essential for a ship to be as steady as possible when a broadside was fired if the fire was to be effective. Only long practice and the seasoning of battle could bring a crew to that peak of efficiency where commands were carried out instinctively and where precise timing made the whole intricate machine function like a living thing, articulate in every beam and spar, every sail and line, gun and musket.

A ship's rigging was made of hemp, which was inclined to stretch under heavy strain, and in bad weather it was apt to provide inadequate support for the masts, which rose from about 175 to 190 feet above the water line with a staggering weight of canvas and yardarms. The chainplates supporting the shrouds and lines not infrequently gave way, further imperiling the masts. In the words of a naval historian, "While the masts and spars were so at the mercy of the gale, they suffered equally in action. It would seem that one had but to fire a gun and a mast went by the board. The cutting of a few shrouds or stays might result in leaving the ship a helpless hulk." The cables holding ships to anchor were likewise of hemp, ten to twenty inches in diameter. When wet and when any length of cable was out, they were enormously heavy and cumbersome, and it would often take an hour or more to bring in an anchor. Thus ships invariably cut their cables when caught at anchor by an enemy vessel. Most fighting ships were crowded, poorly ventilated pestholes.

One of the many hazards facing the American warship of whatever category was that it might, and often did, pursue what appeared to be a tempting prize only to find it was one of a squadron of enemy vessels, the other members of which might be below the horizon. Sometimes American ships hung on the edges of British convoys, picking off ships that dropped behind or were scattered in a storm. On other occasions, they sailed boldly into a convoy, sought out the armed vessels protecting it, and engaged them, knowing that by putting them out of action they would have the whole fleet at their mercy.

In November, 1775, the naval committee of the Continental Congress purchased four vessels to be converted into warships. They were named the *Alfred,* "in honor of the founder of the greatest navy that ever existed [the British navy, of course]," as John Adams put it, the *Columbus,* the *Cabot,* and the *Andrea Doria,* after the great Genoese admiral.

A month later, the naval committee came forward with an even more ambitious program calling for the construction of thirteen ships, five of thirty-two guns, five of twenty-eight, and three of twenty-four. One was to be built in New Hampshire, two in Massachusetts, one in Connecticut, two in Rhode Island, two in New York, four in Pennsylvania, and one in Maryland. The cost was to be not more than $66,666⅔ per vessel on the average (how that rather bizarre figure was arrived at, the records do not disclose). The names of the ships are suggestive: The *Raleigh,* the *Hancock,* the *Boston,* the *Warren,* the *Providence* (which was built at Providence), the *Trumbull,* the *Montgomery,* the *Congress,* the *Randolph,* the *Washington,* the *Effingham,* the *Delaware,* and the *Virginia.* The guns that the frigates carried were, with only a few exceptions, twelve-pounders. Smaller vessels carried four- and six-pounders. They were all "long guns," heavy pieces from three or four to six or seven thousand pounds in weight. These were generally supplemented by small mortars and cohorns or swivels—light guns mounted on pivots and used, with the mortars, against crews and gunners, while the heavier caliber cannon were employed against the planks and rigging of the enemy ship. The most conspicuous feature of such vessels was perhaps the figurehead. We have a description of that of the *Hancock,* which depicted a man (Hancock) with "yellow Breeches, white Stockings, Blue Coat with Yellow Button Holes, small cocked Hat with a Yellow Lace. . . ." A rattlesnake was carved around the stern of the *Hancock,* and the hull of the ship was painted black and yellow. It was a hundred and forty feet long and thirty-five feet wide at its widest point; it drew fourteen feet of water and had a burden of seven hundred and sixty-four tons. The *Boston* had as its figurehead "an Indian Head with a Bow and Arrow in the Hand, painted White, Red and Yellow."

The British merchantman the *Nancy* was captured in May, 1776, with a rich load of muskets and military supplies, and this coup was followed by the seizure of the British supply ship *Hope,* with a large number of entrenching tools and fifteen hundred barrels of powder. The *Hope* was taken by the *Franklin,* one of the vessels in Washington's little navy, Captain James Mugford in command. The British, furious at Mugford's success, which took place almost under the eyes of the British fleet in Boston Harbor, put out thirteen boats carrying more than two hundred men to board the *Franklin* at night and seize the master and his crew of twenty-one. The little company of sailors, armed with muskets and spears, drove off the attackers after a furious struggle in which Mugford was killed, just as he cut off the hands of a British sailor trying to board his ship.

After the British evacuation of Boston, British supply vessels and transports continued to arrive at the harbor after crossing the Atlantic, unaware that it was no longer occupied by the British fleet. It was here that Washington's fleet, in conjunction with a number of privateers, reaped a substantial harvest. Three transports carrying some four hundred Scottish Highlanders were brought into Boston; two more were captured by a Rhode Island privateer and two by the newly commissioned brig, *Andrea Doria.* Washington's fleet continued to cruise in the waters off Massachusetts Bay throughout 1776, and Captain Tucker in the *Hancock* took thirty or forty prizes, but British frigates captured a number of prizes in their own right, including the *Warren,* and retook some of those that had been captured by patriot captains. In the winter of 1777 the fleet was decommissioned and a number of its officers transferred to the Continental Navy.

It was not enough, of course, to commission vessels. Officers had to be found to command them (and, preferably, to supervise their construction) and crews engaged to man them. Old Ezek Hopkins, brother to Stephen Hopkins, long-time governor of Rhode Island and delegate to Congress, was appointed commander of the infant fleet, and John Paul Jones was made senior lieutenant.

John Paul Jones had been born plain John Paul in Scotland in 1747. The son of a gardener, he was apprenticed to a shipowner in White-haven. He visited his older brother William, who was a tailor in Frederick, Maryland, on his first voyage, and when he was relieved of his apprenticeship by the bankruptcy of his master, he joined the crew of a slave ship. After several voyages, he became first mate at the age of nineteen. On the way back to England, where the young man planned to seek a more congenial maritime berth, the captain and the first mate both died of fever; John Paul took command of the ship and brought it safely into port for which service the grateful owners gave him and the crew 10 percent of the value of the cargo and signed Paul on as captain of one of their ships. During one voyage on the *John,* John Paul had the ship's carpenter so severely whipped for neglect of duty that the man died a few weeks later, and Paul was charged with murder and imprisoned. Cleared and given another ship, the *Betsy* of London, he carried cargoes to the West Indies. In 1773, at Tobago, where he had earlier had the carpenter whipped, he was faced with a mutiny by his crew. He killed the ringleader and restored order. Afraid to face a civil court in the Indies, he escaped to America and added Jones to his name. In Philadelphia his friendship with Robert Morris and Joseph Hewes, both delegates to Congress, and his obvious knowledge of maritime matters helped to get him a commission in the newly formed navy.

John Paul Jones was a thin, wiry, active man, five feet five inches tall, with brown hair and bright hazel eyes. He had a sharp, inquisitive nose, rather foxlike; a cleft, emphatic chin; and high cheekbones. He was a spiritual brother to George Rogers Clark, to Anthony Wayne, and, minus of course the impulse to treason, to Benedict Arnold—one of those fiercely ambitious natural geniuses of war, determined on glory and renown and possessed of imagination and energy to force the hand of Providence. By the middle of October, 1776, he had taken sixteen vessels, sent in eight, and "sunk, burned or destroyed the rest. . . ." His advice to Robert Morris (and it was hardly disinterested advice) was to encourage the growth of the navy by a policy of giving all the prizes that were captured to the men and officers who manned the ships, since "the common class of mankind are actuated by no nobler principle than that of self-interest. This, and this only, determines all adventurers in privateers, the owners as well as those they employ." The "infallible expedient" was to "inlist the seaman during pleasure and give them all the prizes. . . . The situation of America is new in the annals of mankind; her affairs cry haste, and speed must answer them," he added.

It was properly ironic that John Paul Jones's first ship should have borne the name of that lady from whom he intended to wrest fame and fortune, Providence. When John Adams met Jones in Paris, he noted admiringly the discipline and neat appearance of Jones's marines, adding, "This is the most ambitious and intriguing officer in the American Navy. Jones has Art, and Secrecy, and aspires very high. You see the Character of the Man in his uniform, and that of his officers and Marines—variant from the Uniforms established by Congress. . . ."

1248 / A NEW AGE NOW BEGINS

Eccentricities and Irregularies are to be expected from him—they are in his Character, they are visible in his Eyes. His voice is soft and still and small, his eye has keeness and Wildness and softness in it."

The other captains serving under Ezek Hopkins were Dudley Saltonstall [brother-in-law of Silas Deane],Abraham Whipple, and Nicholas Biddle. The pay of the commander in chief was set at a hundred and fifty dollars a month. From this modest beginning the roster of officers in the Continental Navy grew to number some three hundred and fifty names during the course of the war. For several years the affairs of the navy were managed, or more often mismanaged, by a succession of committees, and indeed several committees operated simultaneously. In October, 1776, John Paul Jones wrote to Robert Morris that only a board of admiralty, established on a permanent basis, could bring any order into the affairs of the navy. William Ellery, serving on the committee, expressed similar sentiments. "The Congress," he wrote a friend in February, 1777, "are fully sensible of the Importance of having a respectable Navy and have endeavoured to form and equip One, but through Ignorance and Neglect they have not been able to accomplish their Purpose yet. I hope however to see One afloat before long. A proper Board of Admiralty is very much wanted. The Members of Congress are unacquainted with this Department. As One of the Marine Committee I sensibly feel my Ignorance in this Respect." However, as with so many other departments of the government, Congress could not bring itself to relinquish any of those powers that, by and large, it exercised so badly, and it was not until October, 1779, that a board of admiralty was finally established by Congress. It turned out to be almost impossible to find qualified members to serve on the board however, and when Congress in 1781, near the end of the Revolution, finally set up the office of secretary of marine, no one could be found to fill the office, and it passed by default into the hands of Robert Morris, the newly appointed superintendent of finances.

An interesting if distinctly minor episode in the creation of a Continental Navy involves the effort of an ingenious Yankee inventor, David Bushnell of Connecticut, to build, with the backing of Congress, an effective submarine.

Bushnell devised a "water machine" to be used against the British ships anchored in Boston Harbor. Samuel Osgood wrote to John Adams in October, 1775: "The famous Water Machine from Connecticut is every Day expected in Camp; it must unavoidably be a clumsy Business, as its Weight is about a Tun." The submarine was "composed of several pieces of large oak timber, scouped out and fitted together, and its shape . . . compares to that of a round clam. It was bound around thoroughly with iron bands, the seams were corked, and the whole was smeared over with tar, so as to prevent the possibility of the admission of water to the inside." It was large enough for one man to sit or stand in it. Six small pieces of thick glass allowed light to enter, and six hundred pounds of lead were fastened to its bottom to give it stability and keep it under water. Two hundred pounds could be dropped in segments to allow it to rise, but the principal reliance in raising or lowering the device was by "two forcing pumps which drove water out of the bottom as well as a valve, operated by a foot-pedal which allowed water to enter, thus carrying the vessel downward." A rudder with a tiller that passed through a water joint guided the machine. Bushnell even had a device that registered how many fathoms down the submarine was. The machine was propelled by two oars or paddles like the arms of a windmill, which revolved by the action of a crank turned by the opera-tor. Cruising on the surface the submarine took in air through three small orifices.

The torpedo was made in a manner similar to that of the submarine itself. It contained a hundred and thirty pounds of gunpowder, a clock, and a gunlock with a good flint. The torpedo was attached to the rear of the submarine by a screw that also prevented the time fuze in the torpedo from being activiated. When the screw was removed, the tor-pedo was released, and the timing mechanism began to operate. The means of attaching the torpedo to the bottom of a British warship was a large screw that entered the submarine through a water joint. The screw had a crank, and when the submarine was brought to rest against the bottom of a ship, the crank would be turned until the screw had taken hold on the hull. It was then disengaged from the submarine itself; the torpedo was likewise set free, held to the screw in the ship's hull by a line. A time fuze was set so that in thirty minutes or so it would explode and blow a gaping hole in the ship's bottom. "I wish it might succeed," Osgood wrote, of the initial experiment "[and] the Ships be blown up beyond the Attraction of the Earth, for it is the only Way or Chance they have of reaching St. Peter's Gate." It was not until almost a year later, however, that Bushnell was ready to try his machine. He brought his little wooden submarine under the hull of a British man-of-war in New York Harbor, but the copper sheathing prevented him from fixing the screw to the hull, and the torpedo drifted away and exploded harmlessly. As a contemporary account put it, "at each essay the machine rebounded from the ship's bottom, not having sufficient power to resist the impulse thus given to it." Two later attempts in the Hudson River also failed, but the next year at Black Point Bay, near New London, Bushnell, defeated in his efforts to fasten his torpedoes to the hulls of the British ships, attached one by a line and sailed off. The line was discovered by two sailors who hauled in the torpedo, which blew up, destroying the schooner and killing three members of the crew.

When Howe was attempting to clear the American defenses from the Delaware early in the winter of 1777, Bushnell once more tried his torpedoes. This time he equipped them with fuzes that were designed to go off on contact with a ship, and he counted on the current in the Delaware River to carry them against the British vessels. In Bushnell's words, "I fixed several kegs under water, charged with powder to explode upon touching anything, as they floated along with the tide. I set them afloat in the Delaware, above the English shipping. . . . We went as near the shipping as we durst venture . . . but as I afterwards found, they were set adrift much too far distant. . . ." The ice on the river impeded their movement, and daylight disclosed them to the British, who fired at the torpedoes until they were all exploded. The episode marked the end of submarine warfare in the American Revolution.

One of the most successful naval operation of the war was the raid on New Providence in the Bahamas to seize a large supply of munitions. A little fleet, commanded by Commodore Hopkins aboard the *Alfred,* sailed from the Delaware in February, 1776. Included were the *Columbus,* the *Andrea Doria,* which had a crew of a hundred and thirty with thirty marines, the *Cabot,* the *Providence,* the *Hornet,* the *Fly,* the *Wasp,* two brigs, two sloops, and two schooners; armament ranged from eight guns on the *Wasp* to twenty-four on the *Alfred.* Compared with a European fleet of the day it was insignificant, yet it was, in effect, the entire American navy, and the forerunner of what, in time, would become a great naval establishment.

Hopkins' instructions were to cruise along the southern coast of the United States, "in such places as you think will most Annoy the Enemy," but he was determined to undertake the raid on New Providence. On the third of March his squadron reached that island, which had originally been settled by New England Puritans and whose present inhabitants were by no means unfavorable to the American cause. Hopkins put ashore two hundred marines and fifty sailors who landed unopposed and announced to the governor of the island that they intended to "take possession of all the warlike stores" but had no designs on the persons or property of any of the inhabitants. The marines seized a fort outside of town with seventeen cannon—thirty-two-pounders, eighteens, and twelves—and then took possession of Fort Nassau, the principal fortification on the island, having secured the keys from the compliant governor. At Fort Nassau Hopkins' men found a rich cache of supplies, including seventy-one cannon, ranging from six-pounders to thirty-twos, fifteen brass mortars, and twenty-four large casks of powder. It took two weeks to load the booty aboard American warships, and a large sloop was commandeered to carry the surplus. On the return voyage to Rhode Island eight or nine small British ships were captured, and one British brigantine, the *Glasgow,* escaped after a hot engagement because, as Hopkins wrote, "I had upwards of 30 of our best Seamen on board the Prizes, and some that were on board had got too much Liquor out of the Prizes to be fit for Duty."

Initially the voyage was hailed as a great victory for Hopkins and his little fleet, and Congress instructed John Hancock to send Hopkins its congratulations. But as more of the details of the engagement with the *Glasgow* became known, a negative reaction set in. Hopkins, who had put into Providence, Rhode Island, with his booty, found himself shorthanded. Washington, appealed to by Hopkins, sent him a hundred and seventy soldiers to fill up his roster, but a week later he was ordered to return them. Providence was a principal recruiting point for privateers, and it was almost impossible to enlist sailors for the navy there. Proposals had been made by the marine committee for an attack on the fleet that Lord Dunmore had assembled in Virginia, or, alternately, for an attack on the Newfoundland fisheries, but nothing could be done without sailors to man the ships. Hopkins became the scapegoat. A congressional committee was appointed to investigate that officer's performance of his duties. The committee found him at fault in sailing to New Providence without orders and in failing, with a superior force, to capture the *Glasgow.* It so reported to Congress, and Congress censured him. It was certainly not a very promising beginning. John Adams, who had worked hard to prevent Hopkins from being cashiered, "which had been the object intended by the spirit that dictated the prosecution . . . had the satisfaction to think that I had not labored wholly in vain in his defense." The raid against New Providence was, it turned out, both the first and last naval campaign of the infant American fleet. Hereafter individual vessels were dispatched on a variety of missions, from convoying supply ships to cruising for prizes. Of these latter operations, the most notable are those of John Paul Jones, who, in the *Providence,* displayed his remarkable talents as a naval tactician and leader. On his first cruise in the fall of 1776, he ruined the fisheries at Canso and Madame in Nova Scotia and captured sixteen prizes. At Canso, Jones burned "an Oil warehouse with the Contents and all the Materials for the Fishery" and captured three transports carrying coal to New York, then rode out a severe storm and got safely home with as many prisoners as crew.

On a subsequent expedition with the *Alfred* and the *Providence,* Jones captured a large transport carrying uniforms for the British army. The men and officers of the *Providence,* discontented with the condition of the ship and resentful of the cold and stormy weather, turned back. "Being thus deserted," Jones wrote, "the Epedemical discontent became General on Board the *Alfred;* the season was indeed Severe and everyone was for immediately returning to port, but I was determined at all hazards, while my provision lasted, to persevere in my first plan."

Another of the captains who distinguished himself in cruising for prizes was John Barry. Barry was an Irishman who had prospered as a Philadelphia shipowner. In the spring of 1776, he engaged a British sloop, the *Edward,* off the Virginia coast. Although he outgunned the *Edward,* the British ship was manned by experienced sailors and marines, and the battle was a fierce one. Barry's ship was battered, and two men were killed and two wounded. The British ship, its rigging riddled and its hull pierced in numerous places between wind and water, finally struck its colors, thus making Barry the first American naval captain to capture a British warship in battle. When the *Effingham,* whose thirty-two guns made it one of the largest American frigates, was commissioned, Barry was appointed captain, but he and his ship were bottled up in the Delaware by Lord Howe's fleet.

Getting the few ships of the Continental Navy to sea proved to be a major problem. They remained month after month in port, delayed first by the difficulty in recruiting crews and then by the apparent determination of Congress to protect them from the dangers of warfare. The officers of the incipient navy were as touchy and rank-conscious as their army counterparts, and Congress was constantly vexed by squabbles over seniority. Washington wrote to John Jay from Middle Brook, "I beg leave to ask what are the reasons for keeping the continental frigates in port? If it is because hands cannot be obtained to man them on the present encouragement, some other plan ought to be adopted to make them useful. Had not Congress better lend them to commanders of known bravery and capacity for a limited term, at the expiration of which the vessels, if not taken or lost, to revert to the States—they and their crews, in the mean time, enjoying the exclusive benefit of all captures they make, but acting either singly or conjointly under the direction of Congress. . . ."

John Jay replied that the problems of the navy resulted from the fact that its affairs were under the direction of a committee that was a highly inefficient one ("It fluctuates, new members constantly coming in, and old ones going out") but that could not be changed because it was supported by "the family compact," the Arthur Lee faction in Congress. "There is as much intrigue in this State-house," Jay wrote, "as in the Vatican, but as little secrecy as in a boarding-school."

One of the problems that beset the ships of the Continental Navy was the counterpart of a problem that plagued the Continental Army: cleanliness, or, more accurately, the absence of it, and the alarming rate of sickness that was quite evidently the consequence of endemic filthiness and improper sanitary measures. The marine committee, doubtless prompted by John Adams, urged Captain Biddle, who was refitting the *Randolph* at Charles Town, to "see the ship thoroughly and perfectly cleansed, aloft and below from Stem to Stern," to "burn Powder [as a disinfectant] and wash with vinigar betwixt Decks, order Hammocks, all bedding and bed Cloaths and Body Cloaths daily into the quarters or to be aired on Deck. . . ." The crew must keep their persons clean and get regular exercise and wholesome fresh food whenever possible: "Fish when you can get it and fresh food in Port. . . . In short, cleanliness, exercise, fresh air and wholesome food will restore or preserve health more than medicine. . . ." The advice was excellent, but discipline on shipboard was too often lax and such advice was seldom followed, with the result that sickness was a major problem on those few American ships that did manage to get to sea. Moreover, the knowledge that sickness was prevalent on naval vessels made it that much more difficult to recruit crews; a sailor who signed onto an American warship was far more apt to die of disease than of enemy gunfire.

What the marine committee could not provide in money or supplies it tried to make up for in a constant stream of orders and instructions, most of which could not be carried out, and in frequent exhortations. On July 25, 1777, it sent Nicholas Biddle, captain of the *Randolph*, lengthy instructions for raiding a fleet of British merchantmen in the

Caribbean and concluded: "Our ships should never be Idle. The Navy is in its infancy and a few brilliant strokes at this Era would give it a Credit and importance that would induce seamen from all parts to seek the employ, for nothing is more evident than that America has the means and must in time become the first Maritime power in the world."

One aspect of the naval affairs of the United States that deserves special attention is the role of a succession of Congressional commissioners in France. First Silas Deane, then John Adams, and finally Benjamin Franklin performed a number of highly important duties, among them building, buying, and equipping vessels in foreign waters, securing naval supplies, commissioning officers, and even giving sailing orders. The sale of naval prizes and the exchange of prisoners captured at sea were among their responsibilities.

In the summer of 1777, the commissioners tried to borrow or buy (with money that would have to be borrowed from the French) eight ships of the line, with the hope that these, in addition to the Continental frigates then abuilding, could break the British blockade of the American coast. The French, already considering the advantages to be gained from an alliance with the American states, not unnaturally refused. They might soon need the ships themselves. In addition to France, the commissioners tried their luck in Holland, Prussia, and Spain. Holland dared not risk British displeasure, and Prussia was likewise unwilling to take any action that might incur the wrath of Great Britain. Only in Spain, still licking wounds inflicted by the English in the Seven Years' War, did the Americans receive any encouragement. Gardoqui, the foreign minister—subtle and ingenious and more influential than the ancient and courtly Count Blanca, the prime minister—was anxious to take advantage of what appeared to be an opportunity to even old scores. Under his prompting, Florida Blanca expressed his opinion to the French ambassador that a long war between England and America would be "highly useful" to France and Spain. "We should sustain the Colonists," he wrote, "both with effectual aid in money and supplies" and "prudent advice." While Blanca was anxious to avoid irritating the British, Gardoqui was charting a much bolder course. American privateers, cruising in European waters, found Spanish ports readily available for refitting and for disposing of their prizes.

Gardner Allen, the historian of the American navy in the Revolution, proved himself a master of understatement when he wrote that "the situation of the United States from a naval point of view . . . was not altogether encouraging" at the end of 1777. Of the thirteen frigates built in American shipyards, one, the *Hancock*, had been captured, and nine others had either been lost to the enemy in the Delaware River or blockaded in New York Harbor and destroyed; two had been shut up in Narragansett Bay; and the *Virginia* had been confined to Chesapeake Bay. Of the smaller Continental vessels the *Andrea Doria* had been destroyed in the Delaware along with two frigates, the *Delaware* and the *Cabot,* and the *Lexington* had been captured by the British. On the other hand, 464 British merchant ships had been captured by American privateers in the course of the year, of which seventy-two were recaptured; the Continental Navy, such as it was, had captured more than sixty merchant vessels. The proportion between 464 and sixty measures quite well the relative effectiveness of the Continental Navy as contrasted with privateers of all categories.

Throughout 1777 and 1778, a series of problems stranded most of the ships of the infant navy. Some, such as the *Warren* and the *Providence,* were kept in port by British blockade. Others were unable to recruit crews. In addition, the captains of the newly built frigates were engaged in petty feuds. Captain Manley of the *Hancock* and Captain McNeill of the *Boston* fell out, and there was much justice in Dr. William Gordon's complaint to John Adams: "Maritime affairs have been most horridly managed. We have bested G. B. in dilatoriness & blunders. Where the fault hath lain I know not, but the credit of the Continent & Congress requires amendment." Despite the fact that there was bad blood between Manley and McNeill, they overtook and defeated the *Fox,* a British frigate of twenty-eight guns. In the words of a seaman on the *Boston,* "Betwixt the hours of 12 and one P.M. Capt. Manly Began to Engage Broadside & Broadside, our ship [the *Boston*] coming up as fast as Posable; at last up we came and gave them a Noble Broadside which made them to strike a medeatly a Bout half after one."

The *Fox* had hardly struck her colors before Manley and McNeill began squabbling. McNeill urged Manley to sail to Charles Town, join Biddle, refit the ships, and cruise in the West Indies until the fall, when most British frigates, unwilling to risk the autumn storms, returned to their home ports. Manley refused and ventured into the dangerous waters off the northern coast at a time when those waters were, in McNeill's words, "so covered with cruisers that there was no escaping them." Sure enough, a few days later Manley and McNeill with their prize, the *Fox,* found themselves pursued by three ships. The vessels turned out to be the British forty-four-gun frigate, the *Rainbow;* the frigate *Flora* of thirty-two guns; and the ten-gun brig, the *Victor.* Manley and McNeill engaged the *Rainbow,* the closest of their pursuers. While the *Hancock* and the *Rainbow* exchanged broadsides as they passed on opposite tacks, the *Boston* fell in on the same tack and exchanged some five broadsides in a running duel. The *Hancock* was heavily outgunned, and the fire of the British ship was so well directed that some shot passed through the *Hancock* "under the wale" (between the gun ports and the water line), so that McNeill had to fall away and plug the holes before he could tack. In this interval the *Rainbow* came down on the *Hancock,* and the *Fox,* instead of tacking with the *Hancock,* got between that ship and the *Rainbow* and took heavy fire from the *Rainbow* and the *Flora,* which had come to the assistance of her sister ship. The *Rainbow,* leaving the badly damaged *Fox* and *Boston* to the *Flora* and *Victory,* put about and chased the *Hancock.* Manley, to get a better fill on his sails, "started all his water forward" and for the moment outsailed the *Rainbow,* but he had put his ship out of trim in so doing, and on the next tack the British vessel made up distance on him, keeping him in sight through the night. At day the *Hancock* was no more than a mile ahead of the *Rainbow.* At four in the morning, Commodore Sir George Collier, in command of the *Rainbow,* opened fire from his bow guns loaded with round and grapeshot and, doing some damage to the *Hancock's* rigging, rapidly overtook her. At half past eight, Collier was within hailing distance and ordered the American ship to strike her colors if she expected quarter. While Manley hesitated and then tried to slip away on a fresh breeze, Collier fired a broadside, and the American ship struck. The chase had lasted almost thirty-nine hours.

Captain Brisbane of the *Flora* had meanwhile pursued and recaptured the *Fox* after a brief exchange of fire, but the *Boston,* crowding on sail, escaped to the windward. The *Fox* and the *Hancock* were taken into Halifax by their captors, and Collier, in his report of the battle, noted that the latter ship was reported to be "the largest and fastest sailing frigate ever built [by the Americans]" and that "Manley seem'd filled with rage and grief at finding he had so easily surrendered to a ship of only 44 guns, believing all along that it was the *Raisonable,* of 64 guns, who was chasing him."

The capture of the *Hancock* was a severe blow to all Americans who entertained high hopes for the patriot navy. John Manley made an initial error in altering his trim, which slowed his ship and prevented his getting off. Then, instead of putting up a stiff fight and making the British pay a price for capturing him, or perhaps disabling the British ship and making his escape, he tamely surrendered. "Every body here," Collier wrote from Halifax, "is overjoyed at the capture of Mr. Manley, esteeming him more capable of doing mischief to the King's subjects than General Lee was." Manley was sent as a prisoner to New York, and the *Hancock,* now the *Iris* in His Majesty's navy, proved her sailing and fighting qualities against her builders on a number of occasions. When Manley was exchanged, a court-martial cleared him of improper behavior but convicted McNeill of not coming to his support and suspended him from the service. It is hard not to believe that McNeill was made a scapegoat for Manley, who had important and influential friends in Congress and out.

The year 1778 saw another American foray against New Providence. By guile and bluff, fifty sailors seized the two forts on the islands, half a dozen ships in the harbor, thirty American prisoners, and military and naval stores including sixteen hundred barrels of powder. When the frigate *Randolph* returned from France, a squadron was organized at Charles Town that included the *Randolph,* under the command of Captain Nicholas Biddle, and four ships of the South Carolina navy, three of which were privateers commandeered for the occasion. A hundred and fifty South Carolina soldiers did service as marines. After a fruitless cruise along the southern coast, the squadron turned to the West Indies and encountered, east of Barbados, a British sixty-four-gun ship of the line, the *Yarmouth.* Biddle, outgunned by more than two to one, engaged the British ship so effectively that her bowsprit and topmasts were carried away and her sails and riggings slashed. Just as Biddle seemed on the verge of a spectacular success, the *Randolph* blew up, showering her opponent with spars and timbers, and "an American ensign . . . blown into upon the forecastle, not so much as singed," in the words of the commander of the *Yarmouth.* The loss of Biddle, twenty-eight years old and one of the most intrepid and experienced American naval officers, was a bitter blow. Two other American ships, the *Raleigh* of thirty-two guns and the *Alfred* of twenty, were routed, due to inept seamanship, by British ships of inferior firepower; the *Alfred* was captured, and the *Raleigh* ignominiously fled the scene.

The *Warren,* which had been shut up in the Providence River for months, escaped through the British fleet in Narragansett Bay and made its way to Boston in the spring of 1778. The *Columbus* likewise tried to slip through the blockade but was caught, run aground, and burned by its own crew to keep it from falling into the hands of the

British. *The Providence,* by now one of the seasoned veterans of the Continental Navy, also escaped from the Providence River, exchanged fire with the blockading British ships, and sailed for France, but the *Virginia,* trying to get out of the Chesapeake, ran aground and was surrendered to British frigates who came down on her. In the Delaware, the arrival of Howe's forces resulted in the Americans burning the *Washington* and the *Effingham* to keep them from being captured. A correspondent of Timothy Pickering reflected a general feeling of chagrin among patriots in a letter recommending a Massachusetts man for the command of a Continental frigate. "I am confident he would not give her away like a Coward as perhaps has been the case with some others, nor lose her like a blockhead as M . . . [doubtless Manley] did his." The only action that a frustrated Congress could take was to court-martial every officer suspected of dereliction of duty. We have already noted that McNeill of the *Boston* was tried for not properly supporting the *Hancock* and suspended and then dismissed. The captain of the errant *Raleigh,* who had failed to engage the British at the time of the capture of the *Alfred,* was likewise court-martialed and dismissed from the navy.

John Barry replaced Thompson on the ill-fated *Raleigh,* and soon after he left Boston two British warships gave chase, the fifty-gun *Experiment* and the twenty-two-gun *Unicorn.* For sixty hours the British ships pursued Barry, gaining on him or falling behind according to the accidents of the wind. Finally Barry saw an opportunity to engage the *Unicorn,* with the heavier-gunned *Experiment* well to the rear. Coming about, Barry ran down on the *Unicorn,* and, in the account of an officer on the *Raleigh,* "we hoisted our colours, hauled up the mizzen sail and took in the stay sails; and immediately the enemy hoisted St. George's ensign." The *Raleigh* and the *Unicorn* then exchanged broadsides, and the British vessel, skillfully handled, tacked under the *Raleigh's* lee quarter, where her guns were elevated by the heeling of the ship, and delivered a second broadside into the *Raleigh's* rigging, which, as the narrator put it, "to our unspeakable grief, carried away our fore top-mast and mizzen top-gallant-mast." Her decks covered with wreckage, the *Raleigh's* crew struggled to cut the sails and spars away and restore some maneuverability to the vessel while the *Unicorn* continued to bombard them. Barry, his own ship badly crippled, decided to try to board the *Unicorn,* but the British captain had no intention of allowing the *Raleigh* to close and veered off, dropping astern and holding the weather gauge until the *Experiment* should come up and finish the job.

By this time it was night and Barry, his ship disabled, decided to head for shore and run his ship aground rather than have her captured by the British frigates. Until midnight the two ships, running on the same course, exchanged occasional broadsides. Then the *Unicorn,* having left the slower *Experiment* far to the stern, broke off an engagement that had lasted some seven hours and waited for her consort to come up. The *Raleigh* was still not out of danger, for with the arrival of the *Experiment* the two British ships, discerning Barry's intention, did their best to cut him off from the shore. The *Experiment* gave the battered *Raleigh* three heavy broadsides and after the American ship had run aground delivered two more, which the *Raleigh* returned.

With his ship aground, Barry proceeded in what was left of the night to get his crew ashore so that he could destroy the *Raleigh,* but the plan went awry. Through confusion or treachery the ship was not set on fire, but was captured by a longboat from the *Experiment.* Barry had got ashore on the island with a hundred and thirty-three men, and most of these got back to Boston with their captain.

The *Raleigh,* under Barry's leadership, had given a good account of herself. She had lost twenty-five killed and wounded, a very high rate of casualties for a naval engagement of this kind, while the *Unicorn* had ten killed and a large number wounded. The *Raleigh* was pulled off the rocks, refitted, and placed in service by the British, but Barry's determination not to strike his colors to a superior force left his reputation untarnished.

Dozens of minor engagements between American and British privateers, between Continental and state naval vessels and privateers on the one side and British naval vessels on the other, took place during 1778. But one in particular suggests how fierce that warfare could become when two determined rivals faced each other. On May 26, off the capes of Delaware, the *Minerva,* a British sloop carrying sixteen six-pounders, ten cohorns, and forty men, encountered an American brigantine, apparently a privateer, mounting fourteen guns, six cohorns, and twenty-four swivels. The ships ran together and exchanged broadsides for two hours at a range so close that at times their riggings were in danger of becoming entangled. The American cannon were loaded with "old iron cut square, old pots, old bolts, etc." In the two hours of fighting the British ship received a hundred and eighty shot through the topmast stay-sail, "9 great shot ... through our ensign, 1 through our pendant, 13 shot in our mizen-mast, our main-mast shot through and our fore-mast greatly damaged," according to the account of a British officer. One American cannonball went through the hull of the *Minerva* and through fourteen casks of rum, starting the rumor that the ship was taking water and sinking. The British ship lost seven killed and nine wounded out of a crew of forty, almost half her complement of men. The anonymous American vessel also suffered severely, but although it did not force the *Minerva* to strike its colors, it clearly had the better of the battle.

Another Boston privateer of twenty guns, the *General Hancock,* (not, of course, the Continental ship *Hancock*), engaged the British privateer *Levant,* of thirty-two guns, for three hours, until the scuppers ran with blood. The British ship blew up when a stray spark ignited its powder magazine, and only eighteen of its crew of a hundred were rescued by the American ship.

Some notion of the eccentric nature of the war at sea can be gained from an episode involving Lieutenant Thomas Simpson and the *Ranger* that occurred in July, 1779. A small squadron of American frigates— the *Providence* under Commodore Abraham Whipple, the *Queen of France,* and the *Ranger* under Simpson—cruising from Boston eastward, fell in, in a dense fog, with a fleet of a hundred and fifty British merchant ships, convoyed by a British seventy-four-gun ship of the line and several smaller frigates and sloops. As the fog lifted, the *Queen of France* found herself near a large merchant ship. Captain John Rathburn of the *Queen,* a wily and experienced officer, pretended the *Queen* was a British warship, sent off a boat, and captured the merchantman. Another ship was captured in the same way, and then another. The other American frigates joined in the sport, without ever alerting the rest of the fleet or their guardians. Meanwhile Whipple on the *Providence,* with twenty-eight guns, some of them twelve-pounders, came up on one of the escorts, the *Holderness,* a three-decker with twenty-two guns. The *Providence* fired several broadsides, and the British ship struck her colors. She was loaded with a rich cargo of rum, sugar, coffee, and allspice.

During the night the American frigates ran on like wolves in a flock of sheep, still undiscovered. They could hear distinctly the bells on nearby ships and the calls of seamen. And so for three days the American ships sailed along with the convoy, capturing in that time eleven prizes, which, manned by prize crews, were dispatched to home ports. Three were recaptured before they made port, but the eight remaining were valued with their cargoes at more than a million dollars—a very large sum for the impoverished patriots.

14

Naval "Militia" and Privateers

L IKE the Continental Army, the Continental Navy had its "militia"—ships outfitted and commissioned by the individual states. By the end of the war, eleven of the thirteen states had their own "navies" or armed vessels. These were generally small vessels, often armed galleys used chiefly for coast defense, but a few states maintained oceangoing cruisers. The navy of Massachusetts, for instance, was made up of fifteen ships large enough for cruising, and Pennsylvania had ten vessels and nearly thirty small boats and galleys for the defense of the Delaware River. Virginia and Maryland had a common interest in defending the Chesapeake and the rivers that provided such ready access to the interior parts of those states. Virginia's navy included seventy-two vessels of all classes and sizes, most of them lightly armed and useful primarily for bay and river commerce. South Carolina, with Charles Town to defend, had about fifteen seagoing vessels, several of them larger than any ships of the Continental Navy.

Two brigantines and a sloop—the *Independence,* the *Rising Empire,* and the *Tyrannicide*—were commissioned by the General Court of Massachusetts and took a number of British prizes in 1776. There were dozens of similar encounters in all the coastal waters from New Breton to Georgia. Few of them found their way into the pages of history, but for those involved, each was as dangerous and dramatic as Bunker Hill or Yorktown. A dozen men on a little sloop armed with a few swivels, contesting control of an inlet on the Jersey or Carolina coast, might employ all the guile and display all the bravery of great navies clashing on the high seas. Their wounds bled as red, and those who died did so as completely as the victims of famous battles. Like the partisan warfare of the Southern interior, the bitter encounters between cowboys and rangers in Westchester or Tryon counties in New York, and the murderous forays of Indians and Tories along the frontier, the naval war, small as it was in detail, involved in the aggregate thousands of men and countless vessels ranging from rowboats to hastily built frigates. Week in and week out, it was a war of attrition, of cunning and cruelty, of ceaseless vigilance and nerve-racking uncertainty. Governor Jonathan Trumbull of Connecticut, a wise and urbane man, could not suppress his bitterness when he wrote of the piratical actions of Tories in the waters of Long Island. Writing to Seth Harding, the captain of a ship in the Connecticut navy, Trumbull spoke of a "a most unnatural and traitorous combination among the inhabitants of this Colony. Possessed of and enjoying the most valuable and important privileges, to betray them all into the hands of our cruel oppressors is shocking and astonishing conduct and evinces the deep degeneracy and wickedness of which mankind is capable." Trumbull urged Harding to do his best to "suppress this wicked conspiracy . . . this blackest treason."

A third class of vessels employed during the Revolution was the privateers or letters of marque. Letters of marque were issued to armed trading vessels, authorizing them to take prizes where they could. Privateers, strictly speaking, were armed vessels that carried no cargo and were intended for preying on enemy shipping. In March, 1776, Congress authorized privateering and drafted a set of instructions to cover the sport. Pennsylvania, before the war was over, sent out 500 vessels under Continental commissions, and 626 Massachusetts privateers sailed under Continental letters of marque, in addition to nearly 1,000 sent out under the commissions of that state. (Massachusetts, with its long maritime tradition, was one of the first states to establish courts for the trial of prizes captured by privateers.) A list exists of nearly 1,700 letters of marque issued by Congress to privateers that, altogether, mounted some 15,000 guns, most of them doubtless light swivels and four- and six-pounders. A rough estimate is that 59,000 men manned these vessels. Allowing for considerable duplication and deducting armed boats and galleys, we may arrive at a figure of perhaps 1,300 seagoing vessels engaged in various forms of privateering under commissions from Congress.

To these must be added those vessels that were commissioned by the states but did their privateering in Europe and the West Indies; the rough total then is well in excess of two thousand. Many of these, of course, were not full time privateers but rather merchant vessels with sufficient armament to capture smaller or more lightly armed ships. When we consider that Washington's army never exceeded fifteen thousand and the state militia not more than twice that number, it is easy to see that privateering represented very serious competition to the Continental Army as well as to the state militia. While most soldiers went without pay and ate wretched food, many privateers made substantial profits from their patriotic activity. A captured British officer, writing from a Boston prison in the spring of 1777, noted, "Boston harbor swarms with privateers and their prizes; this is a great place of rendez-vous with them. The privateersmen come on shore here full of money and enjoy themselves much after the same manner the English seamen at Portsmouth and Plymouth did in the late war. . . ."

One of the special problems of the privateer—shared by all ships that took prizes—was that although it might start its voyage with a larger-than-necessary crew, if it was lucky and took a number of prizes it had to put crews on board to sail these ships home, so that by the time it neared the end of its cruise it was dangerously undermanned. Thus it might capture ten prizes and put ten men on each (for a total of one hundred) to sail them to port. A number of the undermanned prizes might be recaptured before they could reach home, and the American privateer, short-handed just when it reached the most dangerous point in its voyage—the American coastal waters, where British frigates cruised—might fall an easy victim to a British warship. Such were the hazards of privateering. That it flourished in the face of such risks is plain evidence of the generous profits to be made from it.

The American privateers often engaged British warships of equal or superior firepower and gave good accounts of themselves. The *Yankee Hero* with twelve guns and twenty-six men, fought a stubborn battle with the much larger British frigate the *Milford* before it surrendered; in May, 1776, the *Camden,* a privateer mounting fourteen guns, fought for three hours with the British brigantine the *Earl of Warwick* and, aided by an explosion on the English ship, forced it to strike its colors. A privateer captain, Henry Johnson of Boston, cruised in the English Channel and captured two prizes, and he was followed into

British waters by other daring privateers. Indeed, as early as 1777 the effect of the privateers was being felt. "It is true," the editor of the *Annual Register* wrote of that year, "that the coasts of Great Britain and Ireland were insulted by the American privateers in a manner which our hardiest enemies had never ventured in our most arduous contentions with foreigners. Thus were the inmost and most domestic recesses of our trade rendered insecure. . . . The Thames also presented the unusual and melancholy spectacle of numbers of foreign ships," since British merchants preferred to send their goods under the colors of neutral nations rather than risk them in British vessels.

In addition to those privateers that came out from America to prowl British waters, British shipping suffered acutely from privateers bought or built in French shipyards. Before the French alliance, the *Reprisal,* the *Lexington,* the *Dolphin,* and the *Revenge* were outfitted and dispatched by the American commissioners with French connivance, over the repeated expostulations of the British ambassador, Lord Stormant. Finally Stormant's protests and the implied threat of retribution by Britain forced Vergennes to bring pressure on the Americans to remove the ships from French ports and send them to America.

The privateers, of course, were not alone in their incursions into British waters. The cases of three ships of the Massachusetts navy will perhaps serve to indicate one aspect of the naval warfare. The brigantines *Tyrannicide, Massachusetts,* and *Freedom* sailed in March, 1777, for the coasts of Ireland, England, and France. The *Freedom,* sailing independently, arrived at the French port of Paimboeuf on May 1, having captured twelve British merchant vessels *en route.* The *Massachusetts* and the *Tyrannicide,* sailing together, captured three British vessels, one of them an armed bark and another a transport carrying sixty-three Hessians. The *Massachusetts* arrived at Nantes on May 21, having barely escaped from four British warships; the *Tyrannicide* got away by jettisoning most of its guns and ship's stores and made port at Bilbao, Spain. The *Massachusetts* got back to Marblehead with eight prizes (and with General Pulaski on board) on July 23, forty-four days out of Nantes. The *Freedom* had arrived two weeks earlier, having taken sixteen prizes, and the *Tyrannicide* got back at the end of August. Within the next three months the three ships cruised the waters off Massachusetts and captured a number of prizes; finally the *Freedom* was itself captured by the British frigate *Apollo.*

Indeed, state naval vessels and privateers were so active during the spring and summer of 1777 that Admiral Montagu wrote to Lord

Germain from St. John's, Newfoundland, "The American privateers have been very troublesome on the banks and have comitted great depredations among the fishermen, notwithstanding I have dispatched the men-of-war as they arrived to the different parts of the fishing bank to cruize for their protection. It gives me great concern to be obliged to inform your Lordship that the privateers cruizing in these seas are greatly superior in number and size to the squadron under my command and without a large force is sent out to me, the bank fishery is at a stand."

The British, of course, had their own privateers, and Governor Hutchinson estimated that seventy thousand British sailors were so employed.

Besides the fact that privateering drew off much-needed manpower from the Continental Army and from the newly formed navy, it had other drawbacks from the point of view of the American cause. William Whipple, a delegate to Congress from New Hampshire, writing to his colleague Josiah Bartlett in July, 1778, observed, "I agree with you that privateers have much distressed the trade of our Enemies, but had there been no privateers is it not probable that there would have been a much larger number of Public Ships than has been fitted out, which might have distressed the Enemy nearly as much & furnished these States with necessaries on much better terms than they have been supplied by Privateers? . . . No kind of Business can so effectually introduce Luxury, Extravagance and every kind of Dissipation, that tend to the destruction of the morals of people. Those who are actually engaged in it soon lose every Idea of right & wrong, & for want of an opportunity of gratifying their insatiable avarice with the property of the Enemies of their Country, will without the least compunction seize that of her Friends." There were five privateers fitting out at Portsmouth at the moment Whipple wrote, and they would take some four hundred men, most of them farmers, since the sailors were already long since drained off. No naval vessel could be manned while this was going on, Whipple added. "The reason is plain: Those people who have the most influence with Seamen think it their interest to discourage the Public service, because by that they promote their own interest, viz., Privateering." Not only did the privateers show an unfortunate tendency to disregard the rights of neutrals, they did clearly, as Whipple charged, impede the organization of a Continental Navy. As one of the members of the navy board at Boston wrote John Adams in December, 1778, while the board was still struggling to get a modest fleet to sea,

"The infamous practice of seducing our Men to leave the ships and taking them off at an out-Port, with many other base methods, will make it impossible to get our Ships ready to Sail in force, or perhaps otherwise than single Ships." The remedy, according to William Vernon, a member of the navy board, was "an Embargo upon all Private Property, whether Arm'd or Merchant ships . . . Until the Fleet is compleatly Mann'd."

We get a vivid picture of the hazards of a seaman on an American privateer from the tale of Christopher Hawkins, a farm boy, apprenticed to a tanner in Providence, Rhode Island, who ran away at the age of thirteen and enlisted in the crew of a privateer. The schooner he was on was captured by a British warship, and young Hawkins was drafted as a messboy by one of the officers on the ship. He escaped while his ship was in New York Harbor and returned to work as a farm hand. Two years later, tired of harvesting and irritated by a bad scythe with which he had to mow, he left his employer and once more signed on a privateer at Providence. This time his career as a sailor lasted barely a week. His vessel was captured leaving Providence Harbor, and young Hawkins experienced the dismal horrors of a British prison ship, the *Jersey*. Crowded into the hold of the vessel, the men kept up their spirits by singing a song with the refrain, "For America and all her sons forever will shine." The singing infuriated the jailers, who threatened to shoot if the prisoners did not keep quiet. "They were often set at defiance," Hawkins recalled, "sometimes in the following words, 'We dare you to fire upon us. It will be only half work for many of the prisoners are now half dead from extreme sufferings.'" The prisoners suffered from dysentery and wholly inadequate toilet facilities. "This," Hawkins wrote, "induced an almost constant running over me by the sick, who would besmear myself and others with their bloody and loathesome filth." In such conditions survival became the only law. Men pilfered wretched bits of food from each other and fought like hungry dogs over unsavory morsels. Every prisoner was infested with lice and vermin, and Hawkins saw prisoners picking them off their clothing and out of their hair and eating them. He and a friend escaped by swimming two miles to shore across Long Island Sound.

Hawkins' adventures in trying to get back to Providence give a dramatic picture of the uneasy relationships in which Tories and patriots lived. On much of Long Island, the British-backed Tories were dominant, but there were numerous rebel sympathizers scattered about who were glad to aid Hawkins. The unnerving thing was that the boy never knew how to distinguish between those men and women he encountered who were loyal to the Crown and those who gave their allegiance to the American cause. Every meeting was thus followed by a cautious and laborious sounding out to determine how Hawkins should present himself to secure help and avoid recapture.

Another prisoner on the *Jersey,* the most notorious prisonship in the British navy, wrote, "The dysentery, fever, phrenzy, and despair, prevailed among [the prisoners] and filled the place with filth, disgust, and horror. The scantiness of the allowance, the bad quality of the provisions, the brutality of the guards, and the sick, pinning for comforts they could not obtain, altogether furnished continually one of the greatest scenes of human distress and misery ever beheld." One prisoner estimated that the chances for survival on the *Jersey* were no better than one out of five. Dead bodies were heaved over the side, and at low tide they were exposed in the mudbanks near the ship, a grim and horrifying sight.

15

John Paul Jones

J OHN Paul Jones, having given up the *Providence* in hopes of a larger ship, languished on shore while various projects were hatched and abandoned. Finally in June, 1777, he was placed in command of the *Ranger,* a new eighteen-gun ship. On June 14, Congress authorized that the official flag of the United States "be thirteen stripes alternative red and white; that the Union be thirteen stars, white in a blue field, representing a new constellation." It was Jones who first hoisted this flag on an American warship.

When the *Ranger* was ready for sea, Captain Jones took her on a shakedown voyage to Nantes, capturing two prizes on the way. The ship proved to be cranky and difficult to handle, "owing," Jones wrote, "to the improper quality of her Ballast and to her being rather over Masted. . . ." He judged lowering the mast and filling her ballast with lead the proper cures, which he effected in Nantes. A more difficult problem, and one shared by other American warships, was the foulness of her bottom. The Americans did not have copper available to sheath the bottoms of their vessels as the British did, and therefore their bottoms, after even a few months at sea, were so fouled with barnacles and marine growths that their speed and maneuverability were greatly reduced—sometimes, as it turned out, fatally. There was no remedy for a foul bottom but putting a ship in dry dock and scraping her hull below the water line, a tedious and time-consuming chore.

The end of the year 1778 was as unpromising for the American navy as for the army. The frigates *Providence, Boston, Deane, Queen of France,* and *Warren* were in Boston Harbor. These ships, four of them recently arrived from France, made up, for all intents and purposes, the American navy. Only the *Deane* was manned and ready to sail. The others could not compete with the privateers for crews and thus lay idle in port.

There was one bright note in the picture, however. Jones, having improved the sailing qualities of the *Ranger,* had been carrying the naval war to the British. From France, Jones had written the marine committee a letter breathing patriotic ardor. "It is my hearts first and favorite wish to be employed in Active and enterprizing Services where there is a prospect of Rendering such Services Useful and Acceptable to America. . . . if a life of Service devoted to America can be made instrumental in securing its Independence," he added, he would regard the approbation of Congress, "as an honor far Superior to the Empty Pagentry which Kings ever did or can bestow." Jones proposed to the American commissioners at Paris that he conduct punishing hit-and-run raids along the British coast with the intention of destroying "the greatest amount of property in the shortest time," and in the early spring of 1778 Jones put his ideas into operation. Throughout the month of April, he cruised the British coastal waters, taking prizes and spreading alarm.

Jones was a severe taskmaster who was exceedingly demanding of the sailors and officers under his command. Each of his midshipmen was invited in turn to dine with him in the great cabin but he had to appear in immaculate dress if he was not to suffer Jones's displeasure. At the same time, there was no condescension in the captain's manner; he talked as freely and openly with the lowest of his officers as with those of higher rank. He required arduous duty from the midshipmen. One was always on duty aloft during the day, lodged in a swaying perch on the main-topgallant yard or cross yard, and if Jones caught one napping, he would let go the topgallant halyards, dropping the officer until he was brought up short by the lifts of the yard.

On April 22, 1778, Jones and thirty-one volunteers from the *Ranger* landed at Whitehaven, England, spiked the cannon in the two forts that protected the harbor, and attempted to set fire to some of the vessels anchored off the town. The candles and wicks that Jones had brought with him guttered out before he could accomplish his purpose. He found fire in a house outside the town and scavenged a barrel of tar. A ship, lying at anchor and surrounded by hundreds of other vessels, was selected, and the tar was poured over its decks and down its hatchways and set on fire while Jones, armed with a pistol, held off a crowd of townspeople running to extinguish the flames. The fire soon leaped to the rigging and climbed the mainmast. Coolly Jones got his own party off. On the hills around the harbor hundreds of silent spectators gathered to watch the blaze while Jones, in a final gesture of bravado, stood alone on the pier—a small, insolent figure in his colorful uniform, his pistol in his hand, daring anyone to challenge him. "After all my people had embarked," he wrote, "I stood upon the pier for a considerable time, yet no persons advanced. I saw all the eminences around the town covered with the amazed inhabitants." It was just the kind of scene that fed Jones's ample ego, and it prefigured a classic American drama—the lone gunman against the town. Jones calculated that if he had gotten ashore an hour or so earlier, he would have put the whole fleet and the town itself to the torch. "What was done, however," he noted, "is sufficient to show that not all their boasted navy can protect their own coasts, and that the scenes of distress which they have occasioned in America may soon be brought home to their own door."

Jones's plans did not stop there. Crossing the bay to the Scottish shore, he landed on St. Mary's Isle, very near where he had been born thirty-one years earlier. The island was owned by the Earl of Selkirk, whom Jones intended to kidnap and take to France as a hostage for American prisoners in England. The earl was absent, but Jones's men insisted on carrying off some booty. The captain gave his permission for them to take all the family plate but forbade them to enter the mansion itself. Jones later bought the plate from the crew and returned it to Selkirk.

Leaving the Irish Sea, Jones came to Carrickfergus, Scotland, where a British warship, the twenty-gun *Drake,* lay at anchor. The *Drake,* observing the *Ranger* and believing her to be a British privateer, prepared to leave the harbor and sent an officer in a longboat to make contact with the captain of the visiting vessel. When the officer from the *Drake* stepped onto the quarterdeck of the *Ranger,* he was startled to find himself a prisoner of the Americans. The captain of the *Drake,* still not aware of the identity of the *Ranger,* came out of the harbor accompanied by five small boats filled with excursionists, but when the sightseers saw the *Drake's* longboat tied to the *Ranger,* "they wisely put back."

The *Drake* made slow going against an unfavorable wind while an impatient Jones tacked back and forth outside the harbor mouth waiting for her. It should be pointed out that the *Ranger,* despite Jones's stiff discipline and dashing leadership, was not a happy vessel. The men, encouraged by the first lieutenant, Thomas Simpson, were in a state bordering on mutiny. Simpson, according to Jones, "held up to the crew that being American fighting for liberty, the voice of the people should be taken before the Captain's orders were obeyed." A less-resolute officer would have doubtless concluded that it was no time to engage a British warship of equal armament whose crew outnumbered his own by a substantial margin (though Jones could hardly have known that). To Jones, the daring gambler, it was precisely the moment to attack. Jones, who was inclined to double his bets when he was in trouble, ordered his disgruntled men to battle stations and prepared for action.

"At length," Jones wrote in his account of the engagement, "the Drake weathered the point, and having led her out to about mid-channel, I suffered her to come within hail. The Drake hoisted English colors and at the same instant the American stars were displayed on board the Ranger." Jones expected the battle to begin, but the *Drake* hailed and asked the name of the ship. "The American Continental ship Ranger, that we waited for them and desired that they would now come on; the sun was now little more than an hour from setting, it was therefore time to begin." That was the Jones flair—a message from one gentleman to another to try a course of arms like two medieval knights. With that Jones ordered the *Ranger's* helm up, came across the bow of the *Drake,* and delivered a broadside. "The action," in Jones's words, "was warm, close, and obstinate. It lasted an hour and four minutes, when the enemy called for quarters, her fore and main-topsail yards being both cut away and down on the cap, the topgallant yard and mizen-gagg both hanging up and along the mast . . . the jib shot away and hanging in the water, her sails and rugging cut entirely to pieces, her masts and yards all wounded, and her hull also very much galled." The *Ranger* had lost an officer and a seaman killed and six wounded; the *Drake* lost more than thirty killed and wounded, and among the dead were her captain and a lieutenant.

While the *Ranger* outgunned the *Drake* slightly, Jones had fought his ship with customary skill and resolution. Moreover, he had administered a sharp defeat to the British in their own backyard and done so before an audience made up of hundreds of Scottish spectators. The *Drake* was taken back to Brest along with some two hundred British prisoners, and an American there, seeing the ships enter the harbor, wrote, "It was a pleasure to see the English flag flying under the American stars and stripes." Six British men-of-war were ordered to search for the *Ranger*.

Jones tried to have the democratic Lieutenant Simpson court-martialed for disobeying orders and inciting to mutiny, but there were not enough American naval officers in France to form a board; instead of being court-martialed Simpson was given command of the *Ranger* (which he had originally been promised on the expectation of Jones's getting a larger ship) and set sail for America. Jones meanwhile waited in Paris for the American commissioners to procure a frigate for him to command.

In France, John Paul Jones spent a year of bitter frustration waiting for a new command. Several of the American commissioners were plainly irritated by this demanding popinjay. He might be a dashing sailor, but on land he was a persistent nuisance. His drafts on the commissioners for the support of his crew and the prisoners he had captured were often returned for lack of funds. He himself received no pay, and there was endless delay in disposing of the prizes captured by the *Ranger* and distributing the monies among the officers and crew. Jones was never popular with his men. While it was true that, like any good commander, he took great pains in their cause, they sensed in him a ruthless determination to use them for his own purposes, and they resented his iron discipline. To Jones the men who served under him were less human beings than tools of his relentless will—the agents of his glorious destiny.

For a time it seemed that he would command the *Indien,* a frigate being built in Holland, but the British got wind of the venture and applied so much pressure on the Dutch government that it refused to allow the ship to leave Holland when it was finished. Another proposal was that Jones should command a squadron of French ships flying the American flag. Franklin, that writer of prescriptions for success, took a paternal interest in Jones. Perhaps the Pennsylvania sage saw in the impatient young captain the model and mirror of the hero of *Poor Richard's Almanack,* the poor boy determined to make his way in the world, the exemplar of many of Franklin's own aphorisms. If Jones was not early to bed and early to rise, it was certain that he lost no opportunity to improve his worldly fortunes. The two men, so different in age, both enjoyed a degree of discreet elegance. Jones was abstemious by nature (lemonade was his common drink at sea) and Franklin by necessity (old age and gout), but both men enjoyed pretty and amiable women, fine wine, and French cooking.

Encouraged by Franklin, Jones carried his case directly to Versailles and there persuaded the French minister of marine, de Sartine, to procure a ship for him. In January, 1779, Sartine purchased an East Indiaman named the *Duc de Duras*. The ship was an indifferent sailer— fourteen years old, it showed quite plainly the effects of particularly arduous service—but it was enough for Jones that she would float and could be fitted with guns. With his flair for the dramatic, he renamed the ship the *Bonhomme Richard* after the famous *Almanack* of his friend and advocate, Franklin. It was Jones's intention that *The Good Man Richard* should demonstrate the soundness of his mentor's maxims. And all that industry and resourcefulness could do to make the *Bonhomme Richard* the terror of the seas, Jones did. No efforts were spared to turn this naval sow's ear into a silk purse. Franklin helped by obtaining for Jones the *Alliance,* a new frigate of thirty-two guns. It was commanded by Captain Pierre Landais, an experienced French naval officer. Although Washington suffered from an epidemic of French military officers, Landais was the only Frenchman to command a Continental warship. He had recently arrived in France, with Lafayette as a passenger, after having suppressed a dangerous mutiny among his crew, most of whom were English sailors captured by American privateers and drafted in the absence of available American seamen. It is difficult to imagine an episode that could better represent the plight of the American navy than the fact that its newest and one of its largest warships had to be manned by captured British sailors. In any event, Franklin detained the *Alliance* and placed it under Jones's command along with three French ships: the *Pallas,* a merchantman fitted out as a privateer with thirty-two guns; the *Cerf,* an eighteen-gun cutter, a swift and agile ship; and the *Vengeance,* a brigantine mounting twelve guns. Originally, the plan was that Lafayette, with fifteen hundred infantry soldiers, some cavalry, and six pieces of artillery, should join in a series of raids against the principal British naval stations at Liverpool, Lancaster, Bristol, Whitehaven, and Bath. Then, while Jones waited impatiently, a joint Spanish-French invasion of England was considered; the scheme called for Jones's squadron to make a diversionary raid in the north of England. A large fleet of transports and warships was collected before the plan was abandoned.

By June, 1779, Jones's squadron was ready to sail, but before he could put to sea he had to deal with a disheartening quarrel between

Landais and his crew. Landais was an autocratic and hot-tempered man who was used to dealing with seamen of a very different character than the outspoken and independent American sailors who had been recruited to replace the mutineers. The *Alliance* thus sailed from L'Orient with a divided and uneasy crew. The *Bonhomme Richard* had troubles enough of its own, though they were largely structural rather than disciplinary. Besides being slow and unwieldly, the ship was too poorly constructed to carry the eighteen-pounders that Jones wished to mount in her battery of twenty-eight guns. As it turned out, the only guns that could be found for her were old cannon, a number of which had been condemned as dangerous. Twenty-eight of these twelve-pounders were mounted on the gun deck. On the quarter-deck and forecastle there were six nine-pounders, and in the gun room, under the main battery, six of the eighteen-pounders that Jones was determined to carry were mounted with ports cut too close to the water line to permit the guns to be fired in a heavy sea. The crew of 227 men and officers was made up of 79 Americans (the greater part exchanged prisoners), 83 English, Scottish and Irish, a handful of Scandinavians, and 28 Portuguese. In addition, the *Bonhomme Richard* carried 137 French soldiers in lieu of marines.

In January, when the *Duc de Duras* had been purchased by Sartine, Jones had drawn up a kind of declaration of intent that opened on a note of perhaps slightly false humility: "I am but a young Student in the Science of Arms and therefore wish to recieve instruction from Men of riper Judgement and greater experience. . . ." The author then went on to lay out the rules of "Partizan War" as he understood them. Five ships would be needed; two of them might be small, fast vessels. The bottoms of all ships should be sheathed in copper to prevent fouling and increase their speed. An expedition of the kind he projected would need two light artillery pieces and a number of scaling ladders. Above all, secrecy was essential. None of those who made up the force should know its intended objective except the commander himself.

In June Jones's squadron put to sea on a shake-down cruise, during which they captured several small ships. Jones also discovered a conspiracy among the British sailors to seize the ship and carry him to England as a prisoner. As many of the conspirators as could be identified were put ashore, and in August forty-three Americans who had been recently exchanged were signed up in their places. Finally, on August 14, the squadron sailed from Groix Roads with the mission, assigned by Franklin in consultation with Sartine, of ranging the northern coasts of the

British Isles and inflicting as much damage on British ships and ports as possible. With little wind, the ships made slow progress. On August 23, they were off Cape Clear, and Jones, concerned that the tide might carry the *Bonhomme Richard* too near the shore, put out a barge to tow her. "Soon after sunset," Jones wrote, "the villains who towed the ship, cut the tow rope and decamped with my barge." Shots were fired to deter them, but they escaped. The master of the *Bonhomme Richard,* without orders from Jones, lowered a boat and set out after the fugitives. Soon he was lost in the fog and darkness. The next day Landais came on board the flagship and abused and upbraided Jones "in the most indelicate manner and language," declaring that Jones had lost his boats through imprudence and, most insolent of all, that "he was the only [true] American in the squadron and was determined to follow his own opinion in the chasing when and where he thought proper, and in every other matter that concerned the service. . . ."

The *Cerf*, sent to try to recover the missing boats, likewise got lost, sprung her mainmast in a storm, and returned to France. A storm scattered the ships, and it was a week before they rendezvoused again off Cape Wrath. A few days later a storm again dispersed the squadron, and when it subsided only the *Vengeance* and the *Pallas* joined Jones. Jones planned a raid on Leith, intending to sail up the Firth of Forth and take the port by surprise. First, however, he had to persuade the French captains on the *Vengeance* and *Pallas.* They raised, in Jones's opinion, all kinds of captious objections and were only converted to the project by Jones's statement that he planned to levy a ransom of two hundred thousand pounds sterling on the town under the threat of blowing it up. This news made the French officers more favorably disposed, but the time spent "in pointed remarks and sage deliberations" (as Jones put it) lost the occasion. Another storm came up, and the squadron was blown away from the mouth of the river. By this time Jones and his ships were being shadowed by cutters fitted out for that express purpose. At Leith one sent a detailed description of the three vessels to the Admiralty.

The French captains, discouraged by the bad weather and poor hunting, pressed Jones to return to L'Orient. Reluctantly, he turned south. On September 21, off Flamborough Head, two brigs were captured, and Jones received word of a large fleet of merchant ships in the mouth of the Humber under convoy of a British frigate. Again, adverse winds prevented Jones from getting into the Humber; returning to Flamborough Head, he picked up the signals of the *Pallas* and the errant *Alliance*, which had reappeared as mysteriously as it had disappeared. On the twenty-third, forty-one sails appeared heading northeast, and Jones and his depleted squadron gave chase. As soon as the merchantmen saw the warships bearing down on them, they made for the shore. Their convoying ships, the *Serapis* of fifty-four guns and the *Countess of Scarborough,* turned out at the same time to engage Jones's force. As Jones crowded on sail he gave the signal to form a line of battle. Landais on the *Alliance* paid no attention but continued on his own course. The line of battle thus consisted of the *Bonhomme Richard* and the *Pallas,* and soon the *Pallas* dropped off, leaving the *Bonhomme Richard* to engage the *Serapis*. On the *Bonhomme Richard* the officers and crew, along with the French soldiers acting as marines, were all at their battle stations. As the *Bonhomme Richard* approached the *Serapis*, Captain Pearson of the British ship hailed: "What ship is that?" in "true *bombastic English stile,* it being hoarse and hardly intelligible," according to Lieutenant Nathaniel Fanning, a midshipman. Jones's answer was, "Come a little nearer, and I will tell you." "What are you laden with?" was Pearson's next question. "Round, grape and double-headed shot," was the response. At this the *Serapis* fired a broadside, and the battle began. Jones took his post on the quarter-deck. On the poop was a French officer with twenty soldiers. Richard Dale, the first lieutenant, had command of the gun deck, while the tops—the main, the fore, and the mizzen—were manned by soldiers and sailors—twenty in the maintop, fourteen in the foretop, and nine in the mizzen. These men were armed with muskets, swivels, and cohorns. Their assignment was to clear the tops of the British ship and then turn their fire on the decks.

The *Serapis* was a new, double-decked ship, of whose fifty-four guns twenty were eighteen-pounders as opposed to the twelves of the *Bonhomme Richard*. The *Serapis* thus discharged 300 pounds of iron to 204 for the *Bonhomme Richard*.

The heavier guns gave the British ship a greater advantage than simply adding up the weight of the respective firepower would suggest. Two eighteen-pounders, for instance, could do much more damage than three twelve-pounders, although the weight of metal discharged by both was the same. Knowing that his ship was clumsy and unresponsive, Jones's tactic was to try to place it across the bow of the *Serapis,* bringing the ships to close quarter and allowing his broadsides to rake the enemy vessel at its point of greatest vulnerability. The captain of the *Serapis* was too skilled and experienced an officer to permit the maneuver, and the two ships sailed side by side, Jones unable, despite holding the weather gauge, to come down on the *Serapis,* as that ship wore away each time Jones tried to close. Meanwhile the eighteen-pounders of the *Serapis* worked fearful damage on the hull of the *Bonhomme Richard* below the water line, and Jones, with much of his rigging torn away, found it increasingly difficult to cover his opponent. The battery of twelve-pounders, in which Jones had placed special confidence, was silenced by the guns of the *Serapis.* The old eighteen-pounders on the lower gun deck did no service at all. Two of the first three that were fired burst and killed most of their crews. The French soldiers stationed in the poop deserted their quarters, and Jones had only two nine-pound cannon on the quarter-deck fit to fire. When the officer who commanded these guns was badly wounded in the head, Jones himself rallied a few men and took command, shifting one of the nine-pounders from the lee to the windward side.

The captain of the *Serapis,* confident of the superior sailing qualities of his ship, started to pull ahead. When her commander thought she had sufficient leeway to cross ahead of the *Bonhomme Richard* and rake her bow with his guns, he turned sharply into the wind. But he miscalculated; he saw he could not cross her bows, and, quite properly afraid of running afoul of her and risking being boarded, he wore away to the lee with Jones following. As the *Serapis* lost sailing speed, Jones ran the bow of his ship into the stern of the *Serapis,* but the sails of the *Bonhomme Richard* lost their wind while those of the *Serapis* filled, and the British ship began to pull away, wearing around on her heel.

Jones ordered the helmsman, Stacy, *"a true blooded yankee,"* to try to catch the enemy rigging. At that moment Stacy put the helm hard aweather; the main and mizzen topsails, which had been braced back, were filled away, and a lucky puff of wind swelled them and shot the ship forward, running her jib between the starboard mizzen shrouds and the mizzen guys running from the standing gaff. It was a neat bit of sailing, and Jones gave a cry of triumph: "Well done, my brave lads, we have got her now; throw aboard the grappling-irons, and stand by for boarding." The grappling irons were hurled over the gunwales of the *Serapis,* but her marines quickly cut them loose. More were thrown and more cut. For a moment it seemed as though the *Serapis* might break loose, but at this point her jibstay was cut and fell on the poop of the *Bonhomme Richard,* practically at the feet of Jones himself; Jones, joined by Stacy, swearing and perspiring, made the end of the jibstay fast to the mizzenmast. At this point Jones, preternaturally self-possessed, delivered a little sermon to his sailing master that might have come right out of *Poor Richard's Almanack:* "Mr. Stacy, it is no time for swearing now, you may by the next moment be in eternity; but let us do our duty." The two ships were now lashed together, bow to stern; the *Serapis,* struggling desperately to get free, dropped her anchor, which brought her head into the wind but did nothing to extricate her from the *Bonhomme Richard.*

Now the outcome of the battle rested on the little groups of sailors and French soldiers in the three tops. They, and especially those in the maintop under the command of Lieutenant Stack, had performed their duties with exemplary skill and courage; they had cleared their counterparts out of the tops of the *Serapis* or supressed their fire and cleared the decks of enemy sailors and marines. Lieutenant Fanning, stationed in the maintop, estimated that the tops of the *Serapis* had been silenced within an hour after the start of the battle. "The topmen in our tops had taken possession of the enemy's tops," he noted, "which was done by reason of the Serapis's yards being locked together with ours, that we could with ease go from our main top into the enemy's fore top; and so, from our fore top into the Serapis's main top . . . we transported from our own into the enemy's tops . . . hand grenades, &, which we threw in among the enemy whenever they made their appearance."

The deck and tops of the *Serapis* were thus cleared, "except one man in her fore-top, who would once in a while peep out from behind the head of the enemies foremast and fire into our tops." Fanning ordered the marines in the maintop to hold their fire until the man stuck his head up again and then let him have it, "which they did, and we soon saw this skulking tar, or marine, fall out of the top upon the enemies' fore-castle."

One of the principal hazards of Fanning's position in the maintop was that the mainmast of the *Bonhomme Richard* had been pierced twice by eighteen-pounder shot from the *Serapis* and was standing erect by virtue of those shrouds that remained and a few splinters of wood. The ships now lay so close that the main batteries could not be fired. There was not room enough to sponge and load them, but the *Serapis* kept up a damaging fire with the four of her bow guns that were farthest aft— two eighteen-pounders on the lower gun deck and two nine-pounders on the upper gun deck. Jones was a major factor here. He directed the fire of one nine-pounder against the mast of the *Serapis* with double-headed shot and ordered the other two loaded with grape and canister.

At this point the light sails over the quarter-deck of the *Serapis* caught fire. The flames spread through the rigging and to the sails and stays of the *Bonhomme Richard,* and for a time the battle stopped while the crews of both ships worked frantically to extinguish the fires that threatened to consume them in a general conflagration.

While the decks and tops of the *Serapis* were cleared, the Americans belowdecks in an inferno of smoke and fire were convinced that the battle was lost. Word spread that Jones himself had been killed with all his officers and that the *Bonhomme Richard,* with five feet of water in the hold, was sinking fast. The crew belowdecks thus prevailed on one of the gunner's mates to go above and beg quarter of the British captain before they were all sunk in the sea. "Three men being thus delegated," Fanning recalled, "mounted to the quarter-deck, and bawled out as loud as they could, 'Quarters, quarter's, for God's sake, quarters! our ship is sinking!'" Fanning, hearing the cry from his post in the maintops, was convinced that it came from the *Serapis*, but he soon saw the three men trying to haul down the colors, still calling for quarter. At this moment Jones, perceiving what was happening, abandoned his injunction against swearing and shouted, "What damn rascals are them—shoot them—kill them!" Abashed, the men headed for a nearby hatch, but not before Jones had hurled his empty pistol at the gunner like a lightning bolt. The man's skull was fractured by the blow, and he lay unconscious at the foot of the gangway ladder until the battle was over. Once more fire leaped through the sails, and flaming pieces of canvas fell on the decks of the *Serapis* and the *Bonhomme Richard.* Once more the battle was interrupted while the frantic crews worked to put out the fire, in some instances taking off their coats and jackets and trying to smother the blaze. With the fires under control, Captain Pearson's aide called out to ask if the *Bonhomme Richard* had indeed surrendered and, if so, why she had not struck her colors. "Ay, ay," Jones replied, "we'll do that when we can fight no longer, but we shall see yours come down first; for you must know, that Yankees do not haul down their colours till they are fairly beaten."

That (at least as Fanning recollected it) was rather a long and somewhat pompous speech for the middle of a desperate battle (The line "I have not yet begun to fight," a considerable literary if not historical improvement, did not appear until an account of the battle by Richard Dale, written in 1825. There is no earlier statement that puts these words in Jones's mouth, and Jones himself did not claim to have said them. If he had turned such a splendid phrase in the midst of the battle he would hardly have failed to remember it. His own version was: "I answered him [Pearson's aide] in the most determined negative. . . .")

The battle thus continued, interrupted from time to time by the flaring up of fires and carried on now by hand-to-hand fighting with hand grenades, stink-pots (the eighteenth-century equivalent of tear gas), lances, and boarding pikes. "With these," Fanning wrote, "the combatants killed each other through the ships' port holes, which were pretty large. . . ."

The British eighteen-pounders continued to fire at pointblank range and with devasting effect. Belowdecks the carnage was terrible to look upon; everything seemed lost. Dead and dying men were everywhere; the bulkheads were spattered with blood and human flesh; fires were raging and water pouring in the splintered hull, so that men hardly knew whether they were to be burned alive or drowned. Parties from both ships made repeated efforts to board each other, but were driven back with heavy losses.

At this point the only hope for the battered *Bonhomme Richard* was to hold fast to her tormentor. The commander of the *Serapis* tried every way to get loose from the grip of her foundering enemy, but the *Bonhomme Richard* clung with a fierce tenacity born of the knowledge that her only hope was to inhabit the body of her opponent.

Where was the *Alliance* all this time? Captain Landais, along with the *Pallas,* had been engaged with the *Countess of Scarborough.* Now he appeared in the knick of time as though to administer the *coup de grâce* to the desperate *Serapis.* Instead he discharged a broadside "full into the stern of the Bonhomme Richard," in Jones's words. In spite of frantic signals from her sister ship, the *Alliance* tacked and fired again. It was now nighttime, but the moon was full. The *Bonhomme Richard* was painted entirely black, while the *Serapis* was yellow. Three lanterns, the *Bonhomme Richard's* signals of identification, were put out, but still the firing continued. At this point, Jones's "treacherous master-at-arms" let loose some two hundred prisoners confined belowdecks, apparently in the conviction that the battle was lost and that they must otherwise go down with the ship. One of the freed officers climbed through the ports of the *Serapis* and told the captain of that vessel [Pearson] "that if he would hold out only a little while longer, the ship alongside would either strike or sink. . . ." Jones could hardly be charged with exaggeration when he wrote, "My situation was really deplorable." His officers urged him to strike his colors, but Jones, with the spirit of the true zealot, was determined to triumph or go down with his whole crew. The frightened prisoners were put to work manning the pumps and were thus neutralized. The mainmast of the *Serapis* began to shake, and the firing of her guns slackened, while the American fire seemed to grow brisker. At this point came one of those chance occurrences that so often determine the outcome of a battle. The British gunners, in serving their eighteen-pounders, had accumulated a number of cartridges on the gun deck. A grenade, dropped down the hatch from the maintop of the *Serapis* by an American sailor in an effort to get at a group of British sailors who were huddled between the gun decks, struck the combings of a hatchway, bounced off, and fell between the decks, where it ignited loose powder around the guns and "made a dreadful explosion." More than twenty gunners and crewmen were blown to pieces, and the clothes were blown off a number of others.

The explosion on the gun deck was the last straw for Pearson. The British captain had done all an experienced and courageous officer could do, and still the teeth of this mad American were fastened on his jugular vein. Pearson, swearing and gasconading, called for quarter and ordered his ship's colors to be struck. But no crewman dared to mount the quarter-deck to pull down the pendant. They were afraid of the American riflemen in the tops, they told Pearson, believing from the accuracy of the American fire that the muskets of the Americans and French soldiers were the legendary rifles. Pearson himself was finally forced to climb to the quarter-deck and haul down "the very flag which he had nailed to the flag-staff a little before the commencement of the battle; and which flag he had at that time, in the presence of his principal officers, swore he would never strike to that infamous pirate J. P. Jones."

The most bitterly fought naval engagement of the Revoultion had come to such an end that it was hard to distinguish the victor from the vanquished. The difference was measured by the margin of a *will;* the unyielding will of John Paul Jones versus the more human will of his opponent. The loss of life and the terrible wounds suffered by men on both sides made a doleful tally. Of the slightly more than three hundred men on board the *Bonhomme Richard,* a hundred and fifty were killed or wounded in the four-hour battle. To sustain such casualties and be able to claim victory was without precedent in naval warfare. The British, out of a crew approximately the same size, listed forty-nine killed and sixty-eight wounded, a total of a hundred and seventeen. The damage to the rickety *Bonhomme Richard* was much greater of course than that suffered by the *Serapis.* Jones reported that both sides of his ship for a considerable distance were entirely shot away, so that cannonballs could pass through without striking anything.

The first thing to attend to after the battle were the wounded. In Fanning's words, "To see the dead lying in heaps—to hear the groans of the wounded and dying—the entrails of the dead scattered promiscuously around, the *(American too) over ones shoes,* was enough to move pity from the most hardened and *callous breast."* At this point in Fanning's narrative of the battle he added, "Although my spirit was somewhat dampened at this shocking sight, yet when I came to reflect that we were *conquerors,* and over those who wished to bind America in chains of everlasting slavery; my spirits revived, and I thought perhaps that some faithful historian would at some future period enrol me among the heroes and deliverers of my country. Pardon me, gentle reader, for this involuntary digression, and let this be my excuse, that I felt the spirit which infused courage into my breast on the night of and during the battle which I have just given you a faithful relation of, even while my pen was tracing the dreadful conflict."

As one of those "faithful historians" Fanning appealed to, I am glad to do my bit to "enrol" him "among the heroes and deliverers" of his country. Certainly he belongs there, for his bravery and for his narrative.

There was only one competent surgeon aboard the squadron, a Virginian named Brooks, and many of the wounded died because of the incompetence of the surgeons who attended them. Fanning tells us that "the greater part of the wounded had their legs or arms shot away, or the bones so badly fractured that they were obliged to suffer under the operation of amputation." There was no anesthetic of course, and men bore the pain of their wounds and operations as best they could.

Jones sent a boarding party headed by Lieutenant Dale to the *Serapis,* and soon after, the British officers followed Pearson on board the *Bonhomme Richard.* Pearson, ungracious to the end, handed his sword to Jones, saying, "It is with the greatest reluctance that I am now obliged to resign you this, for it is painful to me, more particularly at this time, when compelled to deliver up my sword to a man, who may be said to fight *with a* halter around his neck!"

To this bit of insolence, Jones replied, "Sir, you have fought like a hero, and I make no doubt but your sovereign will reward you in a most ample manner for it," thereby winning the battle of words as decisively as he had won the naval encounter. Pearson, chastened by Jones's gallant reply to his rudeness, then asked "What countrymen his crew principally consisted of." "Americans," Jones answered.

"Very well," said Pearson, with another bit of snobbery, directed this time at the French, "it had been *diamond cut diamond* with us"; the two captains then withdrew to Jones's cabin, where, after the custom of the day, "they drank a glass or two of wine together," and complimented each other on the bravery of their respective officers and crews, a bravery to be accounted for, presumably, by the fact that they were all Englishmen in the marrow of their bones and the corpuscles of their blood.

Pearson, however, had a final bit of rudeness to deliver. His silver service and plate aboard the *Serapis,* along with his personal belongings (clothing excepted), belonged, according to the rules of war, to his captors, but Jones, in a courteous gesture, sent Pearson's things back to him by one of his officers. The officer returned with Pearson's trunks and the word that he could not receive such a favor from a rebel officer, intimating that he would accept them if they were sent in the name of the captain of the *Pallas,* who held a legitimate commission from the king of France. Jones requested Captain Cottineau to perform the mission. The Frenchman did so, returning with word that Pearson had accepted the trunks "but had not condescended to return any thanks or complements to [Jones]," which in Fanning's very proper opinion "shewed a great want of good breeding and politeness. . . ."

When Fanning went belowdecks with several fellow officers to get the officers' trunks in anticipation of the sinking of the *Bonhomme Richard,* he discovered that there was hardly a piece of clothing as large as a paper dollar left. "Tis true," he wrote, "we found several shirts, coats, etc. but so shockingly were they pierced with the enemy's shot, round and grape, that they were of no value." The hull was so shattered that, in Fanning's judgment, a coach-and-six could have driven right through it. "Upon the whole," Fanning wrote, "I think this battle, and every circumstance attending it minutely considered, may be ranked with propriety, the most bloody, the hardest fought, and the greatest scene of carnage on both sides, ever fought between two ships of war of any nation under heaven." It was certainly the bloodiest and most stubbornly fought naval battle of the American Revolution.

The *Countess of Scarborough* had been engaged by the *Pallas,* with the *Alliance* giving little or no help. For two hours the more heavily armed *Pallas* exchanged broadsides with the British ship, until all the British ship's braces, much of her rigging, and her main and mizzen topsails were shot away, seven of her twenty guns dismounted, and four men killed and twenty wounded. At that point she was surrendered to the *Pallas*. The action of Captain Landais and the *Alliance* can only be explained by the cowardice or jealousy of that officer. His vindictiveness against Jones appears to have been so great that he was willing to see the *Bonhomme Richard* destroyed (and indeed to contribute to its destruction) in order to be able to attack the *Serapis* and claim credit for the victory. Landais, charged by Jones with cowardice and treachery, first challenged the captain of the *Pallas* to a duel in which he wounded him seriously, and then sent a challenge to Jones who "perhaps not thinking it prudent to expose himself with a single combatant, who was a complete master of the small sword," declined the challenge and ordered Landais arrested.

Reading Jones's or Fanning's account of the battle, one gets the impression that the batteries of the *Bonhomme Richard* were relatively ineffective and were soon put out of action except for the three nine-pounders that Jones himself directed, two of which were loaded with grape and canister to sweep the decks of the *Serapis*. However, the damage sustained by the *Serapis,* which, like her opponent, was a "mere wreck" after the battle, suggests that the lighter American guns had played havoc aboard the British vessel. The three masts of the *Serapis* fell into the water soon after the end of the engagement, and the ship was so badly hulled that, in Fanning's estimation, a ton of water a minute was pumped out of the hold for four hours as the carpenters worked to plug the holes.

The *Bonhomme Richard* had taken five feet of water in its hold; one pump had been destroyed by enemy fire and the other three were barely able to maintain that level. There were numerous fires, one so close to the powder magazine that Jones ordered the powder brought on deck so it could be jettisoned if necessary. The next day the ship's carpenters declared the vessel beyond salvaging, and twenty-four hours later, with a freshening sea making it impossible to keep the *Bonhomme Richard* from taking more water, the ship was abandoned and sank. The problem now was to make sufficient repairs to the *Serapis* to enable her to get back to a French port before she was recaptured by British warships. The twenty-fourth and twenty-fifth were given over to making the most essential repairs, but the ship drifted before the wind and could not be sailed until the twenty-eighth, when a jury-rigged mainmast was "gott up" and the squadron made sail to the eastward. It was just in time. Eight British war ships were on Jones's trail, or wake, but although the squadron was "tossing about to and fro in the North Seas for ten days in contrary winds and bad weather," waiting to gain the port of Dunkirk in order to unload the prisoners, the British failed to find them, and the squadron dropped anchor at the Dutch port of Texel on the third of October.

The triumph of the *Bonhomme Richard* over the *Serapis* brought Jones all the glory he had so coveted. To a country starved for victories, Jones's epic battle was like food to a starving man. The feast was made the sweeter because it had happened in the enemy's own waters, under the very nose of the British navy. Every detail was eagerly sought and relished to the full. Captain John Paul Jones, already respected as a naval officer, became a national hero overnight; his name was on every tongue. The victory produced a spate of patriotic ballads, poems, and eulogies. In England the enemies of the government used the occasion to ridicule Lord Sandwich, "Jeremy Twitcher," and Lord North:

> If success to our fleets be not quickly restor'd
> The leaders in office to shove from the board,
> May they all fare alike and the d'il pick their bones,
> Of Germain, Jemmy Twitcher, Lord North and Paul Jones.

Another ballad that was widely circulated hailed Jones as a hero:

> An American Frigate, call'd the *Richard* by name
> Mounted guns forty-four, from New York she came,
> To cruise in the channel of old England's fame,
> With a noble commander, Paul Jones was his name.

The ballad then went on to describe the meeting of the *Bonhomme Richard* and the *Serapis:*

> We fought them four glasses, four glasses so hot,
> Till forty bold seamen lay dead on the spot
> And forty-five more lay bleeding in gore,
> While the thund'ring cannons of Paul Jones did roar.

> Our carpenter being frightened, to Paul Jones did say,
> Our ship leaks water, since fighting today,
> Paul Jones made his answer, in the height of his pride,
> If we can do no better we'll sink alongside.

Paul Jones he then smiled and to his men did say
Let every man stand the best of his play,
For broadside for broadside they fought on the main,
Like true British heroes we return'd it again.

The *Serapis* wore round our ship for to rake,
Which made the proud hearts of the English to ache,
The Shot flew so hot we could not stand it long,
Till the bold British colours from the English came down.

"A New Song of Paul Jones," perhaps written to counteract the ballads in praise of him, began:

Come, each loyal Briton of courage so bold
As annals can shew, you would ne'er be controul'd;
It vexes my patience, I'm sure night and day
To think how that traitor, *Paul Jones* got away.
Derry-down, down, hey! derry down.

Several penny novels were produced that purported to tell the story of the battle. One was entitled *The True History of Paul Jones the Notorious Sea Pirate,* and another, which sold for sixpence, *The Life, Voyages and Sea Battles of that Celebrated Seaman, Commodore Paul Jones still remembered by some of the Old Inhabitants now living in Wapping, he being originally in the Coal-Trade.* It is interesting that one of the stories dug up about him was that in reaction to a thrashing given him for not learning his lesson, he took a club, knocked his schoolmaster senseless, and then fled to a man-of-war.

The reaction in Paris to the news of Jones's victory was almost as enthusiastic as it would be in America when word of the engagement reached there a month later. Franklin, who rejoiced in the success of his protégé, wrote Jones, "For some days after the arrival of your express scarce anything was talked of at Paris and Versailles but your cool Conduct & perservering Bravery during the terrible Conflict." John Adams noted dryly that "the cry of Versailles and the Clamour of Paris became as loud in the favour of Monsieur Jones as of Monsieur Franklin, and the inclination of the Ladies to embrace him almost as fashionable and as strong."

When Abigail Adams met Jones in Paris after his victory over the *Serapis* and at the height of his fame, she found him "soft in his speech, easy in his address, polite in his manners, vastly civil, understands all the etiquette of a lady's toilette as perfectly as he does the mast, sails, rigging of his ship. Under all this appearance of softness he is bold, enterprising, ambitious and active. . . he is said to be a man of gallantry and a favorite amongst the French ladies. . . . He knows how often the ladies use their baths, what color best suits a ladies complexion, what cosmetics are most favorable to the skin."

For Americans Jones's victory bore fruit for years to come. Lieutenant Fanning, for instance, whenever he had to listen to Englishmen make bombastic claims about the prowess of the British navy, observed that "on my merely mentioning in their hearing the battle between the Good Man Richard and the Serapis will shut their mouths and walk off humming for some time to themselves as though they did not hear me."

16

The Continuing War at Sea

W HILE Jones refitted and repaired the *Serapis* at Texel, the British
ambassador to Holland demanded "that these ships and their crews may
be stopped and delivered up, which the pirate Paul Jones of Scotland,
who is a rebel subject and a criminal of the state, has taken." The Dutch
procrastinated. Landais was sent to Paris to be court-martialed, and
Jones took command of the *Alliance*. The wounded were cared for, and
arrangements were made for the sale of the prizes and the exchange of
prisoners. In human terms the prisoner exchange was worth the
voyage and the victory that climaxed it. The squadron had taken
enough British prisoners to procure "the release by exchange of all the
Americans confined in England."

At Texel, the men and officers grew impatient for their share of the
prize money realized from the sale of the *Serapis* and the *Countess of
Scarborough*. Jones promised to do his best to procure the money. Finally
it arrived, but when it was distributed it came to only five ducats each for
the officers and one for the sailors and marines (a sum equal to about
five or ten dollars). Some of the sailors "in a fit of rage threw them as far
as they could from the ship into the sea." The rumor spread that Jones
had kept most of the money for himself, and the men were very near to
mutiny. Many of them had had a bellyful of Jones's glory-seeking. They
wanted their money, and they wanted to go home. There was a fierce

clash of wills between the officers and men on one side and Jones on the other. The crew was adamant. They would not sail to any port other than L'Orient, and there they must be paid the money that had been promised them. Jones appeared to give in. They would sail for L'Orient.

The Dutch, under British pressure, finally ordered Jones to sail with the first favorable wind, and it is a commentary on the age of wind-driven sailing vessels that it was four weeks before he could get out of the harbor. Slipping through the British blockade at Texel—intended specifically to hold him in that port or catch him leaving it—Jones and the *Alliance* sailed through the Strait of Dover in sight of the British fleet anchored in the Downs, passed the Isle of Wight "in view of the enemy's fleet at Spithead," and then cruised the Spanish coast off Cape Finisterre. "I believe those John Englishmen who now saw us," Fanning wrote, "thought we were pretty saucy fellows, and they were perhaps the first American colours some of them had ever seen."

As soon as the *Alliance* was at sea, Jones called his officers to his cabin and told them that he intended to cruise at sea for some twenty days before putting into L'Orient. "And he says, with a kind of contemptuous smile, which he was much addicted to: 'Gentlemen, you cannot conceive what an additional honour it will be to all of us, if in cruising a few days we should have the good luck to fall in with an English frigate of our force, and carry her with us . . . this would crown our former victories and our names, in consequence thereof would be handed down to the latest posterity, by some faithful historian of our country.'" This was more glory than the officers wished for, and they were shrewd enough to know that the name that would be passed down to posterity would be Jones's not theirs. They wanted money, not whatever crumbs of fame would be left from their captain's renown. Fanning added a dry little footnote: "Jones had a wonderful notion of his name being handed down to posterity."

With his officers and crew "in a state bordering on mutiny" Jones once more bluffed his way through. His face flushed with anger, he stamped his foot and declared to his officers, "I mean to cruise as long as I please. I do not want your advice. . . . You know my mind. Go to your duty, each of you, and let me hear no more grumbling." The cruise continued, but when Jones came up with a thirty-two gun British frigate, his crew refused to go to battle stations, and Jones had no choice but to turn and run. Fanning could see him "much agitated," biting his lips and muttering to himself as he walked the quarter-deck. It was bitter medicine for him to swallow.

Back in L'Orient, the crew of the *Bonhomme Richard* (Fanning always called it *The Good Man Richard*) had no more luck drawing their prize money. There seemed to be plenty available to refit and indeed reconstruct the *Alliance* to Captain Jones's specifications, but no money for the crew, who were told by the French that it was an American matter and by the Americans that it was all in the hands of the French; in consequence, "a number of Americans became beggars in a foreign country, especially such as had lost their arms and legs in fighting gloriously under the banners of America," as Fanning put it.

The victory of the *Bonhomme Richard* over the *Serapis* proved to be the highpoint of John Paul Jones's career. His ambition and his violent temper involved him in a series of unpleasant episodes and cost him, at least among his officers and crew, much of the popularity that resulted from his great triumph. While he waited for alterations to be made in the *Alliance,* Jones spent his time in Paris. There he had a passionate affair with Delia, the wife of a Scottish expatriate named Count William Murray, who called herself La Comtesse de Nicolson, as well as affairs with La Comtesse de Lowendahl and other glamorous French ladies who were bowled over by the famous Captain Jones. When Franklin directed him to sail for America at once to convoy ships bearing arms and clothing for Washington's army, Jones did not return directly to L'Orient but dallied at Nantes, where he was lavishly entertained by a week of fetes and parties. When one French lady asked him if he had ever been wounded, he replied, "Never at sea, but I have been hit by arrows that were never discharged by the English!" In response the lady presented him with a cockade, which he promised to wear in battle.

While Jones pleased himself by partying and romancing, Captain Landais, with the active connivance of Arthur Lee, plotted to regain command of the *Alliance.* It was enough for Lee that Jones was Franklin's protégé. He persuaded Landais that his commission from Congress was still good. Landais came to L'Orient and, drawing on the loyalty of some of his former officers and sailors and on the dissatisfaction of many of the men who had sailed under Jones, prevailed on 115 of them to sign a statement saying that they wished Landais to take command of the ship. The letter was sent to Franklin, and with that Landais boarded the *Alliance* and took command of the vessel. Franklin wrote at once to warn Jones of what was afoot: "You are likely to have great trouble. I wish you well through it."

When Jones finally got back to L'Orient and found that his treacherous subordinate had outwitted him, he was beside himself. "Never, I am confident," Fanning wrote, "was a man so dreadfully enraged. His passion knew no bounds; and in the first paroxysm of his rage he acted more like a mad man than a conqueror." Jones immediately began to try to recover the command of his ship, but to his fury Landais and the *Alliance* got safely out of the harbor and made sail for America.

On the return voyage of the *Alliance,* according to the Chevalier de Pontgibaud, Landais was carving a turkey and Arthur Lee helped himself to the liver and was about to eat it "when Landais rose in a fury, and threatened to kill him with the carving-knife." There was a scene of wild confusion, Lee trying to elude the knife while his nephews ran off to find some sailors to prevent their uncle from being murdered by Landais, who shouted that "the best morsel belonged by right to the captain." When Pontgibaud roared with laughter, Landais started after him, "raving mad." Landais was disarmed and bound and confined to his cabin, and the ship proceeded under the command of the first mate. There was ample irony in the fact that Landais had turned on his fellow plotter and principal advocate, Arthur Lee. It might be considered only a proper reward for all the Virginian's troublemaking. In America, Landais was court-martialed and dismissed from the navy.

If Jones had been attending to business, he would not have had his ship stolen out from under him. The episode seems to have served only to make him more choleric and unpredictable. He was given another ship, the *Ariel,* and sailed it to America to bask in the adulation of his adopted country and receive the gratitude of Congress. Although senior officers blocked the move to make him a rear admiral, he was given command in June, 1781, of the still-unfinished *American,* which was to be armed with seventy-six guns, thus becoming by far the largest ship in the navy.

One issue on which Jones was vulnerable was the delay in the sailing of the *Alliance*, which had been filled with desperately needed supplies for the American army. There was more than a suspicion that Jones had delayed the sailing of the *Alliance* in order to pursue his own interests in France. The navy board asked very pointed questions of Jones when he arrived in the United States, among them, "What prevented your sailing with the Alliance when you last commanded her, from the time she was refitted and ready to put to sea to the time Capt'n Landais retook possession of her? . . . Were any vessels taken up before his sailing to bring over the clothing and military stores of the United States to America?" These were serious charges. They raised the question of whether Jones, in his desire for naval glory, had held up supplies destined for Washington's army. If this was the case, it helps to explain Arthur Lee's activities in aiding and abetting Landais in seizing the *Alliance*. In all, the navy board had forty-seven embarrassing questions to ask Jones about his failure to expedite the sailing of the *Alliance* and about his highly irregular and independent actions in regard to the series of ships that had passed under his command, from the *Ranger* to the *Ariel*. It is clear that Jones was, to a degree, a victim of the feud between the supporters of Arthur Lee and the adherents of Franklin. Nonetheless, it seems equally clear that he persistently placed his own interests and ambitions ahead of those of his adopted country. Jones replied, item by item, to the queries of the board of admiralty, giving answers that were plausible enough but that left a good many points unresolved. The board, however, exonerated both Franklin and Jones himself of any blame in the delay of the military material, found the fault in Landais's seizure of the *Alliance*, and ended its report to Congress with the statement that Captain Jones had "made the flag of America respectable among the flags of other nations," and that "returning from Europe he brought with him the esteem of the greatest and best friend of America . . . ," the king of France.

The outfitting of the *American* dragged on until the following year, when the war was to all intents and purposes over. To complete and finish the outfitting was too expensive an undertaking for Congress. The ship was turned over to the French, and Jones' career as an American naval officer was over. Like George Rogers Clark and Henry Lee, Jones could not accommodate himself to a peacetime existence. Increasingly eccentric and embittered, he accepted a commission from Catherine the Great to serve in the Russian navy and commanded a squadron in the Black Sea, but his bad temper and sexual aggressiveness kept him in hot water. He was accused of having raped a young girl and was relieved of his command amid scandal and recrimination. He returned to Paris in bad health and perhaps more than a little mad. Two years later, in 1792, he died in France. His body was placed in a lead coffin filled with brandy and buried in an obscure grave. It was exhumed in 1905, brought to the United States, and placed in a handsome crypt at the United States Naval Academy.

We like to believe that our heroes are exemplary figures. That is certainly not the case with John Paul Jones. From the beginning his career was clouded by acts of intemperance and violence. A fever of ambition raged in him and brought him, finally, the fame that he sought, but it ravaged him like a disease, alienated most of his friends (among them many of the men who had sailed with him and knew his genius at first hand), and finally destroyed him. The history of the American navy in the last two years of the war is overshadowed by the exploits of Jones and by the controversies that surrounded him. Of those few geniune American military or naval geniuses that the Revolution produced, perhaps only Benedict Arnold is a less admirable figure.

While Jones's stunning victory over the *Serapis* was the most famous naval engagement of the Revolution, it was by no means the only notable triumph. In June, 1780, the *Protector*, a twenty-six gun frigate built and commissioned by the state of Massachusetts and captained by John Foster Williams, was cruising off the coast of Newfoundland when it encountered the *Admiral Duff*, a British privateer of thirty-two guns out of St. Kitts loaded with tobacco and sugar. When a typical Grand Banks fog lifted, the officers and crew of the *Protector* saw the large British ship to the windward. To the nervous Americans it appeared as big as a seventy-four-gun ship of the line. All hands were piped to quarters, and hammocks were brought out and stuffed in the nettings alongside the ship's gunwales to provide additional protection against enemy cannonballs. The decks were wetted and sanded to give a better footing to the crew, and the guns were run forward into firing position. The *Admiral Duff* tried to pull ahead of the *Protector* and then hove to under fighting sail. The American ship, flying British colors, came about on the stern of the *Admiral Duff* and pulled up under her lee quarter. There her aft guns could be warped to bear on the enemy, and Williams gave the order to fire a broadside and run up the American flag. The *Admiral Duff* replied with a volley and three cheers. The British vessel, riding much higher than the *Protector,* overshot her, cutting the rigging, while the American cannonballs buried themselves in the hull of the *Admiral Duff* between wind and water. In this fashion, only a pistol shot away from each other, the two ships exchanged broadsides for half an hour. Lieutenant Luther Little, a midshipman on the *Protector,* saw a fellow midshipman struck in the head by a cannon shot—"his brains flew over my face and my gun."

As in the battle between the *Bonhomme Richard* and the *Serapis* a year earlier, the American marines drove their counterparts from the tops and killed the helmsman. The *Admiral Duff,* without a hand at the rudder, swung down on the *Protector,* her cathead—a heavy iron piece projecting from the forecastle to support the anchor—staving in the quarter galley. In a remarkable reenactment of the earlier battle, Williams ordered the jib boom lashed to the main shrouds. The marines, firing into the portholes, kept the British sailors and marines from attempting to board. Just as the Americans were about to board the *Admiral Duff,* the lashings broke and the British ship swung away. As it did, the *Protector* fired another broadside that cut away the enemy's mizzenmast "and made great havoc." The main topgallant sail caught fire, dropped down the rigging, and ignited a hogshead of cartridges on the quarter-deck, which, blowing up, added to the confusion and demoralization on board the *Admiral Duff.* At the port near the stern where Lieutenant Little directed the crew of his fourteen-pounder, a charge of grape wounded him and scattered his men. One grapeshot passed between his backbone and windpipe and one through his jaw, lodging in the roof of his mouth and taking off a piece of his tongue. Another penetrated his upper lip, "taking away part and all my upper teeth." He had fired his gun nineteen times during the course of the battle. He was carried off, bleeding profusely, as one mortally wounded, to the cockpit, and there he was left to die while those less seriously injured received the attention of the ship's surgeon.

A few minutes later the *Admiral Duff* sank, all colors flying. Fifty-five sailors and marines, half of them wounded, were rescued out of a crew numbering more than two hundred. Some of those rescued by the boats of the *Protector* tried to jump out, preferring to die rather than be captured. Lieutenant Little recovered to tell the dramatic story. Another midshipman, Edward Preble, went on to become commander of the American squadron in the Mediterranean during the Tripolitan War.

The American losses were one killed and five wounded out of two hundred officers and men.

The battle was perhaps the most notable success of a state-commissioned vessel during the war. The *Admiral Duff* was a larger ship than the *Protector,* with more guns. We do not, however, know the caliber of the guns of the *Duff,* though we know that the *Protector's* main batteries were fourteen-pounders. In any event the *Protector* clearly outsailed and outfought the *Duff* and won a lopsided victory that was hailed with the greatest enthusiasm in Massachusetts, where John Foster Williams was enthusiastically applauded and songs and poems were written in his honor. When Massachusetts ratified the Federal Constitution in 1788, a ship was built on wheels to be dragged through the streets of Boston, and John Foster Williams, as the most distinguished naval figure of the town, commanded it:

John Foster Williams in a ship
Joined in the Social band, sir,
And made the lasses dance and skip
To see him sail on land, Sir.
Yankee Doodle, keep it up!
Yankee Doodle, dandy,
Mind the music and the step,
And with the girls be handy.

In home waters, the naval operations of the minute American fleet centered, in 1780, on the siege of Charles Town by the British. Sent to assist in the defense of that city, the frigates *Providence, Boston, Queen of France,* and the *Ranger* passed into the Charles Town Harbor, where they were trapped by the British fleet. The *Queen of France,* along with ten other vessels, most of them belonging to the South Carolina navy, was sunk in the Cooper River; the other frigates withdrew up the river and were captured when Charles Town surrendered. The *Providence, Boston,* and *Ranger* were taken into British service. The *Trumbull,* which had been launched in 1776 and had lain in the Connecticut River for three years, unable to pass over the bar at the mouth of the river, finally got out in 1779 and began cruising in April, 1780, under Captain James Nicholson. A few weeks after she put to sea, she joined battle with a heavily armed British privateer, the *Watt.* Outgunned, the *Trumbull* fought a long and bloody battle in which she lost all her masts and had eight men killed and thirty-one wounded, of whom nine later died. The British ship was badly damaged, with eleven men killed and seventy-nine wounded, and the battle, which lasted for five hours, ended in a draw, as neither ship could continue the action. An officer on the *Trumbull* counted 62 shots through the ensign sail, 157 through the mizzen, 560 through the mainsail, and 180 through the foresail. Nicholson had special praise for his crew, "almost the whole of them green country lads, many of them not clear of their sea-sickness. . . ."

Had the *Watt* been a ship of the British navy, the bravery and persistence of Nicholson in this engagement would have been more celebrated. As it was, the encounter did little except to demonstrate what hardly needed demonstrating, that Americans, under the proper conditions, could sail and fight every bit as well as their former masters.

At the end of 1780 the American navy consisted of the frigates *Alliance, Confederacy, Deane,* and *Trumbull,* the latter in the process of being practically rebuilt after her battle with the *Watt.* The British navy had, in the same time, grown from 480 ships to 538. But if the American navy languished, privateering flourished, and Congress issued over 300 letters of marque to private enterprisers who captured 596 British vessels, of which 262 were recaptured. The British, for their part, captured 237 vessels including 34 privateers; only four American vessels were recaptured. Thus the tally stood 334 British merchantmen captured as opposed to 233 American vessels, giving the Americans a favorable balance of 100, although it may well be that the British ships were of substantially greater tonnage than the American.

The *Trumbull,* which had given such a good account of herself in her encounter with the *Watt,* did not get to sea again until August, 1781, when she sailed with a convoy of twenty-eight merchantmen. The day the fleet left port, three sails were sighted to the northeast. A squall carried away the *Trumbull's* foretopmast and main topgallantmast. In such condition she was easily overtaken by two enemy ships, which turned out ironically to be the former *General Hancock,* now the British frigate *Iris* of thirty-two guns, and a former American privateer, the *General Washington,* now renamed the *General Monck* and carrying eighteen guns.

When Captain Samuel Nicholson, brother of the James Nicholson who had commanded the *Trumbull* in the battle against the *Watt,* ordered his men to their battle stations, three-quarters of them ran below and extinguished the lights and matches used to fire the cannon. With the handful of loyal men and officers of the ship, Nicholson attempted a feeble defense that lasted for an hour and thirty-five minutes before the American captain, seeing that any further resistance was futile, struck his colors. The men who had betrayed the ship were mostly British prisoners pressed into service when American sailors could not be lured from their more lucrative service aboard privateers. The loss of the *Trumbull* completed the roster of the thirteen frigates commissioned in 1775. Only the *Alliance* and the *Deane,* built later, remained afloat to represent the United States Navy.

But the privateers swarmed more numerously than ever, and the British suffered, in consequence, their heaviest losses of the war in 1781. Five hundred and eighty-seven merchantmen were captured and 38 privateers; of these, 217 were recaptured or ransomed, leaving a gain of 408. England in turn captured 317, including 40 privateers, of which ten were recaptured. The Americans thus ended the year with a modest balance in their favor of 101—small return, really, for the enormous effort and energy expended. The most significant point was that as the navy dwindled away, what we might call "the private sector" largely took its place. The simple fact was that all of the efforts of the British navy, growing more formidable each year, were not enough to prevent American privateers from exacting an increasingly heavy toll of merchant shipping. On the sea as on land, the power of Great Britain could not crush a resistance that waxed rather than waned as the months passed.

It could be argued in retrospect that the sporadic efforts of Congress to create a Continental Navy were an exercise in futility; that the resources expended on the navy, modest as they were, might have been better spent in supplying Washington's army, or supporting the navies of the individual states. On the other hand the United States was made up from Maryland northward of states whose prosperity depended on ocean-going commerce. It thus seemed to many members of Congress essential to establish a navy of some kind. Had the "militia" navies of the various states been placed under the Continental flag, the result would have certainly been a navy formidable in numbers, but it would still have been unable to contest the control of the Atlantic waters with the great ships of the line that led the British fleet. If to the navies of the respective states could have been added the men and ships absorbed by privateering, the American navy would, again in numbers, have been formidable indeed. But this was never a practical possibility. The large profit to be made (and lost) in privateering made that activity irresistibly attractive to great numbers of sailors and entrepreneurs. The cruises of the privateers, endlessly renewed, corresponded to the militia or guerrilla warfare of the South or the partisan fighters of the Western frontier, where civilian levies, mowed down by British regulars, seemed to spring from the soil in successive crops, each one more stubbornly resistant than the last. So while the Continental Navy, rather like the Army, declined in numbers, the ubiquitous privateers grew more numerous with each passing year.

There are, certainly, striking analogies between the anonymous privateers and their endless struggle with the elements as well as with the British, and the equally anonymous groups of patriots who, largely on their own initiative, continued to resist British domination in fields and forests, towns and hamlets, far from the center stage where the Revolution is presumed to have been fought out. What finally defeated the British was not so much the surrender of Cornwallis at Yorktown as what that event symbolized—that America was determined to fight on, forever if need be, in order to be master of its own destiny. And in the slow and reluctant awareness of that sobering fact, the ceaseless activities of the privateers, as well as the resilience of the farmers of the Southern pine barrens, the over-the-mountain men of the Holston and Watauga valleys, and the yeomen of New England and the Mohawk Valley, played a crucial part.

It is also significant that while Yorktown brought a virtual end to formal military operations, hostilities continued on the sea and between patriot and Tory until the Treaty of Paris, almost two years later.

PART IX

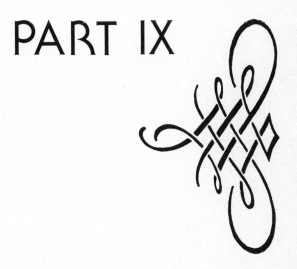

From Savannah to Briar Creek

A FTER the events of 1778—the Battle of Monmouth and the abortive operation against Newport—the scene of the war shifted to the Southern states. The British ministry, having seen its armies defeated in the North at Saratoga and fought or maneuvered to a standstill in the Jerseys and Pennsylvania, now placed its hopes on a successful campaign in Georgia and the Carolinas, where, they were assured, tens of thousands of Loyalists waited only for some sign of encouragement from the mother country to rise and rout the rebels.

In Georgia, at least, there was ample reason for British optimism. The key to Georgia politics during the early years of the Revolution lay in the bitter opposition between Button Gwinnett and Lachlan McIntosh. Gwinnet, who is known to posterity chiefly as the signer of the Declaration of Independence with the fewest surviving (and thus most valuable) signatures, was leader of the radical Whigs. He was indignant when the conservative Whigs, who still controlled the legislature, elected McIntosh as colonel of Georgia's Continental battalion. Gwinnett was president of the state and McIntosh commander of the state's Continental forces when an expedition was undertaken against St. Augustine with McIntosh as commander in chief. The rivalry of the two men had much to do with the failure of the enterprise and led to bitter recrimination between them. The arrest of McIntosh's brother, George, by Gwinnett on the charge of treason (he was later exonerated by Congress) increased the hostility between Gwinnett and McIntosh until the state of Georgia was virtually paralyzed by the struggle for power between them and their adherents. The Georgia assembly, by that time firmly under Gwinnett's control, undertook to adjudicate the dispute about the expedition against St. Augustine. When Gwinnett was vindicated, McIntosh denounced him before the assembly as "A Scoundrell & lying Rascal." In Georgia such an insult could only be wiped out by a duel, and Gwinnett challenged McIntosh. The duel was fought in a field outside Savannah; both men were wounded, Gwinnett the more seriously. He died three days later, thereby helping to insure the rarity of his autograph.

The movement among Gwinnett's friends to have McIntosh removed from his command was thwarted when McIntosh's friends in Congress arranged to have him transferred to Washington's staff for reassignment. Class rivalry was certainly an element in the dispute. Gwinnett represented the "new men," and McIntosh the established leaders of the state.

The bitterness of the division in Georgia is suggested by a letter from John Wereat, a supporter of the McIntosh faction, to a friend in August, 1777. "Honesty, integrity and love of justice," Wereat wrote, "had now become crimes sufficient to secure [an individual] the hateful name of Tory." The laws of Georgia, he charged, had been determined at "a nightly meeting in a tavern," by a group of self-appointed legislators. "We now have another Nocturnal Society established, who have arrogated to themselves the name of the *Liberty Society*. The business of this Cabal," Wereat wrote, " . . . seems to be principally to poison the minds of the people throughout the State, and to set them at enmity with every Man who is not of their party. They . . . bellow Liberty but take every method in their power to deprive the best part of the Community of even the shadow of it. Those wretches seem to me to have a manifest intention to destroy the reputations of their neighbors in order to raise themselves—fortunes and political fame upon the ruins of the real friends of their Country, and the American cause. . . ." As the reader might by now have suspected Gwinnett's friends had attacked Wereat himself as well as McIntosh.

For several months in the summer of 1778, Georgia was virtually without a government. On August 10, after several fruitless attempts to form one, some members of the assembly met at Augusta and elected nine of their number to constitute a supreme executive council, headed by John Wereat. Wereat at once appealed to General Benjamin Lincoln for assistance. Georgia was in a desperate way, Wereat wrote; some evidence of support from Congress was essential if the spirits of the people were to be kept up. The "great defection" of the interior country of the Carolinas was well known. The Indians were only waiting for the arrival of presents to join forces with the British. If the British advanced into the interior country, "the greatest part of the inhabitants, worn out with fruitless opposition, and actuated by fear of losing their *all,* would make terms for themselves; and, as the human mind is too apt to be led by a natural gradation, from one step of infamy to another," it would not be long until they joined the enemy, "against their countrymen in any other state. . . ." In addition, "a great many families, harassed, & unsupported, would remove far northwardly, for which they are already thinking of preparing. . . ." The Georgia militia were indignant that the Carolina militia received thirty dollars a month while they received only six, "which is so perfect a trifle, that they scarcely think it worth receiving." In short, Georgia desperately needed money, supplies, and a force of Continental soldiers in order to defend the state against the expected British attack.

It was hardly surprising under such circumstances that Clinton had high hopes for his "Southern Campaign" and chose as its first objective the town of Savannah. Lieutenant Colonel Archibald Campbell left Sandy Hook, New Jersey, on November 27 with thirty-five hundred troops in a squadron commanded by Commodore Hyde Parker. A month later the fleet anchored near Tybee Island at the mouth of the Savannah River. The little army was made up of the Seventy-first Regiment, two battalions of Hessians, four battalions of Loyalist troops, and a battery of artillery. General Augustine Prevost, British commander in East Florida, had been ordered by Clinton to march north to join forces with Campbell in the attack on Savannah.

The American force defending the city consisted of about seven hundred regulars and perhaps half as many militia under the command of General Robert Howe, Howe was a North Carolinian, whose family owned one of that colony's great plantations on the Cape Fear River. He had been educated in Europe and had fought as a militia captain in the southern campaigns against the Indians back in 1766 and 1769. In Governor William Tryon's expedition against the Regulators—North Carolina back-countrymen who had rebelled in 1771—Howe had served as an artillery colonel. But like Sullivan and many others, Howe was essentially a political general—that is to say, he received his command more for his prominence as a leading Whig than because of any clearly demonstrated military gifts. He had done well in helping the Virginians take Norfolk and was rewarded by being placed in command of the Southern Department, but his campaign against the British forces in East Florida had been a disaster. The fault was not entirely his. The South Carolinians, whose contempt for their immediate neighbors to the north was hardly less than that of Virginians for, say, the Yankees, or of New Englanders for Pennsylvanians, and who were, in any event, famous snobs, resented being under Howe's direction. The Georgians, likewise, made it clear that they would have preferred to serve under one of their own officers. Christopher Gadsden was one of those whose harassment and criticism Howe particularly resented. When Gadsden refused to retract remarks that Howe considered insulting, Howe challenged him to a duel, and Southerners were treated to the unedifying spectacle of two prominent patriots shooting at each other instead of at the British. Howe's shot grazed Gadsden's ear, and Gadsden fired into the air. Then, honor satisfied, the two became close friends.

Howe was succeeded as commander of the Southern Department by Lincoln in September of 1778, but he remained in command of the defenses of Savannah. Heavily outnumbered, Howe would have been well advised to have joined forces with Lincoln and to have avoided a direct battle with Campbell.

Campbell sent Captain Sir James Baird of the grenadiers ashore with a light infantry company on the night of December 25. Baird encountered two men who have him a convincing account of the defenses of the city and "the most satisfactory intelligence concerning the state of matters at Savannah." From their reports it was clear that Howe's force was a small one, less than half the size of the British army; that he had nevertheless made dispositions to defend the city; and that Lincoln, with a force approximatley the size of Howe's, might be expected to try to join Howe in operations against the British as soon as word of Campbell's arrival reached him.

Under the circumstances, Campbell decided to attack without waiting for the arrival of General Prevost who, when he arrived, would, as Campbell's superior, be in command. Howe had established his main line of defense about half a mile southeast of the town, across a road that led from the point where, judging from the location of the British transports, it seemed most likely that Campbell would land his troops. The road crossed a swamp and was flanked on the river side by a flooded rice field and on the other by a thickly wooded and apparently impenetrable swamp. The American left was made up of Georgia militia under the command of Colonel Samuel Elbert. On the right Colonel Isaac Huger commanded the First South Carolina Rifles and Lieutenant Colonel William Thompson's Third Rangers. Farther to the right Colonel George Walton occupied some buildings with a hundred riflemen of the Georgia militia and a cannon. Two artillery pieces were emplaced in the center of the American lines and one on the left flank. A stream that ran diagonally across the American front from two hundred yards in advance of the defensive positions was extended by a trench dug "at a critical spot between two swamps."

Howe plainly expected that the British would have no choice except to make a frontal attack on the American lines, and while his force was outnumbered almost four to one, he had confidence in the excellent marksmanship of his riflemen; moreover, he had the clear advantage of the ground and every reason to anticipate another Bunker Hill. The initial dispositions of the British for the attack seemed to bear out Howe's assumption.

But Commodore Hyde Parker, commanding the British fleet, was directed by Campbell to drop down the river to a high point of land between Tybee Island and Savannah at Girardeau's Plantation, some two miles below Savannah. The British reached the plantation about four o'clock in the afternoon of the twenty-eighth and routed two American galleys, but the tide turned, several transports were grounded, and the British had to wait until dawn to land. Then Lieutenant Colonel John Maitland, the First Battalion of the Seventy-first Regiment, and the Loyalist company of the New York Volunteers were carried in longboats to a levee. From the levee a narrow causeway led across flooded rice fields to Brewton's Hill, where a small detachment of South Carolina Continentals were deployed. The South Carolinians gave a good account of themselves initially, killing the captain of the leading infantry company and wounding six privates; but it was clear they could make no sustained resistance to the much larger attacking force, and the Scottish Highlanders of the Seventy-first Regiment drove them back, thereby securing a beachhead for the landing of the rest of the British army. In the middle of the afternoon of the twenty-ninth, the advance guard of British light infantry formed some eight hundred yards from the American positions for the attack on the road, with the main body approximately two hundred yards in the rear. "I could discover from the movements of the enemy," Campbell wrote, "that they wished and expected an attack upon their left and I was desirous of cherishing the opinion."

What Howe of course did not know was that Campbell, quite by chance, had come upon an old Negro, a slave named Quamino Dolly, who had offered to guide him to a secret path through the wooded swamp that protected the American left. Colonel Walton, who knew the region intimately, had warned Howe of the hidden trail, but Howe thought that the chances of the British discovering it were too remote to even take account of, and in a sense he was right—the revelation of Quamino Dolly was one of those chance incidents that so often overturn the best-laid plans. Sir James Baird, whose Scottish Highlanders and New York Volunteers had earlier in the day driven back the outpost of the South Carolina Continentals, had withdrawn from the battlefield and moved around to the hidden path on the American flank. While the attention of the American defenders was fixed on the awesome panoply of the main British force deploying for the attack, Baird's detachment reached the White Bluff Road undetected and rushed forward on Walton's flank and rear. Walton was wounded and taken prisoner in the first moments of the engagement, and a large part of his demoralized brigade was wounded or captured.

Campbell timed his attack on the American front to coincide with Baird's assault, and the Americans, after a scattered volley that did little damage, withdrew on orders from Howe. The withdrawal was much closer to a rout than an orderly retreat, although some units, not under direct British pressure, preserved their order in commendable fashion and saved the precious artillery pieces. Indeed Howe, perceiving the disaster that had fallen on Walton's brigade, began the retreat of the troops in the center of the American line so precipitously that a large part of the American left was trapped by the British. The only line of retreat was the causeway over Musgrove's Swamp west to the town. The British drove forward to take the causeway and block the American retreat. Howe and the American center reached it ahead of the British. The American right also got across, although a number of soldiers were wounded by enfilading fire; the remainder of the Americans found the route of escape sealed and took to the rice fields, abandoning their weapons in a desperate attempt to escape. Most of those who could not swim died trying to cross Musgrove Creek, and the majority of those who did not drown were made prisoners. The British captured 38 officers and 415 soldiers, 48 pieces of cannon, and 23 mortars, besides a large amount of ammunition and the shipping in the harbor. Eighty-three Americans were killed and 11 wounded, according to Campbell's count, at the cost of seven British killed and 19 wounded.

The roads leading out of Savannah swarmed with refugees, that always pitiful debris of war. General William Moultrie wrote of seeing "many thousands" of "the poor women and children and Negroes of Georgia" trudging along the dusty roads laden with what few possessions they could carry or trundle in carts and wheel barrows, "traveling to they knew not where, (a spectacle that even moved the hearts of the soldiers)." In the formal accounts of battles and campaigns, the thing most difficult to convey is the tide of human misery and the distress that is the grim and perpetual accompaniment of warfare—the endless tale of homes burned or pillaged, possessions looted, families scattered; of hunger and filth and wretchedness, of fright, anxiety, and the feeling of abandonment.

In Henry Lee's words, "Never was a victory of such magnitude so completely gained, with so little loss. . . ." Whether this was strictly true or not, it was a crushing defeat for Howe, who, although he was later exonerated by court of inquiry, had clearly failed to take proper precautions against surprise.

Pursuing Howe's shattered force through Savannah, the British bayoneted a number of them, including some noncombatants who were not agile enough to get out of the way. Howe, with what was left of his force, retreated up the Savannah River to Zubley's Ferry and there crossed the river into South Carolina. Meanwhile Prevost, advancing from St. Augustine with about two thousand soldiers, including Indians, in two divisions—one on land, the other in small armed boats—reached Sunbury, Georgia, where Major Joseph Lane commanded a small fort manned by some two hundred Continental troops and militia. Prevost demanded that the garrison surrender, but Lane refused. Prevost then emplaced his cannon and began a bombardment of Fort Morris. Only a few months earlier Lane had been the messenger of Colonel John McIntosh, who had replied to the demand of the British that he deliver Fort Morris "and remain neuter until the fate of America is determined" with the words: "We, sir, are fighting the battles of America, and therefore disdain to remain neutral till its fate is determined. As to surrendering the fort, receive this laconic reply, *Come and take it!*" But Lane, although he commanded twenty-four pieces of cannon, was overawed by the display of British artillery and, realizing that he had little chance of prevailing in an extended battle or of escaping, surrendered to Prevost. The Americans had one captain and three privates killed and seven wounded; the British, one killed and three wounded. Before calling the surrender an ignominious one, which it certainly appeared to be, it would be necessary to have a better knowledge of what Lane might have accomplished by a determined and costly defense. Certainly in terms of the defense of Georgia and the South against the British invasion, fighting, against whatever odds, would have served the cause much better than capitulation. On the other hand, the Sunbury garrison was thoroughly demoralized by the news of Howe's crushing defeat at Savannah and by the knowledge that Prevost, if by any remote chance he were to need reinforcements, could be readily supplied from Campbell's army.

At Savannah, the captured Americans were given the choice of enlisting in a Loyalist brigade or being imprisoned in Commodore Parker's ships riding in the harbor. When the great majority refused to fight for the British, they fell victims to Parker, who was brutal and highhanded, and to disease, which carried off most of them by summer. In Benson Lossing's words, "The bodies of those who died were deposited in the marsh mud, where they were sometimes exposed and eaten by buzzards and crows."

Thus in three weeks the British had seized effective control of the entire eastern portion of the state of Georgia. Almost eight hundred Americans, the greater part of the force assigned to defend the state, had been killed, wounded, or captured. The legislature, which had moved in 1776 to Augusta, was largely dispersed. John Wereat, president of the executive council of the state, issued a proclamation calling for a new election of legislators who were to re-assemble at Augusta, some seventy-five miles up the Savannah River. Sir James Wright, the royal governor who had been deposed by the patriots, was declared by the British to be once more the governor of Georgia and established himself in Savannah.

At Augusta, George Walton, one of the signers of the Declaration of Independence, was chosen patriot governor. He was censured for having written a letter to the president of Congress harshly criticizing Colonel McIntosh, and the attorney general of the state was instructed to prosecute him, but the awkward fact was that Governor Walton had also been appointed chief justice by the legislature and thus would have to hear the case against himself. The incident suggests a good deal about the general chaos in that portion of the state still at least nominally under the control of the Americans.

Campbell had issued a proclamation "to encourage the inhabitants to come in, and submit to the conquerors, with promises of protection on condition that, 'with their arms, they would support the royal government.'" Georgians in alarming numbers took advantage of Campbell's promise of amnesty; and many of the rest, finding that their despised Tory neighbors, whom they had energetically suppressed, now had the whip hand, moved to the northwestern part of the state, out of the range of Tory vengeance and British supervision.

Prevost, arriving in Savannah, took command of the combined British forces there and sent messages to the Tories of South Carolina, urging them to take up arms and cross the Savannah River at Augusta, there to join forces with a strong detachment under Colonel Campbell and seize this patriot stronghold. About eight hundred North and South Carolina Tories gathered at the Broad River under a Captain Boyd and proceeded to the Savannah, plundering and despoiling as they went. Although the Americans fought a series of skirmishes that delayed Campbell, the British reached Augusta on January 29, 1779, and occupied the town, which had been abandoned just before their arrival. With Augusta in the hands of the British and several military posts established to the west, the whole state had been secured for the Crown with disconcerting ease. Those patriots who were sufficiently mobile took refuge in South Carolina; the British were most industrious in administering the oath of allegiance to His Majesty George III and in seizing the property and sometimes the persons of those who refused to sign. The houses of people identified as unrepentant rebels were usually burned to the ground.

From the main American camp at Purrysburg, some thirty miles north of Savannah, General Moultrie wrote: "We are all in good spirits and ready to receive the enemy but are not strong enough to pay them the first visit." It was Moultrie's opinion that Lincoln would need at least five thousand militiamen before he attempted to cross the Savannah River to engage the enemy. Too many of the Americans were, he wrote Charles Cotesworth Pinckney, "undisciplined and . . . unarmed." On January 10, two weeks after the Battle of Savannah, Moultrie wrote to the president of the South Carolina senate urging that the senators take measures to keep open the lines of communication between General Lincoln's camp at Purrysburg and the city of Charles Town: "For God's sake, let not your legislative or executive economy border too much on parsimony! Be generous to your militia. Allow them everything necessary to take the field. It is now time to open your purse strings. Our country is in danger. . . . Have the modesty to allow that very few of you have the least idea of what is necessary for an army, and grant what the officers shall ask for that purpose. They are certainly the best judges."

One of the few successes of the winter was that of Moultrie's expedition to Beaufort, a small port town on the Carolina coast below Charles Town. Moultrie, with three hundred South Carolina militia, entered the town early in February, and word soon arrived that "the enemy were in full march for Beaufort and not more than five miles off." Moultrie's men were turned out, paraded, and prepared for battle. Not waiting for the British, Moultrie led his men out of town toward the advancing enemy, looking as he went for suitable terrain on which to form a line of defense. The British veered off toward the ferry and then, as Moultrie moved to intercept them, turned back. They beat Moultrie's force to a nearby swamp, where they took defensive positions while Moultrie, halting his men two hundred yards from the British, brought up his fieldpieces (two six-pounders and a two-pounder). With the American soldiers in the open field and the British firing from the shelter of the trees and bushes that ringed the swamp, the engagement was brisk. Moultrie, feeling that his men were too exposed, "ordered them to take trees." The firing continued raggedly for three-quarters of an hour with little damage to either side until the cry rang out along the American positions, "No more cartridges." Moultrie then withdrew his troops, "which was done in tolerable order for undisciplined troops." The British had already begun a hasty retreat, leaving a wounded officer and four enlisted men behind "and their dead lying on the field."

It was a very modest victory, if indeed it could be called a victory at all, but contrasted with the misfortunes that had preceded it, it seemed to the Americans a striking triumph.

The British soon found, as they had in New England and New York, that it was one thing to rout outnumbered and ill-trained soldiers and another to preserve control of those areas not actually occupied by sizable numbers of British soldiers. In South Carolina, Colonel John Dooley collected a force of several hundred patriots and crossed into Georgia to do battle with a comparable force of Tories under Colonel M'Girth. One of M'Girth's officers, Major Hamilton, drove Dooley back across the Savannah, where he was joined by Colonel Andrew Pickens and another band of patriot militia, making a combined force of some three hundred and fifty men. Pickens and Dooley then recrossed the river, followed Hamilton to Car's Fort, and were about to attack him there when word came to Colonel Pickens from his brother at Ninety-Six that the Tory leader Colonel Boyd and his "infamous banditti" were in the vicinity. The depredations of Boyd's Tory irregulars had caused special bitterness among the patriots, and Pickens turned to meet him at Cherokee Ford.

Boyd tried to escape across the ford, but it was guarded by eight men with two swivel guns, who checked Boyd there and forced him to cross farther up the river. The delay allowed time for a detachment of Pickens' men under Captain Anderson to overtake Boyd and ambush him in a canebrake. There was a brief and bitter fight in which Boyd lost a hundred men killed, wounded, and missing to sixteen Americans killed. Boyd shook off Anderson's smaller force and got across the Broad River just before Pickens arrived with the balance of his force. Pickens followed and caught up with Boyd on February 14 at Kettle Creek, where Boyd, unaware that the Americans were still on his heels, had turned his horses out to forage and had ordered cattle to be killed to make a meal for his weary men. As the Americans emerged from the woods, Boyd's pickets fired and fled for camp, where the startled Tories tried to rally and offer some opposition to their attackers. For two hours the confused contest continued, breaking down into small bands of patriots and Tories and even into individual encounters. Some seventy Tories were killed and the same number captured. Boyd, badly wounded, died during the night, as did twenty-nine Americans, in addition to nine who had died during the fighting. The captured Tories were taken to South Carolina and tried for treason, and five of their leaders were hanged.

In terms of the numbers engaged, the battle at Kettle Creek was certainly a minor one, but it had a marked effect on the course of events in the area of the Georgia–South Carolina boundary and indeed throughout both states. It was the first real victory that the patriots could claim since Howe's abortive foray into Florida, almost six weeks earlier. In the intervening weeks, the Americans had suffered one setback after another, the most severe, of course, being Campbell's victory at the Battle of Savannah. Now the patriots took heart, and the Tories, whose support was so crucial to the whole Southern strategy, lost confidence. The British had encouraged them to believe that they could be sure of British protection if they made themselves and their families vulnerable to patriot retribution by taking up arms in active support of the British invasion. The encounter at Kettle Creek showed how empty the British assurances were. The battle itself, though small in scale, was fought with unrelenting savagery on both sides; its aftermath was one of bitter recrimination. "The Tories," David Ramsay wrote, "were dispersed all over the country. Some ran to North Carolina, some wandered not knowing whither. Many went to their homes, and cast themselves on the mercy of the new government."

Prevost was concerned by this display of rebel resistance and by the exposed position of Campbell. Lincoln, whose army at Purrysburg was growing daily by the addition of militia rounded up by the indefatigable exertions of Governor Walton, had sent General John Ashe up the Savannah River with fifteen hundred North Carolina militia and several companies of Georgia Continentals to join General Andrew Williamson with nearly a thousand men for an attack on Augusta. Campbell got word at the same time of Boyd's rout, and, fearing that he himself would be trapped in Augusta, he decamped at night for Savannah, leaving behind him a substantial amount of arms and provisions. At Hudson's Ferry, fifty miles below Augusta, he considered making a stand but thought better of it and resumed his withdrawal. General Lincoln, meanwhile, ordered Ashe to cross the river and pursue Campbell as far as Briar Creek.

Campbell, still withdrawing toward Savannah, was a dangerous opponent. At Briar Creek he saw an opportunity to turn on his pursuers. After he had crossed the creek, he destroyed the bridge and then, confident that Ashe must be detained there, he sent Lieutenant Colonel James Mark Prevost, a younger brother of the commanding general, on an encircling movement, a fifty-mile march around the American flank. It was a difficult maneuver, skillfully executed.

General Griffith Rutherford meanwhile was at Black-Swamp on the north side of the Savannah River, a few miles above Ebenezer Creek, with seven hundred militia; General Williamson remained near Augusta to protect that town.

Ashe crossed the river on February 25 and reached Briar Creek two days later to find the bridge, which ran through a swamp some three miles wide, destroyed. At this point Rutherford, with part of his brigade, was some five miles away at Mathew's Bluff on the Carolina side of the river, while Colonel Marbury, with a detachment of Georgia cavalry, was a few miles farther up Briar Creek. Ashe's detachment was made up of General Bryant's brigade, Lieutenant Colonel Lyttle's light infantry, and some Georgia Continentals—a total of some twelve hundred men. He had for artillery one four-pound brass fieldpiece and two iron two-pound swivels.

Ashe ordered the bridge repaired and crossed the river to confer with Lincoln, whose headquarters were on the Carolina side of the

Savannah. When Ashe got back to his encampment, he found that the work on the bridge had hardly begun. In his absence little or nothing had been done to prepare his brigade for either offensive or defensive operations. The fact was that Ashe's force was caught in the angle formed by Briar Creek, with its marshy extensions, and the Savannah River. Prevost, who had received intelligence of the American movements from the network of Tory spies, moved rapidly to engage Ashe. Williamson, who had crossed Briar Creek some fifteen miles above the destroyed bridge, moved down from Savannah to join Ashe, sending word ahead that Prevost was only some eight miles away; Marbury's dragoons had already encountered the advance units of Prevost's army. The warning failed to reach Ashe. As a consequence, Prevost was able to take Ashe's unsuspecting troops by surprise at three o'clock on the afternoon of February 28.

At the first shots exchanged between Prevost's scouts and the American pickets, drums called the scattered Americans to arms. Cartridges had first to be distributed. Ashe had kept the cartridges in a general magazine rather than pass them out to the soldiers, because, as he said after the battle, the men lacked proper cartridge boxes and carried cartridges "under their arms; others in the bosoms of their shirts; and some tied up in the corner of their hunting shirts." As a result many of the cartridges were ruined on the march, and Ashe had therefore decided to distribute them only prior to an engagement. It is also likely (though Ashe did not mention it in his account of the battle) that he retained the ammunition to keep his poorly disciplined soldiers from firing at random, thereby giving away their movements. In any event precious minutes were lost and much confusion created by the soldiers' need to draw ammunition when they should have been hurrying to form a line of battle.

With retreat impossible, Ashe's officers hastily gathered their men and began an advance toward the British. Colonel Elbert, who had already proved his and his regiment's coolness under fire at Savannah, and Colonel Perkin's regiment led the advance. The British formed from columns into line some hundred and fifty yards from the Americans, and as they did so Elbert's and Perkin's men, many of them sharpshooting riflemen, opened a heavy fire. The Georgians, having fired two or three rounds, began a movement to the left that masked the fire of a regiment of North Carolinians who were moving forward. The Edenton Regiment, another North Carolina unit, at the same time moved to the right, leaving a gap in the American lines that the British were quick to exploit, starting forward on the run with bayonets fixed and giving a fearsome shout as they came. It was, as always with a charge by British regulars, an awesome sight—the long lines of brightly uniformed soldiers maintaining their order remarkably well even at the double over uneven ground, accompanied by the thump of supporting artillery and the wicked flashing of bayonets. It was enough to intimidate seasoned soldiers, and it was too much for the poorly trained militia. The Halifax Regiment on the left took to its collective heels without firing a shot. The Wilmington Regiment advanced, fired several volleys, and then turned and retreated toward the almost impassable barrier of the swamp and creek. The New Bern and Edenton Regiments of the North Carolina militia followed suit, and soon all the North Carolina units were in full flight, abandoning their arms and equipment as they went. General Ashe did his best to rally his men; the Georgia Continentals, the best trained of the American troops, held their ground resolutely, but the collapse of their flanks made it possible for the British to surround them, and Colonel Elbert and most of his men were made prisoners. The majority of Americans escaped as best they could, some by swimming the Savannah, some by means of hastily improvised rafts that were often no more than logs pushed into the river. Many drowned or were killed by the British—some hundred and fifty by rough count. Almost two hundred men were taken prisoner, along with all the American artillery and supplies and five hundred muskets and rifles. The British loss was reported as one commissioned officer killed and fifteen privates killed or wounded. What is most surprising is not the British victory, which everything favored—the relative size of the two forces, the element of surprise, the lack of any prepared line of retreat, and the vastly superior discipline and training of the British—but the startling disparity in the casualties between the two forces. It is hard to understand how the Americans, whose principal claim to any measure of military fame was their accuracy with musket and rifle, could have done as much firing as the account of the battle composed by Ashe suggested. There were, after all, over a thousand Americans engaged in the brief battle. If a third of them had fired their muskets or rifles even once at those British within range, they should have inflicted far heavier casualties than fifteen killed and wounded.

The truth seems to be that there was much less order than the official account suggests. Many soldiers must have fled without forming into units or firing their weapons except perhaps at excessive range. It may also very well be that in the confusion of the unexpected appearance of the British, a number of soldiers never even received the cartridges that had been withheld from them. All in all the engagement at Briar Creek was one of the most disastrous American setbacks of the war. Four or five principles of good military practice were plainly violated by General Ashe and his superior, General Lincoln. In the first place, Lincoln was ill advised to divide his rather meager forces, the more so since he had, of necessity, to place them under the command of officers with whose judgment and military skill he was unfamiliar. General Williamson, for example, who commanded the detachment at Augusta, later went over to the British, and there is evidence that he was in treasonable contact with the enemy before his defection. Ashe and Marbury were brave men, but inexperienced and lacking those special gifts that would have made up for their conspicuous deficiencies. They were, like so many other political generals, good patriots but poor soldiers. Ashe was weak, as American generals so often were, in his reconnaissance and security. He should not have left his command to confer with Lincoln until he was satisfied that those steps that he considered essential to the proper order of his camp had been taken or were at least well advanced. Sensible as his reasons sounded for not distributing ammunition to his soldiers, the fact remained that he was operating in terrain where a surprise encounter with enemy units was always a possibility, and he ran, as events were certainly to prove, an unacceptable risk in not giving the soldiers under his command an adequate supply of cartridges. When on the morning of March 3, his own pickets exchanged fire with a British reconnoitering party, Ashe and his subordinates, warned that enemy units were in the vicinity, failed to take at once the steps that such an encounter should have suggested to them. Once the battle, if we could call it that, had begun, Ashe apparently attempted maneuvers that he might have known inexperienced troops would have little chance of carrying out. The greatest advantage of militia or lightly armed troops living, to a degree, off the country is speed and mobility. Ashe sacrificed both these when he lingered for three days at Briar Creek. This delay, inexcusable in terms of any proper military doctrine, allowed Campbell to devise the tactics for Ashe's defeat and Prevost time to execute them.

Despite all the American errors and deficiencies, the British certainly deserve great credit for the operation. Campbell and Prevost stole from the Americans just those assets—speed and mobility—that should have distinguished the Americans' movements.

The toll of four hundred killed or captured at Briar Creek was swollen by the loss of some six hundred militia who simply scattered to their homes. Some four hundred of Ashe's command eventually found their way back to Lincoln's main force at Purrysburg, but he had lost men and supplies he could ill afford to lose. The defeat squandered whatever gains might have been made for the cause by Pickens' victory at Kettle Creek. It raised Tory morale once more and opened a line of communication among the British, Tories, and Indians in western Georgia, Florida, and the Carolinas. Ashe was so widely denounced for the defeat that he requested a court-martial, which cleared him of the charges of cowardice and inefficiency but did judge that he had failed to take proper precautions.

Ashe, of course, had a different explanation for his defeat: "The little attention paid to order, both by officers and soldiers," he wrote bitterly, "the several mutinies of the Halifax regiment, and desertions from the brigade, and Genl. Bryan's unhappy temper . . . have rendered my command very disagreeable. . . ." General Bryan, commander of the South Carolina militia, claimed that Ashe was "both a traitor and coward." But perhaps the most basic error of all was Lincoln's in sending too small a force to accomplish the task. This was an error repeated by American commanders time after time. The reasons for it are obvious: intelligence of the enemy strength was usually highly inaccurate (thereby often tempting the Americans to assume a balance of strength in their favor far out of accord with the facts), and beyond that, militia had to be employed in some military action or they would soon grow restless and melt away or, what was perhaps worse, demoralize the regulars by their poor order and lack of discipline.

The simple moral to be drawn from the Briar Creek disaster was that there is no real substitute for military training and experience. What British officers would, in most instances, do automatically, often did not even occur to their American counterparts. The armies of the Southern Department had to learn their lessons in the painful and often tragic school of military defeat. As Lee wrote of Lincoln, "His stock of experimental knowledge, of course, could not have been very considerable." The acquisition of that knowledge was costly, indeed; Briar Creek was part of the price.

2

Prevost Threatens Charles Town

GENERAL Lincoln, in command of the Southern Department, with headquarters at Purrysburg, encountered the same problems with the militia levies and even with the Continental soldiers that Washington had struggled with at Cambridge in 1775. Personally courageous, austere, and taciturn in the proverbial manner of his native New England, Lincoln was far less able to cope effectively with them than Washington had been. Lincoln, it will be recalled, had been second-in-command to Gates at Saratoga and had performed satisfactorily if not brilliantly. "Upright, mild, and amiable," in the words of Henry Lee, "he was universally respected and beloved; a truly good man, and a brave and prudent one, but not a consummate soldier."

As David Ramsay described the problem: "Their [the militias'] numbers were considerable, but they had not yet learned the implicit obedience necessary for military operations. Accustomed to activity on their farms, they could not bear the languors of an encampment. Having grown up in the habits of freedom and independence on their freeholds, they reluctantly submitted to martial discipline. When ordered on command, they would some times enquire 'whither they were going?' and 'how long they must stay?'. . . . Unexperienced in the art of war, the Americans were frequently subject to those reverses of fortune which usually attend young soldiers. Unacquainted with military stratagems, deficient in discipline, and not thoroughly broken to habits of implicit obedience, they were often surprised, and had to learn, by repeated misfortunes, the necessity of subordination, and the advantage of discipline."

In the winter of 1779, the Southern army had no Valley Forge. It was a scattered, heterogeneous force spread out over four large, thinly populated states. The South had no social structure like the New England town, with its well-developed institutions and close-knit community life. And the individualism that characterized the American people and that we have already observed in its most striking form in the riflemen of the Virginia and Pennsylvania frontier was rampant in the South. Combined with a semifeudal code of personal honor, it made all forms of common action exceedingly difficult. Southerners seemed constitutionally touchy, arrogant, and combative. But if the Southern soldier was even more of an individualist than his Northern counterpart, this was compensated for to a degree by the fact that the Southern officer, almost invariably a "gentleman," assumed and, paradoxically enough, was granted by virtue of his social class a degree of respect, deference, and loyalty from his men that few Northern officers could claim except as a consequence of long-tested leadership in battle.

At this period perhaps the most notable development in the Southern Department was the election of John Rutledge as governor of South Carolina with almost dictatorial powers. Given a mandate to "do everything that appeared to him [and his council] necessary for the publick good," he gave particular attention to the task of raising a large body of militia and equipping it. "A profound statesman, a captivating orator, decisive in his measures, and inflexibly firm," in Henry Lee's words, Rutledge gave new spirit and vigor to the patriot party. The militia poured into Lincoln's base camp at Purrysburg. In addition Rutledge established a kind of militia reserve with its headquarters at Orangeburg in the center of the state, a mobile force that could be dispatched to any point where it was needed. A regiment of mounted dragoons was also recruited to increase the mobility of the militia.

In a remarkably short time Lincoln found himself with a sufficient force to protect Augusta, where the legislature was about to convene. Taking four thousand men, Lincoln marched there on April 23. Prevost's countermove was to cross the Savannah and make an attempt to attack Charles Town with twenty-four hundred men and a number of

Indians. The British general guessed quite rightly that Lincoln would not let him advance on that important port city unopposed. Colonel John McIntosh, who was in command of a few Continentals at Purrysburg, fell back and evacuated the post, joining Moultrie at Black-Swamp. Prevost's intention was to surprise Moultrie much as Campbell had surprised Ashe a few weeks·before, but Moultrie, getting wind of Prevost's intentions and feeling that his post at Black-Swamp was difficult to defend against a much larger force, slipped away a few hours before Prevost arrived and deployed his troops at Tulifinny Bridge, hoping to block the British advance on Charles Town. Lincoln's response to the word that Prevost was advancing with the apparent intention of attacking Charles Town was to detach three hundred light infantry with orders to hasten to the defense of Charles Town. He himself crossed the Savannah River near Augusta and then marched down the south bank toward Savannah. His thought was to call what he considered Prevost's bluff by threatening the British garrison in Savannah. Such a line of march would, moreover, carry him in the general direction of Charles Town, so that he could keep open the option of going to the support of that city.

At Tulifinny Bridge Moultrie dispatched John Laurens, who had begged him for the command, to help extricate his rear guard of some hundred men who were guarding the crossing at Coosawhatchie. Laurens was given command of a force of approximately a hundred men, with a hundred and fifty riflemen to cover his flanks. Including the rear guard itself, some three hundred and fifty men, or a quarter of Moultrie's little army, were involved in the withdrawal of the troops at Coosawhatchie. Laurens who, as Washington's staff officer had longed to lead his "dear Continentals" into battle, had to make do with militia, but he was nonetheless determined to effect some bold stroke that would win fame for himself and deal a blow to the British. Disregarding Moultrie's orders, he collected the whole force of some three hundred and fifty men and crossed to the east side of the river, drawing up his men with their backs to the creek. But he failed to clear a group of houses on a hill overlooking his own force, and these were promptly occupied by British infantrymen who opened fire on Laurens' men. In Moultrie's indignant recital of the episode, he wrote: "In this situation did he expose his men to [the British] fire, without the least chance of doing them any injury; after remaining some time he got a number of the men killed and wounded; and was wounded himself." The command fortunately devolved on a Captain Shubrick, who immediately pulled the little force out of an increasingly precarious situation and began a hasty retreat to Tulifinny.

When Laurens, wounded in the arm, reached Moultrie's headquarters, Moultrie said, "Well, Colonel, what do you think of it?" "Why, sir," answered Laurens, demoralized by the failure of his first combat command, "your men won't stand."

If that was indeed the case, Moultrie felt it would be futile for him to try to block the British advance at Tulifinny, and he ordered his command to resume their retreat to Charles Town. If Colonel Laurens had not "discouraged the men by exposing them so much and unnecessarily," Moultrie wrote Lincoln, "I would have engaged Gen. Prevost at Tulifinny, and perhaps have stopped his march to Charlestown: we were all at our posts on a very commanding ground and expected every moment to be engaged." Laurens was a brave and devoted officer, but "he was too rash and impetuous."

From Ashpoo, Moultrie wrote to Colonel Charles Cotesworth Pinckney in Charles Town, urging him to make every possible exertion to strengthen the defenses of the city.

As Prevost's army advanced, they committed those depredations that, although now a familiar part of British strategy, never failed to rouse the bitter resentment of the local inhabitants. Moultrie continued to fall back toward Charles Town. Once again, Prevost kept constant pressure on the American rear guard, sending cavalry and light infantry far in advance of the main party to harass Moultrie every mile of the way, and making good use of the superior mobility afforded by his cavalry to take a toll of Moultrie's rear. Instead of receiving reinforcements from the countryside as he had hoped, Moultrie found that a good many of the militia, officers among them, slipped quietly away. Their families and their farms and plantations lay in the path of the British army. The plundering of Prevost's army and the threat of Indian rapine produced the desired effect of frightening many of the inhabitants of the area into applying to the British for protection of their property and their lives.

Governor Rutledge made use of his own Flying Camp at Orangeburg to draw reinforcements in support of Moultrie. He set out with some six hundred men to join Moultrie, but before he reached Tulifinny, Moultrie had already begun his retreat to Charles Town. Meanwhile Lincoln, finding that Prevost refused to be deflected by his feint at Savannah, crossed the river once more and took up the pursuit of the

British. There were thus four forces headed for Charles Town: Moultrie was in the lead, with Prevost in pursuit of him and Lincoln some distance in the rear; and Rutledge was hurrying from Orangeburg to try to make connections with Moultrie.

In Charles Town, the news that Prevost was on the way with a substantial force of British, Tories, and Indians galvanized that normally rather lethargic city. Its defenses had been left in a poor state, the ferry places were unguarded, and the neck between the Cooper and Ashley rivers was inadequately protected. Under the direction of an experienced French engineer, the Chevalier de Cambray-Digny, the citizens of the town and their slaves worked around the clock to strengthen its defenses. The houses in the suburbs, which might have provided cover for an attacking force, were burned down to open fields of fire; a line of fortifications with abatis was constructed on the neck, and several cannon were emplaced to command the approaches. Colonel Francis Marion, in command of the garrison at Fort Moultrie, was reinforced.

Fortunately for the defenders of Charles Town, Prevost, who had moved with such expedition up to this point, hesitated for three days when his force was within striking distance of the city. He was confused by conflicting intelligence that suggested that Lincoln might be on the point of attacking Savannah with a large force. While Prevost waited for further word of Lincoln's movements, Moultrie's little army, Rutledge's Orangeburg militia, and the detachment dispatched by Lincoln all arrived at Charles Town on the ninth and tenth of May.

When Moultrie reached Charles Town with his diminished army— he reported to Lincoln that it had shrunk from "1200 to 600 men"—he found, despite De Cambray's efforts, "a strange consternation in the town: people frightened out of their wits. . . ." The same condition existed in the parishes and savannas that lay along the Cooper and Ashley rivers. "There never was a country in greater confusion and consternation," he wrote General Lincoln, urging him to hurry to Charles Town with his army; "and it may be easily accounted for, when 5 armies were marching through the southern parts of it, at the same time, and all for different purposes. . . ."

The next day, nine hundred British soldiers crossed the Ashley and took up positions in front of the city. The same day, Count Pulaski arrived with a modest detachment of a hundred and fifty "legionnaires." Pulaski, who was obstreperous and moody by turns, had presented Washington with one of his most worrisome foreign-officer problems.

The solution had been to authorize him to recruit his own "legion." This consisted of the staff of Polish officers he had brought with him and, for the most part, of Hessian deserters whose language he could at least speak. As finally constituted it was made up of about two hundred cavalry and approximately the same number of infantry.

Two hours after his arrival, Pulaski placed eighty men beyond the American lines in a small breastwork that was situated in such a manner as to take the advancing British under enfilade fire. A mile beyond the crude breastwork he stationed a platoon of Continental cavalry and some mounted militia volunteers. With these the count, setting an example of personal courage, engaged the British cavalry until he was forced back. He had intended to lead the pursuing British past the American ambush where he had placed his infantry, but the soldiers had been drawn from their positions by the sound of the skirmish, and the ambush failed as the British infantry came up in large numbers and forced Pulaski's advance guard to retreat into the town. Pulaski, by his own report, made a brilliant figure, darting about the battlefield and personally engaging British cavalrymen. Moultrie's account is less flattering: "In this skirmish he [Pulaski] lost his Col. (Kowatch) killed and most of his infantry killed, and wounded, and prisoners; and it was with difficulty, the remainder got in. . . ."

While the physical defenses of the city had been greatly strengthened, an air of confusion prevailed. Rutledge insisted that the militia were under his command. Moultrie, whose command of the handful of Continental soldiers was unchallenged, felt that an integrated command of militia and Continentals alike was essential to any proper defense of the city. He and Rutledge had a disagreeable squabble, and the divided command soon resulted in a minor tragedy. On the night of May 10 Rutledge sent out a party led by Major Benjamin Huger to fill in a gap in the American lines. In the darkness Huger's detachment was mistaken for the British, and nervous militiamen and artillerymen poured out a volley of fire that killed Huger and killed or wounded twelve of his men. Moultrie was furious. Who, he demanded, had given the order for Huger's men to move ahead of the lines? Rutledge, who was standing nearby with members of his council, denied that he had given such orders. "Gentlemen," Moultrie replied, "this will never do; we shall be ruined and undone, if we have so many commanders; it is absolutely necessary to chuse one to command. . . ." If the responsibility for military matters was placed in Moultrie's hands, he would, he assured Rutledge and the council, remain entirely out of civil matters. The governor and council gave in and directed Moultrie to take command of all military operations. With this obstacle surmounted, Moultrie turned his attention to strengthening the American positions. Moultrie's dispositions placed the Charles Town militia on the right of the American line and the "country militia" on the left, with Pulaski's infantry held in reserve and three redoubts held by soldiers from McIntosh's, Marion's, and Harris's units.

Since Lincoln was assumed to be advancing in Prevost's rear, Governor Rutledge came up with the strategy of buying time by entering into negotiations with Prevost. Moultrie, who had confidence in the defenses of the city, was dismayed. He favored encouraging Prevost to attack. But Rutledge persisted. He was convinced that the total American force numbered no more than 1,800 men (although Moultrie tried to persuade him that there were closer to 2,200), while he estimated Prevost's army as "7 or 8,000 men at least," adding that if the British and their Indian allies forced the American lines, "a great number of citizens would be put to death." Moultrie should, therefore, send out a flag of truce to find out what terms could be obtained. "I told him," Moultrie wrote, "I thought we could stand against the enemy, that I did not think they could force the lines, and that I did not chuse to send a flag in my name, but if he chose it and would call the council together, I would send my message."

Moultrie later charged that Rutledge had proposed giving up Charles Town to the British in return for the promise that the state would be regarded as neutral and that no warfare would be carried out there by the British. At that suggestion, according to Moultrie, John Edwards, one of the leading merchants of the city, "was so affected as to weep, and said, 'What, are we to give up the town at last?'" The governor's council then voted, over the protests of the military officers present, to "propose a neutrality during the war between Great-Britain and America, and the question of whether the state shall belong to Great-Britain or remain one of the United States be determined by the treaty of peace between those two powers."

It is hard to imagine that Rutledge and his council could have conceived of a worse bargain. With South Carolina neutralized, Georgia and North Carolina would almost certainly have been easily secured by British and Tory arms. The lower South would thus have been, for all practical purposes, lost to the confederacy, with consequences that, if difficult to calculate, would unquestionably have been devastating to the patriot cause as a whole and more particularly to the hope of ending the war on terms favorable to American unity. Of course, Rutledge and the council, regardless of whatever dictatorial powers may have been granted to them, could not have bound the patriots of South Carolina by such an agreement with Prevost. The more determined adherents to the cause would have doubtless fought on, but the effect on their morale, on that of their neighbors, and, indeed, on that of all friends to liberty would have been most serious.

The persistent question is: what could have brought the governor and his "privy council" to propose such a capitulation? They were apparently ready to trade away the principal port in the South for nothing more than a local and humiliating truce with the enemy. The answer, I believe, lies to a considerable degree in the social structure of the state. Most prominent residents of Charles Town owned large plantations along the quiet waters of the Ashley and Cooper rivers, but for much of the year these were run by overseers while their masters and mistresses enjoyed the sophisticated social life of the city, where they maintained handsome houses. The interior of the state was for many of these wealthy and indulgent men and women an unknown territory, the western portions of which teemed with rough and half-civilized Tories, whose hostility was symbolized by the Regulator War a decade earlier.

The leaders of South Carolina had, moreover, been thoroughly demoralized by the alacrity with which large numbers of slaves on their plantations had deserted to the British army. It was difficult, under the circumstances, to see how domestic order could be restored and resistance to the British carried on at the same time. A policy of neutrality was tempting from two points of view: first, it would give the leaders of the state—the great slaveholders and their merchant allies in Charles Town—a chance to re-establish control over their own affairs; secondly, and perhaps as important, it would avoid the danger of the British destroying the city and imprisoning the leading patriots, thereby, in effect, neutralizing the state in any event. In no other American state were the individuals and those agencies through which resistance to Great Britain was carried on so concentrated as in South Carolina. New England had given evidence of its capacity to carry on the struggle with its major city, Boston, in the hands of the British. New York and Pennsylvania had done likewise. But with Charles Town in British hands, it is hard to imagine that the state could have mustered much effective resistance; and this, of course, was to prove the case when the city was eventually captured by the British. These points must be emphasized in order to explain, if not excuse, a decision that to many minds came close to treason.

Moultrie asked John Laurens, scion of one of the state's most prominent families, to deliver the message to General Prevost, but Laurens, aware of the contents, declined—"he would do anything to serve his country; but he would not think of carrying such a message as that."

Finally Colonel McIntosh and Colonel Smith were prevailed upon, against their wishes, to carry word of the unsavory bargain. They met Colonel Prevost and several other officers a quarter of a mile in front of the American lines, and there a tense and awkward conference took place. The British officers had not come with any bargaining powers, Prevost declared. The best they could do was carry the proposal to his brother, the general. He would bring his response at noon. When the two groups of officers met again, General Prevost's short reply was that he "had nothing to do with the governor, that his business was with General Moultrie, and as the garrison was in arms, they must surrender prisoners of war. . . ."

The reply played skillfully upon Rutledge's fears, referring to "the evils and horrors attending the event of a storm (which cannot fail to be successful). . . ." Four hours would be allowed for an answer, "after which your silence . . . will be deemed a positive refusal." The message was received at 11 A.M. on May 11. As soon as Rutledge had read it he summoned a council of war, made up of Count Pulaski, Colonel Laurens, and Moultrie himself. Prevost's message was read aloud; "the governor and council," Moultrie wrote, "looked very grave and steadfastly at each other and on me, not knowing what I would say." There was a long, uncomfortable pause. Finally Moultrie broke it: "Gentlemen, you see how the matter stands. The point is this: Am I to deliver you up prisoners of war, or not?" Moultrie asked for a tally of the soldiers available for defense of the city and went through the numbers, corps by corps, with Rutledge, writing the figures down on the back of Prevost's letter. They came, by a conservative estimate, to 3,180. The officer in command of a reconnoitering party that had surveyed the British lines likewise gave a tally, unit by unit, of the British army, which was noted by Rutledge on the back of the same letter—3,620 men. In addition there were perhaps a thousand Tories who had recently joined Prevost's army. What then was to be done? The governor and council looked glummer than ever. Their strategy had misfired, and their fate was now in Moultrie's hand. Moultrie, savoring the moment, declared, "I am determined not to deliver you up as prisoners of war—WE WILL FIGHT IT OUT." At this dramatic utterance, John Laurens, his arm still in a sling, jumped up and said, "Thank God! We are upon our legs again."

As Moultrie was leaving the tent where the council had been meeting, Christopher Gadsden, one of the councilors, came up to him and said, "Act according to your own judgment, and we will support you." Moultrie ordered the truce flag to be waved, signaling the end of negotiations and the rejection of the British demand for surrender; and when the British officers, apparently not seeing it, remained at the spot where they had delivered Prevost's message, Moultrie sent a courier to inform them "that all conference was at an end."

That night the soldiers manning the American lines slept on their arms, when they slept at all. The British would doubtless attack at dawn. Each infantryman was issued a hundred rounds of ammunition, and the matches were kept burning by the cannon. But at dawn the exultant word ran along the lines, "the enemy is gone." Under cover of a small force of light infantry, Prevost had withdrawn his main body as soon as the conference was terminated. Pulaski, always a showoff, mounted his horse and dashed out, making "two or three circuits at full speed." Not finding any sign of the British, he collected a group of cavalry and started in pursuit, but the British had by this time crossed the Ashley River, and Moultrie gave Pulaski the job of trying to locate General Lincoln and his army, who might come on the British unaware. Meanwhile Moultrie gave orders to hold a large detachment ready to march "at a moment's warning" if word arrived that Lincoln was under attack. Apparently the British withdrawal was hastened by the interception of a message from Lincoln to Moultrie, assuring him that he was making for Charles Town by forced marches and ending with the exhortation: "DO NOT GIVE UP, OR SUFFER THE PEOPLE TO DESPAIR."

To avoid Lincoln's army, approaching Charles Town from his rear, General Prevost moved off to the Sea Islands that extended in an almost unbroken line from North Carolina to Georgia. The greater part of his command was collected on James and Wappoo islands, not more than two or three miles from Charles Town, where they waited for supplies from New York and posed a constant threat to the city.

Small forays and skirmishes were frequent. A detachment of eighty Americans posted on John's Island directly across from James Island were surprised by a British landing party, who extorted from a terrified sentinel the password and, thus armed, bayoneted a second sentinel before he could give the alarm, then rushed on the home of the local plantation owner, bayoneting everyone not quick enough to make his escape. Young Robert Barnwell, cornered by the soldiers, received seventeen bayonet wounds but survived—"an ornament to his country," in David Ramsay's words.

Eliza Wilkinson, at her plantation on Stono Road, noted the comings and goings of the patriots and the redcoats. She was touched by the condition of the American soldiers. "The poorest soldier, who would call at any time for a drink of water," she wrote, "I would take a pleasure in giving it to him myself, and many a dirty ragged fellow have I attended, with a bowl of water, or milk and water; and with utmost compassion beheld their tattered raiment and miserable situation; they really merit every thing who will fight from principle alone; for, from what I could learn, these poor creatures had nothing to protect, and seldom get their pay; and yet with what alacrity they will encounter danger and hardships of every kind."

A few weeks later Lincoln planned an attack on a British force entrenched at Stono Ferry. It was to be a combined attack, with a body of militia—carried by boat from Charles Town—making a feint against James Island while General Lincoln's force advanced from the mainland. Lincoln should have learned by that time that such coordination is difficult to execute with highly trained troops and virtually impossible with inexperienced recruits. The Charles Town diversionary attack was not even launched until two hours after Lincoln's maneuver.

The American detachment was a substantial one—something in excess of a thousand troops, half of whom were Continentals. For several nights prior to the attack, small parties carried out raids that served to allay British suspicions of a major assault. On June 20, Lincoln advanced with the North Carolina militia on his right and the regulars on his left, his flanks covered by light troops, his reserve composed of cavalry with a small brigade of Virginia militia. The Scottish Highlanders occupied the British defensive positions on the right. They were alerted by their pickets and formed for battle. The Seventy-first Regiment was on the British right, and a regiment of Hessians was on the left. The British flanks appeared to be secured by a morass on one end and a deep ravine on the other. The morass was, in fact, firm enough at that time of year to support the movement of soldiers, and the ravine, though steep, was by no means impassable.

As the advancing Americans drove in the British pickets, two companies of the Seventy-first Regiment rushed out to cover their withdrawal and were badly mauled by the Continentals. Encouraged by this modest success, Lincoln ordered a bayonet charge on the British lines. The British held their fire until the Americans were within sixty yards and then opened up with massed musket and artillery fire. Instead of pressing the attack by bayonet and reserving their fire, the Americans stopped and returned the British volley. A general fire fight followed. For a time the British left seemed about to give way under the pressure of the North Carolina militia led by General Butler, but Colonel Maitland responded quickly to the threat by shifting the Seventy-first to the left and filling the gap with his reserve. The Scottish Highlanders stiffened on the left, and the Hessians, who had fallen back, were rallied by their officers.

At this point in the battle Lincoln tried to reassert his control over the action. The Americans had failed to press their bayonet charge. They must, Lincoln insisted, load, reserve their fire, and make the bayonet charge. The order was futile. The moment for such a charge had passed, if indeed it had ever existed. The action resumed, and after another hour of intermittent fire the opposing forces held substantially the positions they had taken at the beginning of the action. By this time, General Prevost's army could be seen moving toward the ferry to reinforce Maitland's detachment. Lincoln ordered the Americans to withdraw. Some confusion and disorder followed inevitably, and Maitland, seizing the opportunity, ordered an attack by the whole British force under his command. The British, "whose zeal in pursuit" had resulted in some disorder, were charged by the American cavalry. Maitland, the experienced officer, quickly drew his men together to present a barrier of bayonets to the advancing horsemen, meanwhile giving them full fire from his rear rank. The charge broke off, and the horsemen withdrew as fast as they had come on.

For a moment it seemed as though the retreating Americans would be overwhelmed; then, in one of those unanticipated but crucial actions that are so often decisive, Colonel Mason with his Virginia brigade, which had been held in reserve, came forward and delivered a heavy fire that checked the British pursuit and allowed the Americans to make their escape. The American losses were some hundred and fifty killed and wounded; the British casualties were approximately the same. The individual American units and soldiers had fought well. Their defeat was due in large part to Lincoln's faulty plan of attack, which was both too rigid and too ambitious. The initial error was in trying to bring off a coordinated attack without an experienced staff and disciplined troops.

This mistake, which as it turned out did not affect the course of the action in any substantial way, was compounded by Lincoln's determination to take the British lines by a frontal assault, depending on the bayonet with whose use American soldiers were notoriously untrained, rather than by flanking movements covered by a base of fire, where the Americans' innate capacity for fighting in woods and over rough terrain could have been used to the best advantage.

Soldiers, though usually lacking a voice, are by no means unaware of the deficiencies of their leaders in terms of tactics, if not of strategy. The militia, feeling that they had been poorly handled in the assault on Stono Ferry, bored and irritated by the routines of camp life, and alarmed by a constant stream of accounts of British depredations in the countryside, began to desert in large numbers.

Prevost withdrew his own army via the inland waterway to Savannah, leaving Lieutenant Colonel Maitland in command of a force at Port Royal Island off Beaufort. Lincoln, his army much reduced by the departure of the militia, established his headquarters at Sheldon, from where he could block any forays by Maitland. In the words of Henry Lee: "The sultry season had set in; which, in this climate, like the frost of the North, gives repose to the soldier. Preparations for the next campaign, and the preservation of the health of the troops, now engrossed the chief attention of the hostile generals."

During Prevost's march to Charles Town and in the months of May and June, while the British had access to the coastal areas of South Carolina, a systematic pillaging took place that is best described by Ramsay, himself a South Carolinian. And in war as in peace, the heaviest burden fell upon black people. "The forces, under the command of general Prevost," Ramsay wrote, "marched through the richest settlement of the state, where there are the fewest white inhabitants in proportion to the number of slaves. The hapless Africans, allured with hopes of freedom, forsook their owners, and repaired in great numbers to the royal army. They endeavoured to recommend themselves to their new masters, by discovering where their owners had concealed their property, and were assisting in carrying it off. All subordination being destroyed, they became insolent and rapacious, and in some instances exceeded the British in their plunderings and devastations." Indeed, slaves seeking their freedom came in such vast numbers to the British camp that their hosts were hard-pressed to feed and house them, and they were collected in large camps, which soon became pestholes where disease and camp fever brought them down by the hundreds and where, in the absence of nurses and medicines, they died at an appalling rate.

A slave in the prime of life was worth two hundred and fifty Spanish dollars, and much of the wealth of the state was invested in this highly mobile form of property. Ramsay estimated that three thousand slaves were carried off by the British to the West Indies, and that another thousand died of camp fever and related diseases. Many were left behind when the British transports departed for the Caribbean, simply because there was not enough space for them. Some, determined to be free and terrified of the punishment that might await them at the hands of their masters if they were recaptured, tied themselves to the sides of the boats or clung to them until soldiers chopped off their fingers and held them off with bayonets and cutlasses. "Many of them," Ramsay wrote, "labouring under disease, afraid to return home, forsaken by their new masters, and destitute of the necessities of life, perished in the woods." Those who were carried from the mainland by British boats were established on Otter Island, where they were again collected in a camp without proper food or sanitation. Hundreds died and were left where they fell, their bodies gnawed by animals and picked clean by birds. Twenty years later, the island was still strewn with their bones.

As the British withdrew down the Sea Islands toward Savannah, their boats were filled to the gunnels with loot. "Many of the horses which they had collected from the inhabitants were lost in ineffectual attempts to transport them over the rivers and marshes. . . . The British also carried with them . . . rice-barrels full of plate, and household furniture in large quantities. . . . Small parties visited almost every house, stripping it of whatever was most valuable, and rifling the inhabitants of their money, rings, jewels, and other personal ornaments." Graves were broken open and bodies despoiled in the lust for possessions. Feather beds were ripped apart for their feathers, and what could not be carried off was destroyed—windows, chinaware, looking glasses and pictures. Livestock were slaughtered wantonly and left to rot in their own gore, and even many cats and dogs, chickens, and rabbits were butchered in an orgy of destruction. In the handsome plantation houses, gardens were laid waste and "their nicest curiosities destroyed."

3

Failure at Savannah

D'ESTAING, who had abandoned the attempt to capture Newport and had departed for the West Indies with the French fleet to wage war on the British islands there, had enjoyed some modest success. British Commodore William Hotham, who had arrived in Caribbean waters ahead of D'Estaing, had captured the French island of St. Lucia. Later Hotham was joined by Admiral John Byron's fleet. But while Byron was absent on convoy duty, D'Estaing captured the British islands of St. Vincent and Grenada, seizing the latter on July 4, 1779. Two days later the outnumbered British fleet, attempting to recapture Grenada, fought an inconclusive battle with D'Estaing, whom Admiral de Grasse had reinforced with a squadron freshly arrived from France.

General James Grant, the British army commander in the West Indies, was instructed by Germain to leave small garrisons on the various British islands in the Indies and to return to New York with the rest of his soldiers. Grant, however, was convinced that the islands could be held only by a superior British fleet stationed in the Caribbean, and he refused to obey Germain's orders. He established three strong garrisons at St. Lucia, St. Kitts, and Antigua, and sailed for England. By the end of the year the 1,600 British soldiers left on St. Lucia by Grant in

July had been reduced by the unhealthy climate and disease to 685 fit for duty and 576 sick.

In early August, D'Estaing received letters from Governor Rutledge and Monsieur Plombard, the French consul in Charles Town, urging him to sail north and assuring him that a strong assault on Savannah would result in the capture of General Prevost and his army. On September 8, therefore, D'Estaing anchored off Savannah with a fleet consisting of twenty ships of the line carrying seventy-four guns or more, two 54-gun ships, and eleven frigates, along with a sizable detachment of French soldiers. The cooler weather was favorable to the resumption of campaigning, and Lincoln, as soon as he heard of D'Estaing's arrival, broke up his camp at Sheldon and started for Savannah, his messenger urging the militia throughout the state to converge on that city.

On the thirteenth of September D'Estaing landed three thousand soldiers at Beaulieu. Two days later he was joined by Pulaski with his reconstituted legion, and the day after by General Lincoln, who had crossed the river at Zubley's Ferry. The combined force took up positions in front of the city. In David Ramsay's words: "The fall of Savannah was considered infallibly certain. It was generally believed that in a few days the British would be stripped of all their southern possessions. Flushed with these romantic hopes, the militia turned out with a readiness that far surpassed their exertions in the preceding campaign." Prevost responded to the situation with his usual energy. Maitland was recalled from Port Royal and Lieutenant Colonel John Cruger from Sunbury. Ships were sunk in the harbor to block the passage of the French fleet, and the British battery on Tybee Island was destroyed to prevent its falling into allied hands.

French troops were landed in Savannah on the twelfth, and four days later D'Estaing called on Prevost to surrender. The British general, doubtless remembering the cost of his negotiation at Charles Town, requested a twenty-four-hour truce in order to give him time to prepare articles of capitulation in the event he should decide to surrender. The confident D'Estaing granted the truce, which gave Prevost time to strengthen his fortifications very substantially and, more important, provided time for Maitland's force from Port Royal to complete its movement to Savannah, a march accomplished with the greatest difficulty. At the end of the twenty-four hours, Prevost replied that he was determined to defend the town "to the last extremity." The arrival of

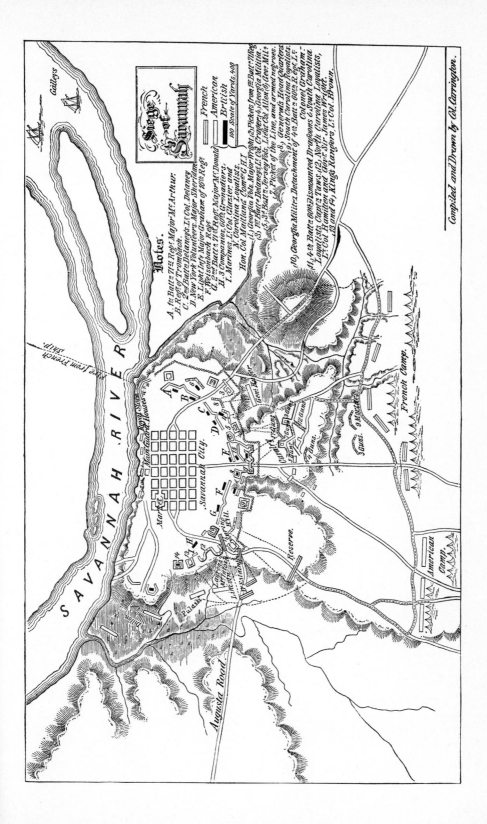

Compiled and Drawn by Col. Carrington.

Maitland, quite literally in the nick of time, increased the numbers of defenders by one-third and raised the spirits of the soldiers because of their confidence in Maitland's fighting qualities.

At Prevost's expression of his intention to fight, the Americans began the formal siege of the city. Heavy artillery had to be hauled from the site of the landing fourteen miles away and it was not until September 24 that sappers began to dig trenches, first horizontally and then laterally; they pushed their lines forward until they had, in the course of twelve days, mounted three pieces of battering cannon and fourteen mortars capable of lobbing shells into the defensive positions. Prevost had not been idle, however, and the British had mounted over a hundred cannon, most of them taken from ships in the river. The allied cannonading, which began on October 4, was so intense that Prevost requested a truce to evacuate the aged, the women, and the children. The allies, once burned by a truce, refused, and the bombardment continued.

The allied cannon fire passed over the British lines for the most part and fell in the city, where it wreaked havoc. Many of the inhabitants took refuge in the Yamacraw Swamp. Before the Loyalist Chief Justice Anthony Stokes could get his trousers on, an eighteen-pound projectile "entered the house, stuck in the middle partition and drove the plastering all about." Taking refuge in the cellar, he found it so crowded with rum and provisions that he and his household slaves could barely squeeze in. Fleeing later to the shelter of the bluffs along the river, Stokes wrote, "Whenever I came to the opening of a street, I watched the flashes of the mortars and guns, and pushed on until I came under the cover of a house; and when I got to the common and heard the whistling of a shot or shell, I fell on my face. . . . The appearance of the town afforded a melancholy prospect, for there was hardly a house which had not been shot through, and some of them were almost destroyed. . . . The troops in the lines were much safer from the bombardment than the people in town. . . . In short, the situation of Savannah was . . . deplorable. A small garrison in an extensive country was surrounded on the land by a powerful enemy, and its seacoast blocked up by one of the strongest fleets that ever visited America . . . numerous desertions daily weakened the force which was at first inadequate to man such extensive lines. . . ."

Prevost's only hope was for relief by a British fleet or an assault by the French and Americans that, if bloodily repulsed, might relieve pressure on the city. The British lines were so heavily defended by redoubts, ditches, abatis, and artillery emplacements that the cost of storming the works seemed sure to prove excessive.

D'Estaing grew more impatient with every passing day. He had been assured by Rutledge that the operation could be completed in a week or ten days, but it had already stretched out to a month. He and his officers grew increasingly uneasy about the state of the fleet. The period of fall storms was approaching, and D'Estaing had already suffered severely off Newport from the fury of such hurricanes. There was always the possibility that a British fleet would arrive to engage D'Estaing and relieve the siege. In addition, D'Estaing had both a personal and racial impetuousness that made him anxious for a speedy conclusion to the siege. In the face of his determination, "Lincoln's wisdom, Lincoln's patience, Lincoln's counsel" were of little effect. D'Estaing issued an ultimatum: the British lines must be stormed at once or the siege raised. Lincoln had little choice. Suppressing his misgivings, he joined with D'Estaing's officers in making plans for an attack.

The allied intention was to approach the British right through a swamp that gave cover along its edge. Two columns of French and Continentals were assigned to this task, while the American militia were to threaten the British center and left and draw Prevost's attention in that direction. The combined French and American assault force consisted of some 3,500 French troops, 600 Continentals, and 350 Charles Town militia. The rest of the militia, numbering several thousand, were directed to the diversionary attack. Prevost put Maitland in command of his right wing, the most vulnerable point in his lines, and held a substantial reserve of the Seventy-first Regiment, two Hessian regiments, a battalion of New Jersey Tories, and a battalion of New York Loyalists.

The attack began on the morning of October 9, with D'Estaing and Lincoln sharing the command of the attacking echelon. An initial error may have been decisive. Count Dillon, a French officer charged with commanding the diversionary attack, lost his way in the dark as he advanced to his line of departure. When daylight came he was still not in position, and the main attack started without the benefit of covering fire from his column. The second misadventure was the delay in the assault forces reaching *their* line of departure. They had advanced in column and were to deploy in a line at the edge of a wood prior to launching the attack. D'Estaing, anxious to have the cover of darkness or the dimmest light of dawn to cover his advance, started the attack with leading elements before the main body of the troops had time to form for an assault. The British, who had been alerted by a spy to the fact that the main allied attack was to be against their right, were waiting, their cannon loaded with grapeshot and their muskets primed. The first wave of attackers thus met with such a withering fire that they broke away to the left to the cover of woods. The second and third French columns, moving forward in the attack as they came on line, suffered much the same fate.

Count Pulaski, leading his cavalry forward with the Continentals, reached the abatis, where he was mortally wounded. John Laurens, with the light infantry, finally had his moment of unclouded glory. With the Second South Carolina Regiment and the First Battalion of Charles Town militia following the light infantry, Laurens stormed the Spring Hill redoubt, got into the ditch, and planted the colors of the Second Regiment there. But the ditch was too deep and the parapet too high for the Americans to penetrate further without ladders. Maitland, observing the Americans, shifted grenadiers and marines to block a further advance and drive them from the ditch. General McIntosh, in com and of the second American line, arrived with his men at the foot the Spring Hill redoubt at the moment that those who remained of the orce under Laurens were trying desperately to extricate themselves fro the ditch. With Pulaski mortally wounded, his mounted lancers broke off and headed for the shelter of the woods on their left, mixing with the men under Laurens' direction, who were retreating from the ditch, and McIntosh's detachment, which was advancing. As young Major Pinckney reached the ditch he saw an indescribable scene of confusion, and found his friend Laurens looking for that portion of his command that had not entered the ditch and apparently had made its way to the woods with the remnants of Pulaski's cavalry. D'Estaing was wounded in the arm, and his staff was apparently reduced to a drummer with whose help he was trying to rally what was left of his shattered force. He ordered McIntosh to move more to the left so as not to obstruct his efforts to collect his troops, and McIntosh and his soldiers, still trying to reach the Spring Hill redoubt, found themselves bogged down in the Yamacraw Swamp, where they came under merciless artillery fire.

At this point it was clear the attack had failed dismally. Those units that had not already been driven off the field were ordered to withdraw. In the words of one participant: "Thus was this fine body of troops sacrificed by the imprudence of the French general, who, being of superior grade, commanded the whole." It was a shattering and unnecessary defeat, which once more raised in many minds the question of whether the advantages of the French alliance were not perhaps outweighed by the military disasters it had occasioned. If the problems of a combined operation had been made clear at Newport, they were heavily underlined at Savannah. Over 700 French and 450 Americans were killed and wounded (of whom 240 were Continentals); total casualties were over 1,100. It was cold comfort that the Americans had fought bravely and well, as their casualties attested. They had been sent on an almost hopeless mission, and they had been once more, by and large, badly led. Officers and men had been lost who could not be easily replaced. As Pinckney wrote after the battle, "If Count D'Estaing had reflected a moment, he would have known that attacking with a single column, before the rest of the army could have reached their position, was exposing the army to be beaten in detail. . . . The enemy, who were to be assailed at once on a considerable part of their front, finding themselves only attacked at one point, very deliberately concentrated their whole fire on the assailing column, and that was repeated as fast as the different corps were brought up to the attack."

The Georgians who had fled Savannah at the approach of Prevost almost a year before had gathered near Lincoln's headquarters to wait for the surrender of the city by the British so that they could return to their homes and plantations in the bays and inlets near the city. After the shattering defeat of the allied army, they were, in Ramsay's words, "for a second time obliged to abandon their country, and seek refuge among strangers." The depreciation of the Continental currency continued at an accelerated pace, "and the most gloomy apprehensions respecting the southern states generally took possession of the minds of the people."

The British losses in killed and wounded were less than one hundred and fifty. In other words, the allies had lost almost ten times as many men as the British and had failed, moreover, to attain their objective. There was triumph and joy among the Tories, and in Britain those who supported the suppression of American independence took new heart. The American cause would have been much better served if D'Estaing had never appeared and if Lincoln had remained encamped at Sheldon with a force too small to do more than intercept raiding parties from Savannah. War-weariness and a few modest American successes had discouraged the supporters of the war in England and had given its opponents high hopes of bringing it to a speedy end, but the spectacular rebel defeat at Savannah strengthened the resolution of the hawks and aroused new hopes that the Americans and their French allies could be finally crushed.

The exultation of the Tories at the abortive attack on Savannah is suggested by a satiric song:

> To Charlestown with fear
>   The rebels repair;
> D'Estaing scampers back to his boats, sir,
>   Each blaming the other,
>   Each cursing his brother,
> And—may they cut each other's throats, sir!

A French officer spoke truly when he wrote, "Our situation had become terrible and disheartening." The wounded soldiers, the cannon used in the siege, and the vast baggage of the French army were laboriously loaded aboard frigates and transports, and D'Estaing sailed away.

When D'Estaing sailed off, General Lincoln was left to pick up the pieces, to patch together an army out of the battered units that were left under his command, and to try to restore a badly damaged morale. He was perhaps better at such a task than at fighting. His stubborn courage and his energy were employed to good effect. In defense of D'Estaing, it must be said that the admiral's anxiety about his ships was well grounded. He had hardly gotten his troops and marines aboard when a violent storm came up and scattered his fleet over a hundred miles of ocean.

Stony Point and Paulus Hook

WHILE the fortunes of war in the South favored British arms and while Clinton squatted in New York, Washington kept his camp at Middle Brook through the winter of 1778–79, a winter that was, for a welcome change, "remarkably mild and moderate." A division that included our friend Joseph Martin was posted, once again, at White Plains. There the camp was laid out in a healthy and delightful spot, and camp discipline was generally good. A strict regimen was established. At daylight the morning gun was fired, answered by three beats of the drum, answered in turn by three beats from every regimental drummer in the whole encampment. The same procedure was followed with the mounting of the guard and at evening roll call. At nine each night, tattoo was the signal for everyone to turn in.

As winter came on at Middle Brook, huts were built as they had been at Valley Forge, but this time more systematic attention was paid to the fundamental principles of sanitation. The army moved into its huts with some little display. Word was given the troops to be ready to strike camp on the firing of a gun. In the words of a Connecticut soldier: "As the gun was fired all the tents, markers and flags were struck down in an instant. Then all went to work packing up tents and baggage, and commenced moving out in different directions, column after column and brigade after brigade, through the whole day . . . the scene was very sublime, the drums and fifes, trumpets and bugle horses, several bands of music all in full sound, and colors flying, horses and cannon moving, and about thirty thousand regular troops [our soldier was wrong by about twenty thousand], all to be seen, as one view moving from the large and beautiful plains to winter quarters."

Many of the units were detached to different areas, where they found dry ground with fresh water nearby and built their huts. The winter was the least arduous of the war for most of the soldiers. There were enough experienced campaigners among them so that they settled quickly and easily into the routines of camp life. The weather was comparatively mild, and it was not until spring that they encountered their worst enemy—snakes. They "swarmed out from the ledge of rocks [near the camp] in platoons and batallions, large black snakes and rattlesnakes surrounded us on every side," one soldier wrote; "but our greatest trouble and fears were in the night, for they would crawl into the huts and into the bunks and snug down by the sides of the soldiers to keep themselves warm; when the soldiers were fast asleep, and in the night we often heard hollowing and screaming and when they awoke and found they had a new sort of bed fellow would create quite a ructor and attack the enemy."

Levies from the states had not arrived in anything like the numbers Washington had hoped for, and sometimes when they did come they had to be turned back because there was no food, clothing, or equipment for them. Horses, so much needed for scouting and reconnaissance missions, not to mention battles, had to be sent away for lack of fodder, and Washington wrote in December that he had not been able to "obtain a farthing of public money for the support of my table for near two months," though this was "a matter of trivial importance because it is of a personal nature." Concerning the prospects of the American cause, he was even gloomier than usual. To believe that anything more could be done in the new year than had been done in the old "would be as unreasonable as to suppose that because a man had rolled a snowball till it had acquired the size of a horse that he might do so till it was large as a house." If the metaphor was Washington's own, it was an apt one. In an effort to strike some blow that might raise patriot spirits, Washington gave Lieutenant Colonel David Humphreys, one of his young aides, the assignment of leading a raid to capture Knyphausen or even Clinton if an opportunity offered. Humphreys, who was a gifted poet and an enterprising soldier, selected four officers and thirty men and embarked on a barge and two whaleboats. But luck was against them. The bitter winter wind blew so hard that the boats were carried past the Battery, one of them to Staten Island and another almost to Sandy Hook. The men could not row against the wind, and the little expedition was forced to make its way up the Raritan to New Brunswick and back to New Windsor by land, arriving on New Year's Day.

Meantime the army drilled and drilled, did the tedious chores of camp duty, and dwindled away, until in May Washington referred to it as "but little more than a skeleton." A few weeks later he wrote to a friend, "I have no scruple in declaring to you that I have never seen the time in which our affairs in my opinion were at so low an ebb as at this present." The military stalemate made it more difficult to recruit new soldiers, and Washington complained: "Excepting about 400 recruits from the State of Massachusetts Bay (a portion of whom, I am told, are children hired at about 1,500 dollars each for nine months service) I have had no reinforcements to this army since last September."

To James Warren he wrote that "speculation, peculation, engrossing, forestalling, with all their concomitants afford too many melancholy proofs of the decay of public virtue." Washington was convinced that the British, having been checked on the military side, persisted in the war largely in expectation of a collapse of the confederation through inflation and a general deterioration of morale.

The fact is that much of our picture of the progress of the Revolution is beclouded by Washington's persistent gloom about the precarious state of the American army. From the moment Washington took command of the Continental Army at Cambridge, he poured out an almost endless succession of letters, each one full of forebodings more dire than the last. Letters written in the fall and winter of 1775 are practically interchangeable with those of any following year. There are the same inventories of complaint and gloom—inaction on the part of Congress, corruption and venality on the part of those charged with supplying the army, selfishness and indifference among officers and soldiers, cowardice and unreliability in the militia, lack of support for the cause from the individual states—and the same anticipations of the collapse of all effective resistance to the British. Most of these charges were, in varying degrees and at different times, true enough, but if we had to depend, as many historians have been inclined to do, primarily on Washington's correspondence for a picture of the state of affairs in America, we should certainly be at a loss to account for the eventual triumph of the cause of independence.

Washington was a great man, and his labors were heroic, but he did not win the war single-handedly, much as that may at times have appeared to be the case. The commander in chief had a deeply morbid or pessimistic vein in him. Of the difficulty of his perpetual struggle to keep at least the semblance of a Continental Army in the field there is certainly no question. That, in itself, was a herculean task. But Washington, in his constant effort to stir Congress and the states to give him adequate support, almost invariably painted the gloomiest picture of the condition of his command. Moreover, it was natural that he mistook the state of his army for the state of the cause itself, and since his army was frequently, if not perpetually, on the verge of disintegration, it seemed to him that the cause was likewise in jeopardy every moment. However, a little reflection on the outcome of Burgoyne's campaign and the war in the South (among a good many other events) will remind the reader that essential as Washington was to the cause and remarkable as his services and his character were, the spirit of independence existed independently of him and had a life and vitality of its own. If this had not been so, all Washington's efforts would have been without effect. In short, the cause was never in as desperate a state as Washington's perpetually apprehensive or despairing letters suggest; the mass of patriots were never quite as corrupt, selfish, or cowardly as one might conclude from reading the general's correspondence.

What the student of the American Revolution must keep in mind is that despite the perpetual optimism of the Loyalists and the chronic despair of Washington, there was in the majority of Americans, and especially those who had made the Revolution, not the slightest indication of a willingness to return, under any circumstances, to a state of dependence on Great Britain. Unless this point is firmly grasped, it is difficult if not impossible to make sense of the Revolutionary struggle. While it is tempting, in dramatic terms if in no other, to see the Revolution as a series of desperate crises in which independence was repeatedly rescued in the hours of its greatest peril by the efforts of one man—Washington—that is simply not the true story.

It was, I think, inevitable that Washington should have felt that the survival of the Continental Army was essential to the preservation of American independence, and it is not surprising that historians subsequently made the same assumption. The capture or destruction of

Washington's army would, of course, have been a terrible setback for the American cause, primarily because of Washington's enormous symbolic importance, and it would certainly have altered the course of the war most significantly. But it would not, I am convinced, have meant an end to the struggle for independence. The decisive defeat or dissolution of the army would have been felt, as I have argued elsewhere, primarily in the problem of forming a nation. The existence of the Continental Army represented the existence of a nation. It was the most powerful unifying principle, the most crucial "national" reality in all the diverse and scattered states.

During the winter of 1778–79, the officers of Washington's staff at Middle Brook entertained themselves as best they could. General Greene, who had his mission in the South still ahead of him, wrote to a friend that he had given "a little dance" at his headquarters, and that Washington and Greene's attractive and vivacious wife had "danced upward of three hours without once sitting down."

On the second of May a full-scale military review was held at Middle Brook, and a few days later Washington noted in his journal, perhaps a little dryly, "Observed a day of fasting, humiliation, and prayer, recommended by Congress." Supplies and money from Congress would have been more welcome.

When the British raided the town of Portsmouth in Virginia, burned nearby Suffolk, and carried off a large quantity of tobacco and "many negroes," Washington noted that he could do little to counter this "predatory war, which the enemy now seem resolved to carry on. . . ."

In June, a British force sailed up the Hudson from New York and captured the American fort at Stony Point. This move forced Washington to march the main body of his army "with all possible expedition to defend West Point." But by the end of the month it was apparent that the always cautious Clinton, whose troops were busy completing the fortifications of Stony Point, had no intention of advancing. The easy British occupation of Stony Point and Verplanck's Point across the river rankled Washington, partly because he was conscious of his own failure to adequately garrison the forts. Furthermore, it would not be too far off the mark to say that Washington was obsessed by the importance to the American cause of West Point, which was only some sixteen miles farther up the river. Washington thus directed Henry Lee to gather information about enemy strength at Stony Point. The fort itself appeared almost impregnable. It stood on a rocky promontory (as one might assume from the name) that thrust out into the Hudson River. When the river was high the main road to the fort was often flooded, and Stony Point was virtually an island. British warships anchored in the river covered the land and water approaches. A swampy area at the base of the rock was watched constantly by sentries. The climb uphill to the fort was through tangled undergrowth and fallen trees. Above were three rows of redoubts in which were emplaced brass twelve-pounders. Beyond the redoubts an abatis ran around the rock, protecting more trenches with cannon.

Early in July Washington wrote to Anthony Wayne urging him "to inform yourself as far as you can, and to give me your opinion of the practicability of an attempt upon this post. If it is undertaken," Washington added, "I should conceive it ought to be done by way of surprise in the night."

Meanwhile, the punitive British raids continued. Tryon, repeating the style of his Danbury foray, raided New Haven, brushing aside the militia who tried courageously but ineffectively to block his advance. The town was plundered and the public stores were burned. Twenty-seven of the militia were killed and nineteen wounded in the defense of the town. From New Haven the British raiders proceeded up the Sound, looting and burning houses as they went. In Fairfield, on the ninth of July, redcoats burned "ninety-seven homes, sixty-seven barns, forty-eight stores, two meeting houses, a church, court-house, jail and two school-houses." At Norwalk two days later these same heroes put the torch to a hundred and thirty houses, eighty-seven barns, and four mills, along with a number of other structures, including two more churches. Again no military objectives were involved; the acts were those of a frustrated bully.

Wayne, acting on Washington's orders, had meanwhile made a careful reconnaissance of the fort at Stony Point. He came away convinced that an attack was practical. Moreover, his light infantry corps of picked troops clearly needed some demanding mission, since they were daily becoming more unmanageable in camp. From inhabitants of the area he had learned that at very low tides in the right quarter of the moon, a sandbar, usually too deeply submerged to permit passage, lay only a few feet below the surface of the water, giving access from the marsh to a point below the fort that was masked from the fire of the defenders. From captured members of a British foraging party, Wayne discovered that the British sentries were unaware of the sandbar and that that particular approach was not guarded.

Wayne sent his best scout, Captain Allen McLane, to the fort under a flag of truce, ostensibily to seek permission for a Mrs. Smith to see her sons who were prisoners there. The usual practice in such circumstances was to blindfold an enemy officer entering fortifications under a flag of truce, but the British commander, a Colonel Johnson, perhaps confident that he had made Stony Point impregnable and that McLane would see this readily enough, did not bother to have him blindfolded. McLane took careful note of the defenses. He observed the grenadiers of the Seventeenth Infantry, the caliber and position of the British guns, and, most striking of all, the fact that the British works, impregnable as they seemed at first glance, were not completed. The central redoubt on the summit of the rock had not been carried beyond a granite outcropping. At the west end there was a gap that a platoon of men could march through abreast.

Washington himself sent Colonel Rufus Putnam, an engineer, to reconnoiter the approaches to Stony Point and to make sketches of the fort and the surrounding country. Then, with Wayne and some of his dragoons, he rode over to Donderberg to review the strategy for the assault. While Washington and Wayne developed their plan of attack, McLane with his company moved down toward Stony Point on July 3 and took up positions in hiding near the British fort. Then followed two weeks of patient waiting and observing. Every detail of the life of the garrison was noted: when guards changed, where sentries were posted, who came and went from the fort to the country beyond, and, most important, when the tides rose and fell. The first low tide that would make the hidden sandbar passable dictated the day and even the hour of attack.

Washington and Wayne agreed on a nighttime bayonet attack. A feint was to be made at Verplanck's Point to prevent reinforcement of Stony Point. When Washington gave Wayne the orders for the attack, Wayne is reported to have replied, "General, if you give me permission, I'll storm Hell itself for you."

On the fourteenth, McLane moved his company to the hills beyond the the fort and intercepted the widow Calhoun and another countrywoman who were on their way to the fort to sell the soldiers "chickens and greens." Other units of Wayne's force lay quietly in the woods, silent and hidden from British eyes. The next day there was a final reconnaissance to be sure that the enemy situation was unchanged, and at eight o'clock in the evening McLane's company cautiously moved near the British sentries to intercept anyone who might try to enter the fort with word that the Americans were taking positions for an assault. The main body of Wayne's light infantry were kept in the dark as to the intended attack until the last minute. At eleven on Thursday morning Wayne called them out on dress parade, and then, instead of dismissing them, he ordered them to march. They moved off down the road along the river and then veered west past the base of Bear Mountain. By three o'clock they were threading their way through hidden ravines near Donderberg. Wayne gave orders that all dogs encountered by the soldiers should be swiftly bayoneted lest their barking alert the British. On the south side of Donderberg in the late afternoon, Wayne told his colonels of the plans for the attack on Stony Point. Their men were to stick pieces of white paper in their hats so that they could identify each other in the dark. Absolute obedience and perfect discipline were essential. No man was to carry a loaded gun except those particularly ordered to do so by Wayne himself. Any man who moved his musket from his shoulder was to be killed. If any soldier retreated a foot, or cringed in the face of danger, the officer next to him was "to immediately put him to Death." (It was not an empty threat. When one young soldier, frightened and confused, paused in the attack to load his musket, his captain ran him through with his sword.) As an added incentive Wayne offered the first man to set foot in the British works a prize of five hundred dollars, the second four hundred, and the third, fourth, and fifth smaller sums.

Six hundred men under Colonels Christian Febiger, Return Jonathan Meigs, and William Hull went to advance on the right. Wayne himself would move with this wing. Another five hundred under the command of Richard Butler, constituted the left; these soldiers too were to use only the bayonet. Colonel Hardy Murfree and his detachment of North Carolinians were assigned to the center. When the American attack was discovered by the British, Murfree's men were to open a sustained, rapid fire to distract the attention of the British defenders from the attacks on their flanks and to give the impression of a frontal assault by a large force. The watchword was "The Fort's our own." Each column was preceded by twenty pioneers armed with axes and billhooks to clear and pull away the abatis that covered the front of the successive British lines. Behind them came a hundred and fifty picked men, the most agile and aggressive in the corps, and behind them the main columns.

By eight o'clock, just after dark, the forward elements stopped at the farm of David Springsteel, two miles from Stony Point, the point of departure for the final phase of the attack. Wayne, who always anticipated death on the eve of a battle, withdrew to the farmhouse to write his last military will and testament. He headed it: "Eleven P.M., near the Hour and Scene of Carnage." It was to be delivered after his death to his closest friend, Sharp Delany. "You have often heard me default the Supineness and unworthy torpidity into which Congress were lulled and that it was my opinion that this would be a Sanguinary Campaign in which many of the choicest Spirits and much of the best blood in America would be lost owing to the parsimony and neglect of Congress," he wrote. "If ever any prediction was true, it is this, and if ever a great and good man was Surrounded with a choice of difficulties it is General Washington. I fear the Consequences, and See clearly that he will be impelled to make other attempts and Efforts to save his Country that his numbers will not be adequate to, and that he may also fall a Sacrifice to the folly and parsimony of our worthy rulers." Wayne commended to Delany the care and education of "my little son and Daughter," and added, "I fear that their mother will not survive this Stroke. . . . I am called to Sup, but whether to breakfast, either within the enemy's lines in triumph or in the other World."

Having prepared himself to meet his Maker, Wayne, like his men, nervously gulped down some food, took up the spear that his officers carried instead of firearms, and gave the order for the advance. The three columns moved out quickly and silently and exactly at midnight reached the swamp at the base of the point. Wayne, with the right wing, moved over the road across the marsh while Butler's men located the sandbar, where the water turned out to be waist-high rather than the foot-or-so deep that they expected. The road itself was soggy and shoe-top deep in mud. Murfree's Carolinians, taking their position in the center, fired before the right and left columns were ready to start their ascent of the rocky slopes. The premature firing turned out to be fortunate. Colonel Johnson, convinced that an attack was being directed at the first line of redoubts and abatis, moved quickly down the hill with a large part of his garrison to man the line. The noise of the British cannon firing in the direction of Murfree's men helped to cover the movement of Butler's and Wayne's flanking units. When Murfree's men failed to advance, the redcoats shouted at them impatiently in the darkness, "Come on, you rebels! Come on and fight!" One ensign shouted back, "Take your time, my lads; we'll be there soon."

The pioneers, who were called the Forlorn Hopes because of their dangerous mission of clearing the abatis with their hooked poles, were too slow for the assault groups who waited with growing impatience, fearful of losing the element of surprise. The men pressed forward, stumbling and falling over tree trunks and interlaced logs. Butler's men, moving through the chilly water that at times was almost neck-high, reached the bank to find a row of sharpened *cheval-de-frise* confronting them. Still undiscovered, they forced their way through the stakes as best they could.

Wayne's men, echeloning to the left as they hit the extreme right of the British first line, floundered in the muddy water but pressed through the British defense works where only a few pickets opposed them. Before Johnson realized what had happened, the Americans were past the first and on to the second line of fortifications. The British commander tried to redeploy his men to turn Wayne's attack, but in the darkness he lost control, and the redcoats milled about in confusion. At the second abatis, Wayne was knocked off his feet by a musket bullet that grazed his head. When he came to, he saw his men moving on ahead of him. "Carry me up to the fort, boys," he called out; "Let's go forward." Two officers lifted him up, and Wayne half walked and was half carried up the hill behind his men.

Christian "Old Denmark" Febiger, a Virginian of Danish birth and a veteran of Arnold's march to Quebec, was also struck by a bullet, which laid open the side of his cheek and nose, but with blood pouring into his mouth from the wound, he too pressed on, exhorting his men to be firm. Wherever the figure of a redcoat could be seen in the moonlight, American bayonets were thrust home, but there was relatively little direct contact between British and American soldiers on the right flank.

With a combination of good luck and good planning, Wayne's assault unit found its way to the gap in the British lines that McLane had reported. They were quickly through it, and even as they breeched this last line, Butler's men, who had encountered only token resistance from startled British soldiers to whom they appeared as silently and unexpectedly as ghosts, from a direction that the defenders thought impregnable, arrived at the trenches and redoubts on the left. For a few moments the parapets stopped them. They had no scaling ladders; their hooked poles were of little use. They seemed stymied until a resourceful soldier, Francis McDonald, climbed on the shoulders of a comrade, got a handhold on the top of the parapet, and, with a spring and an agile wiggle, disappeared over the top. In the dark, he dropped down virtually in the middle of the British defenders. Before he could be recognized or apprehended, he had thrown the bolt on the heavy gate

1348 / A NEW AGE NOW BEGINS

that gave access to the summit of the British works and had opened it to admit his fellows. The British soldiers who had remained behind when Johnson dashed down the hill to repel the attack he believed was developing in his front, were heavily outnumbered. The night was filled with triumphant shouts: "We've got the fort! It's ours!" The British flag was hauled down, and Ludwig Gutbreath, a Pennsylvania German boy, handed it to his colonel.

The American cries from the top of the hill were Johnson's first word that the inner lines had been breeched. He collected what men he could and started up the hill, but before he had gone far he was intercepted by Americans led by the bloody-faced and frightening figure of Old Denmark. Johnson surrendered his sword to the American officer and called to his men to drop their arms, which they did readily enough. Only one British soldier escaped: a Lieutenant Roberts, a strong swimmer, dived into the river and swam a mile or more to the frigate *Vulture,* where he gave the news of the capture of Stony Point by the Americans.

The fierceness of the fighting at Stony Point is indicated by the fact that Wayne's elite corps of light infantry killed twenty redcoats and wounded seventy-four, all by the bayonet, while losing fifteen dead and eighty-four wounded. Their booty was impressive—543 prisoners, fifteen guns, and three Negro servants, as well as thirty-one tents, two works on the construction of fortifications, and a speaking trumpet. The cannon were turned on Verplanck's Point and on the *Vulture,* at anchor in the river.

Wayne, with his hero's wound bound up, wrote a hasty note to Washington: "The fort and garrison with Col. Johnson are ours. Our officers and men behaved like men who are determined to be free." The race for the honor (and the prize) of being the first to penetrate the British works was won by Fleury, the young French nobleman who had fought as a volunteer after Congress refused to give him a commission; he had attached himself to Lieutenant George Knox, who commanded the Forlorn Hopes, in order to be in the forefront, and he had dashed into the interior works and torn down the British flag. Knox himself had been second in the race, followed by Sergeant Baker of Virginia, who, although wounded four times, managed to be the first enlisted man to reach the citadel. Fleury and Knox gave their prize money to be distributed among the enlisted men, who, in addition, each got $140 as their portion of the value of the stores at the fort. The officers took for their prizes the three Negro boys, intending, Wayne explained, to free them "after a few years' service."

Stony Point was rightly accounted a brilliant victory, displaying all the elements of a classic attack: excellent intelligence and thorough reconnaissance in the preparation, and speed, surprise, shock, precise coordination, envelopment, and aggressiveness in the attack itself. It was immediately recognized as one of the most skillfully executed operations of the war. Washington was enthusiastic in his praise. Von Steuben declared that no European general could have done better. General Greene, with perhaps a touch of envy, spoke of "the perfection of discipline" (that rarest of qualities in any American force). "It will," he declared, "forever immortalize General Wayne." Colonel Alexander Spotswood of Virginia called the capture of Stony Point "the greatest stroke that has been struck this war." General John Armstrong, Wayne's fellow Pennsylvanian, wrote to him: "Once in an age, or in the course of some great Revolution, Heaven marks out some particular leader for an acquisition like yours at Stony Point."

Mad Charles Lee, living in his ruined Virginia mansion with his dogs, roused himself to write extravagantly to Wayne: "I do most sincerely declare that your action on the assault of Stony Point is not only the most brilliant, in my opinion, through the whole course of this war on either side, but that it is one of the most brilliant I am acquainted with in history." Pennsylvania at last had a hero to place alongside of the most renowned American generals. Benjamin Rush in Philadelphia noted, "Our streets for several days ring with nothing but the name of General Wayne. You are remembered constantly next to our great and good General Washington. . . . You have established the national honor of our country."

Perhaps the most flattering words were those of a British naval officer, Commodore George Collier, who wrote a detailed account of the action in his journal, describing the "enterprise" as "really a gallant one, and as bravely executed." Moreover, although entitled by the laws of war to put to death all those with weapons in their hands, the Americans, who "had made the attack with a bravery they never before exhibited," showed at the moment of victory "a generosity and clemency which during the course of the rebellion had no parallel."

Wayne's victory belongs with the few clear triumphs of American arms—with Washington's attack on Trenton, the Battle of Bennington, the defense of Fort Mercer against the Hessians, Kings Mountain, and

Cowpens (leaving aside Saratoga and Yorktown as engagements of a different magnitude). It came during a dry year, when events in the South were discouraging and there was little to sustain American hopes for an end to the war. Unfortunately it was somewhat clouded by an unseemly quarrel over those officers singled out in Wayne's official dispatches as having made outstanding contributions to the capture of the fort. Fleury was highly praised and on the basis of that praise was given one of only nine Congressional medals awarded in the course of the entire war. It might be questioned whether it was entirely appropriate for a lieutenant colonel to race ahead of his own soldiers to win such a prize. Field-grade officers, by good military practice, have more serious duties to perform than dashing in front of their junior officers to win a personal glory. On the other hand, it must be said that Fleury had displayed great skill and fortitude during the defense of Fort Mifflin, and he was clearly more than a showoff and adventurer. What especially annoyed those officers who failed to be mentioned in Wayne's dispatches (most of whom, perhaps not incidentally, were New Englanders) was the special mention given to Benjamin Fishbourn and Henry Archer, Wayne's aides, whose contribution to the victory was simply to help their wounded commander up the hill. Old Denmark, although he had been mentioned, felt that Wayne had failed to give him full credit for his part in the victory and wrote an anonymous letter to a Philadelphia newspaper enumerating errors in Wayne's account of the battle. Colonel Isaac Sherman went so far as to challenge Wayne to a duel.

The victory at Stony Point was a shock to the British, and of course to no one more than to Clinton, who, disheartened at the loss of the fort and its garrison and at the failure of the government to send him sufficient troops to subdue America, asked Germain to replace him with Cornwallis. His program of calculated devastation, which had been ordered by the government, was very little to his taste, but raiding parties continued to range the Connecticut coast. New London, already blockaded by British ships, was the next town marked for punishment by fire, along with Jersey seacoast towns. But when word of Stony Point reached Clinton, those operations were immediately abandoned. Clinton collected all available men-of-war and on the seventeenth started up the Hudson to recapture Stony Point and block an attack on Fort Lafayette at Verplanck's Point. As soon as word reached Washington of Clinton's movement, he ordered Wayne to burn and abandon Stony Point and carry off its cannon. Clinton's forces occupied the fort once more and began the laborious work of reconstructing its ruined defenses.

The *Annual Register,* in its account of the events of 1779, wrote of the capture of Stony Point that "it would have done honor to the most veteran soldiers," and a French officer noted: "Plan, execution, address, energy, in short, the most rare qualities were found united there, and I am convinced that this action will . . . elevate the ideas of Europe about the military qualities of the Americans. . . ." Moreover, for those preoccupied with Revolutionary numerology, there was a mystical significance in the fact that the attack had been made by troops (or so it was said) from thirteen states, and had taken thirteen hours. Rumor had it that Wayne had thirteen teeth in each jaw and that after Stony Point he grew three extra toes.

The Tories of New York, thoroughly disillusioned with General Howe, had looked forward to Clinton's assumption of command and the return of the main British army to the city, making New York once again the center of British operations in America. But the event itself proved, as had so many others, a bitter disappointment. Clinton soon proved as indolent and pleasure-loving as Howe and a good deal more oppressive. One of his first acts was to organize a fox hunt on the outskirts of the city. Since foxes were scarce, a Hessian soldier rode ahead of the handful of hounds dragging a bone at the end of a line; the hounds in turn were followed by Clinton and a few of his officers, dashing through fields and gardens and leaping fences in a parody of an English fox hunt. This exercise was derided by New Yorkers of every political persuasion.

Clinton's headquarters was a kind of perpetual open house, with a staff of twelve to wait on the swarms of guests. There were plays, as there had been in Boston and Philadelphia, sometimes written by Major André, and concerts by an orchestra in which Sir Henry played the violin. Clinton had four houses and a farm in various parts of the city. His pay was twelve thousand pounds a year in expense account and salary, but he complained that his fuel bill was two thousand pounds for one winter. "If this lasts," he wrote, "I shall be ruined notwithstanding the greatest economy." Clinton's housekeeper was a pretty young woman, Mrs. Mary Baddeley. The daughter of an Irish country gentleman, she had married a carpenter who had joined the army. When he was sent to America, Mary came with him and soon attracted Clinton's attention. Baddeley, like Burgoyne's quartermaster and many another ambitious lower-class Englishman, encouraged his wife's liaison, and he was promoted in consequence to the rank of captain. Mary was not a splendidly efficient housekeeper or an easy recruit to the general's bed. "Though she admitted me to certain liberties," Clinton wrote, with disarming candor, "I never could prevail on her to grant the last—until resentment did what . . . a warm attachment could not effect. She detected her husband in an intrigue with a common strumpet. She came to me directly—told him she would—and surrendered." Perhaps she was, all in all, the general's most notable conquest. She remained with him until his death and was mother to a number of his illegitimate children.

In addition to living in a lavish style that made him an object of ridicule even to those who enjoyed his hospitality, Clinton grew increasingly moody and snappish. He despised old James Robertson, who was governor of New York, and wrote that he was "smelling after every giddy girl that will let him come nigh her, and retailing amongst his female acquaintances the measures of headquarters when he can come at them." Robertson, for his part, had no very high opinion of Clinton: "He has not the understanding necessary for a corporal. He is inconstant as a weathercock and knows nothing." It seemed to some as though New York was under the joint direction of a nincompoop and a dirty old man.

The military government of the city was, as it had been in Philadelphia, riddled with graft and corruption. Robertson, once a quartermaster and barracks master, was, in the opinion of the patriots, "an accomplished thief." He established police courts in place of the civil courts and appointed the judges, who, in William Smith's words, "did what they were ordered, behaved as submissively as spaniels." Robertson and Oliver DeLancey, the adjutant general, "lavished away, and squandered upon favourites, upon little misses, upon strumpets, panderers and hangers-on; in balls, in dances, in rents, and feasts, in making walls, laying walks, illuminating trees, building music galleries, and in every other kind of dissipation that two old souls could imagine."

When Clinton himself was called to account for the ruinous expenses of his command, he replied cynically and doubtless truthfully, "That the expense is enormous is certain . . . that commissioners and contractors make fortunes—true. But in what war have they not done so?"

Clinton's suspension of the civil courts and with them the rights of many New Yorkers of Loyalist sympathies was especially galling.

Thomas Jones, a Loyalist judge of the superior court of the Province of New York, was convinced that "no General, nor Governor, whatever, had a right to abolish the law, shut up the courts to justice, declare the city a garrison, exercise military law, and establish arbitrary, illegal, courts of police, for the administration of justice within the limits and jurisdiction of the city." Indeed, no patriot writer could have been more critical of Clinton than was Jones. Through Clinton's "pussillanimity, misconduct, irresolution, and want of spirit, the honour of the nation was sacrificed, the blood of the loyalists with impunity shed, the empire dismembered, and the property of loyal Americans given up to rebellion. . . . To the timidity of Clinton, the honour, the glory, and dignity of Britain fell sacrifices, and she is bound to execrate him. . . ."

Henry Lee, who like Wayne commanded a special corps, though at the lower rank of major, had played a minor role in the capture of Stony Point. He yearned now to emulate Wayne's brilliant operation and persuaded Washington to approve his plan for an attack on Paulus Hook, a fort in British hands directly across the Hudson from New York. In that company of brilliant young staff officers who served Washington—Alexander Hamilton, Timothy Pickering, Tench Tilghman, Benjamin Tallmadge, and John Laurens—Lee was outstanding, a charming young man with a genius for military matters.

Sally Wister, the young Quaker diarist, had met Lee when Washington's army was camped near Winter Hill and had found him "not remarkable one way or the other." He sang "prettily" and talked "a great deal." His conversation, she wrote her friend Debbie, was about "how good turkey hash and fried hominy is (a pretty discourse to entertain the ladies)." Egged on by Sally, Lee and a fellow officer extolled Virginia and abused Maryland while Sally "ridiculed their manner of speaking" and teased them unmercifully. "They were not, I am almost certain," she wrote Debbie, "first-rate gentlemen. But they are gone to Virginia, where they may sing, dance, and eat fry'd hominy and turkey hash all day long, if they choose. Nothing scarcely lowers a man, in my opinion, more than talking of eating, what they love, and what they hate." But that was a Virginian.

The Paulus Hook garrison was an isolated one, and there were reports that discipline and security were lackadaisical among the two hundred or so soldiers in the fort. Washington had considered an attack on it but had decided the risks were too great. Lee, working with Captain McLane, whose information about the defenses of Stony Point had been

of such vital importance in planning that attack, made a careful reconnaissance of the approaches to Paulus Hook. They were, on the face of
it, simple enough and thoroughly disheartening. The fort stood on a
low sandspit that projected out into the river. From the north and
northwest, it could be approached across a salt marsh. A tidal creek,
Harsimus Creek, too deep to wade, ran across its front and was deep-
ened and extended by a man-made moat. A circle of strong abatis,
commanded by two small redoubts, provided the main line of defense,
while the heart of the position was a larger redoubt containing five guns
and situated near the center of the fortification. Three barracks and a
powder magazine completed the works. The garrison was commanded
by Major William Sutherland, who had under him a portion of the
Sixty-fourth Light Infantry under Captain Thomas Dundas, forty-one
Hessians under Captain Von Schaller, a body of invalid soldiers, and
some Tories from Cortlandt Skinner's New Jersey Volunteers. There
were some ordnance men and a few ladies of easy virtue who provided
distraction for those soldiers fortunate enough to enjoy their favors.

Washington, persuaded by Lee that an attack was feasible, assigned
four hundred soldiers to the operation: two hundred Virginia Continentals, McLane's partisans, and Captain Levin Handy's two Maryland
companies.

McLane, a rich and aristocratic young Philadelphian, was a particularly interesting character. He had inherited a sizable estate on the death
of his father just at the beginning of the war, and he had thereupon
undertaken to raise a company of soldiers. By the end of 1777 he had
spent most of his fortune (some £115,000) to buy handsome uniforms
for his men and pay their wages. For a time the uniforms seemed worth
the effort; McLane had captured a British patrol on Long Island
because, among the informally clad American forces, the British had
mistaken McLane's men for Hessians. At White Plains, in the retreat
through New Jersey, and at Trenton and Princeton, he had fought with
such bravery and enterprise that Washington gave him a battlefield
commission. In the winter of Valley Forge, his men were so successful at
harassing British and Tory foraging parties that they became known as
the "market stoppers." At the end of 1778, McLane's detachment of
soldiers was incorporated into the Delaware Regiment, which in turn
became part of Henry Lee's "Legion"—modeled, in large part, after
Banastre Tarleton's "Loyal Legion."

McLane was indeed the beau ideal of a handsome and dashing
young officer, with all the gifts of a born military leader; and he was

adored by his men, whose comfort and well-being he placed before his own. Yet he was too forthright and independent, too impetuous and indiscreet to be advanced in any systematic way through the military hierarchy. His dislike and indeed suspicion of Benedict Arnold, which began when he observed Arnold's highhanded and corrupt rule of the city of Philadelphia, simply served to get him in trouble with Washington. When McLane tried to tell Washington about Arnold's profiteering and, in McLane's opinion, treachery, Washington gave him a sharp rebuke.

On the morning of August 18, Lee left Paramus with the two companies of Marylanders and several wagons to create the impression that he was starting out to forage for supplies. The rest of his force joined him at New Bridge, and late in the afternoon he moved off toward Bergen. During McLane's reconnoitering of the approaches to Paulus Hook, he had encountered a deserter who had given him detailed information about the garrison. The distance from New Bridge to Bergen was sixteen miles, with another two miles to Paulus Hook. The timing of the attack was crucial not only because of the importance of the element of surprise but because it was thought that the moat could only be crossed at low tide. Lee's plan was to attack at midnight, just after the turn of the tide. This would presumably give him time to seize the fort, destroy the works, and carry off its defenders as prisoners. Washington took steps to be sure that boats were available across the Hackensack, west of Bergen, to assist in the escape of Lee's force in the event of pursuit.

The first misadventure of the expedition came when Lee's guide took him on a long and apparently unnecessary detour through rough country, so that Lee and his detachment reached their assembly point near Bergen three hours behind schedule. In the difficult and often exhausting march, half the Virginia troops under Major Clark had disappeared. There was the suspicion that Clark, who was furious at being under the command of Lee, an officer junior to him by some months, had dragged his feet or encouraged his men to drag theirs. In any event it was a blow to Lee to learn that his small force was so seriously depleted just at the moment when he was preparing for the assault. Washington, aware of Lee's hell-for-leather propensities, his impetuousness, and his desire for military glory, had been emphatic about one point: Lee must not carry through the attack if he lost the element of surprise. To stop now to try to locate the missing Virginians would be to delay the attack until daylight, which would put an end to any hope of surprise. Lee decided at once to push ahead without Clark's missing men.

The most uncertain element was the height of the water in the moat. Lieutenant Michael Rudolph was sent ahead to determine whether the moat was still fordable. The word that he brought back was that there was a narrow stretch where a crossing could be made. Lee immediately deployed his men in two columns, led by the Forlorn Hopes with their hooked poles that were meant to drag away the abatis. Behind the Forlorn Hopes on the left came the advance party under the command of Lieutenant Armstrong, and behind him a very modest "main body" led by Captain Forsyth. On the right Major Clark commanded those Virginians who remained, while Handy's Marylanders constituted the reserve. The deployment was almost exactly the same as that used at Stony Point, and again the soldiers were ordered not to fire their muskets under any circumstances until ordered to do so. The muskets were loaded, but no powder was put in the firing pans. The muskets were to be shouldered; each soldier was to hold his hat in his right hand until the ditch had been crossed; officers were instructed to kill any man who tried to fire without orders.

Rudolph, who had scouted out the best crossing place, splashed into the water with his men close behind him, and Lieutenant Mc Allister, in command of the other Forlorn Hopes, followed suit some twenty yards to the right. The Forlorn Hopes scrambled up the opposite bank and rushed forward to the abatis as a British sentry shouted the alarm and a few scattered shots were fired. It was McAllister's Forlorn Hopes who first found a gap in the abatis that had been left open for people coming to and from the fort. The lieutenant dashed through, followed closely by Clark and his men, who headed for the main redoubt, bayoneting any soldiers who seemed inclined to offer resistance.

Meanwhile Forsyth and McLane overran another blockhouse. Handy, sizing up the situation quickly, assigned his men to wherever the sounds of fighting indicated they were most needed. A number of British and Hessians were captured or killed in the first encounter, but Captain Schaller held out in the main redoubt with some twenty-five Hessians. He had six heavy cannon that could be brought into action as soon as there was enough light to see. The British in New York had caught the alarm, and there would certainly be a relief force on the way soon. Lee realized that he had little choice but to withdraw, and hastily, taking with him the captured British and Hessian soldiers. He had intended to set fire to the barracks, but he was told they sheltered women and children as well as soldiers. Collecting his prisoners, and not even pausing to spike the cannon, Lee beat a quick retreat.

At Hackensack the boats that were to carry them to safety over the river were missing. When Lee's troops had not appeared, the weary boatmen had dispersed. It was a dangerous situation. Lee's men had gotten their powder wet crossing the moat, they were desperately tired from their long forced march of the night before and from the strain and anxiety of the attack, and they were encumbered by prisoners who were almost as numerous as they were. Lee started his men for New Bridge, and near Weehawken they met Captain Thomas Catlett with fifty stragglers from the Second Virginia Regiment. Their powder was distributed so that each man in the combined force had enough for several rounds, and the soldiers pushed on. A few miles farther they met a relief column that had been sent out as soon as word had been received that the rendezvous with the boats had been missed. The column arrived just in time. Abram van Buskirk's New Jersey Volunteers, a Tory regiment on a foraging expedition, attacked Lee's left rear near the Liberty Pole Tavern (now Englewood), but they were beaten off, and Lee carried his prisoners back in triumph.

The Americans, by Captain Handy's calculation, bayoneted some fifty British and Hessians in their assault. They carried off with them 158 captives, one of whom had represented himself to Lee as Major Sutherland, commander of the fort, but who turned out to be in fact a private soldier masquerading as his commanding officer. The Americans lost less than ten men killed and wounded; and while the action was far from being, as the enthusiastic Handy reported to his father, "the greatest enterprise ever undertaken in America," it was a skillful raid carried out with a verve that proved an augury of the future career of Henry Lee. The fact that so much was made of such a modest triumph indicates, more than anything else, how starved the patriots were for military success in the summer of 1779.

Henry Lee and Alexander Hamilton, comrades-in-arms, had narrowly escaped capture when they had been dispatched to destroy some flour mills after the Battle of Brandywine in 1777. Lee later wrote of their escape: "Thus did fortune smile upon these two young soldiers, already united in friendship, which ceased only with life." Now, when Hamilton heard of Lee's raid, he wrote to Laurens: "The Philadelphia papers will tell you of a handsome stroke by Lee at Powle's Hook. . . . Lee unfolds himself more and more to be an officer of great capacity, and if he had not a little spice of the Julius Caesar or Cromwell in him, he would be a very clever fellow."

There was the same kind of unpleasant aftermath to Paulus Hook that had followed Stony Point. Several Virginia officers, Clark among them, were jealous of Lee's success and turned on their fellow Virginian, bringing charges against him for having taken precedence over officers who outranked him. Lee was, of course, cleared by a court-martial, and Congress sent him a letter of thanks and awarded him a gold medal, similar to that given to Wayne for his victory at Stony Point. But the incident showed once more the degree to which pride of rank and preference so often outweighed revolutionary ardor.

Perhaps the gloomiest event of the year for the New Englanders was the failure of a major expedition against Penobscot Bay. The little settlement of Bagaduce, now Castine, Maine (which was then part of Massachusetts), had been occupied in June by eight hundred British soldiers. From the large, sheltered harbor of Penobscot Bay, the British had mounted raids against American shipping, exercised control over the fisheries, threatened New England with the possibility of a military invasion, and undertaken to establish a new province for the settlement of Loyalists. The seizure of Bagaduce brought an immediate, almost frenzied reaction from the Massachusetts General Court. It was determined that the town must be attacked and wiped out before the British could make it impregnable. Three Continental vessels were borrowed from Congress, New Hampshire contributed one, and the remainder of the fleet of nineteen armed vessels and twenty frigates was collected by the state, with a number of privateers being pressed into service. Two thousand militia were assembled (almost a fourth of the entire force available to Washington), although less than a thousand apparently embarked with the fleet. The militia were under the command of General Solomon Lovell. General Peleg Wadsworth was second-in-command, and Lieutenant Colonel Paul Revere directed the artillery. The fleet was commanded by Dudley Saltonstall, who was instructed "to take every measure & use your utmost Endeavours to Captivate, Kill or destroy the Enemies whole Force both by Sea & Land. . . ." From the first there were the usual failures and disappointments. Despite impressive exertions by all concerned, the expedition was short on men, supplies, and ships. Lieutenant John Trevett, an officer on the sloop *Providence*, declined to accompany the force, noting that he had "no particular inclination to go to Penobscot, for I think the British will get information either at New York or Newport before our fleet can get ready to sail and if they do, I know that three or four large British ships can block them in and that will be the last of all our shipping."

Actually, the fleet got off without interference from the British, who got word late at New York, and it reached Penobscot at the end of July. There were three British sloops of war in the harbor, one of twenty and two of eighteen guns. Nine American ships sailed in to engage them, but there was an unfavorable wind, and the battle was inconclusive. Valuable time was lost in councils of war, but Nautilus Island at the entrance to the bay was seized and a battery was mounted, aimed at the channel between the island and the fort at Bagaduce that was being strengthened by the British. At that point the naval and military branches of the operation fell into a squabble about the tactics that were to be used in reducing the fort. While Saltonstall procrastinated, his junior officers petitioned him to take action. "We think," they wrote, "Delays in the present Case are extremely dangerous, as our Enemies are daily Fortifying and Strengthening themselves & are . . . in daily Expectations of Reinforcement." Their recommendation was "to go Immediately into the Harbour & Attack the Enemy's Ships." After agreeing, Saltonstall changed his mind, and when Lovell's men landed on July 28 on the southwest side of the peninsula where the fort protecting Bagaduce was situated, they had no naval support. The fighting was sharp, and the Massachusetts militia gave a good account of itself in fighting over precipitous terrain. At the end of the day the Massachusetts men held commanding ground above the fort, some five hundred yards away. Still Saltonstall, apparently unwilling to risk damage to his ships from the cannon in the fort, hung back. He would go in, he told Lovell, when the militia had stormed and taken the fort. Meanwhile he would write back to the General Court for instructions. It was a hopeless situation. Less than a thousand militia had no chance of capturing a fort armed by some eight hundred British regulars and reinforced by the three sloops of war. There were further councils of war and further dispatches to Boston, while the fort at Bagaduce was constantly strengthened and reinforcements were hastened from New York. August 13, one British ship of the line and five frigates were sighted. There was another council of war; to fight or to retreat up the Penobscot River was the point at issue. It is not surprising that the demoralized little navy decided to avoid an engagement. The militia hurried on board the transports and joined the Massachusetts navy in its flight up the river. There, to avoid capture by the British, most of the ships were abandoned and set afire, and the soldiers were forced to make their way by land back to Massachusetts. The fiasco was over. Mismanaged and ineptly led, especially by Saltonstall, the expedition against Penobscot Bay was a shattering setback to Massachusetts and a disheartening defeat for the Continental cause. Money and men that would much better have gone to the support of Washington's army had been thrown away. The venture is of interest primarily because it showed the capacity of a state, apparently already strained to the limit of its resources by four long years of war, to mount a large-scale operation where it considered it necessary to do so. In this respect, the expedition against Penobscot Bay, unsuccessful as it was, may be placed alongside examples of the remarkable recuperative powers displayed by the Southern states under the pressure of British invasion.

It was also a practical demonstration, if any were needed, of the need for able military and naval leadership and the difficulty of finding officers who were competent to carry out the tasks assigned them.

5

"Fort Wilson"

THE problems faced by Congress were as perplexing as ever. From the early months of 1779, the delegates were under constant pressure from Conrad Gérard, the French minister, to frame their requirements for a peace treaty. This proved to be a most complex and delicate subject. Two strong positions appeared at once. The Southerners wished to have assurances that they would have free navigation of the Mississippi River, and the New Englanders were determined that they should have guaranteed access to the fishing waters off Newfoundland and Nova Scotia, where generations of New England fishermen had spread their nets and set their lines and which were firmly believed to be essential to the prosperity of the region.

The issue was complicated by Gérard's hints that Spain was about to enter the war on the side of France and the United States and was simply waiting to be reassured by Congress about a few small matters like the ultimate ownership of the Floridas and the control of the Mississippi River. In other words, Spain wished some of the booty that might be available on a victorious termination of the present conflict, and France was plainly anxious to abet her, even though Spain's gains would come at the expense of the United States.

From the first days of Gérard's arrival, he had discovered a group of delegates to Congress who, simply out of gratitude for French support, were most anxious to be his dutiful agents. (James Lovell referred to them contemptuously as the "Lickspittles of the Plenipo.") The issue of the fisheries, first raised in early February, continued to be "agitated" until the middle of August. While the divisions that it produced were fairly straightforward ones, the debate over whether any treaty between England and the allies must have as an absolute condition recognition of the American right to the northern fisheries inherited the animosities aroused by the Deane affair. To many of the delegates, the New Englanders seemed selfishly stubborn in insisting on a provision in the treaty that would benefit only one section of the country. The New Englanders replied that no other section was so economically dependent on a single industry that might, as a result of the achievement of American independence, be withdrawn from it. Among their few allies south of New York were Richard Henry Lee, still true to his alliance with the Massachusetts radicals who, after all, had supported him staunchly in his attacks on Deane, and Henry Laurens, who had also been a bitter opponent of Silas Deane.

Gérard, who soon perceived the New Englanders as the principal impediment to the treaty arrangements favored by the French Court, worked assiduously behind the scenes to push the delegates along and to modify or compromise the proviso on the fisheries. On June 15, Congress replied to a letter from His Most Christian Majesty Louis XVI announcing the birth of a royal princess. These honest Republicans sent effusive congratulations on the happy event and asked the king "to oblige us with portraits of yourself and royal consort, that, by being placed in our council chamber, the representatives of these states may daily have before their eyes the royal friends and patrons of their cause." Along with the portraits, Congress would also be obliged for the loan of several million more *livres*.

By the middle of the summer, the wrangle in Congress over the fisheries clause was an open secret; in the press, a writer who signed himself "O Tempora! O Mores!" attacked the club or junto in Congress that was selfishly impeding the proper business of that body and delaying the appointment of a "person or persons to repair to Europe, with ample powers" for the purpose of concluding a treaty. It was the end of September before the essential requirements for a treaty were finally agreed upon. The next, almost equally arduous, task was that of selecting an individual to negotiate such a treaty, which was of course to be done in concert with France or, as the French hoped, under the tutelage and direction of the Comte de Vergennes. The two principal candidates were John Jay and John Adams. Jay was at this time president of Congress, which could be viewed as an asset or liability, while Adams was in Holland as an agent of Congress trying, among other things, to arrange a loan. It was Jay who wrote to Washington: "There is as much intrigue in this State House as in the Vatican but as little Secrecy as in a boarding school." Since the New Englanders had softened their ultimatum on the fisheries, they were determined to have the appointment of peace commissioner go to one of their own—a man who could be counted on, despite rather waffling instructions, to fight to the bitter end for the fisheries. The deadlock between Jay and Adams was finally broken by making Jay minister to Spain and Adams the peace commissioner.

"The Embarrassments Difficulties and Delays attending this Business in consequence of the Disputes between the late Commissioners," Elbridge Gerry wrote to John Adams, "have exceeded every thing of the Kind, which I have before met with: So far have some of their Friends in Congress been influenced by Attachments and Prejudices as to render it impossible to preserve their Friendship and Confidence, and at the same Time to act with becoming Freedom and Independence." After the election, James Lovell wrote that "some of us look as calm as if we were sure we had *laid the Devil*. Others look as much relieved as David when he became *certain* that the little Innocent was beyond hope, dead. . . ." He also noted that "there seems to be an Infinity of Good Humour in Consequence of the late Elections," and he was confident that the delegates would "go on swimming in the smooth pool of Complacency," at least for the time being.

With Adams chosen commissioner and Jay departing for Spain, the air in Congress grew clearer, but a host of practical problems that had been shoved aside while the delegates chewed over the terms of a possible peace treaty crowded in on them. The most insistent problem, of course, was money, and by late summer the delegates were in as desperate a plight as the end of the previous years had found them. William Floyd, delegate from New York, wrote, "Our treasury nearly Exhausted, Every Department out of Cash, no Magazines of provision laid up, our army Starving for want of Bread, on the Brink of a General Mutiny, and the prospect of a Spedy Supply is very Small. This is a melancholy Situation and would give our Enemies great pleasure, if they knew it." An additional irony lay in the fact that the city of Philadelphia had become a ruinously expensive place to live, largely because of Congress's constant emissions of paper money and the consequent inflation. As Floyd wrote to George Clinton, "when you are informed of the amazing Expense of living here . . . it seems as if the Devil was with all his Emmisaries let loose in this State to Ruin our money."

One delegate observed that he had paid £537 for a suit of clothes and had spent £21 to buy buttons for a servant's coat and have them sewn on. The only solution that Congress could come up with was to draw bills of draft or credit on John Jay and Laurens in the hope that they would in the meantime have been able to borrow money in Europe. This could not be called financing by any stretch of the imagination. It amounted to little but kiting checks on a national scale—drawing on money that did not exist in the declared but most remote hope that it would be available when the checks were finally presented for payment.

When Congress had first debated the issue of price control in February, 1777, James Wilson, among others, had opposed price-fixing on the practical grounds that it would not work. "There are certain things . . . ," he declared, "which absolute power cannot do. The whole power of the Roman emperors could not add a single letter to the alphabet. Augustus could not compel old bachelors to marry," and Congress could not fix prices. When Richard Henry Lee called inflation the "malady of the continent," Dr. Benjamin Rush replied "It is not a spasm, but a dropsy." Rush added: "I beg leave to prescribe two remedies for it. (1) Raising the interest on the money we borrow to six percent. This, like a cold bath, will give an immediate *spring* to our affairs; and, (2) *taxation*. This, like *tapping* [bloodletting], will diminish the quantity of our money, and give a proper value to what remains."

With Congress and the state assemblies unwilling or unable to take any effective steps to control prices, people took the matter into their own hands. Vigilante groups sprang up everywhere to force prices into line. In many of these, women were the leaders. A group of housewives in Fishkill, New York, visited a merchant whose prices they considered excessively high, weighed their own purchases, and paid the price of the goods to the Dutchess County Committee. In Boston a "female mobility" called Thomas Boylston to account for high prices, and a cartload of profiteers and suspected Tories who had refused to accept paper money were ridden out of the city, accompanied by a crowd of some five hundred citizens and a drum and a fife; the procession was led by a young man on horseback with a red coat, white wig, and drawn sword. The villains were taken to Roxbury, dumped out of the cart, and warned, on danger of their lives, not to return to Boston. In the same city the ladies, indignant at the prices of sugar and coffee and convinced that certain merchants were hoarding their supplies to force the prices up, organized their own remedy. "It was rumored," as Abigail Adams wrote to her husband, "that an eminent, wealthy, stingy merchant (who is a bachelor) had a hogshead of coffee in his store, which he refused to sell to the committee under six shillings per pound. A number of females, some say a hundred, some say more, assembled with a cart and trucks, marched down to the warehouse and demanded the keys, which he refused to deliver. Upon which, one of them seized him by his neck and tossed him into the car. Upon his finding no quarter, he delivered the keys, when they tipped up the cart and discharged him, then opened up the warehouse, hoisted out the coffee themselves, put it into the truck and drove off. . . . A large concourse of men stood amazed, silent spectators of the whole transaction. . . ."

The rapid inflation (which, by and large, hurt the poor man more than the well-to-do and the rich—as indeed almost everything does) and the wild speculation that it encouraged fanned class resentment in Philadelphia in the spring and summer of 1779. By November the depreciation of Continental paper had reached thirty-nine to one. Many ordinary citizens, artisans, and laboring men were convinced that corrupt fortunes were being made, very largely at their expense and at that of the patriot cause. In addition, popular emotions were further inflamed by the efforts of the Pennsylvania moderates (or conservatives), now calling themselves the Republicans, to overthrow the radical state constitution of 1776, whose supporters called themselves the Constitutionalists. The Republicans were embarrassed, they declared, to be ruled by such an awkward and misshapen body as a unicameral legislature, which every man of learning knew to be a political monstrosity. The Constitutionalists fought back with the charge that the Republicans wished to fasten a House of Lords on the honest, democratic government of Pennsylvania.

These political tensions and resentments were increased by the continued rise of prices. Self-appointed committees of citizens seized cargoes of wheat going down the Delaware and returned them to the city. The stores of Philadelphia merchants were inventoried by the same committees, and wagons leaving the city with tea, sugar, and rum were sequestered by the radicals. This dangerous brew fermented through the summer, to the dismay of the delegates to Congress, who felt themselves caught in the middle. "This City," Gouverneur Morris wrote, "is now the scene of politics high and low. I may add it is the scene of faction anarchy and distraction. . . . A storm is gathering and will burst upon the heads of our enemies, perhaps of our own. Would to God that the desire of that great luxury to be free was the great desire of my countrymen, but other luxuries more alluring have influenced but too much upon their conduct. The torrent of *paper money* hath swept away with it much of our morals and impaired the national industry to a degree truly alarming." Richard Henry Lee feared that "the innundation of money . . . will bury the liberty of America. . . . The demon of avarice, extortion, and fortune-making seizes all ranks."

In the early days of October, all these matters came to a head in a dangerous riot. The city was full of unpaid and angry militia, a number of them Germans from the western parts of the state. In addition, there were unemployed artisans, and "foolish, reckless boys," the ingredients of a mob. Collected at Burn's Tavern, where their irritations were fanned by rum and beer, the leaders of the mob decided to hunt down some of the exploiters and profiteers, who were, in their minds, largely synonymous with the Republican party. One target of their wrath was James Wilson, an active and articulate opponent of the popular party who had also had the temerity to serve as lawyer for two highly unpopular Quakers who had been charged with treason. It was also rumored that Wilson had speculated in commodities, a rumor that was apparently groundless.

The leaders of the mob, two militia officers named Bonham and Pickering, proposed marching to Wilson's house to express the people's displeasure with its owner. Word was brought at once to Wilson, who immediately applied to the assembly for protection. The assembly referred him promptly to the president and the council, but the time was short, and Wilson and other Republicans who knew themselves to be among those proscribed by the mob decided to trust to their own resources to defend their lives and property. A group of twenty or so Republicans collected at Wilson's house on Walnut and Third streets and organized themselves into an armed garrison. It was a reckless and ill-considered act, if an understandable one. Among the defenders of "Fort Wilson" were Colonel Stephen Chambers, a militia officer and a member of Supreme Executive Council of Pennsylvania; Robert Morris, the so-called "financier of the Revolution," who made a great fortune in that role; General Thomas Mifflin, one of the senior military officers of the state; John Mifflin, a relative of the general; Sharp Delany, a druggist; Daniel Clymer; and William Lewis. The only thing most of the men had in common was that they were active Republicans, committed to reforming the constitution of 1776.

The mob, made up primarily of disgruntled militia, eventually approached Walnut Street, where Captain Allen McLane, the brilliant young Philadelphia officer who had raised and equipped a company at his own expense, and Colonel William Grayson, a respected officer of the Pennsylvania Line, intercepted them and tried to persuade them to disperse. Pickering threatened McLane with his bayonet and then forced him aside as the tide of men swept on down the street to the Wilson house. When the crowd drew abreast of the house, one of its defenders, a militia captain, called out peremptorily from an upstairs window, ordering the militia to move on. The order and tone in which the command was delivered brought an immediate response—a musket shot that killed the officer. The men in the house returned the fire, and what followed was a small battle, with the militia besieging the substantial brick house and the occupants fighting for their lives. Grayson and McLane managed to slip into the house while the militia, driven off by heavy fire that left five of their number killed or wounded in the street, sent for a cannon to fire on the "fort." General Mifflin, at a second-floor window, identified himself and shouted to the soldiers to disperse, trying to make himself heard above the noise of firing and the shouts of the besiegers. The only response was a bullet that smashed the sash by the general's head and showered him with splinters of wood and glass.

A few moments later, an assault party—stripped to their shirts and armed with sledges and bars—dashed out of a side street, covered by a brisk fire from their companions, and battered down a door in the rear of the house. As the men rushed through the door they were met by fire from the stairs. A colonel who wounded one of the invaders with his pistol was dragged down and bayoneted before he could reload. But the attackers were outnumbered, and the expected support from their fellows was not forthcoming. The militia therefore withdrew, while the defenders rushed to shore up the doorway with tables and chairs.

Before the attack could be resumed or the fieldpiece brought into action, President Joseph Reed arrived with two mounted dragoons of the City Light Horse; his knee buttons were unfastened and his boots unlaced, and he carried a pistol in his hand. The sight of the chief executive officer of the state descending on them like an avenging fury had a sobering effect on the rioters. Even before the rest of the City Troop clattered up under the command of Major Lenox, who was in his shirt-sleeves, most of the militia had faded away. The troopers seized twenty-seven stragglers and clapped them in the prison behind the State House. The dead included four militiamen plus a Negro boy who had joined the mob; fourteen were wounded. Within the house, the militia officer who had given the initial order for the crowd to disperse was the only one killed, although three men were wounded.

The end of the battle was not the end of the affair. The principal defenders of "Fort Wilson" were persuaded to go into hiding, while rumors circulated through the city that the militiamen were determined to free those of their companions who had been imprisoned. The City Troop was kept on the alert, but the bad blood between Benedict Arnold (then in command of Philadelphia) and Joseph Reed hampered efforts to take proper security measures. On the morning following the riot, the militia officers appeared at the courthouse to demand that the prisoners be released. Word came that the militia of Germantown were on the march to Philadelphia to free their fellows. President Reed left Timothy Matlack, one of the radical leaders, to cope with the angry militia and rushed off to intercept the Germantown soldiers. Matlack meanwhile decided to release the prisoners.

When Reed returned from Germantown, where he had persuaded the militia to disband, he called leaders from both factions together to try to prevent further disorder. As Robert Morris wrote Wilson, "The Storm is over for this day without any mischief except Mr. Lewis is in Gaol. . . . The President I am told is determined to put the Laws in force or resign. . . . The Ferment is particularly high against you. . . . The poor unfortunates who lost their lives yesterday have been buried this evening with the Honours of War—a Circumstance not Calculated to allay the Passions of Men in a Ferment."

"I wish I had time to speak of the awful state of our national debt and credit," Henry Laurens wrote John Adams on the day of the riot, "the field is too wide for the compass of a letter. . . . We are at this moment on the brink of a precipice, and what I have long dreaded and often intimated to my friends, seems to be breaking forth—a convulsion among the people. Yesterday produced a bloody scene in the streets of this city . . . and from circumstances which have come to my knowledge this morning, there are grounds for apprehending much more confusion. The enemy has been industriously sapping our fort, and we, gazing and frolicking. . . ." Perhaps the "bloody scene" of yesterday would bring about some belated reforms, "but," Laurens continued, even more gloomily, "what shall we do by and by, and not far distant, for quieting a hungry and naked army?"

Wilson was indignant at being forced to remain outside the city while his enemies came and went as they pleased. He met Captain John Barry, the naval officer who had just won praise from Washington for "gallantry and address," and the two made plans for a counteroffensive against the Philadelphia mobs. Wilson was determined, he wrote Robert Morris, to take "further Steps for our Security, and to prevent repeated and continual Insults." A group of citizens must join together to "give some Stability to our Defense of the first Rights of Man." When enough men had been recruited, their names could be submitted to President Reed "with a Tender of the Services of the Subscribers in support of the Government." Such measures, Wilson noted, "will unite and strengthen us, and will awe the Insurgents."

Reed preferred another course. The defenders of Wilson's house were ordered to post very high bail with the assembly for court appearance, but the case never came to trial, and five months later the executive council passed "an act of free and general pardon" to all concerned.

While the particular conditions that produced the "Fort Wilson Riot" were peculiar to Pennsylvania and had their origin in the bitter struggle over independence and over the radical constitution of the state, the riot was only an extreme manifestation of class resentments and animosities that had their counterparts in almost every state. This is certainly not surprising, since at the heart of the Revolution was a stubborn resistance to all forms of privilege and status that denied full opportunity to able and ambitious men, however humble their origins might be, provided of course that they were not black slaves.

That the "Fort Wilson Riot" did not result in large-scale disorders in Philadelphia and perhaps throughout the state was due, more than anything else, to the fact that the Constitutionalists who made up the popular radical party were in power. Had the Republicans been in control of the state, the toll of four militia dead and fourteen wounded might very well have provoked open civil war; the Germantown militia were, after all, ready to march to the city, and James Wilson talked darkly of a paramilitary group to defend the lives and property of the Republican leaders.

6

Parliament Takes Stock

W HEN Parliament convened on November 25, 1779, His Majesty's speech from the throne called upon all Britons "to exert their united efforts in the support and defence of their country, attacked by an unjust and unprovoked war and contending with one of the most dangerous confederacies that was ever formed against the crown and the people of Great Britain." To meet the ruinous expenses of the war, the king relied "on the wisdom and public spirit of the commons for the requisite supplies." In the House of Lords, Lord Chesterfield "entered into a panegyrical analysis of the several parts of it [His Majesty's speech]. He bestowed high encomiums on his Majesty's benevolent attention to the interests of his people. . . . He concluded, after taking notice of the dangerous schemes which appear to be forming by foreign powers against this kingdom, with pressing unanimity on every side of the house, as the only possible means of averting the dangers and evils with which the nation was surrounded."

Rockingham rejected these banalities. "Was there a noble lord in that house," he asked, "who could lay his hand on his heart, and fairly congratulate his Majesty on the blessings enjoyed by his government? It was impossible: no bias, no prejudice, no temptation, could so far confound truth and reason with their opposites, as to convert the very cause of our misfortunes into blessings." Rockingham took "an abstract view of his Majesty's reign," contrasting the peace and happiness of its beginning "with the misery, the distresses, the degradation, and the present diminution of the British dominions. This fatal chain of ruin and destruction to every part of the empire," he said, "he had early foreseen in the present reign." Rockingham ended by proposing a motion that stated that "only new councils and new counsellors" could save the state from "public ruin." The young Lord Lyttleton, counted as one of the king's party because he held a lucrative office of the Crown, joined in the attack on the ministry. No one, he declared, could even say what the government they were urged to support with unanimity stood for. "Fatal experience had shown the futility of their late policy: America stared them in the face; it shewed the folly of the ministers in a rash, a mad war, in which it was evident success was unattainable. . . ." Ireland, he said, was in an equally desperate and rebellious state because of the load of taxes it had to bear and the repressive rule of English officials.

Lord Shelburne came to the support of Rockingham and Lyttleton. He refused to be silenced by the argument that criticism of the king and his ministers would give comfort to the enemy. Shelburne indicted the ministry for the loss of Dominica, St. Vincent, and Grenada in the Caribbean, as well as for its inattention to Jamaica. The Duke of Richmond also attacked the speech and its makers, with special attention to the Earl of Sandwich, who, he said, should be ashamed to remain in office "when every day's experience afforded fresh proofs of his total unfitness for that important station." Lord Camden joined in the call for a new government and gave "a compendious history of the whole course of the American war" and the mistakes and blunders of the North ministry in pursuing it. But on a division of the House, Rockingham's vote of no-confidence lost by a two-to-one margin, 41 to 82.

In the House of Commons, Lord Cavendish and David Hartley proposed a motion similar to Rockingham's, and a warm debate followed. Much was made of the fact that Plymouth, "the great naval key of the kingdom, and the second naval arsenal, was left without defence to the mercy of our enemies." England had blundered in Ireland with highhanded and greedy exactions; it had failed in the Caribbean and in the Mediterranean; Gibraltar was besieged by the Spanish and British trade "annihilated." The situation in America was "so gloomy, that the ministry had cautiously drawn a veil over it, to keep it from the public eye." The army was enormously expensive, poorly used, and riddled with corruption and favoritism. "The experienced veteran was obliged to make way for the raw subaltern, who had more friends or fortune, than merit or claim from long service, to recommend him. Thus murmurings, jealousies, and grievances were created, among those who were fighting the battles of their country and undergo all the fatigues and perils of war. . . ."

Most dangerous of all was the fact that the government was becoming, increasingly, the creature of the king. It was said that "the King was his own minister, his own admiral in chief, his own general, his own secretary, his own president of the council, his own financier." His ministers thus hid behind the shield of the king's invulnerability, which concealed every "knavery, servility, and every species of native folly, treachery, and villainy," saying, when challenged, "I but obey the orders of my sovereign. . . . This doctrine, by which the responsibility of the servants was transferred to the personal and political character of the master, directly tended to overthrow the constitution, and ought to be checked, or instantly censured, in the most positive terms."

In the debate that followed, North defended his ministry tenaciously. He was answered by Charles James Fox, who placed particular emphasis on the improper authority of the Crown. "It was not the mere rumor of the streets, that the king was his own minister," Fox said, "the fatal truth was evident, and had made itself visible in every circumstance of the war carried on against America and the West Indies." After a very long debate, the House divided: for the amendment, 134, against it, 233. A Scot named Adam switched from the Whig to the government side, whereupon Fox ridiculed him as a turncoat "in a strain of very poignant satire." Adam challenged him to a duel and wounded him, "but not dangerously."

The problems of Ireland took up a great part of the time and attention of the delegates during this session of Parliament, but David Hartley brought the discussion back to the American war with a proposal that negotiations be undertaken to effect a truce. He was informed on good authority that many Americans wished to escape from the French alliance, having found it more of a burden than a help. When he had urged North to undertake such negotiations, North had replied that he would never "submit or consent to treat with America upon the footing of an equal." When the Americans were ready to petition as "subjects aggrieved," North had no doubt but that Parliament would receive their petition in a frank and generous spirit. But to enter into negotiations as though America were an independent nation would be to abandon the very principle of Parliamentary authority.

In the debate that followed, the opposition members came back repeatedly to the question of Ireland, where, it was reported, forty-two thousand men were in arms against the government. Burke "also adverted to the consequences of the unhappy contest with America, and the calamitous state of the whole empire. America was lost, we were stripped of our West-India possessions . . . we were divided in our counsels and the administration was incapable and unpopular. But still the same obstinate perseverance was to be adhered to, so long as we had a man, a shilling, or a foot of land. It appeared to be finally determined by the cabinet, that every unfortunate man who had been sent to America upon the romantic and impracticable plan of the conquest or subjugation of that country should either fall by the sword, or be led captive by a victorious enemy."

The Irish had declared for nonimport of British goods and had asserted their own claim to be "free and independent." They had raised a mob in Dublin, and nothing short of free trade would appease them. Why, Burke asked scathingly, had the ministry not followed the same disastrous policy it had pursued in America? Why had they not shut up the port of Dublin and prohibited popular meetings? "Sad and dear-brought experience had taught them the folly, as well as impracticability of such measures: the danger of the present awful moment had made insolence and arrogance give way to fear and humiliation."

Charles James Fox, recovered from his dueling wound, followed Burke, speaking with "uncommon force and energy." He, like Burke before him, "introduced into his speech many observations concerning the American war; and spoke of that as the source of all the public calamities. It was that war, he said, which had led us gradually, step by step, into all our present misfortunes, and national disgraces. What was the cause of our wasting forty millions of money, and sixty thousand lives? The American war. What was it that produced the French re-script, and a French war? The American war. What was it that produced the Spanish manifesto, and a Spanish war? The American war. What was it that had armed forty-two thousand men in Ireland, with arguments carried on the points of forty-two thousand bayonets? The American war. It was that war which had already lost us the empire of America. It was that war which had caused the disgrace of the British flag. . . . It was that war which had already rendered us contemptible to all Europe, which had caused us to be deserted by friends and allies, and despised and trampled upon by our enemies." All these ills stemmed from the same cause, "this increasing, this alarming influence of the crown," and the noblemen and gentlemen in both houses had resolved that "nothing would ever content them, but reducing the influence of the crown within due and constitutional bounds."

Day after day the debate dragged on, entangled in Commons with the question of approving the vast expenditures requested by the government to carry on the war. The arguments of the Whigs were bitter ones. They felt that they had reason and justice on their side, but the Court party, through graft and corruption, held tight to the votes. Sir Charles Bunbury seemed to put his finger on the matter quite precisely. "On one side of the house," he declared, "a minority, great part of which were sunk into despondency, from a deep sense of the wretched situation of the nation; and another part roused to the loudest expressions of rage and indignation against those whom they considered as the authors and provokers of the public calamities. On the other side of the house was a sullen majority, silent within the doors, and loquacious without." In the House of Commons this majority suppressed their misgivings and voted obediently with the government, but outside, under the influence of a little Madeira or port, they did not hesitate to admit quite freely that the situation of the country was a desperate one. England was already a hundred and ninety million pounds in debt, on top of which were crushing new charges; and it had been amply demonstrated that an army of seventy thousand men could not subjugate America. "To entertain an idea now of the probability of our being able to conquer America," Bunbury declared, "was as absurd as any idea of a lunatic in Bedlam could be."

Fox then questioned North and Lord Germain as to whether the war in America for the coming year was to be a defensive or an offensive one. Germain replied that "as far as he knew, the American war was not abandoned." Fox called it a quibble. Apparently, the administration intended to "strike some blow against the revolted colonies, to reduce them to obedience by force of arms. But though this might be their design, it was certainly not in their power. They might as well think of subduing Turkey, as conquering America."

In the days following, the debate focused on the subject of military expenditures. Here the government was most vulnerable, because there were innumerable pockets into which money was put to be hauled out at the discretion of the king's ministers, which was to say, generally, by the king, without any check or review by Parliament. The most conspicuous such pocket was the "army extraordinaries," whereby any deficits that might appear in army accounts were made up out of a special grant. Such a provision was, of course, an invitation to inefficiency and venality, since it was almost impossible to control or to audit effectively. In 1777 alone the "extraordinaries" had come to one million, two hundred thousand pounds.

It was not, Burke pointed out, simply that money spent in such a reckless way was lost to the public treasury. "It was the source of much positive evil. . . . It introduced . . . a kind of slovenliness, a correspondent want of care, and a want of foresight, into all the national management. What is worst of all, it soon surrounds a supine and inattentive minister with the designing, confident, rapacious, and unprincipled men of all descriptions. They are a sort of animal tenacious of their proper prey: and they soon drive away from their habitation all contrary natures. A prodigal minister is not only not saving, he cannot be either just or liberal."

There the matter rested for the time being. Parliament, having consumed almost a month on rancorous and inconclusive debate, voted to renew the king's right to suspend habeas corpus and then adjourned until January 27, scattering to their estates to hunt, drink, and feast for the holidays.

At last, though the Whig opposition did not yet have a clear intimation of it as they left for home, the country was stirring out of a kind of desponding lethargy. The issue was money, but behind that lay a general sense of national malaise; a feeling that the king was indeed holding the country's nose in a mess that he had made; an instinct that government, behind all its assurances and calls for national unity, had taken the wrong course and would not give it up. The Parliamentary debates, which at the time had seemed just another exercise in futility, had awakened the country to its true situation. The lethargy turned almost overnight into a mood of angry frustration. A meeting at the Guildhall in London passed a motion attacking "the present increased, enormous, and undue influence of the crown" and supporting Shelburne's proposed motion for the appointment of a committee to examine the public expenditures. The Duke of Cumberland, the king's brother, wrote an open letter supporting "a fair and candid investigation of the expenditure of the public money" with a view to reform so that, in the future, such money should be spent "in such exertions by sea and land, as might restore his Majesty's dominions to their former splendour. . . ." The freeholders of York petitioned Commons on December 30 for a reform of public spending. Much public money had been squandered, the address to Commons declared, and that in a time when the nation was nearly impoverished, and this money had been used to give the king "a great and unconstitutional influence, which, if not checked, might prove fatal to the liberties of this country." The House was called upon "to reduce all exorbitant emoluments, to rescind and abolish all sinecure places and unmerited pensions. . . ." Moreover, a committee of sixty-one gentlemen was appointed to carry on the agitation for fiscal reform "and such other measures as might conduce to restore the freedom of Parliament."

Middlesex followed suit on the seventh of January, and numerous other counties and cities framed similar addresses and petitions to Parliament. Committees of correspondence were appointed by many counties and towns to develop a plan of common action and to write letters to members of Parliament, pressing for reform. Many of the meetings were attended by members of Parliament who defended their actions or, in many instances, encouraged their constituents to take steps designed to curtail the powers of the king. The issue of the American war came up repeatedly in these meetings, and almost invariably in a spirit prejudicial to the policy of the administration. At the meeting of the freeholders of Whiltshire, Fox himself addressed the gathering, saying that he had never before spoken "to an uncorrupt assembly," a plain slap at the king's men in the House of Commons. It was up to those present, he told them, to show a resolute concern for their own rights. They must insist on a redress of their grievances. "It would not be in the power of the best or ablest minister to make them great or happy, unless they had themselves the spirit and will to become so." In Essex, a large company heard Thomas Day, a "respectable character before little known," speak most eloquently of the plight of the kingdom. "If there was ever a period," he declared, "which called upon every independent man to speak his sentiments, that period was now come: . . . the affairs of the nation were hopeless, except for the rising spirit of the people, exasperated by an unexampled series of provocations and disgraces."

North and his ministers were so dismayed at these signs of growing resistance to the government and the expressions of open hostility to the king that considerable pains were taken to try to stir up the friends of the Court party to hold meetings on their own account and pledge their support to the king and his ministers. "It was contended by those who opposed the petitions and associations," we are told by the editor of the *Annual Register* (doubtless Burke himself), "that the true sense of the counties could not be collected, nor the matters proposed duly examined in such meetings, so new in their form, and so void of regularity, or any known or established authority . . . that the committees of correspondence were apparently intended to over-awe the legislature . . . and that the petitions and resolutions, which were framed in the county meetings, were calculated to produce diffidence and suspicions in the minds of his Majesty's subjects, at a time when unanimity and confidence in government were essentially necessary." The editor noted, in a kind of an aside: "It was, however, observed, that a great part of the persons, by whom protests to this purpose were signed, were placement pensioners, and others connected with government." The spirit of the meetings may be familiar to the reader. The British, it seemed, had gone to school with their cousins, the rebels of America. Popular protest was apparently becoming a new mode of political action.

In March a kind of congress, though no one of course called it that, came together in London. The gathering was made up of deputies from the committees of correspondence in thirteen counties, the cities of London and Westminster, and the towns of Nottingham and Newcastle. A Yorkshire clergyman "of distinguished character and large fortune" was appointed chairman, and the deputies drew and published a plan for a national association. This document called for "popular jealousy to . . . awake, and popular virtue to assert itself. . . ." By "popular" was meant, of course, only the substantial property holders—freeholders— of England, not the landless tenants and the workers and artisans of the cities and towns, not to mention the urban poor whose plight was often desperate. If it was exaggerated to declare that "the very vitals of the constitution had received a mortal wound," the phrase nevertheless served to exemplify the degree of dissatisfaction that existed among those who had the means of expressing their discontent. "A venal majority might . . . be seen . . . in the House of Commons, session after session, moving obsequious to the nod of the minister . . . while every effort of reason and argument, urged by an independent few, had only been answered by numbers, dumb to every other reply."

Reforms, it was agreed, should be pressed by direct representations to Parliament, carried by the deputies plus a hundred more representatives of the counties, chosen in proportion to the population. The deputies, moreover, were charged with preparing a "circular letter, recommending a plan of national union and association, to be dispersed throughout the kingdom. . . ." To many Englishmen such words recalled the beginnings of the American opposition to the authority of Parliament, but now the opposition was directed against the king's abuse of his powers.

Even in the ranks of the government there were some alarming defections. In November, 1779, Lord Gower, who had been one of the strongest supporters of the North ministry, resigned his office on the ground that the policy being pursued in America "must end in ruin to his Majesty and the country." North, describing his efforts to prevail on Gower not to resign, wrote the king, "In the argument Lord North had certainly the disadvantage, which is that he holds in his heart, and has held for three years past, the same opinion with Lord Gower." They were poignant and revealing words, the words of a man held prisoner by his sense of duty to his monarch.

It was abundantly clear that the enemies of the ministry and the friends of America were constantly impeded by the French alliance. The editor of the *Annual Register,* recapitulating the events of the close of 1779 and the early months of 1780, made a shrewd analysis of that unhappy union: "Though no great probability had hitherto appeared of a reduction of the British colonies in America, yet the campaign of 1779 had been in many respects favourable to the royal arms, nor had the Americans derived those advantages from their alliance with France which might have been expected. The difference of manners and of religion between the French and the Americans appears to have excited some jealousy in the latter; nor had they found the French very sincere, or at least very useful allies. It was the interest of the Americans to have put as speedy an end to the war as possible, and to have entirely removed the British troops from the continent. But this seems not to have been the intention of the French: or, if they had such a design, they executed it with very little judgment. The rashness and ill conduct of D'Estaing in Georgia, in 1779, have rendered abortive all his efforts in favour of the Americans. . . ."

In the editor's view a loan of money, of which the Americans were in great need, "would have been much more beneficial to them, than any other aid they were likely to derive from that quarter." If France had, for example, lent or given to the Americans the sum required to equip *one* French fleet, it would doubtless have been a greater help to Congress than all the French ships, sailors, and soldiers that entered American waters. But France, of course, had no interest in such a policy. She wished to use the Revolution, as we have frequently indicated, to advance her own interests, which, under the circumstances, was not unnatural or reprehensible. To have given the Americans a large sum of money that might have enabled them to bring the wasting and destructive war to an early end would have been counter to French aims.

"But whatever the inconveniencies they might labour under," the writer for the *Annual Register* added significantly, "whatever might be their wants, and however wearied with the long continuance of the war, the American colonies yet discovered no disposition to submit again to the authority of Great Britain."

7

The Surrender of Charles Town

T HE British success at Savannah encouraged Clinton to press ahead with a plan for an attack on Charles Town, a move that he would hardly have dared undertake had Savannah fallen to Lincoln and D'Estaing. Pursuing what appeared to be a successful "Southern strategy," he withdrew three thousand British soldiers from Newport and, supplementing them with Hessians and Tories, assembled an expeditionary force of 3,500 soldiers to make an amphibious assault on the leading city of the South. Some 5,000 sailors and marines were also aboard the fleet that sailed from New York on December 26, 1779, under the command of Admiral Marriot Arbuthnot.

The same seasonal storms that before had wreaked havoc with both French and British fleets hit Arbuthnot's ships with such force that they were heavily damaged; many horses were so badly injured by the tossing of the ships that they had to be destroyed; seasickness, terror, and misery afflicted sailors and soldiers alike, and the fleet was dispersed over a large area. The voyage from New York to Edisto Inlet off Charles Town took six weeks, and it was February 11, 1780, before the British force landed. As one Hessian officer wrote: "It may be said that the most strenuous campaign cannot be as trying as such a voyage; for (1) one cannot prepare a decent meal; (2) one takes every morsel with the

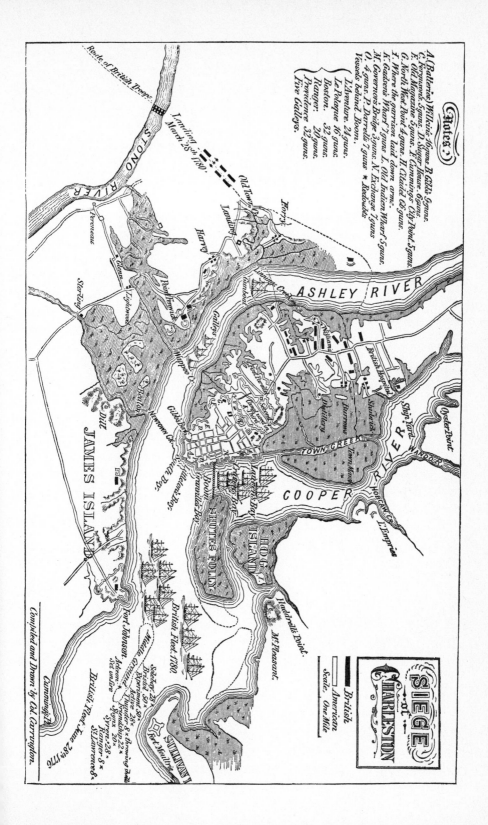

**SIEGE
of
CHARLESTON**

British ▄▄▄
American ▭▭▭
Scale. One Mile

Notes :—

A. Batteries; W. Belleisle 16 guns. B. 6&18s 5 guns.
C. Ferguson's 5 guns. D. King James.
E. Old Magazine 5 guns. F. King James 5 guns.
G. North West Point 4 guns. H. Cummings City Point 5 guns.
I. Where the garrison laid down arms. H. Citadel 68 guns.
K. Gadsden's Wharf 7 guns. L. Old Indian Wharf 5 guns.
M. Governors Bridge 5 guns. N. Exchange 7 guns.
O. 4 guns. P. Darrell's 7 guns. * Redoubts
Vessels behind Boom.

L'Aventure, 24 guns.
Le Polygne 16 guns.
Boston. 32 guns.
Ranger. 20 guns.
Providence 32 guns.
Five Galleys.

Compiled and Drawn by Col. Carrington.

British Fleet June 28th 1776

British Fleet, 1780.

JAMES ISLAND

ASHLEY RIVER

COOPER RIVER

WANDO

STONO RIVER

TOWN CREEK

HOG ISLAND

SHUTES FOLLY

SULLIVANS I.

Fort Moultrie

Mt. Pleasant.

Fort Johnson

Route of British Troops

Landing March 28th 1780

greatest difficulty and discomfort; (3) one enjoys not a moment of sleep because of the fearful rolling and noise. . . ." A week later he wrote, "Everything the same! . . . Terrible weather! Snow, rain, hail, storm, foaming waves and bitter cold."

Lincoln, after the defeat at Savannah, had joined Moultrie in Charles Town. He had hardly arrived before an epidemic of smallpox, the first in twenty-five years, broke out in the city and hampered preparations for its defense. Many of the militia refused to enter Charles Town, saying that "they dreaded that disorder more than the enemy." The defenses of the city, recently reorganized and strengthened by the Chevalier de Cambray, had already started to deteriorate. Slaves, who in the South normally did such work, were unavailable, and little was done to shore up the defenses. South Carolina's six Continental regiments, which had a nominal strength of twenty-four hundred, had wasted away through death, wounds, desertion, and the expiration of enlistments to no more than eight hundred. The South Carolina government, in Ramsay's words "had neither the policy to forgive nor the courage to punish" those militia who, "in the preceding campaign, deserting their country's cause, had repaired for protection to the royal standards of General Prevost. Those who stayed at home and submitted, generally saved some part of their property. Those who continued with the American army were plundered of every thing that could be carried away, and deprived of the remainder . . . by wanton destruction." Congress, appealed to for assistance, could think of nothing better than proposing that the slaves be armed to aid in the defense of the city. Since the desertion of slaves to the British had been one of the most demoralizing aspects of the war to the Southerners, this advice was greeted unenthusiastically. In any event, the Carolinians argued, there were not enough weapons available to arm the slaves even if such a dangerous course were to be followed.

Fifteen hundred North Carolina and Virginia Continentals were sent to bolster the city's defenses, along with two frigates. The South Carolina assembly, discovering a far bolder spirit than the governor and his council had displayed eight months earlier, voted unanimously to defend the city "to the last extremity." One is tempted to observe that when the defenders of Charles Town should have been resolute, they were ready to abandon the cause, and when they should have made a hasty withdrawal, they displayed a foolhardy resolution. Nevertheless, to abandon the city without resistance would have doubtless had a devastating effect on an already low morale.

Once Clinton had landed part of his force at Savannah and the rest on James and Johns Islands at the mouth of Charles Town Harbor, he moved with such speed to block the avenues of withdrawal from the city that the Americans seemed to be able to do little but sit and watch, like a bird mesmerized by a snake coiling to destroy it. Clinton, cautious as always, followed the classic siege techniques. James Island was fortified, and the laborious task of digging trenches to emplace siege guns was started. Meanwhile an American emissary was dispatched to Havana, Cuba, to try to get help from the Spanish governor there. The assembly, having taken steps to preclude any such bargain as Rutledge had earlier offered General Prevost, once again gave him and his council virtually dictatorial powers to organize the defenses of the city. When Rutledge's appeal to the militia to come to the defense of the capital of the state produced hardly a trickle of soldiers, he issued a much sterner admonition, ordering "such of the militia as were regularly draughted, and all the inhabitants, [and] owners of property in the town to . . . join the garrison immediately under pain of confiscation." This edict had little more effect than the previous appeal to patriotism, but Rutledge, with the assistance once more of De Cambray and of Colonel Jean Baptiste Joseph, Chevalier de Laumoy, another French engineer, extended and strengthened the fortifications around the city. Strong abatis were constructed in front of the lines; most effective of all was a water-filled moat or "wet ditch," which was covered by heavy guns in a series of redoubts.

The forces under Lincoln's command numbered some 3,600, plus the 1,500 Continental Virginians and North Carolinians. Clinton, meanwhile, kept sending to New York for more reinforcements, until he had collected over 10,000 men. He had, in addition, a very formidable armament of cannon and mortars, plus the guns of the frigates and galleys that moved freely about the harbor.

Lincoln's weaknesses as a general were now painfully evident. His worst mistake was to keep open no adequate line of retreat for his army. Not able to reinforce his army or to extricate it once the British siege lines had formed, he was caught in the kind of a trap that Washington had always managed to avoid. In his defense it must be said that he was under constant pressure from Lieutenant Governor Christopher Gadsden and the council not to abandon the city. The problems of the Americans were compounded by the cavalry raids of Banastre Tarleton. Tarleton, commanding a blood thirsty Tory regiment that was attired in dashing green uniforms and was known, somewhat inaccurately, as the British Legion (it was also called the Loyal Legion), made a series of ruthless raids into the countryside beyond the British positions.

Colonel Francis Huger, the younger brother of Benjamin, commanded three regiments of the new Continental cavalry and a "body of militia" that had been assigned by Lincoln to hold the "forks and passes" of the Cooper River. It was Huger's impossible mission to keep a line of communication open to the north so that men, arms, and munitions could be gotten into the city and, what was more important, so that the defenders could escape if their position became untenable. To close this line Clinton sent a detachment of fourteen hundred men under Lieutenant Colonel James Webster. Tarleton's British Legion, reinforced by a corps of Tory riflemen under Major Patrick Ferguson, was sent on ahead to try to take the American position at Monck's Corner on the upper Cooper by surprise.

Tarleton, confident of the training and discipline of his men, determined to make a night attack with the hope of securing the bridge over the Cooper. Moving under the strict discipline of silence, Tarleton's scouts caught a slave just as he was about to slip into the woods. He was carrying a letter from one of Huger's officers that gave valuable information about the location of the American camp. "The contents of the letter," Tarleton wrote in his account of the action, " . . . and the Negro's intelligence, which was purchased for a few dollars, proved lucky incidents at this period."

The American cavalry was posted along the banks of the river, with the militia in a meetinghouse that covered the bridge. At three in the morning, Tarleton's advance guard of dragoons and mounted infantry reached the American positions. Tarleton gave the order to charge, and before the startled Americans could collect their wits, his cavalry were on top of them. Major Pierre-François Vernier of Pulaski's Legion and a handful of officers and men who tried to fight back were all killed or wounded. Huger, Colonel William Washington (the general's second cousin once removed), and most of the rest of the American force took refuge in a nearby swamp. The British booty included four hundred horses with saddles and equipment, along with almost a hundred prisoners and fifty wagons loaded with arms, ammunition, and clothing.

With the cavalry cleared out of the way, the British light infantry charged the militia with bayonets, scattered them, and took possession of the bridge, the last link between besieged Charles Town and the outside world. The British losses were one officer and two men wounded and five horses lost. It was one of the most spectacular and one-sided victories of the war; and if the fate of Lincoln's force in Charles Town was not already sealed, this event sealed it.

Three days earlier Admiral Arbuthnot, who had been anchored off

Morris Island at the mouth of Charles Town Harbor, had taken advantage of a strong favoring wind to bear down on Forts Moultrie and Sullivan, guarding the entrance of the harbor. Spectators lined the wharfs and parapets of the city, and British soldiers crowded the shore of James Island to watch the contest. It was a brilliant sight—the white sails spread against the blue waters, the brisk wind whipping up the waves, the puffs of smoke from the cannons' mouths—but soon it was over. The British ships suffered little damage. (The British frigate *Richmond's* foremast was toppled and twenty-seven seamen were killed or wounded.)

The ease with which the British fleet of eight vessels, the largest the *Renown* of fifty guns, had slipped past Forts Moultrie and Sullivan, which the Americans had thought virtually impregnable, was a heavy blow. As the enemy frigates sailed into the harbor, the watchers in the city disappeared, well aware that their situation was increasingly precarious. Soon small boats laden with passengers and personal belongings could be seen putting off from the city to cross the Cooper and land on the north bank of the river.

Before Tarleton, followed by Colonel Webster, had closed the line across the Biggin Bridge at Monck's Corner, seven hundred Continental soldiers under Colonel William Woodford, who had marched five hundred miles in twenty-eight days, arrived to reinforce the Charles Town garrison. They might better have stayed away. Of a thousand North Carolina militia whose terms of enlistment expired at the end of March, only three hundred could be persuaded to stay; the rest departed like rats leaving a sinking ship, or so it must have seemed to those who remained behind.

The first parallel trench, some six to eight hundred yards from the American lines, was begun by Clinton on the third of April and completed on the tenth. It consisted of six main works that covered a line of approach to the second parallel. On the twelfth the batteries mounted in it, consisting of fifteen 24-pounders, two howitzers, and a mortar, began a heavy fire on the town, while sappers working during the short nights, pushed the construction of the second parallel. Hot shells called carcasses were used liberally, along with shrapnel and solid shot, and the town was set afire in three different places.

Each night the trenches were pushed closer to the beleaguered city. Working parties of several hundred men dug away, extending the traverse trench twenty or so yards a night. By April 17 the approach trenches were within three hundred yards of the city, and a small traverse trench was dug from which the Hessian riflemen exchanged shots with their counterparts in the American lines. It was near maximum range for the riflemen, and little damage was done, although one jaeger was shot in the eye and a Continental rifleman was wounded. But the cannon fire was another matter. Although the American gunners were more accurate, they were heavily outgunned. The British had more heavy-caliber cannon, and their constant fire, particularly from the mortars, dismounted American guns and caused casualties among the gunners.

Inside the city, battered every day by British artillery, a warm debate went on over whether to attempt to evacuate in the face of the enemy, despite the risks involved, or to surrender to Clinton. A third alternative was to get as many men as possible across the river under cover of darkness. While the debate went on, British ships entered the east side of the harbor and cut off communication with Fort Moultrie.

The discussion between Lincoln and his officers and the civil authorities of the town was an excruciating one. As Ramsay, himself a native of Charles Town, put it, "to surrender the garrison prisoners of war, appeared to many a disaster of such magnitude as to be nearly equal to any that could take place in attempting the evacuation." It would seem "ungenerous," not to say cowardly, to abandon the citizens of the town "to the mercy of an enraged enemy," but it would be foolhardy to attempt to bring them off with the garrison itself. There seemed to be no alternative to being starved or bombarded into submission.

The field officers under Lincoln's command tried to stiffen his spine by urging him in writing to "take absolute command of every person in this Garrison," and to be "governed either by your own judgment, or the advice of such military councils as you may think proper to call upon. . . ." The officers pledged themselves to support him. There were, moreover, they wrote, "many people in this town, whites as well as blacks, . . . idle, who might be usefully employed upon the works in fatigue, or manning our lines where weak, and sharing the hardships of the Continental troops, already worn down with duty and fatigue. . . ." The manifesto to Lincoln ended with the suggestion that since there were many officers without commands, it might be well to let them escape from the city rather than be captured by the British.

The document is a revealing one. It shows that morale was low in the city, that the military and civil authorities were at odds, that Lincoln's command of the situation was precarious or nonexistent, and that the garrison expected to be captured when the British besiegers finally stormed the city. Meanwhile, according to Ramsay, citizens of Tory inclination stirred up substantial sentiment for surrendering the city to the British before more damage was done. When the word got out that the council of war was considering ways by which the soldiers could be evacuated from the city, however, some of the inhabitants "came into council and expressed themselves very warmly, and declared to General Lincoln that if he attempted to withdraw the troops and leave the citizens, they would cut up his boats and open the gates to the enemy." That was the end of all plans to evacuate the troops.

As early as the middle of March, John Laurens understood very well the precariousness of the American situation. "As the enemy is determined," he wrote Washington, "to proceed by regular approaches, all the operations are submitted to calculation, and he can determine with mathematical precision that with such and such means, in a given time, he will accomplish his end. Our safety . . . must depend upon the seasonable arrival of such a re-enforcement as will oblige him to raise the siege. . . . Your Excellency, in person, might rescue us all. . . . The glory of foiling the enemy in his last great effort and terminating the war ought to be reserved for you." Laurens indeed raised the inevitable question. Why did Washington fail to place himself at the head of as large an army as he could muster and march to raise the siege? The answer is the same as the answer to so many versions of that question asked on a number of occasions. There had been little indication that the South could muster sufficient resources to make a substantial resistance to the British. Washington's principal pool of manpower and supplies was the New England states and Pennsylvania. He dared not venture too far from his base of operations; he dared not expose New England and the middle states to Clinton's army. Clinton, with command of the seas, had much greater mobility than Washington and would like nothing so much as to trap him in South Carolina and force a conclusive battle that would hopefully shatter the American army beyond repair. Washington thus had little choice but to await with growing apprehension the outcome of Clinton's siege.

So it went, day after day. The navy set up guns at the mouth of the Wapoo on James Island and from there fired into the town "whenever the fancy strikes them." When the second parallel was completed on the twentieth, it was only a hundred yards from the main American positions. A capitulation was proposed by Lincoln, with the inhabitants and garrison being permitted to leave in return for "the quiet possession of the town." Clinton, not unexpectedly, rejected this proposal immediately.

Toward the end of April a resident of Charles Town wrote to his wife on their plantation that it was only a matter of time before the city surrendered to Clinton. "This," he added, "will give a rude shock to the independence of America: and a Lincolnade will be as common a term as a Burgoynade. But I hope in time we shall recover from this severe blow." The writer hoped soon to be home. "But a mortifying scene must first be encountered; the thirteen stripes will be levelled in the dust, and I owe my life to the clemency of the conqueror."

The Americans had one last effort left in them. On April 24, Lieutenant Colonel William Henderson, with three hundred Virginians and North Carolinians, made a surprise dawn attack on the approach trenches for the third parallel. Lincoln should have kept the British sappers under constant harassment in an effort to slow down the construction of the trenches. Now, at least, he caught by surprise a group of jaegers and almost a company of the Seventy-first Regiment, who were guarding the approaches and the partially finished third parallel. The Americans were into the trenches with their bayonets before the defenders were able to rally. There was a brief and furious fight in which Captain Moultrie, a young relative of the general, was killed and two Americans wounded while twenty British soldiers were bayoneted to death and twelve captured. The soldiers occupying the second parallel began to press forward and the Americans quickly withdrew, their retreat covered from the main American redoubt with a hail of canister fire made up of shell fragments, broken shovels, pickaxes, hatchets, flatirons, pistol barrels, and broken firelocks. The British, and especially the Hessians, were equally ingenious. An artillery officer, Captain Johann Hinrichs, adapted two brass swivels into grenade launchers and with one of them threw a hand grenade eighteen hundred feet. He used the same contraption to lob hundred-bullet canisters and three-pound case shot, all with devastating effect, on the gunners manning the remaining artillery pieces.

By the time the third parallel was completed, the British lines ran within a hundred yards of the American batteries. It was now possible for the British, and especially the jaegers with their more accurate rifles, to keep up such a heavy fire that it was increasingly hazardous for the defenders to serve their cannon.

One minor incident provided comic relief. On the night of May 3, a British boarding party rowed silently up to a three-masted American schooner anchored close to the town. The men slipped quietly on deck and, finding the ship apparently unguarded, cast off the moorings and towed it back under the guns of the British frigates. When they examined their prize, they found that they had captured a hospital ship full of smallpox patients.

On the sixth, Clinton renewed his demands for surrender. Lincoln again asked for more generous conditions. "No other motives but those of forbearance and compassion," Clinton responded on the ninth, "induced us to renew offers of terms you certainly had no claim to. The alterations you propose are all utterly inadmissible, hostilities will in consequence commence afresh at eight o'clock." After Clinton's letter was received, "we remained near an hour silent," General Moultrie recalled, "all calm and ready, each waiting for the other to begin." Finally, the Americans opened fire in the darkness "and immediately followed a tremendous cannonade." The mortar shells arched through the sky like lethal Roman candles. The effect was that of a brilliant fireworks display. Even with cannonballs falling around him, Moultrie and many others "found it a glorious sight to see [the shells] like meteors crossing each other and bursting in air; it appeared as if the stars were tumbling down." The whole night long there were shells whizzing and hissing, "ammunition chests and temporary magazines blowing up, great guns bursting, and wounded men groaning along the lines. It was a dreadful night! It was our last great effort, but it availed us nothing."

It was a pointless barrage that served only to vent the pent-up frustration of the trapped defenders. "We began to cool," Moultrie wrote, "and we cooled gradually. . . ." On the twelfth of May some fifteen hundred Continental troops marched out at eleven o'clock in the morning to where Clinton, his staff, and his veteran regiments were drawn up in full parade array. The Americans piled their arms, and the officers marched their men back to their shattered barracks, where British soldiers guarded them. The British artillery captain who inventoried the artillery supplies told Moultrie, "Sir, you have made a gallant defence, but you have a great many rascals among you, who came out every night and gave us information of what was passing in your garrison."

After the regulars had surrendered their arms, the militia did likewise. But their ranks seemed unduly thin. It was plain that many had stayed in Charles Town, doubtless hoping to merge with the civilian population of the city and slip away at the first opportunity. The next day the militia were ordered "to parade near Lynch's pasture and to bring all their arms with them, guns, swords, pistols, etc., and those that did not strictly comply were threatened with having the grenadiers turned among them." "This threat," Moultrie wrote, "brought out the aged, the timid, the disaffected and the infirm, many of them who have never appeared during the whole siege." There were, Moultrie noted grimly, three times as many militia prisoners as there had ever been militia present for duty. Of the Continental soldiers who manned the defensive lines, 89 were killed and 138 wounded. Some twenty inhabitants of the town were killed by British artillery fire, some thirty houses were burned, and many were damaged by shells.

The worst casualties suffered by the British came after the American surrender. The arms of the Continental soldiers and the militia were collected in wagons to be taken to the powder magazine in Charles Town, where four thousand pounds of ammunition were stored. Despite a warning that many of the muskets were loaded, the British soldiers handled them carelessly, "throwing them into the magazine." A musket went off and ignited the powder. The result was a terrific explosion that shook the city and the countryside and killed more than fifty soldiers—"their carcasses, legs and arms were seen in the air and scattered over several parts of the town. One man was dashed with violence against the steeple of the new independent church, which was a great distance from the explosion, and left the marks of his body there for several days."

The British were convinced that the Americans had set fire to the magazine, and a Hessian officer, red with rage, accused General Moultrie of having given the order. "You, General Moultrie," he declared, "you rebels have done this on purpose, as they did at New-York," and he placed Moultrie under house arrest.

The fall of Charles Town, like the repulse of the French and Americans at Savannah, was vastly encouraging to the British ministry and seemed, more than ever, to vindicate the Southern strategy. As I have pointed out earlier, the American cause would have been much better served had Lincoln been able to avoid the bloody assault on Savannah and, of course, the defense and capitulation at Charles Town. Each was, in its own way, a particularly rankling defeat. At Savannah, D'Estaing's initial delay and subsequent understandable impatience had snatched defeat from the jaws of victory. Nothing had been gained at the cost of very heavy casualties, and the French alliance had been further tarnished. At Charles Town the case was quite different but possibly more humiliating. A large American force had surrendered, in effect, without a battle. The best hope for an end to the war was the gradual attrition of British resources and of the British will to maintain the fight. To achieve this a dramatic American victory was necessary, or, perhaps more important and certainly more likely, there must be no notable victories for the British, but simply a series of limited and inconclusive engagements such as Washington had, in fact, been carrying on in the middle states since he had taken command of the Continental Army.

The surrender of the Continental soldiers and the militia in Charles Town was one of the major setbacks of the war for the Americans. In no other engagement were so many men lost to the British. In conjunction with the repulse of the French and the Americans at Savannah, it left the seacoast of the lower South securely in British hands. In the interior, roving bands of Tory and patriot irregulars conducted a fierce and bitter partisan warfare to which pillage and murder were the constant accompaniment. Hundreds of Americans of both persuasions died, for the most part, unheralded and indeed unnoticed. Raids and counter-raids went on ceaselessly without a chronicler. Acts of cruelty were performed on both sides, communities were devastated, houses burned, and stock destroyed. Clinton was convinced the South had been dealt a blow from which it would never recover. "The inhabitants from every quarter," he wrote, "declare their allegiance to the King and offer their services in arms. There are few men in South Carolina who are not either our prisoners or in arms with us." And Horace Walpole, hearing the news, declared, "We look on America as at our feet."

It is tempting to place the blame for the surrender at Charles Town on General Lincoln's amiable shoulders. Charles Town was, in fact, the only major American city that was defended against the British during the Revolution. (Washington had made a halfhearted attempt to defend New York, and had merely considered defending Philadelphia.) The reasons were obvious. With the British, until the arrival of the French fleet, in complete command of the sea, the dangers and difficulties of defending a besieged town against a superior force, well trained in siege techniques and well provided with cannon and with experienced engineers, were all too evident. The question is, why did Lincoln allow himself to be trapped in Charles Town? In partial exculpation, it must be said that he found himself forced into the position of defending the city almost before he fully realized what had happened. He was not a notably decisive man, and he was under great pressure from the inhabitants of the city and the officials of the state, especially Rutledge and the privy council, to defend the city. They, in turn, wished to eradicate the memory of their earlier offer to General Prevost to declare the state neutral for the balance of the war.

A bad conscience is usually a poor basis for policy; it was certainly so in this case. Rutledge was a much stronger personality than Lincoln, and he was on his own ground. If Lincoln, as a New Englander, had abandoned the principal city of the South without an effort to defend it, he would certainly have been severely criticized by many Southerners on whom he, as commander of the Southern Department, depended for cooperation, men, and supplies. Moreover, Congress put considerable pressure on him to defend the city and promised him far more than it delivered—nine thousand men, among other things. As Ramsay puts it: "Before the batteries were opened, and for two or three days after, the regular army might have retired from the town; but had the measure been attempted within that period, the most brilliant success would not have prevented the severest censures. . . . Great praise is due to general Lincoln for his judicious and spirited conduct in baffling, for three months, the greatly superior force of sir Henry Clinton and admiral Arbuthnot. Though Charlestown and the southern army were lost, yet by their long protracted defence, the British plans were deranged, and North-Carolina . . . was saved for the remainder of the year 1780."

The judgment is too charitable. Lincoln was still alive when Ramsay's book was published, a venerable hero of the Revolution, and Ramsay had no wish to offend the old warrior. The three-month delay was certainly not due to Lincoln's "judicious and spirited conduct"—he did very little compared with what a vigorous and enterprising commander might have done—but to Clinton's excessive caution and the siege tactics that he adopted in consequence. What Lincoln cannot be excused for is failing to keep open (or at the very least attempting to keep open) lines of retreat for his army. In effect, he surrendered the bulk of the Southern army to the British without a last-ditch fight. It is impossible to imagine an officer of Washington's or Greene's caliber making such an error. In military matters there are always ample reasons for every failure, but in the ruthless calculus of war, excuses can never make up for failures.

Clinton claimed well over five thousand prisoners captured at Charles Town, but this total included every adult male of the town (slaves excepted) and between two and three thousand sailors who had been drafted off their ships to help man the defenses of the city. Perhaps the principal blow to a cause that was always desperately short of experienced officers was the number of them captured by Clinton.

Besides Lincoln himself, six brigadier generals were captured, nine colonels, fourteen lieutenant colonels (John Laurens among them), fifteen majors, and eighty-four captains, as well as numbers of officers of lower rank. This was, in large part, because the militia officers, "influenced by a sense of honor," came to the defense of the city even when they could recruit few enlisted men to accompany them.

On May 1, 1780, the British strength was as follows: In New York there were 7,711 British soldiers; 7,451 Hessians; and 2,162 Provincials, for a total of 17,324. In South Carolina there were 7,041 British soldiers; 3,018 Hessians; and 2,788 Provincials, for a total of 12,847. Another 3,500 were in Nova Scotia, the great majority of them British regulars, and 536 regulars were in garrison in East Florida. Fourteen hundred and fifty-three troops were stationed in West Florida; and there were 862 Hessians and 1,016 Provincials in Georgia, mostly at Savannah. The grand total was some 37,500, of whom roughly 31,000 were British and Hessians.

Several things might be pointed out here in connection with these statistics. The Hessians—slightly in excess of 11,000—made up almost a third of the force of regulars, and the Provincials, the Loyalist troops, approximately a sixth. By far the largest British force, more than 17,000 men, were stationed in New York, where they accomplished no more than to keep Washington on the alert against the possibility of any movements into New England or the Jerseys. Clinton was widely criticized for his inactivity and for letting such a large force lie unused. But the simple fact was that there was little that he could do with it. The almost uninterrupted series of British successes in the South gave the illusion that British arms were prevailing and that the American cause was losing ground almost daily. But the real facts were quite otherwise.

What was evident to the discerning observer was that the defeats, crushing as they were, had brought the British no closer to suppressing American independence than they had been before the Southern campaign started. That issue, clearly, would not be settled by any number of British victories. The fact that after five years of warfare the British troops were, to all intents and purposes, bottled up in three provincial cities was the most dramatic evidence that their task was impossible. Yet, as we have pointed out, the Southern triumphs allowed those British who were determined to do so to preserve a while longer the illusion that the American states could be forced to be once more dependencies of Great Britain; and, perhaps more important, they made it possible for the ministry of Lord North to remain in office.

8

From the Waxhaw
Massacre to Ramsour's Mill

As Prevost's troops had scoured the land on their march from Savannah to Charles Town a year before, so Clinton's army,without any effective American force to restrain them, now began a systematic collection of the spoils of war. The plantations along the Ashley and Cooper rivers were stripped of indigo and cotton. The British, as Ramsay put it, "plundered by system, formed a general stock, and appointed commissaries of captures." In addition, individuals, from colonels down to privates, lined their pockets with the profits derived from selling their loot. As before, thousands of slaves flocked to the British—two thousand were shipped off at one embarkation—and were again crowded into malodorous camps where fever and this time small-pox killed hundreds of them. Many died in such desperate circumstances that in several camps infants were found still nursing on their dead mothers.

The more intelligent and articulate of the freed slaves were quite frequently used by the British as guides in rading parties or assigned to the commissary, where their knowledge of the countryside was valuable in rounding up cattle and livestock. Stedman, the Tory staff officer and historian of the Revolution, mentions that in the march of the British army from Charles Town to Camden, "a number of negroes, mounted on horses, were employed under proper conductors in driving in cattle for the support of the army, and . . . the army was plentifully supplied."

From the letters of Eliza Wilkinson we have a vivid account of a British foraging party. Eliza was at her plantation when a slave girl ran up crying, "O! the King's people are coming! It must be them, for they are all in red." A few moments later Eliza heard "the horses of the inhuman Britons coming in such a furious manner that they seemed to tear up the earth, and the riders at the same time bellowing out the most horrid curses imaginable, oaths and imprecations, which chilled my whole frame. . . . They were up to the house—entered with drawn swords and pistols in their hands. Indeed, they rushed in, in the most furious manner, crying out, 'Where're these women rebels.'" They snatched the caps off the heads of Eliza and her female companions, "only to get a paltry stone and wax pin, which kept them on our heads; at the same time uttering the most abusive language imaginable and making as if to hew us to pieces with their swords." What was even more distressing to Eliza was that "they had several armed Negroes with them, who threatened and abused us greatly." Leaving the terrified women, the soldiers plundered the house "of every thing they thought valuable or worth taking," including the women's clothes. "I ventured to speak to the inhuman monster who had my clothes," Eliza Wilkinson wrote, ". . . . I begged him to spare me only a suit or two; but I got nothing but a hearty curse for my pains; nay, so far was his callous heart from relenting that, casting his eyes towards my shoes, 'I want them buckles,' said he, and immediately knelt at my feet to take them out, which, while he was busy about, a brother villain, whose enormous mouth extended from ear to ear, bawled out, 'Shares there! I say, shares!' So they divided my buckles between them" Eliza Wilkinson's sister had her earrings taken from her ears, the buckles from her shoes, and the wedding ring from her finger. When she begged to be allowed to keep the ring, "they still demanded it, and, presenting a pistol at her, swore that if she did not deliver it immediately, they'd fire." Finally, they departed, "each wretch's bosom stuffed so full they appeared to be afflicted with some dropsical disorder."

Eliza was fortunate. A neighbor's plantation was totally destroyed by raiders, "all his fine iron-works, mills, dwelling-houses and buildings of every kind, even his Negro-houses, reduced to ashes, and his wife and children in a little log hut."

With Charles Town in the hands of the British, Banastre Tarleton extended his forays into the interior of the state, searching for parties of rebels to rout and thereby add to his military laurels. Through spies, word reached the British that a force under Colonel Abraham Buford had been on its way to try to reinforce Charles Town when news of Lincoln's capitulation reached them. Buford had turned his men around and had headed for Hillsboro and the North Carolina line and had then camped near Waxhaw Creek, some nine miles from the Lancaster Courthouse. Buford's force consisted of 380 Continental infantry of the Virginia Line, a detachment of Colonel Washington's cavalry, and two six-pounders.

A force made up primarily of Tarleton's Loyal Legion was immediately dispatched to pursue Buford. The weather was so fiercely hot that a number of horses died on the road. Tarleton commandeered horses from adjacent farms and plantations and pressed on. The determination of the young officer is worth commenting on. On this occasion, as on a number of others, Tarleton displayed that quality essential to successful military leaders—the resolution to force an issue by sheer power of will, ignoring or overcoming the obstacles and complications that would provide ample excuse for a less aggressive commander to break off the action. Fortune seems almost invariably to be on the side of such officers; the truth is that by their undaunted aggressiveness they make that fickle lady their obedient servant.

When Tarleton caught up with Buford, he sent a messenger, who was instructed to greatly exaggerate the number of pursuers and to demand that the Virginians surrender. "If you are rash enough to reject the term," Tarleton wrote, "the blood be upon your head."

"I reject your proposals," Buford answered, "and shall defend myself to the last extremity."

As Tarleton formed up his men for the attack on May 29, he could hear the American officers, only a few hundred yards away, calling to their men to hold their fire until the British were no more than ten paces away. Buford formed his line in an open wood to the right of the road on which his men had been marching, ordering his cannon and baggage to continue their withdrawal. Tarleton dismounted his infantry to form a base of fire in support of the attack of his cavalry. The initial attack, however, was directed against the American right and rear, which was commanded by Lieutenant Pearson.

The rear guard of half a dozen soldiers was quickly overwhelmed, and every man was killed or wounded. As Pearson lay on his back, severely injured, he was slashed in the face, nose, and lip, and his jaw was split open. For five weeks he had to be fed on milk drawn through a quill. He survived, but he could never speak distinctly again.

The furious assault on his rear was the first warning that Buford had of Tarleton's actual attack. He had chosen his ground badly, and there was little protection for his infantry against a cavalry charge. Tarleton's men came at gallop "with the horrid yells of infuriated demons." The Virginians stood firm and turned the charge, but a few minutes later the evidence of the collapse of his rear made Buford realize that further resistance could only result in the slaughter of his men. He therefore hoisted a white flag and ordered his men to ground their arms. Just as he did so, Tarleton's horse was killed under him. Tarleton chose to ignore the flag of surrender. The young ensign carrying it was shot as he advanced toward the British lines, and a continuing British fire made it all too clear that the British officer intended to give no quarter. The Americans were overrun by the Tory cavalry, who, in the words of a contemporary account, "commenced a scene of indiscriminate carnage never surpassed by the ruthless atrocities of the most barbarous savages . . . not a man was spared . . . for fifteen minutes after every man was prostrate [Tarleton's men] went over the ground plunging their bayonets into every one that exhibited any signs of life. . . ."

One of the Virginia officers, Captain John Stokes, survived twenty-three wounds. Attacked by a dragoon with a heavy sword, Stokes parried the blows until he was assaulted by another soldier who with one stroke cut off Stokes's right hand through the metacarpal bones. As he raised an arm to defend his head, his forefinger was severed and his arm hacked from wrist to shoulder. His scalp was laid open by another blow, and he fell to the ground. Another soldier came up as he lay there and asked if he expected quarter. Stokes answered, "I have not, nor do I mean to ask quarters. Finish me as soon as possible." The soldier's reply was to thrust his bayonet twice into the helpless officer. Another did likewise before a sergeant intervened and, seeing that Stokes was still alive, found a surgeon who reluctantly dressed his wounds.

Stokes survived, and "shortly after the adoption of the United States, he was promoted to the bench in the Federal Court—married Miss Pearson—and settled on the Yadkin River, where the county is called Stokes, after his name."

Young Andrew Jackson, his brother Robert, and his cousin Tom Crawford were in a company of thirty or forty patriots captured by the

British in the Waxhaw meetinghouse. A lieutenant in Tarleton's light dragoons ordered young Andrew to clean his boots. "Sir," Jackson replied, "I am a prisoner of war, and claim to be treated as such"; at this the officer brought his sword down. The boy raised his arm instinctively to protect himself, and the sword slashed his arm and head. He and his brother were then put in jail in Camden, where, Jackson recalled, the British "starved me nearly to death and gave me the smallpox." Finally Jackson's mother prevailed on Lord Francis Rawdon to release Andrew and his brother, "on account of our extreme youth and illness." The fourteen-year-old Jackson had been carrying a pistol given him by Colonel William Davie and a small fowling piece lent him by his uncle when he was captured. Jackson lost his weapons with his liberty. Not long afterward, while Andrew was still in jail, some of Colonel Davie's men captured a band of Tories. One of them, a man named Mulford, had Jackson's fowling piece and pistol. They were recognized and cost Mulford his life, since they were taken as evidence that he had been in the party that had attacked a patriot's house, "sacked and burned it and insulted the women-folk of his family." Mulford pleaded that he bought the guns from another man, but the patriots "told him it would do no good to add lying to his other crimes, hanged him forthwith and afterward restored the gun and pistol to their proper owners."

At Waxhaw Creek, the British lost two officers killed and one wounded, three privates killed and thirteen wounded, and thirty-one horses killed and wounded. According to Tarleton's own account of the battle, it was a rumor that he had been killed that "stimulated the soldiers to a vindictive asperity not easily restrained." Over a hundred American men and officers were killed, and two hundred prisoners were captured, "with a number of waggons containing . . . quantities of new clothing, other military stores and camp equipment."

Tarleton naturally played down the indiscriminate slaughter of wounded soldiers—in fact he only alludes to it as "vindictive asperity." Equally understandably, the Americans, horrified by the wanton brutality of many of the British soldiers, gave the story of the "Waxhaw Massacre" wide circulation, exaggerating what was already grim enough. Henry Lee expressed the American point of view when he wrote: "This bloody day only wanted the war dance and the roasting fire to have placed it first in the records of torture and death in the West." The phrase "Tarleton's quarter" became a battle cry of patriot guerrillas warring with their Tory neighbors. The brutality of the soldiers obscured the fact that inept leadership had helped to produce another

American debacle, albeit a minor one; although certainly much of the success of the operation was due to Tarleton's brilliance.

On June 5, Clinton returned to New York, leaving Lord Cornwallis in command at Charles Town. Cornwallis proceeded to establish posts at various points through the interior of the state, and despite a bold proclamation from Governor Rutledge exhorting every South Carolina patriot to carry on the struggle, the British effectively controlled Georgia and South Carolina by midsummer of 1780. Rutledge, writing to Abner Nash, the governor of North Carolina, had to admit that he "could expect no other service from the militia [than suppressing Tories]; they are so apprehensive of their families being killed (and their properties destroyed) by the Tories and Indians, who daily threaten hostilities, while they are absent from their districts." If the British sent regular troops into the frontier areas of the state, Rutledge told Nash, "the disaffected will certainly flock to them." Only the "immediate and greatest exertions of the Northern States" could prevent "the desolation and ruin of this State and Georgia."

With Georgia and South Carolina well in hand, Cornwallis turned his attention to North Carolina. Here, as in South Carolina, there was a potentially valuable source of strength in the Tories, clustered for the most part in the western part of the state.

The principal force detached from Cornwallis's army at Charles Town was that of Lord Rawdon, who proceeded first to Camden, South Carolina, with a substantial division composed of the Twenty-third and Thirty-third Regiments, the Irish Volunteers (a Loyalist corps), Brown's and Hamilton's Loyalist regiments, a legion of cavalry, and an artillery detachment. Major McArthur, with two battalions of the Seventy-first, was stationed beyond Camden at Cheraw on the Pee Dee River to keep communication open with the loyal Scottish community at Cross Creek in North Carolina. The line between Camden and Ninety-Six, where three battalions of Loyalists and some companies of light infantry were stationed, was defended by a strong post at Rocky Mount, garrisoned by some New York volunteers. Between these British posts mobile units traversed the country from the Wateree to the Saluda rivers.

Throughout the Carolinas, disheartened inhabitants, convinced that the war was, in effect, over and that the British had triumphed, collected to give assurances of their allegiance to the Crown. Before his departure for New York, Clinton had issued a slightly ambiguous proclamation that promised pardon, upon their laying down their arms, to all those whose "past treasonable offences" had made them subject to punishment as traitors to the King. They were promised "all those rights and immunities which they heretofore had enjoyed under a free British government, exempt from taxation except by their own legislatures." By these words, Clinton seemed to be conceding what the patriots had thought they were fighting for. Signing such statements was the only way individuals could protect themselves from the ruthless sequestering of their belongings and their property and indeed, in some instances, their lives. It is not surprising that under the circumstances, many communities made overtures to Cornwallis. The militia in the area south of Charles Town sent a flag of truce to the commanding officer at Beaufort and got terms similar to those granted the militia at Charles Town—security for themselves and their possessions on their word not to take up arms again against the British. The inhabitants at Camden negotiated similar terms for themselves. At Ninety-Six, a debate among the citizens of that community ended when most of them signed articles of capitulation.

Hearing the news from the South, Richard Henry Lee in Philadelphia wrote in the gloomiest terms to Arthur Lee. "The enemies design seems to be by great distress and much delusion to bring over the minds of the people. It must be confessed that they have the fairest opportunity, for we have no press in the country, we have received next to no assistance from our sister States or from our ally, whilst our veteran regulars have all been sacrificed in the common cause. . . ." The British quite shrewdly "affect to leave harmless the poor and they take everything from those they call the rich. Tis said that 2 or 3000 Negroes march in their train, that every kind of stock which they cannot remove they destroy. . . . Cornwallis is the scourge—and a severe one he is."

As we have noted before, the summer months in Georgia and Carolina were considered unsuitable for the conduct of campaigns, just as the winter months were unsuitable in the North. Cornwallis thus delayed his movement into North Carolina until the deadly summer heat should break, but the North Carolina Tories, less affected by the weather, were too impatient to wait. John Moore collected some thirteen hundred Tories and made a camp near Ramsour's Mill in Lincoln County. Colonel Locke, determined to crush the Tory serpent in the egg, advanced on Moore's camp on June 20 with a much smaller force of slightly more than four hundred militia, a number of them mounted and formed hastily into an improvised cavalry unit.

The unexpected is always most difficult to cope with, and the appearance the next day of mounted men initially threw the Tories into confusion. They were well situated on a hill some three hundred yards east of the mill itself. The hill sloped gently downward, affording almost unobstructed fields of fire. At the foot of the hill was a glade with thick undergrowth on one side. A rail fence extended from the glade to a point opposite the right of the Tory line. A dozen pickets constituted an outpost some six hundred yards from the Tory camp.

Three companies of patriots were mounted, and the balance of the troops were lined up two-deep along a road. There would be, it was decided, no effort at an overall direction of the battle. The patriot units were to advance individually, their own action guided by those of the companies on their left and right, and by the initial success or failure of the mounted men. To identify each other, Locke's militiamen put pieces of white paper in the front of their hats.

The horsemen surprised the pickets, who fired to alert the main camp and fled. The cavalry pursued them and, carried along by their own momentum, rode to within thirty yards of the Tory lines. At first there was considerable confusion at this unexpected sight, and then, seeing that the horsemen were relatively few in number, the Tories rallied and drove them back. The horsemen retreated in disorder, riding through the infantry who were advancing. Anxious to keep up with the horsemen, the infantry had become widely scattered as the slower men fell to the rear.

As the horsemen withdrew or, rather, fled headlong, it was the turn of the Tories to attempt a counterattack. Those rebel infantrymen who were in the lead took positions between the glade and the corner of the fence, opposite the Tory center. From here they met the advancing Tories with a heavy fire. Reaching the glade, the Tories moved to the right "and came into action without order or system." In some places the Americans "were crowded together in each other's way" and in other places there were large gaps in their line. As the slower militia came up, they found their places beside their fellows. The Tories were similarly reinforced by additions from the top of the ridge, but there was virtually no direction or control of the battle. It dissolved into savage contests between small groups, with those Tories who had ventured beyond their lines gradually being outnumbered and forced back up the hill. On the ridge they could take positions in defilade, largely covered by the crest, and from there they poured a deadly fire down on the patriots. When the patriots withdrew to the cover of the bushes at the edge of the glade, the Tories once more sallied forth, convinced that they had the rebels on the run.

At this point another company of militia came up and took positions under the cover of the fence, which took the Tories in a heavy flanking fire on their right. Other militiamen, finding that the ground on the right gave them better firing positions, worked their way to the east end of the glade, where they could catch the Tories in the left flank. Forced back toward their own lines, the Tories found another party of militia blocking their line of retreat. "In that quarter," Joseph Graham, one of the combatants, tells us, "the action became close, and the parties mixed together in two instances, and having no bayonets, they struck at each other with the butts of their guns." In this savage fighting, some badly battered Tories were taken prisoner, and others, "divesting themselves of their mark of distinction (which was a twig of green pine stuck in their hats)," mixed in with the militia "and all being in their common dress . . . escaped unnoticed."

The Tories, with their left occupied by the Americans, retreated down the hill, crossed the creek at Ramsour's Mill, and there collected their scattered forces. The militia, in possession of the ridge, tried to re-form their units with the notion of defending the hill against a counter-attack or of pursuing the Tories if they continued to withdraw, but the course of the fighting had so dispersed the patriot units, so many men had been wounded, and so many of their companions had stopped to minister to them that only 86 men could be gathered together initially and finally, after strenuous efforts, only 110 out of some 400 could be collected.

"In this perilous situation of things," there was a hasty council of officers and men, and two officers were dispatched to urge General Griffith Rutherford, who was moving toward Ramsour's Mill, to hurry some units forward in support of Colonel Locke's force. Meanwhile a game of bluff between the Tories and the militia was played out. The Tories, believing that they were faced with a much larger number of rebel militia than in fact they were, decided that retreat was the only sensible course of action. In hopes of forestalling pursuit and gaining time to escape, Moore sent a messenger to Locke asking that a truce be arranged to allow them to bury their dead and tend to the wounded. Locke, afraid that the messenger would reveal how weak his force actually was, sent two officers out ahead of the lines. The officers, as anxious to buy time as their enemy, took a bold line and insisted that the Tories must surrender in ten minutes or see the battle renewed. While the officers talked, most of the Tories hurried off on horse or foot as quickly and stealthily as they could. When word of the ultimatum came, fifty of the remaining Tories surrendered, and the rest took to their heels. The patriots had proved much better bluffers, as well as better fighters.

Of the 400 North Carolina militia under Colonel Locke's command, no more than 275 saw action, and of these, 150 were killed or wounded, more than half the men engaged in the battle. The Tory losses were approximately the same, out of a much larger force, and it was the Tories who abandoned the field and fled to Camden. The fact that the casualties of the militia were so disproportionately high is very revealing. In the words of one of the officers who was present: "In this battle neighbors, near relations and personal friends fought against each other, and as the smoke would from time to time blow off, they would recognize each other. In the evening, and on the next day, the relations and friends of the dead and wounded came in, and a scene was witnessed truly afflicting to the feelings of humanity."

The cold facts speak very eloquently both of the bravery of the militia when they were fighting in their home territory and, quite literally, in defense of their homes and families, and of the bitterness and cruelty of such internecine warfare. In no other engagement of the Revolution did the militia sustain such casualties and fight on to victory. The reason seems to have been, in large part, that no effort was made to force the militia to fight in conventional formation. Nor was there any centralized command, so that individuals and units had nothing to inhibit them from using their own wits and judgment. They fought in a way that was natural to them, like Indians (but much more tenaciously), adapting their tactics to the immediate situation on the battlefield. They did not have to wait for orders; they did not have to undertake maneuvers devised by someone not actually on the contested terrain. They did not fear their enemy; they knew them to be plain men like themselves, not the seasoned veterans of famous regiments, and they knew that they would be merciless in victory. In addition, since their casualties were scattered over a large area, the militia had no idea of how heavy their losses actually were and were thus spared, for the most part, one of the most demoralizing aspects of combat—the sight of a large number of dead and wounded. What was perhaps most remarkable was that "few either of the officers or men had ever been in battle before."

The battle of Ramsour's Mill, modest as it was, has never received the attention it deserves. It was the archetypal battle of the "new man," the American, whether Tory or patriot; it was the supreme military expression of individualism. It was the analogue of the Protestant maxim of "every man a priest"; here every man was a general in the sense that he fought, to a very large degree, in response to his own best judgment of what should be done. No other soldier in the world could have fought as the North Carolina militiaman (and similarly his Tory opponents) did at Ramsour's Mill, just as no American regiments could have come on again and again in the face of devastating fire as the British redcoats did at Bunker Hill. The action at Ramsour's Mill gave a tantalizing glimpse of what the often-maligned militia might have done if they had been free "to do their own thing." It is tempting to argue from this, and from a handful of other similar cases, that Washington's greatest error was in trying to use militia like trained and disciplined troops; that he would have been much better off adapting his tactics to the peculiar talents and capacities of the militia rather than making them fight continually under circumstances that were thoroughly uncongenial to their temperament, their character, and their training. I have already discussed the fallacies in this argument. Washington had to form an army and keep it in being for reasons that were as much political as military. The weakness of the militia style of fighting is demonstrated more by what happened after the battle than during its progress.

When Colonel Locke, whose control of the course of the battle was slight or nonexistent, tried to round up soldiers after the occupation of the ridge to pursue the fleeing Tories or, more important, to defend the hill against the counterattack that he initially expected, he could find only eighty-six out of some four hundred soldiers. While it was true that this was due, in part, to his excessive casualties, the fact was that neither he nor his officers had any clear notion of what had happened on the field of battle or of where the units under his command were. If the Tories had realized how much the advantage of numbers lay with them and had made a determined counterattack, the remnants of the American force, scattered as they were, would certainly have been decisively defeated. In other words, luck was a very large element in the American victory.

What was notable about the engagement was far less the tactical skill of the militia than the fierceness and persistence with which they fought and the very heavy casualties that they sustained without breaking off the fight. The point is that once the individual egos of the combatants had been engaged, they were fighting less to achieve "military victory" than to validate themselves. To turn and run under such circumstances meant to abandon, in a very particular and excruciating way, some essential element of self on the field of action. When inexperienced and poorly trained militia were deployed in a mass and ordered about by officers in whom they had, for the most part (and usually rightly) very little confidence, their inclination was to break and run. But their tendency was to stand and fight when they fought largely as self-directed individuals, as they did at Ramsour's Mill.

When Moore's beaten army reached the British camp at Camden, Moore was roundly denounced for undertaking to launch a campaign without waiting for orders from Cornwallis. For a time he was threatened with a court-marial for disobeying orders "by marching out before the time appointed by the commander-in-chief. He was treated with disrespect by the British officers, and held in a state of disagreeable suspense; but it was at length deemed impolitic to order him before a court-martial."

In addition to revealing a great deal about the psyche of Americans, the battle at Ramsour's Mill had important practical consequences. For one thing, it threw off Cornwallis's schedule for a coordinated attack by Tories and British forces on North Carolina. More important, it virtually destroyed the effectiveness of the Tory irregulars in that state. They never entirely recovered their morale after that defeat, which was so narrow and yet so crushing.

Another "mill," Musgrove's Mill, was the scene of a battle as fierce, and far more conclusive, than the engagement at Ramsour's Mill. Colonel Issac Shelby and Colonel Elijah Clarke and their combined forces attempted an attack on Major Patrick Ferguson's rear near Musgrove's Mill on the Enoree River. When Ferguson turned to attack them, the frontier sharpshooters inflicted heavy casualties on the Loyalist unit. Sixty-three were killed, ninety wounded, and seventy captured, while the patriot losses were only four killed and eight wounded. In terms of the number of killed and wounded on each side, the battle at Musgrove's Mill was one of the most decisive defeats of the Loyalist or British forces in the Southern theater of operations. Yet one seldom hears of it, the reason apparently being that no prominent American military leaders were involved and that none of the participants wrote a narrative of the engagement on which historians could base a detailed account of the action. Moreover the action took place early in August, just prior to the disaster at Camden, which completely overshadowed the striking if minor success at Musgrove's Mill and the seizure a few weeks earlier by Shelby and six hundred of his "over the mountain men" of Thickety Fort, a Loyalist post in South Carolina whose defenders had surrendered to Shelby without firing a shot.

Emboldened by the success at Ramsour's Mill, Colonel Thomas Sumter, with South Carolina militia who had fled the state rather than sign Clinton's articles of capitulation and some three hundred Mecklenburg militia, decided to attack the British post at Rocky Mount. The plan was for a diversionary movement against nearby Hanging Rock, while the main assault was to be directed at Rocky Mount. The defenses of that village consisted of two log houses and a building with firing slots, surrounded by a strong abatis of fallen trees and stakes. The stronghold was situated on high ground with clear fields of fire. When Sumter and his men reached the little fort, small parties of riflemen moved forward under the cover of rocks and three stumps and kept up a fire on the embrasures of the buildings while several companies of men tried to advance, under cover of this fire, close enough to set the buildings ablaze. The attackers, however, were driven back repeatedly by heavy fire from the houses and were finally forced to withdraw.

Meanwhile Colonel Davie, in charge of the diversionary attack on Hanging Rock, arrived there at one o'clock in the afternoon with some forty mounted riflemen and the same number of mounted dragoons. While he was reconnoitering the enemy positions, which centered on his own house, he received word that three companies of mounted Loyalist infantry, returning from a raid, had halted at a farmer's house nearby. The Davie house was located in the intersection of a right angle formed by "a lane of staked and ridered fence," one end of which ran to the positions defending Hanging Rock and the other to a clump of woods. Davie moved forward to the end of fence that ran to the woods, and, according to his own account, "as the riflemen were not distinguishable from the Loyalists," they were sent to the other end of the lane with orders to rush the enemy from there. The rifle company passed the Loyalist sentries without even being challenged, dismounted in the lane, and opened fire on the enemy. When they did, the startled Loyalists fled toward the spot where Davie's mounted dragoons were concealed in the woods and there were charged by the dragoons at full gallop. Finally, they were driven into the angle of the fence where they were, again in Davie's words, "literally cut . . . to pieces. As this was done under the eye of the whole British camp, no prisoners could be safely taken, which may apologize for the slaughter that took place on this occasion." Doubtless Davie and his men had in mind "Tarleton's quarter." His men captured sixty horses and saddles and one hundred muskets and rifles. The British camp at Hanging Rock beat to arms, summoning the soldiers in the garrison, but before they could do anything to support the Loyalist raiders, Davie's little force had ridden off.

Again, the action was a minor one, but it was carried out with a skill worthy of a Tarleton; along with Ramsour's Mill and Musgrove's Mill it served notice on the Tories and the British that any notion that they might have that the patriots were near the end of their resources was, to say the least, premature.

While partisan warfare raged, Baron von Steuben undertook to reconstruct a regular army out of the remnants that remained in the Southern Department after Lincoln's surrender at Charles Town. New companies were to be formed around a nucleus of twenty-five veteran soldiers drawn from existing regiments. "To render the recruits anywise serviceable," Von Steuben wrote, "it is absolutely necessary they should be exercised as much as possible, for this purpose the Baron has agreed with Genl. Howe, that none of them are to be employ'd, either on Guards or Fatigue." They were to drill twice daily; for the first six weeks they would do so without arms, "learning to carry themselves well, to march and dress." These exercises were, in every instance, to be conducted by the officers. Slowly the nucleus of an army was formed.

9

Camden

W HATEVER the problems and difficulties, Washington and Congress could not afford to let the South go by default. With the capture of Lincoln and his army, the Southern Department had, at one stroke, been destroyed. For the moment at least, Georgia and South Carolina must be written off. But if North Carolina and Virginia could be defended against the British, they might become bases from which the two southernmost states could be retrieved. The news that caused Clinton to hurry back to New York—that a formidable French fleet was on its way to America with a large force of soldiers under the command of Comte de Rochambeau—raised American hopes. The only question was who should replace Lincoln in the onerous if not impossible task of repairing American fortunes in the South. Nathanael Greene was Washington's choice, but Congress, meddling as it was so often inclined to do, preferred the victor of Saratoga, Horatio Gates.

Washington had already dispatched Baron de Kalb to Virginia in command of a small force of Virginia and North Carolina Continentals. Gates subsequently departed for North Carolina. On June 27 he was joined at Charlotte by Continental and militia troops under Kalb, Richard Caswell, and Griffith Rutherford. Gates's adjutant general, Colonel Otho Williams, had the first hint of trouble to come immediately after Gates took command of the so-called Southern army from Baron de Kalb. In Williams' rather cynical words, Gates, "as though actuated by a spirit of great activity and enterprise, ordered his troops to hold themselves in readiness *to march at a moment's warning.*" The order was "a matter of great astonishment to those who knew the real situation of the troops. But all difficulties were removed by the general's assurances that plentiful supplies of *rum* and *rations* were on the route, and would overtake them in a day or two—assurances that certainly were too fallacious, and that never were verified."

The principal British magazine for the intended campaign in North Carolina and Virginia was established at Camden, a hundred miles or so from Charles Town. It was therefore to Camden that Horatio Gates directed his army. His friend Charles Lee had warned him, "Take care lest your Northern laurels turn to Southern willows." Whatever that rather inscrutable sentence meant, disaster and defeat hung over the enterprise from its beginning. Gates's frame of mind on taking command of the Southern Department is suggested by a letter to Benjamin Lincoln, who had been paroled: "I feel for you; I feel for myself; who am to succeed to, what? To the command of an army, without strength; a military chest, without money; a department apparently deficient in public spirit; and a climate, that increases despondency, instead of animating the soldier's arm." It was hardly a frame of mind that augured success on the battlefield. Gates also dispatched a stream of querulous and gloomy letters to the not-very-effective governor of Virginia, Thomas Jefferson, deploring "the multiplied and increasing wants" of his troops. The difficulty of securing corn and meat "must eventually break up our camp," he added.

Williams and others who knew the region did their best to try to persuade Gates to advance on Camden by way of Charlotte, but Gates was determined to take a shorter route through rough and unfriendly country intersected by swamps, dense woods, and sandy plains. Williams protested the "precipitate and inconsiderate step he was taking," and when that failed, he presented a note from the officers in Gates's command who knew the country best, urging the general to take the route across the Pee Dee through Salisbury, "a fertile country and inhabited by people zealous in the cause of America." But Gates was obdurate, and the little army plunged into a desolate and barren terrain where the way was impeded by creeks and marshes and where little food was to be found. When the army reached the banks of the Pee Dee, they came upon green corn, which the hungry soldiers cut and boiled with

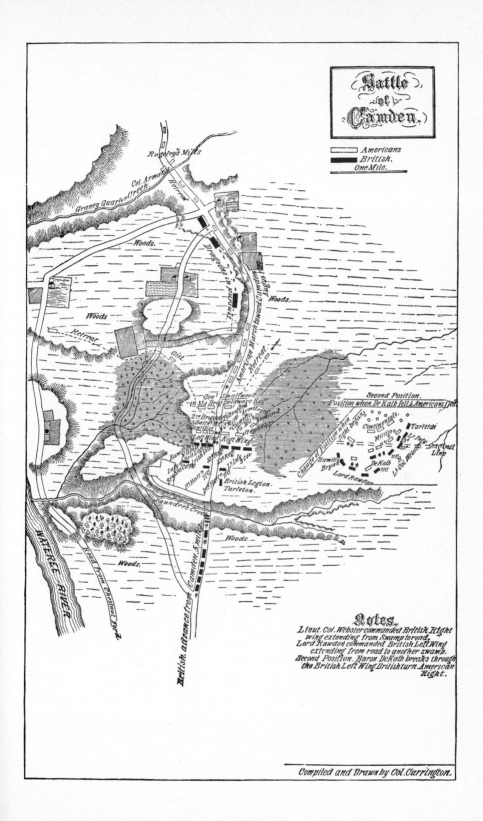

Battle
of
Camden.

Americans
British.
One Mile.

Rugeley's Mills

Col. Armand

Graney Quarter Creek

Retreat

Woods.

Dragoons in pursuit.

Woods.

Woods

American March toward Camden Aug 15

Retreat

Retreat

Glad

Second Position.
Position when De Kalb fell & Americans fled.

Gen' Smallwood
in M'd Brig
Delaware Reg't

2nd brigade Gen'
Stevens Militia
under Gist.

Gen'l Armstrong

Gen'l Gregory

Change of Position when fight begins.

Continentals.

Tarleton.

Militia

Lt. Inf.
Dragoon
Line

Hamilton
Bryan

De Kalb
71st

Lt. Col. Webster.

Hamilton

Left Wing   Rig't Wing

Int. 23rd British

33rd Brit.

N.C. Cont'l British

Volun'rs Irish

33rd Reg.

71st Reg.

Br. Art. Reg. of Ind'l Cos.

British Legion.
Tarleton.

Lord Rawdon

Saunder's Creek

Woods.

WATEREE RIVER

Road from Christie York

British advance from Camden, 5 miles

Woods

Notes.
Lieut. Col. Webster commanded British Right
wing extending from Swamp to road.
Lord Rawdon commanded British Left Wing
extending from road to another swamp.
Second Position. Baron DeKalb breaks through
the British Left Wing British turn American
Right.

Compiled and Drawn by Col. Carrington.

lean beef from gaunt cows and steers running loose in the woods. The meal, while palatable, "was attended with painful effects." In lieu of bread, many soldiers ate green peaches and paid for their folly with severe cramps. Again in Williams' words, "The troops, notwithstanding their disappointment in not being overtaken by a supply of *rum* and provisions, were again amused with promises, and gave early proofs of that patient submission, inflexible fortitude and undeviating integrity which they afterwards more eminently displayed."

Across the Pee Dee, Gates was joined by Colonel Charles Porterfield who, after the fall of Charles Town, had managed to collect a small band of militia and live off the country. Colonel Marion, whose fame lay ahead of him, also joined Gates, "attended by a very few followers, distinguished by small black leather caps and the wretchedness of their attire"—some twenty men and boys, "some white, some black, and all mounted, but most of them miserably equipped; their appearance," Williams added, "was in fact so burlesque that it was with much difficulty the [hilarity] of the regular soldiery was restrained by the officers." Gates took the first opportunity to rid the army of this motley band by sending them "to watch the motions of the enemy and furnish intelligence," which in fact they did with notable skill.

When the army arrived at May's Mill, where they had been assured they would find an ample supply of provisions, they found that larder bare. There were, for the first time, angry murmurings and open threats of mutiny that were only quelled "when the regimental officers, by mixing among the men and remonstrating with them appeased murmurs, for which unhappily," as Williams noted, "there was too much cause." The officers, "by appealing to their own empty canteens and mess cases, satisfied the privates that all suffered alike." Fortunately for the sake of everyone's morale, some corn was found, brought into the camp, and ground at the mill, "and so, in rotation, they were all served in the course of a few hours—more poor cattle were sacrificed—the camp kettles were all engaged—the men were busy but silent until they had each taken his repast; and then it all was again content, cheerfulness and mirth."

Lord Rawdon, with ample warning of Gates's approach, sent for the four companies of light infantry stationed at Ninety-Six and moved forward some fourteen miles from Camden to a natural defensive position on high ground behind the west branch of Lynch's Creek. When Gates's advance elements encountered the British force, the American commander made another of a succession of errors. He stopped and spent several days probing the British positions. Having driven his men to the limit of their endurance to reach the vicinity of Camden, he then dawdled away the days that he had gained. He was thus hasty when he should have conserved the strength of his army, and dilatory when he should have taken full advantage of his superior force by an immediate attack. Rawdon ordered a British post on his right evacuated—the detachment dropped back to Camden—and then, afraid that Gates might move around his right and outflank him, Rawdon fell back himself from Lynch's Creek toward Camden, taking a position at Logtown.

Colonel Sumter, dispatched to try and cut off the British line of supply to Camden, moved up the north side of Lynch's Creek to the recently abandoned Rugeley's Mills, planning to march from there to Camden by the Waxhaw Road. Cornwallis, well aware of Rawdon's exposed position, set out from Charles Town with a small detachment of cavalry on the tenth of August and arrived at Camden on the thirteenth. The situation he found there was far from encouraging. Nearly 800 soldiers of Rawdon's command were sick at Camden and not fit for duty. Of the remaining 2,000, some 1,500 were regulars and the rest Loyalists of varying degrees of reliability. Opposed to his force was Gates's army of between 3,000 and 5,000 men. Moreover, in Stedman's words, "almost the whole country seemed upon the eve of a revolt." Sumter's force was augmented daily by militia and disaffected Loyalists, many of whom were disgruntled because their produce and especially their horses were requisitioned by the British, and they were left with "certificates" or "receipts" that were bought in turn by speculators. For a time Cornwallis considered a retreat, but the sick and a large quantity of stores would have had to be abandoned.

It was typical of Cornwallis that, having decided that retreat was impolitic, he determined to advance and attack Gates's superior force rather than wait for the American general to take the initiative. His own intelligence indicated that the Continentals were in a position difficult to defend, and Cornwallis decided to aim the main weight of his attack at that point, confident that if the Continentals gave way, the militia would follow suit.

At the same time, Gates finally decided to attack the British positions. Over the objections of his staff, he determined on a night march. "I will breakfast tomorrow in Camden with Lord Cornwallis at my table," he is reported to have told his officers, who were unimpressed by this bit of bombast. He then ordered a gill of molasses to be issued to the men, in lieu of rum, with a ration of half-cooked beef and cornmeal. If he had prescribed an emetic, the effects on the intestinal tract of his soldiers could hardly have been more devastating.

It was apparent to Gates's officers that the general did not even know the number of troops under his command. The count on the night before the battle showed that the effective strength of his army was 3,052. When the figures were presented to Gates "as he came from a council of officers, he turned to his chief of staff and said, 'Sir, the numbers are certainly below the estimate made this morning [when the estimated figures had been closer to 5,000].' There was no dissenting voice in the council where the orders have just been read; there are enough for our purpose." Without further consultation with his officers, Gates issued the orders for the advance against the British.

First in Cornwallis's order of march was a division commanded by Lieutenant Colonel James Webster and made up of four companies of light infantry plus the Twenty-third and Thirty-third Regiments, preceded by twenty cavalrymen and mounted infantry of the Loyal Legion. The second division was made up of the Irish Loyalists, the legion infantry, John Hamilton's North Carolina regiment, and Colonel Bryan's Tory refugees. Two battalions of the Seventy-first followed as a reserve, and another detachment defended the town of Camden itself.

Colonel Charles Armand, who commanded an American cavalry advance guard of sixty horsemen (in itself a blunder, since the noise of cavalry movement could not be effectively muffled), received absurd and pompous orders, of the kind so favored by Gates. He was, "in case of an attack by the enemy's cavalry . . . not only to support the shock of the enemy's horse, but to *rout* them; and to consider the order, to stand the attacks of the enemy's cavalry, be their numbers what they may, as positive." In the first clash between the forward units of the advancing armies, at two-thirty in the morning of August 16, Armand's cavalry were driven back by elements of the British Legion. When Colonel Porterfield, on Armand's right flank, tried to hold his ground, he was fatally wounded as elements of the Twenty-third and Thirty-third Regiments came up in quick support of the cavalry.

Armand's cavalry, retreating in the dark, ran into the First Maryland Brigade and threw it into disorder. Both armies then broke off the action until daylight. Gates called another council to discuss the proper course of action. When Colonel Williams went to call de Kalb to the council, that veteran officer greeted him by saying, "Well, and has the general given you orders to retreat the army?" A prisoner, captured in the initial skirmishing, informed the Americans that the British force, now commanded by Cornwallis himself, numbered three thousand men, virtually the same size as the American army. Under the circumstances, the wise course for Gates would have been a cautious withdrawal to stronger defensive positions. But Gates himself seemed incapable of making a decision. He asked his officers what was to be done, and the boldest, or most reckless, advice prevailed. "All were mute for a few moments," Colonel Williams recalled, "when the gallant Stevens exclaimed, 'Gentlemen, is it not too late *now* to do anything but fight.'" De Kalb kept silent, doubtless unwilling, as a foreign officer, to seem to advocate a timid policy. As for Gates, he acquiesced.

The lay of land at the point where the two armies met was highly favorable to Cornwallis. His flanks were protected by swamps that had a kind of funnel effect, so that the Americans were forced into a narrow stretch of open land with limited room to maneuver.

Webster's division took up a position on the British right, while Rawdon moved into line on the left. Two six-pounders and two three-pounders were also brought on line. One battalion of reserves was posted behind each wing. Gates also deployed his force in two lines, with General Mordecai Gist's brigade of Continental troops on the right, the North Carolina militia in the center, and the Virginia militia, which had joined Gates only the day before, on the left along with the light infantry and Porterfield's corps. The First Maryland Brigade formed the second American line. In Williams' words, "the General seemed disposed to await events—he gave no orders." Williams suggested a sharp attack on the British right, and Gates replied, "Sir, that's right; let it be done." This was the last order that his adjutant general received and the last order, apparently, that Gates issued. Edward Stevens' militia were to charge the British right with bayonets. To cover the deployment of Stevens' men, Williams sent forward skirmishers with instructions "to take to single trees and thus annoy the enemy as much as possible." It was at this point that Cornwallis ordered Webster's division to charge the American left held by the Virginia militia.

The British advanced, "*firing* and *huzzaing*." The sight of the British regiments in battle order, with bands playing, flags flying, and bayonets at the ready was too much for the Virginia militia to bear; they broke under the first assault, threw down their arms, and fled, followed quite promptly by part of the North Carolina militia. Gates and General Caswell tried to rally the terrified militiamen, but they "ran like a torrent," flowing past the officers "and . . . spread through the woods in every direction." Among them were some of the same men who had fought so bravely and tenaciously at Ramsour's Mill. All men in all armies are doubtless, taken in the mass, brave and cowardly in roughly the same proportions. More important, the same men are alternately brave and cowardly. What determines whether they are to be, individually and collectively, brave or cowardly on a particular day in a particular action (and sometimes they will be both in the same day) depends on many complex factors: the state of their training, of course; their confidence in their officers, in themselves and in each other; the visual aspects of the battle as it unfolds (whether it discloses frightening or surprising sights); the noise, certainly; and perhaps, above all, the physical and psychological state of the individual soldiers (for these two are very closely related). A cold or hot, hungry, wet, exhausted soldier is much more apt to turn and run for his miserable life than one who is dry, cool or warm, well fed, and reasonably rested. Otho Williams, in his account of the battle, was disposed to reflect upon the panic that spread so quickly among the soldiers. "Like electricity," he wrote, "it operates instantaneously—like sympathy it is irresistible where it touches."

Certainly the militia were not inherently cowards. It is more likely that their officers, starting with Gates himself, had failed to infuse them with the confidence and determination so essential to success on the battlefield. Weakness and uncertainty in the commanding officer is, as we have said before, almost instantly communicated through the ranks to the lowest private. Indeed, the lowest private may often feel it when his officers, because of personal loyalty to their commander, fail to feel it, or, if they do, manage to repress the feeling. It is thus safe to say that if you wish to know the prospects for success in battle of any military unit, talk to the privates, not the officers.

With the American left in full flight, Rawdon's division advanced. The Maryland Brigade was brought up from its position in the reserve to try to restore the line. The American right, anchored by Gist's Continental brigade, held firm, and those North Carolina militia who remained were equally resolute. The American artillery at the same time inflicted substantial casualties on the British, but the Maryland Brigade found the task of trying to shore up the left of the American position too exacting. The British light infantry broke off its pursuit of the militia to turn Gates's left flank. Cornwallis, seeing the Americans hard-pressed there, threw in a portion of his reserve, both cavalry and infantry, and "after a brave resistance for near three quarters of an hour" what had been the American right broke and "gave way in all quarters." The rout was complete. Williams estimated that "At least two-thirds of the army fled without firing a shot."

Few were as precipitous in their flight as the commanding general. One of the grimmest consequences of Gates's abandoning the field was that the outnumbered Continentals had no one to order their retreat. When the officers of the First Maryland Brigade looked for their commanding officer to urge that he give the order to withdraw before the brigade was overrun, they could not find him or any member of the general's staff except Colonel Williams, the adjutant general who, himself without authority to order a retreat, devoted his efforts to trying to rally the soldiers and persuade them to stand firm. When he called to the commander of his own regiment (the Maryland Sixth), that officer answered, "They have done all that can be expected of them. We are outnumbered and outflanked. See the enemy charge with bayonets!" In Williams' words, the men never received any order to retreat, "nor any order from any *general* officer, from the commencement of the action until it became desperate."

The North Carolina militia fled "different ways, as their hopes led or their fears drove them. Most of them, preferring the shortest way home, scattered through the wilderness which lies between the Wateree, and the Peedee rivers, and thence toward Roanoke." One incident tells volumes about the nature of the internecine warfare. Those soldiers who retraced their steps in the Carolinas encountered militia ostensibly coming up to reinforce Gates. But when the militia discovered that Gates's army had been routed and that the British were victorious, they fell on the fleeing soldiers "and captivating some, plundering others and maltreating all the fugitives they met, returned, exultingly home. They even added taunts to their perfidy." One of a party who robbed Brigadier General John Butler of his sword consoled him by saying, "You'll have no further use of it."

The baggage and equipment of the American army had begun to withdraw as soon as the first broken ranks of militia appeared. A few wagons, pulled by the strongest horses, got clear; the "cries of the women and the wounded in the rear and the consternation of the flying troops so alarmed some of the waggoners that they cut out their teams and, taking each a horse, left the rest for the next that should come. Others were obliged to give up their horses to assist in carrying the wounded, and the whole road, for many miles, was strewed with signals of distress, confusion and dismay."

Members of Armand's cavalry legion were among the first to flee, and some of them were seen plundering the baggage train of their own army, with special attention to the officers' baggage. A captain who tried to keep them from carrying off his portmanteau had his hand slashed for his pains. Another officer, his sword broken in the battle, had to stand by and watch his luggage borne off by American soldiers; when he protested, he was answered by threats and abuse. Williams himself, whose account of the action is the most complete, came on the group of soldiers clustered around General Caswell's mess wagon. They had found a pipe of good Madeira wine, and, exhausted and thirsty, they were helping themselves to liberal portions. It was not, Williams realized, a moment to upbraid them for thievery and to stand on military punctilio. He dismounted and joined the soldiers, "the only refreshment he . . . received that day."

Only General Gist was able to keep together part of his command, a hundred men or so who escaped through a swamp. The British cavalry pursued the beaten and exhausted Americans as far as Hanging Rock, twenty-two miles from the field of battle, killing some on the road and capturing hundreds of prisoners.

Stedman, who was in charge of the commissary at Camden and present at the battle, tells us that "the road for some miles was strewed with the wounded and killed who had been overtaken by the legion in their pursuit." (Again Tarleton's Loyal Legion was accused of killing wounded men and those who tried to surrender.) In Stedman's words: "The number of dead horses, broken waggons, and baggage, scattered on the road, formed a perfect scene of horror and confusion: Arms, knapsacks, and accoutrements found were innumerable; such was the terror and dismay of the Americans." The number of Americans killed, wounded, and taken prisoner exceeded the number of regular British troops in the action. A hundred and fifty wagons, loaded with military supplies, were gathered in by the British, along with most of the colors of the units involved and seven cannon. In the bitter words of John Marshall, "Never was a victory more complete, or a defeat more total." The British casualties were heavy for the number of men engaged, but the American casualties were staggering. Henry Carrington gives an estimate of almost 1,000 men killed and wounded, besides those missing and made prisoner. Accepting the fact that a number of Americans were killed or wounded by pursuing British and Tories as they fled from the battlefield, the figures nonetheless indicate the tenacity with which some Americans, primarily the Continentals of the First and, more especially, the Second Maryland Brigades, fought. The Maryland troops lost between 300 and 400 in killed and wounded out of a total of 1,500 men engaged. Indeed, whatever laurels were to be distributed to the Americans certainly went to the Second Maryland Brigade, which charged and broke through the British formations once and finally, deserted by the rest of the American army, was enveloped and overwhelmed. It suffered and inflicted the heaviest casualties of the battle. Undoubtedly the performance of the Marylanders was attributable directly to de Kalb's leadership.

DeKalb, who had led a courageous bayonet charge by the Second Maryland Brigade on the left wing of the British army that temporarily forestalled its envelopment of the American center and left, was wounded eleven times and taken prisoner. Refusing at first to believe that his beloved Continentals had been defeated by the British, he died several days after the battle from his wounds.

The British losses were 325: 69 killed, 245 wounded, 11 missing. The burden of the battle on the British side was borne by the Thirty-third Regiment of Webster's division and the Irish Loyalists, who lost two-thirds of their strength.

Gates, fleeing to Charlotte, was overtaken by an officer from Sumter's detachment who reported that Sumter's force had seized the enemy post on the Wateree, opposite Camden, and had taken forty wagonloads of goods being sent from Charles Town and almost a hundred prisoners. The news came too late, but it suggested what might have been accomplished if Gates had taken a line of action more in keeping with his own resources and the exposed position of the British force at Camden. He sent orders to Sumter to retire as best he could before Cornwallis's victorious army turned on him.

Gates, riding as though pursued by furies, performed the rather remarkable feat of reaching Charlotte, a distance of almost sixty miles, by nightfall. That was the end of his military career. The bubble was pricked. The flight made him an object of almost universal scorn and ridicule. Had he escaped with Gist, or taken refuge at Hanging Rock with the remnants of his army, or found his way to join Sumter's force across the Wateree River, he might have survived the defeat and been given another opportunity to display his ineptness as a military leader. But it was the sixty-mile flight that finished him. Again it was a matter of sending the wrong man to do the job. As we have seen, Washington was by no means free of this failing. But in this instance the fault was clearly Congress's.

Gates's behavior inevitably puts us in mind of his coadjutor, Charles Lee. Lee, to be sure, never turned tail and ran, but he displayed many of the traits that characterized his fellow Englishman. He was boastful and pessimistic by turns, giving some indications of what we would call today a manic-depressive cycle. Where Lee was plainly mad, Gates was merely incompetent—a man always inadequate to the tasks assigned him, with the notable exception of the Burgoyne campaign, which, after all, he did win, however much it may be argued that the principal credit should go to his subordinates. Whatever merit that argument has must rest, paradoxically, on Gates's performance at Camden. Men generally do not change drastically within the space of a few months or even years. The Gates who displayed such poor judgment at Camden was the same Gates who commanded the American forces that defeated Burgoyne. If a number of his actions in that campaign could be interpreted in rather different lights, according to the sympathies of the writer, the events leading up to and including the disaster at Camden certainly tip the scale decisively against Gates.

Lee and Gates shared much of the same background as Englishmen. One need not be a student of English social life to be aware that as the son of the Duke of Leeds's housekeeper (perhaps by the duke himself), Gates must in his youth have suffered innumerable snubs and slights and must all his life have felt the mark of social inferiority because of his origins. When he took the field against General *Earl* Cornwallis and *Lord* Rawdon, can he have been immune to that corrosive sense of class inferiority that to such a large degree sustained the British system? Could Lee, the son of a professional soldier without the wealth and titles that insured the rapid advancement of British officers who were merely competent over more able officers who were their social inferiors? I wonder if it is too far-fetched to see in the rather similar character-type represented by these two men, and in their somewhat comparable actions when exercising independent commands, marks of a debility that was as much the product of caste and class as of inherent weaknesses of character? The question is, to be sure, academic. Whatever the sources of their weakness, the effects on the American cause were deleterious ones.

In the abuse and ridicule heaped on Gates, a mock handbill printed in Rivington's *Gazette* was notable. It read: "REWARD—Strayed, deserted or stolen from the subscriber, [Gates], on the 16th of August last, near Camden, a whole ARMY . . . to the amount of TEN THOU-

SAND . . . with all their baggage, artillery, wagons and camp equipage." The reward was "THREE MILLION of PAPER MONEY as soon as they can be spared from the public funds."

Alexander Hamilton expressed a more than personal bitterness when he wrote to the New York delegate to Congress, James Duane, "What think you of the conduct of this great man? . . . Did ever any one hear of such a disposition or such a fight? His best troops placed on the side strongest by nature, his worst on that weakest by nature, and his attack made by these. 'Tis impossible to give a more complete picture of military absurdity. It is equally against the maxims of war and common sense. . . . But was there ever an instance of a general running away, as Gates has done, from his whole army? And was there every so precipitate a flight? One hundred and eighty miles in three days and a half. It does admirable credit to the activity of a man at his time of life. But it disgraces the general and the soldier. . . . But what will be done by Congress?" Would Gates be relieved of his command? If so, Hamilton wrote, "for God's sake overcome prejudice, and send Greene. You know my opinion of him. I stake my reputation on the events, give him but fair play."

10

Kings Mountain

L EARNING of Sumter's seizure of the British convoy after the battle of Camden, Cornwallis quickly dispatched Lieutenant Colonel George Turnbull with a detachment of New York Loyalists and Major Patrick Ferguson's provincials to intercept Sumter. Sumter, informed of Gates's defeat, broke camp and eluded Turnbull, but Cornwallis was determined to capture him and recover the British provisions, so he also sent Tarleton and his legion in pursuit. Sumter, having gotten as far as Rocky Mount, spent the night there, moved on for eight more miles the next day, and then, putting out only skimpy security, allowed his weary men to stack their arms and bathe in the nearby stream, rest, or forage for food in the woods and adjacent farms. It was in this condition that Tarleton found him at Fishing Creek, South Carolina.

Again Tarleton had carried out his pursuit with his accustomed vigor. When some of his troops were too exhausted by the late summer heat to continue, he left half his force behind and pushed on with a hundred and sixty men. He crossed the Catawba at the Rocky Mount Ford and moved around to Sumter's rear. When he broke upon the startled militia, there was a brief, desperate effort to make some resistance, and then frantic flight. Sumter's force, many of whom were half-clothed and virtually all of whom were without their weapons, was estimated at nearly eight hundred men; some were killed and wounded, the others hopelessly scattered. Sumter escaped with three hundred and fifty men. Once more Tarleton had carried out a brilliant operation. His name, more than ever, carried the threat of sudden and devastating force.

In writing of the attack on Sumter, Henry Lee, himself a highly successful cavalry officer, could not resist pointing out a moral about the use of militia. "Unhappily for America," he wrote, "her soldiers were slaughtered, sometimes from the improvidence of their leaders, more often from their own fatal neglect of duty, and disobedience of order." Only the severest discipline could instill the proper habits into soldiers— "execution on the spot, of a faithless or negligent sentinel, is humanity in the end." But militia would not "endure this rigor," Lee noted, "and are therefore improperly intrusted with the sword of the nation in war. The pursuance of that system [militia] must weaken the best resources of the state, by throwing away the lives of its citizens. . . ."

Hillsboro, North Carolina, was chosen as the gathering point for what remained of the shattered army of the South. The dispersed Continentals first gathered under Smallwood and Gist at Salisbury. Efforts were made to raise a force of North Carolina cavalry under Colonel Davie, and gradually the nucleus of a small army was drawn together. Colonel Davie recruited eighty dragoons, and Major George Davidson assembled two companies of mounted riflemen, establishing himself on the Waxhaw, some thirty-five miles from Charlotte.

In the aftermath of the battle of Camden, Cornwallis appointed a commissioner to take possession of the estates of all enemies of the Crown. After provisions were made for wives and children, the proceeds from the sale of the properties were to be turned over to the paymaster general of the British forces. Death was declared to be the penalty for those Americans who, having pledged allegiance to England and received protection, had taken up arms against the king's soldiers; some militia captured at Camden who fell into this category were hanged.

By September 8, the weather was suitable for military operations, and Cornwallis was ready to press his campaign into North Carolina and then, hopefully, into Virginia, whose capture would, it was assumed, break the back of the American resistance and bring the war to an end. "Elated with these flattering expectations," as Lee put it, "Cornwallis took his route through those parts of the State distinguished for their firm adherence to their country." As the main body of Cornwallis's army marched toward Charlotte, Tarleton with his legion and a body of light infantry moved on its flank, west of the Wateree; Ferguson marched even farther to the west, at the head of his corps of provincials. The advance of Cornwallis, whom Tarleton joined at the Waxhaws, forced Davie and his dragoons back to Charlotte.

The country around the Waxhaws had been so stripped of food by the successive tides of troops who had moved through it that Cornwallis was forced to send a number of foraging parties on a wide sweep to collect provisions for his troops. This he did with complete confidence, convinced that the defeat at Camden had destroyed all effective opposition to his forces. Colonel Davie, informed by spies that Cornwallis's main army was north of the Catawba River while some of his light infantry and Loyalist companies were still on the south bank, decided to attempt a raid by moving far around Cornwallis's left flank, crossing the river, and taking the British there by surprise. Guided by soldiers in his command who were inhabitants of the area and "whose property, wives and children were now in the possession of the enemy," Davie and his little force came on the British encampment at Wahab's Plantation early the next morning, just as the redcoats were preparing to mount their horses. Here Davie repeated the tactics that he had used so successfully at Hanging Rock. He sent Major Davidson through a cornfield with orders to seize the plantation house, and with the rest of his force, including Captain Wahab, he blocked the lane leading from the house. The surprise was complete. Davie had at last turned the tables on a sizable portion of the Loyal Legion. Sixty were killed or wounded at the cost of one patriot casualty, and the rest fled. Captain Wahab "spent the few minutes halt in delicious converse with his wife and children, who ran out as soon as the fire ceased, to embrace their long lost and beloved protector," as Lee put it. Included in Davie's booty were ninety-six horses with their saddles and equipment, and a hundred and twenty muskets and rifles. The patriot force got away just ahead of British troops, coming belatedly to the relief of the now scattered legion. In rage and frustration, the British officer in command ordered Wahab's house burned to the ground.

Davie returned with his bounty to his base camp at Providence on the Charlotte Road, having covered sixty miles and fought a sharp battle in a period of twenty-four hours. At Providence he was joined by Sumter and Major Davidson, with almost a thousand militiamen they had rounded up; with Davie's two hundred dragoons and mounted infantry, these men made up the better part of what might be rather too generously called the army of the South. That it existed at all was a miracle.

Cornwallis, so confident that effective opposition had been destroyed at Camden, may have seen a portent in the clash at Wahab's Plantation. What was increasingly evident in the South was that the Revolution there was truly a Hydra. Where one head was lopped off, two, albeit smaller ones, seemed to appear in its place. That was what the British could never quite grasp—the extraordinary ability of the rebel army to rise like a phoenix from the ashes of defeat, to reconstitute itself almost before the smoke of battle had drifted away. In that strange tenacity—that remarkable gift for organization and reorganization, apparently without end—lay the inevitable defeat of the British. Without effective central authority, determined and energetic individuals like Davie and a dozen others simply created new units out of the bits and pieces of old ones and returned to the battle. The tally of victories and defeats meant little; it was simply the continued and renewed existence of these militia, ill-trained, wretchedly equipped, and haphazardly led as they so often were, that was ultimately unnerving to the British professionals. They were like the teeth of the gorgon; they seemed to spring out of the earth.

Tarleton's own comments are revealing: "It was evident," he wrote, "that the counties of Mecklenburg and Rohan were more hostile to England than any others in America. The vigilance and animosity of these districts checked the exertions of the well-effected [the pro-British], and totally destroyed all communications between the king's troops and the loyalists in the other parts of the province. No British commander could obtain any information; the foraging parties were every day harassed by the inhabitants. . . . Individuals, with expresses, were frequently murdered. Notwithstanding their checks and losses, they continued their hostilities with unwearied perseverance."

Four days after the Wahab foray, Cornwallis resumed his march to Charlotte. Lurking on the British flanks, Davie took a few prisoners and reached Charlotte near midnight. The town consisted of some twenty houses grouped at the intersection of two streets and located on a slight rise. A stone courthouse stood at the center of the town. The town common, on the right of the main street running through the town, was covered with low bushes and bounded by gardens. On the left was an open field. Davie chose this spot to make an organized resistance to Cornwallis's march. He dismounted his cavalry, who, in addition to swords and pistols, carried muskets, and posted them at the courthouse behind a chest-high stone wall. He placed his dismounted infantry some eighty yards in front of the dragoons on both sides of the street, protected to a degree by the fences of the village. As Davie was making the final disposition of his men, the Loyal Legion, under the command of Major George von Hanger because Tarleton was ill, appeared at the end of the common in a column formation, flanked by detachments of light infantry. Hanger had the charge sounded, and the column rode forward toward the courthouse, moving slowly enough to give the infantry time to clear out the advance militiamen. As these groups began a firefight, Hanger came on to the courthouse at a gallop. Davie's dismounted cavalry met the legion with such a heavy and well-directed fire that the column broke and curled back to the edge of the common. The militia on the right of the street were driven in on the stone-fence line, and Davie ordered the infantry on the left to fall back. The center held its fire for the cavalry, and when Hanger charged once more he was again driven back. By this time the pressure of the British infantry had driven in Davie's right flank. He therefore withdrew from the courthouse and took new defensive positions at the east end of the village. This time, Davie's dragoons were mounted. When the legion was ordered back into action by Cornwallis, who came up with the main force, and attacked for a third time, the patriots were driven back once more. As more of the weight of the British infantry was deployed, Davie broke off the engagement and withdrew in the direction of Salisbury. The American losses were five killed and twelve wounded, and the British lost more or less the same number. Again the action was a minor one, but Davie handled his little force skillfully, and his men fought with courage and determination. And Cornwallis was put on notice that he could not look forward to an uninterrupted march through conquered country.

In Georgia, Colonel Elijah Clarke and his mountain riflemen threatened the British post at Augusta, whose garrison was under the command of Thomas Brown, a Tory leader. Clarke, knowing he might need some special incentive to persuade his men to attack Augusta, waited until he heard that the annual payments of the Crown to the loyal Indians were about to be delivered to that town. Arms, ammunition, blankets, salt, liquor, and many other attractive items were included in the present, and Clarke had little difficulty prevailing on his men to make the attack. In Lee's phrase, "the warriors of the hills shouted for battle." In two hours Clarke's riflemen were ready to move, provisions, bullets, and powder having been distributed among them.

Augusta was defended by only a hundred and fifty men and a few score Indians. Brown therefore judged Augusta indefensible against Clarke's much larger force of almost seven hundred men, and he withdrew to Garden Hill with two small brass artillery pieces. Clarke tried to block his movement, but Brown used his artillery to drive the patriots back and then forced his way to the top of the hill by bayonet. In Brown, Clarke had met an opponent as determined and resourceful as himself. Brown was determined to hold out until Colonel John Harris Cruger arrived with reinforcements from Ninety-Six. His chances seemed slim until the Americans ran out of ammunition. Clarke then tried to force Brown to surrender by cutting off his water supply, but Brown ordered his men to save their urine in earthen vessels, "and when cold it was served out with much economy to the troops, himself taking the first draught." Although Brown was wounded in the leg and the wound had become so badly infected that it was torture to wear a boot, he held out for four days until Cruger appeared and Clarke and his men were forced to withdraw.

A combination of events now produced another dramatic encounter. Tarleton and Ferguson, with their respective Loyalist forces, had been moving on roughly parallel lines along the Broad and the Catawba rivers. When word reached Ferguson that Clarke was attacking Brown at Augusta, he set out to come to that officer's assistance; he missed Clarke, however, and returned to Gilbert Town. There he captured a rebel militiaman and instructed him to carry the word to Colonel Isaac Shelby that if he did not surrender, "he [Ferguson] would come over the mountains and put him to death, and burn his whole country." The British officer then visited patriot families in the vicinity and, assuming a kindly and solicitous air, advised them to urge their sons and husbands who were "out liers"—hiding out to avoid taking the oath of allegiance to the Crown—to give themselves up and receive the protection of His Majesty's armed forces. From Gilbert Town, Ferguson began to march to Kings Mountain, on the border of the two Carolinas.

Far from being intimidated by Ferguson's threats, the rebellious pioneers of the frontier settlements resolved to teach the British major humility. The nucleus of the patriot force consisted of Shelby's experienced campaigners and the riflemen rounded up by Nolichucky Jack

Sevier, the Indian fighter. The two men pledged themselves responsible for whatever money they took out of the public treasury to finance the recruiting and arming of their men. They also appealed to Colonel William Campbell, a Virginia militia colonel, and to two Carolina militia colonels, Charles McDowell and Benjamin Cleveland, who operated along the North Carolina border, to bring troops to a rendezvous at Sycamore Shoals on the Watauga on September 26. At Sycamore Shoals more than 1,000 men showed up, most of them mounted and armed with the long rifle. William Campbell, married to Patrick Henry's sister, was the most impressive figure there, a huge man who towered over his fellows and who was a renowned marksman and fighter. He brought 400 Virginians with him. McDowell brought his brother and 160 North Carolinians, while Shelby and Sevier together contributed some 500 to the little army.

The over-the-mountain men were a tough breed. Armed with their long rifles, to which they gave such names as "Hot Lead" and "Sweet Lips," they constituted a formidable fighting force. Henry Lee described them aptly as "a hardy race of men, who were familiar with the use of the horse and rifle, were stout, active, patient under privation, and brave. Irregular in their movements, and unaccustomed to restraint, they delighted in the fury of action, but pined under the servitude and inactivity of camp." It is interesting to note that Lee considered the white settlers of the coastal regions, a group that in large part came to be known as poor whites, "less capable of labor, and less willing to endure it" because of that "dreadful evil," Negro slavery.

The Reverend Samuel Doak preached a sermon to this motley force on Gideon's uprising against the Midianites and suggested that their battle cry be, "The sword of the Lord and of Gideon." One problem that arose almost at once was who should play the role of Gideon. Which of these tough and aggressive men should command the combined force? Campbell, Shelby, and Sevier were the principal candidates. Before this touchy issue was decided, they were joined on the march by three or four hundred more recruits made up of militia from North and South Carolina under the command of Cleveland.

When Ferguson learned of the size of the patriot force on his trail, he sent a request for reinforcements to Cornwallis and Cruger. On the fifth of October he wrote to Cornwallis from Tate's Plantation of Buffalo Creek, some ten miles from Kings Mountain: "I am on my march toward you, by a road leading from Cherokee Ford, north of

Kings Mountain. Three or four hundred good soldiers, part dragoons, would finish this business. [Something] must be done soon. This is their last push in this quarter and they are extremely desolate and cowed."

It was clear that Ferguson took his pursuers too lightly. His actions, in any event, were certainly not those of a man who considered himself in peril. On October 2, he moved his force only four miles, and although he had ample opportunity to join Cornwallis at Charlotte, he decided instead to take up defensive positions on Kings Mountain and, in doing so, to challenge the patriot force to attack him. With the Musgrove's Mill battle still rankling, Ferguson hoped to subject his pursuers to the same kind of punishment that his forces had suffered in that action. Then, with the patriots beaten and demoralized, he might finish them off and thereby close, once and for all, that particular chapter of rebel resistance.

Ferguson was a proud and arrogant man, and, as his message to Shelby reveals, he sought vengeance. This emotion, while often an exemplary one for troops, is one in which a commander dare not indulge. A commander's decisions should all be as cool and deliberate as possible and directed only to one end: the most effective use of the forces under his direction in attaining the desired strategic ends. Pride, determination to chastise, hunger for glory—all such emotions are not only irrelevant to the task at hand, they are filled with danger for any commander who indulges in them. But since they are emotions common to most of us, they often infect the most skilled and experienced soldiers, and they almost as often bring with them disaster.

Ferguson had one other problem. He was an Englishman leading American Tories. He was the scion of an aristocratic Scottish family who had been kept out of the military service initially because of bad health. In 1768 he had bought a commission as captain in the Seventieth Foot and had served in that unit in the West Indies, helping to put down a slave revolt on the island of Tobago. Impressed with the marksmanship of the rebelling Americans in 1776, and trying to find a way to offset it, Ferguson, who was then just thirty years old, invented the first breech-loading rifle used in the British army and secured a patent on it. The weapon could be fired much more rapidly than a muzzleloading piece, was highly accurate, and was reliable in wet weather when the flintlock was simply unusable.

In the advance at Brandywine, Ferguson, who was an excellent shot himself, was close enough to Washington to have easily shot him, but he did not fire because, in the code of the British officer-gentleman, it was bad form to kill enemy officers. In Ferguson's own words, "It was not pleasant to fire at the back of an unoffending individual who was acquitting himself very coolly of his duty, so I let him alone." At Brandywine Ferguson's right elbow was shattered with a musket ball and his arm was permanently crippled. During his convalescence, his corps was broken up by Howe, who, it was said, resented the young officer's invention of the breechloading gun and his inclination to independent action. Those rifles that had been manufactured were put into storage, and the muzzleloading flintlock musket remained the standard arm of the British infantryman for decades to come. Later, Ferguson joined with Tarleton in the brilliant victory at Monck's Corner, but he was afterward glad to operate independently of "Bloody Ban," whose ruthlessness offended an officer too gentlemanly to shoot George Washington in the back.

Ferguson's successes had all been in open warfare, almost invariably raids and forays where speed and surprise were essential. He had no experience with a different defensive operation, and his men were likewise untried in such a situation. On October 6, Ferguson again wrote to Cornwallis, informing him that he had decided to make a stand. Ferguson presumably still hoped for reinforcements from Cruger and from Tarleton's legion. Cruger, however, could not spare men from his post at Ninety-Six, and Tarleton was ill with malaria. Hanger, his second-in-command, was also ill, and Cornwallis himself was in bed with a "feverish cold." Thus Ferguson had to stand on his own feet, which he was confident he could do. "I arrived this day at Kings Mountain," he wrote, "& have taken a post where I do not think I can be forced by a stronger enemy than that against us."

For several days the patriot force was thrown off the track by Ferguson's deceptive maneuvers, but on the sixth Sevier picked up his trail and marched twenty-one miles to Cowpens, a place so called because it consisted largely of pens where half-wild cows, which had been allowed to graze in the woods, were collected to be driven to the coast and there slaughtered for their meat and hides. At Cowpens the army was further augmented by some four hundred Carolina militia recruited by Colonel James Williams. Here, again, was a remarkable demonstration of the capacity for resourceful individuals to gather on their own initiative men willing to fight in the face of inadequate equipment, meager supplies, and many earlier defeats and discouragements. Such moral stamina, often taken for granted by historians writing of the Southern campaigns, was, as we have argued earlier, one of the most striking manifestations of that "new consciousness" that distinguished Americans from other breeds.

The same day, a spy named Joseph Kerr brought the Americans definite word of what had before been rumor—that Ferguson had taken a defensive position on Kings Mountain. By dawn of the seventh the pursuing riflemen were weary to the bone and soaked by a chilly rain that had fallen during the night. There were some mutterings about it being time for a break, but Shelby was determined to push on. Two enemy scouts and a messenger were captured during the morning. The messenger provided a bit of information that probably proved fatal to Ferguson: the British officer could be identified by a checkered shirt that he wore over his uniform to prevent his being a target for rebel marksmen. Thus Ferguson, the man too gallant to shoot Washington, was to become a special target for patriot rifles.

The expeditionary force crossed Broad River some two and a half miles below Tate's Plantation, where Ferguson had, a few days earlier, written so confidently to Cornwallis. From there they took the Ridge Road past the Antioch church, turned north to a point some four miles north of Kings Mountain, and then turned once more toward the "mountain," actually a hill that rose some sixty feet above the heavily wooded surrounding countryside. The summit of Kings Mountain was a rocky area with a few scattered trees. The wooded and boulder-strewn slopes afforded ample cover for an attacking force. The sides of the hill were so steep in places that Ferguson felt confident he could not be attacked in those areas and consequently prepared inadequate defenses there. The British positions on the hill were like a toe and heel with a saddle or arch between them; the toe was the larger and slightly higher promontory, and the heel was the smaller, with more precipitous slopes.

As the Americans approached, some two hundred of Ferguson's men were out on a foraging expedition, leaving him with nine hundred men, eight hundred militia, and a hundred elite soldiers from the King's American Rangers, the Queen's Rangers, and the New Jersey Volunteers, the first two being among the most famous Tory regiments. A mile from Ferguson's position the patriot riflemen dismounted and deployed in four columns, as had been agreed the night before. The Americans were split into three divisions for the assault. Once more the issue of command came up, now with obvious urgency. After some wrangling, it was decided to have Campbell act as "commander of the day," and the attack proceeded under his at-least-nominal direction. Each officer in command of a division "made a short speech in his own way to his men," Private James Collins recalled, "desiring every coward to be off immediately." Collins' own feelings "were not the most pleasant." He was sixteen years old, but he "could not swallow the appellation of coward." He looked around; "every man's countenance seemed to change." "Well, thought I, fate is fate; every man's fate is before him and he has to run it out. . . ." At this point a dispatch rider carrying a message from Ferguson to Cornwallis was intercepted. The message, which declared, "I hold a position on the King's Mountain that all the rebels out of hell cannot drive me from," was read to the American troops waiting to attack. As the advance began, the word was passed along the line of soldiers, "Tie up overcoats, pick touch-holes, fresh prime, and be ready to fight."

Before the men moved forward, they put four or five rifleballs in their mouths, "to prevent thirst, also to be in readiness to reload quick." Cleveland's men were the first to make contact; they opened a heavy fire from the shelter of trees, moving obliquely with Sevier's division to surround the hill while Campbell's and Shelby's men, constituting the center, kept up a galling fire on the defenders. Ferguson, realizing that his men, armed with muskets, were no match for the riflemen, ordered a bayonet charge. Shelby's men, who bore the brunt of the onslaught, had no bayonets, but they nonetheless "obstinately stood until some of them were thrust through the body, and having nothing but their rifles by which to defend themselves, they were forced to retreat."

Ferguson's main guard, posted halfway down the mountain, was finally driven in. In the words of young Ensign Robert Campbell, who was with the North Carolina troops, "The enemy annoyed our troops very much from their advantageous position." Colonel Shelby, "observing . . . what a destructive fire was kept up from behind . . . rocks," ordered the ensign to post some riflemen "opposite to the rocks and near to the enemy, and then return to assist in bringing up the men in order, who had been charged with the bayonet." Ensign Campbell's platoon kept up such a smart fire that Ferguson ordered a company of regulars to face them and cover those Loyalists who were posted behind rocks. Colonel Campbell's Virginians meanwhile approached from the opposite side of the hill. "Here they are, boys!" the towering Campbell cried, "Shout like hell and fight like devils."

Private Collins had the frightening but strangely exhilarating experience of hearing the bullets of the enemy hum overhead as he and his companions began the laborious climb, and he was "soon in profuse sweat" from fear and exertion. Near the summit of the hill, the enemy charged again with bayonets, and Collins and his fellows in the center of the American line were forced to fall back to the base of the hill. Again they came on and once more were driven back. Finally, on their third try, the enemy fire dwindled, and they found themselves just below the summit of the hill at the "toe." "When we had gotten near the top," Collins recalled, "some of our leaders roared out, 'Hurrah, my brave fellows! Advance! They are crying for quarter.'"

Ferguson ordered Captain Abraham de Peyster, the New York Loyalist, to reinforce a post in the heel with a company of British regulars. To reach the position, De Peyster had to march his men across the saddle or arch of the hill, and here they came under such heavy fire that De Peyster, "to his astonishment . . . had almost no men when he arrived at the place of destination. . . . He then ordered his cavalry to mount, but to no purpose. As quick as they were mounted they were taken down by some bold marksman."

Meanwhile Sevier and Shelby tightened their grip on the heel, forcing its defenders across the arch to the larger defensive position, where the Loyalist camp was now virtually surrounded by the forces under McDowell and Cleveland. Here Ferguson hoped to make a stand and drive off his tormentors, but his men were by now thoroughly demoralized. The defenses on the toe were too skimpy to afford much protection. Its defenders were exposed to fire from all sides and surrounded by dead and wounded companions. Some companies tried to surrender, but Ferguson, conspicuous on his horse, cut down the white flags that appeared and worked like a demon to rally his men, blowing constantly on the silver whistle with which he had so often before summoned his troops. Finally, seeing that the contest was hopeless, he and a few of his officers tried to ride through the rebels and escape, but Ferguson was shot from his saddle as eight bullets struck him. Both his arms were broken, "and his hat and clothing were literally shot to pieces."

Captain De Peyster was left in command of those Tories who tried to fight on, taking cover behind the provision wagons and firing at the patriots like the defenders of a wagon train trying to hold off hostile Indians in a movie Western. Finally, De Peyster had no choice but to raise the white flag or see the remainder of his force wiped out. For a brief time, it appeared that the patriots would not honor the flag of surrender. Doubtless thinking of the episode at the Waxhaw and of "Tarleton's quarter," the poorly disciplined riflemen continued to fire at the Loyalists who were trying to give themselves up as prisoners of war. After Shelby and Campbell had prevailed upon their men to stop firing and the Loyalists had been herded together, a stray shot, coming from no one knew where, struck and killed Colonel Williams. At this the riflemen—acting, some said, on an order from Campbell—fired point blank into the mass of prisoners. "We killed near a hundred of them and hardly could be restrained from killing the whole," one officer said after the battle.

Whatever the circumstances, it seems clear that many men who had thrown down their weapons were killed or wounded. Shelby's own account states that it was difficult to effect "a complete cessation of firing. . . . Our men who had been scattered in the battle were continually coming up and continued to fire, without comprehending in the heat of the moment what had happened; and some who had heard that at Buford's defeat the British had refused quarters . . . were willing to follow that bad example." Others who had had their homes burned and their property stolen were doubtless determined to "get them a Tory bastard" by whatever means.

The battle had lasted little more than an hour. Only a handful of Loyalists escaped. Thirty prisoners, most of them known to have been actively involved in looting and pillage, were convicted by a drumhead court-martial of crimes against patriots; twelve were condemned to death, and nine were actually hanged. The shooting of prisoners and the execution of the nine captured Tories besmirched the American victory and added fuel to the fires of bitterness that raged between Loyalist and patriot in the South. To the British it was simply another indication of the barbarity of the Americans, hardly removed in savagery from the native Indians.

The Americans lost 28 killed and 64 wounded. The Loyalists lost 157 killed, 163 too badly wounded to be evacuated, and another 689 who were taken prisoners. Thus the Loyalist losses totaled something in excess of a thousand men.

After the surrender, Collins noted, "The situation of the poor Tories appeared to be really pitiable; the dead lay in heaps on all sides, while the groans of the wounded were heard in every direction. I could not help turning away from the scene before me with horror and, though exulting in victory, could not refrain from shedding tears. . . ." Next morning, Sunday, the scene on the top of Kings Mountain became, in Collins' words, "really distressing" as "the wives and children of the poor Tories came in, in great numbers. Their husbands, fathers and brothers lay dead in heaps, while others lay wounded or dying—a melancholy sight indeed!"

It remained to bury the dead, that grim postlude to every battle. "It was badly done," Collins recalled. "They were thrown into convenient piles and covered with old logs, the bark of trees, and rocks; yet not so as to secure them from becoming a prey to the beasts of the forest or the vultures of the air; and the wolves became so plenty, that it was dangerous for any one to be out at night, for several miles around; also, the hogs in the neighborhood gathered to the place to devour the flesh of men, inasmuch as numbers chose to live on little meat rather than eat their hogs, though they were fat. Half the dogs in the country were said to be mad and were put to death. I saw myself, in passing the place a few weeks after, all parts of the human frame lying scattered in every direction."

The survivors of Kings Mountain were marched off to Hillsboro in the interior of North Carolina, where, in the words of one captured British officer, they were forced to listen to a Presbyterian sermon, "stuffed as full of Republicanism as their camp is of horse thieves." It is perhaps worth noting that Lieutenant Anthony Allaire of Ferguson's legion, who escaped from the prison camp near Salem, North Carolina, was passed along through a Tory underground until he finally got to the British lines at Charles Town. Since there was no adequate prisoner compound in Hillsboro or soldiers to guard them, all but sixty of the prisoners escaped within a few months, most of them doubtless with the blessings of their captors, who had enough to do to feed and clothe themselves. The patriots retained, however, fifteen hundred captured muskets and rifles, and a quantity of supplies.

The defeat was a crushing one with consequences far beyond the mere loss of men and materiel. What the battle did most conclusively was demonstrate, beyond question, the complete failure of Lord North's "Southern strategy." After a succession of victories, the best of the Loyalist auxiliaries had been destroyed. The Southern strategy had never contemplated occupying the entire South. Such an undertaking would have doubtless required fifty thousand British soldiers when there were not thirty thousand to be had on the whole continent of North America. The Southern strategy was based on the conviction that a British expeditionary force could defeat any Continental Army put into the field against it, intimidate the patriot militia, and encourage the far more numerous Loyalists (as it was thought) to take control of their own states in the name of His Majesty's government. If this assumption proved false, then the capture of Savannah, the seizure of Charles Town, the capture of the Southern army, the defeat of Gates at Camden—all these, ultimately, added up to nothing. They were mere military exercises, in varying degrees glorious, but of no enduring strategic significance.

At Kings Mountain what might properly be called a spontaneous, or self-created, patriot army had risen to wipe out one of the best-officered and most successful provincial units in the British military establishment. (When Claude Blanchard, the French commissary officer with Rochambeau's army, heard of Campbell's defeat of Ferguson at Kings Mountain, he wrote, "We cannot conceive how regular troops and they superior in numbers allowed themselves to be beaten by peasants. . . .") The thousand men killed and captured counted for little beside the symbolic significance of Kings Mountain. What had already been suggested by Davie's spirited and defiant defense of Charlotte was now posted for the world to read: Southern patriots could be beaten but not conquered; the Southern Loyalists, without the active support of a nearby British army, could not maintain themselves for a month.

Kings Mountain was understood to be a turning point from the moment that news of it swept through the country. Sir Henry Clinton later called it "the first link of a chain of evils that followed each other in regular succession until they at last ended in the total loss of America." It was to the Southern campaign what Burgoyne's defeat at Saratoga had been to Germain's grandiose scheme for splitting the Northern states along the line of the Hudson.

To a striking degree the battle of Kings Mountain was a re-enactment of the engagement at Ramsour's Mill on a much larger scale. It underlined the point, already made in the earlier engagement, that militia and irregulars performed with remarkable courage and tenacity in situations where they were, in effect, released from the constraints of conventional military operations. What is common to both these battles—Ramsour's Mill and Kings Mountain—is that problems of coordination and control did not exist, essentially because the attackers were moving toward enemy positions established on high ground. In both instances, the enemy had no room for maneuver of any but the most limited kind. All the patriot militia had to do was advance toward an unmistakable objective. It was the simplest possible military exercise, requiring in the main those talents most conspicuous in such irregular forces: marksmanship, mobility, and individual initiative. In both engagements artillery played a negligible role or was not employed by either side.

At Bunker Hill and Fort Mercer, the Americans also had had simple missions; they had only to stand fast and fire their muskets. For the most part they found their own cover, chose their own targets, and, after the first volley, fired without command. There was no problem of maneuver and thus no problem of control, and such authority as there was was exercised more on the level of exhortation and encouragement than direction.

The striking success of militia in these four engagements—two offensive and two defensive—demonstrates very dramatically their limitations as well as their strengths. In virtually every battle of maneuver on open ground, the militia at the very least failed to distinguish itself, and often proved more than useless; their tendency to run away frequently exposed the Continentals to being outflanked and overrun by the British.

It must also be said of Kings Mountain that Ferguson, through his inexperience in defensive fighting, chose the worst possible position. He was, in the first place, misled by the precipitousness of the slopes leading to the top of Kings Mountain. All he could envision was the rebel militia slowly climbing over the steep and rugged terrain while his soldiers, safe behind rocks, fired down on them. What he did not sufficiently take into account was that most of the hill's inclines were so steep that his own men would have to expose themselves to fire at their attackers, and that the hill's roughness provided cover for anyone making the ascent. In the words of a private soldier after the battle, "their great elevation above us has proved their ruin. They overshot us altogether, scarcely touching a man, except those on horseback, while every rifle from below seemed to have the desired effect. . . ."

A patriotic nineteenth-century account of the battle ended with these words: "A wild, terror-stricken shriek rose above the battle—a yell for quarter. A white flag was run up, arms thrown down, and God's champions shouted, 'Victory! Liberty!' That shout echoed from the mountain to the sea, and far along the shore to where the majestic Washington sat almost weeping over the sad horrors of the South. His great heart leaped with prophetic joy as this beam of hope came borne on the triumphant voice of his beloved and trusted men of 'West Augusta. . . .'"

Greene Takes Command

O N the day of the battle of Kings Mountain (October 7, 1780), Nathanael Greene was appointed commander of the Southern Department. It was early December, however, before he arrived to take charge of the force that Gates had scraped together at Hillsboro after the Camden disaster. Meanwhile, partisan or guerrilla warfare, whose first successful practitioners had been, ironically, Tarleton and Ferguson, became the patriots' mode of waging war.

Cornwallis, dissatisfied with Clinton's cautious strategy, appealed over his head to the British ministry for permission to launch an aggressive campaign in North Carolina and Virginia. Endorsing Cornwallis's plan, Germain instructed Clinton to dispatch part of his force in New York under Major General Alexander Leslie to undertake a combined action with Cornwallis. Leslie sailed for the Chesapeake on October 16 with twenty-five hundred men, including the British Guards, the Eighty-second and Eighty-fourth Regiments, and Bose's Hessian regiment, and landed at Portsmouth, Virginia, early in November. There Rawdon, acting on behalf of an ill Cornwallis, met Leslie and conveyed to him Cornwallis's instructions to sail to Charles Town. Leslie therefore left Portsmouth on November 23 and, fighting the contrary winds and bad weather that had so troubled Cornwallis the year before, arrived at Charles Town on December 16.

1435

The simple logistics of Leslie's move from New York to Charles Town are worth noting. It had taken him two months to get from one city to the other. In the meantime his troops had consumed a considerable quantity of food and drink, and the ships that had transported them and the frigates and ships of the line that had guarded the transports had sustained a battering from the elements; a number of them needed to be repaired and refitted. It took another week or so to equip Leslie's force for the campaign ahead. Then, encumbered by a large baggage train, the detachment moved slowly inland, arriving at Camden on January 4, 1781. By contrast, Shelby and Sevier had rounded up over a thousand men, supplied them, and marched some of them over a hundred and fifty miles in just a few weeks to catch Ferguson at Kings Mountain.

While Leslie was making his laborious journey to join Cornwallis, the latter was forced to turn his attention to the increasingly bold forays of partisan bands. Francis Marion and his grimy and bizarrely attired little band of patriots, appearing to join Gates before Camden, had been sent off on a mission designed more to get rid of them than to accomplish anything substantial. Marion, however, made skillful use of his own and his followers' knowledge of the swamps that dotted the region to attack isolated British posts and melt back into the swamps before the British could apprehend him. On October 28, Marion heard that a Colonel Tynes was recruiting Tory militia nearby. Marion and his band of some hundred and fifty men made a forced march under the cover of darkness and attacked Tynes shortly after midnight. The Tories scattered to the woods, and Marion bagged twenty-three prisoners and counted three Tory dead and fourteen wounded, in addition to eighty confiscated horses, saddles, bridles, and new muskets—all at no loss to his own men. Tynes's effort to raise a Tory militia was thus nipped in the bud; in fact, some of the unhappy Tories enlisted in Marion's band of raiders. His next foray was out of the Black River swamps, across the High Hills of the Santee, to cut the British supply lines at Singleton's Mills.

Marion then moved to try to intercept a Tory force of four hundred men under Colonel Watts, marching from Georgetown to Camden. He set a careful ambush, and his men were rewarded by the sight of Watts at the head of his force, marching down the road, as one of Marion's lieutenants wrote, "with great show and magnificence (hoping, no doubt, to terrify and conquer the country). . . ." Catching sight of Marion's men, Watts dispatched his cavalry to surround them. Marion, anticipating the move, withdrew some four hundred yards to a patch of woods and prepared to receive the attack. Watts's cavalry dashed up, "expecting to find us all in confusion and disorder, but to their astonishment we were ready for the attack." While Watts's soldiers hesitated, Marion ordered a charge. Colonel Daniel Horry, who had a bad stammer, tried in vain to get out the word "Charge!" and finding he could not, "leaned forward, spurred his horse, waved his sword for fifty or sixty yards" and "bawled out, *'Damn it, boys you . . . you know what I mean. Go on!'"*

Before the British cavalry could regain the main body, their pursuers "slew a goodly number of them." Watts in turn unlimbered his cannon, which tore "down the limbs and branches of the trees, which fell about us like hail," Captain Tarleton Brown wrote, "but did no other damage than to wound one of our men. . . ." Marion's force was too small to hope to press the attack against Watts, but he "guarded the bridges and swamps in his route, and annoyed and killed his men as they passed."

Marion's tactics were the classic tactics of guerrilla warfare. Making the greatest possible use of the mobility of his little force, he never camped two nights in the same spot. He marched under the cover of darkness from one friendly woods or swamp to another, setting off at sunset, making camp at dawn, and resting his men in the daytime with sentinels constantly on the alert. One of the officers who served under him wrote admiringly: "Upon him depended almost solely the success of the provincial army of South Carolina, and the sequel has proved how well he performed the trust reposed in him. His genuine love of country and liberty, and his unwearied vigilance and invincible fortitude . . . has endeared him to the hearts of his countrymen, and the memory of his deeds of valor shall never slumber so long as there is a Carolinian to speak his panegyric."

Born into a French Huguenot family, and "small enough at birth to be put into a quart mug," Marion had been a frail, almost deformed child with malformed knees and ankles. Like Ferguson, his closest British counterpart, he was quiet and withdrawn, rather austere, and with a scrupulous piety that was part of his Huguenot background. At the same time, a fierce fire burned in him; it showed in his quick glance and the nervous movements of his hands. After a brief career as a sailor, he had shown exemplary courage as an officer in the Cherokee Expedition, led by Moultrie in 1761, and he had afterward become a prosperous planter and a member of the provincial congress of South Carolina.

He had commanded a regiment at the beginning of Clinton's siege of Charles Town. There, soon after his arrival he attended a dinner party given by Moultrie's adjutant general, Captain Alexander McQueen. In Lossing's words, "the host, determined that all of his guests should drink his wine freely, locked the door to prevent their departure. Marion would not submit to this act of social tyranny, and leaped from a second story window to the ground." He broke his ankle in the jump, and since it was still possible at that point to leave Charles Town, Marion was taken on a litter to his plantation in St. John's parish. Thus he was saved from capture when the city was surrendered six weeks later.

After Marion's attack on Watts's column, he sent detachments across the Santee to strike at enemy posts at Scott's Lake and Monck's Corner. Finding Scott's Lake too well fortified, the party turned to Monck's Corner, where Tarleton had earlier inflicted such heavy losses on Buford; there Marion caught the Tory camp so by surprise that they never had time to fire a gun. The booty was thirty-three prisoners and "twenty-odd hogsheads of old spirits" (which may have been why Marion's men were so successful in catching the enemy by surprise). When the garrison at Scott's Lake heard of the attack on Monck's Corner, they marched to the relief of their fellows—whereupon Marion's raiders returned to Scott's Lake in their absence, burned the fort there, and slipped back across the Santee.

This minor action was typical of Marion's hit-and-run tactics, and Cornwallis, in a letter to Clinton, gave a telling account of the effect of such operations. Mentioning Marion's destruction of Colonel Tynes's militia force, Cornwallis added, "Col. Marion had so wrought on the minds of the people, partly by terror of his threats and cruelty of his punishments, and partly by the promise of plunder, that there was scarce an inhabitant between the Santee and Peedee that was not in arms against us."

The story of one of Marion's raiders summons up a vivid picture of the life of a partisan fighter. Paul Hamilton, on a raid with a party of guerrilla fighters, passed near his grandfather's home at Jacksonboro and heard that his mother was there with his grandmother, who was ill with smallpox. Hamilton waited by a fence near a swamp and sent word to his mother that he was there. "What our meeting was I cannot describe," he wrote. He had not seen his mother for twelve months, and she had frequently heard rumors that he was dead. "At length a flood of tears on her part enabled her to break silence, when such affectionate expressions were poured out as I can never forget, nor the warmth of that maternal embrace in which I was clasped to her aching bosom." She gave him a pillowcase filled with clothes and food that she had gathered, and he tied it behind his saddle and departed, "with her blessing on my head. . . ." That night the raiding party encountered a body of British cavalry and were routed after a brief battle. As Hamilton fled, the white pillowcase that he had tied behind his saddle made him a special target for the pursuing British.

When the little partisan force had been reassembled, the colonel in command led them against Fort Balfour at Pocataligo. In Hamilton's words, "Colonel Harden, knowing that we had some staunch friends who had been compelled to enter and garrison the fort, thought that if he could destroy the cavalry, he might induce a surrender of the remainder of the garrison, which were militia, and perhaps one half of them friendly to the American cause; some of whom were men of considerable influence and weight." Harden set an ambush and assigned twelve "well-mounted young men," Hamilton among them, to decoy the cavalry out of the fort. They were ordered to ride toward Von Bitter's Tavern, in full view of the fort. At the tavern the decoys surprised two officers and fifteen cavalry privates and quickly made them prisoners. As a result, the cavalry in the fort were too reduced in number to sally out after the decoys. Harden demanded surrender of the garrison under threat of attack, and Hamilton, accompanying the officer under a flag of truce, recognized friends in the fort and got the impression of confusion among the defenders, confusion doubtless stirred up by the patriots whose services had been commandeered. Colonel Harden then made preparations for an attack and sent Hamilton to carry the word to the commander of the garrison that ten minutes would be allowed "to consider of a surrender, after which, if he refuses, you are both to return immediately to me and, by God, I will be in the fort." The fort, consisting of ninety-two militia (half of them of patriot sentiment), twenty-five British regulars, and a platoon of light dragoons, surrendered without a shot being fired.

Cornwallis, determined to put a stop to Marion's marauding ventures, sent Tarleton after him, but Marion, as elusive as quicksilver, slipped into his familiar swamps. After days of fruitless searching, Tarleton was summoned back by Cornwallis to deal with Sumter, who had taken advantage of Tarleton's absence to badly maul a force under Major James Wemyss. When Tarleton, who had pursued Marion for seven hours through twenty-six miles of gumbo-like swamp, received Cornwallis's order to return, he is reported to have said, "Come, my boys! Let us go back and we will find the Gamecock. But as for this damned old fox, the devil himself could not catch him!" (Marion was forty-eight years old, which must have seemed very ancient to Tarleton, still in his mid-twenties.)

Wemyss had asked Cornwallis's permission to track down Sumter who, he had heard, was at Moore's Hill within a few miles of Fishdam Ford. Wemyss had "good guides . . . and he made no doubt of being able to surprize and rout him." The chance to defeat "so daring and troublesome a man as Sumter," Cornwallis wrote, "and disperseing such a banditti, was a great object." Cornwallis gave Wemyss his blessing and forty of Tarleton's dragoons, who had been left behind when the latter set out after Marion.

Wemyss marched "so early and so fast" on the night of November 8 that he reached Moore's Hill soon after midnight. But Sumter was not there. He had moved earlier in the evening to Fishdam Ford on Fishing Creek. Wemyss pushed on, determined to catch up with his prey, and came on Sumter's new camp at dawn. The British attacked and were among Sumter's men while many of them were still asleep around their fires. As Cornwallis wrote, "as Major Wemyss rode into the camp at the head of the dragoons and the 63rd followed them on horseback, the enemy's arms were not secured and some of them recovering from the first alarm got their rifles and with their first fire wounded Major Wemyss in several places and put the cavalry into disorder." At this point the Sixty-third dismounted and opened fire on the badly scattered Americans, who took refuge in the surrounding woods and from there began a deadly fire on Wemyss's soldiers, who were silhouetted against the abandoned campfires. The fire was too galling to resist. The British withdrew, leaving the major and twenty-two wounded soldiers in a nearby farmhouse. Sumter's own account of the battle indicates that Wemyss, at the head of his detachment, stumbled into one of Sumter's picket posts, and that it was the fire of these pickets, that wounded Wemyss in the arm and knee and knocked him from the saddle. Cornwallis had warned Wemyss not to use Tarleton's cavalry at night because of its vulnerability, but the young lieutenant on whose shoulders the command devolved when Wemyss fell had not heard any such instructions, and he charged into Sumter's bivouac at the head of Tarleton's dragoons; the militia, by now thoroughly awake, shot them up badly and forced them to withdraw.

At the start of the action five dragoons, who had been assigned the mission of taking Sumter dead or alive, were led to his tent by a Tory spy. As the dragoons entered the front of the tent, Sumter exited under the back flap, and he spent the night hiding under a bank of the Broad River. At daylight, with the British withdrawn, Sumter ventured out of his hiding place, gathered his men together, and returned to his camp-site. He found Wemyss and the wounded soldiers in the farmhouse where they had been left, and on Wemyss's pledge that he would not take up arms again, Sumter permitted the wounded officer to be evacuated to Charles Town. (Major Wemyss had in his pocket a list of the men he had hanged and the farmhouses and plantations he had burned on an expedition to the Cheraw, but Sumter looked at the list without realizing its significance and then threw it in the fire.)

Besides the twenty-three British wounded, another ten or fifteen were probably killed during the battle, against American casualties of no more than five or six. The striking thing about the clash is that the patriots, in the absence of Sumter, held their ground and inflicted substantial casualties on their attackers. (Wemyss commanded approximately a hundred and fifty men.) Much of the credit must go, of course, to the officers who took charge after Sumter's hasty departure. But again the resolution of the patriots was undoubtedly due, in large part, to the fact that they knew they were being attacked by Tarleton's legion and were determined to give as good as they got.

The capture of Major Wemyss and the higher rate of British casualties enabled the Americans to cry victory, and, in Cornwallis's words "the whole country came in fast to Sumter." Alarmed by the growth of Sumter's force and concerned for the safety of the British post at Ninety-Six, Cornwallis summoned Tarleton back from his pursuit of Marion. "I wish you would get three Legions," he wrote to Tarleton, "and divide yourself in three parts. We can do no good without you." The accolade was certainly a well-deserved one. The interesting thing about it is that Cornwallis, with his well-equipped veterans, his excellent staff, his trained cavalry, his engineers, and all proper appurtenances of warfare, was almost entirely dependent on an officer in his twenties and a motley collection of Loyalists who, under Tarleton's leadership, were all that stood between Cornwallis and disaster. If it had not been for the British Legion, or the Loyal Legion as it was also called, Cornwallis's position would have been a far more precarious one.

Forced to drop his pursuit of Marion, Tarleton followed Sumter, hoping, by pressing up the Enoree River, to come up behind him.

Sumter's intention had been to attack the British at the Little River post, fifteen miles from Ninety-Six, but he soon realized that Tarleton was after him. At Brierly's Ford on November 18, the British Legion drew fire from a hundred and fifty mounted men when they went down to the river to bathe and water their horses. Tarleton, thus alerted to the fact that he was on Sumter's heels, crossed the Pee Dee at the ford and hurried on. On the night of the nineteenth a deserter from Tarleton's legion came into Sumter's camp with the information that Tarleton was close behind him. Sumter broke camp at once and began a hasty retreat, while Tarleton, aware that he could not move his whole force fast enough to overtake him, pushed on with a hundred and ninety dragoons and eighty mounted infantry of the Sixty-third Regiment.

An hour later, at dusk, Tarleton came up with Sumter's rear guard as the main patriot force was about to cross the Tyger River. A woman who had hidden herself and watched while Tarleton detached his advance party came into Sumter's camp and told him that the British artillery and the main body of infantry were well behind. At this point Sumter had little choice. He had no chance of getting his force across the river under the pressure of Tarleton's legion. There was commanding ground nearby at the Blackstocks Plantation, and Sumter decided to make a stand there. The river was in his rear and also, by a sharp bend, covered his right flank. On the hill were five log houses in an open field. Colonel Wade Hampton's riflemen were detailed to occupy the houses, and Georgia riflemen were placed along a rail fence, running diagonally from the house to a thick woods on the left. The balance of Sumter's troops were posted on the high ground above the cabins, with a company in reserve and the mounted militia covering the right flank at the river.

When Tarleton came up, he realized that Sumter's position at Blackstocks Plantation was too strong to attack before the arrival of the rest of his command. He therefore dismounted and deployed the Sixty-third on the right, overlooking a small creek that ran across the front of Sumter's defensive line. The dragoons were formed on the left. The total enemy force was perhaps two hundred and seventy men, including a cavalry detachment that Tarleton kept in reserve. Sumter realized that it would be a serious tactical error to wait for the main body of British infantry and their three-pounder to arrive on the scene. Colonel Elijah Clarke, the veteran of Musgrove's Mill and numerous other guerrilla raids, was ordered to turn the right of the enemy line and block the advance of the infantry. Sumter, meanwhile, led some four hundred men in an attack on the Sixty-third. They crossed the creek and advanced up the hill beyond it, but here their inexperience was their undoing; they fired too soon, and before they could reload their rifles, the eighty British regulars charged with bayonets and drove the attackers back beyond the log cabins.

At this point Sumter ordered a regiment of mounted infantry under Colonel Edward Lacey to strike at the left flank of Tarleton's dragoons. Lacey's men, their movement covered by the noise and confusion of the battle, slipped to within seventy-five yards of the dragoons and opened a fire that killed or wounded twenty of them. The rest quickly rallied and drove Lacey and his men back. Sumter, riding toward the center of the American positions, was hit by a musket ball that entered his shoulder, traveled along the shoulder blade, and nicked his backbone. It was a painful and disabling wound, and Colonel Twiggs, who commanded a regiment of Georgia troops, took charge. The infantrymen of the Sixty-third, who had penetrated so recklessly into the American positions in pursuit of Sumter's men, suffered heavy casualties both from the log cabins and from the Americans on their right and left. Tarleton, seeing that the soldiers were in danger of being cut off and slaughtered, led a desperate charge against the American lines to cover the withdrawal of the survivors of the Sixty-third.

It was now dark and the British and the Americans disengaged, each side claiming victory. Sumter, badly wounded, conveyed to his officers with difficulty his decision to withdraw his force across the Tyger while he was still able to do so. The bullet had affected Sumter's speech and left him almost entirely paralyzed, and his men, despairing of his life, wrapped him in a bullhide and carried him over the river. Tarleton pursued Sumter's force for two more days, and with their chieftain apparently mortally wounded, his army scattered under Tarleton's relentless pressure. At the Pacolett River, the British leader turned back to Cornwallis's main army, collecting, as he went, refugees from the Kings Mountain debacle.

Sumter's astonishing recovery was like a parable of the nature of patriot resistance. Within two and a half months, he was campaigning again. (He lived fifty-two more years, dying in 1832 at the age of 98.) The American losses at Blackstocks Plantation were three killed and five wounded, while Tarleton lost some fifty killed and wounded out of two hundred and seventy engaged. The American casualties hardly suggest a bitterly fought battle, although Tarleton, to be sure, took heavy losses. They suggest that had Sumter not been severely wounded, the Americans might well have routed or captured the major part of Tarleton's force.

Greene arrived at Charlotte on December 2 and took command of the battered remnant of the Southern army the next day. When word had reached him in late October that Washington had chosen him to command the Southern Department, Greene had written to his wife: "My dear Angel What I had been dreading has come to pass. His Excellency General Washington . . . has appointed me to the command of the Southern Army. . . . This is so foreign from my wishes that I am distressed exceedingly: especially as I have just received your letter of the 2d of this month where you describe your distress and sufferings in such a feeling manner as melts my soul into the deepest distress. I have been pleasing my self with the agreeable prospect of spending the winter with you. . . . How unfriendly is war to domestic happiness! . . ."

In addition to the appointment of Greene, the most notable event of the winter of 1780–81 was the return of Daniel Morgan to the ranks of Continental officers. Morgan had resigned in July of 1779, primarily out of indignation at not being given command of a light infantry brigade that was assigned to Anthony Wayne. Although Congress ordered him to report to Gates prior to the battle of Camden, Morgan, still nursing an understandable resentment at not being promoted to general rank, refused to join a general with whose shortcomings he was already familiar and one who, in Morgan's opinion, had failed to give him full credit for his part in the defeat of Burgoyne. After the debacle at Camden, Morgan searched his soul, and the battle-scarred warrior, like a modern Achilles, joined Gates at Hillsboro, helped him to organize an elite corps of light infantry, was commissioned as brigadier general by Congress, and took command of the corps shortly before the arrival of Greene.

When General Greene took command of the army at Charlotte, he found it short of almost every item needed to conduct a military campaign. On his way south he had stopped in Maryland and Virginia and had urged the legislatures of those states to do all in their power to support the army, "but such was their poverty, even in their capitals," he wrote Joseph Reed, "that they could not furnish forage for my horses." General Gist, a native of Maryland, had been left in that state to forward "recruits and supplies," and Baron Von Steuben was left in Virginia on a similar mission. In the country he passed through, Greene had found that "the people engaged in matters of interest and in pursuit of pleasure, almost regardless of their danger, public credit totally lost, and every man excusing himself from giving the least aid to Government, from an apprehension that they would get no return for any advance"—in other words, they feared that neither Congress nor the state legislatures would pay for goods supplied the army, except perhaps in worthless Continental currency. "The appearance of the troops" at Charlotte was, in Greene's words, "wretched beyond description, and their distress, on account of provisions, was little less than their sufferings for want of clothing and other necessities." General Gates had lost the confidence of his officers, and the troops, in turn, had lost "all their discipline, and [were] so addicted to plundering that they were a terror to the inhabitants." It was like Valley Forge all over again, except that it is more difficult to restore discipline, once lost, than to create it from scratch.

Greene, in addition to devising and carrying out a military strategy to thwart Cornwallis, had to act virtually as his own quartermaster general. The fact that Cornwallis, operating in generally hostile territory, was much better supplied with food than his enemy indicates how important efficient staffwork was. As Washington had once been forced to designate Greene, his best fighting general, as quartermaster, so Greene prevailed on Colonel Edward Carrington, one of the most experienced combat officers in his command, to undertake those duties, "without which I foresee we must starve," he wrote, adding, "I am endeavouring to bring everything into order and perfect our arrangements as much as possible but it is all an up-hill business."

One of the most serious problems was that each state had the right to enlist as many militiamen as it wished and to place them on the Congressional payroll. "I am persuaded," Greene wrote Reed, "North Carolina has militia enough to swallow up all the revenues of America, especially under their imperfect arrangements, where every man draws and wastes as much as he pleases. . . . The ruin of the State is inevitable if there are such large bodies of militia kept on foot," for the militia stripped the country of food like locusts and often seemed more interested in their private vendettas against Tory enemies than in the defeat of the British army.

"We are living upon charity and subsist by daily collections," Greene wrote gloomily. "Indian meal and beef is our common diet, and not a drop of spirits have we had with us since I came to the army. An army naked and subsisted in this manner, and not more than one-third equal to the enemy in numbers, will make but a poor fight, especially as one has been accustomed to victory and the other to flight. It is difficult to give spirits to troops that have nothing to animate them."

Under the circumstances, the best strategy seemed to Greene to be an extension of the guerrilla warfare already being waged so successfully by Marion and Sumter. Such forays might keep Cornwallis off-balance and, even more important, relieve some of the pressure on Greene's commissary, since the raiders, for the most part, lived off the land.

Greene's major problem was that he could not prevail upon the civil authorities to recruit enlistments for the Georgia Line. They seemed determined to depend on a militia force of wildly fluctuating size, "scattered over the face of the whole earth, and generally destitute of everything necessary to their own defence. The militia in the back country are formidable," Greene noted, "the others are not, and all are very ungovernable and difficult to keep together." There might be twenty thousand of them on the rolls but not five hundred ready for battle.

Greene did not know, quite literally from one day to another, how many militia he had in his command. There were, he wrote Joseph Reed, almost daily skirmishes in which the British suffered from constant attrition through casualties, "but the militia coming out principally on the footing of volunteers, they fell off daily after every skirmish and went home to tell the news."

Writing to Thomas Jefferson to appeal for supplies and support, Greene observed, "On your exertions hang the freedom & independence of the southern states." The only hope of protecting Virginia from the ravages of war, he wrote, was to check the enemy in the Carolinas. Thus good policy as well as patriotism dictated an all-out effort to back up the army of the Southern Department. Greene was pleased "to see the enterprise and spirit with which the militia have turned out lately in all quarters to oppose the enemy; and this great bulwark of civil liberty promises security & independence to this country, if they are not depended upon as a principal, but employed as an auxiliary. But if you depend upon them as a principal, the very nature of the war must become so ruinous to the country that the numbers for a time may give security yet the difficulty of keeping this order of men long in the field, and the accumulated expense attending it must soon put it out of our power to make further opposition, and the enemy will only have to delay their operations for a few months to give success to their measures." The army must be filled up with regular troops, "men of a proper size, perfect in their limbs, of a good sound constitution and not exceeding forty five years of age. . . . Officers are the very soul of an army: and you may as well attempt to animate a dead body into action, as to expect to employ an army to advantage when the officers are not perfectly easy in their circumstances, & happy in the service."

One of Greene's first moves was to dispatch Morgan with his elite corps of six hundred men to carry on operations in the Catawba region of South Carolina. Colonel Carrington, in addition to his duties as quartermaster general, was assigned to the related task of reconnoitering routes into Virginia in the event that Cornwallis should move in that direction. Greene also ordered Generals Kosciusko and Stevens to reconnoiter the Catawba and Yadkin rivers, and to collect or build boats that could be carried on wagons from one river to another to transport troops.

Before Morgan was detached to check the Loyalists, Colonel Washington's cavalry set out after an enemy foraging party. A friendly farmer told Washington that a party of almost a hundred Loyalists were holed up at Rudgley's Farm, twelve miles from Camden. Unable to resist the opportunity to tweak the nose of the enemy, Washington led his men to the post, hoping to capture it by surprise. He found that Rudgley and his friends were in a barn, surrounded by abatis and secure from a cavalry attack. Convinced that the Loyalists could be frightened into surrender, Washington had a fallen tree trunk shaped into the form of a cannon, and "bringing it up in military style, affected to prepare to cannonade the barn." When the defenders were thoroughly alarmed, Washington sent in a flag, warning the garrison of the impending destruction, which could be only avoided by immediate submission. Not prepared to resist artillery, "Colonel Rudgley seized with promptitude the auspicious opportunity," Henry Lee wrote, "and, with his garrison, one hundred men, surrendered. . . ."

Meanwhile Greene, with eleven hundred men, established his own camp on December 26 at Cheraw, a site chosen by Kosciusko. From here he was in a position to counter any move by Cornwallis. If Cornwallis committed his army of some four thousand regulars and provincials to an attack on Greene at Cheraw, Greene would retreat, using delaying tactics, while Morgan attacked Ninety-Six. A move by Cornwallis against the highly mobile Morgan would expose Charles Town. If Cornwallis resumed his original strategy of advancing into Virginia, he would have Greene and Morgan dogging his steps, while the Carolinas would be left to Marion's and Sumter's raiders. If Cornwallis remained at Winnsboro, not far from Camden, Greene and his lieutenants would be given valuable time to strengthen their own forces.

The actions of Greene on taking command of the Southern Department are in striking and instructive contrast to those of his predecessor. The true measure of a commanding officer is revealed by how fully his imagination engages the real situation; and with what speed and assurance he moves to establish, at least so far as possible, his control over the complex problems created by the existence of his own forces and their relationship to the enemy. Within a week or two of Greene's arrival on the scene, every soldier and officer in the Southern Department knew that a firm and skillful hand was at the helm. What Henry Lee described as Greene's "vivid plastic genius" was soon much in evidence. "A wide sphere of intellectual resource enabled him to inspire confidence, to rekindle courage, to decide hesitation, and infuse a spirit of exalted patriotism in the citizens of the State," Lee wrote. "By his own example he showed the incalculable value of obedience, of patience, of vigilance, and temperance."

"No man was more familiarized to dispassionate and minute research than General Greene," Lee continued. "He was patient in hearing every thing offered, never interrupting or slighting what was said." Having considered all aspects of the problem and made his decision, "he would enter into a critical comparison of the opposite arguments, convincing his hearers, as he proceeded, of the propriety of the decision he was about to pronounce."

12

Cowpens

Daniel Morgan, commanding 320 Maryland and Delaware Continentals, 200 Virginia riflemen, and 80 light dragoons, was directed by Greene to join the North Carolina militia under General William Davidson and to gather supplies, protect patriot lives and property, and, where expedient, attack the enemy. Cornwallis, alarmed at reports that reached him at Winnsboro, South Carolina, of American troop movements, wrote to Tarleton, who was operating near the Broad River, to inform him that "Morgan and Washington have passed the Broad river" and requesting "all possible intelligence of Morgan." A week later he received word that Morgan was advancing on Ninety-Six with 3,000 men (approximately four times the number of men actually under Morgan's command). Tarleton was ordered to do his best to defend Ninety-Six and to locate Morgan. "Let me know," Cornwallis wrote, "if you think that moving the whole, or any part of my corps, can be of use."

The letter gives an interesting insight into Cornwallis's state of mind. It was plainly written by an anxious and uncertain man who offered, in effect, to leave to the judgment of a very junior officer the crucial decision of where and when to move the main British army. It seems evident that Cornwallis's increasing dependence on Tarleton was an indication of his own sense that he was rapidly losing control of the situation. Indeed, at this point his plight was not too dissimilar to that of Burgoyne on his ill-fated expedition from Canada. Cornwallis, like Burgoyne, had proposed a bold strategy. Now that he was well-launched on it, he was overcome with disquiet. The situation was not at all as he had assumed it to be. He felt surrounded and beleaguered, and somehow vaguely betrayed; and he was fed a constant stream of information that, if not plainly false, he had no confidence in. The numbers of the enemy multiplied beyond understanding. Where one patriot fell, two seemed to spring up; where one Tory fell, two deserted to the patriot cause. Where, for example, could Morgan get three thousand men, unless they had indeed sprung out of the ground?

Morgan reached the Pacolett River on Christmas Day after a brutal fifty-eight mile march, much of it in a cold rain that left the ground a quagmire. There he dispatched Colonel Washington with eighty dragoons and two hundred mounted militia, with orders to attack a detachment of Tories who were wreaking havoc in the neighborhood of Fairfort (or Fair Forest) Creek, between the Pacolett and Enoree rivers. After a forty-mile ride, Washington and his men surprised the Tories near Hammond's Store and killed or wounded a hundred and fifty and captured forty. Once again "Tarleton's quarter" prevailed. Men were shot or stabbed as they struggled to rise from their blankets, and little attention was given to those who tried to surrender. In part the raiders could be exonerated on the grounds that the action of individual soldiers in such an encounter is almost impossible to control. Like the British at the so-called Paoli Massacre, Washington's men struck out at everyone around them; they were not inclined, or, indeed, dared not try to take prisoners in the confused melée. There was also, of course, ample evidence of the bitterness so evident in all clashes between patriot and Tory. The Tories, after all, had been devastating the homes and farms of some of the very men who attacked them.

Again, little mention has been made in histories of the Revolution of the affair at Hammond's Store. It was hardly a battle, and its outcome was not particularly creditable to the patriots. It was, nonetheless, a daring and skillful foray of the kind that had added so much to "Bloody Ban" Tarleton's laurels.

The next day, Colonel Joseph Hayes with forty dragoons headed for Fort William—an impressively named stockaded log cabin near Ninety-Six; it was to that post that Sumter had been marching when Tarleton overtook him at the Tyger River. The handful of defenders of

Fort William, hearing the blood-chilling story of the fate of their fellows at Hammond's Store, had no stomach for holding out. They decamped for Ninety-Six, and Cornwallis got word a few days later from Major Archibald McArthur, whose Seventy-first Highlanders were posted at Brierly's Ford, that "General Cunningham and his people quitted the fort [William] on Saturday night and mounted for 96 & the Rebels took possession of it ye Sunday morning at eight o'clock."

When the British received this disheartening word, Cornwallis's headquarters were sunk in gloom. It seemed that the last hope for an effective Loyalist militia was lost.

Tarleton was aware that Cornwallis hesitated to move north until Morgan had been disposed of. He therefore suggested that he, Tarleton, with reinforcements from the main army, pursue Morgan across the Pacolett River and try to engage him in battle or drive him toward Kings Mountain. Meanwhile the main army would advance from Winnsboro to try to trap Morgan if he escaped from Tarleton. Cornwallis accepted the suggestion and started his army on the march. General Leslie, who had been stationed at Camden, was directed to move along the eastern side of the Wateree and Catawba in a line parallel to Cornwallis's advance.

Morgan meanwhile wrote to Greene that forage for his horses and men was so scanty that he would have to retreat or turn south toward Georgia. Greene replied, urging him to "hold your ground if possible," and mentioning the "disagreeable consequences that will result from a retreat." Morgan, he suggested, might move toward Ninety-Six in search of supplies. "Col. Tarleton is said to be on his way to pay you a visit," Greene concluded. "I doubt not but he will have a decent reception and a proper dismission."

Heavy winter rains brought the rivers to flood stage and delayed Tarleton's pursuit of Morgan. While his force waited at Duggin's Plantation on Indian Creek from January 6 to the 9, Cornwallis began his own tedious advance, averaging five miles a day through the disheartening rain and thick red mud. It was January 16 before Cornwallis got to Turkey Creek, and at that time he was unaware that Tarleton had crossed the Enoree River two days earlier and was close on Morgan's heels. Tarleton, likewise, was unaware of the slow progress of Cornwallis's army. At eight o'clock on the morning of January 16, Tarleton sent a message to Cornwallis: "My Lord, I have been most cruelly retarded by the waters. *Morgan is in force and gone for Cherokee Ford.* I am now on my march. I wish he would be stopped."

Morgan, learning that Tarleton had crossed the Tyger with twelve hundred men, wrote to Greene that his own force of no more than seven hundred was "inadequate to the attempts you have hinted at." Tarleton, on January 15, searched for a spot along the Pacolett where he could get his men across, but all the fords were guarded by Morgan's men. During the night, he pretended to march up the river to Wofford's Iron Works, and when Morgan, taking the bait, moved up the river to block his crossing, Tarleton hurried downstream to Easterwood Shoals and crossed unopposed, although, fortunately for Morgan, not undetected. Morgan was just sitting down to breakfast when scouts brought him word that he had been outmaneuvered; he decamped immediately, and Tarleton arrived so soon thereafter that he ate Morgan's meal.

As Morgan moved up the river, trying desperately to elude his pursuers, Tarleton's scouts were only five miles behind him. Morgan knew that his chances of eluding so tenacious a pursuer were poor. Some of Morgan's officers were familiar with the "cowpens," the open area of fenced pasture where cattle owned by a family in Camden were penned for the winter. By midafternoon Morgan was ten miles from the Broad River; his tired men had marched all day on empty stomachs. More important, the horses could not continue much longer without forage. Morgan therefore decided to turn to the cowpens and take a defensive position there. Sending word to Andrew Pickens and the other militia officers to join him, Morgan rode on to reconnoiter the spot and lay out in his mind defensive dispositions.

The field that Morgan approached was dotted with trees, and it inclined gently for some four hundred yards to a ridge and then another three hundred yards to the summit of the hill, which rose some seventy feet above the surrounding countryside. The ground then dipped and rose to another crest some six hundred yards beyond the first, and then fell off to an open meadow reaching four or five miles to the Broad River. Included in Morgan's command were William Washington's light infantry and dragoons. Three hundred of these were Continental veterans of the Maryland Line who had performed so stoutly at Camden, and some two hundred were Virginia riflemen who had served out terms in the Continental Army and had then enlisted in their state's militia. Some militia had joined Morgan on the march, and Pickens had brought a contingent with him. Morgan's own estimate of the troops under his command on the eve of the battle was eight hundred, although the total may have been nearer a thousand.

The men were glad to finally make camp. Fires were lit, damp

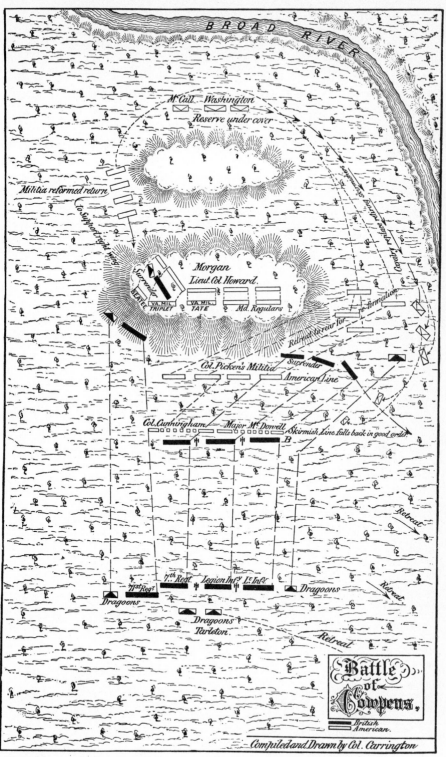

BROAD RIVER

M°Call   Washington
Reserve under cover

Militia reformed return

Morgan
Lieut. Col. Howard.

VA. MIL
TRIPLET

VA. MIL
TATE

Md. Regulars

Surrender
BEATEE

re-formation

Retreat to rear for

Surrender

Col. Picken's Militia

American Line

Col. Cunningham   Major M°Dowell

B

Skirmish Line falls back in good order

Retreat

7th Regt   Legion Infy   Lt Infy

71st Regt

Dragoons

Dragoons

Retreat

Dragoons
Tarleton.

Retreat

Battle
of
Cowpens.

British
American.

Compiled and Drawn by Col. Carrington

clothing dried out, additional ammunition issued, food distributed from the wagons, and rations prepared for supper and breakfast. Small groups of militia straggled in, and a screen of scouts, pickets, and mounted patrols guarded the approaches to the encampment. Morgan, the "Old Wagoner," although troubled by wounds and rheumatism, moved among the militia companies all night long, speaking in his rough, plain way to the nervous soldiers. The sight of Morgan, huge and rugged, with his cheery, confident way, his deep voice and battered countenance, was enough to put heart in the men. His battle plan was a thoroughly eccentric one, but simple enough to be mastered by his poorly trained soldiers. He knew Tarleton to be a slapdash fighter who depended on speed and shock effect for his successes and who scorned conventional maneuvers. He thus assigned a forward line of picked militia riflemen, most of them Georgians and North Carolinians under the command of Major John Cunningham and Major Charles McDowell, to take places behind trees and stumps. They were to let the enemy get within fifty paces before they fired. They were to "Look for the epaulets! Pick off the epaulets!" After that initial volley, instead of trying to stand fast in the face of the dreaded bayonet charge, they were to move, individually, back to the second line of Pickens' militia, firing as they went. Pickens' men would be stationed on the ridge a hundred and fifty yards or so behind the rough first line of Cunningham and McDowell. Pickens' men were also to fire and fall back, or rather sideways; they were to move off to the left, uncovering the fire of the Maryland Continentals, who were again a hundred and fifty yards in the rear and just below the summit of the hill. Major John Eager Howard was in command of this contingent, some four hundred and fifty men, covering a line roughly four hundred yards long.

The reserve—Washington's eighty dragoons and half as many mounted Georgia infantry armed with sabers under Lieutenant Colonel James McCall—were posted half a mile in the rear in defilade, ready to move forward at Morgan's command.

In Lee's words, Morgan "on the verge of the battle . . . availed himself of the short and awful interim to exhort his troops." He addressed himself first, "with his characteristic pith," to the apprehensive militia, praising them for the "zeal and bravery so often displayed by them, unsupported by bayonet or sword." He was, he reminded them, a general accustomed to winning. With his famous "corps of riflemen" he had often before "brought British troops, equal to those before him, to submission." His words to the Continentals were much briefer, as befitted veteran soldiers. He had entire confidence in their "skill and courage," victory was certain "if they acted well their part"; they must not be demoralized by the retreat of the militia in front of them; that was part of the plan of battle.

The dispositions were brilliant ones. In making them Morgan defied most accepted rules of contemporary warfare. More important, he showed remarkable resourcefulness in employing the militia to maximum advantage. Usually assigned to the least hazardous positions or given tasks that they were untrained to and unsuited for, they almost invariably performed badly. It was Morgan's genius to use their genius—which was for accurate fire and quick movement—in such a way as to allow him to employ his regulars most effectively. Once a battle is over and the historians have taken charge of it, it is often difficult to recapture the quality of imagination that has gone into successful strategies. The problem, almost invariably, is for the reader to understand what a remarkable effort of the imagination is required to make even relatively minor breaks with convention. Although it is by now a cliché, it is nonetheless true that Morgan's plan of battle was fertile in just that kind of inspired improvisation that the character of American life was supposed to encourage.

Before dawn on January 17, 1781, Morgan's men, rested and refreshed, ate their breakfast rations and quietly took their battle positions. Despite the courage planted in them by Morgan during the early evening, they were apprehensive. Banastre Tarleton, young, handsome, brilliant, ruthless, was surrounded by an aura of invincibility; he seemed truly to have a charmed life. Patriot mothers frightened their children by evoking him—"Ban Tarleton will get you if you don't be good." So the patriots, veterans and raw recruits alike, undoubtedly felt more than an ordinary portion of that sweating, cold fear that every soldier knows before battle.

Tarleton had reveille beat at two in the morning and broke camp an hour later. He led three light infantry companies in the van with the infantry of the Loyal Legion, the Seventh and Seventy-first Regiments, the legion cavalry, and fifty troopers of the Seventeenth Light Dragoons. The advance units reached Thicketty Creek an hour before dawn, and, having made contact with an American patrol and calculated that Morgan was some five miles away, Tarleton pressed on and debouched from the woods into the open fields that led to the American lines. As the sun rose the American positions became visible. Tarleton knew only one tactic—attack with full force. He dispatched Ogilivie's fifty dragoons to drive in and scatter the skirmishers.

Young James Collins, who had had his baptism of fire at Kings Mountain less than four months before, was in the forward elements down the hill with the rest of the militia, and he felt dreadfully exposed as he saw the enemy advancing just at sunrise, a "sight, to me at least, . . . somewhat imposing," he wrote with classic understatement. Tarleton's men halted for a brief time "and then advanced rapidly as if certain of victory," shouting and hallooing as they came. Tarleton had deployed his troops to the right, intending to turn the American line. This disconcerted and hurried the riflemen. "We gave the enemy one fire," Collins recalled; "when they charged us with their bayonets, we gave way and retreated for our horses."

A detachment of Tarleton's cavalry pursued them. "Now," thought Collins, "my hide is in the loft." Just as the militia got to their horses, the Tory cavalry was among them, making "a few hacks at some," but doing little real damage. As the British cavalry scattered in pursuit of the militia, Washington's dragoons and mounted infantry came down on them "like a whirlwind, and the poor fellows began to keel from their horses without being able to remount. The shock was so sudden and violent," Collins wrote, "they could not stand it and immediately took themselves to flight. There was no time to rally, and they appeared to be as hard to stop as a drove of wild Choctaw steers going to a Pennsylvania market." The militia marksmen had done their work well, however; half the officers in the attacking echelon had fallen before their fire.

With the militia apparently cleared away, Tarleton had started his second attack, confident that he had shattered the American line. As the British passed the line where they had encountered Pickens' militia, they broke into triumphant cheers, but ahead of them were the main American lines manned by Howard's Continental soldiers. Already weary from their advance up the long slope of the hill, the British received volley after volley from the Americans, who fired by ranks, the first firing, while the second loaded and then stepped forward to fire in turn. Tarleton's forces began to falter and drop back at the heavy fire from the top of the hill. At this point Tarleton played his trump card. The feared Highlanders were ordered to attack the American right, and two hundred of them, bagpipes whining, began to ascend the hill. Meanwhile Lieutenant Hughes, an officer "of remarkable fleetness of foot," overtook the fleeing militia, flailed at them with his sword, and denounced them sulfurously until at last, with the aid of Washington's cavalry, he managed to halt their flight. The militia, with the legion driven off by Washington's cavalry, reformed and, as Collins put it, prepared "to redeem our credit." At this point, Morgan rode up waving his sword and shouted, "Form, form, my brave fellows! Give them one more fire and the day is ours. Old Morgan was never beaten." This is the kind of talk soldiers like to hear. Collins and his fellows moved forward on the double to envelop the right flank of the enemy. Howard, seeing that his right flank was under heavy enemy pressure, attempted to realign the Virginia regulars in that direction. The result was initial confusion as some soldiers thought that a retreat had been ordered and began to leave their positions. The movement spread, and officers along the line, "supposing that orders had been given for a retreat, faced their men about and moved off." At this point Morgan, who had been devoting his attention to stiffening the backbone of the militia, rode up to Howard and, in Howard's words, "expressed apprehension of the event" (What he doubtless said was, "What the hell is going on here!"). Howard pointed to the orderly movement of the soldiers as evidence that there was no panic. Morgan replied that Howard should bring the Continentals forward toward the high ground where Washington's cavalry was stationed; he would reconnoiter for the best spot to place them in line. "In a minute," Howard wrote, "we had a perfect line. The enemy were now very near us. Our men commenced a very destructive fire, which they had little expected, and a few rounds occasioned great disorder in their ranks." Washington, after helping to rally the militia, sent word to Morgan, "They're coming on like a mob. Give them one fire and I'll charge them."

It was at this point that Howard's men reached the new positions Morgan had chosen for them. He ordered them to turn and fire, and then, as the badly hit Highlanders stopped, Howard ordered his Continentals to charge with the bayonet and Washington drove hard on their flank. The troops of the Seventh Regiment threw down their muskets; the troops on the left turned to flee, but the cavalry rounded them up. The Highlanders and the dragoons fought on until the full weight of the Americans pressed them down. Pickens' men, reformed, completed the demoralization of the British when they suddenly appeared on the left of the Seventy-first and added their fire to that which had already riddled their ranks. The fighting was brief and bitter and often hand-to-hand before the Highlanders, with nine of their sixteen officers killed or wounded, threw down their arms and cried "quarter!"

Howard, who had dismounted to accept the sword of a captain of the grenadiers, remounted and found the captain clinging desperately to his saddle. When Howard asked him what in blazes he thought he was doing, the terrified officer said that he had been told to give and expect no quarter, "and as my men were coming up, he was afraid they would use him ill." It was not unlikely, Howard admitted, placing the officer in the charge of a sergeant.

When Tarleton rode back to round up the rest of his feared legion for a final counterattack, two hundred of them galloped off and abandoned their leader. Tarleton collected some fifty men and officers to try to carry off one of the grasshoppers—small brass artillery pieces—that was still firing, but before they could reach the gun it was overrun by Howard's men. Seeing that it was too late to save the day, Tarleton started to flee; Colonel Washington was hot after him, thirty yards ahead of his men. Tarleton and two of his officers turned back to try to cut Washington down; Washington slashed at one officer and broke his sword off at the hilt. Just as the officer was about to bring his sword down on Washington's head, a fourteen-year-old bugler hit the officer in the shoulder with a pistol shot. Washington's sergeant major deflected the saber of another British officer and wounded him while Tarleton dashed at Washington, who parried his thrust with his broken sword. Then "reining his charger in a circle, Tarleton snatched his pistol and fired. The ball missed Washington but wounded his horse." Tarleton then turned and fled. When he and a handful of his cavalry reached the camp from which he had set out a few hours earlier, he found some of his Tory supporters looting his baggage train. Those who did not escape were shot on the spot, and Tarleton, gathering up the members of his once-feared legion who had deserted him on the battlefield, rejoined Cornwallis.

The battle, which lasted little more than an hour, netted Morgan and his men 100 enemy killed and 229 wounded. The casualties among the British officers were shocking, 39 killed and 27 wounded. Six hundred of Tarleton's force were captured unwounded, among them 60 Negro batmen, brought along to attend to the needs of the British officers. Included in the spoils of war were 100 horses and 800 muskets, 35 wagons, two captured artillery pieces, and the musical instruments of the enemy. The American losses were 12 killed and 60 wounded.

Major McArthur, captured with his Highlanders, made no bones of his dislike for the brash young officer who had led the fight against the patriots. He told John Eager Howard bitterly that "he was an officer before Tarleton was born; that the best troops in the service were put under '*that boy*' to be sacrificed; that he flattered himself the event would have been different, if his advice had been taken. . . ." And McArthur of course was right. The fault for the disaster at Cowpens was Cornwallis's for sending a boy to do a man's job. At Cowpens Tarleton, and even more the men he commanded, were the victims of his earlier successes. Reckless and arrogant by nature, Tarleton had been made more so by his triumphs. No seasoned officer would have launched a frontal attack on a force roughly equal in size to his own. The most elementary knowledge of tactics called for very different maneuvers—a base of covering fire, flanking movements, and so on. Conventional tactics are conventional tactics because, by and large, they work. If a military genius improvises, he does so as the result of a careful calculation in which he starts with conventional tactics and discards them because of particular circumstances. In just this way, Morgan, who certainly knew the tactics called for in a situation such as he found himself in, deliberately put his money on or, more accurately, bet his little army on the predictability of Tarleton's simple-minded tactics. That is military genius. To be able to isolate just that element—in this case Tarleton's commitment to a particular mode of operation—that is decisive, ignoring all those elements that one is trained to take into consideration, and which, in this case, are irrelevant. A person less of a gambler, less of an inspired improviser than Morgan, would have been obsessed by the question: "But what if Tarleton in this instance, does not do what he has always done before? What if wiser heads among his officers prevail? What if, confronted by a new situation, he reverts to conventional tactics?"

If the original fault was Cornwallis's in placing too much confidence in an officer whose brilliant successes obscured his lack of all-round experience and the absence of that judiciousness that must temper even the most impetuous commander if he is not to bring disaster on himself and his men, Tarleton did all he could to compound the original error. It was not simply the defeat—that might have been expected, once the decision had been made by Tarleton to attack a roughly equal force in open country (and this, after all, was Cornwallis's directive to Tarleton, to seek out and destroy Morgan's army)—it was the dimensions of the defeat that were staggering: 329 killed and wounded, 600 captured, and 200 of Tarleton's own Loyal Legion fled from the field of battle. In proportion to those engaged, the British losses were the highest of any battle since Bunker Hill. Indeed, Cowpens was soon called the Bunker Hill of the South.

Yet many questions about the battle remain unanswered. Despite the deceptively simple plan of battle pursued by both Morgan and Tarleton, there are, as with every other engagement of the Revolution, serious gaps and troubling contradictions in the accounts of the battle. If we accept the account of Private Jámes Collins as substantially correct, and if we assume that he was part of Pickens' militia (he would hardly have been chosen as one of the advance sharpshooters, and if he had been, he surely would have mentioned it in his report of the battle), it appears that a considerable portion of Pickens' force must have been mounted light infantry. Collins speaks of the militia firing and then, under the pressure of a bayonet attack, dashing for their horses, being overtaken by a British cavalry charge as they were mounting, and then being rescued by Washington's horsemen who had charged in turn. How do we reconcile this episode—a portion at least of Pickens' militia having their horses close enough for them to use in their flight—with Morgan's instructions to Pickens, which most historians assure us were followed almost to the letter: to fire two volleys and then file off to the left and retire from the action. Collins, moreover, speaks of the fleeing militia being rounded up with some difficulty and exhorted by Morgan to return to the fray. Yet by other accounts, we have Pickens making an elaborate circuit of the entire battlefield in order to appear on the left of the Highlanders, just at the moment when they were most hotly pressed by Howard's Continentals. It certainly seems unlikely that Pickens was able to reorganize his scattered and fleeing troops and bring them from the extreme left of the American positions, around by a circuitous route, to the extreme right—a maneuver that must have covered the better part of a mile and been carried out in not much more than half an hour, since the whole battle lasted no more than an hour.

Morgan himself, in his official account of the battle written to Greene two days later, makes no mention of such a spectacular maneuver on the part of Pickens, and it is hard to believe that he would not have referred to it had such a march been made. John Eager Howard makes no mention of "Pickens' circuit," nor does Henry Lee in his *Memoirs*. What Lee, who had access to more firsthand information than any other writer on the subject, does say is that at the attack of the British, "the American light parties quickly yielded, fell back, and arrayed with Pickens. The enemy shouted, rushed forward upon the front line, which retained its station, and poured in a close fire; but, [the British] continuing to advance on our militia, they [the militia] retired, and gained with haste the second line. Here with part of the corps, Pickens took post on Howard's right, and the rest fled to their horses. . . ." This narrative reconciles Collins' account with Howard's and is not at odds with any other account by participants. It destroys once and for all the curious myth that Pickens, with his raw and inexperienced militia, carried out a spectacular "circuit" of the battle-field, arriving in the nick of time to seal the fate of the Highlanders. The point is a minor one and is only worth mentioning as an example of how errors become embedded in secondary accounts of battles. The most recent maps of the battle have traced out on them Pickens' imaginary "circuit," which quite plainly never took place except in the imagination of some ingenious historian.

Morgan later defended his choice of the battleground. In the Southern theater, swamps were the preferred "anchors" for defensive positions. They presumably (and actually) prevented one's flank from being turned (which was the constant preoccupation of every com-mander), but Morgan had observed something less desirable about swamps—they had an almost irresistible appeal to frightened militia-men, to whom they appeared not as an obstacle but as a sanctuary. "I would not have had a swamp in view of my militia on any considera-tion," he wrote; "they would have made for it, and nothing could have detained them from it. And as to covering my wings, I knew my adversary, and was perfectly sure I should have nothing but downright fighting. As to retreat, it was the very thing I wished to cut off all hope of. I would have thanked Tarleton had he surrounded me with his cavalry. It would have been better than placing my own men in the rear to shoot down those who broke from the ranks. When men are forced to fight, they will sell their lives dearly; and I knew that dread of Tarleton's cavalry would give due weight to the protection of my bayonets, and keep my troops from breaking as Buford's did. Had I crossed the river, one-half of the militia would immediately have abandoned me." What is perhaps most striking about Morgan's words is the utter lack of any illusion about the militia. But this was only half the story; the other half was his capacity to use them in such a way as to take best advantage of them.

The loss of Tarleton's force at Cowpens was a staggering blow to Cornwallis. He had, as we have seen, become heavily dependent on the young officer who had become almost like a son to him. Tarleton was both his eyes and his principal means of keeping at arm's length such tireless partisan fighters as Marion and Sumter. With that officer's effectiveness greatly diminished and the legend of his invincibility shattered beyond repair, Cornwallis's own range of action was drastically curtailed. Perhaps conscious that he had given Tarleton an assignment beyond his means, he wrote that "the disaster of the seventeenth of January can not be imputed to any defect in my conduct, as the detachment sent was certainly superior to the force against which it was sent. . . ." Cornwallis then added a few revealing sentences. "I believed," he wrote later, "my remaining force to be superior to that under the command of General Greene," but "our hopes of success were not founded only upon the efforts of the corps under my immediate command . . . but principally upon the most positive assurances, given by apparently credible deputies and emissaries, that upon the approach of a British army in North Carolina, a great body of the inhabitants were ready to join and to cooperate with it, in endeavouring to restore his Majesty's government." The fact was, he added, that out of the population of North Carolina, "a very inconsiderable number could be prevailed upon to remain with us, or to exert themselves in any form whatever."

I have earlier compared the American Revolution to a Greek tragedy where each fateful destiny had to be acted out although the audience knew its inevitable conclusion. The Southern campaign fits most appropriately into this metaphor. Since the British ministry lived in a world of illusion, each illusion had in turn to be shattered before the North government and those who supported its policies could be brought to face the reality of American independence, a reality that had existed, in a sense, since the Stamp Act and most certainly since the battles of Lexington and Concord and Bunker Hill. Their final illusion, as we have seen, was that the great majority of the people of the South were loyal to the Crown and would, with a little encouragement, avow that loyalty and take up arms, if necessary, to vindicate it. There was just enough truth in this particular illusion (as I suppose there is in most illusions) to require that it be played out to the end. There were in fact, for the reasons we have described, more Tories in the states of the lower South than in any other part of the confederation. Moreover, while there were large numbers of Tories in every state, it was only in the South (and in parts of New York State) that they existed in groups and communities that were capable of coalescing into military units, regular or irregular. It is a striking fact that the only provincial detachments from the North that had enough coherence and tenacity to hold together were those from New York and New Jersey. Many individual Tories in the middle and northern states were recruited into provincial companies, so that at various times they made up a substantial part of the British armies in America, but it was only in the South that Tories were present in sufficient numbers to carry on sustained guerrilla warfare on their own; that is to say, to recruit, arm, and provision irregular bands of civilian soldiers in much the same fashion as the patriots. The South was, to put it another way, full of self-sustaining Loyalists, men (and women of course as well) whose loyalty to the Crown or, more typically, whose hatred of those who held power—the patriots—was so great that they could be counted on to risk their lives as well as their usually modest fortunes in the British cause.

If the American Revolution had ended, as it might well have, with the British evacuation of Philadelphia, what, one wonders, would have been the state of affairs in the South? The northern and middle states would, in effect, have won, largely on their own, the war for independence. They would have made the major sacrifices and suffered the major losses. Under such circumstances, latent prejudices, never far from the surface, would undoubtedly have made themselves evident—the North condescending toward the South, which had done so little to secure American freedom; the South suspicious of the "republican" principles and democratic attitudes of the North, and sullen because it had had so small a share in the glory of victory. And, far more serious, the Carolinas and Georgia would have been filled with people who still considered themselves, in spirit if not in fact, subjects of His Majesty, George III—an angry, rebellious element, difficult if not impossible to assimilate in the new union, potentially dangerous and posing a constant threat of civil disturbance.

Perhaps, therefore, the most notable purpose served by the British invasion of the Southern colonies was that it served to unmask the Tories and produce what was, in effect, a civil war within the war against England. In addition to fighting the British, and doubtless in the long run more important, the patriots ruthlessly suppressed the disaffected elements in the population: groups and individuals who were, perhaps misleadingly, lumped together under the category of Tory. Among these Tories were unquestionably some of the most "democratic" inhabitants of the Southern states. As contrasted with the patriot leaders, few of them held any substantial number of slaves; many had no slaves at all and abhorred the institution. In the civil war that was the accompaniment of the war against British domination, the "Tories" were destroyed as an important factor in the postwar political life of those states that made up the lower South and that had witnessed the most prolonged and bitter fighting of the "Southern campaigns."

13

Greene Runs

A FTER the battle at Cowpens, Morgan, who was well aware that Cornwallis was in the vicinity, did not loiter. Burying the dead and leaving the
wounded of both armies under a flag of truce, he decamped a few hours
after the battle and, covered by his cavalry, crossed the Broad River.
The next morning he moved on to the Catawba, arriving there on
January 24. The same day, Cornwallis reached Ramsour's Mills on the
road from Cowpens. By then Morgan was two days ahead of him.

Appalled at the laborious progress of his army over rutted, muddy
roads, Cornwallis decided, in effect, to turn his cumbersome army of
some three thousand men into light troops that might move fast enough
to run Morgan to ground. He thus ordered all supplies and baggage
destroyed except for the barest essentials. His troops burned all their
tents and wagons, sparing only those sufficient to carry ammunition,
medical supplies, and the ill and wounded. Everything that could not be
stuffed into the soldiers' packs was disposed of, including the precious
supply of rum. (It is not recorded whether Cornwallis went so far as to
include in his order the very considerable personal and military paraphernalia carried by every properly equipped British officer—that
impedimenta alone would have been enough to slow the progress of any
army.) It was a foolish and quixotic gesture, and it tells more about

Cornwallis's state of mind than about his military judgment. The destruction of so much equipment, including so many of those items that in some modest measure alleviated the misery and discomfort of such a campaign, had a very bad effect on the morale of the soldiers, already depressed by the disaster at Cowpens; it is not surprising that a large number of desertions occurred in the two days Cornwallis stayed at Ramsour's Mills, a spot that already had very unhappy associations for all Loyalists.

While Cornwallis was busy destroying his "surplus" supplies, heavy rains, which added to the discomfort and gloom of his troops, caused the Catawba to rise so high that when Cornwallis reached the river on the twenty-ninth, he found that it was unfordable. Morgan, who had crossed four days earlier, was safely on the other side. From there he dispatched his British prisoners under guard for Virginia.

Greene received word of Morgan's victory on the twenty-third, and he immediately set out from Cheraw to join forces with him. Colonel Huger was ordered to move his wing of the army toward Salisbury in an effort to make contact with Morgan, while Colonel Carrington was instructed to collect boats on the Dan to carry Greene's men across the river if such a move became necessary.

Morgan's advice was to withdraw westward into the mountains, forcing Cornwallis to come after them; if, on the other hand, the British turned north into Virginia, the patriots would be in a position to move towards Charles Town. Greene preferred the strategy of withdrawing ahead of Cornwallis, harassing him and looking for favorable conditions to engage him in battle. Meanwhile Cornwallis, some eighteen miles away, was still delayed on the banks of the Catawba by high water. Greene sent out parties to recruit local militia and posted guards at the various fords on the Catawba where Cornwallis might attempt to cross. The effort was abortive. The river fell, and James Webster and Tarleton crossed it easily at Beattie's Ford. General Davidson, with three hundred men, tried to check Cornwallis's own division at McCowan's Ford and was killed in the skirmish that followed. Greene sent Morgan on ahead, and Morgan crossed the Yadkin on February 3. Cornwallis, confident that he could at last overtake Greene and bring him to a battle, burned most of his remaining baggage and wagons and used the horses to mount a portion of his infantry as part of a light corps under General Charles O'Hara.

Now the rain began again, making life miserable for pursued and pursuer alike. Greene, coming along behind Morgan, realized that the

Yadkin would soon be flooded by water draining out of the mountains. He got his cavalry across, and through his foresight in collecting boats he was able to get the balance of his force over the rapidly rising river. O'Hara's vanguard came up in time to capture Greene's last wagon. There was nothing Cornwallis could do but fire off some of his artillery and wait until the river dropped. It was four days before he could cross; by then Greene had brought his entire command together at Guilford Court House. His men had marched forty-seven miles in forty-eight hours. Having already joined forces with Morgan, Greene now met Lee and Huger and called a council of senior officers, who advised against risking a battle with only some two thousand men, many of them inexperienced militia; Cornwallis was thought to command a third more, most of them seasoned troops. Morgan, miserable with rheumatism acutely aggravated by the cold and damp (and never happy at taking orders), resigned his command and set out for home to warm his aching bones by his own fireside.

At Guilford Court House, Greene was some twenty-five miles away from Cornwallis's army at Salem, but he had still another river to cross, the Dan, before he could be confident of eluding his pursuer. Carrington appeared at this point with the reassuring word that boats had been located and hidden so that they could be brought together on a few hours' notice to get the army across the river. Kosciusko was sent ahead to throw up breastworks at the crossing point, and a detachment of seven hundred light infantry and cavalry were placed under Williams, Carrington, Howard, Washington, and Lee to cover the withdrawal of Greene's main force to the Dan.

The soldiers of both armies were in wretched condition. The midwinter rain alone was enough to dampen the most ardent spirits. For the Americans, food was, as always, in short supply and of poor quality, and the men's clothes were in rags. Even the British uniforms were faded and tattered and usually wet. "The hardships suffered by the British troops," Tarleton wrote, "for want of their tents and usual baggage, in this long and rapid pursuit through wild and unsettled country, were uncommonly great." Cornwallis suffered especially from the destruction of "almost the whole of his light troops" at Cowpens. Tarleton still commanded his legion, but it was greatly reduced in size and effectiveness.

Colonel Otho Williams, given command of Morgan's detachment after the latter refused to serve, managed to place his force across the path of Cornwallis, making it necessary for the British general to close his ranks and reconnoiter actively. Satisfied that Williams' troops constituted a small rear guard, Cornwallis started in pursuit, and for two days Williams drew Cornwallis after him. The three columns—Greene's, Williams', and Cornwallis's—moved on parallel routes, echeloned to the left and rear. Greene's division was in advance, marching by a course that would take it to that stretch of the Dan that was unfordable and that Cornwallis was confident Greene could not cross. Williams marched to Greene's left rear, and Cornwallis, in turn, moved to the left rear of Williams, whose own rear was protected by Henry Lee's light horse. Although the British cavalry was more numerous, they were, Lee wrote, "far inferior in regard to the size, condition and activity of the horses." Nonetheless, it was a grueling march for men and horses alike. Lee's men, riding or standing picket duty, got only a few hours' sleep in twenty-four. Indeed, during the retreat each man "was entitled to but six hours repose in forty-eight. Notwithstanding this privation," Lee wrote, "the troops were in fine spirits and good health." Williams always broke camp before dawn and pushed his men forward so that they would have time to stop for a decent breakfast, "their only meal during this rapid and hazardous retreat."

The men's shoes, Lee reported, were generally worn out, "the body clothes much tattered, and not more than a blanket for four men." The light corps, Lee's own, was better off, "but among its officers there was not a blanket for every three: so that among those whose hour admitted rest, it was an established rule, that at every fire, one should, [in turn] keep upon his legs to preserve the fire in vigor." Tents were never used during the retreat. "The heat of the fires was the only protection from rain, and sometimes snow: it kept the circumjacent ground and air dry, while imparting warmth to the body." Bacon and cornmeal, "good in quality and very nutritious," Lee noted, was the only food.

On the morning of February 13, Williams' force had stopped for breakfast; "the morning was cold and drizzly; our fires which had been slow in kindling, were now lively; the meat was on the coals, and the corn-cake in the ashes," Lee wrote. At this juncture a farmer rode up to say that a British force was only four miles away. Williams, unwilling to deprive his hungry men of their only meal, dispatched Lee with a detachment of cavalry to discover whether Cornwallis was indeed in such close pursuit. Lee, hiding with his detachment in a little copse, sent an officer with two dragoons down the road to look out for the British. In a few minutes Lee heard the clatter of galloping hoofs, and the American officer and dragoons appeared, pursued by a troop of Tarleton's light horse. Lee waited until the enemy had gone past and then, as they were overtaking and sabering his bugler, came down on them in a quick charge. The British turned to face Lee, but their "worn-down ponies were as ill calculated to withstand the stout, high-conditioned, active horses opposed to them, as were the intoxicated, inexpert riders unfit to contend with dragoons always sober and excelling in marksmanship," Lee wrote. "The enemy was crushed on the first charge: most of them were killed or prostrated; and the residue, with their captain, tried to escape." Eighteen British were killed in the brief clash. A few minutes later, musket fire announced the approach of the British advance guard, and Williams set his corps in motion. For the rest of the march to the Dan, O'Hara's advance guard and Lee's rear guard were almost constantly in sight of each other, often within rifle range. Eventually, a strange kind of affinity developed between the two opposing forces. Constrained by mutual interest not to fire on each other, "the demeanor of the hostile troops," Lee wrote, "became so pacific in appearance, that a spectator would have been led to consider them as members of the same army." But appearances were deceiving. Cornwallis was so determined to catch Greene in his trap that, as the two armies approached the Dan, he pushed his march through the night, giving the Americans no respite. On the British and Americans slogged; the roads, frozen into lacerating spines in the morning, soon turned to a muddy goo that dragged at each weary step. At noon on the fourteenth Colonel Williams received word from Greene that he had safely crossed the Dan on the previous day. With this news that their exhausting hegira was near its end and had accomplished its purpose, "the whole corps," Lee wrote, "became renovated in strength and agility; so powerful is the influence of mind over body." Greene's army had covered forty miles in sixteen hours over rutted, miry roads.

Protected by Lee, Williams got his main body over the river by nightfall, and the cavalry, or as Lee preferred to call them, the dragoons, arrived at the riverbank just as the boats that had carried over the last elements in Williams' command were returning. Carrington, who was directing the crossing, ordered the horses to be unsaddled and driven into the water to swim across, while their weary riders, clutching their saddles and bridles, crowded into the boats. Lee and Carrington were the last to leave.

Less than an hour later O'Hara came up to find the quarry gone. All the weary miles, the burned baggage and wagons, the destroyed tents, the short rations had gone for nothing. Greene was across the

Dan. The boats were the secret of the narrow escape—they, and the enterprising Carrington. They were the nail of the horse's shoe without which the battle must surely have been lost. "Generaling" begins with infinite attention to details; only then can courage and brilliant tactics play their part. "Thus ended," .Lee wrote, " . . . this long, arduous, and eventful retreat. . . . Happily for these States, a soldier of consummate talents guided the destiny of the South." Greene's total retreat covered two hundred and thirty miles "without the loss of either troops or stores." A notable record, indeed.

One may demur at the importance Lee gives to Greene's escape across the Dan—"Destroy the army of Greene, and the Carolinas with Georgia inevitably become members of the British empire"—but important it certainly was. The army of the South had, after all, already been destroyed three times; once at Savannah with the defeat of Robert Howe; once at Charles Town with the capture of Lincoln and his army; and again at Camden with the destruction of Gates's army. It could doubtless have been destroyed once more, and once more risen from the ashes of its destruction. On the other hand, there are, presumably, limits to the capacity of any people to persist in struggles and sacrifices. The destruction of Greene's army, any more than the destruction of its predecessors, would not have meant the end of American independence, and, indeed, Lee does not suggest that it would; but it is certainly possible that it could have broken the spirit of patriot resistance in the South and thereby made it vastly more difficult to end the war and establish peace and order in the southern half of the confederacy.

Safe at last in Virginia, "Enjoying wholesome and abundant supplies of food in the rich and friendly county of Halifax," Greene could relax for the moment. Among his soldiers, Lee assures us, "joy beamed in every face," and much time was spent, as soldiers will, "in mutual gratulations; with the rehearsal of the hopes and fears which agitated every breast during the retreat; interspersed with many simple but interesting anecdotes with which every tongue was strung."

But Greene had no intention of relaxing in the enjoyment of his brief leisure or of allowing Cornwallis to enjoy his. He had less than two thousand men under his command; these made up the entire army of the South. Cornwallis, with Leslie's detachment, had perhaps twice as many in the army at Hillsboro. Including those at Charles Town and Savannah and scattered in posts in Georgia and the Carolinas, Cornwallis commanded nearly eight thousand soldiers, provincials, and regulars.

He was far from controlling those states, however. After more than five years of fighting and the expenditure of many lives and enormous sums of money, the British occupied three major American seacoast cities—New York, Charles Town, and Savannah—and that, by and large, was the extent of their "conquest" of America.

In the face of such facts it is difficult to understand how historians have managed to regard the outcome of the American Revolution as somehow in doubt; as dependent on the outcome of this or that battle, or as the consequence of the entry of France into the war. In a certain sense, however, the South, because of the number and energy of its Tories and because those Tories were motivated by a compact and self-conscious set of grievances against the existing social order, was the most crucial theater of the war. As we have argued, a joint British-Tory "victory" there, or even an indefinitely protracted state of warfare, would have seriously compromised the creation of a new union of the American states.

Greene, determined to re-enter North Carolina and once more engage Cornwallis, did all he could to stimulate recruiting of militia. He appealed to Governor Jefferson of Virginia to "press forward the long-expected aid" and encouraged General Stevens' efforts to round up more soldiers.

Scarcely two weeks after he had crossed the Dan, Greene sent Lee and his cavalry, augmented by two companies of Maryland veterans under Colonel Oldham and a corps of South Carolina militia under Pickens, back across the river into North Carolina with orders "to place themselves as close to [Cornwallis] as safety would permit, in order to interrupt his communications with the country, to repress the meditated uprising of the Loyalists, and, at all events, to intercept any party of them which might attempt to join the enemy."

Lee's "Legion," as he preferred to call it, with the other elements in the detachment "sat down" across the road between the Haw River and Hillsboro and began aggressively patrolling the adjacent countryside. The same day, Greene himself, with a detachment of Washington's cavalry, arrived on the scene and conferred with his officers. He intended, he told them, to cross the Dan in a few days with the rest of his army and to move in the direction of Salem and Guilford Court House. Before dawn, a scouting party returned with word that Tarleton had been observed moving from Hillsboro to the Haw with cavalry, infantry, and artillery, presumably to round up Tory recruits. Pickens and Lee immediately set out after Tarleton while Greene returned to his main camp. From a farm boy the American officers learned that Tarleton planned to cross the Haw the following morning.

The little expedition of Lee and Pickens was a dramatic illustration of the value of careful reconnoitering and quickness of movement. The Americans crossed the Haw soon after Tarleton, whose force of some five hundred men was approximately the same size as that of his still undetected pursuers. A few miles from Tarleton's camp, Lee deployed his units: his infantry in the center, Pickens' militia on the left, and the cavalry of the legion, under the command of Major John Rudolph, on the right in column. Oldham's Virginians were in reserve. Rudolph had orders to charge at a full gallop if he came on Tarleton undetected.

As the Americans advanced, they met "two well-mounted young countrymen" who, mistaking the Americans for Tarleton's force (Lee's legion was dressed, like Tarleton's, in short green coats), reported that Colonel John Pyle with four hundred Loyalists was on his way to join forces. The two were sent to Lee, who, it may be imagined, played the role of Tarleton with considerable pleasure, listening attentively to the young men's story and congratulating them on their "laudable spirit." They should, Lee told them, return to Colonel Pyle, who was not far off, and request him to stop his march and move his men to the side of the road so that "Colonel Tarleton" (Lee) could ride by with his "much fatigued troops" to make camp for the night. The message was carried. Pyle moved his men to the side of the road to allow "Tarleton" to pass, and Lee, at the head of his column of horse, "with a smiling countenance, dropping, occasionally, expressions complimentary to the good looks and commendable conduct . . . of his friends," rode past the mounted Loyalists until he came abreast of Pyle, who sat on his own horse at the head of the line. Grasping Pyle's hand, Lee was just about to demand his surrender when a Loyalist officer, catching a glimpse of Pickens' militia concealed in the woods, realized the Loyalists had been duped and ordered his men to open fire on the rear of the cavalry column.

The rear immediately attacked the Tories, and the rest of the column followed suit. Before the startled Tories could recover their wits, ninety of them had been killed and many of the rest seriously wounded. Again it was a matter of "Tarleton's quarter." With other British units so close by, it would have been dangerous to have tried to take prisoners. In Lee's own words, "in some parts of the line the cry of mercy was heard, coupled with the assurance of being our best friends;

but no expostulation could be admitted in a conjuncture so critical." The British promptly termed the encounter a massacre, and the scrupulous Stedman declared that "between two and three hundred . . . were inhumanly butchered while in the act of begging for mercy," adding that "cold and unfeeling policy avows it as the most effectual means of intimidating the friends of royal government." Lee's losses were one horse wounded.

Lee, writing after the war, was at some pains to defend himself, emphasizing that his intention had been to prevail on Pyle to surrender his force. It is difficult to see what other course he could have followed. Greene had ordered him to intercept any Tory detachment that might try to join Cornwallis. Tarleton, the most feared cavalry leader in the British army, was only a mile or so away. Any protracted engagement or any effort by Lee to carry off a body of prisoners almost equal to his own force must have resulted in the Americans being overtaken by Tarleton under the most adverse possible circumstances. If, indeed, Lee did intend to give Pyle an opportunity to surrender with his men, he would have done so at great risk, and he could only have been relieved when the firing on his cavalry gave him the pretext to destroy Pyle's force.

The engagement was a minor one, but its effects were far-reaching. While Lee is undoubtedly right in his argument that the destruction of Pyle's band was a mixed blessing in that it enabled the bigger prize to escape, it is also clear that it virtually put an end to Cornwallis's effort to recruit any substantial number of Tories in North Carolina. If Pyle had joined Cornwallis at Hillsboro, it is by no means unlikely that, encouraged by his example, as many more Tories might have come in, thereby very substantially increasing Cornwallis's army and tipping the scales decisively against Greene in terms of available manpower. As to the killing of Pyle's men, Andrew Jackson perhaps hit nearest the truth when he wrote: "In the long run, I am afraid the Whigs did not lose many points in the game of hanging, shooting and flogging. They had great provocation, but upon calm reflection I feel bound to say they took full advantage of it."

Having dispatched Pyle and his men, Lee and Pickens pressed on to Tarleton's bivouac. It was near sundown, and the British, alerted by the sounds of the encounter, were in a state of confusion. For some moments, Lee and Pickens debated the advisability of attacking at once. But their troops had been on the march since dawn and had already fought a brief but inevitably wearing battle; they decided to make camp, post pickets, put out patrols, and "postpone battle until the morning."

They blocked Tarleton's line of retreat; he had to either fight or flee farther from his base at Hillsboro.

During the night, Lee learned from some farmers that a band of militia were camped a few miles away under the command of Colonel Preston, who was on his way to offer his support to General Greene. Preston did not know that Greene had already crossed the Dan into Halifax County, and he was quite unaware of the proximity of Tarleton's force, or, of course, of Lee and Pickens. Preston was urgently requested to join these officers, and he soon appeared with a "battalion" of some three hundred riflemen from the mountains of western Virginia, a tough and hardy crew. The Virginia militia were especially pleased with the "cheering looks of [Lee's] dragoons, and the high condition of their stout horses." Like all militia, they feared a cavalry charge with cavalrymen slashing at their heads with their sabers; consequently, they were reassured to see such well-equipped and confident horsemen. Indeed Lee was convinced that no country in the world had better riders than could be found in the South. "The boys from seven years of age begin to mount horses," he wrote; "riding without saddle, and often in the fields, when sent for a horse, without bridle. They go to the mill on horseback, and perform all the other small domestic services mounted. Thus they become so completely versed in the art of riding by the time they reach puberty, as to equal the most expert horsemen anywhere." It was, indeed, in cavalry warfare that the South made its principal contribution to the tactics and strategy of the Revolution. New England had nothing to match it. This was, in part, because New England youths, living in villages, did not ride as much as their Southern counterparts, who were raised on scattered farms and plantations. In addition, there was in the South, even in the eighteenth century, a kind of chivalric ideal, in which expert marksmanship and horsemanship were evidences of "manhood." (Out of this tradition came the mythos of the American cowboy of the late nineteenth century, a Southern cavalier reincarnate.) Including cavalry, dragoons, and mounted infantry, probably between a third and half of all Southern militia forces were mounted.

Having satisfied themselves that the soldiers under the command of Lee and Pickens would be worthy companions in combat, the Virginia militia, "these welcome auxiliaries," as Lee wrote, "retired to their post, responding with ardor to the general wish to be led to battle with the dawn of day." The next morning, several hours before daybreak, the Americans, who had slept in the positions that they were to assume in the attack, started to advance. The legion infantry, led by Lee himself, had the special assignment of knocking out the British artillery. Oldham, with his Marylanders, moved on Lee's right, and beyond Oldham Pickens advanced through a wooded area. The cavalry were held in reserve. As the Americans moved forward, word came from the advance scouts that the British were withdrawing. Inquiries at the houses where the British officers had been quartered disclosed that not one but three messages had arrived during the night from an anxious Cornwallis, directing Tarleton to rejoin him as quickly as possible. The order was a blow to Tarleton. He and his lieutenants, drinking and laughing over an "abundant supper," had been anticipating the battle; they were determined to take complete revenge for the loss of Pyle; and, assured of victory," were already looking forward to dividing up Lee's "stout horses" among them.

Lee and Pickens pressed after Tarleton, who was headed for one of the three ferries or fords over the Haw. Making torches out of pitch pine, the lead scouts of the infantry legion picked up Tarleton's trail in the dark. It became clear, as they studied the tracks, that Tarleton had made a feint toward the upper ferry crossing, the nearest at hand; had then slipped off to the right, as though to try the second ferry; and finally had taken the road to the ford, seven miles farther downstream.

With cavalry and mounted infantry in the van, Lee's detachment caught up with Tarleton's rear guard a few miles from the ford. For a while the patriots debated crossing at the second ferry and trying to intercept Tarleton on the other side of the river before he could gain the Hillsboro road. The scheme was a risky one—they could easily be trapped themselves—and they wisely abandoned it and made camp in a little settlement along the river where their men could get food and shelter and much-needed rest. Their expedition had clearly accomplished its purpose. In Lee's words, that "capricious goddess [Fortune] gave us Pyle and saved Tarleton."

The crowded events of the three days demonstrate very well indeed the role of the "capricious goddess" in military affairs. First, at the commencement of their expedition, the Americans had the luck to learn that Tarleton was on a foray across the Haw; then they discovered Pyle in the vicinity before the planned surprise attack on Tarleton. If Lee and Pickens had found Tarleton in his first bivouac, as they confidently expected to do, and had attacked, Pyle would have certainly been drawn by the noise of battle to the support of Tarleton, and his unexpected appearance might well have turned the tide of battle against the Americans. Had Lee and Pickens not been in striking distance of Tarleton, they would never have found Colonel Preston and his Virginians, and this important addition to Greene's small army would almost certainly have been discovered and destroyed by Tarleton and Pyle before it reached Greene, especially since the Virginians had no idea of where Greene was and since they had no cavalry to act as their eyes and ears.

These events underline not only the role of luck or chance in such operations, but the importance of the indefatigable gathering of intelligence and of the capacity of leaders to adapt themselves instantly to changing circumstances. In this respect, the foray of Lee and Pickens is a model for the student of military history.

On February 23, Greene crossed the Dan, according to his plan, and was joined by Lee and Pickens. Their expedition had exceeded his hopes for it. Cornwallis, dismayed by the destruction of Pyle's force and the manner in which it was effected, decided to move his army to the area between the Haw and Deep rivers, which was an especially fruitful ground for recruiting Loyalist auxiliaries. As soon as Cornwallis began his march, Greene sent Colonel Williams, who had protected his rear so effectively on the retreat to the Dan, to keep in close touch with the movements of the British army. Under Williams' command were Lee, Pickens, and Preston. Cornwallis, in turn, still hoping to bring Greene to a decisive battle, decided that the best tactic would be an attack on Williams' comparatively large covering force, which would bring Greene into battle to prevent the destruction of these essential units. Greene had also decided to seek an encounter. He followed Cornwallis across the Haw and placed his army between Troublesome Creek and Reedy Fork. At the same time he kept his men in constant movement, advancing toward Williams one day and withdrawing the next, so that Cornwallis was thoroughly mystified by his intentions. In this situation the superiority of the American cavalry, both in their mounts and in their skill as horsemen, was plainly evident.

What followed was a series of moves and countermoves as elaborate as a chess game. Cornwallis dispatched Webster, one of his most trusted and experienced officers, to try to pin Williams down. Williams' left was in charge of Colonel Campbell, the larger-than-life hero of Kings Mountain, who outranked Pickens and took over his command. Webster's first move, under cover of fog, was against Campbell, who he almost took by surprise. But Lee came up with his light infantry and checked Webster until Williams had time to extricate his main force. At Reedy Fork, Williams prepared to block Webster's advance, and at every point the American cavalry complicated Webster's deployment by their speed of movement.

For a day the British pushed slowly forward, the Americans gradually falling back, but doing so in such an orderly way that no opportunity was presented for Webster to press an attack. One incident occurred during the retreat that is worth mentioning. At the ford on Reedy Fork, Lee had posted twenty-five riflemen, chosen for their skill as marksmen, in a nearby log schoolhouse with instructions to fire through the chinks between the logs at any likely target, especially a British officer. When the British, led by Webster himself on horseback, pushed across the stream, the riflemen, concealed in the schoolhouse not more than thirty or forty yards from the stream, began to fire at him. Since the stream was quite deep at this point, Webster and the infantry accompanying him moved so slowly that some riflemen had a chance to reload and fire a second time. Lee calculated that thirty-two or thirty-three shots must have been fired at Webster's conspicuous figure without one bullet striking him. The battlefield is not the rifle range. Skilled as the American soldier was in the use of his musket or rifle, a careful analysis of the numbers of men engaged and the number of casualties suffered by the British in various engagements will make it abundantly clear that the skill of the American marksman was comparative; in the stress of combat he, like the riflemen in the schoolhouse, had a surprisingly low degree of accuracy.

By the end of the day, Webster had suffered a substantial number of casualties and had achieved nothing of strategic value. Cornwallis, convinced that the superiority of the American cavalry made it impossible to force Greene to an action, recalled Webster and fell back himself toward Bell's Mill on Deep River. A few days later a contingent of Continentals under Colonel Christopher Greene, the general's cousin and hero of the defense of Fort Mercer, arrived along with a fresh contingent of Virginia militia under Brigadier General Robert Lawson. The militia were divided into two brigades, one commanded by General Lawson, the other by Stevens, who had been recruiting successfully in Halifax County. Lawson, like Christopher Greene, had served with distinction in the regular army.

Pickens, unhappy at being outranked by Campbell, marched off with his corps, but a North Carolina force under Generals Butler and Eaton more than made up the deficit. By the end of the month, Greene had under his command some forty-five hundred men—cavalry, infantry, and artillery—of which sixteen hundred were Continentals. While Greene's army grew and was organized into manageable units, Lee and his legion kept such a close check on Cornwallis that he could hardly supply his army and was forced to march from Bell's Mill to New Garden, a Quaker community that, as its name suggested, was "abounding with forage and provision."

14

Guilford Court House

G REENE was now ready for the contest that Cornwallis had so persistently sought. He moved once more to Guilford Court House, twelve miles from Cornwallis's camp at New Garden. Again Lee's cavalry moved out, this time some six miles to a Quaker meetinghouse on the road to New Garden. There, at two in the morning of March 14, Lee's scouts brought him word that a large party of British cavalry was approaching. Lee informed Greene at once and sent scouts to try to determine whether the entire British force was advancing. The scouts soon reported, significantly, that they could not get behind the British advance guard because of British patrols ranging far from the line of march. When this word was conveyed to Greene, he ordered Lee to move forward with his legion and to try to force Cornwallis to reveal his intentions. Lee did this with his usual skill, routing a troop of enemy dragoons under Tarleton in the process, killing and wounding a dozen or so, and capturing twice that number. At another Quaker meetinghouse four miles from Guilford Court House, the Americans and British became so heavily engaged that Lee was convinced that the main army was advancing for battle and "that the long avoided, now wished-for hour was at hand."

Lee withdrew his cavalry, covered by the infantry under Colonel William Campbell, and fell back to Guilford Court House. The Court

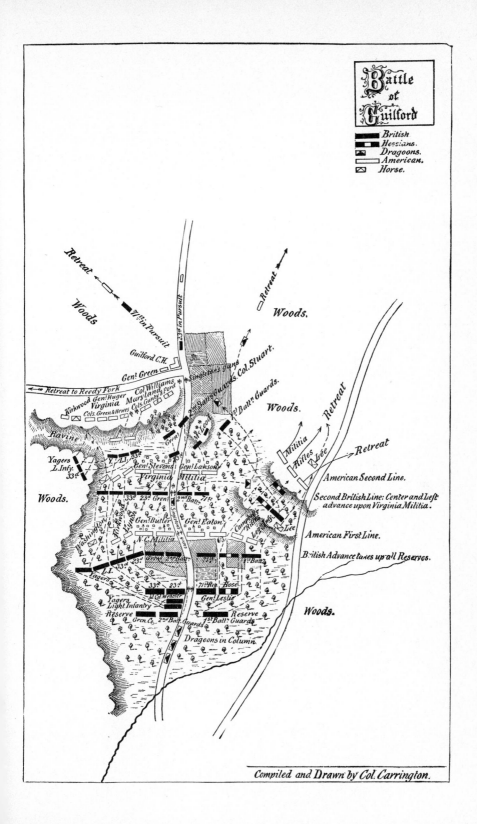

Battle
of
Guilford

British
Hessians.
Dragoons.
American.
Horse.

Retreat

Woods.

Woods.

Retreat

27th in Pursuit

23d in Pursuit

Guilford C.H.

Gen! Green

Retreat to Reedy Fork

Singleton's guns

Retreat

2d Batt? Guards Col. Stuart.

Col Williams
Maryland
Cols. Gunby & Ford

Gen! Huger
Kirkwood Virginia
Cols. Green & Hewes

Woods.

1st Batt? Guards.

Ravine

Militia

Rifles

Retreat

Lee

Yagers
L. Infy.
33d

V. L.I.

Gen! Stevens Gen! Lawson

Virginia Militia

American Second Line.

Second British Line: Center and Left
advance upon Virginia Militia.

Woods.

33d 23d Gren! 2d Batt? 71st

Washington
Kirkwood
Lynch

Gen! Butler Gen! Eaton

N.C. Militia

Campbell
Rifles

Lee

American First Line.

British Advance takes up all Reserves.

Gren! 2d Batt?

1st Batt?

L.I.
33d 23d

Yagers
33d 23d

71st Reg? Bose

Lt Col. Webster

Gen! Leslie

Woods.

Yagers
Light Infantry
Reserve

Gren. Co. 2d Batt. Guards

1st Batt! Guards.

Dragoons in Column.

Compiled and Drawn by Col. Carrington.

House was situated on high ground that sloped gently for half a mile in the direction of New Garden. On the right of the Great State Road was open ground with scattered groves of trees. At the foot of the incline leading to the Court House was a small creek, and here the underbrush was thick and tangled. To the left of the road was a dense forest running down to an open cornfield. Greene placed an advance line at the foot of the slope, with two six-pounders covering the creek. Supporting the artillery pieces was the North Carolina militia under Butler and Eaton. At some distance behind this line was the Virginia militia, commanded by Stevens and Lawson. And behind the Virginia militia, in the large field to the right of the road, were four regiments of Continentals: the two Virginia regiments, led by Christopher Greene and Samuel Hawes, on the right under the command of Huger; and the Maryland regiments led by Colonel John Gunby and Lieutenant Colonel Benjamin Ford, on the left against the road, with Williams as the brigade commander. Washington with his cavalry and the veteran Delaware company of Continentals, along with Colonel Charles Lynch and a battalion of Virginia militia, were charged with protecting the American right. Lee, with Campbell and his Virginia riflemen, covered the left flank. The rest of the artillery were distributed along the rear line formed by the Continentals.

The dispositions were strikingly like those of Morgan at Cowpens, and this was not of course accidental. Greene, like any good general, was always ready to profit from the experience of others. Morgan had indeed written to Greene on February 20 suggesting such a deployment. "I expect Lord Cornwallis will push you until you are obliged to fight him, on which much will depend," Morgan had observed. "You'll have, from what I see, a great number of militia. If they fight, you'll beat Cornwallis; if not, he will beat you, and perhaps cut your regulars to pieces. I am informed that among the militia will be a number of old soldiers. I think it would be advisable to select them from the militia and put them in the midst of the regulars. *Select the riflemen also and fight them on the flanks, under enterprising officers who are acquainted with that kind of fighting, and put the remainder of the militia in the center with some picked troops in their rear with orders to shoot down the first man that runs.* If anything will succeed, a disposition of this kind will. I hope you will not look upon this, as dictating; but as my opinion, in a matter I am much concerned in." The advice was good; it had behind it the weight of Morgan's brilliant success at Cowpens, and such of it as was applicable Greene adopted at Guilford Court House.

The British right, as Cornwallis advanced, consisted of Von Bose's Hessian regiment and the Seventy-first British, with General Leslie in command and the first battalion of guards in reserve; the left was made up of the Twenty-third and Thirty-third, with Webster commanding, and the grenadiers and the Second Battalion of the guards in reserve under O'Hara. Tarleton's dragoons constituted a strategic reserve to be used as the development of the battle suggested. The entire force consisted of hardly more than two thousand men, but most of them were seasoned veterans.

The morning of March 15 was a clear, cold day. Shortly after daylight the British advance guard made contact with the American pickets. The British approach to the first American line was through a defile that forced the advance units together and made it impossible to fully deploy them. The engagement opened with a brisk exchange of artillery. Here the fire from the American six-pounders should have been most effective, but the moment the head of the British column—the Hessians and the Seventy-first Infantry—passed the creek, deploying right and left to form a line of battle, the North Carolina militia, behind a stout rail fence, fired a hasty volley at a range of over a hundred yards and then broke and ran back up the road toward the Court House. Their officers were unable to check "this unaccountable panic." (Not a man had been killed or wounded.) Even Lee's threat to attack them with his cavalry was unavailing. Abandoning muskets, knapsacks, and even canteens, they fled into the woods, which, in the absence of a swamp, promised refuge. The artillery pieces thus exposed had to be quickly withdrawn. The flight of the North Carolina militia also exposed the Virginia militia, who constituted the second American line. On the left, Webster, leading the Twenty-third and Thirty-third Infantry Regiments, brought heavy pressure on Colonel Stevens. That officer, still smarting from the flight of the Virginia militia at Camden, had placed a line of Continental soldiers in the rear of the militia "with orders to shoot every man that flinched." The Virginians fired at maximum range and stood their ground, but the British came on, as always, with their field bands playing and their flags flying.

Leslie, quick to take advantage of the rout of the North Carolinians, directed his Hessians, with the battalion of Guards, to attack Lee and Campbell; he also ordered his reserve to fill the gap in the British lines made by echeloning right. He himself turned left with the Seventy-first Infantry to assist Webster, who was encountering stubborn resistance from the Virginia militia. Washington supported the militia by ordering Lynch's battalion of riflemen to attack Webster's left. O'Hara moved forward from his position in reserve to reinforce Webster, and this movement freed Webster to turn on Lynch's battalion. O'Hara's grenadiers and Guards then joined forces with the Seventy-first in a bayonet charge that finally dislodged the Virginians. With Stevens wounded, his brigade fled, as did Lawson's, and the militia "no longer presented even a show of resistance."

In spite of the panic of the North Carolina militia, the units on the American flanks—Lee's and Campbell's infantrymen on the left and Lynch's battalion on the right—had seriously impeded the British attack and inflicted substantial casualties. More important, the British had been forced to bring their reserves into action and were now completely committed with the exception of Tarleton's dragoons.

Having routed the second line, Cornwallis pressed the attack against the Continentals. The Hessians and Guards were still engaged on. the American left with Lee's and Campbell's infantry. At this point the situation seemed favorable for the Americans. Greene passed along the line of Continentals encouraging them to stand firm; the victory, he assured them, would be theirs. Webster meanwhile led the attack on the First Maryland Regiment. These were Howard's men, who had fought so well at Cowpens, and they once more stood their ground and drove the British back with heavy losses. Webster waited for reinforcements to come up, and when the First Battalion of guards arrived, they charged the portion of the line held by the Second Maryland Regiment. These soldiers, although Continentals, had not been seasoned by combat. Unlike their sister regiment, they gave way quite promptly, abandoning in the process two artillery pieces. Howard's men saved the day by turning on the British as they pursued the Second Marylanders. And now, while the guards and the Maryland Line struggled desperately to dominate the action, Washington charged into the melee with his cavalry. The guards began to give way, and Howard's veterans, charging with fixed bayonets, completed their rout; the British officer in command was struck down by an American officer's sword.

Cornwallis, with one horse shot from under him, mounted one belonging to a dragoon and started to ride toward the guards, who, driven back by Howard's bayonet charge, were in danger of being overwhelmed. The dragoon's saddlebags had slipped around the horse's belly; they caught in the underbrush and frightened the horse.

Just in time, Sergeant Lamb of the Welsh Fusiliers caught the animal's bridle and turned it away, guiding the horse and Cornwallis back to the cover of the woods where the Twenty-third had been rallied.

Determined to save the guards, Cornwallis gave his artillery the order to fire. O'Hara protested that the fire would kill the guards as well as their pursuers. "True," Cornwallis replied, "but this is a necessary evil which we must endure to arrest impending destruction." The decision proved a wise one; the artillery fire, while killing and wounding some of the guards' own men, forced Washington and Howard to abandon their pursuit.

The British now regrouped. The guards who had survived the American counterattack were joined with the Twenty-third and Seventy-first Regiments and the grenadiers by General O'Hara, who was himself painfully wounded.

At the moment when Colonel Alexander Stewart appeared to have routed the Second Maryland, Webster had turned his attention to the American left, attacking Hawes's Virginia Continentals while the force reconstituted by O'Hara resumed the attack on Howard. During all this action, Lee and Campbell had fought the Hessians and guards to a standstill, trying at the same time to maneuver in such a way as to link up with the Continentals fighting on the high ground near the Court House. Lieutenant Colonel Norton, the British officer commanding the force opposed to Lee and Campbell, was aware that other units were under heavy pressure; he therefore left the Hessians to contain Lee and Campbell and moved to join the Seventy-first in their renewed assault on the American right. This was the opportunity that Lee and Campbell had been waiting for. They forced the Hessians back, and Lee, leaving Campbell to engage them, moved to join his own cavalry. Crossing the battlefield, he and his infantry encountered Norton's guards at the point where the Virginia militia had fought so resolutely and at once attacked them, driving them back on the Hessians, hard pressed by Campbell.

The way was now open for Lee to rejoin his cavalry legion near the Court House. When he arrived there he found that Greene, discouraged by the flight of the Second Maryland and his failure to bring them back to the field, alarmed at his inability to make contact with Lee and Campbell on the American left, and concerned at reports that ammunition was running low, had begun a withdrawal. It was carried out in good order, with Christopher Greene's Virginia regiment assigned to secure the line of retreat. If Lee and Campbell had extricated themselves somewhat earlier from the left, Greene might have decided to maintain his position. But his first responsibility was to preserve his army more or less intact.

The Guilford Court House battle had no military significance. For Greene, victory meant inflicting on the British casualties they could ill afford, while avoiding the destruction of his own army. For Cornwallis, the possession of the Guilford Court House battlefield had no meaning if Greene's army survived to fight another day. As Lewis Morris, Jr., Greene's aide-de-camp, had written during the retreat to the Dan, the destruction of "the army was evidently the object of the enemy, and while we can keep that together the country can never be conquered—disperse it, and the people are subjugated."

For a brief time the Seventy-first and Twenty-third Regiments and Tarleton's cavalry followed Greene's retreating troops as though to attack them, but Cornwallis called them back, and Greene stopped some three miles from the battlefield to collect stragglers and re-form and rest his men; from there the exhausted army made its way back to the ironworks at Troublesome Creek, some ten miles from Guilford Court House. "Never," Greene wrote, "did an army labour under so many disadvantages as this; but the fortitude and patience of the officers and soldiery rise superior to all difficulties. We have little to eat, less to drink, and lodge in the woods in the midst of smoke." Greene, burdened with a thousand cares and weakened by lack of sleep and hasty and indigestible meals, fainted from fatigue the day after the battle.

The battle of Guilford Court House was one of the bloodiest of the war. General Charles O'Hara, as we have seen, was wounded. His young brother, a lieutenant in the Royal Artillery, was killed. The guards suffered the severest losses, with their commander, Lieutenant Colonel Alexander Stewart, killed. James Webster, who had fought with his usual skill and courage, was so badly wounded that he died shortly after the battle, and Tarleton was also wounded, though not seriously. The loss of Webster was perhaps the bitterest blow. He was not only one of the most accomplished of Cornwallis's officers, he was also one of the most beloved, uniting, in Tarleton's words, "all the virtues of civil life to the gallantry and professional knowledge of a soldier." His good spirits and fortitude in adversity and his generosity in victory were the best qualities of his class.

British casualties came to 554 killed and wounded out of fewer than 2,000 men engaged. It was a devastating setback for Cornwallis, who claimed the victory on the grounds that Greene's army withdrew from the battlefield. Greene put the matter more accurately when he wrote the day after the battle: "The enemy gained his cause, but is ruined by the success of it." Tarleton regarded "the victory as the pledge of ultimate defeat." When word of the battle reached England, Charles James Fox declared in Commons, "Another such victory would ruin the British army," and Pitt spoke of Guilford Court House as the "precursor of ruin to British supremacy in the south."

Of the American casualties, the largest proportion by far were in the category of "missing." In actual killed and wounded, the American figures were substantially smaller than the British. The Continentals took the heaviest losses; of somewhat more than 1,000 engaged (including the Second Maryland), 144 were killed or wounded. The militia listed 83 casualties, for a total of 227 Americans killed or wounded (less than half the British casualties). A thousand and eighty-four Americans were listed as missing, of whom 552 were the North Carolina militia.

If the thousand or so soldiers who fled the field of battle had stood fast, the Americans would have won a crushing victory that would have ended Cornwallis's campaigning months before Yorktown. Lee accounts for the disproportion in the British and American casualties in these words: "We had great advantage in the ground, and were sheltered in various points until the enemy approached very near; while he was uncovered and exposed from his first step to his last. We had spent the previous day in ease, and the night in rest; he had been preparing during the day, and marching part of the night. We were acquainted with wood and tree fighting; he ignorant of both. And lastly, we were trained to aim and fire low, he was not so trained; and from his cause, or from the composition of his cartridge (too much powder for the lead), he always overshot."

Lee, rightly enough, had praise for the British soldier as well as the American. The Englishman was better clothed and thus better able to endure the cold, and "in every other respect he equalled [the American]—bearing incessant toil, courting danger, and submitting to privation of necessary food with alacrity; exhibiting upon all occasions, unquestionable evidence of fidelity, zeal, and courage. . . ."

The British soldiers, well led as always, had fought with great courage and tenacity, as they had been trained to do. Faced by a force twice as large on unfavorable terrain, they persisted until they possessed the bloody field. But fact remains that if we count only those Americans who stayed to fight, the two forces were roughly equal in size, and the Americans inflicted far heavier casualties than they suffered themselves. It is instructive to contrast the Battle of Guilford Court House with the engagement between patriots and Tories at Ramsour's Mill. At Ramsour's Mill, two irregular bands fought the most desperate engagement of the war in terms of the proportion of casualties to men involved on each side. The point seems clear: American regulars could more than hold their own against British regulars when they fought in a manner "natural" to them.

After the battle, Greene wrote to the president of Congress, Joseph Reed, "The horse at different times in the course of the day, performed wonders. Indeed, the horse is our great safeguard, and without them the militia could not keep the field in this country."

The night after the battle was rainy, dark, and cold. On the battlefield, in Lee's words, "the dead [lay] unburied, the wounded unsheltered" through the bitter night, the British too exhausted and demoralized to provide much aid for the wounded of either side. Some fifty of the injured died before daybreak. After the battle, Cornwallis wrote to Clinton, "many of the inhabitants rode into camp, shook me by the hand, said they were glad to see me and to hear that we had beat Greene, and then rode home again, for I could not get 100 men in all the Regulator's country to stay with us, even as militia." Cornwallis described his army as bearing one-third "sick and wounded, which I was obliged to carry in waggons or on horseback, the remainder without shoes and worn down with fatigue." At Cross Creek, Cornwallis found "there was not four days forage within twenty miles."

It was now his view, he wrote, that the principal efforts of the British should be concentrated in Virginia, even at the cost of abandoning New York.

15

Hobkirk's Hill

A FTER Guilford Court House it was plainly impossible for Cornwallis to resume his pursuit of Greene. His shattered army could not sustain another battle. Instead of following Greene he issued a proclamation, claiming a glorious victory for British arms and urging all Loyalists to come to his support. Then he turned toward Wilmington, North Carolina, the country of the Scottish Highlanders, where he hoped to rest and equip his battered army.

Stedman tells of falling in on the way to Wilmington with a North Carolina Quaker who told him that "it was the general wish of the people to be united to Britain," but that they had so often been deceived in promises of support by the British, that they feared retribution at the hands of the patriots when Cornwallis left the province. Some Tories had lived in the woods like animals for two or three years without daring to go to their own homes. "Others, having walked out of their houses on a promise of their being safe, have proceeded but a few yards before they have been shot." Some had been severely whipped. When Stedman argued the advantages of being subjects of Great Britain over those of a tyrannical Congress, the Quaker answered, in the classic words of civilians who have undergone for a long time the desperate ravages of war: "The people have experienced such distress that I believe they would submit to any government in the world to obtain peace."

When the army of Cornwallis approached Cross Creek, it encountered a figure wilder than Robinson Crusoe, "who had hardly the appearance of being human. He wore the skin of a raccoon for a hat, his beard was some inches long, and he was so thin he looked [like a walking skeleton]. He wore no shirt; his whole dress being skins of different animals. . . . He said that he had lived for three years in the woods, under ground . . . that acorns served him as bread." He was sure that if the Americans had found him they would have killed him. His only crime was that he was a Loyalist.

Greene, who certainly had his own problems—among them the fact "the militia is leaving us in great numbers to return home to kiss their wives and sweethearts," as he put it—nevertheless started after Cornwallis, reaching the Deep River crossing at Ramsay's Mill the day after Cornwallis had crossed the river. There he decided to dismiss most of the militia and give his weary soldiers a rest.

Cornwallis, writing to General William Phillips from Wilmington on April 10, expressed his own view of the situation quite succinctly: "Now, my dear friend, what is your plan? Without one we cannot succeed and I assure you that I am quite tired of marching about the country in quest of adventures. If we mean an offensive war in America, we must abandon New York and bring our whole force into Virginia; we then have a stake to fight for, and a successful battle may give us America. If our plan is defensive, mixed with desultory expeditions, let us quit the Carolinas (which cannot be held defensively while Virginia can be so easily armed against us) and stick to our salt pork at New York, sending now and then a detachment to steal tobacco, etc."

The passage demonstrates very well the weakness of the British position. *There was no plan.* Everything was improvised. The simple fact of the matter was that no one in the British ministry, least of all, of course, Germain, had any idea of the proper strategy to reduce America. Clinton in New York was equally baffled. Suppose he were to evacuate New York and join Cornwallis in Virginia? The effect would be to surrender even the pretense—and the occupation of New York was little more than that—of exercising some domination over the middle and New England states in exchange for a long and uncertain campaign in the South, which had already displayed a disconcerting talent for partisan warfare. Certainly the combined forces of Clinton and Cornwallis could have marched where they wished. But what would such marching have in fact accomplished except to wear out men and waste equipment? The British held Charles Town and Savannah, and it did them precious little good. Moreover, the armies of Greene, Washington, and Rochambeau might well have defeated Clinton and Cornwallis or at least fought several of those bloody and inconclusive engagements that the British could so ill afford and that for the Americans constituted victory, wherever the laurels might be technically placed.

Cornwallis decided on his own to head for Virginia. His army, desperately short of supplies and feeling the effects, practically and psychologically, of having earlier destroyed their baggage, was delighted to abandon North Carolina. On the eve of his departure, Cornwallis sent a message to Lord Rawdon at Camden warning him that Greene would, in all likelihood, invade South Carolina (Rawdon, incidentally, never got the message).

When word reached Clinton of Cornwallis's move into Virginia, he wrote, "My wonder at this move of Lord Cornwallis will never cease, but he has made it, and we shall say no more but make the best of it." Yet he could make little sense of Cornwallis's tactics. "His first object will of course be Lafayette," he wrote, " . . . what his next object will be God knows."

In addition to Cornwallis's independence, Clinton had to cope with Marriot Arbuthnot. The admiral was almost seventy years old when he took command of the American station and not in the best of health. In the words of one historian, "Arbuthnot was pompous, incompetent, and unpredictable, given to absurd schemes of campaign. He resisted Clinton at every turn, now friendly, then hostile, but uncooperative throughout."

In June Arbuthnot simply disappeared with his fleet, without so much as a by-your-leave. "I know not where our old Admiral is gone," Clinton wrote; "I fear he has opened Rhode Island. I tremble while connected with this old gentleman." Arbuthnot's description of his own condition was certainly not a reassuring one. He had lost, he confessed, "almost totally the sight of one eye, and the other is but a very feeble helpmate. . . . Beside, I have lately been seized with very odd fits . . . almost instantly I faint, remain senseless and speechless sometimes four hours and sometimes longer . . . cold sweats for two or three days after. . . ."

With Cornwallis gone, Greene's campaigning was seriously inhibited by the scarcity of supplies of all kinds, particularly, of course, food. Without money to pay for it, food had to be requisitioned. Years of guerrilla warfare as well as, more recently, the marches and countermarches of substantial armies had stripped the country bare. Farmers showed considerable ingenuity in hiding what little was left. As Lee put it very well, "nothing but the gleanings of an exhausted country were left for our subsistence." Greene had thus frequently to adjust the movement of his army to the availability of provisions.

At Ramsay's Mill on Deep River, Greene's army got what respite it could. As Lee put it: "The meagre beef of the pine barrens, with corn-ash cake, was our food, and water our drink; yet we were content; we were more than content—we were happy. The improved condition of the South, effected by our efforts, had bestowed the solace of inward satisfaction on our review of the past; and experience of the lofty genius of our beloved leader, encouraged proud anticipations of the future."

Much time was spent during the days of rest at Ramsay's Mill in discussing the strategy that Greene's little army should adopt: to advance on Cornwallis at Wilmington, to pursue him into Virginia, or to take the opportunity offered by his withdrawal to drive the British and Loyalist garrisons out of the lower South and free the Carolinas—and hopefully Georgia as well—from the last traces of British domination. It soon became evident in discussions among Greene and his officers that the last course of action was clearly the most practical, given the limited capacities of Greene's army. Washington and the French would have to look after Virginia. A campaign into South Carolina would make use of the Southern patriots' talent for partisan warfare, especially raids by cavalry and mounted infantry. The forays of Marion and Sumter could be reinforced and supplemented by Lee's seasoned legion and William Washington's cavalry.

It was decided that the main army under Greene would advance on Camden, where Lord Rawdon commanded a mixed force of Northern Loyalists and British regulars. Lee, joining Marion, "should break down all intermediate posts, completely demolishing communications between Camden and Ninety-Six with Charlestown," thereby isolating these British strongpoints. Lee was the principal advocate of such a plan, perhaps in part because it would give his beloved legion a prominent and quasi-independent role in the kind of operation best suited to their capacities and his tastes. Lee did not, however, prevail without a struggle. A number of the officers maintained that the preservation of Virginia was the most important responsibility, and that Greene, more than any other American general except Washington, had demonstrated his ability to meet the British army on equal terms. The discussion, which Lee recapitulates in great detail, was an interesting and important one that demonstrated the political as well as the military sophistication of those who argued the contending points of view. It is reasonable to assume that Greene's decision to follow Lee's plan was based in large part on his desire to utilize most effectively the proven capacities of Sumter and Pickens and the western militia, which was so quick to rally to their standards. In other words, the South Carolina campaign was ultimately irresistible because it had what we might call a "multiplier effect"; that is to say, Greene's own force would be multiplied by a factor of greatly increased mobility and a substantial augmentation in numbers.

As soon as a decision had been made, Greene detached Lee and Oldham to join Marion and sent word to Sumter and Pickens of his plan of campaign, which hinged directly on their cooperation. Sumter was asked to join Greene at Camden, and Pickens was directed to seal off Ninety-Six. Greene wrote to General Washington on March 29, 1781, "I am determined to carry the war immediately into South Carolina. The enemy will be obliged to follow us or give up their posts in that State. . . . If they leave their posts to fall, they must lose more than they can gain here. . . . The manoeuvre will be critical and dangerous, and the troops exposed to every hardship. But as I share it with them, I hope they will bear up under it with that magnanimity which has already supported them, and for which they deserve everything of their country."

As Lee moved toward Drowning Creek off the Little Pee Dee to join forces with Marion, his legion, in bivouac, was alarmed by the fire of sentries—first to their rear, then to the side, and finally in front of them. Convinced that the British were in the offing, Lee formed up his men and gave them a splendid fight talk, exhorting them to sell their lives dearly in the battle that must surely come at dawn. In the morning the troops moved off in battle order, expecting every moment to hear the thump of British muskets, only to discover by tracks in the mud that their midnight visitors had been a pack of wolves that had circled the camp and had by their noise in the underbrush, alarmed the sentries and drawn their fire. When the men discovered this, Lee tells us, agitation was succeeded "by facetious glee. . . . Nowhere do wit and humor abound more than in camps. Never was a day's march more pleasant, being one continued scene of good humor, interspersed with innocent flashes of wit." Lee came in for his own share of ribbing, along with the pickets, the patrols, the sentinels, and the officer of the day. "Wonderful that not one of the many could distinguish between the movements of wolves and soldiers! They were charged with disgraceful ignorance, shameful stupor, bordering close on rank cowardice." There was almost as much comment on the military prowess of the wolves. The cavalry could learn much from the "acute reconnoitering" of "an enemy in force, well understanding his own views."

After several days' march, Lee found the partisan leader in his natural habitat, the Black River swamp, and there he was received "with joy" by Marion and his band. The two men had cooperated before in an attack on Georgetown, which, although it had proved abortive when the British troops had remained in their barracks instead of coming out to fight, was a model of that most difficult of maneuvers—a skillfully executed, coordinated attack. They thus trusted one another and looked forward to the coming campaign. The dark days of grim resistance and successive defeats seemed at last over. "The ethereal spirit," as Lee put it, "which had animated Marion, Sumter and Pickens, and year after year had sustained, through their example and efforts, the unequal conflict, had long been subsiding." The end was now in sight.

The two officers chose as their first objective a small fort, erected on an Indian burial mound by Lieutenant Colonel John Watson, who had been sent by Rawdon with five hundred cavalry to root Marion out of his swamp. The fort seemed too strong to attack directly. The only hope was to cut off the supply of water from a nearby lake. When the defenders of the fort devised a trench from an adjacent creek to supply the fort, Lee and Marion were ready to abandon the siege. At this point Major Hezekiah Maham proposed building a tall tower out of trees, with a platform on top from which American riflemen could pick off the defenders of the fort one at a time. As soon as "Maham's Tower" was completed and a few of the defenders were killed or wounded, the fort surrendered. Lee and Marion then turned to meet Watson, who was on his way to relieve the fort.

Meanwhile Greene was advancing on Camden with some fifteen hundred men, expecting to be joined by Sumter. But Sumter inexplicably "held off, much to the surprise, regret and dissatisfaction" of Greene, thereby demonstrating one of the particular dangers and frustrations of working with partisan troops: they commonly consult their own sentiments rather than responding to instructions or orders. Thus, however brave and skilled, they are notoriously unreliable. Greene's best hope seemed to be to try to starve Camden into submission by cutting off the foraging parties that scoured the country in increasingly wide sweeps to find food for the garrison. With Watson off searching for Marion, Rawdon had less than nine hundred men to oppose Greene.

Learning from Tory spies that Lee had joined forces with Marion, realizing that this combined force would pose a serious threat to Watson, and wishing him back, in any event, to aid in the defense of Camden, Rawdon sent orders for Watson to return. Greene, equally anxious to try to intercept Watson and to place his own army in a position where Lee and Marion could readily join him if necessary, moved his troops from the north to the east side of Camden. Then, learning that Marion and Lee expected to be able to check Watson's return to Camden and hoping still to be reinforced by Sumter, Greene returned to the north side of the town and took a position on Hobkirk's Hill, athwart the road to Salisbury, with his flanks protected by large swampy areas. The regulars were formed into one line centered on the road, with some two hundred and fifty militia in reserve with the cavalry. Pickets were established in front, and patrols covered the flanks.

On the twenty-fourth, Greene learned of the surrender of "Fort Watson," and the next day the prisoners captured there were brought into camp under guard. Among them were several ex-Continentals, including a former drummer in the Maryland Line. They explained that they had only accepted service with the British so that they might avoid being sent to a prison ship, and that they had planned to take the first opportunity to make their escape back to their units. The Americans accepted this explanation, and the prisoners joined their old outfits. The drummer deserted in the night and informed Rawdon of Greene's position, as well as of the fact that a substantial detachment under Lieutenant Colonel Carrington, which had been assigned to cover the recent movements of Greene's army and which carried his artillery, had not yet rejoined Greene. Sumter's expected brigade, Rawdon was also told, had not arrived either.

Rawdon realized that he could only weaken his own position by delay. His supply of food was dangerously low, and Greene's army was bound to be augmented soon. He decided that his best defense would be a surprise attack on Greene, and he immediately set in motion a plan for an assault the next day. At nine in the morning of the twenty-fifth, with some nine hundred men—a motley collection of Loyalists, stiffened by a few regulars—he began a covered advance along the Waxhaw Road, where heavy woods concealed the movement of his army. At Hobkirk's Hill, Carrington's arrival with provisions and artillery was welcome; extra rations were distributed, and many of the soldiers went down to Pine Tree Creek to wash their clothes. Rawdon was almost on the American positions before the pickets discovered him. They fought

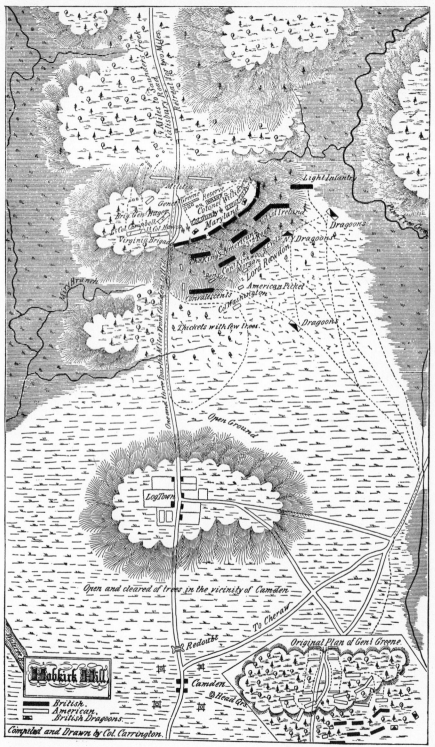

Miles to Rawden's Creek

Salisbury Road to Rugeley's Mills

4 Miles to Road

Militia

General Greene Reserve

Colonel Williams

Brig. Gen. Huger

Lt. Col. Campbell

Virginia Brigade

Lt. Col. Howard

Maryland

Light Infantry

Dragoons

Vol. of Ireland

The Kings American Reg.

Capt. Kirkwood

N.Y. Dragoons

Beaver

Morgan

Lord Rawdon

Convalescents

American Picket

Col. Washington

Dragoons

Mill Branch

One and three fourth Miles to Pond Cul. de Ville

Thickets with few trees.

Open Ground

Log Town

Open and cleared of trees in the vicinity of Camden

To Cheraw

Redoubt

Original Plan of Gen'l Greene.

Camden

Head Qrs.

Hobkirk Mill

British.
American.
British Dragoons.

Compiled and Drawn by Col. Carrington.

stubbornly to allow time for their companions to man their lines at the top of the hill. It was fortunate that Greene had already laid out defensive positions. General Huger took command of the American right with the Virginia brigade. Lieutenant Colonels Campbell and Hawes, in charge of the Maryland brigade—consisting of the indomitable First and the rehabilitated Second Regiments—formed the backbone of the left; Williams was in command, seconded by Gunby, Ford, and Howard. The artillery was placed in the center.

Rawdon's advance line was formed by the King's American Regiment on the right, the New York Volunteers in the center, and the Sixty-third on the left. The convalescents corps constituted the reserve on the right, and the Volunteers of Ireland did so on the left. The general reserve was made up of a South Carolina Loyalist regiment and all the available cavalry.

Watching Rawdon's attack develop, Greene noticed that it was being made on a narrow front that offered the possibility of an envelopment by the American right and left. He thus ordered Campbell on the extreme right of the American line and Ford on the left to move against the flanks of the British, and the center was ordered to advance with fixed bayonets on the attackers. Washington with his cavalry was dispatched to attack the enemy rear. Rawdon immediately countered Greene's move by bringing up the Irish Volunteers to extend his line, but the Americans advanced in good order, and Greene's battle plan seemed about to be vindicated.

At this point, John Gunby's battle-tested Maryland regiment, which had initially joined in the firing in defiance of orders, halted, and its right began to fall back. Gunby, intending to "compact" his battalion, made the error of calling back his leading elements rather than pressing forward to join them. The result was considerable confusion among soldiers who had been caught by surprise in the first place and who had hardly had time to form up before they found themselves attacked. The British right took advantage at once of the disorder among the Marylanders, and came on at a quickstep with a triumphant shout. The Marylanders, "the bulwark of the army," men who had stood fast at Cowpens and proved steady as a rock at Guilford Court House, panicked. That strange terror that can possess the most seasoned troops fell on them, and they ran for their lives. The Second Maryland, which had fled at Guilford Court House, now stood firm, along with the Virginia brigade. But with its flanks exposed and its commanding officer, Ford, wounded, the Second Maryland began to waver and then to fall back, though in far better order than its sister regiment. The British light infantry and the Volunteers of Ireland were soon on the summit of the hill, flanking Hawes's regiment. Greene recalled Hawes, whose regiment by now was the only unbroken one, ordered it to cover the retreat, and withdrew from the hill, leaving the battlefield in possession of Rawdon. The threat of Washington's cavalry prevented Rawdon from pressing his pursuit. "The enemy's cavalry being superior to the British," Tarleton wrote, "their dragoons could not risk much."

The defeat was a bitter one for Greene. He had invited the battle, even though Rawdon's attack had caught him by surprise. With Guilford Court House in mind, he had felt sure that his army, a third again as large as Rawdon's, must prevail. The American casualties were 271, of whom 133 were listed as missing. Of the missing, 47 were known to be wounded and prisoners. In other words, 86 Americans were missing and unaccounted for; presumably they had fled the field. If we subtract this number from the American casualties, the total in dead and wounded would be 185. The British casualties were 258 killed, wounded, and missing. Since it seems reasonable to assume that comparatively few of Rawdon's victorious army fled, the British suffered substantially heavier casualties than the Americans—which makes all the more unaccountable the poor behavior of so many of the patriots. The British lost, in dead and wounded, more than a quarter of the men engaged; the Americans, approximately 12 per cent. Lieutenant Colonel Ford died of his wounds, and Captain Beatty of the First Maryland was killed.

Rawdon, having won himself, as it turned out, a five-month breathing spell, returned to Camden. "The victory at Hobkirk's Hill," Stedman writes, "like that at Guilford Court House . . . produced no consequence beneficial to the British interest." Greene knew this, of course, but his pride as a soldier and his pride in his soldiers was deeply wounded. "No military event had occurred in the course of the war," Lee wrote, "whose issue was so inexplicable as that of [Hobkirk's Hill]." Rawdon had gambled the existence of his little army on one throw of the dice and had won. Greene had, perhaps, been overconfident. His order to counterattack Rawdon was clearly the result of an impulse, but it was the kind of impulse that is inseparable from the highest order of generalship —the ability to see an opening and take advantage of it. It might be said in rebuttal that at this opening stage of the battle the order to Campbell and Ford was premature because of the virtual certainty that it would prompt Rawdon to commit his reserve; thus it was an illusory advantage. In addition, Washington's foray deprived Greene of his services at a critical stage in the battle. Even so, the Americans would doubtless have prevailed if it had not been for the inexplicable collapse of the First Maryland Regiment. Indeed, given the behavior of the American troops on this particular day, there is no reason to believe that a simple defensive stance by Greene, allowing the British to come on in the face of American fire, would have been more successful. The fault was not in Greene's tactics but in the morale of the soldiers.

The days after Hobkirk's Hill were the gloomiest of Greene's career. For a time he considered abandoning his Southern strategy and, very humanly, was disposed to blame Lee for talking him into it. He ordered Lee back to join him at Rudgley's Mills, when Lee might much better have pursued his efforts with Marion to catch Watson. But misery loves company, and none so much as that which it believes has occasioned the misery. So Lee had to return to face a commander "soured by the failure of expected succor from Sumter, . . . deeply chagrined by the inglorious behavior of a favorite regiment," which had converted "his splendid prospects into the renewal of toil and difficulty, of doubt and disgrace. . . ."

On receiving Greene's orders, Lee set out with his legion of infantry and dragoons and marched thirty-two miles in a day. But it was characteristic of Greene that he fought his way out of his despondency, resolved to press on with his campaign, and sent an officer to Lee to countermand his order, along with the very welcome present of a six-pounder and crew to aid in the operations of Lee and Marion. Greene himself returned to the vicinity of Camden and "sat down in a strong position." Rawdon thus found himself in much the same situation he had been in before his striking success at Hobkirk's Hill. His position at Camden was, if not untenable, at least without notable advantage to the British cause, and Rawdon decided to abandon Camden and consolidate other posts in face of the threat from Lee and Marion. He thus ordered John Cruger to evacuate Ninety-Six and join Thomas Brown at Augusta. Maxwell at Fort Granby was directed to fall back to Orangeburg, but Greene was so thoroughly in control of the countryside that none of the messages reached the officers to whom they were sent. On May 10, Rawdon evacuated Camden, burning the jail, the mills, and some private houses; destroying all the stores he could not carry; and bringing off "four or five hundred negroes, and all the most obnoxious loyalists. . . ."

16

Greene Turns South

Wɪᴛʜ Cornwallis headed for Virginia and Rawdon left with the responsibility for maintaining the British "presence" in the South, Greene and his lieutenants began the laborious task of rooting up the various British-Tory posts in North and South Carolina.

Fort Motte was a depot and transfer point for supplies being convoyed from Charles Town to Camden, Fort Granby, and Ninety-Six. The "fort," which took its name from its owner, Mrs. Motte, was actually a large mansion, situated on commanding ground; palisades had been erected around it, and a deep ditch had been dug. When Rawdon began his withdrawal from Camden, almost two hundred men garrisoned the post. Opposite the fort on another hill was an old farmhouse occupied by Mrs. Motte, who had been "dismissed from her mansion."

After their efforts to intercept Watson had failed and Greene had countermanded his order to Lee to return to Rudgley's Mills, Lee and Marion had laid siege to Fort Motte; Lee had stationed himself at Mrs. Motte's farmhouse, and Marion had placed his men on the reverse slope of the hill on which the fort stood. The six-pounder was emplaced to rake the north side of the palisades. When the gun was in position, a flag of truce was sent to the commander of the fort, "admonishing him to avoid the disagreeable consequences of an arrogant temerity," by promptly surrendering. The commander of the fort, a Captain Mc-Pherson, was confident that Rawdon was on his way and therefore refused. Then followed a series of events that read like a suspense story. Word came from Greene urging Lee and Marion to persist in their seige and to try to bring it to a successful conclusion. He was, he told them, hurrying to their support. This was followed by the appearance in the distance of Rawdon's force, coming to raise the seige. There was clearly no time for Lee and Marion to attack and reduce the fort by conventional methods. As at Fort Watson, something had to be improvised. Even while Rawdon's campfires blazed on the skyline, consoling the defenders and promising relief the next morning, the patriots hit on an expedient; they decided to burn the defenders out. Bows and arrows were prepared "with missive combustible matter." Although the "destruction of private property was repugnant to . . . the two commandants," as Lee reported a bit piously, that course of action seemed best. Mrs. Motte, who had extended the hospitality of her little farmhouse to the American officers and whose oldest daughter was married to Major Pinckney, now a prisoner of the British, was a good sport about it. "With a smile of complacency this exemplary lady listened to the embarrassed officer," Lee reports, and declared "that she was gratified by the opportunity of contributing to the good of her country, and that she would view the approaching scene with delight." Indeed, she even contributed a bow and arrow that had been imported from India. Another messenger was sent to McPherson with a final demand for surrender. It was refused, and the arrows were fired, and the roof set ablaze; when soldiers climbed on it to extinguish the burning shingles, they were driven off by grapeshot from the six-pounder. McPherson surrendered, and "mercy was extended, though policy demanded death, and the obstinacy of McPherson warranted it."

Greene came up with his army soon after Fort Motte's surrender, and Rawdon, seeing that he was too late to affect the course of things, crossed the Santee River at Nelson's Ferry and moved toward Charles Town. Greene ordered Lee to attack Fort Granby and Marion to proceed against Georgetown. Sumter, acting independently, undertook to block communication with Ninety-Six and took a small British post at Orangeburg.

Granby was situated on the southern bank of the Congaree near Friday's Ferry, and Lee realized that any prolonged siege of the fort, which was well protected by abatis, earthworks, and palisades, would give Rawdon time to relieve it. He therefore moved quickly and secretly and, covered by morning fog, erected his six-pounder at the end of the woods to the west of the fort. The fort was defended by some three hundred and fifty men, mostly loyal militia under Major Maxwell, a refugee from the Eastern Shore of Maryland and, in Lee's opinion, a trimmer, an opportunist, a man more interested in the spoils of war than in contesting for its laurels. Lee decided to try and bluff Maxwell into surrendering. When the fog lifted, several rounds from the six-pounder announced "our unexpected proximity." Lee sent an officer under a flag of truce to demand that Maxwell surrender, and at the same time the legion infantry advanced (strictly illegal during negotiations) and occupied very favorable ground for an attack.

Maxwell confirmed Lee's judgment of him by consenting to surrender with the understanding "that private property of every sort, without investigation of title . . . should be confirmed to its possessors," and that "the possessors" be allowed to go with their goods to Charles Town—a proviso quite apparently meant to preserve Maxwell's own loot. Lee, knowing that Rawdon was not far off, consented, and three hundred and forty men, sixty of them Hessian regulars, surrendered without resistance, leaving behind them large stores that included ammunition, salt, and liquor, all much appreciated by the victors in this bloodless encounter.

The course of events seemed to vindicate Lee in his advocacy of the South Carolina campaign. In less than a month Greene, despite the defeat at Hobkirk's Hill, had compelled Rawdon to evacuate Camden and had captured, with no losses, Fort Watson, Fort Motte, Fort Granby, and the fort at Orangeburg, along with some eight hundred men (almost the size of Rawdon's whole army) and a large quantity of supplies.

Only Ninety-Six and Augusta remained in British hands, and their days there were numbered. Greene ordered Lee to cooperate with Pickens in an attempt to capture Augusta. Lee began his march on May 15, the same day that Maxwell surrendered Fort Granby, and made thirteen miles before nightfall. The next day he pressed on, having ordered his rather disgruntled dragoons to alternate with the infantry in walking and riding. Lee's ostensible reason for such haste was fear that Cruger, who commanded at Ninety-Six, would abandon that post after hearing of Rawdon's withdrawal from Camden (as indeed Rawdon had instructed him to do in the message that had never reached him) and would reinforce Brown at Augusta. In fact, the remarkable mobility of Lee's force was a great source of pride to him and to his men. It was a principle with him, proof of the hardihood and good discipline of his legion, to astonish everyone with his speed of movement. In three days his detachment covered seventy-five miles.

At the point where his line of march to Augusta approached most closely to Ninety-Six, Lee sent a squadron of horse under Major Rudolph to Ninety-Six to capture some prisoners if possible and discover Cruger's intentions. Rudolph failed to capture any members of the garrison, but two farmers told him that Cruger, far from planning to abandon Ninety-Six, was busy strengthening its defenses in anticipation of an attack. Lee also learned that the annual royal present to the Indians had arrived at Fort Galphin, about twelve miles south of Augusta on the Savannah River, which was garrisoned by two companies of infantry. Taking a detachment of his dragoons with a picked group of infantry mounted behind them, Lee started at daylight for Fort Galphin and arrived a few hours later at the pine barrens that skirted the field surrounding the fort. The day was stiflingly hot. The men had had no water and many were weak from dehydration, but Lee was determined to persevere. A small detachment of infantry was directed to advance on the fort from the opposite direction, with the hope of drawing the defenders out in pursuit of them. The ruse worked as Lee had intended; the garrison sallied forth to capture the little band of infantrymen, and Lee's infantry, or those not too exhausted for one final effort, rushed the fort while the dragoons, supported by the remainder of the infantry, went to the rescue of the militia. The demoralized defenders surrendered at once. Lee lost one man from heat prostration; the enemy suffered only three or four casualties in the brief skirmishing. The Indian gift was a welcome haul—powder, ball, small arms, liquor, salt, blankets, "with sundry small articles" dear to the Indians.

Lee next undertook to make contact with Colonel Clarke and a body of Georgia militia rumored to be in the area, and he sent a bold message to Brown at Augusta demanding that he surrender the post. Brown was tougher than Maxwell. He refused to even answer Lee's letter "and forbade the renewal of such communication." By the twenty-second of May, Lee, along with Clarke and Pickens, who were almost as mobile as Lee, had taken up a position west of Augusta and on the south side of the river. The town itself lay in the midst of an oblong plain, with the river to the east and a dense woods on the west. It was dominated by Fort Cornwallis, a stout, well-built structure surrounded by abatis and a ditch and garrisoned by regulars under the command of Brown. A half mile up the river was another smaller fort, Fort Grierson; occupied by militia, it guarded the water approaches to Fort Cornwallis. Lee's strategy was to drive out the defenders of Fort Grierson and intercept them if they tried to take refuge in Fort Cornwallis. Pickens was to attack from the north and west, while a battalion under Major Pinketham Eaton, passing down the river, was to advance from the south. Lee, with the six-pounder, was also to place himself to the south of the fort to support Eaton's attack and intercept Brown if he ventured out to try to rescue the defenders of Fort Grierson. The cavalry were stationed near Fort Cornwallis in concealment, ready to attack Brown's rear if he should come after Lee. The attack began much as Lee had planned it. Brown did indeed advance from Fort Cornwallis, but, uncertain as to the number of enemy soldiers opposed to him, he was afraid to venture far from his home base. Fort Grierson, attacked on all sides by a much superior force, was quickly overrun. Again there was a grim episode of "Tarleton's quarter." Despite the efforts of the patriot officers, Grierson was killed, along with his major and a number of the Loyalist militia, by the enraged Georgia militia after their surrender. A few escaped to the river and reached Fort Cornwallis. The American casualties were some dozen killed or wounded.

While Brown worked feverishly to strengthen the fort's defenses, Lee began a formal investiture and the construction of a succession of trenches to starve the defenders into submission. On two successive nights, Brown attacked the troops guarding the sappers and each time was driven back after a sharp fight. Lee, unable to find ground from which his six-pounder could command the fort, recalled Maham's tower for riflemen at the siege of Fort Watson and decided to adapt the idea for his artillery piece. The tower was constructed under the cover of an old house; it was brought to a point of ground where the platform at its top was nearly level with the enemy's parapet, and its body was filled with earth, stones, and brick to give strength and solidity to the structure. Lee felt sure that Brown would attempt a sally to destroy the tower, and he heavily reinforced the infantry assigned to guard it. The same night, Brown directed a feint at the trenches running from the river and made his major attack against the tower. Pickens's militia gave a good account of themselves, but they could not stand against the bayonets of the British regulars. Colonel Handy with his Maryland Continentals came to Pickens's rescue with a bayonet attack, and the British were driven back into the fort.

Brown, defeated in the field, began the construction of a tower of his own, from which artillery could be directed at the men working on "Maham tower." But Lee's tower was completed on the first of June, and the next day the six-pounder was drawn up by a block and tackle. The artillery officer in charge, Captain Finley, gave his attention first to destroying Brown's tower and dismounting his cannon. That night Brown sent a Scottish sergeant of the artillery, posing as a deserter, to Lee. He professed to be disenchanted with Brown, gave what was apparently full and candid information about the condition of the fort, and proposed to Lee that the six-pounder should fire hot shot in an effort to blow up the fort's powder magazine and force its surrender. Since the Americans were unfamiliar with the technique of heating and loading red-hot balls, Lee asked the deserter to instruct Finley in the proper procedure and sent him off to the artillery tower. Lying down to sleep, Lee began to worry about the possibility that the sergeant had really been sent to sabotage the six-pounder. Without it, the reduction of the fort would be much more difficult, if not impossible. Lee got up and sent a message to take the sergeant from the tower and place him under guard, and then went back to sleep with an easier mind.

Between the American positions and Fort Cornwallis were five deserted houses that Lee had anticipated using for cover in the final assault. That same morning, Brown's soldiers stole out before daylight and set three of them on fire. The question that Lee puzzled over was why two houses had been left; one in particular was in an excellent position to command the parapets of the fort.

The fire from the six-pounder was now directed at the enemy palisades facing the river, because it was from this direction that the intended attack was to take place the next morning and it was here that the trenches had been extended farthest towards the walls of the fort. Handy's Marylanders and Lee's infantry legion were to carry the main assault. During the night Lee sent a party of selected riflemen to the house nearest the fort. They were told to scout out firing positions on the second floor of the building (from which they could fire into the fort in support of the attack), determine the number of riflemen the building could hold, and then return to the American lines. The plan was to send back the requisite number of riflemen before dawn to take up firing positions in the house. About three o'clock in the morning, as the soldiers waited in their assigned positions for the signal to begin the attack, the house that the riflemen were to occupy in a few minutes blew sky-high, blinding watchers with the glare and filling the air with planks, bricks and plaster. Brown had left the house intact, while burning the others, in hopes that the Americans would use it as a firing point—precisely what they intended to do. By blowing it up, Brown had hoped not only to kill the soldiers in it, but also to divert and demoralize the entire attack.

Pickens and Lee decided to give Brown one final chance to surrender. An officer was sent to the fort under a flag of truce. Brown repeated his determination to defend his post, but there was a hint that his resolution was weakening, and the American commanders decided to delay their attack for another day. The next day an officer from the fort appeared under a flag of truce with an offer to surrender under conditions that were unacceptable to Pickens and Lee. Another day was spent in negotiations, which saved Brown the embarrassment of capitulating on the king's birthday. Actually twelve messages passed between Brown and Lee and Marion before final terms were agreed to. At eight o'clock on the morning of June 5 the British garrison, except for Brown himself, marched out. Lee feared that the Georgia militia could not be prevented from murdering Brown if he appeared on the field; he thus ordered a company of dragoons to defend him. In Georgia, which had so long been left to its own devices, the warfare between Tories and patriots had reached its bitterest point, until, in Lee's words, "at length in this quarter a war of extermination became the order of the day." Georgians of both factions neither gave nor expected quarter but fought like cornered animals, knowing that the outcome of capture would almost invariably be death. Safe in Lee's headquarters, Brown admitted that he had sent the sergeant-deserter to attempt to burn down the Maham tower under the guise of directing the fire of the six-pounder.

While Pickens and Lee were occupied in the siege of Fort Cornwallis, Greene had moved against Ninety-Six, arriving in front of that strong fort on May 22. Greene had about a thousand men under his command. Marion remained near Georgetown after capturing it, and Sumter, who had finally joined Greene at Friday's Ferry, was detached to cover the area south and west of the Congaree. Ninety-Six, which got its name from the fact that it was ninety-six miles from the main town of the Cherokee Indians, was the principal town between the Saluda River, a branch of the Congaree, and the Savannah, which marked the southern boundary of South Carolina. With Camden to the north and Augusta to the south, the three posts secured, to a degree at least, British control of the Western Carolinas. Camden had been abandoned; Augusta was under siege. Now Greene prepared to invest and reduce Ninety-Six, the last post in the lower South held by the British, aside from the coastal cities of Savannah and Charles Town. Lieutenant Colonel Cruger, a New York Tory, commanded at Ninety-Six a garrison that amounted to five hundred and fifty men, of whom three hundred and fifty were American regulars—Tories who, like Cruger, had enlisted in the British army. The rest of the defenders were South Carolina Loyalists.

To the left of the village a small creek furnished water to the garrison. The fort defending the village was a stockade with stout palisades built in the form of a star with "sixteen salient and re-entering angles, with a ditch, fraise, and abatis." Cruger had erected blockhouses at strategic points, with covered communication trenches between the various works, and had done everything that an energetic and experienced officer could do to strengthen the fortifications. Kosciusko, the most experienced engineer in Greene's army, was given the task of directing the siege operations. Ignoring the opportunity to cut off the fort's supply of water, which Lee clearly thought the best move, Kosciusko concentrated his efforts on the star, which was the strong point in the defensive system. His efforts to approach it by a trench were blocked, however, by Cruger's movement of three artillery pieces that covered an attack on the American working parties. The soldiers guarding the sappers were routed and a number bayoneted, with the loss of only one British officer. The American trenches were destroyed, and Kosciusko had to begin once more from a less exposed position.

Day after day the tedious work went forward. Lee, after the surrender of Fort Cornwallis, had left Pickens behind, and he joined Greene at Ninety-Six on June 8. Although a lot of earth had been moved, discouragingly little progress had been made toward reducing the fort. It was Lee's opinion that Kosciusko was much too conventional in his thinking. He had no imagination, as Lee put it, "not a spark of the ethereal in his composition." He knew only conventional siege techniques. Lee's corps, assigned to a position on the left of the fort, pushed its trenches so rapidly that within a few days a battery was ready for the six-pounder. Cruger, watching the trenches inching their way slowly towards his fortifications, realized that his only hope lay in a series of forays that would seriously disrupt and delay the siege works: by "nocturnal sallies . . ." to "destroy with the spade whatever he might gain by the bayonet." But Greene was ready for him, and every sally was turned back. Nevertheless, the attacks "became extremely harassing to the American army," Lee wrote, "whose repose during the night was incessantly disturbed, and whose labor in the day was as incessantly pressed." The American cannon was moved forward to the second parallel, and Cruger was exhorted to surrender. He refused with a flourish, expressing a "perfect disregard of General Greene's promises or threats." The cannonading and the digging continued.

Meantime Lord Rawdon at Charles Town received reinforcements—three regiments from Ireland—and set out on the seventh of June to raise the seige of Ninety-Six. The army under his command consisted of some two thousand men. Afraid that Cruger might despair of help and surrender the fort, Rawdon did everything he could to get word to him that he was on his way.

Sumter sent word to Greene of the arrival of the regiments from Ireland and of Rawdon's advance to Ninety-Six. Since the distance from Charles Town to Ninety-Six was over a hundred miles, it was not likely that Rawdon could reach his destination in less than six or seven days at the earliest. If Sumter could delay Rawdon's advance, Greene might still force the surrender of Ninety-Six. William Washington was sent to reinforce Sumter, Marion was summoned in from his position, and Pickens, who arrived from Augusta, was also sent to support Sumter. So far, Cruger had no knowledge of Rawdon's advance—no messenger had been able to get through the American lines to the fort. Then one day a farmer appeared, riding along the American lines, chatting with the soldiers. He was taken to be one of the local countrymen who were accustomed to visiting camp, going "wherever their curiosity led them" and often bringing food for sale or barter. But before anyone could make a move to intercept him, the "farmer" spurred his horse and dashed to the gates of the fort, triumphantly waving a letter from Rawdon urging Cruger to hold out and promising him speedy relief. On the seventeenth, the garrison's water was finally cut off and a Maham tower was completed that would enable the American artillery to command the parapets. Two patriot trenches and a mine had nearly reached the ditch running around the fortifications. Just when success seemed near, however, word came that Rawdon had eluded Sumter and was within a day's march of the American positions. Greene's choices were to fight Rawdon, make an immediate assault on the fort, or withdraw.

Greene's own choice was the last alternative, but, according to Lee, the troops were dismayed at the prospect of wasting more than three weeks of backbreaking labor and marching off when the prize was so nearly in hand: "they supplicated their officers" to urge Greene to order an attack. "This generous ardor could not be resisted. . . ." Orders were issued for an attack at noon on June 19.

The American formation had William Campbell with the First Virginia Regiment on the left, along with a detachment from the Maryland and Virginia brigades. Lee, with his legion infantry and Robert Kirkwood's Delawares, was to advance on the right. The attacking echelons were furnished with fascines to fill up the enemy's ditch and long poles to pull down the sandbags on top of the parapets. At eleven o'clock the third parallel was manned as the jump-off point of the attack, and the riflemen mounted their Maham towers. The signal for the attack was the firing of the American artillery in the center, and the Americans rushed to the attack with a shout. The patriots were quickly under the parapets, and the issue at once appeared to hinge on whether the poles with hooks would succeed in pulling off the sandbags and thereby making a breech through which Campbell's Virginians could force their way. Cruger now concentrated the fire of three artillery pieces on the point where Campbell's men were trying to open a passage, and the officer in command of the star redoubt, seeing how close the attackers were to success, ordered a bayonet counterattack. His men issued through a sally port at the rear of the redoubt, split right and left, came around through the ditch, and converged on the Americans. Campbell's men thus suddenly found themselves attacked from three directions. The American officers commanding the attack were wounded, and the Virginia and Maryland brigades on the right were forced back with very heavy losses.

The situation on the left took a different course. Rudolph and his men reached the ditch and fought their way into the fort, not having to climb as precipitous a wall. The defenders in that part of the fortifications fled, and Lee was preparing to exploit the penetration when Greene, alarmed by the casualties that had been suffered by the troops on the right, decided to "return to his cardinal policy, the preservation of adequate force to keep the field," and called off the attack. A hundred and eighty-five Americans had been killed and wounded in the course of the siege, most of them during the attack. The garrison had lost eighty-five. The only American officer killed was Captain Armstrong of the Maryland Line, one of the army's best junior officers.

There was deep gloom among the Americans. Three days more would have doubtless been enough to insure the reduction of the fortifications. Greene, on the other hand, although disappointed at failing to reduce the fort, was delighted with the performance of his soldiers. They had attacked a strongly fortified position with great spirit, had sustained a heavy counterattack, had refused to panic, and had on every score given a good account of themselves. The memory of Hobkirk's Hill was, if not eradicated—it could never be that—in large measure relieved. It was as though an errant son had been restored to the good graces of his father. Greene's confidence in his soldiers revived. That was the only benefit, but not an inconsiderable one, of the abortive siege of Ninety-Six.

Now Greene had to run again. But he ran in much better humor, a fact that soon conveyed itself to his troops, who marched through the dust and heat of a South Carolina June with a lighter step. Rawdon, at first determined to pursue Greene and if possible force a battle, found himself so busily engaged with Lee and Washington, who formed Greene's rear guard, that he returned to Ninety-Six and made plans to evacuate the post. He could not remain there to defend it himself, and his withdrawal would simply expose it once more to an attack by Greene's army. Thus Rawdon and Cruger began their march by different routes to Charles Town, with Lee's cavalry close on their heels and Greene himself only a day's march behind. At Friday's Ferry, Lee's dragoons under the command of Captain Joseph Eggleston surprised an enemy foraging party and captured forty-five dragoons without a single American casualty. Rawdon and Cruger joined forces at Orangeburg and established headquarters there.

The soldiers of Greene's army suffered from heat and hunger in almost equal degrees. Their rations had been reduced to a few handfuls of rice a day. It was impossible to get beef; some of the more enterprising tried alligator meat, and giant bullfrogs from the swamps were soon incorporated in the soldiers' ration. Greene decided to go into "summer quarters" in High Hills of the Santee, where the climate was cooler and food more abundant. There "the troops were placed in good quarters, and the heat of July was rendered tolerable by the high ground, the fine air, and the good water of the selected camp."

Greene's South Carolina campaign, after the bitter disappointment of Hobkirk's Hill, had brought an almost unbroken succession of triumphs, minor ones to be sure, but of considerable importance in the aggregate. "Defeat," Lee wrote, "had been changed . . . into victory, and our repulse [at Hobkirk's Hill] had been followed by accession of territory. The conquered states were regained, and our exiled countrymen were restored to their deserted homes,—sweet rewards of toil and peril. Such results can only be attributed to superior talents, seconded by skill, courage, and fidelity. Fortune often gives victory; but when the weak, destitute of the essential means of war, successfully oppose the strong, it is not chance but sublime genius which guides the intermediate operations, and controls the ultimate event."

For all intents and purposes the war was over in the South. There was to be a dramatic last act a few months later at Eutaw Springs, South Carolina, but the issue had been decided, by and large, at Guilford Court House, where the victor, thoroughly defeated, turned away to campaign in more congenial country.

The Southern campaigns are less well known than the campaigns in the North, perhaps in part (as some Southerners have suggested) because the history of the Revolution has been most commonly written by Yankees, but it is every bit as interesting and as important as the better-known operations in the middle and eastern states. It is full of striking and dramatic episodes, of heroic actions and villainous acts. A vast area, far from the center of the stage in Boston, New York, and Philadelphia, was seized by the British. The patriots, without anything but hindrance from their French allies, met initially with disastrous setbacks but finally, in a campaign that is a textbook study in the tactics and techniques of partisan warfare, recovered, for all practical purposes, the Carolinas and Georgia. The use of cavalry was developed there more successfully than by either side in any other theater of the war. Indeed, it is not too much to say that only a few other cavalry officers in history have shown the skill and resourcefulness of that remarkable youth, "Light-Horse Harry" Lee. In Greene, the Southern campaign had its general, pre-eminent in those qualities which make for military success; in Lee it had, besides its dashing young cavalry leader, its great chronicler, a man who wrote a classic history worthy of a place beside the greatest military annals.

Lee had graduated from Princeton at the age of seventeen and had been about to leave for England to study law at the Middle Temple when the war broke out. After the war he fell into a despondency bordering on melancholia. Having commanded a skilled and devoted company of men in a series of brilliant engagements, he had passed through experiences of such intensity that peacetime society seemed pallid by comparison. Lee was a born soldier who at the age of twenty-six found no more play for his genius. He was like a great actor barred from the stage after his first dazzling success. Greene, who was like a father to Lee, wrote in January, 1782, "I have beheld with extreme anxiety, for some time past a growing discontent in your mind, and have not been without my apprehensions that your complaints originated more in distress than in the ruin of your constitution. Whatever may be the source of your wounds, I wish it was in my power to heal them." In the words of his son, Robert E. Lee, he left the army "in sickness and sorrow."

Back in Virginia after the war, Henry Lee, following what was almost a tradition in that state, married his cousin, Matilda Lee, heiress of the great mansion at Stratford. He served in Congress from 1785 to 1788, was active in the political affairs of Virginia as a Federalist, and when his wife died in 1790, seriously considered going to France and seeking a commission in the French republican army. It would, indeed, have been a strange turnabout if "Light-Horse Harry" Lee had distinguished himself as a soldier in France and perhaps become, in time, an officer under Napoleon. He was prevailed on to run for governor of Virginia instead, and he served in that office from 1792 to 1795. Washington placed him in command of fifteen thousand troops raised to suppress the Whiskey Rebellion in 1794. In 1793 Lee remarried, this time to Anne Hill Carter of Shirley, heiress of another great Virginia family (Robert E. Lee was the son of this marriage), and six years later he was back in Congress in time to pronounce the brief but timeless eulogy of Washington as "first in war, first in peace, and first in the hearts of his countrymen."

From this point on Lee followed the path by no means unfamiliar to many Virginia aristocrats. Living with that openhanded lavishness characteristic of his class and engaged in numerous speculative ventures, he found himself deeper and deeper in debt. In 1808 he was imprisoned for debt and wrote his great *Memoirs of the War in the Southern Department of the United States.* Most ironically, the old soldier of the Revolution (he was then fifty-six) was badly injured by a Baltimore mob in one of the bitter riots caused by Jefferson's policy of embargo. He went to the West Indies to convalesce (his enemies said to escape his creditors), and when it was apparent, three or four years later, that he was dying, he was shipped back to the United States and landed in Savannah, where Nathanael Greene's daughter nursed him through the last months of his life on her plantation on Cumberland Island, Georgia.

Lee's coadjutor, Francis Marion, was as skillful and tenacious as the Virginian. It was a credit to both men that they marched and fought together in complete harmony. As for the Carolinian's contributions to the patriot cause in the Southern campaign, General Greene can perhaps be allowed to speak the conclusive word. Greene wrote to Marion on April 24, 1781, "When I consider how much you have done and suffered, and under what disadvantages you have maintained your ground, I am at a loss which to admire most, your courage and fortitude or your address and management. Certain it is no man has a better claim to the public thanks or is more generally admired than you are. History affords no instance wherein an officer has kept possession of a country under as many disadvantages as you have. Surrounded on every side with a superior force, hunted from every quarter with veteran troops, you have found means to elude all their attempts, and to keep alive the expiring hopes of an oppressed militia. . . . To fight the enemy bravely with a prospect of victory is nothing; but to fight with intrepidity under the constant impression of defeat, and inspire irregular troops to do it, is a talent peculiar to yourself."

PART X

Morristown, 1779–80

AFTER Harry Lee's raid on Paulus Hook in August, 1779, and the abortive expedition to Penobscot Bay (in which Washington and the Continental Army, had, of course, no part), Washington prepared to go into winter quarters. "The operations of the enemy this campaign," he wrote to Lafayette in Paris, where the young Frenchman was trying to recruit more French aid, "have been confined to the establishment of works of defence, taking a post at King's Ferry, and burning the defenceless towns of New Haven, Fairfield, and Norwalk . . . where little else was or could be opposed to them, than the cries of distressed women and helpless children; but these were offered in vain." The British evacuated Newport, Rhode Island, under the threat of a new French fleet and abandoned Stony Point, which they had reoccupied unopposed after Anthony Wayne's withdrawal in July.

Washington decided to establish his own headquarters once more in the Ford home at Morristown, with the main body of his army in tents some three miles from town. His army had shrunk to a few more than three thousand men, and on December 16 he wrote to Joseph Reed, president of Congress: "The situation of the Army, with respect to supplies, is beyond description, alarming. It has been five or six weeks past on half-allowance, and we have not more than three days bread at a third allowance, on hand, nor any where within reach. When this is exhausted, we must depend on the precarious gleanings of the neighboring country. . . . We have never experienced a like extremity at any period of the war."

Nathanael Greene, who was then functioning as quartermaster general at Middletown and was often too outspoken for his own good, wrote John Sullivan in Morristown, "Our military exertions however great, leave us but a dull prospect, while administration is torn to pieces by faction, and the business of finance is in distress. False pride & secret enmity poison our councils, & distract our measures; indeed the States are so local in their policy, that we are more like individuals than a united body."

Joseph Martin, freezing and starving, confirmed Washington's account of conditions at Morristown: "Provisions failed more and more," he wrote, "till ¼ pound of meat or bread per day was all we could get to live upon. . . . At last provisions wholly failed and 4 days passed without a mouthful to eat, on the 5th day we drew a gill of wheat measured out to each maw; this only sharpened up their appetites, but had to endure another 4 days of fasting, we had now got beyond hunger but faint & weak."

On the fifth day, before sunrise, there was noise in the camp. It was Washington, "wading in the snow, leading his horse and calling at every hut, speaking kindly to all the soldiers & saying the first he knew of their sufferings was the night before, and he had not slept a moment during the night, but . . . was on his way to see & sympathize with the suffering soldiers." Touched by their general's presence among them, the men "rejoiced to see him & hear his voice." Washington, in turn, was so moved by their fortitude and loyalty that "tears rolled down his cheeks in torrents." Before nightfall enough beef had arrived to give each soldier a quarter of a pound. When the stewards passed out the slim portion, most of the men gulped it down raw, and "it so sharpened their appetites they were almost raving mad," Martin reported. The next day there was a quarter of a pound of bread. It was not surprising that there were bitter complaints from the soldiers. Washington wrote: "There has never been a stage of the war in which dissatisfaction has been so general and alarming," and a week later he noted, "We see in every line of the army the most serious features of mutiny and sedition." The officers of the New Jersey Line dispatched a memorial to the state assembly declaring that "four months' pay of a private would not procure for his family a single bushel of wheat; that the pay of a colonel would not purchase oats for his horse; that a common laborer received four times as much as an American officer."

While Washington struggled to survive another winter, far more bitterly cold than the one at Valley Forge two years earlier, the British garrison in New York watched uneasily as the waterways surrounding the island of Manhattan froze to such a depth that, for the first time in the memory of any living person, heavy carriages could drive across to the mainland. By the same token, American soldiers and cannon could make their way to the city from the Jersey shore. Knyphausen, in command of the city, issued a call for civilian volunteers from ages sixteen to sixty to take up arms in defense of New York. In a few days forty companies had been formed and armed, amounting to nearly three thousand men, "many substantial citizens serving in the ranks of each company. Other volunteer companies were formed: and the city was put into a very strong posture of defence." Indeed the civilian volunteers almost doubled the size of the garrison Clinton had left behind when he sailed for South Carolina in December, and they unquestionably served to discourage Washington from his plans to attack the city. It must have been maddening for him to find his plans frustrated by the alacrity with which Americans had rallied to the British standard, when he was so desperately trying to recruit soldiers for the defense of American independence.

Afraid to risk his poorly equipped army in an attack on the city, Washington contented himself with a raid led by Lord Stirling against Staten Island, which was garrisoned by some eighteen hundred British soldiers. Stirling attacked with twenty-seven hundred men supported by artillery and mortars. After seizing some two hundred head of cattle, he withdrew, alarmed by news of an expedition that had set out from New York under Knyphausen with the intention of coming to the aid of the British garrison.

Martin, who was with Lord Stirling in his raid on Staten Island, had vivid memories of the hardships of that winter foray. After a few brief skirmishes, Martin and his fellows "fell back a little distance and took up our abode for the night upon a bare bleak hill, in full rake of the northwest wind, with no other covering or shelter than the canopy of the heavens, and no fuel but some rotten old rails which we dug up through the snow, which was two or three feet deep. The weather was cold enough to cut a man in two."

As the Americans withdrew to Morristown, the British pursued and harassed them. "We arrived in camp," Martin noted, "after a tedious and cold march of many hours, some with frozen toes, some with frozen fingers and ears, and half-starved into the bargain." Camp was hardly better than the field. In one stretch of four days almost four feet of snow fell. "We were absolutely, literally starved," Martin wrote. "I do solemnly declare that I did not put a single morsel of victuals into my mouth for four days and as many nights, except a little black birch bark which I gnawed off a stick of wood, if that can be called victuals. I saw several of the men roast their old shoes and eat them, and I was afterwards informed by one of the officer's waiters, that some of the officers killed and ate a favorite little dog that belonged to one of them. . . . The fourth day, just at dark, we obtained a half pound of lean fresh beef and a gill of wheat for each man; whether we had any salt to season so delicious a morsel, I have forgotten, but I am sure we had no bread, except the wheat, but I will assure the reader that we had the best of sauce; that is, we had keen appetites. When the wheat was so swelled by boiling as to be beyond the danger of swelling in the stomach, it was deposited there without ceremony."

The Connecticut troops, the reader will recall, had earlier been on the verge of mutiny; Joseph Martin told of the angry mood of his fellow soldiers early in the winter of 1778–79, which had been alleviated in part by furloughing many of the rebellious men. Now the Connecticut Line was in a rebellious mood once more. The most immediate grievance was short rations. Martin notes that there was a little beef but no bread, some rice but no flour.

By May Martin, who had been on outpost duty at Elizabethtown, where American and British patrols clashed constantly and where a close friend of his was bayoneted to death in such an encounter, had joined the main army at Basking Ridge. "Here," he wrote, "the monster Hunger, still attended us. He was not to be shaken off by any efforts we could use, for here was the old story of starving as rife as ever. . . . For several days after we rejoined the army, we got a little musty bread and a little beef, about every other day, but this lasted only a short time and then we got nothing at all. The men were now exasperated beyond endurance; they could not stand it any longer. They saw no alternative but to starve to death, or break up the army, give all up and go home."

It was a bitter dilemma. In Martin's words: "Here was the army starved and naked, and there their country sitting still and expecting the army to do notable things, while fainting from sheer starvation. All things considered, the army was not to be blamed. Reader, suffer what he did and you will say so, too."

At the end of their patience, "the men spent most of their time upon the parade [grounds] growling like soreheaded dogs. At evening roll call they began to show their dissatisfaction by snapping at the officers and acting contrary to orders." On May 25, a flare-up between the adjutant and a soldier, in which the officer called the soldier a "mutinous rascal," resulted in the soldier calling out, "Who will parade with me?" His whole regiment fell in and was joined by two others. They wished to have no particular soldier in charge who might later be court-martialed, so they instructed the drummer to give orders on the drums. "At the first signal," Martin wrote, "we shouldered our arms, at the second we faced, at the third we began our march to join with the other two regiments, and went off with music playing."

As word of the actions of the Second Connecticut Regiment spread, other regiments were called out without guns by their officers. When the soldiers of the Sixth Connecticut tried, in opposition to their orders, to get their guns, Colonel Return Jonathan Meigs barred the way. There was a sharp scuffle, and Meigs, who had always considered himself "the soldier's friend," was badly slashed in the side by a bayonet. Thwarted in their effort to join with the other Connecticut regiments, the Second Connecticut marched back to its regimental area, followed by officers haranguing the men for their mutinous behavior. When one soldier called out the order to halt, "the officers seized upon him like wolves on a sheep and dragged him out of the ranks, intending to make an example of him for being 'a mutinous rascal,' but the bayonets of the men pointing at their breasts as thick as hatched teeth, compelled them quickly to relinquish their hold of him."

The men were now urged to return to their quarters, and when they refused, an officer ran up and announced, "There is good news for you, boys, there has just arrived a large drove of cattle for the army." But the stratagem failed. "Go and butcher them, then," one of the soldiers called out, amid general laughter.

Lieutenant Colonel John Sumner now had his turn at trying to persuade the men to return to their quarters. "After a good deal of palaver, he ordered them to shoulder their arms," and when they refused he began to denounce them in the bitterest terms, with "a whole quiver of the arrows of his rhetoric." There was no more response than before, and the colonel "walked off to his quarters, chewing the cud of resentment all the way. . . ."

Meanwhile the soldiers of the Pennsylvania Line were ordered out by their officers on a "secret expedition" and were distributed in such a way as to surround the Connecticut regiments without either themselves or the Connecticut men being aware of what was afoot. When the Pennsylvanians learned "what was going on among the Yankees"—that is to say, that they had mutinied because of the lack of food—some called out, "Let us join them. Let us join the Yankees; they are good fellows, and have no notion of lying here like fools and starving." At this the Pennsylvanians were quickly withdrawn by their officers before they could become directly involved in the mutiny. While some of the Connecticut soldiers returned to their huts to get what sleep they could, others stayed on the parade ground, "venting our spleen at our country and government, then at our officers, and then at ourselves for our imbecility in staying there and starving in detail for an ungrateful people who did not care what became of us, so they could enjoy themselves while we were keeping a cruel enemy from them." Martin continued, "While we were thus venting our gall against we knew not who," Colonel Walter Stewart of the Pennsylvania Line, so handsome he was called "the Irish Beauty" by the ladies of Philadelphia, came with two or three officers to make another effort to placate the soldiers. Like the others he chided the men for their unsoldierlike conduct. Why hadn't they taken their grievances to their officers? Stewart asked.

They had done that, the men replied, but had gotten no satisfaction.

"But," Stewart said, "your officers suffer as much as you do. We all suffer. The officers have no money to purchase supplies with any more than the private men have, and if there is nothing in the public store we must fare as hard as you. I have no other resources than you have to depend upon. I have not a sixpence to purchase a partridge that was offered to me the other day. Besides . . . you know not how much you injure your own characters by such conduct. You Connecticut troops have won immortal honor to yourselves the winter past, by your perseverance, patience, and bravery, and now you are shaking it off at your heels."

The talk had its effect. There was no mutiny in the men's hearts, just bitterness and despair. They gave up their "mutiny" as quickly as they had raised it. "Our stir," Martin noted, "did us some good in the end, for we had provisions directly after, so we had no great cause for complaint for some time." It was a strange mutiny, as brief and frustrating as the earlier one.

As usual, Washington was much preoccupied with Congress, in addition to trying to preserve his army at Morristown.

In January, buoyed up by the earlier American successes at Stony Point and Paulus Hook and by an apparent stalemate in the South, the North Carolina delegates to Congress wrote the governor of their state that although the quota of supplies assigned to North Carolina for the Continental Army was "far beyond what is their supposed proportion" (every other state thought the same), it should be promptly provided. Failure to comply, they wrote, "might be ruinous to the Cause we are engaged in; and which is now happily drawing to a glorious conclusion."

The concluding comment was a familiar one. Congress had been expecting British acknowledgment of American independence since the spring of 1778—from the time, roughly, of the evacuation of Philadelphia by Howe, the French treaty, and the Battle of Monmouth. The Carlisle commission had played a crucial part in the formation of such a feeling. If the British had been willing to make concessions just short of independence *before* they knew of the French treaty, surely they would grant independence once the treaty was concluded.

The problems of financing the Revolution were certainly enormous, perhaps even insurmountable, but time after time Congress procrastinated, afraid of trying to apply the most radical remedy, taxation. On the ninth of January, Washington wrote to General William Irvine, "Our affairs are in so deplorable a condition (on the score of provisions) as to fill the mind with the most anxious and alarming fears ... men half starved, imperfectly cloathed, riotous, and robbing the country people of their subsistence from sheer necessity." Justifying his requisitions to the counties for supplies, Washington wrote the New Jersey officials, "For a Fortnight past the Troops, both officers and men, have been almost perishing for want. They have been alternately without Bread or Meat the whole time. . . . They are now reduced to an extremity no longer to be supported." As General Greene noted, "It is folly to expect that this expensive department can be long supported on credit. A further attempt would only bring ruin and distress upon ourselves, without affording any substantial advantage, either to the public or the army." Congress had issued a call to the states for certain categories of supplies, but in Greene's view the measure "falls far short of the general detail of the business, the difficulty of adjusting which, between the different agents as well as the different authorities from which they derive their appointments, I am very apprehensive will introduce some jarring interests—many improper disputes as well as dangerous delays."

The baffling part of the whole business was that there were provisions aplenty. "I have authentic reasons to conclude," Greene wrote, "that the country is more plentifully stored with every material necessary for the provision and support of an army, than it has been for three years past. The defect lies in the want of a proper means to draw them into public use." The president of Congress was of the same opinion. "The country abounds with the necessary Resources," he wrote, "but private gain seemed the only object of too many Individuals, without any concern for the public safety." As a delegate from North Carolina put it in a letter to that state's assembly, "The exertions of Congress are no longer competent; and, unless the States exert themselves the Cause is utterly lost; and we shall be left in a situation the most wretched among human beings—that is, exposed to all the Oppressions and Insults of the enraged, Victorious, and avaricious Tyranny."

There was constant tension between Congress and the commander in chief. Washington wanted more men, and, of course, more supplies, but some delegates felt that he had cried wolf too often. Since all efforts to supply his army adequately had failed, perhaps the size of the army should be reduced. Great Britain could not in any event reduce America to its former state of subordination, so it was only necessary to persevere until the inevitable fact of American independence had finally penetrated the consciousnesses of the king and his ministers. Nothing was to be gained by more costly and inconclusive military campaigns. The initiative should be left to the British, who would finally tire of the effort to conquer a land that would not be conquered.

The congressmen who held such views resented the pressures from the French Court to press ahead with military campaigns. Since the French were far more interested in whittling down the military power of England than in American independence, they plainly preferred a war of attrition in which the resources of Great Britain would be gradually—or even better, rapidly—exhausted. Vergennes and the French ministers wished to use the Continental Army as the principal instrument in this attrition. For their purposes it was necessary that the American army should fight as often and as fiercely as possible. It was for this reason that they provided large quantities of supplies and substantial amounts of money. In Elbridge Gerry's words, the failure to undertake active campaigning in 1780 would "renew the uneasiness of the Court of France, who last year remonstrated in very friendly but *expressive* Terms, against the Delays of our military preparations for that Campaign."

Robert Livingston, on the other hand, went so far as to move that all Continental troops whose enlistments expired in April should be dismissed, and that the eighty battalions of the army be reduced to sixty. In the midst of the discussion of Livingston's motion, Chevalier de la Luzerne, who had replaced Gérard as French minister at Philadelphia, pressured Congress to support Washington. "The present situation of the affairs of the alliance in Europe," he declared, "announces the necessity of another campaign, which is indispensable to bring England to an acknowledgement of the independence of the thirteen United States." In Luzerne's (and his government's) view, "the only means of putting an end to the calamities of war is to push it with new vigour; to take measures immediately for completing the army, and putting it in condition to begin an early campaign." If Congress had grown impervious to Washington's pleas, they still responded to French pressure. They hastened to assure Luzerne that they intended to build the army up to twenty-five thousand men. James Lovell, who had no love for the French, put the matter sardonically: "We must cut our Throats for another year at least, and we ought to do it vigorously."

Responding to Luzerne's prodding, Congress on February 9 requested the states "to furnish, by draughts or otherwise, on or before the first day of April next, their deficiencies of the number of 35,211, exclusive of commissioned officers, which Congress deem necessary for the service of the present year." As with the allocation of quotas for provisions and supplies for the Continental Army, there was much wrangling among the states over the numbers of men they were each charged with raising. Samuel Huntington, the president of Congress, anticipated some of the states' disgruntlements by writing in a circular letter that "the Quotas apportioned to each State may be supposed to be not exactly Just."

In March Congress, in reply to another letter from Washington warning that the army showed an inclination to enter into "seditious combinations," decided to send a committee to reside at Washington's headquarters for the express purpose of reforming the army; the committee was to bring some order into the various staff departments (primarily those involved in procurement of supplies) and remove, where possible, various inequities that were a source of constant irritation to the soldiers and officers. Referred to alternately as the committee of cooperation, the committee at camp, or the committee at headquarters, it was welcomed by Washington, who saw that such a committee, if made up of sympathetic members, could be a great asset in dealing with Congress. "Their authority," he wrote, "should be plenopotentiary, it should draw out men and supplies of every kind and to give their sanction to any operations which the Commander-in-Chief may not think himself at liberty to undertake without it. . . . The Committee can act with dispatch and energy [which, Washington knew by painful experience, Congress could not]—by being on the spot it will be able to provide for exigencies as they arise and the better to judge of their nature and urgency. . . . Circumstanced as we are, the greatest good or the greatest ill must result. We shall probably fix the independence of America if we succeed, and if we fail the abilities of the states will have been so strained in the attempt, that a total relaxation and debility must ensue and the worst is to be apprehended."

The most conspicuous result of these events was to put an end, at least for the moment, to efforts to reduce the size of the army. But it is interesting that sentiment for a reduction existed, and it is evident that those members of Congress who wished to whittle down the Continental forces were convinced that Great Britain could never subdue America and must in time come to accept that fact. Meanwhile, they felt that the United States should avoid bankrupting itself completely to support an army that had done very little fighting for two years and would perhaps best serve the cause by fighting very little in the future.

As Washington had hoped, the Congressional committee soon identified itself wholeheartedly with the army and began to exhort the delegates. They reported "that something more is necessary than mere recommendation, or they will lose an army, and thereby risk the loss of an Empire. Time and exigencies render it sometimes necessary," the committee wrote, "for governing powers to deviate from the strict lines of conduct which Regular Constitutions prescribe. We intreat Congress seriously to consider Whether such times and exigencies do not now exist. If they do, shall Posterity say, that those who directed the affairs of America, at this era, were less intrepid, more attentive to personal consequences than their Predecessors. Heaven forbid the thought!"

On May 31, 1780, Washington wrote to Joseph Jones, a Virginia delegate responsive to Washington's own views, declaring his conviction that unless Congress acted with "more energy than they hitherto have done . . . Our cause is lost. We can no longer drudge on in the old way. By ill-timing the adoption of measures, by delays in the execution of them, or by unwarrantable jealousies we incur enormous expences and derive no benefit from them. One State will comply with a requisition of Congress, another neglects to do it, a third executes it by halves, and all differ either in the manner, the matter, or so much in point of time, that we are always working up-hill and ever shall be unable to apply our strength or resources to any advantage. . . . I see one head gradually changing into thirteen. I see one army branching into thirteen, and instead of its looking up to Congress as the Supreme controuling power of the United States are considering themselves as dependent on their respective States. In a word, I see the powers of Congress declining too fast for the consequence and respect w'ch is due to them as the great representative body of America and I am fearful of the consequences."

Jones was in agreement with Washington. At present, he wrote, Congress was primarily a communications system, "little more than the medium through which the wants of the Army are conveyed to the States. . . ." To Congress itself Washington issued new bulletins of alarm. Unless there was immediate reform in the means of recruiting and supplying the army, he wrote, "our affairs must soon become desperate beyond possibility of recovery." "Indeed, I have almost ceased to hope," Washington added. "The country in general is in such a state of insensibility and indifference to its interests, that I dare not flatter myself with any change for the better."

In its quandary, Congress considered for a time asking the states to give it specific powers for calling up men, requisitioning supplies, and collecting taxes, but there was such deep-seated resistance to the proposal that it was dropped. "Congress in general," one delegate wrote in July, "appears exceeding easy in the present situation of affairs. There doth not appear the most distant wish for more powers, but rather on the contrary, a wish to see their States without control (as the term is) free, sovereign, and independent." The appeal to the states to fill their respective quotas of men and supplies failed, as most people had anticipated, to bring anything like the numbers requested.

"Surely, Sir," Oliver Ellsworth wrote to Governor Trumbull, "they do not expect the war to be carried on without means, nor can they mean to let it drop here. Does it not then behove them to adopt some effectual measures for drawing forth their resources, and that without a moments delay. Can it, Sir, be the design of Heaven, that has roused us to exertions thus far, and armed mighty nations for our support and brought us in sight of the promised rest to leave us after all to destruction, and to lament also the best blood of our land as spilt in vain? I trust not."

By November, 1779, the depreciation of paper money had gotten entirely out of hand. In March, 1780, Congress, at long last took the only course left open to it besides bankruptcy and retired the paper money in circulation by accepting it in payments due from the states at one-fortieth of the face value of the notes. As a writer in the *Independent Chronicle* put it, "The only sovereign remedy that can produce a radical cure is the lessening of the currency. . . . The matter is near to a crisis: we have our choice either to part with our paper and so to save our estates and liberties, or to retain it and so doing lose all. We must either submit to the necessity of the day and tax ourselves voluntarily, or we must submit to the parliament of Great-Britain and be taxed for the little property they may leave us, just as their *omnipotence* shall direct. . . ." The news of Congress's recall of paper money delighted the Tories, of course, and gave fresh hope to those Englishmen who were determined to find hope where they could. An English newspaper reported that "gayety and dissapation" were sought as the antidotes for the latest American disaster. "The Congress has fallen into general contempt, for their want of credit and power; the army is absolute and has declared it will not submit to a peace made by Congress; the people grumble, but are obliged to surrender one piece of furniture after another, even to their beds, to pay their taxes. After all," the writer concluded, "a power drawn from such distant and dissonant parts cannot form a permanent union. The force of this kingdom, moving uniformly from one centre, must in all human probability ultimately prevail; or an accident may produce, in an instant, what the most powerful efforts require time and perseverance to accomplish."

At Morristown, Washington and his staff of eighteen officers were crowded in with Mrs. Ford's own family until there was hardly room to turn around, and "scarce one of them," the general wrote, "able to speak for the colds they have caught." Gradually food was accumulated and the most pressing needs of the army met, but it was the middle of February before the chilblained soldiers had moved out of tents and into huts. The cold remained a cruel foe, however. The snow fell until it was waist high and piled in drifts four and five feet deep. "But guards must be mounted every day," Joseph Martin noted, "and as they marched to their different stations they might be traced by the blood of their feet, they were so destitute of shoes & other clothing it seems cruel to drive them out this hard winter." "The oldest people now living," Washington reported to Lafayette, "do not remember so hard a winter. . . ."

It was April before the snow melted and the army stirred to life once more. The soldiers' spirits revived, as they invariably did, with the return of spring. Baron Von Steuben resumed his drills, and Luzerne arrived with Don Juan de Miralles, "a gentleman of distinction from Spain," for a visit with Washington. Four of the baron's best-clad and best-drilled battalions "were presented for review, by the French minister," who was saluted by thirteen cannon. That night there was a ball at the Morris Hotel, "at which were present a numerous collection of ladies and gentlemen of distinguished character." The only incident to mar the occasion was that Don Juan de Miralles caught pneumonia and died four days later. He was given a handsome funeral, "dressed in rich state, and exposed to public view as is customary in Europe." Washington, with his staff "and numerous respectable citizens, formed a splendid procession," Thacher reported, "extending about one mile."

If warmer weather relieved the suffering of the army, their situation was still a deplorable one. The Congressional committee found that "the men often went for days at a time without meat, that forage for horses was unavailable, and that the hospitals were without sugar, tea, coffee, chocolate, wine or liquor of any kind; that every department of the army was without money, and had not even the shadow of credit left; that the patience of the soldiers, borne down by the pressure of complicated sufferings, was on the point of being exhausted."

Everyone felt better when the Marquis de Lafayette arrived in camp on the fourteenth of May with the welcome news (communicated at once by Benedict Arnold to Sir Henry Clinton) that another French fleet and some six thousand soldiers were on their way to America.

2

Springfield and After

While Clinton was still at Charles Town, General Knyphausen, who had been left in command at New York, received word through his spies that Washington's soldiers were disgruntled and mutinous. It was certain that they were, as usual, underpaid and underfed. To Knyphausen it seemed a most propitious time to make a bold attack on the demoralized Americans. The Hessians had for so long played second fiddle to their British employers—feeling always the sharp edge of British condescension, given the most unpleasant posts, and, as at Fort Mercer, sent on difficult missions improperly supported—that the Hessian officer would have been less than human if he had not wished to bring off a coup that so far had evaded every British commander, the complete route or capture of the Continental Army.

Knyphausen's spies were full of assurances that the Tories of New Jersey were at last ready to rise and give substantial aid to their prospective liberators. Their bitterness over the indiscriminate looting of British soldiers in earlier campaigns had evaporated; their resolution had returned. Since intelligence systems usually provide the intelligence that those who maintain them wish them to provide, Knyphausen's intelligence convinced him that he could do successfully that which he wished to do. He thus made preparations to transport some five thousand men

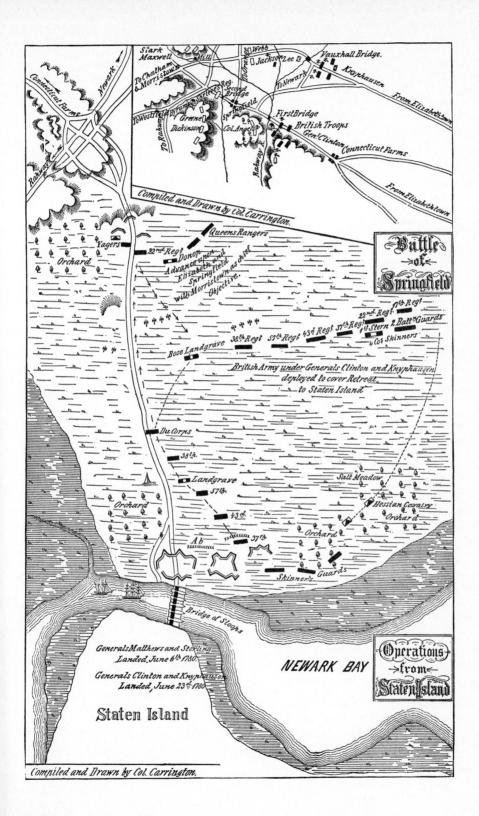

Compiled and Drawn by Col. Carrington.

Battle of Springfield

Siark
Maxwell

To Chatham
& Morristown.

Webb

Jackson

Lee

Vauxhall Bridge.

Knyphausen

From Elizabethtown

To Newark

To Westfield by James

Matticis Reg.

Second
Bridge

To Richmond

Greene
Dickinson

Springfield

Col. Ange.

Col. Angel.

First Bridge

British Troops
Gen. Clinton

Connecticut Farms

From Elizabethtown

Connecticut Farms

Newark

Railway

Railway R.

Yagers

22nd Regt.

Queens Rangers

Orchard

Donop
Advance upon
Elizabeth and
Springfield, as chief
Objective.

7th Regt.

22nd Regt.

1st Stern 2 Batt. Guards

38th Regt.

57th Regt.

43d Regt.

37th Regt.

4 Cos. Skinners

Bose Landgrave

British Army under Generals Clinton and Knyphausen
deployed to cover Retreat
to Staten Island

Du Corps.

38th.

Landgrave

57th.

Salt Meadow

Orchard

43d.

Hessian Cavalry

Orchard

Ab

37th.

Orchard

Skinner's

Guards

Bridge of Sloops

Generals Matthews and Sterling
Landed, June 6th 1780.

Generals Clinton and Knyphausen
Landed, June 23d. 1780.

NEWARK BAY

Operations from Staten Island

Staten Island

Compiled and Drawn by Col. Carrington.

on what was to be, in effect, a large-scale raid. Clinton had left Knyphausen in command of some six thousand soldiers, and Knyphausen had been most active in recruiting additional men, drafting sailors and civilians in such numbers that he almost doubled the size of the force under his command by the spring of 1780. By contrast Washington's entire army numbered scarcely seven thousand, only approximately half of whom could be spared from the duties of camp and garrison life for operations in the field.

On March 22, 1780, Knyphausen had sent a raiding force of four hundred German and English soldiers to the undefended town of Hackensack, New Jersey. There the raiders had broken indiscriminately into private houses, loaded themselves with loot, made prisoners of all men in the town, and then set fire to the courthouse and a number of homes. One of the Ansbach musketeers wrote, "We took considerable booty, both in money, silver watches, silver dishes and spoons, and in household goods, fine English linen, silk stockings, gloves, and neckerchiefs, with other precious silk goods, satin, and stuffs. My own booty which I brought safely back, consisted of two silver watches, three sets of silver buckles, a pair of woman's cotton stockings, a pair of man's mixed summer stockings, two shirts and four chemises of fine English linen, two fine table cloths, one silver tablespoon and one teaspoon, five Spanish dollars and six York shillings in money. The other part, viz., eleven pieces of fine linen and over two dozen silk handkerchiefs, with six silver plates and a silver drinking-mug, which were tied together in a bundle I had to throw away on account of our hurried march, and leave them to the enemy that was pursuing us." By such means did the English expect to reconcile or subdue the rebels!

By the first week in June, Knyphausen, acting on the word of his spies, was ready for more serious business. On the sixth, the first of five British divisions began to land at DeHart's Point near Elizabethtown. The force, when ashore, was made up of almost all of the regulars at Knyphausen's disposal: the British Guards; the Twenty-second, Thirty-seventh, Thirty-eighth, Forty-third, and Fifty-seventh Regiments; Cortlandt Skinner's West Jersey Volunteers; two Ansbach regiments; the Ansbach and Jaeger Corps; the Seventeenth Light Dragoons; Von Diemar's Hessians; the Queen's Rangers (mounted); the Leib Regiment; and the Landgraf, Donop, Bunau and Bose Regiments. They were reinforced by the Forty-second Regiment. Knyphausen explained his plan of action to Clinton: "Having received intelligence that Washington's army was very discontented, that many of them wished to have an opportunity given them to come in to join the royal army, and that he had detached the York Brigade toward Albany to oppose the incursions of the Indians—these reasons induced General Knyphausen to make a move into Jersey with 6,000 men."

The next day, Knyphausen began his march toward Washington's headquarters in Morristown, sending out three hundred dismounted chasseurs as an advance party. Word of the raid reached Washington the same day, but before he could put his own forces into action, Colonel Elias Dayton's regiment of General Maxwell's brigade had already moved to intercept Knyphausen. Most significant of all, the Jersey militia reacted with remarkable alacrity and rallied to support Maxwell's regulars. Colonel Sylvanus Seeley, of the New Jersey militia, noted in his diary: "Had an alarm and the enemy came out as far as Springfield Bridge. The Militia collected fast and joining Maxwell's brigade stopt the enemy. . . ." The enemy thus checked were the three hundred chasseurs who made up Knyphausen's advance guard.

The first warning of what was ahead for the British came on the march from Elizabethtown to Connecticut Farms, a distance of seven miles, when sharpshooting militiamen harassed the British column from behind trees and stone walls. As the British approached Springfield, they could see on the other side of the Rahway River the men of Maxwell's brigade, drawn up to meet them. The British tried to pass over the Rahway bridge. An adjutant took the colors and began to lead the attack, but he had hardly put a foot on the bridge when he was shot dead. Another officer sprang forward and took up the flag and was likewise cut down. Still a third officer suffered the same fate. The leading elements of the British force finally got across the bridge, leaving it covered with the fallen bodies of their comrades, but they had hardly formed a line of battle when the Americans, led by Samuel Parson's brigade, made a fierce bayonet charge and drove the British back. The American casualties were one dead and three or four wounded.

Under harassing fire from trees and stone walls, the chasseurs began to fall back, and Knyphausen, startled by the determination of the American defense, ordered hasty field entrenchments thrown up at Connecticut Farms, some two and a half miles southeast of Springfield. There Knyphausen relieved his frustration by burning some thirty buildings, including the meetinghouse. In Seeley's words, the militia "had about 15 killed and 40 wounded among the latter my brother

Saml, slightly. I had orders and marched my regiment to Thompsons Mills whare we lay all night."

Among a substantial number of British and Hessians wounded in the day's fighting was the British General Stirling. What was perhaps most disheartening to Knyphausen was the word that the Americans, having fired on his vanguard with considerable effect, had then advanced with bayonets. The German commander realized that his entire expedition had been based on erroneous assumptions. Instead of Tory support, he had found unnervingly fierce resistance. It was as though the whole countryside had sprung to arms. What was most notable about Knyphausen's raid at this point was that a large British force had been beaten back by militia before it had even engaged Washington's main army. The memory of Bennington must have been in Knyphausen's mind as he began his withdrawal. His chasseurs had lost fifty-five men killed and wounded during the day's fighting.

During the night of the seventh, Knyphausen and his staff could see hundreds of campfires and signal fires on nearby hills and could hear alarm guns spreading the news of his invasion to patriots. Long before dawn, Knyphausen had decided to abandon his expedition; the problem that remained was how to extricate the large force that had marched out so confidently that morning. The Hessian general ordered his men to withdraw to Staten Island, but the tide was out, the shore was covered with mud, and the bridge of boats was inaccessible. In Charles Stedman's perhaps sardonic words, "It was determined for the credit of the British arms to remain some days longer in New Jersey, lest their precipitate retreat should be represented as a flight."

The next morning, before his defensive works were far advanced, Knyphausen was attacked by the American advance guard, led by Lord Stirling. The attack was more a probe than a true assault, and with the reinforcement of the British line by two German regiments, the Americans withdrew. But constant pressure was maintained on the British positions, and there were frequent skirmishes in the days that followed. One Hessian noted bitterly in his journal, "It is almost impossible to surprise the enemy on any occasion, because every house that one passes is an advanced picket, so to speak; for the farmer, or his son, or his servant, or even his wife or his daughter fires off a gun, or runs by the foot-path to warn the enemy."

Clinton reached Staten Island on the seventeenth of June, while Knyphausen was still at Elizabethtown. Fresh from his triumph at

Charles Town, he readily fell in with the idea of an attack on Morris-town. The British general was convinced that the capture of Charles Town meant, in effect, an end to the war in South Carolina and perhaps in the South as well. It was clearly time for a decisive blow at Washington.

Washington was thoroughly baffled by Knyphausen's strange maneuvers. On the fourteenth, with the British still at Elizabethtown, he wrote: "Our situation is as embarrassing as you can imagine. . . . When they [Knyphausen and Clinton] unite their force, it will be infinitely more so." While Knyphausen was waiting for Clinton's return, Washington took advantage of the interval to recall Henry Lee's light horse, which he had earlier ordered to start for South Carolina, and to direct Lee to carry out extensive and continuous reconnaissance in an attempt to determine the intentions of the British.

Wishing to keep Washington unsettled on the score of a possible British attack on West Point, Clinton made a feint by sending a squadron of six frigates up the Hudson to Verplanck's Point.

In his own account of his strategy, Clinton spoke of "the alarming desertion of [Washington's] troops [which] had combined with the diminuition of their European credit . . . to depress the friends of independence and make them heartily tired of the war. . . ." Thus if Clinton could "at so critical a juncture, by a sudden unexpected move, seize upon their great depot of military stores at Morristown and capture or disperse the forces that covered them, not only every plan of cooperation with their expected French reinforcement must be disconcerted, but other happy consequences would probably follow that might ultimately even lead to a general submission of the whole continent."

Washington responded to the appearance of the British frigates by moving his main army to Pompton, nearer to West Point but only sixteen miles from Springfield. Greene was left at Springfield Bridge with a thousand Continentals to keep an eye on Knyphausen. When Clinton heard that Washington had started his army on the march as though for West Point, he decided to make his move against Springfield and Morristown.

On the twenty-third, Clinton and Knyphausen once again began a march to Springfield at five o'clock in the morning, moving in two columns, one by the Vauxhall Road and the other by the Springfield Road. The force consisted of five thousand infantry, with supporting cavalry and eighteen pieces of artillery, substantially the same force that Knyphausen had started out with two weeks earlier. The column on the

Springfield Road formed into a line of battle near the Matthews House, where a rise gave a good field of fire to the artillery. At the left of the bridge over the Rahway, Colonel Israel Angell's Rhode Island Regiment, supported by one gun, held an orchard that gave them control of the bridge. The British gunners aimed their pieces too high initially, but under the cover of their fire, a company of light infantry forded the stream—only a dozen yards wide at that point—and turned the flank of the American position, forcing Angell to withdraw his men to a second bridge, where Colonel Shreve of the New Jersey Line was fighting tenaciously. Finally British pressure forced William Shreve's and Angell's regiments back to a point where the brigades of Stark and Maxwell had taken up a position. In Isaac Dayton's regiment, Chaplain Caldwell, whose wife had been killed in the fighting on the seventh, passed out Watts's psalms and hymn books to the soldiers when they found themselves short of wadding for their muskets, with the admonition, "Put the Watts into them, boys."

The other British column was directed to gain the pass to Chatham and Morristown. Henry Lee's legion was posted at Little's Bridge on the Vauxhall Road, with Colonel Matthias Ogden's regiment covering them. Greene, however, soon drew them in to stronger defensive positions. Maxwell's and Stark's brigades occupied the high ground near Thompson's Mill, with John Dickinson's militia on their flanks. For forty minutes the Americans stood their ground, twice forcing the British back, before the weight of numbers made them give ground. As the Americans withdrew, they were covered by Colonel Smith, whose regiment was divided between an orchard in the center of the town and a stone house. Checked by fire from the building, the British were halted long enough to allow the Americans to reform, unlimber their artillery, and resume a heavy fire on the advancing redcoats. Once more they were driven back by British artillery fire. The patriots watched from a distance as Springfield was set fire to by the British, who then started back to Elizabethtown with the Americans close on their heels. From Elizabethtown, the British withdrew over their bridge of boats to Staten Island, and the Springfield campaign was over. The Americans lost one officer and twelve soldiers killed, exclusive of the militia, and five officers and fifty-six privates wounded. There were no official British casualties reported, but it was estimated that the British suffered some one hundred and fifty killed and wounded, in addition to the death of General Stirling in the engagement of June 7.

Although one historian has written, "Outnumbered five or six to one, the Americans had fought the British and Hessian troops to a standstill," the operations of June 7 to June 23 are not that easily summed up. The most significant engagement was that of June 7. It was then that Knyphausen, with a substantial force of British regulars and Hessians under his command, was taught by the readiness with which the New Jersey militia responded to his challenge that his hope of a quick and easy campaign was an illusion. Clinton, with a force not substantially larger than Knyphausen's, and with the imminent arrival of the French on his mind, can hardly have intended to make a serious and sustained attack on Washington. When Clinton's complicated strategy failed, Clinton, with Washington remaining at Pompton, had little to gain by pressing the attack. In Stedman's words, "The opposition made at Springfield was an indication to the commander in chief, that every mile of his future march through a country naturally difficult, and abounding with strong passes, would be not less obstinately disputed, . . . determined him to abandon an enterprise, which, even if it should be successful, might cost him too much. . . ." Writing some years after the event, Clinton presented a convincing picture of his own plans, which, according to him, envisioned a combined operation with Knyphausen, advancing in two columns from Perth Amboy and Elizabethtown to envelop Washington's army and capture his supplies. In Clinton's version Knyphausen jumped the gun by his foray on June 7, so that "instead of finding Mr. Washington totally *hors de combat* (as I had the greatest reason to expect) and in a state of unsuspecting security in his camp at Morristown, and the bold, persevering militia of that populous province quiet at their respective homes, it was most likely the whole country was now in arms and every preparation made for opposing me with vigor. . . ." According to Clinton, Knyphausen's venture was an "ill-timed, *malapropos* move," which defeated Clinton's well-laid plans by alerting Washington and the New Jersey militia. The principal impetus for the abbreviated campaign of Knyphausen apparently came from the Board of Associated Loyalists, headed by William Franklin, Benjamin's son, which had been established by Clinton on instructions from the ministry to organize and direct Loyalist raids along the coast.

When Clinton had reached Knyphausen, he had found him, as he wrote, "menaced by a considerable force which held him at bay. . . . This," he added, "was a very unpleasant and mortifying situation, which entirely precluded every idea of the enterprise I had in contemplation." The movement of July 23 was thus, if we can rely on Clinton's words, simply designed to cover the extrication of "the King's troops out of the

Jersies without affront." The fact is there is no reason to believe that Clinton's estimate of the situation in New Jersey was or would have been substantially different from Knyphausen's. Indeed, he says specifically that he intended an expedition, when he returned from South Carolina, that would have been directed at just those ends that Knyphausen proposed to accomplish by the expedition of June 7. And there is no reason to believe that Clinton would have been any more successful than Knyphausen was. The Hessian general managed to preserve an initial element of surprise. His failure was not due to any conspicuous tactical errors on his part but to a complete misreading of the political and military situation in New Jersey. And this misreading the British staff, like the British ministry, made time and time again—which is not really surprising, since, as we have seen, Washington made it frequently himself. To put the matter quite simply, it was "the bold, persevering militia" of New Jersey who really decided the issue. It was not Washington's main army that turned back Knyphausen, it was Knyphausen's and Clinton's conviction that they were faced by a countryside in arms that would impede their movement at every step of a futile and dangerous pursuit of Washington's elusive army.

Clinton was so far from comprehending the situation that he continued to importune Germain for ten thousand more men. Then, he declared, he could bring a speedy end to this interminable war. Clinton, like Howe before him, could only fumble along, improvising strategy as he went, succeeding sometimes and failing at other times. No success seemed to bring the British any nearer their goal, and every failure outweighed, in its effects, all the successes that had preceded it. One is tempted to propose a rough formula: one American victory outweighed five British successes. It is difficult, under such circumstances, to win a war or, more properly, to defeat a revolution.

Not long after the Battle of Springfield, New England underwent an eclipse of the sun. In Boston the day dawned "lowery and drisly," and at nine o'clock "an uncommon darkness came on, without any appearance of a thick cloud . . . it seemed as if a veil was drawn over the city. . . . The darkness increased until [the inhabitants] were obliged to light candles, & this continued until 3 O'Clock P.M. when it lightened up a little, but before Sunset the darkness returned and the Night resembled the darkness of Egypt which might be felt—it was so intense that many persons both in Boston and in the Country, were bewildered in going from house to house, where they were intimately acquainted. . . . During the darkness, in the day, the Green Grass appeared of a deep blue Color & the next Morning, both the Water and the Land were covered with a dark, greasy or oily substance." The darkness was noted as far south as New York and as far westward as Lake Champlain. Tories entertained themselves with the notion that "it was the Devil spreading his Wings over the northern rebelling colonies—and if they dont repent the next time he will certainly fly off with them all."

The arrival of the first division of French troops in mid-July brought an admonitory letter from Washington to Congress. "The eyes of Europe generally, and those of all America," he wrote, "are intently turned to Congress, and to the operations of their Army in this Campaign. . . . We cannot contemplate without horror the Effects of disappointment, as we apprehend that it will be experienced from a want of exertion in some states." A member of Congress gave it as his opinion that "a general languor hath spread itself over all our public transactions," and once again the notion was advanced of appointing Washington dictator of America as "the only means under God by which we can be saved from destruction."

The tension between the army and Congress came to focus on Nathanael Greene's duties as quartermaster general. He wished to have broad discretionary powers, but Congress was unwilling to grant them. "Congress always destroy with their left hand," he wrote resentfully, "what they begin with their right. People that will not learn Wisdom by suffering and experience cannot be saved." Greene resigned when Congress failed to give him the powers he felt were essential to the proper functioning of his office, and in the unpleasant spat that followed, Congress, invariably sensitive to its own dignity, discharged the committee at camp for overstepping its authority and insulting Congress (the committee had supported Greene's cause). The basic problem, as one member of Congress wrote a friend, was that "the committee at some times wrote plainly to us, and pressed our difficultyes close upon us, which is another matter many of us cannot bear altho founded on the greatest truths. . . ." The committee had made substantial progress in the matter of reforming the departments of the army. With its dismissal, the work done was wasted, and Congress had to start all over again. One of the members of the committee responded to its demise in sardonic tone. "I once read of a people," he wrote a friend, "who were sometimes led by a Cloud; And I have known a people whose *Grand Multiform'd Sanhedrin* [Congress] were oftentimes in the midst of a Fog."

Typical of those who saw the committee as a step toward military dictatorship was Major John Armstrong, who wrote to his father, the general, that "speculative knowledge seems to be all that's aimed at [by Congress] and in the diversity of opinion about the medicine, the patient may perish. Dont be astonished," Armstrong added, "if in the abounding *public Weakness or Wickedness*—a certain Gen [Washington]—be raised to the obnoxious name and place of Dictator. It has been proposed, and is now in agitation. This amounts to a little less than a plea of Insolvence. C———s confess themselves bankrupt in credit, sense, honesty and spirit; for in giving up the Sword to one and the Purse to another [Robert Morris] they anihilate their own authority."

Washington, meanwhile, was faced with a rapidly multiplying host of problems. If provisions were not forthcoming, he would have to send back the militiamen who had begun to straggle into camp. "Every day's experience," he noted, "proves more and more that the present mode of obtaining supplies [by appeals to the states] is the most uncertain, expensive, and injurious, that could be devised. It is impossible for us to form any calculation of what we are to expect, and consequently to concert any plans of future execution." "To me," Washington concluded, "it will appear miraculous if our affairs can maintain themselves much longer in their present train. If either the temper or the resources of the Country will not admit of an alteration, we may soon expect to be reduced to the humiliating condition of seeing the cause of America, in America, upheld by foreign arms. The generosity of our allies has a claim to all our confidence and all our gratitude, but it is neither for the honor of America nor for the interest of the common cause, to leave the work entirely to them. . . . On the whole if something satisfactory be not done, the army . . . must either cease to exist at the end of the campaign, or it will exhibit an example of more virtue, fortitude, self-denial, and perseverance, than has perhaps ever been paralleled in the history of human enthusiasm." On August 27, Washington sent a letter to the various states informing them that the greater part of the army had been without meat for six days, while there was only one day's supply of flour in camp. His army had literally become a mendicant one, and when begging failed, it "must assume the odious character of the plunderers instead of the protectors of the people."

Congress, having dismissed the committee that had at least forced it to pay some attention to the needs of the army, occupied itself with other less urgent matters. Ezekiel Cornell, a new delegate from Rhode Island, wrote, "I have seen many new scenes before I came to this place but what I experienced since, exceeds anything I have ever seen before. I never saw a set of men that could quietly submit to every kind of difficulty that tended to the ruin of their country, without making one effort to remove the obstruction. I believe they wish their country well, but suffer their time almost wholly to be taken up in business of no consequence." It was a familiar complaint. It had been heard before, and it would be heard again and again in the future. It was less a particular characteristic of Congress than of deliberative bodies generally, bodies that, as their name might suggest, seldom display a notable capacity for quick and decisive action.

In the midst of Washington's dilemma—how to muster an army to cooperate with the military and naval force momentarily expected from France—word came of a kind of deliverance. The French fleet had been blockaded in the harbor of Brest by the British. It was apparent that it could not arrive in time for a joint campaign against the British during what remained of the year. As soon as the word reached Washington, he dismissed the militia—whom he could not feed in any event—and concurred in the decision of Congress to send Horatio Gates, the hero of Saratoga, south to re-establish the army of the Southern Department, which Benjamin Lincoln had surrendered at Charles Town. So Gates left for the Battle of Camden and a crushing defeat. He was succeeded by Nathanael Greene, and the war in the South entered a new phase.

Edmund Burnett, the great scholar of the Continental Congress, very aptly describes the situation at Washington's headquarters. "It was now time to begin preparations for the next campaign. It had come to be an annual affair. One year repeated another. Washington would begin betimes with his plans and his requests for needful measures, Congress would putter and dally over them for weeks or months, the states would procrastinate still further, and before the army could be got ready the fighting season was over. Troops had come and troops had gone, but troops fit to fight and in sufficient numbers were never available. Supplies laboriously obtained and costly had been consumed, precious time had been lost, and there was nothing to show for it all. Wasted efforts everywhere. Only heartburnings and vexation of spirit."

As we have said before, the loosely united states had, strictly speaking, only to endure. Great Britain had to carry the war to America. As long as America was not subdued, it was independent, and it was, in consequence, winning the war, however many battles or even armies it might lose. Indeed, the principal drawback to losing battles and armies was that it encouraged some Englishmen in the illusion that America might still be subdued and thus postponed the day when they must finally face the fact that it could not be. Washington was at least partially aware of this. He also knew that an army exists to fight, and in turn that America existed, however precariously, as the United States because it had an army to provide for, however badly. It was evident to Washington that the country would soon be, if it was not already, unwilling to support an army that never seemed able to undertake a campaign. It mattered little that the army was unable to undertake campaigns and fight battles primarily because Congress and the states were unwilling or unable to support it; to the states, the Continental Army appeared increasingly as a ruinous and unnecessary expense. They had their own problems, and they were tired of being exhorted month in and month out to muster up men whose principal function seemed to be to consume supplies without bringing the war a day nearer to a conclusion.

A convention of New England states meeting at Hartford in the fall of 1780 made a depressing report. They found the situation of the American cause "truly critical and alarming. Our Army is already or will be shortly reduced in point of numbers as not to be able to furnish competent garrisons for the requisite posts, their pay in arrear for many months, frequently during the campaign totally without provisions, and their present supplies very precarious, no magazines provided—the public treasuries destitute of cash and public officers destitute of credit, and almost the whole Northern and Western frontiers exposed and undefended."

The delegates to the Hartford convention were convinced that "our present embarrassments" arose "in great measure from a defect in the present government of the United States. All government," the delegates declared in a circular letter to the governors of the other states, "supposes the power of coercion; this power however in the general government of the continent never did exist, or which produced equally disagreeable consequences, have never been exercised." Indeed, the powers of Congress had "never been explicitly defined," and had now, by virtue of the fact that various states had defied Congress's requisitions with impunity, "become questionable." "It must be evident to every sensible mind," the delegates continued, "that under these circumstances the resources and force of the country can never be properly united and drawn forth." The delegates therefore proposed that Congress be granted by the states the power to enforce its enactments and requisitions. If these measures appeared to be "rather harsh," the states should keep in mind "that weak, inefficient governments incapable to answer the great end of society, defence against foreign invasion, must and will end in despotism, and that the states individually considered while they endeavor to retain too much of their independence, may finally lose the whole." The delegates, in fact, went so far as to state plainly that whatever the outcome might be on the field of battle, "we shall . . . be without a solid hope of peace and freedom, unless we are properly cemented among [ourselves]. . . ." Despite "the calamities of war . . . we have not sufficient inducements to wish a period to them until our distress if other means cannot effect it have, as it were, forced us into a union." That was putting the matter plainly enough: The states were so divided, jealous, hostile, and suspicious that some delegates saw the continuation of "the calamities of war" as the only hope of forcing them to accept any genuine union.

Perhaps the most notable Congressional reform of 1780 was the establishment of permanent boards of war, treasury, and marine. These functions had been carried on by committees of Congress augmented by "lay members," committees whose membership fluctuated constantly as old delegates left and were replaced by new ones. The setting up of boards whose members were appointed by Congress as a kind of civil service put these important departments for the first time on a professional basis. Robert Morris was chosen superintendent of finance, Alexander MacDougall was appointed secretary of marine, and Benjamin Lincoln, exchanged by the British after the capture of Charles Town, was named secretary of war.

The committee on foreign affairs had dwindled, by the summer of 1780, to one active member, James Lovell, who understandably took the criticism of his fellow delegates with poor grace. "The weather is murderous hot," he wrote to John Jay, "and I cannot go up and down to the offices, in search of those authenticated papers, which ought to be regularly forwarded to you, and other dignified officers abroad." Jay in reply hit the nail on the head when he wrote, "One good private correspondent would be worth twenty standing committees, made up of the wisest heads in America, for purposes of intelligence." In January, 1781, a department of foreign affairs was created, headed by a secretary, charged with carrying on correspondence with United States ministers in various European countries.

James Duane, writing to Washington, expressed his feeling of encouragement that Congress had, at long last, attended to "the Establishment of Executives or Ministers in the departments of Finance, War, the Marine and Foreign Affairs, an accomplishment of the Confederation, the procuring to Congress an Augmentation of power and permanent Revenues for carrying on the War." It seemed to him that "the day is at length arrived when dangers and distresses have opened the Eyes of the People and they perceive the Want of a common head to draw forth in some Just proportions the Resources of the several branches of the federal Union. They perceive that the deliberate power exercised by states individually over the Acts of Congress must terminate in the common Ruin; and the Legislature, however reluctantly, must resign a portion of their Authority to the national Representative, or cease to be Legislatures." But the day was further off than Duane anticipated, some seven years, to be precise.

Early in 1781, Congress ratified the Articles of Confederation. Gradually those Virginians who were able to rise above provincialism had swung around to the view that Virginia should give up its claim to half the continent. Joseph Jones and James Madison used their influence with the Virginia assembly, and Jones wrote, "From the sentiments of the most intelligent persons which have come to my knowledge, I own I am pretty sanguine that they [the states with large western land claims] will see the necessity of closing the union in too strong a light to oppose the only expedient that can accomplish it." And Edmund Pendleton, who carried great weight in Virginia, wrote "that 'twas high time the confederation was compleated," adding, "I would not hesitate to yield a very large portion of our back lands to accomplish this purpose, except for the reason which Shakespeare has put into the mouth of Hotspur:

> 'I'll give thrice so much land
> To any well deserving friend:
> But in the way of bargain, mark ye me,
> I'll cavil on the ninth part of a hair.'"

Jones, as part of his motion to concede the western land claims, of which Virginia's was by far the largest, made the cession contingent on the land being "formed into distinct republican states, which shall become members of the federal union, and have the same rights of sovereignty, freedom and independence, as the other states." Designed to reassure the land speculators as well as the frontier settlers themselves, it was nonetheless one of the most significant resolutions passed by Congress during the Revolution, a classic case of the conjunction of idealism and self-interest. It established the principle of a generous and enlightened policy toward the western lands (and those who were to settle on them) that reached its culmination in the Northwest Ordinance.

Governor Thomas Jefferson, sending word to Congress of the action by the Virginia assembly in ceding its land claims to Congress, wrote, "We flatter ourselves that the liberal Spirit which dictated them will be approved and that the public will not be disappointed of the advantages expected from the measure." "I shall be very happy," Jefferson added, "if the other states of the Union, equally impressed with the necessity of that important convention [the ratification of the Articles of Confederation], shall be willing to sacrifice to its completion. This single event, could it take place shortly would outweigh every success which the Enemy have hitherto obtained and render desperate the hopes to which those successes have given birth."

Parliament

CONGRESS, depressed by its own futility, might have taken heart from the state of Parliament. The British were clearly bogged down in an expensive war that served,with each passing year, to exacerbate feelings between parties and classes.

To the government's perplexities was added the problem of Holland. The Dutch had remained cautiously neutral despite the energetic efforts of John Adams to push them in the direction of recognizing American independence. Since this would have constituted a declaration of war against England, the Dutch were understandably reluctant to take such a decisive step, but Adams did manage to procure substantial loans from Dutch banking houses with the acquiescence of the government. Far more irritating to the British, however, was that John Paul Jones was allowed to refit and equip his ships in Dutch ports and to bring the *Serapis* and the *Countess of Scarborough* with him as prizes of war. When the British ambassador demanded that Holland honor her treaty agreements with Great Britain and yield up the captured ships, he was answered with a volley of equivocations and excuses that added up to a refusal.

On the first of January, 1780, Commodore Fielding, cruising with a British squadron off Portland, fell in with a number of Dutch merchantmen, convoyed by five Dutch ships and frigates of war. Fielding demanded the right to search the Dutch ships for contraband, and when Count Byland, the Dutch commander, refused and fired on the boats sent to board the merchant vessels, Fielding opened fire on Byland, and the outmanned Dutch officer struck his colors. Fielding brought the convoy—accompanied by Byland—in to Spithead, and a *casus belli* plainly existed.

When John Adams heard of the incident he was delighted. This, he thought, would push the Dutch the last step to recognition of American independence and open war with Great Britain. The States-General of Holland demanded the release of the ships, but Great Britain refused and declared that the Dutch, by their failure to observe the provisions of the treaty of 1674, had made their ships subject to search and seizure.

The recalcitrance of the Dutch, whose merchants were determined to profit as much as they could from the War for American Independence, was echoed by Her Imperial Majesty, Queen Catherine of Russia, who announced that the ships of her nation would respect only *de facto* blockades and would resist by force of arms all searches of her vessels on the high seas. Catherine invited the Dutch States-General as well as the Danes and the Swedes to join in her policy of "armed neutrality."

The threat of "armed neutrality" made Lord North even more stubborn in his determination to push the war to a victorious conclusion; and his hand was strengthened by a series of British naval successes in the West Indies. Within less than a month, British captains captured a French merchant convoy of nine ships; three French frigates of forty-two, thirty-six, and twenty-eight guns, respectively; and a Spanish fleet of twenty-one ships, including seven naval vessels. On the sixteenth of January, Sir George Brydges Rodney came up with eleven Spanish ships of the line off Cape St. Vincent, captured four of them, and scattered the rest. The largest prize was the *Phoenix* of eighty guns and seven hundred men. The *Monarcha* and the *Diligente* of seventy guns and six hundred men, including the admiral of the Spanish fleet, were also captured. Three other seventy-guns ships were destroyed in the battle or driven ashore.

From Cape St. Vincent Rodney sailed for the West Indies, but even before he arrived, Commodore Sir William Cornwallis had engaged a French squadron under De La Motte Picquet that was convoying a fleet of merchantmen. A running two-day battle was inconclusive, with the French breaking off the action. On April 17, after Rodney's arrival, the combined British fleet of twenty ships of the line encountered Comte de

Guichen off the Leeward Islands. The French had twenty-three ships. Rodney, on the *Sandwich*, engaged the French at close quarters and sustained such heavy damage to his flagship that it came near to sinking. Again the action was inconclusive, with both sides claiming victory. A month later the two fleets again tried the test of battle, and once more the action ended "without any material advantage on either side." The French gave their losses in the three battles as one hundred and fifty-eight killed and eight hundred and twenty wounded. The British losses were even more severe, and the editor of the *Annual Register* noted "that the decided superiority on which the English had been accustomed to reckon, in naval encounters, when their force and that of the enemy were nearly equal, was not now exhibited. Whatever inferiority there might be on the part of the common seamen of the French fleet, there appeared to be no inferiority with respect either to naval skill, or courage, in the French officers."

But in a series of individual engagements between single English and French frigates, the English ships were uniformly victorious, and these triumphs, plus the inability of the combined French and Spanish fleets to accomplish much in the West Indies against Rodney, gave rise to a great resurgence of national pride in England. A strong Spanish attack on Gibraltar was repulsed with heavy losses to the attackers, and suddenly the military picture looked much brighter than it had at the beginning of the year. The most important consequence of the reversal of British fortunes was that the pressure for peace slackened almost at once, and although the determination for reform of financial expenditures persisted, it was separated from the opposition to the war itself.

Clinton's capture of Charles Town revived the hope that the Southern Tories would flock to the British standard and that the South would soon be safely and permanently in British hands. While the Whigs in and out of Parliament continued to call for an end to the war and to reiterate their conviction that America could never be subdued, they found that they had lost a considerable portion of their supporters, whose hopes for a swift military solution were once more aroused by the news of the capture of the army of the Southern Department and its commanding general, Benjamin Lincoln.

When the House of Commons convened in January, 1780, the matter of Ireland was the most pressing bit of business. The problems of the war in Continental America and the West Indies were shelved for the time being while both Houses gave their attention to the condition of that province. Lord North brought before the House a bill that freed

Irish trade from the most onerous of the restrictions placed upon it. The members were assured that the fires of rebellion had guttered out, that the actions of Parliament for relief of the Irish "had been received by the parliament of that kingdom with satisfaction and with gratitude: and that there was every reason to hope that the connections between the two kingdoms would be more intimate and firm than ever. . . ."

With the Irish question disposed of, at least for the time being, the House once again turned its attention to the matter of the public expenditures, specifically to the reform of the placemen and pensioners of the Crown. The Whig strategy at this point was to focus attention on this one issue as having the greatest public support and leave the ancillary question of the war and a change in government to another day. When Sir George Savile rose to present the petition of the county of York, the House itself was "unusually full, and the gallery was crowded." The members sat in silent expectation; there was none of the familiar murmur of private conversations and noisy interjection as Savile spoke. Savile finished with a direct challenge to North. Did he or did he not intend to undertake to redress the grievances enumerated in the petition? North was plainly uncomfortable with the question. What was at issue was his loyalty to the king. That, at least, was clearly the way that George III would view the matter. North replied evasively that any petition must be thoughtfully considered and the interests of the petitioners weighed against those of the kingdom as a whole.

While the House of Commons gingerly handled the flood of petitions, of which that of York was simply the precursor, the House of Lords debated the Earl of Shelburne's proposal for a joint committee of Commons and Lords "to examine without delay into the public expenditures, and the mode of accounting for the same." After Shelburne, in an able speech, had presented his motion, the peers found themselves in a prolonged and rancorous debate. The Earl of Chesterfield contended "that the majority of the people were extremely well contented under the present government, and that the county petitions and associations were the last struggles of an expiring faction, who, by inflammatory speeches and misrepresentations, had endeavoured to promote insurrections in Ireland; and, having failed in that attempt, now sought, by similar means, to sow dissension in this kingdom." The Marquis of Rockingham was more plainspoken than Shelburne. He had noted from the first moment of the reign of George III that the king had "a fixed determination to govern this country under the forms of law," and for sixteen years he had fought in vain against such a "dangerous and alarming tendency." What had resulted was such "a system of corruption, public venality, and despotism, as never before took place in any limited government." During his own ministry, Rockingham declared, he had done his best "to oppose and defeat this unnatural and unconstitutional influence of the crown, but to very little purpose. . . ."

Again the weight of argument was with the Opposition, but the votes were with the government. Shelburne's motion lost in a division, 101 to 55. In Commons, Burke took up the fight. Here it could not be argued, as it had been in the House of Lords, that the issue was an improper one since finances were not the business of the peers. "In a speech of great length, replete with information, and embellished with all the beauties of eloquence," Burke covered much the same ground traversed in Lords by Shelburne and Rockingham. Burke was at his witty best in describing the royal household, which "had lost all that was stately and venerable in the antique manners, without retrenching any thing of the cumbrous charge of a Gothic establishment. It was shrunk into the polished littleness of modern elegance and personal accommodation. It had evaporated from the gross concrete, into an essence and rectified spirit of expense, where you might have tuns of ancient pomp in a vial of modern luxury. But when the reasons of old establishments was gone, it was absurd to preserve nothing but the burthen of them." The ancient offices, no longer used for ceremonial purposes, served merely as places for supporters of the Court party.

When Burke, after three hours and twenty minutes, at length concluded, "this most eloquent and elaborate speech . . . obtained him the warmest and most unreserved applause from all parties." Even North declared that "a more able speech had never been delivered in that house. . . ."

Burke's plan of reform was contained in five separate bills, and these were placed before the House toward the end of February. North, unable to rally enough members in Parliament to block an investigation into the public expenditures, came up with the notion of a commission, appointed of course by the government, to examine the accounts of public monies. By this means he hoped to intercept the clear intention of the House to appoint a committee of its members. Barré complained that North's stratagem—to "now snatch the business" from the House "and take it all upon himself"—was "extremely unfair and unparliamentary." Throughout March the House wrangled over the question of how the public accounts were to be audited, and over Burke's bills to reduce the number of superfluous officeholders and pensioners. The debates were protracted and wearisome as the government exhausted one recourse after another to deflect or impede the intended reforms: move and countermove, retreat and delay. To reveal the names of the pensioners would, it was argued, embarrass many worthy individuals and expose them to public ridicule and abuse. In the midst of the debates, the matter of the budget for the navy was brought forward by the government. A row ensued about whether to vote the required money or to wait until there had been some evidence of fiscal reform by the government. Here once more the Opposition went down to defeat. A substantial majority of the members were unwilling to make the navy at least theoretically vulnerable to enemy action for the sake of reforming the finances of the state. On the fifteenth of March a list of new taxes was brought in: taxes on malt, Portuguese and French wines, salt, and tea, a stamp duty of six pence on all advertisements in newspapers, and stamp duties on a variety of legal papers. So the result of weeks of inconclusive debate about the reckless wasting of government funds ended with no progress toward reform, but with the House instead docilely approving a whole new set of taxes to support a war that many Englishmen felt had long since been lost.

On April 6, 1780, William Dunning brought to Commons an explosive motion: Resolved, "The influence of the Crown has increased, is increasing, and ought to be diminished." This motion was only one of a number intended to establish some constitutional limitation on the power of the Crown. Dunning's second motion read: "That it is competent to this House, to examine into, and to correct, abuses in the expenditure of the civil list revenues, as well as in every other branch of the public revenue, wherever it shall appear expedient to the wisdom of this House so to go." If the House could establish its control over expenditures, it might bring the war to an end by cutting off the flow of funds. As early as 1742, Dunning pointed out, David Hume had foreseen the increasing influence of the Crown and had predicted that it would bring the destruction of the constitution.

Thomas Pitt supported Dunning. The very presence of Lord North was "an indubitable proof of the enormous influence of the crown." Had not North by his bungling already lost America? He had spent millions of public money, "and wasted rivers of blood of the subjects of Great Britain. And yet, the noble lord [North] now that the whole country with one voice cried out against and execrated the American war," still held his place, purely and simply through the improper influence of the Crown. "The whole business of the minister, for a series of years, had been to make excuses, and devise expedients, to find supplies from year to year," without developing any permanent system of financing the war.

The opposition was ready to deal what it hoped would be a decisive blow. On the chairman's table were some forty petitions subscribed with thousands of names calling for an end to the war and to the king's abuse of his powers.

When a member named Rigby tried to defend the government, Burke declared that his ideas were hopelessly outmoded—that he was "more fit for the British Museum than the British House of Commons." The country gentlemen, the basis of the king's power in Parliament, were at last ready to abandon him. The beleaguered North, seeing his control of the House about to slip from him, shouted at his tormenters, and the House was in a tumult.

When the Dunning motion came to a vote, it carried 233 to 215. The effect was to establish a committee to review all petitions and consider the question of the king's misuse of his authority. Horace Walpole wrote to Sir Horace Mann, "The law seems to me decisive; for this committee is to continue sitting on the petitions, will exclude any other business, will extract from the petitions whatever propositions its pleased . . . and will carry along all those who have already voted on that foundation." If North and his ministry attempted to make a further stand, they would be swept aside. "To combat on the same field of battle after being vanquished," Walpole added, "will, in my opinion, be frenzy." He wished the ministers to retreat before it was too late in order to "prevent very great mischief. . . . A Torrent opposed may damage the foundations of the constitution itself. . . ."

That was precisely the dilemma. The prosecution of the unpopular if not disastrous war against America might very well, thoughtful men believed, bring down the whole British constitution and create a revolutionary situation in England itself. Indeed, there were many who thought that moment was already at hand.

On May 5, 1780, General Henry Conway brought in "A bill for quieting the troubles now reigning in the British colonies in America, and for enabling his Majesty to appoint commissioners, with full powers to treat, and conclude upon terms of conciliation with the said colonies." Britain, hard pressed by its enemies, had "little but our pride and passions left to support us . . . a fatal rebellion . . . preying upon our vitals." Even the little powers "pecked and insulted us," Conway declared. "To such a pitch had our faults and our follies, our ignorance and our presumption brought us." He recalled, as he had every right to, the night when "the taxation of America; a system foolishly . . . and fatally conceived, equally impolitic and unjust" was brought forward in a poorly attended House, and "in a dark and evil hour, like a band of black conspirators," the members had resolved "to rob three millions of British subjects of their liberty and property." It was his "pride and consolation" that he would carry to his grave the knowledge that he had been one of the few who had opposed that infamous bill, the root of all England's present troubles. Conway believed that a full and fair offer of conciliation might still bring the Americans back into the fold. But both sides of the House clearly believed that the time had passed for half-measures. The motion was rejected by a majority of 123 to 81, with a number of Whigs voting against it as inadequate to the realities of the situation.

A similar bill by David Hartley was defeated the next day, as was one proposed by Thomas Pownall, former governor of Massachusetts Bay and a leading expert on American affairs. Pownall's bill proposed to give His Majesty power to "make peace, truce, or convention with America." Like its predecessors, it was handily defeated. But its defeat was less notable than the fact that within the space of three days, three such private bills had been proposed.

Burke's bills for doing away with obsolete or honorific offices that were filled by the king and that paid large stipends were defeated, one after another, and on May 18, his bill to abolish the 67 offices of master of buckhounds, foxhounds, and harriers and paymaster of the pensions was also rejected. Having cleared their consciences by voting that the influence of the king should be reduced, the members of the House of Commons thus proceeded, on virtually every vote, to maintain or augment those powers. The clear implication, according to one member, was that a number of the renegades had had such pressure applied to them that they quickly abandoned their newly asserted independence and returned dutifully to the government fold.

In the midst of these perplexities, Lord George Gordon, "a whimsical and eccentric" peer from Ireland, emerged as the leader of those Protestants who were opposed to any relief for Catholics. The act for relieving "his Majesty's subjects professing the Romish religion, from certain penalties and disabilities on them . . . in the reign of William III" had passed unanimously in 1778, "it being the general opinion of liberal minded men, of all parties, that the laws against the papists were abundantly too rigorous, and that in an enlightened age, in which the principles of toleration so much prevailed, they were a disgrace to our statute-books." Lord George Gordon denounced the Catholic Relief Bill as a betrayal of Protestantism and in doing so fanned all the ancient prejudices of the London populace against "papists." Catholic property and Catholic chapels were destroyed by a mob that at times numbered over sixty thousand people. Members of Parliament were besieged in the House of Commons and had to be rescued by soldiers. The home of Sir George Savile, who had brought in the Relief Bill, was systematically demolished, and unpopular peers and prelates were beaten and abused by angry rioters. Civil authority was completely incapable of coping with the mobs who, in effect, took possession of the city for almost a week. After adjourning on June 2, Parliament, with the protection of troops, convened again on Tuesday, June 6. Lord Sandwich, especially detested for his arrogance and his prominent role in the North ministry, was dragged from his carriage on the way to Westminster. His carriage was torn to pieces, and he was bruised and cut and only rescued with difficulty by the Horse Guards. The house of Lord North was attacked, but a troop of light horse defended it. Then the mob proceeded to Newgate prison, a symbol of the bitter repressiveness of English society. Here they mounted an assault that was as determined and as well organized as a military siege. Scaling ladders appeared, as did sledge-hammers and axes. The house of the chief jailer was broken open and a bonfire made of his furniture, which, piled against the prison gate, burned that gate off its hinges. Cells were broken open and the pris-oners turned out, while the strongest prison in England burned to blackened walls. Parties were detailed to burn and pillage the mansions of unpopular political figures, in addition to the homes of Catholics. The house of the Earl of Mansfield, the dean of the British bench, was assaulted, with Lord and Lady Mansfield barely escaping out the back door. The magnificent furniture of the house was thrown out of the windows and burned in the street, along with valuable paintings, a large law library, and many of Mansfield's own legal writings. A party of guards arrived as the mob was giving its attention to the earl's wine cellars. The Riot Act was read, the crowd was ordered to disperse, and when its members refused, the soldiers opened fire and shot six men and a woman and wounded a number of others.

The following day rumors spread that the rioters intended to destroy the Bank of England, the remaining prisons, and the royal palaces. By this time, troops had been collected and assigned to protect the principal public buildings. One Londoner wrote, in the midst of a city besieged, with many buildings ablaze, "This is the fourth day that the metropolis of England (once of the world) is possessed by an enraged, furious and numerous enemy. Their outrages are beyond description, and meet with no resistance. . . . What this night will produce is known only to the Great Disposer of things. . . . Children are plundering at noonday the City of London." Samuel Johnson, riding to view the ruins of Newgate, saw some hundred men plundering the sessions house of Old Bailey, another prison. "They did their work," Johnson noted, "at leisure, in full security, without sentinels, without trepidation, as men lawfully employed in full day."

Rumors circulated that the mob intended to let loose the lunatics in Bedlam and the lions in the Tower of London. In the evening the King's Bench Prison, Fleet Prison, the new Bridewell, St. George's Church, and a large number of private houses were set on fire. To one witness it was the classic "picture of a city sacked and abandoned to a ferocious enemy." Large supplies of arms had been seized by the mob at the artillery grounds, and these were used in an attack on the Bank of England and on the Pay Office. Both places were guarded by soldiers, who returned the fire of the mob, and many were killed and lay bleeding in the streets or were carried off by their fellows.

Gradually, the rioters were sealed off. Heavy chains, protected by soldiers, were placed around the area where the activities of the mob had been centered. Fires did the greatest damage and threatened for a time to spread through the whole city. When fire engines came to extinguish the flames, the rioters blocked them, cut their hoses, and drove the firemen off. Near St. Andrew's Church, a distillery was attacked and burned. In Lecky's words, "Such a scene of drunken madness had perhaps never before been exhibited in England." Many men and women killed themselves by drinking denatured alcohol. The alcohol gushed into the streets, caught fire, and burned many of the rioters to death. In the midst of the pillaging and destruction, Wilkes, who had been the occasion of an earlier riot, helped to defend the Bank of England and protected several families of Catholics, thereby winning the thanks of the Privy Council.

All told, seventy-two private houses and four jails were destroyed. Two hundred and eighty-five rioters were killed. The historian Edward Gibbon, well aware of the events incident to the decline and fall of a great power, wrote after order had been restored, "Our danger is at an end, but our disgrace will be lasting and the month of June 1780 will

ever be marked by a dark and diabolical fanaticism which I had supposed to be extinct."

While the Catholic Relief Bill had been the occasion of the riots, and
while the riots undoubtedly contained a large ingredient of that fanaticism that Gibbon very properly condemned, there was much more to
them than hostility to the Catholics. The rough treatment given unpopular politicians and the shift of the mob's attention from Catholic
homes and chapels to prisons and public buildings gave ample evidence
of a deep and bitter hostility among the common people of London
toward the government, toward the war itself, and toward what we
today would call "the Establishment"—in other words, all those people
and agencies of government that bore so heavily on the depressed poor,
the working and the criminal classes of London. The anti-Catholic
nature of the initial rioting undoubtedly saved many of the great public
buildings of the city from the fury of the mobs. By the time rioters
turned on these buildings, some hasty defenses had been organized.

The main point of the riot was that a potentially revolutionary
situation existed in England, and that civil authority had proved unable
for four days to cope with one particular manifestation of that revolutionary temper—the Lord George Gordon Riots. Although they were
explained away by some as the unholy fruits of religious fanaticism, they
plainly raised in the minds of every member of the British ruling class
the grim spectre of a general uprising of the lower orders of society.

Certainly the editor of the *Annual Register* was convinced that much
of the violence of the riots was occasioned by "the unpopularity of the
administration" with "the common people," and that such disorder
could not have taken place "under any administration which had been
universally respected by the common people."

Perhaps the most unfortunate consequence of the Lord George
Gordon Riots, as they came to be known, was that the "alarm and terror"
stirred up by them put an immediate damper on the "ardor which had
appeared for promoting popular meetings and associations, and for
opposing the measures of government. The county meetings were
represented by some as having a tendency . . . to bring on insurrections
and rebellion. Many began to consider all popular meetings as
extremely dangerous." Especially among merchants and businessmen,
the recollection of furious mobs roving the city, burning and looting,
was so vivid that their concern for constitutional reform seemed to
evaporate overnight. If the menace of the French-Spanish alliance had

not served to rally these classes behind the government, the specter of civil uprisings effected that transformation. Thus in Britain the first stirring of popular political activity, tentative and limited as it was, was frustrated, first by the string of British naval successes in the winter and spring of 1780, then by the capture of Charles Town, and finally by the shock of the Lord George Gordon Riots. By the same token, the hope for an end to the American war, which was tied so directly to hope for constitutional reform and to the fall of the North government, was again delayed. In addition to the intractability of the king, North was simply too preoccupied trying to fend off Opposition attacks to have much time for other matters. While every month that the war was prolonged meant further hardship and suffering in America, the war frequently slipped to the back of the minds of politicians of both parties as they struggled on the one side to overthrow the government, and on the other, to maintain an increasingly precarious hold on the reins of government.

The British devotion to the restraints of law was strikingly indicated by the controversy that followed the riots and centered on the question of whether the king had exceeded his constitutional authority by order-ing soldiers to suppress the riots without the approval of a civil magis-trate. The editor of the *Annual Register* noted that the use of such power even in so desperate a situation "was a novel idea."

In the midst of a warm debate on the subject, the king prorogued Parliament on June 28 and dissolved it on September 1, 1780. Thus ended any hope for Parliamentary reform or for steps to end the American war. Until a new Parliament could be elected, the direction of affairs remained firmly in the hands of the king and his ministers. The king, of course, was greatly encouraged by the news of Cornwallis's crushing defeat of General Gates at Camden and the destruction of the third army of the Southern Department in the space of less than two years. Now, at last, the Southern Tories should take heart and throw off the chains the patriots had shackled them with; there must be some limit to this perpetual renewal of Southern armies. What North thought is less certain. Perhaps his heart sank at the thought that the success of Cornwallis served, in effect, to further delay His Majesty's acceptance of the reality of American independence and thereby extended his own purgatory as the king's first minister.

Thus the war went on. Stubbornly George III persisted in his ruinous course. The mood of the country subsided from rage to frus-trated bafflement. Those very constitutional barriers and limitations that every middle- and upper-class Englishman revered as the bulwarks of his most precious liberties seemed to make the king immune to popular feeling or to the persistent if futile pressures of the Opposition benches in the House of Commons. The king was adamant in his refusal to accept American independence or even to accept a compromise that would constitute a *de facto* recognition of independence. "I can never suppose," he wrote, "this country so lost to all ideas of self-importance as to be willing to grant American independence." A few months later he denounced all efforts at reconciliation as simply strengthening "the demogogues in America in their arts to convince the deluded people that a little further resistance must make the mother country yield; whilst at this hour every account of the distresses of that country shows that they must sue for peace this summer if no disaster befalls us." In the king's view, far more was at stake than simply American independence. "The giving up the game," he wrote, "would be total ruin; a small state may certainly subsist, but a great one mouldering cannot get into an inferior station, but must be annihilated. . . . The French never could stand the cold of Germany; that of America must be more fatal to them. America is distressed to the greatest degree."

Like all men in positions of great power, George III had no way of knowing the truth about the situation of the British armies in America. His subordinates, like their counterparts in every place and time, were afraid, if indeed they themselves knew better, to tell him what he plainly did not wish to know. Out of the flow of intelligence about the situation in America, confused and contradictory as it was, they and the king simply chose those items that confirmed them in their own prejudices.

The king, moreover, would not enter negotiations with France "whilst the House of Bourbon make American independency an article of their propositions. . . ."

In England a constant flow of optimistic reports, most of them from Tories who dreaded above all else that Britain might abandon them, encouraged the delusion that the war almost was won. In February, 1780, even before the capture of Charles Town, Governor Tryon wrote to England that "the friendly part of America keep up their spirit and are sanguine. . . . That the reunion of the Empire will be yet happily accomplished, and those who have been with circumstances of cruelty drove from their estates and families restored." Other Loyalists declared that "the majority on the west side of the Connecticut are desirous of the restoration of the King's authority, and that in many towns and districts both in New York, Connecticut and Massachusetts Bay they are nearly all so." Lord George Germain said in Parliament that all the personal letters from America were unanimous in describing the patriot cause as being at its lowest ebb. The general population was suffering from the requisitions of the army, the army in turn was suffering acutely from the inadequacy of supplies, the troops were rebellious, and there was a universal desire for peace.

4

General Arnold and the British

IN the fall of 1779, Benedict Arnold, whose name was to become an American synonym for traitor, entered into treasonable correspondence with the British.

A resourceful and courageous military leader, Arnold was also a ruthlessly ambitious man who would stop at nothing to advance his own interests. Yet Washington, who so desperately needed generals, had an almost inordinate admiration and regard for him; indeed, Arnold was one of Washington's "sons," the eldest and most brilliant son among that little company that included Alexander Hamilton, John Laurens, and Henry Lee.

On the surface it would seem strange that Washington, who was usually a shrewd judge of men (though he certainly was wrong at times, as in the case of Charles Lee), was so taken in by Arnold, who was hardly an attractive character. Washington was, however, no more immune to flattery than the next man, and Arnold was assiduous in his attentions to the man on whom his military preferment depended. What spoke most eloquently for Arnold, of course, were his brilliant successes on the field of battle—or what were at least accepted as his brilliant successes. To a commander whose generals failed him so often, the boldness of Arnold, which was plainly a crucial facet of his ambition, was greatly esteemed.

Washington is so often depicted as an austere and virtually emotionless man that it is important to take note of how often he gave his admiration and affection to younger officers under his command.

The first gift that Arnold sought and received from Washington was the military command of Philadelphia. The wound that Arnold had received at the battle of Freeman's Farm had not healed sufficiently for him to return to the field, so on May 28, 1778, Washington designated him as commander of the forces in Philadelphia. It was an important post. The city was the capitol of both the state and the federal government, and Arnold thus had three sets of officials to deal with: those of the city, the state, and the Continental Congress. His arrogant and impatient nature, his basic contempt for civilian authority, and his greed and ambition made him the worst possible choice for such a sensitive job, a job that required tact and diplomacy as well as firmness. Almost from the moment he assumed his office, there were rumors that he was involved in speculation. He lived with a degree of luxury that startled the burghers of a city in which fine living was common if not notorious. He made an enemy of Joseph Reed, Washington's former aide and confidante, sometime president of Congress, and one of the most influential patriot leaders. He seemed to prefer wealthy Philadelphians of Tory sympathies to the company of patriots, and he paid assiduous court to beautiful Peggy Shippen, whose rich and conservative father had been chief justice of Pennsylvania under the Crown. Peggy, the reader will recall, had been much involved in the gay social life of Philadelphia during the British occupation, and only the express orders of her father had prevented her from attending the Meschianza. She had particularly enjoyed the high spirits and charm of young Major John André. Now she encouraged the attentions of a man twice her age—Arnold was thirty-eight—to whose boundless ambition her own desire for luxury and prominence responded.

Arnold wrote to Peggy Shippen in words that he had used in an earlier courtship: "Twenty times have I taken up my pen to write to you, and as often my trembling hand refused to obey the dictates of my heart. . . . My passion is not found on personal charms only; that sweetness of disposition and goodness of heart, that sentiment and sensibility which so strongly mark the character of the lovely Miss P. Shippen, renders her amiable beyond expression and will ever retain the heart she has once captivated." In another letter he told her, again in almost the same words that he had used in courting her predecessor,

"On you alone my happiness depends. . . . And will you doom me to languish in despair? Shall I expect no return to the most sincere, ardent, and disinterested passion?" He then wrote to her father for permission to press his suit, declaring, "Our difference in political sentiments, will, I hope, be no bar to my happiness. I flatter myself the time is at hand when our unhappy contests will be at an end, and peace and domestic happiness be restored to every one." To Peggy he vowed: "May I perish if I would give you one moment's inquietude to purchase the greatest possible felicity to myself." The courtship was finally successful; although Peggy Shippen for a time put up a stout defense, she was at last "Burgoyned" by "her adoring general." They were married in her home on April 8, 1779. A soldier supported Arnold during the ceremony, and at the reception the groom sat with his leg on a campstool. Sometime after the marriage, Arnold wrote to General Robert Howe, who had congratulated him on his domestic felicity, that he had "enjoyed a tolerable share of the dissipated joys of life, as well as scenes of sensual gratification incident to a man of nervous constitution; but, when set in competition with those I have since felt. . . . I consider the time of celibacy in some measure misspent."

His marriage did not, however, improve Arnold's relations with the Philadelphia leaders. In addition to Joseph Reed, Arnold made a bitter enemy of Timothy Matlack, leader of the popular party in the city. Eventually the city council charged him with having been "oppressive to the faithful subjects of this state, unworthy of his rank and station, highly discouraging to those who have manifested their attachment to the liberties and interests of America, and disrespectful to the supreme executive authority." These were vague charges. They were supported by eight specifics that included using public wagons for transporting private property and "showing favour to Tories." Matlack, under the initials T. G., attacked Arnold relentlessly in the *Pennsylvania Packet*. "When I meet your carriage in the street," he wrote, "and think of the splendour in which you live and revel, of the settlement which it is said you have proposed in a certain case, and of the purchases you have made, and compare these things with the decent frugality necessarily used by other officers in the army, it is impossible to avoid the question: From whence have these riches flowed if you did not plunder Montreal?"

Congress was plainly embarrassed by the charges that Pennsylvania pressed so determinedly. Arnold, as a successful general and a protégé of Washington, had many supporters in Congress. Thomas Burke of North Carolina declared that the Pennsylvania council had been "waspish, peevish, and childish" in its persecution of Arnold.

Through all Arnold's troubles with the Pennsylvania officials, Washington stood staunchly behind him. Even his affection for Reed could not bring him to question the motives or actions of Arnold. When the young Philadelphia officer Allen McLane tried to persuade Washington of Arnold's misuse of his office, the general rebuked him sharply. Arnold knew very well that his best chance to avoid punishment for his maladministration was to wrap himself in the mantle of Washington's prestige, and he perceived that the best way to accomplish this was to offer repeatedly to take the full brunt of criticism on himself lest any blame be attributed to Washington for appointing him to his post. "If your Excellency thinks me criminal," he wrote Washington on May 5, "for heaven's sake let me be immediately tried and, if found guilty, executed. I want no favour; I ask only justice. If this is denied me by your Excellency, I have nowhere to seek it but from the candid public, before whom I shall be under the necessity of laying the whole matter. Let me beg of you, Sir, to consider that a set of artful, unprincipled men in office may misrepresent the most innocent actions and, by raising the public clamour against your Excellency, place you in the same situation I am in. Having made every sacrifice of fortune and blood, and become a cripple in the service of my country, I little expected to meet the ungrateful returns I have received from my countrymen; but as Congress have stamped ingratitude as a current coin, I must take it. I wish your Excellency for your long and eminent services, may not be paid in the same coin. I have nothing left but the little reputation I have gained in the army."

Within a few days of the writing of this letter, Arnold entered into a treacherous correspondence with Clinton. This shameless letter to Washington is thus one of the most cold-blooded and indecent missives on record. Arnold knew he was guilty as charged, and he knew, moreover, that treasonous impulses were in his own heart (or had already been expressed—depending on the date, now unknown, of his first contact with the British). The arrogance and presumption of trying to compare, by implication, his own case with that of Washington is literally breathtaking. Carl Van Doren, in his *Secret History of the American Revolution*, calls the letter "hysterical"; it seems to me to be one of the most calculated and shameless acts in history. Arnold was not only in the process of betraying his country, he was betraying a man who had treated him as a friend and even, as we have suggested, as a son, and he was doing so in the most cold-blooded way imaginable.

Hardly knowing how to cope with the charges against Arnold, Congress finally decided, as a kind of a compromise, to dismiss four of the charges and refer the others to a court-martial. A fourteen-man court, which included Generals Henry Knox, Robert Howe, and William Woodford, met on June 1 at Middle Brook, New Jersey, but had to adjourn when word came that the British were advancing up the Hudson. It was December before the court reconvened, and by then its membership had changed substantially. The new board found substance in two charges—that Arnold had improperly written a pass for a ship, the *Charming Nancy*, to leave Philadelphia at the time of its evacuation by the British, and that he had been careless in using military wagons to transport private property. He was sentenced to "receive a reprimand from his Excellency the commander-in-chief."

After a good many months had passed, Washington, at last, wrote to Arnold: "The Commander-in-chief would have been much happier in an occasion of bestowing commendations on an officer who has rendered such distinguished services to his country as Major General Arnold; but in the present case a sense of duty and a regard to candour oblige him to declare that he considers his conduct in the instance of the permit as peculiarly reprehensible both in a civil and military view, and in the affair of the wagons as imprudent and improper." "Peculiarly reprehensible" was perhaps accurate enough, but it was certainly harsh. It seems, however, to have glanced off the armor of Arnold's impenetrable self-esteem. Writing to Silas Deane, he spoke as though his conduct had been vindicated.

It should be pointed out that well before Arnold's treasonable correspondence with Clinton, the British had made efforts to corrupt American officers. In June of 1777 a letter from Peter Livius, chief justice of Canada, to General John Sullivan, urging him to defect to the British, was found in the false bottom of a captured messenger's canteen. The American cause was certainly lost, Livius pointed out, and Sullivan, as one of "the first men in active rebellion," must be "one of the first sacrifices to the resentment & justice of government, your family will be ruined, & you must die with ignominy; or if you should be so happy as to escape, you will drag along a tedious life of poverty, misery and continual apprehension in a foreign land. . . . Now Sullivan," the writer continued, "I have a method to propose to you, if you have resolution & courage, that will save you & your family & estate from this imminent destruction; it is in plain English to tread back the steps you have already taken, & do some real and essential service to your king & country. . . ." Sullivan could send all the most ardent patriots out of New Hampshire and then declare the colony's loyalty to the king. If he pursued such an enlightened course he could expect to be "amply rewarded" by a grateful monarch, and all his past sins would be forgiven. "What is all this expence of human life for?" Livius asked at the end of his letter, "these deluges of human blood? very probably only to set afloat some lawless despotic tyrant in the room of your lawful king."

Germain seemed obsessed with the notion of trying to bribe American generals. If the rebels could not be beaten, they might be bought. At his direction William Eden, in charge of the British secret service, wrote to Sir Henry Clinton in May, 1779: "Our spirits in general with regard to your prospects are not very high; therefore if by any fortunate or able stroke you can get us out of our scrape you will be worshipped by a very grateful country." If there were signs of divisions among the American leaders over the course of the war, Eden wrote, Clinton was not to "hesitate at any expense, promises, threats, management, etc., etc., etc., that may tend to carry the point or disarm the rebellion before the mischief makers [the Whig Opposition] on this side of the water can interfere." Germain likewise was pleased to hear "that the dissensions and jealousies among the members of Congress continue to increase, and that the people's repugnancy to serve in their army becomes every day greater." Clinton was urged to try "gaining over some of the most respectable members of that body, or officers of influence and reputation among their troops. . . ." Sir Henry was thus ready to bite at Arnold's lure.

Arnold's first approach to the British was through a well-known Tory, Joseph Stansbury. "General Arnold sent for me," Stansbury recalled, "and, after some general conversation, opened his political sentiment respecting the war between Great Britain and America, declaring his abhorrence of a separation of the latter from the former as a measure that would be ruinous to both." Arnold then "communicated to me, under a solemn obligation of secrecy, his intention of opening his services to the commander-in-chief of the British forces in any way that would most effectually restore the former government and destroy the then usurped authority of Congress, either by immediately joining the British army or co-operating on some concealed plan with Sir Henry Clinton."

Stansbury, who had been born in England and now kept a glass and china shop on Front Street, had been an active supporter of the British during Howe's occupation of Philadelphia. After its evacuation, however, he lay low and avoided doing anything to draw the attention of patriots to himself, although he privately circulated verses exhorting the Loyalists:

> Think not, though wretched, poor, or naked,
> Your breast alone the load sustains;
> Sympathizing hearts partake it:
> Britain's monarch shares your pains.
> This night of pride and folly over,
> A dawn of hope will soon appear.
> In its light you will discover
> Your triumphant day is near.

"In order to facilitate the completion of his wishes," Stansbury wrote later of Arnold, "I went secretly to New York with a tender of his services to Sir Henry Clinton." (Arnold had chosen for his code name that of the Scots General George Monk, who had helped to overthrow the Long Parliament and restore the Stuart monarchy in the person of Charles II.) In New York Stansbury made contact with Major André. One of the assurances that Arnold wanted from the British was that they intended to pursue the war to a victorious conclusion. The message that André sent back by Stansbury stated that the British had met his overtures "with full reliance on his honorable intentions," and that furthermore Arnold could be confident "that no thought is entertained of abandoning the point we have in view. That, on the contrary, powerful means are expected for accomplishing our end."

One of Stansbury's most definite instructions was to find out how much the British were prepared to pay for treason. André, making a record of his discussions with the go-between, wrote, "We likewise assure him that in the very first instance of receiving the tidings or good offices we expect from him, our liberality will be evinced. . . ." The rewards would be generous in proportion to the services performed. "Should the abilities and the zeal of that able and enterprising gentleman amount to the seizing an obnoxious band of men, to the delivery into our power or enabling us to attack to advantage and by judicious assistance completely to defeat a numerous body, then would the generosity of the nation exceed even his most sanguine hopes." If such an attempt were to fail and Arnold were forced to flee, he could be assured that "the cause for which he suffers will hold itself bound to indemnify him for his losses and receive him with the honours his conduct deserves."

André sent Stansbury back to Philadelphia with a list of items that the British would be pleased to have: "The Counsels of [Congress]. Contents of dispatches from foreign abbetors. Original dispatches and papers. . . . Channels through which such dispatches pass, hints for securing them. Number and position of troops. . . . Influential persons of rank with the same favourable disposition in the several commands in different quarters. . . . Magazines—where any new are forming."

Blackstone's *Commentaries,* a famous work on English law popular in America, was the code book to be used in ciphering and deciphering correspondence. Each word would have three numbers—the page of Blackstone, and the line and the number of the word in a particular line. Invisible ink might also be used, with the notation "F" or "A" to indicate that the writing might be brought out by fire or acid. André proposed that Peggy Shippen Arnold write to him on frivolous social matters, with messages written between the lines in acid by Mrs. Arnold's friend Peggy Chew or by Arnold himself. "This will come by a flag of truce exchanged officer, etc.," André noted, "every messenger remaining ignorant of what they are charged with. The letters may talk of the Mischianza or or other nonsense." André then wrote down an account of his discussion with Stansbury and sent it to Clinton, with the suggestion that if he agreed to it, he should seal it and send it to Germain.

André promptly wrote to Peggy Chew, who had been his partner at the Mischianza, a letter full of chitchat, expressing his hope that he was "yet in the memory of the little society of Third and Fourth Streets and even of the *other Peggy,* now Mrs. Arnold, who will I am sure accept of my best respects. . . ." The letter was marked "A" for acid, but it apparently brought no response from Peggy Chew; neither she nor Peggy Shippen Arnold figured in the correspondence that followed.

Arnold's first effort to send a letter in invisible ink was botched, and the letter came out a blur when held over the fire. There were numerous other misadventures and confusions, but Arnold nevertheless managed to dispatch a fairly regular flow of political and military information to Clinton. "General Washington and the army," he wrote in cipher in one letter, "will move to the North river [the Hudson] as soon as forage can be obtained. Congress have given up Charles Town if [attacked]. They are in want of arms, ammunition, and men to defend it." Seizing documents, he wrote André, was impossible. "Their contents can be known from a member of Congress." But Arnold did not say what member, though he was at pains to assure André that "Could I know S.H.'s intentions he would never be at a loss for intelligence. . . . Madam Arnold," he added, "sends her particular compliments." André would not send him such information, but he assured him once more, "with the strictest truth that the war is to be prosecuted with vigour, and that no thought is entertained of giving up the dependency of America. . . ."

Through André, Clinton sent a specific suggestion to Arnold: "Join the army, accept a command, be surprised, be cut off: these things may happen in the course of manoeuvre, nor you be censured or suspected. A complete service of this nature involving a corps of five or six thousand men would be rewarded with twice as many thousand guineas." This was the sort of thing that Clinton had in mind. "It is such as these he pledges himself shall be rewarded beyond your warmest expectations. The colour of the times favours them, and your abilities and firmness justify his hopes of success."

Such vague promises were not sufficient for Arnold. He made clear in his next letter, written through Stansbury to a fellow Tory poet, the Reverend Jonathan Odell, and through Odell to André, that he wished to have agreement on a specific sum, specifically £10,000 to be "engaged to him for his services" as well as "any loss he may sustain in case of detection." The £10,000 was a substantial sum, perhaps the equivalent of between two hundred and fifty thousand and a half-million dollars in today's currency. Arnold plainly did not intend to be a traitor for nothing. The balance of his letter contained information about the size of Washington's army and the state of supplies ("Plenty of everything at camp—supplied from everywhere") and news of Sullivan's campaign against the Iroquois.

What followed were a series of letters between Clinton and Arnold, all in cipher and sent by complicated and circuitous routes, in which the principals debated the price of treason. Ten thousand pounds, Clinton instructed André to write, was certainly not too much for some services, but "real advantage . . . or a generous effort" must be evident; it could not be paid out for a mere hope or promise. André added, "Permit me to prescribe a little exertion. . . . It is the procuring an accurate plan of West Point, New Windsor [Washington's headquarters], Constitution [the fort opposite West Point], etc. . . . The army as brigaded with the commanding officers in form commonly called the order of battle. Sketches or descriptions of harbours to the eastward which might be attacked, and where stores and shipping might be destroyed."

André reminded Arnold once more that he would be of much more potential use to the British cause if he had a command. It seemed to the British officer important that he and Arnold meet: "I am convinced a conversation of a few minutes would satisfy you entirely and I trust would give us equal cause to be pleased." That was all very well, Arrold replied in effect, but what about the ₤10,000? He hoped to have a command in a few weeks, and then perhaps he could arrange an interview with André. For the moment he had no plan of West Point; the only one in existence was in Washington's hands. So the correspondence lapsed. André wrote to Peggy Arnold, instead of her husband, offering to "enter into the whole detail of capwire, needles, gauze, etc., and to the best of my ability, render you in these trifles services from which I hope you would infer a zeal to be further employed." One wonders if the letter was searched for an "F" or an "A" and subjected to fire and acid without success.

Peggy Arnold replied, thanking André for his offer to be of service and assuring him "that her friendship and esteem for him is not impaired by time or accident."

Meanwhile Jonathan Odell, finding himself at least temporarily unemployed in the spy business, turned to his poetry and wrote:

> Seen or unseen, on earth, above, below,
> All things conspire to give the final blow.
> Heaven has a thousand thunderbolts to dart;
> From hell ten thousand living flames will start;
> Myriads of swords are ready for the field;
> Myriads of lurking dangers are concealed;
> In injured bosoms dark revenge is nursed.
> Yet but a moment and the storm shall burst.

Doubtless he took special pleasure in his insider's reference to "injured bosoms" where "dark revenge is nursed."

In the period between the end of his correspondence with Clinton and his return to active service as commander of West Point, Arnold tried first to get Congress to pay a padded expense account, then to get Washington to grant him a furlough from the army so that he could undertake a privateering expedition in the hope of getting money to support the lavish style of life that he and his wife seemed determined to maintain. There are also indications that he applied for a loan to the French minister, the Chevalier de La Luzerne, and was haughtily rebuffed.

By May 25, 1780, Arnold had already begun to maneuver for the command of West Point, and he wrote to General Philip Schuyler to enlist his support. He had earlier requested a leave of absence from Washington, he noted, in the belief that it would be an inactive summer, but now with the prospects of some campaigning, he was determined to return to the field, "though attended with pain and difficulty" because of his wound. "I wish," he added, "to render my country every service in my power, and with the advice of my friends am determined to join the army. . . ." Arnold asked Schuyler to serve as his intermediary with Washington, and Schuyler wrote back that the general had "expressed himself with regard to you in terms such as the friends who love you could wish. . . . He expressed a desire to do whatever was agreeable to you, dwelt on your abilities, your merits, your sufferings, and the well-earned claims you have on your country. . . . I believe you will have an alternative proposed, either to take charge of an important post . . . or your station in the field. . . . If the command at West Point is offered, it will be honorable; if a division in the field, you must judge whether you can support the fatigues, circumstanced as you are."

At the same time Arnold wrote to Schuyler, angling for the command of West Point, he reopened his correspondence with the British. Now, at last, he might have a prize to deliver that would be worth the £10,000 that he had earlier insisted upon. André had departed with Clinton on the expedition against Charles Town, and Arnold now wrote to General Knyphausen, commanding the New York garrison in Clinton's absence. His cover name was now Mr. Moore. Mr. Moore renewed his request for a specific guarantee of money or, as Arnold put it, "security . . . for his family." In addition, he needed "a small sum of ready money to employ in a particular channel. . . . He particularly desires to have a conference with an officer of confidence. He will take a decisive part in case of an emergency or that a capital stroke can be struck."

Knyphausen, understandably, felt that he did not have authority to enter into such negotiations. He would pass on the word as promptly as possible to Clinton, and meanwhile he was "happy in cultivating the connexion and in giving Mr. Moore every testimony of his regard, from the persuasion which the general entertains of his rectitude and sincerity." Arnold immediately began sending information that he thought might be of use to the British command, especially information given him by Lafayette about the impending arrival of a French fleet and eight thousand French soldiers. He also continued his efforts to secure command of West Point. But he was disconcerted to discover that Washington planned to leave that fort in the hands of a few invalids and to protect it by keeping his own army in position to attack any British force moving against it. Thwarted for the moment, Arnold traveled to West Point, which was under the command of General Robert Howe, the officer who had botched the defense of Savannah the year before. "I called on General Howe at West Point," he wrote from Fishkill to Washington on the sixteenth of June, "which I never saw before, was greatly disappointed both in the works and the garrison. There is only 1,500 soldiers, which will not half man the works." A quick attack by the British would surely be successful. "This place has been greatly neglected," he continued. "General Howe tells me there is not ten day's provision for the garrison. . . . The works appear to me, though well executed, most wretchedly planned to answer the purpose designed: viz., to maintain the post and stop the passage of the river." In talking with Howe, Arnold dwelt so persistently on the vulnerability of Rocky Hill, the highest point in the fort, which commanded all the other works, that Howe thought it peculiar.

Back in Philadelphia, Arnold once more, through Stansbury, contacted the British. He no longer spoke of the probability of his taking command of West Point, but he now had a drawing of the defenses on both sides of the river, prepared by a French engineer-officer, "and thinks he could settle matters with a proper officer that you might take it [West Point] without loss, and also lay down a plan of communication whereby you should be informed of everything projected at Headquarters."

Again, much of the correspondence was about payment. "My stock in trade (which I have before mentioned)," he wrote Clinton, "is ℥10,000 with near an equal sum of outstanding debts. . . . I expect you will pay into the hands of the bearer [a new emissary this time, one Samuel Wallis] 1000 guineas to be invested in goods suitable for our market. . . ." A year of secret negotiations was beginning to tell even on Arnold's steely nerves. "If you have any regard for my safety," he wrote in conclusion, "by no means trust to any conveyance that is not known or proved. You may be deceived by false friends. Mention no names. Write me in cipher and through some medium."

The following day Arnold wrote again, this time assuring Clinton that he would be given command of West Point— "a post in which I can render the most essential services"—and making suggestions for a meeting with a British officer. "The mass of the people are heartily tired of the war," he added, "and wish to be on their former footing. They are promised great events from this year's exertion. If disappointed, you have only to persevere and the contest will soon be at an end. The present struggles are like the pangs of a dying man but of short duration."

Clinton's reply, taking up Arnold's suggestion of a meeting with a British officer, said nothing about money, which was so plainly Arnold's principal preoccupation. Arnold wrote back on the fifteenth that he wished property valued at £10,000 sterling "to be paid to me or my heirs in case of loss; and, as soon as that shall happen, 500 pounds per annum to be secured to me for life, in lieu of the pay and emoluments I give up. . . . If I point out a plan of co-operation by which Sir Henry shall possess himself of West Point, the garrison, etc., etc., etc. £20,000 sterling I think will be a cheap purchase for an object of so much importance. . . . I request a full and explicit answer."

To hedge his bets, Arnold at the same time applied to Congress for back pay and allowances, "that I may be enabled to take the field," and Congress replied by ordering five thousand dollars to be advanced against his pay. Meantime Clinton replied to Arnold's letter of the fifteenth. Twenty thousand pounds sterling would be paid to Arnold if West Point with its three thousand defenders fell into British hands through Arnold's efforts. On the other hand, if the plan failed, he would be generously provided for. However, the ten thousand pounds down and the promise of an "annuity of 500 whether services are performed or not . . . can never be made."

Clinton's reply to Arnold was delayed a month in transmission. It went, by a most circuitous route, through Odell, Wallis, Stansbury, Peggy Arnold, and then on to Arnold, who was with Washington near King's Ferry. On July 31, Washington, preparing to cross the Hudson, encountered Arnold and told him that he was giving him command of the light troops "which was a post of honour . . . which his rank entitled him to." Arnold's face fell. His whole plan was imperiled. He turned away without speaking or thanking Washington for the appointment. The next day he once more asked Washington for the West Point command. His wounds were troubling him; he did not feel capable of campaigning in the field. At last Washington acceded, and on the third of August Arnold was ordered to "proceed to West Point and take the command of that post and its dependencies," which included the forts of Stony Point and Verplanck's Point and the positions on the east side of the Hudson from Fishkill to King's Ferry.

Washington had moved in response to Clinton's clear intention of attacking the French at Newport; an attack there would expose New York and give Washington an opportunity to assault the city with its much-reduced garrison. But the unpredictable Clinton got only as far as Huntington, Long Island, and then, uneasy about the defenses of New York, turned around and sailed back. At this unexpected maneuver, Washington recrossed the Hudson to the Jersey side and put his army into a defensive position at Tappan, thereby blocking Clinton's access to the posts on the Hudson.

As commander of West Point, Arnold set out to strengthen that post and put it in good order. It was essential that he do nothing to raise the slightest suspicion that he did not intend to defend the fort. He received additional enforcements, including a corps of engineers, "Sappers and Miners," among whom was Joseph Martin. Martin had left Dobbs Ferry most reluctantly. He had found there a charming and amiable girl. "Many young men have, doubtless felt the same upon similar occasions, . . ." he wrote, but that time has long since gone by and my affections with it, both 'gone with the years beyond the flood' never more to return." At West Point he found, for company "rats enough had they been men, to garrison twenty West Points."

Arnold meanwhile carried on his own minor speculations, which he seemed as unable to resist as a kleptomaniac could forbear stealing. He again traded in public supplies for his own benefit and filled his headquarters with goods that he could hardly have expected to use. He sold pork, salt, and wine and kept the money. His justification was that the army owed him money that it had never paid. His temper increasingly short, he waited for some word from Clinton that the British commander was still interested in buying West Point.

The main point to be effected now was the meeting between Arnold and André. This was the most complex and the delicate part of the whole scheme. Arnold could not run the risk of trying to enter the British lines, and it was difficult to see how he could receive André and have sufficient time to talk with him about the betrayal of the fort without arousing the suspicions of his own aides. To Arnold, the simplest solution seemed to be to have André come to West Point disguised as a spy for the Americans. Such men came and went constantly. It was, moreover, fairly common knowledge that Arnold had been anxious to make contact with such agents who could keep him supplied with information about enemy intentions. With this in mind Arnold told his aide, Colonel Richard Varick, that he was writing a letter to a certain

John Anderson (André's cover name) "in a merchantile style . . . to establish a line of intelligence of the enemy's movements." That seemed reasonable enough to Varick, and the next day Arnold ordered an officer, Lieutenant Barber, to "proceed in a barge with a flag, one sergeant, and seven privates to Fort Washington . . . taking with you Mary McCarthy and her two children . . . who have my permission to enter the British lines. . . ." Mrs. McCarthy carried a letter from Arnold to André, proposing that the British officer visit West Point in disguise to confer with Arnold. André's reply implicitly rejected Arnold's notion—this at the insistence of Clinton, who wished the meeting to take place somewhere on neutral ground, near the river and close to British warships so that if anything went wrong, André would have a good chance to make his escape. Above all, Clinton rejected the idea that André should go in any sort of disguise. That would make him liable to be hanged as a spy rather than simply captured as a prisoner of war.

André's letter to Arnold, ostensibly written by a secret agent, John Anderson, had to pass through the hands of one of the officers in Arnold's command, Colonel Sheldon, who was in charge of a post on the Lower Salem Creek; it was therefore phrased in most elliptical sentences. Arnold had told Sheldon that he was expecting to contact a spy, but Sheldon was mystified by André's (or Anderson's) reference to the possibility that an officer (André) might appear at Dobbs Ferry "Monday next, the 11th, at Twelve o'clock" in place of the spy, John Anderson. This, of course, was in conformity with Clinton's insistence that André not disguise himself, but the idea that Arnold might be conferring with a British officer about military secrets seemed to Sheldon very odd. Arnold professed to be equally surprised, but he wrote Sheldon that he would go to Dobbs Ferry and confer with the spy John Anderson, coming under a flag of truce, or, if the spy failed to appear, with the officer who might appear in his place.

Arnold then wrote to André, using the pen name Gustavus and preserving in his letter the fiction that John Anderson was an American agent, in case the letter was intercepted. In the letter he once more urged André to come as a spy. "You must be sensible," he wrote, "my situation will not permit my meeting or having any private intercourse with such an officer." André must come "to our lines by stealth. If you can do it without danger on your side," Arnold added, "I will engage you shall be perfectly safe here."

Then, just in case the message did not reach André, or in case he persisted in coming as a British officer to Dobbs Ferry, Arnold visited a Tory friend down the river on Sunday night and the next morning set out by barge for Dobbs Ferry. The British plan, as it turned out, was for Beverley Robinson, in whose house Arnold had his headquarters, to come under a flag of truce to make arrangements for the furnishings of his house and to be accompanied by André, who would take the occasion to meet privately with Arnold.

5

Treason

THREE days before the scheduled meeting with André, Benedict Arnold rode out alone on the road to Dobbs Ferry and was observed there by Joseph Martin. Unaware that he was being watched attentively by the sergeant, Arnold sat on his horse a long time, examining the road. Martin "thought it strange to see him quite alone in such a lone place." He had been acquainted with Arnold from childhood, he noted later, "and never had too good an opinion of him." It was a strange meeting between the treacherous general from Connecticut, famous all over the world for his military exploits, and the obscure enlisted man from the same state. Martin's great narrative was still far in the future, but it would rank with the great military accounts of history and give him a much fairer fame than Benedict Arnold's.

A British gunboat took Robinson and André up the Hudson on September 11 and landed them at Dobbs Ferry, where they waited for Arnold. At this point the conspirators had their first misadventure. British gunboats on the river sighted Arnold's barge and opened fire on it. Arnold's soldiers rowed across to the west side of the river, where Arnold took refuge in a blockhouse. With a river between them, André and Arnold each waited for the other to appear; their plan frustrated, Arnold returned to West Point, André to New York.

On Friday, the fourteenth, Arnold once more wrote André, again urging him to come "by stealth" to the American lines. "If you have any objections to this plan," he added, "I will send a person in whom you may confide, by water, to meet you at Dobb's Ferry on the Wednesday the 20th instant . . . who will conduct you to a place of safety where I will meet you. . . . It will be necessary for you to be disguised. . . ." Arnold had a final piece of treachery. He had received that day from Washington a letter telling him that he was on his way to Hartford to meet with General Rochambeau and asking for a guard of a captain and fifty men. "You will keep this to yourself, as I want to make my journey a secret," Washington concluded. Arnold included this information in his letter to André and Clinton.

Again, Clinton made an effort to arrange a meeting between Robinson and Arnold, with André presumably present, but Arnold felt that the plan was too risky and vetoed it. Peggy Arnold and the three children, one their own and two by Arnold's first marriage, had arrived and were staying in the Robinson house during the final stages of the effort to arrange the meeting between André and her husband. Clinton told Admiral Rodney of the negotiations with Arnold, and orders were issued for soldiers and transports to be ready for a quick strike up the Hudson as soon as the final arrangements between André and Arnold, or John Anderson and Mr. Moore, had been concluded.

On Wednesday, September 20, André went to Dobbs Ferry with instructions from Clinton to the commander of the British frigate *Vulture* to carry André down the river to a prearranged point; there Joshua Smith, a Tory sympathizer and a friend of Arnold's, was supposed to pick up André—or rather John Anderson, a spy with valuable information for the Americans. Smith had also agreed to allow Arnold and André to confer at his house. On Wednesday morning, however, Smith could not procure a boat, and André had to wait impatiently all through the day, contriving to get word to Arnold that he was still aboard the *Vulture* waiting for Arnold's emissary. Finally, with a boat lined up, Smith and Arnold could not get men to man the oars. At last two young farmers, the Cahoon brothers, were bullied into undertaking the expedition by Arnold; they were quite unaware, of course, of what was afoot.

With Smith in the boat and their oars muffled, the brothers rowed some six miles down the river and across Haverstraw Bay to the *Vulture*. "We were hailed by the vessel," Samuel Cahoon recalled, "and Mr.

Smith answered 'Friends,' and said we were from King's Ferry and bound to Dobbs Ferry, and we were ordered alongside immediately."

Smith delivered his messages from Arnold, who made it clear that he wished André to come without Robinson. André, after a few moments of reflection, threw a blue cloak with a hood over his red uniform coat and settled in the stern with Smith, who steered the boat while the Cahoon brothers rowed. The boat landed at the foot of Long Clove Mountain, some two miles below Haverstraw. Arnold was waiting with a horse for André. The first point to be settled, in Arnold's view, was the price that he was to be paid by the British for betraying the fort and the cause. They did not go to Smith's house but "hid among firs" and discussed their business like any plotters in the night. While the two men, the charming and clever young Englishman, who doubtless felt like an actor in one of his own romantic melodramas, and the saturnine traitor, greedy and remorseless, talked, Joshua Smith and the two coerced oarsmen waited nervously in the boat. Finally Smith "deemed it expedient to inform them of the approaching dawn of day." Arnold then came to the riverbank and tried to persuade the Cahoon brothers to row André back to the *Vulture,* but they, independent countrymen as they were, had had enough of the mad night's venture. They were tired and annoyed with themselves for having been persuaded to go in the first place. Their shrewd farmers' sense told them that something foul was in the air. In Samuel Cahoon's words, "Mr. Smith said if we could not go we must do as we thought best, and would leave it to us. . . ." So there, at the most crucial point of the whole dangerous rendezvous, plans were thwarted by the obduracy of two farmers, immune to threats or bribes, who simply wished to go home and to bed. In a strange way, that was the story of the American Revolution—stubborn and intractable farmers who were determined to be independent and to do as their consciences or simply their inclinations prompted them.

After a hasty conference, Arnold and André rode off to find a temporary refuge in Smith's house, where they could make plans to get André back to the *Vulture* or to the safety of the British lines. Smith and his oarsmen were left to return the borrowed boat to Haverstraw Creek, where they arrived at sunup, 5:59 A.M.

André, riding to Smith's house with Arnold, passed a guard, which, as he declared later, "I did not expect to see, having Sir Henry Clinton's direction not to go within an enemy's post." It was against "my stipulation, my intention, and without my knowledge beforehand," André later told the court-martial board. It also indicated Arnold's basic indifference to André's safety. He knew, as well as anyone, that the fact of being, if only technically, within the American lines made André, if captured, subject to the charge of being a spy rather than simply a prisoner of war who, as an important officer, would be readily exchanged. Indeed, it is not too much to say that Arnold, by so casually carrying André off to Smith's house, killed him as surely as if he had put a bullet in his heart himself.

At the house the two men were joined by Smith and the Cahoons (Smith's family had been sent away in expectation of just such an emergency). André now had to wait until nightfall before he could attempt to return to the *Vulture*. Meanwhile Colonel James Livingston, commanding at King's Ferry, had just that morning acquired a four-pounder and a howitzer that he was itching to fire at the enemy, and there was the *Vulture,* an ideal target, riding at anchor well within range of his guns. Livingston, displaying admirable initiative, gave the order to fire. The tide was slack with no wind, so although the *Vulture* immediately upped anchor and tried to make way, she lay becalmed and was soon a crippled bird, her hull pierced by six shots "between wind and water." "Many others," Beverley Robinson reported, "struck the sail and rigging, and boats on deck. Two shells [explosive rather than solid shot] hit us, one full on the quarterdeck, another near the main shrouds." The only person injured, however, was Captain Andrew Sutherland, who was hit on the nose by a splinter.

Arnold and André could, of course, hear the firing, and they watched apprehensively from Smith's house, which overlooked the river, as the shelling continued. The irony of the situation can hardly have escaped the two men. The independence of the Cahoons had kept André from returning quickly and safely to the *Vulture*. Now the enterprise of Livingston and the accuracy of his gunners were posing another unexpected hazard. Not until about eight or nine o'clock in the morning did the *Vulture* draw slowly out of range of Livingston's miniature battery and proceed down the river.

It was plain that André would have to find another way home. Even if the *Vulture* should make its way back at nightfall, the ship was now the object of close American attention, and it would be very difficult for André to regain it. Arnold, who had all along urged André to come to West Point disguised as an American spy, now proposed that he assume such a disguise to get back to the British lines by land, after being gotten across to the east bank by boat. André had the sense to protest strongly, but Arnold argued that there was no other way. Equipped with a pass from Arnold, André would be entirely safe; no American soldier would presume to question General Arnold's pass. Having overcome André's better judgment, as well as his instructions from Clinton, Arnold then insisted that André carry in his boot the plans of the West Point fortifications that he had brought with him. If Arnold's object had simply been to deliver the fort into British hands, he could certainly have reviewed the plan with André until it was firmly fixed in his head and thereby have avoided the obvious danger of having him carry such an incriminating document. It was dangerous enough to send André back through territory controlled by the Americans; it infinitely compounded that danger to send him with an incriminating document, poorly concealed on his person. In André's words, Arnold "made me put the papers I bore between my stockings and my feet. Whilst he did it, he expressed a wish, in case of any accident befalling me, that they should be destroyed, which I said of course would be the case, as when I went into the boat I should have them tied about with a string and a stone."

Arnold insisted on the map, which André could have reconstructed adequately from memory, because it was "the merchandise," the tangible goods for which Arnold intended to be handsomely paid. It was therefore important that it arrive in Clinton's hands as irrefutable evidence that Arnold had performed his part of the bargain.

The notion of the stone and the string sounds almost like children playing spy games. Certainly the whole enterprise was plagued by amateurism. If André was to be equipped with a stone and a piece of string while he crossed the Hudson, how was he to dispose of the incriminating document on land? And even on water, removing his boot and stocking, extracting the map, tying it up, and throwing it overboard would have been a rather awkward and time-consuming process.

The final error, of course, was the disguise. If André had returned in his uniform, he could not have been executed as a spy. He might have carried a flag of truce, so that if stopped and questioned he could have purported to be returning from a conference on the exchange of prisoners or some other official mission. So one error was compounded by another. André declared that he had no choice but to go in disguise after Smith's "refusal to reconduct me back the next night as I had been brought. Thus become a prisoner, I had to concert my escape." The chances are that despite his initial protest, the idea of slipping through the American lines in disguise appealed to the thespian in André. It would be a fitting and appropriate end to an exciting adventure: he would thereby become an actor in his own real-life play.

Arnold was uneasy that his long absence from headquarters might arouse the suspicions of his aides, who seemed to him to be constantly prying into his affairs. He therefore left André with two alternate plans for returning to New York, providing passes for both contingencies. One, for Joshua Smith, gave him "permission to pass with a boat and three hands and a flag to Dobb's Ferry, on public business, and to return immediately." This would enable Smith to row out to the *Vulture* wherever that vessel lay. Another pass authorized Smith to "pass the guards to the White Plains, and to return; he being on public business by my direction." Thus equipped, Smith could accompany André on a land route, crossing the river at King's Ferry and going down the east bank, where he should be able to avoid American outposts.

The third pass read: "Permit Mr. John Anderson to pass the guards to the White Plains, or below, if he chooses; he being on public business by my direction." This pass could be used by André, when Smith left him, to continue on to the British lines. The escape by water to the *Vulture* was the safest and most practical from André's point of view; it depended, however, entirely on Arnold. Arnold would have to secure a boat, again through Smith, and find, with Smith's help, men to row it. This apparently simple task was much more difficult than it seemed, as the reader can judge from the trouble that Smith and Arnold had had in originally procuring a boat and persuading the Cahoons to row it out to the *Vulture*. Arnold was preoccupied and impatient, and he did not have the time or the inclination to hunt about for two oarsmen, thereby running the risk of arousing suspicion. If escape by the *Vulture* in his character as a British officer was much the safest course for André, his escape by land and in disguise was much the simpler solution for Arnold. But of course what Arnold did not reflect sufficiently upon was that André's safety was also his. André's capture would almost inevitably lead to Arnold, most obviously through the map if that were discovered, or, failing that, through the pass that bore Arnold's signature. The mistake was that of a selfish and tired man. Arnold thought primarily of himself and failed to take account of the fact that André's fate was inextricably entangled with his own. We must also remember that Arnold had been under very heavy strain for days, indeed for eleven days, ever since the first abortive effort to make contact with André. It was now Friday, September 22. Arnold had been up all night and doubtless a good part of the night before. His wound, which was often painful when he was tired, throbbed, and cool and self-possessed as he was, he found it difficult to think clearly.

Leaving André, who was still uncertain as to how he was to make his way back to New York, Arnold rode off with Smith to Stony Point, where his barge waited to take him the fifteen miles upriver back to West Point. On the way to Stony Point, according to Smith (who, of course, was desperately anxious to clear himself of the charge of being a coconspirator), Arnold told him that André was a New York merchant who, out of pride, had borrowed a British officer's uniform and who should not be allowed to continue in such false plumage, for his own safety. If Arnold really told Smith this and if Smith believed him, he was a simple goose indeed. It is possible that Arnold told him the story and that Smith accepted it, suspecting it to be false but having nothing to gain by saying so. In any event, at this crucial point Arnold abandoned André to Smith and, in so doing, sealed his own fate as well as that of the young British officer.

When Smith returned, André still believed that he had the option of being rowed out to the *Vulture* that night. But Smith clearly had no stomach for the *Vulture* venture. When, to André's "great mortification," Smith "persisted in his determination of carrying me by the other route [that is by land]," the Englishman abandoned his scarlet coat for a purple one with gold-laced buttons. He kept his own waistcoat, which had no military markings on it, and his handsome white-topped riding boots. He also wore a round civilian hat. At dusk he got on the horse that Arnold had left for him and rode with Smith and his Negro servant the short distance down to the King's Ferry landing. The men at the ferry recalled that the figure later identified as André was silent and aloof while Smith was garrulous, having a drink with the officers and, once they were on the water, urging the ferrymen to row faster. At Verplanck's Point Smith talked to Colonel Livingston and told him he was going "up towards General Arnold's, or that route; and I gave him one letter to be delivered to General Arnold," Livingston recalled; "I then urged him to stay awhile and take supper or a drink of grog. He then informed me that there was a gentleman waiting for him who had just rode on, and was in a hurry to get off, and informed me that his business was very urgent, and I did not insist on his staying any longer. He then rode off and I did not see the person who was with him, it being dark and he having rode forward."

André wanted to ride to White Plains, but a platoon of militia, headed by a captain, stopped them at Crompond, eight miles from

Verplanck's Point, and began to question them. The captain knew Smith as a Tory sympathizer, and he was disposed to give him trouble. Where were they going? To Major Strang's. Major Strang was not at home, the militia captain replied. Then to Colonel Drake's. Drake had moved away. Where was Smith's pass? Smith produced it. The Christian name on the pass was Joshua, but the captain knew Smith as Joe, which he took to be Joseph. Smith explained patiently that his name was in fact Joshua. What was he up to riding about the country in the dead of night? He was going to White Plains with his companion, Smith said, to try to get intelligence from the enemy. The persistence of the militia captain's questions must have unsettled Smith, and André even more. In any proper army, a pass was a pass; there were no inquisitive countrified captains to ask rude questions about things that were none of their business.

His suspicions apparently allayed, the captain advised the two men, Smith and his silent companion, to spend the night at a nearby farmhouse. "Riding in the night would be dangerous when they got below Croton river, from the Cowboys," the Loyalist raiders. Smith decided to accept the militia captain's advice. He and André shared the same lumpy bed in the little farmhouse, André turning and muttering in his sleep.

Smith and André were up and off before dawn, making seven miles to Cat Hill before they stopped at a farm for breakfast. There Smith turned back, leaving André to ride alone the last fifteen miles to White Plains. Smith was afraid of the cowboys, while André, of course, would have welcomed them. It seemed unlikely to both men that André would encounter any rebels beyond Pine's Bridge.

As André rode on down Hardscrabble Road past Chappaqua and Pleasantville, he encountered a country boy who told him that scouts were operating in the area, and in consequence he turned onto the Tarrytown Road. The fact was that one road was little safer than the other. Cowboy raiders had been ranging through the countryside the day before, and now patriot "skinners" were out in considerable force, hunting down Loyalists. John Paulding, Isaac Van Wart, and David Williams were hiding in the woods near the Tarrytown Bridge. As soon as they saw the small, elegant figure of André, sitting his horse like a gentleman, they sensed something exotic, something not generally encountered on the Tarrytown Road. They emerged from the brush with their muskets at the ready and stopped André sometime between nine and ten o'clock of a cool, fall Saturday morning.

André's first assumption—that the men were Loyalist cowboys—induced him to speak to them in terms that fanned their suspicions. Furthermore, as soon as he opened his mouth, his accent told them that they had caught no ordinary bird. The clipped, cultivated voice rang in their ears with a decidedly foreign sound. "I hope, gentlemen, you belong to the lower party [British Loyalists]," André said.

One of the men replied, "We do." "So do I," André responded, "and by the token of this ring and key you will let me pass. I am a British Officer on business of importance, and must not be detained." As evidence André had proffered his watch with its attached seals and his military ring. One of the men took his watch and then ordered him to dismount. André realized at once that he had made the wrong assumption. He was in the hands of rebels. He tried a different tack. "I am happy, gentlemen, to find that I am mistaken. You belong to the upper party [the Whigs] and so do I. A man must make use of any shift to get along, and to convince you of it here is General Arnold's pass. . . . I am in his service."

"Damn Arnold's pass," one of the bushmen answered. "You said you was a British Officer, where is your money?"

"Gentlemen, I have none about me."

"You are a British Officer, and no money. . . . Let's search him."

The three men searched André and found not a shilling.

"I bet he has his money in his boots," one of the men said. So André had to remove his boots, with rough help from his captors. There was no money for the disappointed rebels, only papers. They searched his saddle, but with no success.

André then decided to try to bribe the men who were so eager to find money. They could, he told them, name their sum to deliver him to the British lines. No, they said shrewdly, they would simply be taken prisoners and probably hanged for their trouble. Well then, said André, seeking desperately for a way out of his predicament, one of them could go forward to King's Bridge with a note from him demanding five hundred guineas (the equivalent of perhaps ten thousand dollars in present currency), while he remained behind with two of his captors. The men considered this suggestion, whispering together and apparently divided in their views. Finally they declared that they would have none of his plan. If one of them went forward with a message from him, the British would doubtless send out a party, and they would all three be taken prisoner. They had decided to take him to the commanding officer at the nearest American post at North Castle.

Officers in charge of posts near the British lines had been ordered to keep an eye out for a John Anderson from New York and to pass him on to West Point when he appeared. At North Castle, Lieutenant Colonel John Jameson had succeeded Sheldon in command. He assumed that André was the John Anderson he had been instructed to look out for. But it was odd that he was stopped on his way to White Plains carrying papers "of a very dangerous tendency" as Jameson wrote to Arnold, preparing to send Anderson on to headquarters. Jameson must have sensed that something was not quite right, because he sent the captured papers to Washington, who was on his way back from his conference with Rochambeau at Hartford and was said to be near Peekskill.

Major Benjamin Tallmadge, head of Washington's secret service, had been out with a party on scouting duty; he appeared at North Castle not long after André's departure and heard Jameson's account of the capture of John Anderson. Tallmadge, whose business it was to be suspicious, at once put two and two together. It was no secret that Arnold had arranged to meet a certain John Anderson, allegedly an American spy. Thus if Anderson had been intercepted on his way to New York with important secret papers concealed on his person, the natural assumption was that Arnold had supplied him with that information. At least Arnold would have some explaining to do. Tallmadge persuaded Jameson to send after André and bring him back to North Castle until matters could be cleared up. If Arnold was guilty of treason, sending Anderson to him would only give both of them an opportunity to make their escape. After a discussion among the officers at the post, Jameson consented reluctantly but insisted on sending word of the capture to Arnold. "I did not think of a British ship being up the river," he wrote later to Washington, in an effort to exculpate himself from the charge of blundering, "and expected that, if he was the man he has since turned out to be, he would come down to the troops in this quarter, in which case I should have secured him." Whatever Jameson's defense, he plainly made a bad mistake in taking half-measures—that is, in having André brought back but also notifying Arnold of his capture.

André and his guards were overtaken at Peekskill, and André was brought back to North Castle. On Sunday morning he was sent to Lower Salem. When André learned that the captured papers had been sent to Washington, he knew that the cause was lost, and he wrote to the general to inform him that "the person in your possession is Major John André, adjutant general of the British army." He did not mention

Arnold's name but stated that he had come between the British and American lines to "meet a person who was to give me intelligence." He had been "betrayed . . . into the vile condition of an enemy in disguise within your posts. . . . I was involuntarily an impostor." André would have been less than human if he had not been thoroughly frightened at the turn of events. The masquerade was over. The gay and charming young man, to whom war was, for the most part, a delightful kind of game with lots of attentive ladies, balls, and parties, with glorious battles and intriguing secret maneuvers, had run out his string. The game had turned more deadly than he perhaps had ever guessed it would.

When Arnold had gotten back to his headquarters at Robinson's house, he had found two thoroughly rebellious young aides. Varick and Arnold's other aide, David Franks, who had been sent to Philadelphia to escort Peggy Arnold and the children to Arnold's headquarters, were both ready to resign. They had expostulated with Arnold over his friendship with Joshua Smith, and they suspected him of being engaged in some dubious mercantile venture with him, "under the sanction of his own command and through the rascal Smith." They were determined to ask for transfers if it turned out that their chief was once more involved in some illegal or barely legal activity, and they begged Peggy Arnold to use her influence with her husband to persuade him to break off the relationship.

But Arnold had more pressing matters on his mind. He had had time, during the long ride up the river from Stony Point, to reflect on how much his own safety depended on André's. Until he knew that André was safe within the British lines he could not rest easy.

The next night at dinner, after Smith had appeared with word for Arnold that he had seen André safely to Pine's Bridge and thus, presumably, home free, an unpleasant scene took place between Smith and Varick. When the butter ran out, Arnold said: "'Bless me, I had forgot the olive oil I bought in Philadelphia. It will do very well with salt fish.' . . . The oil was procured, and, on Arnold's saying it cost eighty dollars, Smith replied, 'Eighty pence' [meaning] that a dollar was really no more than a penny; upon which [Varick] said with some warmth . . . 'That is not true, Mr. Smith.'" It was not so much what he said as the way in which he said it that made it clear that Varick deliberately intended to insult Smith.

In Varick's words, "A very high dispute took place," in which Franks joined with his friend in baiting Smith. "You as well as myself," Varick later wrote Franks, "were cavalier with Smith till Mrs. Arnold (who also thought ill of Smith), observing her husband in a passion, begged us to drop the matter."

After dinner, when Smith had left, the furious Arnold gave his two aides a severe dressing-down. "If he asked the devil to dine with him, the gentlemen of his family should be civil to him." To which Franks replied boldly that if Arnold had not been at the table, he would have thrown a bottle at Smith's head. When Varick tried to divert some of Arnold's wrath by taking the blame for attacking Smith, Franks, in a temper of his own, declared that Arnold had been hypercritical of late and that he wished to be discharged as his aide. Franks stormed out of the room "in a passion," out of the headquarters, and rode off to Newburgh, where he stayed for two days. Varick, left on the field of battle with Arnold, gave vent to all his anger and dismay over his commander's slippery dealings and bad temper, cursing Smith "as a scoundrel, a damned rascal, and a spy," and telling Arnold that his reputation had already suffered "by an improper intimacy with Smith."

Arnold, doubtless sobered by hearing his most trusted aide denounce Smith as a spy and aware of what thin ice he was skating on, got the better of his temper at last. He was, he told Varick, "always willing to be advised by the gentlemen of his family, but, by God, [he] would not be dictated to by them. . . ." That same evening, Varick received a letter from a member of Governor Clinton's staff expressing distrust of Smith's "loose character." Varick considered the letter a vindication of his own attitude, took it to Arnold, "and then told him," as Varick put it, "that I considered his past conduct and language to me unwarrantable . . . and that I could no longer act with propriety [as his aide]."

At this Arnold capitulated completely. He would, he assured Varick, "never go to Smith's house again or be seen with him but in company." We know Smith primarily through the eyes of Varick and Franks and, on their testimony, through Peggy Arnold's, but he must have been a thoroughly unsavory character to arouse such strong feelings in the three of them. Ironically, it was their loyalty to Arnold and their protectiveness toward him that brought the whole issue to its strident climax. And it was typical of Arnold that, using any tool, clean or dirty, that came to hand, he as casually discarded it when it had served its purpose. So with Smith.

The officer in charge of taking André to Arnold had returned with him to North Castle, and it was Sunday before, after much further discussion, he started out once more with the message from Jameson to

Arnold. Meanwhile the captain who had been dispatched with the secret papers to find Washington came back without having found the general and was sent off again to West Point, where Washington was by now presumed to have arrived. Thus two messengers, one to Arnold, with news of André's capture, and one to Washington with the captured papers that told the whole story of the treason, were on their way simultaneously.

The messengers did not reach Arnold's headquarters until Monday. Washington spent Sunday night at Peekskill, and Smith, by chance, dined at the house where Washington stopped. Meanwhile Beverley Robinson and Captain Sutherland were waiting with growing anxiety on the battered *Vulture* for some sign of André. Thoroughly alarmed, they sent word on Sunday to Clinton in New York that André had not appeared.

At his headquarters, Arnold had to survive a long Sunday, during which he, too, must have felt increasingly uneasy. On Monday morning, before breakfast, he went to his office and asked Varick if he had replied to some dispatches from Jameson and Tallmadge. Varick said he had not and that he felt too sick to answer them now. Arnold left the office, and Varick never saw him again.

Arnold had made arrangements to give breakfast to Washington and his staff, but at nine o'clock Alexander Hamilton arrived with word that Washington had been delayed and that breakfast should be served without him. While the headquarters party was eating, the letters from Jameson were delivered to Arnold. He broke the seals and read them, and then, without displaying a trace of emotion, he excused himself and "ran out and ordered an horse saddled, and sent a servant down the hill to order his barge's crew to man the boat." Franks, back from Newburgh, had gone to pick some peaches in Robinson's orchard for breakfast. Arnold dashed upstairs, conferred briefly with Peggy, and then came back down. At the foot of the stairs, he encountered Franks with his hands full of peaches. Arnold told him to tell Washington that he had gone over to West Point "and would return in about an hour." A man with less nerve would doubtless have panicked. Washington, the man he had betrayed, was probably only a few minutes away, and he might already know of Arnold's treachery. Arnold had only minutes to extricate himself from a situation that, if he were captured, must mean certain death.

Leaving the house, Arnold mounted his horse and dashed off down a precipitous trail to the river, where he threw his saddle and pistols into the barge and ordered the men to carry him down to Stony Point. At Stony Point, he told the bargemen that his "particular business from Washington to the Captain of the *Vulture* obliged him to go on board," promising the sailors two gallons of rum for their services. When he reached that vessel—so aptly named, it seemed to patriots—he directed that the men who had obeyed his orders be arrested as prisoners of war, a minor villainy but a revealing one.

Meanwhile Washington arrived, had breakfast, and departed for West Point to meet with Arnold. At West Point there was, mysteriously, no Arnold. While he was conferring with his staff, Washington received Jameson's letter and the map found on André. He realized at once that Arnold intended to betray West Point, but he seemed as self-possessed as ever; there was no break in the famous composure. He sent Hamilton off at once with a detachment of soldiers to try to intercept Arnold at Verplanck's Point and gave orders to his staff to look to the defenses of the fort. Then, as Lafayette told Robert Dale Owen, the English reformer, years later, Washington left the room with the marquis and once outside, out of sight and earshot, "giving way to an uncontroulable burst of feeling" threw his arms around Lafayette's neck and wept unabashedly. "I believe," Lafayette told Owen, "this was the only occasion throughout that long and sometimes hopeless struggle, that Washington ever gave way, even for a moment, under a reverse of fortune; and, perhaps I was the only human being who ever witnessed in him an exhibition of feeling so foreign to his temperament." We know Washington certainly gave vent to his emotions on a number of other occasions, but certainly never more poignantly. The initial despair was quickly followed by a cold fury. In the words of the unhappy Joshua Smith, who was promptly arrested and charged with treason, Washington "was the more enraged at the defection of General Arnold than [he] could have been at the treasonable conduct of any general officers under his command . . . and . . . he was led to suspect all around him. . . ."

Washington immediately sent word to Anthony Wayne to march to reinforce West Point against a possible British attack. Wayne wrote a typically bombastic account to a friend: "I am confident that the perfidy of Gen. Arnold will astonish the multitude. . . . The dirty, dirty acts which he has been capable of committing beggar all description, and are of such a nature as would cause the *Infernals to blush*." West Point, Wayne continued, was occupied by Americans "of a spiritless miserable *Vulgus* in whose hands the fate of America seemed suspended. In this situation his Excellency [Washington] (in imitation of Caesar and his Tenth Legion) called for his *veterans* . . ."—none other, of course, than General Wayne and his troops. And Wayne did, it must be admitted, respond like a veteran. He roused his men and within an hour had them on the march in the dead of night, hurrying them sixteen miles in four hours "without a single halt or a man left behind." It was an impressive performance by a man who, if he was vain and boastful and often rash, was one of the few real soldiers among Washington's generals. Washington, according to Wayne, thought the march "fabulous" and "when convinced of the reality . . . received us like a god, and retiring to take a short repose exclaimed, 'All is safe, and I again am happy.' May he long, very long, continue so!"

Similar reaction was expressed by General Greene's orders of the day to his troops on September 26: "Treason of the blackest dye was yesterday discovered"; Arnold had been about to surrender West Point to the British. "Such an event," the orders read, "must have given the American cause a deadly wound, if not a fatal stab. Happily the scheme was timely discovered to prevent the final misfortune. The providential train of circumstances which led to it affords the most convincing proofs that the liberties of America are the object of divine protection. . . . Our enemies, despairing of carrying their point by force, are practicing every base art to effect, by bribery and corruption, what they cannot accomplish in a manly way."

Across the river, at Arnold's headquarters in the Robinson house, his two young aides were still unaware of their commander's treachery. Around noon, Franks came to the window of the room where Varick lay sick in bed and, raising the window, told his friend he had just heard "a report that one Anderson was taken as a spy on the lines and that a militia officer had brought letters to Arnold and that he had been enjoined to secrecy by Arnold." It had occurred to Franks that Arnold might be involved with the mysterious John Anderson, but the two aides recoiled from the idea, "instantly reflecting," Varick recalled, "that I was injuring a gentleman and a friend of high reputation in a tender point. . . . It was uncharitable and unwarranted even to suppose it."

Even when Varick heard during the day that Arnold's barge had gone down the river instead of to West Point, that "circumstance made no impression on me," so firmly had he dismissed the idea of Arnold's treason. Peggy Arnold, abandoned in the flight of her husband and burdened with news of the catastrophe, waited in bed until Washington had left the house. The day before, she had spent an hour with the sick

Varick, "while I lay in a high fever, made tea for me, and paid me the utmost attention in my illness." Now she sent her housekeeper to see how Varick was, and as soon as the housekeeper had brought word that the patient was better, Peggy, "with her hair dishevelled and flowing about her neck," summoned him. "Her morning-gown with few other clothes remained on her—too few to be seen even by gentlemen of the family, much less by many strangers. . . . She seized me by the hand," Varick recalled, "with this—to me—distressing address and a wild look: 'Colonel Varick, have you ordered my child to be killed?' Judge you of my feelings at such a question from this most amiable and distressed of her sex, whom I most valued. She fell on her knees at my feet with prayers and entreaties to spare her innocent babe. A scene too shocking for my feelings, in a state of body and nerves so weakened by indisposition and a burning fever. I attempted to raise her up, but in vain." Franks at this point arrived with a doctor, and the three men carried her to her bed, "raving mad."

Varick remained with her, and after a few minutes she burst into a storm of weeping and exclaimed to the young officer seated by her on the bed "that she had not a friend left here." Varick replied that she had Franks and himself and General Arnold, who would soon be home back with General Washington from West Point.

"No, General Arnold will never return; he is gone, he is gone forever; there, there, there, the spirits have carried [him] up there, they have put hot irons in his head."

At last, Varick began to suspect that something, perhaps treason by Arnold, lay behind Peggy Arnold's hysterics. As soon as she heard that Washington had returned to the house without Arnold, she cried out that "there was a hot iron on her head and no one but General Washington could take it off, and wanted to see the General."

The doctor left the room with Varick and Franks and told them that Arnold must be sent for or his wife would surely die. Franks and Varick then told the doctor what they suspected—that Arnold had fled to the British. But they still could not bring themselves to speak their suspicions to Washington, and Washington, in turn, had enough question in his own mind as to whether the two aides had been involved in the plot to keep silent. After a hasty conference, Varick and Franks decided that perhaps the way to break the news to Washington was to let him see Peggy Arnold's condition and perhaps draw from it the same conclusions that they had drawn. Varick thus went to Washington, told him that Mrs. Arnold was out of her wits, went with Washington to her room, and told her that Washington was there. "She said no, it was not. The General assured he was, but she exclaimed; 'No, that is not General Washington; that is the man who was a-going to assist Colonel Varick in killing my child.'" Arnold, she declared once more, had been carried away by evil spirits—which, one is tempted to say, was true enough.

At this point Hamilton appeared with a letter from Arnold, safe aboard the *Vulture,* to Washington. "The heart which is conscious of its own rectitude," it read, "cannot attempt to palliate a step which the world may censure as wrong. I have ever acted from a principle of love to my country, since the commencement of the present unhappy contest between Great Britain and the colonies. The same principle of love to my country actuates my present conduct, however it may appear inconsistent to the world, who very seldom judge right of any man's actions." He asked no favor for himself. "I have too often experienced the ingratitude of my country to attempt it. But from the known humanity of your Excellency, I am induced to ask your protection for Mrs. Arnold from every insult and injury that a mistaken vengeance of my country may expose her to. It ought to fall only on me; she is as good and innocent as an angel, and is incapable of doing wrong. I beg she may be permitted to return to her friends in Philadelphia, or come to me, as she may choose. . . ." The letter, plus Peggy Arnold's hysterics, convinced Washington that she was innocent. Thus Arnold used Washington for the final time. Knowing Arnold and his wife and perhaps, above all, the involvement of André, it is difficult to believe that she was not fully aware of the conspiracy and had not encouraged and abetted it as best she could. It is also hard to believe that, in the brief and frantic period when Arnold was upstairs with her before his flight, they did not plan her wild seizure, as they had planned so much else. Varick, at least, came to believe that she had been acting all along.

The letter from Arnold was, in a way, the final effrontery, but it is striking that the first thing that Arnold did on reaching the haven of the *Vulture* was to write this curious epistle to Washington, the man whom above all others he had wronged. It was perhaps the most human thing he had done throughout the long period of intended treachery.

Hamilton, who was engaged to General Schuyler's daughter, was treated to another convincing scene in Peggy Arnold's mad act. "It was the most affecting scene I was ever witness to," he wrote his fiancée. "One moment she raved, another she melted into tears. Sometimes she pressed her infant to her bosom and lamented its fate, occasioned by the imprudence of her father, in a manner that would have pierced sensibility itself. All the sweetness of beauty, all the loveliness of innocence, all the tenderness of a wife, and all the fondness of a mother showed themselves in her appearance and conduct. We have every reason to believe that she was entirely unacquainted with the plan, and that the first knowledge of it was when Arnold went to tell her he must banish himself from his country and from her forever." If such was the case, she showed astonishing restraint until her husband was well out of harm's way.

The next day the charming and appealing invalid remembered nothing of what had gone before. She received Washington and Lafayette propped up in bed, and Hamilton lingered a long time trying to comfort and reassure her: "Her sufferings were so eloquent," he wrote Betty Schuyler, "that I wished myself her brother, to have a right to become her defender." The next day, having succeeded spectacularly in disarming suspicion, Peggy Arnold set off for Philadelphia, attended by the devoted Franks.

Here it is necessary to retrace some steps. When Washington arrived at Robinson's house on his return from West Point, he did not, as we have seen, mention to Varick or Franks that he knew of Arnold's treachery. Even at the initial scene with Peggy Arnold he did not disclose his knowledge. At four o'clock, he sat down to dinner with members of his staff: Lafayette, Knox, two French engineers who had been busy strengthening the defenses of West Point, and Colonel Lamb, the artillery officer. Despite his fever, Varick, in Arnold's absence, acted as host. Franks was also present. No one seemed to have much appetite, but Washington, entirely self-possessed, "behaved with his usual affability and politeness." Sometime after dinner, Washington asked Varick to take his hat and "walk out with him. . . . He thus declared he had the most indubitable proofs of Arnold's treachery and perfidy . . . he said he had not the least cause of suspicion of Major Franks or myself, but that his duty as an officer made it necessary to inform me that I must consider myself a prisoner, in which I, as politely as I could, acquiesced. It was what I expected. I then told him the little all I knew."

At seven in the evening Washington sent out his first orders. André was to be brought to Robinson's. He was to be "most closely and narrowly watched . . . André must not escape." When Jameson, about midnight, received Washington's dispatch, he sent off Major Tallmadge with André in the charge of a hundred mounted dragoons. The party arrived at Robinson's at dawn. Washington also dispatched officers he knew could not have been involved in the plot to take command at

Verplanck's Point and Stony Point. The West Point garrison was alerted, and word was sent to Nathanael Greene to move the main army to King's Ferry and await further orders. Word began to spread through the various echelons of the army of Arnold's treason. Major William North later recalled "the dark moment . . . in which the defection of Arnold was announced in whispers. It was midnight, horses were saddling, officers going from tent to tent ordering their men, in suppressed voices, to turn out and parade. No drum beat; the troops formed in silence and darkness. I may well say in consternation, for who in such an hour, and called together in such a manner, and in total ignorance of the cause, but must have felt and feared the near approach of some tremendous shock." Washington, who felt for Arnold a hatred that he could never feel for any other person, also interested himself in André's fate. André was taken from Robinson's house—where Washington had not seen him—down the river on a barge to Stony Point and there imprisoned in Mabie's Tavern under heavy guard; Washington then undertook to convene a board of general officers to examine André and "as speedily as possible to report a precise state of his case, together with your opinion of the light in which he ought to be considered and the punishment that ought to be inflicted."

The board, which consisted of Lord Stirling, Lafayette, Baron von Steuben, St. Clair, Robert Howe, the major generals, and seven briga-dier generals, among them Glover, Stark, and Knox, was headed by Nathanael Greene. It met on September 29 in the Dutch church at Tappan. André was interrogated by the board, with special attention to the question of whether he had knowingly come within the American lines and to the matter of his disguise. He was candid in his answers, basing his defense on the argument that his intention had always been to appear as a British officer and to remain outside the American lines, however vaguely they were defined. The board then read letters from Beverley Robinson, Arnold, and Sir Henry Clinton, all arguing that André had in fact come under a flag of truce and that he had been under Arnold's order while in the American lines and thus could not properly be considered a spy. While Arnold insisted that André had come under a flag, André himself made no such claim. Had he been willing to lie, and had his lie been supported by Clinton and Arnold, the board might have had a pretext for giving him a sentence short of death. As it was, the facts seemed clear beyond serious cavil. There could be no question about the disguise, or about the fatal papers that Arnold had so needlessly saddled him with. André had, in fact, convicted himself out of his own mouth. After a period of deliberation, the board reached a verdict that every member signed: "that Major André, adjutant general to the British army, ought to be considered as a spy from the enemy; and that, agreeable to the law and the usage of nations, it is their opinion he ought to suffer death."

In general orders the next day, Washington approved the sentence and ordered the execution to take place at five o'clock the following day. In spite of his sympathy for André, a sympathy apparently shared by many members of the board and by a number of his guards and captors, Washington had little choice but to confirm the unanimous verdict of his board. To do otherwise would have seemed weak and sentimental. The crime existed independently of the character or charm of the man who had committed it, and the rules of war were clear enough.

It was not until Friday, the twenty-ninth—the day that the board met and made its recommendation that André be executed as a spy— that Clinton received definite word from Washington as to André's situation. Accompanying it was a letter from André himself, freeing Clinton of any blame for his capture and stating that "changing my dress, which led to my present situation," was "contrary to my own intentions as they were to your orders. . . . I am perfectly tranquil in mind and prepared for any fate to which an honest zeal for my King's service may have devoted me." André thanked Clinton "for your Excellency's profuse kindness to me," ending with the assurance that "I receive the greatest attention from his Excellency General Washington, and from every person under whose charge I happen to be placed."

Clinton in his anxiety summoned William Smith, the royal chief justice, and quizzed him about the legal aspects of André's role, rambling on from that subject to a review of his plans to capture West Point "and putting an end to the war, for he had boats of all draughts for proceeding to Albany." "I said little," Smith noted in his account of the conversation, "for he spoke much. . . . I enlarged upon the idea he now had of the importance of the Hudson and the acquisition of it as the end of the war. . . . I almost suspect that he still has designs upon the Hudson." Clinton told Smith that there were other American generals who were ready if the opportunity offered to aid the British, and when Smith nodded his head in agreement, Clinton asked him to name anyone he had in mind.

Clinton next convened a general council of civil and military officers and extracted from them an opinion that André had not, in fact, acted as a spy. Clinton then sent off a commission to meet, under a flag of truce, with Washington, in order to present the arguments in support of a different interpretation of André's role.

The appointment of the commission to present a special plea to Washington gave the general a pretext to delay André's execution until Monday, "at twelve o'clock precisely."

Hamilton, in disguised handwriting but certainly at Washington's behest, then wrote to Clinton that since André "was captured in such a way as will according to the laws of war justly affect his life. . . . Perhaps he might be released for General Arnold, delivered up without restriction or condition. . . . Arnold appears to have been the guilty author of the mischief; and ought more properly to be the victim, as there is great reason to believe he meditated a double treachery, and had arranged the interview in such a manner that if discovered in the first instance, he might have it in his power to sacrifice Major André to his own safety." The postscript read, "No time is to be lost."

Washington said little about Arnold's treachery, but his actions were eminently expressive of his emotions. Above everything else, he wished for vengeance on his betrayer. Only a very compelling emotion could have persuaded Washington to propose such a dubious negotiation. Hamilton himself was plainly embarrassed by his own role in the matter. Writing to his friend and intimate, John Laurens, he noted that "a gentleman" had suggested exchanging André for Arnold, but that he had refused to mention such a dishonorable proposition to André, "which must have placed me in the unamiable light of supposing him capable of meanness, or of not feeling myself the impropriety of the measure." The "gentleman" could only have been Washington, the man of ultimate rectitude. No one else had the authority to propose such a scheme. Hamilton must have expostulated with Washington, and indeed, as he told Laurens, he refused to speak to André about the suggestion. However, he did write reluctantly to Clinton, implying that Arnold had not been above sacrificing André to save his own hide, which although undoubtedly true was hardly relevant at this point. Carl Van Doren, who has told the most complete and accurate account of Arnold's treachery, notes that there is nothing to "indicate whether Washington approved of Hamilton's letter, or even knew of it." It seems to me inconceivable that Hamilton, Washington's loyal aide, who was repelled by the whole idea of such a transaction, would have proposed it to Clinton except at Washington's direction. To guard against the possibility that the letter would not reach Clinton before André's execution, Captain Ogden, who carried the letters to Clinton, was instructed to sound out the British by dropping a hint that André's life would be spared if Arnold were returned to the Americans. He did as he was instructed. The officer to whom he addressed the question went immediately to Clinton, who rejected the idea out of hand.

Washington, brooding over how he might be revenged on Arnold, conceived a scheme almost as far-fetched as the proposal for exchanging André for Arnold. To carry it out he needed, above all, time. Washington sent General Greene to meet the British delegation, headed by the governor of New York, General Robertson. Greene and Robertson conferred alone for some time, while Murray, Robertson's aide, talked to Hamilton. Much of the discussion between Greene and Robertson revolved around the conflict between the testimony of Arnold and of André himself. When Robertson produced a letter from Arnold in which Arnold took all the blame on himself (which was easy, since he was safe within British lines), Greene produced André's very different statement and declared that "Arnold was a rascal and André a man of honour whom he believed; and they would consent to no conference for additional evidence. Greene repeated the suggestion that Arnold be given up in return for André, and Robertson replied with no more than a scornful look.

While the British waited on the *Greyhound* off Dobbs Ferry, Greene returned to confer with Washington and the next morning brought word that Washington remained unmoved. Now Robertson, in a letter to Washington, began to hint at retaliation against American prisoners of war in British hands. A letter from Arnold was delivered to Washington with the explicit threat to execute forty Carolinans charged with betraying their parole if the sentence against André were carried out. "Suffer me to entreat your Excellency," Arnold had written, "for your own and the honour of humanity, and the love you have of justice, that you suffer not an unjust sentence to touch the life of Major André. But if this warning should be disregarded, and he should suffer, I call heaven and earth to witness that your Excellency will be justly answerable for the torrent of blood that may be spilt in consequence."

On Sunday, October 1, Washington rejected any further conference or delay in André's execution. André's personal servant was permitted to come out to Tappan, and André requested, in a letter to Washington, that he be shot instead of hanged like a common criminal. Washington refused the request, since, as he later explained to Congress, André was either a spy, in which case he should die the death of a spy, or he was a prisoner of war, in which case he should not be executed at all. To mitigate the sentence would be to raise the question of whether he had been fairly condemned.

Sometime before noon on October 2, André, in the splendid full-dress uniform of a British officer, was brought to the gallows on the hill above Tappan with Major Tallmadge at his side and a guard of soldiers. Tallmadge, who had come to like and admire the young Englishman, turned away, "entirely overwhelmed with grief that so gallant an officer and so accomplished a gentleman should come to such an ignominious end."

With as large and attentive audience as any actor could wish, André climbed on the coffin resting in the baggage wagon and adjusted the rope around his neck and the handkerchief over his eyes. He was asked if he had some final word to speak. At this, "he raised the handkerchief from his eyes and said, 'I pray you to bear me witness that I meet my fate like a brave man.'" The driver lashed his horses, and the one plain victim of Benedict Arnold's treachery was hanged by his neck until dead. Many of those who watched wept openly.

Dr. James Thacher recorded in his journal: "Major André is no more among the living. I have just witnessed his exit. It was a tragical scene of the deepest interest. During his confinement and trial, he exhibited those proud and elevated sensibilities which designate greatness and dignity of mind. . . ." On the day of his execution, breakfast was sent to him from Washington's own table, and "he partook of it as usual, and having shaved and dressed himself, he placed his hat on the table and cheerfully said to the guard officer, 'I am ready at any moment, to wait on you.'"

The execution was that kind of pageant that the eighteenth century was so adept at staging. In this instance, the pageant was about the death of a brave man, and it was made all the more poignant by the fact that a brave man died for a traitor. The eighteenth century, like the nineteenth, was immensely preoccupied by the manner of dying, by how people looked and deported themselves and what they said, whether they died on the battlefield or home in bed. And we know that many people, well aware of the drama of death, rehearsed the scene in their minds and prepared some final words of exhortation, encouragement, or simple wisdom to comfort those who clustered about them to see how they would meet this most final and dramatic moment. Before his absorbed and critical watchers, André did very well indeed.

Alexander Hamilton wrote a few days later: "Among the extraordinary circumstances that attended him [André], in the midst of his enemies, he died universally esteemed and universally regretted."

A Tory lady poet, Ann Seward, wrote "A Monody on the Death of André":

> Oh Washington! I thought thee great and good,
> Nor knew thy Nero thirst for guiltless blood:
> Severe to use the power that fortune gave,
> Thou cool, determined murderer of the brave.
> Remorseless Washington! the day shall come,
> Of deep repentance for this barbarous doom. . . .

On the patriot side, John Paulding, who was one of André's captors, was singled out for glory in a song that lamented André's death:

> Now Arnold to New York is gone,
>   A-fighting for his king,
> And left poor Major André
>   On the gallows for to swing;
> When he was executed,
>   He looked both meek and mild;
> He look'd upon the people,
>   And pleasantly he smil'd.
>
> It mov'd each eye with pity,
>   Caused every heart to bleed,
>   And every one wish'd him releas'd
>   And Arnold in his stead.
> He was a man of honor,
>   In Britain he was born;
> To die upon the gallows
>   Most highly he did scorn.
>
> A bumper to John Paulding!
>   Now let your voices sound,
> Fill up your flowing glasses,
>   And drink his health around;
> Also to those young gentlemen
>   Who bore him company;
> Success to North America,
>   Ye sons of liberty!

André's hanging was not the last chapter in the Arnold drama. Washington conceived a daring plan for vengeance on the man who had betrayed him as well as the cause. He sent for Henry Lee and instructed him to find a reliable noncommissioned officer to enter the British lines in disguise and kidnap Arnold. Arnold was not to be hurt, but he was not to be permitted to escape unless the only alternative was killing him. "His public punishment," Washington told Lee, "is the sole object in view."

Lee came up at once with the name of a Virginia sergeant in his legion, a man whose courage and resourcefulness had been proved in half-a-dozen demanding campaigns, Sergeant Major John Champe, "rather above the common size—full of bone and muscle; with a saturnine countenance, grave, thoughtful, and taciturn. . . ." Lee undertook to persuade Champe that his mission would be an honorable one. It was clear that such underhanded doings were uncongenial to the soldier, especially since the plan called for him to appear to desert the American cause and then enlist in the British army in order to be in a position to arrange Arnold's kidnaping. Lee told Champe that if he succeeded "in the safe delivery of Arnold," he would not only gratify Washington "in the most acceptable manner, but he would be hailed as the avenger of the reputation of the army, stained by foul and wicked perfidy." Champe agreed to make the attempt, and Lee gave him detailed instructions, including the names of agents that he could contact in New York to aid him in carrying out the plan. The riskiest part of the venture turned out to be Champe's desertion from the American army at Tappan. He was almost apprehended by a patrol of dragoons and barely got away ahead of his pursuers, dashing to the shore near Bergen and swimming out to two British galleys anchored offshore. The circumstances of his escape argued better for his authenticity as a deserter than he could have done himself. He was interrogated at length and then taken to Sir Henry Clinton, whom he assured that many American soldiers, weary and disillusioned, were simply waiting for opportunities to follow in his footsteps.

Clinton, according to Lee's account, gave Champe several guineas and referred him to General Arnold—who was engaged in raising a legion of loyal Americans—with a letter telling the circumstances of his desertion. Arnold assigned Champe to the quarters of his recruiting sergeants, near his own headquarters.

Several days after he reached New York, Champe made contact with the agent who was to assist him in his mission. By means of letters smuggled out of the city, Champe informed Lee of his progress, and Lee in turn passed word along to Washington, who parcelled out money for the expenses of the enterprise while warning Lee that Champe should not show specie for fear of arousing suspicion. Champe scouted Arnold's habits carefully. Every evening, he learned, the general stepped into the little garden in back of his headquarters before retiring. By loosening several palings on the fence, Champe and an accomplice could gain access to the garden before Arnold appeared, gag him, throw a thick canvas over him, and carry him a few hundred yards to where two other men would wait with a boat to carry him over to the Jersey shore.

The plans were carefully laid, the night set. But luck was once more with Arnold. The day of the kidnaping, too late to notify the men who manned the boat, Arnold and his small contingent of soldiers and noncommissioned officers were ordered to depart for Virginia. Champe had no choice but to sail off with his mission aborted. It was not until the end of Arnold's campaign in Virginia that he found an opportunity to rejoin the Americans. Even though the venture, on which Washington had placed such hopes, failed, Washington "munificently anticipated every desire of the sergeant, and presented him with a discharge from further service, lest he might in the vicissitudes of war, fall into the enemy's hands; when if recognized he was sure to die on the gibbet."

Historians have been inclined to dismiss Lee's story of the Champe mission as fantasy. Douglas Freeman ignores it, and Carl Van Doren calls it vastly inflated in the telling, though on what specific evidence it is not clear. Certainly Sergeant Major Champe did exist and was discharged from the army under circumstances similar to those described by Lee in his *Memoirs of the War in the Southern Department.* Lee reprints letters to him from Washington concerning the kidnapping scheme, letters whose authenticity has never been questioned. Finally, Lee was not given to fanciful tales and would hardly have made up such a story out of whole cloth. One can only assume that the uneasiness or incredulity of historians is related to the fact that the whole episode is "out of character" for Washington, or at least out of that character that historians have, as though by covert agreement, attributed to Washington. To see Washington so implacable in his desire for revenge ill comports with the picture of a man whose emotions were always under iron control. Yet it is true that Arnold's desertion was undoubtedly the bitterest blow that Washington suffered in the course of the war, and knowing him as a man capable of terrible passions of anger, it is not to be wondered that he responded as he did, first with proposals for a dishonorable bargain, and then with a cloak-and-dagger scheme worthy of the present-day CIA.

The defection of Arnold brought a reaction of patriotic fervor. Effigies of Arnold were dragged through the streets of Philadelphia and other towns and cities and were burned to the accompaniment of bitter denunciations. The British, on the other hand, found great encouragement in Arnold's desertion. A rumor spread that "General Greene had gone over to Cornwallis with 700 men." The British intercepted a letter from Arthur Lee in which Lee denounced an anonymous New York patriot in terms that seemed to reflect on his loyalty. The contentious Lee had James Duane in mind, but the British assumed it was General Schuyler, and since Elizabeth Schuyler had just married Alexander Hamilton, they entertained themselves with the thought that Schuyler, through his daughter's marriage to Hamilton, might "gain a sway over Washington or be in the military plot with him to surrender America back to Great Britain and become Monks themselves."

New York, always a hotbed of rumor, buzzed with stories that other defections were imminent. If Schuyler could not corrupt Washington, one story ran, he might "use his sway to ruin both Washington and the Congress and this seems most probable." William Smith, who was a perpetual optimist, even found solace in the thought that Washington himself might return to his allegiance to the Crown. Smith had talked, several years before, to "Washington's physician and confidant," John Cochran, and had "hinted my confidence that these commotions would not separate us from Great Britain; that Washington would one day bring about the reunion and be rewarded with an Irish peerage. I have no doubt of his repeating it to him, nor but that the idea was flattering to his vanity. His wrath at Arnold may be far outrunning him in that race." There was, it seemed, no limit to the delusions with which the British could comfort themselves or avoid the unpleasant necessity of facing the truth.

I have spent what may seem to the reader an inordinate amount of time on Arnold's treachery. It is, of course, one of the most familiar stories in American history, but it only reveals itself in its real fascination of plot and intrigue when it is told in some detail (and there is, of necessity, a good deal that has been omitted). Why, one is bound to ask, did this event loom so large in the minds of American patriots then and in the popular imagination in later generations? For one thing, the theme of loyalty and treachery touches the sentiments of everyone who is loyal to a party, a country, a community, or a person. It has to do with the principle of order in the social universe of man. If there is no loyalty, how is civilized life to be preserved? So the story of Benedict Arnold's treachery is, in symbolic representation, entangled in the threads of our existence. It is, moreover, a remarkable suspense story whose effect historians have tried to heighten by suggesting that if the plot had not been discovered and Arnold had delivered West Point into Clinton's hands, the American cause would have been lost, as Clinton himself so confidently believed it would have been. The fact is that nothing is less likely than that the capture of West Point by Clinton—assuming that he would indeed have captured it—would have brought an end to the war. There is simply no basis for such a conclusion.

The fact that Arnold wished to betray his country for the most sordid of all motives—money—made comparisons with Judas Iscariot's betrayal of Christ inevitable and made the event resonate with vivid Scriptural implications for contemporaries. Of course, there was also the fact that Arnold was a dashing and heroic soldier, a genuine hero in the eyes of most Americans, which made his defection all the more shocking. Arnold's treachery has also produced, in every generation since it was disclosed, historians who have tried manfully but vainly to redeem Arnold's reputation by arguing, in the main, that he was badly treated by Congress and thus somehow forced into treason.

There have certainly been few acts of treason in history that have been as spectacular as that of Benedict Arnold. It was, one is tempted to say, the *archetypal* act of treachery; and that, ultimately, might be the final solace for the proud, greedy, ambitious man who was a little mad in his unshakable conviction that his country had treated him ill. The world will never forget Benedict Arnold, as it has forgotten many far worthier spirits. That, at least, he accomplished.

Lafayette, in an account of Arnold's treason that he wrote to the Chevalier de La Luzerne, expressed very effectively the nature of that act: "In the course of a revolution such as ours it is natural that a few traitors should be found, and every conflict which resembles a civil war of the first order . . . must necessarily bring to light some great virtues and some great crimes. Our struggles have brought forward some heroes (General Washington for instance) who would otherwise have been merely private citizens. They have also developed some great scoundrels who would otherwise have remained merely obscure rogues. But that an Arnold, a man who, although not so highly esteemed as has been supposed in Europe, had nevertheless given proof of talent, of patriotism, and especially of the most brilliant courage, should at once destroy his very existence and should sell his country to the tyrants whom he had fought against with glory, is an event . . . which confounds and distresses me, and, if I must confess it, humilitates me to a degree that I cannot express. . . . This is the first atrocity that has been heard of in our army. . . ." Lafayette was sure that the dishonored Arnold would "blow his brains out." That was almost as bad a calculation as William Smith's prediction that Washington would one day betray the American cause.

The approach of winter brought an end to the campaign of 1780, if indeed the military events of that year in the North deserved the name of a campaign. The year that had begun with the rebuff of Knyphausen and later Clinton at Springfield, had, in Washington's words, "appeared pregnant with events of a favorable complexn," so far so that he had dared to anticipate an end "to my military pursuits" and a return to "domestic life. . . . We have been half the time without provision," he added, "and are likely to continue so. We have no magazines, nor money to form them; and in a little time we shall have no men, if we had money to pay them. We have lived upon expedients till we can live no longer. In a word the history of the war is a history of false hopes and temporary devices, instead of system and economy."

6

The Mutiny of the Pennsylvania Line

I N the winter of 1780–81, the Continental Army faced what was almost certainly its greatest crisis, a crisis that came, ironically, not on the battlefield but in the camp, not because of the enemy but because of the army's own bitter sense of alienation—because, more specifically, of its hunger and misery, aggravated by a deep feeling of injustice. Washington had warned Congress so often that the army's hardships might lead to mutiny that his warnings had lost their force. But now the wolf was finally at the door.

With the onset of winter, Washington began to make plans to place his army in winter quarters. Wayne's Pennsylvania Line was assigned to Mount Kemble, near Morristown. As always, the equipment of the Continental soldiers was wretched. There were not enough shoes, blankets, coats, tents, medical supplies, stockings, or shirts, nor was there money to pay the men or enough food to sustain them. There were none of the small luxuries that in most wars help to make a soldier's life bearable; there were no entertainments or distractions to take their minds off their miseries. Around them the men saw civilians living, by the standards of the soldiers, in positive luxury, and they saw, with increasing bitterness, that some Americans had grown fat and prosperous on the needs of others.

Farmers who professed to have nothing to sell to commissary officers in exchange for worthless Continental currency smuggled food to the British and sold it for good sterling. It seemed to the soldiers that the whole burden of the struggle for American independence fell on their thin and chilblained shoulders. Congress, mired in bickering and futility, was contemptible to them. All they got from that body were visits from investigating committees, promises, and occasional doles of worthless money.

In the ardor of patriotism, or because of a promised bounty or the blandishments of a pausible recruiting officer, they had in many instances enlisted for the duration of the war, which had now gone on longer than anyone, British or American, could have imagined; nor was the end in sight. As we have already seen, the patriot soldiers suffered terrible pangs of homesickness; they yearned for wives and children who would hardly know them, for friends and parents and comfortable firesides and good food. They were willing to fight, but to sit and rot, to be weakened by malnutrition and to die of disease, of camp fever, pneumonia, or influenza, seemed insupportable. To be expected to undergo terrible privations simply so that the Continental Army could continue to exist seemed to the ordinary soldier much too much to ask. The soldiers had no doubt in their own hearts that America was and must remain independent; the British could never subdue them or ever again rule them. But it was difficult for them to see the relationship between that simple, fundamental fact and the necessity of their living and dying in hunger and filth and misery, huddled together under the scourge of bitter winters.

Washington, concerned as always for his men, sent "the bad clothed men of Pennsylvania" to Morristown because huts were left there from previous winter encampments, huts that might give the soldiers some protection from the elements. However, when an advance party arrived at Mount Kemble on November 28, they discovered that many of the huts had been torn down to furnish firewood and lumber for the local inhabitants. On December 1, the remaining huts were allocated to the various units by the officers. The previous winter the Connecticut and Maryland Lines, along with Hand's mixed brigade, had occupied the huts, which were aligned in two parallel rows. They had been built on the model developed at Valley Forge three years earlier. They were sixteen feet long by fourteen feet wide, with the side walls some six or seven feet to the eaves; the roofs were made of smaller logs or split slabs running down from a low ridgepole. In some huts there was a window or two, and in each was a fireplace made of lath and clay. Ten or twelve men slept in double-deckered bunks with straw for bedding. Each regimental area was arranged in lines, with a front of three hundred feet on parade, running back a thousand feet in depth. Together the huts made up a sizable town, one much larger, in fact, than any but the principal cities of America. Since Valley Forge, much attention was paid by the officers to cleanliness and sanitation. Men were not allowed to build huts below ground (which would have been warmer) because of problems of ventilation and dampness. Latrines, which were not a serious problem in cold weather (except of course for the difficulty of digging in frozen ground), were kept apart from the men's living and eating areas.

In addition to the soldiers, there were about a hundred women and children in the camp at Mount Kemble. These were the families of men who had no other way to provide for them. They drew rations along with the men and lived in the huts in areas that were rudely partitioned off. Washington knew that the men would desert if he rejected such an unmilitary arrangement. The women, moreover, performed some very practical functions, acting as laundresses and as nurses in the hospitals. Their presence in all encampments during the war was officially recognized by occasional orders declaring that women must not throw soap-suds on the parade ground, that they must make use of the latrines, and that they must not ride in the baggage wagons in the march.

Lieutenant John Bigham of the Fifth Pennsylvania Regiment was sent to the Mount Kemble camp with $14,068 in state paper to pay bounties due new recruits in the line. The lieutenant and the money never arrived, and when he was hauled before a court-martial, he claimed that he had spent the money for expenses on his trip to the camp. At a time when ten head of cattle cost $27,733, the charge was perhaps not as preposterous as it seemed.

An effort was made to raise hard money by solicitation to pay the Pennsylvania Line, and on December 27 a member of the Pennsylvania council started for Mount Kemble with 4,842 shillings that included 80½ English guineas, 3 French guineas, 5¼ moidores, 5 Spanish pistoles, 4 ducats, 43½ Spanish dollars, and 99 Portuguese johannes.

As the month ran out, the men in their huts began to plan demonstrations to drive home their discontent and their rankling sense of the injustice done them in the matter of their enlistments. When the Pennsylvania councilor arrived on the twenty-ninth with his piddling little collection of hard money, the inadequacy of the sum, coupled with the news that Bigham had absconded with money intended for soldiers, added to the soldiers' discontent. With this the last hope for any real response to their grievances seemed lost.

Wayne, so proud of his veterans, badgered Joseph Reed, president of Pennsylvania, until Reed wrote a sharp reply, and then Wayne, more tactfully, acknowledged that Reed had doubtless done as much as "the exhausted state of the treasury and other circumstances would admit of, although they were not equal to your wishes or [his soldiers'] merits and expectations. . . ." The fact was that his men were once more "reduced to dry bread and beef for our food, and to cold water for our drink. Neither officers nor soldiers have received a single drop of spirituous liquors from the public magazines since the 10th of October last, except one gill per man sometime in November; this, together with the old worn out coats and tattered linen overalls, and what was once a poor substitute for a blanket (now divided among three soldiers), is but very wretched living and shelter against the winter's piercing cold, drifting snow and chilling sleets."

As the Pennsylvania general put it, "Our soldiers are not devoid of reasoning faculties, nor are they callous to the first feelings of nature, they have served their country with fidelity for near five years, poorly clothed, badly fed and worse paid; of the last article, trifling as it is, they have not seen a paper dollar in the way of pay for near *twelve months*." Wayne was full of gloomy forebodings. If the government were to give "your soldiery a landed property, making their interest and the interest of America reciprocal . . . I will answer for their bleeding to *death,* drop by drop, to establish the independence of this country." On the other hand, if something was not done immediately to express in a material way the appreciation of the country for the sacrifices and hardships of its soldiers, "to give them a local attachment to this country and to quiet their minds, we have not yet seen the worst side of the picture." The officers, Wayne concluded, worked along with "the poor naked fellows" at their huts and redoubts, "in order to produce a conviction to their minds that we share and more than share every vicissitude in common with them, sometimes asking to participate of their bread or water."

The day after he wrote to Reed, Wayne encouraged his men to cut off the tails of their coats "to repair the elbows and other defective parts." Some ingenious soldiers discovered that they could make three decent infantry caps out of "one tolerable and two very ordinary hats," and they were now trying to "make three short coats out of three tattered long ones."

In addition to no pay, little food, and threadbare clothing, many members of the Pennsylvania Line were convinced that they had been tricked by Congress, that they were the victims, as they put, of a "fine deception." Although they had enlisted for three years *or* the duration, these men had believed (or said they had been told) that "duration" meant that if the war was over *before* the three years were out, they would be discharged. Thus when their three years of misery were up, they insisted that they be given the choice of leaving the army or re-enlisting for the duration of the war and being paid the new bounties that the state had been paying for enlistment since July—three johannes (Portuguese gold coins worth some twenty-seven dollars in silver) and two hundred acres of land after the war. The request was certainly not an unfair one, and Wayne, in his letter to Joseph Reed, completely associated himself with it. Veterans of the Pennsylvania Line who had served three bitter years could see no justice in new recruits getting more than they had gotten. Prisoners from the Philadelphia jails, pardoned when they agreed to enlist and sent off to the camp at Mount Kemble to fill up the depleted company rolls, had more hard money in their pockets than the veterans had seen in three years of arduous campaigning.

Much of the soldiers' resentment was directed against officers who abused and bullied them, men who, not born to authority or trained to it, used it clumsily and roughly, arousing the hostility of soldiers who, in many instances, knew themselves to be better men than those who ordered them about.

January 1, 1781, was the day on which, in the view of many soldiers, their three-year enlistments were up. On that day they were determined to go home or draw a bounty for re-enlistment. As the time grew shorter, Wayne became increasingly anxious about the mood of the soldiers and the possibilities of serious trouble. "I sincerely wish," he wrote to the colonel of the Fifth Regiment, "the Ides of January was come and past. I am not superstitious, but can't help cherishing disagreeable ideas about that period." The state of Pennsylvania must "adopt some effectual mode and immediate plan to alleviate the distress of the troops and to conciliate their minds and sweeten their tempers, which are much soured by neglect." But Congress and the Pennsylvania council dillied and dallied. It would not do to seem to yield to pressure and threats from the soldiers, they assured themselves; to do so would be to set a dangerous precedent. While it is true that Congress did not have the money the soldiers wanted, the desired land could have been promised to the men.

On the thirtieth of December, Wayne wrote to the assistant clothier general of the army: "The distressed condition of the soldiery for clothing beggars all description. For God's sake send us our dividend of uniforms, overalls, blankets."

Monday, January 1, was clear and brisk. Wayne and his staff were preoccupied with the reorganization, ordered by Congress, of the regiments. That night the officers of the Tenth Regiment, many of whom would be reassigned as a consequence of the reorganization, had "an elegant regimental dinner and entertainment. . . . We spent . . . the evening till about ten o'clock as cheerfully as we could wish, when we were disturbed by the huzzas of the soldiers upon the Right Division, answered by those on the Left," one of the officers wrote.

Lieutenant Enos Reeves, who was at the party, ran out to the parade ground with his fellow officers and found there "numbers in small groups whispering and busily running up and down the line. In a short time a gun was fired upon the right and answered by one on the right of the Second brigade, and a skyrocket thrown from the center of the first, which was accompanied by a general huzza throughout the line, the soldiers running out with their arms, accouterments and knapsacks." Each officer ran off to his own company to try to persuade the men to return to their huts and put down their arms. The central parade ground was apparently the rendezvous point, and despite the efforts of the officers, the men began to move from all directions toward that central point. Lieutenant White, trying to turn back one contingent, was shot through the thigh, and "Capt. Samuel Tolbert in opposing another party was shot through the body. . . . They [the soldiers] continued huzzaing and fireing in a riotous manner," Lieutenant Reeves reported, "so that it soon became dangerous for an officer to oppose them by force."

The soldiers seized the artillery pieces in the camp and broke open the magazine where powder and balls were stored. At that point a dispute broke out between those who wished to fire the cannon as a kind of alarm signal and others who feared that it would frighten people in the country roundabout. While the soldiers argued, one man skipped up and put a match to the cannon. That decided the issue. The roar was irresistible, and the other pieces were immediately fired, "every discharge of the cannon . . . accompanied by a confused huzza and a general discharge of musketry."

Wayne, who had declined an invitation to dinner in order to be on hand in case of trouble, now appeared on horseback with one of his regimental commanders "and spoke to [the men] for a considerable time, but it had no effect. Their answer was, they had been wronged and were determined to see themselves righted." Wayne assured them he would do all in his power to see their wrongs redressed. The answer from the soldiers was that their business was with Congress and the governor and council of Pennsylvania. They had no quarrel with the officers. "With that, several platoons fired over the General's head. The general called out: 'If you mean to kill me, shoot me at once, here's my breast,' opening his coat."

They had no intention of harming any officer, they reiterated, "two or three individuals excepted." Up to this point, the firing of the cannon and the huzzaing had failed to turn out a majority of the camp in support of the mutiny. The mutineers, realizing that their success depended on rallying their fellows, turned to Colonel Stewart's regiment. The "Irish Beauty," who had been largely responsible for talking the Connecticut Line out of their own incipient mutiny in May, was so respected and beloved by his men that they were not disposed to join their comrades, and a number of them had to be forced to come over at the point of bayonet.

Some soldiers of the Fourth Regiment who had hesitated to cast their lot with the mutineers were ordered by their captain to recapture the cannon. In Reeve's words, "They charged but would not advance, then dispersed and left the officer alone." One soldier dashed out as though to bayonet Lieutenant Colonel Richard Butler, who ducked between two huts to evade him. As Butler went around one hut and the soldier went the other way to head him off, Captain Bettin came down the alley between the huts, saw the soldier rushing toward him, raised his sword to strike him, and received a musket bullet through his body.

Late that night Wayne drafted "an order" that was sympathetic and conciliatory in tone. "Agreeably to the proposition of a very large proportion of the worthy soldiery last evening," he wrote, "General Wayne hereby desires the noncommissioned officers and privates to appoint one man from each regiment, to represent their grievances to the General." These grievances the general would do his best to redress, "and he further plights . . . that no man shall receive the least injury on account of the part they shall have taken on the occasion. . . . The General hopes soon to return to camp with all his brother soldiers who took a little tour last evening." The order did not check the mutiny, but it may have persuaded some soldiers who had not yet joined to remain with what was left of their units.

After he had written his appeal to the soldiers, Wayne, at four-thirty in the morning, began a letter to Washington. It was not an easy letter for that proud soldier to write. "It is with inexpressible pain," he declared, "that I now inform your Excellency of the general mutiny and defection which suddenly took place in the Pennsylvania Line, between the hours of nine and ten o'clock last evening. Every possible exertion was made by the officers to suppress it in its rise, but the torrent was too potent to be stemmed." One officer was dead and two apparently mortally wounded. "A very considerable number of the field and other officers are much injured by strokes from muskets, bayonets, and stones. Nor have the revolters escaped with impunity. Many of their bodies lay under our horses' feet, and others will retain with existence the traces of our swords and espontoons." Wayne did not send the letter. Perhaps, on reflection, he felt that in his exhausted and depressed state he had exaggerated things. It was not true, for instance, that "many" soldiers' bodies "lay under our horses' feet," bold as the phrase sounded. Wayne felt that the question that would immediately be raised by everyone who heard news of the mutiny, and by none more appropriately than Washington, was: "What did General Wayne and his officers do to suppress this upheaval?" Certainly Wayne had responded bravely and tactfully to the crisis, but that was not readily conveyed in a letter.

That Wayne was not entirely candid with the mutineers is not surprising. While he offered clemency and the redress of their grievances, he also had taken pains to notify the Continental brigade at Pompton to make haste to Chatham and had alerted the militia to join with them there to try to contain the mutineers and to intercept them if they marched to Trenton or Philadelphia. Wayne also sent word to Congress that the rebellious soldiers might be on the way to Philadelphia for a confrontation with the members of Congress. Under the circumstances, it might be well for Congress to leave the city for a time.

At nine in the morning, Wayne wrote another letter to Washington with a less feverish account of the events of the preceding night. "As a last resort," he noted, "I am advised to collect them and move slowly on towards Philadelphia. . . . Their general cry is, to be discharged, and that they will again enlist and fight for America, a few excepted."

By noon the mutinying soldiers had taken effective control of the camp. They posted their own guards and sentinels, and then, marching down the company streets, they turned men out of their huts and made them join the mutiny. "They continued huzzaing and a disorderly firing till they went off, about two o'clock, with drums and fifes playing, under command of the sergeants, in regular platoons," in good military order, with advance and rear guards out.

Marching out of camp, they met General Wayne, who once more fruitlessly expostulated with them. Which way, he asked, did they intend to go? Trenton or Philadelphia, their leaders replied. Well, at least he hoped they would not disgrace the cause of their country by going over to the enemy. Not only was that not their intention, they replied, but they would hang any man who attempted it, and indeed, if the enemy were to "come out in consequence of this revolt, they would turn back and fight them." They were injured men, seeking redress of their grievances, not traitors to their country, however ungrateful that country might be for their services.

"If that is your sentiments," Wayne replied, "I'll not leave you, and if you won't allow me to march in your front, I'll follow in your rear." These bold words were answered with a cheer, and Wayne, joined by Butler and Stewart, rode with the mutineers. When the men intercepted a drove of some hundred head of cattle, they left a few behind for the use of the officers. What astonished many of the officers, frightened and dismayed as they were by the uprising, was the good discipline of the soldiers. In Reeves's words, "The men went off very civilly last night to what might have been expected from such a mob. They did not attempt to plunder our officers' huts or insult them in the least, except those who were obstinate in opposing them. They did not attempt to take with them any part of the State stores, which appears to me a little extraordinary, for men when they get but little want more."

The first night's march took them only four miles to Vealtown, now Bernardsville, where they made camp and slaughtered some of the cattle they had acquired. All during the night more groups straggled in until there were some fifteen hundred in the bivouac area. Early Tuesday morning they were on the way to Princeton. Cornelius Tyger, a New Jersey Tory, "stood and saw them all march by. . . . They were in high spirits. They marched in the most perfect order and seemed as if under military discipline." As Wayne hurried after them, he overtook numerous small groups of soldiers with the same purpose. At the bridge over the Raritan, "some honest fellows advised the General not to go to the main body, many being intoxicated and very ill-disposed." But Wayne pushed on and overtook the troops just after they had made camp at Middle Brook, where many of them had wintered in 1778–79. Wayne called the sergeants together, read them his order, and asked them to prevail on their men to let him address them the next morning.

This the sergeants ostensibly tried to do, but the men were adamant. They had heard enough promises and exhortations. On Wednesday, "very early, not waiting for the General, in contradiction to the solicitations of the commanding and other sergeants," they broke camp and resumed their march. Finally they were prevailed upon to form up in a field by the side of the road, and there Wayne addressed them, but with no more success than before. The men took to the road, as a spy reported to the British, with "the greatest order . . . if a man takes a fowl from an inhabitant he is severely punished." Indeed the soldiers, leading themselves and enforcing their own improvised rules, showed better discipline as mutineers than they had often done under their own officers. And that was, in simple fact, remarkable. It showed once more what we have already seen so often: that the individual American soldier was self-motivated to a degree unknown in the professional armies of the day. In addition, the rank and file of enlisted men had, within their own ranks, leadership necessary for an exacting march that required great self-discipline. It is not surprising, under the circumstances, that the people of the towns and hamlets through which they passed seemed more inclined to treat them like conquering heroes than as riotous mutineers.

A "board of sergeants" constituted the democratic leadership of this strange mutiny. Under the board was an informal staff with a mock major general and other "officers," appointed from the ranks. The sergeants from the ten infantry regiments and one from the artillery elected a twelfth to be president of the board. He, oddly enough, appears to have been a deserter from the British army. He was apparently a Pennsylvanian who had been captured early in the war, had enlisted in a Loyalist regiment in order to get out of prison, and then had deserted to the Americans.

On Wednesday, at Princeton, there was another conference between the sergeants and Wayne, Butler, and Stewart. The officers had settled on a strategy of trying to persuade the mutineers to send a committee to meet with Congress rather than to go themselves. The board of sergeants established their headquarters in Nassau Hall on the campus of the College of New Jersey, and the men camped on Prospect Farm outside of town.

When Washington received word from Wayne's aide of the mutiny of the Pennsylvania Line, his immediate fear was that the mutiny would spread through other units of the army. He knew that there was active discontent among the New England soldiers at West Point. The Connecticut Line had already, on two separate occasions, behaved in a mutinous manner. In a mutiny the only practical course, generally speaking, is to surround the mutineers with a superior force, compel them to surrender their arms, and hang a few of the ringleaders as an example to the rest. But the New Jersey Line was not large enough or reliable enough to quell the mutiny, and Washington hesitated to call on other units for fear that, if it came to a showdown, they would join the mutineers before they would fire on them. Washington therefore sent trusted officers to try to ascertain the mood of the other Continental troops, while he himself prepared to ride to Philadelphia. He instructed Wayne to try to remain with the troops if they would permit him and to do his best to convince them of the folly of their course when the "first transports of passion had evaporated." It seemed to Washington, very wisely, that to attempt to check their march by placing reliable troops (if there were any) across their path would do more harm than good and would "tempt them to turn about and go in a body to the enemy, who by their emissaries will use every argument and mean in their power to persuade them that it is their only asylum. . . . If they could be stopped [by argument] at Bristol or Germantown, the better. . . . I look upon it, that if you can bring them to a negotiation matters may afterwards be accommodated; but that an attempt to reduce them by force will either drive them to the enemy or dissipate them in such a manner that they will never be recovered."

Washington's program was one that Wayne had already embarked on, but Washington objected strongly to Wayne's suggestion that Congress leave Philadelphia. "The mutineers, finding the body before whom they were determined to lay their grievances fled, might take a new turn and wreak their vengeance upon the persons and properties of the citizens. . . ." The fact was that there were many Tories in Philadelphia who would be glad to abet them in such work. "I would therefore wish you," Washington concluded, "if you have time, to recall that advice and rather recommend it to them to stay and hear what propositions the soldiers have to make."

Washington doubtless had mixed feelings about the mutiny. He had anticipated one for several years and had constantly warned Congress that a mutiny was imminent if adequate support was not mustered for the army. Congress had been unable to respond adequately, and month after month the poor, wretched army had to struggle along as best it could with a trickle of supplies where it needed a stream. Serious as the implications of the mutiny were for the Revolutionary cause, some shock might stir Congress to fresh efforts to meet the needs of the Continental Army.

News of the mutiny spread quickly to New York. Clinton got word from a spy as soon as Washington did, and on the fourth of January, Captain Frederick Mackenzie wrote in his diary an accurate précis of the event. He even knew that the troops, passing Wayne's quarters, had huzzaed "for officers and soldiers without pay, clothing or provisions; then for Thirteen Kings without breeches." The boats along the Delaware, Mackenzie noted, had been "secured so as to prevent the mutineers from making use of them to pass the river to Philadelphia." Mackenzie, like his general, drew the wrong conclusions, adding, "The country is in great confusion, and the persons in authority under Congress dread the effects of this revolt, as the people in general are tired of the oppression and difficulties they suffer and earnestly wish for a return of peace and the old Government."

As for Clinton, he took steps, as soon as he had confirmed the reports of the mutiny, to take whatever advantage of it he might. The British grenadiers and the light infantry were alerted to be ready to march, along with three battalions of Hessian grenadiers and jaegers. Clinton's plan was to land his force at South Amboy, New Jersey, "to favor the revolt and keep the militia back." Clinton also drafted a letter "to assure the mutineers that in this struggle for their just rights and liberties, they will be assisted by a body of British troops, that if they will lay down their arms they will be pardoned for all past offenses, be paid all the pay due them by Congress, and not be required to serve [in the British forces] unless they chuse it." The mutineers were invited to send commissioners to Amboy to negotiate for them and "to consider the total inability of Congress to satisfy their demands, even if they were inclined to grant them," and they were warned "of the severity with which numbers of them will be punished, if they suffer themselves to be satisfied with the promises of Congress, and return to their service." The principal problem was not drawing up the British proposals to the mutineers but getting them into their hands. Mackenzie dispatched some eight or nine copies by five different routes in the hope that at least one would reach the soldiers of the Pennsylvania Line at Princeton. Privately Clinton was not too hopeful of the outcome. His informants had already brought word that the Americans had shown no disposition to join the British.

An American spy in New York reported the same day to Washington that the British knew of the mutiny: "Nothing could possibly have given them more pleasure," he reported. "Every preparation is making among them to come out and make a descent on Jersey. I think South Amboy is their object. They expect those in mutiny will immediately join them. . . . If they come out it will be with considerable force, and may be expected within twenty-four hours from this time."

Mackenzie, as prone to catch at straws as his superiors, wrote in his diary, "Ethan Allen and the Vermonters appear to be inclined to declare for us, and 'tis reported some of them have joined the King's troops at Ticonderoga. . . . We have the most sanguine hopes that the loyalists in Maryland and the other Southern provinces, on hearing of the mutiny of the Pennsylvania troops, will immediately rise up and declare themselves. . . . I do not see how the rebellion can possibly exist much longer. . . . The people," he added, "are so much oppressed, and long so earnestly for a return of peace and the re-establishment of their former mild government, that they only wait to see a beginning made, when they will join heartily in overturning the tyrannical and oppressive government under which they now suffer. . . ." In Mackenzie's opinion, if Congress by some miracle satisfied the Pennsylvanians, "the rest of the Continental troops in the same situation will make the same demands and expect like satisfaction. . . . Should the insurgents join us, the matter must be at an end. The rebels will find it impossible to raise another army, all strength and confidence will be lost among them, and a general defection must be the consequence."

On Thursday, January 4, at Princeton, the mutineers' board of sergeants talked with Wayne and the two colonels about the demands of the soldiers. The men who had enlisted in 1776 and 1777 were to be "without any delay discharged; and all arrears of pay and depreciation of pay be paid to the said men, without any fraud, clothing included." Men who had enlisted in 1778 or since then were also to be entitled to "their discharge at the expiration of three years from the said enlistment." New recruits, who had clearly enlisted for the duration, were to receive the bounty, pay, and clothing that had been promised to them. Those men discharged and furnished with their pay and clothing were to be free to re-enlist or not. They were "not to be compelled to stay by any former officers commanding. . . ," and those who wished to stay "for a small term as volunteers" were to be "at their own disposal and pleasure." Six days would be allowed "to complete and settle every such demand."

If the demands, fair as they were from the soldiers' point of view, had been met, the result would have been the virtual dissolution of the

Pennsylvania Line, which constituted more than a quarter of Washington's army. Wayne's reply was thus somewhat evasive: "All such non-commissioned officers and soldiers as are justly entitled to their discharges shall be immediately settled with, their accounts promptly adjusted, and certificates for their pay and arrearages of pay and clothing given them. . . ." The issue centered around the words "justly entitled." Congress and the officers of the line insisted that those soldiers who had served for three years were not "justly entitled" to be discharged, having in fact enlisted for the duration. Wayne concluded: "These propositions are founded in principles of justice and honor, between the United States and the soldiery, which is all that reasonable men can expect. . . . If the soldiers are determined not to let reason and justice govern on this occasion, he [Wayne] has only to lament the total and unfortunate situation to which they will reduce themselves and their country."

While the negotiations were conducted in good spirit, and the men of the line, adequately fed for the first time in months, seemed well disposed, they grew increasingly restless during the day. The strain of being mutineers, uncertainty about the future, and conflicting counsels wore on their nerves. Some had been opposed to any discussions at Princeton or elsewhere. Their business was with Congress, and they were afraid of being once more cozened and bamboozled. The officers with their fancy words and glib promises, with their emotional evocation of old battles and old loyalties, were not to be trusted. The men had gone too far to settle for a little thin gruel. Word trickled in that eighty officers had gathered with arms at nearby Allentown; that the New Jersey militia were blocking the road to New York, and that other militia units were between them and Philadelphia. In such circumstances, it is small wonder that they were somewhat paranoid. Many soldiers believed the talks were simply stalling tactics to allow Washington to trap the mutineers.

The soldiers promptly fastened on the phrase "justly entitled" and demanded that Wayne be more specific. Was he referring to the men whose three-year terms had, in their opinion, expired? In reply Wayne, hoping to draw the soldiers off from Philadelphia, stated that he had no authority to decide the point in question and proposed a meeting between the soldiers' board and the Pennsylvania council at Trenton to get "a full and explicit answer."

The soldiers rejected the proposed meeting at Trenton out of hand and declared, rather ominously, that the officers should not "think that we cannot settle these matters by such a formidable body of men as we are." If the officers could not settle the issue on the spot they were simply wasting the soldiers' time, and the soldiers must then "take some measures that will procure us our own happiness."

During the day word reached Princeton of a British movement, specifically of British vessels and barges in the Raritan waiting to evacuate the mutineers to New York if they so desired. At this the soldiers assured Wayne that if the British came out with aggressive intentions, they would "act with desperation" against them.

Meanwhile, in Philadelphia, an alarmed Congress had appointed a committee consisting of General Sullivan of New Hampshire, lately retired from the army and back in Congress, the Reverend John Witherspoon, a representative from New Jersey and president of the college at Princeton, and John Mathews of South Carolina to confer with the Pennsylvania council on what action might be taken with regard to the mutiny. General St. Clair headed for Princeton with Lafayette and John Laurens, who was in Philadelphia on Washington's business, and arrived at Trenton in the middle of the afternoon of January 4. They found the town full of conflicting rumors and of the uncertainty produced by those rumors. No one knew what the mutineers would do next, which was not surprising, for the men did not know themselves. Lafayette, always the romantic, believed that he could end the mutiny with an inspiring speech to the troops. That evening he sat down to write an account to Luzerne. "The insurgents are more devilish than ever," he declared. "A deputation was sent to them from Trenton to beseech them not to move to this town. Some persons believe they will be here tomorrow." Others believed that "they will remain at Princeton as an intermediate point from which, if the militia should show signs of attacking them, they could go to New York, after putting the country to fire and sword without distinction of age and sex. But if they are left at peace, they say they will not turn to the enemy. . . . The sentries and pickets have orders to let no Continental officer pass; and nobody is permitted to address the soldiers. Everything is done through committees." To Lafayette this proved that the British, through spies and agents, were "determined to prevent any effect which influence or eloquence might have." Yet he was determined to try the issue. Colonel Stewart had reported that the soldiers, hostile to almost all generals, made an exception of Lafayette. He would go "and see if they can interrupt my passage or my eloquence."

St. Clair and Lafayette, with three light horse as escort, rode from

Trenton to Princeton on Friday afternoon. At the lines they were stopped, asked to identify themselves, and then sent with a guard to the board of sergeants at Nassau Hall. "We talked with them," Lafayette reported, "and they showed us what had been written between General Wayne and themselves. From there we went to General Wayne's quarters, where at various times we saw the chosen leaders." It was soon plain to Lafayette that he would have no chance to exhort the soldiers. When John Laurens arrived, the soldiers took alarm. Too many officers meant, in their view, trouble. It was time for all of them to depart except those needed in the negotiations—Wayne and his two colonels, who were perhaps as much prisoners as guests of the mutineers. The sergeants thus sent a message to Laurens, Lafayette, and St. Clair giving them an hour and a half in which to depart, "for fear of evil consequences."

The three officers set off for Mount Kemble, where St. Clair intended to take command of those troops who had not joined the mutiny. On the way they met a party of some thirty soldiers coming to join their comrades at Princeton. At last Lafayette had an audience: "After many effusions of the heart, and fine words," he wrote, "they at last consented to return to their huts. . . . All these people tell me that they would follow me wherever I might need them . . . that they would die to the last man under my orders; but that I do not know all they have suffered; that they will have justice from their country."

There matters rested for the time being. In Philadelphia steps were taken to audit the accounts of the Pennsylvania Line with a view to settling "the pay and depreciation of the Line." Joseph Reed, with the Congressional committee and the Philadelphia Light Horse—a troop of gentlemen militia, handsomely dressed and mounted, who had done some occasional fighting but whose principal duties were ceremonial—set out for Princeton. In the meantime, battalions of the New Jersey Line took their positions at Morristown, Pompton, and Chatham, and bodies of militia began to gather at South Amboy (where Clinton intended to land his force), at Brunswick, and at Elizabethtown, as well as at Hopewell and Crosswicks. But there was so much sympathy among these soldiers for the mutineers that they could hardly have been used aggressively. The situation was summarized by Washington in a letter to the governors of all the New England states. "At what point," he wrote, "this defection will stop, or how extensive it may prove, God only knows. At present the troops at the important posts in this vicinity remain quiet, not being acquainted with this unhappy and alarming affair [a very doubtful statement, indeed]. But how long they will continue so cannot be ascertained, as they labor under some of the pressing hardships with the troops who have revolted. . . . The circumstances will now point out more forcibly what ought to be done than anything that can possibly be said by me on the subject." In other words, the states had better show a little more initiative in collecting and forwarding supplies and money, or the mutiny might well become general. It was "vain to think an army can be kept together much longer under such a variety of sufferings as ours has experienced. . . . unless some immediate and spirited exertions are adopted to furnish at least three months pay to the troops as money that will be of some value to them, and at the same time ways and means are devised to clothe and feed them better (more regularly I mean) than they have been, the worst that can befall us may be expected."

One interesting point that emerged in the discussions at Princeton was that the mutineers were determined, in whatever settlement might be effected, not to have their old officers back, even in the event that the British attacked and that the Pennsylvanians engaged them as they continued to insist that they would. It is not clear whether they harbored particular resentments against their officers as a whole or whether, having found they could get along quite well as a democratic army, they intended to continue to function in that manner.

When Joseph Reed reached Princeton, he sent a letter to Wayne requesting him to meet him at Maidenhead, a few miles from Princeton, for a conference. In the letter he declared that he was willing to hear the complaints of the soldiers and to redress all legitimate grievances. The pay would be made up and the clothing furnished at the earliest possible moment. The sergeants allowed the letter to be delivered to Wayne, then asked for it. Wayne let them take it away but insisted that he must be the one to read it to the troops. The sergeants consented to this and promised that the men would be assembled in the morning to hear the letter read. The board of sergeants also wrote to Reed, assuring him that he would be welcome in Princeton and "need not be in the least afraid or apprehensive of any irregularities or ill treatment, that the whole Line would be very happy how expedient your Excellency would be in settling this unhappy affair."

On Saturday night or Sunday morning one of the British agents, a Loyalist named Mason, who was wanted by the patriots for murder and robbery, got through the lines with a guide and delivered Clinton's message to Williams, the "major general" of the insurgents. Williams at once took the messenger and the message to the board of sergeants, who, in turn, decided to deliver them to Wayne. At four o'clock in the morning two sergeants awakened the general and gave him Clinton's offer as well as the two agents. In Wayne's words, "the soldiery in general affect to spurn at the idea of turning Arnolds (as they express it)." The general, greatly reassured by the reaction of the board of sergeants, promised the two sergeants who had brought the prisoner a reward of fifty guineas of gold, which was an odd and impulsive gesture. They had simply carried out the instructions of the board. Obviously, the reward was a measure of Wayne's relief; the event settled once and for all the rumors that had circulated all week that the mutiny had been stirred up by British agents. Wayne then prevailed on the sergeants to send Mason and his guide, James Ogden of Brunswick, to Trenton, where Reed could deal with them as British spies. The same night another spy entered the town and, perhaps hearing of the fate of Mason, simply dropped Clinton's offer outside the door to the room where the sergeants customarily met. A third man, apparently a double agent, delivered a copy of the letter to St. Clair at Morristown.

Reed conferred with Wayne and the colonels at Maidenhead and was reassured by what they told him as well as by the fact that the sergeants had turned over the British agents without hesitation. He decided it was safe enough for him to go to Princeton, but he embellished the situation rather dramatically, writing to the Pennsylvania council: "The consequences of their [the mutineers'] defection to the enemy are so great and alarming that I think nothing ought to be left unattempted to improve the good disposition. I have but one life, and my country has the first claim for it."

Before he could set out for Princeton, Reed received a disconcerting letter from the mutineers asking that Mason and Ogden be returned to Princeton and kept prisoner there.

As Reed approached the outskirts of Princeton, he was greeted by the whole line, drawn up at attention with the artillery ready to fire a salute in his honor. Reed reluctantly returned the salute of the sergeants, who took the place of officers in each company. "We did not apprehend," he wrote Washington, "it would be prudent or politic to risk anything . . . on account of ceremony . . . as we were then fully in the power of the mutineers, it did not seem prudent to give cause of offense on unessential points."

At the conference, the sergeants presented one plain grievance: the veterans who had enlisted in 1776 and 1777 must be discharged with their arrears in pay and clothing. When Reed demurred, on the grounds that this amounted to a general release without regard to terms of enlistment, the sergeants gave an angry inventory of the subterfuges that they claimed had been used to get them to enlist for the duration. "Rigorous severity," they declared, had been "frequently exercised, especially when they requested an inquiry into the terms of their enlistment and corporal punishment inflicted without court martial or inquiry." Their obvious sincerity and depth of feeling convinced Reed that "some undue methods have been taken to engage many in the service." He therefore consented to the proposition "that all those whose times were expired, and who had not freely entered again knowing the duration of the service, should be discharged," but to no others.

The agreement, which would clearly be accepted by the men, dismayed Wayne and the colonels. They felt it would be better to disband the Pennsylvania Line entirely than to discharge some soldiers and keep others, especially since it was evident that this would probably have to be done on the basis of the individual soldier's own word. It seemed to them that Reed had accepted the soldiers' statements regarding the terms of their service, rather than their own.

On Monday, a week after their uprising, the mutineers of the Pennsylvania Line agreed to the terms proposed by Reed and marched to Trenton to take up quarters there. The two spies, Mason and Ogden—the latter had left a bride of two months at home—were tried and hanged, Mason affirming his loyalty to George III and dying like a brave man, Ogden like a terrified youth unwittingly caught in a deadly game. For five days their bodies swung in the winter wind.

The sergeants, wheedled a bit by Reed, rejected Wayne's rash offer of an award of fifty guineas apiece, which was a vast relief to Wayne, who had promised it, and to Reed, who would have been responsible for producing it. "As it has not been for the sake or through any expectation of receiving a reward," they wrote, "but for the zeal and love of our country that we sent them [the spies] immediately to General Wayne, we therefore do not consider ourselves entitled to any other reward but the love of our country. . . ." The letter, Reed wrote to Washington, "would have done credit to persons of more elevated stations in life."

The mutiny was now, in effect, at an end. The soldiers had gotten much of what they had originally demanded. They were promised that a commission would be appointed to hear all cases in dispute concerning periods and terms of enlistment, and that their arrears would be settled. The British had continued making frantic efforts to open negotiations with the insurgents, but with a notable lack of success. By the twelfth, they were still looking for "people of property" to volunteer for "from one to two hundred guineas each" to make contact with the leaders of the mutineers. It is probably safe to say that the British secret service was never as helpless, or Clinton as poorly informed or as misinformed, as they were about the events of the January mutiny.

General Sullivan, a member of the Congressional committee who had accompanied Reed to Trenton, wrote to Luzerne on January 13, giving an analysis of the mutiny that it would be difficult to improve upon. After describing the course of the uprising, he noted, "Thus, Sir, has this surprising affair been brought to a happy issue. Perhaps history does not furnish an instance of so large a body of troops revolting from the command of their officers, marching in such exact order, without doing the least injury to individuals, and remaining in this situation for such a length of time, without division or confusion among themselves, and then returning to their duty as soon as their reasonable demands were complied with." Such behavior, Sullivan pointed out, should convince the British how much they mistook the disposition of the majority of Americans when they declared that the Americans would readily give their support to the Crown "if they were not overawed by their tyrannic rulers." Among the mutineers were "a large body . . . of foreigners, as well as natives, having no officer to command them and no force to prevent their joining the enemy for which they had repeated invitations, yet, though they well knew they were liable to the severest punishment for their revolt, they distained the British officers with a firmness that would have done honor to the ancient Romans, and through the whole have shown the greatest respect to the Committee of Congress, to the Governor and members of the Council for the State of Pennsylvania . . . and have not deviated through the whole from that order and regularity which upon other occasions must have done honor to military discipline."

It was, for a fact, a remarkable mutiny; one, as Sullivan suggested, without a parallel in the history of armies. The sad gap in our knowledge of it lies in the complete absence of any records or reminiscences of the debates and discussions among the soldiers involved. A buried and almost wholly inaccessible part of the Revolution—the lives and minds and temperaments, the thoughts, prejudices, and emotions of the ordinary Revolutionary soldier—suddenly made itself manifest in the most startling and dramatic form, and in doing so gave us hints of the richness, complexity, and originality of that hidden life; of the remarkable resources and potentialities that lay in a group of men who could instantly discard their own officers and replace them with men they trusted and obeyed better than those regularly appointed to command them. The mutiny can be taken to reveal, as Sullivan partially understood, that under the formal structure of the army, imposed from above, lay another nascent structure with its own identity, its own inherent logic and order. Only one thing was lacking—the test of battle. One cannot repress a twinge of regret that Clinton did not so far misread the situation as to take the occasion for an advance that would have brought the mutineers of the Pennsylvania Line into combat under their own "officers." At least the suspicion is sown (a suspicion supported by the course that the mutiny took) that the often-abused common soldier was perhaps better than the men who led him.

As with any major earthquake, there were numerous aftershocks following the formal end of the mutiny.

The commissioners appointed to hear the cases of men whose terms of enlistment were in dispute began to hear them without waiting for the records to be sent from Philadelphia; and since, in the absence of records, the sworn word of the soldier was to be accepted, many soldiers perjured themselves and swore that they had enlisted only for three years and were therefore entitled to discharges.

It is perhaps revealing that the discarded officers, furious at the threats and insults from their men, wished, almost without exception, to see the mutiny suppressed by force of arms and the leaders hanged. Instead they saw the mutineers sympathized with and even praised, while they waited in a kind of exile for the issue to be resolved. Moreover, the men bitterly resented the fact that they were forced to take back the officers whom they had so emphatically rejected. There were angry scenes, abuse, and disobedience. "The men," Reed wrote, "certainly had not those attachments which the officers supposed, and their fears being now at an end, they give loose to many indecencies, which are very provoking to those who have long been accustomed to receive unconditional submission." Some officers were excluded from the camp, and others threatened with physical violence.

Trenton seethed with discontent. Back pay did not arrive, and men who had been dismissed hung about camp waiting for their money. There were others who were willing to re-enlist, but there was no money to pay their bounties. "The soldiery are full," Wayne wrote to the Pennsylvania council on the fifteenth, "in the spirit of re-enlisting. Had we money and instructions we could improve it to great effect. On the contrary we shall lose the chief part of them." One advantage in discharging the most militant of the mutineers was that they were obliged to turn in their muskets before they departed, and thus disarmed they were far less of a threat. In addition to those discharged, many more were furloughed until "the Ides of March," when they were to reassemble at specific locations, regiment by regiment. "I am now fully convinced," Wayne wrote to Washington, "that there is no situation in life but admits of some consolation. Ours at one period appeared very gloomy indeed. But more lucid and pleasing prospects begin to dawn. The soldiery are as impatient of liberty as they were of service, and are as importunate to be re-enlisted as they were to be discharged. Money is fast collecting for the purpose and I trust that a few weeks will put it into my power to announce to your Excellency a reclaimed and formidable Line."

But trouble was not over. The New Jersey Line, which had complaints of its own, was fired by the example of the Pennsylvania Line, and at Pompton, where they were camped, word came to their commanding officer, Colonel Israel Shreve, that the men intended to leave their hutments and march to Trenton to make demands of the state assembly, which was in session there. When Shreve tried to stop them, they simply ignored him. There was no violence, and the mutineers went off in reasonably good order, Shreve trailing along behind. At Chatham, where there was another detachment of the line, they stopped to recruit for the mutiny, but here they also learned that the assembly had already passed laws for their relief. A firm but conciliatory line was taken by the officers and the commissioners appointed by the assembly to inquire into the matter of enlistments. The sergeants who, in emulation of the Pennsylvania Line, had taken charge now petitioned for a general pardon, and Colonel Dayton replied that since they had "neither shed blood nor done any violence to any office or inhabitant; he hereby promises a pardon to all such as immediately without hesitation shall return to their duty and conduct themselves in a soldierly manner. Those who shall, notwithstanding this unmerited proffer of clemency, refuse obedience, must expect the reward of such obstinate villainy."

When the pardon was read to the soldiers, they gave three cheers and returned, obediently enough, to their encampment at Pompton, but the spirit of mutiny was still in the air; soldiers disobeyed orders or obeyed them in a grudging spirit and with muttered threats against their officers. General Robert Howe had meanwhile been dispatched from West Point by Washington with a strong contingent of New

England troops and orders to put down the mutiny by whatever means necessary. He arrived after a grueling forced march through deep snow, and at dawn the men of the New Jersey Line awoke to find their camp surrounded. They were ordered to "parade without arms," and when some protested, a regiment of Massachusetts soldiers was ordered to advance on them and the New Jerseymen were given five minutes to comply with their orders. "This had its effect," Howe wrote, "and they to a man marched without arms to the ground appointed for them." Howe was provided with a list of "the most atrocious offenders" and selected one from each regiment to be executed on the spot by a firing squad made up of twelve of the "most guilty mutineers."

As Dr. Thacher, the Connecticut physician, noted in his journal, "This was a most painful task; being themselves guilty, they were greatly distressed with the duty imposed upon them, and when ordered to load some of them shed tears. The wretched victims, overwhelmed by the terrors of death, had neither time nor power to implore mercy and forgiveness of their God, and such was their agonizing condition that no heart could refrain from emotions of sympathy and compassion." The first man was led a few yards away from the silent troops and was placed on his knees, and at the command of an officer, three fired at his head and three at his breast, "the other six reserving their fire in order to dispatch the victim should the first fire fail. It so happened in this instance," Thacher reported, "the remaining six then fired and life was instantly extinguished." A second man was executed in similar fashion, and the third was pardoned on the recommendation of his officers and "to his unspeakable joy."

After the executions the men were once more paraded and were required by platoons to promise "by future good conduct to atone for past offenses." They showed, Howe wrote Washington, "the fullest sense of their guilt and such strong marks of contrition that I think I may venture to pledge myself for their future good conduct."

Washington, appropriately, had the last word in his orders, thanking Howe and his men for their "march through rough and mountainous roads, rendered almost impassable by the depth of the snow," and for the good spirit with which they had performed such a terrible duty. "The General," Washington continued, "is deeply sensible of the sufferings of the Army. He leaves no expedient unessayed to relieve them, and he is persuaded Congress and the several States are doing everything in their power for the same purpose. But while we look to the public for the fulfillment of its engagements, we should do it with proper allowance for the embarrassments of public affairs. We began a contest for liberty and independence ill provided with the means for war, relying on our own patriotism to supply the deficiency." There were many mercenary armies in the past that had suffered even greater distress than the Continental Army. "Shall we who aspire to the distinction of a patriot army, who are contending for everything precious in society against every thing hateful and degrading in slavery; shall we who call ourselves citizens discover less constancy and military virtue than the mercenary instruments of ambition?" Believing the mutiny to have been prompted "by the pernicious advice of a few who probably have been paid by the enemy to betray their associates, the General is happy in the lenity shown in the execution of only two of the most guilty after compelling the whole to an unconditional surrender."

There were some troubling implications in the general's statement. The actions of the New Jersey mutineers had been much milder, it might be argued, than those of the Pennsylvania Line, who, after all, had killed several officers and been far more obdurate in their mutiny than their fellows from New Jersey. There was, moreover, not the slightest shred of evidence that any New Jersey soldiers had been paid by the British to foment mutiny. To say so was to demean the motives of those unhappy men who had been singled out as examples. What was plain enough, between the lines, was that the New Jersey soldiers had been made examples of. What Washington and the civil authorities dared not do to the more culpable Pennsylvanians, they had done to the soldiers of the New Jersey Line. But these are the fortunes of war. In circumstances so strained and dangerous, evenhanded justice is seldom achieved. What Washington feared more than anything else was that the spirit of revolt might spread like a disease through the army and destroy it in a few weeks, where the British had failed to do so in five years of warfare. Desperate situations require desperate remedies. The fact that the Pennsylvanians could not be punished did not mean that the New Jerseymen should not. The soldiers of Pennsylvania, furthermore, took, as they well knew, a desperate risk. One is inclined to argue that they deserved the clemency that the authorities were forced, however reluctantly, to give them. Perhaps their imitators deserved what they got.

7

Lafayette in Virginia

Washington, as we have seen, was obsessed with the treason of Benedict Arnold. Like a vengeful father, he was determined to do his best to capture and humiliate the man who had betrayed his trust. He therefore sent another "son" to effect this purpose. Lafayette was assigned to the command of units assembled at Peekskill with orders to march to Virginia and capture Arnold, who had been sent by the British to Virginia to destroy that state as a base of supplies and provisions for the Continental Army.

In May, 1779, a British expedition from New York under the command of Major General Edward Mathew and Admiral Sir George Collier had made an amphibious landing at Hampton, Virginia, and had occupied Fort Nelson, collecting large quantities of tobacco, ordnance, and naval supplies. The Americans burned an almost completed twenty-eight-gun frigate on the stocks and two French merchantmen to keep them from falling into British hands. In addition, a hundred and thirty-seven vessels of all kinds and sizes trapped in the Hampton Roads were burned or captured by the raiders. Having struck a devastating blow at the principal supply depot in America, the British returned to New York without losing a man. They had inflicted losses estimated at over £2,000,000, which would probably be the equivalent of several hundred million dollars today.

Nineteen months later Arnold, given the task of once more destroying military supplies in Virginia, left New York with sixteen hundred
soldiers. He was also ordered to give support to the Loyalists of that
state and to check the flow of Virginia soldiers to Greene in North
Carolina. On December 20, 1780, he sailed out of New York Harbor
and into a violent storm that scattered his fleet and drove some of his
transports ashore; he lost almost a quarter of his force. Nevertheless,
Arnold landed at Hampton Roads on December 30 and, proving that he
was as vigorous a traitor as a patriot, immediately pushed up the James
River in captured boats to Richmond.

Simcoe's Rangers, who made up part of Arnold's force, were sent
toward the Chickahominy River, where they learned that a detachment
of General Thomas Nelson's militia was at the Charles City Court
House. Led by a captured Negro slave, forty mounted Rangers caught
some hundred and fifty militia by surprise, killed several, and captured
about fifty.

There was an inescapable irony in the fact that Benedict Arnold
was ravaging Virginia almost unopposed. Virginia had been a leader,
with Massachusetts, in the agitation that preceded the Revolution. It had
provided the commander of the American army and a number of the
most notable political and military figures of the Revolution, as well as
many soldiers and an endless stream of supplies. To see it prostrate and
humiliated by a traitor was a bitter cup for all patriots, but bitterest, of
course, for the inhabitants of the Old Dominion.

Washington, however, now saw an opportunity to trap Arnold with
the help of the French fleet. If the French could block Arnold's evacuation by sea, Lafayette might be able to run him to ground, isolated as he
was in patriot territory. With three light-infantry regiments made up of
New Jersey and New England Continentals, Lafayette started south,
expecting to be joined by those regiments of the Pennsylvania Line that
had mutinied a few months before.

Lafayette's New Englanders and New Jerseyites resented being sent
south, where the summer climate was notoriously oppressive and the
people and their ways thoroughly alien. Since the mutiny of the Pennsylvania Line, the threat of soldiers taking matters into their own hands
had hovered over the entire Continental establishment. Soldiers were
weary of the protracted and inconclusive struggle; there had not been a
major battle or campaign north of Virginia for more than a year. The
routines of camp life grew particularly abrasive, and officers and men
clashed repeatedly over small points of discipline. Lafayette, marching

to Virginia, had to contend with numerous desertions. He ordered that one apprehended deserter be hanged, but then, unnerved by his sense that his army was near mutiny, he pardoned and dismissed another offender, following which he issued an order to his troops declaring that "he was setting out for a difficult and dangerous expedition; but that he hoped soldiers would not abandon him; but that whoever wished to go away might do so instantly." Lafayette had learned something of the psychology of the American soldier. "From that hour," he wrote in his memoirs, "all desertions ceased, and not a man would leave."

Washington, meanwhile, sent word to Rochambeau requesting that the French join in a combined operation with the intention of trapping Arnold in Virginia. It was a rather ill-considered move on Washington's part—to employ the French fleet and a substantial part of the French army to capture Arnold; it was perhaps the only time that his personal feelings beclouded his military judgment. Actually, Washington's request for the cooperation of French troops reached Newport after Rochambeau had already dispatched a small fleet for Virginia under Captain Le Gardeur de Tilly. De Tilly captured the forty-four-gun British frigate *Romulus* in Lynnhaven Bay, as well as ten other prizes, but Arnold withdrew up the Elizabeth River to Portsmouth, where the river was too shallow for De Tilly to follow him. The Frenchman therefore sailed back to Newport.

The American commander in chief visited Newport on March 6, 1781, for a general discussion of strategy with Rochambeau. The French general, having belatedly received Washington's request for soldiers to aid in the operation against Arnold, had already loaded 1,140 men aboard transports ready to set sail under the command of Chevalier Destouches. The need to repair a frigate had delayed the sailing, but the squadron of eight ships of the line and four frigates sailed on the eighth.

Lafayette reached Head of Elk, Maryland, on the third of March and continued south to Annapolis, where he waited for Destouches. While he waited, Lafayette proceeded by canoe up the Elizabeth River to reconnoiter the route for an attack on Arnold, who had established his headquarters at Portsmouth. Lafayette also had a warm reunion with Baron von Steuben, who was confident that he could turn Virginia militiamen into soldiers as well drilled as those that he had produced at Valley Forge. Von Steuben, always the optimist, assured Lafayette that five thousand militia could be recruited.

Von Steuben's optimism proved ill-founded. His normally cheerful disposition was strained to the utmost in Virginia. Riding to a county courthouse to take command of a band of five hundred militia, he found only five, three of whom promptly deserted. Finally some six hundred men of indifferent quality were rounded up. Von Steuben found them an intractable lot. But to Benjamin Harrison, a Virginian, they were "600 fine men under Baron Steuben which he will not carry into action. . . . His conduct gives universal disgust. . . . I believe him a good officer on parade but the worst in every other respect in the American Army." Von Steuben, for his part, was far from enchanted with the Virginians. "I am not less tired of this State than they are of me," he wrote, adding, "I shall always regret that circumstances induced me to undertake the defense of a country where Caesar and Hannibal would have lost their reputation, and where every farmer is a general, but where nobody wishes to be a soldier." That was uncomfortably close to the mark.

Lafayette, like Von Steuben, found it difficult to comprehend Southerners or to cope with their polite evasiveness. "There is a great slowness and great carelessness in this part of the world," he wrote Washington. "But the intentions are good, and the people want to be awakened." He wished for Washington's presence, which might arouse the Virginians from their lethargy. Lafayette also had some unpleasant personal news for Washington: when the British came to Mount Vernon, "many Negroes deserted to them." Moreover, Lund Washington, Washington's brother, according to Lafayette, had then gone on board the British sloop of war and offered to give them provisions, his idea apparently being to dissuade them from burning the plantation house. This action, Lafayette wrote, "will certainly have a bad effect, and contrasts with spirited answers from some neighbours that had their houses burnt accordingly."

Washington promptly wrote, rebuking Lund. He was sorry to hear of the loss of his slaves, but "that which gives me most concern," he wrote, "is, that you should go on board the enemys Vessels, and furnish them with refreshments. It would have been a less painful circumstance to me, to have heard, that in consequence of your non-compliance with their request, they had burnt my House, and laid the Plantation in ruins." Washington was sure that his brother had acted from his best judgment; "But to go on board their Vessels; carry them refreshments, commune with a parcel of plundering Scoundrels, and request a favor by asking the surrender of my Negroes, was exceedingly ill-judged. . . ." Washington was convinced that the British would return in other raids and warned his brother that he should make no accommodation to them, even if it resulted "in the loss of all my Negroes, and in the destruction of my houses." What Lund might do was remove some of "the most valuable and least bulky articles" to a place of safety.

Washington's hope of capturing Arnold proved abortive when the unpredictable British Admiral Marriot Arbuthnot reached the Chesapeake before Destouches, even though the French fleet had had a thirty-six hour head start. Each admiral had eight ships, but the British outgunned the French vessels. For an hour the two fleets inflicted heavy damage on each other. The British were pursuing the French in a line of battle when Destouches came about to the leeward and sailed on a new tack past the British ships, both fleets exchanging broadsides as they passed. The lee gauge was conventionally to be avoided, but in this instance the wind was so strong that it made the French ships keel over enough to lift their windward sides out of the water; the French gunners could therefore bring their lower tiers of guns into action. The effect on the British was just the opposite; keeled over to the leeward, the guns on their lower tiers could not be elevated sufficiently to fire at the French. The British superiority in firepower was thus nullified and their windward advantage worse than useless. Neither Destouches or Arbuthnot were naval commanders of genius. The battle was inconclusive, with, if anything, some advantage to the French. But Destouches, as D'Estaing before him, sailed for home, leaving Arbuthnot in control of the "sea of battle." Arbuthnot sailed into the Chesapeake and made contact with Arnold.

Lafayette, assuming that Arbuthnot had with him forces to strengthen Arnold, remained at Annapolis for almost a week. As it turned out, Arbuthnot had brought supplies for Arnold but no reinforcements of troops. It was not Clinton's intention to make Virginia a major theater of operations, and he had little confidence in Arnold's reliability. Arnold, more aware of his own vulnerability than the Americans, was alarmed by the news of Lafayette's proximity and begged Clinton for more men.

Having failed to deliver the troops that Lafayette needed if he was to have any hope of proceeding against Arnold, Destouches arrived back at Newport on March 26. Lafayette in his original orders had been instructed to "return to the main army, in case Arnold quitted Virginia, or the French lost superiority of naval force." He thus withdrew to Head of Elk and asked for further directions. Washington wrote to him on April 5: "While we lament the miscarriage of an enterprise which bid so fair for success, we must console ourselves in the thought of having done everything practicable to accomplish it. . . ." Once more the hope of substantial assistance from the French had proved illusory, but Washington was careful not to express disappointment or to criticize Destouches. "The point upon which the whole turned, the action with Admiral Arbuthnot, reflects honor upon the chevalier and upon the marine of France," he wrote. Lafayette was directed to return to Philadelphia. The next day, however, Washington ordered him to join forces with Greene in South Carolina. When he later learned that Clinton had sent General William Phillips with two thousand men to reinforce Arnold, he again countermanded his orders and placed Lafayette under Greene's command, with instructions to assume the direction of the campaign in Virginia and to report to Greene as well as to him. Greene received word from Washington that Lafayette was being placed under his command a few weeks after the battle of Guilford Court House. "I am happy to hear the Marquis de La Fayette is coming to Virginia," Greene wrote, "though I am afraid from a hint in one of Baron Steuben's letters that he will think himself injured in being superseded in the command [that is, placed under Lafayette]. Could the Marquis join us at this moment, we should have a most glorious campaign. It would put Lord Cornwallis and his whole army into our hands."

From his base of operations at Annapolis Lafayette marched to Baltimore, where a ball was given to honor him, and where he prevailed upon the belles of that city to make shirts for his soldiers and upon the young men to recruit a troop of dragoons to join his army. On his own promissory note he borrowed two thousand guineas from the merchants of the city to equip his ragged soldiers "with shirts, overalls, hats and boots." Thus refurbished, their mutinous impulses were allayed, and they marched south in good spirits. As Lafayette wrote Washington, "their honor having been interested in this affair . . . murmurs as well as desertions, are entirely out of fashion."

From Baltimore to Alexandria, Virginia, and then to Fredericksburg, Lafayette advanced with high hopes of engaging Arnold on favorable terms. At Fredericksburg, however, he learned that General Phillips had landed near Petersburg with the reinforcements requested by Arnold, had taken command of the combined forces, and was advancing up the James, leaving a train of burned homes and pillaged plantations on the way. While Arnold had burned and destroyed some of the supplies at Richmond, much was left. The city was obviously the goal of Phillips' army, and Lafayette, unencumbered by artillery and baggage, made a dash for Richmond, entering the city on April 29, just ahead of Phillips. The British general arrived to find Richmond in Lafayette's hands. In the battle of Minden, Phillips had commanded the battery that had fired the cannon that killed Lafayette's father; now he withdrew down the James and vented his chagrin by writing a series of insolent letters to the marquis. The Americans, he charged, had fired on a flag of truce. "You are sensible, sir, that I am authorized to inflict the severest punishment in return for this bad conduct, and that towns and villages lay at the mercy of the King's troops, and it is to that mercy alone you can justly appeal for their not being reduced to ashes." Lafayette must deliver the culprits to Phillips. "Should you, Sir, refuse this, I hereby make you answerable for any desolation which may follow in consequence." Clinton, having sent a traitor to pillage Virginia, had reinforced him with a fool.

Lafayette replied that the tone of Phillips' letter precluded any further correspondence. A few days later Phillips came down with a malarial fever, and the command of his force devolved on Arnold. Lafayette and his men were at Wilton on the other side of the James River a few days after that when an officer came under a flag of truce with a letter from Arnold requesting an exchange of prisoners. Phillips, it turned out, had died of the fever, doubtless augmented by bad temper, but Lafayette was no more ready to receive a communication from Arnold than he had been from Phillips. He sent a chilly rebuke, and Arnold in turn threatened to send the American prisoners to the West Indies. Lafayette continued to rebuff Arnold and forwarded the correspondence to Washington, who wrote, "Your conduct upon every occasion meets my approbation, but in none more than your refusing to hold a correspondence with Arnold."

At this point the arrival of Cornwallis at Petersburg, Virginia, put the marquis in a precarious position. He had less than a thousand Continentals, with some fifty horse, the Baltimore dragoons, quite untested, and some militia. Opposed to him was Cornwallis with some five thousand well-equipped and seasoned troops. Cornwallis, utilizing Tarleton's legion—now grown to eight hundred men mounted on Virginia thoroughbred hunters instead of the undersized ponies of which Lee had been so contemptuous—had far more mobility. Lafayette did not see how he could hope to escape, but he wrote to Hamilton that he was "determined to be beaten with some decency. . . . Their

command of the waters, the superiority in cavalry and the great disproportion of forces, gave the enemy such advantages that I durst not
venture to listen to my fondness for enterprise." The fact that he had a
detached command had made him more cautious, and he was sure that
if the Pennsylvania Line arrived in time, "Lord Cornwallis shall pay
something for his victory."

Hamilton had shortly before had a spiteful and unpleasant quarrel
with Washington over who should go up or down the stairs first, and the
New Yorker had resigned from Washington's staff. Lafayette thought
Hamilton was wrong, but if Hamilton was determined to leave the
commander in chief, Lafayette wanted that other "son" of their common father to join him. "Come here, my dear friend," he wrote, "and
command our artillery in Virginia. I want your advice and your exertions." Indeed, he was, at the moment, less the Marquis de Lafayette,
"the very high and very mighty Lord Monseigneur Marie Joseph Paul
Yves Roch Gilbert du Motier de La Fayette" (as he had been christened),
than a frightened and uncertain young man. He wrote to his brother-in-
law, Vicomte Louis de Noailles, a member of the expeditionary force at
Newport: "None of my friends in the North, except General Washington send me any news; if they do not know any more about what
concerns us, I fear I shall be judged severely, even unjustly. . . ." He
counted on Noailles to put the record straight: "If you write to France,
mon ami" he added, "give news to me . . . tell them that your poor
brother-in-law is devilishly busy getting himself licked."

It was not the speed and agility of Lafayette's army that saved him.
Cornwallis inexplicably abandoned his pursuit of Lafayette and turned
west to Charlottesville, the seat of the House of Burgesses. He sent
Tarleton and his legion on ahead to try to capture the members of the
assembly. As Tarleton, sticking to back roads, rode on with his legion
undetected, he passed, at midnight, the Cuckoo Tavern, near Louisa.
At the tavern Jack Jouett, a tall, powerful man, famous as a rider and
marksman, heard the rumble of Tarleton's cavalry and, going to the
window, saw them trotting by in the faint moonlight. He guessed at once
that they were on their way to Charlottesville and set out to spread the
warning. At the Louisa Inn he stirred up the fat landlord who lived day
and night in a great armchair, and by morning he had wakened Dr.
Thomas Walker, a leading patriot in the area, and enlisted his help in
passing on the news of Tarleton's raid. He woke Jefferson at Monti-
cello, and Mrs. Jefferson and her three small children were bundled

into a coach and driven to a hideaway in the mountains. At Charlottesville, Jouett found the legislators at breakfast. They convened at once in order to officially recess to Staunton and then took to the hills.

Tarleton stopped at the Walker plantation for breakfast, and Mrs. Walker, aware that every minute counted to allow the assemblymen at Charlottesville to get out of town, took her sweet time preparing a typically ample meal of salt herring, salt beef, and johnnycake.

At Charlottesville, Tarleton's men rounded up seven dilatory legislators and gathered in a thousand flintlocks and four hundred barrels of powder, along with clothing and tobacco intended for Greene's army in South Carolina. "Like birds of prey, they seized on everything that they could find," a patriot wrote. The British cavalry officer moved so rapidly that he almost bagged the governor, Thomas Jefferson, who reportedly was observing the events in Charlottesville through his spyglass.

Tarleton maintained that his prisoners "generally and separately avowed that if England could prevent the intended co-operation of the French fleet and army with the American forces during the ensuing autumn, both Congress and the country would gladly dissolve the French alliance and enter into treaty with Great Britain." These recollections were long after the event itself, but two points might be made in regard to them. First, on the matter of dissolving the French alliance: it had been, to this time, a bitter disappointment to the Americans. Nothing positive had resulted from it in the military or naval spheres, and it had inhibited the opening of treaty discussions between the British and the Americans. The second point is that Tarleton did not say (though he doubtless meant to imply) that his American prisoners would have entered into treaty negotiations with the British if those negotiations were aimed at returning the states to the status of British colonies.

While Tarleton raided Charlottesville, Cornwallis dispatched Simcoe's Rangers to crush Baron von Steuben, who was guarding the military supplies at Point of Fork on the James. Simcoe made such an impressive parade of his forces at the river that Steuben beat a hasty retreat, leaving the bank of the river covered with arms and stores. Convinced that Cornwallis was close behind him, Steuben fled fifty miles before stopping. Like many another officer, the baron was apparently better at drilling than fighting.

Tarleton, outside of the raid on Charlottesville, was relatively inactive. It is difficult to guess why Cornwallis did not use him more aggressively against Lafayette, who was acutely conscious of his vulnerability to "an army mounted on race-horses," as he described Tarleton's legion. Perhaps the legion had never entirely recovered from Kings Mountain, or had been so often blunted by Lee that it had lost irretrievably the dashing *esprit* that had made it so dangerous. Moreover Cornwallis was reluctant to risk his "eyes"—Tarleton's cavalry—on the early stages of a campaign whose outcome he could not yet discern.

Trying to augment his small army, Lafayette paid a visit to Daniel Morgan, who lived in nearby Winchester nursing his arthritis and his grievances, complaining of "the infirmities of age" and of being "blind as a bat." Yet, beguiled by the young Frenchman, Morgan agreed to join him with a company of riflemen from the Shenandoah Valley, and a few days later he hobbled into Lafayette's camp with his mountaineers. "Mon Dieu!" Lafayette exclaimed, "What a people are these Americans; they have reinforced me with a band of giants." A few days later, Morgan's riflemen were instrumental in turning back an attack by Tarleton's dragoons; during the march, Lafayette wrote Washington with astonishment, "the riflemen ran the whole day in front of my horse without eating or resting." But Morgan's old pains and aches were too much for him. "I am afraid I am broke down," he said, and he left reluctantly for home.

The only course that made sense for Lafayette to follow was the one that he described in a letter to Washington. "Were I to fight a battle," he wrote, "I should be cut to pieces, the militia dispersed and the arms lost. Were I to decline fighting, the country would think itself given up. I am therefore determined to skirmish, but not to engage too far, and particularly to take care of their immense and excellent body of horse, who the militia fear as they would so many wild beasts. . . ." Cornwallis was, in fact, already advancing. He had crossed the James River, wide and slow, at Westover, the great Byrd plantation, and Lafayette's scouts had intercepted one of his letters, in which Cornwallis had written: "The boy cannot escape me!" Lafayette was determined to try. Leaving his artillery behind—"a strange whim," he wrote, "but it saved Richmond"—he began a series of moves, feints, twists, and turns that baffled Cornwallis and Tarleton's cavalry. The marquis bivouacked in the woods at night and fought rear-guard actions during the day. In this manner he reached the Raccoon ford of the Rapidan River on June 7. He was joined there three days later by Wayne, commanding three regiments of the Pennsylvania Line, some nine hundred men.

It had been a calculated risk to send the Pennsylvania Line to reinforce Lafayette. Few other generals could have carried it off, but Wayne, a Pennsylvanian himself, had just that combination of amiable cajolery and tough-minded discipline needed to keep some control over his morose troops, who marched along "mute as fish," their ammunition carried in guarded wagons. They slogged through warm summer rain and mud, making only ten or twelve miles a day; Wayne seemed determined to march the mutiny out of them if he could not coax it out.

In the plantation country near Richmond, one of the Pennsylvania officers got his first glimpse of Southern slavery. White women, swathed in silk and linen against the sun, lined the road to watch the soldiers pass by. Lieutenant William Feltman noted, "They will have a number of blacks about them, all naked, nothing to hide their nakedness. I am surprised this does not hurt the feelings of the fair sex to see these young boys of about Fourteen and Fifteen years Old to Attend them. . . ." Naked slaves also waited table in the handsome plantation houses along the river where Feltman and his fellow officers were several times invited to dine.

The British, as they withdrew, had left Negroes with smallpox along the road to give the pox to their pursuers. They lay "starving and helpless, begging of us as we passed them for God's sake to kill them as they were in great pain and misery." The picture was seared into the young lieutenant's memory.

With Wayne's force, Lafayette felt strong enough to at least try a cautious advance. Inexplicably, Cornwallis, hitherto so aggressive, fell back. Lafayette was now joined by an embarrassed Von Steuben, riding in his now-familiar sulky and smoking the inevitable long pipe; he commanded his eighteen-months men (soldiers who had refused to enlist for the duration but had accepted a kind of intermediate enlistment period) and a body of militia. Von Steuben got a cold reception when he joined Lafayette. His precipitous flight at Point of Fork had shattered what vestiges of reputation were left of him. "The militia left him. His new levies deserted. All Virginia was in an uproar against him. The enemy laughed at him, and I cannot describe to you what my surprise has been," Lafayette wrote. Lafayette, it must be said, had his own critics. A militia officer under his command wrote, "I fear the Marquis may lose his credit. Deserters, British, cringing Dutchmen and busy little Frenchmen swarm about HDQuarters. The people do not love Frenchmen, every person they can't understand they take for a Frenchman."

While Cornwallis attempted to give the impression that the British were in complete control of the state, Lafayette, close on his heels, tried "to give his [Cornwallis's] movements the appearance of a retreat. God grant that there may be an opportunity to give them the appearance of a defeat," he added. The addition of Von Steuben brought Lafayette's force to almost five thousand, two thousand of whom were Continentals. He felt able to press harder on Cornwallis, who first withdrew to Richmond and then a few days later evacuated that city and moved down the James toward Williamsburg.

It is difficult to understand why Cornwallis dropped back down the peninsula formed by the James and the York rivers. He might at any time have established defensive positions and made an effort to draw Lafayette and Wayne into battle. They were both notoriously hotheaded and eager for action, and they could probably not have resisted a challenge, since the respective armies were now roughly equal in numbers. Cornwallis had doubtless by this time a bellyful of chasing American armies and of fighting them too. The best strategy seemed to be to draw Lafayette down the peninsula after him and then hope that British frigates and transports could sail up the rivers, land troops in the Frenchman's rear, and trap his whole army.

Dropping back through Richmond, Cornwallis's men had burned two thousand hogsheads of tobacco, and the fragrant smoke still hung over the town as Lafayette's men marched in. Harnesses, uniforms, food, six hundred bushels of flour, and five thousand muskets had all been destroyed.

The most gratifying espisode came on the twenty-sixth of June. Wayne dispatched four platoons of Richard Butler's infantry and Major William MacPherson's cavalry against Simcoe; they caught a regiment of the Queen's Rangers by surprise at Hot Water Plantation, chased them five or six miles, killed forty men, and captured a number of prisoners as well as horses and cattle. The Battle of Hot Water was a minor engagement, but it was tonic to the spirits of Virginians who had grown resigned to having Cornwallis "sport through the country without opposition."

Lafayette himself seemed surprised at his good fortune in having eluded Cornwallis and having managed to join forces with Wayne. Undoubtedly the decisive moment of the Virginia campaign came when Cornwallis, hot in pursuit of Lafayette's exhausted and much smaller army, stopped at Bottom's Bridge and undertook the Charlottesville diversion, a "Quixotic expediton," Tarleton called it. At that point Lafayette had a force of some one thousand Continental light infantry plus perhaps three thousand militia, who came and went so constantly that it was almost impossible to keep track of them. Against this force Cornwallis commanded in the neighborhood of seven thousand men, British regulars and Tories, of whom over eight hundred were Tarleton's cavalry legion. Lafayette's most critical disadvantage was in fact in cavalry; he did not have enough to perform the routine tasks of reconnoitering. The arrival of Colonel John Francis Mercer (who had been on General Lee's staff and had retired from the army in disgust after Lee's court-martial) with fifty young Virginia gentlemen, mounted and equipped at their own expense, gave Lafayette his only effective scouting force.

It is not too much to say that the survival of Lafayette's army hinged on his ability to elude Cornwallis, with his large detachment of cavalry, and to join forces with Wayne's mutinous Pennsylvanians. In Mercer's opinion, "it was . . . utterly impossible for the Marquis to escape, if diligently watch'd & harass'd by so formidable a corps of horse." Tarleton, who made a demonstration against Lafayette, had only to station himself on Lafayette's flank to prevent him from marching and allow Cornwallis to come up with his main body and destroy him or force his surrender. In Tarleton's words, "At this period, the superiority of the [British] army, and the great superiority of the light troops, were such as to have enabled the British to traverse the country without apprehension or difficulty, either to destroy stores and tobacco in the neighborhood of the rivers [the Potomac, the Rappahannock, the Mattaponi, and the Pamunkey], or to undertake more important expeditions." The destruction of Lafayette's army and the penetration by the British up the parallel lines of the Rappahannock and the Potomac, at one point only eight miles apart, would have brought them to Fredericksburg and Falmouth, where there was an arms factory and large depots of vital American supplies. Such a movement would have left Virginia not only virtually defenseless but unable to play any role in supporting Greene's campaign in the South. More important, such action by Cornwallis would, of course, have made Yorktown impossible and would have effectively severed the Northern states from those to the south, thus vastly complicating the war from the point of view of Congress. But Cornwallis, who had fought so often and so well, failed to take advantage of the opportunity presented to him.

8

Congress

Wᴴɪʟᴇ Lafayette and Cornwallis maneuvered in Virginia, issues that would have a bearing on the fate of America were being discussed elsewhere—in Congress, in Parliament, in the French court.

Early in 1781, Vergennes had hinted that France had had enough of the war and was ready to negotiate a long-term truce, under which the British would give up New York but retain possession of Georgia and South Carolina. John Adams, who was the only American commissioner present in Paris at the time, made clear his indignation at the suggestion. In exasperation, Vergennes instructed Luzerne to bring pressure on Congress to force Adams into line. The French minister to the United States obediently "communicated . . . several observations respecting the conduct of Mr. Adams: and in doing justice to his patriotick character," he declared to the committee on foreign affairs that Congress must put its confidence "in the king's friendship and benevolence . . . his inviolable attachment to the principle of the alliance, and . . . his firm resolution constantly to support the cause of the United States. . . ." Congress should give Adams, Luzerne said, "the principal and most important outlines for his conduct" and then "order him, with respect to the manner of carrying them into execution, to receive his directions from the Count de Vergennes" or whomever Vergennes might indicate.

Thus Adams was the victim of a squeeze play. In America Luzerne, acting as the agent of Vergennes, attempted to prevail on Congress to tell Adams what Luzerne wished him to do, and in Paris Adams was to ask Vergennes how to do it. And Congress tamely acquiesced. On only one point were Adams and the other commissioners who joined him— Franklin and young John Jay—free to insist, and that point was the British acknowledgement of American independence *prior* to serious treaty discussions. On all other matters they were "to be ultimately governed by the advice of the French Court." There was a move, led by the New Englanders, to strike out this clause as being, in Thomas Rodney's words, "too abject and humiliating," but the French faction prevailed, and the clause remained intact. (Rodney wrote, "I was against the clause because I think it must convince even the French Court that we are reduced to a weak and abject state and that we have lost all that spirit and dignity which once appeared in the proceedings of Congress. . . .")

When John Jay, then Congressional commissioner in Spain, read the instructions, he wrote to Thomas McKean, the president of Congress, that he found it "difficult . . . to reconcile myself to the idea of the sovereign independent States of America submitting, in the persons of their ministers, to be absolutely governed by the advice and opinions of the servants of another sovereign. . . . This instruction, besides breathing a degree of complacency not quite republican, puts it out of the power of your ministers to improve those chances and opportunities which in the course of human affairs happens more or less frequently to all men. Nor is it clear that America, thus casting herself into the arms of the King of France, will advance either her interest or reputation with that or other nations. . . ." When John Adams received word of the new instructions at The Hague, where he was negotiating a loan from the Dutch, his initial reaction was surprisingly mild. "I am a sheep," he wrote to a friend, " . . . and I have been fleeced, but it gives me some pleasure to reflect that my wool makes others warm. . . . I am a bird, that my feathers have been plucked and worn as ornaments by others. Let them have the plumage if they will, it is but a geegaw." He was better suited, he wrote James Warren, for making war than peace.

In defense of Vergennes, it must be said that he was not always well advised. Admiral de Ternay had written to him in the summer of 1780 that "the fate of North America is yet very uncertain, and the Revolution is not so far advanced as it has been believed in Europe." Count Hans Axel von Fersen, aide-de-camp to Rochambeau in Rhode Island, described New England as engaged in a kind of civil war between Tories and patriots, with the propertied classes anxious for return to the British fold. The Whig faction in Rhode Island, he wrote, "was composed of people of the basest extraction who possessed little property. . . . The Tories are for the English or to put the matter more accurately, for peace without caring much about freedom or dependence."

It was small wonder that in the face of such reports, Vergennes hesitated to send fresh contingents of French soldiers to America. Lafayette wrote to him in January, 1781, reminding him of how little the French military and naval assistance had weighed so far in the war. "Since the hour of the arrival of the French," he wrote, "their inferiority has never for one moment ceased, and the English and Tories have dared to say that the French wished to kindle, rather than extinguish the flame. This calumny becomes more dangerous at a period when the English detachments are wasting the South; when, under the protection of some frigates, corps of fifteen hundred men are repairing to Virginia without our being able to get to them." Control of the sea was the crucial point, Lafayette argued. America could never make real headway against the British as long as the British were free to shift their men about by water as they pleased, to make sudden raids like that of Arnold's in Virginia, or to mount sustained invasions like Cornwallis's investment of South Carolina. The result was a kind of impasse. If the British were willing to pay the price, they could harass the states indefinitely as long as they controlled the seas, but there were not enough soldiers in all Britain and Germany to "conquer" and permanently occupy the confederated states.

It thus followed, Lafayette argued, that it was necessary to "give us, both by vessels sent from France and by a great movement in the fleet in the islands, a decided naval superiority for the next campaign." Ships and, equally important, money to pay the American soldiers and maintain the Continental Army—these were absolutely necessary if the war was not to drag on for years and in the end prove more injurious than helpful to France. Indeed the only clear advantage that the French had lay in their ability to make use of the Americans for the attrition of the British military forces and the exhaustion of the British treasury. At the point where active American resistance virtually ceased, the full weight of the war would fall upon France, and the calculations of profit and loss would doubtless tilt sharply in favor of England.

In America, Lafayette told Vergennes, "all that credit, persuasion and force could achieve has been done. . . . That miracle, of which I believe no similar example can be found, cannot be renewed." Ten thousand more French soldiers were needed.

Swayed by the persistent importunings of the American commissioners and by Lafayette's arguments, Vergennes decided to dispatch two more divisions of infantry and artillery to America (far short, of course, of the ten thousand soldiers proposed by Lafayette), bringing the total of French troops to somewhat over six thousand men and officers supported by a large fleet, or, more accurately, by two fleets—one under De Barras to be stationed at Newport, and the fleet under De Grasse that had been operating in the West Indies.

The Congressional plans for the year 1781 varied principally from those for 1780 in that the states were urged to bring the regiments of their respective lines up to full strength by recruiting for the duration of the war; if this failed, they were asked to draft the requisite number of men for a year and as long thereafter as it took to secure replacements for them. New appeals were made to the states for supplies and provisions. "Applications to the contiguous States on the subject," Madison wrote to Joseph Jones, in Virginia "have been repeated from every quarter, till they seem to have lost all their force."

Finances continued to perplex the delegates. A committee appointed to make recommendations to Congress "for arranging the finances, paying the debts and economizing the revenues of the United States" decided that "most of our Difficulties have arisen from an Ignorance of Finance," and they undertook to give themselves a crash course in financial theory, reading such authorities as David Hume and Sir William Temple. The fruit of their deliberations was a proposal that the states be asked to pass laws allocating to Congress a duty of 4 per cent on all imported goods. After some debate, it was resolved that the states be requested "as indispensably necessary" to grant Congress the power "to levy for the use of the United States a duty of five per cent, *ad valorem*" on all imports and a duty of 5 per cent "on all prizes and prize goods condemned in a court of admiralty of any of these states. . . ."

What was so baffling and disheartening was that the country was plainly able to support the army adequately, but parochialism and jealousy undermined all efforts. A desperate Congress followed one fruitless exhortation with another. Appealing once more in January, 1781, for the states to fill the requisitions made on them by Congress, the president of Congress repeated the all-too-familiar tale of woe: "However great may be the burthens which we are called upon to sustain," he wrote, "let us remember that they are the price of liberty; and that they have been common to every people who have dared to struggle for social happiness against violence and oppression. Let us reflect on our solemn engagements to devote our lives and our fortunes to the best of causes; and we shall find that we cannot be destitute of resources. . . . Will a people whose fortitude and patriotism have excited the admiration of Europe, languish at the bright dawn of triumph, and endanger the public happiness by a selfish parsimony?" The answer, apparently, was "yes."

Among the problems facing Congress in 1781 was the one posed by General Burgoyne and the British troops captured at Saratoga. Congress finally persuaded itself that Burgoyne was complaining about the treatment of himself and his officers as a pretext for violating the terms of his surrender, and that Congress would therefore be wise to violate them first. "All the great writers on the law of Nature & nations," Eliphalet Dyer wrote somewhat optimistically to Jonathan Trumbull, "will Vindicate us in a Suspension of our part till he can and does remove those just grounds of suspicion & fear." Burgoyne refused to give Congress a list of the names of the soldiers under his command; so that if the men, having been released by the Americans, were used again in contravention of the terms of surrender, they could not be identified. Congress fastened on this as an excuse to refuse to let the captured soldiers and officers be embarked on British transports at Rhode Island. On the other hand, the delegates were tormented by the thought that violation of the convention might "kindle anew the expiring flame, call forth fresh Vigor & Exertions" among the British and "arouse some friendly powers in Europe, to furnish them with greater aid and Supplies to Crush if possible this New & as they will say perfidious rising Empire, in whom there is no trust, nor faith. . . ." In addition, the British armies in America might be stirred "to more desperate exertions," since they "will not ever think again in any Circumstances to Enter into any Capitulation or Convention with any of our Generals." One solution seemed to be for Congress to require renewed assurances from Burgoyne that it felt he would not or could not give, and under this pretense to retain the prisoners of Saratoga. The other was to hold up their return until such time as "the Court of Great Britain should ratify & Confirm the Convention & proper Notice thereof be Given. . . ." The latter course was followed by Congress, and the "character" of the United States suffered somewhat in consequence. Another provision of Congress was that General Burgoyne was not to embark for England until "he paid off in Silver or Gold all the Expenses for his support & his Troops since the Convention."

The disaffection of the army with Congress is suggested by a letter from Alexander Hamilton, probably written to Governor George Clinton at the time when Congress was reigning on the Saratoga convention. "These men," Hamilton wrote of the members of Congress, "seem . . . to have embraced a system of infidelity. They have violated the convention of Saratoga; and I have reason to believe that the ostensible motives for it were little better than pretences, that had no foundation." They had also overturned Washington's arrangements with Howe for an exchange of prisoners. To commit "such frequent breaches of faith," Hamilton wrote, was "to ruin our national character." The result must be "to bring government at home into contempt, and of course to destroy its influence." "I would ask," Hamilton added, "whether in a republican state and a republican army, such a cruel policy as that of exposing those men, who are foremost in defence of their country to the miseries of hopeless captivity, can succeed. For my own part I have so much of the milk of humanity in me, that I abhor such *Neronian* maxims; and I look upon the old proverb, *that honesty is the best policy* to be so generally true, that I can never expect any good from a systematical deviation from it. . . . I dwell upon the faults of Congress, because I think they strike at the vitals of our opposition and of our future prosperity. . . ."

With the news that Maryland, its conditions at long last met, had voted to ratify the Articles, Congress set March 1, 1781, as the official date for the announcement of "the final ratification of the Confederation of the United States of America." The ceremonies were modest ones: thirteen rounds of cannon fire, toasts, and fireworks. Everyone was aware that there was a bit of the anticlimactic about the ratification. Maryland's obduracy, which had so irritated many delegates, appeared in retrospect as simple wisdom. Had the Articles been accepted without cession of the western land claims of the various states, there could have been only endless trouble and contention over the issue. It is perhaps not too much to say that the most substantial asset of the United States under the Articles of Confederation, and the element that most clearly bound the states together in a common interest, was Congress's ownership of that vast western region toward which so many dreams and hopes were directed. Indeed, it would not be too far off the mark to say that it was the *only* tangible asset of the United States. Enthusiasm over the final ratification of the Articles was tempered by the conviction, held by many people in and out of Congress, that the Articles, which had in fact been taken to define the powers of Congress vis-à-vis the states, had long before they were ratified, been shown by events to be plainly inadequate to the exigencies of the federal union.

With the Articles of Confederation at last ratified, the representatives of Vermont, who appeared in Philadelphia to argue their case for being admitted to the union, took the shrewd line that if the principle of their statehood was accepted, they would willingly leave the actual determination of their boundaries to the judicial arbitration provided for by the Articles. The New Yorkers were outraged when Congress accepted the proposal, and one of the delegates wrote bitterly to Governor Clinton "that so flagrant a breach of faith and violation of the Confederation, so soon after its ratification . . . has a direct tendency to destroy all confidence in that body [the new "Confederation Congress," as it was now properly called]."

The proposal of the Hartford convention that Congress be given the power to coerce the states cropped up once more. Jesse Root, a Connecticut delegate, was convinced that, "it is as necessary that Congress should exercise the powers of Coercion over particular states for the general purposes of the confederacy, as it is . . . that each state should exercise such power over its particular citizens for the weal of the State." Alexander Hamilton, so far as his duties as a member of Washington's staff would permit him, joined forces with his father-in-law, General Schuyler, to urge that a convention be called to draft a new constitution that would give adequate powers to Congress; and General Sullivan allied himself with such exponents of Congressional power as James Madison and James Varnum of Rhode Island.

Varnum was aware of "An extreme tho perhaps well-meant Jealousy, in many Members of Congress," especially the veterans of that body, which served to "frustrate every Attempt to introduce a more efficacious system." While "Prudent Caution against the Abuse of Power is very requisite for support of the Principles of republican Government; . . . when that Caution is carried too far, the Event may, and probably will prove alarming." He, like Hamilton, was convinced that a general convention was the most practical means of augmenting the powers of the central government. In May, 1781, Congress gave its attention to a report drafted by the "strong government" group among the delegates. The report listed seven areas in which Congress should have greater powers, but the general sentiment of Congress was so clearly opposed to the recommendations that they were abandoned.

With infinite weariness of spirit, Congress turned once more to the painful matter of finances. Inflation was once again the nightmare that haunted their dreams and deliberations. The efforts to "sink" or retire the vast sums of paper money issued by Congress had failed. The "new money" was proving as unstable as the old. "Never," Samuel Johnston of North Carolina wrote in April, "was a poor fly more completely entangled in a cobweb than Congress in their paper currency." Word came from Virginia that "in a few days the old Continental money has depreciated from two hundred to seven, eight, and some say nine Hundred for one."

Almost inadvertently, Congress had taken the most significant step in solving its financial problems by appointing Robert Morris superintendent of finances. Morris was certainly the nearest thing to a financial genius that the Revolution produced, and while Congress brewed grandiose schemes to cope with the economic crisis, Morris took any number of direct, practical measures. He prevailed on Congress to establish a national bank; he abandoned the procedure of requisitioning specific supplies from the states, sold off large quantities of supplies that could not be moved because of a lack of transportation, and put the purchasing of provisions for the army on a cash basis. He used his considerable personal credit where necessary. Most important of all perhaps, he was fortunate to have another French loan arrive just in time to prevent complete insolvency.

Washington, hearing of the intention of Congress to send John Laurens to France for the purpose of trying to round up more money (a job that Laurens at first declined), wrote to him in April, 1781, "If France delays a timely and powerful aid in the crucial posture of our affairs, it will avail us nothing, should she attempt it hereafter. We are suspended in the balance. . . . We are at the end of our tether, now or never our deliverance must come."

It seemed to the Tories that the Americans were indeed at the end of their tether. In May, 1781, Rivington's *Royal Gazette* reported exultantly, "The Congress is finally bankrupt! Last Saturday a large body of the inhabitants with paper dollars in their hats by way of cockades, paraded the streets of Philadelphia, carrying colors flying, with a DOG TARRED, and instead of the usual appendage and ornament of feathers, his back was covered with the Congress paper dollars. This example of disaffection, immediately under the eyes of the rulers of the revolted provinces, in solemn session at the State House assembled, was directly followed by the jailer, who refused accepting the bills in purchase of a glass of rum, and afterwards by the traders of the city, who shut up their shops, declining to sell any more goods but for gold or silver. It was declared also by the popular voice that if the oppositon to Great Britain was not in future carried on by solid money instead of paper bills, all further [resistance] to the mother country were vain and must be given up."

The fact was that although Congress in March of 1780 had finally decided to retire the inflated state and Continental currencies, a year later the old bills were still unredeemed in some of the states, where their depreciation had continued to two, three, and four hundred for one. As James Madison put it in a letter written in July, 1781, "The new bills, which were to be issued only as the old ones were taken in, are . . . in a great degree still unissued; and the depreciation which they have already suffered has determined Congress and the States to issue as few more of them as possible."

Yet despite the apparent insolubility of the financial problem, the feeling grew in Congress that the year 1781 might be the crucial year of the war. The news from the South—Kings Mountain, Cowpens, Hobkirk's Hill—bred optimism. It seemed that the third army of the Southern Department might at least survive under Greene's skillful and determined leadership, and that, under the circumstances, was tantamount to victory. Clinton lay in New York like one paralyzed. French military and naval forces were hourly expected in force; indeed one division of the French army had already arrived. John Sullivan, a better legislator than a general, wrote to Washington: "Amidst all those flattering prospects we are called upon to make our last desperate struggle to pave the way to that peace and Independence for which we have so long contended." Even Washington himself sounded a cautiously optimistic note: "The game is yet in our own hands; to play it well is all we have to do. . . . A cloud may yet pass over us . . . but certain I am, that it is in our power to bring the war to a happy conclusion."

9

The Episode at Green Spring Farm

LAFAYETTE, in Virginia, was delighted by news of the reception accorded the first division of the French army on its arrival at Newport. The Tories, he wrote Governor George Clinton, "dont know how to account for the behavior of those men whom their grandmothers and the British Gazetteers had represented to them under the shape of everything that is bad." Lafayette saw "dispositions . . . on both parts for union and good understanding." He assured Clinton "that the second division will arrive . . . and that France means to keep, pay and subsist in this country a French division wholly submitted to Gnl. Washington's orders, which aided by a naval force will not leave us till it has effectually put an end to the war."

In New York, Sir Henry Clinton noted the arrival of the French expeditionary force with apprehension. "I owe it to my country & I must in justice to my own fame declare to your lordship," he wrote Germain, "that I become every day more sensible of the utter impossibility of prosecuting the war in this country without reinforcements." To place any hope in the Tories, Clinton warned, was "visionary." They were numerous but "fettered." Forays accomplished little except to arouse the countryside, "and to possess territories demands garrisons. The acquisition of friends," Clinton continued, "unless we occupy the country they inhabit, is but the addition of fresh examples to the list of pensioned refugees." If Germain were to review the number of troops and compare them with the task that they were expected to accomplish, he could hardly avoid the conclusion "that we are by some [thousands] too weak to subdue this formidable rebellion."

The French officers at Newport were attentive observers of everything American. But above all, they were fascinated by the character of Washington. They had heard much of the great American general and they paid close attention to him, but it was plain they did not know quite what to make of him. He was, in the first place, so thoroughly non-French. Comte Charles-Francis de Broglie wrote, " . . . he preserves that polite and attentive good breeding which satisfies everybody, and that dignified reserve which offends no one. He is a foe to ostentation and to vainglory. . . . He does not seem to estimate himself at his true worth." Another Frenchman was impressed by Washington's ability "for grasping the whole scope of a subject." The Swedish Count Axel von Fersen, an officer in the French army, noticed, "A tinge of melancholy affects his whole being, which is not unbecoming, it renders him more interesting."

Claude Blanchard, the commissary officer for Rochambeau's army, took careful note of the dinner he had with Washington: "vegetables, roast beef, lamb, chicken, salad dressed with nothing but vinegar, green peas, puddings and some pie, a kind of tart [doubtless mince pie], greatly in use in England and among Americans. . . . They gave us on the same plate beef, green peas, lamb, etc." Dinner was followed by numerous toasts. Blanchard noted Washington's "physiogonomy" as containing something "grave and serious; but," he added, "it is never stern, and, on the contrary, becomes softened by the most gracious and amiable smile. He . . . converses with his officers familiarly and gaily."

Blanchard, who spent much of his time collecting wood for Rochambeau's army, found the Americans "slow and mistrusting." He observed that they seemed to spend most of their time at the dinner table, where they preferred boiled and roasted meat and a variety of vegetables. "They drink nothing but cider and Madeira wine with water," he noted, and dessert was usually "preserved quinces or pickled sorrel," the latter often being eaten with the meat dish. Coffee, much weaker than French coffee, was usually served, along with strong tea, several hours after the meal. Breakfast was far from "French." "Besides tea and coffee, they put on the table roasted meats with butter, pies and ham; nevertheless they sup [have a heavy noon meal] and in the afternoon they again take tea. Thus the Americans are almost always at the table; and as they have little to occupy them, as they go out little in winter and spend whole days along side of their fires and their wives, without reading and without doing anything, going so often to table is a relief and preventive of *ennui*."

Blanchard was also struck by the neat, pleasant houses of the inhabitants of Newport; "with the mechanic and the countryman as well as with the merchant and the general, their education," he wrote, "is nearly the same; so that a mechanic is often called to their assemblies, where there is no distinction, no separate orders." The inhabitants owned and tilled their own land. "This way of living and this sweet equality," the French officer added, "have charms for thinking beings. These manners suit me pretty well."

The commissary officer visited a school and found a "very worthy man," who "had not the air of a missionary but the tone of a father of a family," teaching a room full of boys and girls. "I saw the writing of these children," Blanchard noted, "it appeared to me to be handsome, among others, that of a young girl 9 or 10 years old, very pretty and very modest and such as I would like my own daughter to be, when she is as old. . . ." Blanchard found the Rhode Islanders "affable, well clad, very cleanly and all tall. The women," he added, "enjoy the same advantages, have fair skins and are generally pretty. They all have oxen and cows at least as handsome as those of our Poitou. . . ."

In June an incident took place that had important consequences. A British officer, Ensign John Moody, captured a mail pouch from a rebel courier near Sussex Court House, New Jersey. Moody took it to Clinton's headquarters in New York City, where the general was as pleased with the booty as any child with a collection of new toys. He called in the governor, old James Robertson, and General Knyphausen, and together they went over the papers. Moody was given a reward of two hundred guineas, and Lieutenant Mackenzie, the indefatigable diarist, wrote "The capture of this Mail is extremely consequential, and gives the Commander in Chief the most perfect knowledge of the design of the Enemy." Included among the letters was one to Colonel Benjamin Tallmadge about spies in New York, a letter from Washington to Lund Washington with a warning that Mount Vernon might be a special object of British vengeance, a letter to Washington's dentist requesting a pair of pliers to adjust his false teeth, and one from Martha Washington to her housekeeper inquiring about "Cotton for the counterpins . . . she desired milly Posey to have the fine piece of linning made white how is

Betty has she been spinning—all winter—is charlot done the worke I left for her To do." (The general's lady was short on punctuation.)

The fact was that the capture of the dispatches was the most fortunate thing that could have happened from Washington's point of view, for they fixed in Clinton's mind the conviction that Washington and Rochambeau had their attention unalterably fixed on New York City. Clinton promptly wrote to Cornwallis directing him to detach some of the troops under his command for the reinforcement of the army in New York, unless he "were engaged in some important movement that might render it important to detain them longer," or unless he intended to carry the war to the "upper part of the Chesapeake." Then followed a series of contretemps that were to prove fatal to Cornwallis and thus serve to administer the *coup de grâce* to the British effort to reduce the American states "to a proper degree of subordination."

Cornwallis, receiving Clinton's instructions, was engaged at the time in no more important an operation than occupying Williamsburg and was decidedly opposed to any foray into Maryland and lower Pennsylvania; he therefore prepared to embark the troops that Clinton had requested. Those who remained, he informed Clinton, would not be sufficient to hold Williamsburg. He was therefore crossing the James and retiring to Portsmouth on the bay. Cornwallis also mentioned in his dispatches to Clinton that he had given careful attention to the terrain at Yorktown and was convinced that it was too extensive a position for him to defend with the troops left to him. Cornwallis, plainly annoyed at having his command trimmed rather than augmented, offered to return to Charles Town and assume command of future operations in South Carolina.

Clinton had already been irritated by Cornwallis's decision to abandon the Carolinas and move into Virginia before he had been ordered to do so by Clinton. He was now doubly irritated by the manner in which Cornwallis complied with his request for reinforcements. "All right," Cornwallis seemed to be saying, "take your damn soldiers, and good riddance, but don't expect anything of me."

Cornwallis then began his movement from Williamsburg across the James to Portsmouth. On the fourth of July, the British army bivouacked at the ford in front of Jamestown, and Simcoe's Rangers passed over to secure the other side. The next day the wagons, bathorses, and baggage were gotten across. Lafayette, who had followed Cornwallis from Williamsburg, hoping to catch him crossing the river, was informed by a Negro slave that the main body of the army had crossed. Cornwallis, hearing of Lafayette's approach, did all he could to encourage this illusion, ordering the pickets to allow themselves to be driven back, thereby giving confirmation to the notion that only the rear guard was on the north side of the river.

At four in the afternoon the British outposts were attacked by militia and riflemen, and the army stood under arms and prepared to receive the attack. While the riflemen drove in the British pickets, Colonel Walter Stewart's battalion of the Pennsylvania Line followed in reserve. The Americans had to cross some four hundred yards to gain the Williamsburg-Jamestown road. There, carried forward by Wayne's urging, they shot three successive rear-guard commanders, pushing the pickets ahead of them.

Wayne, with Major MacPherson's cavalry, some riflemen, volunteer dragoons, and three pieces of artillery, moved forward to a plantation near the river called Green Spring Farm and launched an attack. Tarleton fell back in such a way as to draw Wayne on, and the Pennsylvanians would surely have fallen into a trap if Lafayette, riding up to view the engagement, had not taken notice of the fact that the British pickets who were killed or driven back were promptly replaced. This suggested that the British were on the north side of the river in much larger force than Lafayette had been led to believe. The marquis rode out to a point of land along the river from which he could see the British soldiers hidden near the riverbank, waiting for the order to attack. Lafayette galloped back to warn Wayne, but Wayne had spotted a British artillery piece, left as a decoy, and had already ordered Major William Galvan's regiment forward on the double to seize the apparently abandoned gun, while he started his main body across a narrow road through the swamp.

Cornwallis, anxious to strike a crippling blow at "the boys," waited until a substantial part of Wayne's force was beyond the swamp before he ordered an attack. Lieutenant Colonel Yorke's light infantry formed the British right, and the left was made up of the Forty-third, Seventy-sixth, and Eightieth Infantry regiments under Lieutenant Colonel Thomas Dundas. The British moved forward in numbers considerably larger than Wayne's force; they came on with their bands playing, the soldiers giving their battle cry—a spectacle that had more than once caused Americans to take to their heels. The British line extended beyond Wayne's own on the left and right and threatened an envelopment.

Galvan's men, hopelessly outnumbered, fired a volley at the

approaching redcoats and them fell back in reasonably good order. Wayne, his plume shot out of his hat, observed Galvan's predicament and knew he had to make an instant decision. The narrow corduroy road leading back to Williamsburg was the only clear line of retreat. There was little hope of bringing his men over that in any proper order, and if they floundered into the swamp they would be cut to pieces. He gave the order to charge and spurred his own horse forward while his men came on yelling at the top of their lungs, their bayonets fixed. At this unexpected reaction, the British faltered. Perhaps the Americans were in greater force than expected. Wayne's men dashed through heavy musket and grapeshot fire to within seventy yards of the British lines while the redcoats, bewildered by the Americans who were "making a devil of a noise of firing and huzzaing," halted their own advance and looked about uncertainly for orders. Wayne at once took advantage of the confusion in the British ranks to extricate his men, while Cornwallis, disconcerted by Wayne's unexpected attack, hesitated to press too hard on his heels. Lafayette, who had been too late to check Wayne's initial advance, played a courageous part in helping to extricate the Pennsylvanian's corps. One of his two extra horses, ridden by his groom, was killed, and the other was wounded.

In the charge of the Pennsylvanians, many of the American officers were cut down. Ebenezer Denny, a red-haired ensign from Carlisle, only twenty years old, saw his captain shot and had to take command of the company. He had been a messenger at Fort Pitt at the age of eleven, but he had never before had such a weight of responsibility on him. "Young and inexperienced, exhausted with hunger and fatigue [I] had like to disgraced myself," he wrote; "—had nothing to eat all day but a few blackberries—was faint and with difficulty kept my place; once or twice was about to throw away my arms. . . ."

Lieutenant William Feltman was struck in the chest by a piece of cannister from the British artillery, but he held his position until his battalion was ordered to withdraw. "Upon our retreat I felt very faintish, but the thought of falling into the enemy's hands made me push on as hard as I possibly could for about five miles. . . ."

The Americans lost twenty-eight killed, ninety-nine wounded, and twelve missing. British losses were seventy-five killed or wounded. Lafayette, lured into a trap, was fortunate to have escaped with the better part of his army intact. Only the impetuosity of Wayne had prevented a major disaster. Also, the fall of darkness had made pursuit difficult if not impossible, and Lee thought this, more than Wayne's daring, was the saving of Wayne's corps. "One hour more of daylight must have produced the most disasterous conclusions," he wrote. That was Cornwallis's conclusion as well. One wonders why he did not attack earlier.

Colonel John Francis Mercer gave an account of Lafayette's generalship at Green Spring that was anything but flattering. He had informed the marquis that the evidence was that the main body of British had not yet passed over the river, and that the Americans were thus greatly outnumbered. Mercer considered the initial dispositions unsound and the battle a hopeless one from the beginning. Ordered forward from the house they had occupied with a small contingent of riflemen, Mercer and his men were soon driven back by British artillery fire; coming on Wayne's brigade, he found them in a wood "drawn up in such close order as to render it utterly impracticable to advance in line & preserve their order—the line was necessarily broke by the trees as they pass'd the wood." The British on the other hand "advanc'd in open order at arm's length & aiming very low kept up a deadly fire." Mercer could not refrain, in his account of the action, from commenting on the ironic fact that the Americans were taking up "the stiff German tactics" of close-order attack taught by Baron von Steuben at the very time when "the British acquir'd the good sense, from experience in our woody country, to lay it aside."

It was Mercer's opinion that Lafayette's force only escaped destruction by good luck. Had the British cavalry charged, "the Marquis's army wou'd have been broken & dispers'd, & Lord Cornwallis wou'd have escap'd the catastrophe at York." It is not hard to imagine Washington's displeasure had such been the outcome. Lafayette's job was to hang on Cornwallis's rear and not to risk his own army by bringing on a full-scale battle under disadvantageous conditions. Most accounts of the engagement have overlooked the role of Mercer's militia in the opening stages of the fighting, a role that Mercer plainly thought was critical, since it forced the British to deploy prematurely and gave them an erroneous notion of the nature of the American attack. At the end of his own account, Mercer added, "Thus terminated one of the most silly & misjudged affairs that took place during the war . . . it required all the bravery of Wayne & his corps & above all, the misconduct of the enemy, to save the whole from capture."

Tarleton's account of the action plainly reinforces Mercer's (it is only fair to say that Mercer had read Tarleton's account of the engagement before he wrote his own). "Too great ardor," Tarleton wrote, "or false intelligence, which is most probable, for it is the only instance of this officer [Lafayette] committing himself during a very difficult campaign, prompted him to cross a morass to attack Earl Cornwallis, who routed him, took his cannon, and must inevitably have destroyed his army, if night had not intervened. His Lordship," Tarleton added, "might certainly have derived more advantage from his victory." If Cornwallis had pushed the pursuit of the defeated Americans, Lafayette's army "must have been annihilated," and "such an exploit would have been easy, fortunate, and glorious, and would have prevented the combination which produced the fall of Yorktown and Gloucester."

Greene was pleased at Anthony Wayne's overly optimistic account of the affair at Green Spring, but he was concerned that Lafayette might be tempted to consider Cornwallis a lion whose teeth had been pulled. "Be a little careful and tread softly," he warned, "for depend upon it you have a modern Hannibal to deal with in the person of Lord Cornwallis."

Lafayette collected his army at Green Spring Farm and fell back during the night to Chickahominy Church. Cornwallis completed the crossing of the James River and moved on to Portsmouth, The units that were to reinforce Clinton in New York were then sent on ahead, while Cornwallis "followed by easy marches with the rest."

As Cornwallis marched to Portsmouth, he carried with him as his servant a Negro named James, who was actually a spy for Lafayette. James reported on the progress of Cornwallis's army, but he was unable to find out anything about future plans. In Lafayette's words, "his Lordship is so shy of his papers that my honest friend says he cannot get at them." (After the war the spy was given his freedom as "James Lafayette" by an act of the Virginia legislature.)

At Portsmouth there was disconcerting news for Cornwallis: Clinton had countermanded the order to sail. If Cornwallis's purpose had been to discomfort his commander in chief, he had succeeded. Indeed, it could be said that the lord had refined to a precise art the technique, on the one hand, of not quite obeying orders (as when he abandoned the Carolinas to move into Virginia), and on the other, of obeying them too well (as in the present instance). By what right, the indignant Clinton inquired, had Cornwallis taken it upon himself to give up Williamsburg? If he was still there, he was to remain there until further orders. If he had left it, he should try to repossess it and establish a defensive post there for the protection of ships of the line that might be anchored near there, either at Old Point Comfort or Hampton Roads or at Yorktown on the York River. As for Cornwallis's suggestion of quitting the Chesapeake, that seemed to disturb Clinton most of all, though he had earlier had serious reservations about any extensive campaigning in Virginia. On the contrary, as soon as the heat of summer was over, it was his intention to "send there all the troops he could spare from the different posts under his command." Having tried New England, New Jersey, and Pennsylvania, and then, those campaigns having proved unproductive, having tried the South, ultimately another exercise in futility, Clinton apparently had convinced himself that the Chesapeake held the key to defeating the stubborn Americans.

Cornwallis should also occupy Yorktown, "or at least to hold Old Point Comfort, if it was possible to do it, without at the same [time] holding York." There is no record of Cornwallis's private feelings at this moment. They may well have been ones of satisfaction. If that was his game, he had bluffed Clinton into restoring the troops that he had requested and promising more. But Old Point Comfort, in the opinion of Cornwallis's engineers, was of little use. It could not command the entrance into Hampton Roads or protect British ships lying in the Roads. Portsmouth was equally useless; ships of the line could not even enter its harbor. It thus seemed to Cornwallis that the only lines open to him were to fortify Yorktown and Gloucester.

Cornwallis's servant James reported to Lafayette that Cornwallis was about to leave Portsmouth but that there was no indication of his destination and Lafayette wrote ruefully that he was forced to "guess at every possible whim of an enemy that flies with the wind and is not within reach of spies or reconnoitrers." At the same time, Lafayette was candid enough to declare, "Lord Cornwallis' abilities are to me more alarming than his superiority of forces. I ever had a great opinion of him. Our papers call him a bad man, but was ever any advantage taken of him where he commanded in person? To speak plain English I am devilish afraid of him."

With Cornwallis clearly ready to evacuate Portsmouth, Lafayette received a message from Washington: "I shall shortly have occasion to communicate matters of very great importance to you." Lafayette at once concluded that Washington's news would be that he was marching with his army to Virginia. He replied to the general, "Should a French fleet now come in Hampton Road, the British army would, I think, be ours." And he wrote to Luzerne, "Mon Dieu, why haven't we a fleet here? . . . If the French army could fall from the clouds into Virginia and be supported by a squadron we should do some very good things. . . ."

Cornwallis sent part of his army by transports into the Chesapeake and then into Hampton Roads, and both villages were seized without resistance on the first of August. By the twentieth, Cornwallis had completed the evacuation of Portsmouth, and two days later he had established his army at Yorktown and Gloucester.

As soon as Lafayette heard that the British had landed at Gloucester and Yorktown he sent word to Washington, adding, "You must not wonder my dear General that there has been a fluctuation in my intelligence. I am positive the British Councils have also been fluctuating." He understood his own mission. He would not, he wrote Washington, take any chance of an engagement with Cornwallis that might bring defeat. "His Lordship plays so well that no blunder can be hoped from him to recover a bad step of ours." What was called for now was caution and patience. Wayne's detachment guarded the road to Richmond, and Lafayette placed the remainder of his force at Malvern Hill, where he could keep a close watch on Cornwallis.

10

To Virginia

ELSEWHERE, other pieces of a complex puzzle were beginning to fall into place. Washington, whose hopes for a major combined operation with the French fleet and then, after Rochambeau's arrival, with the French expeditionary force had survived three years of disappointment, now began to think once more of a joint attack on Clinton. The Comte de Barras had arrived in May to take command of the French fleet at Newport, bringing with him dispatches that empowered Rochambeau to cooperate with Washington in a campaign under Washington's command. Washington therefore met Rochambeau in Wethersfield, Connecticut, on May 21 to discuss plans to attack Clinton at New York. Admiral de Grasse, De Barras informed Rochambeau, was on his way with a substantial number of warships to reinforce the French fleet at Newport in anticipation of an attack on New York, or on some other city if New York seemed impractical. Washington at once wrote letters to the assemblies of all the New England states requesting that sixty-two hundred militia be called up for what would hopefully be a final and conclusive campaign with the French against Clinton.

After the conference at Wethersfield, Washington had written in his diary: "Fixed with Count de Rochambeau upon plan of Campaign

. . . to commence an operation against New York, . . . or to extend our views to the southward as circumstances and a Naval superiority might render more necessary. . . ." When Rochambeau returned to Newport, his officers in a council of war persuaded him to change the plan of the coming campaign. Duc de Lauzun, who brought word of the change in plans to Washington, saw him in one of his rare but famous rages. For three days Washington could not trust himself to speak to the French officer. "It was only on the third day," Lauzun wrote, "and then out of regard for me, that he gave me an answer, a very cold one, in which he said that he held to the plan he had signed."

Rochambeau gave way gracefully, but he continued to urge Washington to give up the idea of attacking New York and to turn his attention to Cornwallis's army in Virginia. To Admiral de Grasse, who had just arrived in the West Indies with a sizable fleet, the worried Rochambeau wrote: "These people here are at the end of their resources. Washington has not half the troops he counted on; I believe, though he is hiding it, that he has not 6,000 men. M. de Lafayette has not 1,000 regulars with the militia to defend Virginia. . . . This is the state of affairs and the great crisis at which America finds itself. . . ." Then Rochambeau quietly sank Washington's plan for an attack in New York. "The southwesterly winds and the distressed state of Virginia," he noted, "will probably lead you to prefer the Chesapeake Bay, and it is there that we think you can render the greatest services. . . ."

On August 14, Washington received a message that De Grasse was headed for the Chesapeake but could not stay there long. Washington was furious. Timothy Pickering and Robert Morris found him "striding to and fro in such a state of uncontrolled excitement" that he paid no attention to his visitors. "Resentment, indignation and despair had burst upon him," Pickering reported. "His hopes were blasted, and he felt that the cause was lost and his country ruined." The two men hastily excused themselves. An hour later Washington had gained control of himself, although it was plain to Pickering that he was "tossing like a suppressed volcano within." "I wish to the Lord," Washington declared passionately, "the French would not raise our expectations of a cooperation [not to] fulfill them."

That night, when he sat down to his journal, he had accepted the inevitable. "Matters having now come to a crisis," he wrote, "and a decisive plan to be determined on, I was obliged, from the shortness of Count de Grasse promised stay on this Coast, the apparent disclination in their Naval Officers to force the harbour of New York and the feeble compliance of the States to my requisitions for Men . . . to give up all idea of attacking New York; and instead thereof to remove the French Troops and a detachment from the American Army . . . to Virginia." The notion of trapping Cornwallis in Virginia had always been in the back of his mind, as conquering New York was in the front of it.

Now, with the matter in a sense decided for him, he seemed relieved and more at ease with the world. Claude Blanchard, who was near Washington as the French troops crossed the Hudson, felt that he had been "exhausted, destitute of resources," but now "seemed to see a better destiny arise." The Abbé Claude Robin, the French chaplain, noted, "He never has more resources than when he seems to have no more." On the other hand Alexander Hamilton, still nursing his grievance over Washington's rebuke, noted scornfully that "The Great Man" was on a wild-goose chase.

On the twenty-first the American army, with part of the French, returned to the familiar territory at King's Bridge. There they drew up in order of battle, while the officers reconnoitered the British positions on the opposite bank. The same charade designed to keep Clinton in some state of uncertainty was repeated several times while Washington and Rochambeau waited impatiently for word from De Grasse.

Rumors meanwhile flew through New York City: Washington and Rochambeau were on their way to attack with nine thousand men; boats were being collected up and down the Hudson for an assault on the city; French engineers were making plans for a fort adjacent to the city; a French fleet was on the high seas headed for American waters. Lieutenant Mackenzie expressed a common anxiety: "We seem," he wrote, "throughout this war to have adhered to the injudicious plan of dividing our Army into numerous detachments . . . we are not formidable in any one place . . . we are now weak and dispersed at most of our posts. Should De Grasse enter the Chesapeak . . . we shall run the risk of losing all the troops in Virginia." The criticism was a valid one. The British had, by scraping the very bottom of the manpower barrel, collected and maintained something in excess of thirty-five thousand men in America, more than three times the largest force that could be brought into the field against them, but this force had, in six long years, accomplished very little in the way of returning the American states to their original status as colonies of Great Britain. The only flaw in Mackenzie's reasoning was that concentrating them all in New York City would not have accomplished anything.

Washington took considerable pains to deceive Clinton, who was only too ready to be deceived. Working parties cleared the roads approaching New York, burning barricades of trees and repairing potholes. A regiment was sent to make a feint toward Staten Island, and the soldiers themselves were kept in the dark as to their general's plans. "If we do not deceive our own men," Washington wrote, "we will never deceive the enemy." "We do not know the object of our march, and are in perfect ignorance," a French officer wrote, "whether we are going against New York, or whether we are going to Virginia to attack Cornwallis," Washington threw himself into the part of an actor with disarming enthusiasm. He stopped an old Tory farmer and questioned him about Staten Island, and then, as if he had let something slip, he said quickly that these were just casual queries, not to be taken seriously.

Among those scouts and skirmishers who were deployed in front of the British fortifications was Joseph Martin now a sergeant. "Sometimes only four or five of us," Martin wrote, "sometimes ten or twelve . . . would drive them into the redoubt, when they would reinforce and sally out and drive us all over the gully. We kept up this sport till late in the afternoon." Then Martin and two friends went down to the Bronx River. From the bank they could see five British horsemen on an island in the river. Martin was in his white hunting shirt, and one of the British horsemen called him "a white-livered son of a bitch." "We then became quite sociable," Martin added; "they advised me to come over to their side and they would give me roast turkeys. I told them that they must wait till we left the coast clear, ere they could get into the country to steal them, as they used to do."

The British reply was that they would give Martin and his friends "pork and 'lasses." The British artillery had recently fired a volley; didn't the Americans wish to borrow the British surgeons to attend the wounded, since their own were "a pack of ignoramuses"?

With all their fire and thunder the British had only wounded a dog, Martin answered, and since "they and their surgeons were of the same species of animals, I supposed," Martin added, "the poor wounded dog would account it a particular favor to have some of his own kind to assist him."

This banter was interrupted when Martin noted a group of men on the island somewhat to one side near a house. Luckily, as he looked at them, he saw the flash of a musket and dropped instinctively to the ground. The bullet hit the tree where he had been standing; "if I had not 'dove at the flash,'" he wrote, "the ball would have gone directly through my body. . . ."

It was here, preparing to lay siege to New York, that Martin suffered his only wound of his many campaigns. He was put in charge of a party of soldiers sent to scout beyond the American lines for cowboys in the area. Martin's officer told him to take his party to a particular spot and if no Tories were encountered to return to camp. The patrol ran its course, saw no cowboys, and then, having rested, decided it would be "a pity to return with our fingers in our mouths and report that we had seen nothing." So they decided to venture on into a small wood that lay ahead of them. They had hardly entered the wood when they found themselves outflanked and outnumbered by a band of thirty or forty cowboys who fired on them at close range, missing them all. The patrol fired back, but before they could reload the cowboys rushed them, and they had no choice but to take to their heels as fast as they could. Their first obstacle was a broken-down post-and-rail fence, which Martin's men got over ahead of him. When Martin tried to blunder through the fence, he caught his foot in the crack of a fallen tree and tumbled headlong, his foot held fast. "Here I hung," he wrote, "as fast as though my foot had been in the stocks, my ham lying across the butt of another tree while my body hung down perpendicularly. I could hardly reach the ground with my hands, and, of course, could make but little exertion to clear myself from the limbs."

The leader of the cowboy band rushed up to the fence and slashed at Martin's leg with his sword, laying the bone bare. "I could see him through the fence," Martin noted, "and knew him. He was, when we were boys, one of my most familiar playmates, was with me, a messmate, in the campaign of 1776. . . ." He had deserted to the enemy, having been, in Martin's words, "coaxed off by an old harridan, to whose daughter he had taken a fancy. . . . He was a smart active fellow and soon got command of a gang of Refugee Cowboy plunderers."

Martin thought his time was up, but with one desperate effort he cleared his foot and scrambled free. His assailant knew Martin as well as Martin knew him, for he called after him by name telling him to surrender and promising that he would be well treated. Martin had to run a hundred yards or more across an open field to the cover of woods to rejoin his patrol, which was waiting for him there. The cowboys never fired at him, and Martin hoped that it was because his former messmate had restrained them. Even so, it was "the only time the enemy drew blood from me during the whole war."

The combined French and American army was in motion by the middle of August. Admiral de Barras had been prevailed upon to sail from Newport to join forces with De Grasse in the Chesapeake, and Duportail had been sent ahead to meet De Grasse and inform him that Washington and Rochambeau were on the way. General Heath, with four thousand New Englanders, was left to protect the Hudson Valley and distract Clinton. Still the greatest secrecy was preserved. Jonathan Trumbull, Jr., son of the governor of Connecticut, was Washington's secretary, and he thoroughly enjoyed his conspiratorial role in keeping the army's destination secret. "No movement perhaps was ever attended with more conjectures," he wrote, " . . . some were indeed laughable enow'; but not one I believe penetrated the real design." Even after the army had begun to march south, Washington hoped to keep up the illusion that he planned an attack on Staten Island. He took Colonel Philip Van Cortlandt "by the arm and went some distance on the road, and gave me his orders both written and verbal," Van Cortlandt wrote. Washington wished the New York officer to carry all his boats and entrenching tools on the march and to constitute the rear guard, so that Clinton might assume that an amphibious assault was intended.

Comte de Deux-Ponts did not learn until the second day of the march, "under the strictest secrecy from one of my friends, well informed, that all the maneuvers by which we threaten New York are only a feint, that Lord Cornwallis is the real object of our marches, and that we are going to direct them towards Virginia."

Dr. James Thacher was disenchanted with all the mummery. "Our situation reminds me of some theatrical exhibition," he wrote in his diary, "where the interest and expectations of the spectators are constantly increasing, and where curiosity is wrought to the highest point. . . . Bets have run high on one side, that we were to occupy the ground marked out on the Jersey shore, to aid in the seige of New York, and on the other, that we are stealing a march on the enemy, and are actually destined to Virginia."

Ovens were built at Chatham for the ostensible purpose of baking French bread for the French soldiers, thus supporting the notion of a siege.

Everywhere on the march south, men, women, and children turned out to catch a glimpse of George Washington. Their manner was quiet and almost reverential, as if a deity had passed. People reached out to touch his horse or his cloak, and women held their children up so they could get a view of the savior of their country. The French officers were astonished and impressed. Once, when they were halted in the street of a town by a crowd that wished to look at Washington, the general turned to the Frenchman Charles William Dumas and said: "We may be beaten by the English; that is the fortune of war; but here is an army that they will never conquer." Observing many such scenes, Abbé Robin wrote, "The Americans, that cool and sedate people . . . are roused, animated, and inflamed at the very mention of his name, and the first songs that sentiment or gratitude has dictated, have been to celebrate General Washington."

One thing that was much on Washington's mind was that his troops might become mutinous when they realized they were to make a march of more than four hundred miles, through the heat of late summer, to Virginia. He wrote to Robert Morris, that almost inexhaustible source of desperately needed funds, one more urgent letter: "I must entreat you . . . to procure one month's pay in specie for the detachment. . . . Part of these troops have not been paid anything for a long time past, and have on several occasions shown marks of great discontent. The service they are going upon is disagreeable to the northern regiments; but I make no doubt that a *douceur* of a little hard money would put them in a proper temper." To Governor Thomas Sim Lee of Maryland, he wrote, "The moment is critical, the opportunity precious, the prospects most happily favorable."

Clinton, absorbed in his own problems, was reluctant to face the possibility that Washington was headed for Virginia. He had recently suffered two brief attacks of blindness, doubtless the product of his perpetual anxieties, and Mary Badderly was about to produce his child. William Smith, the Tory chief justice of New York, found Clinton seized by "gusts of passion . . . insensible of his danger." "I despair of Clinton, . . ." Smith wrote, "He will make the apprehension of a French fleet an excuse for inactivity."

The British had a remarkably efficient intelligence system, far better, on the whole, than that of the Americans. (On August 18 a spy reported to Clinton that Rochambeau's son, the Viscount de Rochambeau, had dispatched his mistress to Trenton, New Jersey, to make a rendezvous with the viscount, since the general, his father, permitted "no kept mistresses.") It brought in a constant flow of information, much of it contradictory. Clinton was thus free, as commanders with ample intelligence sources invariably are, to choose out of the endless supply of particulars those that supported his own view of the enemy's intentions and to ignore the rest. And Washington had certainly been careful to provide him with ample information to suit his predilections.

Clinton's own officers, the Hessians, and, more vocally, the Tories were indignant at the general's inaction. On August 25, Clinton called in

Lieutenant Mackenzie to present to that startled young officer a plan for a raid on Newport, and two days later he wrote to Cornwallis that he could not fathom Washington's strange maneuvers; apparently he was returning to his former headquarters at Morristown. At the end of August, Clinton got word from one of his most trusted spies, "Squib," who wrote simply: "The Chesapeake is the Object—All in motion." The next day, as Washington rode into Philadelphia, Clinton wrote to Cornwallis, "Mr. Washington's force still remains in the neighbor hood of Chatham and I do not hear that he has yet detached to the southward."

By the twenty-ninth the secret could not longer be kept (except perhaps from Clinton). Dr. Thacher noted in his diary: "The British army under Cornwallis is unquestionably the object . . . the deception proved completely successful . . . the menacing aspect of an attack on New York will be continued till time and circumstance shall remove the delusive veil from the eyes of Sir Henry Clinton, when it will probably be too late. . . ."

Today the combined French and American army could be moved by jet transports the distance from New York to Yorktown in an hour, or by car or rail in a few days. In the late summer of 1781, the army moved like a great, lethargic serpent, fifteen or twenty miles a day, day in and day out, its head twenty miles beyond its tail; it wound over dusty roads, across bridges, over hills, past woods and open fields, towns and farms. Eventually everyone, even Clinton, knew its destination. But there was nothing anyone could do to check or substantially impede its movement. Cornwallis, busy constructing his defenses, knew it was coming, as slowly and inevitably as fate, but he trusted in the British navy to get him and his men off, if necessary, or in Clinton to reinforce him. Clinton waited in New York while his spies brought him daily reports on Washington's progress. And in the weeks that passed, as the army crawled south, America waited, not privy to the entire plot but dimly aware that things were moving to some striking dénouement.

Washington reached Philadelphia on August 30 at one o'clock in the afternoon. He was met at the outskirts of the city by a cavalry troop and escorted to the City Tavern. There he held an informal court, with the members of Congress and other dignitaries coming to pay their respects. Washington was to stay with Robert Morris in his handsome house on Walnut Street, while Rochambeau and his staff were quartered in the home of Chevalier de La Luzerne.

The next day Washington visited Congress and spoke briefly and soberly to the delegates. That body had tried him sorely, and on occasion, vice versa. But he did not chide them; and they, although they may at times have doubted him, knew him for what he was—the soul of American independence. It was a little-noticed but poignant moment in the steady flow of events that made up the Revolution. Washington seemed to say by his presence—grave, austere, formidable, wearing like an aura all that he had suffered at their hands in terms of vacillation, delay, petty plotting, inadequate support—"I have been your faithful servant so far as it lay within me to be. I have endured."

At the Morris mansion that night there was as splendid a feast as the city could provide. Rochambeau and the Marquis de Chastellux, Thomas McKean, president of Congress at the moment, and Generals Moultrie, Knox, and Sullivan were honored guests. They drank toasts to the United States, to the King of France, "His Catholic Majesty" (that one went down a little hard), to the allied armies, to the arrival of De Grasse. McKean made a hit with his toast, "When lilies flourish, roses fade," an allusion to the rise of France and the decline of England.

The ships on the Delaware fired salutes, and the city was illuminated after dark. Washington walked through the streets, followed by a crowd, "eagerly pressing to see their beloved general," one of the French officers noted. A Tory who watched silently wrote, "I saw this man, great as an instrument of destruction and devastation to the property, morals and principles of the people . . . walking the street, attended by a concourse of men, women and boys who huzzaed him and broke some of my father's windows and others near us."

The next morning there was troubling news. The British fleet under Graves and Hood—twenty warships—had left New York. The British might intercept De Barras on his way from Newport and rout him before he had a chance to join De Grasse. It was equally possible, if De Grasse by chance had not yet reached the Chesapeake, that the British ships might slip in ahead of him and force De Grasse to come into the more confined waters of the bay after them. There the French admiral's superiority in ships and firepower might be negated.

Continental and French troops were to enter Philadelphia after Washington and Rochambeau, but for a time it seemed they might have to remain on the north bank of the Delaware. Washington had sent ahead orders to have boats collected to ferry seven thousand men across the river, but only enough had been rounded up to accommodate two thousand; the rest were forced to march on to Head of Elk in Maryland. Morris, trying desperately to get money to pay the troops and food to fill their bellies, wrote to the commissary general, "Should the operations against Cornwallis fail for want of supplies the states must thank their own negligence. If they will not exert themselves upon the present occasion, they never will."

There were only twelve wagonloads of ammunition, musket cartridges as well as shot and powder for the artillery pieces. Knox estimated that he needed 300,000 cartridges, 20,000 flints, and 1,000 powder horns among numerous other items. He had bitter words about "the vile and water-gruel governments" who failed to respond to his pleas, and Washington noted ruefully, "Certainly, certainly, the people have lost their ardor in attempting to secure their liberty and happiness."

The American troops entered the city of Philadelphia wearing sprigs of evergreen in their ragged hats. Sergeant Joseph Martin, now detailed as a sapper and miner, was among them. They were led by Scammel's light infantry. It had not rained for days; "We raised a dust like a smothering snow-storm," Dr. Thacher wrote, "blinding our eyes and covering our bodies with it; this was not a little mortifying as the ladies were viewing us from the open windows of every house as we passed." The Continentals were certainly not a very reassuring sight, marching in not the best of military order to the music of fifes and drums. The soldiers, who had not been paid for months, could not help contrasting the appearance of the plump, well-dressed Philadelphians with their own poor state. "Great symptoms of discontent . . . appeared on their passage through the city," one of their officers wrote. But a French onlooker noted, "The plainly dressed American army lost no credit in the steadiness of their march and their fitness for battle," and Claude Blanchard observed that "the soldiers marched pretty well, but they handled their arms badly. There were some fine-looking men; also many who were small and thin, and even some children twelve or thirteen years old."

Washington sat on his great white horse as the troops passed on review, man and horse as still and massive as a great statue. A man who did not like to gamble, or who did not trust himself to gamble, he had staked everything on one throw of the dice. Would he find the trap empty, and if he did, would his poorly clothed, badly fed, unpaid army march back all those weary miles? But his anxiety did not show. To the soldiers who passed by the "old man" or the "Old Hoss," as some of the irreverent frontiersmen called him, there was only the emanation of perpetual strength and untiring resoluteness of purpose in those composed and heroic features.

After the army—actually, only a token portion of it—had passed in review, Washington sat down to write to Lafayette, the boy he had sent to do a man's work and who had indeed done it: "... my dear Marquis, I am distressed beyond expression to know what has become of the Count De Grasse, and for fear that the English fleet, by occupying the Chesapeake ... frustrate all our flattering prospects.... Should the retreat of Lord Cornwallis by water be cut off, I am persuaded you will do all in your power to prevent his escape by land.... You see how critically important the present moment is ... adieu, my dear Marquis if you get any thing new from any quarter, send it I pray you, *on the spur of speed* for I am almost all impatience and anxiety."

The day after the Americans had marched through Philadelphia, their allies, the French appeared. Brilliant as butterflies in their splendid uniforms, "they marched through the town, with the military music playing before them, which is always particularly pleasing to the Americans; the streets were crowded with people, and the ladies appeared at the windows in their most brilliant attire. All Philadelphia was astonished to see people who had endured the fatigues of a long journey, so ruddy and handsome, and even wondered that there could possibly be *Frenchmen* of so genteel an appearance." Behind the dazzling show there were some less appealing realities. Count Fersen wrote, "Our army, unfortunately, is as little disciplined as the French army always is under ordinary circumstances.... Our chiefs are very strict, and not a day passes that there are not some two or three officers placed under arrest, I have myself seen some lamentable scenes where a whole corps of men ought to have been cashiered, but as we only number five thousand we cannot afford to lose a man...."

Rochambeau, interestingly enough, had to double the guard to prevent these magnificently attired, well-fed French peasants and workmen, dressed as soldiers, from deserting, from slipping away to share the fortunes of the ragged, gaunt, unpaid Continental troops of Washington's army. The men of Deux-Ponts' regiment had many relatives living in Pennsylvania who came to their camp outside the city to visit them and, merely by their presence, to tempt them to try to escape into the endless countryside, where counties were as big as provinces and individual states were large enough to hold comfortably all the Frenchmen in France.

Rochambeau's army made their camp in a meadow by the Schuylkill, and the Soissonnais Regiment put on a drill before twenty thousand spectators who applauded ecstatically at their maneuvers. In the evening, Luzerne commandeered thirty cooks from the French army to prepare a feast for a hundred and eighty guests. Joseph Reed, president of Pennsylvania, scored a culinary coup with a ninety-pound turtle caught in the Delaware, which Baron Ludwig von Closen described as "sumptuous, spectacular. . . . The soup was served in an immense shell, and the fat, seasoned and peppered, had the taste of consommé."

The French were lionized by the ladies of Philadelphia, Chastellux was shown twenty-two hundred shirts that had been made by the women of the city for the soldiers of Pennsylvania; "on each shirt was the name of the married or unmarried lady who made it. . . ." (Perhaps Martin, even though a New Englander, got one.) Chastellux also met Mrs. Robert Morris, the reputed social leader of Philadelphia, and noted, "Her taste is as delicate as her health: an enthusiast to excess for all French fashions, she only waits for the termination of this little revolution, to effect a still greater one in the manners of her country."

Chastellux, during his days in Philadelphia, was a tireless observer of the city and its citizens, of American customs, manners, and principles, and particularly of its numerous sects. He went to a Quaker meeting and heard a man who "talked a great deal of nonsense about internal grace . . . to the brethren and the sisterhood, who had all of them a very inattentive and listless air. After seven or eight minutes of silence, an old man went down on his knees, dealt us out a very unmeaning prayer, and dismissed the audience." "On quitting this melancholy homespun assembly," Chastellux went to an Episcopal service, which, he wrote, "appeared to me as sort of *opera,* as well for the music as for the decorations: a handsome pulpit placed before a handsome organ; a handsome minister in that pulpit, reading, speaking, singing with a grace entirely theatrical, a number of young women answering melodiously from the pit and boxes. . . . All this, compared to the quakers, the anabaptists, the presbyterians, etc., appeared to me rather like a little paradise itself, than as the road to it."

While Morris racked his brains to try to scrape together money to pay the soldiers, Colonel John Laurens, who had been sent to Paris to make one final pitiful supplication to the French monarch for more money, arrived with the intoxicating word that His Most Christian and Catholic Majesty had come through with 2,500,000 silver livres. This was not quite as grand as it sounded—a livre was worth about nineteen cents—but it was clearly much, much better than nothing. The trouble was that the money had been landed at Boston, and it would take weeks to get it into the hands of the soldiers. Robert Morris thus met with

Rochambeau and begged for a loan of twenty thousand dollars to be repaid out of the silver livres at Boston. The French pled poverty; they had the equivalent of only forty thousand dollars in their treasury, which was not enough to pay their own troops. Moreover, the treasurer of the army had already left the city.

At the same time, a courier reached Washington at Chester, Delaware, with word that De Grasse had arrived with his fleet off the mouth of the Chesapeake. Washington had sometimes shown a rage that singed those about him; now he displayed what no one had ever seen him display before—joy. The startled and delighted French officers saw his "naturally cold" demeanor vanish. " . . . his features, his expression, his whole carriage were changed in an instant. . . . A child whose every wish had been granted, could not have revealed a livelier emotion." Count Dumas wrote, "I have never seen a man moved by a greater or sincerer joy."

It would be hard to improve on that. Washington set out at a trot for the wharf at Chester to give Rochambeau the news. Rochambeau had not arrived yet, and Washington dismounted and waited for the French general's boat to appear. As soon as it came in sight, Rochambeau's aide saw the startling spectacle of Washington "standing on the shore and waving his hat and white handkerchief joyfully." When the boat came within earshot Washington began shouting the good news, still waving his hat and handkerchief, and when Rochambeau stepped ashore Washington threw his arms around the portly Frenchman in a gesture more Gallic than American.

The news spread everywhere as though carried on the air. Philadelphia gave itself over to noisy celebration; crowds dashed through the streets, firing off blank charges and hallooing for their allies. In this happy atmosphere the loan of money to pay the American soldiers was quickly negotiated, and Morris took steps to get the money forward to the marching men.

At Head of Elk, Washington wrote an order to his army: "It is with the highest pleasure and satisfaction that the Commander-in-chief announces to the Army the arrival of Count de Grasse in the Chesapeak . . . he felicitates the army on the auspicious occasion, he anticipates the glorious events which may be expected . . . the general calls upon the gentleman officers, the brave and faithful soldiers . . . to exert their utmost abilities in the cause of their country, to share with him . . . the difficulties, dangers, and glory of the enterprise." A few days later, the troops were mustered for payday, the payrolls were read, and the men stepped forward to receive their pay (or rather a modest token of it) from barrels of silver half-crowns. This was no Continental paper, unsubstantial as tissue; this was hard money. Major William Popham of New York wrote, "This day will be famous in the annals of History for being the first in which the Troops of the United States received one month's Pay in specie." The hundred and forty-four thousand livres was not enough to cover all that was owed, and another appeal was made to Robert Morris, who wrote in despair: "The late movements of the army have so entirely drained me of money that I have been obliged to pledge my personal credit very deeply . . . besides borrowing money from my friends and advancing . . . every shilling of my own. . . ."

Meanwhile Morris did all he could to hurry on the French money from Boston. Strongboxes of oak were built, and from fifteen hundred to two thousand crowns were packed in each box. Groups of twenty boxes were then placed in huge chests made of oak boards, the tops were nailed down, and the chests were fixed to the axles of oxcarts with welded iron straps. One horse and four oxen pulled each of the chests. The trip turned out to be almost two months long.

At Baltimore, a tumultuous reception awaited Washington. Again he was met by a cavalry company and the officials of the city; cannons were fired, and there were speeches, toasts, and illuminations, all of which the general bore with good grace. The next morning he was up before daylight and off with his aides on a hurried side trip to Mount Vernon. He had last been to the plantation in which he took such pride and to which he had given such devoted attention six years ago, on May 4, 1775, when he had left for Philadelphia. Even Mount Vernon had felt the war. There were inevitable changes; things had deteriorated, as they will without the firm directing hand of a master. But Martha and her retinue of slaves had kept the place in remarkably good order, and Washington's stepgrandchildren were there, the children of Martha's son by her first marriage, Jacky Custis. Washington noted in his journal simply enough: "I reached my own Seat at Mount Vernon (distant 120 Miles from the Hd. of Elk). . . ." Anyone who has come home from war will know what a depth and variety of emotions lay behind that sentence.

Rochambeau and Chastellux had been invited to visit Mount Vernon, and the next morning, after Washington had met with his slaves and talked to them, he conferred with his farm manager, and he and Martha made plans for entertaining the French officers.

Jonathan Trumbull, Washington's young secretary, was impressed by the plantation. "A numerous family now present. All accommodated,

An elegant seat and situation," he noted, "great appearance of opulence and real exhibitions of hospitality and princely entertainment." Washington dictated a stream of letters to Trumbull: one to the Governor of Maryland pressing him to collect supplies for the army; another to militia commanders asking help from their men in repairing the roads the army must march over; and another to Benjamin Lincoln with instructions to push the army on as fast as possible. "Every day we now lose is comparatively an age. . . . Hurry on then, my Dear Genl, with your Troops on the wing of Speed."

To Lafayette he wrote, "We are thus far, my Dear Marquis, on our way to you. The Count de Rochambeau has just arrived. . . . & we propose (after resting tomorrow) to be at Fredericksburg on the night of the 12th.—the 13th. we shall reach New Castle & the next day we expect the pleasure of seeing you at your encampment. . . . P.S. I hope you will keep Lord Cornwallis safe, without Provisions or Forage until we arrive. Adieu."

Chastellux, when he arrived with Rochambeau, found the dinner excellent; "tea succeeded dinner, and lasted until supper. The war was frequently the subject. . . ." Chastellux asked Washington which works on military history and tactics he had found most instructive, and the general replied, "the King of Prussia's Instructions to his Generals, and the Tactics of M. de Guibert; from whence," Chastellux added, "I concluded that he knew as well how to select his authors as to profit by them."

With a little advance guard of trusted slaves riding ahead to give word at Fredericksburg that Washington and Rochambeau would be arriving the next day, Washington started out on the twelfth accompanied by his aides, his secretary, and Jack Custis, who wanted to see for himself what war was all about. On the road the party met a courier who had unsettling news. De Grasse had sailed out of Lynnhaven Bay to do battle with the fleet of Graves and Hood. No one knew the outcome of the engagement. Washington's brief interlude of relaxation was over. Once more anxiety descended like a cloud. The brief excursion to Mount Vernon was the only time during the war that Washington, on the eve of a crucial campaign, was not constantly with his army, doing, as we have so often seen, much of the routine staffwork, checking hundreds of small but important details. The situation was, to be sure, different now. The army was in the hands of competent general officers. Nothing could be done until its arrival at Williamsburg. He might, to be sure, have hurried on to that town to join Lafayette and begin to make plans for the siege of Cornwallis, or, perhaps more important, to assure himself that Cornwallis would not take alarm and move out of his stronghold on the York. If Cornwallis, brushing Lafayette and Wayne aside, had set out for Charles Town, Washington's strategy would have been upset. Although the allied army might, in that case, have followed him and eventually, with Greene's assistance, have shut him up in Charles Town, the siege of that city would have been a prolonged affair, and the chances for the British fleet to evacuate the British army, if that had proved necessary, would have been greatly increased. In any event, the visit to Mount Vernon gave a fresh buoyancy to Washington's spirit. He was almost lighthearted as he rode on with his staff and Rochambeau to Williamsburg.

Sergeant Joseph Martin had been left behind in Philadelphia with a detail of sappers and miners to make cartridges for muskets and cannon. His men also had an opportunity to draw "a few articles of clothing, consisting of a few tow shirts, some overalls and a few pairs of silk-and-oakum stockings." They also, with the other soldiers, got a month's pay. "This," he wrote, "was the first that could be called money, which we had received as wages since the year '76, or that we ever did receive until the close of the war . . . as wages."

Martin and his men, when they had finished their task, set off down the Delaware on the *Birmingham,* a schooner whose hold was filled with ammunition, to join the army. As they passed Mud Island, Martin reçalled vividly the terrifying bombardment he had endured there in the fall of 1777, almost four years ago. At Head of Elk the *Birmingham* joined a "mosquito fleet" of small vessels and set sail for the James River. The passengers were lucky enough to have on board a thirty-gallon hogshead of rum, which the officers, "who loved a little of the 'good creature' as well as the men," contrived to place in the bulkhead adjacent to their cabin; they nailed up the wall and left only a spigot protruding, by means of which they could very freely imbibe. Martin and his messmates promptly discovered that the other end of the barrel rested against the bulkhead in the ship's hold, and they, with a brace and bit, broached the hogshead on the other end, "so that while the officers in the cabin thought they were the sole possessors of its contents, the soldiers in the hold had possession of at least as good a share as themselves." As the little fleet approached the mouth of the James it passed the French men-of-war lying in Lynnhaven Bay, their masts like "a swamp of dry pine trees."

The Battle of the Capes

CORNWALLIS's first intimation of serious trouble came on August 29. By that time, Washington's army had been on the march for ten days. The twenty-eight-gun *Guadeloupe,* carrying dispatches for Clinton, had just dropped past the Hampton Roads when its captain saw a large fleet of what were plainly frigates, approaching from the southeast. More and more ships appeared on the horizon until the skyline was white with sails. The formidable fleet furled their canvas and anchored inside Cape Henry. When the *Guadeloupe* carried the news back up the river to Cornwallis at Yorktown, that gentleman's heart may well have skipped a beat or two. There was no more leisurely digging. A Hessian noncommissioned officer complained, "We hardly have time for eating. Often we had to eat raw meat." Cornwallis also sent a volley of urgent communiqués north by small, fast schooners, by galleys, and even by whaleboats rowed by crews of eight or ten. They all carried the same message: "An enemy's fleet within the Capes, between thirty and forty ships of war, mostly large."

De Grasse, meanwhile, put ashore some French troops commanded by the Comte de Saint-Simon; troops who, Cornwallis assured his men, were "raw and sickly, ... enervated by a hot climate." Cornwallis watched them land without interfering, and Clinton later, when everyone was blaming everyone else for the Yorktown disaster, wrote that he could not understand why Cornwallis had not "cut up Monsieur St. Simon's three thousand enervated troops on their landing within a few miles of him . . . or placing himself between them and Lafayette's small corps."

On September 1, four French frigates sailed up the York River and anchored below Yorktown. It was clear to the British that defenses must be built facing the river side as well as the land, and the next day soldiers began constructing them. "I am now working very hard at the redoubts of the place," Cornwallis wrote Clinton. "The Army is not very sickly, Provisions for six weeks. I will be very careful of it." The soldiers had a somewhat different view of the matter, however, and one British junior officer wrote apprehensively of a "fatal storm, ready now almost to burst on our heads." An American officer had a different metaphor. General George Weedon, writing to Nathanael Greene on September 5, declared, "The business with his Lordship [Cornwallis] in this State will very soon be at an end, for I suppose you know e'er this that we have got him handsomely in a pudding bag with 5,000 land forces and about 60 ships including transports. . . . If our star dont most wonderfully deceive us, we shall shortly do his business. . . . Count de Grasse has 27 line-of-battle ships and six frigates besides the Rhode Island fleet, and I think, my dear fellow, there is little risque of our ever being the juniors at sea again. . . ."

On the Gloucester side of the York River, British engineers directed slaves in building a palisade and small fort. The British and German soldiers could or would do little digging in the August heat, and a number of the Germans deserted whenever an opportunity offered. Cornwallis counted under his command some seven thousand soldiers, by far the larger portion on the Yorktown side of the river. Charles O'Hara, "a most perfect specimen of a soldier and a courtier of the past age," a "black" Irishman and a friend of Horace Walpole, had recovered from the wounds he had received at Guilford Court House and was a very welcome addition to Cornwallis's army. The British commander calculated that it would take some six weeks to build proper fortifications around the camp. After that, he wrote Clinton, he could send some of his men to New York to aid in the defense of that city.

A German soldier from Bayreuth, Johann Conrad Doehla, who had been brought with his Hessian comrades from the garrison in New York to reinforce Cornwallis, found the women of Virginia much more affectionate to German soldiers than those in other provinces and marveled over the fact that the Virginians took "crabs from dry land and hay grows on trees [Spanish moss]. It is like this," he noted; "there are found here many little crabs which are called sand crabs. they stay in the sandy soil of this locality—which has many small holes—and as soon as it rains a little these come out of their holes in abundance, so that the ground swarms with them. We have collected and boiled whole kettles. They are a variety of water crabs only somewhat smaller; they boil red and taste like ours. . . . There is in this country a long, smooth moss which grows abundantly on the trees and hangs down from the boughs . . . it is gathered by the inhabitants by the cart load and put into piles, from which the cattle are fed during the winter."

The cotton was blooming, and the fields were white with bolls, "They bloom very beautifully," Private Doehla wrote, "reddish, white and sky-blue all mixed together. One stalk often bears 10, 12, 15 bolls as large as hen's eggs or chestnuts. . . . We make ourselves coverlets for the beds and couches in our tents, where we slept on it, but we had little time for more than that."

The British and American picket lines were so close that, as a Hessian soldier noted, "one could hear every relieving of watch and patrols; and now French, now English or German, calling out: 'Who's there?' 'Friend' . . . Everything must proceed quietly. One dares call out neither to sentry nor patrol except only to give the agreed signal. Nor does one dare smoke or make a fire." Desertions from the British lines were constant, especially among the Hessians. "Tonight Private Roessler of Wunsiedel from the Colonel's Company deserted his post on the Ansbach Regimental picket. . . . Private Friedlein of Eyb's Company deserted from a picket post." A few were recaptured and severely punished. "The erstwhile deserter Froelich . . . ran the gauntlet 16 times through 300 men . . . He was quite pitifully cut and beaten, and he had to be led all day by 2 non-coms because he could not walk."

The British and the Hessians in Yorktown suffered terribly from the heat. Men died every day, and a Hessian wrote in his journal, "we get terrible provisions now, putrid ship's meat and wormy biscuits that have spoiled on the ships. Many of the men have taken sick here with dysentery or the bloody flux and with diarrhea. Also the foul fever is spreading, partly on account of the many hardships from which we have had little rest day or night, and partly on account of the wretched food; but mostly the nitre-bearing water is to blame for it."

On September 5 there was noise of firing beyond the Capes. The firing marked the opening of the decisive engagement of the Yorktown campaign, the naval battle between the recently arrived British and French fleets. The British fleet under Graves and Hood had sailed for the Chesapeake on September 1, weeks after it was supposed to have left New York. Much of the delay was due to the lack of effective communication between Clinton and Graves, or, more basically, to any real trust or confidence between those two commanders. Graves was openly contemptuous of Clinton's constant air of anxiety bordering on desperation. It seemed to him close to plain cowardice.

When Graves and Hood finally set sail, they knew only that the fleet of the Comte de Barras was somewhere about, a fleet considerably smaller than their own and one with which they would have welcomed a battle. There were rumors that De Grasse was on his way from the Indies, but Graves had no notion that the French admiral had the Chesapeake Bay as his destination. Bad luck dogged the British from the outset. Hood's *Terrible,* a seventy-four-gun ship of the line, was leaking badly, although five pumps were worked constantly. Inexplicably, it turned out that two frigates, the *Ajax* and the *Montagu,* had sprung masts and leaks. The whole fleet had to lay by while emergency repairs were made. The ships then made way again, and on the fifth, at dawn, Graves's lookout raised the Capes of the Chesapeake, and, running before the wind, the British fleet bore into Lynnhaven Bay.

But someone, of course, was there before them. The French ships lay at anchor in three lines, with scouting vessels covering the waters outside the Capes. News of the arrival of the British fleet, signaled by the scouting ship the *Aigrette,* found eighteen hundred sailors and ninety officers ashore collecting wood. Nonetheless, there was an instant celebration among the crewmen remaining aboard the French men-of-war, and frantic preparations were started to entertain the approaching British. Graves, having no ship ahead to signal a warning, was slower to discover the real situation. It was 9:30 A.M. before a shout from the crow's-nest on his flagship, the *Solebay,* gave the news that French frigates were anchored inside the Capes, some ten miles ahead. The captain of the ship at first discounted his lookout's report. "It must be the charred pines that you see," he called up, "they burn them for tar and leave the trunks standing." The lookout persisted, and the captain climbed aloft himself. What he saw reassured him. He could count only eight ships, and he concluded that they must be the squadron of De Barras, arrived from Newport.

At eleven o'clock, seven or eight more French ships were counted anchored in the bay. Graves ordered his supply ships and those small vessels that accompanied any considerable fleet to draw off, and he formed his own line for battle. De Grasse was ready to weigh anchor not long after Graves had given his initial orders to prepare for battle, even though many of his men were still ashore; but the tide was running in, and until it turned the French fleet had to wait. It turned at noon, after almost half an hour of tense waiting. The great ropes holding the ships were cut, and they began the exacting maneuver of getting around Cape Henry and into the open sea to meet the oncoming British. The line was led by Commodore Louis Antoine de Bougainville—a sailor who had started life as a soldier—on the *Auguste*. It was Bougainville who, after the death of Montcalm, had surrendered Canada to the British at the end of the Seven Years' War. Turning sailor, he had explored the South Pacific and had brought back with him the vivid paperlike flower that bears his name. Now he commanded the advance squadron. De Grasse was on the *Ville de Paris,* the towering flagship of the French fleet, and behind him the French frigates struggled to form a proper line of battle. The *Souverain* and the *Citoyen* almost ran aground and had to make several extra tacks to clear the channel.

The forward echelon was made up of the *Pluton* of seventy-four guns, the *Bourgoyne* of eighty guns, and the *Marsaillais* and the *Diademe* of seventy-four. A mile and a half astern were the *Reflechi* and the *Caton;* the rest of the fleet labored far behind. De Grasse, despite getting off to an awkward, scrambling start, had the advantage of a far heavier armament—four hundred more guns on five more ships—than the combined fleets of Graves and Hood. The British had one clear asset: their copper-bottomed vessels were decidedly faster and more maneuverable than the foul-bottomed French warships. Moreover the British fleet, coming off an open sailing formation, was arrayed in a far more orderly line of battle, nineteen ships in a line some five miles long, and, most important of all, they had the weather gauge. Hood in the *Barfleur* was in command of the leading squadron; Graves commanded the center in the *London;* and Drake in the *Princessa* commanded the rear.

The two lines approached each other swiftly in a steady breeze, the British to the windward. The convergence of the two lines brought the ninety-gun British lead vessels, the *Barfleur* of Hood's division and the *London* of Graves's, against the much-lighter-gunned ships of Bougainville. As one French officer with grudging admiration for British seamanship wrote, "They came down upon us with a following wind and an assurance which made us think they did not know our strength." Such indeed was the case. Graves still thought he had only to contend with the modest squadron of De Barras. Graves did not open fire, however. Like a medieval knight, searching out his rival for personal combat, he waited for the French admiral (De Barras, he thought) to come up in his flagship. It was a grand gesture. By it Graves lost the opportunity to inflict crippling damage on the French van and perhaps lost, in consequence, the battle, Yorktown, and the war. But gestures were important. This one had the effect of disconcerting the French and enraging Hood.

For an hour the British sailed toward land and the French toward open sea on opposite tacks. By two o'clock, the leading ship in the British line, the *Alfred,* was dangerously near Middle Ground Shoal, and Graves ordered his fleet to come about. By this time he had sailed the French line and realized that he was not contending with the fleet of De Barras but with a much larger fleet that probably outgunned his own. The tack, moreover, brought him in line with and roughly parallel to the French center, with his rear strung out behind the French rear and considerably to the windward. Hood's division, which had been in the van, was now in the rear. Drake, who now led the British line of battle, had the *Terrible,* rendered hardly terrible at all by her leaky bottom, and the *Ajax,* also leaking.

For a moment it seemed to the French as though the British had decided to fight among themselves. The fact was that Drake had signaled to the crippled *Terrible,* which seemed about to drop out of the action, to take her place in line, and when his signals had been ignored he had fired three shots across her bow. Then came one of the most inexplicable of all Graves's orders. The first four or five of Bougainville's ships were far in front of the main body of his division and thus most vulnerable to British attack, but Graves ordered his sails dropped and lay dead in the water until the gap in the French line had been closed. The log of the *London* carried the entry: "Brought to in order to let the Center of the Enemys Ships come a Brest of us."

Graves waited an hour and a half and then, when the French were finally all straightened out, he led the advance, coming down on the French from the windward gauge in an odd obliquing maneuver that brought the converging fleets together at their apex so that, initially, only the lead ships were engaged. The French rear still lagged far behind, effectively out of the action for the time being. The line-ahead signal—a white flag—was augmented by a blue and white checkered flag, meaning "Ships to bear down and engage close." Graves's failure to lower the white "line ahead" when running up the signal to engage the enemy confused some of his captains. Graves's own maneuver was even more unorthodox. The *London* was in the center of the British line, and Graves turned her abruptly to starboard and bore down on the French line head on. Other captains followed him, thus breaking the British line. Graves bore off before he was within range of the French, fired a broadside that fell short, and then, trying to untangle the mess, ran up a series of signals that left his captains more in the dark than ever. By 4:15 most of the great ships were within a hundred yards or so of each other, and they opened fire almost simultaneously, crashing broadsides of deadly cannon fire into each other's vitals, splintering great oaken planks, tearing off limbs, splattering the decks with blood and entrails.

Naval warfare in the eighteenth century, much like land warfare, counted heavily on a devastating initial shock at close range, a brutal battering force too much for human flesh and blood to endure, too much for a ship, however stout, to withstand. From thirty to forty-five cannon of large caliber, throwing projectiles that weighed as much as fifty pounds, belched forth destruction. Often it was destruction to their own crews, as guns exploded under the pressure and were turned into murderous shrapnel, or broke loose from their fittings and hurtled backward, smashing bulkheads into kindling. Some guns fired shrapnel to clear marines from the rigging, and others fired chains to tear the enemy's shrouds and lines to shreds. Indeed it was the French practice to fire initially at the rigging in the hope of making it impossible for the enemy to maneuver his ship.

Thus on the first exchange the hulls of the French ships and the bodies of their seamen took the heaviest battering, while the masts and sails of the British ships were riddled. Drake's lead ship, the seventy-four-gun *Shrewsbury,* was the first British casualty. The fire of the *Pluton* tore off the leg of her captain and killed his first lieutenant and thirteen seamen. As the two ships continued to exchange fire, twelve more sailors were killed and forty-eight wounded. The *Shrewsbury* took five balls below her water line, and her topmast was shot through in three places. She fell out of the line, and when the *Intrepid* sailed up to cover her, she, in turn, came under such heavy fire from the *Marsaillais* that she was forced out of line with sixty-five shots in her starboard side. On the French side, the *Reflechi* was badly battered and her captain killed by a broadside from Drake's *Princessa.* She, and then the *Pluton* and the *Caton,* withdrew, badly damaged.

Bougainville's division found itself heavily outgunned as four of its ships were engaged with seven to eight British vessels at close range. The rest of the French fleet was too far in the rear to offer help, and while the British efforts to cut off the French van were unsuccessful, they gave the *Diademe* a fearful working over so that only four of its 36-pounders and nine 18-pounders were fit for use; the *Saint-Esprit* came to her assistance, however, and drove off her attackers, commencing a fire "that the gentlemen of Albion could not stand and had to haul their wind."

The outnumbered Bougainville, realizing that he would be cut to pieces at ordinary range, pulled so close to Drake's *Princessa* that their hulls almost touched, and the fighting for a time raged at such close quarters that the expressions of the sailors and marines were plainly visible and the shouts and orders on both ships could be easily heard. Drake bore off to uncover the fire of the nearby British frigates, and Bougainville took advantage of the lull to give the *Terrible* a broadside. That ship was already taking five feet of water an hour in its hold, and the pumps could not keep up with it. Bougainville's own ship also suffered heavily, with ten killed and fifty-eight wounded. Twice the *Auguste's* foretop bowline was shot away so that the mainsail could not be properly trimmed, and twice the sailors who went aloft to repair it were shot out of the rigging by musket fire from the *Princessa*. The third time Bougainville called for volunteers, none came forward. The French officer then held up his purse and offered it to anyone who would undertake to replace the line. A sailor who scrambled up the mast and out on the yardarm called down, "General, we do not go there for money," and secured the line, returning unscathed through heavy enemy fire.

An hour after the vans had begun firing on each other, the center divisions came within range and began firing, the delay being due to the strange angle at which Graves had elected to engage the French. The *Europe* and the *Montagu,* the first two ships in the British center, suffered heavily in the initial exchange. The masts and rigging of the *Europe* were badly shattered, and her hull was holed dozens of times. The *Montagu* took heavy losses in her crew and dropped out of the line with her masts ready to topple at any moment. The ships that followed suffered relatively light damage; they engaged at maximum range in a falling wind. The *Royal Oak,* the *London,* the *Bedford,* the *Resolution,* the *Centaur,* and the *Monarch* were comparatively unscathed; the *London* had the heaviest losses with four men killed, eighteen wounded, and "one large shot through the main mast and two in the foremast; a number of shot in the side . . . sails and rigging much cut. . . ."

When Graves hauled down his signal flag for "line ahead," it was

5:25, and the ships of his rear were almost within range of De Grasse's last division. The flag "engage the enemy" still flew, and Hood turned to starboard to try to engage the French ships. The captain of the *Citoyen* noted that at 5:45 the *Barfleur* (Hood's flagship) "came up, as well as the two ships ahead of her . . . they hove to and experimented to see whether their cannon balls would reach our ships. The enemy admiral began by firing several shots and the other ships . . . followed suit . . . their fire became general up as far as my ship but it did not last long . . . I had much the better of the exchange with the three-decker [the *Barfleur*], for it appeared to me that nearly all her cannon balls fell into the sea. . . ."

Thirty-five minutes after Hood's division closed with the French rear, Graves lowered the "engage the enemy" flag from the masthead, and the day's battle was at an end.

In his account of the engagement, De Grasse gave Bougainville full praise for saving a confused and indeed desperate situation. "The laurels of the day," he wrote, "belong to de Bougainville . . . for having led the van and having personally fought the *Terrible*." Bougainville calculated that his gunners had fired 684 cannonballs during the engagement and had taken 54 in the hull and 70 hits in the rigging. Drake's *Princessa* reeled back from her encounter with the *Auguste* with three shot in the mainmast and the mizzen-topmast, topsails, and gaffs shot away. All that remained for that night was to make such repairs as were possible, to stuff gaping holes near the water line with great wads of oakum, to man the pumps, brace masts, refit rigging, sew the dead in their shrouds, and patch together the wounded. This last was the grimmest part of all. The crude surgery of the day was performed without any anesthetic except a slug of fiery rum, so shattered limbs were severed and wounds stitched while men groaned and screamed in pain. Biting a lead bullet was a poor substitute for morphine.

Besides the efforts to patch up men and ships, preparations had to be made to resume the battle on the following day, for the battle of September 5 was inconclusive. The real issue, to be decided through the long night, was which fleet, come morning, would be in the best shape to renew the battle. That fleet would be counted the victor in the engagement off the Capes. For another hour or so the two fleets sailed along in parallel lines perhaps a mile apart, leaving the ocean dotted with disabled vessels whose crews worked frantically to make them, if not seaworthy, at least capable of moving under their own sail. After darkness fell, the French sailors and marines remained at their combat stations, lanterns lit and matches burning. In the words of one of De Grasse's officers, "The fleet passed the night in the presence of the enemy in line of battle, the fires in all the vessels lighted." It made a strange scene, the two great war fleets sailing in silent company under the night sky, each vessel's intricate interior life pulsing within it, each beautiful but deadly machine readied for the concluding act of the terrible drama.

The British still clung tenaciously to the weather gauge, though as the battle had developed it had given them an initiative of which they had made poor use. The order from Graves was to hold the line of battle through the night, with two cable lengths between ships. By ten o'clock, Graves knew the condition of his fleet. The *Shrewsbury*, the *Montagu*, and the *Intrepid* had fallen out of the line hours earlier; the topmast of the *Princessa* was near collapse; the *Terrible* was losing ground, or, more accurately gaining water; and the *Ajax* was barely holding its own with double pumping. Six of Grave's fifteen ships had been put out of action for all practical purposes.

On the French side the *Diademe*, the *Pluton*, and the *Reflechi*, along with the *Caton*, had been forced out of the fire fight by the battering that they had taken, and the *Auguste*, Bougainville's flagship, had sustained serious damages. But the French vessels, even those that had suffered the heaviest casualties, had been less affected in their sailing capabilities than their British counterparts. The French strategy of directing fire at the masts, riggings, and upper works of the enemy had proved successful. It was easier to patch a riddled hull than to replace the delicate and complicated rigging of a sailing ship. The French had lost 209 men killed and wounded; the British, 336 of whom 90 had been killed.

The fact that darkness found the French fleet less seriously wounded than the British was the result in large part of two elements: the courage and skill with which Bougainville handled the van—especially the example he set in fighting his own ship, *the Auguste*—and a whole series of errors, most of them inexplicable, committed by Graves and to a degree compounded by Hood. Like Yorktown itself, the British failure resulted in years of unpleasant mutual recrimination between Graves and Hood, each of whom blamed the other for the blunders of the day. There was certainly enough blame to go round. Graves and Hood, like Cornwallis and Clinton, carried on their discreditable wrangles for years in Parliament, in pamphlets and books, and in the newspapers. The public, the political factions, the statesmen of the day tried their cases in a hundred courts, formal and informal. Since there was no glory to be gained in any event, it became of paramount importance to fix the blame. But that was all in the future.

On the night of September 5, while men's ears still rang from the hideous concussions of the great cannon, the British errors could be quite simply listed. The first and probably, when all was said and done, the conclusive error was in allowing the French fleet to get out of Lynnhaven Bay and into a line of battle unmolested—in fact, falling off to give them time to do so. This initial error meant that the British lost the opportunity to engage the French on equal terms, or, indeed, with the odds very much in their favor. The next error was for the British to sail parallel to the French fleet on the opposite tack so that when the fleet was forced to come about, the heavier-gunned ships of the British van, under Hood, who was an experienced and aggressive commander, were out of reach of Bougainville's division. Graves's decision to come down on the French line diagonally was another mistake, less serious perhaps than the preceding one, but one that resulted in the piecemeal engaging of the French fleet and squandered most of the advantage of the weather gauge. Having flown the flag "line ahead," Graves, by not striking it when he flew "engage the enemy," gave Hood grounds for continuing to sail ahead with his division until, an hour or more after his lead and center divisions had been hotly engaged, Graves struck the "line ahead" as though by a kind of afterthought. The other British captains read the same signals, but they engaged, and Hood could plainly see that they had. Why did Hood, except perhaps out of pique and disgust at Graves's clumsy maneuvers, remain aloof from the battle so long? And why, when he closed on the French, did he hang off at extreme range where his fire did little damage? Hood's reputation rested on being a tough fighter with an instinct for the enemy's jugular. Why then did he dance about out of effective range?

Every battle, on land or water, is, as we have seen by abundant evidence, a riddle, never to be entirely unraveled. The mistakes that Graves and Hood made were mistakes planted, in a sense, in their neurological systems. They were the mistakes, as we like to say today, in the curious recesses of their psyches, mistakes that traveled some delicate circuitry from their brains to the smallest fibers of their nerve ends and back, errant couriers, carrying the wrong messages. The system that put Graves in command of the fleet at this crucial juncture of world history, with Hood as his disgruntled second-in-command, was perhaps, ultimately, the guilty party.

The more or less stupefying thought is that it took this hopeless compounding of British errors to give the much larger French fleet a narrow margin of superiority—one could not call it victory—after the smoke of battle had blown away. And one must keep in mind of course that the issue was far from settled when the sun popped up over the horizon on the morning of the sixth.

Graves, a basically rather timid and indecisive man, was somewhat in awc of Hood. His instincts told him to break off the fighting, collect his battered ships, and sail back to New York with the excuse that he had been overwhelmed, after a valiant fight, by De Grasse's superior fleet. If that was not in the best tradition of the British navy, it was a better course than ending up at the bottom of the sea. Moreover, he was confident that he could place the blame squarely on Hood's shoulders, because of his inexplicably dilatory conduct during the battle. He had a scapegoat and the greater part of his fleet; what more could he, in good conscience, want? Nonetheless, the commander of the fleet sent an officer to his second-in-command, who in his own mind he had already indicted for the failure of the day before, to inquire if, in Hood's opinion, the battle should be renewed.

At the moment the message arrived, Hood was writing a bitter criticism of *Graves's* direction of the battle. The fact that the fate of thousands of men was at stake did not prevent Hood from indulging in a snit. "I dare say Mr. Graves will do what is right. I can *send* no opinion, but whenever Mr. Graves wishes to see me, I will wait upon him with great pleasure." Then Hood went back to finishing his critique of the battle, entitled, resoundingly, "Sentiments upon the Truly Unfortunate Day": "Yesterday the British fleet had a rich and most plentiful harvest of glory in view, but the means to gather it were omitted in more instances than one," he wrote. The first "means" omitted was Graves's allowing the French to get out of Lynnhaven Bay. If the British had attacked as they were clearing the Capes, "several of the enemies ships must have been cut to pieces." The "Sentiments" were extensive and explicit and, for the most part, correct. Of his own excessive scrupulosity in regard to the *London's* signal, he had little to say.

The morning of the sixth was clear and fair, with very light air. The work on the ships of the two fleets went ahead, with jerry rigs of every kind devised to repair the damaged masts and rigging. Five British ships replaced topmasts while the French watched. Here, one would have thought, De Grasse might at last have taken the offensive. His fleet was in much the better condition. Why did he sail idly along while the British worked frantically to get their damaged ships in condition to resume the battle?

Graves called Drake and Hood to his flagship in midmorning for a council of war, but the discussion began badly with mutual recriminations between Graves and Hood. "Why didn't you bear down and engage?" Graves asked as soon as Hood was aboard.

"You had the signal up for the line," Hood replied.

"Why did *you* bear down on the enemy?" Graves asked Drake.

"On account of the signal for action."

"What say you to this, Admiral Hood?"

"The signal for the line was enough for me." A lame answer.

The two admirals could not agree on how long and at what particular times the "line ahead" flag had flown, and outside of Graves's cabin the staff officers of Hood's ship and Graves's abused each other while their commanders squabbled within. So the day passed without decision, and a growing mood of despondency settled over the British fleet. Nothing is so demoralizing for a soldier or sailor as waiting, especially when one is surrounded by the terrible consequences of an earlier engagement in the form of dead or seriously wounded companions. The two fleets continued to sail on a southwest course, De Grasse covered by Graves and making no effort to take the weather gauge or to renew the battle. While it is true that having the British to the windward sharply limited the French commander's room for maneuver, he could at any time have come about and, with his substantial superiority in numbers, forced Graves either to engage or draw off.

On the seventh, a breeze rose from the south-southwest, and De Grasse finally felt himself in a position to contest the weather gauge, but he was satisfied to wage a harmless enough war of tacking without closing on the British, who were now some eight miles away. By nightfall the two fleets were nearly a hundred miles from the Chesapeake, near Cape Hatteras, North Carolina. De Grasse had written, during the day, a strange letter to Bougainville, which seemed to urge him to fight his division as though it were an independent command. "If the wind continues and the English do not escape us tonight, we shall meet them at closer range tomorrow morning. I hope the day will be a happier one, which will permit us to go back and take those Johnnies in the Chesapeake. What a joy it will be to have the ships of de Barras united with ours!"

The last sentence is a revealing one. It gives the clue to De Grasse's reluctance to engage the British on the sixth and seventh. If he could draw Graves off from the Capes of the Chesapeake, De Barras would have an opportunity to slip inside, unmolested by Graves's superior fleet, or, conversely, to come down the coast after De Grasse and join with him to administer the *coup de grâce* to the British fleet. De Grasse was apparently aware that he had little to congratulate himself on in the handling of his fleet. The fact that he had received no adequate warning of Graves's approach was the fault of De Grasse himself and it was a fault that might easily have proved fatal. It must be said in defense of De Grasse that he had no way of knowing the exact state of the British fleet or the damage that had been inflicted on it by Bougainville's division. That information, though known to us, was concealed from him. His basic mission in the last extremity was to prevent Graves from reinforcing, supplying, or taking off Cornwallis's army. To accomplish that mission he had only to prevent Graves from defeating him; he did not have to defeat Graves. As long as his fleet was more or less intact, Graves would not help the beleaguered Cornwallis. Augmented by De Barras, De Grasse's fleet would so far outgun the British that they would hardly dare contest the issue. So De Grasse continued to sail southward, leaving the initiative to Graves, who was clearly reluctant to take it.

September 8 was dark and windy, with menacing clouds and scattered thunderstorms sweeping across the water. The seas grew heavy, and the *Terrible* flew a distress signal. The *Intrepid* had lost her maintopmast, and the forearm seemed about to be carried away momentarily. Graves wrote, "These repeated misfortunes in sight of a superior enemy who kept us all extended and in motion, filled the mind with anxiety and put us in a position not to be envied." Finally, on the ninth, De Grasse began to be anxious about the ships and seamen he had abandoned in Lynnhaven Bay. The British might, at any moment, swing about and make for the Capes, arriving ahead of the French. "It is what we ought to have been doing since the battle," Bougainville wrote in his journal; "That is, our very best to get back into that bay, recover our ships, barges and boats. . . ." Best of all, De Grasse might find De Barras there.

De Grasse was readily persuaded. As soon as it was dark, he came about for the Chesapeake under full sail. Hood, who apparently observed the maneuver, wrote, "I was distressed that Mr. Graves did not carry all the sail he could also, and endeavor to get to the Chesapeake before him; it appeared to me to be a measure of the utmost importance to keep the French out, and if they did get in they should first beat us."

At first light, Hood's fears (if he had had them) were confirmed.

There was no sign of De Grasse's fleet. The admiral wrote Graves at once, "I flatter myself you will forgive the liberty I take in asking whether you have any knowledge of where the French fleet is, as we can see nothing of it from the *Barfleur*. . . . I am inclined to think his aim is the Chesapeake . . . if he should enter the Bay . . . will he not succeed in giving most effectual succour to the rebels?"

Graves's response was to waste valuable time by calling another council of war, in order to, in effect, say that he had no idea where the French were. It is not unfair to say that Graves committed the final and irretrievable error of this particular series when he followed De Grasse for two days without trying to engage him and without at the same time staying close enough to discern any change in the Frenchman's course. If he had covered De Grasse's turn northward, he could have forced him to fight off the Capes or before he arrived there, under circumstances where the superior sailing qualities, or what were at least thought to be the superior sailing qualities, of the British ships might very well have carried the day. By letting De Grasse slip away, he compounded all his earlier mistakes and sealed the fate of Cornwallis's army.

Graves was further delayed in his pursuit of De Grasse by the death agonies of the *Terrible*. She continued to take water; the pumps broke down; the lower deck guns were pushed overboard to lighten her; provisions were transferred to other ships; but it was clear nothing could be done to save her, and finally the decision was made to burn and sink her. The sea cocks were opened and the fire set; she made a brilliant blaze, blew up, and sank. Graves then turned his fleet for the Chesapeake. But De Grasse had already raised Cape Henry and seen the welcome sight of ships' masts. It was De Barras, who had sailed in a wide circle to avoid the British, almost making contact with De Grasse off Cape Hatteras. De Barras's fleet brought the ships under De Grasse's command to thirty-five battleships.

On September 13, while Graves was on course for the Chesapeake, a British ship appeared and told him that De Grasse was back in Lynnhaven Bay, his fleet joined to that of De Barras. Graves sent Hood a message: "Admiral Graves presents his compliments to Sir Samuel Hood and begs leave to acquaint him that the *Medea* has just made the signal to inform him that the French fleet are at anchor . . . in the Chesapeake, and desires his opinion what to do with the fleet. . . ." To which Hood replied: "Rear Admiral Sir Samuel Hood . . . is extremely concerned to find . . . that the French fleet is at anchor in the Chesapeake . . . though it is no more than what he expected . . . Sir Samuel would be very glad to send an opinion, but he really knows not what to say in the truly lamentable state we have brought ourselves." The council of war that followed concluded that because of "the position of the enemy, the present condition of the British fleet, the season of the year so near the equinox, and the impracticability of giving any effectual succour to General Earl Cornwallis . . . it was resolved, that the British squadron . . . should proceed with all dispatch to New York."

It took Graves two weeks to reach New York with his fleet, and word sped ahead of him that he had been defeated by De Grasse, which was not, of course, strictly true; he had defeated himself. There were three thousand inhabitants of New York waiting at the docks when a small, fast-sailing packet brought the first official word on September 17. When Graves's fleet straggled into port two days later, many Tory families began to pack their most cherished possessions, and Frederick Mackenzie wrote, "I fear the fate of the Army in Virginia will be determined before our fleet can get out of the harbour again. . . ." Clinton, of course, was not disposed to take any of the blame himself. "All depended on a fleet," he wrote later. "Sir Henry Clinton was promised one. Washington had one." When George III received the news, he at last was ready to face facts. "I nearly think," he wrote the Earl of Sandwich, "the empire ruined . . . this cruel event is too recent for me to be as yet able to say more."

At this point it is perhaps appropriate to reflect briefly on the *narrowness* of the margin by which De Grasse accomplished his mission, and, in turn, of the odds against Washington's gamble. It is hard not to believe that it was Graves's bungling that prevented the British from scoring a decisive naval victory on the fifth of September. Subsequently any course would have been better than the one that Graves followed. If he had vigorously renewed the attack on the morning of the sixth, he might still have saved the day. If, eschewing battle, he had posted himself at the entrance to the bay, he would have been able to make contact with Cornwallis, cut up the remainder of De Grasse's supply ships and transports already in the bay, and disrupt Washington's plans generally. If De Grasse had sailed off, Graves might have been able to drive off or decisively defeat the fleet under De Barras. If De Grasse had remained in the vicinity, Graves must eventually have brought him to a contest on his own terms. So, strictly speaking, Washington undertook the most hazardous of operations—a combined naval-military maneuver that also involved cooperation with the French, cooperation that had twice before brought disappointment if not disaster—with only a remote chance of success. If De Grasse had been delayed even a week or so by storms, by an engagement in the West Indies, or by unfavorable winds, Graves and Hood would have been in Lynnhaven Bay before him. If Rochambeau's message had gone astray, which was by no means unlikely, De Grasse would certainly have headed for New York or Newport, and again Washington's plans would have proved abortive. The fact was that, against all the odds, luck favored Washington at every turn. Everything that could go right for the Americans did; and for the British everything possible went wrong.

But British wrong-headedness lay behind British bad fortune. The odds for the patriots were not in fact as bad as they looked. Washington clearly had to do something. The one thing he could not do was what the British proved themselves so adept at doing—nothing. And given the fact that he had to do something, what he did was probably as good as anything else he could have done, and maybe, in the light of events, better. In military matters action does wonders; as we have seen time and again, it creates luck. To have the initiative is usually much more than half the battle; it is, in general military terms, "the weather gauge." The confusion, the mistakes, errors, wrangles, personal vendettas, stupidities, and blunders that characterized the British actions or, more generally, inactions were, in very large part, the natural consequences of the fact that the British were fighting a war that had become loathesome to them and that they had long since lost any hope of winning. From this simple fact, all the rest followed.

On the same day, September 8, that the Battle of the Capes was concluded, the final engagement in the South took place. Lord Rawdon had left some two thousand soldiers under the command of Lieutenant Colonel Alexander Stewart in North Carolina, on the west side of the Congaree near the Wateree. Greene was in the high hills of the Santee, some sixteen miles to the north. Recent rains had brought the Congaree and the Wateree to flood stage, and Greene was forced to make a circuitous march of seventy miles to approach Stewart. He came on Stewart by surprise and deployed his units much as Morgan had done at Cowpens. The North Carolina militia were placed in the center, with the South Carolinians on either side. Lee was posted with his legion, on the right and on the left was Wade Hampton. The second line was made up of Greene's Continentals, with William Washington's cavalry and the light infantry of Robert Kirkwood in reserve. When Stewart finally received word of Greene's advance, he drew up his troops some two hundred yards west of Eutaw Springs, in a single line running from Eutaw Creek to and beyond the River Road. Eutaw Creek covered his right, and his left was covered by Captain John Coffin's cavalry and a detachment of infantry, held in reserve in the woods.

The British line was in a sparse wood; a short distance in the rear, in an open field, was a large, three-story brick house with garden and palisades extending to Eutaw Creek. Stewart selected the house as a strongpoint to cover the possible retreat of his army, and he placed some three hundred men under Major John Majoribanks in thickets along the creek to watch the American left and be prepared to attack if an opportunity offered. The skirmishers engaged and dropped back, and the six-pounders and three-pounders opened up a heavy fire down the River Road on the British lines; the British battery returned fire. The American militia, led by Andrew Pickens on the left and Francis Marion on the right, advanced "steadily and without faltering . . . with shouts and exhortations into the hottest of the enemy fire, inaffected by the continual fall of their comrades around them." Finally, the militia faltered under heavy fire, and having fired seventeen rounds while moving forward resolutely, they stood fast.

General Jethro Sumner was ordered to reinforce them and push the attack once more. Stewart responded by bringing his reserve into action on the American right, opposite Sumner. On the left, General William Henderson's troops of the North Carolina Line were exposed to heavy fire from Majoribanks' men in the thickets along the creek. Henderson asked for permission to charge and clear the enemy from his left and front, but Greene was afraid to expose the flank of the militia and leave his artillery unprotected. Henderson was wounded, but Wade Hampton preserved order among the soldiers of the brigade.

Meanwhile, Sumner's men, under heavy pressure from the British left, began to fall back; the British "sprang forward as to certain conquest, and their line became deranged." At this point Greene ordered the remainder of his reserve under Colonel Otho Williams to "advance and sweep the field with his bayonets." Williams' brigades replied to the command with a shout that echoed across the battlefield. They moved forward at once, holding their fire until they were within forty yards of the enemy lines. Here the Virginians fired a volley, and the rest of the brigades, with trailed arms, advanced on the double. For a moment the issue of the battle hung in the balance, as such engagements almost invariably did. Then the British left, which had dashed forward so precipitantly, began to withdraw in some confusion. Here Lee helped to turn the tide by advancing with his legion on the retreating British left. The left fled, thoroughly demoralized, but the British center stood firm until the Maryland Continentals delivered a volley. At this point the whole enemy line gave way and fell back on the brick house. Lee's cavalry, which was in the cover of the woods on the American right, failed to join the action. Majoribanks' men still held their positions along the river, and Greene, noting that if not uprooted they would take the Marylanders under dangerous enfilading fire, ordered Washington to charge the British right in conjunction with an advance by Hampton's detachment. Washington's cavalry reached the thicket well in advance of Hampton's infantry and, attempting an attack, found that they could not penetrate the heavy underbrush that provided cover for the British. Wheeling around to take Majoribanks in the flank, many of Washington's officers were killed and a number of his men were killed or wounded by the deadly fire from the thicket. Washington's men, without officers, were badly scattered, "routed and flying, horses plunging as they died or coursing the field without their riders. . . . In the foreground, Hampton was covering and collecting the scattered cavalry, while Kirkwood, with his bayonets, rushed furiously to revenge their fall, and the road was strewed with the bodies of men and horses and the fragments of dismounted artillery." The scene was one of "indescribable confusion" in which the only element of order was the sight of the American second line advancing. Robert Campbell, the giant leader of the Virginia riflemen, had been mortally wounded in the attack on the British left, and his son supported him in his saddle. The British seemed in full retreat, and refugees, flying from the battle, spread the word as far as Charles Town that the rebels were on their heels. Stores were destroyed along the road, and commissary supplies in the British camps were set afire.

But Majoribanks still held out in his riverbank stronghold. The remnants of Washington's command, joined with Hampton, renewed the attack, but it was only the added pressure of Kirkwood and the general withdrawal of the British line that forced Majoribanks back as far as the garden palisades. At this point the whole complexion of the battle changed. Stewart's foresight in ordering the brick house turned into a garrison saved his command—that and the impulse of the Americans to stop in the British encampment and loot the abandoned tents of the fleeing soldiers. In the words of one officer, the tents "presented many objects to tempt a thirsty, naked and fatigued soldiery to acts of

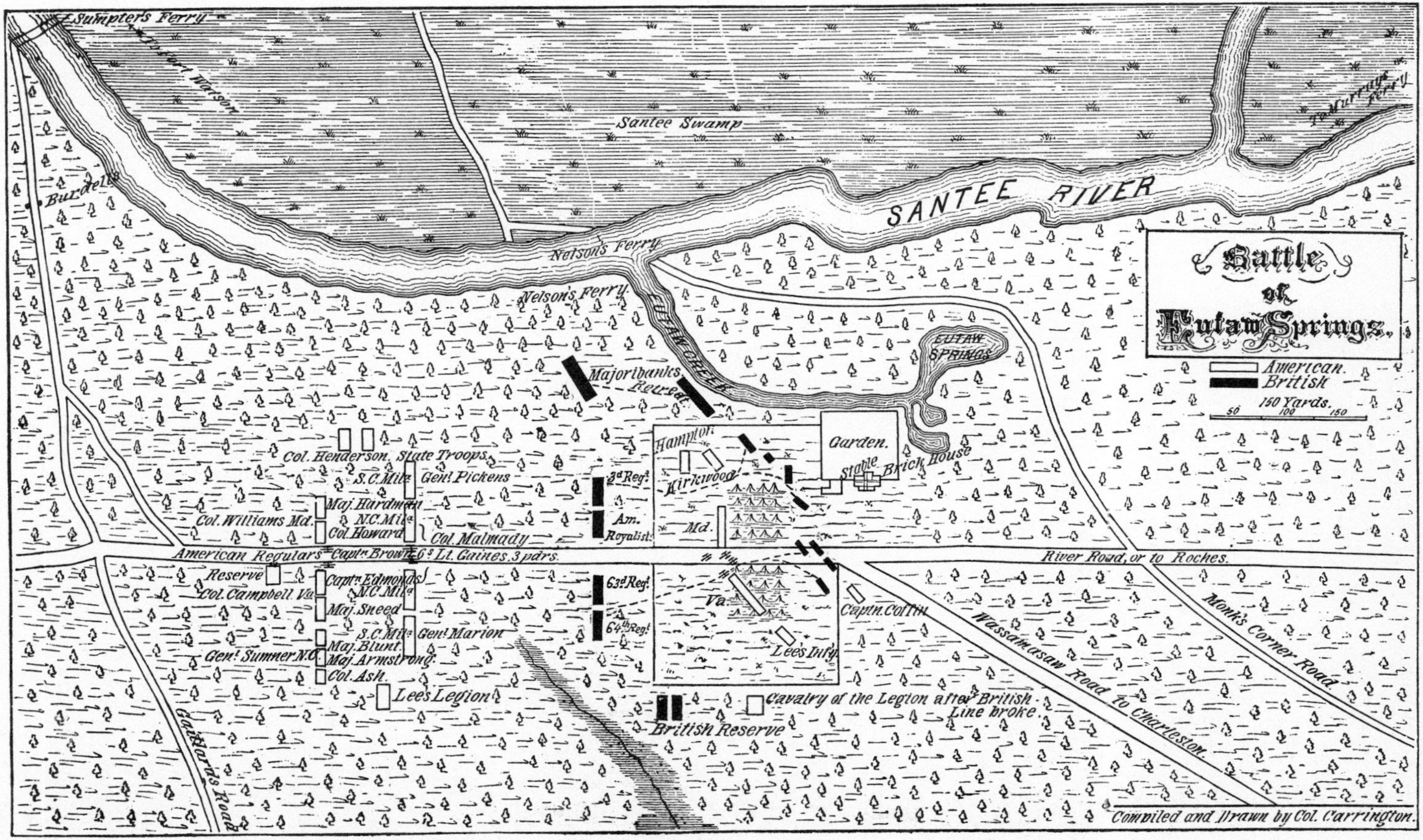
Battle of Eutaw Springs.
American.
British
150 Yards.
50
100
150
Sumpters Ferry
To Fort Watson
Santee Swamp
SANTEE RIVER
To Murrays Ferry
Burdells
Nelson's Ferry
Nelson's Ferry
EUTAW CREEK
EUTAW SPRINGS
Majoribanks Retreat
Hampton
Garden.
Stable
Brick House
Kirkwood
Md.
Va.
Capt'n Coffin
Lee's Infy.
Col. Henderson. State Troops.
S.C.Mil'a
Gen'l Pickens
Maj. Hardman
N.C.Mil'a
Col. Williams Md.
Col. Howard
Col. Malmady
3d Reg't
Am. Royalist
American Regulars
Capt'n Brown
6s Lt. Gaines. 3 pdrs.
River Road, or to Roches.
Reserve
Capt'n Edmonds
N.C.Mil'a
Col. Campbell Va.
Maj. Sneed
63d Reg't
64th Reg't
S.C.Mil'a
Gen'l Marion
Maj. Blunt.
Gen'l Sumner N.C.
Maj. Armstrong.
Col. Ash.
Lee's Legion
British Reserve
Cavalry of the Legion after British Line broke.
Wassamasaw Road to Charleston.
Monk's Corner Road.
Gaillards Road
Compiled and Drawn by Col. Carrington.

insubordination." Here the American line "got into irretrievable confusion," and the officers were left without soldiers to command and exposed to a devastating fire from the brick house, which now functioned much like the Chew mansion at the Battle of Germantown. The Americans, "unconscious or unmindful of consequences. . . bent on the immediate fruition of [their] advantages, dispersing among the tents, fastened upon the liquors and refreshments they afforded and became utterly unmanageable." Many were shot down in the act of looting.

In this situation the British counterattacked. Hampton met the counterattacking force and after a sharp battle drove it back. He then pursued it to the palisaded garden, where he came under such "fatally destructive" fire that his men were killed or driven off in full retreat. At this point the American artillery had been brought up to fire on the house, but it was brought too near, and the defenders killed or wounded the artillerymen before they could deliver effective fire. At this moment Majoribanks' men rushed forward, seized the artillery, and dragged it under the cover of the house. The Americans had no choice except to withdraw. The casualties on both sides had been unusually heavy. Once again Greene had been denied a victory. This time his little army had fought, on the whole, with exemplary bravery in the field. But that lack of discipline that had so often proved fatal before once more overtook him when victory seemed in his grasp. A triumph at Eutaw Springs would have crowned Greene's long and heroic struggle in the South with the laurels that he so well deserved.

The concluding large-scale engagement in the South, Eutaw Springs inspired the poet of the American Revolution, Philip Freneau, to write a poem entitled, "At Eutaw Springs the Valiant Died."

> At Eutaw Springs the valiant died;
> Their limbs with dust are covered O'er—
> Weep on, ye springs, your tearful tide;
> How many heroes are no more!
>
> If in this wreck of ruin, they
> Can yet be thought to claim a tear,
> O smite your gentle breast and say
> The friends of freedom slumber here!
>
> They saw their injured country's woe:
> The flaming town, the wasted field;
> Then rushed to meet the insulting foe;
> They took the spear—but left the shield.

Led by thy conquering genius, Greene,
The Britons they compelled to fly;
None distant viewed the fatal plain,
None grieved in such a cause to die—

But like the Parthian, famed of old,
Who, flying, still their arrows threw,
These routed Britons, full as bold,
Retreated and retreating slew.

Now rest in peace, our patriot band;
Though far from nature's limits thrown,
We trust they find a happier land,
A brighter sunshine than their own.

12

The Siege of Yorktown

A T Williamsburg, the soldiers of the Continental Army were hardly aware that the fate of Cornwallis was being settled by a battle between the French and British fleets; even in Lieutenant Feltman's diary there is no mention of the engagement. But by the time Washington arrived in Williamsburg at four o'clock on the afternoon of September 15, everyone knew that Graves and Hood had sailed off and had abandoned the British troops at Yorktown to their fate.

The arrival of Washington and Rochambeau called, of course, for a full-scale military review. Colonel St. George Tucker, hurrying back to his camp to form his brigade on parade, saw the Marquis de Lafayette dash up impetuously to Washington and throw his arms about him "with an ardor not easily described."

The Comte de Saint-Simon invited Washington to ride through the French lines, and the soldiers, in their immaculate uniforms, "cut a most splendid figure." The general came next to the Continental line, where he was saluted by cannon. By now he had acquired a considerable retinue of men, women, and children, drawn by the news that the savior of his country had reached his army.

Washington made George Wythe's house his headquarters. "Cornwallis may now tremble for his fate," Tucker wrote his wife, "for nothing but some extraordinary interposition of his guardian angels seems capable of saving him and his whole army from captivity. . . ."

It is not hard to imagine Washington's feelings when De Grasse sent word on September 23 that, with the season of coastal storms coming on, he felt obliged to leave Lynnhaven Bay and head for the Indies. Knowing Washington's temper, we can hardly doubt that he had a few bitter thoughts about the French alliance, which had promised so much and delivered so little. If, with his trap ready to be sprung and Cornwallis caught in the "pudding bag," De Grasse sailed away, everything would go for nought—the elaborate stratagems at New York, the weary march south, the weeks of planning and waiting.

"I cannot conceal from your Excellency," Washington wrote several days later when he had had a chance to get possession of himself, "the painful anxiety under which I have labored since the receipt of the letter with which you honored me on the 23rd inst. . . . Give me leave in the first place to repeat to Yr Excellency that the enterprise against York under the protection of your Ships is as certain as any military operation can be rendered by a decisive superiority of strength and means . . . and that the surrender of the british Garrison will be so important in itself and its consequences, that it must necessarily go a great way towards terminating the war, and securing the invaluable objects of it to the Allies." The departure of De Grasse from the Chesapeake area would permit the evacuation or reinforcement of Cornwallis and thus "would frustrate these brilliant prospects, and the consequences would be not only the disgrace and loss of renouncing an enterprise, upon which the fairest expectations of the Allies have been founded, after . . . uncommon exertions and fatigues; but the disbanding of the whole Army for want of provisions." In the course of his long letter, Washington "earnestly entreated" De Grasse not to undo all that had been so painstakingly done. There would never again be such an opportunity to strike a decisive blow. Even "momentary absence" of the French fleet could have the most disastrous consequences.

Lafayette, who undoubtedly helped frame the letter, was the messenger, and he added his considerable powers of persuasion to Washington's. All he could say as a Frenchman and as a soldier he must have said to De Grasse, and if he did the Revolution no other service, he would have placed America in his debt for his role in helping to persuade De Grasse not to abandon their common task.

At Williamsburg, Ebenezer Denny noted that "the presence of so many general officers, and the arrival of new corps, seemed to give

Siege
of
Yorktown.

American.
French.
British.

YORK RIVER.

Legion of Rangers
Reg* of Gloucester

Guadaloupe
Charon

F* Fusileers
St Simon

Reg* of Touraine
Reg* of Agenois
Reg* of Hainenois

Sunken Vessel taken by Americans.
Redoubt taken by French.
Redoubt taken by French.

Four British Redoubts occupied by French

F
Parallel
Second Parallel

Saintonge
Soisonnois
Deux Ponts
Bourbon

F
A
A
A

Moors House

First Parallel
American Hospital

WORMELEY'S CREEK

Place of Surrender.

L* Infantry.
Virginia Militia
Gov* Nelson
American Hospital

Baron Viomenils

French Artillery

MARYLAND
VIRGINIA
PENN'S
Lafayette
Baron Steuben
NEW YORK

American Artillery

Road to Hampton.

Rhode Island
New Jersey
Sappers and Miners
Gen* Clinton

Adj* Gen*
Guards
Rochambeau

Qr Master Gen*

Washington

☐ Artificers
☐ Laboratory
☐ Magazine

Compiled and Drawn by Col. Carrington

additional life to everything; discipline the order of the day. In all directions troops seen exercising and manoeuvring. Baron Steuben, our great military oracle. The guards attend the grand parade at an early hour, where the Baron is always found waiting with one or two aids on horseback. These men are exercised and put through various evolutions and military experiments for two hours—many officers and spectators present; excellent school, this. At length the day of the parade comes on. The guards are told off; officers take their posts, wheel by platoons to the right; fine corps of music detailed for this duty, which strikes up; the whole march off, saluting the Baron and field officer of the day, as they pass. Pennsylvania brigade almost all old soldiers, and well disciplined when compared with those of Maryland and Virginia [Denny was from Pennsylvania]. But the troops from the eastward [New England] far superior to either."

Joseph Martin, as usual, devoted much of his time to trying to scrounge food. He and another sergeant set off with the company cook to collect some provisions from the commissary. There was a long line ahead of them, so they bought a haslet of beef from the butchers and sent the cook off with it, with instructions to have it ready for them when they got back to camp with the supplies. When the two sergeants got back to their tents late at night, they found the cook fast asleep "and not the least sign of cookery going on." They woke him rather rudely.

"Where is the pluck you brought home?"

"I sold it."

"Sold it! What did you sell if for?" Martin asked, though the cook's breath told well enough.

"I don't know."

"If you sold it what did you get for it?"

"If you will have patience, I will tell you," the frightened cook answered, stalling for time.

"Patience," Martin's friend broke out, "it is enough to vex a saint. Here we sent you home to get something in readiness against our return, and you have sold what we ordered you to provide for us and got drunk, and now we must go all night without anything to eat, or else set up to wait a division of the meat and cook it ourselves. What, I say, did you get for it? If anything we can eat at present, say so."

"I will tell you," the cook said; "First, I got a little rum, and next I got a little pepper and—and—then I got a little more rum."

"Well, and where is the rum and pepper you got?"

"I drank the rum," he said; "there is the pepper."

"Pox on you," said the sergeant, "I'll pepper you." He started for the cook, but Martin, perhaps in anticipation of future meals, intervened to save the cook from a drubbing.

A few days later, in Martin's words, "we prepared to move down and pay our old acquaintance, the British, at Yorktown, a visit. . . . They thought, 'The fewer the better cheer.' We thought, 'The more the merrier.' We had come a long way to see them and were unwilling to be put off with excuses."

It was the twenty-eighth before the American and French armies were deployed at Yorktown. That night Washington and his staff "slept in the field without any other covering than the canopy of the heavens and the small spreading branches of a tree." The American troops took up their positions on the right, the French on the left. On the thirtieth, the British quite inexplicably retired from their outer works at Pigeon Quarter and the high ground adjacent to it, leaving a redoubt that was promptly occupied by the Americans. The same day Colonel Alexander Scammel, who had fought bravely in half a dozen engagements, was captured by the British while he was reconnoitering and was shot in the back after he had surrendered.

Work now started in earnest on parallel trenches, which were under heavy fire from British eighteen-pounders. Over three hundred and fifty shells were counted from sunrise to sunset one day, and the British also kept up a heavy fire through the nights. Colonel Richard Butler of the Pennsylvania Line noted that the Americans had yet to fire an artillery piece at the British lines. "Indeed," he wrote, "I discover very plainly that we are young soldiers in a seige; however, we are determined to benefit ourselves by experience, one virtue we possess, that is perseverance. . . ." On October 4, as the trenching went forward doggedly, the British fire slackened, and deserters brought the encouraging word that many of the British troops were ill, that they were crowded together in close and uncomfortable quarters, and that their cavalry were very short of fodder.

The American soldiers were still clad in rags, and one of them "ventured to prophesy . . . that if the war is continued through the winter, the British troops will be scared at the sight of our men, for as they never fought with naked men, the novelty of it will terrify them."

During the siege of Yorktown, Joseph Martin saw "in the woods herds of Negroes which Lord Cornwallis (after he had inveigled them from their proprietors) . . . had turned adrift, with no other recompense for their confidence in his humanity than the smallpox for their bounty and starvation and death for their wages. They might be seen scattered about in every direction, dead and dying, with pieces of ears of burnt Indian corn in the hands and mouths, even of those that were dead."

As the preparations for the siege progressed, one-third of the army worked on fatigue each day, making gabions, fascines, and saucissons and building bases for the heavy artillery. Covering parties, up to a regiment in strength, "lay all night on their arms" to protect the working parties. There was constant patrolling by both the Americans and the British. American engineers went out to reconnoiter, accompanied by escort parties; there were frequent exchanges of fire. "This business," Denny wrote, "reminds me of a play among the boys, called Prison-base."

At Gloucester the Duc de Lauzun, whose romantic and erotic memoirs give such a vivid picture of life at the French Court, was second in command to General Weedon—"a good enough soldier," Lauzun wrote, "but one who hated war . . . and went in deadly fear of coming under fire." At Lauzun's urging Rochambeau sent artillery and eight hundred French soldiers under the Marquis de Choisy, who, as an officer senior to Weedon, took command of the troops around Glouces-ter. Lauzun described Choisy as "a good and gallant man, ridiculously violent, always making scenes with everyone, and entirely devoid of common sense." He began inauspiciously by "finding fault with General Weedon and all the militia, told them they were cowards, and in five minutes had them almost as frightened of himself as of the English, which is certainly saying a good deal." At Gloucester Tarleton came seeking "the French duke," and Lauzun's cavalry engaged sharply with the leader of the famous Loyal Legion. As Tarleton rode toward Lauzun with his pistol raised, his horse was knocked down by one of his own dragoons. Before Lauzun could capture him, Tarleton's cavalry rode to his rescue. But the honors of the day clearly went to the Frenchman.

On October 5 Joseph Martin, with his sappers and miners, went forward in a heavy rain to assist the engineers in laying out the works. The engineer officers marked out the proposed trenches and indicated to the sappers, who followed them with their arms full of pine lathes, where to place the sticks. The officers then told Martin and his men to stay where they were until they returned, and they disappeared into the darkness. The sappers and miners crouched in the rain, feeling alarm-ingly exposed hardly a hundred yards from the British lines; they knew that under the rules of warfare they could expect no quarter if they were captured. While they waited, a large figure in a greatcoat loomed up out of the blackness, asked them what they were about, warned them not to reveal they were miners and sappers if captured, and went off in search of the engineers. A few minutes later he returned with the officers, and the men discovered that their interrogator had been Washington himself. "Had we dared," Martin wrote, "we might have cautioned him for exposing himself so carelessly to danger at such a time, and doubtless he would have taken it in good part if we had."

The rain interrupted the work, but the next night, October 6, the rest of the trenches were outlined, and soldiers began to dig after Washington had struck a few ceremonial blows with a pickax. While fires were built in another section to distract the attention of the British, the soldiers worked quickly and silently in the sandy soil, and by morning they had dug deep enough to afford themselves protection from enemy fire. When morning came the British discovered the Americans "literally under their noses and tried firing artillery but without effect. As each shot was fired from one particular piece a large bulldog chased the projectile out toward the American trenches. Some soldiers wanted to capture the animal and fix an insolent message to its collar, but," Martin noted, "he looked too formidable for any of us to encounter."

Slowly the noose was tightened. Gabions were made in great numbers and carried forward under the cover of darkness to provide protection for the sappers. By the seventh, batteries were ready to have artillery implaced in them and the trenches to be occupied with soldiers. A ceremony was made of the occasion, with drums beating and colors flying. The light infantry division was given the honor of occupying the trenches, and the flag was planted on the parapet with the motto, *Manus haec inimica tyrannis*. Then with a show of bravado that startled the British, the light infantry mounted the parapet above the trenches and there, within easy range of the British guns, went through the manual of arms: shouldering arms, presenting arms, aiming, and then grounding their pieces. To the British who watched this bold maneuver, it must have seemed a portent of things to come. The order for this bit of showmanship had been given by Colonel Alexander Hamilton. At least one officer (and doubtless many men) thought it a reckless and ill-considered gesture. James Duncan of the Pennsylvania Line noted, "Although I esteem him [Hamilton] one of the first officers in the American army, must beg leave in this instance to think he wantonly exposed the lives of his men. . . ." He also undoubtedly exposed his own career. If British cannoneers had been waiting by their pieces with lighted matches and the Americans had been riddled by a volley of grapeshot, Hamilton's reputation would hardly have survived the incident. On the other hand, I suppose it could be said in Hamilton's defense that he realized that the chances of the British artillery being loaded and ready to fire at that particular moment were relatively slight; it was even less likely that they would have been loaded with grape and cannister.

On the following night, in the face of a continuing cannonade, a large battery was emplaced on the British left; it consisted of three 29-pounders, three 18-pounders, two 10-inch mortars, and two 8-inch howitzers. The French the same night mounted a battery of eight 18- and 12-pounders, two mortars, and two howitzers. In the center a grand battery was mounted of twelve 32-, 24-, and 18-pounders, with six mortars and six howitzers. Even from the American lines it was evident that the British were "embarrassed, confused and indeterminate." The next day, at three o'clock in the afternoon, the French and American batteries were at last ready to fire. The honor of touching the first match to the cannon fell to the commander in chief. Washington laid the match on the touchhole of a thirty-two pounder, and the three batteries began their fire. Those of General Lamb and the Comte de Saint-Simon "opened with great elegance. . . . The shot and shells flew incessantly through the night, dismounted the guns of the enemy and destroyed many of their embrasures." It was a brilliant pyrotechnic display, the greatest by far of the war.

According to Martin, the signal to open fire in the line of batteries was the hoisting of the American flag. "I confess I felt a secret pride swell my heart," Martin wrote, "when I saw the 'star-spangled banner' waving majestically in the very face of our implacable adversaries; it appeared like an omen of success to our enterprise. . . ."

When the American bombardment began, it was more severe than anything the British had hitherto experienced in America. Bombs of a hundred to two hundred pounds were fired by howitzers. Many of these burst in the air or on impact with devastating effect. The cannonballs were also of large caliber—eighteen, twenty-four and thirty-six pounders that shredded the British defenses. Those civilians who remained in Yorktown fled with such possessions as they could carry to the sandy cliffs along the river and there dug into the banks to try to protect themselves from the bombardment. "But there also," a Hessian soldier noted, "they did not stay undamaged; for many were badly injured and mortally wounded by the fragments of bombs, which exploded partly in the air and partly on the ground, their arms and legs severed or themselves struck dead." Several British ships in the river were set afire by hot shot from the French batteries.

On October 11, the French and Americans fired 3,600 shots, "at the town, our line, and at the ships in the harbor," according to Private Doehla of the Ansbach Regiment. "The bombs and cannonballs," he wrote, "hit many inhabitants and negroes of the city, and marines, sailors, and soldiers. One saw men lying nearly everywhere who were mortally wounded and whose heads, arms, and legs had been shot off. . . . Likewise on watch and on post in the lines, on trench and work details, they were wounded by the fearfully heavy fire. . . . I saw bombs fall into the water and lie there for 5, 6–8 and more minutes and then still explode, which was so repulsive and horrible in the water that one can scarcely believe it. It showered upon the river bank the sand and mud from below; if one sat there, it felt like the shocks of an earthquake." A constant stream of wounded men were "continually dragged and carried down by the water and loaded on boats to be rowed out to hospital ships, where they were scarcely safer than they had been in the town. Some cannonballs flew over Yorktown and pierced the hulls of several ships before they lost their momentum. Some skipped across the river like flat stones thrown by a boy and struck soldiers on the Gloucester side."

"A tremendous and incessant" fire was kept up from the American batteries, in the phrase of Dr. James Thacher. Red-hot shells from the French batteries on the left of the American lines near the river set three British vessels on fire including a forty-four-gun frigate, making a "splendid conflagration." The ships were enwrapped in a torrent of fire, according to Thacher, who saw flames "spreading with vivid brightness along the combustible rigging, and running with amazing rapidity to the tops of the several masts, while all around was thunder and lightning from our numerous cannon and mortars, and in the darkness of night, [it] presented one of the most sublime and magnificent spectacles which can be imagined. Some of our shells, overreaching the town, are seen to fall into the river, and, bursting, throw up columns of water like the spouting of the monsters of the deep."

While the bombardment of the British fortifications went on, the trenches of the second parallel were completed and batteries emplaced within three hundred yards of the British lines. At daylight the British increased their cannonading in a frantic effort to dismount the American guns. Each day Cornwallis's situation deteriorated. While casualties were suffered on both sides (Thacher had to take time from his journal to amputate a wounded soldier's leg above the thigh), the British took much the heavier losses, without any apparent hope of extricating themselves. Thacher, taking his turn in the trenches every other day, watched the artillery duel in awe: "The bombshells from the besiegers and the besieged are incessantly crossing each others' paths in the air. They are clearly visible in the form of a black ball in the day, but in the night they appear like a fiery meteor with a blazing tail, most beautifully brilliant, ascending majestically from the mortar to a certain altitude and gradually descending to the spot where they are destined to execute their work of destruction."

Thacher was amazed at the accuracy of the artillerymen. He noted that "an experienced gunner will make his calculations, that a shell will fall within a few feet of a given point, and burst at the precise time [this depended on calculating the time of flight of the projectile and cutting the fuse at the right length to go off shortly after impact] . . . When a shell falls, it whirls round, burrows, and excavates the earth to a considerable extent and, bursting, makes dreadful havoc around."

The work of pushing the siege lines was impeded by two large British redoubts, well in front of the main British works, which threatened to enfilade the trenches at one point. It was thus decided to make an assault on them. The one on the left of the British lines near the river was assigned to a brigade of light infantry under the command of Lafayette, with the assault wave led by Alexander Hamilton. The attack was to be by bayonet, and at eight o'clock in the evening, the Americans, behind heavy supporting fire, placed fascines (or gabions) over the ditch and mounted the works. The fighting was brief and bitter. With the redoubt breeched, the outnumbered British fled for their own lines. Eight Americans were killed and thirty wounded. Thacher, called up to attend the injured, saw the British commander of the redoubt, Major Campbell, who was already wounded, being threatened with death by an infantry captain in retaliation for the killing of Colonel Scammel; but Hamilton intervened, and in Thacher's words, "not a man was killed after he ceased to resist." The British lost nine or ten killed, several wounded, and thirty captured.

During the attack the whole British line poured out artillery and musket fire to protect the redoubt. Washington, Lincoln, and Knox, who stood watching the attack, seemed to Colonel David Cobb, one of Washington's aides, to be dangerously vulnerable to enemy fire.

"Sir," Cobb said, "you are too much exposed here. Had you not better step a little back?"

"Colonel Cobb," Washington replied, "if you are afraid, you have liberty to step back."

While the Americans attacked the redoubt on the left, the French attacked the one on the right; that assault was led by Baron de Vioménil. The French, anxious to prove that they were even more valorous than their allies, attacked so recklessly that they lost almost a hundred men killed and wounded, while the defenders of the redoubt had eighteen killed and forty-five men and officers captured.

On October 13, the allies pushed their lines closer. "All day there were many killed and wounded in all regiments," Doehla wrote, "but especially among the light infantry." The attrition continued—the dead, the wounded, and the deserters. "Since this siege," Doehla wrote, "there have altogether many men deserted to the enemy from us, the English, and the Hessians."

If the beleaguered Cornwallis still clung to the hope of being rescued from his predicament, he dreamed in vain. It was true that a relief expedition of five thousand troops had been embarked in New York, ready to sail at a moment's notice. Fire ships had been prepared with the intention of using them to spread confusion in the French fleet, under the cover of which the British transports might sail up the York and disembark their troops. The damaged ships of Graves's fleet had been repaired, and Admiral Robert Digby had arrived with additional vessels to reinforce Graves and Hood. Even with Digby's squadron, the combined fleet fell well short of the naval force under De Grasse's command, but as Hood wrote to a friend in the British Admiralty, "*Desperate* cases require *bold* remedies." Hood, who was determined to try to go to the aid of Cornwallis, blamed the delay on the vacillation of Graves, of whose ability he thought "very meanly. . . . I know he is a *cunning* man," he added, "he may be a good theoretical man, but he is certainly a bad practical one," as he had proved in the action off the Capes of the Chesapeake.

At Yorktown, meanwhile, the second parallel was immediately connected with the two redoubts, and plans were made to emplace batteries in them to help "convince his lordship that his post is not invincible, and that submission must soon be his only alternative. . . . Many of the enemy's guns are entirely silenced, and their works are almost in ruins."

Early in the morning of the sixteenth came the inevitable counterattack. Three hundred and fifty men under the command of Lieutenant Colonel Robert Abercromby were ordered to attack the two most advanced American batteries and spike the guns. Lieutenant Colonel Gerard Lake with a detachment of guards and grenadiers attacked one battery, and Major Armstrong, leading the light infantry, assaulted the other. Both positions were forced, and eleven guns in the French battery were spiked, with a number of French soldiers killed and wounded. It was a hollow victory, however. In Cornwallis's own words, it "proved of little public advantage, for the cannon having been spiked in a hurry, were soon rendered fit for service. . . ."

Boudinot relates that Washington, failing to prevail on De Grasse to hold his blockade, decided on a stratagem to hasten Cornwallis's surrender before the restless De Grasse could sail away. He devised some pretext to send Hamilton and several other officers under a flag of truce to discuss "some business." Hamilton's party carried food and drink and met a similar group of British officers between the lines. There, in a polite picnic, Hamilton mentioned casually that Washington had decided to storm the British lines, expressing at the same time regret that so many gallant officers and men must be killed in such an assault. Unfortunately, Hamilton added, the temper of some of the Southern soldiers was such that Washington might find it difficult to prevent them from slaughtering the British soldiers and officers once they had entered the enemy lines. "They knew Gen. Washington's humane Temper, and his wish to avoid the unnecessary shedding of blood." The Americans then suggested, according to Boudinot, what terms of surrender would be acceptable to Washington. The tale is an engaging one. Boudinot, as occasional chief of Washington's intelligence service, plainly liked such stories of intrigue.

To Cornwallis, waiting for help that did not come, the only hope for escape appeared to be to abandon all his military equipment and try to carry the bulk of his army by boat across the York under the cover of darkness. Once on the Gloucester side, he could retreat to Head of Elk and await assistance there, or perhaps begin the campaign in Virginia and Maryland that he had advocated so strongly. In any event he would buy time, and time was what he desperately needed. It was inconceivable that the French naval supremacy in American waters would remain long unchallenged; even at that moment, Cornwallis believed, British ships must be assembling. Almost half of his command were sick or injured. Morale was as low as the dwindling supplies of food. While the endless allied bombardment did more damage to the spirits than the bodies of the defenders, the gradual attrition of the British army through death and injury with no end in sight increased the general demoralization. Cornwallis felt abandoned and betrayed. Against his better judgment he had done what he had been told to do (or at least what he thought he had been told to do), and Clinton had left him high and dry.

Plans went forward to slip across the river under the cover of darkness. Word was sent to Tarleton to prepare to join in an attack on Choisy before daybreak. The commanding officers of regiments were informed of the intended movement, and sailors and soldiers from Gloucester were dispatched with boats to bring off the Yorktown garrison. Everything went with the smooth efficiency of experienced soldiers. By eleven o'clock at night on the sixteenth, the light infantry and part of the brigade of guards had already crossed the river without intervention by the allies. Cornwallis was ready to cross with the second echelon and had written a letter to be sent to Washington soliciting his care for the British sick and wounded who would have to be left behind. Part of the second division had already embarked when a heavy squall blew up, scattering the boats and making passage of the river almost impossible. While the storm raged, Cornwallis waited with a sinking heart for it to subside. When it did, several hours later, precious time had been lost. There was no longer any hope of completing the evacuation before daylight. Reluctantly, Cornwallis sent word to the troops who had crossed the river to return to Yorktown. Again there was a delay, because the boats were on the Yorktown side of the river and had to be rowed over to Gloucester, then the troops had to be embarked and carried back to Yorktown by the weary crews. It was daylight before the movement was completed, and the boats came under allied artillery fire as they approached the Yorktown side. In Tarleton's words: "Thus expired the last hope of the British army."

It was another day before Cornwallis could bring himself to accept the fact that there was no alternative to surrender except to see his soldiers die before his eyes of disease, cannon fire, and starvation.

Thus on the morning of October 17 Ebenezer Denny and the troops manning the American lines "had the pleasure of seeing a drummer mount the enemy's parapet, and beat a parley, and immediately an officer, holding up a white handkerchief, made his appearance outside their works; the drummer accompanied him, beating. . . . An officer from our lines ran out and met the other, and tied the handkerchief over his eyes. . . . Firing ceased totally."

That same morning the Hessian Doehla noted: "Early at the break of day, the bombardment began again from the enemy side even more horribly than before; they fired from all the redoubts without stopping. Our detachment, which stood in the hornwork, could scarcely avoid the enemy's bombs, howitzer shot, and cannon balls any more; one saw nothing but bombs and balls raining on our whole line." Cornwallis, convinced at last that there was no way out of the trap he had placed himself in, sent out a flag of truce.

There was only sporadic firing during the rest of the day, and the next morning the batteries on both sides of the lines were silent. "We greatly enjoyed ourselves," Doehla wrote, "after the great loss of sleep, the work, and hardships which we had experienced day and night with the greatest danger to our lives. . . . I for my part," the private added, "had indeed just cause to thank my God that He was my Protector, mighty Helper, and Deliverer, who had so graciously preserved my life throughout the siege, and had guarded my body and all its members from sickness, wounds and every enemy shot. Oh! how many 1,000 cannon balls have I escaped, with danger to my life dangling before my eyes!"

Cornwallis proposed a cessation of hostilities for twenty-four hours in order that representatives of the respective armies might meet at the Moore House to discuss the terms of surrender. Washington replied with an offer of a two-hour suspension of hostilities; he may have privately doubted that he had twenty-four hours to spare. Cornwallis responded by proposing that the British troops be sent back to Britain and the Germans to Germany "under engagement not to serve against France, America, or their allies" for the duration of the war.

On the eighteenth, Washington replied by emphatically rejecting Cornwallis's proposal to return the prisoners of war to their home countries. The same terms would be granted to the British that had been granted to the American prisoners at Charles Town. The British army should surrender to the Americans, the British navy to the French. Officers were to keep their side arms and personal belongings. The British troops would be sequestered for the remainder of the war in Virginia, Maryland, or Pennsylvania. Cornwallis and other senior officers were to be allowed to return to England. "The garrison at York," the terms of surrender read, "will march out to a place to be appointed in front of the posts, at two o'clock precisely with shouldered arms, colours cased, and drums beating a British or German march. They are then to ground their arms, and return to their encampments, where they will remain until they are dispatched to the places of their destination." The garrison at Gloucester was to surrender an hour later. Cornwallis had two hours to reach a decision before hostilities would be renewed. Cornwallis negotiated safe passage for certain of his officers and for his dispatches to Clinton, and that concluded the matter.

Word of the negotiations and the impending capitulation spread through the American camp like wildfire, and Dr. Thacher spoke for many of his fellows when he wrote exultantly in his journal on the morning of October 19, "This is to us a most glorious day, but to the English, one of bitter chagrin and disappointment. Preparations are now making to receive as captives that vindictive, haughty commander and that victorious army, who, by their robberies and murders, have so long been a scourage to our brethren of the Southern states."

Two hours before the British were due to march out, the French and the American soldiers were drawn up in lines extending for over a mile, the Americans on the right side of the road, the French on the left. The two armies made a striking contrast: the handsomely attired French soldiers with their elegant and aristocratic officers, resplendent in gold and silver braid; the Americans affecting a kind of tattered jauntiness, their uniforms, if they had them, patched and faded. At least they were, for one of the few times in the war, adequately shod, and their muskets and bayonets flashed in the sun. In the front line were the soldiers of the Continental Line, who "appeared tolerable enough." Behind them stood the militia, mainly those of Virginia and Maryland, "who looked rather badly tattered and torn." At the head of the American line, "the great American commander, mounted on his noble courser, took his position, attended by his aides." It was the ultimate moment for Washington, a moment that was balm to all the wounds of frustration, disappointment, and outright despair that he had suffered; all the defeats, the embarrassments, the humiliations endured by a proud and ambitious man would now be washed away. As he sat astride that "noble courser" he did not look like a gambler who had staked everything on one lucky throw of the dice and now claimed the pot. Those who viewed that impassive countenance could not have guessed at the intensity of the feelings within, or that the outcome was anything but the carefully contrived and inevitable consequence of an impeccable strategy.

At the head of the French line was Comte de Rochambeau. The French band played sprightly music featuring the timbrel—"a delightful novelty . . . [which] produced . . . a most enchanting effect." Every French regiment flew while silk colors bearing three silver lilies. The drummers and fifers made spirited music, and the soldiers "appeared very well, they were good looking, tall, well-washed men" with white gaiters, their uniform facings red, white and green.

Behind the long lines of soldiers were clusters of civilians, men, women and children, who had come from miles away to witness the glorious event.

Finally, after a long hour of waiting, the British troops marched out "with slow and solemn step," the drums and fifes playing the dirgelike tune of "The World Turned Upside Down," a tune that had been heard at Saratoga. One of the final ironies was in the splendid appearance of the British soldiers. The night before the surrender Cornwallis had "opened his stores and directed that every soldier be furnished with a new suit complete." But "in their line of march," Thacher noted with obvious satisfaction, the beauty proved only uniform-deep; "we remarked a disorderly and unsoldierly conduct, their step was irregular and their ranks frequently broken." The soldiers were defeated, however their uniforms might belie it.

As the British marched out of their fortifications at Yorktown, they looked away from the Americans and fixed their eyes on the French as though to say, "We are surrendering to you, the French, true soldiers and worthy enemies, and not to this American rabble." Lafayette, observing this "affectation," ordered the band to play "Yankee Doodle," and noted with satisfaction that the British "turned their heads at the sound of the tune."

Claude Blanchard also observed that "the English displayed much arrogance and ill-humour during this melancholy ceremony." After the surrender, the Hessian troops maintained much better order than the British, who, Blanchard noted, "were proud and arrogant. There was no call for this," he added; "they had not even made a handsome defense, and, at this very moment, were beaten and disarmed by peasants who were almost naked, whom they pretended to despise, and who, nevertheless, were their conquerors."

What Thacher quite rightly called "the last act of the drama" was the bitterest. "Here their mortification could not be concealed." Their lieutenants choked on the command "ground arms," and Thacher was "a witness that they preformed this duty in a very unofficer-like manner; and that many of the soldiers manifested a *sullen temper,* throwing their arms on the pile with violence, as if determined to render them useless."

General Lincoln, who had had to surrender to Clinton at Charles Town, now saw the tables reversed and superintended the details of the surrender. Another matter for satisfaction was that the friction between the French and American soldiers, which had broken out from time to time in violent brawls, was notably absent from the Yorktown operation. "Harmony, confidence and friendly intercourse" took the place of the usual tensions.

It was not surprising to Thacher to see the British chagrin at their humiliation, "as they have always entertained an exalted opinion of their own military prowess and affected to view the Americans as a contemptible and undisciplined rabble." Cornwallis, who had enjoyed so many triumphs, sulked in his tent, given up "entirely to vexation and despair." Pleading bad health, he sent General Charles O'Hara, now his second-in-command, with instructions to deliver his sword, if possible, to Rochambeau rather than to Washington. It was a gesture so "ungentlemanly," so grudging and ungracious, as to reveal once more, in the hour of defeat, the deeper feelings of the British for the "rebels." The Americans were, in simple fact, still presumptuous upstarts to most of the members of the British ruling class. The career of Lord Cornwallis, a peer of the realm, a tough and skillful soldier, had reached its bitter nadir. Rochambeau refused to accept the proffered sword, and O'Hara had to turn, with all eyes upon him, and cross the road to present Cornwallis's sword to Washington.

After the British and Hessian troops had passed between the two lines, they came to a large field encircled by a squadron of French cavalry. There the British and Hessian regiments in succession stacked their arms. Many of the men and officers wept as they did so.

"As everything was now over," Doehla wrote, "we marched back through the two armies—but in silence into our lines and camp, having nothing more than our few effects in the packs on our backs. All spirit and courage which at other times animated the soldiers had slipped from us, especially inasmuch as the Americans greatly jeered at us like conquerors as we marched back through the armies." The 7,171 soldiers and officers who surrendered were accompanied by 63 wives and 14 children. Among the captured booty were military chests containing over five thousand pounds sterling. In addition, 191 guns of all calibers were captured, including 29 mortars throwing shells of from 25 to 120 pounds, and 31 heavy cannon and siege guns. Four frigates and thirty-nine transports were among the eighty-two British ships in the river that surrendered, and the officers, sailors, and marines on board added another 1,140 to the number of prisoners.

That night Denny noted in his journal, "much confusion and riot among the British through the day; many of the soldiers were intoxicated; several attempts made in the course of the night to break open the stores; an American sentinel killed by a British soldier with a bayonet. . . . Negroes lie about sick and dying, in every stage of the smallpox. Never was in so filthy a place. The supplies of clothing in the town were divided among the officers to the value of sixty dollars a piece."

The next day Cornwallis wrote to the superior for whom he had a cold contempt to inform him that he had surrendered the troops under his command, and by implication to blame Clinton and vindicate himself. He would, he told Clinton, never have remained at Yorktown to be caught in a trap if he had not been "assured by your Excellency's letters that every possible means would be tried by the navy and army to relieve us."

The day after the surrender, when Lafayette visited Cornwallis with a party of officers, the British general took him aside and showed him a map with a route traced on it by which, Cornwallis declared, he would have crossed the river and marched to South Carolina and the safety of Charles Town. Lafayette assured Cornwallis "that all his efforts would have been in vain, that the Americans would have pursued him and cut off his retreat before he could have escaped from Virginia." Lafayette then went aboard De Grasse's flagship and tried to persuade the commander to sail against Charles Town with an army commanded by Lafayette; De Grasse refused, declaring that his orders required him to go to the West Indies. "Naval officers," Lafayette observed to Jared Sparks, many years later, "are always impatient to be on their own element, and never contented to act in concert with land forces."

The Duc de Lauzun was chosen by Rochambeau to carry the news of Yorktown to France. When the French Revolution came eight years later, Lauzun, then Duc de Biron, first commanded a Revolutionary army and then, falling from favor, was sentenced by the Revolutionary tribunal to go to the guillotine. When the executioner came for him, the duc was found eating oysters; the lover of some of the most fascinating women of the French Court won himself a modest immortality by saying to his executioner, with entire self-possession, "Citizen, allow me to finish," and holding out a glass of wine, added, "take this wine, you must have need of courage, in your calling."

The captured British and Hessian soldiers were marched to Frederick, Maryland, and Winchester, Virginia, the latter a march of two hundred and forty miles. There they were put into abandoned barracks,

"20–30 men to a hut, where we hardly had room to stand. We were imprisoned like dogs," Doehla wrote, "and our rooms were worse than pigstys and dog kennels in Germany."

In these crowded and unhealthy conditions, the prisoners made out as best they could. A number went to work as hired hands for the farmers in the surrounding countryside, for labor was hard to come by and prisoners were in demand for "threshing, spinning, woodcutting and whatever the countrymen have to do." The food was poor; little meat, coarse Indian bread, and half-ground oatmeal were the staples of the prisoners' diet, but most of the soldiers had money and were thus able to supplement their meager fare with "bread, cheese, butter, eggs, and all other kinds of provisions like turnips, potatoes, cabbages, brandy, punch, cider, rum and beer in abundance.... Many of the English bargained and exchanged for rum, brandy, and whisky their entire uniforms from head to foot and covered themselves afterwards only with their blankets or made themselves coats from the same, which they pulled over their bodies or made into greatcoats." Indeed, by contrast with the victorious Americans, now wintering at Newburgh, the prisoners lived very well indeed.

As the events that were to culminate in the surrender of Cornwallis had slowly unfolded, patriots everywhere had waited in a state of hopeful anticipation. Suddenly it appeared that a war that so often seemed destined to drag on interminably until it guttered out like a spent candle might be won by a decisive victory. To those aware of Washington's complicated strategy to trap Cornwallis at Yorktown, the latter days of September and October passed slowly indeed—and nowhere more painfully so than in the halls of Congress. On the sixteenth of October, word reached Philadelphia that Cornwallis had offered to surrender but on terms that were unacceptable to Washington. Finally, at three o'clock on Monday morning, October 22, a messenger rode into the city with word of the capitulation of the British army at Yorktown. It was as though an enormous burden had been lifted from the shoulders of the members of Congress. Euphoria prevailed. Elias Boudinot, writing to his brother, proclaimed that "the glorious Success of the allied Arms" must mark "a Day famous in the annals of american History.... would to God, that a deep sense of Gratitude may follow this remarkable Smile of Heaven at the critical Era."

Boudinot also tells us that when the messenger brought word of Cornwallis's surrender, there was not enough hard money in the

Congressional coffers to pay him for his expenses, "and the Members of Congress, of whom I was one, each paid a Dollar to accomplish it."

On the twenty-fourth, Congress went in a body to the Lutheran Church, "where divine service (suitable to the occasion) was performed" by one of the chaplains of Congress. The supreme executive council and the assembly of the state of Pennsylvania, the minister of France and his secretary, and a large number of the citizens of Philadelphia attended as well. In the evening the city was illuminated with candles and made bright with fireworks, and a large portrait of Washington painted by Charles Willson Peale was hung above Market Street. Everywhere there was a deep conviction that Yorktown must mark the end of Britain's effort to subdue America. "If these severe doses of ill fortune [Yorktown and the British setbacks in the South], do not cool the phrenzy and relax the pride of Britain," James Madison wrote, "it would seem as if Heaven had in reality abandoned her to her folly and her fate. . . . With what hope or with what view can they try the fortune of another campaign?"

The president of Congress, Thomas McKean, wrote in his official capacity to Washington, tendering the congratulations of Congress on Cornwallis's surrender. He then added: "Words fail me when I attempt to bestow my small tribute of thanks and praise to a Character so eminent for wisdom, courage and patriotism and one who appears to be no less the Favorite of Heaven than of his country; I shall only therefore beg you to be assured that you are held in the most grateful remembrance; and with a particular veneration, by all the wise and good in these United States." Washington would always know that he had been the principal instrument "to annihilate the British power in America, which you have so effectually broken by this last capital blow; that you may be ever hailed The Deliverer of your Country, and enjoy every blessing Heaven can bestow, is the sincere and ardent Prayer of one, who professes himself to be, with every sentiment of regard and all possible attachment."

Yorktown, in addition to fixing in the popular mind the image of France as the indispensable instrument of American independence, set the picture of Washington as the victorious "Deliverer" of his country. If, through a different outcome of any of the complex chain of events that left Cornwallis marooned at Yorktown, the British general and his army had been able to escape from Washington's trap and peace had nonetheless come (as it inevitably must have sooner or later) without any dramatic climax, Washington's own reputation would not have stood so high. His perseverance, courage, moral stamina, and qualities of leadership would all have been praised and admired and he himself venerated as the most important single figure in the patriot ranks. But the fact would have remained that from Monmouth, in the spring of 1778—an engagement in which he was more distinguished for personal courage than wisdom or sound strategy—to the end of the war, he had fought and won no major engagement with a British army. This was no fault of Washington's, but it was a fact nonetheless. The most decisive events would then have appeared to be the battles in the South, beginning with Kings Mountain and ending with Greene's victory at Eutaw Springs. And had the battles in the South been the last major engagements of the Revolution, Nathanael Greene, rather than Washington, might well have appeared as the "Deliverer" of America. Certainly Greene's reputation would have stood much higher in relation to that of Washington than it has, and the campaigns of the South would have occupied a much more prominent place in our knowledge of the Revolution than they presently do. In short, important as it undoubtedly was, the victory at Yorktown served to distort our understanding of the Revolution in significant ways.

The Tories were, of course, dismayed at the news of Yorktown. In Philadelphia Anna Rawle, Tory daughter of Tory parents, recorded in her diary the news of Cornwallis's surrender "as surprizing as vexatious." Various members of the family gathered to comfort each other; Joshua Howell, her uncle, looking "as though he had sat up all night. . . . [said] as there is no letter from Washington, we flatter ourselves that it is not true. . . ." Next day the news was official. When the word of the celebration was spread, along with instructions to illuminate all windows, the Rawles left theirs unlighted, and Anna recorded the consequences in her diary to send to her mother. "I suppose, dear Mammy, thee would not have imagined this house to be illuminated last night, but it was. A mob surrounded it, broke the shutters and the glass of the windows, and were coming in, none but forlorn women here. We for a time listened for their attacks in fear and trembling till, finding them grown more loud and violent, not knowing what to do, we ran into the yard. . . . We had not been there many minutes before we were drove back by the sight of two men climbing the fence." The men proved to be friends who ran into the house and "fixed up lights at the windows, which pacified the mob, and after three huzzas they moved off." Other

Tories were forced to illuminate their windows by the same tactics, and Anna wrote that "it was the most alarming scene I ever remember. For two hours we had the disagreeable noise of stones banging about, glass crashing, and the tumultuous voices of a large body of men, as they were a long time at the different houses in the neighbourhood. At last they were victorious, and it was one general illumination throughout the town. As we have not the pleasure of seeing any of the gentlemen in the house, nor the furniture cut up, and goods stolen, nor been beat, nor pistols pointed at our breasts, we may count our sufferings slight as compared to many others."

John Drinker lost half the goods out of his shop. Mrs. Gibbs, who tried to cover the retreat of her fleeing husband, was given a bloody nose. John Waln lost his pickles, which were thrown about the street, and barrels of sugar were stolen from his warehouse. "It seems universally agreed," Anna Rawle wrote, "that Philadelphia will no longer be that happy asylum for the Quakers that it once was. Those joyful days when all was prosperity and peace are gone, never to return; and perhaps it is as necessary for our society to ask for terms as it was for Cornwallis. Juliet says all Uncle Pennington's fine pictures are broken; his parlour was full of men, but it was nothing . . . to Nancy's illness, who was for an hour to two out of her senses and terrified them exceedingly."

The Yorktown victory inspired the following ballad.

> Cornwallis led a country dance,
>   The like was never seen, sir.
> Much retrogade and much advance,
>   And all with General Greene, sir.
> . . . .
> Now hand in hand the circle round
>   This ever-dancing pair, sir:
> Their gentle movements soon confound
>   The earl as they draw near, sir.
> His music soon forgets to play—
>   His feet can move no more, sir,
> And all his bands now curse the day
>   They jigg'd to our shore, sir.
>
> Now Tories all, what can ye say?
>   Come—is not this a griper,
> That while your hopes are danced away,
>   'Tis you must pay the piper?

Philip Freneau, on hearing the glorious news, sat down and wrote "An Ancient Prophecy":

When a certain great king whose initial is G.
Shall force stamps upon paper, and folks to drink tea;
When these folks burn his tea and stampt paper, like stubble,
You may guess that the king is then coming to trouble.
But when a petition he treads under his feet,
And sends over the ocean an army and fleet;
When that army, half starved, and frantic with rage,
Shall be cooped up with a leader whose name rhymes to cage;
When that leader goes home dejected and sad,
You may be assured the king's prospects are bad.

But when B. and C. with their armies are taken,
The king will do well if he saves his own bacon.
In the year seventeen hundred and eighty-two,
A stroke he shall get that will make him look blue
In the years eighty-three, eighty-four, eighty-five,
You shall hardly know that the king is alive;
In the year eighty-six the affair will be over,
And he shall eat turnips that grow in Hanover.
The face of the lion shall then become pale,
He shall yield fifteen teeth and be sheared of his tail.
O king, my dear king, you shall be very sore;
The Stars and the Lily shall run you on shore,
And your lion shall growl—but never bite more.

I have placed considerable emphasis on the fact that the fate of American independence by no means rested on the outcome of the Yorktown campaign. If luck had not been with Washington at every turn, Cornwallis would have gotten off scot-free. But there is no basis for arguing that failure to trap Cornwallis would have brought about a collapse of the struggle for independence and the return of the American states to their former dependence upon Great Britain. The independence of the colonies was irreversible. The Revolution, or, if one prefers, the war, might have dragged on several years longer. In fact, it did drag on several years longer, while the British government absorbed the full implications of the Yorktown disaster and fussed interminably about whose fault it was.

The fact was, as we have said, that the British army had been sent on an impossible task; they had been sent to fight a war against a revolution. Thus all their precious "victories" turned out to be illusory. But since they could not understand this, or since they understood it only dimly (and they can hardly be blamed for this, since historians subsequently have understood it very little better), they kept on fighting. The rebel soldiers in the field understood the situation rather well; and many Englishmen understood it. It was North and his cabinet who could not get the truth through their heads.

This then provides the answer to the question of the role of the French in "winning American independence." We have already presented considerable evidence that the formal French alliance, with the appearance on the American scene of French fleets and French soldiers, represented a distinct setback for the American cause. This may appear ungrateful; the "Lafayette, we are here" syndrome is so deeply rooted that it is not easily plucked out; but for three years the French military and naval alliance was, if not a disaster, a plainly negative element in the Revolutionary struggle. It may be argued that Yorktown redeemed all that. Yorktown was certainly much more a French victory than an American one; even the strategy had been basically Rochambeau's. But Yorktown did not "win American independence"; Yorktown was simply the culmination of a long, long series of frustrations and disappointments interlarded with British "victories" that brought the North ministry finally to the realization that they could not "win" the American Revolution.

The importance of Yorktown has been enhanced by British historians, of course, since by and large they have much preferred to believe that their great rival, France, a foe proved worthy of—if not quite up to—their metal on many a battlefield, was the cause of their undoing, rather than an army of scruffy rebels led by clerks and farmers. To understand this is to banish at once the ancient myth that the French won independence for the Americans at the Battle of Yorktown. It would be much more accurate to say that (by a long sequence of bad decisions) the British won it for the Americans at Yorktown, but even this would misstate the case rather seriously. It would imply that everything—sixteen long years of unremitting struggle to be free and independent—hung on the outcome of one battle, which of course was not really a battle but a siege. It would suggest that one of the great movements of modern history would have been deflected or aborted if De Grasse had not survived Graves's inept attack; and that of course is nonsense, as any reader who has come this far will know. The Americans were to be independent. That was written in the inscrutable ledger of history; the only question to be settled was when and how—this year or next, Yorktown or some other town, Carolina or New York?

If Louis XVI, who certainly didn't give a damn about American freedom and independence, had decided to cut his losses and get out of the game, had decided not to send De Grasse and to order Rochambeau and his troops home, would that have been the end of American independence? You know the answer as well as I. In the words of Elias Boudinot: "The Siege of York Town was merely accidental. . . ."

Having said this, we must still give Yorktown its due. It was a splendid, dramatic way to terminate the large-scale fighting of the Revolution. Instead of simply petering out, in the midst of increasing bitterness and acrimony, the war seemed to have ended in one glorious, smashing victory, a victory that was a tonic for the American spirit and brought with it a revival of patriotic ardor that helped to carry the country through the lengthy period of scattered, minor actions and long, drawn-out negotiations that concluded with the formal treaty of peace more than a year later. From Burgoyne's surrender at Saratoga, which has often (and wrongly, I think) been called "the turning point of the Revolution," to Yorktown was a long three years; a very slow "turning point," one might say. It is true that the news of Saratoga helped to persuade the French to enter into a formal alliance with Congress, but, as we have seen, that was a very mixed blessing. Indeed, if it had not been for Yorktown, one would have to judge the military and naval aspect of the alliance a complete failure. Yorktown saved the reputation of the alliance, so to speak, and gave the American patriots a triumph that they had long hungered for.

Certainly it would have been uncivil as well as ungrateful for Americans to have publicly declared that the French help, so generously given, had fallen far short of expectations. So the myth has persisted, and as myths go it is a relatively harmless one. The only reason to shatter it is to give the full measure of credit to those men and women who labored and sacrificed and often spent their lives to free the American states from a condition of dependence and subordination that, seeming inconsistent with the dignity of free men, had become intolerable to them.

13

Parliament Reacts

Nᴇᴡs of the battle between Graves and De Grasse and of Cornwallis's besieged army reached England by the middle of November. North and his cabinet were at once apprehensive. In the words of Sir Nathaniel Wraxall, the English diarist, "Lord George Germain in particular, conscious that on the prosperous or adverse termination of the expedition must depend the fate of the American contest, his own stay in office as well as probably the duration of the Ministry, felt, and even expressed to his friends, the strongest uneasiness on the subject."

On Sunday, November 25, official word of Cornwallis's surrender arrived at the house of Lord Germain in Pall Mall. Germain's worst fears had been realized; he had at last reaped the fruit of six years of bungling and ineptitude. He scurried off with the dismal news to Lord Stormant, and then to Lord North in Downing Street. North turned pale at Germain's report. The inconceivable had happened. He took the news, as Germain put it, "as he would have taken a ball in his breast," talking wildly, waving his arms, and pacing up and down the room, repeating "O God! it is all over!"

Indeed, it seemed that much was over—the effort to subdue the American colonies, North's own ministry, and possibly, most dire of all, England's hard-won hegemony in the world. It is doubtful, however, that North blamed himself or his ministers for this dark hour. Like most men in such a plight he probably blamed everyone else (certainly there was blame enough to go around): Clinton, Cornwallis, Graves, his enemies in Parliament, the French, and that final resource for victims of their own folly, the fates.

The first question that North and his anxious ministers had to decide was whether to postpone the opening of Parliament, scheduled for two days hence. But that was impractical; members from distant boroughs were on their way, and many had already arrived in London. It was, of course, essential to rewrite the king's address, which "had already been drawn up and completely prepared for delivery from the throne." Meanwhile, word had to be sent to the king, who was at Kew.

After his meeting with North, Germain returned home for dinner with his three daughters, Lord Walsingham, Wraxall, and several other members of his household. None of the other guests knew of the fateful news, and Germain seemed composed if preoccupied. During the meal a message arrived from the king. Germain opened it and read it without comment. When the ladies had withdrawn, Germain told his guests that word had arrived that the first minister of France, the old Comte Maurepas, was near death. To this Wraxall replied, "It would grieve me to finish my career, however far advanced in years, were I First Minister of France before I had witnessed the termination of this great contest between England and America."

"He has survived to witness that event," Germain said.

Wraxall was puzzled. Perhaps Germain referred to the inconclusive naval action between De Grasse and Graves. "My meaning," he replied, "is that if I were the Count de Maurepas, I should wish to live long enough to behold the final issue of the war in Virginia."

"He has survived to witness it completely," answered Germain. "The army has surrendered, and you may peruse the particulars of the capitulation in that paper." Taking a letter from his pocket, he handed it to Wraxall, "not without visible emotion."

Wraxall read it aloud to the rest of the company, and there was some desultory and gloomy conversation about the implications of the surrender. Wraxall was probably not alone in his curiosity about the king's response. It was, after all, the intractability of the king that had, in the last analysis, kept the war going for so long. Germain consented to read the king's letter, "observing, at the same time, that it did the highest honour to his Majesty's fortitude, firmness and consistency of charac-ter"—all, it might be said, the most unfortunate of attributes.

The king's words, which displayed the same stubborn and intractable temper that had so long sustained the war, burned themselves into Wraxall's memory. The king particularly lamented the news "on account of the consequences connected with it and the difficulties which it may produce in carrying on the public business or in repairing such a misfortune. But I trust that neither Lord George Germain nor any member of the Cabinet will suppose that it makes the smallest alteration in those principles of my conduct which have directed me in past time and which will always continue to animate me under every event in the prosecution of the present contest." It is a pity that such indomitable spirit was expended on such a poor cause. The king seemed to be saying that he was determined to carry on the war despite the capitulation of Cornwallis. The faint-hearted might despair, but not their king. Wraxall's comments were filled with an unconscious irony: "What ever opinion we may entertain relative to the practicability of reducing Americans to obedience by force of arms at the end of 1781, we must admit that no sovereign could manifest more calmness, dignity or self-command than George III displayed in his reply."

When Parliament convened on November 27, Lord North, who had tried to resign a half-dozen times since Saratoga, had the thankless task of trying to stave off the attacks of the opposition. All that had been prophesied by his enemies had come to pass, and he, who had long had no stomach for the war, had once more to face the political music, a cacophony of indignant accusations and recriminations. His days and the days of his government were numbered, and this could only have been welcome to him.

The king's address urged an energetic prosecution of the war: "I have no doubt but that by the concurrence and support of my Parliament, by the valour of my fleets and armies, and by a vigorous, animated and united exertion of the faculties and resources of my people, I shall be able to restore the blessings of a safe and honorable peace to all my dominions."

The speech was followed by a barrage of angry questions, and when Parliament took up the matter of supplies, Sir James Lowther rose to ask whether, as a preliminary to such a discussion, it was not proper to inquire whether the ministry was still resolved "to persevere in this war and feed it with more British blood." The fact was that "it had been obstinately, fatally pursued. The country was drained, exhausted, dejected. Their hearts were against it. They considered it as a struggle against nature, in which everything was to be hazarded and nothing to be got. The Speech from the Throne had given them a most serious alarm, it shewed them that ministers were determined to persevere in spite of calamity: that they were bigotted to the prosecution of the contest. . . ." It was the responsibility of the members of Parliament "to do their duty and to discharge their trust to their constituents" by coming to "a specific delcaration on the point" and putting "an end to the war by a preemptory resolution." Lowther thereupon proposed a motion that read: "That it is the opinion of this House that the war carried on in the colonies and plantations of North America has proven ineffectual either to the protection of his Majesty's loyal subjects in the said colonies, or for defeating the dangerous designs of his enemies. . . ."

A member named Powys seconded the motion. "We had," he declared, "persevered in this war against the voice of reason and wisdom, against experience that ought to teach, against calamity that ought to make us feel." The war had become "the idol of his Majesty's ministers, to which they had sacrificed the interests of the empire and almost half the territories: they bowed before it, they made the nation bow. . . . The illusion which had filled the minds of some gentlemen with the hope of seeing America reduced to her former obedience to this country was now no more." He could understand how many honest men had been at first misled by the hope that America could be subdued by arms, but "he could not conceive how it came to pass that now, when the illusion was at an end, when repeated disasters and calamities had proved that the reduction of America by force was impracticable, there could be found a set of honest, independent gentlemen who could persevere in supporting those measures by which the empire had been dismembered and destroyed. That ministers should persevere in the mad plan of pursuing the phantom of conquest in America was not at all surprising to him; on the contrary, it was extremely natural, because to the war they owed their situations and their emoluments, and by a peace they must lose them. . . ." But this was certainly not the case with the at least theoretically "independent gentlemen" who still supported them. Under what delusion? It was plain that England's course had left her without a friend in the company of nations. "We were left to contend alone with our enemies," Powys declared; "abandoned by all the world, we could not find a friend from pole to pole."

Everywhere there were abundant signs "of the decay and fall of a great empire." England at the present moment was comparable to Rome in Gibbon's great history, Powys argued. The war with America was not like ordinary wars "between two rival or two neighboring states about a barrier or a boundary. . . . It was a war in which every conclusion was against us; in which we had suffered every thing without gaining any thing. . . . He called upon gentlemen to say if there was still any hopes, after the disaster in Virginia; if there was still any disposition in their minds to go on? What ray of hope was not blasted! What prospect had not failed! What object was not abandoned!" Nothing could be gained but the perpetuation of the party in power. "It was time, therefore, for parliament to interfere, and to prevent the total ruin which the measures of administration could not fail to bring on, if they should remain unchecked." Lowther's motion for putting an end to the war made no accusations, did not "clog the wheels of government . . . it only asserted a fact which nobody could dispute; of the truth of which the whole world was perfectly acquainted. . . . It went no further than to say that among the operations of the war, America should not be the theatre. . . ."

North, under such fire, tried once more to resign, but the king refused and went so far as to draft a statement of abdication, a remarkable document in which he stated what he doubtless believed to be the case: that he had "had no object so much at heart as the maintenance of the British Constitution. . . ." The difficulties he had encountered from "His scrupulous attachment to the Rights of Parliament" were proof of his devotion to this principle. The rebelliousness of the House of Commons had, he declared, "totally incapacitated Him from either conducting the War with effect, or from obtaining any Peace but on conditions which would prove destructive of the Commerce as well as the essential Rights of the British Nation." It was the constant clamor for peace that the king suggested, was undermining his own plan for bringing the war to an honorable conclusion. George clearly felt that the true enemies of Great Britain were not those determined to pursue a costly, destructive, and ultimately hopeless war, but those who insisted that the war was folly and agitated for an end to it. Attacked and denigrated by Parliament, his effectiveness at an end, he had, he wrote, no choice except to resign.

The rumor of the king's intended abdication, which promptly circulated in the higher circles of government and in Parliament, had a sobering effect on the opposition. For the first time in modern history a British monarch had threatened to abdicate. Such an act would have produced the severest kind of constitutional crisis, a crisis for which Whigs such as Burke, Shelburne, and Fox certainly had no stomach. That George III even considered such a step was an indication of the extremity to which the war had driven his country. Knowing the temperament of George III, his stubbornness and pride, it is unlikely that the draft was simply a bluff. It took some persuasiveness on the part of his ministers to turn him from a course of action that they finally convinced him would be disastrous for the nation, Whig and Tory alike.

Parliament adjourned for Christmas, and when it reconvened the bitter debates in the House of Commons were resumed. Finally, on March 4, 1782, the antiwar members pushed a resolution through the House that characterized as enemies of the country and of the king anyone who made an attempt to continue the war. The resolution was followed by an "enabling act" that enabled, since Parliament could not order it, the king to make a peace or truce with the American states. Two weeks later, on March 19, North, hearing rumors of motions to be made in Parliament that seemed to him little short of treasonous, wrote to the king "in the most decided terms, resigning his employment." The letter reached the king as he was setting out to hunt. He read it without comment, put it in his pocket, and mounted his horse. A page ran after him to say that Lord North requested a reply.

"Tell him," the king said, "that I shall be in town tomorrow morning, and will then give Lord North an answer." Then, turning to his companions on the hunt, the king said, "Lord North has sent me in his resignation; but I shall not accept it."

The word of North's resignation had not spread in London, where gossip usually flew faster than the birds. There "few individuals of either party entertained a doubt of the continuance of the struggle." They were, it might be said, reconciled to a nightmare from which the king refused to let them awake, despite Parliament's opposition. But this time North was adamant; "from weariness and disgust, or apprehension of the consequences that might accrue to his sovereign, to himself and to the country," he was determined to step down as first minister. The fact was that in some quarters the disenchantment with the war (and in others a profound repugnance) had, in the opinion of some experienced observers of the political scene, brought feeling to such a point that some general uprising against the king and his ministers was by no means out of the question. It was this latter point that North undoubtedly emphasized in his meeting with the king. For over an hour George III and his first minister met in camera; when the meeting was over, North was still fixed in his determination to resign.

By this time word had spread that something of a momentous nature was afoot. Usually, as is the custom the world over with legislators, the members of the House straggled in for several hours after the body was called to order in the late afternoon; but on this occasion at least four hundred members had taken their seats before five o'clock. One of the few members missing was North himself. Every time the door at the end of the hall opened, all eyes were directed toward it in anticipation of the first minister's arrival.

Finally North entered in full dress, his ribbon of the Order of the Garter over his coat. Amid cries of "order and places" as the members scurried for their seats, North walked to the Treasury Bench and attempted to address the chair. Lord Surrey, who had given notice of his intention to introduce a motion, had priority and insisted on his right to speak first once the House was called to order. There were cries and shouts from members in every quarter of the room and moments of pandemonium while the chair tried in vain to restore order. North, flushed and tense, finally managed to communicate, above the uproar, that he had an announcement of utmost importance to make, and the opposition bench consented at last to permit him to speak.

"His object was to save the time and trouble of the House," he declared, "by informing them that the administration was virtually at an end; that His Majesty had determined to change his confidential servants; and that he should propose an adjournment, in order to allow time for the new ministerial arrangements which must take place."

The scene that followed North's brief statement was more frantic by far than the one that had preceded it. The opposition benches erupted in cries of triumph and hoots of derision. There were expressions of surprise and delight on the part of the enemies of North, and surprise and dismay on the part of the supporters of the government. It was Wraxall's opinion that "a more interesting scene had not been acted within the walls of the House of Commons since . . . Sir Robert Walpole retired from power" in 1743. Amid all the clamor, Burke gained the floor long enough to urge his friends to temper their "vociferous joy." But, in Wraxall's words, "scarcely could he obtain a hearing amidst the impatience of men who for the first time beheld before their eyes the promised land" of political power and preferment. When one of the friends of the government attempted to pronounce a panegyric on "the personal virtues and amiable qualities of the First Minister," the opposition gave "violent indications of dissatisfaction."

North was at his best in defeat and humiliation. He retained his "equanimity, suavity and dignity" in a way that impressed all but the blindest partisans. Since the members of the House had expected a long session, lasting until midnight, most of them had not ordered up their coaches, and there was a confused milling at the entrance to Parliament while messengers were sent to fetch the vehicles. Lord North, knowing that his request for adjournment would, under the circumstances, undoubtedly be granted, had had the foresight to order his coach to wait. Now, as he stepped forward to enter it, he enjoyed this modest triumph. He turned to the solicitous friends who had accompanied him from the House and said, "Good night, gentlemen, you see what it is to be in the secret."

Horace Walpole wrote to Lady Ossory, "Were I young, and of heroic texture I would go to America."

14

Peace Negotiations

FOLLOWING the news of Yorktown and the resignation of North, which was accepted by Parliament without a division, Charles James Fox, leader of the opposition and supporter of American independence, appeared to be North's logical successor. The King refused to accept Fox as his first minister, however, and offered the government to Lord Shelburne. But Shelburne was unable to form a government, and he was replaced by Rockingham, who formed a new government with Shelburne as secretary of state for the Southern Department (which included home, Irish, and colonial affairs). Fox was appointed secretary of state for the Northern Department, which dealt with foreign affairs. The result was considerable confusion and rivalry between Fox and Shelburne. Did treaty negotiations with America fall properly under the heading of colonial affairs or foreign relations?

Both Fox and Shelburne began to make independent overtures to those Americans who were thought to be authorized to enter into negotiations. Shelburne, after a hint from Franklin that the time might be ripe for discussing terms, dispatched Richard Oswald, a Scottish merchant who had made a fortune in the slave trade and who had spent his youth in Virginia, to France to make contact with Franklin.

Oswald and Franklin began informal discussions in Paris. Franklin enumerated points that in his view were essential in any treaty negotiations with America, among them the acceptance of American independence, the withdrawal of British troops, and "a freedom of Fishing on the Banks of Newfoundland and elsewhere as well as fish for Whales." Franklin had another list of desired though not necessary items, designed, he said, to effect a speedy reconciliation between Britain and the United States. The first point under this heading was the indemnification of all the citizens of the towns that had been burned and destroyed by the British—"This sum not to exceed five or six hundred thousand pounds." If such a settlement were accompanied "by some of acknowledgment . . . of Parliament or otherwise" of the British error "in distressing those countries so much as we had done," such words would "do more good than People could imagine," Franklin wrote. Another conciliatory measure would be to give American ships and merchants the same privileges enjoyed by the merchants of Britain and Ireland. Finally, Franklin suggested that the British give up "every part of Canada." Shelburne was astonished at the presumption of Franklin's suggestions, but the preliminary discussions nonetheless continued.

Oswald's advice to Shelburne was to be tough with France and the other allies and accommodating with America. "They have," he wrote, "shewn a desire to treat and to end with us on a separate footing from the other Powers, and I must say in a more liberal way, or at least with a greater appearance of feeling for the future interests and Connections of Great Britain than I expected . . . and therefore we ought to deal with them tenderly, and as supposed conciliated Friends . . . and not as if we had any thing to give them that we keep from them, or that they are very anxious to have. . . I really believe the Doctor [Franklin] sincerely wishes for a speedy settlement, and that after the loss of Dependence, We may lose no more; but on the contrary, that a cordial Reconciliation may take place over all that country." Oswald was convinced that the American commissioners would not demand the desired articles of the treaty if the necessary terms were readily granted.

Oswald talked at length, confidentially and comfortably, with Franklin, but when, on Franklin's suggestion, Oswald talked with John Jay, the Englishman got a long harangue from that commissioner about the sins of the British. "You seem," Jay said to Oswald, "to think that France ought to consider the Independence of our states as sufficient indemnification for all her expenses in the War." (Although Oswald had never said this to Jay, he had said it on several occasions to Franklin.) "But," Jay continued, "that ought not to be admitted, as it in the first place, puts us under a greater obligation to France than we incline to as if to her alone we are indebted for our Independence." France had made conquests during the war, and Britain could not expect to get back all she had lost in the course of the conflict. Quite true, Oswald replied, but surely America, once independence had been acknowledged by Great Britain, could not be expected to remain at war in order to secure France her conquests.

It had been Oswald's very clear impression, in his conversations with Franklin, "that having got the Grant of Independence, their Treaty with France was at an End. . . ." Thus his "unpleasant reception from Mr. Jay" was thoroughly disconcerting. The exchange is an interesting one because Jay is often depicted as the member of the commission most jealous of France and most determined to pursue an independent course in the treaty negotiations. Here, according to Oswald, he appears most solicitous for the interests of France and quite hesitant about following an independent course. Jay then went on to discuss the nature of the alliances with France, Spain, and Holland, giving Oswald the impression that "the Commissioners of the Colonies would agree or refuse to close with Us according as they should consider the terms which those two last powers shall insist on, to be reasonable or unreasonable."

In a résumé of his conversations with Jay and Franklin, Oswald made a significant comment: "From what has been said, and from any thing I could learn here, there is good reason to apprehend, that the colony Commissioners think much less of their own concerns than of those of Foreign Nations; or rather that they consider their Business as good as settled. . . ." While the dignity of Congress required a formal statement of "Release from their Dependence on Great Britain," the commissioners did not seem concerned enough about that particular issue to "prepare to give peace to G. B. but on condition of our settling with those other Nations. At first France was only named, but now Spain and Holland are included. . . . The Business therefore of those Commissioners at this Place, seems to point at Superintendency over the General Peace, and not only to bring it to a conclusion but upon such terms and conditions, as to them shall seem just and reasonable." Oswald guessed, quite shrewdly, that America had recently concluded treaties with Spain and Holland, which accounted for its new solicitude for those countries.

What seemed increasingly plain to Oswald was that the commissioners saw themselves as dictating a general peace. He had entered into negotiations confident that the grant of independence to the former colonies, plus "a few exchanges or concessions of little consequence," would produce peace between the United States and Great Britain. "But the Affair seems to have taken a different turn," Oswald noted. France had disclaimed any role in the negotiations over independence and had left that to the commissioners and the agents of the British ministry authorized to speak for the government. If Britain (in the person of Oswald) remonstrated with the commissioners over their apparent determination to tie peace to a general settlement, "they plead Treaties, Conscience and Character. . . ."

In addition to his discussions with Franklin, Oswald talked with Vergennes. From his conversations with Franklin and Vergennes, Oswald picked up one other odd and interesting notion. This was that the two men, representing their respective countries, wished a solid and enduring peace, and that Franklin at least believed that such a peace, once agreed to, could be secured by the power of the Congress of the United States. Thus Congress would become the "guarantor of the general Peace"; the commissioners, Oswald wrote, were "convinced that Congress can make it stand for any length of time they please, as believing the united Power of their confederacy will be of such weight as to make it the Interest of either of the belligerant Powers to desist from War whenever they chose to interpose: and consequently that the same being once understood, the said Powers would perceive that it would not be for their Interests to break the peace." There was certainly a kind of breathtaking audacity about the notion—that the United States, devastated by seven years of war, debt-ridden and insolvent, deeply divided by sectional jealousies and not yet master in her own house, should believe that it might soon have the capacity to dictate to the two greatest military powers of the age. It was an idea not incompatible with the new nation's notion of its own potential power and importance in the world. It would not be many years before Thomas Jefferson was attempting just such a policy.

Whether the idea existed outside of the imagination of Oswald it is impossible to say, but it is striking that he believed it to be in the minds of the commissioners and of Vergennes as well. It did not seem far-fetched to Oswald, who indeed conjectured that if England, France, Spain, and Holland were at war among themselves and Congress should declare "against any one, or more of them," that country or countries would "be obliged to give way, and put an end to the Quarrel. . . . This Capacity in the American Colonies," Oswald wrote, "if admitted to exist at this time must continue to increase and become more decisive from year to year, in proportion to the quick increase of Population in that Country. . . ." It had been this thought above all others that, Oswald confessed, had made him tremble "ever since I came to dispair of recovering" the colonies.

The prospects of peace revived in Congress those factions that on the one hand wanted the American peace negotiators to allow themselves to be guided by the French, and on the other were suspicious of the French and wished the American commissioners to have as much independence of France as possible. James Lovell, who belonged in the latter camp, wrote to John Adams complaining of those delegates who wished to keep Adams and his fellow negotiators, John Jay and Benjamin Franklin, in "leading strings." "Blush, Blush! America, Consult and ultimately concur in every thing with the Ministers of his Most Christian Majesty, the Independence of the United States according to the Tenor of our alliance kept the sole ultimatum!"

An "antigallic ferment" appeared in Congress, primarily represented by Arthur Lee's efforts to have the commission of June 15, 1781, appointing "the Ministers Plenipotentiary to negotiate a Treaty of Peace with Great Britain," reconsidered, together with the instructions to the commissioners. Throughout much of August, 1782, the members of Congress debated the question of how far its commissioners were to be required to submit to the "leading strings" of Vergennes and the French Court. James Madison effected a compromise designed to give the commissioners "sufficient latitude in reporting without implying on the part of Congress a desire to alter past instructions." Luzerne, of course, knew very well through his friends in Congress what was going on in that body, and he kept Vergennes informed of the "antigallic ferment." Certainly, although the Lee faction thought the instructions to the commissioners much too inhibiting, there was little sentiment for a separate peace with Great Britain. "They will be much disappointed," one delegate wrote, "if they expect a separate peace with America. . . . Our Independence and the alliance with France must go Hand in Hand."

When Luzerne, late in September, placed before Congress a report on the proceedings of the peace negotiations, Congress replied "*unanimously*" that it would "inviolably adhere to its alliance" and "conclude neither a separate peace or truce with Great Britain. . . . Congress will not enter into the discussion of any overtures for pacification but in confidence and in concert with his Most Christian Majesty."

When Adams, still in Holland attempting to secure a Dutch loan, received word of the informal discussions between Franklin and Oswald, he was offended. It was undignified, in his view, to receive "any agent about peace, who had not a commission and full powers to treat with the United States of America." But Franklin, Adams wrote, "must make himself a man of consequence by piddling with men who had no title. But thus it is that men of great reputation may do as many weak things as they please, and to remark their mistakes is to envy them."

Jay shared Adams' suspicions of Vergennes and Franklin. Arthur Lee, his capacity for troublemaking only partially diminished by distance and by the opposition he aroused in Congress, wrote to Adams that Robert Livingston, the newly appointed secretary of foreign affairs, was "as devoted a partisan of Count Vergennes and Dr. Franklin as any that exists." The instructions to the commissioners, which directed them to be guided by Vergennes, Lee asserted, "give great offense and uneasiness to many in Congress no one more than to myself. I think it most dishonorable and dangerous. It is a surrender to our independence and sovereignty and an acknowledgment that we are unequal to either."

There was more than a little truth to Lee's allegations. Luzerne considered Livingston his man, and Livingston in turn was grateful to the French minister and employed a Frenchman as his secretary. Adams, alarmed by Lee's letter, wrote Livingston a long lecture on international diplomacy. In this arena every nation pursued its own interests. It was foolish and romantic to believe otherwise. To think that France would put the interests of America before her own or even on a par with her own was simply naive. It was the part of wisdom to protect the United States in every way possible, while keeping faith with France and maintaining the most open and friendly relations with her. The important thing was to take a realistic view of the matter, and to base American policy not on instructions from Vergennes but on a cool appraisal of how America's interests could best be served, consistent with the letter and spirit of the alliance. All Adams asked of Livingston was that he "insist upon seeing with your own eyes, using your own judgment and acting an independent part."

Henry Laurens, on his way to Holland to replace Adams in 1780, had been captured on the brig *Mercury* by the British and had been held in the Tower of London "on suspicion of high treason" for almost fifteen months. Now he was released under heavy bail put up by Richard Oswald and was sent by Shelburne to sound out John Adams.

When the old friends met, Laurens, who was understandably embittered by his treatment at the hands of his captors, told Adams that he had "a very poor opinion of both the integrity and abilities of the new ministry. . . . He thinks," Adams wrote, "they know not what they are about, that they are spoiled by the same impurity, duplicity, falsehood and corruption, with the former." But Laurens believed that "the nation and the best men in it are for universal peace and express acknowledgement of American independence, and many of the best are for giving up Canada and Nova Scotia." Both Adams and Laurens agreed that negotiations must be preceded by an open, or at least tacit, recognition of American independence. Adams wrote Franklin in Paris an account of the meeting with Laurens.

Fox, meanwhile, had sent his own agent, Thomas Grenville, to Versailles to sound out Franklin and Vergennes on the matter of a treaty. Fox hoped that France would set such terms as would alienate America and make it possible to negotiate a separate peace with the former colonies. Vergennes blocked this move, however, by proposing that Britain and the United States should carry on one set of negotiations and France and Great Britain another; the final signing, however, should have the concurrence of all parties.

Before these maneuvers had progressed very far, Rockingham died on July 1, 1782. Shelburne became prime minister, and Fox resigned from the government. Shelburne then took the entire negotiations into his own hands.

It soon became evident that the death of Rockingham and the resignation of Fox represented a setback for the United States. Not only did the commissioners lose the opportunity to play Fox's emissary off against Shelburne's, they lost two members of the British government most sympathetic to their cause. In addition, their own punctilio about the recognition of independence as a prior condition delayed formal negotiations until after a Spanish attack on Gibraltar had been attempted and repulsed. Shelburne was thus encouraged to take a stronger line. Oswald was instructed to fight for articles indemnifying the Loyalists for confiscated property and guaranteeing the payment of debts that had been owed to British creditors by American merchants prior to the outbreak of hostilities.

When Adams, having concluded a treaty with Holland, arrived in Paris in October to join Jay and Franklin, he found that little had transpired there. The crisis in the British government brought on by the death of Rockingham and the succession of Shelburne had delayed formal negotiations. Franklin had made clear that there must first be "a full and complete" recognition of independence by Great Britain, and that the commissioners had been instructed to insist upon the freedom of fishing on the Grand Bank of Newfoundland. Also, the boundaries between Canada and the United States must be properly drawn. These were the essentials. Franklin, who had told Oswald that acknowledgment of independence must be the first article, was persuaded by Jay and Adams to insist that recognition of independence must *precede* any formal treaty discussions.

It turned out that Adams' misgivings about Franklin were groundless. He seemed no more inclined than his fellow commissioners to be strictly bound by the instructions from Congress of April, 1781, to "ultimately . . . govern youselves by the advice and opinion of the French ministry." "Mr. Jay as well as Mr. Franklin and myself," Adams wrote a friend, "are exceedingly embarrassed by some of our instructions."

In Paris Adams, who had only heard reports of the new instructions, read the obnoxious sentence for the first time and immediately wrote a letter of warm protest to Livingston. Strictly interpreted, he noted, the article would take from the commissioners "all right of judging for ourselves," and oblige them "to agree to whatever the French ministers should advise us to, and to do nothing without their consent." If that was in fact the intent of the instruction, Adams declared, "I hereby resign my place in the commission and request that another person may be immediately appointed in my stead."

The commissioners decided, in Adams' words, "to construe our instructions as we do all other precepts and maxims, by such limitations, restrictions and exceptions as reason, necessity and the nature of things point out."

Adams discovered that Jay, who visited him soon after his arrival in Paris, had an almost pathological dislike of the French in general. He considered them a shifty and immoral people. "He don't like any Frenchman," Adams observed. Jay was convinced, and he tried to convince Adams, that Vergennes was plotting with the British behind the backs of the American commissioners to rob the United States of the fisheries, the Western lands, and the navigation of the Mississippi. Adams was disconcerted by the evident animus behind Jay's suspicions. "These whispers ought not to be credited by us," he declared a little stiffly.

Soon after Adams joined Franklin and Jay, Oswald was reinforced by another British negotiator, Henry Strachey, a much stronger character, "as artful and insinuating a man as they could send," Adams noted; "he pushes and presses every point as far as it can possibly go; he has the most eager, earnest, pointed spirit," a far cry from the compliant Oswald.

Strachey started off by stating his government's determination that debts owed by Americans to British merchants should be paid. When Franklin protested that the commissioners could not commit the individual states to such a provision, Adams bridled. Certainly as a commissioner he had no disposition to oppose the collection of lawful debts. Strachey was obviously pleased and relieved to find on this point an ally among the American commissioners. After the session, Adams explained to Jay and Franklin his view of the matter. While it was true the commissioners could not commit the states, Congress could certainly recommend that the states open their courts to British creditors for the purpose of recovering legitimate debts. Shelburne could thus appear as the champion of the merchants. Moreover, Great Britain might be less inclined to try to exclude American merchants from her trade. From their initial opposition, Jay and Franklin "gradually fell into this opinion."

The next thorny issue was that of compensation to the Tories for property confiscated by the patriots. "We cannot stipulate for such compensation," the commissioners declared, "unless on your part it be agreed to make retribution to our citizens for the heavy losses they have sustained by the unnecessary destruction of private property. . . . We should be sorry if the absolute impossibility of our complying further with your propositions should induce Great Britain to continue the war for the sake of those who caused and prolonged it." Strachey's answer was equally emphatic. Some provision for the refugees was a condition for continuing the treaty discussions. "It effected equally the honor and humanity of your country and of ours."

Strachey gave poor advice to Thomas Townshend, Shelburne's colonial secretary, when he wrote, "I venture to tell you, that I am inclined to think, if you make the restitution or indemnification to the refugee, a sine qua non, the American Commissioners will accede rather than break off the Treaty upon such a point. . . ." Oswald, who by this time knew the commissioners' minds almost as well as they themselves did, had a different opinion. He had long talks with Jay and Adams independently and found them adamant on the subject of the Loyalists. If there could be peace on no other terms, the war must go on—even if it were for seven years more. If Great Britain persisted, the American response might well be to demand restitution for all that its citizens had suffered at the hands of the British.

Adams, informed by Lafayette that Vergennes was offended that he had not called on him since his arrival in Paris, rode out to Versailles to see the count. They talked amiably enough, both well aware of the instructions of Congress of April, 1781, and aware too that the commissioners were not observing them. Vergennes offered no reproof, however. Indeed he could not, for to do so would reveal that he knew the instructions, which were supposed to be secret. He asked Adams how the negotiations were proceeding, and Adams told him that the commissioners and the British negotiators differed on two points only—the northern boundaries of Maine and the treatment of the Tories. Vergennes declared that he was not surprised that the British had made a point of compensation for the Loyalists. All precedents were in favor of it. In rebuttal Adams cited the case of Ireland. The Tories "by their misrepresentations had deceived the nation . . . and now that very nation was thought to be bound in honor to compensate its dishonorers and destroyers."

Adams came away from his meeting with Vergennes convinced that Vergennes wished the issue of the Tories to be a sticking point between the English and Americans that would delay the negotiation of a treaty. These suspicions were increased by word that Vergennes' secretary, Rayneval, was making frequent secret trips to England.

At the end of November Franklin and Adams had a long talk that cleared the air and produced a new confidence in each other's principles, if not each other's character. Adams expressed his uneasiness at the disposition of a faction in Congress to abandon the Mississippi boundary and the fisheries, and the encouragement that the French seemed to give to this group. Adams declared, in his blunt way, "that he paid no regard to [Vergennes'] opinion or recommendation on the subject and could guess at his motive for interfering as intending to prevent a speedy Agreement with Great Britain so as in the Interim they might bring forward their own Treaty, and those of their Allies, to a more favorable conclusion." Franklin heard him out, did not try to exonerate Vergennes, and agreed that the commissioners should stand firm on these points.

In the meantime Jay entered into informal conversations with Aranda, the Spanish ambassador to Versailles, over the western and southern boundaries between the United States and the Spanish territories of Louisiana and West Florida. Jay insisted that the Mississippi River should constitute the western boundary of the United States as far south as the thirty-first degree of latitude. Aranda appealed to Vergennes to use his influence in support of the Spanish position. A further complication arose from the fact that Spain wished to prolong the war and keep America actively engaged in it until it had made good its intention of recapturing Gibraltar from the British. Vergennes in fact was inclined to favor the Spanish side of the matter, and he let word reach Shelburne to that effect. Jay heard rumors that Vergennes had sent word to the British minister, and it increased his suspicion of French motives.

To push the negotiations along, Jay and Franklin decided to give way on the issue of British recognition of independence as a precondition. Oswald's instructions to treat with the "commissioners of the United States" would be accepted as *de facto* recognition of American independence. The way was now cleared, a year after the surrender of Cornwallis at Yorktown, for serious negotiations. On October 5, Jay, on behalf of his fellow commissioners, presented Oswald with a draft treaty that, in addition to Franklin's "necessary articles," contained a paragraph making clear America's claim to the Mississippi River.

At this point Henry Laurens arrived, burdened by word of the death of his brilliant son, who had been killed in a skirmish with Tories in August, 1782. "Thank God, I had a son, who dared to die in defense of his country," he had said on hearing the tragic news. At the conference table he took his place opposite Richard Oswald, a business associate and a close friend.

With the talks stalemated over the issue of the Tories, another British emissary, Benjamin Vaughan, appeared in Paris with word that the ministry was much embarrassed over the matter and wished for some face-saving formula that would prevent the negotiations from breaking down. The formula was finally found in these rather ambiguous words: "It is agreed that the Congress shall earnestly recommend it to the legislatures of the respective states to provide for the restitution of all estates, rights, and properties which have been confiscated . . . and that persons . . . shall have free liberty to go into any part or parts of any of the thirteen of the United States and therin to remain twelve months unmolested in their endeavors to obtain restitution of such of their estates, rights, and properties as may have been confiscated."

With the Tory issue resolved at least for the moment, the matter of the fisheries proved unexpectedly awkward. How close were American fishermen to be allowed to the shores of Newfoundland and Cape

Breton? Were they to have the privilege of drying their fish on shore? Since there were no means of refrigeration, it was of great importance that fish, especially cod, should be dried before it turned bad. To have to sail back to American territory to dry their fish and then return to the Grand Bank would greatly diminish the profits of the New England fishermen. Adams was determined that the treaty should guarantee Americans the same rights in the fisheries that they had always enjoyed, that "the United States shall continue to enjoy unmolested the right to take fish of every kind . . . and in all places where the inhabitants of both countries used at any time before to fish" and to cure their fish on the shores of Newfoundland.

Fitzherbert, one of the British negotiators, declared, "'Right' is an obnoxious expression." At this Adams burst forth, "Gentlemen, . . . can there be a clearer right? . . . When God Almighty made the Banks of Newfoundland at three hundred leagues' distance from the people of America and six hundred leagues' distance from those of France and England, did he not give as good a right to the former as to the latter? If Heaven in the Creation gave a right, it is ours at least as much as it is yours. If occupation, use, and possession give a right, we have at least as much as you. If war and blood and treasure give us a right, ours is as good as yours."

The English conceded that Adams' point was well taken, but their instructions, they insisted, gave them no choice in the matter.

"That is perfectly all right," Adams replied. "We can wait. Send a courier back to London."

"No, no!" Fitzherbert answered, dismayed at the thought of having "all laid loose before Parliament."

Strachey suggested leaving the article on the fisheries to the definitive treaty, but Adams was adamant. "I never could put my hand to any articles without satisfaction about the fishery," Adams insisted.

Laurens and Jay supported Adams. After some tense exchanges, a compromise gave the Americans "liberty" to fish on the coast of Newfoundland and a "right" to fish on the Bank. The American commissioners agreed to a clause that protected the Tories from "any future confiscations" or "any prosecutions . . . against any person or persons, for or by reason of the part which he or they may have taken in the present war."

At the end of the day, the Americans had reason to feel that they had gotten a good bargain. The negotiators adjourned with the final draft agreed upon. The next day they would meet to sign it. That night at dinner Adams was asked if he would like fish. "No," he replied, "I have had a pretty good meal of them today." "I am glad to hear it," one of the guests said, "as I know that a small quantity would not satisfy you."

To his friend Elbridge Gerry, Adams wrote, "Our Tom Cod are safe in spite of the malice of enemies, the finesse of allies, and the mistakes of Congress."

The next day, November 30, the British and American negotiators met twice more, first at Jay's house, then at Oswald's. Henry Laurens added a stipulation that the British troops, upon evacuating American posts, should carry off no Negroes or other American property. The British still held Charles Town and Savannah, and Laurens knew from experience that many former slaves would wish to depart with the British when they left. The point was agreed to and incorporated in the treaty. As soon as Britain reached an agreement with France, the preliminary articles were to go into effect and hostilities would cease.

The various copies were then signed and sealed. After the signing, which "passed in the simplest manner with great civility and decorum on all sides," the negotiators rode out to Passy to have dinner with Franklin. There they were joined by some Frenchmen, one of whom expatiated to the British on "the growing greatness of America," declaring that "the Thirteen United States would form the greatest empire in the world."

"Yes, sir," Caleb Whitefoord, the secretary to the British commissioners, replied, "and they will *all* speak English; every one of 'em."

Franklin was not impressed by Henry Laurens' prediction that he would be "called blessed by all the grateful of the present generation" for his part in "the great work." The worldly-wise doctor replied, "I have never yet known of a peace that did not occasion a great deal of popular discontent, clamour, and censure on both sides. . . . The blessings promised to peacemakers, I fancy relates to the next world for in this they seem to have a greater chance of being cursed." Laurens, doubtless with Franklin's lesson in mind, teased Adams about the possibility of their all being hanged by their indignant countrymen on their return to America. "John Adams & Co. may be hanged, but no damage will arise to the United States," Laurens added. The joke stung Adams. "I cannot think our country will hang her ministers merely for their simplicity in being cheated into independence, the fisheries and half the Great Lakes," he answered. "Our countrymen love buckskins, beaverskins, tom-cod, and pine trees too well to hang their ministers for accepting them, or even for purchasing them by a little too much 'reciprocity' to the tories."

With the treaty signed, there were still of course many possible pitfalls. The British ministry might not accept the work of its agents, or Parliament might reject the treaty. Similarly, Congress might raise difficulties. Vergennes, despite the instructions of Congress, had not been consulted on the negotiations, and the preliminary articles had been signed without his concurrence.

On the other hand, the terms were, on the whole, generous ones. The American had gained every essential point. Vergennes, who doubtless knew very well what had been going on, even to the specific details of the treaty, was perhaps as pleased as the Americans. He had Spain to contend with, however; he could not approve of treaty arrangements objectionable to that country. It was better if he could plead ignorance and assure the Spanish that he had had no part in the negotiations. The *fait accompli* with which the Americans presented him enabled Vergennes to plead innocent to Spain, and at the same time brought considerable pressure on that power to agree to reasonable terms in the joint negotiations that she was conducting with France to end the war between those two nations and Great Britain.

The American accomplishment was perhaps best measured by a letter from Vergennes to Rayneval: "You will notice," Vergennes wrote, "that the English buy the peace more than they make it. Their concessions, in fact, as much to the boundaries as to the fisheries and the loyalists, exceed all that I could have thought possible. What can be the motive that could have brought terms so easy that they could have been interpreted as a kind of surrender?"

Without attributing duplicity to Vergennes or arguing that he was inclined to deliberately betray American interests, his letter makes clear beyond any shadow of a doubt that he had thought that the Americans were entirely unrealistic in their demands and that England would not make such concessions. Therefore, if consulted, he would most assuredly have urged the American commissioners quite sincerely, as he did on the issue of the Tories, to trim their sails. At every point in his long contact with the representatives of Congress, Vergennes did his best to moderate their demands and guide their steps, and it would have been remarkable if he had not. The result of the independent action of the commissioners—the preliminary treaty—and Vergennes' astonishment at it, went further to vindicate their course of action than volumes of disputation could ever do. (Similarly, Aranda, the Spanish ambassador, was surprised and indignant at the concessions that the British had made to the Americans.)

With Congress, the shrewd French minister took the line of a betrayed and properly indignant friend. "Our opinion could not influence the negotiations," the count wrote Luzerne, "since we knew nothing of their details, and because they were completed in the most sudden, unforeseen, and, I might say, extraordinary manner." What most concerned Vergennes was the clause on the fisheries, which, in his opinion, conflicted with the exclusive rights of the French that had been contained in the existing treaty of commerce with America.

It was left to Franklin to give Vergennes formal notification of the preliminary articles. The count waited almost two weeks to reply, and then his answer was a cold rebuke. "I am at a loss, sir, to explain your conduct and that of your colleagues on this occasion," he wrote Franklin. "You have concluded your preliminary articles without any communication between us, although the instructions from Congress prescribe that nothing shall be done without the participation of the King. . . . You are wise and discreet, sir; you perfectly understand what is due to propriety; you have all your life performed your duties. . . . I am not desirous of enlarging these reflections; I commit them to your own integrity."

Vergennes and the king were not as offended as the count's rebuking letter suggested. Franklin went to make his personal amends to the French minister, and that evening he wrote to request a further French loan of six million livres, which the king granted.

Having concluded their own preliminary treaty, the American commissioners now had to wait on the progress of the negotiations between England on the one hand and France, Spain, and Holland on the other. These proved complicated and delicate, and if the Spanish ambassador, Aranda, had not, like the Americans, ignored or stretched his instructions, they might have dragged on interminably. As it was, by January 20 the various parties were ready to sign the general treaty. That document was the consequence, more than anything, of Vergennes' mastery of the art of diplomacy. The count and his secretary, Rayneval, had shown the greatest skill and patience, especially in dealing with the inflexibility of the Spanish Court, which was determined to gain Gibraltar as the price of its relatively modest contribution to "victory." To Rayneval, who had borne the brunt of the negotiations with Shelburne, the treaty was "a miracle," and he wrote triumphantly to a friend: "So at least we have peace. . . . It renders infinite honor to our respected Minister. England had been plucked all over; but to pluck the bird without making her squawk, *voilà le grand art!* This is what our chief has done, and he is truly honored here in this country."

The first word that the British public had of the preliminary treaty came with the king's speech from the throne at the opening of Parliament on December 5, 1782. The galleries of the House of Lords were filled with distinguished visitors, among them the young son of Vergennes, a number of American Loyalists who had gotten wind of the treaty, and Rayneval.

The buildings of Parliament were wrapped in a blanket of fog, and the members of both houses, crowded with the spectators into a single chamber, waited for two hours for the king's arrival. Finally he entered, announced by a volley of artillery, and took his seat on the chair of state, his right foot resting on a stool. It was clear to his audience that he was in a state of considerable perturbation. He had, he declared to his hushed audience, given orders to halt the war on the North American continent. His aim had always been "an entire and cordial reconciliation." Finding it "indispensable to the attainment of this object," he continued, "I did not hesitate to go the full length of the powers vested in me, and offer to declare them—" (at this point the king hesitated as though to gain command of himself and then continued), "—and offer to declare them *free and independent States,* by an article to be inserted in the treaty of peace." It was his "humble and ardent prayer to Almighty God" that Britain would be spared "the evils which might result from so great a dismemberment of the Empire, and that America may be free from the calamities which have formerly proved, in the mother country, how essential monarchy is to the enjoyment of constitutional liberty." Language, religion, common interests, and affection, he hoped, would "yet prove a bond of permanent union between the two countries."

The voice was George III's, but the conciliatory words were those of Shelburne, and to pronounce them was doubtless the hardest thing that monarch ever had to do. "He hesitated, choked, and executed the painful duties with an ill grace which does not belong to him," an American visitor wrote. "In pronouncing the word 'independent' the King of England did it in a constrained voice," Rayneval told Vergennes. If the words were conciliatory, as was Shelburne's way, they were also duplicitous, which was a less admirable quality of the first lord of the treasury. The preliminary treaty, which had already been signed, was nowhere mentioned, and it was not clear from the king's address in what terms the former colonies had been declared "free and independent States." The speech was hardly finished before London was filled with speculation about what it had, in fact, meant.

That night, Elkanah Watson, a New England merchant who had been a witness of the episode in the House of Lords, visited John Singleton Copley, who had been painting his portrait. In the background Copley had painted a ship delivering to America the news that independence had been recognized. The American flag, caught in the rays of the sun, had been left unfinished, awaiting the official word of independence. Now Copley, Watson reported, "with a bold hand, a master's touch, and I believe an American heart," added the Stars and Stripes.

Viscount Stormant, the denigrator and bitter enemy of America, attacked Shelburne in the House of Lords. Did not the king's speech say, he asked, "that, without any condition, any qualification, any stipulation whatsoever, America shall be independent whenever France chooses to make peace with us?" Shelburne himself had not long ago declared that the sun of Great Britain must set when America became independent. "That sun is set," Stormant declared. "There is not a ray of light left. All is darkness."

Fox, who was a friend to America but the implacable enemy of Shelburne, could not resist the opportunity provided by that minister's ineptness to attack him. Fox, and Burke with him, took the line that independence had indeed, according to the king's speech, been granted unconditionally; and while Shelburne in the House of Lords was rebutting this charge, young William Pitt, the worthy successor to his famous father and captain of Shelburne's forces in the House of Commons, was admitting that "unqualified recognition" of American independence was "the clear indisputable meaning of the provisional treaty." With a rift apparent in his own cabinet, Shelburne took refuge in the need for secrecy. Negotiations with France and Spain were at a critical stage; he could not disclose the details of the provisional treaty.

Horace Walpole found an occasion to produce one of his devastating thrusts. Shelburne's "falsehood was so constant and notorious," he declared, "that it was rather his profession than his instrument. It was like a fictitious violin, which is hung out of a music shop to indicate in what goods the tradesman deals; not to be of service, nor to be depended on for playing a true note."

The American commissioners were disconcerted by the hue and cry raised in Parliament and by Shelburne's equivocation. They had been drawing up propositions for inclusion in the definitive treaty that would have given the United States in effect "free trade" with England and the various parts of the British Empire. They had reason to believe that Shelburne was a warm advocate of such a policy, but the rancorous attacks on his government indicated that there was little chance of such a liberal line prevailing.

On January 27, a week after the preliminary treaties with France and Spain had been concluded, Shelburne revealed their terms along with those of the American treaty to both houses of Parliament. Inside and outside of Parliament, the treaties were attacked by different groups and factions.

The refugee Tories were especially outraged. The treaty had betrayed them by offering a shadow instead of substance. "The misery which American independence has brought to individuals is inexpressible," one declared, "and I assure you that I am one of the most ill-used." Adams, who had good friends among the Tories, most notably Jonathan Sewall, had some sympathy for their unhappy plight, but Franklin, whose son William was the leader of those Tories who besieged Shelburne's ministers with complaints and reproaches, was unmoved. He wrote a fable about mongrel dogs who had corrupted faithful dogs and then abandoned them. Now that the faithful dogs were victorious, the mongrels wished to be rewarded by the lion, king of the forest. In a council of beasts, summoned to adjudicate the matter, the wolves and foxes sided with the mongrels, while the horse, maintaining that King Lion had been persuaded by bad advisors "to war unjustly upon his faithful subjects," urged the other animals to reject the mongrels' claim.

The particular fire of Shelburne's enemies was concentrated on the American treaty. The boundary line with Canada was badly drawn, they charged; the fur trade had been abandoned and the Indians deserted. A member of Shelburne's own cabinet wrote that the Americans "had evidently been too cunning for us in the negotiation." In the House of Lords Shelburne made an eloquent defense of the treaty, failing to mention his hopes for a speedy reconciliation with the former colonies and stressing the crisis in public credit, the low estate of the navy, and the general disillusionment with the war among all classes of Englishmen. In a vote on the king's speech, Shelburne carried the Lords by a thirteen-vote margin, but in Commons the tide ran heavily against the government. Burke and Fox joined forces with North—an odd alliance—to denounce the treaties, with particular attention to the articles of the American treaty. There was a brief moment of comic relief when a dog that had wandered into the House began to bark. There were shouts of "Hear! hear!" and North, turning to the chair, said, "Sir, I was interrupted by a new Speaker, but as his argument is concluded, I will resume mine."

On February 21, Shelburne's opponents proposed a resolution that accepted peace and approved the recognition of independence but denounced the concessions contained in the provisional treaty. After an all-night debate, the motion carried by 207 to 190, and Shelburne, after approaching North and Charles James Fox for help in preserving his ministry and being coldly rebuffed, resigned. Pitt, aware of the Fox-North alliance, denounced it as "the unnatural coalition" and told the members of the House, "I know a just and lawful impediment, and, in the name of public safety, I here forbid the banns."

"We have demolished the Earl of Shelburne," Burke wrote, "but in his fall he has pulled down a large piece of the building." For the moment the ship of state was rudderless, and all the treaty arrangements, so carefully pieced together, seemed in peril. What followed was an interregnum of seven weeks, with affairs at a standstill. Fox, who had so long and so mercilessly denounced North, now plotted with him to take control of the government, while the king, with grim reflections on the frailty of politicians, tried to circumvent their maneuvers. George III had reason to resent Fox. Not only had Fox been a tireless critic of his government, but Fox had done his best to corrupt the Prince of Wales and turn him against his father. The fact was that the prince had good reason to dislike the king. In the words of Christopher Hobhouse, "His father had ruled him exactly as he ruled the Bostonians, and with as little success." The Prince of Wales, taking his cue from his hedonistic mentor, often ridiculed his father in public, and word, of course, promptly reached the king. It was said that George had declared that "he would have no peace till his son and Fox were secured in the Tower." Now, instead of seeing Fox in the Tower, he was faced with the prospect of having him share the leadership of his government with the man who for so long had been his dutiful and uncomplaining servant. It is small wonder that the king delayed that moment as long as possible. It was a pill only slightly less difficult to swallow than American independence, and one dose followed closely upon the other. Rather than yield, he declared, he would "go to Hanover" (that is, abdicate) and return to the ancient principality of his family. Rather than accept a coalition government in which Fox held an important cabinet post, he would accept North, or Pitt, "or Mr. Thomas Pitt or Mr. Thomas anybody." Finally he accepted in April a new government under the nominal leadership of the Duke of Portland, in which Lord North and Fox were secretaries of state with the effective powers of the administration in their hands.

In his attack on Shelburne, which had been largely responsible for bringing down his ministry, Fox had denounced the preliminary treaties as "more calamitous, more dreadful, more ruinous than war could possibly be." Now he replaced Shelburne's emissaries with his own men, most conspicuously the Duke of Manchester, whom Vergennes found "as cunning as he is weak and callous." But the new negotiators made little headway in obtaining revisions of the original treaties, and Fox was characteristically loosetongued in denouncing his predecessors. To the French ambassador he expressed his contempt for "those devils" who had made the preliminary treaties, and he castigated Shelburne and his colleagues "as pusillanimous ministers without any shred of character." There had been a poor peace because "those villainous persons have tied my hands in every conceivable manner."

With the Dutch, Fox, once their professed friend, proved particularly obdurate, doubtless because they were in the poorest bargaining position and because in his negotiations with them he might win concessions that would compensate for his failure with France and the United States. From the time of Lexington and Concord, Fox had appeared in Parliament as the champion of American independence. Now, instead of picking up Shelburne's enlightened policy of *rapprochement* with Great Britain's colonies, he took a harsh and vindictive line, apparently for no better reason than party politics. Fox's chief negotiator, David Hartley, whom Adams described caustically as "talkative, disputatious and not always intelligible," had long been a friend of the American cause, and he warmly endorsed the American commissioner's proposal for "one simple and invariable principle . . . viz., reciprocity. . . ." He was sharply rebuked for his pains by Fox, who stood on the principle that no American manufactured goods could be imported into England, a principle that John Adams later denounced as "the first link in that great chain of Orders in Council which have been since stretched and extended, till it has shackled the commerce of the globe."

This restraint was followed by another order-in-council excluding American ships from trade with the British West Indian Islands. Noting the growing disparity between Hartley's personal beliefs and professions and the policy of the ministry, John Adams wrote, "Mr. Hartley is probably kept here if he was not sent at first merely to amuse us and to keep him out of the way of embarrassing the coalition." The guess was close to the fact. The story is worth recounting not only because it is replete with irony but because it demonstrates both the good fortune of the American commissioners in securing such a favorable treaty and the missed opportunity to have restored close relations between the United States and Great Britain. In the words of a recent historian of the treaty, the policy of Fox and North "opened up a grievous and festering wound in Anglo-American relations."

Finally, on the morning of September 3, almost a year after the signing of the preliminary articles, the definitive treaties were signed at David Hartley's quarters in the Hôtel d'York. Hartley, perpetually optimistic, was confident of the "reciprocal advantage" that would accrue to England and America by their joining "in one common cause for, the reunion of all our ancient affections and common interests."

15

The Aftermath of Yorktown

Wʜɪʟᴇ the American commissioners in Paris began their protracted discussions with the emissaries of first the Rockingham and then the Shelburne governments, Washington marched his victorious army north, where it could intercept any move by Clinton from New York. His stepson, Jacky Custis, who had served as his aide during the siege of Yorktown, had contracted camp fever, and he died on November 5 at Eltham, thirty miles from Yorktown; he left two children, Eleanor Parke Custis and George Washington Parke Custis, who were adopted by Washington.

Having started the army on the long march north, Washington stopped in Fredericksburg to visit his mother; then he rode on to Mount Vernon for a week's respite. From his home he wrote to Lafayette, who planned to return to France, sending him "my ardent Vows for a propitious voyage . . . and a safe return in the spring." He wrote to General Greene at the same time, instructing him to keep a close watch on the British at Charles Town. "My greatest fear," he added, "is, that Congress, viewing this stroke in too important a point of light, may think our work too nearly closed, and will fall into a state of languor and relaxation." The words proved prophetic.

The trip from Mount Vernon to Philadelphia was a triumphal

procession. At Annapolis the governor and assembly of Maryland, along with the citizens of the town, acclaimed him. The newspaper reported that even notorious Tories joined "feebly in applauding the man, whose late successes had annihilated their hopes. . . . The evening was spent at the governor's elegant and hospitable board with festive joy, enlivened by good humour, wit and beauty. Every heart overflowed with gratitude and love, and every tongue grew wanton in his praise. . . . 'Unrival'd and unmatched shall be his fame, And his own laurels shade his envied name.'"

In Baltimore the general was received with, if possible, even greater enthusiasm, and when he arrived at Philadelphia on November 26, the *Pennsylvania Journal* discovered that the glory of the moment outran even its editor's extravagant pen: "All panegyrick is vain and language too feeble to express our ideas of his greatness," the editor confessed. "May the crown of glory he has placed on the brow of the genius of America, shine with untarnished radiance and lustre, and in the brightness of its rays be distinctly seen—WASHINGTON, THE SAVIOUR OF HIS COUNTRY!"

Charles Willson Peale, who was later to fashion a set of false teeth for the general, had painted a number of transparent pictures as "expressions of . . . respect and gratitude to the conquering Hero." One showed Washington and Rochambeau "with rays of glory and interlaced civic crowns over their heads, framed with palm and laurel branches, and the words of transparent letters, SHINE VALIANT CHIEFS. . . ."

A week of celebrations, of balls and parties and festivities of all kinds, followed. Washington and the other officers in the city were entertained by The Society of the Friendly Sons of St. Patrick at a splendid dinner, and the general attended a play by "the celebrated M. Beaumarchais . . . extremely well acted by the young gentlemen, students in that polite language," from the College of Philadelphia.

At the end of March, Washington moved his headquarters to Newburgh, New York, where the main army, under the command of General Heath, had taken up winter quarters.

Among the soldiers who moved north after Yorktown was Joseph Martin, with his contingent of sappers and miners. After being employed as quartermaster troops in Virginia, they sailed to Head of Elk, Maryland, and then marched on to Philadelphia and eventually to Burlington, New Jersey. There Martin's detachment at last found comfortable quarters in a mansion that had once belonged to the British governor of the colony. He and his fellow noncommissioned officers shared "a neat room in one of the wings," while his men occupied the rest of the house.

After Yorktown, General Arthur St. Clair, with regulars from Virginia, Maryland, and Pennsylvania, marched south to reinforce Greene. The British force at Wilmington withdrew hastily to Charles Town, but even with his augmented army Greene was too weak to assault the city; he had to content himself with cutting off all land communication. Anthony Wayne meanwhile surrounded Savannah. When the British evacuated that city in July, 1782, they took with them four thousand Tories and five thousand slaves.

The countryside around Charles Town showed clearly the ravages of war. When Lieutenant Ebenezer Denny was sent to Georgetown (almost one hundred miles to the north) with a convoy of wagons loaded with rum, the few people he saw "fled from us and in some instances hid themselves." The farms looked poor and neglected. In camp "deaths [were] so frequent," Denny noted, "the funeral ceremony [was] dispensed with." The beef brought from the North Carolina backcountry was "poor indeed, and . . . unwholesome." When Denny met a companion coming from the commissary one morning and asked him how the beef was, the other replied "that it took two men to hold up the creature until the butcher knocked it down." The troops lived chiefly on rice, which was fine for the sick "but rather washy for duty men."

As the time approached for the evacuation of Charles Town, those Tories who had taken refuge in the city and were now unable or unwilling to leave with the British tried to return to their homes. "Some very miserable objects came out," Denny noted, "—whole familes, battered and starving." But they were turned back, "an unnecessary cruelty," in Denny's opinion.

A number of the leading patriot plantation owners of the state, whose slaves had run away to the British or, as they preferred to put it, had been stolen by the British, brought pressure on the governor to intercede with General Leslie under the terms of the treaty to prevent their property from being carried off. Threatening to confiscate whatever British or Loyalist property had not yet been seized, Governor John Mathews secured an agreement with Leslie "that all the slaves of the citizens of South-Carolina, now in the power of the honourable lieutenant-general Leslie, shall be restored to their former owners, as far as is practicable, except such slaves as may have rendered themselves particularly obnoxious on account of their attachment and services to the British troops, and such as had specifick promises of freedom." In return the governor promised not to withhold the settlement of any British debts—a small concession, since the final word in such matters lay with the legislature and the courts. Another article specified that no slaves who were restored to their former masters were to be punished "for having attached themselves to the British troops." This clause is particularly interesting since it concedes, in effect, that far from having been "stolen," a large number of slaves did indeed "attach" themselves to the British.

Procedures were set up by the governor and his staff to return the errant slaves to their masters as quickly and efficiently as possible. As David Ramsay wrote, "Great were the expectations of the suffering inhabitants, that they would soon obtain re-possession of their property; but these delusive hopes were of short duration." Only 136 ex-slaves could be found on board the British fleet when it was loaded and ready to sail, and of these only "seventy-three landed for delivery"—seventy-three out of thousands known to have been within the British lines. At this point the agreement collapsed completely. There were rumors that Colonel James Moncrieff had appropriated eight hundred slaves and sent them off to the West Indies for sale; actually, Leslie could not bring himself to return the blacks to slavery, and many were freed. Ramsay estimates that from the beginning to the end of the war, in the state of South Carolina alone, twenty-five thousand slaves were lost to their owners. Many, as we have noted, died of disease and neglect in British encampments. Many more performed services for the British in various capacities, and some served in Loyalist military units or sailed on British privateers.

Finally, on December 13, 1782, the British departed from Charles Town, taking with them some four thousand Tory refugees and a disputed number of slaves. The Americans "found the town very quiet—houses all shut up," and it was several days before the frightened inhabitants who remained dared to show themselves.

It should be said that despite the great exodus of Tories, many remained. These were the courageous or persistent or desperate ones. In South Carolina, for example, thirty-one prominent Loyalists were, on application to the legislature, fully restored to "their property and citizenship." Thirty-three were given their property back but forbidden to hold any office of public trust for a period of seven years; sixty-two others were "relieved of confiscation" on the payment of a 12 per cent property tax.

Two weeks after the evacuation of the city, the Americans broke camp and went into winter quarters. "The Pennsylvanians," Denny wrote, "have been reduced, by deaths, desertions, etc." to a single regiment of six hundred men. These, with the remaining Maryland, South Carolina, and Virginia units, found housing on James Island: "Officers and men all in comfortable quarters. Provisions good; very little occasion for fire through the winter. . . . Plenty of fish and oysters all round us, and what the folks here call stone crabs, very fine; they are like the common crabs but much larger, and soft shells. Officers in rotation dine with General Greene, at his house in the city." In April, 1783, word finally arrived of the preliminary treaty of peace. "Great rejoicing—grand review—dinner—fire works, and dance at the cantonment" with ladies and gentlemen from Charles Town, Denny noted. On June 15, Denny was at last back in Philadelphia, where he and his men were left to cool their heels until the final treaty was concluded.

Paradoxically, the surrender of Cornwallis at Yorktown had the effect of increasing rather than diminishing the bitter partisan warfare that raged between patriot and Tory irregulars, especially in the Jerseys. As Roger Lamb, the British soldier-historian, said, "The spirit of political rancor in America had at this period risen to an uncommon height." In the words of another contemporary observer: "The malignity, virulence, and savage barbarity, that . . . pervaded all ranks, classes and denominations, whether in the civil or military line, cannot be delineated in any terms, but such as must agonize the heart of sensibility. . . ."

Tory raiders in New Jersey—the Associated Loyalists—seized a well-known patriot leader, Captain Joshua Huddy, took him to a prison ship in the Hudson, and fifteen days later hanged him and left him swinging with a message pinned to his breast: "We the refugees having long with grief beheld the cruel murders of our brethren, and finding nothing but such measures daily carrying into execution; we therefore determine not to suffer without taking vengeance, for the numerous cruelties, and thus begin, and have made use of captain Huddy as the first object to present to your view, and further determine to hang man for man, while there is a refugee existing. Up goes Huddy for Philip White."

White was a Tory, obnoxious to the patriots, who had been captured by a company of militia and shot trying to escape. The execution of Huddy caused, as it was intended to do, a storm. Sir Henry Clinton ordered a court-martial of the Loyalist leader, a Captain Richard Lippincott, who had authorized the hanging, but the court adjourned without delivering a verdict; Washington then sent an indignant letter to Clinton describing Huddy's death as "the most wanton, cruel, and inprecedented murder that ever disgraced the arms of a civilized people." The officer who was in command at the execution of Huddy, he demanded, must be delivered up or a British officer would be hanged in retribution. Clinton replied stiffly. He had of course not sanctioned the killing of Huddy; he would not surrender those involved to Washington. They would be tried and punished according to British law.

Sir Guy Carleton, who arrived in New York to replace Clinton in May, 1782, took up the matter with Washington at once, expressing in strong terms his regret at the hanging and promising to do all he could to prevent such actions in the future. But Washington persisted in his plan to execute a British officer of comparable rank. Thirteen captains serving in Cornwallis's army had been captured at Yorktown, and Washington ordered them to draw straws to determine which one should be executed in revenge for the hanging of Huddy. Captain Charles Asgill, a member of a titled English family, drew the fatal straw, which had the word "unfortunate" written on it. Asgill, who was seventeen years old, was brought under heavy guard to New Jersey.

Carleton at once suggested to Asgill's parents that they take up the fate of their son with the king and queen of France and Vergennes and try to prevail on them to use their influence with Washington to prevent the execution.

At the court martial of Captain Lippincott there was testimony that William Franklin had instructed the captain to hang Huddy and that Lippincott had simply been carrying out orders. He was thus acquitted, and the fate of Asgill seemed sealed.

As the time for the execution approached and there was no sign that the British intended to surrender Lippincott (Franklin was safe in England), Washington began to try to find a way out of his unpleasant dilemma. Finally he wrote Congress "that . . . he would stay the Execution of Capt. Asgill without an express order from Congress to the Contrary." The result was a bitter debate in that body extending over three days, "during which," Elias Boudinot reported, "more ill blood appeared in the House, than I had ever seen." A majority were clearly in favor of ordering Asgill executed. The minority, led by Boudinot, managed to delay the final vote a day, and on that very day a letter from the king and queen of France arrived, along with one from Vergennes, urging clemency. "This operated like an electrical shock," Boudinot noted. "In short it looked so much like something supernatural that even the minority, who were so much pleased with it, could scarcely think it real . . . and thus," Boudinot concluded, "We got clear of shedding innocent Blood, by a wonderful intervention of Providence." Asgill was pardoned on November 7, 1782, and Washington wrote to inform him, stating that "through the whole . . . of this unpleasant affair, I was never influenced by sanguinary motives, but by what I conceived a sense of my duty, which loudly called upon me to take measures, however disagreeable, to prevent a repetition of these enormities. . . ."

The incident does not place Washington in a very favorable light. To try to stop the mutual killing that went on among patriots and Tories by hanging an innocent man—one protected, it could be (and was) argued, by the terms of Cornwallis's capitulation—seems far-fetched. Clearly Washington wished to focus attention upon the activities of the Associated Loyalists in such a dramatic way that the British would take measures to check their depredations. It was at best a radical remedy for a grievous problem.

The French army stayed on until the conclusion of the preliminary treaty, and while a number of its officers returned to France, others, like the Marquis de Chastellux, traveled through the states and enjoyed the hospitality of grateful Americans wherever they went. Chastellux expressed his intention of writing a book about America. Although, in the opinion of Lauzun, he was "too hot-headed ever to stick to one idea for any length of time," he plunged with characteristic enthusiasm and uncharacteristic determination into his study of America and Americans. The American Philosophical Society for Promoting Useful Knowledge to be Held at Philadelphia elected him an associate member, and he visited and corresponded with a number of the leaders of the Revolution, Jefferson and James Madison among them. He reported to Claude Blanchard that he had "collected some notes respecting the American revolution, that he would not content himself with mere observations, and that he would publish a complete work."

What resulted was, in Blanchard's ill-natured opinion, a superficial work containing "some agreeable details . . . but many trifling matters, mediocre pleasantries and eulogiums, often but little deserved, or persons who had flattered him." The modern reader will judge otherwise. Chastellux's *Travels in North America in the Years* 1780, 1781, *and* 1782 is one of the most engaging and perceptive books written by a foreigner about Americans. Besides keen observations, it contains much advice, as good today (or better) than when it was first offered. "Your fellow citizens live and will continue to live," Chastellux wrote Madison, "in the vicinity of Nature; she is continually under their hands; she is always great and beautiful. Let them study her; let them consult her, and they can never go astray. Caution them only, not to build too much on the pedantic legislations of Cambridge, of Oxford, and Edinburgh, which have long assumed a sort of tyranny in the empire of opinion, and seem only to have composed a vast *classic* code for no other purpose than to keep all mankind in class, as if they were still children. . . . Let the universities, always too dogmatical, always too exclusive, be charged only to form good scholars, and leave to unrestrained philosophy the care of forming good men."

The marquis, an amateur anthropologist, stated it as a principle "that the character, the genius of a people, is not solely produced by the government they have adopted, but by the circumstances under which they were originally formed. . . . *Thus everything that is, partakes of what has been;* and to attain a thorough knowledge of any people, it is not less necessary to study their history than their legislation. If we then wish to form an idea of the American Republic, we must be careful not to confound the Virginians, whom warlike as well as merchantile, and ambitious as well as a speculative genius brought upon the continent, with the New Englanders, who owe their origin to enthusiasm; we must not expect to find precisely the same men in Pennsylvania, where the first colonists thought only of keeping and cultivating the deserts, and in South Carolina where the production of some exclusive articles fixes the general attention on external commerce, and establishes unavoidable connexions with the old world."

The Chevalier de Pontibaud, who sailed for Europe soon after Yorktown, was convinced that it was during this period that the younger and more impressionable French officers acquired those "false ideas of government and philanthropy" that they later "propagated in France with so much enthusiasm and such deplorable success,—for this mania of imitation powerfully aided the Revolution, though it is not the sole cause of it. . . ." "We are bound to confess," Pontibaud added, "that it would have been better both for themselves and us, if these young philosophers in red-heeled shoes had stayed at the Court."

The surrender of Cornwallis of course produced despair among the Tories of New York, who blamed the failure of British arms and all their consequent troubles on Clinton. William Franklin, whose vindictiveness Clinton had attempted to restrain, wrote spitefully, "The Commander in Chief is gallant to a proverb and possesses great military knowledge in the field, but he is weak, irresolute, unsteady, vain, incapable of forming any plan himself, and too weak or rather too proud and conceited to follow that of another [such as, presumably, Franklin]. . . . Since the death of André he has not had a man of abilities about him, never were there a set of men more eminently ill-qualified for the offices they occupy. In consequence there is confusion in every department though offices are multiplied without number. . . . If folly herself had presided at the helm, she could not take more effectual measures to overturn everything we had been doing."

The Tories were delighted when Clinton, who naturally tried to free himself from blame for the Yorktown disaster, was replaced by Carleton. Carleton was a very different kind of person. He had already had a distinguished career in America, as an officer under the revered Wolfe in the French and Indian War and as the able and energetic governor of Canada at the time of Arnold's invasion. Now he showed a generous and conciliatory spirit. He made clear to the Loyalists that he "had been all along with the opposition," that is to say, that he had always opposed the policy of trying to subdue America by force of arms. "He sees everything with his own eyes and hears everybody," an admiring Tory wrote. "He is up and about before four in the morning. Before the quarter part of his army have opened their eyelids, he has perhaps rode ten or a dozen miles; he comes almost every day to the parade, which is a signal that immediately after he will have a levee, where every one may tell their story, or request a private hour. . . . And those who have had conversations with him go away very much satisfied with his patience and condescension. In short, his conduct has procured him the respect of the army, and the love of the Loyalists."

The more realistic of the Tories understood that the war was near an end and that their enemies had triumphed. The England on which they had placed their fortunes and their hopes had failed them. Some prepared to move to Canada or Nova Scotia, others made plans to sail for England. Those simpler men and women, unable or unwilling to leave, began to cut their ties to the British army and to hope by their very inconspicuousness to avoid punishment at the hands of their fellow Americans. Still others clung in the face of all the odds to the illusion that Yorktown was simply a passing setback. James Rivington's *Royal Gazette*, the bellwether of Tory sentiment, exhorted the faint-hearted: "The melancholy catastrophe that has befallen my Lord Cornwallis and his gallant army is justly bewailed by every real lover of his country. But . . . we ought not to despond or despair. The spirit of the nation is too high, its resources too many, not to urge us to repair his loss and revenge his fate. Such accidents only stimulate the powerful and brave to a further persecution of the war."

There was further encouragement from England. In a letter written in January, 1782, a supporter of North wrote to a friend in New York, "Government here does not intend to give up the contest, and I am convinced that they will send out all the force that can be spared from this country and Ireland early in the spring. . . . So confident am I that this country will strain every nerve for the recovery of America, that I shall not think of any arrangements in my concerns which some panic struck creatures might be induced to adopt after the Chesapeake affair." Then in March word came that the ministry had given orders that offensive war should not be carried on in America. Five weeks later word arrived of the overthrow of the North ministry, and with that news even the most optimistic Tories began to give up hope.

There was brief revival of the New Yorkers' optimism in May with the news that Admiral Rodney had beaten and scattered De Grasse's fleet in the West Indies, taking the commander himself prisoner. The British artillery company paraded with their fieldpieces, along with two battalions of the Loyalist Kingston Regiment of foot militia; there were fireworks and illuminations and toasts to the defeat of the rebels and their allies.

Finally, however, the fatal word came—the articles of the preliminary treaty. A New York Tory, Beverley Robinson, whose house Benedict Arnold (who, by the way, had sailed for England with Cornwallis after Yorktown) had used as his headquarters and from which he had fled minutes before his plot was discovered, wrote to Clinton: "And, oh my dear Sir, what dreadful and distressing tidings does she [the ship that brought the news] bring us—the independence of America given up by the King without any conditions whatever, the Loyalists of America to depend upon the mercy of their enemies for the restoration of their possessions, which we are assured they will never grant, the greatest part of the estates that have been confiscated by them are already sold."

Another Tory wrote, "Never was despair and distraction stronger painted than in the countenances I momentarily see, and I do declare that I am often obliged to retire to my room to avoid hearing aspersions against my country too justly founded. The militia, who have been performing the military duties of the Crown have declined further service . . . and went to their different homes to console their wretched fates. . . . Papers are every night stuck up in every corner of the town with the most vindictive fury against those who advised our Sovereign to accede to the independence of this country."

Robinson, who had been proscribed by an act of the New York assembly, wrote, "I must . . . prepare to go to England with my wife and daughters, and I still comfort myself with the hope that the government of Great Britain will not suffer us to starve but allow us a small pittance to support us the remainder of our lives." The leading Loyalists of the city drew up a remonstrance that they presented to Carleton, protesting independence and speaking of the "inexpressible misfortune of being forever cast out from the protection of his Majesty." In addition, they drew up another appeal and gave it to William Franklin to present to the king.

In the words of one Tory, "It is the most awful moment of uncertainty. The extreme dejection of some, the fear of others, the anxiety and suspense of all is so strongly marked it checks the ardor of the stoutest hopes and forces you to participate in their alarms."

"Judge Bayard has given £300 for a cabin to transport himself and family to England. Billy says, 'God d—n them, I thought it would come to this. What is to become of me, sir. I am totally ruined, sir. I have not a guinea, sir.' Thomson, who . . . casts his eyes generally on the dark side of the picture, has worried himself into a settled illness. Coxe is struck dumb . . . Shoemaker says Providence will work good out of evil, Colonel Morris that if had remained in the army he should now have been an old Lieutenant General."

Carleton undertook to give all the assistance he could to those Tories who wished to go to Nova Scotia. Some six hundred persons, including women and children, were prepared to try their fortunes there, and Carleton made provisions for each family to receive a grant of five to six hundred acres and issued them clothing, tools, medicines, arms, and ammunition from the royal supplies.

Others clung on, hoping against hope. Beverley Robinson was sure that if the ministry were to offer "a proper and reasonable constitution to America at large without having anything to say to Washington or Congress," the great majority of Americans would gratefully accept it. On March 25 word came that the preliminaries to a general peace had been signed at Paris, "in consequence of which hostilities by sea and land were to cease. . . ." The proclamation for the halting of hostilities was read to a large crowd in front of Carleton's headquarters. "When the reading was concluded, no one huzza'd or showed any mark of joy or approbation," and "nothing but groans and hisses prevailed, attended by bitter reproaches and curses upon their king for having deserted them in the midst of their calamities."

When Robinson and his friends read the articles having to do with the restitution of Tory property, they felt that the final blow had fallen. "A greater cruelty could not have been laid upon any set of men whatever," he wrote to Clinton, "for we poor provincials are entirely excluded and not even allowed to be British subjects. . . . My dear sir, the cruel and hard treatment we have received from the Ministry of Great Britain is ten times more afflicting and cuts deeper to the heart than all the Americans can do to us. We have made them our enemies by adhering to and endeavoring to support the constitution and government of England, for which cause we are slighted and cast off as beggars."

Along with the exodus of Loyalists, hundreds of patriots who had abandoned their homes in advance of Howe's seizure of the city in 1776 poured back into New York to reclaim what was left of their possessions. Most were in for a keen disappointment. Carleton allowed them "to view their estates, take inventories and unmolested or insulted to return," but the British army still occupied the city, and the Americans who entered New York found they could not dispossess the occupants so readily as they had imagined. Many expressed their resentment by denouncing Tories they encountered on the streets, and such exchanges were usually especially bitter when former friends and neighbors met. Captain Tilton, an Associated Loyalist known to have burned "grist mills and meeting-houses," carried a spear to protect himself.

The *London Chronicle* printed a letter from an American Tory that described his plight in lurid terms: "Our fears at present surpass all description. Never was there upon the face of the earth a set of wretches in a more deplorable situation. Deprived of all hope of future comfort or safety, either for themselves or their unhappy wives and children, many have lost their senses, and now are in a state of perfect madness. Some have put a period to their miserable existence by drowning, shooting and hanging themselves, leaving their unfortunate wives and helpless infants destitute of bread to support them."

Meanwhile Washington and Carleton, joined by Governor George Clinton, met to discuss the evacuation of the city. "When all were seated Washington opened the business," speaking "without animation with great slowness and a low tone on voice." The general expressed his concern that the British troops not carry away with them property belonging to Americans, especially such slaves as had run away from their masters. On this point Carleton was emphatic. The British had promised them their freedom, and they therefore could not be forced back to slavery.

The evacuation proved more complicated than Carleton had anticipated. It appeared that many more Tories wished to leave with the British than anyone had guessed. In part this was based on the experience of those Tories who tried to return to their homes behind the American lines. "The violence of the Americans," Carleton wrote to Elias Boudinot, president of Congress, " . . . increased the number of their countrymen who look to me for escape from threatened destruction. Almost all within these lines conceive the safety both of their property and their lives depend upon their being removed by me, which renders it impossible to say when the evacuation will be completed."

The case of Joshua Booth was not atypical. He was seized near Goshen by patriots who bound him, cut off his hair, shaved his eyebrows with a penknife, tarred and feathered his head, and stuck a sheepskin cap on it. Then they hung a cowbell around his neck and pinned a paper on him that read:

> Look ye Tory crew
> and see what George
> your King can do.

Cavalier Jouett, a Tory who had been a prisoner at Woodbridge, New Jersey, and had been decently enough treated by the residents of that town, returned with his family "to speculate on the spirit of the times there"—in other words, to sound out the citizens and see if he might settle there. He was told, however, in no uncertain terms that "the case was altered now. . . . He had no right or title to come there." Some of the more intractable men of the town gathered around him with sticks and whips and threatened to give him a "continental jacket" if he did not depart promptly. When Jouett asked if he had ever injured any of them, the reply was that he had been a traitor to his country and "that no such damn rascal should ever enjoy the benefits of the country again."

Major Benjamin Tallmadge, the head of Washington's secret service, had agents in New York who were considered to be notorious Tories, and he feared for their safety after the British evacuation. Tallmadge thus asked for and received permission from Washington to enter the city under the cover of a flag of truce while the British were still there. In New York, Tallmadge wrote, "I was surrounded by British troops, tories, cowboys and traitors." Tallmadge was treated courteously by Carleton and besieged by Loyalists who begged him for "protection against the dreaded rage of their countrymen." Tallmadge contacted all his agents and took the necessary steps to protect them from punishment at the hands of the patriots.

In the face of the hostility of the patriots, many Tories who had been no more than passive adherents of the Crown feared to remain on American soil, and every British transport that could be pressed into service carried them off by the hundreds to Nova Scotia, England, or the West Indies. One group sailed for the Bahamas with six months' provisions for two thousand persons. A party of some two hundred went to Fort Frontenac in Canada to enter the fur trade there. But by far the largest number headed for Nova Scotia. The provincial troops— the King's American Dragoons and the Queen's Royal Rifles, among others—who had often fought so valiantly alongside British regulars, felt that they were in an especially dangerous situation. Many of the young officers and men had virtually grown up in the British service and now felt themselves entirely abandoned, without trades or professions to maintain themselves and their families. They petitioned Carleton for arms, ammunition, tools, provisions, building materials, three hundred acres of land, and three years' pay for every private and proportionately more for officers.

The Associated Loyalists, who, because of their constant raids and excursions, enjoyed the particular emnity of the Americans, also headed in large numbers for Nova Scotia. One of them wrote, "I can't bear the idea and it is distressing to me to think I should be drove with my wife in our old age and my two dear daughters to begin a settlement in a cold climate, and in the woods where we are to cut down the first tree. I can hardly expect to live to see the settlement so far advanced as to be in a tolerable comfortable way and then what a situation I shall leave my dear wife and daughters in."

A large fleet of transports arrived in April, and thousands of people, with all the worldly possessions they could carry with them, poured down to the docks to board the vessels. Carleton gave orders to the port officers and ships' captains that they should be allowed to take everything they wished, including farm implements, horses, and cattle. He had allowed American officers to be present on the wharves to make sure that no property belonging to patriots was carried off, and these officers, finding that dozens of Negroes were boarding the British ships, protested to Carleton that they were being carried off in violation of the terms of the peace treaty. Carleton's reply was that the blacks had been freed by British proclamation and were going aboard not as stolen property but as free men. "The Negroes I found free when I arrived at New York," he declared, "I had therefore no right, as I thought, to prevent their going to any part of the world they thought proper." At Nova Scotia, a "black town" adjacent to Port Roseway contained about twelve hundred free blacks, many of whom had served with the British forces during the war.

At the end of April, when the fleet sailed, it carried some seven thousand men, women, and children with it. Day after day more people applied for transportation; by the middle of August there was a list of over five thousand persons waiting to depart. In September a large fleet carried off most of the provincial regiments—Tarleton's British Legion, the New York Volunteers, the Loyal Americans, De Lancey's Volunteers, the Queen's Rangers, and the King's American Regiment—and other Loyalists, a total of eight thousand. In five months, a hundred and seventy-five ships of all kinds sailed out of the harbor of New York for the Bay of Fundy.

Meanwhile more and more Americans entered the city, often to buy up Loyalist property at bargain prices. Thomas Wertenbaker, in his history of New York during the Revolution, gives a vivid picture of the city during these months. "Down on the docks army commissioners were selling surplus stock—cattle, wagons, horses, firewood; on Queen Street there was one auction after another, as the departing merchants disposed of all goods they could not take with them; here one dealer was selling bricks, here another a pile of heavy timbers, there . . . barrels of sugar, molasses and rum. It was bargain day for the buyers." "There is no end to auctions and vendues," a returning patriot wrote, "everything, is selling off, and I believe a great deal more than the vender can make a good title for."

By the time the tide of humanity had ebbed, more than twenty-seven thousand Loyalists had made the passage to Nova Scotia and other towns and cities of Canada and had started their new lives. It must be said that the king and Parliament did their best for the loyal subjects. A commission was appointed to make a survey of the losses suffered by the Loyalists in "their rights, properties and professions." By 1790, they had received over three million pounds, which today would be equal to perhaps sixty or seventy million dollars. Pensions had been given to 588 persons, and some of the more prominent New York Tories came out quite well. Oliver de Lancey received £ 24,940; Beverley Robinson got an almost equal amount; and the Reverend Charles Inglis and Isaac Low, who had played an active part in Arnold's treachery, got £ 3,670 and £ 5,667 respectively.

In addition to the Loyalists, the British and Hessian regulars had to be evacuated; conspicuous among them were the troops captured at Yorktown, who were sent to New York as the port of embarkation. Carleton dispatched some of the New York garrison to England and requested another fleet to transport "the Anspach, Waldeck, Hanau and Anhalt Zerbst troops," to be followed by the Hessians. The stream of refugees seemed endless. In June, three thousand more Loyalists boarded fourteen transports for Nova Scotia, and a month later twenty-six crowded transports carried off "the Hessian and other foreign troops taken with Burgoyne."

As the Hessian officer John Charles Philip von Krafft, now a lieutenant, sailed out of the New York Harbor, he noted in his journal, "My whole heart is full of sadness when I see fading from my view the receding landmarks and house-tops, in whose midst I leave my whole happiness behind me."

16

Congress: A Rope of Sand

I N Congress the most serious problem was, as always, finances. During 1782 the states, with the exception of New Jersey, had not, Robert Morris wrote, "given me one shilling." New Jersey, which had been assessed $485,679, had contributed $5,500, considerably less than 1 per cent. "They have been deaf," Morris continued, "to the calls of Congress, to the clamors of the public creditors, to the just demands of a suffering army, and even to the reproaches of the enemy, who scoffingly declare that the American Army is fed, paid, and clothed by France."

The most critical point, of course, was the army. Since there was no official peace the army could not be safely disbanded, and even when peace came, the army could not be dismissed until the officers and men had been paid their wages. The issue was so delicate and crucial that Congress dispatched representatives to the various state legislatures to personally emphasize the desperateness of the situation. At the beginning of June, 1782, Morris reported that all pleas and exhortations had produced only twenty thousand dollars, one day's expenses. Four million dollars was due from the states on July 1, but only fifty thousand dollars was paid. The question at the back of every delegate's mind was whether, at the end of a long and exhausting war, with victory in sight, the United States was going to collapse into its component parts—

individual states, jealous, divided, parochial in their interests; not the nucleus of a great nation but a discord of petty states, contending for preferment and advantage. Even more likely was a prostrate Congress, overawed by a mutinous army made desperate by the neglect and indifference of the states.

"On the general subject of supplies," the South Carolina delegates wrote home in late October, "we need hardly inform you that our Army is extremely clamorous, we cannot pay them—we can hardly feed them. There is no money in the Treasury and we are obliged to draw upon the Foreign Loans before they are perfected."

Writing a month later, Alexander Hamilton noted, "There are good intentions in the Majority of Congress, but there is not sufficient wisdom or decision. There are dangerous prejudices in the particular states opposed to those measures which alone can give stability and prosperity to the Union. There is a fatal opposition to Continental views. Necessity alone can work a reform."

Congress had earlier proposed to the states a 5 per cent impost on all manufactured articles imported into any state, but according to the Articles of Confederation, all thirteen states had to ratify the amendment before it could become law. Eleven states ratified quite promptly, but Rhode Island and Georgia took no action, and in November, 1782, Congress gave a nudge to those states, calling, in its extremity, for "an immediate definitive answer." The Rhode Island delegates were embarrassed by the recalcitrance of their state. They had written in September to their legislature: "When we assure you that not a Farthing of money has been paid into the General Treasury from any of the states, excepting Pennsylvania, for more than a Year Since, you will agree with us that permanent Revenues are absolutely necessary."

The Rhode Island legislature did not agree, and two new delegates from that state came to defend its position. "The object of a seven years war," they wrote "has been to preserve the Liberties of this Country, and not to assume into our own hands the power of governing tyrannically." On December 6, Congress voted to dispatch a delegation to Rhode Island to urge the importance of the measure and made one more futile appeal to the states to fill the requisitions of Congress. Before the delegation got very far, it was overtaken by word that Virginia had repealed her approval of the impost, and that Maryland was reported about to follow suit. It was clear that a reaction had set in and that the impost was doomed. Parochialism had won out once more. Two years of effort had come to nothing.

At the same time, Washington called to the attention of Congress once again the discontent in the army caused by "the total want of money or the means of existing from one day to another, the heavy debts they have already incurred, the loss of credit, the distress of their families at home, and the prospect of poverty and misery before them." At last, in December, the army sent a deputation of officers to make representations directly to the delegates. The demands of the officers were reasonable enough: an advance of at least part of the pay due the men; a firm commitment to the balance; and, for the officers, the commutation of half-pay for life into full pay for a specific number of years or else a lump sum. "Our embarrassments thicken so fast," the petition read, " . . . that many of us are unable to go further. Shadows have been offered to us while the substance has been gleaned by others. The citizens murmur at the greatness of their taxes, and are astonished that no part reaches the army. We have borne all that men can bear." The documents concluded by suggesting that "further experiments" on the patience of the soldiers "may have fatal effects."

James Madison expressed very well the situation of the delegates in a letter to Governor Benjamin Harrison of Virginia. "Your Excellency will readily conceive the dilemma in which Congress are placed," he wrote, "pressed on one side by justice, humanity and the public good to fulfill engagements to which their funds are incompetent, and on the other left without even the resource of answering that every thing which could have been done had been done." In a letter to a friend, Madison wrote bitterly, "But what can a Virginia Delegate say whose constituents declare they are unwilling to make the necessary contributions, and [are] unwilling to establish funds for obtaining them elsewhere."

The pressure from the army meanwhile increased. Officers called on to testify before another of the interminable committees appointed by Congress to try and find a way out of its quandry declared "in very high-colored expressions . . . that if a disappointment were now repeated the most serious consequences were to be apprehended," and General Alexander McDougall stated that "the army were verging to that state which we are told will make a wise man mad."

It is important to note that at this point Washington's insistance on creating and maintaining a Continental Army received its ultimate vindication. The issue of state particularism versus national unity was joined on precisely the question of providing for the army. If the army had been allowed to disband and the responsibility for paying the soldiers had been shifted to the respective states from which those soldiers came (as some members of Congress wished), it is hard to believe that the principle of unity could have survived. Against all the forces pulling the states apart, one force, in essence, held them together: the necessity of coping with the Continental Army. It was also among the officers and men of the army that the strongest spirit of nationalism could be found. As MacDougall put it, "The most intelligent and considerate part of the army were deeply affected at the debility and defects of the federal Government, and the unwillingness of the States to cement and invigorate it." The creditors of the Congress, of course, were also strongly nationalistic; their best, if not only, hope for payment lay with a strengthened Congress. But this group was too scattered and lacking in political leverage to achieve its purpose unaided.

The advocates of a strong national government were well aware of the importance of the army in "cementing and invigorating" the federal government. "The great *desideratum*" Hamilton wrote to Washington in February, 1783, "is the establishment of general funds, which alone can do justice to the creditors of the United States (of whom the army forms the most meritorious class), restore public credit, and supply the future wants of government. This is the object of all men of sense; in this the influence of the army, properly directed, may cooperate." Hamilton was recommending a dangerous game when he hinted to Washington that he might "properly direct" the army to help secure "the establishment of general funds," but it is easy to appreciate the feelings of those who saw the so-recently-formed union on the verge of disintegration.

A land tax, a poll tax, a house tax, a window tax, a tax on salt, on imported wines, on coffee, in short, virtually every tax that had been known to societies of men was proposed and debated. But the trouble with all of them was that they required the concurrence of every state, and there seemed no prospect of securing such unanimity. "Every engine is at work here," Arthur Lee wrote a friend, "to obtain permanent taxes and the appointment of Collectors by Congress, in the States. The terror of a mutinying Army is played off with considerable efficacy."

The spirit that prevailed among unionists in most of the states at this time is suggested by Benjamin Lincoln's observation that a "heavy cloud [is] gathering over the United States . . . that, unless the greatest precautions are taken . . . will burst and sweep away our feeble confederation, and endanger, if not overturn, the union of these states." To Lincoln it appeared that the states were taking the position "that they have borne more than their proportion of the expenses of the war, and that the United States are greatly indebted to their inhabitants, who, they say, look to *them* for protection, justice & relief. I find that those states have it in contemplation, to settle the debts due from the United States to their own inhabitants, charge the United States with the sum, and deduct it from any requisition of Congress, which has been made upon them. . . . The moment the several states think they have this right, and think proper to exercise it, we may date the loss of the confederation, the annihilation of the Union, and the ruin of the states."

One of the few accomplishments of Congress, waiting bemusedly for the end of the war in 1782, was the adoption of the Great Seal of the United States. The matter had been under consideration since July, 1776, when a committee made up of Franklin, John Adams, and Jefferson had been charged with bringing in proposals for a design. One that was suggested and abandoned showed the Children of Israel fleeing across the Red Sea, pursued by the Egyptians, led by a pharaoh who looked rather like George III. The committee brought in another design on August 20, but the delegates were unenthusiastic and the matter was laid aside, although certain elements of the design, among them *E Pluribus Unum* and "the Eye of Providence in a radiant Triangle," would appear in subsequent versions. In March, 1780, a new committee, made up of James Lovell, John Morin Scott, and William Houston, had been appointed, and several months later they submitted a design that Congress, after some debate, had recommitted.

In the spring of 1782, a committee made up of Arthur Middleton and John Rutledge of South Carolina and Elias Boudinot of New Jersey took up the task once more. The committee enlisted the help of a Philadelphia amateur of heraldry, William Barton, who submitted a design showing an eagle with arrows and an olive branch in its talons. It also included a pyramid on the reverse side. Charles Thomson, the secretary of Congress, apparently added the mottoes *Annuit Coeptis* ("He, God, favors our undertakings") and *Novus Ordo Seclorum* ("A New Age Now Begins") to the reverse side. On June 20, 1782, Thomson placed the design before Congress, and it was adopted the same day.

Before dispatches arrived from the American commissioners announcing the preliminary peace, a letter circulated in the press that purported to be from the secretary of Parliament to the lord mayor of London. Dated December 3, it referred to "the preliminary articles for a peace, signed on the 30th of November, by the Ambassadors on the part of England, and those on the part of the United States. . . . It now only remains to sign the articles between Great-Britain and France, to constitute a general peace." This encouraging note was followed by a report from France that the war might continue indefinitely, since the negotiators could not agree. A month later word came of the king's speech in Parliament, in which it was stated that the preliminary treaty with "the American Colonies" had been signed. But what did "American Colonies" mean? Was this some dodge? Did it conceal a persistent unwillingness to acknowledge independence? Congress remained "in a very disagreeable state of suspense." It was over ten weeks since Livingston had heard any word from the American commissioners.

"Here," a member of Congress wrote on March 11, "we wait with anxiety for the stage from Elizabethtown, and at New York, the shores are crowded, the evening they are to hear from Philadelphia." By then it was five months since any dispatches had arrived from the Congressional commissioners. Finally, on March 12, Captain Joshua Barney arrived with official word of the provisional treaty signed on November 30. The news had taken three days short of three-and-a-half months to cross the Atlantic.

For four days after the arrival of the preliminary treaty, the delegates to Congress spent their time reading and discussing the dispatches. Of course the treaty was not to go into effect until the conclusion of a treaty between Great Britain and France, but most members felt that the war was, indeed, at an end. "Upon the whole." one delegate wrote, "if we have not peace, there has been a game played that will be the wonder of ages yet to come; however, I have great hopes and small fears." Most of the delegates were surprised and pleased by the generous terms of the treaty. "The terms granted to America," James Madison wrote, "appeared to Congress on the whole extremely liberal." A member from New Hampshire noted that the articles covering the boundaries and fisheries "are Ample and I believe Equal to the most Sanguine Expectation." The provision in regard to the Tories was at once discerned to be full of loopholes, clearly designed to enable the British ministry to say to the Loyalists "that they had attended to their Interest as far as Lay in their power on the Settlement of a peace."

What did raise a storm in Congress was the very evident fact that the commissioners had not followed their instructions "to undertake nothing in the negotiations for peace or truce without [French] knowledge and concurrence." The course followed by the commissioners, Madison noted, "affected different members of Congress very differently." As might have been expected, those of the pro-French party were furious and wished to censure the commissioners. The anti-French were, on the whole, pleased. Defeated in Congress, they had triumphed in Paris. The secret article on West Florida, which provided that if England had wrested West Florida from the Spanish by the time peace was concluded, it should remain in English hands, was "most offensive." It was the clearest and most unjustifiable violation of the commissioners' instructions. A good many delegates judged it "inconsistent with the spirit of the Alliance, and a dishonorable departure from the candor, rectitude, and plain dealing professed by Congress."

Congress was thus in a quandary, a position "infinitely perplexing," as Madison wrote in cipher to Edmund Randolph. One of the problems was that Congress had applied for a grant from the French king of twenty million livres that it desperately needed; the delegates were dismayed by the thought that the Court, offended by the action of the American commissioners, might refuse it. Luzerne, indignant at the failure of his own long and assiduously pursued policy, expressed his displeasure to Livingston and to those members of Congress who were his pliant tools. Word that the king had given America six million livres relieved that anxiety and suggested that the French Court was perhaps not as displeased as it professed to be.

The course recommended by Livingston to Congress was that the commissioners be instructed to inform the minister of France of the secret article "in such a manner as will best tend to remove any unfavorable impression it may make on the court of France of the sincerity of these States or their ministers." Alexander Hamilton, now a delegate from New York, offered a resolution in Congress to give effect to Livingston's proposal, and a warm debate followed. Some delegates wished to censure and recall the commissioners, while others wished to commend them.

If the delegates had hoped that word of the preliminary articles would relieve them of pressure from the army, they were quickly disabused. Some Continental officers, their patience exhausted, had started to circulate papers calling on the soldiers to take matters into their own hands. This was the moment of which there had been so many warnings. The Newburgh Addresses, as the papers were called, proposed that the officers of the army notify Congress that unless their grievances were promptly redressed they would refuse to disband when peace was concluded, and if the war were to continue they would "retire to some unsettled country," leaving Congress without an army. It was at this point that the "conspiracy," if it was that, came to Washington's attention.

Mild or temporizing action would have brought the incipient mutiny to full flower, but Washington acted quickly and firmly. He denounced the "disorderly proceedings" of the previous day (March 10, the day of the first Newburgh Address) in general orders and directed that representatives of every regiment meet on the fifteenth "to discuss how best to attain the just and important object in view." The second Newburgh Address, which appeared on the twelfth, stated that Washington's general orders had indicated support for the conspirators. It was an agonizing moment for Washington. He was the last person to have illusions about Congress or about the willingness of the states to make their proportionate contributions to any system of national finances. Yet he had set as his star the principle that the military power must always be subordinate to civil authority. In the name of that principle, he had a hundred times accommodated himself to the wishes of Congress when they were contrary to his best judgment. He had stoicly endured petty harassments, jealousies, the failure to fulfill promises, and perhaps above all, starvation rations for his officers and his men over eight long, bitter years; now, with the final, triumphant end in sight, he was tested once more.

He had feared mutiny from his sorely pressed troops, for years had warned against it, and he had prevented it, in large part, because of his own awesome presence and the veneration in which he was held by those who served under him. The army had survived at least two minor uprisings and one major one—the mutiny of the Pennsylvania Line. The spirit behind the Newburgh Addresses was more deadly and implacable than any earlier movement of revolt. The previous episodes had been limited to the ranks of the enlisted men. Now officers and men were united in a determination to win redress of their grievances from Congress, which of course had no means to remove them. Major John Armstrong, son of the general, was apparently the ringleader. While Washington had the deepest sympathy for the plight of his soldiers, he was determined to suppress the movement before it got out of hand.

Never an easy or spontaneous speaker, the general appeared at the meeting of officers on the fifteenth with a carefully prepared address. His appearance was in itself startling and unexpected to the conspirators. Even the boldest of them must have realized that their cause was lost when the commander in chief arrived with his aides and asked to speak. "Gentlemen," he began, "By an anonymous summons, an attempt has been made to convene you together; how inconsistent with the rules of propriety! how unmilitary! and how subversive of all order and discipline, let the good sense of the army decide."

He read the words with difficulty and with obvious emotion, and then, pausing at the end of the opening paragraph, he took out his glasses "and begged the indulgence of his audience while he put them on, observing at the same time that he had grown grey in their service and now found himself growing blind. There was something so natural, so unaffected, in this appeal," one of the officers present recalled, "as rendered it superior to the most studied oratory. It forces its way to the heart, and you might see sensibility moisten every eye."

With his glasses on and his audience now thoroughly his, Washington continued. The address, he told his listeners "was calculated to impress the mind, with the idea of premediated injustice in the Sovereign power of the United States, and rouse all those resentments which must unavoidably flow from such a belief." He had always put the interests of the army first. "It can *scarcely be supposed* at this late stage of the War," he said solemnly, "that I am indifferent to its interests. But, how are they to be promoted?" "The anonymous Addresser" had recommended withdrawing from the United States; "this dreadful alternative, of either deserting our Country in the extremest hour of her distress, or turning our Arms against it . . . has something so shocking in it, that humanity revolts at the idea. My God! what can this writer have in view, by recommending such measures? Can he be a friend to the Army? Can he be a friend to this Country?

"For myself . . . the sincere affection I feel for an Army, I have so long had the honor to Command," Washington continued, "will oblige me to declare in this public and solemn manner, that, in the attainment of compleat justice for all your toils and dangers, and in the gratification of every wish, so far as may be done consistently with the great duty I owe my Country, and those powers we are bound to respect, you may freely command my Services to the utmost of my abilities."

At the close, Washington exhorted his officers to express their "utmost horror and detestation of the Man who wishes, under any specious pretences, to overturn the liberties of our Country, and who wickedly attempts to open the flood Gates of Civil discord, and deluge our rising Empire in Blood." By so doing "[you] will give one more distinguished proof of unexampled patriotism and patient virtue, rising superior to the complicated sufferings; And you will . . . afford occasion for Posterity to say, when speaking of the glorious example you have exhibited to Mankind, 'had this day been wanting, the World have never seen the last stage of perfection to which human nature is capable of attaining.'"

Washington is sometimes depicted as a rather simple person of limited intellectual range, a blunt, plainspoken man, a doer rather than a thinker. Be that as it may, his handling of the potential revolt indicated by the Newburgh Addresses was masterly. That is not to say it was artificial or contrived. Certainly the contrary is true. But the commander in chief handled the episode with the keenest political instinct and the wisest judgment. Most commanders in such circumstances would have tried to crush the incipient uprising by ferreting out and arresting the ringleaders. Washington certainly had the means of finding out who the principal culprits were. But he was too astute to react in such a manner. To have singled certain individuals out would have been to risk making martyrs of them; it would, if the persons exposed were popular officers, have almost certainly stiffened the resistance of the army as a whole; it would have had the effect of seeming to ally Washington with Congress and those at whose hands the army felt it had suffered.

It would have been equally fatal, as we have suggested, to have done nothing and thereby seem to have given tacit approval to the movement. Washington's strategy of simply appearing at the meeting of the mutinous officers was a brilliant one. He let two tension-filled days pass in which he appeared to have taken no position, and then he appeared and spoke in the most powerful and compelling way. The little incident with the glasses at the beginning of his speech was doubtless spontaneous, but it was also the consequence of unerring instinct. Then, with many of his officers already in tears, Washington did not upbraid or attack them; he confined his indictment to the single officer who had written the address, as though only he were guilty of treasonable thoughts. Instead of putting them on the defensive by seeming to question their loyalty, he invited the officers to join him in condemning one individual who was attempting to mislead them all. He recalled their long and arduous service together, spoke vividly of the dangers of such a course of action as that proposed by the author of the address, and then appealed to that ultimate judge—posterity. In that final sentence he touched on one of the deepest chords that vibrated in the American soul. If the officers were to lead the army in a revolt against Congress and thereby throw the United States into turmoil, posterity would never know the outcome of that great struggle for liberty through which they had so recently passed; the great experiment would be aborted, and the world would never see the results of "the last stage of perfection to which human nature is capable of attaining," the dream of a new and better age for mankind.

When Washington had finished his speech, he withdrew. The shamefaced officers competed with each other in resolutions of loyalty, of confidence in the good intentions of Congress, and of their rejection of the "infamous propositions . . . in a late anonymous address." Major Samuel Shaw, our most reliable source for the meeting, added a most perceptive comment. "On other occasions," he wrote, Washington "had been supported by the exertions of an Army and the countenance of his friends but in this he stood single and alone. . . . He appeared, not at the head of his troops, but as it were in opposition to them; and for a dreadful moment the interests of the Army and its General seemed to be in competition! He spoke—every doubt was dispelled, and the tide of patriotism rolled again in its wonted course."

It is difficult to sufficiently emphasize the symbolic importance of the so-called Newburgh conspiracy. Not only did Washington's action have the very important practical effect of nipping the conspiracy in the bud; it provided just that striking occasion for him to complete the transition from a military chieftain to a civil leader. His handling of the Newburgh conspiracy killed further serious talk of mutiny and thereby preserved the army, its morale not only intact but undoubtedly considerably improved (as a result of Washington's reminder that they were heroes and the makers of a new order). The episode also demonstrated that Washington was a greater power than Congress; by his courage and his political genius, he had rescued it if not from extinction at least from embarrassment and humiliation. In so doing he had effected a subtle but critically important change in the nature of American politics. That change would bear fruit in the Federal Constitution and in his own administration as the first president.

Washington's success in quelling the Newburgh conspiracy did not result, as he undoubtedly had hoped it would, in renewed efforts to create an adequate system of national finances. "We are still hammering," wrote Stephen Higginson of Massachusetts on April 7, "on a strange, though artful, plan of finance, in which are combined a heterogeneous mixture of imperceptible and visible, constitutional and unconstitutional taxes. . . . This connection and dependence of one part on another is designed to produce the adoption of the whole." Higginson, who was a strong advocate of state sovereignty, was suspicious of all such efforts. Besides, he noted, "Congress have not yet tried the strength of the Confederation." He believed that "there must be a thorough disposition in the States . . . to take their respective shares of the common burden, and to adhere strictly to the principles of the Confederation, or the Union will necessarily be dissolved." The North Carolina delegates put the matter more trenchantly: "We have promised but have not yet been able to pay them [the army] one month's pay. . . . Promises, even those which are spacious, are found to be very light food. . . . For whatever has been fabled concerning the Chamelion, it is generally believed that no animal can live on the air. Money, or good securities are desired, we have neither."

Hamilton summed up the situation in a letter to Washington: "There are two classes of men Sir in Congress of very different views— one attached to state the other to Continental politics. The last have been strenuous advocates for funding the public debt upon solid securities, the former have given every opposition in their power and have only been dragged into the measures which are no nearer being adopted [through] the clamours of the army and other public creditors."

Finally, after much thrashing about, Congress decided on April 18 to ask the states for the power to levy an *ad valorem* tax on articles imported into the United States. "It has been the most difficult and perplexing question," Virginia's Joseph Jones wrote Washington, "of any that has engaged the attention of this body for some time. The various objects to be combined, and the different interests to be reconciled, to make the system palatable to the States was a work not easily or speedily to be effected; and altho' it was the wish of many to settle the plan upon clear and unquestioned principles of finance, yet such were the prejudices of some States, and of some individuals, and such their jealousies, we were obliged to take a middle course with respect to its duration, and the appointment of Collectors, or hazard ultimately the loss of the measure. As it stands it will answer the purposes intended, if the States will grant their concurrence."

That proved to be the difficulty. James Madison wrote an eloquent address to accompany Congress's request to the states for "concurrence." It was the same theme played upon by Washington in his response to the Newburgh Addresses. After describing in vivid terms the desperate needs of the army and of Congress, Madison added, "Let it be remembered finally, that it has ever been the pride and boast of America, that the rights for which she contended, were the rights of human nature. . . . No instance has heretofore occurred, nor can any instance be expected hereafter to occur, in which the unadulterated forms of Republican government can pretend to so fair an opportunity of justifying themselves by their fruits. In this view the citizens of the United States are responsible for the greatest trust ever confided to a political society. If justice, good faith, honor, gratitude, and all the other qualities which ennoble the character of a nation, and fulfill the ends of government, be the fruits of our establishments, the cause of liberty will acquire a dignity and lustre which it has never yet enjoyed; and an example will be set which cannot but have the most favourable influence on the rights of mankind." If the reverse should take place, Madison concluded, "the great cause which we have engaged to vindicate will be dishonored and betrayed; the last and fairest experiment in favour of the rights of human nature will be turned against them, and their patrons and friends exposed to be insulted and silenced by the votaries of tyranny and usurpation."

But the impost, even if conceded by the states, would not solve the immediate dilemma, which was how to pay the army. "Our circumstances," a delegate wrote to Baron von Steuben, "afford an odd contrast to those we have heretofore experienced. The Difficulty which heretofore oppress'd us was how to raise an Army. The one which now embarrasses us is how to dissolve it."

The problem that Congress faced can be simply stated. Every day that the army remained in existence represented an increased expense, an expense that Congress was unable to meet and which thus constituted a charge against any future revenues. Justice and good policy demanded that some step be taken to provide for the soldiers who had received no pay for months on end and for the officers whose future status was still unsettled. Until the definitive treaty was signed, the war was not officially over. It would therefore be reckless to totally disband the army, even if it were possible to persuade the men and officers of the Continental Army to return to their homes with their demands unmet. The expedient that a desperate Congress decided upon was to send home on furlough all those noncommissioned officers and men who had enlisted for the duration of the war. In lieu of pay they were to carry with them what were in effect promissory notes, issued in the name of Congress and pledging three months pay when Congress should procure the money. To the relief of Congress, the furloughing proceeded "with perfect good order," as Washington put it, and the men departed "without a settlement of their accounts, or a farthing of money in their pockets." It was certainly shabby treatment for the men who had carried the principal burden for the cause of liberty.

The case with the officers was somewhat different. They submitted, through Washington, what Madison called "a pathetic representation," stating that they were soon "to retire from their subsistence without receiving the means of subsistence elsewhere." At the same time, Washington wrote a letter to the president of Congress stating that he himself was preparing "to return to that domestic retirement, which, it is well known, I left with the greatest reluctance, a Retirement for which I have never ceased to sigh through a long and painful absence, and in which (remote from the noise and trouble of the World) I meditate to pass the remainder of life in a state of undisturbed repose." The contest now approaching a successful conclusion had been an unequal and a doubtful one, and the victory of the Americans "will afford infinite delight to every benevolent and liberal mind . . . and we shall have equal occasion to felicitate ourselves on the lot which Providence has assigned us, whether we view it in a natural, a political or moral point of light." The citizens of the new nation "had been placed in the most enviable condition, as the sole Lords and Proprietors of a vast Tract of Continent, comprehending all the various soils and climates of the World, and abounding with all the necessaries and conveniences of life," and now had secured the most precious of gifts, "absolute freedom and Independency."

Washington then proceeded to develop the theme he had opened with his officers at the time of the Newburgh Addresses. Americans must be considered, from this time forth, he wrote, "as Actors on a most conspicuous Theatre, which seems to be peculiarly designated by Providence for the display of human greatness and felicity. . . ." Not only did Americans have an abundance of all the material things needed "for private and domestic enjoyment, but Heaven has crowned all its other blessings, by giving a fairer opportunity for political happiness, than any other Nation has ever been favored with. . . . The foundation of our Empire was not laid in the gloomy age of Ignorance and Superstition, but at an Epocha when the rights of mankind were better understood and more clearly defined, than at any former period, the researches of the human mind, after social happiness, have been carried to a greater extent, the Treasures of knowledge, acquired by the labours of Philosophers, Sages and Legislatures, through a long succession of years, are laid open for our use, and their collected wisdom may be happily applied to the Establishment of our forms of Government, free circulation of Letters, and the unbounded extension of Commerce, the progressive refinement of Manners, the growing liberality of sentiment, and, above all, the pure and benign light of Revelation, have had a meliorating influence on all mankind and increased the blessings of Society."

That was the situation in which the citizens of the United States found themselves, and such were their prospects for helping to spread political and social justice and enlightenment around the world. The real question, as Washington saw it, was whether the United States had the courage and enterprise to seize the opportunity presented to it, "whether they will be respectable and prosperous, or contemptible and miserable as a Nation. This is the time of their political probation, this is the moment when the eyes of the whole World are turned upon them, this is the moment to establish or ruin [our] national Character forever, this is the favorable moment to give such a tone to our Federal Government, as will enable it to answer the ends of its institution, or this may be the ill-fated moment for relaxing the powers of the Union, annihilating the cement of the Confederation, and exposing us to become the sport of European politics, which may play one state against another to prevent their growing importance, and to serve their own interested purposes. . . . It is yet to be decided whether the Revolution must ultimately be considered a blessing or a curse, not to the present age alone, for with our fate will the destiny of unborn Millions be involved."

If one had to select a single document to sum up the dreams and aspirations or perhaps, the presumptions of the Revolution, and one that contained in its rhetoric the seed of the new nation, it would be difficult to find a better one than Washington's letter to the president of Congress. Its eloquence was all the more moving since the author had acted out, in the most dramatic terms, his own commitment to the great hope of redemption—first for Americans and then for the world that watched so anxiously the outcome of the struggle between Great Britain and her erstwhile colonies. Here again was posterity in the form of those "unborn Millions," endless legions stretching as far into the future as the mind could reach, who would curse or bless their progenitors as they were false or true to their trust, which was no less than the happiness and prosperity of the human species.

With the letter, Washington placed the weight of his enormous prestige on the side of a strong national government and against a narrow and parochial notion of America as a loose confederation of sovereign states. But not even that great reputation, which grew daily, was enough to tip the scales decisively toward nationalism. The champions of a federal union succeeded in having Washington's letter sent out to all the states along with that of the officers. "I doubt not," wrote Elias Boudinot, who was serving a second term as president of Congress, that the states "will rejoice in an opportunity of rewarding their [the officers'] Toils by a strict fulfilment of all the public engagements." It was a pious hope; Boudinot certainly knew the states well enough by now to know that Congress was whistling in the wind.

If Boudinot did not know it, the soldiers did. On June 13th, one of the furloughed regiments, stationed in Philadelphia, sent a "mutinous remonstrance" to Congress. Signed by the sergeants, it was reminiscent of the mutiny of the Pennsylvania Line, but it was more threatening since the complainants were quite literally within a stone's throw of the halls of Congress. Benjamin Lincoln and General St. Clair managed to placate the soldiers, but a few days later word reached the city that some eighty men of the Third Pennsylvania Regiment at Lancaster were on the march for Philadelphia to place their demands before Congress. When Congress applied to John Dickinson, president of the supreme council of the state, for militia troops to protect the delegates, Dickinson replied that he did not believe the militia could be relied on to take up arms against the soldiers unless there were some actual outrage; "it would hazard the authority of government," he declared, to attempt to stop the soldiers from entering Philadelphia.

When the men arrived they established themselves in an empty barracks and announced that they had come to secure a settlement of their accounts with Congress. Their mood did not seem overly belligerent, and the situation was judged, at least for the moment, to be "tolerably easy." It being Friday, Congress adjourned for the weekend. But Saturday morning, with evidence of trouble brewing, Boudinot summoned Congress into emergency session. The number of angry soldiers had grown to four or five hundred, and these "very unexpectedly appeared before, and surrounded, the State House, with fixed Bayonets, the Supreme Executive Council, sitting also in the same House."

The soldiers' attention was first directed to Dickinson; from him they demanded commissions so that they could appoint their own officers with "full powers to adopt such measures as they may judge most likely to procure us justice. You will immediately issue such authority and deliver it to us," their letter stated, "or otherwise we shall instantly let those injured soldiers upon you, and abide by the consequences. You have only twenty minutes to deliberate on this important matter." Dickinson simply handed the missive to Congress, and that body found itself in a most unpleasant quandary. Dickinson, called on once more to take action against the mutineers, protested his inability to do so. General St. Clair was directed to use his influence, which turned out to be nil. Hamilton then urged St. Clair to "take order for terminating the mutiny," in other words, to use force. But there was no force to use. Finally it was decided to remain in cession, to take no notice of the mutineers surrounding the State House, and to adjourn at the normal hour of three o'clock. So for several uncomfortable hours, the delegates sat, waited, and wondered if they would find themselves prisoners of their own soldiers when they tried to leave the State House. When, at very long last, the delegates filed out of the hall, some of the bolder soldiers pretended to block the way but then withdrew. There was a barrage of boos and catcalls, but the members passed unharmed through the mob of angry soldiers and curious spectators.

Boudinot, on the advice of Congress, sent off a letter to Washington at Newburgh, asking him to march toward Philadelphia with his most reliable troops in the event his intervention should be needed. After several emergency meetings had failed to decide upon a proper course of action, Congress voted to adjourn and meet three days later at Princeton. At this point, as unexpectedly as they had risen, the mutineers laid down their arms, asked for clemency, and blamed the whole affair on their officers. Substance was given to the charge by the fact that two of the officers fled from the city and boarded packets for England. One of them left a message justifying his conduct as the consequence of "a series of injuries and . . . incessant indignities" that the army had experienced. "Let what bad men there are at the helm of Government observe from this instance how dangerous it is to drive men of honor to desperation. . . . All we regret is failing in a noble attempt."

On the eve of Congress's departure for Princeton, a delegate from North Carolina wrote to the governor of his state, describing the plight of that body as "without the means of paying those Debts they Constitutionally contracted for the safety of the United States, responsible for every thing, and unable to do any thing, hated by the public creditors, insulted by the Soldiery and unsupported by the citizens." Major John Armstrong, the author of the Newburgh Addresses, who had been in Philadelphia during the mutiny and may well have had a hand in it, wrote to Horatio Gates, "I have had my share of sweat, dust and watching. I have scarcely spirits to hold up my head. . . . The grand Sanhedrin of the Nation, with all their solemnity and emptiness, have removed to Princeton, and left a state, where their wisdom has been long question'd, their virtue suspect, and their dignity a jest." For Congress, it was the nadir of its short but troubled life.

In Princeton, Congress proceeded to wrangle for months over the question of where blame belonged for their humiliation in Philadelphia. To Benjamin Rush, who blamed Congress, a Pennsylvania delegate, John Montgomery replied: "Wou'd not the Charge lay with more propriety against the States who have withheld their taxs and have Defeated Evry Salutary measure proposed by Congrass of Establishing revenues in order to do Justice to the Soldier and Criditor." Rush wrote back, "The Congress is abused, laughed at and cursed in every company."

It was soon evident that the delegates missed the amenities of Philadelphia, the well-appointed taverns, and the agreeable social life; but they had been virtually driven from the city, and their pride was wounded. They would not return unless they were invited. As Montgomery put it, "will you proud Philadelphians Condessend to invite them to return or will you rather say that they went without our Knowlage and they may return without an invetation. We will not stoop to do it." If Congress were invited back, "things will Come to rights again, mens tempers will Cool and thire fears Subside and Congrass will strut on the pavements of the grand metropolaiss and talk those Woundefull thing over and Congratulate Each other on the mervolous Esscape we made and the great Wisdom and prudence in Conducting affair to a happey Esue." But no invitation was forthcoming. Congress remained at Princeton, and the delegates expressed their disenchantment with that provincial village by not attending. For most of the period that Congress met there, only six states were represented, so that no business of consequence could be conducted. One delegate withdrew to his farm in disgust, writing to a friend, "I am much the happiest when I hear or think nothing of the erratic meteor which rose with so much splendor and I fear will set with no small disgrace."

Congress, when it did meet, gave a good deal of its attention to the matter of a permanent home. Maryland offered to be host. In August, Philadelphia at last proposed that Congress return, but it was decided to adjourn to Annapolis for six months or a year, and then go to Trenton, New Jersey, for a like period, "so that," in Boudinot's wry phrase, "we are to be in future wandering Stars and to have our Aphelion and Perihelion." Perhaps in this fashion they would not wear out their welcome in any one spot.

On November 4 Congress adjourned to meet at Annapolis on the twenty-sixth. At this point an embarrassing situation developed. The terms of the definitive treaty, which arrived on the eve of Congress's departure, were almost identical with those of the preliminary treaty, but the treaty provided that it should be signed by both parties within six months. The problem was to assemble delegates from a sufficient number of states to ratify the treaty in time for it to get back to England before the six-month period should expire. On December 13 delegates from seven states assembled in Annapolis, but the Articles of Confederation stated that no important action—and ratification of the definitive treaty was assuredly that—could be taken by Congress without the concurrence of nine states. With the most conclusive act of the Revolution about to be performed, sufficient states could not be mustered to perform it. On December 16, Jefferson wrote to Edmund Pendleton, "We have no certain prospect of nine states in Congress and cannot ratify the treaty with fewer, yet the ratifications have to be exchanged by the 3d of March." Meanwhile the delegates conducted what business they could and waited for the arrival of their colleagues.

On several occasions the departure of delegates on private business shrank the number of states represented to six and once to five. Jefferson wrote to Madison, "We have never yet had more than 7 states and very seldom that, as Maryland is scarcely ever present, and we are now without a hope of it's attending till February, consequently having six states only, we do nothing." Richard Bereford, a delegate from South Carolina, was ill in Philadelphia. In desperation, Jefferson proposed adjourning Congress to Bereford's sickroom so that the treaty might be ratified before it was too late, but this suggestion was deemed impractical. Some of the frustrated delegates proposed finally that the seven states ratify the treaty and conceal from Great Britain the fact that the ratification was unconstitutional. Jefferson opposed the notion. Word would leak out, and America would appear ridiculous in the eyes of the world.

Finally, on January 13, two delegates from Connecticut arrived; the next day the convalescing Richard Bereford attended, and nine states ratified the treaty. The next question was: Could the treaty be taken to England in time to meet the deadline, only six weeks away? The chances were certainly slim. Three copies were immediately prepared and dispatched on three different vessels. Colonel Josiah Harmar, secretary to the president of Congress, was given the original, and he dashed to New York to catch a French packet that was about to sail. Robert Morris was given a copy with instructions to get it to England any way he could, and a third copy was given to Colonel David Franks with instructions to get the first ship he could find sailing for Europe. Harmar's packet, which sailed on January 21, ran aground leaving New York Harbor and was forced to return to port. It was five weeks after they left Annapolis before either Harmar or Franks were on the ocean. Jacob Read of South Carolina comforted himself with the assurance that "As the greatest good faith has been observed on our part and Nought but the Act of God has prevented the Ratification getting to Europe in Time I trust no ill will result to the Union from the delay." Harmar, who reached London first, was a month late, but the British ministry had no inclination to haggle, and the ratifications were exchanged on May 12.

The story is worth relating because it shows the condition to which Congress, under the Articles of Confederation, had sunk. Those political leaders in every state who were already convinced of the need for reform were able to add another arrow to their quiver.

Having at last ratified the definitive treaty and thus brought a formal end to a war that had, for most practical purposes, ended after the surrender of Cornwallis at Yorktown, it seemed to the weary patriots that the time had arrived for celebration. There was, inevitably, something anticlimactic about such an event, but plans were nonetheless entered into with enthusiasm. Philadelphia, while not the present seat of Congress, was plainly the most appropriate place for the main celebration.

The Pennsylvania assembly appropriated six hundred pounds for a triumphal arch to be erected at the upper end of Market Street, and Charles Willson Peale was put in charge of its construction. On his direction a Roman arch forty feet high and fifty feet wide was constructed of canvas and adorned with appropriate paintings and mottoes. January 22 was set as the night for the celebration. Eleven hundred lamps were lit at dusk to illuminate the city. But as Peale climbed to the top of the arch to set the highest lamp, a rocket, prematurely discharged, ignited the arch. With his clothes on fire, Peale fell twenty feet to the street, breaking two of his ribs. A number of spectators, crowded around the arch, were burned by pieces of flaming canvas, and a sergeant of artillery was killed.

Plans were immediately made to build a new arch, and the celebration was rescheduled for May 10. On that night there was a new arch, "a marriage of classic Rome and modern Peale." Over the center, in Latin and English, was written the line from Vergil taken from the reverse side of the Great Seal of the United States: *Novus Ordo Seclorum.* A bust of Louis XVI was conspicuous on one side, and a cenotaph in honor of those who had died for their country appeared on the other. A sun, for France, and thirteen stars for the United States were painted on the frieze. Other scenes and symbols represented peace and commerce, the loyalty of the army, the Christianizing of the Indians, and the growth of the arts and sciences. Below was a painting of a large tree with thirteen branches, heavy with fruit and bearing the motto, "By the Strength of the Body will these ripen." Another panel showed Cincinnatus, the Roman farmer-general, returning to his plow crowned with laurel, obviously a tribute to George Washington.

17

The Army Disbands

O N May 13, 1783, with the war at an end and the disbanding of the army imminent, a group of officers led by Baron von Steuben, Henry Knox, and Edward Hand met to form a society to preserve the bond between officers of the Continental Army. "It has pleased the Supreme Governor of the Universe," the constitution of the society read, " . . . to cause the separation of the Colonies of North America from the domination of Great Britain, and . . . to establish them free, independent, and sovereign States, connected by alliances founded on reciprocal advantages. . . . To perpetuate, therefore, as well the remembrance of this vast event, as the mutual friendships which have been formed under the pressure of common danger, and in many instances cemented by the blood of the parties, the officers of the American army do hereby . . . associate, constitute, and combine themselves into one society of friends, to endure as long as they shall endure, or any of their eldest male posterity."

Like Cincinnatus, the citizen-general who left his plow to command the armies of Rome, the officers of the Continental Army were "returning to their citizenship." The new Society of Cincinnatus was pledged to uphold "those exalted rights and liberties of human nature for which they have fought and bled" and to "promote and cherish between the respective States, that union and national honor so essentially necessary to their happiness and the future dignity of the American Confederacy." In addition the members were to display "brotherly kindness in all things" to each other and give aid to those officers and their families in need of assistance. Washington was chosen president of the society, and branches were organized in every state.

On October 18, 1783, Washington issued the last general order to his troops: "It remains only for the Commander-in-Chief to address himself once more, and that for the last time, to the armies of the United States, however widely dispersed the individuals who composed them may be, and to bid them an affectionate, long farewell. But before the Commander-in-Chief takes his final leave of those he holds most dear, he wishes to indulge himself a few minutes in a brief review of the past." Washington then spoke of American independence—"the object for which we contended against so formidable a power"—as cause for "astonishment and gratitude." In the general's view, the endurance of the army "through almost every possible suffering and discouragement, for the space of eight long years, was little short of a standing miracle." The men and officers of the army had participated in "astonishing events . . . events which have seldom if ever before taken place on the stage of human action; nor can this probably ever happen again." No one who had not been a witness to the scene "could imagine that the most violent local prejudices would cease so soon, and that men who came from the different parts of the continent, strongly disposed by the habits of education to despise and quarrel with each another, would instantly become one patriotic band of brothers." This, of course, was somewhat overstating the case. Washington himself, as we have seen, had not been free of sectional prejudices. Perhaps it was his consciousness of the prejudices that he had once held that led him to place such emphasis on the overcoming of them.

It was generally acknowledged that independence had brought with it such "enlarged prospects of happiness" as "almost exceed the power of description." Washington gave an inventory of the variety of jobs that would be available to the retired soldier—in farming, fishing, commerce, and the settling of the West. The war, he reminded his soldiers, had inevitably produced some unfortunate prejudices against the military. These the discharged soldiers must bear in mind and do their best to mollify—"they should carry with them into civil society the most conciliatory dispositions. . . ." They must not allow their indignation at the fact that there were some "envious individuals, who are unwilling to pay the debt the public has contracted," to poison their minds against their countrymen.

For his officers, Washington had a special injunction. "Unless the principles of the federal government were properly supported, and the powers of the Union increased, the honor, dignity, and justice of the nation would be lost forever. . . ." They must, therefore, do their best, as citizens, to achieve "these great and valuable purposes on which our very existence as a nation so materially depends." To each branch of the army and each rank he had some special word of commendation; finally, he praised the private soldiers for their extraordinary patience in suffering, as well as their invincible fortitude in action. He assured all those who had served under him of his "inviolable attachment and friendship," and called down the blessings of Heaven on those who had "secured innumerable blessings for others."

Washington could not say straight out that the army have been sacrificed to the provincialism and suspicion of the states, but that could be read plainly enough between the lines. What he could and did say was that the future of the independent American states rested on their union, and that sentiment he implanted in the hearts and in the consciousness of every officer and soldier who had served under him through the weary years of the war. He thus sent them forth into civilian life full of ardor for the union that he embodied and that so clearly possessed him.

Major Benjamin Tallmadge can be forgiven if he believed that the struggle for independence had been "attended with more appalling hardships and sufferings than have heretofore been borne by any body of military men; sustained with more firmness and perseverance than history accords to any other army. . . ." That, indeed, was his general's view. "No language," Tallmadge wrote, "can express the feelings of the army when the foregoing general orders were read. The most hardy soldiers were unable to restrain the copious flow of tears; and to some of us who had been honored with peculiar tokens of confidence and favor, the scene was absolutely overwhelming. For myself, the thought of being separated from my General, whom I loved with filial affection, and obeyed with perfect readiness and delight, was heartrending in the extreme." It was forty-five years after the event when Tallmadge wrote down his recollections of that moment, but they remained as vivid as if they had happened yesterday. "No change of situation, no engagements in business, nor any new friendships have ever been permitted," he wrote, "to abate that high regard, that profound respect, that ardor of affection, and that entire devotion of all my powers to the views and wishes of this illustrious man. I loved and venerated him. . . ."

It might be well, at this point, to view the end of the Revolution through the eyes of our friend Joseph Martin. In the summer of 1782 Martin and his men had been sent to Constitution Island, in the Hudson River off West Point, and there they spent most of their time blasting rocks for repair of the fort and the building of new barracks. There was little to relieve the monotony except playing pranks on the "old man," the captain of the company who was heartily disliked by the soldiers for his severity and bad humor. Martin and his fellows waited anxiously for an official end to the war so that they could at long last return to their homes, but it would be another year before they were discharged.

In the fall they cut firewood and then, in Martin's words, "having provided our wood for the winter, built our barracks, stowed ourselves away snugly in them. . . ." It was the end, Martin noted, of his seventh year of service in the army. And once more food was in short supply. "I lived, half the winter," Martin noted, "upon tripe and cowheels, and the other half on what I could get. . . . We passed this winter as contentedly as we could, under the hope that the war was nearly over, and that hope buoyed us up under many difficulties which we could hardly have surmounted without its aid." Finally, on April 19, 1783, confirmation came of the rumors that had been circulating for several weeks—that the long years of war were at last over "and the prize won for which we had been contending. . . ." Instead of exultation, there was a strange feeling of anticlimax. "The soldiers," in Martin's words, "said but very little about it; their chief thoughts were more closely fixed upon their situation as it respected the figure they were to exhibit upon their leaving the army and becoming citizens. Starved, ragged and meager, not a cent to help themselves with, and no means or method in view to remedy or alleviate their condition. . . . All that they could do was to make a virtue of necessity and face the threatening evils with the same resolution and fortitude that they had for so long a time faced the enemy in the field."

On June 11, "the old man" came into the barracks with his arms full of discharge, or rather furlough, papers. He ordered the men to empty their cartridge boxes on the floor. Out of the habit of obedience they did so, but when the captain told them that those who needed them might take them back again, "they were all immediately gathered up and returned to our boxes." Indeed, it seemed little enough for the services they had performed for their country—a handful of cartridges and a furlough. It was furlough rather than discharge because "to discharge us absolutely in our present pitiful, forlorn condition, it was feared, might cause some difficulties which might be too hard for the government to get easily over." Many of the cartridges were soon fired, without bullets, from muskets that were aimed at the officers in a "salute" that was less than affectionate. Martin confessed that he felt as much sadness as joy. "We had lived together," he wrote, "as a family of brothers for several years, setting aside some little family squabbles, like most other families, had shared with each other the hardships, dangers, and sufferings incident to a soldier's life; had sympathized with each other in trouble and sickness; had assisted in bearing each other's burdens or strove to make them lighter by council and advice; had endeavored to conceal each other's faults or make them appear in as good light as they would bear. In short, the soldiers, each in his particular circle of acquaintance, were as strict a band of brotherhood as Masons and, I believe, as faithful to each other. And now we were to be, the greater part of us, parted forever; as unconditionally separated as though the grave lay between us. . . . I question if there was a corps in the army that parted with more regrets than ours did. . . . Ah! it was a serious time." Martin himself, anxious to get his "settlement certificates," signed up again for a six-month period, collected his certificates at the end of that time, "purchased some decent clothing," and took his leave of the army.

At this point in his narrative, written when, in his view, people cared very little for the hardships and sufferings of the old Continental soldiers, Martin stopped to review those hardships and sufferings, contrasting what had been promised to soldiers on enlistment with what they had in fact received. Few of them, for instance, ever received the hundred acres of land that they had been promised on enlistment. Since "no agents were appointed to see that the poor fellows ever got possession of their lands," most of it fell into the hands of speculators, "who were driving about the country like so many evil spirits, endeavoring to pluck the last feather from the soldiers." "When," Martin wrote, "the country had drained the last drop of service it could screw out of the . . . soldiers, they were turned adrift like worn-out horses, and nothing said about land to pasture them on."

The lot of the discharged soldiers was often a hard one. Separated in April, 1783, Elijah Fisher looked for work without success. "There was so meny that Come from the army and from see that had no homes that would work for little or nothing but there vitels that I Could not find any Employment. . . . I could git into no bisnes neither by see nor

Land. . . . I Com Down by the markett" he wrote in his diary, "and sits Down all alone, allmost Descureged, and begun to think over how that I had been in the army, what ill success I had met with there and all so how I was ronged by them I worked for at home . . . and now that I could not get into any besness and no home, which you may well think how I felt; but then Come into my mind that there ware thousands in wors sircumstances then I was, and having food and rament, be Content, and that I had nothing to reflect on myself, and I[resolved] to do my endever and leave the avent to Provedance, and after that I felt as content as need to be."

When Washington entered New York at the end of November, 1783, he had already discharged a large portion of his army "in so judicious a way, that no unpleasant circumstances occurred." The triumphant, if not victorious troops marched into the city with General Knox at the head of a "select corps," followed by Washington and Governor Clinton with their staffs. The officers of the army marched eight abreast, followed by leading citizens of the town on horseback and then by citizens marching eight abreast. "Entire tranquillity prevailed and nothing occurred to mar the general joy," Tallmadge wrote. "Every countenance seemed to express the triumph of republican principles over the military despotism which had so long pervaded this now happy city. . . . The joy of meeting friends, who had long been separated by the cruel rigors of war, cannot be described." Some patriots in the city had already anticipated the entry of the Continental Army by flying American flags. William Cunningham, one of the most militant Tories in the city, amused himself by tearing them down, but he got his comeuppance when he tried to remove the flag at Day's Tavern on Murray Street. The robust Mrs. Day met him at the door and boxed his ears until the powder flew from his wig, to the delight of the spectators.

A considerable crowd had gathered in the Bowery, displaying their union cockades with sprigs of laurel in their hats. They watched as first a corps of dragoons marched by, followed by light infantry, a corps of artillery, and then other units in order. The slender column, all that remained of the Continental Army, was spruced up to look its rather faded and worn best. It marched down Broadway amid cheers and waving flags and drew up in front of Cape's Tavern. There the men remained at ease while a detail continued on to raise the flag over Fort George.

The British had one final joke to play. They had cut the halyards of the flagpole and greased the pole itself when they had taken down the Union Jack. Now, when the Americans tried to raise The Stars and Stripes, the sailors who attempted to shinny up the pole could not make it, and the last boatload of British soldiers in the harbor watched their efforts and jeered. Finally some cleats were found, the pole was scaled, and the flag was raised to the accompaniment of the firing of thirteen cannon.

That night there was a lavish public dinner given by Governor Clinton for Washington, his officers, and the leading citizens, and on the following evening there was "a most splendid display of fire-works," which, in Tallmadge's words, "far exceeded anything I had ever seen in my life."

On December 4, Washington met with his general officers at Fraunces Tavern in New York for a farewell party. It was a moment of sentiment and nostalgia that only an old soldier could understand. The fraternity of comrades-in-arms, formed by the hardships and dangers of war, has no counterpart in civil life. Men who have risked their lives in a common cause are bound together by the strongest of ties. They share the incommunicable memories that will die only with them and that, in not a few instances, merge with the common memory of their nation, passed on from generation to generation. The elegant tavern was filled thus with feelings too deep to speak of. With all their faults and shortcomings, this small band of heroes had, in the end, prevailed against the mightiest power on earth. They had suffered and sacrificed and persevered. For them their leader had come to seem, in his passion and his patience, in his rocklike endurance, in his majestic benignity, the embodiment of all that they had fought for for so long and at such cost. He had been sustained through all defeats and disappointments by his grand vision of "freedom and Independency," of the benefactions to be won for all mankind, and he had communicated that vision to those who did not already have it and had supported it in those who did whenever it faltered. Now it was all at an end—the misery of it and the glory; the ineffable mystery of it. It was part of history. Words were inadequate, but they were all that was available.

The officers were waiting at the tavern when Washington entered. There was a "slight refreshment" that no one had much heart for. It was consumed "in almost breathless silence," and then the general filled his wine glass, "and turning to the officers, he said, 'With a heart full of love and gratitude, I now take leave of you. I most devoutly wish that your latter days may be as prosperous and happy as your former ones have been glorious and honorable.'"

The officers wept without embarrassment, and Washington, in a voice thick with emotion, said, "I cannot come to each of you, but shall be obliged if each of you will come and take me by the hand."

Knox was nearest to Washington. He turned to his commander in chief who, "suffused in tears, was incapable of utterance, but grasped his hand; then they embraced each other in silence." In the same manner, "every officer in the room marched up, kissed, and parted with his general in chief." "Such a scene," Tallmadge recalled, "of sorrow and weeping I had never before witnessed. . . . It was indeed too affecting to be of long continuance—for tears of deep sensibility filled every eye— and the heart seemed so full, that it was ready to burst from its wonted abode." For Tallmadge "the simple thought . . . that we should see his face no more in this world seemed to me utterly insupportable." But the time of parting had come, and "waiving his hand to the *grieving children* around him, he left the room. . . ."

From the tavern, Washington and his staff went to join the governor of New York and the council of the city, and there the general took his formal leave. A corps of light infantry was drawn up in a line, and Washington, resplendent in his blue and buff uniform, passed the line to Whitehall and embarked there in his barge for Paulus Hook, accompanied by Baron von Steuben. His journey south to Annapolis seemed alternately like a triumphant procession and a funeral cortege. Gratitude and affection poured over him, mixed with a kind of heart-rending sorrow, sorrow akin to that felt by Major Tallmadge when he reflected "that we should see his face no more in this world. . . ." It was this feeling that he was "leaving"—going away to "that domestic retirement" that he had so longed for—and that his departure would leave a great chasm, an unfillable void, in the heart of America that touched the hushed crowds who turned out to look upon the savior of America with a strange kind of sadness.

Every great enterprise begins in love, not in political arrangements or legal definitions. "Nothing great is accomplished without passion," is the way Hegel expressed it. As the philosopher Eugen Rosenstock-Huessy said, the question is, what are we to fall in love with once the old love has lost its power over us? The Americans had loved England, the mother country—fabulous, powerful, intricate, venerable. They had loved the king as the symbol of that ancient, splendid empire.

When the king had lost their love, it had flowed, as water finds its level, to the majestic figure of George Washington. And it was in Washington's love for his men—for the soldiers and officers of the Continental Army—and in their love for him that the federal union had its beginning. All political unions must begin in a union of hearts.

The day before Washington was to deliver his commission to Congress, a ball was given in his honor. Washington, who loved to waltz, was a graceful dancer. "The general," one guest noted, "danced every set, that all the ladies might have the pleasure of dancing with him, or as has been handsomely expressed, *get a touch of him.*"

On the morning of December 23, Washington appeared before Congress and was escorted to a seat. "Sir," entoned Thomas Mifflin, "the United States in Congress assembled are prepared to receive your communications." At this Washington rose and bowed to the twenty or so delegates who represented what there was of the United States—more, some thought, a shadow than a reality. They, in turn, lifted their hats in a kind of republican salute. Washington, nervous and awkward, had difficulty reading the manuscript he held in a shaking hand. His voice faltered repeatedly as he informed the delegates that he wished to "surrender in their hands the trust committed to me, and to claim the indulgence of retiring from the Service of my Country." He had a special word of gratitude for the members of his personal staff: "It was impossible the choice of confidential Officers to compose my family should have been more fortunate." One of the members of that family, Alexander Hamilton, sat before him as a delegate from New York; two other delegates, Richard Henry Lee and Arthur Lee, were uncles of Light-Horse Harry Lee.

"I consider it indispensable to close this last solemn act of my Official life," Washington concluded, "by commending the Interests of our dearest Country to the protection of Almighty God, and those who have superintendence of them to his holy keeping." As Washington commended "our dearest country to the protection of Almighty God," his voice, hardly audible under the stress of emotion, "faltered and sank and the whole house felt his agitations." As at Fraunces Tavern in New York, many of the spectators and delegates wept openly. Washington paused to gain control of himself and then continued "in a most penetrating manner." "Having now finished the work assigned me, I retire from the great theatre of Action, and bidding an Affectionate farewell to this August body under whose orders I have so long acted, I here offer my Commission, and take my leave of all the employments of public life." Then he drew his commission from his breast pocket and handed it to Mifflin. (It was ironic that it was Mifflin who, as president of Congress, received it; his loyalty to Washington had more than once been in doubt.)

Mifflin replied for Congress, but beside the directness and simplicity of Washington's brief remarks, the president's address sounded windy and pretentious, "without," as one member wrote, "any show of feelings." At last the ceremony was over, and Washington withdrew. After the adjournment of Congress there were greetings and farewells to delegates who were old friends, and then Washington rode off for Mount Vernon, where, as it turned out, he had little "domestic retirement." Dozens of politicians sought his advice, and promoters of every plan for the reform of the Articles of Confederation tried to enlist his support. Even at Mount Vernon, he represented inescapably what there was of unity and thus of possibility in the United States.

In the words of Jefferson, " . . . we have a *Washington* whose memory shall be adored while liberty shall have votaries, whose name will triumph over time, and will in future ages assume its just station among the most celebrated worthies of the world. . . ."

To the ordinary American, George Washington more than made up for a lost king. I have been at such pains to distinguish the Revolution from the all-encompassing shadow of Washington that I feel I must be at some pains to make clear my view of the Virginian's role. First of all, there is, as I trust I have made sufficiently explicit, the fact that he *embodied* the Revolution. He did not win it single-handed as John Adams believed history would report (and as it very largely has). I believe American independence would have been won without him. But the form that independence would have taken could certainly have been very different. Washington knew that he was the leading actor in one of the great dramas of world history and that, as a consequence, he was always on stage. From his own officers and men to the emissaries of the British, those who encountered Washington felt in that passionate and yet thoroughly self-possessed man the force of a great genius. His genius was the ability to endure, to maintain his equilibrium in the midst of endless frustrations, disappointments, setbacks, and defeats. The American colonists had only to likewise endure to become their own masters—free and independent—and George Washington became the symbol of that determination to endure. He was bound to create and sustain a Continental Army and in the process to destroy or at least mute the deep-rooted parochialism of the states. So he not only symbolized the will of Americans to persevere in the cause of liberty, he symbolized the unity of the states; he embodied the states united, or the United States. From the winter of 1776, when he virtually created the Continental Army in the face of obstacles that would have defeated any man of lesser physical and moral stamina, to the Battle of Yorktown, his greatest achievement was that he kept·the Continental Army in existence, feeble and precarious as that existence usually was. The fact that he kept it in existence during the period from 1778 to the fall of 1781, when it never fought a major battle or embarked on a major campaign, was, if anything, more remarkable than its creation. The existence of the Continental Army assured the existence of Congress and thus of an actual agency of national government, however weak and inefficient. If Washington's army had disintegrated, as it seemed so often on the verge of doing, Congress might very well have followed suit; it was the need to provide, one way or another, for Washington's army that more than anything else kept Congress together. If Congress had disbanded, the problem of creating a viable nation out of thirteen disparate and jealous provinces would have been infinitely more difficult. Above all, if Washington had not in his splendid erectness, his imperturbable Roman countenance, his manner, his bearing, his figure, and his presence *embodied* the union, it is doubtful that unification could have been accomplished on the practical political level.

Washington was a consummate politician in what would emerge as the new style, or the American style. He could project an image, an image of which he was the artificer; he could placate, compromise, adjudicate, effect his ends by subtle but persistent pressure, make skillful use of the strengths and the weaknesses of those on whom he was dependent for help and support. And he could do this while preserving his own integrity and keeping his ultimate objectives always in view. He was seldom distracted by the trivial or irrelevant. He was patient but firm, stern but kind, demanding but just—in short, he was the archetypal father, "the father of his country."

How was he as a general? His greatness plainly rests on other grounds, but the question is not irrelevant. Generaling is not simply fighting; there is much more to it than that. An army has to be organized, staffed, trained, drilled, fed, clothed, disciplined, embued with an *esprit* that will make it fight. If the existence of the Continental Army in the face of enormous difficulties was the most important thing about it, Washington must receive high marks as a general. But it had also to fight. In fighting Washington showed the most important instinct of a general—an awareness of the limitations of the tool at his disposal. If the individual American soldier was far more enterprising than his British counterpart, more highly motivated, and a much better shot, he was also lacking in the machine-like discipline that was the essence of conventional eighteenth-century military tactics. Moreover, the Continental soldier, with of course notable exceptions, was poorly led. There was no military caste or tradition in America. There was no class, outside the South, accustomed from birth to giving orders; nor was there one accustomed from birth to receiving them, except in the slave population of the South. Company-grade officers—ensigns, lieutenants, and captains—were almost invariably lacking in experience and self-confidence. Nor did they have a group of professional noncommissioned officers, corporals and sergeants of various ranks, to lean on. These men are the backbone of any professional army. In most armies officers come and go, but these tough and seasoned individuals are always there with an accumulation of practical military wisdom to pass on to the newest recruit or the rosiest-cheeked young lieutenant. It is they, normally, who break in the new officers, and they were, for the most part, missing in Washington's army.

In the next level of command, the field-grade officers—majors, lieutenant colonels, and colonels—Washington was better served. Here there were a number of officers who had fought, if only in modest capacities, under British officers in the French and Indian War. It was here also that the heaviest casualties were usually suffered. This was in part the consequence of the nature of eighteenth-century warfare. In addition, wherever there is conspicuous weakness in the lower levels of command, the casualties among the next higher levels are apt to be disproportionately large. This is because these officers must take exceptional risks to make up for the deficiencies of their subordinates. So Washington constantly lost outstanding field-grade officers, who were killed or wounded or promoted to the rank of brigadier. It was by the brigadier generals that Washington, as time passed, was perhaps best served. After the first group, veterans of the French and Indian War, had passed from the scene because of age or incompetence, a younger and more vigorous generation advanced on merit from field-grade rank, took their places, and provided the brightest spot in the officer corps.

Among the original major generals the matter was quite different. Richard Montgomery, the best by far of the initial contingent, died in the attack on Quebec. Charles Lee was a disaster. Horatio Gates, who was a child of fortune at Saratoga, was very little better. Thomas Conway was devious, deceitful, and insubordinate. John Sullivan was energetic but incompetent. Considering his age and inexperience, Lafayette, who, of course, was not one of those originally commissioned, acquitted himself with honor if not with brilliance. Benjamin Lincoln was popular and conscientious but no more. Israel Putnam, who conducted himself with great energy and enterprise at the Battle of Bunker Hill, never reached such heights again; he was old and fussy. William Heath was adequate for certain military chores, but he was no man to exercise an active command. And so it went. If we except Daniel Morgan, whose services, due to health or temperament, were intermittent, the only general officer to emerge as a military leader of the first rank was Nathanael Greene. Greene was, without question, the American general who came closest to deserving the title of military genius. His campaign in the Carolinas in 1780–81 was the most successful British or American campaign of the war.

Washington was not an infallible judge of men by any means. He thought far better of Charles Lee than that unhappy man deserved; he had complete faith in Benedict Arnold, although it took no special discernment to recognize that Arnold was an ambitious intriguer. The instances could be multiplied, but the point is not an essential one.

On one level at least, Washington was served incomparably well. His own personal staff, his aides, were brilliant young officers (his "sons") who adored him. From Joseph Reed to Alexander Hamilton, Henry Lee, and John Laurens, no commander could have been better or more faithfully served. His general staff was another matter. Only Nathanael Greene, drafted in desperation, was able to bring any semblance of order or system into the office of quartermaster general, and he soon fell out with Congress. Commissary, ordinance, and transportation were, for the most part, woefully inadequate to the demands placed upon them. Perhaps their greatest shortcoming was that they were hopelessly entangled with Congress, which interfered without helping.

This review of Washington's officer corps is necessary in order to answer the question about Washington's own generalship. An army is only as good as its officers. On balance, the officer corps under Washington's command was sadly deficient when compared with that of the enemy. As a general Washington was severely limited by that simple fact, and it is greatly to his credit that there were few instances where he did strain that very imperfect instrument, the Continental Army, beyond its limited capacities. If the first objective of a commanding officer is to win a victory, his second is to avoid defeat. As we have said often before, Washington had only to avoid defeat in order to assure an eventual triumph of the American cause. Aside from the brilliant raid at Trenton, an imaginative and daring foray in which Washington's personal presence insured the success of the mission, he performed no dazzling strategic or tactical feats. As might have been expected, he made a number of mistakes, most of them of minor importance (the exception being the Battle of Monmouth), and some of these (again Monmouth would be the classic example) he repaired by his own personal courage, which was always beyond question.

In summary, it must be reiterated that Washington, if he did not single-handedly "win" the American Revolution, or, in a certain sense, "win" it at all, and if he did not appear as a brilliant military strategist or an ingenious tactician, nonetheless represented the principle of *union* in a most powerful and dramatic form and very well deserves to be what he perhaps in fact no longer is—"first in the hearts of his countrymen."

In a curious way, as the epitome of the Protestant ethos, his greatness lay less in what he did than what he did not do; what, in essence, he denied himself. He did not try to extend his army beyond its capacities in order to win military laurels for himself. He did not entirely lose patience with Congress and take matters into his own hands, as he so well might have done. He did not allow the adulation of the public to persuade him that he was more than human. He did not exhaust himself physically and mentally by the awesome burdens that he bore, but seemed able to constantly draw on fresh reserves of physical and moral strength. He did not, except on rare occasions, lose his temper. He survived, which under ordinary circumstances might be considered a negative virtue, but which, in the American Revolution, turned out to be the essential achievement.

It will be recalled that John Adams said, with perhaps more than a twinge of envy, that the history of the Revolution would be a lie from one end to the other, the gist of it being that Franklin smote the earth with his electrical rod, George Washington sprang out of the ground, Franklin electrified him, and the two between them conducted all the war and diplomacy of the Revolution. It proved, in fact, a remarkably accurate prophecy. The American Revolution has been written about for the most part, and is certainly firmly fixed in the popular mind, as the personal achievement of George Washington. As important and decisive a figure as Washington was in many ways, *he was not the*

Revolution, and it is crucial, if that event is ever to be properly understood, to separate the man and the event, closely intertwined as they may be. It need not diminish Washington a cubit to demonstrate that he had nothing to do with many of the most important events of the Revolution. Lexington and Concord and Bunker Hill, three decisive engagements, took place, of course, before he appeared on the military scene. He had no role in the surrender of Burgoyne's army, and most important of all, he was not involved in the critically important campaigns in the South or in the prolonged war of attrition along the Western frontier.

In a sense it was Washington's restraint, more than Washington's actions, that determined his greatness. He cast himself as the "Father of his Country"—wise, patient, stern, austere—and played that essential role with a profound sense of its significance, its potentialities, and its limitations. Greatness consists, as we have said before, in being appropriate to the requirements of the hour. By this measure Washington, as commander in chief of the Continental Army and perhaps even more as the first President of the United States, was a very great man.

18

Blacks in the Revolution

As we approach the end of this work, it is perhaps appropriate to discuss the role in the Revolution of those Americans who have most recently asserted their right to be full beneficiaries of the principles for which the Revolution was fought. Blacks, slave and free, played a significant part in the events we have been describing. If the response of slaves to Lord Dunmore's appeal to them to flee to the British at the beginning of the war, and the flight of tens of thousands of blacks to the British during the course of the conflict shattered Southern illusions and hardened Southern attitudes toward slavery, the Revolution had a very different effect in the North. As we have seen, many Americans— Southern and Northern alike—were deeply troubled by the paradox of fighting for freedom while holding a substantial portion of the population in slavery.

The fact that almost a thousand slaves answered Dunmore's call was less significant than the fact that many thousands more had planted in their minds the notion that they might be free. There were reports of a black mother in New York naming her infant Dunmore, and it was reported that a black man in Philadelphia jostled whites on the street and told them to wait until "lord Dunmore and his black regiment come, and then we will see who is to take the wall."

Very early in the period of Revolutionary agitation, free blacks in the North were quick to point out the disadvantages under which they labored and to ask, in the name of liberty, for their full rights as citizens. In Rhode Island, always liberal or radical in its leanings, the Reverend Samuel Hopkins, minister in the First Congregational Church of Newport, became the leader in an antislavery movement. He went from door to door among his neighbors and the members of his congregation pressing masters to free their slaves, and he gave numerous sermons to the same effect. When one man replied to Hopkins that his slave was quite happy with his situation, Hopkins asked if could question him. The master consented; Hopkins asked the slave if he was happy and the slave replied cheerfully enough that he was. "Would you be happier if you were a free man?" Hopkins asked. "O yes, Massa—me would be much more happy!" His master, convinced, freed him immediately.

In 1773, Hopkins recruited Ezra Stiles, a fellow minister and future president of Yale College. Hopkins had a plan to train a number of free blacks to be sent to Africa as Christian missionaries, and Hopkins and Stiles raised enough money to buy the freedom of an intelligent and pious young slave, Bristol Yamma, who was a member of Hopkins' own congregation. He and a free black, John Quaumino, were both sent to the College of New Jersey at Princeton. After a year at the college they had "made such proficiency, and in such a measure qualified for the mission proposed, that they would enter upon it directly," Hopkins reported, "were there opportunity to send them to Africa!"

In Philadelphia, the Quaker printer Anthony Benezet wrote and printed numerous antislavery tracts. Patrick Henry was one of many Americans touched by Benezet's writings. After reading a Benezet tract, Henry declared that although he was a slaveholder himself he could not justify the institution since it was "repugnant to humanity . . . inconsistent with the Bible," and contrary to the principle of liberty. Benezet started a racially integrated school in Philadelphia in 1770, and five years later there were five whites and forty blacks enrolled. The Quaker reformer put persistent emphasis on the incongruity of Americans claiming liberty for themselves while at the same time denying it to black men and women. "Anthony Benezet," wrote Dr. Benjamin Rush, himself an enthusiastic convert to the antislavery cause, "stood alone a few years ago, in opposing negro slavery in Philadelphia; and now three-fourths of the province, as well as of the city, cry out against it. . . . A spirit of humanity and religion begins to awaken in several of the colonies in favor of the poor Negroes." Rush's observations were made in 1773, and in the same year Rush himself published a pamphlet entitled "An Address to the Inhabitants of the British Settlements in America upon Slavekeeping . . . designed to shew the iniquity of the slave trade." Rush joined other reform-minded citizens of Philadelphia to form The Society for the Relief of Free Negroes Unlawfully Held in Bondage. When Rush was offered a thousand guineas a year to practice medicine in Charles Town, South Carolina, a large sum for that day, he refused, declaring that he was unwilling to live "where wealth has been accumulated only by the sweat and blood of Negro slaves."

Rush and Benezet found a ready ally in a newcomer to Philadelphia. Thomas Paine's first publication in America was an abolitionist tract entitled "African Slavery in America." "That some desperate wretches should be willing to steal and enslave men by violence and murder for gain, is rather lamentable than strange. But that many civilized, nay, christianized people should approve, and be concerned in the savage practice, is surprising," the pamphlet began.

Negroes themselves began to go to court in the Northern colonies as early as 1776 to sue for their freedom. A number of them were successful; indeed there is apparently no instance of a black man who sued for his freedom failing to receive it. Such a procedure was slow and expensive, however, and few blacks could afford it. It was soon replaced by petitioning the legislatures of the respective states. In Massachusetts in 1773 "many slaves" requested relief from the Great and General Court. "We have no property! we have no wives! we have no children! no city! no country!" their petition read. After appointing a committee to consider the petition, the assembly tabled it, a favorite political device for delaying sticky issues, but the next session the petitioners were back again, describing themselves as "a Grate Number of Blacks . . . who . . . are held in a state of slavery within the bowels of a free and christian Country." Many of them had been "stolen from the bossoms of our tender Parents and from a Populous, Pleasant and plentiful country and brought hither to be made slaves for Life in a christian land." These were hard words that touched the consciences of many whites, but again, after some debate, nothing was done.

As early as 1766, the General Court had began to struggle with a bill to "prohibit the importation and purchasing of slaves." Such a law was passed in 1771 but vetoed by Governor Hutchinson. In 1774 Connecticut passed "an Act for prohibiting the Importation of Indian, Negro or Molatto Slaves." The Rhode Island legislature the same year adopted a law restricting the slave trade, and prefaced it with the statement that "those who are desirous of enjoying all the advantages of liberty themselves, should be willing to extend personal liberty to others." The act provided that any slave brought into the colony should immediately become free. Pennsylvania limited the importation of slaves in 1773 by imposing a tax of £20 on every slave brought into the colony. In the South, Virginia, North Carolina, and South Carolina passed legislation against the importation of slaves as part of the nonimportation agreements.

With the outbreak of the war, there came a new series of petitions from slaves in the Northern states, addressed to the respective legislatures. Together they made an impressive and moving chorus. In a petition of January, 1777, a group of slaves in Massachusetts reminded the legislature that they had submitted one petition after another. The principle on which the Americans had opposed Great Britain "pleads stronger than a thousand arguments in favor of your humble petitioners," the document read. The life of a slave was "far worse than Nonexistence." In New Hampshire a similar group urged the legislators of that state to free them so "that the name of slave may not more be heard in a land gloriously contending for the sweets of freedom." It was not a matter of bad treatment, but rather that they wished to know "from what authority they [their masters] assume to dispose of our lives, freedom and property."

Either the slave petitioners had the help of sympathetic whites in framing their applications, or there were a number of very literate individuals among them. In Connecticut in 1779, eight slaves of William Browne of Salem—Great Prince, Little Prince, Luke, Caesar, and Prue, with her three children, "all friends to America"—petitioned for freedom. "We hope," they wrote, "that our good mistress, the free State of Connecticut, engaged in a war with tyranny, will not sell good honest Whigs and friends of freedom and independence, as we are." There was a deep poignance about such requests by slaves who called themselves "good honest Whigs." While legislators delayed and equivocated, caught between the sacred rights of property and the call of humanity, the arguments of the slaves penetrated the consciences of more and more whites.

Three free blacks were particularly active both in the patriot agitation against Great Britain and in behalf of their enslaved brothers and sisters. Prince Hall, born in Barbados, came to Massachusetts in 1765 and prospered. He encouraged, signed, and doubtless helped to draft petitions from slaves asking for their freedom. (Before Bunker Hill, a

British military lodge of the Masonic order initiated Hall and fourteen other blacks.)

Paul Cuffe, a free black, ran a shipyard in Massachusetts and served as a captain on one of his own vessels. In 1780, he and six other blacks drew up a petition to the state legislature asking that blacks be relieved from paying taxes since they had "no voice or influence in the election of those who tax us."

Phillis Wheatley was raised by a Boston family as their own child and soon showed unusual gifts as a poet. She published her first book of verse in 1770, entitled *Poems on Various Subjects, Religious and Moral.* Soon she was known on both sides of the ocean. Voltaire complimented her "very good English verse," and she was pointed to by reformers as evidence that blacks were not innately inferior to whites and could, if properly educated, rival them in literature and letters as well as in other fields of endeavor. When Washington was appointed commander in chief of the Continental Army, Phillis Wheatley wrote an effusive poem to commemorate the occasion, expressing the hope that "your Excellency would be successful in the great cause you are so generously engaged in."

> Thee, first in place and honours,—we demand
> The grace and glory of thy martial band.
> Fam'd for thy valour, for thy virtues more,
> Here every tongue thy guardian aid implore.

John Paul Jones, aboard the *Ranger,* wrote a friend in Boston, "I am on the point of sailing—I have to write to you—pray be so good as to put the Inclosed into the hands of the Celebrated Phillis, the African Favorite of the Muse and of Apollo—should she reply, I hope you will be the bearer."

In New Jersey, Governor William Livingston in 1778 requested the legislature of that state to pass an act freeing all slaves, declaring that slavery was "utterly inconsistent with the principles of Christianity and humanity; and in Americans who have idolized liberty, peculiarly odious and disgraceful." The earliest state to abolish slavery was Rhode Island in 1774, followed by Vermont in 1777 and Pennsylvania three years later.

The British, of course, were very ready to comment on the incongruity of Americans professing to be fighting for liberty while at the same time holding other human beings in servitude.

When the British landed in Maryland in 1777, Ambrose Serle got his first view of Negro slavery. "Scarce a white Person was to be seen," he noted, "but negroes appeared in great abundance. These live in Huts or Hovels near the Houses of their owners, and are treated as a better kind of Cattle, being bought or sold, according to Fancy or Interest, having no Property not even in their Wives or Children. Such is the Practice or Sentiment of Americans, while they are bawling about the Rights of *human Nature,* and oppose the freest Govt. and most liberal System of Polity known upon the Face of the Earth!"

Du Roi, the Hessian officer captured at Saratoga, was shocked at his first sight, as a prisoner in Virginia, of slavery. He saw a slave girl six years old sold for six hundred pounds. "At the sale they are examined by the purchaser," he wrote, "exactly like cattle. They must walk up and down for him, move their limbs and do everything they are asked to do, so he can see if they are capable of work. It is terrible to see these slaves say good-bye to their comrades and relations, sometimes parents and wives, when sold to a master living in another province, and when there is no prospect of seeing their dear ones again."

At the same time it must be said that the British, while always ready to appeal to slaves to desert their masters, seldom showed much compassion for or understanding of the blacks who sought refuge with them. They were herded into camps, where great numbers of them died of a multiplicity of diseases. When smallpox broke out among escaped slaves in Virginia, General Leslie wrote to Cornwallis, "About 700 Negroes are come down the River in the Small Pox. I shall distribute them about the Rebell Plantations."

The attitude of white American soldiers toward blacks is difficult to assess. In scattered references in diaries and journals, there is a quality of superiority or outright antagonism. Not infrequently, officers or civil officials in their comments lump blacks with whites of inferior character and ability in an indiscriminate category. Blacks carried out, by and large, the more menial tasks of the army, but there are suggestions that black sailors on privateers and Continental vessels enjoyed a substantially greater degree of equality then their fellows in the army.

The condescending tone of Joseph Martin's account of a black soldier's capture of a British officer is probably quite typical of the attitude of most white soldiers towards their black comrades-in-arms.

Martin tells of "an aged Negro who was head of the camp" and carried a rusty old cutlass. On a scouting expedition, Scipio, as he was called, established himself at a crossroads, and when a British officer "mounted on a fine horse" came cantering towards him, the black man darted from the bushes as the officer passed, grabbed the reins of his horse, drew out his old cutlass, "and set cutting and told him, 'you no surrender, I kill ye.'" The officer tried to draw his own sword, "but the old soldier cut on so he could not; he then tried to draw his pistols, but the old veteran determined to have him or kill him on the spot, at last the officer surrendered and old Scipio led him up to the troops all covered with blood and delivered him to Col. Meggs with his horse and sword and pistols; with as much pride as any general who conquered an army."

As the war dragged on, with its endless need for new recruits, more and more slaves in the Northern states found freedom through enlisting in the army. When General Sullivan told his slave to be prepared to travel with him to join in the fight for liberty, the slave is reported to have remarked that "it would be a great satisfaction to know that he was indeed going to fight for *his* liberty." Slaves enlisted by the hundreds to secure their freedom, and, most touchingly, many took the name of "Liberty." Thus, in one Connecticut regiment, the forty-eight blacks included Jeffrey Liberty, Pomp Liberty, Sharp Liberty, Cuff Liberty, Dick Freedom, Ned Freedom, Cuff Freedom, Peter Freedom, Jube Freedom, and Prinnis Freedom.

Recruiting officers, who received ten dollars a head for every man they enlisted, did not hesitate to sign up blacks. Likewise the states, called upon time after time for new levies, were acting more from self-interest than humanitarian principles when they sent off blacks to join the Continental Army. Blacks, slave and free (the latter belonging to the bottom stratum of American society), also found the bounty offered for enlistment attractive, and they doubtless often bore better than their white companions the hardships of military life. In April, 1778, for example, the town of Medford, Massachusetts, enlisted a black man and paid him a bounty of one hundred dollars. Hingham enrolled Plato McLellan and a man named Jack. Andover signed up Cato Freeman with the provision that he should be what his name implied after three years of service.

Rhode Island was the leader in enlisting slaves as soldiers. The state legislature proposed the formation of a battalion, composed primarily of slaves, to augment Washington's depleted army at Valley Forge. Slaves were to be bought from their masters and freed upon "passing muster." Although few slaves were enlisted for the projected battalion, substantial numbers of blacks were found in the Rhode Island Line of the Continental Army by the end of the war. A French officer with Rochambeau noted that one Rhode Island regiment was two-thirds black.

At the Battle of Rhode Island, Colonel Christopher Greene's First Regiment had a hundred and twenty-five Negro soldiers, of whom more than thirty were free blacks. They were among the soldiers who for some four hours repulsed a strong attack by a detachment of Hessians and inflicted heavy casualties.

Another strong incentive to enroll blacks in the Continental Army or in the state militia was that they could often be prevailed on more easily than whites to enlist as substitutes for whites who were drafted. If a white man who owned a slave was drafted, it was very tempting for him to send his slave instead, and many slaves undoubtedly obtained their freedom in this way.

In the South, which felt the same desperate manpower shortages as the North, there was constant agitation to enlist slaves. In 1779, when the cause seemed on the verge of disaster in South Carolina and Georgia, Congress urged those states to enlist three thousand slaves. The owners would be paid at the rate of a thousand dollars per able-bodied young black, and the slaves, if they performed "well and faithfully," would be freed at the end of the war and receive fifty dollars. The principal advocate of this plan was John Laurens. Young Laurens' father, Henry, had given up the slave trade in 1770, and at the outbreak of the war, perhaps under his son's urging, he wrote him that he was "devising means for manumitting many of them and for cutting off the entails of slavery."

A resolution of Congress observed that South Carolina could make little contribution to the manpower needs of the army "by reason of the great proportion of citizens, necessary to remain at home to prevent insurrections among the negroes, and to prevent the desertion of them to the enemy." Congress proposed that "a force might be raised . . . from among the negroes which would not only be formidable to the enemy . . . but would also lessen the danger from revolts and desertions, by detaching the most vigorous and enterprising from among the negroes."

Laurens' close friend, Alexander Hamilton, had supported the project with Washington, writing, "The contempt we have been taught to entertain for the blacks, makes us fancy many things that are founded neither in reason nor experience. . . . The dictates of humanity and true policy, equally interest me in favor of this unfortunate class of men." Laurens hurried to his home state, eager to improve the condition of "those who are unjustly deprived of the rights of mankind," and to support "the defenders of liberty with a number of gallant soldiers." Laurens' hopes were doomed to disappointment. Governor John Rutledge wrote him that the council had rejected the notion; in the lower house the idea "was received with horror by the planters, who figured to themselves terrible consequences." Laurens wrote to Washington that the proposal had been "drowned by the howlings of a triple-headed monster, in which prejudice, avarice and pusillanimity were united."

Figures are difficult to come by, but there is no question that many blacks served in the Continental Army, in the militia of the Northern states, in the Congressional and state navies, and, perhaps above all, on privateers. An official return on the Continental Army in the summer of 1778 showed 755 blacks in fourteen brigades. Samuel Parson's Connecticut brigade led the list with 148 blacks. At Ticonderoga in 1776, a Pennsylvania officer, describing the Yankee regiments to his wife, noted they were made up of "the strangest mixture of Negroes, Indians and whites, with old men and mere children, which together with a nasty lousy appearance make a most shocking spectacle."

Some blacks who enlisted in the army or navy were runaways; others, as we have seen, were slaves who were, in effect, bought from their masters; some were sent as substitutes for their drafted masters; others, free blacks, enlisted to get a handsome bounty or out of genuine devotion to the cause of liberty. It has been estimated that more than five thousand blacks of all categories served in the Continental Army or in the navy. Most of them were slaves, fighting to earn their freedom. The majority were privates in the army; many were orderlies, wagoners, pioneers, and service troops of all kinds. A substantial number were fighting soldiers, and a number of them fought with courage and tenacity.

The unmistakable lesson taught by the defection of slaves to the British was that slaves wished freedom as much as white men, and far from being the happy, childlike primitives that their masters believed them to be, they were willing to risk their lives to escape from perpetual servitude. This lesson was not lost on men like George Mason, Patrick Henry, and Thomas Jefferson, but they were at a loss as to how the lesson, once learned, might be applied. The mass of slave owners interpreted the lesson after their own fashion. Since the slaves harbored this dangerous desire for freedom that could not be granted, they must be rigorously repressed, watched, guarded, and systematically intimidated. Thus the institution of slavery grew harsher and more bitter after the war fought for liberty. Where before the war many Southerners of consequence condemned slavery in the most emphatic terms, after it fewer and fewer dared speak out against it.

If the Revolutionary War hardened the South in its fear and anxiety about slaves, it gave thousands of slaves their freedom, marked the definite end of slavery as an institution in the North, and awakened the consciences of a great many Northern whites to the iniquity and, above all, the inconsistency of black servitude in a country that had won its independence in the name of freedom. It might thus be justly said that one of the consequences of the American Revolution was the Civil War. While many Americans felt a deep sense of shame that slavery persisted in a free country and were determined that it should be somehow eradicated, many others grew increasingly rigid and indeed paranoid in their defense of "the peculiar institution."

19

Women in the Revolution

THE revolutionary spirit that infected slaves in the North and the South, and that emboldened the Baptists, among others, to press for religious toleration, had its effect on feminine patriots as well. Not only did women share in every aspect of the struggle, but they raised some pointed questions about their own status. In the winter of 1776, Abigail Adams, knowing of her husband's preoccupation with independence, wrote John that Congress should take up the question of independence for women, as well as for the colonies. A new code of law should not "put such unlimited power into the hands of husbands." Since all men "would be tyrants if they could," particular care and attention should be paid to the rights of the ladies who might otherwise "foment a rebellion, and . . . not hold ourselves bound by any laws in which we have no voice or representation."

John's reply was not particularly sympathetic. "I cannot but laugh," he answered. "We have been told that our struggle has loosened the bonds of government everywhere; that children and apprentices were disobedient, that schools and colleges were grown turbulent; that Indians slighted their guardians, and Negroes grew insolent to their masters. But your letter was the first intimation that another tribe, more numerous and powerful than all the rest, were grown discontented." So-called masculine domination, Adams believed, was more theory than fact. "We are obliged to go fair and softly, and, in practice, you know we are the subjects. We have only the name of masters, and rather than give up this, which would completely subject us to the despotism of the petticoat, I hope General Washington and all our brave heroes would fight."

Undertaking to recruit Mercy Otis Warren, sister of James Otis and wife of James Warren, in her campaign to get Congress to pass laws that "would put it out of the power of the arbitrary and tyrannic to injure us with impunity by establishing some laws in our favor upon liberal principles," Abigail told her friend that John had replied to her request in a haughty and imperious way and that she had taken the occasion to inform him that she had been testing "the disinterestedness of his virtue [which],when weighed in the balance," she had found wanting. To John himself she wrote, "I cannot say that I think you are very generous to the ladies, for, whilst you are proclaiming peace and good will to men, emancipating all nations, you insist upon retaining an absolute power over wives." But arbitrary power, like other things, is apt to be broken, and "notwithstanding all your wise laws and maxims, we have it in our power, not only to free ourselves, but to subdue our master, and, without violence, throw both your natural and legal authority at our feet." The tone was playful, but there was seriousness behind it. Despite the fact that, as we have seen earlier, American women enjoyed more important freedom than women anywhere else in the world, they still moved in "lead strings" held by men.

In another exchange of correspondence on the subject of education, Abigail reminded her husband that those who suffered most seriously from the inadequacies of the present system were the women. She dared to hope that "some more liberal plan might be laid and executed for the benefit of the rising generation. . . . If we mean to have heroes, statesmen, and philosophers," she wrote, "we should have learned women. . . . If much depends, as is allowed, upon the early education of youth, and the first principles which are instilled that the deepest root, great benefit must arise from literary accomplishments in women."

On this score at least, John Adams was at one with his wife. "Your sentiments of the importance of education in women are exactly agreeable to my own," he replied. In history, he noted, there was hardly an instance of a great man who did not have about him some unusual woman—mother, wife, or sister—to whom, in large measure, he owed his eminence.

There was certainly a measure of condescension in Adams' reply, but it evoked no protest from Abigail. Their relationship was, indeed, a model of mutual respect and affection. Abigail Adams had a fine mind and a keen wit. If she was not as erudite as her husband, she was as broadly read, and she discussed political, moral, and philosophical issues with him as an equal. And she was only one among thousands of wives whose relations with their husbands were characterized by deep affection and a sense of mutuality often missing from marriages in later generations. General Knox had his adored Lucy, to whom he wrote long letters filled with such military and political information as he dared commit to paper. Esther De Berdt Reed—"My dearest beloved"—was a sturdy support to her husband, Joseph Reed. Samuel Adams' wife had much the same relationship with her husband that Abigail Adams had with her husband John. Mercy Otis Warren was a student of political theory capable of crossing swords with John Adams. She was also a poet, playwright, and historian, a lady of considerably more talent than her diligent if somewhat plodding husband.

Eliza Wilkinson of South Carolina was an independent young lady who declared in a letter to a friend that "men say we have no business with [political matters]. It is not our sphere! And Homer (did you ever read Homer, child?) gives us two or three broad hints to mind our domestic concerns, spinning, weaving, etc. and leave affairs of higher nature to men; but I must beg his pardon—I won't have it thought, that because we are the weaker sex as to *bodily* strength, my dear, we are incapable of nothing more than minding the dairy, visiting the poultry-house, and all such domestic concerns; our thoughts can soar aloft, we can form conceptions of things of a higher nature; and have as just a sense of honor, glory, and great actions, as these 'Lords of the Creation.' What contemptible *earth worms* these authors make us! They won't even allow us our liberty of thought, and that is what I want." She was indignant at having her opinions brushed aside with reminders "of our spinning and household affairs as the only matters we are capable of thinking or speaking of with justice or propriety. I won't allow it, positively won't."

Esther Reed raised three hundred thousand pounds in Philadelphia for the soldiers of the Pennsylvania line. Patriotic ladies in other cities performed similar services. And there were literally thousands of others, famous or obscure, who played their roles, just as the men did, in the Revolutionary crisis. Many of them, such as Sally Wister and Eliza Wilkinson, we know through letters and journals. We also know their Tory counterparts, who braved and suffered as much as the female patriots, and in the end, of course, more. Everywhere that men went, women went too, even, as we have seen in the dramatic story of Molly Pitcher, into battle. Lieutenant Thomas Anburey, reconnoitering in front of the British lines after the battle of Freeman's Farm, came on the bodies of three dead Americans, two men and a woman, in a strange tableau of death. The woman had cartridges in her hands, and her arms were extended as though to give them to one of the men.

Women were of course used as spies and secret agents by both sides. At Valley Forge, Washington forbade women from Philadelphia coming into camp because there were indications that they had been persuading soldiers to desert. A country girl who had volunteered to visit Philadelphia to sell eggs and collect information was almost captured by a British patrol when she was reporting to Major Benjamin Tallmadge not far from the city. Tallmadge pulled her up behind him on his horse and, pursued by British dragoons, carried the girl off to the safety of the American lines.

When Elias Boudinot was in charge of military intelligence for the American army at Valley Forge, he stopped at Rising Sun for dinner. "After Dinner," as Boudinot told the story, "a little poor looking insignificant Old Woman came in & solicited leave to go into the Country to buy some flour—While we were asking some Questions, she walked up to me and put into my hands a dirty old needlebook, with various small pockets in it." Boudinot told the woman, whose name was Lydia Darragh, to return for her answer, and when she had left he examined the needle book. In the last pocket was a piece of paper rolled up like a pipestem. On it was the information that General Howe planned to march out of the city the next morning with five thousand men and thirteen pieces of cannon. Boudinot hurried off to headquarters with the information, which tallied with other bits and pieces that had come to him. Washington listened thoughtfully to Boudinot's report and made a shrewd prediction of Howe's intentions: Howe would march against the American lines at Chestnut Hill. He warned Boudinot to move his staff headquarters. The old woman's information proved correct. Howe came out of the city but after several days of inconclusive skirmishing withdrew to Philadelphia.

Today one could read a hundred monographs on the American Revolution without getting more than a hint that women were involved at all. It is interesting to note, however, that in the popular *Romance of the Revolution,* a collection of anecdotes about Revolutionary heroes published in the early nineteenth century, women figured very prominently. One such lady was Deborah Sampson, a young woman of a rather questionable background, who made herself a set of men's clothing and enlisted in October, 1778, under the name of Robert Shirtliffe. She served for three years as a soldier and was wounded twice, the first time suffering a sword cut on the side of her head, the second time a bullet wound in her shoulder. Finally she got camp fever, and her sex was discovered by a Doctor Birney, who, instead of revealing her secret, had her taken to his own house in Philadelphia. The doctor's niece helped to care for "Robert Shirtliffe" and in the process fell in love with "him." When Deborah had recovered, Birney, so the story goes, sent her to General Washington with a letter that told of her deception. Washington discharged her with some kind words "and a sum of money sufficient to bear her expenses to some place where she might find a home."

In 1780 a poem was addressed to the "females of Pennsylvania and New Jersey . . . who illustrated the nobility of their sentiment and virtue of their patriotism, by generous subscriptions to the suffering soldiers of the American army." The poem was entitled "Our Women," and it began:

> All hail! superior sex, exalted fair,
> Mirrors of virtue, Heaven's peculiar care;
> Form'd to enspirit and enoble man
> The immortal finish of Creation's plan!
>
> Accept the tribute of our warmest praise
> The soldier's blessing and the patriot's bays!
> For fame's first plaudit we no more contest
> Constrain to own it decks the female breast.

Further perfervid verses praised the "sister angels of each state," declaring they would "live admired from age to age":

> With sweet applauses dwell on every name,
> Endear your memories and embalm your fame,
> And thus the future bards shall soar sublime,
> And waft you glorious down the stream of time;
> Then freedom's ensign thus inscribed shall wave,
> "The patriot females who their country save;"
> Till time's abyss absorb'd in heavenly lays,
> Shall flow in your eternity of praise.

John Marshall, in his life of George Washington, mentioned that the women of Philadelphia had subscribed large sums for the relief of "suffering soldiers," and that patriotic women in other towns and cities had followed suit. "This instance of patriotism on the part of our fair and amiable country women," Marshall added, "is by no means single. Their conduct throughout the revolutionary war was uniform. They shared with cheerfulness and gaiety, the privations and sufferings to which the situation of their country exposed them. In every stage of this severe trial, they displayed virtues which have not always been attributed to their sex, but which it is believed they will, on every occasion calculated to unfold them, be found to possess. With a ready acquiescence, with a firmness always cheerful, and a constancy never lamenting the sacrifices which were made; they not only yielded up all the elegancies, delicacies, and even conveniences, to be furnished by wealth and commerce, relying on their farms and domestic industry for every article of food and raiment; but, consenting to share the produce of their labour, they gave up without regret a considerable portion of the covering designed for their own families, to supply the wants of a distressed soldiery; and heroically suppressed the involuntary sigh, which the departure of their brothers, their sons, and their husbands, for the camp, rended from their bosoms."

Women were wives, mistresses, camp followers, sisters, and mothers, occasionally nurses, sometimes spies, and often heroines, such as the young women who went so lightheartedly to the spring to deceive the Indian raiders at Bryan's Station. Perhaps the most important function they performed as a sex was running farms (and sometimes businesses, as in the case of Esther Reed) while their husbands went off to fight the war. As the mistresses of farms and plantations, they struggled to make ends meet, to raise the children, and to pay the taxes for support of the war. When the war came their way, they risked fire and plunder, bullying and insult, and, in a few cases, death. They were, not infrequently, the victims of atrocities that, though mild enough by present-day standard, seemed horrifying to our forefathers.

It is hard to say with any confidence what the war meant to them in terms of their place in American society. While we have noted the cases of independent women who wished for greater opportunities and protections under the law for their sex, it would be a mistake to suggest that such feelings ever took the form of anything like a movement. The problem is complicated by the fact that American women, having enjoyed greater respect and having been valued higher by men than women had in any other modern society, were paradoxically losing some of the status and dignity that had earlier been theirs. The Revolution drew them more fully than before into the political and social life of an emerging nation, but at the same time an increasingly rigid moral code, centering on the sexual relation between men and women, served to diminish their freedom and their importance. So it must be said that for women the Revolution was an ambiguous legacy—they were of great importance and prominence in it; but they had less dignity and importance, for the most part, in the decades following it. Once more we might listen to the advice of the Marquis de Chastellux, who wrote in a letter to James Madison: "I know not, Sir, whether the following principle be that of a philosopher, or only of a Frenchman; but I am of the opinion that every amusement which separates the women from the men, is contrary to the welfare of society, is calculated to render one of the sexes clownish, and the other slovenly, and to destroy, in short, that sensibility, the source of which Nature has placed in the intercourse between the sexes."

Americans would have done well to have been more attentive to the marquis. First business and then leisure separated the sexes. If American men did not become "clownish" and the women "slovenly," it was certainly the case that both suffered in "sensibility."

20

Novus Ordo Seclorum

N ow, dear reader (to employ that amiable convention of nineteenth-century authors), having accompanied me on this long journey, you deserve a "conclusion," which, indeed, any proper history should have. I only trust that the American Revolution in its best spirit is still *unconcluded.* It has been my purpose to take it away from the academic historians, the professors, and return it to you. It has, after all, produced us—you and me—and I began this work with the conviction that we must try to understand what it was all about and what it means to us today. Although the reader may doubt it at this point, much, much more might have been said. This work, large as it is, is, for a certainty, only a sampling, though I trust a faithful one, of the enormous body of material extant on the years that saw the birth of this republic.

What does it all mean?

Every schoolchild who has been victimized by deadly textbook histories of the United States knows what we have already seen ample evidence of—that the Articles of Confederation were completely inadequate to define the government of a nation as large and variegated and complex as the newly united States. Yet provincialism had had over a hundred years of growth in America under the aegis of Great Britain, and it was not easily uprooted. The advocates of a strong national government found it a tedious and difficult task to lead the individual states in the direction of a federal union that would have some energy and force. Even the suggestion of a stronger union alarmed some champions of state sovereignty, such as Patrick Henry, who heard the iron march of despots behind the mildest suggestions for constitutional reform.

In 1786, the long-standing (and still continuing) dispute between Maryland and Virginia over fishing rights in the waters of the Potomac provided an occasion for the Annapolis Convention, at which delegates from five states called, in carefully veiled language, for a subsequent convention to be held in Philadelphia the following summer for the purpose of making certain necessary alterations in the Articles of Confederation. Under this dubious imprimatur, delegates from twelve states met in the Pennsylvania State House in May, 1787, and there, through the long, hot summer, fashioned the Federal Constitution, which established a new and far stronger national government. That convention was by general agreement composed of the most able and learned group of political theorists and practical politicians in history. All of the ideas and most of the practical forms discussed by the delegates were the common intellectual currency of the time. They had been debated in the assemblies that had drafted the particular state constitutions, and there were few notions that had not been given practical form in one state constitution or another. The task that faced the delegation in 1787 was primarily one of applying what were by and large generally agreed upon principles of sound government to a totally new situation.

For virtually the first time in history, as the delegates constantly reminded each other, men had an opportunity to meet and deliberate and frame a constitution designed to meet the needs of men for a just, stable, and orderly government. Certainly no other nation in the modern world had had such an opportunity. Most of mankind had lived under governments that they had inherited—ill-defined governments that had emerged from the mists of antiquity, governments in which the powerful oppressed the weak and the cunning exploited the guileless. Now there might be a new beginning, not just for Americans, but for all those who lived and labored under harsh and despotic rulers, whether kings and their courts or aristocracies (oligarchies, the Greeks called them) where the many labored for the welfare of the few.

The reverse side of the Great Seal of the United States told the story succinctly. The eye of God in a triangle represented the trinity, hovering above a pyramid, the perfect geometric form. The pyramid also symbolized the perfect governmental form, with the three branches of government—executive, legislative, and judicial—that the framers aspired to create, as fixed and permanent as the three persons of the trinity. The pyramid was still unfinished as the country was unfinished, as the great uninhabited spaces that would one day be filled were unfinished. *Annuit Coeptis,* "He, God, favors our undertaking." From the first the Puritans had yearned to be God's instruments for the redemption of the world. That vainglorious hope had seemed presumptious indeed in the hearts of a handful of settlers in a remote wilderness. Now it was restated. "God favors our undertakings"; we do this in His name and through Him it will flourish and bear fruit among all the nations of the earth.

We evoke again those images, drawn largely from the Bible, that spoke so powerfully to our forebearers: "But they shall sit every man under his vine, and under his fig tree, and none shall make *them* afraid: for the mouth of the LORD of hosts hath spoken it." The passage is in Micah, as are so many that echoed in the hearts of the Americans, but "man under his own vine and under his fig tree" is one of the most common phrases in the Bible, standing for freedom and independence under the eye of the Lord.

It is perhaps worth repeating here the three verses in Micah that precede that passage: "But in the last days it shall come to pass, that the mountain of the house of the Lord shall be established in the top of the mountains . . . and people shall flow into it. And many nations shall come and say, Come and let us go up into the mountain of the Lord . . . and he will teach us of his ways and we will walk in his paths; for the law shall go forth from Zion, and the word of the Lord from Jerusalem. And he shall judge among many people, and rebuke strong nations far off, and they shall beat their swords into plowshares and their spears into pruning forks: nation will not lift up a sword against nation, neither shall they learn war any more."

At the bottom of the Great Seal are the three words from Vergil's *Eclogues, Novus Ordo Seclorum,* "a new age now begins." It was that that the American Revolution and its consummation, the Federal Constitution, was to accomplish: a new age, a new human order, in which no man was sentenced by the chance of birth to subordination and exploitation and no class of men was ordained to rule over others. These were America's revolutionary credentials—a new dispensation for the human race, a new hope for humanity. And so the world indeed understood it.

The American Revolution, standing in the line of inheritance of the English Civil War and the Glorious Revolution of 1688–89 and soon to be followed by the French Revolution, was the first of the so-called democratic revolutions of modern times (though there were certainly conspicuous and powerful democratic elements in the English Civil War). And whether or not it was "the mountain of the house of the Lord . . . established in the top of the mountains," people did indeed "flow into it" in an endless tide from every nation of the world so that America became, in a strange way, not a nation (though that is what it called itself, since it could define itself in no other way) but a unifying principle, a congress, a gathering or a family of nations. Or at least that was what it aspired to be at its best, however badly and repeatedly it failed of its professions. Indeed it often doubted the rightness of its professions, since it was not always easy or pleasant to be the receptacle into which poured the despised and disinherited of the earth as well as the aspiring and ambitious. It would have certainly been easier and more convenient to have been a nation in the ordinary and traditional sense, instead of a kind of holding company whose fate it was to reenact, again and again, the drama of the rise of the subordinate and dependent to dignity and equality.

The interesting thing is that it was seldom the native-born Americans who saw their country as a refuge for those in every part of the world who were oppressed and yearned to be free. For example Thomas Jefferson, with all his concern for democracy, was not especially interested in extending its benefits. He was opposed to unlimited immigration on the grounds that settlers from the Old World would bring with them vices and prejudices that would corrupt their new home. George Grieve, the English translator of the Marquis de Chastellux's *Travels,* took a very different point of view. Immigration, he argued, would prove the future strength of the country. In his words: "Men of small, or no fortune, who cannot live with comfort, nor bring up a family in Europe; labourers and artizans of every kind; men of modesty and genius, who are cramped by insurmountable obstacles in countries governed by cabal and interest; virtuous citizens compelled to groan in silence under the effects of arbitrary power; philosophers who pant after liberty of thinking for themselves, and of giving vent, without danger, to those generous maxims which burst from their hearts, and of contributing their mite to the general flock of enlightened knowledge; religious men, depressed by the hierarchial establishments of every country in Europe; the friends to freedom; in short, the liberal, generous, and active spirits of the whole world. —To America, then, I say with fervency, in the glowing words of Mr. *Payne,* who is himself an English emigrant—'O! receive the fugitives, and prepare in time an asylum for mankind'"

It is striking that two "foreigners," Thomas Paine and George Grieve, had the most powerful vision of America as "the asylum of mankind." Against the provincialism of Jefferson and many other citizens of the new nation, they predicted the true future of the United States.

Of course they were not without their American counterparts. Governor Jonathan Trumbull of Connecticut, trying to enlist the support of the Dutch in 1782, summoned up the same vision for his friend Baron Van der Capellen den Pol, a leader of the republican faction in Holland. America, Trumbull said, was a land that called out to the dispossessed of other nations. Land was readily available, "12,000 acres situate most advantageously for future business, selling for 300 guineas English—i.e. little more than six pence sterling the acre. Our interests and our laws teach us to receive strangers, from every quarter of the globe, with open arms. The poor, the unfortunate, the oppressed from every country, will find here a ready asylum;—and by uniting their interests with ours, enjoy in common with us, all the blessings of liberty and plenty. Neither difference of nation, of language, of manners, or of religion, will lessen the cordiality of their reception among a people whose religion teaches them to regard all mankind as their brethren."

After World War II an eccentric Englishman, Wyndham Lewis, who had hated America the better part of his life, had an odd September romance with it and wrote a curious little book in praise of us, entitled *America and Cosmic Man.* Many Englishmen have commented on the United States, much of that comment unfavorable and almost all of it condescending. So it is perhaps suitable at the end of this story of bitter conflict between Englishmen and Americans to quote from a present-day English critic. "For a political mind, it [American history]," Lewis wrote, "is one of the most attractive histories of all: it reads like a lesson in politics. . . . At the foundation of the American State, when many very able minds contended with one another in this initial act of creation, the theory of human government is brought into a clear distinct light. We see the State built up from the bottom as if it were a demonstration in political science. . . . There is a logic and congruity, I think, in this vast place," Lewis wrote, "so recently a kind of *tabula rasa* physically, this world that is still new, being the cradle of a new type of man: not a man that is Mongol, or African, or Celt, or Teuton, or Mediterranean, but the sum of all these. Its situations—an island with Asia on one side, and Europe and Africa on the other—is propitious." After discussing what it means to be a "good Englishman" or a "good European," Lewis declares, "as to a good American, he, it appears to me, cannot but be a universalist (the term internationalist is conditioned too much by its past use to be a feasible alternative, though if you are not a nationalist, you are surely an internationalist of some sort)."

"To make of America merely another nationality, neither more nor less—like the German or French—would be an ambition limited indeed. The destiny of America is not to be just another 'grande nation': but to be the great big promiscuous grave into which tumble, and there disintegrate, all that was formerly race, class, or nationhood." This fate was, Lewis argued, contained in America's beginning, "that the great abstract reservoir of human beings labelled American (black, white and yellow, Irish, Polish, Syrian, Swedish, Russian, German, Italian) the first great 'melting-pot,' should be instrumental in bringing about the melting of *other* pots, where the various elements had so far remained obstinately intact. . . . The logic of the geographical position and history of the United States leads only, I believe, to one conclusion: namely, the ultimate formation of a society that will not be as other societies, but an epitome of all societies. . . . It has been built or is being built from outside, many different peoples and cultures converging on it—either, as that regards the people, as refugees, or as slaves or as what not: people have moved in to make it, it has not moved out, like a spider constructing its web, to embrace all outside itself. Nor is it an endemic culture, moving out to modify other cultures, and subdue them to one standard, namely its own. . . . This is, I repeat, the only possible meaning of the U.S.A.—to be the place where a Cosmopolis, as the Greeks would call it, is being tried out. Either the United States is (1) a rather disorderly collection of people dumped there by other nations which did not want them—a sort of wastepaper basket or trash-can; or (2) a splendid idea of Fate's to provide a human laboratory for the manufacture of Cosmic Man. It is, I feel, quite certainly the second of these alternatives."

Even if one is slightly uneasy with Wyndham Lewis's "Cosmic Man," it is clear that he has grasped an important point. The United States is a kind of interim stage between the old parochialism of the nation-states and a more universal society. The important point is that while the Founding Fathers certainly would not have put the matter this way, they were more preoccupied with the principle of universalism (which I, like Wyndham Lewis, like much better than internationalism) than any other generation of Americans down to the present. I believe that they would have responded warmly to the notion of the "United States" (which is, after all, a description, not a name) as a society that would be the vector of a new human order rather than simply a nation among other nations. A Frenchman (the French, far more than the British, have been sympathetic observers of the American scene, perhaps because it is so thoroughly un-French) has recently argued that a world revolution is presently taking place, led, largely against its will, by America, and that only America can sustain that revolution and bring it to fruition. Whether that is true or not (the recent *détente* with China has opened our eyes, formerly blinded by fear and prejudice, to the fact that China may well have most important contributions to make to any world revolution), I believe that the first American Revolution has an inexhaustible capacity to illuminate our own "soul" or "spirit" as well as the dilemmas of our times; and that America, forged once in the fires of adversity, may be forged once more and in that forging merge its great talents and energies, its gift for self-criticism and for visions of a better world, with the common metal of humanity.

We might here review the major premises of this work. The condition of life in colonial America had produced a man with a new consciousness—self-reliant, independent, basically democratic. The reader will recall that Captain Evelyn of the Fifty-second Light Infantry, stationed in Boston in the spring of 1775, wrote to his father that in his opinion the trouble with the colonies was "to be found in the nature of mankind; and that it proceeds from a new nation, feeling itself wealthy, populous, and strong; and being impatient of restraint, are struggling to throw off that dependency which is so irksome to them." A substantial number of Americans wished to be masters of their own destiny. Once this process had begun and it was clear that Americans were willing to stake their lives on the outcome, the Revolution was, in a real sense, accomplished.

The Revolution began, in essence, with the Stamp Act, which revealed clearly that a large number of colonial Americans were no longer willing to occupy a subordinate and dependent role in relation to the mother country; they were no longer willing to be powerless and to have their fate and their fortune decided, in many instances quite arbitrarily, by a group of men geographically remote and perhaps more remote in awareness of and sympathy for the problems and needs of

Americans. Moreover, this determination that each man should sit under his own fig tree and under his vine and that no one should disturb him—that no one should say how his money was to be spent or what he should or should not do—was not created and manipulated by a group of middle-class radical intellectuals but was the most profound expression of a large and decisive portion of the American people, from the farmers of New England and the merchants and sailors of Boston to the lawyers and artisans of New York and Philadelphia and the yeoman farmers and great plantation owners of the South. Perhaps never again as united, these American colonists suddenly and unexpectedly rejected the Stamp Act. And from this position they never retreated. To be sure, some dropped away, unable to face the implications of resistance to Great Britain, or more realistically aware of those implications than their fellows. But from the Stamp Act to Lexington and Concord, a major-ity—or perhaps, since there was no colonial Gallup Poll, we should say a sufficient number—of Americans maintained this "revolutionary" stance without flinching. That was the Revolution. The wavering and uncertainty was on the other side of the ocean. The Stamp Act was repealed, but the Declaratory Act was passed to take some of the sting out of what was otherwise an awkward capitulation. The Townshend Duties were tried and, in the face of resourceful and determined resistance, dropped. Troops were sent to preserve order, and then were withdrawn. And finally, when it almost seemed as though a kind of *modus vivendi,* a practical compromise that would constitute a *de facto* recognition of the right of the colonists to be free from British taxation in any form, might develop, Lord North had the fatal inspiration to use the colonists to bail out the inept and rapacious management of the East India Company, and Thomas Hutchinson used that misstep to precipi-tate the American Revolution.

The military (and the moral and spiritual) leadership of this Revo-lution fell to George Washington. Washington did not "win the Revolu-tion." He preserved the Continental Army as the symbol of the union of the thirteen colonies. If there had been no Washington, Great Britain would, in time, have wearied of the impossible task of trying to subdue several million stubborn Americans, and the colonies would have become independent. But as certainly as we can say anything about the past, we can say that America would have been made up, in that event, of thirteen loosely confederated and often bitterly quarrelsome, essen-tially sovereign states. The French did not win the American Revolution any more than Washington did. The French entry into the war hardened the hearts of the British and probably prolonged the war; the active military operations of the French in America had a negative effect prior to the Battle of Yorktown. Even if there had been no Yorktown, the British would not have "won" the American Revolution.

Popular history has persisted in making George III the villain of the American Revolution, and in fact he was; the one consistent element was the stubborn pride of the king. Whenever his ministers wavered he stiffened their spines, and when their spines proved immune to his stiffening he got rid of them, until at last he found that doggedly faithful instrument of his will, Lord North. There is no question that in the acts undertaken to punish the town of Boston for its insolence in dumping the tea into the harbor, North had behind him the great mass of British public opinion in all levels of society but the lowest, where sympathy for the American cause was deeply rooted. But when it became apparent that the issue was not simply chastising Boston but subduing by force of arms and at enormous expense a territory vastly larger than Great Britain herself, public sentiment, as we have seen, gradually abandoned the king and his ministers; and when his ministers wavered, only the implacable determination of the king prolonged the inevitable outcome of the contest. So George III was indeed the villain, though a very decent sort of villain as villains go. But it is not necessary, of course, to be wicked to be a villain; it is only necessary to persist in a wrong policy when that policy, however reasonable it may have originally appeared, has become destructive of the values by which all decent societies of men seek to live.

As these comments make clear, and as I trust I have made abundantly clear in the body of this work, I believe that after the Stamp Act there was never any serious chance that Americans would accept the unlimited authority of Parliament to legislate for them. The only real question was whether Parliament would discover an enlightened enough spirit to concede to the colonists sufficient independence and autonomy to keep them as loyal members of the British Empire, or whether, in the name of principle, they would drive them into complete independence. It was due largely to the temper and personality of George III that England followed the latter course. One suggestive aftermath of the war was that the British people, as represented in Parliament, were so dismayed by the disastrous consequences of having left sufficient power in the hands of a single executive officer, the king, that they saw to it that no king would ever have such power again.

Historians are great "if-ers," and the revolution offers them a field day. They point out that *if* Howe in Boston had been more aggressive, Washington's ill-trained army must have been scattered far and wide and the Revolution brought to an abrupt halt. *If* Howe had been more alert at Long Island, more persistent at White Plains, more tenacious in the Jerseys, more resolute at Brandywine, more sagacious at Germantown, more enterprising at Philadelphia, Washington's army would have been defeated and/or captured and the Revolution would have been over. If Howe had reinforced Burgoyne on his march from Canada; *if* Clinton had been skillful at Monmouth or had taken greater advantage of his opportunities, or *if* he had shown more initiative in New York; *if,* once again, he had pressed his campaign in the Jerseys or campaigned in New England, or supported Cornwallis more generously in the South, or divined Washington's intention of trying to trap Cornwallis in Virginia, Washington's and Rochambeau's army might have been defeated and/or captured and the Revolution would have been over.

And, then of course, the ultimate "if"—*if* the French had not entered the war! Historians can hardly be blamed for such little touches, designed to heighten the drama of the Revolution (although, God knows, it needs no heightening); indeed the historian quite properly keeps this eternal "if" very much in the front of his mind. But the result has been a serious distortion of the nature of the Revolution itself. One consequence of the work of the "if-ers" is that the Revolution has commonly been treated as a "war" rather than as a "revolution." This of course was the British mistake as well. In a war, especially in the eighteenth-century variety, when one side has absorbed a sufficient number of defeats, lost a sufficient number of soldiers, and surrendered a sufficient number of towns and cities, it adds up the profits and losses, finds that the debit column far outweighs the gains, and petitions for peace, or, more abjectly, surrenders. But a revolution is a different matter. A revolution is for keeps. A true revolution is not reversible; it cannot be "defeated" in any conventional sense. The people can be decimated, starved, virtually destroyed, and in the right circumstances, by means of utter ruthlessness, the revolution can be suppressed. But "suppressed" is different from "defeated."

There must have been some reason why America was the graveyard of British military reputations; why no British general emerged with his laurels untarnished. After all, these were the same men, or at the very least the same type of men, who had administered a decisive drubbing to the French and Spanish during the Seven Years' War. They made up the best military and naval force in the world. As we have seen, it never occurred to any but a handful of congenital optimists that they could be defeated by a ragtag citizen army of untrained levies. And properly speaking they weren't. They "won" almost every engagement. From the "battle" of Lexington and Concord, which wasn't, properly speaking, a battle at all, to Yorktown, the British claimed an almost unbroken series of victories.

The American "victories" were modest ones for the most part. Harlem Heights, a victory of a kind; Trenton a very brilliant one and standing almost by itself; Germantown, a near thing; Cowpens and Kings Mountain undeniably victories, but definitely minor engagements in terms of the forces engaged; Eutaw Springs quite clearly a victory. And finally, a rather ambiguous victory, Yorktown. The surrender of Burgoyne was not preceded by any clear-cut American "victory," except that at Bennington; Burgoyne simply drowned in a sea of rebels, and this clearly was what would have happened to any such force that ventured too far from its base of operations, be it Boston, Montreal, New York City, Philadelphia, Charles Town, or Savannah. Great Britain could have gone on winning battles for another decade and never have won the war, for the "war" was not a war but a revolution.

Wendell Phillips, the nineteenth-century reformer, wrote: "Revolutions are not made, they come." The American Revolution was not "made" by a small group of radical intellectuals; it was formed in the consciousness of Americans in every colony and every walk of life, perhaps even more strongly in the plain people of the colonies than among their leaders. And when it was formed, not even knowing itself formed, it manifested itself with startling force and unanimity at the time of the Stamp Act. Never again so unequivocal in its response to what it judged to be the abuse of the authority of Parliament, the violation of its "covenant," that American consciousness nonetheless found within itself the resources to make good its determination that the covenant between America and Great Britain be scrupulously observed or, failing that, that the colonies be free and independent.

The American Revolution was, in modern parlance, the first "people's liberation movement." In order to make any sense out of the question of whether Great Britain could have "won the war," we have to rephrase the question in a different form: Could Great Britain, after, let us say, the battle of Bunker Hill, and after, certainly, the Declaration of Independence, have reduced the colonies to a "proper state of subordination"? Could they, in short, have turned off the revolution? Could they have restored the *status quo ante bellum,* as the military and diplomatic historians put it? And the answer, of course, is an emphatic no. It is quite literally impossible to imagine Thomas Hutchinson returning to Massachusetts to guide its affairs and squabble with his council once again; or William Tryon back in North Carolina or New York, or, indeed, any other governor directing the affairs of this or that colony. In 1779, with the Carlisle commission, Great Britain went as far as it could have possibly gone short of granting complete independence in meeting the American grievances that had brought on the "war"; and while Washington and Congress "feared it like the devil," it caused hardly a stir among the rank and file of patriots. No peace movement developed in the states to barter for a return to the parental fold, which had once appeared such a haven of security. It was indeed as Washington had said of the people crowding around him on the march from New York to Virginia: "We may be beaten by the English . . . but here is an army they will never conquer."

American independence was not a precarious issue, hanging always in the balance, resting on a victory here or there, on this alliance or that, on the preservation of Robert Howe's army of the Southern Department, or Benjamin Lincoln's army of the Southern Department, or Horatio Gates's army of the Southern Department—each of which were successively obliterated—or even on the survival of Nathanael Greene's army, or the Continental Army of George Washington himself. The Revolution was, quite simply, the first and one of the most powerful expressions of the determination of a people to be free.

Beyond this the Revolution exists as an extraordinary dramatic episode in and of itself. It is an absorbing story in which heroism, devotion, sacrifice, and herculean labors contend with arrogance, greed, cruelty, selfish ambition, and cowardice; and these virtues and sins are by no means distributed in any simple way between Britons and Americans or even between patriots and Tories.

And *beyond that* the American Revolution is one of a great chain of revolutionary events that began with the English Civil War and the Glorious Revolution and ran through the French Revolution, the Russian Revolution, and most recently, the Chinese Revolution; one of a series of cataclysmic events that changed the world. The English Civil War was against arbitrary authority exercised by a king over his subjects; the American Revolution was waged against arbitrary authority exercised by the mother country against her colonies. One of the consequences of the American Revolution was the defining of political relationships and the development of safeguards to prevent the exercise of arbitrary power; another was the reform of English political life; another was, to a substantial degree, the French Revolution, which was certainly influenced by and in a sense flowed out of the American Revolution. But where the American Revolution had been political, the French Revolution set out to destroy hierarchical social relations between classes in the name of equality, liberty, and fraternity. The Russian revolutionists maintained that the basis of man's subordination of other men was economic, and that the economic structure of capitalism had to be destroyed before men could be truly free.

The Chinese, for their part, have declared for total and perpetual revolution—revolution as a way of life. But already they have made dramatic modifications of that doctrine in order, presumably, to find an ally against the senescent Russian Revolution. The truth is that technology, and the relentless competition between nations that it has brought in its train, has forced us by such practical matters as the devaluation of the dollar, the unfavorable United States trade balance, and the energy crisis to recognize that we live in an age when economics are more important than ideology. The modern world has been remade by a series of revolutions that began with the English Civil War of 1640. We are now one revolutionary world. Or to put the matter in a familiar maxim: We are all in the same boat.

It is thus of particular importance for all the nations of the modern world to understand our common revolutionary tradition and to recognize that the brute force of modern technology must be mastered and humanized, whether we call ourselves capitalists, socialists, communists, republicans, or democrats.

As I remarked in the introduction to this work, it is a commonplace today to say that we are in the midst of a "revolution"; indeed, when I mentioned to people that I was writing a book on "The American Revolution," they almost invariably said, "Which American Revolution?" I do not have the space or the inclination to end this work with a detailed critique of contemporary American society, but it does seem to me that there is taking place a transformation of that consciousness that brought about and fought the American Revolution, established the Federal Constitution, and sustained the "filling up" of America and the creation of a great industrial and technological society that, with all its failures, has remained in many ways a remarkably open society. To say that a new consciousness is being born and to welcome it, with numerous cautious reservations to be sure, but nonetheless to welcome it, is in no way to denigrate the old consciousness from which it has issued and which, at the moment, it seems to be so stridently rejecting. It is a modern heresy to believe that the human type that emerged from the revolutionary struggles of the later eighteenth century was the final form of human development. The Founding Fathers did not say so. They simply said that a "new age now begins," as it most surely had.

A new consciousness, to free itself of the ubiquitous, pervasive presence of the old, must fiercely reject it, overreact, overstate (and pay a heavy price for doing so, like soldiers in a war in which no quarter is asked or given); but eventually they must always come back to make peace with all in the old order that gave them life and gave them the ideals in the name of which they wage war against it. This transformation of consciousness is so vast and so omnipresent, so much a part of our daily awareness, that it is both impossible and unnecessary to trace it in detail. That consciousness is certainly, to a degree that is hard now to estimate, a by-product of the Vietnam War. The reader will hardly have missed, as I certainly did not, the striking analogies between Great Britain in the middle years of the eighteenth century and the United States in the middle decades of the twentieth. As Britain—powerful, enlightened, the most advanced and liberal nation in the world— proceeded, full of self-righteousness, to put down riot and rebellion among her ungrateful subjects across the sea, we, full of our own power and righteousness, declaring to the world our devotion to international justice, to self-determination, to democracy, undertook to check the progress of "Godless Communism" in a small country half a world away. Like Great Britain we persisted, out of stubbornness, pride, and inertia, long after our intervention had turned into a disastrous war that we could not win. And in our rage at not being able to win, we—enlightened, democratic nation that we profess to be—embarked on a policy of senseless devastation, that most bankrupt of all policies, the punitive. If we could not defeat our enemy, we would punish him severely.

George Mason, a slaveholder himself, said in the Federal Convention in reference to the evil of slavery, "As nations cannot be rewarded or punished in the next world, they must be in this. By an inevitable chain of causes and effects, Providence punishes national sins, by national calamities." The "punishment" that followed that particular "sin" of slavery was plainly the terrible tragedy of the Civil War. It would be vain to guess what our "punishment" may be for the Vietnam War, or even *if* it will be. We have already been punished substantially in the tearing of the bonds of generation and community; we have paid in a hundred large and small ways by loss of the comity and good faith that bind a people together. On the other hand, we might take heart from the future of Great Britain after the catastrophic failure of its "American policy." England went on to its greatest age of power and importance in the nineteenth century. Yet it might be said that England's punishment was contained in its defeat: it lost, as Burke and others had predicted it would, "several millions of as loyal and industrious people as lived" and the jewel of its empire, the American colonies.

America (and the world) may become green (as in "the greening of"), blue (collar), Red, black, brown, or even yellow (as in the yellow hordes of Asia), but the American Revolution will remain one of the most crucial, if not *the* most crucial episode in modern history. It would be presumptuous to try to divine God's plans for Man—indeed some theologians have suggested that He Himself may be uncertain—but I do believe that there is much truth in Rosenstock-Huessy's statement that we can only go as far forward in history as we are willing or able to go back. History, the collective memory of the race, must be preserved, purified, and refined. Like the old crone in the fairy tale who had to be carried over the river by the hero despite her crushing weight and who turned, in the passage of the stream, into an enchanting maiden, we have to bear the burden of history, however heavy; otherwise we cannot escape from the pathless forest.

To many members of my generation, it is disconcerting to see young men and women turning away from the "serious" concerns of life; instead of becoming doctors and lawyers, legislators, scholars, and diplomats, they are turning to potting, weaving, painting, sculpting, carpentering, baking bread, and writing poetry. In my own moments of disquiet, I find considerable comfort in words John Adams wrote to his wife: "I must study politics and war, that my sons may have liberty to study mathematics and philosophy. My sons ought to study mathematics and philosophy, geography, natural history and naval architecture, navigation, commerce and agriculture, in order to give their children a right to study painting, poetry, music, architecture, statuary, tapestry and porcelain." This seems to me one of the most extraordinary utterances of the era of the American Revolution. In John Adams's iron soul there lay this dream of a gentler day when the arts of war and politics would be replaced by higher and fairer expressions of the human spirit. In Adams's ascending order lay prefigured at least the better portion of that new consciousness struggling presently to be born. In a society that one feared had lost the capacity to create and appreciate beauty, a new generation is striving, however ineptly at times, to give substance to Adams' vision.

When Joseph Martin sat down, as an old man, to relive his experiences as a private in the Continental Army, he felt very keenly that a growing, bustling America had forgotten much of what he and his fellow soldiers had fought for and had, above all, forgotten the hardships they had suffered in the long years of war. Congress must have thought "her soldiers had not private parts," he wrote, for they often had no trousers and nothing but shirts to cover their nakedness. Even the blankets were of the cheapest baize, "thin enough to have straws shot through [them] without discommoding the threads." Many a cold, stormy night Martin had to lie "in a wood, or a field, or a bleak hill, with such blankets . . . with nothing but the canopy of the heavens to cover me. . . . Almost every one," he wrote, "has heard of the soldiers of the Revolution being tracked by the blood of their feet on the frozen ground. This is literally true, and the thousandth part of their suffering has not, nor ever will be told."

With food as with clothing, it was all promises. "Oftentimes," Martin reminded his readers, "have I gone one, two, three, even four days without a morsel, unless the fields or forests might chance to afford enough to prevent absolute starvation." Until August, 1777, some pretense was made of paying the Continental soldiers the six and two-thirds dollars a month they were supposed to receive. But the pay was in constantly depreciating paper currency, and when it was paid it was hardly enough to buy a square meal. From August, 1777, to the end of the war Martin received one month's pay in specie, on the march to Yorktown. "The country," he wrote with an uncharacteristic edge of bitterness, "was rigorous in exacting my compliance to *my* engagements to a punctilio, but equally careless in performing her contracts with me, and why so? One reason was because she had all the power in her own hands and I had none. Such things ought not to be."

"How many times have I had to lie down like a dumb animal in the field, and bear 'the pelting of the pitiless storm,' cruel enough in warm weather, but how much more so in the heart of winter. Could I have had the benefit of a little fire, it would have been deemed a luxury. But when snow or rain would fall so heavy that it was impossible to keep a spark of fire alive, to have to weather out a long, wet, cold, tedious night in the depth of winter, with scarcely clothes enough to keep one from freezing instantly, how discouraging it must be, I leave to my reader to judge."

To suffer so was to envy the hogs in their warm sties. People who had never been in an army thought the fighting the worst of it, but in battle you could only be wounded or killed. The worst was the long, long, endless weeks that rolled into months and then years of suffering from cold and hunger in camp, and of marching, marching, marching. Martin had often marched until he had been "so beat out . . . that I have fallen asleep while walking the road and not been sensible of it till I have jostled against someone in the same situation; and when permitted to stop and have the superlative happiness to roll myself in my blanket and drop down on the ground in the bushes, briars, thorns, or thistles, and get an hour or two's sleep. . . . Reader, believe me, for I tell a solemn truth, that I have felt more anxiety, undergone more fatigue and hardships, suffered more every way, in performing one of those tedious marches than ever I did in fighting the hottest battle I was ever engaged in. . . ."

So the last word is Private—later Sergeant—Joseph Martin's. If there has been one spirit that has guided us through the seemingly interminable anguish of the War for American Independence, it is this entirely captivating character, so full of wit and good humor, of courage and high spirits, as solid and tough-grained as a Connecticut maple and as enduring as the rocks of his adopted state of Maine. He speaks to us over all those intervening years as vividly and freshly, as shrewdly and idiomatically, as if we sat in his own parlor long ago and listened as he carried us back in time to the "Adventures, Dangers and Sufferings of a Revolutionary Soldier," as he subtitled his *Narrative*. If the famous military and political leaders of the day had not had the Joseph Martins to lead—the common soldiers, faithful and tenacious in the cause of liberty—there would have been no American Revolution. Politicians debated, squabbled, contended, and proposed, and generals and colonels disposed, but Martin and his fellow soldiers endured through every hazard and every defeat and even more notably through the desperate privation of army life. And in so doing, they gave America its freedom and its task. The vast land waited for its fulfillment, to be filled up by those "millions yet unborn" that haunted the dreams and filled out the rhetoric of Revolutionary statesmen.

On July 4, 1796, the Reverend Samuel Thacher, a Congregational minister, gave a sermon at Concord, Massachusetts. His theme was that liberty was "a pure, original emanation from the great source of life." It had been almost obliterated from the earth "when AMERICA, indignant at oppression, rose and proclaimed it with a voice which broke the spell of the confining nations . . . and struck like thunder upon the ears of despots." Arbitrary government, oppression, and exploitation must give way all over the earth to the determination of peoples to be free and equal. "All hail! Approaching Revolutions!" Thacher proclaimed: "Americans, we have lived ages in a day. Pyramids of lawless power, the work of centuries, have fallen in a moment!"

The advantages of the American Revolution could not be adequately described in the time allotted to him. It was enough to say that "its effects are not confined to one age or one country." Its influence would, in the years ahead, be extended "beyond calculation." Those of his countrymen who had assembled at Concord to commemorate the Revolution were, in practical fact, also marking "the consequent emancipation of a world."

In 1961, a hundred and sixty-five years later, an Englishman, Arnold Toynbee, speaking to an American audience at the University of Pennsylvania, said:

"The American Revolution has gone thundering on. Nothing can stop it, no, not even the American hands that first set it rolling. But, during these last . . . years, your revolution has gone on without you. The leadership has fallen into other hands. These non-Americans could never have seized the leadership of your revolution if you had not dropped it." America's power and affluence, Toynbee contended, had estranged her from her own ideals and pushed her into the position "of being the leader of the very opposite of what America's World Revolution stands for. . . . But the future is still open. Your role in the coming chapter of the World's history is not yet irrevocably decided. It is still in your power to re-enter into your heritage. It is still within your power to re-capture the lead in your own revolution."

The future is still open. . . .

Bibliographical Note

The identifying characteristic of academic history is footnotes. They are the classic imprimatur of scholarly respectability. Systematic footnoting would, however, greatly extend the length and cost of this already long and costly enterprise, and it would serve little scholarly purpose. Beyond that I confess to a certain ingrained prejudice against footnotes. Originally a modest and useful means of giving the source of specific quotations in the text, they have progressed (or regressed) to being contentious, expository, and didactic, a sort of cumbersome vehicle, full of scholarly impedimenta, which is dragged along with the text and from which the author pulls forth for display endless exhibits of his erudition, fending off critics with frequent asides designed to demonstrate his knowledge of the literature of the field, and making snide comments about rival historians (as, "For a different point of view see J. D. Pendant's ineptly argued and weakly supported *The Investiture Controversy Investigated,* chapters VI-VIII, and *passim, op. cit., ibid.,* etc.").

I believe most of this is absurd. So-called didactic footnotes are usually better placed in the text or abandoned. Furthermore, they are often an invitation to dubious scholarly tactics. The historian who encounters a particularly indigestible fact that does not fit his theory or that casts an unfavorable light on the subject of his biography can, and very often does, tuck it away (and explain it away) in a footnote. Hence, a footnote such as this: [5]"Jones [a contemporary observer] declares that X cursed and swore like a madman, but we must dismiss this because we know that Jones was angry with X and that it was quite out of character for X to curse and swear." This scholarly dodge seems to me to be perilously close to cheating. I suspect we would all be better off if expository and didactic footnotes were banned from scholarly texts.

Be that as it may, I can say for this work that the primary sources for the history of the era of the American Revolution are well known to historians familiar with the field. I have in most places in the text stated the work from which a particular quotation has been taken, as, "Light Horse Harry Lee noted in his *Memoirs of the Southern Campaign* . . . ," or "Dr. Thacher recorded in his diary. . . ." Beyond that I have, wherever practical, given the name of a letter writer, the date or approximate date of the letter, and often the name of the recipient. With such evidence, a serious or even an interested amateur wishing to track down the full text of letter or document will be able to do so with little difficulty.

I would like to review here the primary source materials used in this work. For anyone interested in the American Revolution from the beginning of the resistance to Parliament down to 1776, one monumental work looms over all others, Peter Force's *American Archives*. This work in nine large volumes is an extraordinary compilation of newspaper articles, public documents, and letters dealing with the period of agitation and the opening episodes of the war. It contains literally thousands of vivid and illuminating items. Just as this present work was getting under way, Arno Books, a subsidiary of *The New York Times,* reprinted almost two hundred volumes of "eyewitness accounts"—firsthand, contemporary narratives by participants in the Revolution. These were, almost without exception, well known, but many were out of print and difficult or impossible to get, and all are expensive in their original editions. This ambitious venture was my most valuable single resource; indeed, I often had the eerie feeling that it had been published for my express benefit. I had the same feeling about another work, more modest in extent, but almost equally valuable; Mark Mayo Boatner III's *Encyclopedia of the American Revolution,* published in 1966. This estimable volume, clearly the result of vast labors, saved me countless hours in reference libraries hunting down information on some obscure but interesting figure in the Revolution or on some minor (or major) battle or engagement.

Also useful was Henry Steele Commager's and Richard B. Morris's *Spirit of 76,* a splendidly comprehensive collection of firsthand accounts of the Revolution accompanied by helpful notes (not footnotes). There are, in addition, many standard primary sources in print. Any quotation from a letter written by a delegate to Congress is almost certainly from Edmund Burnett's great collection of *Letters of Delegates to Continental Congress,* in seven volumes. The *Journals of Congress* have also been printed, but they contain only the barest record of daily business.

For the military campaigns, the principal sources are to be found in the letters and papers of the general officers involved. First and foremost, of course, is Washington's own voluminous correspondence. The (John) *Sullivan Papers* were very helpful, as were William Moultrie's *Memoirs* (especially for the seige of Charles Town) and, to a lesser degree, those of General William Heath. I have already mentioned the greatest military history to come out of the Revolution, Henry Lee's *Memoirs of the Southern Campaign.* In addition, there are numerous journals and diaries, most of them by officers—American, British, and Hessian. Some of the most striking, however, are by enlisted men. Joseph Plumb Martin's *Narrative* was a kind of autobiographical recollection of the events in which he had participated, and what little it may have lost in immediacy it doubtless gained in literary style.

There are four contemporary formal histories of the Revolution that are still extremely useful. William Gordon's *History,* published in 1788, is a very good one, as is that of David Ramsay, which is still unexcelled in its account of the origins of the Revolution. Ramsay's *History of the Revolution in South Carolina* is also very helpful. Charles Stedman, who was a member of Howe's staff, wrote perhaps the best overall contemporary military account of the war, especially reliable of course for those campaigns in which he participated. In addition, Banastre Tarleton wrote a kind of British counterpoint to Henry Lee's *Memoirs—A History of the Campaigns of 1780 and 1781 in the Southern Provinces of North America,* and John Burgoyne, William Howe, and Henry Clinton wrote lengthy and tendentious accounts of their campaigns that were intended to vindicate their actions (usually by putting the blame on their fellow officers). Of these Clinton's is the most successfully sustained narrative.

For the British side, Hansard's *Parliamentary Debates* and the *Annual Register* were the most useful. The nature of the *Annual Register* is perhaps best suggested by its full title, *The Annual Register or General Repository of History, Politics, and Literature, for the Year* [whatever the year was]. This remarkable work, which was edited through a considerable portion of its life by Edmund Burke, gave a year-by-year résumé of principal events in the Western world. The 1780 edition was prefaced, for example, by a "Review of the Principal Transactions of the present Reign," which had a subdued Whig note to it. This was followed by twenty chapters on "British and Foreign History," much of it based on parliamentary debates with lengthy extracts from those debates, many of which were devoted to the American war. The next section entitled "Principal Occurrences," was devoted primarily to firsthand accounts of naval and military engagements, along with the births, marriages, promotions, and deaths among the great lords of the realm. Then followed a section of "Public Papers" and a section entitled "Biographical Anecdotes and Characters," which reviewed the theater season and the leading books published during the year, and which contained a very complimentary "Sketch of the Life and Character of General Washington." ("Candour, sincerity, affability, and simplicity, seem to be the striking features of his character, till an occasion offers of displaying the most determined bravery and independence of spirit," the author concluded.) Sections on the "Manner of Nations," "Philosophical Papers," "Antiquities," and, finally, a selection of "Poetry" completed the *Annual Register* for 1780. We certainly have nothing so interesting or comprehensive today.

W. E. H. Lecky's great eight-volume *History of England in the Eighteenth Century,* while not a primary source, contains, of course, a great amount of material on America and the Revolution, most of which has been abstracted in a single volume.

The best sources for the diplomatic history of the period are Francis Wharton's *Diplomatic Correspondence of the American Revolution* in six volumes and Benjamin F. Stevens' *Facsimiles of American Documents Relating to the Revolution in Foreign Archives* in twenty-five volumes. Also used, though more sparingly, were the numerous editions of the letters and writings of the leading figures of the Revolution. In addition to often quite adequate collections of such papers edited in the nineteenth century, there are a number of large-scale editions of these papers presently under way, among them the papers of Thomas Jefferson in a projected seventy-five volumes, the Adams Papers in an even larger number of volumes, and the papers of Hamilton, Madison, Franklin, Marshall, and Mason, each in a multivolume edition.

In addition to the printed primary source materials, there is an enormous amount of primary material that has not been printed. All of the original thirteen states have historical societies and libraries. Many university libraries, especially those at the older Eastern universities such as Harvard, Columbia, Princeton, and Yale, have large collections of manuscript materials relating to the Revolution. The William Clements Library at the University of Michigan, the Houghton Library at Harvard, the Beinecke Library at Yale, the American Antiquarian Society at Worcester, Massachusetts, and the Institute of Early American History and Culture at Williamsburg, Virginia, are among the most prominent of such manuscript repositories, with collections covering much more than the Revolution. There are, also of course, the Library of Congress at Washington and the National Archives. As I mentioned in the introduction, there are literally millions of letters, papers, and documents having to do with the era of the Revolution. No one person could absorb them in a long lifetime. It seems safe to say, however, that with, I am sure, many exceptions, the most interesting and important primary source materials have been published.

At the beginning of this work, my research assistant, Lester Cohen, and I made a journey through the most important repositories of manuscript materials on the East Coast to get a notion of what unused or little-used materials might be found in these libraries and historical societies. Lester Cohen then spent the better part of a year collecting nine large volumes of manuscript material, reproduced by xeroxing. He struck his richest veins in the Jared Sparks manuscripts in the Houghton Library at Harvard and in the George Bancroft Papers at the New York Public Library; in the Historical Society of

Pennsylvania's Laurens Papers; and in the Connecticut Historical Society's Jonathan Trumbull Papers. The Sparks and Bancroft collections were especially helpful because they were the product of years of assiduous collecting by those two nineteenth-century historians.

The American Antiquarian Society has the most complete collection of colonial newspapers. Newspapers were, as is clear from the text, used extensively.

Most, if not all, of the thirteen states have their own historical magazines. These contain many contemporary letters and other important documents. Although others were consulted, the two most useful were the *Pennsylvania Magazine of History and Biography,* with an excellent index, and the *William and Mary Quarterly.*

Still another category of works was used. These were so-called monographs, specialized studies on a single topic. The term is a loose one that covers what are essentially narrative accounts of small segments of a larger topic (although the monographs themselves may bulk very large), as well as works that are essentially analytical and interpretive. An example of the first type of monograph would be Carl Van Doren's *Mutiny in January,* an account of the mutiny of the Pennsylvania Line that was very detailed and, in consequence, very helpful in this work. In the same category would be Van Doren's *Secret History of the American Revolution,* a study of the spies, double agents, and traitors on both sides. It is here that the story of Arnold's treachery is perhaps most carefully and scrupulously told. Allen French's splendid monograph *The First Year of the Revolution* is outstanding narrative history. Of the relatively few monographs used, virtually all were in this category. The other category (and what is usually more generally meant by the term "monograph") is, as I have said, the analytical or interpretive study. Examples of this type would be *Sceptre and Mitre* by Carl Bridenbaugh, a work which purports to show that religious conflicts were at the heart of the Revolution; or Gordon Wood's more recent *Political Ideas of the American Revolution.* Most monographs of this kind extract from the complex tangle of episodes and ideas that characterize a major historical event certain themes or topics for detailed examination. The danger in such studies is that their authors are tempted to claim more importance for their particular "theme" than a comprehensive and balanced perspective justifies. Thus a famous and very influential monograph by Arthur Schlesinger, entitled the *New England Merchants and the American Revolution,* argued very learnedly that the Revolution really came about because the New England merchants were determined to protect their trade. This doctrine, supported by an infinite number of footnotes, proved so persuasive that it was taught to several generations of graduate students of history as simple fact.

At worst the monograph is very apt to muddy the historical waters and draw attention away from the primary issues. At best it serves an important if transient purpose by relating historical events to the "spirit of the times," and thus keeping them accessible, at least on a scholarly level, through "reinterpretation." The writing of them also serves to keep historians occupied and to get them promoted in institutions preoccupied by "scholarship." If it is true, as I believe it is, that the truth of an event is to be found in the full and careful telling of it—that, as Erich Auerbach said, the event, properly told, contains its own interpretation—standard monographic history has little meaning for a work of this kind. It was thus little used, an omission that had the incidental benefit of saving an enormous amount of time, since literally hundreds of monographs have accumulated on the era of the American Revolution.

Hopefully, at this point the reader interested in the matter of sources (which is certainly a very interesting matter) has some idea of how this history was assembled. My primary commitment from the first moment of undertaking this task has been to consult the primary sources, the words and actions—as recorded in letters, diaries, journals, newspapers, public documents, and memoirs—of the men and women who were involved in the event out of which this nation was born. I have tried at all times to be attentive to them; to listen carefully and to reflect upon the meaning of their words and actions. Whatever virtues this work may have is the consequence of that essentially simple process—listening.

INDEX

Abbott, Edward, 1173
Abercrombie, James, 585
Abercrombie, Robert, 992, 1703
Acland, John, 933–934
"Act Concerning Religion" (Calvert), 24
Actaeon, 631–634
Active, 630
Acts of Trade and Navigation, 136, 179, 248
Adams, Abigail, 380, 552, 565, 683, 845, 1132
  on independence for women, 1808–1810
  on John Paul Jones, 1286–1287
  on women's education, 1809
  on women's group action against high
    prices, 1365
Adams, Andrew, 842, 1055
Adams, Hannah, 486, 490
Adams, John, 198, 258, 285, 417, 1829–1830
  on animosity between congressional agents
    in France, 1139–1140
  and Battle of Lexington, 473
  and Boston Massacre, 345–348, 351–357,
    359
  and Boston Tea Party, 381–382, 384
  and *Common Sense,* 682–683
  concludes peace treaty with Holland, 1731
  and Continental Navy, 1239, 1240, 1253,
    1255
  on Coudray, 976
  criticizes Washington, 961

  on Crown vs. colonies, 180
  and Declaration of Independence, 693–695,
    699–704
  on education for women, 1809–1810
  estimation of popular war sentiments by,
    656
  on evacuation of Philadelphia, 987
  and Ezek Hopkins, 1251
  on failure of Canadian campaign, 617–618,
    620
  and First Continental Congress, 418–429,
    431, 433, 435–437, 439, 442, 444, 446
  on framing of constitutions, 544–546
  in France, 843
  and Franklin, 544, 1050–1051, 1731–1734
  on French alliance, 1045, 1046
  on genesis of Revolution, 2, 175
  and Gerry, 1737
  and Great Seal, 1766
  on Hartley, 1744
  on "history" of Revolution, 1796
  and Holland, 1541
  and Howe brothers, 756–758
  and independence, 685–687, 689–695
  on independence for women, 1808–1809
  on Indians, 112, 562
  and Jay, 1731–1733, 1736
  and Jones, 1247–1248, 1286
  and Lafayette, 1734

Adams, John (cont.):
  and Laurens, 1730–1731, 1737
  on legislatures, 849
  on Lexington and Concord, 489
  and Livingston, 1732
  on Maryland, 691
  on meeting of Franklin and Voltaire, 1050
  and Minutemen, 464
  on murder of Christopher Seider, 328
  on New England envy of superiority, 94
  and New York constitution, 856
  and Oswald, 1733–1734
  on Otis, 321
  as peace commissioner, 1363, 1729–1734, 1736, 1737
  on physical fitness of troops, 499
  on powder problem, 581
  on proposal of American navy, 644–645
  on reformation of militia into army, 575–576
  on Reformers' emphasis on education, 155
  on rise of America and British decline, 131, 158
  and Second Continental Congress, 543–548, 553, 555, 558–561, 563, 595, 845
  and Sewall, 666, 1742
  and Stamp Act, 204–205, 212, 247, 250
  and state constitutions, 847–851, 861
  and Strachey, 1733, 1736
  Thoughts on Government, 848–850
  vs. Tories, 448–449, 1742
  and Vergennes, 1637–1638, 1734
  and Virginia constitution, 850–851
  and Warren, 536
  on Washington, 551, 1792
  vs. Washington, 1025
Adams, John Quincy, 258, 536
Adams, Joseph, 486
Adams, Samuel, 201, 217, 234, 258, 287, 507, 893
  and Battle of Lexington, 473, 475, 478
  and Boston Massacre, 344, 346, 348, 358, 359
  and Boston Tea Party, 381, 388
  and British troops, 302–303, 309–310, 320
  and committees of correspondence, 368, 585, 586
  and Common Sense, 683, 684
  and First Continental Congress, 418, 423, 426, 433, 439, 442
  and funeral of Seider boy, 328, 329
  vs. Hancock, 840
  and independence, 686, 687, 691
  on Lee (Arthur), 1142
  and Lee (Charles), 1103
  and Lee (Richard Henry), 1143

  and Liberty case, 284
  and nonimportation, 298–299
  on Quartering Act, 265
  and Second Continental Congress, 543, 547, 548, 553
  and Sugar Act, 179
  vs. Washington, 1019, 1025
Administration of Justice Act, 417
Admiral Duff vs. Protector, 1293–1294
"Adventurers," 374
African Slavery in America (Paine), 1800
Agnew, James, 951, 968
Aigrette, 1675
Aix-la-Chapelle, Treaty of (see Treaty of Aix-la-Chapelle)
Ajax, 1675, 1677, 1681
Alamanace, Battle of, 661
Alarm Companies, 460
Albany Congress, 124–125
Albemarle, Lord, 24
Alden, Ichabod, 1158–1159, 1167
Alexander, William, 712–713
  (See also Stirling, Lord)
Alfred, 1245, 1250, 1252, 1257, 1258, 1677
Allaire, Anthony, 1432
Allen, Andrew, 668, 670
Allen, Ethan, 561, 585, 587–592, 607, 1145, 1612
  and invasion of Canada, 598–602, 604
Allen, Gardner, 1254–1255
Allen, James, 668–671, 674, 987, 1035, 1085
Allen, John, 668, 670
Allen, William, 581, 668, 1037
Allen, William, Jr., 668, 670
Alliance, 1283–1284, 1296
  fires on Bonhomme Richard, 1280
  under Jones's command, 1273–1274, 1276, 1288, 1291
  Landais takes command of, 1290–1292
Allston, Joseph, 96
Alsop, George, 84–85
Alsop, John, 422
Alsop, Joseph, 779
America and Cosmic Man (Lewis), 1819–1820
American, 1291, 1292
American Club (London), 143
Ames, Nathaniel, 130–131
Amherst, Jeffrey, 554, 1213
Amyot, Jacques, 7
Anaka (slave), 88
Anburey, Thomas, 895–897, 899, 903, 905
  at Freeman's Farm, 925–927, 929–930, 1811
  at Saratoga, 935–937
Anderson, Captain, 1311
Anderson, Enoch, 960

Anderson, Mrs. William, 147–148
André, John, 604, 1032–1033, 1039–1040,
    1351, 1556, 1754
    and Arnold, 1561–1564, 1568–1577, 1581,
        1582, 1589
    captured by patriots, 1578–1580
    and Clinton, 1573, 1583, 1589–1592
    examined by board of general officers, 1589
    execution of, 1593
    and Peggy Arnold, 1587
    reaction to execution of, 1594
    and Smith, 1572–1578
    and Washington, 1580–1581, 1589–1593
Andrea Doria, 1245, 1246, 1250, 1255
Andrew (slave), 351, 354
Andrews, John, 654
Angell, Israel, 1531
Annapolis:
    Congress meets in, 1780
    welcomes Washington, 1747
Annapolis Convention, 1816
Anne, queen of England, 139
Annual Register, 1377–1379
Antislavery movement, 81, 103–105, 1799
Antrobus, Captain, 171–172
Apollo vs. *Freedom*, 1264
Aranda (Spanish ambassador to France):
    and Jay, 1734–1735, 1738, 1739
    and Vergennes, 1735
Arbuthnot, Marriot, 1380, 1383–1384, 1391,
    1488, 1628, 1629
    and Arnold, 1628–1629
Archer, Henry, 1350
Areopagitica (Milton), 56
Ariel, 1291, 1292
Aristocracy vs. democracy, 94
Armand, Charles, 973, 990, 1411, 1414
"Armed neutrality," 1542
Arminius, Jacobus, 52
Armstrong, General John, 628–630, 956, 959,
    1349
    at Germantown, 964, 965, 967, 970
    sees committee at camp as step toward
        military dictatorship, 1535
Armstrong, Major John, 1505, 1703, 1769,
    1778–1779
Armstrong, Lieutenant, 1356
Army, Archibald, 770
Army, British:
    attempts of, to corrupt American officers,
        1559
    in Boston, 301–312, 319–330, 455–458,
        464–465, 501–502
    corruption in, 455–456
    desertions from, 306–307, 456–457
    discipline in, 307–308

hostility toward, 306–309, 457–458, 465
inaction of, 648
after retreat from Concord, 501, 506
women and children with, 456
in New York, 313–318, 885, 1084
    evacuation of, after Yorktown, 1760–
        1761
in Philadelphia, 1032–1041
    corruption in, 1036
    destructiveness of, 1034–1035
    social life of, 1032–1033, 1035
strength of (May 1, 1780), 1392
at Yorktown, 1696–1710
    and surrender ceremony, 1706–1708
(*See also* British troops)
Army, Continental:
    annual futility of attempts to organize, 1536
    company-grade officers of, 1794
    composition of, at evacuation of Brooklyn,
        752
    and Congress, 579–580, 839, 846, 1519–
        1524, 1536–1537, 1601, 1604, 1610–
        1611, 1642, 1762–1765, 1768, 1774–
        1779, 1793, 1795
    democracy in, 1001, 1004, 1015
    desertions from, 570, 779–780, 963, 990–
        991, 1037
    discipline problems in, 566–573, 752, 775–
        776
    and encumberment of troops, 712, 785
    field-grade officers of, 1794
    formation of, 564–583
    hardships of men in, 991, 1445–1446,
        1488–1489, 1830–1831
        (*See also* Valley Forge)
    importance of survival of, 745–746, 1341–
        1342, 1537
    lack of provisions for, 581–582, 991, 1444–
        1446, 1488–1489, 1519–1521, 1525,
        1535, 1537, 1600, 1603, 1605
    and lot of discharged soldiers, 1787–1788
    major generals of, 1794–1795
    marches from Boston to New York, 711–
        712
    marches north from Yorktown, 1746–1747
    vs. militias, 777–778
    and mutinous conduct of troops:
        at Basking Ridge, 1516–1518
        at Danbury, 1128–1129
        of New Jersey Line, 1621–1623
        of Pennsylvania Line, 1605–1623
        in Philadelphia, after Yorktown, 1777–
            1778
    and Newburgh Addresses, 1768–1772
        (*See also* Newburgh Addresses)
    officers in, 1133–1134, 1794

Army, Continental (*cont.*):
  parochialism undermines efforts to support,
      1640, 1785
  political vs. military considerations in, 1113
  promises vs. realities of, 1787
  proposals to reduce size of, 1520, 1522
  receives pay in specie, 1668–1669
  recruitment problems of, 1133–1136
  re-enlistment problems of, 574–577, 579–
      580, 775, 777–778, 804, 828–829, 875,
      877
  sectional animosity in, 1134–1135
  sickness in, 754, 785, 803–804
  size of (1780), 1527
  and states' support, 1537
  sustained by Washington, 1792–1793, 1822
  as symbol of nation, 1342, 1537, 1764–1765,
      1822
  winters in Morristown (1777), 875–880
  winters in Morristown (1779–1780), 1513–
      1525
  winters in Valley Forge (*see* Valley Forge)
Army, French:
  arrival of, 1534
  marches through Philadelphia, 1666–1667
  in Savannah, 1332
  at Yorktown, 1696–1697, 1699–1700,
      1702–1703, 1706–1708
Arnold, Benedict, 491, 561, 877, 907, 1039,
      1293
  absolves André of blame, 1592
  and André, 1561–1564, 1568–1577, 1581,
      1582, 1589
  and Arbuthnot, 1628
  in assault on Quebec, 614–617, 620
  bargains with British for rewards, 1561–
      1567
  vs. British in Connecticut, 882–883
  and Burke, 1558
  and Clinton, 1525, 1555, 1559, 1561–1563,
      1566, 1567, 1569, 1572, 1628, 1629
  code used by, 1562
  commands Philadelphia, 884, 1085, 1556–
      1557, 1566
  commands West Point, 1567–1570
  commits treason, 1555–1599
  court-martial of, 1559
  and Deane, 1559
  escapes to *Vulture*, 1583–1584
  at Fort Stanwix, 913–914
  at Freeman's Farm, 923–929
  vs. Gates, 928–929
  and Hamilton, 1583, 1584, 1587
  and Howe, 1557, 1559, 1566
  indifference of, to André's safety, 1573–
      1576

  insists that André carry West Point plans in
      boot, 1575
  and invasion of Canada, 594–596, 598, 605
  and Knuyphausen, 1565
  and Lafayette, 1565, 1598–1599, 1624–
      1626, 1628
  vs. Lafayette, 1624–1626, 1628–1630
  maneuvers for command of West Point,
      1565–1566
  marches to Quebec, 606–613, 619
  vs. Matlack, 1557
  and New Jersey campaign, 807, 808
  notified of André's capture, 1580, 1583
  passed over for promotion, 878
  and Peggy Shippen, 1556–1557
  persuades André to dress as spy, 1574–1575
  and Phillips, 1629, 1630
  plot to kidnap, 1595–1596
  public reaction to treason of, 1597
  vs. Reed, 1368, 1556, 1557
  sails for England with Cornwallis, 1755
  at Saratoga, 933, 935
  and Schuyler, 1565
  speculations of, 1556, 1568
  and Stansbury, 1560–1563, 1566, 1567
  submits padded expense account, 1564
  suspected by McLane, 1355
  threatens to execute 40 Carolinians if André
      is hanged, 1592
  at Ticonderoga, 561, 585–593
  treason of, Lafayette on, 1598–1599
  in Virginia, 1624–1632
  and Washington, 606–607, 878, 1555–1556,
      1558–1559, 1564–1567, 1572, 1583–
      1589, 1591, 1592, 1594–1595, 1624–
      1626, 1795
Arnold, Peggy, 1562, 1564, 1567, 1572, 1581–
      1583, 1585–1586
  and André, 1587
  and Hamilton, 1587–1588
  and Lafayette, 1588
  and Washington, 1586–1588
  (*See also* Shippen, Peggy)
Articles of Confederation, 843, 844, 846, 1066,
      1143–1144, 1642–1643
  inadequacy of, 1815
  provisions of, 1763, 1780
  ratified by Congress, 1539
  ratified by last state, 1642
Asgill, Charles, 1751–1752
Ashe, John, 1312–1316
Asia, 640
Associated Loyalists, 1750, 1752, 1759
Association of the Colonies, 443–444
"At Eutaw Springs the Valiant Died"
      (Freneau), 1691–1692

Atlee, Sam, 737, 740
Atley, Charles, 38
Attucks, Crispus, 339, 340, 347, 353, 354
Auchmuty, Robert, 352
Augusta:
    engagement at, 1423–1424
    occupied by British, 1309
Auguste, 1676, 1679–1681
Austin, Jonathan W., 334, 354
Ayers, Captain, 378–379

Baddeley, Captain, 1352
Baddeley, Mary, 1351–1352, 1662
Bagaduce, 1358–1359
Bailey, James, 353
Baird, James, 1304, 1306
Baker, Sergeant, 1348
Balcarres, Earl of, 935
Baltimore, Lord, 24, 152, 660
Bancroft, Edward, 1139
Bangs, Isaac, 706–707, 713–714
Baptists press for religious toleration, 1808
Barber, Lieutenant, 1569
Barber, William, 486
Bardeleben, Captain, 733, 742
Barfleur, 1676, 1680, 1686
Barker, John, 484, 486
Barnard, Rev., 466–467
Barney, Joshua, 1767
Barnwell, Robert, 1327
Barr, James, 467
Barré, Isaac, 192–193, 224, 241, 294, 619,
    1064, 1156
    opposes Lord North, 1545
Barrell, William, 428
Barren Hill, Lafayette at, 1079–1081
Barrett, James, 483
Barrington, William, 312
    on Americans as fighting men, 463
    on Boston convention, 302, 304
    and Dickinson "letters," 279
    dispatch to, on Battle of Bunker Hill, 533
    and *Liberty* affair, 286, 287
    opposes land speculation, 168
    opposes policy toward colonies, 871
    opposes policy of scattering troops in
        colonies, 264
Barroll, Joseph, 492
Barry, John, 1252, 1258–1259, 1369
Barter, 63–64
Bartlett, Josiah, 578, 1265
Barton, William, 880–890, 1766
Basking Ridge, 1516–1518
Basset, James, 333, 336, 343
Baum, Friedrich, 916–918
Bayard, John, 962

Baylor, George, 1124
Bayonet drills, 1013
Beatty, Captain, 1494
Beaufort, Ga., attack on, 1310
Beaumarchais, Pierre Augustin Caron de, 867,
    878, 1008, 1139, 1140
    on American Revolution, 1047
    and French-American alliance, 1047–1049,
        1051
Beaver, 380, 383
Becom, Samson, 113
Bedford, 1679
Bedford, Duke of, 129, 166, 303
Belknap, Jeremy, 566
Belknap, Joseph, 341–342
Bellinger, Peter, 909
Benezet, Anthony, 1799–1800
Bennington, Battle of, 915–921, 1825
    Indians at, 916–917
Bentham, Jeremy, 371
Bereford, Richard, 1780
Berkeley, Lord, 24
Bernard, Francis, 226, 227, 275
    and British troops, 302–303, 305, 306, 310–
        312, 319–321
    and Circular Letter, 286–287
    as governor, 288–291
    and *Liberty* incident, 284–285
    praises "Farmer's Letters," 279
    and Stamp Act, 200–201, 232
    and Stamp Act Congress, 221
    and Stamp Act riots, 203, 268
    and Townshend Duties, 273–274, 293
Bethlehem, Pa., 1002
Betsy, 1247
Bettin, Captain, 1606
Biddle, Nicholas, 1248, 1253–1254, 1257
Bigham, John, 1602–1603
Bill of Rights (English), 1, 58, 120–121
Bill of Rights Society, 406
Bills of credit, 141
Billy (Washington's slave), 999
Bird, Henry, 1215–1216
Birmingham, 1671
Birmingham Meetinghouse, 955
Birney, Dr., 1812
Bissel, Israel, 491
Black-white marriages, 101–102
Blacks (*see* Negroes; Slave trade; Slavery;
    Slaves)
Blackstocks Plantation, engagement at, 1442–
    1444
Blanca, Count, 1254
Blanchard, Claude, 1433
    on Americans, 1647–1648
    and Chastellux, 1752

Blanchard, Claude (*cont.*):
  on English arrogance at Yorktown
    ceremony, 1707
  on Washington's optimism, 1658
  on Washington's troops in Philadelphia,
    1665
Bland, Richard, 369, 427, 432
Bland, Theoderick, 952–954
Blennerhassett, Lieutenant, 731
Bliss, Theodore, 338
Blowers, Sampson Salter, 354
Blue Jacket, 1152
Blue Licks, battle at, 1229–1230
Board of Associated Loyalists, 1532
Board of Trade and Plantations, 47, 59, 121,
    137–138, 167–168
Board of War and Ordnance, 842–843
  and Conway Cabal, 1021–1023
Boardman, Oliver, 906–907
Bolingbroke, Lord, 165–166
Bolton, Lieutenant Colonel, 1166
Bonhomme Richard, 1273–1286
  crew of, deprived of prize money, 1290
  vs. *Serapis,* 1276–1285
Boone, Daniel, 1213, 1230, 1232
Booth, Benjamin, 394, 395, 434, 446
Booth, Joshua, 1758
Bordentown, N.J., 807
Border war, 1234–1237
  (*See also* Clark, George Rogers; Moravian
    Indians, atrocities against; Sandusky
    expedition)
Bordon, Reverend, 651
Borre, Prudhomme de, 955, 956, 991
Bose, von, 1480, 1527
Boston, 1245, 1255–1256, 1258, 1269
  at siege of Charles Town, 1295
Boston, 67–69, 132
  after Battle of Bunker Hill, 531–532, 538
  British troops in, 301–312, 319–330, 455–
    458, 464–465, 501–502
    (*See also* Boston Massacre)
  British vessels captured at, 1246
  British withdrawal from, 653–655
  eclipse of the sun at, 1533–1534
  French-American brawl in, 1120
  Liberty incident in, 281–286, 300
  and nonimportation, 274–275, 298–299
  as patriot headquarters, 464
  and Quartering Act, 267
  siege of, 506–509, 648–649
  and Stamp Act, 200–205, 208–209, 212,
    225–227, 244–246, 252
  Tories in, 659, 1364–1365
  and Townshend Duties, 281–284, 298–299
Boston Massacre, 317–318, 331–342
  aftermath of, 343–363

Boston Neck:
  bombardment of, 650
  fortification of, 458
Boston Port Bill, 385–400, 407, 408, 410–411
Boston Tea Party, 373–384
  English debate over, 385–389
Bostwick, Elisha, 818
Boswell, James, 865, 1158
Botta, Carlo, 750, 837
Boucher, Jonathan, 87
Boudinot, Elias, 1026, 1082
  and Carleton, 1758
  on Congress' reception of French
    plenipotentiary, 1137–1138
  on Congress without permanent home,
    1779–1780
  on congressional debate on execution of
    Asgill, 1751–1752
  and Great Seal, 1766
  on joy of Congress at news of Cornwallis'
    surrender, 1710
  on Lee (Charles), 1103–1104
  and mutiny of furloughed troops, 1777,
    1778
  on payment of officers, 1777
  and Washington, 1778
  and woman spy, 1811
  at Yorktown, 1703, 1716
Bougainville, Louis Antoine de, 1676–1682,
    1685
  and De Grasse, 1684
Bound Brook (*see* Middle Brook)
Bouquet, Henry, 166
Bowdoin, James, 306, 418, 543
Boyce, David, 466
Boyd, Captain, 1309
Boyd, Colonel, 1310–1311
Boyd, Thomas, 1170
Boylston, Thomas, 1364
Boyne, 639
Braddock, Edward, 126, 549
Bradford, William (editor), 227
Bradford, William (governor), 16–18, 22, 29
Bradstreet, Anne, 72–73
Bradstreet, Simon, 72
Brandywine, Battle of, 948–957, 1013
  Ferguson at, 1426–1427
  French volunteers at, 956
  Hessians at, 951–952, 954
Brant, Joseph, 596, 910–912, 914, 1189, 1228
  raids Cherry Valley, 1158–1160, 1181, 1184
  raids Mohawk Valley, 1158, 1160–1162,
    1180–1181, 1184
  raids Ohio Valley, 1181–1182
  vs. Sullivan, 1165, 1168, 1169
Brant, Molly, 596, 1154
Brantley, John, 1015

Bravery vs. cowardice, 1413
Braxton, Carter, 690, 851
Breed's Hill (see Bunker Hill, Battle of)
Brewer, James, 339
Brewton, Miles, 96
Breyman, Heinrich von, 917, 919, 929, 935
Briar Creek, Battle of, 1312–1316
Brisbane, Captain, 1256
Bristol, 630, 632, 633, 635
British fleet (see Navy, British)
British Legion, 1441–1442
    (See also Loyal Legion)
British prisoners after Yorktown, 1709–1710
British troops:
    desertions among, 306–307, 456–457, 639,
        915, 1099, 1674, 1696, 1702
    encumberment of, 905
    treatment of, after Saratoga, 942–943
Brodhead, Daniel, 1163, 1165, 1176, 1178,
        1179, 1218
    at treaty meeting with Doonyontat, 1179–
        1180
Broglie, Charles-François de, 1004, 1647
Brooklyn, evacuation of, 745–753
    Hessians at, 751
Brooks, Dr., 1282
Brooks, John, 1003
Brooks, Lieutenant Colonel, 913–914
Broome, Robert, 32
Broome, Samuel, 597
Broughton, Nickolson, 643
Brown, John, 586, 587, 599, 601
    attacks Johnson's Indian forces, 1183
Brown, Joseph, 955
Brown, Peter, 530
Brown, Robert, 16
Brown, Tarleton, 1437
Brown, Thomas, 1423, 1424
    and South Carolina campaign, 1495, 1498–
        1502
Browne, William, 323, 1801
Bryan, Colonel, 1411
Bryan, General, 1312, 1316
Bryan, George, 220, 863
Bryan's Station, attack on, 1229
Buford, Abraham, 1395–1396, 1431, 1438
Bull, William, 96
Bülow, Friedrich Wilhelm von, 837
Bumpstead, Stephen, 38
Bunau, von, 1527
Bunbury, Charles, 1374
"Bundling," 69–70
Bunker, Rachel, 74
Bunker Hill, Battle of, 488, 510–539, 743,
        1074, 1433–1434
    aftermath of, 531–534, 538–539
    American desertions at, 514, 527, 528, 568

American lack of organization at, 517–520,
        525, 528–529, 534
    American retreat from, 530–531
    British assessment of American forces at,
        533
    British casualties at, 532–533
    British errors at, 532–533, 536–538
    first attack, 522–524
    preparations for, 510–521
    second attack, 524–525
    third attack, 528–530
Burd, Edward, 738, 740
Burdick, Benjamin, 332, 340
Burgh, James, 144, 255–256, 676
Burgoyne, 1676
Burgoyne, John, 5, 501, 506, 725
    on Admiral Graves, 637–638
    Americans cut supply line of, 932
    at Bennington, 915–917, 919–921
    blames Clinton for defeat, 940
    in Boston, 582
    at Bunker Hill, 517, 526, 530, 539
    and Clinton, 932–933, 937
    early career of, 504–505
    in England following surrender, 943
    failure of Howe to make contact with, 879–
        880
    at Freeman's Farm, 922–926, 929, 930
    Hessians with, 895, 905
    and Indians, 895–897, 899, 901–903, 906,
        908–912, 922, 924, 929
    invades New York from Canada, 725, 780,
        891–908
    in New Jersey campaign, 886
    receives message from Clinton in silver
        bullet, 939
    at Saratoga, 932–933, 936, 938
    as scapegoat, 943–944
    and Schuyler, 942
    surrenders, 127, 938–942, 1051, 1417,
        1716, 1825
    at Ticonderoga, 898–899
    violates terms of surrender, 1641–1642
Burk, John, 195
Burke, Edmund, 271, 294, 371, 619, 865,
        1723, 1829
    on "army extraordinaries," 1375
    attacks Shelburne, 1741
    on British public opinion on America, 867
    challenges North on French-American
        treaty, 1063
    on colonial liberties, 385–386, 453–454
    on defeat of Hessians at Trenton, 827
    introduces reform plan, 1545, 1547, 1548
    joins North in denouncing American treaty,
        1742
    on repeal of Stamp Act, 243

Burke, Edmund (*cont.*):
on resignation of Shelburne, 1743
ridicules Burgoyne's speech to Indians, 897
speaks against colonial representation in
Parliament, 186–187
on "unhappy contest with America," 1373
warns against British policy, 869
Burke, Thomas, 841, 956–957, 1027–1029,
1143
and Arnold, 1558
Burnaby, Andrew:
on Boston in 1759, 68
on "bundling," 69
on lack of education in Maryland, 84
on New York, 75
on Philadelphia, 77–80
on Rhode Island, 71
on Virginia, 89, 91, 93
Burnett, Edmund, 1536
Burr, Aaron, 72, 129, 609, 722, 816
at Valley Forge, 997
Burr, Esther, 72
Burr, Mrs. Thaddeus, 881
Burr, Theodosia, 72
Bushnell, David, 1248–1250
Bute, Earl of, 146, 166, 177, 202, 650
Butler, John, 1189, 1328, 1414, 1476
at Fort Stanwix, 910–912
at Guilford Court House, 1479
vs. Sullivan, 1165–1168, 1171
at Wyoming Valley Massacre, 1156–1157
Butler, Richard, 1345–1347
at Battle of Hot Water, 1635
and Pennsylvania mutineers, 1606, 1608–
1609
at Yorktown, 1696
Butler, Walter, 914
at Cherry Valley Massacre, 1159–1160
vs. Sullivan, 1166, 1168, 1170
vs. Willett, 1187–1189
Butler, William, 1171
Butler, Zebulon, 1156–1157
Byland, Count, 1542
Byles, Mather, 345
Byrd, William, 85, 88
Byrd, William II, 88, 91, 142, 146
Byrd, William III, 90
Byron, John, 1121–1122, 1331

Cabot, 1245, 1250, 1255
Cadwalader, John, 794, 795, 1030
and Battle of Princeton, 830
at Trenton, 813, 815–817, 822–824
Caesar, 1107
Cahokia, 1192, 1193, 1197–1198
Cahoon, Samuel, 1572–1574
Caldwell, Chaplain, 1531

Caldwell, William, 1228
Callender, Amos, 588
Callender, John, 568
Calvert, Cecilius (*see* Baltimore, Lord)
Calvert, Leonard, 24
Calvin, John, 48, 52, 153–157
Calvinists (*see* Presbyterians; Puritans)
Cambray-Digny, Chevalier de, 1321, 1381,
1382
Cambridge, army at, 496–501
lack of authority in, 500
provisioning of, 499–501
and Stockbridge Indians, 498–499
Washington assumes command of, 564–
582
Camden:
Battle of, 1407–1418, 1469, 1536
Rawdon evacuates, 1498
Camden, Lord, 242, 254–256, 1371
Camden vs. *Earl of Warwick,* 1263
Campbell, Archibald, 1303–1309, 1312, 1315
Campbell, Arthur, 662
Campbell, Lieutenant Colonel, 1493, 1494
Campbell, Major, 1701
Campbell, Robert, 1429, 1690
Campbell, Samuel, 1158
Campbell, William (British), 624, 633
Campbell, William (Virginian):
at Guilford Court House, 1478, 1480–1482
at Kings Mountain, 1425, 1428–1431, 1433
at Ninety-Six, 1505
vs. Webster, 1475, 1476
Canada:
importance of British retention of, 129–130
invasion of, 594–620
as possible ally of colonies, 584–585, 618–
619
Washington considers invasion of, 1130
Canadians at Saratoga, 924
Canajoharie, 1185, 1186
Canceaux, 645
Cannon, James, 857, 863
Cape Henry, 1672
Capes, Battle of, 1672–1692
British errors in, 1682, 1687–1688
and Cornwallis, 1685
Carleton, Guy, 585, 877, 941, 1165, 1173
aids Tories who wish to go to Nova Scotia,
1756
on Arnold, 586
and Boudinot, 1758
and Burgoyne's invasion, 891–893
discusses evacuation of New York with
Washington and Gov. Clinton, 1757–
1758
and evacuation of New York, 1758–1761
and Huddy affair, 1751

and invasion of Canada, 595, 596, 598–599, 604, 605, 614, 616, 617
and Negroes who wish to leave with British, 1758–1760
and patriots in New York, 1757
replaces Clinton in New York, 1754
and Tallmadge, 1759
and Tory refugees, 1759
Carlisle, Earl of, 1065, 1071, 1072
Carlisle peace commission, 1065–1076, 1102, 1519, 1826
influenced by Tories, 1074
report of, to North, 1073–1074
Carmichael, Dr., 1139
Carolinas:
founding of, 24–25
individuals and communities surrender to British in, 1398–1399
(See also North Carolina; South Carolina)
Carr, Maurice, 332, 342, 343
Carr, Patrick, 339, 340, 345, 354
Carrington, Edward, 1445, 1447, 1465, 1466, 1468, 1469
at Hobkirk's Hill, 1492
Carrington, Henry, 989, 1415
Carroll, Charles, 717
Carroll, John, 337
Carroll of Carrollton, Charles, 1000, 1147
Carter, Anne Hill, 1508
Carter, Landon, 683, 690
Carteret, Lord, 24
Cary, Archibald, 851
Cary, Jonathan, 339
Castle William, 343–345, 358, 455
Caswell, Richard, 624–625, 1081
at Camden, 1407, 1412, 1415
Catherine, queen of Russia, 1292, 1542
Catholic-Protestant riots in London (see Lord George Gordon Riots)
Catholic Relief Bill, 1549, 1551
Catlett, Thomas, 1357
Caton, 1676, 1678, 1681
Cavalry warfare, 1473, 1475, 1476, 1507
Greene on, 1485
Cavendish, Lord, 1371
Cazneau, Andrew, 335
Centaur, 1679
Cenway, Henry, 864
Cerf, 1273, 1275
Chambers, Stephen, 1366
Champe, John, 1595–1596
Chance, role of, 1474–1475, 1687–1688, 1714
Chandler, J. B., 448
Chandler, John, 881
Charles I, king of England, 1, 29, 51–55, 257
Charles II, king of England, 23, 26, 29, 55, 57
Charles X, king of France, 975

Charles Town, S.C., 95–97, 209–211, 246
attack on, 624–636, 1295
British occupy, 1487–1488
evacuated by British, 1749
French-American brawl in, 1121
Hessians at, 1380–1381, 1385, 1387, 1389
Prevost's threat to, 1318–1322
Rutledge proposes neutrality for, 1323–1325
siege of, 1380–1392, 1469
strengthens defenses, 1321
surrender of, 1388–1389
Charlotte:
engagement at, 1420–1423
wretched condition of troops in, 1445
Charlottesville, Cornwallis and Tarleton at, 1631–1632, 1635
Charming Nancy, 1559
Chase, Samuel, 438, 702, 717, 1068
Chase, Thomas, 302
Chastellux, Chevalier de, 973, 1236–1237, 1664
against amusements that separate men from women, 1814
and Madison, 1752–1753, 1814
at Mount Vernon, 1669–1670
on Quaker and Episcopal services, 1667
Travels in North America in the Years 1780, 1781, and 1782, 1752
Chatham, Lord, 240, 944, 1064–1065
death of, 1065
on use of Indians against patriots, 1155
(See also Pitt, William [the Elder])
Cheeshateaumuck, Caleb, 112
Cherokee Expedition, 1437
Cherokees, 1213–1214
Cherry Valley, Indian attacks on, 1158–1160, 1166, 1173, 1181, 1184
Chester, John, 527–528, 530–531, 534
Chesterfield, Lord, 1370, 1544
Chestnut Hill, engagement at, 992–993
Chevaux-de-frise, 979–980
Chew, Benjamin, 436, 965
Chew, Peggy, 1562
Chew mansion, 965–968, 970
Chinese Revolution, 1, 1826, 1827
Choiseul, Duc de, 129, 974
Choisy, Marquis de, 1697, 1704
Christian, William, 1214
Christina (Mohegan), 1220
Church, Benjamin, 302, 347, 474, 555
Cilley, Joseph, 924, 1096–1097
Circular Letter, 273–274, 286–287, 294
Citoyen, 1676, 1680
Civil War, 1828
Clarendon, Lord, 24, 54, 278
Clark, Captain, 1178

Clark, Colonel, 629
Clark, George Rogers, 5, 1181, 1190–1211, 1215–1218, 1231–1235
 as archetype of Western hero, 1233
 attacks Chillicothe villages, 1231–1232
 on battle at Blue Licks, 1231
 vs. Bird, 1215–1216
 captures Cahokia, 1197–1198
 captures Kaskaskia, 1196–1197
 captures Vincennes, 1198, 1205–1211
 commissioned to lead attack on Detroit, 1216–1217
 condition of forces of, 1218
 defeats Shawnees and allied tribes, 1216, 1228
 desertions from forces of, 1217–1218
 early life of, 1190–1191
 life of, after peace, 1233–1234
 loses Vincennes, 1199
 marches to Vincennes, 1201–1205, 1210–1211
 organizes militia for defense of Kentucky country, 1192
 recruits men for expedition, 1194–1195
 secures Indians' allegiance, 1198–1199
 secures Virginia sponsorship for Old Northwest expedition, 1192–1194
Clark, Major, 1355–1356, 1358
Clark, William, 1234
Clarke, Elijah, 1404, 1423, 1424, 1442
 in South Carolina campaign, 1499
Clarke, John, 531
Clarke, Jonas, 475, 478
Clarke, Richard, 377–378
Clayford, James, 720–723
Clerke, Francis, 933
Cleveland, Benjamin, 1425, 1429, 1430
Clinton, George, 504, 716, 939, 1646
 attacked by Cornwallis, 879
 celebrates victory in New York City, 1788–1789
 discusses evacuation of New York with Washington and Carleton, 1757–1758
 as governor of New York, 930–931, 1180
 joins attacks against Indians, 1183–1184
 takes command at Fort Montgomery, 931
Clinton, Henry, 501, 504, 505, 582–583, 800, 803, 1543
 and André, 1573, 1583, 1589–1592
 anxieties of, 1662
 and Arnold, 1525, 1555, 1559, 1561–1563, 1566, 1567, 1569, 1572, 1575, 1595, 1628–1630
 assumes command in Philadelphia, 1038, 1039
 at attack on Charles Town, 624–631, 635–636
 and Battle of Bunker Hill, 510, 515, 526, 531, 537
 at Battle of Long Island, 730–731, 734, 738, 739, 741
 at Battle of Monmouth, 1087, 1090–1092, 1095, 1098–1101
 and Battle of Rhode Island, 1111, 1119
 and Battle of Saratoga, 933, 937, 939
 blamed by Cornwallis for defeat at Yorktown, 1709
 blamed by Tories for defeat at Yorktown, 1753
 and captured mail pouch, 1648–1649
 in command of New York, 1351–1353
 and Cornwallis, 1653–1654, 1673
 on Cornwallis' disaster at Yorktown, 1672–1673
 on Cornwallis' move to Virginia, 1488
 deceived by Washington in New York, 1658–1659
 on defeat at Kings Mountain, 1433
 on desertion of Washington's troops, 1530
 directs Cornwallis to detach troops for reinforcement of New York, 1649
 dispatches troops to Cornwallis, 1435
 encourages attack on Springfield, 1529–1530, 1532
 and evacuation of Philadelphia, 1084–1085
 fails to reinforce Cornwallis, 1661–1663, 1704
 on failure of British fleet, 1687
 inaction of, 1662–1663
 in Georgia, 1303
 and Germain, 1562
 vs. Graves, 1675
 holds New York, Staten Island, and Newport, 1107
 vs. Howe, 946–947
 with Knuyphausen in New Jersey, 1529–1533
 and lack of knowledge of proper strategy, 1487
 at Lechmere Point, 649
 and Lee, 1082, 1083
 makes feint at West Point, 1530
 and mutiny of Pennsylvania Line, 1611, 1616–1617, 1619
 on need of reinforcements, 1646–1647
 occupies New York City, 1107–1109, 1398, 1645
 promises pardon to patriots who surrender, 1398–1399
 reoccupies ruins of Stony Point, 1350–1351
 seizes Forts Montgomery and Clinton, 930–932, 939
 sends message to Burgoyne in silver bullet, 939

at siege of Charles Town, 1380, 1382–1388, 1390–1392
at Stony Point, 1342
stripped of forces at New York, 1124
and surrender of Charles Town, 1390, 1530
suspends civil courts in New York, 1352–1353
and Tory refugees after Yorktown, 1750–1751
urged to bribe American officers, 1560
vs. Washington, 1529, 1530, 1532, 1590–1591, 1656, 1658, 1659
Clinton, James, 716, 771, 930
in expedition against Indians and Tories, 1163–1168, 1176
Closen, Ludwig von, 1667
Clymer, Daniel, 1366
Cobb, David, 1133–1134, 1701–1702
Cochran, John, 1597
Cock Hill Fort, 793, 794
Cockle, James, 179
Coddington, William, 21
Coercive Acts, 407, 451, 865
(See also Intolerable Acts)
Coffin, John, 1689
Coffin, William, 408
Coke, Edward, 254
Colden, Cadwallader, 207, 212, 313, 315
College of New Jersey, 84, 144, 1799
Indians at, 1153
Negroes at, 1799
College of William and Mary, 112–113
Collier, George, 758, 1256–1257, 1349
occupies Fort Nelson, Va., 1624
Collins, James:
at Cowpens, 1455, 1456, 1459, 1460
at Kings Mountain, 1429–1432
Colonies, British view of, 185–188
Columbus, 1245, 1250, 1257–1258
Combs, Thomas, 143
Committee at camp, 1521–1522, 1525, 1534–1535
Committee of cooperation (see Committee at camp)
Committee at headquarters (see Committee at camp)
Committee of Secret Correspondence, 843
Committees of correspondence, 368–369, 409, 471
in England, 1376, 1377
and Massachusetts Government Act, 405
and tea monopoly, 375–376
Committees of Public Safety, 463, 500–501, 510
and Tories, 663
Common Sense (Paine), 677–686, 804–805, 857, 1044

on America as part of British Empire, 680–681
attacks kingship, 679–680
attributed to John Adams, Sam Adams, and others, 683–684
on society vs. government, 678
Conciliatory bills, 1062–1065, 1067–1069, 1072–1073
Chatham on, 1064–1065
Dalrymple on, 1067
Germain on, 1067
Laurens on, 1068
Morris on, 1068, 1069
Washington on, 1069
Concord, Battle of, 482–484
British retreat from, 484–489
(See also Lexington and Concord, Battle of)
Confederacy, 1295
Congress, 1245
Connecticut:
constitution of, 854
founding of, 23
Hessians in, 881–882
prohibits importation of Indian or black slaves, 1800
Stamp Act riots in, 206–207, 209, 231–232
war preparations in, 460
Conolly, John, 622
Consciousness, transformation of, 1827–1828
Constitution, U.S., 2, 1816
and state constitutions, 861–863, 1816
and Virginia constitution, 853
Constitutional Convention, 1816
Constitutions, colonial, 544–546
Constitutions, state, 847–863
and Adams, 847–851, 861
Connecticut, 854
Georgia, 855, 856
Maryland, 855
New Hampshire, 856–857, 859
New Jersey, 854
New York, 855–857
North Carolina, 854
Pennsylvania, 857–863, 1050
Rhode Island, 854
South Carolina, 854–855
and U.S. Constitution, 861
Virginia, 850–854, 862
Continental Army (see Army, Continental)
Continental Congress, First, 4, 417–418, 430–444
achievements of, 445–446
and Association of Colonies, 443–444
Declaration and Resolves of, 442–443
delegates to, 446
English reactions to, 450–454
and Galloway Plan of Union, 439–441, 445

Continental Congress, First (*cont.*):
  invites Canada to join American cause, 585
  and manner of voting, 431–432
  and nonimportation, 434–440, 443, 445
  and Parliament's right to regulate trade,
    441–442
  social life of delegates, 436–437
  and Suffolk Resolves, 434–435
Continental Congress, Second, 543–563, 839–
    846
  accomplishments of, 842–844
  in Annapolis, 1780
  appeals to states to fill requisitions, 1640–
    1641
  appoints commander in chief, 546–548
  appoints commissioners of Indian affairs,
    1151
  appoints committee at camp, 1521
  appoints committee to deal with
    Pennsylvania mutineers, 1614
  appoints Continental Army officers, 553–
    556
  and army, 579–580, 839, 846, 1519–1524,
    1536–1537, 1601, 1604, 1610–1611,
    1642, 1762–1765, 1768, 1774–1778
  and Arnold, 1557–1559, 1564, 1567
  and Articles of Confederation, 843, 1143–
    1144, 1763, 1780, 1781
  augments Washington's powers, 811, 825
  authorizes official flag of United States,
    1268
  authorizes privateering, 1262, 1296
  and Board of War and Ordnance, 842–843,
    1021–1023
  and Burgoyne, 1641–1642
  and Carlisle commission, 1068–1072, 1519
  commissions George Rogers Clark to lead
    attack on Detroit, 1216–1217
  and committee to negotiate with Howe
    brothers, 756–758
  and Committee of Secret Correspondence,
    843
  and conflicts with Washington, 1026–1029,
    1057, 1146, 1407, 1520–1523, 1534,
    1746
  and constitution, 844
  and Continental Army, 579–580, 839, 846,
    1519–1524, 1536–1537, 1601, 1604,
    1610–1611, 1640, 1642, 1762–1765,
    1768, 1774–1779, 1793, 1795
  and Conway Cabal, 1020–1026, 1029–
    1030
  critics of Washington in, 961, 1019–1020,
    1025
  debates execution of Asgill, 1751
  debates pensions for officers, 1026–1029,
    1146
  debates proposal that Congress be
    empowered to coerce states, 1643
  debates treatment of captured Tories, 1027,
    1029
  and Declaration of Independence, 693–707
  denies Washington knowledge of French
    treaty, 1057
  difficulties of, 839–841, 846, 1519–1524
  dilatory members of, 841–842
  and diplomacy, 843
  discharges committee at camp, 1534
  discusses terms of preliminary treaty with
    England, 1767–1768
  disputes fisheries issue, 1361–1362
  establishes department of foreign affairs,
    1538
  establishes navy, 1239–1240, 1248
  establishes permanent boards of war,
    treasury, and marine, 1538
  establishes procedure for admission of new
    states, 843
  and European soldiers of fortune, 1138
  and exchange of prisoners, 1026–1027,
    1146
  expects British acknowledgment of
    American independence, 1519
  factions within, 840, 843, 1729
  and financial affairs, 1132, 1145, 1147–
    1149, 1363–1364, 1519, 1523–1524,
    1640, 1644–1645, 1762–1766, 1772–
    1775
  flees to Baltimore, 806, 811
  flees to Princeton, 1778
  and formation of navy, 644–645, 647, 834,
    843
  and framing of constitutions, 544–546
  and French alliance, 1044–1046, 1048–
    1049, 1054–1055, 1143
  furloughs troops, 1774–1775
  vs. Greene, 1534
  as guarantor of peace terms, 1728
  handling of, by Washington, 760–761
  and Indians, 1151–1154
  and invasion of Canada, 594–596, 618–620
  lack of effective effort by, 1535–1537
  and land speculation, 845–846
  lays foundation for Supreme Court, 843
  learns of Cornwallis' surrender, 1710
  leaves Philadelphia, 963
  and Lee-Deane controversy, 1138–1143,
    1146
  letters of marque issued by, 1262–1263
  logrolling in, 842
  and Luzerne, 1637–1638
  and manner of voting, 844–845
  and Marine Committee, 834, 1248
  moves toward independence, 685–693

and mutiny of furloughed troops, 1777–
1779
and Newburgh Addresses, 1768
and North's conciliatory bills, 1072
orders Adams to accept Vergennes's terms,
1637–1638
parochialism in, 1640, 1763–1764, 1772–
1773, 1776–1777
passes resolution ceding Western land
claims, 1539–1540
and peace negotiations, 1728–1730, 1732–
1735, 1738
and peace treaty, 1780–1781
and pressure from France for more military
campaigns, 1520–1521
ratifies Articles of Confederation, 1539
receives French plenipotentiary, 1137–1138
and representation of slaves, 844
returns to Philadelphia, 1137
scheme for seizing members of, 1031–1032
sends Laurens to France to secure money,
1644
and Ticonderoga, 591–592
and Tories, 660
and Vermont-New York dispute, 1144–
1145
and Virginia, 622
Washington visits, 1131–1132, 1663–1664,
1791–1792
vs. William Thompson, 1146–1147
Continental Navy (see Navy, Continental)
Conway, Thomas, 961, 964, 966, 1015, 1079,
1795
at Brandywine, 1020
on contempt of Southerners for New
Englanders, 1134
as inspector general, 1022–1024
submits resignation, 1022, 1029–1030
on Washington, 1020–1021
Conway, H. Seymour, 226, 232
resigns from cabinet, 272
and Stamp Act, 193, 240, 241, 264
Conway, Henry, 1547–1548
Conway Cabal, 994, 1019–1030, 1146
Cooper, Anthony Ashley (see Shaftesbury, Earl
of)
Cooper, Samuel, 288–289, 302, 348, 357
Cooper, William, 719–720
Copley, John Singleton, 150–151, 346, 380,
1740–1741
Corey, Judith, 74
Cornbury, Lord, 198
Cornell, Ezekiel, 1535–1536
Cornplanter, 1182
Cornstalk, 1152
Cornwallis, Charles, 294, 731, 871, 963, 1445
abandons starving Negroes, 1696–1697
attacks George Clinton, 879
attempts to escape from Yorktown, 1704
attempts to recruit Tories in North
Carolina, 1470, 1472
avoids attendance at surrender ceremony,
1708
bargains over surrender terms, 1705
and Battle of Capes, 1685
and Battle of Cowpens, 1449–1452, 1455,
1458, 1460–1461
in Battle of Long Island, 730, 733–734, 741
and Battle of Princeton, 830–832, 834–835,
837
and battle at Ramsour's Mill, 1404
and Battle of Trenton, 822
blames Clinton for defeat at Yorktown, 1709
at Brandywine, 951–953
at Camden, 1410–1413, 1416, 1417
captures Yorktown, 1655
at Charlotte, 1421–1423
at Chestnut Hill, 992
and Clinton, 1653–1654, 1673
and Clinton's attack on Charles Town, 624,
625
as Clinton's second in command, 1068
in command at Charles Town, 1398, 1399
constructs defenses at Yorktown, 1663, 1673
denies Parliament's right to tax colonies, 294
enters Philadelphia, 963
at Fort Lee, 797
at Fort Mercer, 988–990
at Fort Washington, 795
and Graves, 1686
at Green Spring Farm, 1650–1653
vs. Greene, 1447–1448, 1465–1470, 1472,
1475, 1476, 1478–1485
at Guilford Court House, 1478–1485
and Kings Mountain, 1425, 1427, 1429
vs. Lafayette, 1630–1636, 1650–1652,
1649–1655
launches aggressive campaign in South,
1435, 1436
vs. Marion, 1438–1440
vs. Morgan, 1449, 1451, 1464, 1465
in New Jersey campaign, 803–804, 806–
807, 828, 830–832, 834–835, 837,
885–887, 1124
in North Carolina, 1398, 1399
options of, 1671
orders all supplies and baggage destroyed
after Cowpens, 1464–1465, 1468
recalls Tarleton, 1474
sends troops requested by Clinton to New
York, 1649, 1653
size of army of, 1469
vs. Sumter, 1419–1420, 1441
surrenders at Yorktown, 1297

Cornwallis, Charles (*cont.*):
  takes possession of estates of patriots, 1420
  and Tarleton, 1441, 1449–1451, 1457,
    1458, 1460–1461
  in Virginia, 1488
  and Wayne, 1650–1651, 1655
  at Wilmington, N.C., 1486–1487
  at Yorktown, 1672–1674, 1701–1708
Cornwallis, William, 1542
Cottineau, Captain, 1283
Cotton, Josiah, 117
Coudray, Tronson de, 959, 975–976
Coulon, Joseph, 124
Coulon de Villiers, Louis, 124
Counter Reformation, 51
Countess of Scarborough, 1276, 1280, 1283–
  1284, 1288, 1541
Courts, effect on, of Stamp Act, 229–230
"Cowboys," 1126, 1578
Cowpens, 1427
  Battle of, 1452–1463, 1825
Cox, Ebenezer, 909, 910
Craddock, Mathew, 33
Crafts, Thomas, 306
Crashaw, William, 15–16
Craven, Lord, 24
Crawford, Tom, 1396–1397
Crawford, William, 167, 1221–1226
Cresap, Michael, 572
Cresswell, Nicholas, 85
Crèvecoeur, Hector St. John, 1156, 1157
Crèvecoeur, Michel Guillaume Jean de, 158–
  161, 1049
Criminals as immigrants, 37–44
Cromwell, Oliver, 1, 26, 29, 54–55
Cromwell, Richard, 55
Crown Point, 584–585, 589, 591, 595
  and Burgoyne's invasion, 895, 897, 898
Crozier, John, 489–490
Cruger, John Harris, 1332, 1424, 1425, 1427
  at Ninety-Six, 1495, 1498, 1499, 1503, 1504,
    1506
Cuffe, Paul, 1802
Cumberland, Duke of, 1375–1376
Cunningham, General, 1450
Cunningham, John, 1453
Cunningham, William, 1036, 1788
Currency, 140–141, 1148
  (*See also* Money, paper)
Curwen, Samuel, 667
Cushing, John, 348
Cushing, Thomas, 302, 324, 369–370
  and First Continental Congress, 418, 423,
    426, 439, 442
  and Second Continental Congress, 543, 548
Cushing, William, 693

Custis, Daniel Parke, 549
Custis, Eleanor Parke, 1746
Custis, George Washington Parke, 1746
Custis, Jacky, 1669, 1670, 1746
Custis, John, 1135
Custis, Martha, 549–550
  (*See also* Washington, Martha)

Dale, Richard, 1276, 1279, 1282
Dalrymple, John, 1067
Dalrymple, William, 305, 306, 308, 322, 325
  and Boston Massacre, 342, 344, 345
  and Lexington and Concord, 494
Dana, Francis, 1070
Dana, Richard, 306, 308, 327, 343
Danbury, Conn.:
  British-Hessian destruction at, 881–883
  mutinous conduct of troops at, 1128–1129
  Putnam in command at, 1124
D'Arendt, Baron, 1023
Darragh, Lydia, 1811
Dartmouth, 379–380, 383
Dartmouth, Earl of, 397, 459, 463
  and Gage, 408–410, 418, 450, 473
  and Southern campaign, 624
Dartmouth College, 113, 144
D'Artoise, Comte, 975
Dashwood, Francis, 145–146, 177
Davidson, George, 1420, 1421
Davidson, William, 1449, 1465
Davie, William, 1397, 1405–1406
  at Charlotte, 1420–1423, 1433
Davis, Benjamin, 336
Dawes, William, 475–476, 478
Day, Thomas, 1376
Dayton, Elias, 955, 1528, 1621
Dayton, Isaac, 1531
Deane, 1269, 1296
Deane, Silas, 420, 554, 843, 1008, 1019
  and Arnold, 1559
  and Continental Navy, 1248, 1254
  and French alliance, 1049, 1051–1053
  and French volunteers, 974–975
  and Lee, 1138–1143, 1146
  and soldiers of fortune, 1138–1139
Dearborn, Henry, 518, 617, 1171
  at Freeman's Farm, 923–924, 928
De Barras, Comte, 1640, 1656, 1660–1661,
  1664
  at Chesapeake, 1675, 1677, 1684–1686
De Berdt, Dennis, 273
Debtors' laws, 859–860
Declaration of Independence, 693–707, 1066
  British view of, 725, 868
  and "happiness," 697–699
  and slavery, 704–705

Declaration of Rights, 58
"Declaration on Taking Up Arms"
    (Dickinson), 571
Declaratory Act, 242–243, 247–248, 266, 311,
    1822
De Fermoy, General, 830, 898
De Grasse, Admiral, 1331, 1658, 1666, 1673,
    1675, 1702, 1703
  announces departure for Indies, 1694
  arrives with fleet off Chesapeake, 1668
  and Bougainville, 1684
  vs. British fleet, 1664, 1670, 1683
    at Chesapeake, 1661, 1676, 1680, 1683–
      1688
  vs. Graves, 1670, 1687–1688, 1715
  and Lafayette, 1709
  puts ashore French troops in Virginia, 1672
  sails to reinforce fleet at Newport, 1656
  in West Indies, 1640, 1657
De Hart, Colonel, 829
De Kalb, Johann (see Kalb, Johann)
De Lancey, Oliver, 728, 1032–1033, 1040,
    1352, 1761
De Lancey's Volunteers, 1760
Delany, Sharp, 1346, 1366
De la Place, William, 584, 589
De Lauzun, Duc, 1657
Delaware, 1245, 1255
Delaware Indians:
  atrocities committed against, 1219–1221
  atrocities committed by, 1226
  with Kirkwood at Ninety-Six, 1505
De Leyba, Fernando, 1215
Demont, William, 792, 793
Denny, Ebenezer:
  on Americans in Southern winter quarters
    after Yorktown, 1750
  on British after surrender, 1708–1709
  at Green Spring Farm, 1651
  on Southern countryside after Yorktown,
    1748
  at Yorktown, 1694–1695, 1697, 1704
Department of Foreign Affairs, 1538
De Peyster, Abraham, 1232, 1430
De Pontiere, 1009
Derby, Earl of, 504–505
Desertion:
  British, 306–307, 456–457, 639, 915, 1099,
    1674, 1696, 1702
  at Bunker Hill, 514, 527, 528, 568
  from Continental Army, 570, 779–780, 963,
    990–991, 1037
  from French army, 1666
  at Guilford Court House, 1484
  among Hessians, 1673, 1674, 1702
  at Hobkirk's Hill, 1484

from Lafayette, 1626
  at Valley Forge, 1001
  at Yorktown, 1696, 1702
D'Estaing, Comte, 1071, 1084, 1107–1108,
    1116, 1117, 1176
  at Battle of Rhode Island, 1109–1111,
    1113–1114
  in Boston, 1120–1122
  at Savannah, 1332, 1334–1337, 1378, 1389
  in West Indies, 1331
Destouches, Chevalier, 1626, 1628, 1629
Detroit, 1192–1194, 1198, 1199, 1216–1217
  schemes for attack on, 1192, 1210, 1216–
    1217
Deux-Ponts, Comte de, 1661, 1666
Diademe, 1676, 1679, 1681
Diaries, 608–609
Dickinson, John, 258, 294, 471, 660
  and Articles of Confederation, 844
  and Boston Port Bill, 396–398
  and Canadian campaign, 617–618
  and Declaration of Independence, 700–702,
    706
  "Declaration on Taking Up Arms," 571
  "Farmer's Letters," 276–280
  on financial problems, 1147
  and First Continental Congress, 425, 436,
    442
  and invasion of Canada, 595
  in London, 146–150
  and mutiny of furloughed troops, 1777–
    1778
  and Pennsylvania constitution, 861, 863
  and rift with Franklin, 560
  and Second Continental Congress, 544,
    561–562
  at Springfield, 1531
  and Stamp Act, 220, 233–234
  Tory sympathizers in family of, 665
Dickinson, Philemon, 1090, 1091
Dictatorship under Washington suggested,
    1534
Diemar, von, 1527
Digby, Robert, 1702
Digby, William, 940–941
Diggers, 55–57
Diligent, 642
Diligente, 1542
Dillon, Count, 1334
Dillon, Robert, 97
Dinwiddie, Robert, 123–124, 549
Diplomacy, 843
  (See also France, alliance with)
Divided loyalties, 668–674
Do-Good Papers (Franklin), 105
Doak, Samuel, 1425

Dobbs Ferry, N.Y., 783
Doehla, Johann Conrad, 1673–1674, 1710
  on Yorktown, 1700, 1702, 1704–1705, 1708
Dolly, Quamino, 1306
Dolphin, 1264
Don, Lieutenant, 925
Donop, Carl Emil Kurt von, 733, 735, 765, 787
  attacks Fort Mercer, 980–983, 987
  in campaign against Morristown, 1527
  at Princeton, 830–832
  at Trenton, 814, 815, 823
Dooley, John, 1310
Doolittle, Ephraim, 460
Doonyontat, 1179
Dorchester Heights, fortification of, 649–651
Douglas, Captain, 588
Downer, Silas, 230
Drake, Colonel, 1578
Drake vs. *Ranger,* 1270–1272
Drayton, William, 626, 628, 1142
  and attack on Charles Town, 632–635
Drinker, Henry, 434
Drinker, John, 1713
Duane, James, 422, 430, 432–433, 400, 687
  advises confiscation of Indians' lands, 1151–1152
  Hamilton appeals to, to substitute Greene for Gates, 1418
  and Lee, 1597
  on necessity of transferral of power from states to Congress, 1538–1539
Du Bois, Lewis, 1183
Duc de Duras, 1273, 1274
Dudingston, William, 364–367
Dudley, Thomas, 72
Duer, William, 1153
Dulany, Daniel, 215–217, 259
Dumas, Charles William, 1661–1662, 1668
Duncan, James, 1698
Dundas, Thomas, 1354, 1650
Dunkers, 45
Dunlap, John, 706
Dunmore, Lord, 168, 621–624, 1251
  and evacuation of Brooklyn, 751
  offers to free slaves, 621–622, 1798
Dunmore's War, 1191
Dunning, William, 1546, 1547
Du Ponceau, Pierre Etienne, 1000, 1009, 1010, 1014
Duportail, 998, 1004–1005, 1084, 1661
Duquesne, Marquis, 123
Du Roi, 895, 941, 943, 1803
Dutch settlements, 23, 29
Dwight, Timothy, 1159
Dyer, Eliphalet, 220, 229, 438, 553, 561, 1641

Eagle, 725, 727–729, 733
East Florida, 1392
East India Company, 373–375, 1822
Easton, James, 586
Eaton, General, 1476, 1479
Eaton, Pinketham, 1500
Eclipse of the sun, Tories' interpretation of, 1533–1534
Eden, Robert, 660–661
Eden, William, 1065, 1067, 1560
Edes, Benjamin, 201, 213
Education:
  American, as seen by Frenchman, 1648
  of Americans in England, 144
  of Indians, 112–113, 116, 144
  in Maryland, 84
  of Negroes, 1799
  in New England, 62, 67
  in Pennsylvania, 144
  and religion, 155
  in South Carolina, 96
  for women, urged by Abigail Adams, 1809
Edward, 1252
Edwards, John, 1323
Edwards, Jonathan, 72
Effingham, 1245, 1252, 1258
Effingham, Lord, 4, 868
Eggleston, Joseph, 1506
Elbert, Samuel, 1305, 1313, 1314
Eleanor, 380, 383
Elfe, Thomas, 96
Eliot, Andrew, 349
Eliot, John, 49, 52, 112
Elizabeth I, queen of England, 48
Elizabethtown, N.J., Hessians winter in, 1807
Ellery, William, 1028, 1248
  on French alliance, 1054–1055
  on paper money, 1147–1148
Elliot, Gilbert, 870
Ellsworth, Oliver, 1523
Emerson, William, 482, 567–568
Empress of Russia, 489
England:
  accession of William and Mary in, 58
  American visitors to, 142–151
  attempts to thwart French-American alliance, 1060–1061
  and Carlisle peace commission, 1065–1076
  champions of colonies in, 175–176, 192–193, 224, 239–243, 294, 385–387, 402–403, 406–407, 452–454, 494, 864–872
  impeded by French alliance, 1378
  Civil War in, 53–55, 215, 257, 1818, 1826, 1827
  vs. colonies, after repeal of Stamp Act, 263–272, 293–299

as commonwealth, 55
and Continental Congress, 450–454
crime in, 31, 37–38
dissatisfaction with government in, 1377–1378
Glorious Revolution in, 1, 58–59, 680, 1818, 1826
influence of Reformation in, 48–49
mercantilist policies of, 133–141
as "mother country," 142–151
offers of conciliation by, 1060–1065
political decadence in, 149–150
political and social ferment in, 55–56
poverty in, 30–32, 145
public frustration in, 1375
public opinion in, 867–869
resistance to Catholicism in, 57–58
Restoration period in, 57
as seen by Americans, 142–151, 184–185
sentiment in, to continue war after Yorktown, 1755
social decadence in, 145–146
social inequities in, 148–149
Stuart kings vs. Parliament in, 48–55
(See also Parliament)
Enlisted man's life, 778, 1127–1130
Enos, Colonel, 611
Enos, Richard, 38
Episcopal service, described by Chastellux, 1667
Equality, American, as seen by Frenchman, 1648
Erskine, William, 831, 883, 1058–1059
Essay on Liberty (Price), 865
Europe, 1679
Eustis, William, 536
Eutaw Springs, Battle of, 1688–1692, 1825
Evelyn, A. Glanville, 490, 1821
Ewing, James, 815, 823, 824
Experiment, 630, 632, 633, 1258–1259

Fairfax, George, 392
Fairfax, Sally, 549–550
Fairfax, William, 549
Fairfield, Conn., raided by British, 1343, 1513
Falcon, 1110
Falmouth, Mass., destruction of, 645–646
Faneuil, Peter, 45–46
Fanning, Nathaniel, 1289, 1290
on Bonhomme Richard vs. Serapis, 1276, 1278–1280, 1282–1284, 1287, 1289
on Jones vs. Landais, 1290–1291
Farewell Address, Washington's, 1784–1785
"Farmer's Letters" (Dickinson), 276–280
Farnsworth, Amos, 508, 530
Fauquier, Governor (Va.), 197, 211

Febiger, Christian, 1345, 1347, 1348, 1350
Fellows, John, 716, 936
Felt, Captain, 466–467
Feltham, Jocelyn, 589
Feltman, William, 1634, 1651, 1693
Ferguson, Adam, 255, 1065–1066
Ferguson, Colonel, 951, 1124
Ferguson, Mrs., 1071
Ferguson, Patrick, 1383, 1404, 1419, 1435, 1437
declines to shoot Washington, 1426–1427
invents first breech-loading rifle, 1426
at Kings Mountain, 1424–1430, 1433, 1434
at Monck's Corner, 1427
at Wahab's Plantation, 1421
Fersen, Hans Axel von, 1638–1639, 1647, 1666
Field, Francis, 317
Fielding, Commodore, 1541–1542
Fifth Monarchy Men, 55
Finley, Captain, 1501
Fishbourn, Benjamin, 1350
Fisher, Elijah, 1787–1788
Fisher, Jonathan, 66
Fisher, Miers, 436
Fiske, John, 85
Fitch, Jabez, 569
Fithian, Philip, 88, 732
Fitzherbert (British peace negotiator), 1736
Fitzroy, Augustus Henry (see Grafton, Duke of)
Flag, U.S., Congress authorizes, 1268
Fleury, Louis Teissedre de, 956, 973
at Fort Mifflin, 983–986, 1350
at Stony Point, 1348, 1350
Flora, 1110, 1256
Florida (see East Florida; West Florida)
Floyd, William, 1363–1364
Flucker, Lucy, 539
Fly, 1250
Flying Camp, 716, 792, 829, 1320
Fogg, Jeremiah, 1175
Foot, John, 72
Foot, Lucinda, 72
Forbes, Gilbert, 719
Forbes, Major, 925–926
Ford, Benjamin, 1479, 1493, 1494
Fordyce, Captain, 623
Forest, James, 345–346
Forlorn Hopes, 1346–1348, 1356
Forsyth, Captain, 1356
Fort Anne, 900–901, 932
Fort Balfour, 1439
Fort Box, 714
Fort de Chartres, 1193
Fort Clinton, 930, 931, 939

Fort Constitution, 715, 775, 931, 1563
Fort Cornwallis, 1499–1502
Fort Dayton, 913
Fort Defiance, 714, 899
Fort Detroit, 1192–1194, 1198, 1199, 1216–1217
Fort Duquesne, 123
Fort Edward, 898, 901, 904, 906–908, 915, 932, 938
Fort Frontenac, 1759
Fort Galphin, 1499
Fort George, 207, 1788–1789
Fort Granby, 1495–1498
    Hessians at, 1498
Fort Greene, 714
Fort Grierson, 1500
Fort Herkimer, 1185
Fort Hunter, 1187
Fort Independence, 782, 876–877, 900, 930, 931
    Hessians at, 876
Fort Jefferson, 1216, 1217
Fort Johnson, 626, 630
Fort Keyser, 1183, 1184
Fort Lafayette, 1350
Fort Laurens, 1178
Fort Lee, 715, 782, 792, 797–798
Fort Massac, 1196
Fort Mercer:
    battle at, 979–983, 1433–1434, 1526
    evacuation of, 989
    Hessians at, 980–983, 987, 989, 990, 1526
    U.S. naval ships at, 979–980
Fort Miami, 1192
Fort Mifflin, battle at, 979, 980, 983–987, 989
Fort Montgomery, 930, 931, 939
Fort Morris, 1307
Fort Motte, 1496
Fort Moultrie, 1321, 1384, 1385
    (See also Fort Sullivan)
Fort Nassau, 1251
Fort Necessity, 124
Fort Nelson, 1217, 1232, 1624
Fort Oswego, 895
Fort Paris, 1183
Fort Pitt, 1163, 1194, 1651
    Indian treaty meeting at, 1152
Fort Putnam, 714
Fort Rensselaer, 1187
Fort Sackville, 1205
Fort St. Joseph, 1192
Fort Schuyler (see Fort Stanwix)
Fort Stanwix, 908–914, 1184, 1185
Fort Stirling, 714
Fort Sullivan, 627, 630, 634, 635, 1166, 1384
    (See also Fort Moultrie)
Fort Ticonderoga (see Ticonderoga)

Fort Washington, 715, 782, 790–801, 808, 898
    Hessians at, 793–795
Fort Watson, 1491, 1498, 1500
Fort William, 1450–1451
"Fort Wilson Riot," 1365–1369
Forty Fort, 1156–1157
Fosdick, Nathaniel, 337, 338
Foster, Benjamin, 642
Fothergill, John, 143
Fowey, 661
Fox, 1255–1256
Fox, Charles James, 372, 619, 864–865, 869–870
    on American war, 1373–1374
    attacks Shelburne, 1741–1744
    and French-American alliance, 1062–1063
    on Guilford Court House, 1484
    and Holland, 1744
    and North, 1742–1743
    vs. North, 1372
    and peace negotiations, 1725, 1731
    refuses to import American goods, 1744
    resigns from government, 1731
    as secretary of state, 1743–1744
    turns against America, 1744
    urges "resolute concern" for citizens' rights, 1376
Fox, Stephen, 402
Fox Mills, 1183, 1184
Fox-North policy, 1744–1745
Foxcroft, John, 668
France:
    alliance with, 944, 1044–1059
        Adams on, 1045, 1046
        American reaction to, 1114–1115
        and Beaumarchais, 1047–1049, 1051
        celebrated by Washington, 1055–1057
        disappointment of, 1132–1133, 1336, 1372, 1378–1379, 1507, 1632, 1634
        English reaction to, 1060–1065, 1074, 1107, 1823
        and Franklin, 1049–1053
        French views of, 1045–1047, 1133
        as impedance to English champions of colonies, 1378
        as mixed blessing, 1716
        as negative factor in Revolutionary struggle, 1715, 1822–1823
        and Spain, 1049, 1052, 1132, 1214
        and treaty of alliance, 1053–1054
        and treaty of amity and commerce, 1053
        and Vergennes, 1046, 1047, 1051–1054
        views for and against, 1044–1046
        Washington on, 1535
    openly supports American cause, 944
    and peace negotiations, 1726–1731, 1737–1739, 1741

preliminary treaty with England, 1741–
1742
presses Congress for more military
campaigns, 1520–1521
reaction in, to Jones's victory, 1286
refuses to supply ships, 1254
sends money to Boston, 1667
and Spain, 1738
supplies military stores to Washington, 877–
878, 1045, 1048
Francis, Turbott, 901–903
Franklin, 1246
Franklin, Benjamin, 68–69, 77, 78, 105, 142–
144, 170, 461
and Adams, 544, 1050–1051, 1731–1734
at Albany Congress, 124–125
animosity between, and congressional
agents in France, 1139
aphorisms of, 156
approached by Hutton, 1061
and Articles of Confederation, 844
and conference with Howe brothers, 756–
758
and Continental Navy, 1254
and Declaration of Independence, 693, 694,
699–700, 702, 704
Do-Good Papers, 105
in France, 843, 1008, 1049–1053, 1061,
1075–1076
and Great Seal, 1766
and Hutchinson letters, 369–372
and Indians, 113–114, 116, 562
inquires about foreign assistance, 1044
on investigating committee to Montreal, 717
and Jay, 1733
and Jones, 1272–1274, 1286, 1290, 1292
and land speculation, 168, 845–846
and Laurens, 1737
to Lee, 1139
meets Voltaire, 1050
and Oswald, 1725–1728, 1732
and Paine, 676, 678, 683
and peace negotiations, 1725–1735, 1737
on peace terms, 1061–1062
Poor Richard's Almanack, 1272
and Pulaski, 998
and rift with Dickinson, 560
and Second Continental Congress, 544
and Shelburne, 1725, 1726
and Stamp Act, 191, 193, 208, 243
and Strachey, 1733
on Tories' attack on peace treaty, 1742
and Vergennes, 1638, 1728, 1739
and Weissenstein, 1075–1076
Franklin, William, 429, 470, 660, 1532, 1756
on Clinton, 1753–1754
and Huddy affair, 1751

opposes nonimportation agreements, 434,
446–447
Franks, David, 1581–1583, 1585, 1586, 1588,
1781
Fraser, Simon, 900–903, 933
at Freeman's Farm, 922, 924–925
at Saratoga, 933–936
Frederick the Great of Prussia, 837, 1008,
1009
Freedom, 1264
Freeman, Cato, 1804
Freeman, Douglas, 991, 1596
Freeman's Farm, Battle of, 922–930
Hessians at, 922
French, colonial wars with, 122–124
French, Jeremiah, 305–306
French-American brawls, 1120–1121
French and Indian War, 79, 124–129
British debt incurred by, 169
as training ground for Washington's
officers, 1794
French navy (*see* Navy, French)
French Revolution, 1, 257, 1818, 1826–1827
French volunteers, 956, 972–977, 989–990,
1321
influences of, on French Revolution, 1753
Freneau, Philip, 675–676, 1691–1692, 1714
Frey, John, 911
Friars of St. Francis, 146
Friedlein, Private, 1674
Friends, Society of (*see* Quakers)
Friendship, 631
Frontiersmen, "separatist" tendencies of,
1235–1236
Frothingham, Dr., 4
Fry, Joshua, 124
Furnival, Captain, 958

Gadsden, Christopher, 265, 1240, 1304, 1382
and First Continental Congress, 424, 438,
840
and Howe, 1304
and Moultrie, 1326
and Sons of Liberty, 211, 258
at Stamp Act Congress, 220, 223
Gage, Thomas, 286, 289, 555
and Battle of Bunker Hill, 515–516, 518–
519, 533, 539
and Battle of Lexington and Concord, 472–
474, 490
and Boston insurrection over Stamp Act,
226–227
and Boston Massacre, 345
and Boston Port Bill, 408–410, 413
and British troops in Boston, 305, 307, 308,
311, 319, 455–456, 582–583, 637
and burning of seaport towns, 645

Gage, Thomas (*cont.*):
  vs. colonists, 458, 463
  exchange of letters with Washington, 582
  on First Continental Congress, 447
  fortifies Boston Neck, 458
  as governor, 418–419, 423, 450, 460, 501–
    502
  and Massachusetts Government Act, 404
  opposes land speculation, 168
  and Putnam, 498
  and Quartering Act, 265
  returns to England, 648
  and siege of Boston, 506–508
  on Stamp Act Congress, 221–222
  on Stamp Act riots, 212
  and Ticonderoga, 584
  and ties to America, 505
  and Warren, 536
Gale, Benjamin, 149
Galloway, Joseph, 258, 426, 429
  at Brandywine, 952
  on dwindling of patriot cause in
    Pennsylvania, 470–471
  and First Continental Congress, 431, 433–
    434, 439–441, 445
  and Howe, 949
  on Mischianza, 1041
  and Pennsylvania state constitution, 863
  and Serle, 799–800, 888, 1031–1032, 1058
  and withdrawal of British from
    Philadelphia, 1058
Galloway Plan of Union, 439–441, 445
Galvan, William, 1650–1651
Gambier, James, 1121
Gansevoort, Peter, 908–909, 912, 913, 1171
Gardenier, Captain, 911
Gardoqui, Diego de, 1254
Garrick, David, 145, 147
Garrick, Edward, 333–334
Gaspee, 602
Gaspee affair, 364–369
Gates, Horatio, 5, 553, 555, 573, 944, 1164,
    1778, 1795
  vs. Arnold, 928–929
  at Battle of Camden, 1407–1414, 1416–
    1418
  and Burgoyne's surrender, 938–940, 1026,
    1417
  and Clinton, 932–933
  before Congress, 919
  and Conway, 1019, 1022–1025, 1029
  at Freeman's Farm, 922–923, 927–929
  and Lee, 1408, 1417
  loses confidence of officers, 1445
  and Marion, 1436
  and New Jersey campaign, 807, 808, 813
  at Saratoga, 933, 938, 944

  vs. Schuyler, 897–898, 919–920
  sent to re-establish army in South, 1536
  vs. Washington, 961, 991, 1026
Gavett, Billy, 466
General Hancock, 1260
General Monck, 1296
General Washington, 1296
Generals, experienced vs. inexperienced, 745–
    746
Generals, Washington's, 1794–1795
Genesee, 1169–1170
George III, king of England, 4, 192, 805
  announces independence of America, 1740
  attempts to destroy factional government,
    165–166
  calls for public support of war effort, 1370
  and Clinton, 636
  colonial attitudes toward, 398–400, 676
  and Cornwallis' surrender, 1718–1719
  dissolves Parliament (1780), 1552
  drafts statement of abdication, 1721–1722
  on failure of British fleet, 1678
  vs. Fox, 1743
  Jefferson's indictment of, for slavery, 704–
    705
  and Lexington and Concord, 494–495
  on Lord Chatham, 945, 1065
  and Lord North, 294, 295, 871, 945, 1074–
    1075, 1722, 1823
  refuses compromise, 1552–1554
  and Stamp Act, 237, 242–243, 245, 247
  takes personal direction of war, 870–871,
    892, 1074–1075, 1372
  as villain of Revolution, 1823
  and Wilkes affair, 177
Georgia, 1301–1316
  British military strength in (1780), 1392
  constitution of, 855, 856
  controlled by British, 1398
  favors independence, 691
  Hessians in, 1392
  Indian raids in, 1152, 1213
  joins patriot camp, 662–663
  joins Union, 563
  Liberty Society in, 1302
  militia of, 1303
  patriot-Tory enmity in, 1502
  politics in, 1301–1303, 1308
  sends expedition against St. Augustine,
    1301–1302
  settlement of, 25–26
  and Stamp Act, 228
  supreme executive council in, 1303
  Tory military action in, 1309–1312
  urged by Congress to enlist slaves, 1805
Gérard, Conrad, 1052–1053, 1137–1138,
    1142, 1144

presses Congress on peace treaty, 1361–
1362
Germain, George, 533, 637, 723, 802, 885
and American privateers, 1264–1265
announces patriot cause as all but lost, 1554
approves Howe's expedition to
Philadelphia, 949
on Boston town meetings, 402
on British defeat at Trenton, 827
and Burgoyne, 891–893, 921, 941
and Clinton, 636, 1646–1647
controversial letter to Howe, 880
and Cornwallis' surrender, 1717–1719
on determination to pursue American war,
1374
on effect of Lexington and Concord on
North ministry, 494
on "generosity" of peace terms, 1067
orders Clinton to attack coastal ports, 1109,
1121
orders Clinton to dispatch troops to
Cornwallis, 1435
orders troops withdrawn from Philadelphia,
1058, 1069
and Southern campaign, 624
tries to bribe American generals, 1560
on use of Indians against patriots, 1155
German immigration, 29, 36, 41–42, 45, 657
German volunteers, 972
Germantown, Battle of, 964–971, 1013, 1051,
1074, 1825
Gerry, Elbridge, 665, 682, 1142, 1363
and Adams, 1737
favors arrest of critical journalist, 1148–
1149
on French displeasure with American
inactivity, 1520
on imminence of independence, 690–691
Gibault, Father, 1198, 1202
Gibbon, Edward, 865, 1060, 1550–1551
Gibbons, Mary, 720–723
Gibbs, Mrs., 1713
Gifford, James, 351
Gill, John, 323
Gill, Moses, 558
Girty, Simon, 1178, 1226, 1228–1230
Gist, Christopher, 123
Gist, Mordecai, 992, 1420, 1444
at Camden, 1412, 1413, 1415, 1416
Glasgow, 1251
Glorious Revolution, 1, 58–59, 680, 1818,
1826
Gloucester, Duke of, 974
Glover, John, 885, 907
and André, 1589–1590
at Battle of Rhode Island, 1110, 1116–1118
and Battle of White Plains, 782–783

and evacuation of Brooklyn, 747, 748
at Freeman's Farm, 923
promoted to brigadier general, 879
at Saratoga, 938
at Trenton, 816, 820–821, 823
Gnadenhütten, 1219–1221
Gold, J., 882
Golden Hill, Battle of, 313–318
Goldfinch, John, 333, 335, 341
Goodman, Paul, 269
Gordon, George, 1548–1549
Gore, Captain, 465
Gower, Lord, 1378
Grafton, Duke of, 264, 269, 272, 864
on Burgoyne's surrender, 944
Graham, Joseph, 1401
Grant, Colonel, 734, 738, 740, 741
Grant, General James, 901, 1080, 1333
Grant, Sir James, 210
Gratz family, 46
Graves, Samuel, 515, 1693, 1702
and burning of seaport towns, 645–646
characteristics of, 637–639
at Chesapeake, 1675–1682, 1685, 1686
vs. Clinton, 1675
and Cornwallis, 1686
vs. De Grasse, 1670, 1687–1688, 1715
fatal errors of, 1686–1688
and Hood, 1683–1688
leaves New York, 1664
at Noodle Island, 507–508
proceeds to New York, 1687
Graves, Thomas, 508
Gray, Harrison, 447–448
Gray, Ned, 464
Gray, Sam, 336, 338–340, 352
Graydon, Alexander, 602, 1020
on Conway, 1103
criticizes treatment of Tories in
Philadelphia, 664–665
on Fort Washington, 792
Grayson, William, 1367
Great Bridge, Battle of, 622–623
Great Protestation, 50–51
Great Seal of United States, 1766, 1816–
1817
Green, William, 332
Green Mountain Boys, 1145
under Ethan Allen, 587–588, 590, 1145
under Seth Warner, 598, 600, 601, 604
Green Spring Farm, engagement at, 1650–
1655
Greene, Ashbel, 1010
Greene, Christopher, 611, 1476
at Battle of Rhode Island, 1118, 1805
at Fort Mercer, 980–982, 989
at Guilford Court House, 1479, 1482

Greene, Nathanael, 5, 538, 883, 884, 1712, 1795
  and André, 1589–1590
  on army administration, 1514
  on army's financial difficulties, 1519
  on Arnold's treason, 1585
  at Battle of Brandywine, 951–953, 955
  at Battle of Germantown, 964–967
  at Battle of Monmouth, 1093, 1095–1096, 1098
  and Battle of Princeton, 830
  at Battle of Rhode Island, 1109, 1112, 1114–1116, 1119
  at Battle of White Plains, 782, 783
  on cavalry, 1485
  in Charles Town, after Yorkville, 1750
  in command of Southern Department, 1435, 1444, 1536, 1645, 1795
  vs. Congress, 1534
  vs. Cornwallis, 1447–1448, 1465–1470, 1472, 1475, 1476, 1478–1485
  criticizes Washington, 961
  on desperate condition of army, 991
  on discipline problems, 570–571
  on engagement at Green Spring Farm, 1653
  at Eutaw Springs, 1688–1691
  at Fort Mercer, 988–990
  and Fort Washington, 790–794, 796, 797
  and guerrilla warfare, 1446
  at Guilford Court House, 1478–1485
  Hamilton on, 1418
  at Harlem Heights, 769
  at Hobkirk's Hill, 1492–1495
  on impoverished condition of Southern army, 1445–1446
  on independence, 675
  and Jefferson, 1470
  and Lafayette, 1629
  on large store of provisions available, 1519–1520
  and Lee, 1448, 1507–1508
  at Middle Brook, 1342
  on militia, 1446
  and Morgan, 1447, 1449, 1451, 1452, 1459, 1465, 1466
  on New Englanders, 566–567
  in New Jersey, 805, 815, 818–820, 886
  in New York, 717, 725, 733, 755, 763
  at Ninety-Six, 1502–1506
  on North Carolina militia, 1445
  ordered to move main army to King's Ferry, 1589
  pursues Cornwallis, 1470–1473, 1475–1477, 1487
  on re-enlistment problem, 576
  reinforced by St. Clair after Yorktown, 1748
  resigns, 1534
  in retreat from Cornwallis, 1465–1469
  and Robertson, 1592
  and scarcity of provisions, 1488–1489
  at siege of Boston, 496–498
  and South Carolina campaign, 1489–1498, 1502–1509
  at Springfield, 1530, 1531
  and Steuben, 1009–1010
  and Sullivan, 1172, 1514
  supplies French fleet, 1123
  urges attack on Clinton, 1083, 1087
  at Valley Forge, 1003, 1005, 1007
  in Virginia, 1469
  and Washington, 1407, 1688, 1690, 1746
  on Wayne's victory at Stony Point, 1349
  and Weedon, 1673
Greene, Mrs. Nathanael, 1000
Greenleaf, Joseph, 474
Gregg, Colonel, 916–917
Grenville, George, 266, 268
  character of, 169
  on concessions to Americans, 1063
  and Revenue Act, 173
  and Stamp Act, 189–191, 193, 240–242
  and Townshend Duties, 293–294
Grenville, Thomas, 1731
Grey, Charles, 951, 993, 998, 1121, 1124
Grey, Colonel, 1080
Greyhound, 723, 1592
Gridley, John, 322–323
Gridley, Richard, 511–513, 515, 519, 536
Grieve, George, 1818–1819
Griffin, Cyrus, 842
Griffin, Samuel, 815
Guadeloupe, 1672
Guerriere, 1107
Guerrilla warfare, 1435, 1437–1441, 1446, 1462, 1507
Guichen, Comte de, 1542–1543
Guilford Court House, Battle of, 1478–1485, 1507
  American desertions at, 1484
  Hessians at, 1480–1482
  vs. Ramsour's Mill, 1484–1485
Gunby, John, 1479, 1493
Gutbreath, Ludwig, 1348
Gwinnett, Button, vs. Lachlan McIntosh, 1301–1302

Hackensack, N.J., looted by Knuyphausen, 1526
Hadden, James, 902
Hair, Benjamin, 663
Hair, John, 663
Haldimand, Frederick, 1165–1166, 1174, 1182
Hale, Matthew, 254

Hale, Nathan, 774–775
Hale, Samuel, 774
Half-pay debates, 1026–1029, 1146
Hall, David, 267, 297, 299
Hall, Prince, 1801–1802
Hallowell, Benjamin, 203, 322, 654
    and Graves, 638–639
    and *Liberty* affair, 283, 285
Hamilton, Alexander, 129, 406, 722, 960, 968,
        1191, 1353, 1795
    on André, 1594
    and Arnold, 1583, 1584, 1587
    at Battle of Brandywine, 950
    at Battle of Monmouth, 1087, 1095, 1101
    at Battle of Princeton, 833
    at Battle of Trenton, 816, 820
    at Battle of White Plains, 787
    as congressional delegate from New York,
        1763, 1765, 1768, 1773, 1778, 1791
    and Conway Cabal, 1024–1025
    and D'Estaing, 1108
    on faults of Congress, 1642
    and Gates, 991, 1418
    on Greene, 1418
    and Lafayette, 1630–1631
    and Laurens, 1591
    and Lee (Charles), 1086–1087, 1105
    and Lee (Henry), 1357–1358
    marries Elizabeth Schuyler, 1597
    and mutiny of furloughed troops, 1778
    on Negroes, 1805–1806
    offers to exchange André for Arnold, 1591
    on parochialism in Congress, 1763, 1773
    and Peggy Arnold, 1587–1588
    and preliminary treaty with England, 1768
    proposes constitutional convention, 1643
    sent to Philadelphia to collect shoes, 960
    and Steuben, 1010, 1015
    suggests use of army to enforce payments of
        funds by states to Congress, 1765
    and Washington, 976–977, 1555, 1631,
        1658, 1765, 1773
    at Yorktown, 1698–1699, 1701, 1703
Hamilton, Dr. Alexander:
    on Bostonians, 69
    on Maryland, 84
    on New York, 75–76
    on Pennsylvania, 79–80
    on Rhode Islanders, 71
Hamilton, Henry, 1192–1193, 1199–1201,
        1205–1210
Hamilton, John, 1411
Hamilton, Major, 1310
Hamilton, Paul, 1438–1439
Hammond, John, 35–36
Hammond's Store, engagement at, 1450
Hampden, John, 47, 53

Hampshire Grants, 920–921
Hampton, Wade, 1442
    at Eutaw Springs, 1688–1691
Hampton Roads, Va.:
    Arnold lands at, 1625
    British raid, 1624
Han Yerry, 1170
Hanbury, John, 147, 149–150
Hancock, 1245, 1257, 1258
    capture of, 1255–1257
    renamed *Iris,* 1257
Hancock, John, 302, 507, 949, 956, 1251
    vs. Adams (Sam), 840
    and Battle of Lexington, 473, 475, 478–479
    and Battle of Rhode Island, 1116
    and Boston Massacre, 344, 348, 358–359
    and Circular Letter, 287–288
    as colonel of Minutemen, 460
    and Committee of Public Safety, 463
    and Declaration of Independence, 706
    and *Liberty* affair, 281–282, 285
    and Mein affair, 324
    and repeal of Stamp Act, 245
    and Second Continental Congress, 543,
        547–548, 562, 840
Hand, Edward, 781, 879, 1192
    at Battle of Long Island, 733, 735, 737, 738
    at Battle of Princeton, 830, 833
    at Battle of White Plains, 786
    and evacuation of Brooklyn, 748–749
    and Society of Cincinnatus, 1783
    on Sullivan's expedition against Indians and
        Tories, 1166, 1167
Handy, Levin, 1354, 1356, 1357
    in South Carolina campaign, 1500, 1501
Hanger, George von, 1423, 1427
Hannah, 643
Hannastown, raid on, 1228
Happiness as human right, 697–699
Harcourt, William, 837–838
Harden, Colonel, 1439
Harding, Lieutenant, 1179
Harding, Seth, 1262
Hare, Henry, 1166
Harland, Si, 1193
Harlem Heights, British defeat at, 768–778, 1825
    Hessians at, 770
Harmar, Joseph, 1781
Harnett, Cornelius, 841
Harper, Alexander, 1180–1181
Harrington, James, 848
Harris, George, 501, 529
Harris, Robert, 702
Harrison, Benjamin, 92, 1131
    at First Continental Congress, 427, 428
    as governor of Virginia, 1217–1218, 1230–
        1231

Harrison, Benjamin (*cont.*):
  and Madison, 1764
  recalls Clark, 1232–1233
  at Second Continental Congress, 562, 563
  on Steuben, 1627
Harrison, Joseph, 282–283, 285
Harrison, Robert, 1021
Harrod, James, 1213
Harry, John, 663
Hartegan, James, 337
Hartley, David, 1371, 1372, 1548, 1744, 1745
Harvard University, 46, 68, 84, 112, 143
Harvey, Edward, 494
Haslet, John, 738, 786, 787, 834
Hason, John, 112
Hathorn, Colonel, 1161
Hawes, Samuel, 1479, 1482, 1493, 1494
Hawkins, Christopher, 1266–1267
Hawley, James, 592
Hawley, Joseph, 665, 682
Hayes, Joseph, 1450
Hays, Mary Ludwig (Molly Pitcher), 1097–1098, 1811
Hazelwood, John, 979, 986
Heard, Nathaniel, 717
Heath, William, 546, 554, 755, 962, 1112, 1795
  at Battle of Lexington, 481
  at Battle of Long Island, 716, 734
  at Battle of White Plains, 783–784, 787
  and Burgoyne's surrender, 939
  distracts Clinton in Hudson, 1661
  and evacuation of Brooklyn, 746
  at Fort Independence, 876–877
  at Fort Washington, 792
  in New Jersey campaign, 803, 804, 879
  winters at Newburgh, N.Y., 1747
Heckewelder, John, 115–116, 1219
Hegel, G. W. F., 1790
Heister, Phillip von, 814, 885
  at Battle of Long Island, 731, 739, 741–742
  at Battle of White Plains, 785
Hell-fire Club, 145–146
Helm, Captain, 1198, 1199
Henderson, Richard, 1213
Henderson, William, 1387, 1689
Hendricks, William, 608
Henley, Robert, 242
Henrietta Maria, Princess, 51
Henry, John, 1068
Henry, John Joseph, 608, 615–617
Henry, Patrick, 92, 369, 661
  on Carlisle commission, 1068–1069
  and Clark, 1193–1194, 1216
  against constitutional reform, 1816
  and Continental Congress, 428–429, 431–432, 440
  on French alliance, 1054
  and land speculation, 845–846
  and slavery, 1799, 1806
  and Stamp Act resolves, 195–197
  and Virginia constitution, 850–851
Herkimer, Nicholas, 909–912
Herrick, Samuel, 918
Hesse, Emmanuel, 1214–1216
Hesse-Cassel, Landgrave of, 827
Hessians, 5, 730–731, 781
  ambushed near White Plains, 1125–1126
  at Battle of Brandywine, 951–952, 954
  at Battle of Long Island, 730–731, 741–742
  at Battle of Monmouth, 1095
  at Battle of Princeton, 830–831
  at Battle of Rhode Island, 1118, 1119
  at Battle of Trenton, 813–814, 819–825, 827
  at Battle of White Plains, 785–788
  in Burgoyne's invasion, 895, 905
  captured by Massachusetts navy, 1264
  at Charles Town, 1380–1381, 1385, 1387, 1389
  at Chestnut Hill, 992
  condescended to by British, 905, 1034, 1526
  in Connecticut, 881–882
  with Cornwallis at Yorktown, 1672–1674
  desertion among, 1673, 1674
  encumberment of, 905
  evacuate Brooklyn, 751
  evacuate New York, 1761
  at Fort Granby, 1498
  at Fort Independence, 876
  at Fort Mercer, 980–983, 987, 989, 990, 1526
  at Fort Washington, 793–795
  at Freeman's Farm, 922
  in Georgia, 1392
  at Guilford Court House, 1480–1482
  at Hackensack, 1527
  at Harlem Heights, 770
  at Kip's Bay, 765–766
  looting and destruction by, 1033–1034
  Martin on, 1106–1107
  in New Jersey, 807, 813–814, 819–825, 827, 830–831, 835–836, 886
  in New York, 1392
  at Paulus Hook, 1354, 1356, 1357
  in Philadelphia, 1032–1034
  as prisoners in Pennsylvania, 943
  as prisoners after Yorktown, 1709–1710
  punishment of deserters from, 1674
  raid Westchester County, 1124
  at Savannah, 1303, 1334, 1392
  in South Carolina, 1392
  at Springfield, 1528–1529, 1532
  at Stono Ferry, 1327–1328
  at Yorktown surrender ceremony, 1707, 1708

Heth, T. Will, 968–969
Hewes, George, 381
Hewes, Joseph, 1247
Hickey, Thomas, 719–722
Higginson, Stephen, 1772–1773
Hill, John, 332
Hill, Wells, 168
    (*See also* Hillsborough, Earl of)
Hillsborough, Earl of, 272, 319, 350
    and Bernard, 289–291
    orders Circular Letter rescinded, 286–287, 294
    and Townshend Duties, 295–298
Hinkley, Joseph, 338
Hinman, Colonel, 592
Hinrichs, Johann, 1387
Hobhouse, Christopher, 1743
Hobkirk's Hill, engagement at, 1492
    American desertions at, 1494
Holderness, 1260
Holland, 1541–1542
    and peace negotiations with English, 1727, 1728, 1739
    signs peace treaty with U.S., 1731
Hollis, Thomas, 143
Holt, John, 231
Holton, Samuel, 841
Holy Ground, 713–714
Home, Henry, 255
Hood, Samuel, 320, 1664, 1693, 1702
    at Chesapeake, 1675–1682
    vs. De Grasse, 1670
    and Graves, 1683–1688
Hood, Zachariah, 211, 212
Hooker, Thomas, 23, 254, 848
Hooper, William, 846–848, 854
Hope, capture of, 1246
Hopkins, Ezek, 647, 1246, 1248
    raids New Providence, 1250–1251
Hopkins, Samuel, 1799
Hopkins, Stephen, 1240, 1246
Hopkinson, Francis, 894–895, 1035
Hornet, 1250
Horry, Daniel, 629, 1437
Horses:
    problems presented by, 1222–1223
    treatment of, by Indians, 916
Hortalez & Company, 1008, 1047–1049, 1139, 1140
Hosmer, Titus, 841–842
Hospital ship, captured at Charles Town, 1387–1388
Hospitals, military, 578, 937, 942, 1002, 1036
Hot Water, Battle of, 1635
Hotham, William, 730, 1331
Houston, William Churchill, 423, 1143
    and Great Seal, 1766

Howard, John Eager, 1453, 1455–1460, 1466
    at Guilford Court House, 1481, 1482
    at Hobkirk's Hill, 1493
Howard, Kenneth (*see* Effingham, Lord)
Howard, Martin, Jr., 205–206
Howe, George Augustus, 502–503
Howe, Richard ("Black Dick"), 502, 800, 980
    at Battle of Rhode Island, 1111, 1117
    and conference with congressional committee, 756–758
    and Continental Navy, 1250, 1252, 1258
    in New York, 723–727, 729, 755
    and peace commission, 1065
Howe, Robert, 5, 623, 1406
    and André, 1589–1590
    and Arnold, 1557, 1559, 1566
    and Gadsden, 1304
    and New Jersey mutiny, 1621–1622
    at Savannah, 1303–1308, 1469
Howe, William, 582, 624, 627, 670, 755
    abandons New Jersey, 887–888
    avoids showdown with Washington, 948–949, 959–960
    and Battle of Brandywine, 948–955
    and Battle of Bunker Hill, 510, 512, 515–517, 521–522, 524–526, 531–534, 537–538
    and Battle of Germantown, 965
    and Battle of Long Island, 730–732, 735, 738, 741
    and Battle of Trenton, 812–814, 824
    and Battle of White Plains, 780–783, 785, 789
    and Burgoyne, 892–893, 920, 921, 938, 941
    at Chestnut Hill, 992–993
    in command at Boston, 648
    and Dorchester Heights, 650–653
    and enticement of American troops, 778
    and evacuation of Boston, 653–655
    and evacuation of Brooklyn, 746, 750
    evaluation of, 1041–1043
    failure to make contact with Burgoyne, 879–880
    failure to press advantage at New York, 758–759
    vs. Ferguson, 1427
    and Fort Mercer, 980, 983, 988
    and Fort Mifflin, 980, 983, 987
    and Fort Washington, 791–797, 799
    inactivity of, in Philadelphia, 1038
    and Mrs. Loring, 1036
    in New Jersey, 802–810, 828, 846, 873, 876, 878, 885–887
    at New York, 712–713, 722–724, 727–728, 761, 765–766, 773, 774, 856
    occupies Philadelphia, 962–963, 1031–1043
    orders Clinton up Hudson, 932

Howe, William (*cont.*):
  and peace negotiations, 756, 1065
  plans of, foiled by woman spy, 1811
  relieved by Clinton in Philadelphia, 1038–
    1039
  and siege of Boston, 501–505
  staff members' assessments of, 1038–1039
  vs. Washington, evaluation of, 1042–1043
  on withdrawal of troops from Philadelphia,
    1058
Howell, Joshua, 1712
Hoylan, Stephen, 643–644
Huddy, Joshua, 1750–1751
Hudson River, chain stretched across, 880, 930
Huger, Benjamin, 1322
Huger, Francis, 1383, 1465, 1466, 1479
  at Hobkirk's Hill, 1493
Huger, Isaac, 1305
Hughes, Lieutenant, 1455–1456
Huguenots, 29, 45–46
Hull, William, 774–775, 1345
Hume, David, 867, 1242, 1546, 1640
Humphreys, Captain, 616
Humphreys, David, 1339–1340
Hunter, Martin, 964, 965
Huntington, Ebenezer, 740, 804
Huntington, Samuel, 1521
Husband, Hermon, 661
Hutcheson, Francis, 144, 254–255
Hutchings, Lieutenant, 1195
Hutchinson, Anne, 21–22
Hutchinson, Thomas, 179–180, 191, 198–199,
    298, 1822
  as acting governor, 225–226, 308, 320–321,
    323–325, 328, 329, 331–332, 341–344,
    348, 350, 357, 363
  and Boston Massacre, 341–344, 348, 350,
    357, 363
  on Boston popular government, 212
  and Boston Port Bill, 390
  and Boston Tea Party, 375–377, 379–383
  on British privateers, 1265
  on British retention of Canada as key to
    American Revolution, 129
  and Governor's Council, 417–418
  and letters to Whately, 369–372
  on Lexington and Concord, 495
  and Massachusetts Government Act, 401
  and Stamp Act riots, 200, 202–205, 212
  vetoes law prohibiting importation and sale
    of slaves, 1800
Hutton, James, 1061–1062, 1064
Hyde, Edward, 54

Immigration, 28–46, 1818–1819
  Dutch, 29
  English, 28, 30–41

  German, 29, 41–42, 45
  Huguenot, 29, 45–46
  Irish, 29–30
  Jewish, 46
  opposed by Jefferson, 1818
  Puritan, 29
  Quaker, 29, 45
  Scotch-Irish, 30, 44–45
  Scottish, 29
  Separatist, 29
  Swedish, 29
  Welsh, 30, 45
Impressment, 201, 282, 291, 292, 638, 1141
Indentured servants, 24, 31–37, 43–44, 86,
    101, 103
Independence, 1261
Independence:
  impossibility of preventing, 1536–1537,
    1714–1715
  role of French in winning, 1715
  sentiment for, 675–676, 685, 1341
  social and psychological vs. political, 398
Indian affairs, commissioners of, 1151, 1155
Indian Charity School, 1158
Indians, 107–119
  allied with Tories, 1150–1151, 1154, 1156–
    1162, 1165–1177, 1181–1189, 1215,
    1229–1230
  attack Kentucky settlements, 1229–1231
  in attack on Vincennes, 1206, 1208–1209
  attempts to educate, 112–113, 116, 144
  attractiveness of life of, 18, 113–116
  at Battle of Oriskany, 908–912, 914
  at Bennington, 916–917
  British attempt to incite, 596
  British feelings about employing, 1150
  in Burgoyne's invasion, 895–897, 899, 901–
    903, 906, 908–912, 922, 924, 929
  and Clark, 1198–1201, 1206, 1208–1209,
    1216–1217, 1231–1232
  at College of New Jersey, 1153
  Congress' appeal to, for peace, 562–563
  in Connecticut, 112
  continued embittered relations between
    Western settlers and, 1234–1237
  in defense of Augusta, 1424
  employment of, against British, 498–499,
    1155, 1505
  employment of, against patriots, 1150–
    1151, 1155–1162, 1173, 1235–1237
  enmity among, 112, 1235
  at Fort Stanwix, 908–914
  at Freeman's Farm, 922, 924, 929
  in Gates's army, 907
  in Georgia, 1152, 1213
  and horses, treatment of, 916
  and land speculation, 168–169

and Maryland settlers, 24
and Massachusetts Bay Colony, 22
patriot attacks against, 1163–1179, 1182–1188
and Plymouth colony, 17–18, 22
and Proclamation Line, 166–167
punitive raids by, promoted by British, 1234
raid Cherry Valley, 1158–1160, 1181
raid Mohawk Valley, 1158, 1180–1181
raid New York settlements, 1151, 1158–1162, 1180–1184
raid Pennsylvania settlements, 79, 1156–1158, 1178–1179
with St. Leger, 908–912
scorched-earth policy against, 1163, 1166, 1168–1177, 1179
as scouting parties for British, 941
sense of humor of, 116, 914
and sexual relations with settlers, 110–111
in South Carolina, 1152, 1155, 1213
Southern campaign against, 1213–1214
style of warfare of, 1150–1151, 1174–1175
Sullivan's expedition against, 1163–1177
in threat to Charles Town, 1319
at Ticonderoga, 903
treatment of horses by, 916
at treaty meetings, 117–118, 1152–1155, 1179–1180
and Virginia, 109–110, 112
and Virginia Tories, 621–622
and Walking Purchase of land in Pennsylvania, 118–119
and Wyoming Valley Massacre, 1156–1158
(See also Cherokees; Delawares; Iroquois Confederacy; Oneidas; Stockbridge Indians)
Indien, 1272
Inflation, 1132, 1147–1148, 1340, 1364–1366, 1644–1645
Morris takes measures to deal with, 1644
and vigilante groups to force prices down, 1364–1365
(See also Money, paper, depreciation of)
Inflexible, 896, 900
Ingersoll, Jared, 189, 193, 209
Ingham, John, 425
Ingils, Charles, 799
Intercolonial hostilities, 160
(See also Parochialism of states)
Intercolonial wars, 122–124, 132
Intolerable Acts, 407
(See also Coercive Acts)
Intrepid, 1678, 1681, 1685
Iris, 1296
(See also General Hancock)
Irish immigration, 29–30, 36
Irish soldiers, drunken brawls of, 1127–1128

Iroquois Confederacy, 1172–1173, 1175
Irvine, William, 992, 1218, 1221, 1228, 1231, 1519
Isle-aux-Noix, 599–600
Izard, Ralph, 1139, 1142

Jacatagua, 609
Jack (free Negro), 351
Jackson, Andrew, 1396–1397
on patriots' killing of enemies, 1472
Jackson, Robert, 1396–1397
Jackson, William, 325–326, 335
James (spy for Lafayette), 1653, 1654
James, Major, 207–208
James I, king of England, 48–51
James II, king of England, 1, 57–58
James Island, Southern army winters in, 1750
Jameson, John, 1580, 1582–1584, 1588
Jamestown settlement, 14–15
Jasper, William, 632–633, 635
Jay, John, 422, 735
and Adams, 1731–1733, 1736
and Aranda, 1734–1735
elected president of Congress, 1149
at First Continental Congress, 430, 432, 438, 440
and Franklin, 1733
named minister to Spain, 1363
on naval problems, 1253
and New York constitution, 855–856
and Oswald, 1726, 1727, 1733, 1735
and peace negotiations, 1726–1737
proposes private correspondent for intelligence purposes, 1538
urges against invasion of Canada, 1131
and Van Schaack, 666
and Vergennes, 1638
Jefferson, Thomas, 92, 94, 197, 561, 848
and Chastellux, 1752
and Clark, 1193, 1194, 1216, 1217
and Committee of Correspondence, 369
and Declaration of Independence, 693–700, 704–705
on difficulties of ratifying peace treaty, 1780
and Gates, 1408
and George III, 676, 704
and Great Seal, 1766
and Greene, 1446, 1470
and Indians, 112, 118
informs Congress that Virginia assembly cedes western land claims to Congress, 1540
and Madison, 1780
opposes unlimited immigration, 1818
and Randolph, 665
on Sidney, 254
and slavery, 104, 704–705, 1806

Jefferson, Thomas (*cont.*):
vs. Tories, 448
and U.S. power, 1728
warned of Tarleton's raid, 1631–1632
on Washington, 551, 1792
Jeffries, John, 354
Jenifer, Daniel of St. Thomas, 1148
Jenkins' Fort, 1156
Jenyns, Soame, 214–215
Jersey, 1266–1267
Jewish immigration, 46
John, 1247
Johnson, Colonel, 1344, 1346–1348
Johnson, Guy, 592, 596, 914, 1156, 1158, 1171
Johnson, Henry, 1263
Johnson, John:
at Fort Stanwix, 909, 910
leads Indian-Tory raids, 1181–1184, 1189
Johnson, Michael (*see* Attucks, Crispus)
Johnson, Samuel, 237, 865, 1550
Johnson, William, 596, 1154, 1189, 1236
Johnson, William Samuel, 149, 194, 312
at Stamp Act Congress, 220, 229
Johnston, Augustus, 205–206, 208, 230
Johnston, Samuel, 854, 1644
Johnstone, George, 1065, 1069–1071
Johnstown, 1187–1189
Jones, Captain, 926
Jones, Hugh, 33
Jones, Ichabod, 641–642
Jones, John Paul, 647, 1238, 1268–1293
attitude of crew toward, 1272, 1289–1290
and *Bonhomme Richard,* 1273–1285
British conspiracy to capture, 1274
and Catherine the Great, 1292
character of, 1292–1293
in command of *Alliance,* 1288–1289, 1291
cruises for prizes, 1252, 1289
death of, 1292
declaration of intent by, 1274
and distribution of prize money, 1288–1289
and Earl of Selkirk, 1270
early life of, 1246–1248
in France, 1272–1274, 1290, 1291
and Franklin, 1272–1274, 1286, 1290
in Holland, 1288–1289, 1541
vs. Landais, 1290–1291
before navy board, 1291–1292
vs. Pearson, 1281–1283
raids Whitehaven, England, 1269–1270
and *Ranger,* 1268–1272, 1802
as taskmaster, 1269
writes to Phillis Wheatley, 1802
Jones, Joseph, 1522–1523, 1539, 1640, 1773
Jones, Thomas, 718–719, 1041, 1353
Joseph, Jean Baptiste (*see* Laumoy, Chevalier
de)

Joucaire, Chabert, 123
Jouett, Cavalier, 1758
Jouett, Jack, 1631–1632

Kalb, Johann, 961, 974–975, 1022, 1023, 1056
at Camden, 1407, 1408, 1411, 1412, 1416
at Valley Forge, 1004
Kalm, Peter, 78
Kames, Lord, 255
Kaskaskia, 1192–1194, 1196–1197, 1200,
1233
Kearsley, Dr., 664–665
Keaton, Patrick, 354
Kemble, Margaret, 505
Kempenfelt, Richard, 1242
Kent, Benjamin, 691
Kenton, Simon, 1193
Kentucky, Indian attacks in, 1229–1231
Kerr, Joseph, 1428
Kettle Creek, battle at, 1310–1312
"Key to Liberty" (Manning), 64–66
Kilbuck, 1152
Killroy, Matthew, 337, 338, 352, 357
King, Rufus, 1117
King-Fisher, 1110
King George's War, 122
King William's War, 122
King's American Dragoons, 1759
King's American Rangers, 1428, 1760
King's College (Columbia), 75
Kings Mountain, Battle of, 1424–1435, 1825
consequences of, 1432–1433
as re-enactment of engagement at
Ramsour's Mill, 1433
Kingston, N.Y., burning of, 932
Kip's Bay, "battle" of, 761–767
Hessians at, 765–766
Kirkwood, Robert, 1505, 1688, 1690
Knight, Dr., 1226
Knowlton, Thomas, 518–519, 769–771
Knox, George, 1348
Knox, Henry, 712, 876, 960, 1664
and André, 1589–1590
and Arnold court-martial, 1559
and Boston Cadets, 408
and Boston Massacre, 334, 337
celebrates French alliance, 1132
and defenses around Boston, 539, 566
at Dorchester Heights, 650
drags cannon from Ticonderoga to Boston,
649
at Germantown, 966
at head of "select corps" marching through
New York City, 1788
on Howe's failure to take Philadelphia, 887
at New York, 725–727
on officer corps, 776

on scarcity of supplies in Washington's
army, 1665
and Society of Cincinnatus, 1783
supports attack on New York, 1083
threatens resignation, 975–976
at Trenton, 816–817, 820, 821
at Valley Forge, 998, 1000
at Washington's farewell party, 1790
at West Point, 1588
at Yorktown, 1701
Knox, John, 255
Knox, Lucy, 1810
Knox, William, 1121
Knyphausen, Wilhelm von, 963, 1648
and Arnold, 1565
attacked by Stirling, 1529
at Brandywine, 951–954
checked at Springfield Bridge, 1528–1529
in command at New York, 1515
at Connecticut Farms, 1528–1529
at Fort Washington, 793, 794
loots Hackensack, N.J., 1527
makes foray into New Jersey, 1526–1533
at Monmouth, 1087, 1090, 1092, 1095
raids Westchester County, 1124
reattacks Springfield, 1530–1531
recruiting activities of, 1527
size of army under command of, 1527
at Trenton, 814, 821, 827
Kosciusko, Thaddeus, 922–923, 1447, 1466
at Ninety-Six, 1503
Krafft, John Charles Philip von, 1761
Kyashota, 1152

Lacey, Edward, 1443
Lady William, 631
Lafayette, James, 1653
Lafayette, Marquis de, 973–977, 991, 1056,
1273, 1795
and Adams, 1734
advises restraint, 1084
and André, 1589–1590
and Arnold, 1565, 1598–1599, 1624–1626,
1628
vs. Arnold, 1624–1626, 1628–1630
on arrival of French army, 1646
attempts expedition against Canada, 1079
in Baltimore, 1629
at Barren Hill, 1079–1081
at Battle of Rhode Island, 1109, 1112, 1114,
1116, 1117, 1119–1120
at Brandywine, 956, 976
and Conway Cabal, 1025
and Cornwallis, 1649–1650
and De Grasse, 1694, 1709
desertions from, 1626
at Fort Mercer, 989–990

at Green Spring Farm, 1650–1653
and Greene, 1629
and Hamilton, 1630–1631
and Lee, 1087–1090, 1101–1102
at Monmouth, 1087–1090, 1095, 1096,
1098, 1101–1102
and Morgan, 1633
at Morristown, 1525
and Peggy Arnold, 1588
and Pennsylvania mutineers, 1614–1615
and Phillips, 1629–1630
at Richmond, 1630
on Southerners, 1627
and Steuben, 1626, 1629, 1634, 1635
and Tarleton, 1632–1633
and Vergennes, 1639–1641
visits Cornwallis after surrender, 1709
and Washington, 976–977, 1079–1081,
1087, 1088, 1133, 1513, 1524, 1627–
1630, 1633, 1654–1666, 1670, 1693,
1746
on Washington's weeping at Arnold's
treason, 1584
and Wayne, 1633–1636, 1650–1651
at Yorktown, 1701, 1707
Lake, Gerard, 1703
Lamb, General, 1699
Lamb, John, 600, 883, 930, 1588
Lamb, Roger, 1750
Lamb, Sergeant, 929, 1482
Land speculation, 168–169, 845–846, 1193,
1787
Landais, Pierre, 1273–1276, 1280, 1284, 1288
vs. Jones, 1290–1291
reclaims command of Alliance, 1290–1292
Landgraf, von, 1527
Landon, John, 90
Lane, Joseph, 1307–1308
Langford, Edward, 334, 339, 352
Langlad, Charles de, 1200
Languedoc, 1107, 1111
La Salle, Robert Cavelier de, 1192
Lathrop, John, 347
Laud, William, 53
Laumoy, Chevalier de, 990, 1382
Laurens, Henry, 96, 246, 258, 626, 1057
and Adams, 1730–1731, 1736, 1737
captured and imprisoned by British, 1730
and Carlisle commission, 1069–1071
in Continental Congress, 840, 841, 1141,
1145–1146
and Conway Cabal, 1020, 1025
and Deane-Lee dispute, 1140–1142, 1362
and Franklin, 1737
on French troops at Newport, 1111
on inflation riot, 1368
on North's conciliatory bills, 1068, 1073

Laurens, Henry (*cont.*):
  and Oswald, 1730, 1735
  and peace negotiations, 1730, 1735–1737
  on pensions for officers, 1027–1029
  resigns as president of Congress, 1141, 1149
  and Shelburne, 1730
  and South Carolina constitution, 855
  and Stamp Act riots, 209–211
  stipulates that British take no Negroes upon
    withdrawal from America, 1737
  Sullivan complains about French alliance to,
    1114–1115
  supports New England's demand for access
    to fishing waters, 1362
  and Washington, 1146
Laurens, John, 966, 1103, 1191, 1353, 1795
  in attack on Savannah, 1335
  at Battle of Monmouth, 1091–1092
  on celebration of French alliance, 1056
  at Charles Town, 1319–1320, 1325–1326,
    1386, 1392
  on Congress' failure to inform Washington
    of secret articles of French treaty, 1057
  on Conway, 1022
  and D'Estaing, 1108
  and Hamilton, 1591
  as line of communication between Congress
    and Washington, 1057, 1146
  obtains money from France, 1667
  and Pennsylvania mutineers, 1614, 1615
  and plan to enlist slaves, 1805–1806
  sent to France to secure money, 1644
  at Valley Forge, 993, 1009, 1010, 1014–
    1016
  and Washington, 1146, 1555
  wounds Lee in duel, 1105
Lauzun, Duc de, 1697, 1709, 1752
Lawson, John, 110–111
Lawson, Robert, 1476, 1479, 1481
Lawyers, as theoreticians of Revolution, 254–
  257
Learned, Ebenezer, 913, 914, 923–924, 936
Lechmere Point, fortification of, 649
Lecky, William:
  on East India Company agents, 374
  on English public opinion (1775–1776), 865
  on English who favor enforcement of Stamp
    Act, 238
  on George III, 870–871
  on Grenville, 169
  on Lord George Gordon Riots, 1550
  on Lord North, 294
  on Pitt the Elder, 239
Lee, Arthur, 280, 843, 1240, 1253, 1791
  British intercept letter of, 1597
  and Deane, 1138–1143, 1146
  and Duane, 1597

  and French alliance, 1047, 1049, 1051–1053
  Houston's evaluation of, 1143
  and Landais, 1290–1292
  and peace negotiations, 1729, 1730
  on taxation by Congress, 1765
Lee, Charles, 555, 564, 919, 1795
  accuses Hamilton of perjury, 1105
  at Battle of Monmouth, 1087–1094, 1098,
    1100, 1101
  at Battle of White Plains, 784
  Belknap's characterization of, 566
  capture of, 809–810, 888, 1032
  and Clinton, 1082, 1083
  in command of Southern Department, 627–
    636
  and Conway, 1019
  court-martial of, 1090, 1092, 1103
  exchanged for Prescott, 890
  and Fort Washington, 791
  and fortification of New York, 712–713
  and Gates, 1408, 1417
  on Howe, 1035
  and Lafayette, 1080–1081, 1087–1090,
    1101–1102
  on loss of Fort Washington, 797
  madness of, 1103–1105
  and New Jersey campaign, 803, 804, 806–
    810
  on readiness of Americans to fight, 413
  and re-enlistment problem, 580
  on riflemen, 573
  treasonous behavior of, 1081–1083, 1102
  and Washington, 1081–1083, 1086, 1087,
    1093–1095, 1102–1103, 1105
  vs. Washington as commander in chief, 546–
    547, 553, 824
  on Wayne's victory at Stony Point, 1349
Lee, Francis Lightfoot, 1141
Lee, Henry ("Light-Horse Harry"), 208, 1191,
  1307, 1342, 1791, 1795
  on attack on Augusta, 1424
  attacks Paulus Hook, 1353–1358
  career of, 1507–1508
  on condition of troops retreating from
    Cornwallis, 1467
  on Cowpens, 1459–1460
  on Green Spring Farm, 1651–1652
  at Eutaw Springs, 1688–1690
  at Fort Cornwallis, 1500–1502
  at Fort Galphin, 1499
  at Fort Granby, 1497–1498
  at Fort Motte, 1496, 1497
  on Greene, 1448, 1469
  at Guilford Court House, 1478–1482
  on Guilford Court House, 1484, 1485
  and Hamilton, 1357–1358
  on Hobkirk's Hill, 1494

impersonates Tarleton, 1471
instructed to kidnap Arnold, 1595
on lack of hostility between Greene's and Cornwallis' forces, 1468
on Lincoln, 1316, 1317
on militia, 1420
on Morgan, 1453–1454
at Morristown, 1530, 1531
at Ninety-Six, 1503–1505
in pursuit of Cornwallis, 1470, 1477
in retreat from Cornwallis, 1466–1469
on riflemen, 1425
on Rutledge, 1318
and slavery, 1425, 1805
in South Carolina campaign, 1489–1492, 1495–1507
on Southern horsemanship, 1473
on success of South Carolina campaign, 1506–1507
on surrender of Rudgley, 1447
vs. Tarleton, 1467–1468, 1470–1475, 1478
on Wahab family, 1421
and Washington, 1508, 1530, 1555, 1595, 1596
on Waxhaw Massacre, 1397
vs. Webster, 1475, 1476
and Whiskey Rebellion, 1508
Lee, Matilda, 1508
Lee, Richard Henry, 369, 683, 848, 1194, 1791
on Articles of Confederation, 1143
on British success in South, 1399
on Burgoyne's invasion, 893–894
and congressional finances, 1148
and Conway, 1021
and Deane, 1141, 1143
on depreciation of paper money, 1366
at First Continental Congress, 427–428, 432–433, 438, 442
and French alliance, 1044, 1054
on inflation, 1364
and Lee's (Charles) court-martial, 1103
and strategy for independence, 686–687, 689, 691–693, 702
supports New England's demand for access to fishing waters, 1362
and Virginia constitution, 851
vs. Washington, 1019, 1025
Lee, Robert E., 1508
Lee, Thomas Ludiwell, 851
Lee, William, 1141–1143
Legge, William (see Dartmouth, Earl of)
Legislatures, Adams on, 849
Leisler, Jacob, 76
L'Enfant, Pierre, 1009
Lennox, Charles, 868
Lenox, Major, 1367
Leonard, Daniel, 404, 448–449

Leonidas, 1148–1149
Leslie, Alexander, 456, 465–467
agrees to return slaves to former owners, 1748–1749
and Cornwallis, 1451, 1469, 1480
frees slaves, 1749
moves from New York to Charles Town, 1435–1436
on Negroes with smallpox, 1803
Leslie, Thomas, 814, 831
Lester, Lucretia, 74
Letters from an American Farmer (Crèvecoeur), 158–160
Letters of marque (see Privateers)
Levant, 1260
Levelers, 55–57
Lewis, Francis, 1081
Lewis, Meriwether, 1234
Lewis, William, 1366, 1368
Lewis, Wyndham, 1819–1821
Lexington, 1255, 1264
Lexington and Concord, Battle of, 470–484, 743, 1074
aftermath of, 489–495
American reaction to, 490–493
English reaction to, 490, 493–495, 866
Liberty incident, 281–286, 300, 321, 324
Liberty Society, 1302
Lilburne, John, 55, 56
Lillie, Theophilus, 326
Lillington, Alexander, 624–625
Lincoln, Abraham, 8
Lincoln, Benjamin, 803, 876, 878, 884, 1160, 1543, 1795
attacks British at Stono Ferry, 1327–1329
at Charles Town, 1319–1321, 1323, 1326, 1381–1383, 1385–1392, 1469
in command of Southern Department, 1304, 1309, 1312, 1315–1317
at Freeman's Farm, 924
and Lafayette, 1079
marches to Augusta, 1318
and mutiny of furloughed troops, 1777
at Saratoga, 936, 1317
at Savannah, 1332, 1334, 1336, 1337
on states vs. Congress, 1765–1766
superintends details of British surrender, 1707–1708
threatens British at Savannah, 1319
and Washington, 1670
Wereat appeals for support to, 1303
at Yorktown, 1701
Lindsay, John, 1158
Line, Colonel, 957–958
Lippincott, Richard, 1750–1751
Little, Luther, 1293–1294
Little Neck, N.J., engagement at, 1124

Littleton, Thomas, 254
Livingston, Henry, 928, 1098, 1117
Livingston, James, 599, 600
Livingston, Colonel James, 1574, 1577
Livingston, Peter, 421, 719–720
Livingston, Philip, 220, 422
Livingston, Robert, 212, 220, 223, 693, 694
    and New York constitution, 855–856
    and peace negotiations, 1730, 1732
    and preliminary treaty with England, 1768
    proposes reduction of army, 1520–1521
Livingston, William, 276, 422, 426, 432, 1028, 1143
    asks New Jersey legislature to free all slaves, 1802
Livius, Peter, 1559–1560
Lochry, Archibald, 1181
Locke, Colonel, 1399–1403
Locke, John, 47, 181, 254, 848
    and *Common Sense*, 680
    and Declaration of Independence, 696–698
    and First Continental Congress' Declaration and Resolves, 443
    and Fundamental Constitutions of Carolina, 25
    as member of Board of Trade and Plantations, 137
Logan, William, 635
Logistics, 781
London, 1676–1679, 1683
Long, Colonel, 900–901, 904
Long Island, Battle of, 730–744
    aftermath of, 745–746
    Hessians at, 730–731, 741–742
Looting and destruction:
    in New Jersey, 836–837
    in Philadelphia, 1033–1035
    in South Carolina, 1330
Lord George Gordon Riots, 1548–1552
Loring, Mrs., 1036
Lossberg, von, 807, 814
Lossing, Benson, 1161, 1308, 1438
Louis XIV, king of France, 57, 122
Louis XVI, king of France, 878, 970, 1052–1053, 1362, 1716
Lovell, James, 898, 1020, 1029, 1149, 1362, 1521
    on election of peace commissioner, 1363
    and Great Seal, 1766
    and Jay, 1538
    and peace negotiations, 1729
    as sole member of committee on foreign affairs, 1538
Lovell, Solomon, 1358–1359
Low, Isaac, 442
Lowendahl, Comtesse de, 1290
Lower Fort, 1181

Lowther, James, 1719–1721
Loyal Americans, 1760
Loyal Legion, 1354, 1382–1383, 1441, 1697
    at Camden, 1411, 1415
    at Cowpens, 1454, 1457, 1458
    at Charlotte, 1423
    leaves America after Yorktown, 1760
    in Virginia, 1630–1633, 1636
    and Waxhaw Massacre, 1395–1396
    (*See also* British Legion; Tarleton, Banastre)
Loyalists (*see* Tories)
Luck, role of, 1474–1475, 1687–1688, 1714
Lumbrozo, Jacob, 34
Luther, Martin, 153–155
Luzerne, Chevalier de la, 1521, 1524–1525, 1564, 1598
    and Congress, 1637–1638
    gives feast in honor of French army, 1667
    and peace negotiations, 1729–1730, 1768
    and Rochambeau, 1663
    and Vergennes, 1637–1638, 1739
Lyman, Simeon, 580
Lynch, Charles, 1479–1481
Lynch, Thomas:
    at First Continental Congress, 424, 425, 430, 438, 441–442
    at Stamp Act Congress, 220
Lynnhaven Bay:
    British fleet in, 1675
    French fleet in, 1670, 1671, 1675, 1676, 1685
Lyon, Ben, 1193
Lyttle, Lieutenant Colonel, 1312
Lyttleton, Lord, 239, 1371

McAllister, Lieutenant, 1356
McArthur, Archibald, 1398, 1451, 1457–1458
McCall, James, 1453
McCarthy, Mary, 1569
Macaulay, Catharine, 866–867
McCauley, William, 337
McClure, David, 63
McCrea, Jane, 906, 920
M'Daniel, Sergeant, 632
Macdonald, Donald, 624–625
McDonald, Donald, 1187
McDonald, Francis, 1347
McDonnell, Captain, 1160
MacDougall, Alexander, 394, 879, 885, 962
    on army's difficulties with Congress, 1764, 1765
    at Battle of Germantown, 964, 967
    at Battle of Golden Hill, 313–315
    at Battle of Princeton, 829
    at Battle of White Plains, 786
    commands forces in Highlands, 1124, 1131

entertains Massachusetts congressional
delegation in New York, 421–422
named secretary of marine, 1538
with Washington in New York, 717, 719
McDowell, Charles, 1425, 1430, 1453
McEvers, James, 208
McGary, Hugh, 1230
McGinnis, Richard, 1156, 1157
M'Girth, Colonel, 1310
Machias-Liberty, 642
M'Intosh, Colonel, 1325
McIntosh, Ebenezer, 201–203, 205
McIntosh, George, 1302
McIntosh, John, 1307, 1308, 1319
McIntosh, Lachlan, 1178, 1179, 1192, 1335
vs. Gwinnett, 1301–1302
Mackay, Colonel, 320
McKean, Thomas, 424, 1070, 1146, 1664
on congressional resolution on
independence, 687
and Declaration of Independence, 701–702
at Stamp Act Congress, 220
Mackenzie, Frederick, 13–14, 486, 715
on captured mail pouch, 1648
on Clinton, 1108–1109
on condition of fighting men, 798
on dividing of army into numerous
detachments, 1658
and Fort Washington, 793
on Graves's fleet, 1687
on Hale, 774
at Harlem Heights, 772
on Howe, 765–766, 781
on New York fire, 773
on Pennsylvania mutineers, 1611, 1612
on state of Continental Army, 780
McLane, Allan, 1191
and Arnold, 1355, 1558
confronts Philadelphia mob, 1367
at Paulus Hook, 1353–1356
at Stony Point, 1344, 1345, 1347
and Washington, 1355, 1558
MacLean, Allan, 614, 1038–1039
McLellan, Plato, 1804
McNeill, Captain, 1255–1258
McPherson, Captain, 1497
MacPherson, William, 1635, 1650
McQueen, Alexander, 1438
Macutte Mong, 1209
Madison, James, 94, 104, 851, 1539, 1640
and Chastellux, 1752–1753, 1814
and Harrison, 1764
on inflation, 1645
and Jefferson, 1780
on parochialism in Congress, 1764
and peace negotiations, 1729
and Randolph, 1768

on republican form of government, 1773–
1774
supports congressional power, 1643
on terms of preliminary peace treaty, 1767–
1768
on Yorktown, 1711
Magaw, Robert, 747
and Fort Washington, 792, 793, 795
Maham, Hezekiah, 1491, 1500
Maine:
British navy threatens, 1358–1359
naval adventures in, 641–642
Maitland, John, 1305, 1328–1329
at Savannah, 1332–1335
Majoribanks, John, 1689–1691
Manchester, Duke of, 1744
Manley, Captain, 1255–1258
Manly, John, 644
Mann, Horace, 1547
Manning, William, 64–65
Mansfield, Earl of, 1549–1550
Marblehead Amphibians, 747, 748
Marbury, Colonel, 1312, 1313, 1315
Marchant, Henry, 1138
Marcy, William, 486
Margaretta, capture of, 641–642
Marine Committee, 834, 1248, 1253–1254
Marion, Francis, 1321, 1323, 1409, 1436–
1439, 1446, 1689
at Charles Town, 1438
at Fort Motte, 1496, 1497
in South Carolina campaign, 1489–1492,
1495–1497, 1502, 1504, 1508–1509
Marsaillais, 1676, 1678
Marseilles, 1111
Marshall, Christopher, 393
Marshall, John, 94, 816, 1000, 1415
on Revolutionary women, 1813
Marston Moor, Battle of, 54
Martin, Joseph, 780, 792, 959
and ambush of Hessians near White Plains,
1125–1126
and Arnold, 1571
on attacks on Fort Mercer, 983, 988
on attacks on Fort Mifflin, 984–988
at Battle of Germantown, 965, 967–968,
970–971
at Battle of Long Island, 736–737
at Battle of Monmouth, 1090–1091, 1093,
1096–1098
at Battle of White Plains, 783–785, 787–
789
on black soldier's capture of British officer,
1803–1804
and Burgoyne's surrender, 939–940
at Burlington, N.J., 1747–1748
on Chestnut Hill, 993

Martin, Joseph (cont.):
  and deception of Clinton at New York,
    1659–1660
  on drunken brawls of Irish soldiers, 1127–
    1128
  on enlisted man's life, 778, 1127–1130
  on end of war, 1786–1787
  and evacuation of Brooklyn, 747
  and evacuation of Philadelphia, 1086
  on fighting in Connecticut, 882–883
  gets smallpox inoculation, 884
  on hardships of soldiers, 1830–1831
  at Harlem Heights, 768–769, 772
  on last winter of war, 1786
  at Morristown, 1514, 1516, 1524
  on mutinous conduct of troops at Basking
    Ridge, 1516–1518
  on mutinous conduct of troops at Danbury,
    1128–1129
  in Philadelphia, 1665, 1671
  re-enlistment of, 880–881
  and retreat from New York, 761, 763–765,
    768
  returns to White Plains, 1106–1107, 1338
  sails down Delaware to rejoin army, 1671
  searches out Tories, 1126–1127
  on sectional animosity, 1134–1135
  at Staten Island, 1515–1516
  on Thanksgiving (1777), 993–994
  at Valley Forge, 997, 1001–1002, 1007–
    1008, 1012
  in Washington's march to Virginia, 1665
  at West Point, 568
  in Williamsburg, 1695–1696
  wounded in engagement with "cowboys,"
    1660
  at Yorktown, 1695–1699
Martin, Josiah, 471, 624, 661–662
Martin's Station, capitulation of, 1215
Maryland, 83–85, 275
  constitution of, 855
  indentured servants in, 36, 38
  opposes independence, 691
  as paradise for women, 84–85
  ratifies Articles of Confederation, 1642
  settlement of, 23–24
  and Stamp Act, 198, 211
Masères, Francis, 186
Mason (British agent), 1616–1618
Mason, Colonel, 1328
Mason, David, 466
Mason, George (Boston Tory), 303
Mason, George (Virginia patriot), 94, 104,
    1121
  and Clark's expedition to Old Northwest,
    1191, 1194, 1195, 1201, 1216
  on repeal of Stamp Act, 247–248

  and slavery, 1806, 1828
  and Virginia Bill of Rights, 696–700, 850
  and Virginia constitution, 851
Masons, 1161–1162
  in Boston, 306, 464
  honor Washington, 1131
  initiate Negroes, 1802
Massachusetts, 1264
Massachusetts:
  commissions privateers, 1262
  delegates to First Continental Congress,
    418–429, 436, 438–439
  delegates to Second Continental Congress,
    543
  Great and General Court, 200–201, 204,
    219, 273, 286–288, 311–312, 320, 323,
    369, 418, 1800
  navy of, 1261, 1264, 1358–1360
  prohibits importation and sale of slaves,
    1800
Massachusetts Bay Colony, 20–23
  (See also Boston)
Massachusetts Government Act, 401–405, 407,
    410
  English debate over, 402–403
Massachusetts Provincial Congress, 458, 463,
    473, 496–497, 500–501, 544
  and friction between Arnold and Allen,
    592–593
Massasoit, 17
Mather, Cotton, 66–67, 157
Mather, Increase, 143
Mather, Samuel, 1055
Mathew, Edward, 1624
Mathews, John, 1144, 1614, 1748–1749
Matlack, Timothy, 857, 863, 1368
  vs. Arnold, 1557
Matthews, David, 718–721, 794–796, 951
Mattoon, Ebenezer, 924
Maurepas, Comte de, 1718
Maury, James, 95
Maverick, Samuel, 339, 340
Mawhood, Charles, 832–833
Maxwell, Major, 1498
Maxwell, William, 829–830, 877, 886, 1083,
    1495
  at Brandywine, 950–952, 956
  court-martial of, 991
  on expedition against Indians and Tories,
    1167
  at Germantown, 964, 966
  harasses Clinton's advance guard, 1085–
    1086
  at Monmouth, 1086, 1087, 1091, 1098
  at Morristown, 1528
  at Springfield, 1531
Mayflower Compact, 154–155

Meals, American, as seen by French commissary officer, 1647–1648
Medea, 1686
Meeker, Major, 1160–1161
Meigs, Return Jonathan, 1345, 1517
Mein, John, 323–325
Mennonites, 45
Mercantilism, 133–141
Mercer, Hugh, 716, 819, 832–834
Mercer, John Francis, 1636, 1652
Mercury, 1730
Meredith, Thomas, 663–664
Meserve, George, 208–209
"Mess," 712, 785
Middle Brook, Washington's headquarters at, 1131–1133, 1338
   (*See also* Bound Brook)
Middleton, Arthur, 424, 1766
Middleton, Charles, 1241–1242
Middleton, Henry, 96
Midwives, 74
Mifflin, John, 1366
Mifflin, Thomas, 396, 397, 424, 428, 436
   and Battle of Princeton, 830
   and Conway Cabal, 1019, 1022, 1024, 1025
   defends Wilson against mob, 1366
   and evacuation of Brooklyn, 747–750
   in Philadelphia, 962
   promoted to major general, 878
   receives Washington's commission, 1791–1792
   requests command, 1081
   at Trenton, 823
   with Washington in New York, 716
Miles, Samuel, 737, 739, 741
Milford vs. *Yankee Hero*, 1263
Military expenditures, British, 1374–1375
Militia, 62–63, 170, 459, 577, 777–778
   atrocities committed by, against Christian Indians, 1220–1221
   vs. Continental Army, 777–778
   desertions from, 1320, 1329
   enlistments in, for attack on Newport, 1109
   gathering of, after Lexington and Concord, 496–501
   and Greene, 1446
   join Philadelphia mob in riot, 1367–1368
   Lee on use of, 1420
   limitations and strengths of, 1434
   Massachusetts, 463
   under Morgan, 1454, 1460
   Negroes in, 1806
   at Noodle Island, 507–509
   sympathy of, with Pennsylvania mutineers, 1615
   Washington's comments on, 754, 777

(*See also* Lexington and Concord, Battle of; Continental Army, formation of; Minutemen)
Miller, Adam, 911
Milton, John, 56, 848
Minden, Battle of, 1630
Minerva, 642, 1259–1260
Minisink, Indian and Tory attack on, 1160–1162
Minnigrode, Lieutenant Colonel, 982
"Minor" encounters, 1124–1125
Minutemen, 459, 463, 464, 491
   as elite corps, 497, 577
   at Lexington and Concord, 479–480, 482, 484
Miralles, Juan de, 1525
"Mischianza" in Philadelphia, 1039–1041, 1556
Misère, 1193
Mitchell, Major, 476–477
Mittelberger, Gottlieb, 42, 80
Moffat, Thomas, 205–206
Mohawk Valley, raided by Tories and Indians, 1158, 1160–1162, 1180–1182, 1184
Molasses Act of 1733, 136–137, 171
Molesworth, Ponsonby, 304–306
Molineux, Will, 327, 343–345, 348, 408
   and Boston Massacre, 342
   and Boston Tea Party, 377–378
Monarch, 1679
Monarcha, 1542
Monck's Corner, 1427, 1438
Monckton, Lieutenant Colonel, 1098, 1099
Moncrieff, James, 1749
Money, paper, depreciation of, 1132, 1145, 1147, 1336, 1364–1366, 1523–1524
   (*See also* Inflation)
Monk, Christopher, 339, 358–359
Monmouth, Battle of, 1086–1105
   British deserters at, 1099
   Hessians at, 1095
   Lee in command at, 1088–1093, 1101
   practical gains of, 1100
   Washington takes command at, 1094
   Washington's mistakes at, 1088–1089, 1094, 1100–1101, 1712, 1796
Monmouth, Duke of, 29
Monroe, James, 816, 820, 822, 1000
Montagu, 1675, 1679, 1681
Montagu, John, 365, 379, 380, 1264–1265
   (*See also* Sandwich, Earl of)
Montcalm, Louis Joseph de, 127
Montesquieu, Baron de, 696
Montesquieu, Baron de (grandson of philosopher), 973
Montgomery, 1245
Montgomery, Hugh, 337, 338, 355–357
Montgomery, John, 1779

Montgomery, Richard, 930, 1794–1795
   in assault on Quebec, 613–615, 618, 619
   and invasion of Canada, 553–556, 595, 598–
      605
Montreal, occupation of, 605, 743
Montresor, John, 652, 1037
Moody, John, 1648
Moore, James, 624
Moore, John, 1399, 1401, 1404
Moore, Sam, 1193
Moravian Indians, atrocities committed
      against, 1219–1221
Moravians, 45, 83, 1002, 1219
More, Comte de, 976
Morgan, Daniel, 95, 920, 962, 1192, 1795
   with Arnold on march to Quebec, 608, 611,
      616–617
   and Battle of Cowpens, 1449–1454, 1456–
      1460
   at Chestnut Hill, 992
   commissioned brigadier general, 1444
   vs. Cornwallis, 1464–1466
   dispatched to South Carolina, 1447
   at Freeman's Farm, 923–926, 928
   vs. Gates, 1444
   and Greene, 1447, 1449, 1451, 1452, 1459,
      1465, 1466, 1479
   and Lafayette, 1633
   at Monmouth, 1086, 1090, 1092, 1101
   in New Jersey campaign, 886
   resigns commission, 1444, 1466
   at Saratoga, 934, 936, 938
   vs. Tarleton, 1449, 1451–1454, 1458
Morris, Gouverneur, 665
   and Carlisle commission, 1070
   on conciliatory bills, 1068, 1069
   and Conway Cabal, 1029–1030
   on French alliance, 1069
   on inflation, 1365–1366
   on Lee court-martial, 1103
   and New York constitution, 855–856
   at Valley Forge, 1000
Morris, Lewis, Jr., 1483
Morris, Robert, 828, 846, 878, 1070, 1247
   defends Wilson against mob, 1366, 1368
   named superintendent of finance, 1538
   and peace treaty, 1781
   and Pennsylvania constitution, 861, 863
   and Rochambeau, 1667–1668
   as secretary of marine, 1248
   on states' failure to pay Congress, 1762
   takes measures to deal with inflation, 1644
   and Washington, 1657, 1662–1665, 1669
Morris, Mrs. Robert, 1667
Morristown, N.J.:
   desperate conditions at (1779–1780), 1513–
      1516, 1519

Knyphausen starts campaign against
      (1780), 1526–1528, 1530, 1532
   mutinous conduct at (1779–1780), 1516–
      1518
   Washington winters at (1777), 875–880
   Washington winters at (1779–1780), 1513–
      1517
Morton, James, 702
Morton, Robert, 1034–1035
Morton, Thomas, 17–18
Motte, Mrs., 1496–1497
Moultrie, Captain, 1387
Moultrie, William, 626, 628–636, 1664
   attacks Beaufort, 1310
   at Charles Town, 1319–1322, 1325–1326,
      1381, 1388, 1389
   and Cherokee Expedition, 1437
   and Laurens, 1319–1320
   on Pulaski, 1322
   takes command at Charles Town, 1322–
      1323
   on war in Georgia, 1307, 1309, 1310
Mount Defiance, 932
Mount Hope, 932
Mount Independence, 899–900, 903, 932
Mount Kemble, 1600–1603
   dissatisfactions of troops at, 602–604
   huts at, 1601–1602
   mutiny at (see Pennsylvania Line, mutiny of)
   St. Clair takes command of nonmutineers at,
      1615
   women and children at, 1602
Mount Vernon:
   British reception at, 1627
   Washington retires to, 1792
   Washington visits, 1669–1670, 1746
Mowat, Henry, 645–647
Moylan, Stephen, 998
Mugford, James, 1246
Muhlenberg, Peter, 951, 1083
Munroe, William, 475, 486
Murfree, Hardy, 1345, 1346
Murray, Delia, 1290
Murray, James, 305, 323, 338, 753
Murray, John (see Dunmore, Earl of)
Murray, Robert, 766
Murray, William, 1290
Musgrave, Thomas, 964–966
Musgrove's Mill, engagement at, 1404
Muskets vs. rifles, 556–557
Mutinous conduct of American troops:
   at Basking Ridge, 1516–1518
   at Danbury, 1128–1129
   at Morristown, 1516–1518
   of New Jersey Line, 1621–1623
   of Pennsylvania Line, 1605–1623
   in Philadelphia, after Yorktown, 1777–1778

Mutiny Act (1765), 264
Myers, Lieutenant, 465

Nancy, capture of, 644, 1245–1246
Nash, Abner, 1398
Nash, Colonel, 634, 964
Natanis, 613
Naval "militia" (*see* State navies)
Naval warfare, 6, 637–647, 1238–1260, 1678
  off Boston, 1246
  and Bushnell's "water machine," 1248–1250
  established pattern of, 1242–1245
  at New Providence, 1250–1251, 1257
  off Southern coast, 1257
  (*See also Bonhomme Richard* vs. *Serapis;*
    Capes, Battle of; Charles Town, siege
    of; *Drake* vs. *Ranger;* Navy, British;
    Navy, Continental; Navy, French;
    Penobscot Bay, expedition against;
    Privateers; *Protector* vs. *Admiral Duff;*
    Rhode Island, Battle of; State navies;
    Trumbull vs. *Iris* and *General Monck;*
    Trumbull vs. *Watt*)
Navigation acts, 135–136, 170–171
Navy, British:
  vs. American privateers, 1296–1297
  attacks coastal towns, 1121
  in Battle of Rhode Island, 1110–1112, 1118
  at Boston, 1121–1122
  captures Dutch ships, 1541–1542
  captures Spanish ships, 1542
  conditions in, 638, 1240–1242
  desertions from, 639, 1241
  at end of 1780, 1295
  vs. French fleet, 1107–1108, 1628
    at Chesapeake, 1674–1688
    in West Indies, 1542–1543
  guerrilla tactics against, 637–647
  number of vessels in, 1240
  at Penobscot Bay, 1358–1359
  prison ship in, 1266–1267
  superiority of, 1132
  in West Indies, 1542–1543
  (*See also* Impressment; Press gangs)
Navy, Continental:
  and Adams, 1239, 1240, 1253–1255
  birth and growth of, 642–645, 647, 843,
    1239–1240, 1245, 1248
  and Bushnell's "water machine," 1248–1250
  condition of, in 1777, 1254–1255
  and cruising for prizes, 1252
  and Deane, 1254
  at end of 1778, 1269
  at end of 1780, 1295
  at Fort Mercer, 979–980
  and Franklin, 1254
  loses *Hancock,* 1255–1257

and Jones, 647, 1238, 1246–1248, 1252
  Negroes in, 1803, 1806
  officers of, 1246–1248
  at Penobscot Bay, 1358–1360
  problems of, 1252–1253, 1255
  raids New Providence, 1250–1251, 1257
  sanitation and health problems in, 1253
  ships' guns and figureheads in, 1245
  use of captured British sailors by, 1273
Navy, French:
  and Arnold, 1625, 1628
  arrives off Chesapeake, 1668, 1672
  at Battle of Rhode Island, 1109–1111,
    1113–1114, 1120
  at Boston, 1120–1122
  blockaded in harbor of Brest, 1536
  vs. British fleet, 1107–1108, 1628
    at Chesapeake, 1674–1688
    in West Indies, 1542–1543
  clashes with American seamen, 1120–1121
  off New York, 1107–1108
Navy, Spanish, vs. British fleet in West Indies,
  1542–1543
Negroes, 1798–1807
  abandoned starving by Cornwallis, 1696–
    1697
  in Arnold's treason plot, 1577
  at Boston Massacre, 355
  British agree not to take, upon withdrawal
    from America, 1737, 1757–1758
  with British forces, 332, 1393–1394, 1399,
    1625, 1798
  at Camden, 1409
  captured by British, 1342
  captured at Camden, 1495
  captured at Stony Point, 1348–1349
  at College of New Jersey, 1799
  in Continental Army, 752, 1118, 1803–1806
  at Cowpens, 1457
  in defense of Charles Town, 628
  desert to British, 622, 1324, 1329–1330,
    1381, 1393–1394, 1798, 1803
  dying of smallpox at Yorktown, 1709
  free, 80, 101, 1799, 1801–1802, 1804, 1806
    ask full rights as citizens, 1799
  Hamilton on, 1805–1806
  in Kaskaskia, 1193
  killed by Indians, 1156
  killed in Philadelphia mob action, 1368
  killed at Yorktown, 1700
  and Lafayette's pursuit of Cornwallis, 1649
  leave with British, 1759–1760
  as Masons, 1802
  in navy and on privateers, 1803, 1806
  petition Massachusetts to be relieved of
    taxes, 1802
  at siege of Charles Town, 1383, 1385

Negroes (*cont.*):
as spies for Continental forces, 1653
sue for freedom in Northern courts,
1800
testify at Boston Massacre trial, 351
at Ticonderoga, 1806
with Tories in New York, 719, 1168
(*See also* Anaka; Andrew; Attucks, Crispus;
Billy; Dolley, Quamino; Jack; James;
Quaumino, John; Sampson; Slave
trade; Slavery; Slaves; Wheatley,
Phillis; Yamma, Bristol)
Neilson's Farm, 933
Nelson, Thomas, 1625
Netherlands (*see* Holland)
New Brunswick, N.J., 805, 807
New England, 61–75, 105
communities of, 61–67, 74–75
education in, 62, 67
English view of, 187–188
Hartford convention (1780), 1537–1538
and mercantilism, 134
military camps of, 566–571
sexual practices in, 69–70
and Stamp Act, 200–209, 211
women in, 72–74
New Englanders:
demand access to fishing waters off
Newfoundland and Nova Scotia, 1361–
1363
fraternization with British by, 569
pressure for independence by, 685, 690
Washington's opinion of, 566
New Hampshire:
constitution of, 856–857, 859
and Indians, 1151
New Haven, raided by British, 1343, 1513
New Jersey:
British invasion of, 802–810
constitution of, 854
Hessians in, 807, 813–814, 819–825, 827,
830–831, 835–836, 886
Knuyphausen's raid into, 1526–1533
looting, destruction, and atrocities in, 835–
837, 881–882
recaptured by Washington, 875–876
settlement of, 23
Tories in, 1462
New Jersey campaign (*see* Howe in New Jersey;
Monmouth, Battle of; Princeton, Battle
of; Trenton, Battle of)
New Jersey Line, mutiny of, 1621–1623
New Jersey Volunteers (Tory), 1428
New Providence, naval raids on, 1250, 1257
New states, establishment of procedure for
admission of, 843

New York:
and Boston Port Bill, 393–395
British military strength in (1780), 1392
constitution of, 855–857
and dispute with Vermont, 1144–1145
Hessians in, 1392
Indian and Tory raids in, 1151, 1158–1162,
1180–1184
and nonimportation, 274–275, 299
opposes independence, 686–688, 691, 693,
702, 703
and Quartering Act, 265–267
settlement of, 23
and Stamp Act, 198, 207–208
Tories in, 657, 766–767, 800–801, 885,
892–893, 904, 1351, 1462
New York City, 75–77
British troops in, 313–318, 885
defies Stamp Act, 228, 231
evacuation of, by British, 1758–1761
fire in, 772–773
fortification of, 712–715
occupied by Clinton, 1107–1109, 1351–
1353, 1487
officers in command at, 716–718
patriots return to, after Yorktown, 1757,
1760
prepares for attack by Washington, 1515
retreat from, 760–767
social life in, under Clinton, 1351
Stamp Act riots in, 207–208, 211, 212, 252
Tories in, 657, 766–767, 800–801, 885,
1351
after Yorktown, 1754–1759
Washington in, 712–727
Washington wishes to attack, 1656–1658
welcomes Washington and victorious troops,
1788–1789
New York Volunteers, 1760
Newberry, William, 1166
Newburgh, N.Y., as Washington's
headquarters, 1747
Newburgh Addresses, 1768–1772
Newburgh conspiracy (*see* Newburgh
Addresses)
Newcastle, Duke of, 150, 504
Newell, Timothy, 654–655
Newlanders, 41–42
Newport, R.I.:
American-French attack on (*see* Rhode
Island, Battle of)
British evacuate, 1513
establishment of, 21
Stamp Act riots in, 205–206
Newtown, destruction of, 1168
Nichols, Moses, 918

Nicholson, James, 1295, 1296
Nicholson, Samuel, 1296
Nicoll, John, 206
Nicolson, Comtesse de, 1290
Ninety-Six, siege of, 1502–1506
Nixon, John, 706, 717–718, 770, 857
  at Freeman's Farm, 923–924
  at Saratoga, 938
Noailles, Louis de, 1631
Nonconsumption agreements, 443
Nonexportation agreements, 443
Nonimportation agreements, 274–276
  cheating on, 323
  effect of, on England, 293, 295
  English reactions to, 450–451
  erosion of, 357–358
  and First Continental Congress, 434–440,
    443, 445
  and repeal of Townshend Duties, 298–299
  and Richardson affair, 326–328
  rifts over, among Boston patriots, 325
  and Second Continental Congress, 644
  and slave trade, 1801
Noodle Island, engagement of, 507–509
Norfolk, Va., burning of, 621–624
Norris, Deborah, 957–958, 1353
North, Lord Frederick, 4, 178, 264, 272, 291,
    865
  admits opposition to king's policies, 1378
  and "armed neutrality," 1542
  attempts to block investigation into public
    expenditures, 1545
  attempts to resign after Saratoga, 945
  and Boston Port Bill, 387
  and Boston Tea Party, 375, 382–383
  and Cornwallis' surrender, 1717, 1719, 1721
  defends his ministry, 1372–1373
  denounces American treaty, 1742
  and East India Company, 1822
  and First Continental Congress, 454
  and Fox, 1742–1743
  and French-American alliance, 1060, 1063
  and George III, 294, 295, 871, 945, 1074–
    1075, 1722, 1823
  and Intolerable Acts, 407
  introduces bill to free Irish trade, 1543–
    1544
  and Lexington and Concord, 494
  on Montgomery, 619
  offer of concession by, 560
  realizes impossibility of winning in America,
    1715
  resigns, 1722–1724
  resists hostility to government, 1376–1377
  ridiculed after Jones's victory, 1285
  as secretary of state, 1743
  sends troops to Boston, 300
  and Southern campaign, 1038, 1392, 1432,
    1461
  and Townshend Duties, 294–299
  on use of Indians against patriots, 1155
  (See also Conciliatory bills)
North, Thomas, 8
North, William, 1589
North Carolina, 83, 94–95
  British carry warfare into, 1398
  constitution of, 854
  Cornwallis attempts to recruit Tories in,
    1470, 1472
  favors independence, 691
  Indians in, 1213–1214
  militia of, 1445
  patriot-Tory battles in, 624–625, 1399–
    1406
  petitioned by Watauga Association for
    annexation to, 1212–1213
  and Stamp Act, 228–229
  Tory military action in, 624–625, 1399–
    1406, 1411, 1471
  (See also Carolinas)
North Castle, 1580, 1582
  André delivered to, 1579–1580
Northington, Earl of, 242
Northwest Ordinance, 1540
Norton, Lieutenant Colonel, 1482
Norwalk, Conn., raided by British, 1343, 1513
Nova Scotia, British military strength in
    (1780), 1392
Nugent, Robert Earl, 149–150

Oblong Redoubt, 714
O'Brien, Jeremiah, 642
Occom, Samson, 144
Odell, Jonathan, 1563, 1564, 1567
Ogden, Aaron, 955
Ogden, Captain, 1591–1592
Ogden, James, 1617, 1618
Ogden, Matthias, 1531
Oglethorpe, James, 122
O'Hara, Charles, 1465–1466, 1468
  at Guilford Court House, 1480–1483
  at Yorktown, 1673, 1708
Ohio Company of Virginia, 1191
Ohio Valley, raided by Brant, 1181–1182
Old Denmark (see Febiger, Christian)
Old Northwest, 1191–1192
  British reluctance to abandon posts in, after
    peace treaty, 1233
  ceded to United States, 1232
  Indians of, 1192
  (See also Clark, George Rogers)
Old Point Comfort, 1654

Oldham, Colonel, 1470, 1471, 1474
  in South Carolina campaign, 1490
Oliver, Andrew, 205, 208, 370, 371
  and Stamp Act riots, 202–203
Oliver, Peter, 348–349, 532, 538
Oneidas:
  form alliance with Sullivan, 1168–1169,
    1171
  settlements destroyed, 1180
Oriskany, Battle of, 909–911
Orne, Joshua, 818
Osgood, Samuel, 1248
Oswald, Richard:
  and Adams, 1733–1734
  and Franklin, 1725–1728, 1730
  and Jay, 1726–1727, 1733
  and Laurens, 1735
  and peace negotiations, 1725–1729, 1731–
    1733, 1735, 1737
  and Shelburne, 1725–1726, 1731
  and Strachey, 1733
  and Vergennes, 1728
Otis, James, 72, 259, 280, 287
  on American representation in Parliament,
    186
  and British troops, 301–304, 309
  and Liberty incident, 284–285
  and Mein affair, 323–324
  and resistance to England, 179–183
  and Robinson affair, 321–322
  and Sons of Liberty, 258
  and Stamp Act, 201, 213, 217, 218, 221, 222,
    234, 237, 245
  and Townshend Duties, 272–273
Otis, Joseph, 520
Otis, Mercy, 72
  (See also Warren, Mercy Otis)
Outacity, 112, 118
Owen, Robert Dale, 1584

Paca, William, 1142
Page, John, 85–86, 763, 771
Paine, Robert Treat:
  and Battle of Lexington, 473–474
  and Boston Massacre trial, 347, 349, 350,
    352, 357
  and First Continental Congress, 418, 423,
    426, 428, 436, 442
  and Second Continental Congress, 543, 548
Paine, Thomas, 676–684, 962–963
  African Slavery in America, 1800
  attacks Deane, 1141
  attempts to rouse Philadelphians to defend
    city, 962–963
  on Battle of Germantown, 969–970
  and Common Sense, 677–684, 857
  and "crisis papers," 805

  early career of, 677–678
  encourages immigration, 1819
  in New Jersey campaign, 804–805
  and proposed history of Revolution, 999
  and Rush, 676–677
  and slavery, 104–105
  at Valley Forge, 998–999
  warns against foreign entanglements, 1044
  on Washington, 805
Paine, Timothy, 404
Pallas, 1273, 1275, 1276, 1280, 1283, 1284
Palmer, Deacon, 683
Palmes, Richard, 335, 338–339, 351
Paoli Massacre, 960–961, 964, 993
Paris, Isaac, 909
Paris, Treaty of (see Treaty of Paris)
Parke, Thomas, 143
Parker, Hyde, 1303, 1305, 1308
Parker, James, 315
Parker, Peter:
  at Charles Town, 624–625, 627, 629–630,
    632, 633, 635–636
  at New York, 723, 730
Parliament:
  debates continuation of war after Yorktown,
    1719–1722
  debates diminution of royal power, 1546–
    1547
  debates navy budget, 1546
  debates war policy, 1370–1375
  defeats motion for offer of conciliation to
    America, 1548
  dissolved (1780), 1552
  petitioned for reform of public spending,
    1376, 1544–1546
  proposed colonial representation in, 186–
    187
  redresses losses of Tories, 1760–1761
  renews king's right to suspend habeas
    corpus, 1375
Parochialism of states, 1134–1135, 1640,
    1763–1764, 1772–1773, 1776–1777,
    1784, 1793, 1815–1816
Parr, James, 1167
Parsons, Samuel, 717, 740, 876, 877, 885
  launches private attack on Ticonderoga,
    586–587
  and Negro troops, 1806
  at Springfield, 1528
Partridge, Oliver, 221
Paterson, John, 726–727, 923, 1098
Patroonships, 76
Patten, Matthew, 63–64
Patterson, Robert, 339
Paulding, John, 1578–1579, 1594
Paulus Hook, Lee captures, 1353–1358
Pausch, Georg, 934–935

Payne, Edward, 339
Peabody, Nathaniel, 841
Peace negotiations, 1725–1745
  on acceptance of American independence, 1726, 1732, 1735
  on agreement of British not to take Negroes, 1737
  on America's claim to Mississippi, 1735
  on Canadian borders, 1732, 1734, 1767
  on ceding of Canada to U.S., 1726, 1731
  on compensation to Tories, 1733–1735, 1767
  on fishing rights, 1726, 1732, 1735–1736, 1739, 1767
  and France, 1726–1731, 1737–1739, 1741
  on future safety of Tories, 1736
  and Holland, 1727–1728, 1739
  on indemnification of citizens of towns destroyed by British, 1726
  on payment of debts to British merchants, 1733
  on privileges of American ships and merchants, 1726
  role of Congress in, 1728–1730, 1732–1735, 1738
  and Spain, 1727, 1728, 1734–1735, 1739, 1741
  on Spanish–U.S. boundaries, 1734–1735
  on West Florida, 1768
  on withdrawal of British troops, 1726, 1737
Peace treaties signed, 1745
Peace treaty ratified by Congress, 1780–1781
Peace treaty, preliminary
  announced by Shelburne, 1742
  discussed by Congress, 1767–1768
  news of, reaches America, 1750, 1755
Peale, Charles Willson, 834, 1000, 1132, 1711, 1747, 1781
Pearson, Captain, 1276, 1279–1280, 1282–1283
Pearson, Lieutenant, 1395–1396
Peck, Thomas Handasyd, 351
Pelham, Henry, 346
Pell's Point, 782
Pemberton, Samuel, 327
Pendleton, Edmund, 851, 1539, 1780
Penn, John, 660, 847–848, 1149
Penn, Richard, 436
Penn, William, 26, 114–115
Pennsylvania, 77–82, 105
  abolishes slavery, 1802
  commissions privateers, 1262
  constitution of, 857–863, 1050
  favors independence, 692
  founding of, 26–27
  hospitality to Indian sachems in, 112
  Indian raids in, 1156–1158, 1178–1179
  legal maneuvering of, 139
  Moravian Indians in, atrocities against, 1220–1221
  navy of, 1261
  opposes independence, 686–688
  protection of frontier against Indian raids, 79
  Republicans vs. Constitutionalists in, 1365, 1369
  settlement of, 30, 45
  and Stamp Act, 228
  Walking Purchase of land in, 118–119
Pennsylvania Declaration of Rights, 858
Pennsylvania Dutch, 45
Pennsylvania Light Horse, 1615
Pennsylvania Line, mutiny of, 1605–1623
  and British efforts to negotiate, 1611, 1616–1619
  Congress appoints committee on, 1614
  consequences of, 1620–1623, 1625
  good order of, 1609
  joined by Wayne, 1608–1610, 1612–1618
  and move to Trenton, 1618–1621
  and negotiations at Princeton, 1609, 1612–1614, 1616–1618
  and offer from Clinton, 1611, 1616–1617
  and Reed, 1615–1618, 1620
  and refusal to accept old officers back, 1616
  (See also Mount Kemble)
Pennsylvania Line, in Virginia, 1633–1636
Penobscot Bay, expedition against, 1358–1360
Pensions for officers proposed, 1026–1029, 1146
Pepperell, William, 122, 718
Pepys, Samuel, 47
Percy, Hugh, 13, 409, 419, 752, 800
  at Battle of Long Island, 731, 738, 741
  at Battle of White Plains, 789
  at Battles of Lexington and Concord, 472, 474, 480–481, 484–485, 487–489
  at Fort Washington, 794, 795
Peters, Daniel, 570
Peters, Samuel, 659
Petition of Right, 51–52
Petty, William (see Shelburne, Earl of)
Philadelphia, 77–79, 105, 425, 805
  Adams' assessment of, 436
  Arnold commands forces in, 1556–1557, 1566
  British occupation of, 1031–1043
  British social life in, 1032–1033, 1035–1036, 1039–1041
  captured by Howe, 962–963
  celebrates ratification of peace treaty, 1781–1782

Philadelphia (*cont.*):
  celebrates repeal of Stamp Act, 246
  celebrates Washington's victory at
    Yorktown, 1711
  citizens seize merchants' goods in, 1365
  citizens wear paper money in hats as
    cockades, 1644
  damage to property in, 1034–1035
  French army marches through, 1666–1667
  Hessians in, 1032–1034
  as home of Continental Congress, 436, 544,
    840, 841
  under Howe, 1031–1043
  inflation riot in, 1366–1369
  military preparation of, 492
  "Mischianza" in, 1039–1041
  and nonimportation agreements, 274–276
  prisoners of war in, 1036–1037
  and repeal of Townshend Duties, 299
  and Stamp Act, 228
  theatrical entertainments in, 1033
  Tories in, 840, 949, 1031, 1033, 1074
  Washington visits, 1131–1132, 1663–1664
  welcomes Washington after Yorktown, 1747
  withdrawal of British from, 1058, 1069,
    1084–1085
Phillips, Deacon, 344
Phillips, Wendell, 1825
Phillips, William, 896, 900, 924, 1487
  and Arnold, 1629, 1630
  at Saratoga, 933, 936
Phoenix (British man-of-war), 724, 761
Phoenix (Spanish ship), 1542
Physick, Phillip, 425
Pickens, Andrew, 1214, 1689
  at Cowpens, 1452, 1453, 1455, 1456, 1459,
    1460
  at Fort Cornwallis, 1500, 1502
  at Kettle Creek, 1310–1311, 1316
  in pursuit of Cornwallis, 1470
  in South Carolina campaign, 1490–1491,
    1498–1500, 1502, 1504
  vs. Tarleton, 1470–1476
Pickering, Timothy, 879, 961, 1258, 1353,
  1657
  at Battle of Germantown, 966–968
  and Board of War, 1021
  at Valley Forge, 999
Pierce, Isaac, 341
Pigot, Robert, 517, 521, 524–525
  at Battle of Rhode Island, 1110, 1117
Pilgrims (*see* Plymouth, settlement at;
  Separatists)
Pillaging by British, 1329–1330, 1393–1394,
  1399
Pinckney, Charles Cotesworth, 1309, 1320,
  1335, 1336, 1497

Piquet, De La Motte, 1542
Pitcairn, John, 462, 530
  at Battle of Lexington, 479–481
Pitcher, Molly (*see* Hays, Mary Ludwig)
Pitt, Leonard, 381
Pitt, Thomas, 1546–1547
Pitt, William (the Elder), 233, 256, 297
  on American liberties, 385–386, 452–453
  champions American cause, 239–243, 293–
    294, 868
  on French-American alliance, 1060–1061
  and French and Indian War, 127, 170
  on Guilford Court House, 1484
  on New York intransigence, 265
  withdraws from public life, 264
  (*See also* Chatham, Lord)
Pitt, William (the Younger), 1741, 1743
Plan of 1764, 167
Plessis, Maduit de:
  at Fort Mercer, 980–982, 990
  at Germantown, 966, 973, 975
Plombard, M., 1332
Pluton, 1676, 1678, 1681
Plymouth, settlement at, 16–18, 23
Pocahontas, 15, 109, 119
Poems on Various Subjects, Religious and Moral
  (Wheatley), 1802
Polish volunteers, 922–923, 972, 997–998
Pollexfen, John, 133
Pollock, Oliver, 1199
Polly, 171–172, 378–379, 383
Pomeroy, Seth, 520, 523, 553
Pontgibaud, Chevalier de, 1291, 1753
Pontiac, 166
Poor, Enoch, 898
  on expedition against Indians and Tories,
    1167, 1168
  at Monmouth, 1083, 1099
  at Saratoga, 923, 936
Poor Richard's Almanack (Franklin), 1272
Poor whites, 1425
Popham, William, 1669
Porterfield, Charles, 951, 1409, 1411, 1412
Portland, Duke of, 1743
Portsmouth, settlement of, 21
Potter, Colonel, 640
Potter, George, 144
Poverty in England, 30–32, 145
Powhatan, 15, 108, 109, 118
Pownall, Thomas, 212, 288, 302, 306, 357,
  1548
Powys, M. P., 1720–1721
Prairie du Rocher, 1193
Pratt, Charles, 168, 865
Preble, Edward, 1294
Pre-Contract, 69–70
Presbyterians, 29, 30, 44, 53, 144–145

Prescott, Richard, 604, 888–890, 1081
Prescott, William, 782
  at Bunker Hill, 511–515, 518–520, 525–
    527, 529–530, 536
Press gangs, 173, 201, 282, 638
Preston, 641, 1111
Preston, Battle of, 55
Preston, Captain, 336–343, 345–347, 349–352
Preston, Colonel, 1473, 1475
Prevost, Augustine, 1309, 1315, 1381, 1391
  at Briar Creek, 312, 313
  at Fort Morris, 1307–1308
  at Savannah, 1303, 1304, 1332–1334
  at Stono Ferry, 1328–1329
  threatens Charles Town, 1318–1322, 1329
  withdraws from Charles Town, 1326
Prevost, James Mark, 1312, 1325
Price, Richard, 865
Priestley, Joseph, 371
Prince, Newton, 351
Prince of Wales, 1743
Princessa, 1676, 1678–1681
Princeton:
  Battle of, 828–838, 1074
    Hessians at, 830–831
  Congress meets in, 1779–1780
  Pennsylvania mutineers at, 1609, 1612–
    1618
Princeton University (*see* College of New
    Jersey)
Prison ship, British, 1266
Prisoners of war, 1026–1027, 1146
  American, in Philadelphia, 1036–1037
  American treatment of, 1431, 1432
  British and Hessian, after Saratoga, 942–
    943
  British treatment of, 1397
  exchange of, after Jones's victory, 1288
  in Philadelphia, 1036–1037
  Tories as, 1027, 1029
Pritchard, Mrs. (actress), 147
Privateers, 1238, 1251, 1255, 1259–1260,
    1262–1266, 1296, 1297
  authorized by Congress, 1262–1263, 1296
  British, 1265
  vs. British Navy, 1296–1297
  in British waters, 1263–1264
  commandeered for foray against New
    Providence, 1257
  commissioned by states, 1263
  vs. Continental Army and state militias,
    1263
  disadvantages of, 1265–1266
  French, 1264
  hazards of, 1263
  welcomed in Spanish ports, 1254
Proclamation Line of 1763, 166–167

Proctor, Thomas, 1167
Proprietary colonies, 23
Protecteur, 1107
Protector vs. *Admiral Duff,* 1293–1294
Protestant Reformation (*see* Reformation,
    effect of)
Providence, 1245, 1247, 1250, 1252, 1255,
    1258, 1260, 1268, 1269
  at siege of Charles Town, 1295
Providence, R.I.:
  as headquarters of Sullivan, 1123
  as recruiting center for privateers, 1251
  settlement of, 22–23
Pulaski, Casimir, 997–998, 1124, 1160, 1264
  at Charles Town, 1321–1323, 1325, 1326
  at Savannah, 1332, 1335
Pultney, William, 1062
Puritan communities, 61–67, 74–75
Puritanism, 153–158
Puritans, 19–23, 29, 48–49, 53, 1817
  sexual practices of, 69–70
Putnam, Israel, 546, 553, 554, 644, 959, 1112,
    1795
  and Battle of Bunker Hill, 511–512, 515,
    518–520, 527, 529, 531, 536
  and Battle of Lexington and Concord, 491
  in Battle of Long Island, 735–736, 738, 740,
    743, 746
  and Boston Port Act, 391
  commands forces at Danbury, 1124
  at Fort Independence, 930, 931
  at Fort Washington, 793–794
  Graydon on, 1134
  at Harlem Heights, 769, 772
  and Howe, 503
  in New Jersey campaign, 886
  at New York, 716, 755, 761, 766
  and siege of Boston, 507, 508
  at Trenton, 815, 817, 822
Putnam, Rufus, 527, 1344
Pyle, John, 1471–1472, 1474, 1475

Quakers, 29, 80, 152
  and antislavery cause, 81
  dominance of, in Pennsylvania, 79, 80
  meeting of, described by Chastellux, 1667
  oppose independence, 657, 688, 857
  and Penn, 26–27, 30
  and prisoners of war, 1036
Quartering Act, 264–267, 294, 313–314
Quaumino, John, 1799
Quebec:
  Arnold's march to, 606–613, 619
  assault on, 614–618, 743
  British victory at, 127, 502, 511
Quebec Act, 401–402, 405–407, 410, 435, 585
Queen Anne's War, 122

Queen of France, 1260, 1269, 1295
Queen's Rangers, 992, 1428, 1527, 1635, 1760
Queen's Royal Rifles, 1759
Quincy, Dorothy, 473
Quincy, Edmund, 327
Quincy, Josiah, 96
    and Boston Tea Party, 381
    defends Captain Preston, 345–349, 351–355
    and Stamp Act riots, 204
Quincy, Samuel, 347, 350, 352–353

Rainbow, 758, 759, 1255–1256
Raisonable, 1256
Raleigh, 1245, 1257–1259
Rall, Johann, 787, 788, 794
    at Trenton, 814–815, 819–822, 824
Ramsay, David:
    on action at Charles Town, 1381, 1385, 1386, 1391
    on attack on Savannah, 1332, 1336
    on Barnwell, 1327
    on British pillaging, 1393
    on capacities drawn forth by Revolution, 256–257
    on dashed hopes of South Carolinians of reclaiming slaves, 1749
    on failure of England to permit freedom while retaining supremacy, 297
    on militia, 1317–1318
    on pillaging of South Carolina, 1329–1330
    on slaves who deserted to British, 1330
    on Tories after Kettle Creek engagement, 1311–1312
    on Tories and patriots, 656–658
Ramsay's Mill, 1487, 1489
    engagement at, 1399–1404
        British desertions at, 1465
        consequences of, 1404
        vs. Guilford Court House, 1484–1485
        significance of, 1402–1404
Randolph, 1245, 1253, 1257
Randolph, Edmund, 92, 851, 1768
Randolph, John, 665–666, 676
Randolph, Peyton, 197, 427, 548
    and Continental Congress, 430–431
Ranger, 1260, 1268, 1269, 1292, 1802
    vs. *Drake,* 1270–1272
    at siege of Charles Town, 1295
Rathburn, John, 1260
Rawdon, Francis, 529, 728, 1397, 1398, 1435
    advances to Ninety-Six, 1504, 1506
    at Camden, 1409, 1410, 1412, 1413, 1417
    evacuates Camden, 1498
    at Hobkirk's Hill, 1492–1495
    in North Carolina, 1688
    in South Carolina campaign, 1489, 1491–1498, 1504, 1506

Rawle, Anna, 1712–1713
Raymond, John, 486
Rayneval, 1734, 1738–1740
Read, Jacob, 1781
Read, Joseph, 782
Redemptioners, 36
Reed, Esther De Berdt, 1810, 1813
Reed, Joseph:
    Adams on, 424
    vs. Arnold, 1556, 1557
    at Battle of White Plains, 786
    and Board of War, 1021
    and Boston Port Bill, 396, 397
    at First Continental Congress, 424, 428, 433
    at Harlem Heights, 769–776
    and Johnstone, 1070–1071
    to Lee, 796–797
    at Luzerne's feast, 1667
    and mob action in Philadelphia, 1367–1369
    at New York, 725
    and Pennsylvania Line mutiny, 1615–1618, 1620
    promoted to brigadier general, 879
    at Second Continental Congress, 544
    at Trenton, 813, 814
    at Valley Forge, 1000
    and Washington, 577, 579–580, 1513–1514, 1795
    and Wayne, 1603–1604, 1616, 1617
Re-enlistment problem, 574–577, 579–580, 777–778
    at Charles Town, 1384
    at Germantown, 963
    after Harlem Heights, 777–778
    in New Jersey, 804, 875, 877
    and Washington's personal appeals and guarantees, 828–829
Reeves, Enos, 1605, 1606, 1608
Reflechi, 1676, 1678, 1681
Reformation, effect of:
    in America, 153–158
    in England, 48–49
Regulator War, 1324
Regulators, 661, 1303
Reid, Thomas, 144
Religion as key to American consciousness, 152–161, 270
Renown, 1384
Representation, American vs. English view of, 214
Reprisal, 1264
Resolution, 1679
Restoration Settlement, 57
Revenge, 1264
Revenue Act (*see* Sugar Act)
Revere, Paul, 306, 390, 408, 458
    ancestry of, 46
    and Battle of Lexington, 475–479

makes engraving of Boston Massacre, 346
and "mechanics," 464
at Penobscot Bay, 1358
punch bowl fashioned by, for patriot
    headquarters, 288
and Warren, 535
Revolution vs. war, 1824–1825
Revolution, political, novelty of, 398
Revolution Settlement, 1
Reynolds, Aaron, 1229
Rhode Island, 70–72
    abolishes slavery, 1802
    Battle of, 1109–1120
        French assistance at, 1109–1111, 1113,
            1120, 1646
        Hessians at, 1118, 1119, 1805
        Negroes at, 1805
    constitution of, 854
    enlists Negro soldiers, 1804–1805
    French assistance to, 1109–1111, 1113, 1120
    and *Gaspee* affair, 364–369
    proposes establishment of navy, 644–645,
        1239–1240
    restricts slave trade, 1800–1801
    settlement of, 21–23
    and Stamp Act, 197–198, 230, 252
    and Sugar Act, 174–175
Richardson, Ebenezer, 326–328, 348–349
Richmond, 1384
Richmond, Duke of, 243, 868, 869, 1065, 1371
Riedesel, Baroness von, 895, 905
    at Saratoga, 936, 937, 939, 942
Riedesel, Friedrich Adolf von:
    at Bennington, 915
    in Burgoyne's invasion, 895, 900, 902, 903,
        905
    at Freeman's Farm, 922, 924, 926, 927, 929
    at Saratoga, 933
Rifle, breech-loading vs. muzzle-loading,
    1426–1427
Riflemen, 557–558, 572–573, 920, 962, 1476
    at Augusta, 1423
    at Chestnut Hill, 992
    at Cowpens, 1452, 1453
    on expedition against Indians and Tories,
        1167
    at Fort Cornwallis, 1501
    at Freeman's Farm, 923–925
    at Guilford Court House, 1479
    at Kings Mountain, 1424, 1425, 1428–1431
    with Lafayette in Virginia, 1633
    at Quebec, 608, 616
    at Reedy Fork, 1476
    at Rocky Mount, 1405
    at Saratoga, 936
    with Sumter, 1442
    vs. Tarleton, 1473
    at Vincennes, 1207

Rising Empire, 1261
Rittenhouse, David, 423, 706
Ritzema, Rudolph, 787
Rivington, James, 1754
Roberts, Lieutenant, 1348
Robertson, Archibald, 652, 1034
Robertson, James, 168, 1212, 1214, 1352, 1648
    and Greene, 1592
    hints at retaliation against American
        prisoners if André is hanged, 1592
Robin, Claude, 1658, 1662
Robinson, Beverley, 1130, 1583, 1589
    after Yorktown, 1755–1757, 1761
Robinson, John (customs commissioner), 171–
    172, 174–175, 206
    and Otis affair, 321–322
Robinson, John (Treasury official), 871, 1075
Robordeau, Daniel, 730
Rochambeau, Comte de, 1407, 1572, 1626,
    1638, 1647, 1664, 1697
    guards against desertion by French troops,
        1666
    and Luzerne, 1663
    and Morris, 1667–1668
    at Mount Vernon, 1669–1670
    and Washington, 1626, 1656–1658, 1661,
        1668, 1670, 1671
    at Williamsburg, 1693
    at Yorktown, 1706, 1708, 1715
Rochambeau, Viscount de, 1662
Rocheblave, 1194, 1196, 1198
Rockingham, Lord, 237, 239, 242, 264, 867,
    869
    death of, 1731
    vs. George III, 1371, 1544–1545
    named prime minister, 1725
Rocky Mount, 1405
Rodney, Caesar, 220, 428, 660, 701–702
Rodney, George Brydges, 1542, 1543, 1572
    scatters De Grasse's fleet in West Indies,
        1755
Rodney, Thomas, 815, 824, 835, 1638
Roebuck, 761
Roessler, Private, 1674
Rogers, Robert, 502, 786, 797
"Rogues and vagabonds" as immigrants, 39–41
Rolfe, John, 15, 101, 109
Rolfe, Rebecca, 109
    (*See also* Pocahontas)
Roman Catholicism, Puritan fear of, 402, 406
Romney, 282–284, 287
Romney, George, 1158
Romulus, 1626
Root, Jesse, 1643
Rose, 642, 724, 761
Rose, John, 1221–1227
Rosenstock-Huessy, Eugen, 1790, 1829
Rosenthal, Baron (*see* Rose, John)

Ross, James, 952–954
Ross, Lieutenant, 341
Rotch, Francis, 380–381
Rouërie, Marquis de la (*see* Armand, Charles)
Rousseau, Jean Jacques, 108, 680
Rowe, John, 322, 328, 381
Rowley, Major, 1187
Royal George, 896, 900
Royal governors, 138–140, 660, 663
Royal Greens, 910
Royal Oak, 1679
Royalists (*see* Tories)
Ruddle, Captain, 1215
Ruddle's Station, 1215
Ruddock, Timothy, 308, 327
Rudgley, Colonel, 1447
Rudolph, John, 1471, 1499, 1505
Rudolph, Michael, 1356
Ruggles, Timothy, 221
Rush, Benjamin, 144, 551, 826, 1349
    and antislavery movement, 1799–1800
    blames Congress for mutinous troops in
        Philadelphia, 1779
    on British vs. American medical service,
        1006
    on depreciation of money, 1148, 1364
    on Lee court-martial, 1103
    and Paine, 676–677
    resigns in protest over condition of military
        hospitals, 1002
    on sanitation, 1006–1007
    vs. Washington, 1019
Rush, Jacob, 143
Russell, Jason, 13
Russian Revolution, 1, 257, 1826, 1827
Rutherford, Griffith, 1213, 1312, 1401, 1407
Rutledge, Edward, 428, 701–702
    Adams on, 444
    and conference with Howe brothers, 756–
        758
    favors Galloway Plan of Union, 440
    favors nonimportation, 438
Rutledge, John, 428, 432, 687, 840, 1144
    and Adams, 424, 546
    and attack on Charles Town, 626, 627, 632,
        635, 636
    and defense of Charles Town, 1382, 1390–
        1391
    as governor of South Carolina, 1318, 1398
    and Great Seal, 1766
    and independence, 855
    and Jay, 856
    proposes neutrality for South Carolina,
        1323–1325
    rejects Laurens' plan to enlist slaves, 1806
    and Savannah, 1332, 1334
    sends reinforcements to Moultrie, 1320

    at Stamp Act Congress, 220
    and threat to Charles Town, 1320–1323

Sabin, James, 366
Sackville, Lord George, 243
St. Augustine, Georgia sends expedition
    against, 1301–1302
St. Clair, Arthur, 821, 833, 878
    and André, 1589–1590
    and Burgoyne's invasion, 898–905
    and mutiny of furloughed troops, 1777,
        1778
    and Pennsylvania mutineers, 1614–1615,
        1617
    reinforces Greene after Yorktown, 1748
St. Croix, 1208
Saint-Esprit, 1679
St. John's, 590, 591, 599–600, 603, 604
St. Leger, Barry, 895, 920
    and Burgoyne's invasion, 891–892
    at Fort Stanwix and Oriskany, 908–914
    Indians with, 908–914
St. Louis, British attack on, 1214–1215
St. Ovary, Baron, 956
Saint Sauveur, Chevalier de, 1120
Saint-Simon, Comte de, 1672–1673, 1693,
    1699
Ste. Geneviève, 1193
Salem, 1219–1220
Saltonstall, Dudley, 1248, 1358–1360
Samoset, 17
Sampson (Negro pilot), 630, 632
Sampson, Deborah, 1812
Sandusky expedition, 1221–1227
Sandwich, 1543
Sandwich, Earl of, 638, 1240–1241, 1371,
    1549
    ridiculed after Jones's victory, 1285
Saratoga, Battle of, 932–938
    Canadians at, 924
    consequences of, 944–947, 1051, 1716
Sartine, de (French minister of marine), 1273,
    1274
Savage, William, 720
Savannah:
    Battle of, 1303–1308, 1469
    British evacuate, 1748
    British occupy, 1487–1488
    French troops in, 1332
    Hessians in, 1303, 1334, 1392
    siege and attack on, 1332–1337
Savile, George, 869, 1063, 1544, 1549
Scammell, Alexander, 748, 749, 1665, 1696
Scarborough, 640
Schaller, Captain von, 1354, 1356
Schebosh, 1220
Schönbrunn, 1219

Schuyler, Elizabeth, 1587–1588
Schuyler, Hon Yost, 914
Schuyler, Philip, 553, 554, 564–565, 627, 877, 916
    and Arnold, 928, 1565
    and Baroness von Riedesel, 942
    and Burgoyne's invasion, 893, 898, 901, 904–905, 907
    on effect of Indian raids, 1183
    vs. Gates, 897–898, 919–920
    and invasion of Canada, 594–600, 602–603, 606–607
    and Lafayette, 1079
    and New Jersey campaign, 806, 807
    rumors about, 1597
    and saving of Fort Stanwix, 913–914
    urges constitutional convention, 1643
Scipio, 1804
Scotch-Irish immigration, 30, 44–45, 657
Scott, Alexander, 633
Scott, Charles, 876
    at Battle of Monmouth, 1086, 1088, 1089, 1091, 1098
Scott, John Morin, 211, 315, 716, 737
    and Great Seal, 1766
    with Massachusetts delegates in New York, 421–422
Scottish Covenanters, 29, 30, 44
Scottish Highlanders, 29
Scottish philosophers, 254–256
Scott's Lake, 1438
Scudder, Nathaniel, 1148
Seabury, Samuel, 447
Sears, Isaac, 316, 394
Sectional animosity, 1134–1135, 1784
    (See also Parochialism of states)
Seeley, Samuel, 1528–1529
Seeley, Sylvanus, 1528–1529
Seider, Christopher, 327–328
Selin, Anthony, 1167
Selkirk, Earl of, 1270
Senter, Isaac, 608–613
Separatists, 16, 19, 29, 51
    (See also Williams, Roger)
Serapis, 1284, 1288, 1541
    vs. Bonhomme Richard, 1276–1285
Sergeant, John, 848
Serle, Ambrose, 684, 758, 804
    on American troops in New York, 723–725, 727–729, 755–756, 763, 764
    on Battle of Long Island, 731–733
    on British withdrawal from Philadelphia, 1058, 1059
    on Burgoyne's defeat, 978
    calculates American manpower, 1037
    on distressed condition of New England, 885

on evacuation of Brooklyn, 751–752
    on evacuation of Philadelphia, 1084
    on French alliance, 1057
    and Galloway, 799–800, 888, 1031–1032, 1058
    on New York fire, 773
    on New York patriots, 798–799
    on New York Tories, 766–767
    on retreat from New York, 762–763
    on slavery, 1803
    on Thanksgiving (1777), 994
Seven Years' War, 124–129, 505, 1824
Sevier, John, 168, 1212, 1214
Sevier, Nolichucky Jack, 1424–1425, 1427, 1429, 1430, 1436
Sewall, Henry, 142
Sewall, Jonathan, 447, 668
    and Adams, 666
    and Liberty affair, 285
    prosecutor at Boston Massacre trial, 347
Sewall, Samuel, 142, 145
Seward, Ann, 1594
Seymour-Conway, Francis, 168
Shaeffe, Susanna, 304–305
Shaeffe, William, 304
Shaftesbury, Earl of, 24–25
Shaw, Samuel, 1772
Shea, John, 747
Shelburne, Earl of, 272, 371–372, 1371
    announces preliminary treaties with America, France, and Spain, 1741–1742
    becomes prime minister, 1731
    and Fox, 1742–1744
    and Franklin, 1725, 1726
    and Laurens, 1730
    and North, 1742–1743
    and Oswald, 1725, 1726
    and peace negotiations, 1725–1726, 1731, 1733, 1741
    proposes committee to examine public expenditures, 1375, 1544–1555
    and Quartering Act, 264–266
    resigns, 1773
    and Vergennes, 1735
    writes king's speech announcing independence of America, 1740
Shelburne, Henry, 221
Shelby, Isaac, 1404–1405, 1436
    at Kings Mountain, 1424, 1425, 1428–1431
Sheldon, Colonel, 1569
Sheldon, Major, 812
Shepard, Samuel, 672–674
Shepherd, Colonel, 782
Sherman, Isaac, 1350
Sherman, Roger, 693–694, 845
Shipley, Jonathan, 402–403

Shippen, Edward, 438
Shippen, Peggy, 1039, 1556–1557
  (*See also* Arnold, Peggy)
Shippen, William, 143, 425, 428
Shirley, William, 170
"Shirtliffe, Robert," 1812
Shreve, Israel, 1621
Shreve, William, 1531
Shrewsbury, 1678, 1681
Shubrick, Captain, 1320
Shuldham, Admiral, 725
Sidney, Algernon, 254, 678, 848
Silver Heels, 1152
Silvester, Richard, 302–303
Simcoe, John, 1124, 1635
Simcoe's Rangers, 1625, 1632, 1649
Simitière, Pierre Eugène du, 1132
Simpson, Captain, 934
Simpson, Thomas, 1260, 1271–1272
Sinclair, Patrick, 1214–1215
Skene, Major, 561
Skene, Philip, 915, 938
Skinner, Cortlandt, 1354, 1527
Slave trade, 71
  and Declaration of Independence, 704–705
  limited by Pennsylvania, 1801
  and nonimportation agreements, 1801
  prohibited in Connecticut and Rhode
    Island, 1800–1801
  prohibited in Virginia, North Carolina, and
    South Carolina as part of
    nonimportation agreements, 1801
  rejection of, by Congress, 443
Slavery:
  abolished in Rhode Island, Vermont, and
    Pennsylvania, 1802
  and Du Roi, 1803
  Henry on, 1799, 1806
  Jefferson on, 104, 704–705, 1806
  and Laurens, 1805
  Lee on, 1425, 1805
  Mason on, 1806
  Paine on, 104–105
  shock of, to Europeans, 1803
  Southern attitudes toward, changed by
    Revolution, 1798, 1807
  Southern indictment of, 103–105
Slaves, 24, 83, 86, 90, 93, 96–97, 101–106
  aid Washington on march to Virginia, 1670
  black vs. white, 86, 103
  British treatment of, 1696–1697, 1709, 1803
  build palisade and fort for British at
    Yorktown, 1673
  Clark's proclamation on, 1197
  conceive notion of freedom, 1798
  dependence of, on plantation system, 102–
    103
  desert to British army, 622, 1324, 1329–
    1330, 1381, 1393–1394, 1798, 1803,
    1806–1807
  freed by Leslie, 1749
  and Livingston, 1802
  nakedness of, 1634
  offered freedom by Dunmore, 621–622,
    1798
  petition state legislatures for freedom, 1800,
    1801
  and representation in Congress, 844
  returned by British to former owners in
    South Carolina, 1748–1749
  and sexual relations with whites, 97, 101–
    102
  with smallpox, 1634, 1696–1697, 1709,
    1803
  stolen by British for sale in West Indies,
    1749
  taken by British from Savannah, 1748
  value of, 1330
  white, 24, 103
    (*See also* Indentured servants)
  Woolman's attempts to free, 81
Smallpox:
  epidemic of, in Charles Town, 1381
  epidemic of, among Wooster's troops at
    Montreal, 717
  among escaped slaves in Virginia, 1803
  inoculations against, 883–884, 1002
  among Negroes with Cornwallis, 1696–
    1697, 1709
Smallwood, William, 957, 1420
  at Battle of Long Island, 738, 741
  at Battle of White Plains, 787, 788
  at Germantown, 964
  on inferiority of American officers,
    776
  at Monmouth, 1098
Smith, Abbott, 33, 36
Smith, Adam, 186
Smith, Colonel, 1325, 1531
Smith, Francis:
  at Battle of Concord, 483–484, 487
  at Battle of Lexington, 474, 478, 480
Smith, Isaac, 481
Smith, Job, 171–172
Smith, John, 15, 108, 109, 118
Smith, Joshua, 1572–1578, 1581–1584
Smith, Lieutenant Colonel, 966
Smith, Matthew, 608
Smith, Michael, 317
Smith, Samuel, 980, 983
Smith, Sydney, 144
Smith, Thomas (patriot), 428, 857–858
Smith, Thomas (Tory), 663, 664
Smith, W. P., 1194–1195

Smith, William, 422, 423, 1352, 1597, 1599
  and André, 1590
  on Clinton, 1662
Smith, Dr. William, 426
Smith, William, Jr., 194
Smuggling, 136–137, 171–172, 174–175, 364
Smyth, J. E. D., 89–90
Social mobility, 156
Society of Cincinnatus, 1783–1784
Society of Friends (see Quakers)
Society for the Relief of Free Negroes
    Unlawfully Held in Bondage, 1800
Soldiers of fortune, 975, 1138–1139
Solebay, 630, 1675
Solemn League and Covenant, 390, 393, 397
Sons of Liberty, 178, 280, 281, 303
  attempt to prevent armed conflict, 225, 231
  and Boston Massacre, 235, 354–355
  vs. British soldiers, 461
  capture Margaretta, 641–642
  and committees of correspondence, 368
  English view of, 237
  and Gaspee affair, 366
  growth of, 234–235, 257–258
  and Liberty affair, 283, 284
  in New York, 207–208, 231, 274, 313–317
  and nonimportation, 274
  origin of name of, 192
  and repeal of Stamp Act, 244–247
  and Stamp Act, 195, 230, 234–235
  and Stamp Act riots, 201, 207–208, 211–213
  and tea monopoly, 377
South Carolina, 95–101, 211, 275
  British looting and destruction in, 1330
  British military strength in (1780), 1392
  constitution of, 854–855
  controlled by British, 1398
  and desertion of slaves to British army, 1324
  elects Rutledge governor, 1318
  favors independence, 691
  Hessians in, 1392
  and Indians, 1152, 1155, 1213
  Legislative Council of, 626
  and Marion, 1437–1441
  militia of, 1318
  naval adventures in, 642–643, 1257
  navy of, 1261
  pillaging of, by Clinton's forces, 1393–1394
  pillaging of, by Prevost's forces, 1329–1330
  planters in, seek return of slaves from
      British, 1748–1749
  Rutledge proposes neutrality for, 1323–
      1325
  social structure of, 1324
  Tories in, after Yorktown, 1749
  urged by Congress to enlist slaves, 1805
  (See also Carolinas)

Southern campaigns, 5, 1038, 1301, 1341,
    1392, 1422, 1432, 1461, 1462, 1507, 1712
Southern colonies, 83–106
  and nonimportation, 275
  and Stamp Act, 211
Southern frontier, 1212–1218
  Cherokees on, 1213–1214
  and Watauga Association, 1212–1213
Southern states:
  cavalry warfare in, 1470, 1475
  Tories in, 657, 658, 661–662, 1461–1463,
    1470
Southerners:
  characteristics of, 1318, 1427–1428
  demand free navigation of Mississippi, 1361
  Lafayette on, 1627
Souverain, 1676
Spain:
  and France, 1738
  and French-American alliance, 1049, 1052,
    1132, 1214
  Jay appointed minister to, 1363
  and peace negotiations, 1727, 1728, 1734–
    1735, 1738, 1739, 1741
  preliminary treaty with England
      announced, 1741–1742
  presses for Floridas and control of
      Mississippi, 1361
  seizes British posts on Mississippi, 1214
  welcomes American privateers, 1254
Spanish moss, 1674
Sparks, Jared, 1709
Spear, Major, 952, 954
Speculation, 1148, 1365
  (See also Land speculation)
Spencer, Joseph, 554, 877
  at Harlem Heights, 769
  with Washington in New York, 716–717,
    755
Spencer, Oliver, 1167
Sphynx, 631, 632, 634
"Spirits," 32–33
Spotswood, Alexander, 1349
Springfield, engagement at, 1528–1532
  Hessians at, 1528–1529, 1532
Springsteel, David, 1345
Spy, 642
Squanto, 17
Stack, Lieutenant, 1278
Stacy (Jones's helmsman), 1277–1278
Stamp Act, 2, 189–199, 225–235, 294, 296, 311
  Barré's speech opposing, 192–193
  colonial reaction to, 193–199
  effects of:
    on colonists, 225–235, 250–259, 1821–
      1822, 1825
    on courts, 229–230

Stamp Act, effects of (*cont.*):
  economic, 232–233
  on merchants, 227–229, 232
  on publishers, 227
  on royal officials, 230–231
  efforts to enforce, 227–228
  English debate over, 236–249
  English vs. American views on, 213–218
  Henry's speech on, 195–196
  provisions of, 191, 227
  repeal of, 235, 243–249
    British Tory reaction to, 268
  and Sons of Liberty, 195, 230, 234–235
  and Virginia resolves, 196–199
Stamp Act Congress, 219–224
  resolves of, 222–223
Stamp Act riots, 200–213, 252
  in Boston, 200–205, 208–209, 212, 225–227, 252
  in Charles Town, 209–211
  in Connecticut, 206–207, 209, 231–232
  in Maryland, 211
  in New York, 207–208, 212, 252
  in Newport, R.I., 205–206
  in Southern colonies, 211
Standish, Miles, 17
Stansbury, Joseph, 1560–1563, 1566, 1567
Stark, John, 491
  and André, 1589–1590
  at Bennington, 916–917, 919
  at Bunker Hill, 517–518, 523, 536, 553
  at Trenton, 816
State navies, 1261–1262, 1264, 1297
Staten Island raided by Stirling, 1515
Stedman, Charles, 887–888, 1034, 1038, 1070
  on American tactics at Monmouth, 1100
  on Camden, 1410, 1415
  on fears of Tories, 1486
  on Hobkirk's Hill, 1494
  on Knyphausen's raid into New Jersey, 1529, 1530
  on Lafayette, 1080
  on Lee vs. Tarleton, 1472
  on Negroes with British troops, 1393–1394
  on Springfield engagement, 1532
Stedman, Mrs., 474
Steele, Andrew, 1230–1231
Stephen, Adam, 814–815, 878, 879, 884
  at Brandywine, 951, 955
  court-martial of, 991
  at Germantown, 964, 967, 968, 970
Steptoe, Dr., 428
Sterling, Colonel, 795, 980
Steuben, Friedrich Wilhelm Augustus von, 1015, 1056, 1444, 1774
  and André, 1589–1590

  at Battle of Monmouth, 1084, 1098
  and Lafayette, 1626, 1629, 1634, 1635
  at Morristown, 1524
  reconstructs regular army in South, 1406
  vs. Simcoe's Rangers, 1632
  and Society of Cincinnatus, 1783
  tactics of, inappropriate at Green Spring Farm, 1652
  trains Continental Army at Valley Forge, 1008–1016
  in Virginia, 1626–1627, 1634, 1635
  and Washington, 1009–1011, 1013, 1015, 1790
  on Wayne's victory at Stony Point, 1349
  in Williamsburg, 1695
Stevens, Edward, 1412, 1447, 1470, 1476
  at Guilford Court House, 1479–1481
Stewart, Alexander, 1482, 1483, 1688
Stewart, Walter:
  at Eutaw Springs, 1688–1690
  at Green Spring Farm, 1650
  and Pennsylvania mutiny, 1518, 1606, 1608, 1609, 1614
Stiles, Ezra, 72, 492, 1799
Stirling, General (British), 1529, 1531
Stirling, Kitty, 1000
Stirling, Lady, 1000
Stirling, Lord (patriot), 755, 1056
  and André, 1589–1590
  attacks Knyphausen, 1529
  attacks Staten Island, 1515
  at Battle of Brandywine, 951, 954, 955
  at Battle of Germantown, 964
  at Battle of Long Island, 733, 734, 737–738, 740–742, 744
  at Battle of Monmouth, 1093, 1095, 1098, 1100
  at Battle of Princeton, 833
  at Battle of White Plains, 784, 786
  and Conway Cabal, 1021–1022
  and New Jersey campaign, 806, 817–819, 823, 826, 833, 878, 884, 887
  at Trenton, 817–819, 823, 826
  urges attacks on Philadelphia and New York, 1083–1084
  with Washington in New York, 715, 717
  (*See also* Alexander, William)
Stockbridge Indians, 464, 498–499, 1151, 1154
Stocking, Abner, 608–609
Stockton, Richard, 701
Stockwell, Major, 913
Stoddert, Major, 958, 971
Stokes, Anthony, 1333
Stokes, John, 1396
Stone, William, 911

Stono Ferry, Lincoln's attack on, 1327–1329
Stony Point, 1342–1351, 1589
    British evacuate, 1513
    burned and abandoned, 1350
    captured by British, 1342
    commanded by Arnold, 1567
    recaptured by Wayne, 1343–1351
    use of pioneers at, 1345–1347
Storer, Anthony Morris, 1067–1068
Stormont, Lord, 1264, 1717, 1741
Story, William, 203
Strachey, Henry, 1733
    and Adams, 1733, 1736
    and Franklin, 1733
Strahan, William, 267, 297, 299
Strang, Major, 1578
Stuart, John, 1155
Sturgis, S., 882
Stuyvesant, Peter, 23
Submarine (see "Water machine")
Suffolk Resolves, 434–435, 450, 459
Sugar Act (1764), 171–176, 180, 219, 223,
    248–249
Sullivan, John, 431, 555, 567, 572, 580, 879,
    1664, 1795
    in Battle of Brandywine, 951–957, 1112
    in Battle of Germantown, 964, 965, 967
    in Battle of Long Island, 733–735, 738–740,
        742, 743, 953
    in Battle of Rhode Island, 1109–1120
    in Battle of Trenton, 813, 815, 817, 819–
        821
    in Battle of White Plains, 784
    as British prisoner, 755–756
    on Conway, 1020
    court-martial of, 991
    forms alliance with Oneidas, 1168–1169
    and Greene, 1514
    on Hamilton, 976–977
    headquarters at Providence, 1123
    leads expedition against Indians and Tories,
        1163–1177, 1184, 1189
    on military hospitals, 578
    in New Jersey campaign, 884, 885
    in New York, 716, 717, 725, 746
    and Pennsylvania mutineers, 1614, 1619,
        1620
    on planned attack on Boston, 652
    on powder problem, 582
    and slave, 1804
    succeeds Lee, 810
    supports congressional power, 1643
    urged to defect to British, 1559–1560
    at Valley Forge, 996–997
    and Washington, 1112–1114, 1119, 1645
Sumner, Jethro, 1689

Sumner, John, 1517
Sumter, Thomas, 1405, 1410, 1416, 1446
    in South Carolina campaign, 1490–1492,
        1495, 1497, 1502, 1504
    vs. Tarleton, 1419–1420, 1439, 1441–1444
    vs. Wemyss, 1439–1441
Supreme Court, U.S., 182, 843
Surprise attacks, 1124–1125
Surrey, Lord, 1723
Sutherland, Andrew, 1574, 1583
Sutherland, William, 1354
Swedish settlement on Delaware, 29
Swiggett, Howard, 1236
Swiss immigration, 36
Symonds, Colonel, 917
Syren, 631, 632, 634

Tallmadge, Benjamin, 1353, 1580, 1583, 1588,
    1593, 1648
    on hardships of fighting men, 1785
    in New York after Yorktown, 1758–1759
    on New York's reception of victorious
        troops, 1788, 1789
    saves girl spy, 1811
    on Washington's Farewell Address, 1785,
        1786
    on Washington's farewell party, 1790
Tarleton, Banastre, 809, 1032, 1354, 1415,
    1424, 1427, 1435, 1760
    at Charles Town, 1382–1384
    and Cornwallis, 1441, 1449–1451, 1457,
        1458, 1460–1461, 1474
    at Cowpens, 1449, 1451–1455, 1457–1461
    vs. Davie, 1421, 1422
    at Gloucester, Va., 1697, 1704
    at Green Spring Farm, 1650, 1652–1653
    vs. Greene, 1465, 1467–1468, 1470, 1471,
        1475
    at Guilford Court House, 1478, 1480, 1481,
        1483, 1484
    on hardships of troops under Cornwallis,
        1466
    at Hobkirk's Hill, 1494
    on hostility of Southern patriots, 1422
    vs. Lee, 1467–1468, 1470–1473, 1475, 1478
    vs. Marion, 1439–1441
    at Monck's Corner, 1427, 1438
    vs. Morgan, 1449, 1451–1454, 1458, 1465
    vs. Sumter, 1419–1420, 1439, 1441–1444
    in Virginia, 1630–1633, 1635, 1636
    and Waxhaw Massacre, 1394–1398
    vs. Wayne, 1650, 1652–1653
    (See also Loyal Legion)
Tarrant, Sarah, 467
Tattamagouche, 642
Tawney, R. H., 131

Taxation:
  by Congress, 1147
  by England, 169–175, 179, 183, 186, 263,
    266, 268–269, 271–276
  "external" vs. "internal," 182, 268
  by Parliament vs. king, 697
  (See also Sugar Act; Stamp Act; Townshend
    Duties)
Taylor, Daniel, 939
Tea, tax on, 295–298, 311
  (See also Boston Tea Party)
Temple, William, 1640
Ternay, Admiral de, 1638
Terrible, 1675, 1677, 1679–1681, 1685, 1686
Thacher, James, 766, 900, 901, 914, 932
  on abandonment of Ticonderoga, 903–904
  on André's execution, 1593
  on British and German surgeons, 942
  on British surrender at Yorktown, 1707,
    1708
  on Burgoyne's surrender, 941
  on Miralles' funeral, 1525
  on New Jersey mutineers, 1622
  on secrecy of Washington's march to
    Virginia, 1661
  on Washington, 1130, 1133
  on Washington's army in Philadelphia, 1665
  on Washington's march to attack Cornwallis,
    1663
  on Yorktown, 1700, 1701, 1706
Thacher, Oxenbridge, 191, 198
Thacher, Samuel, 1831–1832
Thanksgiving (1777), 993–994
Thayendanegea (see Brant, Joseph)
Thayer, Major, 983
Theoreticians of Revolution, 254–257
Thirty Years' War, 51
Thomas, John, 497, 554–555, 650
Thompson, Benjamin, 573
Thompson, Captain, 1258
Thompson, Colonel, 629, 631, 632
Thompson, William, 1146–1147, 1305
Thomson, Charles, 396, 430, 436, 560, 706,
  1766
"Thoughts of a Freeman," 1020
Thoughts on Government (Adams), 848–850
Throgs Neck, 781–782
Thunder, 630–631
Ticonderoga, 584–593, 597
  Allen and Arnold's attack on, 585–593, 743
  and Burgoyne's invasion, 898–900, 903–904
  Dickinson advocates return of, to British,
    595
  Indians at, 903
  Knox drags cannon from, to Boston, 649
  Parsons' raid on, 586
  and Second Continental Congress, 591–592

Tilghman, James, 671–672
Tilghman, Matthew, 855
Tilghman, Philemon, 671
Tilghman, Tench, 671–672, 771, 1054, 1353
  on Indian treaty meeting, 1153–1154
Tilly, La Gardeur de, 1626
Tilton, Captain, 1757
Time, American attitude toward, 156–157
Tocqueville, Alexis de, 94
Tolbert, Samuel, 1605
Tonnant, 1107, 1111
Tooke, John Horne, 494, 868
Tories, 468–472, 656–668
  accompany British from Savannah, 1748
  afraid of retribution by patriots, 1486–1487
  allied with Indians, 1150–1151, 1154, 1156–
    1162, 1165–1177, 1181–1189, 1215,
    1229–1230
  and Battle of Bunker Hill, 531–532
  at Bennington, 916–918, 921
  blame Clinton for Cornwallis' defeat, 1753–
    1754
  in Boston, 659, 1364–1365
  captured, congressional debate on, 1027,
    1029
  captured at Westchester, 1126–1127
  in Charles Town, 1386, 1748, 1749
  and Continental Congress, 840
  and eclipse of the sun, 1533–1534
  at Freeman's Farm, 922, 924
  at Kings Mountain, 1428, 1430–1433
  leave with British, 1749, 1758–1761
  in Maine, 641
  and Marion, 1436, 1438
  military actions of, 1461–1462
    in Georgia, 1309–1312
    in North Carolina, 624–625, 1399–1406,
      1411, 1471
    in South Carolina, 1450. 1455
    in Virginia, 621–623
  in New Jersey, 1428, 1462
  in New York, 657, 766–767, 800–801, 885,
    892–893, 904, 1351, 1462
  in North Carolina, 854, 1309
  opinions of patriots among, 461–463
  and patriots, relations between, 656–658,
    1266–1267, 1390, 1397, 1502, 1750–
    1752
  in Philadelphia, 840, 949, 1031, 1033, 1074
  piracy of, 1262
  at Saratoga, 924
  satiric song sung by, at abortive attack on
    Savannah, 1337
  and siege of Boston, 506
  in South Carolina, 1309
  in Southern states, 657, 658, 661–662,
    1461–1463, 1470

treatment of, 663–666
  at Waxhaw Massacre, 1396
  after Yorktown, 1712–1713, 1748–1757
  (*See also* King's Rangers; New Jersey
      Volunteers; Queen's Rangers)
Town meetings, 62
Townshend, Charles, 176–177, 191–192, 242
  and taxation of colonies, 264, 266, 268–269,
      271–272
Townshend, Thomas, 1733
Townshend Duties, 272–276, 281, 286, 300,
      311, 1822
  Boston riot against, 281–284
  repeal of, 293–299
Toynbee, Arnold, 1832
"Transylvania," 1213
*Travels in North America in the Years 1780, 1781,
    and 1782* (Chastellux), 1752
Treaty of Aix-la-Chapelle, 122
Treaty meetings with Indians, 117–118
  at Fort Pitt, 1152–1153
  in Northern Department, 1153–1154
  in Southern Department, 1154–1155
Treaty of Paris (1763), 1192
Treaty of Paris (1783), 1233, 1234
  hostilities continue from Yorktown to, 1298
Treaty of Ryswick, 122
Treaty of Utrecht, 122
Trenton:
  Battle of, 811–827, 1074, 1825
  British and Hessians winter in, 807
  Pennsylvania mutineers at, 1618–1621
Trevelyan, George, 53
Trevett, John, 1358
Troup, Robert, 1025
Trowbridge, Edmund, 348, 349
Trumbull, 1245, 1295, 1296
  vs. *Iris* and *General Monck,* 1296
  vs. *Watt,* 1295
Trumbull, Benjamin, 764
Trumbull, John, 1118
Trumbull, Jonathan, 312, 553, 561, 597, 808,
      841
  on British troops in Boston, 301
  on enlistment of militia, 1109
  favors immigration, 1819
  on Mount Vernon, 1669–1670
  on re-enlistment problem, 574
  on Tory piracy in Long Island Sound, 1262
Trumbull, Jonathan, Jr., 1661
Trumbull, Joseph, 1029
Tryon, William:
  and Clinton, 932
  as governor of New York, 565, 660, 1155
  as governor of North Carolina, 95, 228, 624
  on high spirits of Tories, 1553
  and Howe, 723

  leads expedition against Regulators, 1303
  and plot to assassinate Washington, 718–
      719
  raids New Haven, 1343
Tucker, Captain, 1246
Tucker, St. George, 1693–1694
Tudor, John, 343
Tudor, William, 683
Tufin, Armand, 973
Turnbull, George, 1419
Tustin, Colonel, 1160–1161
Twiggs, Colonel, 1443
Twiss, Lieutenant, 899
Tyger, Cornelius, 1608
Tyler, Moses Coit, 682
Tyler, Royall, 344
Tynes, Colonel, 1436, 1438
Tyrannicide, 1261, 1264

Underhill, John, 112
Unicorn, 1258–1259
Universalism, 1820–1821

Valley Forge, 993–1018
  building of huts at, 998–999
  clothing problems at, 1001
  code of drill at, 1010–1014, 1016
  desertion from, 1001
  discipline problems at, 1001
  failure of Howe to attack, 1042–1043
  fraternization between officers and enlisted
      men at, 1001
  hunger at, 1002–1003, 1007
  McLane's company at, 1354
  May Day at, 1017
  medical problems at, 1002, 1006–1007
  Paine at, 998–999
  resignation of officers at, 1005
  social life at, 1000
  soldiers' occupations at, 1005–1006
  women forbidden at, 1811
Van Buskirk, Abram, 1357
Van Cortlandt, Philip, 1171, 1661
Van der Capellen den Pol, Baron, 1819
Van Doren, Carl, 1591, 1596
Van Rensselaer, Robert, 1182–1183
Van Schaak, Peter, 666
Van Schaick, Goose, 1165
Van Wart, Isaac, 1578–1579
Vane, Henry, 56–57
Varick, Richard, 1568, 1581–1583, 1585–1588
Varnum, James M., 996, 1083, 1090, 1098
  at Battle of Rhode Island, 1110, 1116
  supports congressional power, 1643
Vaughan, Benjamin, 1735
Vaughan, John, 932
Vengeance, 1273, 1275

Vengeance, in commanders, 1426
Vergennes, Comte de, 944, 1046, 1047, 1051–1054
  and Adams, 1734
  and American privateers, 1264
  and Aranda, 1735
  on Battle of Germantown, 970
  disillusionment of, with French-American alliance, 1133
  on Duke of Manchester, 1744
  and Franklin, 1728, 1739
  and Lafayette, 1639–1641
  and Luzerne, 1637–1638
  and peace negotiations, 1728–1732, 1734, 1735, 1738, 1739
  and peace treaty, 1363, 1738
  proposes British give up New York but retain Georgia and South Carolina, 1637–1638
  and Raynevel, 1738, 1740
  sends more troops and ships to America, 1640
  and Shelburne, 1735
  and Spain, 1738
  urges clemency for Asgill, 1751
  wishes to use Continental Army to exhaust British power, 1520, 1639
Vermont, 1144–1145, 1643
  abolishes slavery, 1802
  British destruction in, 1184
Vernier, Pierre-François, 1383
Vernon, William, 1266
Verplanck's Point, 931, 1342, 1344, 1348, 1350, 1589
  commanded by Arnold, 1567
Victory, 1256
Vietnam War, 1828
Vigo, 1200
Ville de Paris, 1676
Vincennes, 1192, 1198–1211, 1217, 1232, 1233
  captured by Clark, 1205–1211
  captured by Hamilton, 1199
  Clark's march to, 1201–1205, 1210–1211
  Indians in Clark's attack on, 1206
Viomenil, Baron de, 1702
Virginia, 1245, 1255, 1258
Virginia, 83, 85–94, 98, 1052
  Arnold in, 1624–1629
  and Boston Port Bill, 392
  cedes western land claims, 1539–1540
  committee of correspondence in, 369
  constitution of, 850–854, 862
    (See also Virginia Bill of Rights)
  and Dunmore's War, 1191
  House of Burgesses, 92, 195–197, 369, 392, 661, 1631

  indentured servants in, 34, 36, 38, 86
  Lafayette vs. Cornwallis in, 1624–1636
  vs. Lord Dunmore, 621–624
  and mercantilism, 134
  navy of, 1261
  and nonimportation, 275
  Ohio Company of, 1191
  as producer of outstanding men, 93–94
  slave defections in, 621–622
  sponsors Clark's expedition to Old Northwest, 1194
  and Stamp Act, 195–199, 228, 237
  Tory military actions in, 621–623
Virginia Bill of Rights, 696–697, 699, 850–852
Virginia Company, 14, 24
Virginia Convention, 622
Virginia Resolves, 196–198, 221, 685, 689, 692
Visscher, Richard, 909, 910
Voltaire, 108, 1050, 1802
Volunteers, foreign, 972–977, 997–998, 1008–1009
  (See also French volunteers; Polish volunteers)
Von Bose (see Bose, von)
Von Bülow (see Bülow, von)
Von Bunau (see Bunau, von)
Von Closen, Ludwig (see Closen, Ludwig von)
Von Diemar (see Diemar, von)
Von Donop, Carl Emil Kurt (see Donop, von)
Von Fersen, Hans Axel (see Fersen, Hans Axel von)
Von Heister, Phillip (see Heister, Phillip von)
Von Kneyphausen, Wilhelm (see Knyphausen, Wilhelm von)
Von Krafft, John Charles Philip (see Krafft, John Charles Philip von)
Von Landgraf (see Landgraf, von)
Von Lossberg (see Lossberg, von)
Von Steuben, Friedrich Wilhelm Augustus (see Steuben, Friedrich Wilhelm Augustus von)
Voss, Jennie, 38
Vulture, 1348, 1572–1574, 1576–1577, 1583, 1584, 1587

Wadsworth, James, 717
Wadsworth, Peleg, 1358
Wahab, Captain, 1421
Waldeck, Philipp, 794
Waldo, Albigence, 995–996, 1003, 1005, 1016–1017
Walker, Patrick, 332
Walker, Thomas, 1631
Wallace, James, 640, 642
Wallis, Samuel, 1566, 1567
Waln, John, 1713

Walpole, Horace, 239, 865, 1062, 1063, 1065, 1390, 1724
   attacks Shelburne, 1741
   on parliamentary committee to review all petitions, 1547
Walpole, Robert, 1723
Walton, George, 1305, 1306, 1308, 1312
Wanton, Joseph, 365, 367
War of the Austrian Succession, 122
War of 1812, 1233
War of Jenkins' Ear, 122
War of the League of Augsburg, 122
War vs. revolution, 1824–1825
War of the Spanish Succession, 122
Ward, Artemas, 546, 711, 879
   and Battle of Bunker Hill, 518, 519, 536
   on riflemen, 573
   as second in command, 552, 553
   at siege of Boston, 497, 500
   vs. Washington as commander in chief, 548
Ward, Joseph, 683
Ward, Samuel, 432, 576, 577
Warfare, eighteenth-century, 127–128, 1012, 1794, 1824
Warner, Seth, 902, 907
   and Battle of Bennington, 916, 917, 919
   and Green Mountain Boys, 598, 600, 601, 604
Warren, 1245, 1246, 1255, 1257, 1269
Warren, James, 72, 348, 429, 465, 489, 491–492, 553, 555
   on Hancock, 840
   on independence, 684
   on Minutemen, 497
   on powder problem, 582
   on Tories, 659
Warren, Joseph, 306, 377, 408, 464
   and Battle of Bunker Hill, 520, 530, 535–536
   and Battles of Lexington and Concord, 474–475, 483, 487
   on Boston Massacre, 358–361, 464–465
   as physician, 328, 536
   and Suffolk Resolves, 434
Warren, Mercy Otis, 380, 458, 465, 1809, 1810
   (*See also* Otis, Mercy)
Warren, William, 337
Washburn, Wilcomb, 118
Washington, 1245, 1258
Washington, George, 5, 104, 168, 637, 1822
   aides of, 1795
   and Allen, 602
   on alliance with France, 1535
   and André, 1580–1581, 1589–1593
   annual futility of attempts to organize army, 1536
   appeals to Morris for money, 1662

   appointed commander in chief, 548
   appoints Greene commander of Southern Department, 1435, 1444
   on Arbuthnot, 1629
   and Armand, 973
   and Arnold, 606–607, 878, 1555–1556, 1558–1559, 1564–1567, 1572, 1583–1589, 1591, 1592, 1594–1595, 1624–1626, 1795
   on arrival of French troops, 1534
   and Asgill, 1751–1752
   assumes command, 564–583
   at Battle of Brandywine, 948–956
   at Battle of Long Island, 730, 734–735, 742
   and battle at Fort Mifflin, 986, 988
   at Battle of Monmouth, 1087–1090, 1092–1095, 1098–1104, 1712, 1796
   at Battle of Princeton, 831–835, 837
   and Battle of Rhode Island, 1109, 1112, 1117
   at Battle of White Plains, 783–786, 788–789
   begs De Grasse not to leave Chesapeake, 1694
   and Boston Port Bill, 392, 425
   and Boudinot, 1778
   on British reception at Mount Vernon, 1627–1628
   on British retreat from Concord, 487
   and Burgoyne, 907, 944
   and Carlisle commission, 1826
   censures Heath, 876–877
   at Chestnut Hill, 993
   chosen president of Society of Cincinnatus, 1784
   and Clark, 1216
   vs. Clinton, 1529, 1530, 1532, 1590–1591, 1656, 1658, 1659
   and committee at camp, 1521–1522, 1525
   on *Common Sense*, 682
   company-grade officers of, 1794
   and conflicts with Congress, 1026–1029, 1057, 1146, 1407, 1520–1523, 1534, 1746, 1764
   considers invasion of Canada, 1130–1131
   vs. Conway, 1019–1025, 1029–1030
   and councils of war, 748
   criticisms of, 961, 994, 995, 1004, 1019–1020
   (*See also* Conway Cabal)
   on danger to Philadelphia, 878
   and Deborah Sampson, 1812
   deceives Clinton in New York, 1658–1659
   decides against attacking Howe at Philadelphia, 990, 993–995
   declares terms of surrender, 1705–1706
   delivers commission to Congress, 1791–1792

Washington, George (*cont.*):
denied knowledge of French treaty, 1057
deploys troops for winter quarters (1778),
    1123–1124
description of, by Dr. Thacher, 1130
on destruction of Falmouth, 646–647
dictatorship under, suggested, 1534
and discipline problems, 566–573
discusses evacuation of New York with
    Carleton and Clinton, 1757–1758
at Dorchester Heights, 649–653
early life and development of, 548–553
as embodiment of Revolution, 1792
equates survival of Continental Army with
    independence, 1341–1342, 1537
errors of, at Monmouth, 1088–1089, 1094,
    1100–1101
and evacuation of Boston, 653–655
and evacuation of Brooklyn, 745–753
and exchange of prisoners, 1026–1027
and farewell party with generals in New
    York, 1789–1790
field-grade officers of, 1794
at First Continental Congress, 438–439
and foreign volunteers, 975
and forming of army, 488
and Fort Washington, 790–798
and French alliance, 1055–1057, 1132–
    1133, 1535
in French and Indian War, 123, 124, 126–127
French officers' estimate of, 1647
vs. Gates, 961, 991, 1026
as general, 1793–1796
genius of, 1792
at Germantown, 959, 964, 966, 967, 969,
    970
gives smallpox inoculations, 883–884, 1002
and Hamilton, 976–977, 1555, 1631, 1658,
    1765, 1773
handling of Congress by, 760–761
at Harlem Heights, 765, 769–770, 773–777
on "history of the war," 1599
honored by Masons, 1131
vs. Howe, evaluation of, 1042–1043
and Huddy affair, 1750–1752
improvises navy, 643–645
and Indians, 1155
instructs Lee to abduct Arnold, 1595
and invasion of Canada, 598
and invasion of New Jersey, 802–810
and Jones, 1522–1523
joy of, at news of French fleet's arrival, 1668
vs. Knuyphausen, 1528, 1530, 1532, 1533
and Lafayette, 976–977, 1079–1081, 1087,
    1088, 1133, 1513, 1524, 1627–1630,
    1633, 1654, 1655, 1666, 1670, 1693,
    1746

and land speculation, 845–846
and Laurenses, 1146, 1555
and Lee (Charles), 1081–1083, 1086, 1087,
    1093–1095, 1102–1103, 1105
and Lee (Henry), 1508, 1513, 1530, 1555,
    1595, 1596
letter to Lund Washington captured, 1648
life spared by Ferguson at Brandywine,
    1426–1427
and light infantry corps, 1134
and Lincoln, 1670
on Lord Dunmore, 622
and McLane, 1558
major generals of, 1794–1795
makes headquarters at Newburgh, 1747
makes headquarters at White Plains, 1106–
    1107
makes personal appeal for re-enlistment,
    828–829
marches north from Yorktown, 1746–1747
marches to Virginia, 1661, 1663–1665,
    1669–1671
and Mary Gibbons, 721–723
at Middle Brook, 884–887, 1131–1133,
    1338
and militia, 754, 777, 1403, 1536
and Montgomery, 604
and Morris, 1657, 1662–1665, 1669
in Morristown (1777), 875–880
in Morristown (1779–1780), 1513–1515,
    1518–1525
at Mount Vernon, 1669–1670, 1746, 1792
on murder of Jane McCrea, 906
and mutiny of Pennsylvania Line, 1609–
    1610, 1615–1616
and naval affairs, 643–645, 1238, 1251–
    1253
on need for aid from France, 1644
on need to reform army, 776–777, 1016
on New Jersey mutiny, 1622–1623
in New York, 712–727
and Newburgh Addresses, 1769–1772
on North's conciliatory bills, 1069
and Ohio Company of Virginia, 1191
orders Wayne to West Point, 1584
outmaneuvered by Howe in Pennsylvania,
    963
and Peggy Arnold, 1586–1588
permits women and children in military
    camps, 1602
persistent gloom of, 1340–1341
in Philadelphia (1778–1779), 1131–1132
plot to assassinate, 718–723
as politician, 1793
praises Wayne's victory at Stony Point, 1349
predicts Howe's intentions from
    information of woman spy, 1811

and problems with officers, 878–879, 991, 1005
on Proclamation Line, 167
and proposed attack on Boston, 648–649
proposes pensions for officers, 1026, 1027
and provisioning of army, 581–582, 1519–1521, 1525, 1535
and Pulaski, 998, 1321–1322
pursuaded by French to carry campaign to Virginia, 1657–1658
rebukes McLane for accusing Arnold of treachery, 1355
and recapture of Stony Point, 1344, 1350
receives augmented powers, 825
receives full power over war operations, 811–812
recruiting problems of, 1133, 1135, 1340
and re-enlistment problems, 574–577, 579–580, 775, 777–778, 804, 828–829, 875, 877
restraint of, 1796–1797
and retreat from New York, 754–756, 760, 763–765
and Rochambeau, 1626, 1656–1658, 1661, 1668, 1670, 1671
says farewell to troops, 1784–1785
at Second Continental Congress, 544, 546–548, 556
on sectional animosity, 1135
sends Gates to re-establish army in South, 1536
sends Pennsylvania troops to Mount Kemble for winter (1780–1781), 1601
sends Sullivan against Indians and Tories, 1163–1165
shadows Howe's army, 959–960
and siege of Charles Town, 1386
and Steuben, 1009–1011, 1013, 1015, 1790
submits to Congress officers' appeal for payment, 1775
suggestion of dictatorship for, 1534
suggestion of dukedom for, 1067
and Sullivan, 1112–1114, 1119, 1172, 1176–1177, 1645
supports Lee's attack on Paulus Hook, 1353–1355
as symbol of federal union, 1791–1793, 1796
and Tallmadge, 1758
at Trenton, 811–827
on union of states, 1775–1776, 1785
at Valley Forge, 993–1018
visits Congress, 1131–1132, 1663–1664, 1791–1792
visits Philadelphia, 1131–1132, 1663–1664
and Wayne, 1346, 1584–1585
weeps at Arnold's treason, 1584

welcomed by New York City after victory, 1788–1789
and West Point, 1565–1566
at Williamsburg, 1693, 1694
withdrawal from Harlem Heights, 782, 783
at Yorktown, 1696, 1698, 1699, 1701–1703, 1705, 1706, 1708
role of luck in, 1687–1688
Washington, John Augustine, 552
Washington, Lawrence, 548–549, 1191
Washington, Lund, 1627–1628, 1648
Washington, Martha, 549–550, 1133, 1648–1649, 1669
at Valley Forge, 1000
Washington, William, 816, 820, 822, 1383, 1395
vs. Cornwallis, 1470, 1466
at Cowpens, 1452, 1453, 1455–1457, 1459
at Eutaw Springs, 1688, 1690
and Greene, 1407, 1688, 1690, 1746
at Guilford Court House, 1479–1482
at Hammond's Store, 1450
at Hobkirk's Hill, 1493–1495
in South Carolina campaign, 1504, 1506
tricks Tories into surrendering, 1447
Wasp, 1250
Watauga Association, 168, 1212–1213
"Water machine," 1248–1250
Watkins, Jacob, 38
Watson, Elkanah, 1740
Watson, John, 1491, 1492, 1495
Watson-Wentworth, Charles (*see* Rockingham, Lord)
Watt vs. *Trumbull*, 1295
Watts, Colonel, 1436–1437
Watts, Stephen, 911
Waxhaw Massacre, 1395–1398
Wayne, Anthony, 879, 886, 1007, 1105, 1444
appeals to mutinous soldiers, 1606, 1608, 1609, 1613
at Brandywine, 950–951, 955, 956
and Cornwallis, 1650–1651, 1655
court-martial of, 991
at Germantown, 964, 966–968, 970
at Green Spring Farm, 1650–1653
on injustice of sufferings of soldiers, 1603
joins mutinous troops, 1608–1610, 1612–1618, 1620, 1621
and Lafayette, 1633–1636, 1650–1651
at Monmouth, 1087, 1088, 1091, 1092, 1095, 1098
at Mount Kemble winter quarters, 1603–1606
mutineers deliver Clinton's message to, 1617
at Paoli, 960–961
recaptures Stony Point, 1343–1351
and Reed, 1603–1604, 1616, 1617

Wayne, Anthony (*cont.*):
　reinforces West Point, 1584–1585
　supports effort to capture Philadelphia,
　　1083
　surrounds Savannah, 1748
　vs. Tarleton, 1650, 1652–1653
　warns Congress of mutinous troops, 1607
　and Washington, 1346, 1584–1585
Weales, Elizabeth, 34
Wealth of Nations (Smith), 186
Webb, Samuel, 649–650
Webster, James, 1383, 1384, 1411, 1412, 1465
　at Guilford Court House, 1480–1483
　vs. Williams, 1475, 1476
Wedderburn, Alexander, 371–372
Weedon, George, 763, 770, 771, 1673
　at Brandywine, 951
　at Gloucester, Va., 1697
　and Greene, 1673
Weissenstein, Charles de, 1075–1076
Welch, Thomas, 485
Welsh immigration, 30, 45
Wemms, William, 337, 357
Wemyss, James, 1439–1441
Wendell, Oliver, 351, 354
Wentworth, John, 458–459, 660, 728
Wereat, John, 1302–1303, 1308
Wertenbaker, Thomas, 1760
Wesley, John, 4, 865–866
West, Colonel, 1116
West Florida, 1392, 1768
West Indies, 1331, 1371, 1372
　British naval successes in, 1542–1543
　United States denies trade with, 1744
West Point, 1342
　André asks Arnold for plan of, 1563
　commanded by Arnold, 1567–1570
　plans for, given to André by Arnold, 1575
　reinforced by Wayne, 1584–1585
Westchester County, raided by Hessians, 1124
Western campaign, 5–6
Western Reserve, 845
Weston, Thomas, 17
Whately, Thomas, 369–371
Wheatley, Phillis, 1802
Wheelock, Eleazar, 1158
Wheelock, John, 144
Whicher, Joseph, 466
Whipple, Abraham, 366, 367, 1248, 1260
Whipple, William, 1115, 1265
Whiskey Rebellion, 1508
Whitaker, Nathaniel, 144
White, Henry, 799
White, Hugh, 333–334, 336–338, 354
White, Lieutenant, 1605
White, Major, 966
White, Philip, 1750

White, Robert, 987
White Eyes, 1152, 1156
White Plains:
　Battle of, 779–789
　　Hessians at, 785–788
　Hessians ambushed near, 1125–1126
Whitefoord, Caleb, 1737
Whitehaven, England, raided by Jones, 1269–
　1270
Whitehouse, Jane, 338
Wiederhold, Andreas, 819, 1032
Wigglesworth, Edward, 1118
Wilkes, John, 177–178, 258, 314, 868, 1156,
　1550
Wilkinson, Captain, 809
Wilkinson, Eliza, 1327, 1394, 1810
Wilkinson, James, 923–924, 934
　and Conway Cabal, 1019, 1021, 1024, 1025
Will, Captain (Shawnee chief), 1213
Willard, Abijah, 518–519
Willett, Marinus, 908–910, 912–913, 1094
　leads defense of western New York, 1185–
　　1189
William (III) and Mary, 1, 58, 137
William of Orange (*see* William and Mary)
Williams ("major general" of Pennsylvania
　mutineers), 1616, 1617
Williams, David, 1578–1579
Williams, James, 1427, 1431, 1466
Williams, John, 283
Williams, John Foster, 1293–1295
Williams, Major, 1033
Williams, Otho, 1407–1409, 1411–1415, 1689
　vs. Cornwallis, 1466–1468, 1475, 1479
　at Hobkirk's Hill, 1493
Williamsburg, Va., 90, 195, 1649, 1693–1695
Williamson, Andrew, 1213, 1222, 1312, 1313,
　1315
Willing, Mr., 428
Wills, Solomon, 737
Wilmot, George, 326–327, 348, 349
Wilson, James, 544, 687–688, 702
　opposes price-fixing, 1364
　target of Philadelphia mob, 1366–1369
　urges autonomy of Congress in dealing with
　　Indians, 1153
Wilson, John, 306
Winstanley, Gerrard, 55–56
Wintermot family, 1156–1157
Winthrop, Hannah, 458
Winthrop, James, 520
Winthrop, John, 19–22, 70
Wise, Captain, 246
Wister, Sally, 957–958, 971, 1353, 1810
Witherspoon, John, 144, 423, 428, 701, 844,
　1614
Wolcott, Oliver, 717, 718

Wolfe, James, 127–129, 192, 502
Women, 1808–1814
  dead in battle, 1811
  forbidden at Valley Forge, 1811
  independence for, urged by Abigail Adams,
    1808–1810
  lose status and freedom after Revolution,
    1814
  Marshall on, 1813
  in Maryland, 84–85
  in New England, 72–74
  in New York City, 76–77
  organize to force prices down, 1364–1365
  as spies and secret agents, 1811
  subscribe large sums for relief of soldiers,
    1813
  with troops at Mount Kemble, 1602
Wood, Major, 1161–1162
Woodford, William, 622–623, 1099
  and Arnold court-martial, 1559
  at Charles Town, 1384
Woodhull, Nathaniel, 717, 742
Woodmason, Charles, 98–101
Woolman, John, 80–82
Wooster, David, 554, 597, 603, 717, 876
  with Arnold in Connecticut, 882–883
Worcester County convention, 459
Work as American obsession, 156–157

Wraxall, Nathaniel, 1717–1719, 1723
Wright, James, 662, 1308
Writs of assistance, 272, 294
Wyandot Panther, 906
Wyllys, Samuel, 737, 739, 741, 764
Wyoming Valley Massacre, 1156–1158, 1173
Wythe, George, 197, 848, 1693

Yamma, Bristol, 1799
Yankee Hero vs. *Milford,* 1263
Yarmouth, 1257
Yorke, Lieutenant Colonel, 1650
Yorktown:
  captured by Cornwallis, 1655
  siege of, 1696–1710
  surrender of, 1297–1298, 1705, 1825
    consequences of, 1711–1712, 1716
    distorts true nature of Revolution, 1716
    importance of, enhanced by British, 1715,
      1716
    surrender ceremony, 1706–1708
    Tory reaction to, 1712–1713
    unimportance of, 1714–1716
Young, Thomas (Boston patriot), 335, 857,
  1145
Young, Thomas (Scottish professor), 77

Zeisberger, David, 1219–1220

Acknowledgments

I wish to acknowledge the assistance of Oliver Allen, who launched me on this venture; David Thomson, for skillful editorial assistance; and Kenneth Leish, for extraordinary labors performed under considerable pressure of time. Charlotte Cassidy and Frances Rydell gave loving care to typing the manuscript.

The most important contribution to this venture was of course that of Lester Cohen, who, as I have noted, collected nine large volumes of source materials for use in this work. Matt Seccombe also made many useful contributions.

About the Author

Page Smith was educated at the Gilman School in Baltimore, Dartmouth College, and Harvard University. He was an infantry officer during World War II, and afterward served as research associate at the Institute of Early American History and Culture, and has taught at the University of California at Los Angeles and at Santa Cruz, where he was Provost at Cowell College. He is now Professor Emeritus of that University as well as Co-director of the William James Association. Dr. Smith is the author of *As a City upon a Hill: The Town in American History, The Historian and History, Daughters of the Promised Land: Women in American History*, and the highly acclaimed two-volume biography *John Adams.* He has been a historical advisor and consultant to the People's Bicentennial Commission, a nationwide citizens' organization preparing programs and activities that reflect the founding principles of the Declaration of Independence, in celebration of the American Bicentennial. Page Smith lives in Santa Cruz, California.

DATE DUE

DISPLAY			
NO7 '9?			
GAYLORD			PRINTED IN U.S.A.